British Railway Steam Locomotives 1948-1968

British Railway Steam Locomotives 1948-1968

Hugh Longworth

OPC

An imprint of
Ian Allan Publishing

Contents

Front cover: Former LM&SR Stanier Class 5 No 44971 seen climbing Shap on 23 March 1967. *G. T. Robinson*

Back cover, main image: Former Southern Railway Bulleid 'West Country' No 34027 *Taw Valley* photographed in rebuilt form between Paddock Wood and Marden on 3 August 1959. *G. M. Kichenside*

Back cover, lower inset: BR Standard Class 9F No 92028 stands alongside No 7029 *Clun Castle* on Southall Shed in 1965. *P. A. Buckland*

Back cover, top inset: Former LNER Gresley Class K3 No 61903 seen ex works at Doncaster on 23 August 1959. *R. Fisher*

Half title: Rebuilt 'Merchant Navy' Pacific No 35017 *Belgian Marine* in 1965.

Title page: GWR Collett '6800' 'Grange' class 4-6-0 No 6826 *Nannerth Grange* at Penzance in August 1953.

Right: Highland Railway Drummond '0P' 0-4-4T No 55053, running alongside Loch Fleet on a train from The Mound to Dornoch on a beautiful sunny day in July 1955.

First published in 2005

ISBN 0 86093 593 0

The right of Hugh Longworth to be identified as the author of this work has been asserted in accordance with the Copyright Designs and Patents Act 1988 sections 77 and 78.

Published by Oxford Publishing Co

an imprint of Ian Allan Publishing Ltd, Hersham, Surrey KT12 4RG.
Printed in England by Ian Allan Publishing Ltd, Hersham, Surrey KT12 4RG.

Code: 0503/A

All pictures from Ian Allan Library unless credited otherwise.

Preface

It may be of some interest to the reader of this book that my own interest in railways began in 1969 when I was eleven years old. Not only do I have no personal experience of the period described in this book, but I was not born until half-way through it!

It was in fact this lack of experience that directly led me to start preparing these lists. I wanted to have in one place a complete list of all BR's steam locomotives so that I could make sense of all the magazines and books that I was reading, and all the photographs I was enjoying. Ian Allan's ABCs were wonderful for their users, but for the historian they fall down because each one is, by necessity, confined to one point in history. The basic locomotive list I compiled eventually grew into the book you have before you now.

This book is the one I always wanted. I couldn't find it so I had to write it myself. I hope you find it useful too.

Hugh Longworth, 2005

This book is dedicated to my wife Doris, and my daughter Heppy.

Thank you Doris, your unfailing love and belief in me has kept me going.

Thank you too, Heppy. I started work on this book before you were born. Do you remember the nights when you couldn't sleep and you sat up on my knee in front of the computer while I was typing all those numbers in? Now you are ten we've graduated from Thomas to 1466!

GNR Gresley 'N2' class 0-6-2T No 69543 at King's Cross shed in October 1955, fitted with condensing apparatus.

BR Standard '9F' 2-10-0 No 92055.

Introduction

The aim of this book is to provide a complete listing of all steam locomotives owned by British Railways from its formation in 1948 until the end of steam in 1968. Full technical details are given for each class, together with a short potted history. For each locomotive, details of its introduction, BR renumbering, withdrawal and scrapping are given, together with any name it may have carried. All major variations in the class are outlined.

In 1923 the Railway Companies of Great Britain were formed into four large groups, the Great Western Railway (GWR), the Southern Railway (SR), the London Midland & Scottish Railway (LMS) and the London & North Eastern Railway (LNER). At midnight on 31st December 1947 these four Railway Companies (together with a few small independent Railway Companies) were nationalised and formed the new British Railways.

For the first few months of 1948 locomotives retained their pre-nationalisation numbers, with the addition of the letter W, S, M or E in front of the number. (Note that the Isle of Wight engines always remained in a separate number series which was also prefixed W). In fact very few locomotives received their prefix letters before March 1948 when a new renumbering scheme was announced, in which most locomotives were renumbered as shown below. In most cases the locomotives were renumbered as they received major overhauls and the last engine was not renumbered until 1956. This meant that many locomotives were withdrawn without receiving their new numbers.

GWR locomotives retained their original numbers. This was because GWR locomotives carried their numbers on a brass or cast iron numberplate which would have been expensive to change. All other groups had painted numbers, which could be changed more easily. SR locomotives were renumbered by the addition of 30000 to their numbers. LMS locomotives were renumbered by the addition of 40000 to their numbers (filling the series 40001 to 59999). LNER locomotives were renumbered by the addition of 60000 to their numbers. In each group there were some exceptions and these are detailed in the lists. The series from 70000 to 99999 was reserved for British Railways standard locomotives which were to be built, and the large numbers of War Department Austerity locomotives which were purchased by BR. The 10000 series was reserved for diesel locomotives, and the 20000 series for electric locomotives.

Layout of the book

There are five main sections in this book as follows:

- Part 1. GWR Locomotives.
- Part 2. Southern Locomotives.
- Part 3. LMS Locomotives.
- Part 4. LNER Locomotives.
- Part 5. BR Standard and Austerity Locomotives.

Each of the first four sections also include locomotives built to pre-nationalisation designs by British Railways.

In addition there are nine appendices:

- Appendix 1. Statistics.
- Appendix 2. Chronological list of classes (listed by Railway Company).
- Appendix 3. Alphabetical list of locomotive names.
- Appendix 4. Chronological list of additions to stock.
- Appendix 5. Chronological list of withdrawals from stock.
- Appendix 6. Youngest and oldest locomotives at time of withdrawal.
- Appendix 7. Locomotives which survived for more than a year after withdrawal before scrapping.
- Appendix 8. Locomotives which still carried their pre-nationalisation number after January 1951.
- Appendix 9. Ex-LNER locomotives 1946 renumbering scheme.

Most locomotives are listed in strict numerical order. The main exception to this is the section covering the Southern Railways locomotives. The Southern Railway continued to use a very haphazard method of numbering its engines, and each class could be scattered over a wide numerical range. Each of the main sections (30xxx, 31xxx and 32xxx) starts with a numerical list and following this the classes are grouped together in alphabetical class order.

The only other exceptions to engines being listed in strictly numerical order, are in cases where a locomotive class was built using the number series of locomotives already withdrawn or renumbered. For example BR continued to build GWR designed '9400' class pannier tanks. Some of these (3400-3409) took the numbers of previously withdrawn 'Bulldog' ('3300' class) locomotives. In this situation the classes are listed one after the other.

In each section there are locomotives which are numbered outside the main series, for example service (departmental) locomotives or preserved locomotives which were still running on BR. These are shown separately at the end of each section.

Sometimes it is easier to describe the development of several classes of engines together, and these Historical Surveys are to be found at the end of each section, and they are referred to from the relevant class headings.

Class Heading

For each class the following information is given in the heading:

1. **Class Type**. Each pre-nationalisation company had a different method of classifying its locomotives. If two different classes in the same section have the same classification then they are differentiated by a numerical suffix, for example $2F^3$. The suffix is only used in this book to simplify cross-referencing with the appendices. It does not form part of the official classification. When referring to other classes in the text the BR number of the first member of the class is often given to avoid confusion.

2. **Number Series**.

3. **Locomotive Type** (4-6-2, 0-6-0T and so on). The following suffixes are used:

   - T Tank Locomotive
   - ST Saddle Tank Locomotive
   - PT Pannier Tank Locomotive
   - CT Crane Tank Locomotive
   - WT Well Tank Locomotive (tank between the frames).

4. **Description.** Original owning company, designer and class name (where appropriate).

Class Details

Following the heading, full technical details of the class are given as follows: (The details given are those which apply to an average member of the class, and while they are as accurate as possible, many minor detail changes could be made to individual members of the class. Wherever possible, locomotives which differ from the rest of the class are noted in the lists.)

1. **Power Classification.** British Railways adopted a modified version of the system of power classifications which was used by the LMS. In this system the locomotives were classified according to their power (from 0 up to 9 for the most powerful). This number had the suffix F for freight locomotives, P for passenger locomotives and MT for mixed traffic locomotives. Mixed traffic locomotives were also known simply by the number (for example class '5' or class '5MT'; they are shown in this book as '5MT'). In addition there were other varieties such as '5XP' (which was a classification halfway between '5' and '6' used by the LMS and later superseded), and combinations such as '6P5F' where locomotives fitted into different classes for freight and passenger working. In some cases locomotives were reclassified, and this is shown in the heading.

2. **Introduced.** This shows the building dates of the class, together with the dates of any major rebuilds.

3. **Designer.** The name of the designer of the locomotives is given, or the name of the locomotive builder if designed by an outside contractor.

4. **Company.** This is the name of the original Railway Company to own the engines. Many classes were built over a period of time by more than one company (for example Midland Railway and LMS) - this can be seen from the building dates.

5. **Weight.** The weight of the engine is given in full working order in tons (t) and hundredweights (cwt). Tender weights (where known) are given separately.

6. **Driving Wheel.** The driving wheel diameter is given in feet (') and inches (").

7. **Boiler Pressure.** The boiler pressure is given in pounds per square inch (psi). Boilers are assumed to be saturated unless they are noted as superheated.

8. **Cylinders.** Details are given of the cylinder position and size. The main types are *Inside* (two cylinders between the frames), *Outside* (two cylinders outside the frames), *Three* (two outside cylinders and one inside) or *Four* (two outside and two inside cylinders). There were other variations (such as compound locomotives) and these are made clear in the notes. The cylinder diameter and stroke are given in inches.

9. **Tractive Effort**. This is an indication in pounds force (lbf) of the haulage power of the locomotive.

   Tractive Effort is calculated as follows:

   $T.E. = (D^2 \times S \times P \times 85)/(W \times 100)$

   T.E. = tractive effort in pounds force, D = diameter of cylinder in inches, S = piston stroke in inches, P = working pressure in pounds and W = diameter of driving wheel in inches. This gives the tractive effort at 85% of the working pressure (a commonly accepted proportion due to the fact that the steam is cut off before the piston has traversed its full stroke). The answer is multiplied by 1½ for three-cylinder engines and 2 for four-cylinder engines. The tractive effort for compound locomotives is based on the dimensions of the low pressure cylinder at 80% of the boiler pressure.

   Tractive effort is purely a theoretical figure and many other factors influenced the relative hauling powers of different steam locomotives.

10. **Valve Gear.** The main types of valve gear in use were *Stephenson*, *Walschaert*, *Caprotti* and *Joy*. The valves were *Slide*, *Piston* or *Poppet*.

Following the technical details a short description of the history of the class is given, together with descriptions of any main variations in the design.

Class Totals. For each class a list is given showing the number of locomotives in stock at the end of each year from 31st December 1947 to 31st December 1967.

Locomotive Lists

The following information is given for each locomotive:

1. The first column shows the locomotive number, normally the number the locomotive was allocated under the March 1948 renumbering scheme. If the number is shown in *italics,* then the allocated number was never actually carried by the locomotive concerned (the locomotive being withdrawn before renumbering could take place). In some cases the first column contains no number; although the locomotive came into BR stock, it was withdrawn early in 1948 before a BR number could be allocated to it. The symbol § after a locomotive number indicates that the locomotive has been preserved.

2. The second column shows the build date and the builder of the locomotive. The dates are shown as follows: 12/75 for December 1875, 08/08 for August 1908 or simply 00 for 1900. In general year build dates of 60 or below refer to the 1900s and numbers above 61 refer to the 1800s. (The only exception to this is 58865, the oldest engine to come into BR stock, which was built in 1858). The name of the locomotive builder is abbreviated. Abbreviations all in upper case are outside builders, those in upper and lower case are the Railway Companies' own workshops. The abbreviations used are as follows:

9Elm	Nine Elms
AB	Andrew Barclay Sons & Co Ltd
AE	Avonside Engine Co Ltd
Asfd	Ashford
AW	Sir W G Armstrong Whitworth & Co Ltd
B	Borsig (Germany)
BM	Beardmore Ltd
Bow	Bow
BP	Beyer Peacock & Co Ltd
Bton	Brighton
CF	Chapman & Furneaux Ltd
CL	Cooke Loco Company
Cow	Cowlairs
Crw	Crewe
D	Dubs & Co
Dar	Darlington
Der	Derby
DM	Davies & Metcalfe Ltd
DL	Dodman & Co, Lynn
Don	Doncaster
Elh	Eastleigh
FE	Falcon Engine & Carriage Company
FW	Fox Walker & Co
Ghd	Gateshead
Gor	Gorton
H	R & W Hawthorn & Co Ltd
HC	Hudswell Clarke & Co Ltd
HE	Hunslet Engine Co Ltd
HKP	H K Porter (USA)
HL	Hawthorn Leslie & Co
Hor	Horwich
Inv	Inverurie
K	Kitson & Co
KS	Kerr Stuart & Co Ltd
Lchg	Lochgorm
Lngh	Longhedge
Mel	Melton Constable
Mlsp	Miles Platting
MW	Manning Wardle & Co Ltd
N	Neilson & Co Ltd
NB	North British Locomotive Co Ltd
NR	Neilson Reid & Co Ltd
NW	Nasmyth Wilson & Co Ltd
P	Peckett & Sons Ltd

RP	Ruston & Proctor Ltd	Str	Stratford
RS	Robert Stephenson & Co Ltd	V	Vulcan Ironworks (USA)
RSH	Robert Stephenson & Hawthorns Ltd	VF	Vulcan Foundry Ltd
S	Sentinel (Shrewsbury) Ltd	W	Woolwich Arsenal
SC	Sentinel-Cammell	WB	W G Bagnall Ltd
Sdn	Swindon	Wlv	Wolverhampton
SF	Societe Franco Belge	YE	Yorkshire Engine Co Ltd
SRlx	St Rollox (Glasgow)	Yrk	York
SS	Sharp Stewart & Co		

3. The third column shows the date that the locomotive received its British Railways number, and the previous number carried by the locomotive. This is usually the pre-nationalisation number, but in some cases it is another British Railways number. In situations like this the engine will be found listed under both numbers.

4. The fourth column shows the dates that the locomotive was in BR ownership. There can be two dates in this column separated by a hyphen (-). The date is in the format MONTH/YEAR for example 12/55 for December 1955. If the date before the hyphen is left blank then the locomotive came into BR ownership at midnight on 31st December 1947. If a date is shown before the hyphen then this is the date the locomotive was built, or was acquired by BR.

   Note that some locomotives were renumbered by BR (this was for a variety of reasons including reclassification, transfer to or from service stock and clearing a range of numbers for new locomotives). This can mean that although a locomotive was in BR stock it did not belong to the class until the date shown before the hyphen. For the WD Austerity locomotives, their date of introduction to stock is either their purchase date by BR (even though many were already on loan) or their date of official transfer from the LNER 'O7' class.

   The date after the hyphen shows the date that the locomotive was finally withdrawn. In some cases of transfer to departmental stock (or again the date of transfer of the 'O7' class) it is the transfer date that is shown here. Note that some locomotives were renumbered within capital stock before that withdrawal date and this will be noted in the notes column.

   If a locomotive was withdrawn and reinstated then this is shown by an entry in the notes column using the ⊠ symbol.

5. The fifth column shows the scrapping date of the locomotive. The information for engines withdrawn after 1957 is fairly well documented, before then less so. The date is given for the month and year of scrapping, or just for the year. A date in *italics* is approximate.

6. The sixth column displays any relevant notes. Codes are used shows any detail differences which are listed in the class header. Any rebuilding or reclassification of locomotives is indicated by the symbol ⇨. This is often prefixed by the date of the rebuilding. If the date is in *italics* then it is an approximate date.

   The notes column also shows any further renumberings which took place. A number preceded by the symbol ➲ indicates that the locomotive was renumbered to the number shown at some time during its BR ownership. This symbol will be preceded by the date of renumbering.

   If a locomotive was withdrawn and later reinstated, then this is indicated by the ⊠ symbol. This is followed by the dates of first withdrawal and then reinstatement, separated by a hyphen, for example ⊠12/62-02/63.

7. If the locomotive is named, then the name is shown indented on the following line. The symbol ➲ is used to indicate a change of name. Dates of naming and removal of names are not usually shown.

A few examples follow to clarify the locomotive lists:

Number	*Built*	*Renumbered*	*BR Dates*	*Scrap*	*Notes*
34001	05/45 Bton	04/49 21C101	-07/67	10/67	WCx
EXETER					11/57⇨r

34001 was built at Brighton in May 1945. It came into BR stock at the beginning of 1948. It was originally numbered 21C101 and it received its BR number in April 1949. It was named EXETER. It was part of the 'WC' ('West Country') class. The 'x' refers to its tender type as listed in the class header. In November 1957 it was rebuilt (see 'r' in the class header) and it was finally withdrawn in July 1967 and scrapped in October 1967.

Number	*Built*	*Renumbered*	*BR Dates*	*Scrap*	*Notes*
67702	01/48 Dar	05/48 *69001*	01/48-10/60	11/60	
69001	01/48 Dar	9001	01/48-10/60	11/60	05/48➲67702

These two entries refer to the same engine, but they come from different parts of the book. It was built in January 1948 at Darlington as LNER number 9001. Although it was allocated the number 69001 it never carried this as it was decided to renumber the class into a range where more numbers were available. So in May 1948 it was renumbered 67702. It was finally withdrawn in October 1960 and scrapped the following month.

Number	*Built*	*Renumbered*	*BR Dates*	*Scrap*	*Notes*
4082	04/24 Sdn		-02/65	06/65	
WINDSOR CASTLE				02/52➲7013	
4082	07/48 Sdn	02/52 7013	07/48-09/64	01/65	m4
WINDSOR CASTLE					

In February 1952 4082 and 7013 exchanged identities (names and numbers). This means that there are two entries for each of these. The first entry is for the original locomotive (which was built in April 1924 at Swindon, was withdrawn in February 1965, and scrapped in June 1965) and the second entry is for the second locomotive to carry this number. 7013 had been built in July 1948 before being renumbered in February 1952 and withdrawn in September 1964.

Number	*Built*	*Renumbered*	*BR Dates*	*Scrap*	*Notes*
48077	12/36 VF	12/49 70611	12/49-03/68	06/68	m
48078	12/36 VF	08/48 8078	-08/65	12/65	m
48079	12/36 VF	08/48 8079	-12/66	06/67	mo
				08/48⇨c	

Notable among these three locomotives (all built at Vulcan Foundry in December 1936) is that 48077 was renumbered from WD 70611 when it was taken into stock in December 1949, and 48079 was converted from oil-burning to coal-burning in August 1948.

Number	*Built*	*Renumbered*	*BR Dates*	*Scrap*	*Notes*
58343	05/81 Crw	10/48 28227	-09/53	*10/53*	
	05/81 Crw	28230	-01/48	*07/48*	
58344	05/81 Crw	28233	-03/49	*49*	
58345	05/81 Crw	28234	-04/48	09/48	
	06/81 Crw	8236	05/50-07/50	10/50	s
58346	06/81 Crw	28239	-03/52	*03/52*	
58347	10/89 Crw	09/48 28245	-02/53	*03/53*	

This section shows a number of interesting features. 58343 and 58347 were the only two of this batch to actually be renumbered. 28230 was withdrawn in January 1948 and was not even allocated a new number (the renumbering scheme being finalised in March 1948). 8236 was a locomotive which was sold by the LMS to the Shropshire and Montgomery Railway before it was able to be renumbered into the LMS duplicate list (20000 added to the number). It came into BR stock with the rest of the stock of the Shropshire and Montgomery in May 1950, and was withdrawn in July of the same year.

Number	*Built*	*Renumbered*	*BR Dates*	*Scrap*	*Notes*
45169	08/35 AW	09/48 5169	-05/63	12/63	
				☒12/62-02/63	

45169 was withdrawn in December 1962, reinstated in February 1963 and finally withdrawn in May 1963. Incidentally, this was just one of a number of engines that were reinstated in the severe winter of 1962-63 when many of the new diesels were failing in the extreme cold.

Accuracy of the information

In a book such as this accuracy is of great importance. However as the book has developed through multiple iterations it has become obvious to me that there will *always* be errors in an undertaking of this size. That raises the question, 'at what point should the book be published, bearing in mind that more information is always becoming available?'. I have taken the decision to release the book now for several reasons. I think that many people will appreciate having all the information to hand in one place. It also will provide a forum for people to add in their own information, or corrections to improve future versions of the book.

There has been some discussion in the railway press recently regarding the need to seek out the original source materials when collating such material as this. There have also been complaints about forcing information into a consistent format (for example listing dates by month and year when many of the authorities gave the information in different formats such as '4 weeks ending'). However much of the original source material is no longer available and I have been aiming in this book for completeness and consistency as the main aim, while maintaining accuracy as far as possible.

The great majority of this information has been collated from previously published material. The material has proved to be of varying degrees of accuracy, and I have corrected any errors as I have found them. I have also decided to give dates in month and year format wherever possible, or simply the year when that is all that is available. Doubtful dates are always shown in *italics*. When dates were originally given within a period that included a month end, then the date given in this book is of the month which includes most days within that period.

The following list shows my perception of the level of accuracy of the data in this book, from the most accurate to the least accurate. (However, I consider even the most inaccurate parts of my data to be more than 99% accurate.)

- Locomotives listed (the only locomotives that are not included are those withdrawn before 1st January 1948, but not scrapped until after that date)
- Year of entry to service or withdrawal (checked against the official returns)
- Month of entry to service or withdrawal (based on reported information at the time)
- Dates of renumbering (based on reported information at the time)
- Builders and build dates (collated from a wide variety of sources such as published histories)
- Scrapping dates (based on contemporary observations – dates before 1957 are not as widely available)

Other information such as class details and historical information are based on information commonly available in other published material.

Selected Bibliography

The following is a list of books that were particularly helpful to me as I prepared this book.

ABC British Railways Locomotives Combined Volume, various editions 1946-1968 *published by Ian Allan*
Allied Military Locomotives of the Second World War *by R Tourret*
Big Four Remembered *by J S Whiteley & G W Morrison*
BR Steam Locomotives from Modernisation to Nationalisation *by Alan Williams and David Percival*
British Locomotive Catalogue 1823-1923 Vols 2-5 *by Bertram Baxter and David Baxter*
British Locomotives of the 20th Century Vols 1 and 2 *by O S Nock*
British Railways Locomotives 1948 *by Chris Banks*
British Railways Locomotives 1955 *by Chris Banks*
British Railways Steaming series *by Peter Hands*
Engines of the L M S Built 1923-1951 *by J W P Rowledge*
From Mainline to Industry *by Frank Jones*
GWR Engines Names Numbers Types and Classes 1911-1946 *published by the Great Western Railway*
GWR Engines Names Numbers Types and Classes (1940 - preservation) *by Brian Whitehurst*
Illustrated History of LMS Locomotives Vols1-3 *by Bob Essery & David Jenkinson*
Journal of the Stephenson Locomotive Society *1946-1968*
Last Steam Locomotives of British Railways *by P Ransome-Wallis*
L B & S C R Locomotives *by F Burtt*
LMS Engines Names Numbers Types and Classes *by J W P Rowledge*
Locomotives at the Grouping Nos 1-4 *by H C Casserley & S W Johnson*
Locomotives I Have Known *by J N Maskelyne*
Locomotive Illustrated Magazine *various editions*
Locomotives of British Railways *by H C Casserley & L L Asher*
Locomotive of the GWR *published by the RCTS*
Locomotive of the LNER *published by the RCTS*
Locomotive Stock Alterations 1952-1954 *published by the RCTS*
Locomotive Stock Books, 1946, 1948, 1950, 1952, 1960, 1963, 1966 and 1969 *published by the RCTS*
Locomotive Stock Changes and Withdrawal Dates Vols 1-4 *by Michael McManus*
Nameplates of the Big Four *by Frank Burridge*
Observer's Book of Railway Locomotives of Britain, various editions *by H C Casserley*
Pictorial Record of Great Western Absorbed Engines *by J H Russell*
Pictorial Record of Great Western Engines, Vols 1 and 2 *by J H Russell*
Pocket Encyclopaedia of British Steam Railways and Locomotives *by O S Nock*
Railway Observer *1948-1968 published by the RCTS*
Steam All the Way *by Nigel Harris*
Steam Locomotives 1955 Vols 1-4 *by Eric Sawford*
Stroudley and his Terriers *by Tom Middlemass*
The Gresley Legacy *by Martin Smith*
The Story of the Q1s *by John Scott Morgan*
The Story of the Southern USA Tanks *by H Sprenger, K Roberton and C Sprenger*
What Happened to Steam Vols 1-50 *by Peter Hands*
Xpress Locomotive Register Vols 1-4 *published by Xpress Publishing*

In addition the British Steam Locomotives website (www.britishsteam.com) by Roy Vandersteen has been helpful in tracking down elusive data on obscure engines.

Part 1
Great Western Railway Group

Part 1. Great Western Railway Group

Locomotive Origins

The Great Western group was different from the other three groups in that it consisted of one main pre-grouping company which absorbed a number of smaller Railway Companies in 1922/23. Locomotives from the following absorbed companies were still running at nationalisation.

AD	Alexandra (Newport & South Wales) Docks & Railway
BM	Brecon & Merthyr Railway
BPGV	Burry Port & Gwendraeth Valley Railway
BR	Barry Railway
Cam	Cambrian Railways
Car	Cardiff Railway
CMDP	Cleobury Mortimer & Ditton Priors Light Railway
Cor	Corris Railway (Narrow Gauge)
L&L	Liskeard & Looe Railway
LMM	Llanelly & Mynydd Mawr Railway
MSWJ	Midland & South Western Junction Railway
PM	Powlesland & Mason, Swansea Docks
PT	Port Talbot Railway & Docks Company
RR	Rhymney Railway
SHT	Swansea Harbour Trust Railways
TV	Taff Vale Railway
VoR	Vale of Rheidol Railway (Narrow Gauge)
W&C	Whitland & Cardigan
W&L	Welshpool & Llanfair Light Railway (Narrow Gauge)
WCP	Weston, Clevedon & Portishead Railway

In addition to the above the following non-GWR locomotives should be noted. Four locomotives from the Shropshire & Montgomery Railway (S&M) were taken into BR (Western Region) stock in 1950. Three of these were ex-LNWR 'Coal Engines' and are thus shown in the LMS section, but the other engine is shown here. One service locomotive was purchased from the Ystalyfera Tin Works in 1948. A number of 'R.O.D.' (Railway Operating Division - First World War) locomotives had been purchased by the GWR. These were identical to the LNER (GCR) class 'O4', with the addition of GWR fittings.

Locomotive Numbering

GWR standard locomotives had a rather unusual method of numbering in that it was usually the second digit rather than the first which determined the locomotive class (that is the 100s digit rather than the 1000s). For example the various 2-6-2T locomotives were numbered in the '3100', '4100', '5100', '6100' and '8100' series and the 'Hall' and 'Modified Hall' locomotives were numbered in the '3900', '4900', '5900', '6900' and '7900' series.

In 1946 the GWR had started a limited renumbering scheme for some of the absorbed locomotive classes. This had not been completed by 1948 and locomotives which had not been renumbered at that date are shown in the lists under both their old and new numbers.

Locomotive Classification

GWR locomotives were classified according to class numbers (for example '5700'), while main line passenger locomotives had class names as well (for example '4073 Castle' class). All absorbed engines were classed according to the originating company and a numerical suffix has been added to enable cross-referencing with the appendices.

Notes

Many locomotives were built to GWR designs after 1948 in the following classes: '2251', '4073', '5101', '5700', '6700', '6959', '7400', '7800' and '9400'. In addition two new 'GWR' classes were introduced by BR, the '1500' and '1600' classes.

In 1957 the 'City' class locomotive CITY OF TRURO was returned to running order in order to run special trains. It also worked ordinary service trains during this period. It is listed at the end of the section under Preserved Locomotives.

The three VoR locomotives (7-9) were the only steam locomotives remaining in BR stock at the end of 1968. They remained in BR stock until 1989 when the Vale of Rheidol Railway was sold by BR.

Hurry Riches Rhymney Railway 'R1' class 0-6-2T No 40, fitted with GWR boiler.

Hurry Riches Rhymney Railway 'A' class 0-6-2T No 70, fitted with GWR boiler.

Hurry Riches Taff Vale Railway 'O4' class 0-6-2T No 280 at Swindon Works in May 1949, fitted with original boiler.

YTW 1
0-4-0ST Ystalyfera Tin Works – Peckett

Power Classification: 0F
Introduced: 1900
Designer: Peckett
Company: Ystalyfera Tinplate Works
Weight: 21t 0cwt
Driving Wheel: 3' 2½"
Boiler Pressure: 140psi
Cylinders: Outside 14" x 20"
Tractive Effort: 12120lbf
Valve Gear: Stephenson (slide valves)

This locomotive was built by Peckett in 1900. It was acquired from the Ystalyfera Tinplate Works in 1948 and worked as a service locomotive in South Wales.

Year End Totals: 'YTW' (service) class

'47	'48	'49	'50	'51	'52	'53	'54	'55	'56	'57	'58	'59	'60	'61	'62	'63	'64	'65	'66	'67
	1	1	1	1	1	1														

Number	Built	Renumbered	BR Dates	Scrap	Notes
1 **HERCULES**	00 P		07/48-01/54	03/54	

Cor 3-4
0-4-2ST Corris Railway (Narrow Gauge)

Power Classification: Unclassified
Introduced: a 1878 (as 0-4-0T) rebuilt (as 0-4-2T) in 1900
b 1921
Designer: a Falcon Engine & Carriage Company
b Kerr Stuart
Company: Corris Railway
Weight: a 9t 0cwt
b 8t 0cwt
Driving Wheel: a 2' 6"
b 2' 0"
Boiler Pressure: 160psi
Cylinders: Outside 7" x 12"
Tractive Effort: a 2665lbf
b 3330lbf
Valve Gear: Stephenson (slide valves)
Gauge: 2' 3"

The 2' 3" gauge Corris Railway was acquired by the GWR in 1930. No. 3 was a survivor of the original three locomotives bought by the Corris Railway. Nos. 1 and 2 were condemned in 1921 when No. 4 was bought.

The Corris Railway was completely closed in 1948 when the Dovey River Bridge was washed away and the two locomotives were left stranded at Machynlleth. They were later purchased by the Tal-y-Llyn Railway in May 1951. These locomotives were unique in that they carried the same numbers while owned by four successive Railway Companies (Corris Railway, GWR, BR and Tal-y-Llyn Railway). No. 3 now carries the name SIR HAYDN and No. 4 the name EDWARD THOMAS.

a Original 1878 built engine.

b 1921 built engine.

Year End Totals: 'Cor' class

'47	'48	'49	'50	'51	'52	'53	'54	'55	'56	'57	'58	'59	'60	'61	'62	'63	'64	'65	'66	'67
2																				

Number	Built	Renumbered	BR Dates	Scrap	Notes
3 §	78 FE		-10/48		a
4 §	21 KS		-10/48		b

WCP 5-6
0-6-0T Weston Clevedon & Portishead Stroudley 'Terrier'

Power Classification: 0F
Introduced: 1872-1880 rebuilt with extended smokeboxes by Marsh 1911 onwards
Designer: Stroudley
Company: LBSCR later sold to Weston Clevedon & Portishead Railway
Weight: 28t 5cwt
Driving Wheel: 4' 0"
Boiler Pressure: 150psi
Cylinders: Inside 12" x 20"
Tractive Effort: 7650lbf
Valve Gear: Stephenson (slide valves)

The Weston Clevedon & Portishead Railway was an independent line until it became bankrupt in 1940. The GWR was one of the principal creditors and it took over these two locomotives. They were Stroudley 'Terriers' built at Brighton in 1877 and 1875 as LBSCR Nos. 43 GIPSYHILL and 53 ASHTEAD respectively. They were sold to the WCP in 1925 and 1937 respectively. See SR class 'A1X' for more details. It is interesting to note that if they had not been sold by the Southern Railway then they could have received the BR numbers 32643 and 32653.

Year End Totals: 'WCP' class

'47	'48	'49	'50	'51	'52	'53	'54	'55	'56	'57	'58	'59	'60	'61	'62	'63	'64	'65	'66	'67
2	1	1	1	1	1	1														

Number	Built	Renumbered	BR Dates	Scrap	Notes
5 **PORTISHEAD**	06/77 Bton		-03/54	03/54	
6	12/75 Bton		-01/48	07/48	

VoR 7-9 (1213)
2-6-2T Vale of Rheidol (Narrow Gauge)

Power Classification: Unclassified
Introduced: 1923-24
Designer: Swindon
Company: GWR
Weight: 25t 0cwt
Driving Wheel: 2' 6"
Boiler Pressure: 165psi
Cylinders: Outside 11½" x 17"
Tractive Effort: 10510lbf
Valve Gear: Walschaert (piston valves)
Gauge: 1' 11½"

The two original locomotives for this line were built as No. 1 EDWARD VII and No. 2 PRINCE OF WALES in 1902. They were fitted with Stephenson valve gear. The Vale of Rheidol was amalgamated with the Cambrian Railways in 1913 and then taken over by the GWR in 1922. The two locomotives lost their names in 1915 and became GWR Nos. 1212 and 1213 in 1922.

Two new locomotives, 7 and 8 were built by the GWR to a modified design with Walschaert valve gear in 1923. In 1924 another new engine was built, although it was officially known as a rebuild of 1213 and it took 1213's number. In 1932 1212 was scrapped. 1213 was renumbered to 9 by BR in 1949 and later had the name of the original engine reinstated.

The three locomotives had the distinction of being the only steam locomotives to remain on British Railways after the end of standard gauge steam in 1968. They also became the only steam locomotives to be painted in the standard BR Blue livery and became BR class '98'. Early in 1989 the Vale of Rheidol railway was sold to the Brecon Mountain Railway Company, and the locomotives finally ceased to be part of BR stock.

Year End Totals: 'VoR' class

'47	'48	'49	'50	'51	'52	'53	'54	'55	'56	'57	'58	'59	'60	'61	'62	'63	'64	'65	'66	'67
3	3	3	3	3	3	3	3	3	3	3	3	3	3	3	3	3	3	3	3	3

Number	Built	Renumbered	BR Dates	Scrap	Notes
7 § 06/56➲ **OWAIN GLYNDŴR**	07/23 Sdn		-04/89		
8 § 06/56➲ **LLYWELYN**	07/23 Sdn		-04/89		
9 § 06/56➲ **PRINCE OF WALES**	24 Sdn	03/49 1213	-04/89		

Class continued with 1213

BM [1] 421-428, (11, 332, 504)
0-6-2T Brecon & Merthyr 4ft 6in

For details see 421

Number	Built	Renumbered	BR Dates	Scrap	Notes
11	12/09 RS		-01/49	49	g ➲421

Class continued with 332

CMDP 28-29
0-6-0PT Cleobury Mortimer & Ditton Priors

Power Classification: 2F
Introduced: 1908
Designer: Manning Wardle
Company: Cleobury Mortimer & Ditton Priors
Weight: 39t 18cwt
Driving Wheel: 3' 6"
Boiler Pressure: 160psi
Cylinders: Outside 16" x 22"
Tractive Effort: 18235lbf
Valve Gear: Stephenson (slide valves)

These were the only two locomotives ever owned by the CMDP and they were used for working granite trains from Abdon Clee Quarries. They were named BURWARTON and CLEOBURY. They were originally built in 1908 as saddle tanks and they were rebuilt in 1931 and 1924 respectively as pannier tanks with GWR boilers. Their names were removed when they were rebuilt. They were later fitted with large spark arresting chimneys.

Year End Totals: 'CMDP' class

'47	'48	'49	'50	'51	'52	'53	'54	'55	'56	'57	'58	'59	'60	'61	'62	'63	'64	'65	'66	'67
2	2	2	2	2	2	1														

Number	Built	Renumbered	BR Dates	Scrap	Notes
28	08/08 MW		-11/53	*53*	
29	08/08 MW		-01/54	*54*	

RR [1] between 30 & 46
0-6-2T Rhymney Railway 'R'

Power Classification: 4F
Introduced: 1907-1909
Designer: Hurry Riches, built by R Stephenson
Company: Rhymney Railway
Weight: 66t 19cwt
g 62t 10cwt
Driving Wheel: 4' 6"
Boiler Pressure: 175psi
g 200psi superheated
Cylinders: Inside 18½" x 26"
Tractive Effort: 24510lbf
g 28015lbf
Valve Gear: Stephenson (slide valves)

These Belpaire boilered locomotives were built for the Rhymney Railway in 1907 (30-32) and 1909 (34 and 46). They were later developed into the 'R1' class (see 35-44).

g Two locomotives were fitted with GWR boilers and were superheated. In addition No. 34 was fitted with a high domed cab roof when it was rebuilt in 1934.

Year End Totals: 'RR [1]' class

'47	'48	'49	'50	'51	'52	'53	'54	'55	'56	'57	'58	'59	'60	'61	'62	'63	'64	'65	'66	'67
5	5	3	1																	

Number	Built	Renumbered	BR Dates	Scrap	Notes
30	12/07 RS		-05/49	07/49	
31	12/07 RS		-02/51	*08/51*	g
32	12/07 RS		-02/50	04/50	

Class continued with 34

RR [2] between 33 & 51
0-6-2T Rhymney Railway 'M'

Power Classification: 4F
Introduced: 1904
Designer: Jenkins, built by R Stephenson
Company: Rhymney Railway
Weight: 62t 11cwt
Driving Wheel: 4' 6"
Boiler Pressure: 175psi
Cylinders: Inside 18½" x 26"
Tractive Effort: 24510lbf
Valve Gear: Stephenson (slide valves)

Six of these engines were built for the Rhymney Railway in 1904. Three came into BR stock in 1948 (the first having been withdrawn in 1935). They were fitted with Belpaire fireboxes. The GWR '5600' class was developed from this class.

g No. 47 was rebuilt with a GWR boiler, high domed cab roof and GWR bunker in 1930.

Year End Totals: 'RR [2]' class

'47	'48	'49	'50	'51	'52	'53	'54	'55	'56	'57	'58	'59	'60	'61	'62	'63	'64	'65	'66	'67
3	2	1	1																	

Number	Built	Renumbered	BR Dates	Scrap	Notes
33	09/04 RS		-02/51	*51*	

Class continued with 47

RR [1] between 30 & 46
0-6-2T Rhymney Railway 'R'

Class continued from 32

Number	Built	Renumbered	BR Dates	Scrap	Notes
34	09/09 RS		-11/49	01/50	g

Class continued with 46

RR [3] 35-44
0-6-2T Rhymney Railway 'R1'

Power Classification: 4F
Introduced: 1921
Designer: Hurry Riches
Company: Rhymney Railway
Weight: 66t 0cwt
g 62t 10cwt
Driving Wheel: 4' 6"
Boiler Pressure: 175psi
g 200psi superheated
Cylinders: Inside 18½" x 26"
Tractive Effort: 24510lbf
g 28015lbf
Valve Gear: Stephenson (slide valves)

This was a development of the Rhymney Railway 'R' class of 1907 (see 30), the only difference being the number of boiler tubes and the heating surface. They were built by Hudswell Clarke and Beyer Peacock and were also known as the 'AR' class.

No. 35 finished its days as a stationary boiler at Worcester (1957-58).

g Some engines were rebuilt with GWR boilers and were superheated in 1925-1949.

Year End Totals: 'RR [3]' class

'47	'48	'49	'50	'51	'52	'53	'54	'55	'56	'57	'58	'59	'60	'61	'62	'63	'64	'65	'66	'67
10	10	10	10	10	10	9	9	8	4											

Number	Built	Renumbered	BR Dates	Scrap	Notes
35	07/21 HC		-11/56	02/58	
36	07/21 HC		-10/57	*10/57*	
37	09/21 HC		-09/56	*10/56*	
38	09/21 HC		-10/57	*10/57*	
39	12/21 BP		-08/55	12/55	g
40	12/21 BP		-10/53	53	
					49⇨g
41	12/21 BP		-05/56	*56*	
42	12/21 BP		-09/57	*10/57*	
43	12/21 BP		-02/57	03/57	
44	12/21 BP		-07/56	*08/56*	g

RR [1] between 30 & 46
0-6-2T Rhymney Railway 'R'

Class continued from 34

Number	Built	Renumbered	BR Dates	Scrap	Notes
46	10/09 RS		-07/50	02/51	

RR [2] between 33 & 51
0-6-2T Rhymney Railway 'M'

Class continued from 33

Number	Built	Renumbered	BR Dates	Scrap	Notes
47	06/04 RS		-04/49	07/49	g
51	08/04 RS		-10/48	*48*	

RR [4] 52-75
0-6-2T Rhymney Railway 'A' & 'A1'

Power Classification: 4F
Introduced: 1910-1918
Designer: Hurry Riches
Company: Rhymney Railway
Weight: 64t 3cwt
g 63t 0cwt
Driving Wheel: 4' 4"
Boiler Pressure: 175psi
g 175psi superheated
Cylinders: Inside 18" x 26"
c Inside 18½" x 26"
Tractive Effort: 23870lbf
c 25210lbf
Valve Gear: Stephenson (slide valves)

There were two different varieties in this class when built; the 'A' class with round topped boilers and the 'A1' class (introduced 1914) with Belpaire boilers. Originally 63-70 were 'A1' class, but there was much swapping of boilers between locomotives. From 1929 onwards many locomotives were rebuilt with GWR superheated boilers. By 1948 all the survivors had either 'A1' boilers or GWR boilers.

Although designed for freight work in the Welsh valleys these engines also performed much passenger work. The 'P' class (82-83) was designed as a passenger version of this class.

c No. 55 had larger cylinders.

g Many engines were fitted with GWR superheated boilers. In addition, No. 70 was fitted with a GWR high domed cab.

Year End Totals: 'RR [4]' class

'47	'48	'49	'50	'51	'52	'53	'54	'55	'56	'57	'58	'59	'60	'61	'62	'63	'64	'65	'66	'67
24	21	19	17	15	10	7	4													

Number	Built	Renumbered	BR Dates	Scrap	Notes
52	05/10 RS		-11/49	*03/50*	g
53	05/10 RS		-06/49	09/49	
54	06/10 RS		-04/48	*48*	
55	05/10 RS		-02/53	*02/53*	gc
56	05/10 RS		-09/53	*53*	g
57	04/11 HC		-04/52	*52*	
58	05/11 HC		-09/54	*54*	g
59	06/11 HC		-07/55	*55*	g
60	07/11 HC		-03/51	*08/51*	g
61	08/11 HC		-02/50	*06/50*	
62	09/11 HC		-12/48	01/49	g
63	06/14 HC		-09/52	*09/52*	g
64	07/14 HC		-05/50	*08/50*	
65	08/14 HC		-01/54	*54*	g
66	03/16 HC		-07/55	11/55	g
67	07/16 HC		-09/52	*09/56*	
68	09/18 RS		-06/54	*07/54*	
69	09/18 RS		-07/55	55	g
70	09/18 RS		-07/55	55	g
71	06/10 RS		-12/48	*01/49*	g
72	07/10 RS		-02/52	*52*	
73	07/10 RS		-06/52	*08/52*	
74	07/10 RS		-01/51	02/51	g
75	07/10 RS		-10/53	*03/54*	g

RR [5] 76-77
0-6-2T Rhymney Railway 'P1'

Power Classification: 3P
Introduced: p 1908, rebuilt 1915
1917
Designer: Hurry Riches
Company: Rhymney Railway
Weight: 58t 19cwt
Driving Wheel: 5' 0"
Boiler Pressure: g 175psi superheated
Cylinders: Inside 18" x 26"
Tractive Effort: 20885lbf
Valve Gear: Stephenson (slide valves)

No. 76 was rebuilt in 1915 from a 'P' class engine (see 82-83) with a Belpaire boiler replacing the round topped boiler. No. 77 was built new in 1917 by Hudswell Clarke to the same design. They were later both rebuilt with GWR superheated boilers in 1929-30 and were thus identical with the similarly rebuilt 'P' class (see 82-83).

g Both engines were fitted with GWR superheated boilers.

p Ex-'P' class locomotive.

Year End Totals: 'RR [5]' class

'47	'48	'49	'50	'51	'52	'53	'54	'55	'56	'57	'58	'59	'60	'61	'62	'63	'64	'65	'66	'67
2	2	2	1	1	1															

Number	Built	Renumbered	BR Dates	Scrap	Notes
76	07/09 RS		-11/50	*11/50*	gp
77	04/17 HC		-11/53	03/54	g

RR [6] 78-81
0-6-2T Rhymney Railway 'AP'

Power Classification: 3P
Introduced: 1921
Designer: Hudswell Clarke
Company: Rhymney Railway
Weight: 63t 0cwt
Driving Wheel: 5' 0"
Boiler Pressure: 175psi superheated
Cylinders: Inside 18½" x 26"
Tractive Effort: 22060lbf
Valve Gear: Stephenson (slide valves)

This was the last class of 0-6-2T locomotives to be built for the Rhymney Railway. Four engines were built by Hudswell Clarke in 1921. They were designed for passenger work and were very similar to the 'P1' class (76-77), but they were fitted with larger side tanks and bunkers and a superheated boiler.

g They were all rebuilt with GWR boilers between 1928 and 1949.

Year End Totals: 'RR [6]' class

'47	'48	'49	'50	'51	'52	'53	'54	'55	'56	'57	'58	'59	'60	'61	'62	'63	'64	'65	'66	'67
4	4	4	4	4	4	4	2													

Number	Built	Renumbered	BR Dates	Scrap	Notes
78	08/21 HC		-07/55	12/55	
					49⇨g
79	08/21 HC		-07/55	55	
					49⇨g
80	11/21 HC		-01/54	*54*	g
81	11/21 HC		-05/54	*54*	g

RR [7] 82-83
0-6-2T Rhymney Railway 'P'

Power Classification: 3P
Introduced: 1908
Designer: Hurry Riches
Company: Rhymney Railway
Weight: 58t 19cwt
Driving Wheel: 5' 0"
Boiler Pressure: g 175psi superheated
Cylinders: Inside 18" x 26"
Tractive Effort: 20885lbf
Valve Gear: Stephenson (slide valves)

These engines were designed for passenger work and were built by R Stephenson in 1908 with larger wheels than the similar 'A' class (52-75). They were also fitted with vacuum brakes.

Three locomotives were built, one of which (76) was rebuilt with a Belpaire boiler replacing the round topped boiler to become a 'P1' class engine.

g The two engines were later rebuilt with GWR superheated boilers in 1926 and 1939 and were thus identical with the similarly rebuilt 'P1' class.

Year End Totals: 'RR [7]' class

'47	'48	'49	'50	'51	'52	'53	'54	'55	'56	'57	'58	'59	'60	'61	'62	'63	'64	'65	'66	'67
2	2	2	2	2	2	2	1													

Number	Built	Renumbered	BR Dates	Scrap	Notes
82	06/09 RS		-05/54	06/54	g
83	08/09 RS		-05/55	55	g

RR [8] 90-92 (605)
0-6-0T Rhymney Railway 'S1'

Power Classification: 4F
Introduced: 1920
Designer: Hurry Riches
Company: Rhymney Railway
Weight: 56t 8cwt
Driving Wheel: 4' 4½"
Boiler Pressure: 175psi
Cylinders: Inside 18" x 26"
c Inside 18½" x 26"

Tractive Effort:	23870lbf c 25210lbf
Valve Gear:	Stephenson (slide valves)

These three engines were built in 1920 by Hurry Riches for the Rhymney Railway. They were built with Belpaire boilers and none of them were rebuilt with GWR boilers. Their original GWR numbers were 604-606. The numbers 90-92 were allocated in the 1946 renumbering scheme, 90 and 92 being re-numbered in 1947 and 91 in 1948.

c 90 had larger cylinders.

Year End Totals: 'RR [8]' class

'47	'48	'49	'50	'51	'52	'53	'54	'55	'56	'57	'58	'59	'60	'61	'62	'63	'64	'65	'66	'67
3	3	3	3	3	3	3														

Number	*Built*	*Renumbered*	*BR Dates*	*Scrap*	*Notes*
90	06/20 HC		-05/54	*05/54*	c
91	07/20 HC	03/48 605	-06/54	54	
92	07/20 HC		-06/54	*06/54*	

Class continued with 605

RR [9] 93-96 (610-611)
0-6-0T Rhymney Railway 'S'

Power Classification:	4F
Introduced:	1908
Designer:	Hurry Riches
Company:	Rhymney Railway
Weight:	54t 8cwt
Driving Wheel:	4' 4½"
Boiler Pressure:	175psi
Cylinders:	Inside 18" x 26"
Tractive Effort:	23870lbf
Valve Gear:	Stephenson (slide valves)

These four engines were built by Hudswell Clarke in 1908. They were built with round-topped boilers and rebuilt with GWR taper boilers from 1930 onwards. The original GWR numbers were 608-611, and the numbers 93-95 were allocated under the 1946 renumbering scheme. Only 95 and 96 remained to be renumbered in 1948 and 1949 respectively.

g All four engines were rebuilt with GWR taper boilers.

Year End Totals: 'RR [9]' class

'47	'48	'49	'50	'51	'52	'53	'54	'55	'56	'57	'58	'59	'60	'61	'62	'63	'64	'65	'66	'67
4	4	4	4	4	4	3														

Number	*Built*	*Renumbered*	*BR Dates*	*Scrap*	*Notes*
93	06/08 HC		-05/54	*06/54*	g
94	07/08 HC		-03/54	*06/54*	g
95	07/08 HC	09/48 610	-09/53	*10/53*	g
96	08/08 HC	12/49 611	-04/54	54	g

Class continued with 610

4073 100A1, 111, 4000, 4016, 4032, 4037, 4073-4099, 5000-5099, 7000-7037
4-6-0 GWR Collett 'Castle'

Power Classification:	6P reclassified 7P in 1951
Introduced:	1923-1950
Designer:	Collett
Company:	GWR
Weight:	Loco 79t 17cwt Tender 46t 14cwt
Driving Wheel:	6' 8½"
Boiler Pressure:	225psi superheated
Cylinders:	Four 16" x 26"
Tractive Effort:	31625lbf
Valve Gear:	Inside Walschaert with rocking shafts (piston valves)

Collett's four-cylinder 'Castle' class was a development of Churchward's 'Star' class ('4000' class) with increased dimensions. Several were rebuilt from 'Star' class locomotives (see below). They were one of the most successful locomotive classes ever built in this country (with a total of 171 engines being constructed), and they greatly influenced locomotive design on the other three main Railway Companies. 4073 was exhibited at the British Empire Exhibition at Wembley in 1924 where it was positioned next to the LNER 4-6-2 No. 4472 FLYING SCOTSMAN. This led to trials between the two types in which the 'Castles' proved to be superior engines. The LNER pacifics were altered to take into account the lessons learned.

The '6000' 'King' class locomotives were directly developed from these engines and were very similar in appearance, although slightly larger.

5005 was partially streamlined in 1935. The streamlining was removed in sections from 1937 to 1947.

There was a lot of name changing within this class as detailed below:

4082 WINDSOR CASTLE and 7013 BRISTOL CASTLE swapped identities in February 1952. The original 4082 had once been driven by King George V on a visit to Swindon. It was felt that 4082 would be a suitable locomotive to haul the late King George VI's funeral train in 1952 from London to Windsor. Unfortunately the locomotive was undergoing repair in Swindon at the time and could not be made ready in time. Therefore 7013 took its name and number and the two locomotives kept their new identities.

4009 SHOOTING STAR was renumbered and named 100 A1 LLOYD'S in 1936 (the A1 was on a separate plate on the cabside underneath the 100). 5043-5063 carried names transferred from 'Earl' class locomotives (9000 class), after some of the Earls concerned complained about their names being applied to such antiquated looking locomotives. 5071-5082 were renamed in 1940-1941 after aircraft which had become household names during the Battle of Britain.

Several other locomotives also changed names at various times including 7007 which was renamed GREAT WESTERN as it was the last passenger express steam locomotive to be built by the GWR. The locomotives renamed after 1948 are shown in the locomotive lists.

The former names carried by locomotives which changed names before 1948 are as follows: 4016 KNIGHT OF THE GOLDEN FLEECE, 4037 QUEEN PHILIPPA, 5043 BARBURY CASTLE, 5044 BEVERSTON CASTLE, 5045 BRIDGWATER CASTLE, 5046 CLIFFORD CASTLE, 5047 COMPTON CASTLE, 5048 CRANBROOK CASTLE, 5049 DENBIGH CASTLE, 5050 DEVIZES CASTLE, 5051 DRYSLLWYN CASTLE, 5052 EASTNOR CASTLE, 5053 BISHOP'S CASTLE, 5054 LAMPHEY CASTLE, 5055 LYDFORD CASTLE, 5056 OGMORE CASTLE, 5057 PENRICE CASTLE, 5058 NEWPORT CASTLE, 5059 POWIS CASTLE, 5060 SARUM CASTLE, 5061 SUDELEY CASTLE, 5062 TENBY CASTLE, 5063 THORNBURY CASTLE, 5064 TRETOWER CASTLE, 5065 UPTON CASTLE, 5071 CLIFFORD CASTLE, 5072 COMPTON CASTLE, 5073 CRANBROOK CASTLE, 5074 DENBIGH CASTLE, 5075 DEVIZES CASTLE, 5076 DRYSLLWYN CASTLE, 5077 EASTNOR CASTLE, 5078 LAMPHEY CASTLE, 5079 LYDFORD CASTLE, 5080 OGMORE CASTLE, 5081 PENRICE CASTLE and 5082 POWIS CASTLE. It can be seen from the above list that many of the displaced names were transferred to other locomotives, in some cases more than once. In addition 5086 formerly carried the names MALVERN ABBEY and then SIR ROBERT HORNE, and 5089 carried the name MARGAM ABBEY when they were still 'Star' class locomotives 4066 and 4069.

The following variations were found within the class:

d These engines had double chimneys fitted from 1956 onwards.

3 These engines were fitted with three-row superheaters. (The original locomotives had two-row low-temperature superheaters).

4 These engines were fitted with four-row superheaters.

s A number of engines were rebuilt from 'Star' class locomotives (4000 class). 100 A1 was formerly 4009 and 5083-92 were formerly 4063-72 retaining their original names.

p No. 111 was rebuilt from the GWR Pacific Locomotive THE GREAT BEAR, retaining the same number. It was the first Pacific type locomotive in Britain, and when built in 1908 it was the most powerful express engine in the country. Because of its weight it was restricted to the main line between London and Bristol. This restricted its usefulness and it was reconstructed as a 'Castle' class locomotive in 1924 and renamed VISCOUNT CHURCHILL.

m The 7000 series were fitted with mechanical lubricators.

o Because of the coal crisis after the war some locomotives were temporarily converted for oil burning in 1946 and 1947. They were later reconverted to coal burning (c)

Year End Totals: '4073' class

'47	'48	'49	'50	'51	'52	'53	'54	'55	'56	'57	'58	'59	'60	'61	'62	'63	'64	'65	'66	'67
141	151	161	170	168	168	167	167	167	167	166	165	162	155	152	97	49	12			

Number	*Built*	*Renumbered*	*BR Dates*	*Scrap*	*Notes*
100 A1	04/07 Sdn		-03/50	05/50	so
LLOYD'S					09/48⇨c
111	02/08 Sdn		-06/53	53	p
VISCOUNT CHURCHILL					

Class continued with 4000

Car [1] 155
0-6-2T Cardiff Railway

Power Classification:	4F
Introduced:	1908
Designer:	Ree, built by Kitson
Company:	Cardiff Railway
Weight:	66t 12cwt
Driving Wheel:	4' 6½"
Boiler Pressure:	g 175psi superheated
Cylinders:	Inside 18" x 26"
Tractive Effort:	22990lbf
Valve Gear:	Stephenson (slide valves)

This was the sole survivor of three locomotives, the first of which was withdrawn in 1930. They were built in 1908 by Kitson and Co. for the Cardiff Railway.

g It was fitted with a GWR superheated taper boiler in 1928.

Year End Totals: 'Car [1]' class

'47	'48	'49	'50	'51	'52	'53	'54	'55	'56	'57	'58	'59	'60	'61	'62	'63	'64	'65	'66	'67
1	1	1	1	1	1															

Number	*Built*	*Renumbered*	*BR Dates*	*Scrap*	*Notes*
155	12/08 K		-09/53	*10/53*	g

PT [1] 184
0-6-2T Port Talbot Railway

Power Classification:	Not classified
Introduced:	1898-1899
Designer:	R Stephenson
Company:	Port Talbot Railway
Weight:	56t 0cwt
Driving Wheel:	4' 6"
Boiler Pressure:	g 180psi superheated
Cylinders:	Inside 18" x 26"
Tractive Effort:	23870lbf
Valve Gear:	Stephenson (slide valves)

This was the last surviving locomotive of a batch of eleven engines built by R Stephenson in 1898-1899. The first engine was sold out of service as long ago as 1901.

g Two locomotives of this class were rebuilt with GWR superheated boilers, 184 being rebuilt in 1925.

Year End Totals: 'PT [1]' class

'47	'48	'49	'50	'51	'52	'53	'54	'55	'56	'57	'58	'59	'60	'61	'62	'63	'64	'65	'66	'67
1																				

Number	*Built*	*Renumbered*	*BR Dates*	*Scrap*	*Notes*
184	09/98 RS		-10/48	01/49	g

AD [1] 190
0-6-2ST Alexandra Docks

Power Classification:	Not classified
Introduced:	1908
Designer:	Andrew Barclay
Company:	Alexandra Docks
Weight:	52t 13cwt
Driving Wheel:	4' 3"
Boiler Pressure:	150psi
Cylinders:	Outside 18" x 26"
Tractive Effort:	21060lbf
Valve Gear:	Stephenson (slide valves)

Three locomotives were bought in 1908 by the Alexandra Docks Company in Newport to handle increasing coal exports through the docks. They were designed for heavy shunting. 190 was the last survivor, the first being withdrawn in 1934. It was rebuilt in 1923 with shorter tanks and a GWR smokebox.

Year End Totals: 'AD [1]' class

'47	'48	'49	'50	'51	'52	'53	'54	'55	'56	'57	'58	'59	'60	'61	'62	'63	'64	'65	'66	'67
1																				

Number	Built	Renumbered	BR Dates	Scrap	Notes
190	09/08 AB		-04/48	48	

TV [1] 193-195 (792-794)
0-6-0T Taff Vale 'H'

Power Classification: 1F
Introduced: 1884
Designer: Hurry Riches, built by Kitson
Company: Taff Vale Railway
Weight: 44t 15cwt
Driving Wheel: 5' 3"
Boiler Pressure: 140psi
Cylinders: Inside 17½ x 26"
Tractive Effort: 15040lbf
Valve Gear: Stephenson (slide valves)

These locomotives were built specifically for working the Pwllyrhebog incline at Clydach Vale Colliery which included a section of 1 in 13. The incline was worked by these engines and a cable which counterbalanced ascending (empty) and descending (full) trains.

The locomotives had a tapered inner firebox and boiler to allow plenty of water over the firebox crown while working on the incline. A large dome was fitted over the firebox to ensure a good quantity of dry steam. They remained in virtually original form throughout their lives and were withdrawn from 1951 when working over the incline was discontinued.

They were renumbered as part of the 1946 GWR renumbering scheme.

193 and 195 were sold into industrial service where they survived until January 1960 and April 1957 respectively.

Year End Totals: 'TV [1]' class

'47	'48	'49	'50	'51	'52	'53	'54	'55	'56	'57	'58	'59	'60	'61	'62	'63	'64	'65	'66	'67
3	3	3	3	2	1															

Number	Built	Renumbered	BR Dates	Scrap	Notes
193	84 K	06/48 792	-02/52	01/60	
194	84 K	09/48 793	-11/53	03/54	
195	84 K	02/49 794	-11/51	04/57	

Class continued with 792

BR [1] 198, 212-213, 231
0-6-2T Barry Railway 'B'

Power Classification: 3F
Introduced: 1888-1890
Designer: Hosgood, built by Sharp Stewart
Company: Barry Railway
Weight: 50t 2cwt
Driving Wheel: 4' 3"
Boiler Pressure: g 150 psi
Cylinders: Inside 18" x 26"
Tractive Effort: 21060lbf
Valve Gear: Stephenson (slide valves)

This was a larger version of the extinct 'A' class. Twenty-five engines were built in 1888-1890, and the first was withdrawn in 1922. The 'B1' class (see 238) was an enlarged version of these engines.

g The survivors were rebuilt with GWR boilers from 1924 onwards.

Year End Totals: 'BR [1]' class

'47	'48	'49	'50	'51	'52	'53	'54	'55	'56	'57	'58	'59	'60	'61	'62	'63	'64	'65	'66	'67
4	2																			

Number	Built	Renumbered	BR Dates	Scrap	Notes
198	12/88 SS		-01/48	04/48	g

Class continued with 212

TV [2] between 200 & 299 (301 & 420)
0-6-2T Taff Vale 'O4'

Power Classification: 4F
Introduced: 1907-1910
Designer: Hurry Riches
Company: Taff Vale Railway
Weight: 65t 5cwt
g 61t 0cwt
Driving Wheel: 4' 6½"
Boiler Pressure: 175psi
g 175psi superheated
Cylinders: Inside 17½" x 26"
Tractive Effort: 21730lbf
Valve Gear: Stephenson (slide valves)

Mr Hurry Riches built a succession of 0-6-2Ts for the Taff Vale Railway including this 'O4' class and the earlier 'O3' class (410-411). These were built in 1907-1910 by Manning Wardle, Beyer Peacock and Vulcan Foundry. Some locomotives had rounded tops to the tanks while others were rebuilt with square tops.

The locomotives numbered in the 200-220 series were renumbered as part of the 1946 GWR renumbering scheme. Those renumbered before 1948 were 200 (300), 204 (311), 205 (313), 207 (315), 209 (318) and 210 (319). 201, 202 and 206 were never renumbered and all the rest received their new numbers in BR days.

g Thirty-six of the forty-one engines in this class were rebuilt with GWR boilers.

Year End Totals: 'TV [2]' class

'47	'48	'49	'50	'51	'52	'53	'54	'55	'56	'57	'58	'59	'60	'61	'62	'63	'64	'65	'66	'67
41	37	30	25	19	12	10	7													

Number	Built	Renumbered	BR Dates	Scrap	Notes
200	07/08 BP		-07/48	48	g
201	07/08 BP	301	-12/48	01/49	g
202	07/08 BP	302	-04/48	04/48	
203	09/10 VF	12/48 310	-01/52	01/53	g
204	09/10 VF		-07/55	55	g
205	09/10 VF		-07/54	07/56	g
206	08/08 BP	314	-12/49	03/50	g
207	09/10 BP		-11/52	08/53	g
208	09/10 BP	09/48 317	-07/55	11/55	g
209	09/10 BP		-08/52	09/52	g
210	09/10 BP		-03/55	04/55	g
211	09/10 BP	05/48 320	-05/55	04/56	g

Class continued with 215

BR [1] 198, 212-213, 231
0-6-2T Barry Railway 'B'

Class continued from 198

Number	Built	Renumbered	BR Dates	Scrap	Notes
212	05/89 SS		-07/48	08/49	g
213	05/89 SS		-01/49	08/49	g

Class continued with 231

TV [2] between 200 & 299 (301 & 420)
0-6-2T Taff Vale 'O4'

Class continued from 211

Number	Built	Renumbered	BR Dates	Scrap	Notes
215	09/10 BP	04/48 321	-07/55	55	g
216	09/10 BP	03/48 324	-01/55	02/55	g
217	09/10 BP	04/49 333	-09/52	10/52	g
218	09/10 BP	01/50 409	-12/52	01/53	g
219	08/10 VF	05/48 414	-06/51	11/51	g
220	08/07 MW	11/48 420	-04/51	08/51	g

Class continued with 236

BR [1] 198, 212-213, 231
0-6-2T Barry Railway 'B'

Class continued from 213

Number	Built	Renumbered	BR Dates	Scrap	Notes
231	02/90 SS		-11/49	01/50	g

TV [2] between 200 & 299 (301 & 420)
0-6-2T Taff Vale 'O4'

Class continued from 220

Number	Built	Renumbered	BR Dates	Scrap	Notes
236	06/08 BP		-01/53	02/53	g

Class continued with 278

BR [2] 238-277
0-6-2T Barry Railway 'B1'

Power Classification: 3F
Introduced: 1890-1900
Designer: Hosgood, built by Sharp Stewart and Vulcan Foundry
Company: Barry Railway
Weight: 55t 3cwt
g 53t 9cwt
Driving Wheel: 4' 3"
Boiler Pressure: 160psi
g 150psi
Cylinders: Inside 17½" x 26"
Tractive Effort: 20825lbf
g 19525lbf
Valve Gear: Stephenson (slide valves)

This was a larger version of the 'B' class (see 198) with increased water and coal capacities. Forty-two locomotives were built in 1890-1900, the first of which was withdrawn in 1932. Several of the class survived for a while after withdrawal as works shunters at Swindon before being broken up.

g Several were rebuilt with GWR boilers from 1924 onwards.

Year End Totals: 'BR [2]' class

'47	'48	'49	'50	'51	'52	'53	'54	'55	'56	'57	'58	'59	'60	'61	'62	'63	'64	'65	'66	'67
20	14	9	7																	

Number	Built	Renumbered	BR Dates	Scrap	Notes
238	07/90 SS		-06/48	48	
240	07/90 SS		-04/51	12/52	g
246	03/92 VF		-01/49	06/50	
248	03/92 VF		-07/48	48	g
258	12/94 SS		-11/49	01/53	
259	12/94 SS		-08/48	10/48	
261	05/00 SS		-08/48	48	g
262	05/00 SS		-03/50	05/50	g
263	06/00 SS		-04/51	11/51	g
265	06/00 SS		-11/49	01/50	g
267	06/00 SS		-04/51	01/52	g
268	06/00 SS		-04/48	48	g
269	06/00 SS		-10/49	05/50	g
270	06/00 SS		-05/51	05/51	g
271	06/00 SS		-05/51	10/52	g
272	06/00 SS		-03/50	05/50	g
274	03/00 SF		-04/51	05/51	g
275	04/00 SF		-04/48	48	g
276	04/00 SF		-04/51	04/51	g
277	04/00 SF		-04/49	07/49	

TV [2] between 200 & 299 (301 & 420)
0-6-2T Taff Vale 'O4'

Class continued from 236

Number	Built	Renumbered	BR Dates	Scrap	Notes
278	07/10 VF		-05/51	51	g
279	07/10 VF		-05/54	02/55	g
280	07/08 BP		-05/49	07/49	
281	08/10 VF		-08/50	10/50	g
282	07/08 BP		-06/54	54	g
283	08/10 VF		-03/49	49	
284	08/10 VF		-11/52	02/53	g
285	04/07 MW		-08/53	10/57	g
286	06/08 BP		-10/50	11/50	g
287	04/07 MW		-12/49	02/50	g
288	09/10 VF		-03/50	50	g
289	07/08 BP		-08/49	10/49	
290	10/10 BP		-07/55	55	g
291	07/08 BP		-01/50	03/50	g
292	07/08 BP		-04/52	52	g
293	06/07 MW		-07/51	51	g
294	07/07 MW		-07/50	02/51	g
295	07/07 MW		-06/51	51	g
296	09/07 MW		-09/49	11/49	
297	07/08 BP		-12/49	08/50	g
298	07/08 BP		-07/48	07/49	g
299	07/08 BP		-06/51	51	g

Number	Built	Renumbered	BR Dates	Scrap	Notes
301	07/08 BP		-12/48	01/49	g ➲201
302	07/08 BP		-04/48	04/48	➲202

Class continued with 310

TV [3] between 303 & 399 (402 & 440)
0-6-2T Taff Vale 'A'

Power Classification:	4P
Introduced:	1914-1921
Designer:	Cameron, built by Hawthorn Leslie, North British and Vulcan Foundry
Company:	Taff Vale Railway
Weight:	65t 14cwt
Driving Wheel:	5' 3"
Boiler Pressure:	200psi superheated a 175psi superheated
Cylinders:	Inside 17½" x 26" a Inside 18½" x 26"
Tractive Effort:	21480lbf a 21010lbf
Valve Gear:	Stephenson (slide valves)

After Mr Hurry Richards death in 1911, J Cameron brought out some more 0-6-2Ts of a similar design to the Taff Vale class 'O4' (see 200). These were known as the 'A' class and they were designed for passenger work and had larger wheels. Some locomotives had rounded tops to the tanks while others were rebuilt with square tops.

The engines numbered in the 303-316 series were renumbered as part of the GWR renumbering scheme. Those renumbered before 1948 were 303 (401) and 305 (403).

g They were all rebuilt with GWR boilers from 1924 to 1931.

a Some of the class varied in cylinder sizes and boiler pressure.

Year End Totals: 'TV [3]' class

'47	'48	'49	'50	'51	'52	'53	'54	'55	'56	'57	'58	'59	'60	'61	'62	'63	'64	'65	'66	'67
58	58	58	58	58	57	55	52	40	15											

Number	Built	Renumbered	BR Dates	Scrap	Notes
303	02/21 HL		-05/56	09/56	g
304	02/21 HL	03/48 402	-08/57	08/57	g
305	02/21 HL		-05/57	57	g
306	12/21 VF	07/49 404	-04/56	04/56	g
307	12/21 VF	07/49 406	-03/56	04/56	ga
308	12/21 VF	12/48 408	-12/55	01/56	ga
309	10/14 HL	06/49 438	-02/53	04/55	ga

Class continued with 312

TV [2] between 200 & 299 (301 & 420)
0-6-2T Taff Vale 'O4'

Class continued from 302

Number	Built	Renumbered	BR Dates	Scrap	Notes
310	09/10 VF		-01/52	01/53	g 12/48➲203

Class continued with 314

TV [3] between 303 & 399 (402 & 440)
0-6-2T Taff Vale 'A'

Class continued from 309

Number	Built	Renumbered	BR Dates	Scrap	Notes
312	08/15 NB	09/49 439	-06/56	08/56	g

Class continued with 316

TV [2] between 200 & 299 (301 & 420)
0-6-2T Taff Vale 'O4'

Class continued from 310

Number	Built	Renumbered	BR Dates	Scrap	Notes
314	08/08 BP		-12/49	03/50	g ➲206

Class continued with 317

TV [3] between 303 & 399 (402 & 440)
0-6-2T Taff Vale 'A'

Class continued from 312

Number	Built	Renumbered	BR Dates	Scrap	Notes
316	08/15 NB	06/50 440	-07/56	08/56	g

Class continued with 322

TV [2] between 200 & 299 (301 & 420)
0-6-2T Taff Vale 'O4'

Class continued from 314

Number	Built	Renumbered	BR Dates	Scrap	Notes
317	09/10 BP		-07/55	11/55	g 09/48➲208
320	09/10 BP		-05/55	04/56	g 05/48➲211
321	09/10 BP		-07/55	55	g 04/48➲215

Class continued with 324

TV [3] between 303 & 399 (402 & 440)
0-6-2T Taff Vale 'A'

Class continued from 316

Number	Built	Renumbered	BR Dates	Scrap	Notes
322	01/15 HL		-09/54	11/55	ga

Class continued with 335

TV [2] between 200 & 299 (301 & 420)
0-6-2T Taff Vale 'O4'

Class continued from 321

Number	Built	Renumbered	BR Dates	Scrap	Notes
324	09/10 BP		-01/55	02/55	g 03/48➲216

Class continued with 333

BM [1] 421-428, (11, 332, 504)
0-6-2T Brecon & Merthyr 4ft 6in

Class continued from 11

Number	Built	Renumbered	BR Dates	Scrap	Notes
332	12/09 RS		-12/49	06/50	g ➲423

Class continued with 421

TV [2] between 200 & 299 (301 & 420)
0-6-2T Taff Vale 'O4'

Class continued from 324

Number	Built	Renumbered	BR Dates	Scrap	Notes
333	09/10 BP		-09/52	10/52	g 04/49➲217

Class continued with 409

TV [3] between 303 & 399 (402 & 440)
0-6-2T Taff Vale 'A'

Class continued from 322

Number	Built	Renumbered	BR Dates	Scrap	Notes
335	11/14 HL		-03/54	06/54	ga
337	12/14 HL		-02/53	12/54	ga
343	12/14 HL		-10/55	11/55	g
344	12/14 HL		-11/52	08/53	ga
345	05/20 HL		-08/55	04/56	g
346	08/15 NB		-10/55	11/55	g
347	12/21 VF		-12/56	05/57	g
348	12/21 VF		-05/56	11/56	g
349	12/21 VF		-03/57	06/57	ga
351	12/21 VF		-07/56	11/56	g
352	08/15 NB		-03/55	06/55	ga
356	08/15 NB		-01/55	06/55	g
357	08/15 NB		-01/56	02/56	g

Class continued with 360

LMM [1] 359
0-6-0ST Llanelly & Mynydd Mawr

Power Classification:	1F
Introduced:	1917
Designer:	Hudswell Clarke
Company:	Llanelly & Mynydd Mawr Railway
Weight:	34t 9cwt
Driving Wheel:	3' 7½"
Boiler Pressure:	160psi
Cylinders:	Outside 15" x 22"
Tractive Effort:	15474lbf
Valve Gear:	Stephenson (slide valves)

This locomotive was acquired from the Llanelly and Mynydd Mawr Railway. It was built by Hudswell Clarke in 1917. It was reboilered by the GWR and was fitted with a warning bell on the top of the tank.

Year End Totals: 'LMM [1]' class

'47	'48	'49	'50	'51	'52	'53	'54	'55	'56	'57	'58	'59	'60	'61	'62	'63	'64	'65	'66	'67
1	1	1	1	1	1	1														

Number	Built	Renumbered	BR Dates	Scrap	Notes
359 HILDA	06/17 HC		-01/54	54	

TV [3] between 303 & 399 (402 & 440)
0-6-2T Taff Vale 'A'

Class continued from 357

Number	Built	Renumbered	BR Dates	Scrap	Notes
360	07/16 VF		-02/55	55	ga
361	07/16 VF		-01/57	07/57	ga
362	07/16 VF		-05/56	56	g
364	07/16 VF		-03/57	08/57	g
365	07/16 VF		-10/55	02/56	g
366	08/16 VF		-10/55	11/55	ga
367	02/19 NW		-03/56	04/56	g
368	05/20 HL		-10/56	56	g
370	02/19 NW		-08/57	08/57	ga
371	03/19 NW		-01/55	04/55	ga
372	03/19 NW		-02/55	55	ga
373	04/19 NW		-08/57	02/58	g
374	04/19 NW		-08/55	02/56	g
375	05/20 HL		-11/54	04/55	g
376	05/20 HL		-01/57	08/57	g
377	05/19 NW		-05/56	08/56	g
378	05/19 NW		-12/56	05/57	g
379	05/19 NW		-02/56	04/56	g
380	07/19 NW		-10/56	11/56	g
381	07/19 NW		-08/57	08/57	g
382	07/19 NW		-04/56	09/56	g
383	05/20 HL		-08/57	08/57	g
384	06/20 HL		-02/56	56	g
385	06/20 HL		-04/57	05/57	g
386	06/20 HL		-04/56	06/56	g
387	07/20 HL		-11/56	11/56	ga
388	08/20 HL		-10/56	02/57	g
389	09/20 HL		-01/56	04/56	g
390	09/20 HL		-08/57	10/57	g
391	10/20 HL		-09/56	11/56	g
393	11/20 HL		-05/57	57	g
394	12/20 HL		-07/56	02/59	g
397	12/20 HL		-04/57	08/57	g
398	01/21 HL		-08/57	10/57	g
399	01/21 HL		-09/56	09/56	g
402	02/21 HL		-08/57	08/57	g 03/48➲304
404	12/21 VF		-04/56	04/56	g 07/49➲306
406	12/21 VF		-03/56	04/56	ga 07/49➲307
408	12/21 VF		-12/55	01/56	ga 12/48➲308

Class continued with 438

Cameron Taff Vale Railway 'A' class 0-6-2T No 309 at Cardiff Cathays in June 1949, fitted with GWR boiler.

Jones Cambrian Railways '15' class 0-6-0 No 849 at Dovey Junction in May 1953.

GWR Collett '1101' class 0-4-0T dock shunter No 1105 at Swansea East Dock.

Midland & South Western Junction Railway 2-4-0 No 1334 at Reading in March 1952.

TV [2] between 200 & 299 (301 & 420)
0-6-2T Taff Vale 'O4'

Class continued from 333

Number	Built	Renumbered	BR Dates	Scrap	Notes
409	09/10 BP		-12/52	01/53	g 01/50➲218

Class continued with 414

TV [4] 410-411
0-6-2T Taff Vale 'O3'

Power Classification: Not classified
Introduced: 1902-1905
Designer: Hurry Riches, built by Kitson
Company: Taff Vale Railway
Weight: 63t 0cwt
Driving Wheel: 4' 6½"
Boiler Pressure: g 160psi
Cylinders: Inside 17½" x 26"
Tractive Effort: 19870lbf
Valve Gear: Stephenson (slide valves)

This class was developed from the 'O2' class of 1899. These were the last two survivors (built in 1904) of a class of fifteen locomotives, the first withdrawn in 1928. The 'O4' class (see 200) was a later version of these engines.

g They were both rebuilt with GWR boilers in 1930. In addition 410 received GWR side tanks, bunker and a high domed cab roof.

Year End Totals: 'TV [4]' class

'47	'48	'49	'50	'51	'52	'53	'54	'55	'56	'57	'58	'59	'60	'61	'62	'63	'64	'65	'66	'67
2																				

Number	Built	Renumbered	BR Dates	Scrap	Notes
410	01/04 K		-03/48	03/48	g
411	02/04 K		-02/48	48	g

TV [2] between 200 & 299 (301 & 420)
0-6-2T Taff Vale 'O4'

Class continued from 409

Number	Built	Renumbered	BR Dates	Scrap	Notes
414	08/10 VF		-06/51	11/51	g 05/48➲219
420	08/07 MW		-04/51	08/51	g 11/48➲220

BM [1] 421-428, (11, 332, 504)
0-6-2T Brecon & Merthyr 4ft 6in

Power Classification: 4F
Introduced: 1909-1914
Designer: Dunbar, built by R Stephenson
Company: Brecon & Merthyr
Weight: 66t 19cwt
g 62t 10cwt
Driving Wheel: 4' 6"
Boiler Pressure: 175psi
s 175psi superheated
Cylinders: Inside 18½" x 26"
Tractive Effort: 24520lbf
Valve Gear: Stephenson (slide valves)

This was the B&M '36' class which was based on the Rhymney Railway 'R' class (see 30) with round topped fireboxes. Eight engines were built by R Stephenson in 1909-1914. The locomotives carried the numbers 11, 21, 332, 504, 698, 888, 1084 and 1113 before the 1946 GWR renumbering scheme. Not all received their new numbers and 1084 (allocated 427) was withdrawn in 1947.

g Some locomotives were rebuilt with GWR taper boilers between 1924 and 1941.

s Two of the GWR boiler fitted locomotives were superheated.

Year End Totals: 'BM [1]' class

'47	'48	'49	'50	'51	'52	'53	'54	'55	'56	'57	'58	'59	'60	'61	'62	'63	'64	'65	'66	'67
7	6	4	1																	

Class continued from 332

Number	Built	Renumbered	BR Dates	Scrap	Notes
421	12/09 RS	11	-01/49	49	g
422	12/09 RS		-06/50	10/50	gs
423	12/09 RS	332	-12/49	06/50	g
424	01/10 RS	504	-01/48	48	
425	03/14 RS		-03/51	05/51	
426	03/14 RS		-03/50	50	gs
428	04/14 RS		-08/50	10/50	

Class continued with 504

BM [2] 431-436 (1372-1375, 1668-1670)
0-6-2T Brecon & Merthyr 5ft

Power Classification: 3F
Introduced: 1915-1921
Designer: Dunbar, built by R Stephenson
Company: Brecon & Merthyr
Weight: 57t 12cwt
g 59t 5cwt
Driving Wheel: 5' 0"
Boiler Pressure: 175psi
g 175psi superheated
Cylinders: Inside 18" x 26"
Tractive Effort: 20885lbf
Valve Gear: Stephenson (slide valves)

These engines were similar to the earlier B&M 0-6-2T class (421-428) but they were fitted with larger wheels. Six engines were built in 1915-1921 by R Stephenson.

The locomotives were renumbered under the 1946 GWR scheme. 433 (1374) was renumbered before 1948.

g Most of the locomotives were rebuilt with GWR superheated boilers between 1927 and 1936.

r 436 (1670) was rebuilt by the GWR with an ex-Rhymney Railway boiler.

Year End Totals: 'BM [2]' class

'47	'48	'49	'50	'51	'52	'53	'54	'55	'56	'57	'58	'59	'60	'61	'62	'63	'64	'65	'66	'67
6	6	6	6	5	5	2														

Number	Built	Renumbered	BR Dates	Scrap	Notes
431	08/15 RS	07/49 1372	-10/53	53	g
432	09/15 RS	11/48 1373	-05/53	53	g
433	09/15 RS		-02/51	51	g
434	02/21 RS	04/49 1375	-09/53	04/54	g
435	02/21 RS	04/50 1668	-01/54	54	g
436	02/21 RS	10/49 1670	-01/54	10/54	r

Class continued with 1372

TV [3] between 303 & 399 (402 & 440)
0-6-2T Taff Vale 'A'

Class continued from 408

Number	Built	Renumbered	BR Dates	Scrap	Notes
438	10/14 HL		-02/53	04/55	ga 06/49➲309
439	08/15 NB		-06/56	08/56	g 09/49➲312
440	08/15 NB		-07/56	08/56	g 06/50➲316

BM [1] 421-428, (11, 332, 504)
0-6-2T Brecon & Merthyr 4ft 6in

Class continued from 428

Number	Built	Renumbered	BR Dates	Scrap	Notes
504	01/10 RS		-01/48	48	➲424

RR [8] 90-92 (605)
0-6-0T Rhymney Railway 'S1'

Class continued from 92

Number	Built	Renumbered	BR Dates	Scrap	Notes
605	07/20 HC		-06/54	54	03/48➲91

RR [9] 93-96 (610-611)
0-6-0T Rhymney Railway 'S'

Class continued from 92

Number	Built	Renumbered	BR Dates	Scrap	Notes
610	07/08 HC		-09/53	10/53	g 09/48➲95
611	08/08 HC		-04/54	54	g 12/49➲96

AD [2] 666-667
0-6-0T Alexandra Docks

Power Classification: 3F
Introduced: 1917
Designer: Kerr Stuart
Company: ROD sold to Alexandra Docks
Weight: 50t 0cwt
Driving Wheel: 4' 0"
Boiler Pressure: 160psi
Cylinders: Outside 17" x 24"
Tractive Effort: 19650lbf
Valve Gear: Stephenson (slide valves)

These locomotives were built during the First World War for the ROD (the War Department) and numbered ROD 604 and 602. They were purchased in 1919 by the Alexandra Docks company.

Year End Totals: 'AD [2]' class

'47	'48	'49	'50	'51	'52	'53	'54	'55	'56	'57	'58	'59	'60	'61	'62	'63	'64	'65	'66	'67
2	2	2	2	2	2	2	1													

Number	Built	Renumbered	BR Dates	Scrap	Notes
666	08/17 KS		-04/55	04/55	
667	08/17 KS		-11/54	54	

AD [3] 680
0-6-0ST Alexandra Docks - Peckett

Power Classification: Not classified
Introduced: 1886-1890
Designer: Peckett
Company: Alexandra Docks
Weight: 26t 17cwt
Driving Wheel: 3' 6"
Boiler Pressure: 140psi
Cylinders: Outside 14" x 20"
Tractive Effort: 11105lbf
Valve Gear: Stephenson (slide valves)

This was the survivor of two locomotives built by Peckett for the Alexandra Docks Railway in 1886 and 1890. The other engine was sold to a colliery in 1929, where it survived until 1953. They were very small locomotives measuring only 23ft. over the buffers.

Year End Totals: 'AD [3]' class

'47	'48	'49	'50	'51	'52	'53	'54	'55	'56	'57	'58	'59	'60	'61	'62	'63	'64	'65	'66	'67
1																				

Number	Built	Renumbered	BR Dates	Scrap	Notes
680	01/86 P		-12/48	12/48	

Car [2] 681-684
0-6-0PT Cardiff Railway

Power Classification: 4F
Introduced: 1920
Designer: Hope, built by Hudswell Clarke
Company: Cardiff Railway
Weight: 45t 6cwt
Driving Wheel: 4' 1½"
Boiler Pressure: 165psi
Cylinders: Inside 18" x 24"
Tractive Effort: 22030lbf
Valve Gear: Stephenson (slide valves)

These were the last engines to be delivered to the Cardiff Railway before its absorption into the GWR. Four engines were built as saddle tanks in 1920, and they were converted to pannier tanks by the GWR between 1926 and 1939.

Year End Totals: 'Car [2]' class

'47	'48	'49	'50	'51	'52	'53	'54	'55	'56	'57	'58	'59	'60	'61	'62	'63	'64	'65	'66	'67
4	4	4	4	4	4	3	1													

Number	Built	Renumbered	BR Dates	Scrap	Notes
681	02/20 HC		-02/55	*06/55*	
682	02/20 HC		-10/53	*04/54*	
683	03/20 HC		-12/54	*02/56*	
684	03/20 HC		-05/54	04/55	

PM [1] 1150-1152 (696, 779, 935)
0-4-0ST Powlesland & Mason - Peckett

For details see 1150

Number	Built	Renumbered	BR Dates	Scrap	Notes
696	07/13 P		-11/52	*09/56* 12/51➲1150	

Class continued with 779

SHT [1] 1140 (701)
0-4-0ST Swansea Harbour Trust - Barclay

For details see 1140

Number	Built	Renumbered	BR Dates	Scrap	Notes
701	04/05 AB		-05/58	07/58 06/48➲1140	

Class continued with 1140

PM [1] 1150-1152 (696, 779, 935)
0-4-0ST Powlesland & Mason - Peckett

Class continued from 696

Number	Built	Renumbered	BR Dates	Scrap	Notes
779	09/16 P		-08/63	04/65 10/50➲1151	

Class continued with 935

BR [3] 783-784
0-6-0T Barry Railway 'E'

Power Classification: 0F
Introduced: 1889-1891
Designer: Hosgood, built by Hudswell Clarke
Company: Barry Railway
Weight: 33t 7cwt
Driving Wheel: 3' 6½"
Boiler Pressure: 150psi
Cylinders: Inside 14" x 20"
Tractive Effort: 11760lbf
Valve Gear: Stephenson (slide valves)

These were the survivors of five small tank engines built by Hudswell Clarke in 1889-1891 for working the breakwater sidings at Barry Island. The first was withdrawn in 1932. 781 and 785 were rebuilt to 0-4-2Ts by removing the rear connecting rods and they were used for auto-train working. They were both withdrawn before 1948.

g 783 was reboilered by the GWR and fitted with a larger bunker and other detail differences.

Year End Totals: 'BR [3]' class

'47	'48	'49	'50	'51	'52	'53	'54	'55	'56	'57	'58	'59	'60	'61	'62	'63	'64	'65	'66	'67
2	1																			

Number	Built	Renumbered	BR Dates	Scrap	Notes
783	01/90 HC		-08/48	*01/49*	g
784	01/90 HC		-08/49	10/49	

TV [1] 193-195 (792-794)
0-6-0T Taff Vale 'H'

Class continued from 195

Number	Built	Renumbered	BR Dates	Scrap	Notes
792	84 K		-02/52	01/60 06/48➲193	
793	84 K		-11/53	*03/54* 09/48➲194	
794	84 K		-11/51	04/57 02/49➲195	

LMM [2] 803
0-6-0T Llanelly & Mynydd Mawr

Power Classification: 2F
Introduced: 1911
Designer: Hudswell Clarke
Company: Llanelly & Mynydd Mawr
Weight: 40t 12cwt
Driving Wheel: 4' 0"
Boiler Pressure: 160psi
Cylinders: Inside 16" x 24"
Tractive Effort: 17410lbf
Valve Gear: Stephenson (slide valves)

This engine was the only one of its class and it was built by Hudswell Clarke in 1911. It was originally named RAVELSTON. It was rebuilt in 1927 with a renovated boiler, Belpaire firebox, GWR smokebox and extended bunker, and the name was removed at the same time.

Year End Totals: 'LMM [2]' class

'47	'48	'49	'50	'51	'52	'53	'54	'55	'56	'57	'58	'59	'60	'61	'62	'63	'64	'65	'66	'67
1	1	1	1																	

Number	Built	Renumbered	BR Dates	Scrap	Notes
803	01/11 HC		-03/51	*51*	

W&L 822-823
0-6-0T Welshpool & Llanfair (Narrow Gauge)

Power Classification: Unclassified
Introduced: 1902
Designer: Beyer Peacock
Company: Welshpool & Llanfair Railway
Weight: 19t 18cwt
Driving Wheel: 2' 9"
Boiler Pressure: 150psi
Cylinders: Outside 11½" x 16"
Tractive Effort: 8175lbf
Valve Gear: Walschaert (slide valves)
Gauge: 2' 6"

These two locomotives were originally Nos. 1 and 2 of the Welshpool & Llanfair narrow gauge railway. No. 2 was originally named THE COUNTESS. The railway was taken over by the Cambrian Railways and then by the GWR and the locomotives were renumbered 822 and 823. They were both rebuilt in 1930 with new boilers.

Passenger working on the Welshpool & Llanfair Railway ceased in 1931, but freight working continued until 1956. The locomotive nameplates were removed about 1952 and latterly only 822 had been in use. The locomotives were then put into store. The line was reopened in 1963 by the Welshpool & Llanfair Light Railway Preservation Company Limited, and the two locomotives are now working again as Nos. 1 and 2.

Year End Totals: 'W&L' class

'47	'48	'49	'50	'51	'52	'53	'54	'55	'56	'57	'58	'59	'60	'61	'62	'63	'64	'65	'66	'67
2	2	2	2	2	2	2	2	2	2	2	2	2	2	1						

Number	Built	Renumbered	BR Dates	Scrap	Notes
822 § THE EARL	09/02 BP		-08/61		
823 § COUNTESS	09/02 BP		-07/62		

Cam [1] 844-896
0-6-0 Cambrian Railways '15'

Power Classification: 2MT
Introduced: 1903-1919
Designer: Jones, built by R Stephenson and Beyer Peacock
Company: Cambrian Railways
Weight: Loco 38t 17cwt, Tender 31t 13cwt
Driving Wheel: 5' 1½"
Boiler Pressure: 160psi some superheated
Cylinders: Inside 18" x 26"
Tractive Effort: 18625lbf
Valve Gear: Stephenson (slide valves)

These were the survivors of the fifteen Cambrian Railways 'Belpaire boilered goods engines'. They closely resembled the GWR 'Dean Goods' class ('2301'). They were built in 1903-1919 and were also known as class '89'. The first locomotive was withdrawn in 1922.

Year End Totals: 'Cam [1]' class

'47	'48	'49	'50	'51	'52	'53	'54	'55	'56	'57	'58	'59	'60	'61	'62	'63	'64	'65	'66	'67
11	11	11	11	11	9	5														

Number	Built	Renumbered	BR Dates	Scrap	Notes
844	10/18 BP		-08/54	*54*	
849	11/18 BP		-09/54	*10/54*	
855	05/19 BP		-09/54	*54*	
864	05/19 BP		-11/52	*52*	
873	06/19 BP		-03/54	*54*	
887	04/03 RS		-11/52	*52*	
892	06/03 RS		-04/53	*53*	
893	03/08 BP		-02/53	*53*	
894	03/08 BP		-04/53	*53*	
895	03/08 BP		-09/54	*54*	
896	03/08 BP		-04/53	*53*	

1854 906-907, between 1705 & 1900
0-6-0PT GWR Dean (Swindon) 4ft 7½in

Power Classification: 3F
Introduced: 1890-1895 embodying parts of earlier engines
Designer: Dean, built at Swindon
Company: GWR
Weight: 46t 13cwt
Driving Wheel: 4' 7½"
Boiler Pressure: 180psi
Cylinders: Inside 17" x 24"
Tractive Effort: 19120lbf
Valve Gear: Stephenson (slide valves)

Refer to the Historical Survey of GWR Pannier Tank Engines at the end of this section for more details of this class.

This class was also known as the '1701' class and originally consisted of 120 locomotives the first being withdrawn in 1928. 1710 and 1756 were sold to the Rhondda & Swansea Bay Railway and 1715 and 1882 to the Neath & Brecon Railway, but all returned to GWR stock in 1922.

All the locomotives were rebuilt as pannier tanks from 1909 onwards.

Year End Totals: '1854' class

'47	'48	'49	'50	'51	'52	'53	'54	'55	'56	'57	'58	'59	'60	'61	'62	'63	'64	'65	'66	'67
36	25	10	2																	

Number	Built	Renumbered	BR Dates	Scrap	Notes
906	05/95 Sdn		-04/48	07/49	
907	05/95 Sdn		-03/51	*51*	

Class continued with 1705

SHT [2] 1141, 1143, 1145 (929, 968, 1098)
0-4-0ST Swansea Harbour Trust - Peckett

For details see 1141

Number	Built	Renumbered	BR Dates	Scrap	Notes
929	06/06 P		-06/52	*07/52* 03/48➲1141	

Class continued with 968

PM [1] 1150-1152 (696, 779, 935)
0-4-0ST Powlesland & Mason - Peckett

Class continued from 779

Number	Built	Renumbered	BR Dates	Scrap	Notes
935	01/12 P		-12/61	03/63 06/49➲1152	

Class continued with 1150

PM [2] 1153 (942)
0-4-0ST Powlesland & Mason - Hawthorn Leslie

For details see 1153

Number	Built	Renumbered	BR Dates	Scrap	Notes
942	03/03 HL		-10/55	*11/55*	
				11/49➲1153	

Class continued with 1153

SHT [3] 1142 (943)
0-4-0ST Swansea Harbour Trust - Hudswell Clarke

For details see 1142

Number	Built	Renumbered	BR Dates	Scrap	Notes
943	06/11 HC		-11/59	04/60	
				11/48➲1142	

Class continued with 1142

SHT [2] 1141, 1143, 1145 (929, 968, 1098)
0-4-0ST Swansea Harbour Trust - Peckett

Class continued from 929

Number	Built	Renumbered	BR Dates	Scrap	Notes
968	06/08 P		-11/60	03/61	
				02/49➲1143	

Class continued with 1098

SHT [4] 1144 (974)
0-4-0ST Swansea Harbour Trust - Hawthorn Leslie

For details see 1144

Number	Built	Renumbered	BR Dates	Scrap	Notes
974	07/09 HL		-01/60	04/60	
				09/48➲1144	

Class continued with 1144

1901 992, 1903-2019
0-6-0PT GWR Dean & Armstrong (Wolverhampton) 4ft 1½in

Power Classification:	2F
Introduced:	1874-1895
Designer:	Dean & G Armstrong, built at Wolverhampton
Company:	GWR
Weight:	36t 3cwt
Driving Wheel:	4' 1½"
Boiler Pressure:	165psi
Cylinders:	Inside 16" x 24"
Tractive Effort:	17410lbf
Valve Gear:	Stephenson (slide valves)

Refer to the Historical Survey of GWR Pannier Tank Engines at the end of this section for more details of this class.

170 locomotives of this class were originally built (including the old '850' class). The first was withdrawn in 1906, and the remainder were rebuilt as pannier tanks from 1910 onwards.

s 1925 and 2007 were never rebuilt and remained as saddle tanks until they were scrapped.

Year End Totals: '1901' class

'47	'48	'49	'50	'51	'52	'53	'54	'55	'56	'57	'58	'59	'60	'61	'62	'63	'64	'65	'66	'67
44	44	31	25	13	7	3	3	3	2	2										

Number	Built	Renumbered	BR Dates	Scrap	Notes
992	09/75 Wlv		-02/51	*51*	

Class continued with 1903

1000 1000-1029
4-6-0 GWR Hawksworth 'County'

Power Classification:	6MT
Introduced:	1945-1947
Designer:	Hawksworth
Company:	GWR
Weight:	Loco 76t 17cwt Tender 49t 0cwt
Driving Wheel:	6' 3"
Boiler Pressure:	280psi superheated Later reduced to 250psi superheated
Cylinders:	Outside 18½" x 30"
Tractive Effort:	32580lbf then 29090lbf
Valve Gear:	Stephenson (piston valves)

These were the ultimate locomotives in the development of GWR two-cylinder 4-6-0 express engines and were descended directly from the 'Saint' ('2900') class. They were the last GWR passenger design built before nationalisation and they were a larger version of the 'Modified Hall' ('6959') class. They were designed during the war for fast mixed traffic work.

The 'Counties' were distinct from all other GWR 4-6-0 designs in that they had one long splasher covering all the wheels and a straight (instead of curved) nameplate. Every locomotive of the class carried the name of a County served by the GWR (some of which had been carried on the previous 4-4-0 'County' class which were all scrapped in the 1930s). They were never as popular as the other main line classes such as the 'Halls', as they fell rather uncomfortably between the express and mixed traffic classifications.

From 1955 onwards they were all rebuilt with double chimneys and the boiler pressure was reduced.

Year End Totals: '1000' class

'47	'48	'49	'50	'51	'52	'53	'54	'55	'56	'57	'58	'59	'60	'61	'62	'63	'64	'65	'66	'67
30	30	30	30	30	30	30	30	30	30	30	30	30	30	30	21	8				

Number	Built	Renumbered	BR Dates	Scrap	Notes
1000	08/45 Sdn		-07/64	12/64	
	COUNTY OF MIDDLESEX				
1001	09/45 Sdn		-05/63	03/65	
	COUNTY OF BUCKS				
1002	09/45 Sdn		-09/63	02/64	
	COUNTY OF BERKS				
1003	10/45 Sdn		-10/62	05/64	
	COUNTY OF WILTS				
1004	10/45 Sdn		-09/62	05/64	
	COUNTY OF SOMERSET				
1005	11/45 Sdn		-06/63	08/64	
	COUNTY OF DEVON				
1006	11/45 Sdn		-09/63	06/64	
	COUNTY OF CORNWALL				
1007	12/45 Sdn		-10/62	11/63	
	COUNTY OF BRECKNOCK				
1008	12/45 Sdn		-10/63	08/64	
	COUNTY OF CARDIGAN				
1009	12/45 Sdn		-02/63	08/63	
	COUNTY OF CARMARTHEN				
1010	01/46 Sdn		-07/64	12/64	
	COUNTY OF CARNARVON				
	11/51➲ **COUNTY OF CAERNARVON**				
1011	01/46 Sdn		-11/64	03/65	
	COUNTY OF CHESTER				
1012	02/46 Sdn		-04/64	12/64	
	COUNTY OF DENBIGH				
1013	02/46 Sdn		-07/64	03/65	
	COUNTY OF DORSET				
1014	02/46 Sdn		-04/64	12/64	
	COUNTY OF GLAMORGAN				
1015	03/46 Sdn		-12/62	05/64	
	COUNTY OF GLOUCESTER				
1016	03/46 Sdn		-09/63	02/64	
	COUNTY OF HANTS				
1017	03/46 Sdn		-12/62	12/63	
	COUNTY OF HEREFORD				
1018	03/46 Sdn		-09/62	11/63	
	COUNTY OF LEICESTER				
1019	04/46 Sdn		-02/63	01/64	
	COUNTY OF MERIONETH				
1020	12/46 Sdn		-02/64	07/64	
	COUNTY OF MONMOUTH				
1021	12/46 Sdn		-11/63	07/64	
	COUNTY OF MONTGOMERY				
1022	12/46 Sdn		-10/62	01/64	
	COUNTY OF NORTHAMPTON				
1023	01/47 Sdn		-03/63	08/63	
	COUNTY OF OXFORD				
1024	01/47 Sdn		-04/64	07/64	
	COUNTY OF PEMBROKE				
1025	01/47 Sdn		-02/63	01/64	
	COUNTY OF RADNOR				
1026	01/47 Sdn		-09/62	01/64	
	COUNTY OF SALOP				
1027	03/47 Sdn		-10/63	06/64	
	COUNTY OF STAFFORD				
1028	03/47 Sdn		-12/63	05/64	
	COUNTY OF WARWICK				
1029	04/47 Sdn		-12/62	09/63	
	COUNTY OF WORCESTER				

SHT [5] 1146-1147 (1085, 1086)
0-6-0ST Swansea Harbour Trust - Peckett

For details see 1146

Number	Built	Renumbered	BR Dates	Scrap	Notes
1085	04/12 P		-01/51	*51*	
				02/49➲1146	
1086	02/13 P		-04/51	*51*	
				03/49➲1147	

Class continued with 1146

SHT [2] 1141, 1143, 1145 (929, 968, 1098)
0-4-0ST Swansea Harbour Trust - Peckett

Class continued from 968

Number	Built	Renumbered	BR Dates	Scrap	Notes
1098	10/18 P		-07/59	01/60	
				01/50➲1145	

Class continued with 1141

1101 1101-1106
0-4-0T GWR Collett dock shunters

Power Classification:	3F
Introduced:	1926
Designer:	Collett, built by Avonside Engine Co.
Company:	GWR
Weight:	38t 4cwt
Driving Wheel:	3' 9½"
Boiler Pressure:	170psi
Cylinders:	Outside 16" x 24"
Tractive Effort:	19510lbf
Valve Gear:	Walschaert (piston valves)

These locomotives were built by the Avonside Engine Company to GWR requirements for dock shunting. They had domed Belpaire boilers and Walschaert valve gear. They were intended to replace older 0-4-0Ts taken over from the Swansea Harbour Trust and they spent most of their lives working alongside the SHT and P&M locomotives in Swansea docks.

Year End Totals: '1101' class

'47	'48	'49	'50	'51	'52	'53	'54	'55	'56	'57	'58	'59	'60	'61	'62	'63	'64	'65	'66	'67
6	6	6	6	6	6	6	6	6	6	6	6	5								

Number	Built	Renumbered	BR Dates	Scrap	Notes
1101	06/26 AE		-11/59	02/60	
1102	07/26 AE		-01/60	04/60	
1103	07/26 AE		-01/60	04/60	
1104	08/26 AE		-01/60	04/60	
1105	08/26 AE		-01/60	04/60	
1106	08/26 AE		-01/60	04/60	

SHT [1] 1140 (701)
0-4-0ST Swansea Harbour Trust - Barclay

Power Classification:	0F
Introduced:	1905
Designer:	Barclay
Company:	Swansea Harbour Trust
Weight:	28t 0cwt
Driving Wheel:	3' 5"
Boiler Pressure:	160psi
Cylinders:	Outside 14" x 22"
Tractive Effort:	14305lbf
Valve Gear:	Stephenson (slide valves)

The Swansea Harbour Trust company had a fleet of small saddle tank engines for working the Swansea

Dock lines, which they worked together with the Powlesland & Mason locomotives.

This was the only survivor of three Barclay locomotives built for the Swansea Harbour Trust, the first being sold out of service in 1915. These were the first locomotives purchased by the SHT. This engine was renumbered in 1948 under the 1946 GWR renumbering scheme. It was fitted with a GWR safety valve casing and other modifications including a bell in front of the cab.

Year End Totals: 'SHT 1' class

'47	'48	'49	'50	'51	'52	'53	'54	'55	'56	'57	'58	'59	'60	61	'62	'63	'64	'65	'66	'67
1	1	1	1	1	1	1	1	1	1	1										

Class continued from 701

Number	Built	Renumbered	BR Dates	Scrap	Notes
1140	04/05 AB	06/48 701	-05/58	07/58	

SHT [2] 1141, 1143, 1145 (929, 968, 1098)
0-4-0ST Swansea Harbour Trust - Peckett

Power Classification: 0F
Introduced: 1906-1918
Designer: Peckett
Company: Swansea Harbour Trust
Weight: 33t 10cwt
Driving Wheel: 3' 7"
Boiler Pressure: 150psi
Cylinders: Outside 15" x 21"
Tractive Effort: 14010lbf
Valve Gear: Stephenson (slide valves)

These three Swansea Harbour Trust Pecketts were virtually identical to the Powlesland & Mason Pecketts (1150-52). They were renumbered under the GWR 1946 renumbering scheme in 1948, 1949 and 1950 respectively.

Year End Totals: 'SHT 2' class

'47	'48	'49	'50	'51	'52	'53	'54	'55	'56	'57	'58	'59	'60	'61	'62	'63	'64	'65	'66	'67
3	3	3	3	3	2	2	2	2	2	2	2	1								

Class continued from 1098

Number	Built	Renumbered	BR Dates	Scrap	Notes
1141	06/06 P	03/48 929	-06/52	*07/52*	

Class continued with 1143

SHT [3] 1142 (943)
0-4-0ST Swansea Harbour Trust - Hudswell Clarke

Power Classification: 1F
Introduced: 1911
Designer: Hudswell Clarke
Company: Swansea Harbour Trust
Weight: 28t 15cwt
Driving Wheel: 3' 4"
Boiler Pressure: 160psi
Cylinders: Outside 15" x 22"
Tractive Effort: 16830lbf
Valve Gear: Stephenson (slide valves)

This Hudswell Clarke engine was the most powerful of the Swansea Harbour Trust 0-4-0STs. It was renumbered in 1948 under the GWR 1946 renumbering scheme. 1142 finished its life working at Clee Hill near Shrewsbury.

Year End Totals: 'SHT 3' class

'47	'48	'49	'50	'51	'52	'53	'54	'55	'56	'57	'58	'59	'60	'61	'62	'63	'64	'65	'66	'67
1	1	1	1	1	1	1	1	1	1	1	1									

Class continued from 943

Number	Built	Renumbered	BR Dates	Scrap	Notes
1142	06/11 HC	11/48 943	-11/59	04/60	

SHT [2] 1141, 1143, 1145 (929, 968, 1098)
0-4-0ST Swansea Harbour Trust - Peckett

Class continued from 1141

Number	Built	Renumbered	BR Dates	Scrap	Notes
1143	06/08 P	02/49 968	-11/60	03/61	

Class continued with 1145

SHT [4] 1144 (974)
0-4-0ST Swansea Harbour Trust - Hawthorn Leslie

Power Classification: 0F
Introduced: 1909
Designer: Hawthorn Leslie
Company: Swansea Harbour Trust
Weight: 26t 17cwt
Driving Wheel: 3' 6"
Boiler Pressure: 150psi
Cylinders: Outside 14" x 22"
Tractive Effort: 13090lbf
Valve Gear: Stephenson (slide valves)

This locomotive was built by Hawthorn Leslie for the Swansea Harbour Trust in 1909. It was renumbered in 1948 under the GWR 1946 renumbering scheme.

Year End Totals: 'SHT 4' class

'47	'48	'49	'50	'51	'52	'53	'54	'55	'56	'57	'58	'59	'60	'61	'62	'63	'64	'65	'66	'67
1	1	1	1	1	1	1	1	1	1	1	1	1								

Class continued from 974

Number	Built	Renumbered	BR Dates	Scrap	Notes
1144	07/09 HL	09/48 974	-01/60	04/60	

SHT [2] 1141, 1143, 1145 (929, 968, 1098)
0-4-0ST Swansea Harbour Trust - Peckett

Class continued from 1143

Number	Built	Renumbered	BR Dates	Scrap	Notes
1145	10/18 P	01/50 1098	-07/59	01/60	

SHT [5] 1146-1147 (1085, 1086)
0-6-0ST Swansea Harbour Trust - Peckett

Power Classification: 1F
Introduced: 1912-1915
Designer: Peckett
Company: Swansea Harbour Trust
Weight: 38t 10cwt
Driving Wheel: 3' 10"
Boiler Pressure: 160psi
Cylinders: Inside 16" x 22"
Tractive Effort: 16650lbf
Valve Gear: Stephenson (slide valves)

These were the largest locomotives owned by the Swansea Harbour Trust, being 0-6-0Ts. Three were built by Peckett in 1912-1915, the first being scrapped in 1926. They were both renumbered in 1949 under the GWR 1946 renumbering scheme.

Year End Totals: 'SHT 5' class

'47	'48	'49	'50	'51	'52	'53	'54	'55	'56	'57	'58	'59	'60	'61	'62	'63	'64	'65	'66	'67
2	2	2	2																	

Class continued from 1086

Number	Built	Renumbered	BR Dates	Scrap	Notes
1146	04/12 P	02/49 1085	-01/51	*51*	
1147	02/13 P	03/49 1086	-04/51	*51*	

PM [1] 1150-1152 (696, 779, 935)
0-4-0ST Powlesland & Mason - Peckett

Power Classification: 0F
Introduced: 1912-1916
Designer: Peckett
Company: Powlesland & Mason
Weight: 33t 10cwt
Driving Wheel: 3' 7"
Boiler Pressure: 150psi
Cylinders: Outside 15" x 21"
Tractive Effort: 14010lbf
Valve Gear: Stephenson (slide valves)

Powlesland & Mason was a firm which operated trains on the Swansea Harbour Trust Lines. Their engines worked alongside the Swansea Harbour Trust's own locomotives. These three Peckett built engines were similar to the Swansea Harbour Trust Pecketts (see 1141). They were renumbered as part of the GWR 1946 renumbering scheme, 1152 in 1949, 1151 in 1950 and 1150 in 1951.

1151 was sold into industrial service where it survived until scrapped in April 1965.

Year End Totals: 'PM 1' class

'47	'48	'49	'50	'51	'52	'53	'54	'55	'56	'57	'58	'59	'60	'61	'62	'63	'64	'65	'66	'67
3	3	3	3	3	2	2	2	2	2	2	2	2	2	1	1					

Class continued from 935

Number	Built	Renumbered	BR Dates	Scrap	Notes
1150	07/13 P	12/51 696	-11/52	*09/56*	
1151	09/16 P	10/50 779	-08/63	04/65	
1152	01/12 P	06/49 935	-12/61	03/63	

PM [2] 1153 (942)
0-4-0ST Powlesland & Mason - Hawthorn Leslie

Power Classification: 0F
Introduced: 1903
Designer: Hawthorn Leslie
Company: Powlesland & Mason
Weight: 26t 13cwt
Driving Wheel: 3' 6"
Boiler Pressure: 120psi
Cylinders: Outside 14" x 20"
Tractive Effort: 9520lbf
Valve Gear: Stephenson (slide valves)

This 1903 Hawthorn Leslie engine was bought by Powlesland & Mason in 1919 from Sir Alfred Hickman of Bilston. It was originally named DOROTHY and it was renumbered in 1949 under the 1946 GWR renumbering scheme. It was reboilered by the GWR.

Year End Totals: 'PM 2' class

'47	'48	'49	'50	'51	'52	'53	'54	'55	'56	'57	'58	'59	'60	'61	'62	'63	'64	'65	'66	'67
1	1	1	1	1	1	1	1													

Class continued from 942

Number	Built	Renumbered	BR Dates	Scrap	Notes
1153	03/03 HL	11/49 942	-10/55	*11/55*	

Cam [2] 1196-1197
2-4-0T Cambrian Railways

Power Classification: Not classified
Introduced: 1866 rebuilt at Swindon 1923-1924
Designer: Sharp Stewart
Company: Cambrian Railways
Weight: 33t 3cwt
Driving Wheel: 4' 6"
Boiler Pressure: 150psi
Cylinders: Inside 14" x 20"
Tractive Effort: 9255lbf
Valve Gear: Stephenson (slide valves)

Three 2-4-0Ts were built for the Cambrian Railways in 1866 by Sharp Stewart. They were numbered 1192, 1196 and 1197 and named MAGNOLA, GLADYS and SEAHAM. 1192 was scrapped in 1929, and the others were rebuilt with Swindon fittings in 1923-1924 to become 'Small Side Tanks'.

Year End Totals: 'Cam 2' class

'47	'48	'49	'50	'51	'52	'53	'54	'55	'56	'57	'58	'59	'60	'61	'62	'63	'64	'65	'66	'67
2																				

Number	Built	Renumbered	BR Dates	Scrap	Notes
1196	05/66 SS		-04/48	06/48	
1197	05/66 SS		-04/48	06/48	

AD [4] 1205-1206
2-6-2T Alexandra Docks

Power Classification: 4MT
Introduced: 1920
Designer: Hawthorn Leslie
Company: Alexandra Docks
Weight: 65t 0cwt
Driving Wheel: 4' 7"
Boiler Pressure: 160psi
Cylinders: Outside 19" x 26"
Tractive Effort: 23210lbf
Valve Gear: Stephenson (slide valves)

These were the last locomotives built for the Alexandra Docks Railway. They were based closely on a Mersey Railway design of 1887 which had been purchased by the Alexandra Docks in 1903 when the Mersey Railway was electrified.

The engines were needed to haul heavy coal trains and yet be able to negotiate sharp curves, and they had a very short coupled wheelbase of 11' 6". They were fitted with Belpaire boilers.

Year End Totals: 'AD [4]' class

'47	'48	'49	'50	'51	'52	'53	'54	'55	'56	'57	'58	'59	'60	'61	'62	'63	'64	'65	'66	'67
2	2	2	2	1	1	1	1	1												

Number	Built	Renumbered	BR Dates	Scrap	Notes
1205	20 HL		-01/56	*02/56*	
1206	20 HL		-01/51	*51*	

VoR 7-9 (1213)
2-6-2T Vale of Rheidol (Narrow Gauge)

Class continued from 9

Number	Built	Renumbered	BR Dates	Scrap	Notes
1213 §	24 Sdn		-04/89		03/49⊙9

L&L 1308
2-4-0T Liskeard & Looe

Power Classification:	1P
Introduced:	1902
Designer:	Andrew Barclay
Company:	Liskeard & Looe
Weight:	32t 0cwt
Driving Wheel:	4' 0"
Boiler Pressure:	140psi
Cylinders:	Inside 14½" x 22"
Tractive Effort:	11470lbf
Valve Gear:	Stephenson (slide valves)

This locomotive was built by Andrew Barclay in 1902. It was acquired by the GWR when they took over the Liskeard & Looe Railway in 1909.

g It was rebuilt with a GWR boiler in 1929.

Year End Totals: 'L&L' class

'47	'48	'49	'50	'51	'52	'53	'54	'55	'56	'57	'58	'59	'60	'61	'62	'63	'64	'65	'66	'67
1																				

Number	Built	Renumbered	BR Dates	Scrap	Notes
1308	11/02 AB		-05/48	*06/48*	g
LADY MARGARET					

W&C 1331
0-6-0ST Whitland & Cardigan

Power Classification:	0F
Introduced:	1877
Designer:	Fox Walker & Co.
Company:	Whitland & Cardigan Railway
Weight:	31t 0cwt
Driving Wheel:	4' 0"
Boiler Pressure:	130psi
Cylinders:	Inside 16½" x 24"
Tractive Effort:	15040lbf
Valve Gear:	Stephenson (slide valves)

This locomotive was built by Fox Walker for the Whitland & Cardigan Railway in 1877. It was acquired by the GWR in 1886 and was withdrawn from ordinary service as long ago as 1902. However it was retained for use as a departmental locomotive still carrying its original GWR number 1387. In 1927 it was rebuilt, renumbered to 1331 and returned to capital stock.

Year End Totals: 'W&C' class

'47	'48	'49	'50	'51	'52	'53	'54	'55	'56	'57	'58	'59	'60	'61	'62	'63	'64	'65	'66	'67
1	1	1																		

Number	Built	Renumbered	BR Dates	Scrap	Notes
1331	01/77 FW		-01/50	03/50	

MSWJ 1334-1336
2-4-0 Midland & South Western Junction Railway

Power Classification:	1MT
Introduced:	1894 rebuilt 1924
Designer:	Dübs & Co.
Company:	Midland & South Western Junction Railway
Weight:	Loco 35t 5cwt Tender 30t 5cwt
Driving Wheel:	5' 6"
Boiler Pressure:	165psi
Cylinders:	Inside 17" x 24"
Tractive Effort:	14740lbf
Valve Gear:	Stephenson (slide valves)

These locomotives were built in 1894 for passenger work on the MSWJR main line as Nos. 10-12. They were rebuilt in 1924 with GWR fittings. They spent most of their lives on the Lambourn branch, usually to be found at Didcot or Reading sheds. They retained their original cabs throughout their lives.

These were among the very few 2-4-0s to come into British Railways stock.

Year End Totals: 'MSWJ' class

'47	'48	'49	'50	'51	'52	'53	'54	'55	'56	'57	'58	'59	'60	'61	'62	'63	'64	'65	'66	'67
3	3	3	3	3	1	1														

Number	Built	Renumbered	BR Dates	Scrap	Notes
1334	01/94 D		-09/52	*10/52*	
1335	01/94 D		-09/52	*52*	
1336	01/94 D		-03/54	04/54	

Car [3] 1338
0-4-0ST Cardiff Railway - Kitson

Power Classification:	0F
Introduced:	1898
Designer:	Kitson & Co.
Company:	Cardiff Railway
Weight:	25t 10cwt
Driving Wheel:	3' 2½"
Boiler Pressure:	160psi
Cylinders:	Outside 14" x 21"
Tractive Effort:	14540lbf
Valve Gear:	Hawthorn Kitson

This was the survivor of two locomotives built in 1898 by Kitson for the Cardiff Railway. The other engine was withdrawn in 1932. It was fitted with Hawthorn Kitson valve gear, which was a form of Walschaert valve gear with the link above the running plate instead of below. No coal bunker was fitted. It finished its days shunting at Bridgwater docks.

Year End Totals: 'Car [3]' class

'47	'48	'49	'50	'51	'52	'53	'54	'55	'56	'57	'58	'59	'60	'61	'62	'63	'64	'65	'66	'67
1	1	1	1	1	1	1	1	1	1	1	1	1	1	1	1					

Number	Built	Renumbered	BR Dates	Scrap	Notes
1338 §	05/98 K		-09/63		

PT [2] 1358
0-8-2T Port Talbot

Power Classification:	Not classified
Introduced:	1902
Designer:	Sharp Stewart
Company:	Port Talbot Railway
Weight:	75t 17cwt
Driving Wheel:	4' 3"
Boiler Pressure:	180psi
Cylinders:	Outside 20" x 26"
Tractive Effort:	31200lbf
Valve Gear:	Stephenson (slide valves)

The Port Talbot Railway had five 0-8-2Ts in total. The first two were built in the USA in 1899 and were scrapped in 1928-29. This locomotive was the survivor of three locomotives built by Sharp Stewart in 1902. They were based on a class of seven engines introduced on the Barry Railway in 1896. The Barry Railway engines and the other two Port Talbot engines were scrapped between 1926 and 1935. 1358 was fitted with a Swindon style boiler and smokebox.

Year End Totals: 'PT [2]' class

'47	'48	'49	'50	'51	'52	'53	'54	'55	'56	'57	'58	'59	'60	'61	'62	'63	'64	'65	'66	'67
1																				

Number	Built	Renumbered	BR Dates	Scrap	Notes
1358	02 SS		-02/48	03/48	

1361 1361-1365
0-6-0ST GWR Churchward

Power Classification:	0F
Introduced:	1910
Designer:	Churchward
Company:	GWR
Weight:	35t 4cwt
Driving Wheel:	3' 8"
Boiler Pressure:	150psi
Cylinders:	Outside 16" x 20"
Tractive Effort:	14835lbf
Valve Gear:	Stephenson (slide valves)

Refer to the Historical Survey of GWR Pannier Tank Engines at the end of this section for more details of this class.

Only three classes of outside cylinder 0-6-0 tank engines were ever built by the GWR, the '1361', '1366' and '1500' classes.

The '1361' class was designed in 1910 for shunting in sidings with severe curves (such as docks), and they had a wheelbase of only 11ft. They were an updated version of the old '1392' class engines which were built for the Cornwall Minerals Railway in 1873 and were taken over by the GWR 1877. They were the last saddle tanks to be constructed at Swindon.

The '1361' class were fitted with round-topped boilers and saddle tanks. The '1366' class was developed from them with Belpaire boilers and pannier tanks.

They were to be found based at Swindon and docks such as Plymouth and Bridgwater.

Year End Totals: '1361' class

'47	'48	'49	'50	'51	'52	'53	'54	'55	'56	'57	'58	'59	'60	'61	'62	'63	'64	'65	'66	'67
5	5	5	5	5	5	5	5	5	5	5	5	5	5	2						

Number	Built	Renumbered	BR Dates	Scrap	Notes
1361	04/10 Sdn		-05/61	11/61	
1362	06/10 Sdn		-05/61	09/61	
1363 §	06/10 Sdn		-12/62		
1364	08/10 Sdn		-01/61	09/61	
1365	08/10 Sdn		-12/62	09/63	

1366 1366-1371
0-6-0PT GWR Collett

Power Classification:	1F
Introduced:	1934
Designer:	Collett
Company:	GWR
Weight:	35t 15cwt
Driving Wheel:	3' 8"
Boiler Pressure:	165psi
Cylinders:	Outside 16" x 20"
Tractive Effort:	16320lbf
Valve Gear:	Stephenson (slide valves)

Refer to the Historical Survey of GWR Pannier Tank Engines at the end of this section for more details of this class.

When the old Cornwall Minerals Railway '1392' class needed replacement in 1934 an updated version of the '1361' class was built. They were fitted with Belpaire boilers and pannier tanks.

They were to be found based at Swindon and docks such as Plymouth and Bridgwater. In 1962 1367, 1368 and 1369 moved to the Wenford Bridge branch to replace the Beattie Well Tanks (30585-87, SR class '0298') when they were withdrawn.

w Several locomotives were fitted with steam heating apparatus and warning bells for working Channel Isles boat trains at Weymouth Quay.

Year End Totals: '1366' class

'47	'48	'49	'50	'51	'52	'53	'54	'55	'56	'57	'58	'59	'60	'61	'62	'63	'64	'65	'66	'67
6	6	6	6	6	6	6	6	6	6	6	6	6	4	3	3	3				

Number	Built	Renumbered	BR Dates	Scrap	Notes
1366	02/34 Sdn		-01/61	11/61	
1367	02/34 Sdn		-10/64	03/65	w
1368	02/34 Sdn		-10/64	03/65	w
1369 §	02/34 Sdn		-11/64		w
1370	02/34 Sdn		-01/60	05/60	w
1371	02/34 Sdn		-11/60	05/61	

BM [2] 431-436 (1372-1375, 1668-1670)
0-6-2T Brecon & Merthyr 5ft

Class continued from 436

Number	Built	Renumbered	BR Dates	Scrap	Notes
1372	08/15 RS		-10/53	*53*	g 07/49➲431
1373	09/15 RS		-05/53	*53*	g 11/48➲432
1375	02/21 RS		-09/53	*04/54*	g 04/49➲434

Class continued with 1668

1400 1400-1474
0-4-2T GWR Collett Motor Fitted

Power Classification:	1P
Introduced:	1932-1936
Designer:	Collett
Company:	GWR
Weight:	41t 6cwt
Driving Wheel:	5' 2"
Boiler Pressure:	165psi
Cylinders:	Inside 16" x 24"
Tractive Effort:	13900lbf
Valve Gear:	Stephenson (slide valves)

These locomotives were designed for light branch work and they were designed to take the place of the old '517' class engines (dating back to 1868) which were life expired. They were built to virtually the same design with a few minor improvements. They were originally known as the '4800' class and were numbered 4800-4874. They were renumbered in 1946 to make way for the '2800' class engines to be renumbered in the 4800 series as they were converted for oil-burning. This class was motor fitted for working push-pull trains. The '5800' class was identical except that the engines were not motor fitted.

They could be seen all over the GWR system on light branch trains until they began to succumb to branch line closures and the introduction of the diesel railcar in the 1950s.

Year End Totals: '1400' class

'47	'48	'49	'50	'51	'52	'53	'54	'55	'56	'57	'58	'59	'60	'61	'62	'63	'64	'65	'66	'67
75	75	75	75	75	75	75	75	75	68	61	49	41	32	27	19	12	2			

Number	Built	Renumbered	BR Dates	Scrap	Notes
1400	08/32 Sdn		-06/57	06/57	
1401	08/32 Sdn		-11/58	11/59	
1402	08/32 Sdn		-10/56	*11/56*	
1403	09/32 Sdn		-11/57	01/58	
1404	09/32 Sdn		-02/56	04/56	
1405	09/32 Sdn		-09/58	10/58	
1406	09/32 Sdn		-03/58	04/58	
1407	09/32 Sdn		-06/60	10/60	
1408	09/32 Sdn		-03/58	04/58	
1409	10/32 Sdn		-10/63	03/64	
1410	03/33 Sdn		-06/61	10/61	
1411	03/33 Sdn		-10/56	*56*	
1412	03/33 Sdn		-06/60	07/60	
1413	04/33 Sdn		-03/56	*56*	
1414	04/33 Sdn		-04/57	05/57	
1415	04/33 Sdn		-02/57	03/57	
1416	04/33 Sdn		-10/56	*07/58*	
1417	04/33 Sdn		-02/59	04/59	
1418	04/33 Sdn		-10/58	04/59	
1419	04/33 Sdn		-04/61	08/61	
1420 §	11/33 Sdn		-11/64		
1421	11/33 Sdn		-12/63	05/64	
1422	11/33 Sdn		-06/57	12/64	
1423	11/33 Sdn		-01/59	11/59	
1424	11/33 Sdn		-11/63	06/64	
1425	11/33 Sdn		-02/56	*03/56*	
1426	11/33 Sdn		-04/62	07/62	
1427	11/33 Sdn		-06/60	10/60	
1428	11/33 Sdn		-06/59	11/60	
1429	11/33 Sdn		-03/59	06/61	
1430	07/34 Sdn		-09/58	02/59	
1431	07/34 Sdn		-04/61	06/61	
1432	07/34 Sdn		-07/63	09/63	
1433	07/34 Sdn		-01/61	11/61	
1434	07/34 Sdn		-07/62	09/62	
1435	08/34 Sdn		-01/62	05/63	
1436	08/34 Sdn		-10/58	04/59	
1437	08/34 Sdn		-02/59	11/59	
1438	08/34 Sdn		-11/62	07/64	
1439	08/34 Sdn		-08/57	09/57	
1440	03/35 Sdn		-12/63	02/64	
1441	04/35 Sdn		-06/60	10/60	
1442 §	04/35 Sdn		-05/65		
1443	04/35 Sdn		-06/57	07/57	
1444	04/35 Sdn		-10/64	04/65	
1445	04/35 Sdn		-09/64	04/65	
1446	04/35 Sdn		-09/58	04/59	
1447	04/35 Sdn		-03/64	07/64	
1448	04/35 Sdn		-06/60	10/60	
1449	04/35 Sdn		-06/60	10/60	
1450 §	07/35 Sdn		-05/65		
1451	07/35 Sdn		-07/64	08/64	
1452	07/35 Sdn		-06/60	10/60	
1453	07/35 Sdn		-11/64	03/65	
1454	07/35 Sdn		-12/60	08/61	
1455	07/35 Sdn		-05/64	07/64	
1456	07/35 Sdn		-02/59	11/59	
1457	08/35 Sdn		-02/59	11/60	
1458	08/35 Sdn		-11/64	02/65	
1459	08/35 Sdn		-09/58	04/59	
1460	02/36 Sdn		-02/56	*03/56*	
1461	02/36 Sdn		-05/58	07/58	
1462	02/36 Sdn		-09/62	11/63	
1463	02/36 Sdn		-04/61	06/61	
1464	02/36 Sdn		-06/60	10/60	
1465	02/36 Sdn		-09/58	04/59	
1466 §	02/36 Sdn		-12/63		
1467	02/36 Sdn		-04/59	08/59	
1468	02/36 Sdn		-03/62	03/65	
1469	02/36 Sdn		-09/58	04/59	
1470	02/36 Sdn		-10/62	10/63	
1471	02/36 Sdn		-10/63	11/63	
1472	02/36 Sdn		-11/64	02/65	
1473	02/36 Sdn		-08/62	09/63	
1474	02/36 Sdn		-09/64	12/64	

1500 1500-1509
0-6-0PT BR (GWR) Hawksworth

Power Classification:	4F
Introduced:	1949
Designer:	Hawksworth
Company:	BR (GWR design)
Weight:	58t 4cwt
Driving Wheel:	4' 7½"
Boiler Pressure:	200psi
Cylinders:	Outside 17½" x 24"
Tractive Effort:	22515lbf
Valve Gear:	Walschaert (piston valves)

Refer to the Historical Survey of GWR Pannier Tank Engines at the end of this section for more details of this class.

The '1500' class did not appear until after nationalisation and was a short wheelbase heavy shunting design. The locomotives were different from all other tank designs on the GWR. Above the running plate level they were similar to the '9400' class, but the '1500' class had no running plate and had outside cylinders with Walschaert valve gear. The pannier tanks did not flank the sides of the smokebox as on most other pannier tanks except the '9400' and '9700' classes.

The locomotives were based in the London and Newport areas. 1501, 1502 and 1509 were sold to the National Coal Board on withdrawal. 1501 survived to be preserved, while the other two were scrapped in October 1970.

Year End Totals: '1500' class

'47	'48	'49	'50	'51	'52	'53	'54	'55	'56	'57	'58	'59	'60	'61	'62	'63	'64	'65	'66	'67
		10	10	10	10	10	10	10	10	10	10	9	9	7	5					

Number	Built	Renumbered	BR Dates	Scrap	Notes
1500	06/49 Sdn		06/49-12/63	05/64	
1501 §	07/49 Sdn		07/49-01/61		
1502	07/49 Sdn		07/49-01/61	10/70	
1503	08/49 Sdn		08/49-12/63	05/64	
1504	08/49 Sdn		08/49-05/63	05/64	
1505	08/49 Sdn		08/49-05/62	06/62	
1506	09/49 Sdn		09/49-12/63	05/64	
1507	09/49 Sdn		09/49-12/63	05/64	
1508	09/49 Sdn		09/49-09/62	11/62	
1509	09/49 Sdn		09/49-08/59	10/70	

1501 1531-1542
0-6-0PT GWR Armstrong (Wolverhampton) 4ft 7½in

Power Classification:	2F
Introduced:	1872-1881
Designer:	Dean & G Armstrong, built at Wolverhampton
Company:	GWR
Weight:	42t 17cwt
Driving Wheel:	4' 7½"
Boiler Pressure:	165psi
Cylinders:	Inside 17" x 24"
Tractive Effort:	17525lbf
Valve Gear:	Stephenson (slide valves)

Refer to the Historical Survey of GWR Pannier Tank Engines at the end of this section for more details of this class.

These were the last survivors of 103 locomotives built at Wolverhampton. The first of these was withdrawn in 1875. They were rebuilt as pannier tanks from 1910 onwards.

Year End Totals: '1501' class

'47	'48	'49	'50	'51	'52	'53	'54	'55	'56	'57	'58	'59	'60	'61	'62	'63	'64	'65	'66	'67
4	2	1	1																	

Number	Built	Renumbered	BR Dates	Scrap	Notes
1531	08/79 Wlv		-12/49	02/50	
1532	09/79 Wlv		-07/48	*48*	
1538	12/79 Wlv		-11/48	*01/49*	
1542	02/80 Wlv		-02/51	*51*	

1600 1600-1669
0-6-0PT BR (GWR) Hawksworth

Power Classification:	2F
Introduced:	1949-1955
Designer:	Hawksworth
Company:	BR (GWR design)
Weight:	41t 12cwt
Driving Wheel:	4' 1½"
Boiler Pressure:	165psi
Cylinders:	Inside 16½" x 24"
Tractive Effort:	18515lbf
Valve Gear:	Stephenson (slide valves)

Refer to the Historical Survey of GWR Pannier Tank Engines at the end of this section for more details of this class.

These were direct descendants of the '1901' and '2021' classes of 1884 and 1897. They were designed for shunting and light branch work and were built to replace the older locomotives. They were noticeably smaller than most other GWR pannier tanks as they were designed for routes with low clearance.

In 1957 1646 and 1649 were transferred a long way from home to work the branch line between Dornoch and The Mound in Scotland. They replaced the two ex-Highland Railway 0-4-4T engines (55051 and 55053, LMS class '0P') which had been specially retained to work that branch.

1600 and 1607 were sold for further service in industry, being finally scrapped in December 1963 and September 1969 respectively.

Year End Totals: '1600' class

'47	'48	'49	'50	'51	'52	'53	'54	'55	'56	'57	'58	'59	'60	'61	'62	'63	'64	'65	'66	'67
		20	30	50	50	50	55	70	70	70	70	64	55	50	39	33	15	3		

Number	Built	Renumbered	BR Dates	Scrap	Notes
1600	10/49 Sdn		10/49-03/59	12/63	
1601	10/49 Sdn		10/49-08/60	03/61	
1602	10/49 Sdn		10/49-09/60	03/61	
1603	10/49 Sdn		10/49-06/59	06/61	
1604	10/49 Sdn		10/49-07/60	10/61	
1605	11/49 Sdn		11/49-02/62	05/62	
1606	11/49 Sdn		11/49-09/61	03/62	
1607	11/49 Sdn		11/49-08/65	09/69	
1608	11/49 Sdn		11/49-09/63	11/63	
1609	11/49 Sdn		11/49-07/62	10/62	
1610	11/49 Sdn		11/49-12/59	03/61	
1611	11/49 Sdn		11/49-10/65	01/66	
1612	11/49 Sdn		11/49-07/65	10/65	
1613	12/49 Sdn		12/49-03/65	07/65	
1614	12/49 Sdn		12/49-02/64	04/64	
1615	12/49 Sdn		12/49-06/61	02/62	
1616	12/49 Sdn		12/49-10/59	03/61	
1617	12/49 Sdn		12/49-11/63	03/64	
1618	12/49 Sdn		12/49-05/62	02/63	
1619	12/49 Sdn		12/49-05/63	02/64	
1620	06/50 Sdn		06/50-06/60	03/61	
1621	06/50 Sdn		06/50-01/63	11/63	
1622	06/50 Sdn		06/50-06/64	07/64	
1623	06/50 Sdn		06/50-06/65	10/65	
1624	06/50 Sdn		06/50-02/62	05/62	
1625	08/50 Sdn		08/50-06/60	03/61	
1626	08/50 Sdn		08/50-08/62	08/63	☒09/61-10/61
1627	08/50 Sdn		08/50-06/64	08/64	
1628	08/50 Sdn		08/50-09/66	01/67	
1629	09/50 Sdn		09/50-06/60	03/61	

GWR Churchward '1361' class 0-6-0ST No 1365.

GWR Collett '1366' class 0-6-0PT No 1368.

GWR Collett '1400' class 0-4-2T No 1466 at Brixham in August 1953.

GWR Dean '655' class 0-6-0PT No 1747 awaiting scrapping at Swindon Works in October 1950.

Number	Built	Renumbered	BR Dates	Scrap	Notes
1630	01/51 Sdn		01/51-06/64	08/64	
1631	01/51 Sdn		01/51-11/64	02/65	
1632	01/51 Sdn		01/51-04/65	08/65	
1633	01/51 Sdn		01/51-10/62	10/63	
1634	02/51 Sdn		02/51-06/61	09/61	
1635	02/51 Sdn		02/51-10/59	03/61	
1636	02/51 Sdn		02/51-06/64	08/64	
1637	02/51 Sdn		02/51-06/60	03/61	
1638 §	03/51 Sdn		03/51-08/66		
1639	03/51 Sdn		03/51-11/64	04/65	
1640	03/51 Sdn		03/51-07/61	11/61	
1641	03/51 Sdn		03/51-11/64	03/65	
1642	04/51 Sdn		04/51-01/62	06/62	
1643	04/51 Sdn		04/51-10/65	01/66	
1644	04/51 Sdn		04/51-10/59	02/61	
1645	04/51 Sdn		04/51-10/62	12/63	
1646	05/51 Sdn		05/51-12/62	10/63	
1647	05/51 Sdn		05/51-04/61	08/61	
1648	05/51 Sdn		05/51-05/63	09/63	
1649	05/51 Sdn		05/51-12/62	10/63	
1650	11/54 Sdn		11/54-02/64	05/64	
1651	12/54 Sdn		12/54-10/65	02/66	
1652	12/54 Sdn		12/54-01/60	07/61	
1653	12/54 Sdn		12/54-12/62	06/63	
1654	12/54 Sdn		12/54-06/64	08/64	
1655	01/55 Sdn		01/55-07/65	10/65	
1656	01/55 Sdn		01/55-06/64	10/64	
1657	01/55 Sdn		01/55-11/64	02/65	
1658	02/55 Sdn		02/55-11/64	04/65	
1659	02/55 Sdn		02/55-10/60	06/61	
1660	02/55 Sdn		02/55-02/66	06/66	
1661	03/55 Sdn		03/55-07/64	12/64	
1662	03/55 Sdn		03/55-12/63	04/64	
1663	03/55 Sdn		03/55-01/65	06/65	
1664	03/55 Sdn		03/55-11/64	05/65	
1665	04/55 Sdn		04/55-07/64	10/64	
1666	04/55 Sdn		04/55-02/64	06/64	
1667	05/55 Sdn		05/55-11/64	02/65	
1668	05/55 Sdn		05/55-01/65	06/65	
1669	05/55 Sdn		05/55-10/65	02/66	

BM [2] 431-436 (1372-1375, 1668-1670)
0-6-2T Brecon & Merthyr 5ft

Class continued from 1375

Number	Built	Renumbered	BR Dates	Scrap	Notes
1668	02/21 RS		-01/54	*54*	g 04/50➲435
1670	02/21 RS		-01/54	*10/54*	r 10/49➲436

1854 906-907, between 1705 & 1900
0-6-0PT GWR Dean (Swindon) 4ft 7½in

Class continued from 907

Number	Built	Renumbered	BR Dates	Scrap	Notes
1705	03/91 Sdn		-11/50	*50*	
1706	03/91 Sdn		-06/48	08/48	
1709	04/91 Sdn		-11/50	*11/53*	
1713	05/91 Sdn		-06/48	*01/49*	
1715	05/91 Sdn		-10/49	*03/50*	
1720	06/91 Sdn		-12/49	*06/50*	
1726	06/92 Sdn		-04/48	51	
1730	07/92 Sdn		-08/48	52	
1731	07/92 Sdn		-06/49	08/49	

Class continued with 1752

655 between 1742 & 1789, 2702-2719
0-6-0PT GWR Dean (Wolverhampton) 4ft 7½in

Power Classification: 2F
Introduced: 1892-1897
Designer: Dean, built at Wolverhampton
Company: GWR
Weight: 46t 13cwt
Driving Wheel: 4' 7½"
Boiler Pressure: 180psi
Cylinders: Inside 17" x 24"
Tractive Effort: 19120lbf
Valve Gear: Stephenson (slide valves)

Refer to the Historical Survey of GWR Pannier Tank Engines at the end of this section for more details of this class.

This class was the same as the '1854' class but the engines were built at Wolverhampton instead of Swindon. These were the survivors of fifty-two locomotives, the first being withdrawn in 1928.

Year End Totals: '655' class

'47	'48	'49	'50	'51	'52	'53	'54	'55	'56	'57	'58	'59	'60	'61	'62	'63	'64	'65	'66	'67
21	14	12																		

Number	Built	Renumbered	BR Dates	Scrap	Notes
1742	03/92 Wlv		-02/50	08/50	
1745	05/92 Wlv		-08/48	07/49	
1747	06/92 Wlv		-05/50	*10/50*	⊠11/49-12/49
1749	07/92 Wlv		-10/48	*11/48*	

Class continued with 1773

1854 906-907, between 1705 & 1900
0-6-0PT GWR Dean (Swindon) 4ft 7½in

Class continued from 1731

Number	Built	Renumbered	BR Dates	Scrap	Notes
1752	10/92 Sdn		-03/50	05/50	
1753	10/92 Sdn		-04/48	*04/48*	
1754	10/92 Sdn		-12/49	02/50	
1758	11/92 Sdn		-03/49	05/49	
1760	12/92 Sdn		-07/50	09/50	
1762	12/92 Sdn		-04/48	*05/48*	
1764	12/92 Sdn		-10/49	*08/50*	
1769	02/93 Sdn		-04/48	48	

Class continued with 1799

655 between 1742 & 1789, 2702-2719
0-6-0PT GWR Dean (Wolverhampton) 4ft 7½in

Class continued from 1749

Number	Built	Renumbered	BR Dates	Scrap	Notes
1773	01/93 Wlv		-03/50	05/50	
1780	05/93 Wlv		-08/48	*48*	
1782	08/93 Wlv		-11/50	*50*	
1789	05/94 Wlv		-10/50	*50*	

Class continued with 2702

1854 906-907, between 1705 & 1900
0-6-0PT GWR Dean (Swindon) 4ft 7½in

Class continued from 1769

Number	Built	Renumbered	BR Dates	Scrap	Notes
1799	06/95 Sdn		-12/49	11/50	

Class continued with 1855

1813 1835
0-6-0PT GWR Dean (Swindon) 4ft 7½in ex-Side Tank

Power Classification: 2F
Introduced: 1882-1884 (survivor built 1883)
Designer: Dean, built at Swindon
Company: GWR
Weight: 44t 8cwt
Driving Wheel: 4' 7½"
Boiler Pressure: 165psi
Cylinders: Inside 17" x 24"
Tractive Effort: 17525lbf
Valve Gear: Stephenson (slide valves)

Refer to the Historical Survey of GWR Pannier Tank Engines at the end of this section for more details of this class.

The '655', '1501', '1813', '1854' and '2721' classes were all very similar, but the '1813' class differed in that the engines were originally constructed as side tanks, before being converted to saddle tanks and finally to pannier tanks.

This locomotive was the last survivor of forty locomotives, the first being withdrawn in 1928.

Year End Totals: '1813' class

'47	'48	'49	'50	'51	'52	'53	'54	'55	'56	'57	'58	'59	'60	'61	'62	'63	'64	'65	'66	'67
1	1																			

Number	Built	Renumbered	BR Dates	Scrap	Notes
1835	03/83 Sdn		-01/49	03/49	

1854 906-907, between 1705 & 1900
0-6-0PT GWR Dean (Swindon) 4ft 7½in

Class continued from 1799

Number	Built	Renumbered	BR Dates	Scrap	Notes
1855	02/90 Sdn		-12/50	*51*	
1858	03/90 Sdn		-10/50	*50*	
1861	03/90 Sdn		-11/51	*03/52*	
1862	03/90 Sdn		-12/50	*51*	
1863	03/90 Sdn		-09/49	11/49	
1867	04/90 Sdn		-11/48	*11/48*	
1870	05/90 Sdn		-10/50	*50*	
1878	11/90 Sdn		-11/49	01/50	
1884	12/90 Sdn		-08/49	10/49	
1888	01/91 Sdn		-12/49	*03/50*	
1889	01/91 Sdn		-12/48	*01/49*	
1891	02/91 Sdn		-12/49	02/50	
1894	07/95 Sdn		-02/49	04/49	
1896	07/95 Sdn		-12/49	02/50	
1897	07/95 Sdn		-01/49	03/49	
1900	08/95 Sdn		-04/48	*03/49*	

1901 992, 1903-2019
0-6-0PT GWR Dean & Armstrong (Wolverhampton) 4ft 1½in

Class continued from 992

Number	Built	Renumbered	BR Dates	Scrap	Notes
1903	09/81 Wlv		-06/52	*07/52*	
1907	11/81 Wlv		-01/50	03/50	
1909	01/82 Wlv		-11/49	*03/50*	
1912	04/82 Wlv		-12/49	02/50	
1917	08/82 Wlv		-03/51	05/51	
1919	09/82 Wlv		-11/49	*10/50*	
1925	12/83 Wlv		-04/51	11/51	s
1930	05/84 Wlv		-08/49	10/49	
1935	08/84 Wlv		-10/53	*53*	
1941	11/86 Wlv		-02/51	*51*	
1943	01/87 Wlv		-03/51	*51*	
1945	02/87 Wlv		-11/49	01/50	
1949	02/88 Wlv		-04/50	*10/50*	
1957	06/88 Wlv		-04/51	*04/51*	
1964	11/89 Wlv		-02/52	*04/52*	
1965	12/89 Wlv		-01/50	03/50	
1967	01/90 Wlv		-06/51	*12/51*	
1968	02/90 Wlv		-09/51	*51*	
1969	02/90 Wlv		-08/49	10/49	
1973	07/90 Wlv		-12/49	02/50	
1979	11/90 Wlv		-08/50	09/50	
1989	06/91 Wlv		-09/50	10/50	
1990	06/91 Wlv		-11/49	01/50	
1991	07/91 Wlv		-01/53	06/55	
1993	08/91 Wlv		-04/51	*05/51*	
1996	10/91 Wlv		-01/53	*53*	
2000	12/91 Wlv		-12/49	02/50	
2001	12/91 Wlv		-08/52	*08/52*	
2002	01/92 Wlv		-02/52	*52*	
2004	09/92 Wlv		-01/52	*52*	
2006	10/92 Wlv		-12/49	*10/50*	
2007	10/92 Wlv		-12/49	*06/50*	s
2008	11/92 Wlv		-03/58	04/58	
2009	04/94 Wlv		-01/51	*51*	
2010	05/94 Wlv		-03/53	05/53	
2011	11/94 Wlv		-08/56	*56*	
2012	11/94 Wlv		-06/58	07/58	
2013	12/94 Wlv		-05/50	07/50	
2014	12/94 Wlv		-11/51	*51*	
2016	02/95 Wlv		-01/52	*02/52*	
2017	02/95 Wlv		-03/51	*01/52*	
2018	03/95 Wlv		-12/49	02/50	
2019	03/95 Wlv		-12/49	*06/50*	

2021 2021-2160
0-6-0PT GWR Dean Wolverhampton 4ft 1½in

Power Classification: 2F
Introduced: 1897-1905
Designer: Dean, built at Wolverhampton
Company: GWR
Weight: 39t 15cwt
Driving Wheel: 4' 1½"
Boiler Pressure: 165psi
Cylinders: Inside 16½" x 24"
Tractive Effort: 18515lbf
Valve Gear: Stephenson (slide valves)

Refer to the Historical Survey of GWR Pannier Tank Engines at the end of this section for more details of this class.

The '2021's were the survivors of 140 locomotives built in 1897-1905 at Wolverhampton. The first was withdrawn in 1907.

2101-2160 were the only GWR 0-6-0ST/PTs to be built with domeless boilers. Many later acquired domed boilers and the domeless boilers appeared on locomotives throughout the whole class. Some locomotives were also superheated.

In 1906 2120 and 2140 were fitted with dummy coach shells covering the locomotive. These were intended to match the coaches used on auto train working. They were converted back to normal in 1911.

s At nationalisation 2048 was still fitted with a saddle tank but it was rebuilt with pannier tanks (p) later that year.

Three engines were sold for further industrial use; 2034 (scrapped in March 1964), 2053 (March 1961) and 2092 (September 1964).

Year End Totals: '2021' class

'47	'48	'49	'50	'51	'52	'53	'54	'55	'56	'57	'58	'59	'60	'61	'62	'63	'64	'65	'66	'67
110	110	100	85	61	38	27	21	9	4	1	1									

Number	Built	Renumbered	BR Dates	Scrap	Notes
2021	02/97 Wlv		-06/51	51	
2022	03/97 Wlv		-12/49	11/51	
2023	04/97 Wlv		-01/52	52	
2025	05/97 Wlv		-05/52	56	
2026	05/97 Wlv		-04/51	51	
2027	06/97 Wlv		-02/57	03/57	
2029	07/97 Wlv		-11/49	01/50	
2030	08/97 Wlv		-02/52	52	
2031	09/97 Wlv		-01/53	02/53	
2032	10/97 Wlv		-06/51	51	
2033	11/97 Wlv		-03/51	51	
2034	11/97 Wlv		-08/55	03/64	
2035	01/98 Wlv		-03/55	04/55	
2037	01/98 Wlv		-07/50	09/50	
2038	02/98 Wlv		-04/53	53	
2039	02/98 Wlv		-04/50	04/50	
2040	03/98 Wlv		-10/56	56	
2042	04/98 Wlv		-04/53	53	
2043	05/98 Wlv		-01/55	02/55	
2044	06/98 Wlv		-07/51	08/51	
2045	06/98 Wlv		-12/49	02/50	
2047	07/98 Wlv		-12/49	11/51	
2048	08/98 Wlv		-05/52	52	s48⇔p
2050	09/98 Wlv		-10/51	51	
2051	10/98 Wlv		-07/51	08/51	
2052	10/98 Wlv		-05/50	08/50	
2053	11/98 Wlv		-04/54	03/61	
2054	12/98 Wlv		-03/51	10/51	
2055	01/99 Wlv		-01/51	02/51	
2056	01/99 Wlv		-03/51	51	
2059	03/99 Wlv		-11/49	01/50	
2060	04/99 Wlv		-12/54	02/55	
2061	04/99 Wlv		-04/55	04/55	
2063	06/99 Wlv		-05/51	05/51	
2064	06/99 Wlv		-11/49	02/51	
2065	06/99 Wlv		-11/49	01/50	
2066	07/99 Wlv		-09/51	04/54	
2067	08/99 Wlv		-11/52	10/59	
2068	08/99 Wlv		-01/53	02/53	
2069	09/99 Wlv		-04/59	05/60	
2070	10/99 Wlv		-08/55	55	
2071	10/99 Wlv		-06/50	08/50	
2072	11/99 Wlv		-07/56	08/56	
2073	11/99 Wlv		-06/51	51	
2075	01/00 Wlv		-03/51	04/51	
2076	02/00 Wlv		-10/51	51	
2079	06/00 Wlv		-11/52	12/52	
2080	09/00 Wlv		-03/52	52	
2081	10/00 Wlv		-09/54	54	
2082	10/00 Wlv		-06/55	06/55	
2083	11/00 Wlv		-11/51	51	
2085	12/00 Wlv		-08/53	53	
2086	01/01 Wlv		-05/52	52	
2088	03/01 Wlv		-08/55	11/55	
2089	03/01 Wlv		-09/51	51	
2090	03/01 Wlv		-03/55	04/55	
2091	04/01 Wlv		-04/50	06/50	
2092	04/01 Wlv		-08/55	09/64	
2093	05/01 Wlv		-01/52	07/52	
2094	05/01 Wlv		-05/52	52	
2095	06/01 Wlv		-04/51	05/51	
2096	07/01 Wlv		-05/50	06/50	
2097	07/01 Wlv		-03/55	55	
2098	08/01 Wlv		-05/51	05/51	
2099	09/01 Wlv		-06/54	06/54	
2100	11/01 Wlv		-06/52	07/52	
2101	01/02 Wlv		-03/56	56	
2102	01/02 Wlv		-11/49	01/50	
2104	03/02 Wlv		-05/51	05/51	
2106	04/02 Wlv		-08/52	09/52	
2107	05/02 Wlv		-06/56	56	
2108	05/02 Wlv		-12/54	55	
2109	06/02 Wlv		-02/52	52	
2110	07/02 Wlv		-07/50	09/50	
2111	07/02 Wlv		-03/53	53	
2112	08/02 Wlv		-09/54	54	
2113	09/02 Wlv		-03/50	03/50	
2114	09/02 Wlv		-12/49	06/50	
2115	10/02 Wlv		-06/52	07/52	
2117	11/02 Wlv		-06/51	08/51	
2121	02/03 Wlv		-06/52	52	
2122	03/03 Wlv		-11/52	11/53	
2123	03/03 Wlv		-10/52	10/52	
2124	05/03 Wlv		-07/50	09/50	
2126	05/03 Wlv		-09/50	10/50	
2127	05/03 Wlv		-09/52	52	
2129	07/03 Wlv		-03/53	53	
2130	07/03 Wlv		-05/50	11/50	
2131	08/03 Wlv		-11/51	51	
2132	09/03 Wlv		-08/50	09/50	
2134	10/03 Wlv		-05/57	06/57	
2135	10/03 Wlv		-01/53	11/53	
2136	11/03 Wlv		-04/55	04/55	
2137	11/03 Wlv		-12/49	02/50	
2138	12/03 Wlv		-05/56	56	
2140	01/04 Wlv		-05/52	52	
2141	03/04 Wlv		-10/50	50	
2144	05/04 Wlv		-05/55	06/55	
2146	06/04 Wlv		-03/53	53	
2147	06/04 Wlv		-03/53	53	
2148	07/04 Wlv		-02/52	08/53	
2150	09/04 Wlv		-01/52	52	
2151	09/04 Wlv		-05/52	52	
2152	10/04 Wlv		-11/51	51	
2153	10/04 Wlv		-12/50	51	
2154	11/04 Wlv		-01/52	02/52	
2155	11/04 Wlv		-11/50	50	
2156	12/04 Wlv		-02/53	53	
2159	02/05 Wlv		-08/51	08/51	
2160	03/05 Wlv		-02/57	57	

BPGV [1] 2162-2168

0-6-0T Burry Port & Gwendraeth Valley

Power Classification:	2F
Introduced:	1909-1919
Designer:	Hudswell Clarke
Company:	Burry Port & Gwendraeth Valley
Weight:	37t 15cwt g 44t 0cwt
Driving Wheel:	3' 9"
Boiler Pressure:	160psi
Cylinders:	Outside 16" x 24"
Tractive Effort:	18570lbf
Valve Gear:	Stephenson (slide valves)

The Burry Port & Gwendraeth Valley Railway had a fleet of small 0-6-0 tank locomotives to work its line. They were all of low height because of the low bridges on the line. These were the survivors of seven locomotives built by Hudswell Clarke in 1909-1919. The first was withdrawn in 1929. 2162 was originally named PONTYBEREM.

g Several locomotives were rebuilt by the GWR with GWR fittings.

Year End Totals: 'BPGV 1' class

'47	'48	'49	'50	'51	'52	'53	'54	'55	'56	'57	'58	'59	'60	'61	'62	'63	'64	'65	'66	'67
5	5	5	5	5	5	4	4	1												

Number	Built	Renumbered	BR Dates	Scrap	Notes
2162	05/14 HC		-03/55	55	g
2165	05/13 HC		-03/55	04/55	g
2166	10/16 HC		-05/55	06/55	
2167	08/19 HC		-02/53	05/53	g
2168	02/16 HC		-05/56	56	g

BPGV [2] 2176

0-6-0ST Burry Port & Gwendraeth Valley

Power Classification:	1F
Introduced:	1907
Designer:	Avonside Engine Co.
Company:	Burry Port & Gwendraeth Valley
Weight:	38t 5cwt
Driving Wheel:	3' 6"
Boiler Pressure:	165psi
Cylinders:	Outside 15" x 22"
Tractive Effort:	16530lbf
Valve Gear:	Stephenson (slide valves)

This locomotive built by the Avonside Engine Company for the Burry Port & Gwendraeth Valley Railway in 1907. It was named PEMBREY until 1927.

g It was rebuilt by the GWR with GWR fittings.

Year End Totals: 'BPGV 2' class

'47	'48	'49	'50	'51	'52	'53	'54	'55	'56	'57	'58	'59	'60	'61	'62	'63	'64	'65	'66	'67
1	1	1	1	1	1	1	1													

Number	Built	Renumbered	BR Dates	Scrap	Notes
2176	01/07 AE		-03/55	04/55	g

2181 2181-2190

0-6-0PT GWR 2021 with modified brakes 4ft 1½in

Power Classification:	2F
Introduced:	1897-1905 rebuilt 1939-1940
Designer:	Dean, built at Wolverhampton
Company:	GWR
Weight:	39t 15cwt
Driving Wheel:	4' 1½"
Boiler Pressure:	165psi
Cylinders:	Inside 16½" x 24"
Tractive Effort:	18515lbf
Valve Gear:	Stephenson (slide valves)

Refer to the Historical Survey of GWR Pannier Tank Engines at the end of this section for more details of this class.

The '2181' class locomotives were converted from standard '2021' class locomotives in 1939-1940. They were given altered brake gear to give them increased braking power for working on heavy gradients. They were converted and renumbered from 2133, 2125, 2074, 2145, 2149, 2118, 2143, 2087, 2105 and 2157 respectively.

Year End Totals: '2181' class

'47	'48	'49	'50	'51	'52	'53	'54	'55	'56	'57	'58	'59	'60	'61	'62	'63	'64	'65	'66	'67
10	10	10	8	7	3	3	3													

Number	Built	Renumbered	BR Dates	Scrap	Notes
2181	09/03 Wlv		-02/52	52	
2182	05/03 Wlv		-08/55	55	
2183	12/99 Wlv		-05/55	55	
2184	05/04 Wlv		-11/50	50	
2185	08/04 Wlv		-12/52	02/53	
2186	11/02 Wlv		-04/55	04/55	
2187	04/04 Wlv		-02/52	04/52	
2188	01/01 Wlv		-02/52	02/52	
2189	04/02 Wlv		-10/50	11/50	
2190	01/05 Wlv		-04/51	51	

BPGV [3] 2192-2193

0-6-0ST Burry Port & Gwendraeth Valley

Power Classification:	1F
Introduced:	1900 s 1901
Designer:	R A Carr, built by Chapman & Furneaux
Company:	Burry Port & Gwendraeth Valley
Weight:	41t 18cwt s 35t 12cwt
Driving Wheel:	3' 8" s 3' 6"
Boiler Pressure:	140psi
Cylinders:	Outside 16" x 24" s Outside 15" x 22"
Tractive Effort:	16615lbf s 14025lbf
Valve Gear:	Stephenson (slide valves)

These two locomotives were built for the Burry Port & Gwendraeth Valley Railway by Chapman & Furneaux in 1900-1901.

s 2193 was a slightly smaller engine.

Year End Totals: 'BPGV 3' class

'47	'48	'49	'50	'51	'52	'53	'54	'55	'56	'57	'58	'59	'60	'61	'62	'63	'64	'65	'66	'67
2	2	2	2	1																

Number	Built	Renumbered	BR Dates	Scrap	Notes
2192	08/00 CF		-04/51	05/51	
ASHBURNHAM					
2193	09/01 CF		-02/52	*52*	s
BURRY PORT					

BPGV [4] 2194-2195
0-6-0ST Burry Port & Gwendraeth Valley

Power Classification: 0F
Introduced: 1903
Designer: Eager, built by Avonside Engine Co.
Company: Burry Port & Gwendraeth Valley
Weight: 31t 7cwt
Driving Wheel: 3' 6"
Boiler Pressure: 150psi
Cylinders: Outside 15" x 20"
Tractive Effort: 13660lbf
Valve Gear: Stephenson (slide valves)

These two engines were built by the Avonside Engine Company for the Burry Port & Gwendraeth Valley Railway in 1903. 2195 was named CWM MAWR until 1929.

g 2194 was rebuilt with GWR fittings in 1923.

Year End Totals: 'BPGV [4]' class

'47	'48	'49	'50	'51	'52	'53	'54	'55	'56	'57	'58	'59	'60	'61	'62	'63	'64	'65	'66	'67
2	2	2	2	2	2															

Number	Built	Renumbered	BR Dates	Scrap	Notes
2194	05/03 AE		-02/53	02/53	g
KIDWELLY					
2195	04/05 AE		-01/53	*11/53*	

BPGV [5] 2196
0-6-0ST Burry Port & Gwendraeth Valley

Power Classification: 1F
Introduced: 1906
Designer: Avonside Engine Co.
Company: Burry Port & Gwendraeth Valley
Weight: 38t 0cwt
Driving Wheel: 3' 6"
Boiler Pressure: 170psi
Cylinders: Outside 15" x 22"
Tractive Effort: 17030lbf
Valve Gear: Stephenson (slide valves)

This engine was built by the Avonside Engine Company for the Burry Port & Gwendraeth Valley Railway in 1906.

Year End Totals: 'BPGV [5]' class

'47	'48	'49	'50	'51	'52	'53	'54	'55	'56	'57	'58	'59	'60	'61	'62	'63	'64	'65	'66	'67
1	1	1	1	1	1	1	1	1	1											

Number	Built	Renumbered	BR Dates	Scrap	Notes
2196	09/06 AE		-01/56	*56*	
GWENDRAETH					

BPGV [6] 2197
0-6-0T Burry Port & Gwendraeth Valley

Power Classification: 0F
Introduced: 1909
Designer: Hudswell Clarke
Company: Burry Port & Gwendraeth Valley
Weight: 36t 8cwt
Driving Wheel: 3' 9"
Boiler Pressure: 160psi
Cylinders: Outside 15" x 22"
Tractive Effort: 14960lbf
Valve Gear: Stephenson (slide valves)

This engine was built for the Burry Port & Gwendraeth Valley Railway by Hudswell Clarke in 1909.

Year End Totals: 'BPGV [6]' class

'47	'48	'49	'50	'51	'52	'53	'54	'55	'56	'57	'58	'59	'60	'61	'62	'63	'64	'65	'66	'67
1	1	1	1	1																

Number	Built	Renumbered	BR Dates	Scrap	Notes
2197	03/09 HC		-10/52	*52*	
PIONEER					

BPGV [7] 2198
0-6-0T Burry Port & Gwendraeth Valley

Power Classification: 1F
Introduced: 1910
Designer: Hudswell Clarke
Company: Burry Port & Gwendraeth Valley
Weight: 37t 15cwt
Driving Wheel: 3' 9"
Boiler Pressure: 165psi
Cylinders: Outside 15" x 22"
Tractive Effort: 15430lbf
Valve Gear: Stephenson (slide valves)

This engine was a slightly larger version of No. 2197 and it was built by Hudswell Clarke for the Burry Port & Gwendraeth Valley Railway in 1910.

g It was rebuilt by the GWR with GWR fittings.

Year End Totals: 'BPGV [7]' class

'47	'48	'49	'50	'51	'52	'53	'54	'55	'56	'57	'58	'59	'60	'61	'62	'63	'64	'65	'66	'67
1	1	1	1	1	1	1	1	1	1	1	1	1								

Number	Built	Renumbered	BR Dates	Scrap	Notes
2198	12/10 HC		-03/59	*59*	g

2251 2200-2299, 3200-3219
0-6-0 GWR Collett

Power Classification: 3MT
Introduced: 1930-1948
Designer: Collett
Company: GWR
Weight: Loco 43t 8cwt
Tender 36t 5cwt
r Tender 47t 6cwt
Driving Wheel: 5' 2"
Boiler Pressure: 200psi superheated
Cylinders: Inside 17½" x 24"
Tractive Effort: 20155lbf
Valve Gear: Stephenson (slide valves)

These locomotives were designed for mixed traffic work to replace the Armstrong and Dean 'Goods' engines which had carried the brunt of the work on the light absorbed lines in Central Wales. They were very similar to the 'Dean Goods' class ('2301' class) in frames, wheels and motion, but they were fitted with a short tapered boiler with no dome. They had large side window cabs and could work over almost all the system. They were frequently used on passenger duties and were lively engines with a good turn of speed. 3218 was the first locomotive to be built at Swindon under the new BR ownership in 1948.

r Some of the class were fitted with large tenders from withdrawn 'ROD' locomotives, the majority of the class being fitted with smaller Churchward or Collett tenders.

w 2211-2240 were built during the war in 1940-1944. They were built without side windows to the cabs in order to assist with the black-out regulations. They were later rebuilt with normal side window cabs.

Year End Totals: '2251' class

'47	'48	'49	'50	'51	'52	'53	'54	'55	'56	'57	'58	'59	'60	'61	'62	'63	'64	'65	'66	'67
118	120	120	120	120	120	120	120	120	120	120	119	92	82	73	53	34	15			

Number	Built	Renumbered	BR Dates	Scrap	Notes
2200	06/38 Sdn		-09/62	06/64	
2201	07/39 Sdn		-06/64	01/65	
2202	08/39 Sdn		-10/60	01/61	
2203	08/39 Sdn		-09/60	11/60	
2204	08/39 Sdn		-12/63	05/64	
2205	08/39 Sdn		-06/59	02/60	
2206	08/39 Sdn		-12/61	05/62	
2207	08/39 Sdn		-04/61	06/61	
2208	08/39 Sdn		-06/59	04/60	
2209	09/39 Sdn		-08/62	07/63	
2210	09/39 Sdn		-06/65	09/65	
2211	05/40 Sdn		-11/64	12/64	w
2212	05/40 Sdn		-12/62	04/64	w
2213	05/40 Sdn		-11/60	02/61	w
2214	05/40 Sdn		-05/65	08/65	w
2215	05/40 Sdn		-10/61	12/61	w
2216	06/40 Sdn		-01/62	06/62	w
2217	06/40 Sdn		-11/64	04/65	w
2218	06/40 Sdn		-11/64	04/65	w
2219	06/40 Sdn		-03/64	06/64	w
2220	06/40 Sdn		-12/61	03/62	w
2221	08/40 Sdn		-11/64	03/65	w
2222	08/40 Sdn		-05/65	08/65	w
2223	08/40 Sdn		-05/62	12/62	w
2224	09/40 Sdn		-09/63	01/64	w
2225	09/40 Sdn		-06/59	01/60	w
2226	09/40 Sdn		-08/59	10/59	w
2227	10/40 Sdn		-04/61	07/61	w
2228	10/40 Sdn		-06/59	12/59	w
2229	10/40 Sdn		-09/62	09/63	w
2230	10/40 Sdn		-01/62	04/62	w
2231	10/44 Sdn		-02/65	02/65	w
2232	10/44 Sdn		-09/64	11/64	w
2233	10/44 Sdn		-11/61	03/62	w
2234	10/44 Sdn		-05/62	10/62	w
2235	10/44 Sdn		-08/59	12/59	w
2236	10/44 Sdn		-05/65	02/66	w
2237	11/44 Sdn		-06/59	04/60	w
2238	11/44 Sdn		-06/59	12/59	w
2239	11/44 Sdn		-05/62	02/63	w
2240	12/44 Sdn		-06/62	11/62	w
2241	03/45 Sdn		-02/64	08/64	
2242	04/45 Sdn		-05/65	08/65	
2243	04/45 Sdn		-01/63	05/63	
2244	04/45 Sdn		-06/65	08/65	
2245	04/45 Sdn		-05/63	05/64	
2246	08/45 Sdn		-12/63	04/64	
2247	08/45 Sdn		-02/64	06/64	
2248	08/45 Sdn		-09/64	12/64	
2249	08/45 Sdn		-09/64	12/64	
2250	09/45 Sdn		-08/62	09/63	
2251	03/30 Sdn		-12/63	05/64	
2252	03/30 Sdn		-12/59	03/60	
2253	03/30 Sdn		-03/65	05/65	
2254	03/30 Sdn		-01/59	11/59	
2255	03/30 Sdn		-05/62	11/62	
2256	03/30 Sdn		-09/62	01/64	
2257	04/30 Sdn		-09/64	12/64	
2258	04/30 Sdn		-12/58	02/59	
2259	04/30 Sdn		-04/59	05/59	
2260	04/30 Sdn		-11/61	02/62	
2261	04/30 Sdn		-09/64	12/64	
2262	04/30 Sdn		-12/59	03/60	
2263	04/30 Sdn		-01/59	03/59	
2264	04/30 Sdn		-09/60	10/60	
2265	05/30 Sdn		-09/60	11/60	
2266	05/30 Sdn		-10/59	03/60	
2267	06/30 Sdn		-11/61	03/62	
2268	06/30 Sdn		-05/65	02/66	
2269	07/30 Sdn		-01/59	03/59	
2270	04/30 Sdn		-09/59	12/59	
2271	08/34 Sdn		-09/62	10/63	
2272	08/34 Sdn		-08/59	01/60	
2273	08/34 Sdn		-12/63	07/64	
2274	08/34 Sdn		-09/60	11/60	
2275	08/34 Sdn		-02/60	05/60	
2276	09/34 Sdn		-09/62	07/64	
2277	09/34 Sdn		-12/63	05/64	
2278	09/34 Sdn		-09/59	03/60	
2279	09/34 Sdn		-01/59	05/59	
2280	09/34 Sdn		-09/59	02/60	
2281	01/36 Sdn		-11/59	12/60	
2282	01/36 Sdn		-05/60	08/60	
2283	01/36 Sdn		-12/63	04/64	
2284	01/36 Sdn		-06/59	02/60	
2285	01/36 Sdn		-11/59	01/60	
2286	01/36 Sdn		-09/64	01/65	
2287	01/36 Sdn		-05/65	09/65	
2288	01/36 Sdn		-12/61	06/62	
2289	01/36 Sdn		-05/64	08/64	
2290	01/36 Sdn		-06/59	03/60	
2291	01/38 Sdn		-09/64	11/64	
2292	02/38 Sdn		-06/62	09/62	
2293	02/38 Sdn		-07/59	10/59	
2294	02/38 Sdn		-09/62	08/64	
2295	02/38 Sdn		-07/62	10/62	
2296	06/38 Sdn		-10/59	01/60	
2297	06/38 Sdn		-09/60	10/60	
2298	06/38 Sdn		-12/63	04/64	
2299	06/38 Sdn		-09/59	01/60	

Class continued with 3200

2301 2322-2579
0-6-0 GWR Dean Goods

Power Classification: 2MT
Introduced: 1883-1899
Designer: Dean, built at Wolverhampton
Company: GWR
Weight: Loco 36t 16cwt
Tender 34t 5cwt

Driving Wheel:	5' 2"
Boiler Pressure:	180psi superheated
Cylinders:	Inside 17" x 24" c Inside 17½" x 24"
Tractive Effort:	17120lbf c 18140lbf
Valve Gear:	Stephenson (slide valves)

This was Dean's standard 0-6-0 engine for mixed traffic work on the GWR. A total of 280 were built in 1883-1899, numbered 2301-2580, the first being withdrawn in 1907. Twenty engines (2361-2380) were built with outside frames, the remainder had inside frames. Most of the class received domed Belpaire boilers from 1911 onwards. In addition nearly all of them (including all those listed here) were fitted with superheaters. Twenty locomotives (2491-2510) were rebuilt as 2-6-2Ts for working in the Birmingham area. They were known as the '3900' class and were all withdrawn between 1930 and 1934.

Sixty-two locomotives were taken over by the Government in the First World War, the majority of which (all except eight) returned safely. Again in the Second World War 108 locomotives were transferred to the military authorities for use overseas (including some which had been overseas in the First World War). Many of these were lost in France and the remainder found their way all over the World - one or two even being reported in China.

c Some locomotives (numbers unknown) had larger cylinders.

Year End Totals: '2301' class

'47	'48	'49	'50	'51	'52	'53	'54	'55	'56	'57	'58	'59	'60	'61	'62	'63	'64	'65	'66	'67
54	52	49	47	44	36	12	4	2	1											

Number	Built	Renumbered	BR Dates	Scrap	Notes
2322	01/84 Sdn		-06/51	08/51	
2323	01/84 Sdn		-06/53	53	
2327	02/84 Sdn		-04/53	05/53	
2339	06/84 Sdn		-03/52	52	
2340	07/84 Sdn		-06/54	06/54	
2343	07/84 Sdn		-02/53	53	
2349	11/84 Sdn		-03/52	04/52	
2350	11/84 Sdn		-01/53	02/53	
2351	11/84 Sdn		-02/53	02/53	
2354	11/84 Sdn		-04/53	53	
2356	12/84 Sdn		-07/48	48	
2382	09/90 Sdn		-04/50	08/50	
2385	07/90 Sdn		-10/51	11/51	
2386	07/90 Sdn		-12/50	51	
2401	10/91 Sdn		-01/53	53	
2407	11/91 Sdn		-01/52	52	
2408	11/91 Sdn		-01/53	02/53	
2409	11/91 Sdn		-04/53	53	
2411	11/91 Sdn		-04/54	54	
2414	12/91 Sdn		-03/53	53	
2426	02/92 Sdn		-12/53	54	
2431	02/93 Sdn		-11/51	12/51	
2444	05/93 Sdn		-11/52	52	
2445	05/93 Sdn		-03/53	53	
2449	07/93 Sdn		-01/53	53	
2452	10/95 Sdn		-10/52	52	
2458	12/95 Sdn		-05/54	54	
2460	12/95 Sdn		-04/54	54	
2462	12/95 Sdn		-01/53	53	
2464	01/96 Sdn		-12/49	02/50	
2468	02/96 Sdn		-01/53	02/53	
2474	03/96 Sdn		-04/55	55	
2482	05/96 Sdn		-12/52	53	
2483	05/96 Sdn		-09/52	10/52	
2484	06/96 Sdn		-05/54	54	
2513	02/97 Sdn		-07/55	55	
2515	03/97 Sdn		-02/53	02/53	
2516 §	03/97 Sdn		-05/56		
2523	05/97 Sdn		-09/49	09/49	
2532	06/97 Sdn		-05/54	54	
2534	07/97 Sdn		-01/53	09/56	
2537	07/97 Sdn		-01/53	53	
2538	08/97 Sdn		-05/57	57	
2541	08/97 Sdn		-06/54	06/54	
2543	09/97 Sdn		-02/53	05/53	
2551	11/97 Sdn		-09/53	53	
2556	11/97 Sdn		-06/53	53	
2568	02/98 Sdn		-05/53	53	
2569	04/98 Sdn		-10/48	10/48	
2570	04/98 Sdn		-01/49	03/49	
2572	11/98 Sdn		-12/52	53	
2573	11/98 Sdn		-02/53	53	
2578	01/99 Sdn		-09/53	53	
2579	01/99 Sdn		-01/54	54	

2600 2612-2680
2-6-0 GWR Dean 'Aberdare'

Power Classification:	4F
Introduced:	1900-1907
Designer:	Dean
Company:	GWR
Weight:	Loco 56t 15cwt Tender 47t 14cwt
Driving Wheel:	4' 7½"
Boiler Pressure:	200psi
Cylinders:	Inside 18" x 26"
Tractive Effort:	25800lbf
Valve Gear:	Stephenson (slide valves)

These were the survivors of a class of eighty-one locomotives, the first of which was withdrawn in 1934.

In 1899 a small class of locomotives was built called the 'Kruger' class. These were extremely ugly and unsuccessful locomotives, and some parts of them were used in building the first few of the 'Aberdare' class in 1900.

The first of the 'Aberdare' class to be built was No. 33 in 1900 (later renumbered 2600). They were distinctive locomotives, having double frames for the coupled wheels, but single frames and bearings for the leading truck. They also had inside cylinders. They were named the 'Aberdare' class because their main duties (until displaced by '2800' class locomotives) involved hauling coal trains from Aberdare to Swindon. Many were later fitted with large 'ROD' tenders.

Year End Totals: '2600' class

'47	'48	'49	'50	'51	'52	'53	'54	'55	'56	'57	'58	'59	'60	'61	'62	'63	'64	'65	'66	'67
12	4																			

Number	Built	Renumbered	BR Dates	Scrap	Notes
2612	07/03 Sdn		-01/48	48	
2620	08/03 Sdn		-08/49	10/49	
2623	04/01 Sdn		-02/48	48	
2643	10/01 Sdn		-07/48	01/49	
2651	12/01 Sdn		-06/49	08/49	
2655	01/02 Sdn		-06/49	08/49	
2656	01/02 Sdn		-03/48	48	
2662	09/02 Sdn		-07/48	01/49	
2665	09/02 Sdn		-01/48	48	
2667	09/02 Sdn		-10/49	12/49	
2669	10/02 Sdn		-05/48	48	
2680	12/02 Sdn		-06/48	01/49	

655 between 1742 & 1789, 2702-2719
0-6-0PT GWR Dean (Wolverhampton) 4ft 7½in

Class continued from 1789

Number	Built	Renumbered	BR Dates	Scrap	Notes
2702	02/96 Wlv		-01/50	03/50	
2704	03/96 Wlv		-03/50	05/50	
2706	04/96 Wlv		-10/48	11/48	
2707	05/96 Wlv		-07/50	09/50	
2708	06/96 Wlv		-07/49	09/49	
2709	06/96 Wlv		-09/48	10/48	
2712	08/96 Wlv		-03/50	05/50	
2713	09/96 Wlv		-09/49	11/49	
2714	09/96 Wlv		-05/48	05/48	
2715	10/96 Wlv		-07/50	09/50	
2716	11/96 Wlv		-09/50	11/50	
2717	11/96 Wlv		-10/48	01/49	
2719	12/96 Wlv		-11/50	11/50	

2721 2721-2799
0-6-0PT GWR Dean (Swindon) 4ft 7½in

Power Classification:	3F
Introduced:	1897-1901
Designer:	Dean, built at Swindon
Company:	GWR
Weight:	45t 13cwt
Driving Wheel:	4' 7½"
Boiler Pressure:	180psi
Cylinders:	Inside 17½" x 24"
Tractive Effort:	20260lbf
Valve Gear:	Stephenson (slide valves)

Refer to the Historical Survey of GWR Pannier Tank Engines at the end of this section for more details of this class.

These were the survivors of eighty locomotives the first of which was withdrawn in 1945. They were identical with the '655' class, the only difference being that these were built at Swindon. 2756 was sold to the Rhondda & Swansea Bay Railway in 1921, but returned to the GWR with its original number in 1922.

2794 was sold into industrial service and it survived until September 1958.

Year End Totals: '2721' class

'47	'48	'49	'50	'51	'52	'53	'54	'55	'56	'57	'58	'59	'60	'61	'62	'63	'64	'65	'66	'67
44	27	15																		

Number	Built	Renumbered	BR Dates	Scrap	Notes
2721	11/97 Sdn		-08/50	09/50	
2722	03/98 Sdn		-11/50	50	
2724	03/98 Sdn		-02/49	04/49	
2728	05/98 Sdn		-04/48	48	
2730	05/98 Sdn		-04/48	05/48	
2734	07/98 Sdn		-08/48	09/48	
2738	08/98 Sdn		-12/49	11/50	
2739	09/98 Sdn		-05/48	48	
2743	04/99 Sdn		-10/50	50	
2744	04/99 Sdn		-11/50	11/50	
2745	05/99 Sdn		-01/50	03/50	
2746	05/99 Sdn		-07/48	01/49	
2748	05/99 Sdn		-04/48	48	
2749	05/99 Sdn		-04/48	01/49	
2751	06/99 Sdn		-04/48	09/48	
2752	06/99 Sdn		-03/48	48	
2754	07/99 Sdn		-10/50	50	
2755	07/99 Sdn		-08/48	10/48	
2756	08/99 Sdn		-05/49	07/49	
2757	08/99 Sdn		-02/50	50	
2760	08/99 Sdn		-10/50	50	
2761	03/00 Sdn		-03/50	05/50	
2764	03/00 Sdn		-07/48	09/48	
2767	08/00 Sdn		-01/49	03/49	
2769	09/00 Sdn		-03/49	05/49	
2771	09/00 Sdn		-06/50	08/50	
2772	09/00 Sdn		-11/49	03/50	
2774	09/00 Sdn		-04/48	48	
2776	10/00 Sdn		-04/48	48	
2780	10/00 Sdn		-07/50	09/50	
2781	01/01 Sdn		-06/48	06/48	
2785	01/01 Sdn		-04/48	48	
2786	01/01 Sdn		-12/49	06/50	
2787	01/01 Sdn		-12/49	02/50	
2789	02/01 Sdn		-05/49	08/50	
2790	02/01 Sdn		-06/50	08/50	
2791	02/01 Sdn		-04/50	06/50	
2792	02/01 Sdn		-06/50	08/50	
2793	02/01 Sdn		-01/48	48	
2794	02/01 Sdn		-11/49	09/58	
2795	02/01 Sdn		-01/49	03/49	
2797	03/01 Sdn		-06/48	48	
2798	03/01 Sdn		-11/49	01/50	
2799	03/01 Sdn		-03/50	05/50	

2800 2800-2883, (4800-4811)
2-8-0 GWR Churchward

Power Classification:	8F
Introduced:	1903-1919
Designer:	Churchward
Company:	GWR
Weight:	Loco 75t 10cwt Tender 40t 0cwt
Driving Wheel:	4' 7½"
Boiler Pressure:	225psi superheated
Cylinders:	Outside 18½" x 30"
Tractive Effort:	35380lbf
Valve Gear:	Stephenson (piston valves)

This was the first 2-8-0 freight engine design to be built in this country, the prototype 2800 (originally No. 97) being built in 1903. The design was much in advance of its time and this class and the slightly modified '2884' class were built from 1903 until 1942. They remained the standard freight design on the GWR for the rest of the company's existence, and were used on the heaviest freight trains.

The earlier locomotives originally had 18" diameter cylinders and were not superheated. They were superheated from 1909 onwards and had the cylinders bored out to 18½" to match the later engines. All the locomotives were later fitted with curved framing over the cylinders and outside steam pipes.

o Twenty of the '2800'/'2884' class locomotives were rebuilt to oil burning during the coal crisis of 1947. They were renumbered in the 4800 series (causing the '4800' class 0-4-2Ts to be renumbered in the 1400 series). By 1950 they were all converted back to coal burning with their original numbers.

Year End Totals: '2800' class

'47	'48	'49	'50	'51	'52	'53	'54	'55	'56	'57	'58	'59	'60	'61	'62	'63	'64	'65	'66	'67
72	75	83	84	84	84	84	84	84	84	84	78	49	35	34	28	10	1			

Year End Totals: '2800' (oil burning) class

'47	'48	'49	'50	'51	'52	'53	'54	'55	'56	'57	'58	'59	'60	'61	'62	'63	'64	'65	'66	'67
12	9	1																		

Number	Built	Renumbered	BR Dates	Scrap	Notes
2800	06/03 Sdn		-04/58	05/58	
2801	09/05 Sdn		-12/58	01/59	
2802	09/05 Sdn		-12/58	02/59	
2803	10/05 Sdn		-04/59	04/59	
2804	10/05 Sdn		-07/59	08/59	
2805	10/05 Sdn		-05/60	08/60	
2806	10/05 Sdn		-03/60	04/60	
2807 §	10/05 Sdn		-03/63		
2808	10/05 Sdn		-09/59	12/59	
2809	10/05 Sdn		-01/60	03/60	
2810	10/05 Sdn		-09/59	12/59	
2811	11/05 Sdn		-10/59	03/60	
2812	11/05 Sdn		-01/59	09/59	
2813	11/05 Sdn		-11/60	04/61	
2814	11/05 Sdn		-08/58	08/58	
2815	11/05 Sdn		-12/59	12/59	
2816	12/05 Sdn		-10/59	12/59	
2817	12/05 Sdn		-03/59	08/59	
2818 §	12/05 Sdn		-10/63		
2819	12/05 Sdn		-01/61	04/61	
2820	12/05 Sdn		-11/58	11/58	
2821	01/07 Sdn		-09/60	04/61	
2822	01/07 Sdn		-11/64	02/65	
2823	01/07 Sdn		-04/59	08/59	
2824	01/07 Sdn		-08/59	12/59	
2825	01/07 Sdn		-03/59	08/59	
2826	01/07 Sdn		-09/59	12/59	
2827	02/07 Sdn		-08/58	06/59	
2828	02/07 Sdn		-01/59	08/59	
2829	02/07 Sdn		-02/59	02/59	
2830	02/07 Sdn		-01/59	08/59	
2831	03/11 Sdn		-01/60	02/60	
2832	04/11 Sdn	04/49 4806	-11/59	04/61	
2833	04/11 Sdn		-03/59	08/59	
2834	05/11 Sdn	01/50 4808	-11/62	05/63	
2835	05/11 Sdn		-05/60	05/60	
2836	09/12 Sdn		-06/64	02/65	
2837	09/12 Sdn		-05/60	08/60	
2838	09/12 Sdn		-08/59	10/59	
2839	10/12 Sdn	10/48 4804	-06/64	02/65	
2840	10/12 Sdn		-06/59	05/60	
2841	10/12 Sdn		-12/63	12/64	
2842	10/12 Sdn		-09/63	07/64	
2843	11/12 Sdn		-06/59	02/60	
2844	11/12 Sdn		-02/60	04/60	
2845	12/12 Sdn	12/49 4809	-07/63	09/63	
2846	12/12 Sdn		-11/60	02/61	
2847	01/13 Sdn	06/49 4811	-03/60	04/60	
2848	01/13 Sdn	07/49 4807	-06/59	02/60	
2849	01/13 Sdn	04/49 4803	-08/62	06/63	
2850	02/13 Sdn		-02/60	03/60	
2851	02/13 Sdn		-06/63	07/64	
2852	02/13 Sdn		-10/63	06/65	
2853	02/13 Sdn	06/49 4810	-05/62	08/62	
2854	02/13 Sdn	02/49 4801	-10/63	07/64	
2855	02/13 Sdn		-12/62	02/63	
2856	04/18 Sdn		-04/64	12/64	
2857 §	04/18 Sdn		-04/63		
2858	04/18 Sdn		-01/63	03/63	
2859 §	05/18 Sdn		-12/64		
2860	05/18 Sdn		-04/62	07/62	
2861 §	05/18 Sdn		-03/63		
2862	05/18 Sdn	09/48 4802	-04/64	02/65	
2863	06/18 Sdn	05/49 4805	-06/59	04/60	
2864	06/18 Sdn		-06/59	04/60	
2865	06/18 Sdn		-01/63	02/63	
2866	09/18 Sdn		-03/63	01/64	
2867	10/18 Sdn		-07/63	05/64	
2868	10/18 Sdn		-06/59	05/60	
2869	10/18 Sdn		-06/59	06/60	
2870	10/18 Sdn		-06/59	04/60	
2871	10/18 Sdn		-05/63	06/64	
2872	11/18 Sdn	09/48 4800	-08/63	06/64	
2873 §	11/18 Sdn		-12/64		
2874 §	11/18 Sdn		-05/63		
2875	11/18 Sdn		-04/64	02/65	
2876	01/19 Sdn		-01/65	02/65	
2877	01/19 Sdn		-01/60	03/60	
2878	01/19 Sdn		-06/59	05/60	
2879	02/19 Sdn		-08/64	12/64	
2880	03/19 Sdn		-06/59	05/60	
2881	03/19 Sdn		-01/60	02/60	
2882	03/19 Sdn		-12/63	03/65	
2883	03/19 Sdn		-11/62	04/63	

Class continued with 4800

2884 2884-2899, 3800-3866, (4850-4857)

2-8-0 GWR Modified '2800' class with side window cabs

Power Classification:	8F
Introduced:	1938-1942
Designer:	Collett
Company:	GWR
Weight:	Loco 76t 5cwt
	Tender 40t 0cwt
Driving Wheel:	4' 7½"
Boiler Pressure:	225psi superheated
Cylinders:	Outside 18½" x 30"
Tractive Effort:	35380lbf
Valve Gear:	Stephenson (piston valves)

This was the Collett version of the '2800' class, built 20 years after the last '2800' class locomotive was built. They were slightly heavier with large side-windowed cabs and outside steam pipes. There was a casing on the left hand side of the locomotive on the running plate (looking like a continuous splasher over the wheels) which was used to store the fire-irons.

o Oil burning locomotives renumbered in the 4850 series. By 1949 they were all converted back to coal burning with their original numbers.

Year End Totals: '2884' class

'47	'48	'49	'50	'51	'52	'53	'54	'55	'56	'57	'58	'59	'60	'61	'62	'63	'64	'65	'66	'67
75	77	83	83	83	83	83	83	83	83	83	83	83	83	83	82	67	34			

Year End Totals: '2884' (oil burning) class

'47	'48	'49	'50	'51	'52	'53	'54	'55	'56	'57	'58	'59	'60	'61	'62	'63	'64	'65	'66	'67
8	6																			

Number	Built	Renumbered	BR Dates	Scrap	Notes
2884	03/38 Sdn		-04/64	04/65	
2885 §	03/38 Sdn		-01/64		
2886	03/38 Sdn		-06/64	04/65	
2887	03/38 Sdn		-06/64	02/65	
2888	03/38 Sdn	09/48 4850	-02/63	06/63	
2889	03/38 Sdn		-04/63	06/63	
2890	04/38 Sdn		-04/65	08/65	
2891	04/38 Sdn		-10/64	02/65	
2892	04/38 Sdn		-05/63	08/63	
2893	04/38 Sdn		-11/64	04/65	
2894	11/38 Sdn		-08/63	04/64	
2895	11/38 Sdn		-04/65	08/65	
2896	11/38 Sdn		-06/64	02/65	
2897	11/38 Sdn		-03/63	01/64	
2898	11/38 Sdn		-10/64	02/65	
2899	12/38 Sdn		-03/65	07/65	

Class continued with 3800

2900 2902-2989

4-6-0 GWR Churchward 'Saint'

Power Classification:	4P
Introduced:	1902-1913
Designer:	Churchward
Company:	GWR
Weight:	Loco 72t 0cwt
	Tender 40t 0cwt
Driving Wheel:	6' 8½"
Boiler Pressure:	225psi superheated
Cylinders:	Outside 18½" x 30"
Tractive Effort:	24395lbf
Valve Gear:	Stephenson (piston valves)
	c Caprotti (poppet valves)

In 1902 the GWR introduced a locomotive which was to become the forerunner of a long line of 4-6-0 express engines. This was No. 100 which was later renumbered 2900 WILLIAM DEAN. It had a high running plate and large domeless boiler, which looked unusual at the time, but set the pattern for future GWR locomotives. It was the first GWR engine to carry outside cylinders. The early locomotives were rebuilt from 1903 onwards with new superheated boilers and the remainder were built as such.

In total seventy-seven locomotives were built, the first being withdrawn in 1931. 2900 itself was withdrawn in 1932. They were numbered 2900-2955, 2971-2990 and 2998. 2971, 2972 and 2979-2990 were constructed as Atlantics (4-4-2s) and were later converted (in 1912-1913) to 4-6-0s. Successive batches were named after Ladies, Saints, Courts and names connected with Sir Walter Scott's novels, but the class was collectively known as the 'Saint' class.

There were many variations in the class. Some had inside steam pipes, while others had outside steam pipes. Some of the earlier engines had the raised running plate extending to the back of the cab.

In 1924 2925 SAINT MARTIN was rebuilt with 6' 0" wheels and renumbered 4900 to become the prototype of the 'Hall' ('4900') class.

Some of the engines were renamed before 1948, including 2979 formerly MAGNET and 2987 formerly ROBERTSON.

a These were originally built as Atlantic locomotives (see above).

c 2935 had Caprotti valve gear and it was the only locomotive ever to run on the GWR with poppet valves.

Year End Totals: '2900' class

'47	'48	'49	'50	'51	'52	'53	'54	'55	'56	'57	'58	'59	'60	'61	'62	'63	'64	'65	'66	'67
47	39	31	26	13	4															

Number	Built	Renumbered	BR Dates	Scrap	Notes
2902	05/06 Sdn		-08/49	10/49	
LADY OF THE LAKE					
2903	05/06 Sdn		-11/49	01/50	
LADY OF LYONS					
2905	05/06 Sdn		-04/48	05/48	
LADY MACBETH					
2906	05/06 Sdn		-08/52	*09/52*	
LADY OF LYNN					
2908	05/06 Sdn		-12/50	*02/51*	
LADY OF QUALITY					
2912	08/07 Sdn		-02/51	*51*	
SAINT AMBROSE					
2913	08/07 Sdn		-05/48	*48*	
SAINT ANDREW					
2915	08/07 Sdn		-10/50	*50*	
SAINT BARTHOLOMEW					
2916	08/07 Sdn		-07/48	*48*	
SAINT BENEDICT					
2920	09/07 Sdn		-10/53	11/53	
SAINT DAVID					
2924	09/07 Sdn		-03/50	05/50	
SAINT HELENA					
2926	09/07 Sdn		-09/51	10/51	
SAINT NICHOLAS					
2927	09/07 Sdn		-12/51	*02/52*	
SAINT PATRICK					
2928	09/07 Sdn		-08/48	*10/48*	
SAINT SEBASTIAN					
2929	09/07 Sdn		-12/49	*03/50*	
SAINT STEPHEN					
2930	09/07 Sdn		-11/49	01/50	
SAINT VINCENT					
2931	10/11 Sdn		-02/51	*51*	
ARLINGTON COURT					
2932	10/11 Sdn		-06/51	*06/51*	
ASHTON COURT					
2933	11/11 Sdn		-01/53	*02/53*	
BIBURY COURT					
2934	11/11 Sdn		-06/52	*07/52*	
BUTLEIGH COURT					
2935	11/11 Sdn		-12/48	*01/49*	c
CAYNHAM COURT					
2936	11/11 Sdn		-04/51	*05/51*	
CEFNTILLA COURT					
2937	12/11 Sdn		-06/53	*53*	
CLEVEDON COURT					
2938	12/11 Sdn		-08/52	*52*	
CORSHAM COURT					
2939	12/11 Sdn		-12/50	*51*	
CROOME COURT					
2940	12/11 Sdn		-01/52	*03/52*	
DORNEY COURT					
2941	05/12 Sdn		-12/49	02/50	
EASTON COURT					
2942	05/12 Sdn		-12/49	02/50	
FAWLEY COURT					
2943	05/12 Sdn		-01/51	*02/51*	
HAMPTON COURT					
2944	05/12 Sdn		-11/51	*02/52*	
HIGHNAM COURT					
2945	06/12 Sdn		-06/53	*53*	
HILLINGDON COURT					
2946	06/12 Sdn		-11/49	01/50	
LANGFORD COURT					
2947	06/12 Sdn		-04/51	*10/51*	
MADRESFIELD COURT					
2948	06/12 Sdn		-11/51	*12/51*	
STACKPOLE COURT					
2949	05/12 Sdn		-01/52	02/52	
STANFORD COURT					

Number	Built	Renumbered	BR Dates	Scrap	Notes
2950	05/12 Sdn		-09/52	10/52	
TAPLOW COURT					
2951	03/13 Sdn		-06/52	08/52	
TAWSTOCK COURT					
2952	03/13 Sdn		-09/51	51	
TWINEHAM COURT					
2953	03/13 Sdn		-02/52	52	
TITLEY COURT					
2954	03/13 Sdn		-06/52	08/52	
TOCKENHAM COURT					
2955	04/13 Sdn		-03/50	05/50	
TORTWORTH COURT					
2979	04/05 Sdn		-01/51	02/51	a
QUENTIN DURWARD					
2980	05/05 Sdn		-05/48	05/48	a
CŒUR DE LION					
2981	06/05 Sdn		-03/51	08/51	a
IVANHOE					
2987	08/05 Sdn		-10/49	12/49	a
BRIDE OF LAMMERMOOR					
2988	08/05 Sdn		-05/48	05/48	a
ROB ROY					
2989	09/05 Sdn		-09/48	10/48	a
TALISMAN					

R.O.D. 3002-3049
2-8-0 Railway Operating Division (GCR) Robinson

Power Classification: 7F
Introduced: 1917-1919, based on a 1911 Great Central Railway design
Designer: Robinson
Company: Railway Operating Division
Weight: Loco 73t 11cwt
Tender 47t 14cwt
Driving Wheel: 4' 8"
Boiler Pressure: 185psi superheated
Cylinders: Outside 21" x 26"
Tractive Effort: 32200lbf
Valve Gear: Stephenson (piston valves)

In 1911 Robinson introduced this 2-8-0 design on the Great Central Railway. (See LNER class 'O4'). They were adopted by the Railway Operating Division of the Royal Engineers as a standard type for service during the First World War. 521 locomotives were built between 1917 and 1919 by many different locomotive builders for service in France. Many stayed in this country and eventually all returned safely to Britain where they were purchased by the GCR (LNER class 'O4'), the LNWR (all withdrawn by 1933) and the GWR.

The GWR bought 3000-3019 in 1919, which were virtually new locomotives. Eighty-four more were hired in the period 1919-1922. In 1925 eighty engines were purchased (including some of those which had originally been hired). The best thirty of these were numbered 3020-3049 and the whole series of engines from 3000 to 3049 were refurbished and fitted with GWR fittings. The remainder (numbered 3050-3099) were in very bad condition and they were used until they were totally unfit and then scrapped (1927 onwards). None of these last fifty lasted into BR days, but their tenders reappeared on 2251 and 2600 class locomotives.

The frames of 3005 were used in 3033 when it was rebuilt in 1949.

They were easily distinguished from all other GWR 2-8-0s by having parallel boilers with a dome as well as a GWR safety valve casing. They also had continuous splashers over the rear three driving wheels.

Year End Totals: 'ROD' class

'47	'48	'49	'50	'51	'52	'53	'54	'55	'56	'57	'58	'59	'60	'61	'62	'63	'64	'65	'66	'67
45	29	29	29	29	29	26	23	20	6	5										

Number	Built	Renumbered	BR Dates	Scrap	Notes
3002	05/19 NB		-04/48	09/48	
3004	05/19 NB		-02/48	03/48	
3005	05/19 NB		-08/48	04/49	
3006	05/19 NB		-06/48	01/49	
3008	05/19 NB		-09/48	01/49	
3009	05/19 NB		-06/48	01/49	
3010	05/19 NB		-03/56	56	
3011	06/19 NB		-10/58	12/58	
3012	06/19 NB		-05/56	56	
3013	06/19 NB		-09/48	10/48	
3014	05/19 NB		-10/55	11/55	
3015	06/19 NB		-10/58	11/58	
3016	06/19 NB		-10/56	11/56	
3017	07/19 NB		-10/56	11/56	
3018	07/19 NB		-01/57	05/57	
3019	07/19 NB		-04/48	48	
3020	19 NB		-06/54	07/54	
3021	19 NB		-07/48	48	
3022	19 NB		-06/56	56	
3023	18 NB		-10/55	11/55	
3024	19 NB		-10/58	01/59	
3025	18 RS		-07/54	54	
3026	18 NW		-12/54	01/55	
3027	17 NW		-05/48	01/49	
3028	18 NW		-08/56	56	
3029	19 NB		-05/56	56	
3030	17 NB		-07/48	48	
3031	17 NB		-05/56	56	
3032	17 NW		-10/55	55	
3033	18 NB		-05/53	53	
3034	18 NB		-02/53	06/53	
3035	18 K		-08/48	01/49	
3036	19 NB		-03/58	03/58	
3037	18 NB		-08/48	01/49	
3038	19 RS		-07/56	08/56	
3039	19 NB		-08/48	01/49	
3040	19 NB		-06/56	56	
3041	19 NB		-03/58	04/58	
3042	17 NB		-10/56	56	
3043	19 NB		-09/56	56	
3044	19 NB		-10/56	11/56	
3046	19 NB		-08/48	01/49	
3047	17 NW		-06/53	53	
3048	19 NB		-05/56	56	
3049	17 NW		-11/48	01/49	

3100 3100-3104
2-6-2T GWR Churchward '3150' rebuilds 5ft 3in

Power Classification: 4MT
Introduced: 1906-1908 rebuilt by Collett 1938-39
Designer: Churchward
Company: GWR
Weight: 81t 9cwt
Driving Wheel: 5' 3"
Boiler Pressure: 225psi superheated
Cylinders: Outside 18½" x 30"
Tractive Effort: 31170lbf
Valve Gear: Stephenson (piston valves)

The GWR was a large user of the 2-6-2T type (the 'Prairie tank'). There were two varieties, the small 'Prairie tanks' ('4400', '4500' and '4575' classes) and the large 'Prairie tanks' ('3100', '3150', '5101', '6100' and '8100' classes).

The '3100' class were rebuilt from '3150' class locomotives with higher boiler pressure and smaller wheels for banking purposes. Their original numbers were 3173, 3156, 3181, 3155 and 3179 respectively. Originally it was planned to convert all the '3150' class and the old '3100' class (see '5101' class), but the Second World War put a stop to the conversion programme. The '8100' class was similarly converted except they were fitted with slightly larger 5' 6" wheels.

Year End Totals: '3100' class

'47	'48	'49	'50	'51	'52	'53	'54	'55	'56	'57	'58	'59	'60	'61	'62	'63	'64	'65	'66	'67
5	5	5	5	5	5	5	5	5	5	5	2	1	1							

Number	Built	Renumbered	BR Dates	Scrap	Notes
3100	10/07 Sdn		-05/57	02/61	
3101	04/07 Sdn		-08/57	02/61	
3102	12/07 Sdn		-10/58	01/61	
3103	04/07 Sdn		-01/60	12/60	
3104	11/07 Sdn		-06/57	10/57	

3150 3150-3190
2-6-2T GWR Churchward 5ft 8in

Power Classification: 4MT
Introduced: 1906-1908
Designer: Churchward
Company: GWR
Weight: 81t 12cwt
Driving Wheel: 5' 8"
Boiler Pressure: 200psi superheated
Cylinders: Outside 18½" x 30"
Tractive Effort: 25670lbf
Valve Gear: Stephenson (piston valves)

The '3150' class was developed from the original '3100' class of 1903 (see '5101' class). They were fitted with larger boilers which were subsequently superheated. There were originally forty-one locomotives; five were converted to '3100' class in 1938, and the first three were withdrawn in 1947.

3150 was rebuilt with the frames from 3184 in 1949.

Year End Totals: '3150' class

'47	'48	'49	'50	'51	'52	'53	'54	'55	'56	'57	'58	'59	'60	'61	'62	'63	'64	'65	'66	'67
33	30	26	23	22	17	15	15	15	13	3										

Number	Built	Renumbered	BR Dates	Scrap	Notes
3150	04/06 Sdn		-09/57	01/58	
3151	04/07 Sdn		-03/52	52	
3153	04/07 Sdn		-02/53	05/53	
3154	04/07 Sdn		-10/50	50	
3157	04/07 Sdn		-10/52	01/53	
3158	04/07 Sdn		-04/48	06/48	
3159	05/07 Sdn		-11/49	01/50	
3160	05/07 Sdn		-06/53	08/53	
3161	05/07 Sdn		-12/52	01/53	
3163	06/07 Sdn		-06/57	07/57	
3164	06/07 Sdn		-03/56	56	
3165	06/07 Sdn		-07/48	09/48	
3167	06/07 Sdn		-08/52	08/52	
3168	06/07 Sdn		-09/50	11/50	
3169	06/07 Sdn		-07/50	09/50	
3170	06/07 Sdn		-08/58	09/59	
3171	10/07 Sdn		-07/57	08/57	
3172	10/07 Sdn		-10/57	11/57	
3174	10/07 Sdn		-03/58	04/58	
3175	10/07 Sdn		-03/49	05/49	
3176	11/07 Sdn		-11/57	12/57	
3177	11/07 Sdn		-10/57	12/57	
3178	11/07 Sdn		-01/51	51	
3180	11/07 Sdn		-10/57	11/57	
3182	12/07 Sdn		-08/49	10/49	
3183	12/07 Sdn		-10/57	11/57	
3184	12/07 Sdn		-07/48	04/49	
3185	12/07 Sdn		-02/56	56	
3186	12/07 Sdn		-06/57	06/57	
3187	01/08 Sdn		-11/57	01/58	
3188	01/08 Sdn		-11/52	01/53	
3189	01/08 Sdn		-09/49	11/49	
3190	01/08 Sdn		-03/58	05/58	

2251 2200-2299, 3200-3219
2-6-0 GWR Collett

Class continued from 2299

Number	Built	Renumbered	BR Dates	Scrap	Notes
3200	09/46 Sdn		-01/65	04/65	
3201	09/46 Sdn		-05/65	08/65	
3202	10/46 Sdn		-06/60	08/60	
3203	10/46 Sdn		-12/63	04/64	
3204	10/46 Sdn		-02/63	10/63	
3205 §	10/46 Sdn		-05/65		
3206	10/46 Sdn		-12/63	05/64	
3207	10/46 Sdn		-12/62	07/64	
3208	10/46 Sdn		-05/65	08/65	
3209	11/46 Sdn		-06/64	08/64	
3210	12/47 Sdn		-11/64	02/65	
3211	12/47 Sdn		-09/62	04/63	
3212	12/47 Sdn		-10/63	12/64	
3213	12/47 Sdn		-12/63	11/64	
3214	12/47 Sdn		-10/63	01/64	
3215	12/47 Sdn		-01/63	01/64	
3216	12/47 Sdn		-12/63	05/64	
3217	12/47 Sdn		-11/64	12/64	
3218	01/48 Sdn		01/48-05/65	08/65	
3219	01/48 Sdn		01/48-12/63	11/64	

3300 3335-3455
4-4-0 GWR Dean & Churchward 'Bulldog'

Power Classification: 3MT
Introduced: 1899-1910
Designer: Dean
Company: GWR
Weight: Loco 51t 16cwt
Tender 40t 0cwt
c Loco 49t 16cwt
Driving Wheel: 5' 8"
Boiler Pressure: 200psi superheated
Cylinders: Inside 18" x 26"
Tractive Effort: 21060lbf
Valve Gear: Stephenson (slide valves)

Dean and Churchward built these locomotives between 1899 and 1910 with outside frames. They were developed from the 'Duke' class ('3252' class) and were later fitted with new boilers and superheaters. 3300-3319 were actually rebuilt 'Dukes', but none of these lasted into BR days. 3300-

Burry Port & Gwendraeth Valley Railway 0-6-0ST No 2196 *Gwendraeth* inside Llanelly shed in July 1950.

GWR Collett '2251' class 0-6-0 No 2253, fitted with a Churchward tender.

GWR Churchward '2800' class 2-8-0 No 2832 at Tyseley in May 1949.

GWR Churchward '4500' class 2-6-2T No 4505.

3340 were built with curved frames and 3341-3455 had straight topped frames. The class was known as the 'Bulldog' class, that being the name carried by 3311, one of the original locomotives. The majority of the class carried miscellaneous names. The last fifteen (3441-3455) were named after birds, and had slightly deeper frames than the others of the class.

In all 156 locomotives were built, the first being withdrawn in 1929. Twenty-nine locomotives were used in the construction of the '9000' class in 1936-1939. 3341 was the last locomotive to carry an old-style combined oval number and nameplate.

Some of the un-named locomotives formerly carried names as follows: 3335 TREGOTHNAN, 3366 EARL OF CORK, 3377 PENZANCE, 3382 CARDIFF, 3383 ILFRACOMBE and 3386 PADDINGTON.

b 'Bird' class locomotives with slightly deeper frames.

c 3335 was the last surviving engine with curved frames.

Year End Totals: '3300' class

'47	'48	'49	'50	'51	'52	'53	'54	'55	'56	'57	'58	'59	'60	'61	'62	'63	'64	'65	'66	'67
45	28	9	8																	

Number	Built	Renumbered	BR Dates	Scrap	Notes
3335	02/00 Sdn		-10/48	*01/49*	c
3341	05/00 Sdn		-11/49	09/50	
BLASIUS					
3363	12/02 Sdn		-10/49	12/49	
ALFRED BALDWIN					
3364	02/03 Sdn		-06/49	08/49	
FRANK BIBBY					
3366	02/03 Sdn		-04/48	*06/48*	
3376	05/03 Sdn		-09/48	*10/48*	
RIVER PLYM					
3377	05/03 Sdn		-03/51	*05/51*	
3379	05/03 Sdn		-06/48	*01/49*	
RIVER FAL					
3382	09/03 Sdn		-11/49	01/50	
3383	09/03 Sdn		-12/49	*03/50*	
3386	09/03 Sdn		-11/49	*02/51*	
3391	01/04 Sdn		-05/48	*01/49*	
DOMINION OF CANADA					
3393	01/04 Sdn		-11/49	*08/50*	
AUSTRALIA					
3395	01/04 Sdn		-08/48	*01/49*	
TASMANIA					
3396	01/04 Sdn		-03/48	*48*	
NATAL COLONY					
3400	02/04 Sdn		-05/49	07/49	
WINNIPEG					
3401	03/04 Sdn		-11/49	*03/50*	
VANCOUVER					
3406	03/04 Sdn		-01/51	*02/51*	
CALCUTTA					
3407	04/04 Sdn		-12/49	02/50	
MADRAS					
3408	04/04 Sdn		-04/48	*04/48*	
BOMBAY					
3417	06/06 Sdn		-04/48	*06/48*	
LORD MILDMAY OF FLETE					
3418	06/06 Sdn		-08/49	10/49	
SIR ARTHUR YORKE					
3419	06/06 Sdn		-08/49	10/49	
3421	06/06 Sdn		-04/48	06/48	
3426	07/06 Sdn		-12/49	02/50	
3430	08/06 Sdn		-12/48	01/49	
INCHCAPE					
3431	08/06 Sdn		-12/48	*12/48*	
3432	08/06 Sdn		-12/49	02/50	
3438	09/06 Sdn		-10/49	12/49	
3440	09/06 Sdn		-06/48	*10/48*	
3441	05/09 Sdn		-02/49	04/49	b
BLACKBIRD					
3442	05/09 Sdn		-07/48	07/49	b
BULLFINCH					
3443	05/09 Sdn		-05/49	*05/49*	b
CHAFFINCH					
3444	05/09 Sdn		-06/51	*08/51*	b
CORMORANT					
3445	05/09 Sdn		-10/48	*01/49*	b
FLAMINGO					
3446	11/09 Sdn		-12/48	*01/49*	b
GOLDFINCH					
3447	12/09 Sdn		-04/51	08/51	b
JACKDAW					
3448	12/09 Sdn		-01/49	03/49	b
KINGFISHER					
3449	12/09 Sdn		-06/51	*06/51*	b
NIGHTINGALE					
3450	12/09 Sdn		-12/49	03/50	b
PEACOCK					
3451	01/10 Sdn		-04/51	*05/51*	b
PELICAN					
3452	01/10 Sdn		-04/48	*48*	b
PENGUIN					
3453	01/10 Sdn		-11/51	12/51	b
SEAGULL					
3454	01/10 Sdn		-11/51	*11/51*	b
SKYLARK					
3455	01/10 Sdn		-06/50	08/50	b
STARLING					

9400 3400-3409, 8400-8499, 9400-9499
0-6-0PT GWR Hawksworth 4ft 7½in

Power Classification: 4F
Introduced: 1947-1956
Designer: Hawksworth
Company: GWR
Weight: 55t 7cwt
Driving Wheel: 4' 7½"
Boiler Pressure: 200psi
s 200psi superheated
Cylinders: Inside 17½" x 24"
Tractive Effort: 22515lbf
Valve Gear: Stephenson (slide valves)

Refer to the Historical Survey of GWR Pannier Tank Engines at the end of this section for more details of this class.

These were taper-boiler pannier tanks designed for heavy shunting. Developed from the '5700' class, they were in fact a tank engine version of the '2251' class. The first ten locomotives (9400-9409) were built at Swindon and were superheated. The remainder appeared after nationalisation and were not superheated. They were built by a variety of different contractors (Bagnall, Yorkshire Engine and Robert Stephenson) and delivery was very slow, with the last few not appearing until 1956. They were the last locomotives of pre-nationalisation design to be built. They had a very short life due to the introduction of diesels to replace them.

These were the last in a long line of GWR pannier tanks, a GWR design dating back to the 1860s. They were very sturdily built engines and their main dimensions were the same as the '5700' class. The pannier tanks did not flank the sides of the smokebox as on most other pannier tanks except the '1500' and '9700' classes.

9424 was sold for industrial use, surviving until 1966.

s Swindon built superheated locomotives.

Year End Totals: '9400' class

'47	'48	'49	'50	'51	'52	'53	'54	'55	'56	'57	'58	'59	'60	'61	'62	'63	'64	'65	'66	'67
10	10	23	76	119	169	180	198	201	210	210	210	181	165	150	108	78	32			

Number	Built	Renumbered	BR Dates	Scrap	Notes
3400	12/55 YE		12/55-11/64	02/65	
3401	01/56 YE		01/56-11/64	02/65	
3402	02/56 YE		02/56-11/64	02/65	
3403	02/56 YE		02/56-09/64	02/65	
3404	03/56 YE		03/56-07/62	10/62	
3405	04/56 YE		04/56-11/64	01/65	
3406	05/56 YE		05/56-11/64	02/65	
3407	08/56 YE		08/56-10/62	11/62	
3408	08/56 YE		08/56-09/62	11/62	
3409	10/56 YE		10/56-10/64	02/65	

Class continued with 8400

3500 3561-3562, 3582-3599
2-4-0T GWR Dean 'Metropolitan Tanks'

Power Classification: 1P
Introduced: 1869-1899 (survivors built 1894-1899)
Designer: Dean
Company: GWR
Weight: 41t 7cwt
Driving Wheel: 5' 2"
Boiler Pressure: 165psi
Cylinders: Inside 16" x 24"
Tractive Effort: 13900lbf
Valve Gear: Stephenson (slide valves)

These were the survivors of a class of 140 locomotives, the first being withdrawn as long ago as 1898. They were known as 'Metropolitan tanks' as many of them were fitted with condensing apparatus for working through the tunnels on the Metropolitan line.

There had been several different versions of the 'Metropolitan tank' of increasing size dating from 1869. Most of them were to be found working on country branch lines, having been replaced in the London area from the early 1920s. The '9700' class later took over their Metropolitan line duties. 3593 was rebuilt as a 2-4-2T in 1905 but was withdrawn before 1948.

Year End Totals: '3500' class

'47	'48	'49	'50	'51	'52	'53	'54	'55	'56	'57	'58	'59	'60	'61	'62	'63	'64	'65	'66	'67
10	7																			

Number	Built	Renumbered	BR Dates	Scrap	Notes
3561	01/94 Sdn		-10/49	12/49	
3562	02/94 Sdn		-02/49	04/49	

Class continued with 3582

1159 3574-3577
0-4-2T GWR Armstrong & Dean (also known as '3571' or '517' class)

Power Classification: 1P
Introduced: 1895-1897
Designer: Dean, built at Wolverhampton
Company: GWR
Weight: 35t 4cwt
Driving Wheel: 5' 2"
Boiler Pressure: 150psi
Cylinders: Inside 16" x 24"
Tractive Effort: 12635lbf
Valve Gear: Stephenson (slide valves)

These were the survivors of several large classes of 0-4-2T locomotives, which were the forerunners of the '1400' and '5800' classes. The earliest had been built in 1876 by G Armstrong. These locomotives were the last of the type, built by Dean in 1895-1897. Ten engines were constructed, being withdrawn from 1928 onwards.

Year End Totals: '1159' class

'47	'48	'49	'50	'51	'52	'53	'54	'55	'56	'57	'58	'59	'60	'61	'62	'63	'64	'65	'66	'67
3	3																			

Number	Built	Renumbered	BR Dates	Scrap	Notes
3574	08/95 Wlv		-12/49	*03/50*	
3575	09/95 Wlv		-10/49	12/49	
3577	10/95 Wlv		-05/49	07/49	

3500 3561-3562, 3582-3599
2-4-0T GWR Dean

Class continued from 3562

Number	Built	Renumbered	BR Dates	Scrap	Notes
3582	02/99 Sdn		-11/49	01/50	
3585	05/99 Sdn		-01/48	*01/48*	
3586	06/99 Sdn		-11/49	01/50	
3588	08/99 Sdn		-12/49	*06/50*	
3589	09/99 Sdn		-08/48	*48*	
3592	09/99 Sdn		-04/49	06/49	
3597	10/99 Sdn		-08/48	*48*	
3599	11/99 Sdn		-10/49	12/49	

5700 3600-3799, 4600-4699, 5700-5799, 7700-7799, 8700-8799, 9600-9682, 9711-9799
0-6-0PT GWR Collett 4ft 7½in

Power Classification: 4F (some LMR based engines were reclassified 3F in 1953)
Introduced: 1929-1949
Designer: Collett
Company: GWR
Weight: 47t 10cwt
m 49t 0cwt
Driving Wheel: 4' 7½"
Boiler Pressure: 200psi
Cylinders: Inside 17½" x 24"
Tractive Effort: 22515lbf
Valve Gear: Stephenson (slide valves)

Refer to the Historical Survey of GWR Pannier Tank Engines at the end of this section for more details of this class.

The '5700' class was the GWR standard type of pannier tank locomotive. They were designed for shunting and light goods work and were developed from the '2021'/'2721' classes. They were built as replacements for earlier saddle tank and pannier tank locomotives dating back to the 1880s. They were very similar to the '2721' class apart from having Belpaire boilers, enclosed cabs, higher pressure boilers and larger bunkers. They had tapered chimneys, and large domes.

The first engine No. 5700, appeared from the North British Locomotive Company works in 1929 and it was to be the first of no fewer than 863 locomotives to be built (including the '6700' and '9700' derivatives). Seven different locomotive builders were used in the construction of these engines.

Between 1956 and 1963 thirteen locomotives were sold to London Transport for departmental duties, where some of them remained working until 1971. Their London Transport numbers and service details were as follows:

Number	Built	Renumbered	LT Dates	Scrap	Notes
L89 §	09/29 Sdn	08/63 5775	08/63-01/70		
L90	03/30 KS	01/57 7711	01/57-09/61	01/62	
L90 §	12/30 NB	01/62 7760	01/62-06/71		
			2nd engine to carry this number		
L91	04/29 Sdn	03/57 5752	03/57-11/60	06/61	
L91	05/29 Sdn	12/60 5757	12/60-12/67	01/70	
			2nd engine to carry this number		
L92 §	01/30 Sdn	04/58 5786	04/58-09/69		
L93	11/30 AW	10/58 7779	10/58-12/67	09/68	
L94 §	11/30 NB	12/59 7752	12/59-06/71		
L95 §	06/29 Sdn	05/60 5764	05/60-06/71		
L96	02/30 NB	01/62 7741	01/62-12/66	09/67	
L97	02/30 NB	12/62 7749	12/62-09/68	01/70	
L98	01/30 NB	12/62 7739	12/62-11/68	01/70	
L99 §	05/30 KS	06/63 7715	06/63-12/69		

Apart from these seven other engines were sold for further use: 3650, 7714, 7754, 9600, 9642 (all since preserved), 3663 (scrapped 1970) and 9792 (scrapped April 1973).

m The later locomotives (also known as the '8750' class, introduced in 1933) were of a slightly modified design. They had detail alterations including increased weight and a modified cab with angular windows on the front and back instead of the original round windows. 8700 had the detail alterations but retained the original style cab. (This was not the original 8700 which was converted to form the prototype for the '9700' class and was renumbered 9700).

o 3711 was converted to oil burning in 1958.

Year End Totals: '5700' class

'47	'48	'49	'50	'51	'52	'53	'54	'55	'56	'57	'58	'59	'60	'61	'62	'63	'64	'65	'66	'67
751	762	772	772	772	772	772	772	772	768	757	728	678	621	563	405	305	166	27		

Number	Built	Renumbered	BR Dates	Scrap	Notes
3600	12/38 Sdn		-12/63	04/64	m
3601	12/38 Sdn		-10/64	02/65	m
3602	01/39 Sdn		-02/62	05/62	m
3603	01/39 Sdn		-07/64	12/64	m
3604	01/39 Sdn		-12/63	03/64	m
3605	01/39 Sdn		-10/66	04/67	m
3606	01/39 Sdn		-12/62	10/63	m
3607	02/39 Sdn		-10/66	04/67	m
3608	02/39 Sdn		-06/65	10/65	m
3609	02/39 Sdn		-08/60	12/60	m
3610	02/39 Sdn		-02/65	05/65	m
3611	02/39 Sdn		-08/62	12/63	m
3612 §	03/39 Sdn		-10/64		m
3613	03/39 Sdn		-05/64	07/64	m
3614	03/39 Sdn		-03/62	05/62	m
3615	03/39 Sdn		-10/65	02/66	m
3616	03/39 Sdn		-09/65	02/66	m
3617	04/39 Sdn		-09/64	11/64	m
3618	04/39 Sdn		-05/64	07/64	m
3619	04/39 Sdn		-09/66	11/66	m
3620	05/39 Sdn		-06/65	10/65	m
3621	05/39 Sdn		-11/64	01/65	m
3622	05/39 Sdn		-09/64	11/65	m
3623	05/39 Sdn		-09/62	09/63	m
3624	05/39 Sdn		-05/62	10/62	m
3625	05/39 Sdn		-07/66	11/66	m
3626	06/39 Sdn		-08/63	01/64	m
3627	06/39 Sdn		-02/63	11/63	m
3628	06/39 Sdn		-01/63	03/63	m
3629	06/39 Sdn		-01/63	06/64	m
3630	06/39 Sdn		-09/62	12/63	m
3631	07/39 Sdn		-07/65	11/65	m
3632	07/39 Sdn		-12/62	11/63	m
3633	07/39 Sdn		-10/63	06/64	m
3634	07/39 Sdn		-07/64	12/64	m
3635	09/39 Sdn		-04/65	08/65	m
3636	09/39 Sdn		-02/62	05/62	m
3637	09/39 Sdn		-10/62	08/63	m
3638	09/39 Sdn		-01/61	04/61	m
3639	10/39 Sdn		-01/63	09/63	m
3640	10/39 Sdn		-05/62	09/62	m
3641	10/39 Sdn		-08/62	10/63	m
3642	10/39 Sdn		-04/65	06/65	m
3643	10/39 Sdn		-11/65	02/66	m
3644	10/39 Sdn		-06/65	10/65	m
3645	11/39 Sdn		-05/62	08/62	m
3646	11/39 Sdn		-05/64	08/64	m
3647	11/39 Sdn		-06/65	10/65	m
3648	11/39 Sdn		-12/63	03/64	m
3649	11/39 Sdn		-01/61	04/61	m
3650 §	12/39 Sdn		-09/63		m
3651	12/39 Sdn		-04/63	12/63	m
3652	12/39 Sdn		-10/63	12/63	m
3653	12/39 Sdn		-10/63	02/64	m
3654	12/39 Sdn		-08/65	02/67	m
3655	01/40 Sdn		-12/62	01/64	m
3656	01/40 Sdn		-02/62	05/62	m
3657	01/40 Sdn		-05/61	09/61	m
3658	01/40 Sdn		-09/65	11/65	m
3659	01/40 Sdn		-10/65	12/65	m
3660	02/40 Sdn		-04/63	09/63	m
3661	02/40 Sdn		-04/65	08/65	m
3662	02/40 Sdn		-08/65	02/66	m
3663	02/40 Sdn		-12/62	70	m
3664	02/40 Sdn		-05/64	07/64	m
3665	03/40 Sdn		-01/64	04/64	m
3666	03/40 Sdn		-12/62	01/63	m
3667	03/40 Sdn		-05/61	09/61	m
3668	03/40 Sdn		-07/63	04/64	m
3669	03/40 Sdn		-09/65	12/65	m
3670	04/40 Sdn		-05/61	09/61	m
3671	04/40 Sdn		-07/65	10/65	m
3672	04/40 Sdn		-04/64	10/64	m
3673	04/40 Sdn		-05/64	08/64	m
3674	04/40 Sdn		-12/62	01/64	m
3675	06/40 Sdn		-12/65	04/66	m
3676	06/40 Sdn		-05/61	08/61	m
3677	06/40 Sdn		-12/65	06/66	m
3678	07/40 Sdn		-12/63	03/64	m
3679	07/40 Sdn		-03/63	06/64	m
3680	07/40 Sdn		-05/64	07/64	m
3681	07/40 Sdn		-03/66	08/66	m
3682	07/40 Sdn		-12/65	06/66	m
3683	07/40 Sdn		-10/64	12/64	m
3684	07/40 Sdn		-05/62	08/62	m
3685	12/40 Sdn		-04/64	01/65	m
3686	12/40 Sdn		-07/65	10/65	m
3687	01/41 Sdn		-06/65	10/65	m
3688	01/41 Sdn		-09/62	12/63	m
3689	01/41 Sdn		-05/64	09/64	m
3690	02/41 Sdn		-06/65	10/65	m
3691	02/41 Sdn		-04/65	09/65	m
3692	02/41 Sdn		-05/64	07/64	m
3693	03/41 Sdn		-07/64	12/64	m
3694	03/41 Sdn		-09/62	01/64	m
3695	08/41 Sdn		-07/64	12/64	m
3696	08/41 Sdn		-11/65	02/66	m
3697	09/41 Sdn		-05/62	09/62	m
3698	09/41 Sdn		-04/64	08/64	m
3699	09/41 Sdn		-02/65	07/65	m
3700	09/36 Sdn		-02/65	02/65	m
3701	09/36 Sdn		-05/64	07/64	m
3702	10/36 Sdn		-04/64	12/64	m
3703	10/36 Sdn		-05/62	09/62	m
3704	10/36 Sdn		-01/61	04/61	m
3705	10/36 Sdn		-03/65	04/65	m
3706	10/36 Sdn		-11/63	01/64	m
3707	10/36 Sdn		-09/64	01/65	m
3708	10/36 Sdn		-07/65	10/65	m
3709	10/36 Sdn		-08/66	12/66	m
3710	10/36 Sdn		-05/63	12/63	m
3711	11/36 Sdn		-05/63	11/63	m 58⇨o
3712	11/36 Sdn		-12/63	03/64	m
3713	11/36 Sdn		-02/62	07/62	m
3714	11/36 Sdn		-12/63	03/64	m
3715	01/37 Sdn		-03/65	07/65	m
3716	01/37 Sdn		-12/63	03/64	m
3717	01/37 Sdn		-06/65	10/65	m
3718	02/37 Sdn		-05/62	10/62	m
3719	02/37 Sdn		-01/63	01/63	m
3720	02/37 Sdn		-12/63	05/64	m
3721	02/37 Sdn		-04/64	05/64	m
3722	02/37 Sdn		-05/62	11/62	m
3723	02/37 Sdn		-04/62	10/62	m
3724	02/37 Sdn		-05/61	08/61	m
3725	06/37 Sdn		-01/65	03/65	m
3726	06/37 Sdn		-01/62	07/62	m
3727	06/37 Sdn		-04/64	03/65	m
3728	07/37 Sdn		-04/65	08/65	m
3729	07/37 Sdn		-03/63	12/63	m
3730	07/37 Sdn		-11/64	02/65	m
3731	07/37 Sdn		-05/64	08/64	m
3732	08/37 Sdn		-05/62	02/63	m
3733	08/37 Sdn		-12/63	03/64	m
3734	08/37 Sdn		-04/64	09/64	m
3735	08/37 Sdn		-09/65	12/65	m
3736	09/37 Sdn		-03/63	07/63	m
3737	09/37 Sdn		-09/64	04/65	m
3738 §	09/37 Sdn		-08/65		m
3739	09/37 Sdn		-10/64	04/65	m
3740	09/37 Sdn		-01/59	03/59	m
3741	09/37 Sdn		-09/62	11/63	m
3742	09/37 Sdn		-11/64	02/65	m
3743	09/37 Sdn		-05/62	10/62	m
3744	10/37 Sdn		-08/66	12/66	m
3745	10/37 Sdn		-12/64	04/65	m
3746	10/37 Sdn		-07/64	12/64	m
3747	10/37 Sdn		-02/65	07/65	m
3748	10/37 Sdn		-05/64	12/64	m
3749	10/37 Sdn		-11/65	05/66	m
3750	11/37 Sdn		-09/62	12/63	m
3751	11/37 Sdn		-09/65	12/65	m
3752	11/37 Sdn		-07/64	12/64	m
3753	11/37 Sdn		-01/65	03/65	m
3754	11/37 Sdn		-11/65	02/66	m
3755	11/37 Sdn		-10/62	01/64	m
3756	11/37 Sdn		-03/63	12/63	m
3757	12/37 Sdn		-05/64	07/64	m
3758	12/37 Sdn		-03/66	08/66	m
3759	12/37 Sdn		-12/65	04/66	m
3760	12/37 Sdn		-09/62	11/62	m
3761	12/37 Sdn		-05/64	07/64	m
3762	12/37 Sdn		-12/63	03/64	m
3763	12/37 Sdn		-06/65	10/65	m
3764	12/37 Sdn		-01/63	01/64	m
3765	03/38 Sdn		-07/63	09/63	m
3766	04/38 Sdn		-08/63	01/64	m
3767	04/38 Sdn		-10/65	12/65	m
3768	04/38 Sdn		-05/64	07/64	m
3769	04/38 Sdn		-10/62	12/63	m
3770	05/38 Sdn		-04/65	10/65	m
3771	05/38 Sdn		-01/63	10/63	m
3772	05/38 Sdn		-06/65	11/65	m
3773	05/38 Sdn		-10/62	11/62	m
3774	05/38 Sdn		-05/62	10/62	m
3775	07/38 Sdn		-12/65	04/66	m
3776	07/38 Sdn		-04/66	08/66	m
3777	07/38 Sdn		-12/63	03/64	m
3778	07/38 Sdn		-03/64	08/64	m
3779	07/38 Sdn		-12/63	04/64	m
3780	08/38 Sdn		-12/62	09/63	m
3781	08/38 Sdn		-08/63	03/64	m
3782	08/38 Sdn		-10/66	04/67	m
3783	08/38 Sdn		-09/62	08/63	m
3784	08/38 Sdn		-06/65	10/65	m
3785	09/38 Sdn		-07/62	09/62	m
3786	09/38 Sdn		-03/63	12/63	m
3787	09/38 Sdn		-01/63	12/63	m
3788	09/38 Sdn		-11/65	03/66	m
3789	10/38 Sdn		-10/65	01/66	m
3790	10/38 Sdn		-06/65	10/65	m
3791	10/38 Sdn		-12/63	06/64	m
3792	10/38 Sdn		-11/65	02/66	m
3793	10/38 Sdn		-09/58	10/58	m
3794	10/38 Sdn		-12/64	08/65	m
3795	11/38 Sdn		-05/63	08/63	m
3796	11/38 Sdn		-03/65	07/65	m
3797	12/38 Sdn		-11/64	01/65	m
3798	12/38 Sdn		-10/64	01/65	m
3799	12/38 Sdn		-01/61	04/61	m

Class continued with 4600

2884 2884-2899, 3800-3866, (4850-4857)
2-8-0 GWR Modified '2800' class with side window cabs

Class continued from 2899

Number	Built	Renumbered	BR Dates	Scrap	Notes
3800	12/38 Sdn		-08/64	12/64	
3801	12/38 Sdn		-08/64	12/64	
3802 §	12/38 Sdn		-08/65		
3803 §	01/39 Sdn		-07/63		
3804	08/39 Sdn		-07/64	12/64	
3805	08/39 Sdn		-09/64	12/64	
3806	08/39 Sdn		-12/63	06/64	
3807	08/39 Sdn		-02/65	03/65	
3808	09/39 Sdn		-07/65	10/65	
3809	09/39 Sdn		-10/64	01/65	
3810	09/39 Sdn		-11/64	03/65	
3811	09/39 Sdn		-09/63	03/64	
3812	09/39 Sdn		-06/65	10/65	
3813	09/39 Sdn	06/49 4855	-07/65	12/65	
3814 §	03/40 Sdn		-12/64		
3815	03/40 Sdn		-05/64	08/64	
3816	03/40 Sdn		-07/65	12/65	

Number	Built	Renumbered	BR Dates	Scrap	Notes
3817	03/40 Sdn		-08/65	03/73	
3818	04/40 Sdn	09/48 4852	-05/65	08/65	
3819	04/40 Sdn		-12/64	04/65	
3820	04/40 Sdn	06/49 4856	-07/65	09/65	
3821	04/40 Sdn		-10/64	12/64	
3822 §	04/40 Sdn		-01/64		
3823	05/40 Sdn		-07/65	10/65	
3824	09/40 Sdn		-06/64	02/65	
3825	09/40 Sdn		-09/64	01/65	
3826	09/40 Sdn		-01/65	03/65	
3827	10/40 Sdn		-11/62	12/62	
3828	11/40 Sdn		-10/64	12/64	
3829	11/40 Sdn		-03/64	07/64	
3830	11/40 Sdn		-06/65	10/65	
3831	12/40 Sdn	05/49 4857	-09/63	04/64	
3832	01/41 Sdn		-04/64	08/64	
3833	01/41 Sdn		-07/63	09/63	
3834	12/41 Sdn		-04/64	02/65	
3835	01/42 Sdn		-01/65	04/65	
3836	01/42 Sdn		-11/65	01/66	
3837	01/42 Sdn	08/49 4854	-07/65	10/65	
3838	01/42 Sdn		-11/64	01/65	
3839	01/42 Sdn	11/49 4853	-12/63	08/64	
3840	01/42 Sdn		-07/65	10/65	
3841	02/42 Sdn		-03/64	08/64	
3842	02/42 Sdn		-07/65	10/65	
3843	02/42 Sdn		-10/63	03/64	
3844	04/42 Sdn		-10/65	01/66	
3845 §	04/42 Sdn		-06/64		
3846	05/42 Sdn		-10/63	04/64	
3847	05/42 Sdn		-03/64	07/64	
3848	05/42 Sdn		-07/65	10/65	
3849	06/42 Sdn		-05/65	08/65	
3850 §	06/42 Sdn		-08/65		
3851	06/42 Sdn		-07/65	10/65	
3852	06/42 Sdn		-04/64	10/64	
3853	06/42 Sdn		-12/63	12/64	
3854	06/42 Sdn		-06/65	10/65	
3855 §	10/42 Sdn		-08/65		
3856	10/42 Sdn		-10/64	01/65	
3857	10/42 Sdn		-03/64	06/64	
3858	10/42 Sdn		-09/63	05/64	
3859	10/42 Sdn		-05/65	09/65	
3860	10/42 Sdn		-08/64	11/64	
3861	11/42 Sdn		-07/65	10/65	
3862 §	11/42 Sdn		-02/65		
3863	11/42 Sdn		-10/65	01/66	
3864	11/42 Sdn		-07/65	10/65	
3865	11/42 Sdn	04/49 4851	-03/65	07/65	
3866	12/42 Sdn		-07/65	12/65	

Class continued with 4850

4900 4900-4999, 5900-5999, 6900-6958, (3900-3955)
4-6-0 GWR Collett 'Hall'

For details see 4900

Number	Built	Renumbered	BR Dates	Scrap	Notes
3900	12/29 Sdn		-07/62	11/62	o
SHOTTON HALL				03/49➲4968	
3901	01/30 Sdn		-08/62	01/64	o
STANWAY HALL				04/49➲4971	
3902	08/29 Sdn		-09/62	04/64	o
NORTHWICK HALL				09/48➲4948	
3903	01/29 Sdn		-08/63	01/64	o
BROUGHTON HALL				04/50➲4907	
3904	01/30 Sdn		-02/64	07/64	o
SAINT BRIDES HALL				10/48➲4972	
3950	12/35 Sdn		-04/65	08/65	o
GARTH HALL				10/48➲5955	
3951	09/38 Sdn		-07/64	12/64	o
ASHWICKE HALL				11/48➲5976	
3952	03/43 Sdn		-10/65	02/66	o
NORCLIFFE HALL				03/50➲6957	
3953	02/43 Sdn		-12/65	05/66	o
LEIGHTON HALL				09/48➲6953	
3954	11/39 Sdn		-09/63	08/65	o
ARBURY HALL				02/50➲5986	
3955	12/42 Sdn		-05/61	06/61	o
HABERFIELD HALL				04/49➲6949	

Class continued with 4900

4073 100A1, 111, 4000, 4016, 4032, 4037, 4073-4099, 5000-5099, 7000-7037
4-6-0 GWR Collett 'Castle'

s Engines rebuilt from 'Star' class locomotives.

Class continued from 111

Number	Built	Renumbered	BR Dates	Scrap	Notes
4000	04/06 Sdn		-05/57	05/57	s
NORTH STAR					

Class continued with 4016

4000 between 4003 & 4062
4-6-0 GWR Churchward 'Star'

Power Classification:	5P
Introduced:	1906-1923
Designer:	Churchward
Company:	GWR
Weight:	Loco 75t 12cwt Tender 46t 14cwt
Driving Wheel:	6' 8½"
Boiler Pressure:	225psi superheated
Cylinders:	Four 15" x 26"
Tractive Effort:	27800lbf
Valve Gear:	Inside Walschaert with rocking shafts (piston valves)

The first four-cylinder engine on the GWR was No. 40, built in 1906 as an Atlantic (4-4-2) engine. It was rebuilt in 1909 as a 4-6-0 engine and renumbered 4000 NORTH STAR. It was the first in a long line of GWR four-cylinder express engines which included the 'Star', the 'Castle' ('4073') and the 'King' ('6000') classes. (It was later converted to a 'Castle' class engine.)

Seventy-two more engines were built between 1907 and 1914 and in 1922 to 1923. The earlier locomotives were subsequently fitted with new boilers and superheaters, while the remainder were built as such. They were named after Stars, Knights, Monarchs, Queens, Princes, Princesses and Abbeys. The unnamed locomotives had their names removed during the war (for obvious reasons) and were formerly named as follows: 4022 BELGIAN MONARCH, 4023 DANISH MONARCH, 4025 ITALIAN MONARCH, 4026 JAPANESE MONARCH, 4028 ROUMANIAN MONARCH and 4030 SWEDISH MONARCH. All the engines named after monarchs (4021-4/6-30) were named THE *xxx* MONARCH in 1927, and then had the 'THE' prefix removed some months later.

There was some changing of names before 1948, and the following names were originally carried by the engines concerned: 4007 RISING STAR, 4017 KNIGHT OF THE BLACK EAGLE, 4021 KING EDWARD, 4022 KING WILLIAM, 4023 KING GEORGE, 4025 KING CHARLES, 4026 KING RICHARD, 4028 KING JOHN and 4030 KING HAROLD. The King names were changed to prevent confusion with the new 'King' class in 1927.

From 1925 to 1929 4000, 4009, 4016, 4032 and 4037 were rebuilt as 'Castle' class locomotives, the 'Castles' being a development of the 'Star' class built by Collett. In 1937-1940 4063-4072 were also rebuilt to 'Castles' and were renumbered 5083-5092. They retained their original names but were officially regarded as new engines.

Three different varieties of steam pipes could be seen fitted to the engines in BR days. Some retained the original inside steam pipes. Others received elbow type steam pipes when the inside cylinders were replaced but the outside cylinders were not. Others had the 'Castle' type of outside steam pipes fitted when they had all four cylinders replaced.

Withdrawal of the class commenced in 1932.

Year End Totals: '4000' class

'47	'48	'49	'50	'51	'52	'53	'54	'55	'56	'57	'58	'59	'60	'61	'62	'63	'64	'65	'66	'67
47	46	43	36	20	8	4	3	3	2											

Number	Built	Renumbered	BR Dates	Scrap	Notes
4003 §	02/07 Sdn		-07/51		
LODE STAR					
4004	02/07 Sdn		-04/48	05/48	
MORNING STAR					
4007	04/07 Sdn		-09/51	10/51	
SWALLOWFIELD PARK					
4012	03/08 Sdn		-10/49	12/49	
KNIGHT OF THE THISTLE					
4013	03/08 Sdn		-05/50	06/50	
KNIGHT OF ST. PATRICK					
4015	03/08 Sdn		-02/51	04/51	
KNIGHT OF ST. JOHN					

Class continued with 4017

4073 100A1, 111, 4000, 4016, 4032, 4037, 4073-4099, 5000-5099, 7000-7037
4-6-0 GWR Collett 'Castle'

s Engines rebuilt from 'Star' class locomotives.

Class continued from 4000

Number	Built	Renumbered	BR Dates	Scrap	Notes
4016	04/08 Sdn		-09/51	*51*	s
THE SOMERSET LIGHT INFANTRY (PRINCE ALBERT'S)					

Class continued with 4032

4000 between 4003 & 4062
4-6-0 GWR Churchward 'Star'

Class continued from 4015

Number	Built	Renumbered	BR Dates	Scrap	Notes
4017	04/08 Sdn		-11/49	01/50	
KNIGHT OF LIÉGE					
4018	04/08 Sdn		-04/51	*05/51*	
KNIGHT OF THE GRAND CROSS					
4019	05/08 Sdn		-10/49	12/49	
KNIGHT TEMPLAR					
4020	05/08 Sdn		-03/51	*04/51*	
KNIGHT COMMANDER					
4021	06/09 Sdn		-10/52	*10/52*	
BRITISH MONARCH					
4022	06/09 Sdn		-02/52	*04/52*	
4023	06/09 Sdn		-06/52	09/52	
4025	07/09 Sdn		-08/50	09/50	
4026	09/09 Sdn		-02/50	04/50	
4028	09/09 Sdn		-11/51	12/51	
4030	10/09 Sdn		-05/50	06/50	
4031	10/10 Sdn		-06/51	*51*	
QUEEN MARY					

Class continued with 4033

4073 100A1, 111, 4000, 4016, 4032, 4037, 4073-4099, 5000-5099, 7000-7037
4-6-0 GWR Collett 'Castle'

s Engines rebuilt from 'Star' class locomotives.

Class continued from 4016

Number	Built	Renumbered	BR Dates	Scrap	Notes
4032	10/10 Sdn		-09/51	*51*	s
QUEEN ALEXANDRA					

Class continued with 4037

4000 between 4003 & 4062
4-6-0 GWR Churchward 'Star'

Class continued from 4031

Number	Built	Renumbered	BR Dates	Scrap	Notes
4033	11/10 Sdn		-06/51	*51*	
QUEEN VICTORIA					
4034	11/10 Sdn		-09/52	*52*	
QUEEN ADELAIDE					
4035	11/10 Sdn		-10/51	*51*	
QUEEN CHARLOTTE					
4036	12/10 Sdn		-03/52	*04/52*	
QUEEN ELIZABETH					

Class continued with 4038

4073 100A1, 111, 4000, 4016, 4032, 4037, 4073-4099, 5000-5099, 7000-7037
4-6-0 GWR Collett 'Castle'

s Engines rebuilt from 'Star' class locomotives.

Class continued from 4032

Number	Built	Renumbered	BR Dates	Scrap	Notes
4037	12/10 Sdn		-09/62	12/62	s
THE SOUTH WALES BORDERERS					

Class continued with 4073

4000 between 4003 & 4062
4-6-0 GWR Churchward 'Star'

Class continued from 4036

Number	Built	Renumbered	BR Dates	Scrap	Notes
4038	01/11 Sdn		-04/52	52	
QUEEN BERENGARIA					
4039	02/11 Sdn		-11/50	12/50	
QUEEN MATILDA					
4040	03/11 Sdn		-06/51	06/51	
QUEEN BOADICEA					
4041	06/13 Sdn		-04/51	05/51	
PRINCE OF WALES					
4042	05/13 Sdn		-11/51	11/51	
PRINCE ALBERT					
4043	05/13 Sdn		-01/52	03/52	
PRINCE HENRY					
4044	05/13 Sdn		-02/53	53	
PRINCE GEORGE					
4045	06/13 Sdn		-11/50	50	
PRINCE JOHN					
4046	05/14 Sdn		-11/51	01/52	
PRINCESS MARY					
4047	05/14 Sdn		-07/51	51	
PRINCESS LOUISE					
4048	05/14 Sdn		-01/53	02/53	
PRINCESS VICTORIA					
4049	05/14 Sdn		-06/53	53	
PRINCESS MAUD					
4050	06/14 Sdn		-02/52	04/52	
PRINCESS ALICE					
4051	06/14 Sdn		-10/50	50	
PRINCESS HELENA					
4052	06/14 Sdn		-06/53	53	
PRINCESS BEATRICE					
4053	06/14 Sdn		-07/54	07/54	
PRINCESS ALEXANDRA					
4054	06/14 Sdn		-01/52	02/52	
PRINCESS CHARLOTTE					
4055	07/14 Sdn		-02/51	05/51	
PRINCESS SOPHIA					
4056	07/14 Sdn		-10/57	57	
PRINCESS MARGARET					
4057	07/14 Sdn		-02/52	02/52	
PRINCESS ELIZABETH					
4058	07/14 Sdn		-04/51	08/51	
PRINCESS AUGUSTA					
4059	07/14 Sdn		-09/52	10/52	
PRINCESS PATRICIA					
4060	07/14 Sdn		-10/52	10/52	
PRINCESS EUGENIE					
4061	05/22 Sdn		-03/57	57	
GLASTONBURY ABBEY					
4062	05/22 Sdn		-11/56	56	
MALMESBURY ABBEY					

4073 100A1, 111, 4000, 4016, 4032, 4037, 4073-4099, 5000-5099, 7000-7037
4-6-0 GWR Collett 'Castle'

Class continued from 4037

Number	Built	Renumbered	BR Dates	Scrap	Notes
4073 §	08/23 Sdn		-05/60		
CAERPHILLY CASTLE					
4074	12/23 Sdn		-05/63	10/63	4 04/59⇨d
CALDICOT CASTLE					
4075	01/24 Sdn		-11/61	03/62	
CARDIFF CASTLE					
4076	02/24 Sdn		-02/63	10/63	
CARMARTHEN CASTLE					
4077	02/24 Sdn		-08/62	12/62	3
CHEPSTOW CASTLE					
4078	02/24 Sdn		-07/62	12/62	4
PEMBROKE CASTLE					
4079 §	02/24 Sdn		-05/64		
PENDENNIS CASTLE					
4080	03/24 Sdn		-08/64	12/64	4 08/58⇨d
POWDERHAM CASTLE					
4081	03/24 Sdn		-01/63	10/63	
WARWICK CASTLE					
4082	04/24 Sdn		-02/65	06/65	02/52➲7013
WINDSOR CASTLE					
4082	07/48 Sdn	02/52 7013	07/48-09/64	01/65	m4
WINDSOR CASTLE					
4083	05/25 Sdn		-12/61	12/61	
ABBOTSBURY CASTLE					
4084	05/25 Sdn		-10/60	11/60	
ABERYSTWYTH CASTLE					
4085	05/25 Sdn		-05/62	11/62	
BERKELEY CASTLE					
4086	06/25 Sdn		-04/62	11/62	
BUILTH CASTLE					
4087	06/25 Sdn		-10/63	06/64	4 02/58⇨d
CARDIGAN CASTLE					
4088	07/25 Sdn		-05/64	09/64	4 05/58⇨d
DARTMOUTH CASTLE					
4089	07/25 Sdn		-10/64	01/65	
DONNINGTON CASTLE					
4090	07/25 Sdn		-06/63	06/64	4 03/57⇨d
DORCHESTER CASTLE					
4091	07/25 Sdn		-01/59	01/59	
DUDLEY CASTLE					
4092	08/25 Sdn		-12/61	12/61	
DUNRAVEN CASTLE					
4093	05/26 Sdn		-09/64	01/65	4 12/57⇨d
DUNSTER CASTLE					
4094	05/26 Sdn		-03/62	08/62	
DYNEVOR CASTLE					
4095	06/26 Sdn		-12/62	04/64	
HARLECH CASTLE					
4096	06/26 Sdn		-01/63	10/63	
HIGHCLERE CASTLE					
4097	06/26 Sdn		-05/60	05/60	4 06/58⇨d
KENILWORTH CASTLE					
4098	07/26 Sdn		-12/63	06/64	
KIDWELLY CASTLE					
4099	08/26 Sdn		-09/62	09/62	
KILGERRAN CASTLE					

Class continued with 5000

5101 4100-4179, 5101-5199
2-6-2T GWR Churchward & Collett 5ft 8in

Power Classification:	4MT
Introduced:	1903-1906, 1929-1949
Designer:	Churchward & Collett
Company:	GWR
Weight:	78t 9cwt a 75t 10cwt
Driving Wheel:	5' 8"
Boiler Pressure:	200psi superheated
Cylinders:	Outside 18" x 30"
Tractive Effort:	24300lbf
Valve Gear:	Stephenson (piston valves)

The large 'Prairie' tanks were all developed from a prototype built in 1903. This was No. 99. It was later renumbered 3100 and thirty-nine others were built in 1905-1906 numbered 3111-3149. This was the old '3100' class. In 1906-1908 forty-one engines were built with larger boilers which formed the '3150' class.

In 1929 the old '3100' class engines were renumbered in the 5100 series and they were then known as the '5100' class. They had been superheated and were rebuilt by Collett with detail alterations and increased weight.

From 1929 onwards new locomotives were built to the modified design and these were known as the '5101' class. The '6100' class locomotives introduced in 1931 were another variation with increased boiler pressure. Ten of the original '5100' class locomotives (including the original 5100) were rebuilt as the '8100' class in 1938-1939.

The first locomotive to be withdrawn was 5149 in 1947, while others were still being built (4160-4179 appearing in 1948-1949).

a '5100' class locomotives (see above).

Year End Totals: '5101' class

'47	'48	'49	'50	'51	'52	'53	'54	'55	'56	'57	'58	'59	'60	'61	'62	'63	'64	'65	'66	'67
149	151	159	157	151	145	143	143	141	140	137	125	119	104	93	71	57	29			

Number	Built	Renumbered	BR Dates	Scrap	Notes
4100	08/35 Sdn		-11/65	02/66	
4101	08/35 Sdn		-07/64	09/64	
4102	08/35 Sdn		-09/62	05/64	
4103	08/35 Sdn		-09/64	12/64	
4104	08/35 Sdn		-05/64	07/64	
4105	09/35 Sdn		-01/64	09/64	
4106	09/35 Sdn		-09/62	09/63	
4107	09/35 Sdn		-06/65	10/65	
4108	09/35 Sdn		-10/64	02/65	
4109	09/35 Sdn		-04/64	07/64	
4110 §	10/35 Sdn		-06/65		
4111	10/35 Sdn		-09/65	02/66	
4112	10/35 Sdn		-08/62	12/63	
4113	10/35 Sdn		-11/65	07/66	
4114	10/36 Sdn		-11/63	03/64	
4115 §	10/36 Sdn		-06/65		
4116	11/36 Sdn		-09/62	09/63	
4117	11/36 Sdn		-09/61	10/61	
4118	11/36 Sdn		-09/62	11/63	
4119	11/36 Sdn		-09/63	08/65	
4120	12/37 Sdn		-11/64	12/64	
4121 §	12/37 Sdn		-06/65		
4122	01/38 Sdn		-06/64	12/64	
4123	01/38 Sdn		-11/61	06/62	
4124	01/38 Sdn		-08/64	12/64	
4125	05/38 Sdn		-06/65	11/65	
4126	05/38 Sdn		-01/62	04/62	
4127	05/38 Sdn		-01/63	05/63	
4128	05/38 Sdn		-06/64	12/64	
4129	05/38 Sdn		-09/62	11/63	
4130	10/39 Sdn		-07/64	12/64	
4131	10/39 Sdn		-09/64	12/64	
4132	10/39 Sdn		-06/64	12/64	
4133	10/39 Sdn		-10/64	01/65	
4134	10/39 Sdn		-05/63	11/63	
4135	10/39 Sdn		-05/64	12/64	
4136	11/39 Sdn		-06/64	12/64	
4137	11/39 Sdn		-10/64	01/65	
4138	11/39 Sdn		-07/58	08/58	
4139	12/39 Sdn		-07/58	10/58	
4140	08/46 Sdn		-11/63	02/64	
4141 §	08/46 Sdn		-03/63		
4142	08/46 Sdn		-12/63	06/64	
4143	09/46 Sdn		-06/64	11/64	
4144 §	09/46 Sdn		-06/65		
4145	09/46 Sdn		-12/62	07/63	
4146	09/46 Sdn		-08/62	07/63	
4147	09/46 Sdn		-09/65	12/65	
4148	10/46 Sdn		-09/65	02/66	
4149	10/46 Sdn		-03/63	12/63	
4150 §	06/47 Sdn		-06/65		
4151	06/47 Sdn		-04/65	09/65	
4152	06/47 Sdn		-09/62	07/63	
4153	06/47 Sdn		-11/64	08/65	
4154	07/47 Sdn		-10/65	01/66	
4155	08/47 Sdn		-09/65	02/66	
4156	08/47 Sdn		-06/65	07/80	
4157	08/47 Sdn		-06/65	10/65	
4158	08/47 Sdn		-06/65	02/66	
4159	09/47 Sdn		-06/64	10/64	
4160 §	09/48 Sdn		09/48-06/65		
4161	09/48 Sdn		09/48-11/65	07/66	
4162	09/48 Sdn		09/48-07/60	09/60	
4163	09/48 Sdn		09/48-10/62	09/63	
4164	09/48 Sdn		09/48-01/60	12/60	
4165	10/48 Sdn		10/48-10/65	01/66	
4166	10/48 Sdn		10/48-06/64	12/64	
4167	10/48 Sdn		10/48-05/64	08/64	
4168	11/48 Sdn		11/48-09/65	02/66	
4169	11/48 Sdn		11/48-05/65	06/65	
4170	10/49 Sdn		10/49-09/60	04/61	
4171	10/49 Sdn		10/49-10/64	01/65	
4172	10/49 Sdn		10/49-01/65	04/65	
4173	10/49 Sdn		10/49-12/64	04/65	
4174	11/49 Sdn		11/49-06/64	11/64	
4175	11/49 Sdn		11/49-10/65	01/66	
4176	11/49 Sdn		11/49-10/65	04/67	
4177	11/49 Sdn		11/49-05/65	08/65	
4178	11/49 Sdn		11/49-10/65	04/66	
4179	12/49 Sdn		12/49-02/65	10/65	

Class continued with 5101

4200 4200-4299, 5200-5204
2-8-0T GWR Churchward

Power Classification:	7F
Introduced:	1910-1923
Designer:	Churchward
Company:	GWR
Weight:	81t 12cwt
Driving Wheel:	4' 7½"
Boiler Pressure:	200psi superheated
Cylinders:	Outside 18½" x 30"

Tractive Effort: 31450lbf
Valve Gear: Stephenson (piston valves)

The increase in mineral traffic in South Wales in the early 1900s meant that there was a need for a tank engine version of the '2800' class. A 2-8-2T was considered, but this was rejected because of the length of the wheelbase.

This class of 2-8-0T engines was designed to work the heavy short-haul coal and mineral trains in South Wales. They were designed using standard GWR parts as used in the '2800' class. A total of 205 engines were built (including the '5205' class) between 1910 and 1940. They were the only 2-8-0Ts to run in this country.

The first engine to be built was 4201 in 1910. (4200 was a later engine, built in 1923). Between 1910 and 1930 195 engines were built numbered 4200-4299 and 5200-5294. 5205 onwards had larger cylinders and other minor alterations and were known as the '5205' class.

In the 1930s during the depression there were more '4200' and '5205' engines in service than were needed for the dwindling coal traffic in South Wales. It was decided to rebuild them as the '7200' class with an extra pair of trailing wheels and a larger bunker so that they could have a wider field of activity. The 4200 class engines which were rebuilt in 1937 were 4202 (7242), 4204 (7243), 4205 (7245), 4209 (7249), 4210 (7252), 4216 (7244), 4219 (7250), 4220 (7241), 4234 (7246), 4239 (7240), 4240 (7251), 4244 (7247), 4245 (7253) and 4249 (7248).

The '4200's were built with inside steam pipes and straight frames over the cylinders. Later many were rebuilt with outside steam pipes and raised framing over the cylinders.

Year End Totals: '4200' class

'47	'48	'49	'50	'51	'52	'53	'54	'55	'56	'57	'58	'59	'60	'61	'62	'63	'64	'65	'66	'67
91	91	91	91	91	91	91	91	91	91	91	91	91	76	74	70	54	33	8		

Number	Built	Renumbered	BR Dates	Scrap	Notes
4200	02/23 Sdn		-03/59	11/59	
4201	12/10 Sdn		-10/59	03/60	
4203	02/12 Sdn		-01/61	09/61	
4206	02/12 Sdn		-12/59	02/60	
4207	02/12 Sdn		-10/61	05/62	
4208	02/12 Sdn		-11/59	01/60	
4211	03/12 Sdn		-08/59	12/59	
4212	08/12 Sdn		-06/59	02/60	
4213	09/12 Sdn		-01/64	06/64	
4214	09/12 Sdn		-05/64	08/64	
4215	09/12 Sdn		-10/59	02/60	
4217	11/12 Sdn		-07/59	03/60	
4218	11/12 Sdn		-09/62	06/64	
4221	12/12 Sdn		-08/59	02/60	
4222	11/13 Sdn		-10/64	02/65	
4223	11/13 Sdn		-08/59	11/59	
4224	11/13 Sdn		-02/59	04/59	
4225	11/13 Sdn		-01/63	09/63	
4226	11/13 Sdn		-03/59	11/59	
4227	11/13 Sdn		-02/65	07/65	
4228	11/13 Sdn		-12/63	03/64	
4229	11/13 Sdn		-03/61	04/61	
4230	11/13 Sdn		-09/62	09/63	
4231	11/13 Sdn		-12/59	01/60	
4232	08/14 Sdn		-10/63	02/64	
4233	08/14 Sdn		-10/64	02/65	
4235	09/14 Sdn		-08/62	10/62	
4236	10/14 Sdn		-09/62	01/64	
4237	10/14 Sdn		-04/64	07/64	
4238	10/14 Sdn		-12/63	12/64	
4241	10/14 Sdn		-04/64	12/64	
4242	02/16 Sdn		-03/64	03/65	
4243	02/16 Sdn		-05/64	08/64	
4246	03/16 Sdn		-12/62	12/63	
4247 §	03/16 Sdn		-04/64		
4248 §	04/16 Sdn		-05/63		
4250	04/16 Sdn		-09/62	09/63	
4251	05/16 Sdn		-06/63	02/64	
4252	03/17 Sdn		-09/63	06/64	
4253 §	03/17 Sdn		-04/63		
4254	03/17 Sdn		-04/65	08/65	
4255	04/17 Sdn		-04/64	01/65	
4256	04/17 Sdn		-01/64	07/64	
4257	04/17 Sdn		-10/63	05/64	
4258	05/17 Sdn		-04/65	09/65	
4259	05/17 Sdn		-03/64	03/65	
4260	05/17 Sdn		-06/59	02/60	
4261	05/17 Sdn		-03/59	11/59	
4262	09/19 Sdn		-04/64	08/64	
4263	10/19 Sdn		-02/64	06/64	
4264	10/19 Sdn		-07/63	01/64	
4265	11/19 Sdn		-06/63	10/63	
4266	11/19 Sdn		-08/62	02/63	
4267	11/19 Sdn		-10/62	06/63	
4268	11/19 Sdn		-08/65	12/65	
4269	12/19 Sdn		-12/62	06/64	
4270 §	12/19 Sdn		-09/62		
4271	02/20 Sdn		-12/63	04/64	
4272	02/20 Sdn		-10/63	07/64	
4273	03/20 Sdn		-10/64	02/65	
4274	03/20 Sdn		-06/62	10/62	
4275	03/20 Sdn		-01/64	04/64	
4276	04/20 Sdn		-12/62	09/64	
4277 §	04/20 Sdn		-06/64		
4278	04/20 Sdn		-07/64	12/64	
4279	05/20 Sdn		-01/64	05/64	
4280	05/20 Sdn		-01/63	02/64	
4281	05/20 Sdn		-12/60	02/61	
4282	06/20 Sdn		-09/63	07/64	
4283	06/20 Sdn		-10/64	03/65	
4284	08/20 Sdn		-09/64	10/64	
4285	08/20 Sdn		-04/65	09/65	
4286	08/21 Sdn		-09/64	10/64	
4287	08/21 Sdn		-01/61	04/61	
4288	09/21 Sdn		-11/60	12/60	
4289	09/21 Sdn		-10/62	01/64	
4290	09/21 Sdn		-02/63	07/63	
4291	09/21 Sdn		-09/62	11/62	
4292	10/21 Sdn		-10/64	12/64	
4293	10/21 Sdn		-08/62	10/62	
4294	11/21 Sdn		-09/64	10/64	
4295	11/21 Sdn		-12/64	03/65	
4296	08/22 Sdn		-12/63	06/64	
4297	08/22 Sdn		-02/65	03/65	
4298	10/22 Sdn		-06/63	10/63	
4299	10/22 Sdn		-12/63	04/64	

Class continued with 5200

4300 4303-4386, 5300-5399, 6300-6399, 7300-7341
2-6-0 GWR Churchward

Power Classification: 4MT
Introduced: 1911-1932
Designer: Churchward
Company: GWR
Weight: Loco 62t 0cwt
Tender 40t 0cwt
w Loco 64t 0cwt
s Loco 63t 16cwt
Driving Wheel: 5' 8"
Boiler Pressure: 200psi superheated
Cylinders: Outside 18½" x 30"
Tractive Effort: 25670lbf
Valve Gear: Stephenson (piston valves)

This was the first modern 2-6-0 design to be built in Britain. They were designed from standard GWR locomotive parts already available and they were virtually a tender version of the '3150' class. 324 locomotives were built, the first being withdrawn in 1936 (for conversion to '6800' and '7800' classes - see below). They were very successful mixed traffic locomotives, being used on semi-main line passenger work and on cross-country routes.

Over the years there were many detail alterations such as different types of chimney, alteration to the frame length at the rear and many were later fitted with outside steam pipes.

It was found that engines working on severely curved routes experienced excessive flange wear on the leading coupled wheels. In 1928, in order to alter the weight distribution, sixty-five engines of the 5300 series had 30cwt castings fixed behind the front buffer beams and they were given corresponding numbers in the 8300 series. From 1944 onwards these were gradually reconverted and they reverted to their 5300 numbers. 8393 was the last one to be reconverted in September 1948.

The last twenty engines to be built in 1932 were fitted with the same weight modification and in addition they had side window cabs and outside steam pipes. They were the '9300' class. Between 1956 and 1959 these too had their ballast weights removed and they were renumbered 7322-7341.

Between 1936 and 1939 eighty-eight locomotives of the '4300' class and twelve locomotives of the '8300' class were withdrawn from service and their wheels and motions were used in the construction of the 'Grange' ('6800') and 'Manor' ('7800') classes. Many more would have been converted, but the war intervened and stopped the rebuilding programme.

o 6320 was converted for oil burning in 1947 and reconverted to coal burning (c) in 1949.

s 7322-7341 were ex-'9300' class locomotives and were fitted with side window cabs.

w 7300-7304 had detail alterations which made them heavier.

Year End Totals: '4300' class

'47	'48	'49	'50	'51	'52	'53	'54	'55	'56	'57	'58	'59	'60	'61	'62	'63	'64	'65	'66	'67
220	212	211	210	204	200	197	197	196	193	194	178	149	122	113	68	35				

Number	Built	Renumbered	BR Dates	Scrap	Notes
4303	06/11 Sdn		-11/52	12/52	
4318	10/11 Sdn		-06/52	*08/52*	
4320	01/11 Sdn		-01/49	03/49	
4326	08/13 Sdn		-03/57	04/57	
4337	10/13 Sdn		-11/51	*51*	
4353	03/14 Sdn		-11/48	*12/48*	
4358	04/14 Sdn		-08/59	12/59	
4365	07/15 Sdn		-04/48	*48*	
4375	11/15 Sdn		-01/58	02/58	
4377	12/15 Sdn		-01/59	09/59	
4381	05/16 Sdn		-05/53	*06/53*	
4386	07/16 Sdn		-04/48	*07/48*	

Class continued with 5300

4400 4400-4410
2-6-2T GWR Churchward 4ft 1½in

Power Classification: 3MT
Introduced: 1904-1906
Designer: Churchward
Company: GWR
Weight: 56t 13cwt
Driving Wheel: 4' 1½"
Boiler Pressure: 180psi superheated
Cylinders: Outside 17" x 24"
Tractive Effort: 21440lbf
Valve Gear: Stephenson (piston valves)

The GWR was a large user of the 2-6-2T type (the 'Prairie tank'). The small 'Prairie tanks' consisted of the '4400', '4500' and '4575' classes.

The original prototype of the '4400' class was No. 115 built in 1904 at Swindon. It was a small version of the old '3100' (later '5100') class which was designed for light branch work. It proved an immediate success over the hilly branch lines in the West Country. No. 115 was renumbered 4400 and ten more were built at Wolverhampton in 1905-1906. All the engines were subsequently superheated.

It was found that their small wheels limited their use for fast running and they were restricted to hilly branch lines such as the Princetown, Liskeard & Looe, Much Wenlock and Tondu branches. The '4500' class were built with larger wheels so as to have a wider sphere of influence.

Year End Totals: '4400' class

'47	'48	'49	'50	'51	'52	'53	'54	'55	'56	'57	'58	'59	'60	'61	'62	'63	'64	'65	'66	'67
11	11	10	10	8	7	4	3													

Number	Built	Renumbered	BR Dates	Scrap	Notes
4400	10/04 Sdn		-04/51	*04/51*	
4401	07/05 Wlv		-09/54	*10/54*	
4402	07/05 Wlv		-12/49	11/50	
4403	10/05 Wlv		-01/53	02/53	
4404	12/05 Wlv		-03/52	*52*	
4405	01/06 Wlv		-08/55	*55*	
4406	02/06 Wlv		-08/55	11/55	
4407	04/06 Wlv		-03/53	*53*	
4408	05/06 Wlv		-01/53	03/53	
4409	06/06 Wlv		-02/51	*51*	
4410	06/06 Wlv		-08/55	*55*	

4500 4500-4574
2-6-2T GWR Churchward 4ft 7½in

Power Classification: 4MT reclassified 3MT in 1953
Introduced: 1906-1915, 1924-1927
Designer: Churchward
Company: GWR
Weight: 57t 0cwt
Driving Wheel: 4' 7½"
Boiler Pressure: 200psi superheated
Cylinders: Outside 17" x 24"
Tractive Effort: 21250lbf
Valve Gear: Stephenson (piston valves)

The ‘4500’ class was developed directly from the ‘4400’ class, but they were fitted with larger wheels and higher pressure boilers. 4500-4519 were built at Wolverhampton in 1906-1908 - the last locomotives to be built there. The earlier locomotives were built without superheaters, but were subsequently superheated.

They were a popular class and were very effective and efficient on branch line work. The first fifty originally were fitted with inside steam pipes but many later received outside steam pipes. There was some variation in the size and shape of the bunkers.

Later engines had larger side tanks to increase the water capacity and had sloping tops to the tanks. These were known as the ‘4575’ class (see below).

Year End Totals: ‘4500’ class

'47	'48	'49	'50	'51	'52	'53	'54	'55	'56	'57	'58	'59	'60	'61	'62	'63	'64	'65	'66	'67
75	75	75	71	68	63	52	52	39	39	36	28	22	17	11	6	2				

Number	Built	Renumbered	BR Dates	Scrap	Notes
4500	10/06 Wlv		-08/53	53	
4501	11/06 Wlv		-03/53	53	
4502	12/06 Wlv		-10/51	51	
4503	01/07 Wlv		-01/51	51	
4504	02/07 Wlv		-06/52	08/52	
4505	02/07 Wlv		-10/57	12/57	
4506	04/07 Wlv		-03/55	04/55	
4507	05/07 Wlv		-10/63	06/64	
4508	06/07 Wlv		-10/59	11/59	
4509	06/07 Wlv		-06/51	08/51	
4510	07/07 Wlv		-03/53	05/53	
4511	09/07 Wlv		-11/53	53	
4512	09/07 Wlv		-02/53	06/53	
4513	10/07 Wlv		-10/50	11/50	
4514	01/07 Wlv		-02/53	53	
4515	12/07 Wlv		-04/53	53	
4516	01/08 Wlv		-12/52	01/53	
4517	02/08 Wlv		-02/53	53	
4518	03/08 Wlv		-10/52	10/52	
4519	04/08 Wlv		-02/59	07/59	
4520	03/09 Sdn		-01/53	02/53	
4521	03/09 Sdn		-12/55	01/56	
4522	03/09 Sdn		-02/55	55	
4523	03/09 Sdn		-10/55	55	
4524	03/09 Sdn		-06/58	08/58	
4525	02/10 Sdn		-06/53	53	
4526	02/10 Sdn		-01/58	03/58	
4527	03/10 Sdn		-03/53	05/53	
4528	03/10 Sdn		-12/50	51	
4529	03/10 Sdn		-03/52	52	
4530	04/13 Sdn		-03/55	55	
4531	04/13 Sdn		-02/50	04/50	
4532	04/13 Sdn		-02/55	55	
4533	04/13 Sdn		-03/55	55	
4534	04/13 Sdn		-02/55	04/55	
4535	05/13 Sdn		-02/55	03/55	
4536	05/13 Sdn		-04/59	04/59	
4537	05/13 Sdn		-02/55	55	
4538	05/13 Sdn		-05/57	06/57	
4539	05/13 Sdn		-10/55	55	
4540	11/14 Sdn		-03/59	08/59	
4541	11/14 Sdn		-10/55	01/56	
4542	11/14 Sdn		-08/55	55	
4543	11/14 Sdn		-08/50	09/50	
4544	11/14 Sdn		-09/52	52	
4545	12/14 Sdn		-09/58	04/59	
4546	12/14 Sdn		-01/58	06/58	
4547	12/14 Sdn		-02/60	05/60	
4548	01/15 Sdn		-11/57	11/57	
4549	01/15 Sdn		-12/61	04/62	
4550	02/15 Sdn		-10/60	05/61	
4551	02/15 Sdn		-02/58	04/58	
4552	03/15 Sdn		-09/61	09/61	
4553	03/15 Sdn		-12/58	08/59	
4554	03/15 Sdn		-09/58	09/58	
4555 §	09/24 Sdn		-11/63		
4556	09/24 Sdn		-06/60	11/60	
4557	09/24 Sdn		-09/62	08/63	
4558	09/24 Sdn		-07/62	10/62	
4559	09/24 Sdn		-10/60	05/61	
4560	09/24 Sdn		-08/59	02/60	
4561 §	10/24 Sdn		-05/62		
4562	10/24 Sdn		-03/60	04/60	
4563	10/24 Sdn		-10/61	02/62	
4564	10/24 Sdn		-09/64	01/65	
4565	10/24 Sdn		-10/61	03/62	
4566 §	10/24 Sdn		-04/62		
4567	10/24 Sdn		-09/62	08/64	
4568	10/24 Sdn		-02/59	05/59	
4569	10/24 Sdn		-07/64	11/64	
4570	01/24 Sdn		-01/63	08/64	
4571	01/24 Sdn		-03/61	04/61	
4572	01/24 Sdn		-12/58	03/59	
4573	01/24 Sdn		-08/61	08/61	
4574	11/24 Sdn		-02/63	11/64	

4575 4575-4599, 5500-5574
2-6-2T GWR Modified ‘4500’

Power Classification:	4MT reclassified 3MT in 1953
Introduced:	1927-1929
Designer:	Churchward / Collett
Company:	GWR
Weight:	61t 0cwt
Driving Wheel:	4' 7½"
Boiler Pressure:	200psi superheated
Cylinders:	Outside 17" x 24"
Tractive Effort:	21250lbf
Valve Gear:	Stephenson (piston valves)

These engines were developed from the ‘4500’ class with larger side tanks which had sloping tops to increase the water capacity.

p In 1953 some engines were motor fitted for working push-pull trains in the South Wales Valleys.

Year End Totals: ‘4575’ class

'47	'48	'49	'50	'51	'52	'53	'54	'55	'56	'57	'58	'59	'60	'61	'62	'63	'64	'65	'66	'67
100	100	100	100	100	100	100	100	100	98	93	77	67	40	32	16	11				

Number	Built	Renumbered	BR Dates	Scrap	Notes
4575	02/27 Sdn		-08/60	01/61	
4576	02/27 Sdn		-09/58	04/59	
4577	02/27 Sdn		-11/59	05/60	
4578	02/27 Sdn		-08/58	10/58	p
4579	02/27 Sdn		-09/58	04/59	
4580	02/27 Sdn		-06/58	08/58	
4581	02/27 Sdn		-04/58	05/58	p
4582	02/27 Sdn		-04/58	05/58	
4583	02/27 Sdn		-01/58	01/58	
4584	02/27 Sdn		-02/59	09/59	
4585	03/27 Sdn		-10/59	02/60	
4586	03/27 Sdn		-04/56	04/56	
4587	03/27 Sdn		-08/60	04/61	
4588 §	03/27 Sdn		-07/62		
4589	03/27 Sdn		-09/60	01/61	p
4590	03/27 Sdn		-10/58	01/59	
4591	03/27 Sdn		-07/64	11/64	
4592	03/27 Sdn		-01/60	04/60	
4593	03/27 Sdn		-09/64	04/65	
4594	04/27 Sdn		-11/60	06/61	
4595	04/27 Sdn		-12/58	01/59	
4596	04/27 Sdn		-09/57	09/57	
4597	04/27 Sdn		-01/58	02/58	
4598	04/27 Sdn		-12/56	57	
4599	04/27 Sdn		-03/59	07/59	

Class continued with 5500

5700 3600-3799, 4600-4699, 5700-5799, 7700-7799, 8700-8799, 9600-9682, 9711-9799
0-6-0PT GWR Collett 4ft 7½in

Class continued from 3799

Number	Built	Renumbered	BR Dates	Scrap	Notes
4600	09/41 Sdn		-07/64	09/64	m
4601	09/41 Sdn		-11/62	11/62	m
4602	10/41 Sdn		-11/64	02/65	m
4603	10/41 Sdn		-04/64	07/64	m
4604	10/41 Sdn		-07/65	10/65	m
4605	01/42 Sdn		-10/62	12/63	m
4606	01/42 Sdn		-02/65	03/65	m
4607	01/42 Sdn		-09/65	12/65	m
4608	01/42 Sdn		-09/64	12/64	m
4609	01/42 Sdn		-05/65	08/65	m
4610	02/42 Sdn		-10/64	04/65	m
4611	02/42 Sdn		-06/65	10/65	m
4612 §	02/42 Sdn		-08/65		m
4613	03/42 Sdn		-12/64	04/65	m
4614	03/42 Sdn		-07/64	12/64	m
4615	04/42 Sdn		-10/64	12/64	m
4616	04/42 Sdn		-10/64	01/65	m
4617	04/42 Sdn		-10/63	02/64	m
4618	04/42 Sdn		-10/63	02/64	m
4619	05/42 Sdn		-09/64	04/65	m
4620	05/42 Sdn		-07/65	10/65	m
4621	05/42 Sdn		-07/65	10/65	m
4622	06/42 Sdn		-05/64	08/64	m
4623	06/42 Sdn		-06/65	10/65	m
4624	06/42 Sdn		-09/64	04/65	m
4625	09/42 Sdn		-05/62	09/62	m
4626	09/42 Sdn		-03/64	01/65	m
4627	09/42 Sdn		-10/64	12/64	m
4628	10/42 Sdn		-05/64	07/64	m
4629	10/42 Sdn		-09/63	12/63	m
4630	11/42 Sdn		-11/65	02/66	m
4631	11/42 Sdn		-06/65	10/65	m
4632	11/42 Sdn		-01/62	05/62	m
4633	11/42 Sdn		-04/63	12/63	m
4634	11/42 Sdn		-09/64	04/65	m
4635	12/42 Sdn		-07/66	11/66	m
4636	12/42 Sdn		-09/65	12/65	m
4637	12/42 Sdn		-05/64	09/64	m
4638	12/42 Sdn		-06/65	12/65	m
4639	12/42 Sdn		-06/65	10/65	m
4640	12/42 Sdn		-12/63	02/64	m
4641	12/42 Sdn		-05/62	09/62	m
4642	01/43 Sdn		-01/64	07/64	m
4643	01/43 Sdn		-04/65	08/65	m
4644	01/43 Sdn		-10/63	03/64	m
4645	02/43 Sdn		-11/65	05/66	m
4646	02/43 Sdn		-11/66	05/67	m
4647	03/43 Sdn		-10/62	11/62	m
4648	03/43 Sdn		-09/64	01/65	m
4649	03/43 Sdn		-09/64	11/64	m
4650	04/43 Sdn		-07/65	10/65	m
4651	04/43 Sdn		-09/63	11/63	m
4652	04/43 Sdn		-04/64	06/64	m
4653	04/43 Sdn		-11/64	08/65	m
4654	04/43 Sdn		-12/63	04/64	m
4655	05/43 Sdn		-06/65	10/65	m
4656	05/43 Sdn		-12/62	03/63	m
4657	05/43 Sdn		-07/64	12/64	m
4658	06/43 Sdn		-05/64	09/64	m
4659	06/43 Sdn		-05/64	04/65	m
4660	06/43 Sdn		-07/64	12/64	m
4661	10/43 Sdn		-12/63	07/64	m
4662	10/43 Sdn		-09/65	12/65	m
4663	11/43 Sdn		-06/65	10/65	m
4664	11/43 Sdn		-07/65	10/65	m
4665	12/43 Sdn		-06/65	09/65	m
4666	12/43 Sdn		-06/65	10/65	m
4667	12/43 Sdn		-04/64	07/64	m
4668	01/44 Sdn		-07/65	11/65	m
4669	01/44 Sdn		-06/65	10/65	m
4670	01/44 Sdn		-10/64	12/64	m
4671	02/44 Sdn		-11/65	02/66	m
4672	03/44 Sdn		-07/63	12/64	m
4673	03/44 Sdn		-06/65	10/65	m
4674	03/44 Sdn		-11/64	03/65	m
4675	03/44 Sdn		-06/65	10/65	m
4676	04/44 Sdn		-10/65	02/66	m
4677	04/44 Sdn		-03/63	04/63	m
4678	05/44 Sdn		-07/64	08/64	m
4679	05/44 Sdn		-05/65	08/65	m
4680	06/44 Sdn		-12/65	06/66	m
4681	11/44 Sdn		-12/63	03/64	m
4682	11/44 Sdn		-09/63	10/63	m
4683	11/44 Sdn		-10/65	04/66	m
4684	12/44 Sdn		-07/65	10/65	m
4685	12/44 Sdn		-05/62	09/62	m
4686	12/44 Sdn		-08/59	08/59	m
4687	12/44 Sdn		-11/64	01/65	m
4688	12/44 Sdn		-12/63	03/64	m
4689	12/44 Sdn		-12/65	04/66	m
4690	01/45 Sdn		-10/63	03/64	m
4691	01/45 Sdn		-09/64	09/65	m
4692	01/45 Sdn		-09/64	12/64	m
4693	01/45 Sdn		-04/64	08/64	m
4694	01/45 Sdn		-06/65	10/65	m
4695	01/45 Sdn		-06/64	12/64	m
4696	02/45 Sdn		-11/66	04/67	m
4697	02/45 Sdn		-07/65	10/65	m
4698	02/45 Sdn		-11/65	02/66	m
4699	02/45 Sdn		-06/64	08/64	m

Class continued with 5700

4700 4700-4708
2-8-0 GWR Churchward

Power Classification:	7F
Introduced:	1919-1923
Designer:	Churchward
Company:	GWR
Weight:	Loco 82t 0cwt Tender 46t 14cwt
Driving Wheel:	5' 8"
Boiler Pressure:	225psi superheated
Cylinders:	Outside 19" x 30"
Tractive Effort:	30460lbf
Valve Gear:	Stephenson (piston valves)

This class was designed at the end of the First World War to meet the need for a large freight engine to work the night vacuum fitted goods services. They were built as mixed traffic engines and were an enlarged version of the ‘4300’ class.

4700 was built with a small boiler in 1919, and was rebuilt with a larger boiler in 1921. 4701-4708 were built with the larger size boiler in 1922-1923. 4700 attended the Railway Centenary at Darlington in 1925.

GWR Churchward '4700' class 2-8-0 No 4707 at Swindon in April 1954.

GWR Collett '5101' class 2-6-2T No 5103.

GWR Collett '5205' class 2-8-0T No 5216 at Port Talbot in July 1950.

GWR Collett '4900' 'Hall' class 4-6-0 No 5999 *Wollaton Hall*.

They were the only mixed traffic 2-8-0s in Britain. Their weight restricted them to working on the main lines. They spent many years working on the West of England main line and between Paddington and Birkenhead, but they were also used regularly on passenger trains at the weekends. The only other 2-8-0s in Britain to work passenger trains regularly were the SDJR 53800 '7F' class.

They were similar in looks to the '2800' class but had larger driving wheels and splashers and the drive was on the second coupled axle, compared to the third on the '2800' class.

Year End Totals: '4700' class

'47	'48	'49	'50	'51	'52	'53	'54	'55	'56	'57	'58	'59	'60	'61	'62	'63	'64	'65	'66	'67
9	9	9	9	9	9	9	9	9	9	9	9	9	9	9	6	4				

Number	Built	Renumbered	BR Dates	Scrap	Notes
4700	03/19 Sdn		-10/62	03/64	
4701	01/22 Sdn		-09/63	08/65	
4702	02/22 Sdn		-06/62	11/62	
4703	03/22 Sdn		-05/64	07/64	
4704	04/22 Sdn		-05/64	07/64	
4705	04/22 Sdn		-12/63	03/64	
4706	03/23 Sdn		-02/64	04/64	
4707	04/23 Sdn		-05/64	07/64	
4708	04/23 Sdn		-10/62	12/63	

2800 2800-2883, (4800-4811)
2-8-0 GWR Churchward

Class continued from 2883

Number	Built	Renumbered	BR Dates	Scrap	Notes
4800	11/18 Sdn		-08/63	06/64	o 09/48➲2872
4801	02/13 Sdn		-10/63	07/64	o 02/49➲2854
4802	06/18 Sdn		-04/64	02/65	o 09/48➲2862
4803	01/13 Sdn		-08/62	06/63	o 04/49➲2849
4804	10/12 Sdn		-06/64	02/65	o 10/48➲2839
4805	06/18 Sdn		-06/59	04/60	o 05/49➲2863
4806	04/11 Sdn		-11/59	04/61	o 04/49➲2832
4807	01/13 Sdn		-06/59	02/60	o 07/49➲2848
4808	05/11 Sdn		-11/62	05/63	o 01/50➲2834
4809	11/12 Sdn		-07/63	09/63	o 12/49➲2845
4810	02/13 Sdn		-05/62	08/62	o 06/49➲2853
4811	01/13 Sdn		-03/60	04/60	o 06/49➲2847

2884 2884-2899, 3800-3866, (4850-4857)
2-8-0 GWR Modified '2800' class with side window cabs

Class continued from 3866

Number	Built	Renumbered	BR Dates	Scrap	Notes
4850	03/38 Sdn		-02/63	06/63	o 09/48➲2888
4851	11/42 Sdn		-03/65	07/65	o 04/49➲3865
4852	04/40 Sdn		-05/65	08/65	o 09/48➲3818
4853	01/42 Sdn		-12/63	08/64	o 11/49➲3839
4854	01/42 Sdn		-07/65	10/65	o 08/49➲3837
4855	09/39 Sdn		-07/65	12/65	o 06/49➲3813
4856	04/40 Sdn		-07/65	09/65	o 06/49➲3820
4857	12/40 Sdn		-09/63	04/64	o 05/49➲3831

4900 4900-4999, 5900-5999, 6900-6958, (3900-3955)
4-6-0 GWR Collett 'Hall'

Power Classification:	5MT
Introduced:	a 1907, rebuilt 1924 1928-1943
Designer:	Collett
Company:	GWR
Weight:	a Loco 72t 10cwt Loco 75t 0cwt Tender 46t 14cwt
Driving Wheel:	6' 0"
Boiler Pressure:	225psi superheated
Cylinders:	Outside 18½" x 30"
Tractive Effort:	27275lbf
Valve Gear:	Stephenson (piston valves)

In 1924 one of the 'Saint' class locomotives (2925 SAINT MARTIN, built in 1907) was rebuilt with 6' 0" driving wheels. It was rebuilt in order to meet the need for a mixed traffic locomotive with higher boiler power and a higher speed than the '4300' class and became the prototype of the 'Hall' class. It was also fitted with a side window cab, but no other major changes were made (until fitted with outside steam pipes in December 1948). It was later renumbered 4900.

Having proved itself as a powerful general purpose locomotive 330 more were built to the '4900' and to the modified '6959' design between 1928 and 1950. These new engines were all named after Halls, and had higher pitched boilers, modified footplating and detail differences compared to 4900.

Apart from 4911 BOWDEN HALL which was destroyed in an air raid in 1941 all of the class survived to become BR locomotives.

In 1944 Hawksworth introduced a modified version of the class known as the '6959' class.

4983 ALBERT HALL was rescued from Barry Scrapyard for preservation, but when it was being restored it turned out to be the engine 4965 ROOD ASHTON HALL. The two engines probably swapped identities in 1962 when 4965 was authorised for withdrawal, but 4983 was found to be in a poor condition and was withdrawn instead. 4965 was returned to service carrying 4983's name and number plates rather than create the additional paperwork of reinstating one engine and withdrawing another. This raises the question as to whether a similar swapping of identities took place on any other engines without being recorded.

- a This was the prototype engine converted from 'Saint' Class engine 2925.
- o Between 1946 and 1950 some of the class were converted to oil burning (as a result of the 1946 coal crisis). They were renumbered in the 3900 series but were later re-converted and reverted to their original numbers.

Year End Totals: '4900' class

'47	'48	'49	'50	'51	'52	'53	'54	'55	'56	'57	'58	'59	'60	'61	'62	'63	'64	'65	'66	'67
247	252	255	258	258	258	258	258	258	258	258	258	256	254	246	173	106	50			

Year End Totals: '4900' (oil burning) class

'47	'48	'49	'50	'51	'52	'53	'54	'55	'56	'57	'58	'59	'60	'61	'62	'63	'64	'65	'66	'67
11	6	3																		

Class continued from 3955

Number	Built	Renumbered	BR Dates	Scrap	Notes
4900 **SAINT MARTIN**	09/07 Sdn		-04/59	04/59	a
4901 **ADDERLEY HALL**	12/28 Sdn		-09/60	12/60	
4902 **ALDENHAM HALL**	12/28 Sdn		-09/63	05/64	
4903 **ASTLEY HALL**	12/28 Sdn		-10/64	04/65	
4904 **BINNEGAR HALL**	12/28 Sdn		-12/63	06/64	
4905 **BARTON HALL**	12/28 Sdn		-11/63	06/64	
4906 **BRADFIELD HALL**	01/29 Sdn		-09/62	10/63	
4907 **BROUGHTON HALL**	01/29 Sdn	04/50 3903	-08/63	01/64	
4908 **BROOME HALL**	01/29 Sdn		-10/63	07/64	
4909 **BLAKESLEY HALL**	01/29 Sdn		-09/62	04/64	
4910 **BLAISDON HALL**	01/29 Sdn		-12/63	04/64	
4912 **BERRINGTON HALL**	02/29 Sdn		-08/62	11/62	
4913 **BAGLAN HALL**	02/29 Sdn		-09/62	04/64	
4914 **CRANMORE HALL**	02/29 Sdn		-12/63	04/64	
4915 **CONDOVER HALL**	02/29 Sdn		-02/63	04/63	
4916 **CRUMLIN HALL**	02/29 Sdn		-08/64	12/64	
4917 **CROSSWOOD HALL**	03/29 Sdn		-09/62	06/64	
4918 **DARTINGTON HALL**	03/29 Sdn		-06/63	03/64	
4919 **DONNINGTON HALL**	03/29 Sdn		-10/64	02/65	
4920 § **DUMBLETON HALL**	03/29 Sdn		-12/65		
4921 **EATON HALL**	04/29 Sdn		-09/62	02/64	
4922 **ENVILLE HALL**	04/29 Sdn		-07/63	01/64	
4923 **EVENLEY HALL**	04/29 Sdn		-05/64	08/64	
4924 **EYDON HALL**	05/29 Sdn		-10/63	06/64	
4925 **EYNSHAM HALL**	05/29 Sdn		-08/62	08/62	
4926 **FAIRLEIGH HALL**	05/29 Sdn		-09/61	10/61	
4927 **FARNBOROUGH HALL**	05/29 Sdn		-09/63	01/64	
4928 **GATACRE HALL**	05/29 Sdn		-12/63	01/65	
4929 **GOYTREY HALL**	05/29 Sdn		-03/65	07/65	
4930 § **HAGLEY HALL**	05/29 Sdn		-12/63		
4931 **HANBURY HALL**	05/29 Sdn		-07/62	11/62	
4932 **HATHERTON HALL**	06/29 Sdn		-11/64	04/65	
4933 **HIMLEY HALL**	06/29 Sdn		-08/64	10/64	
4934 **HINDLIP HALL**	06/29 Sdn		-09/62	07/64	
4935 **KETLEY HALL**	06/29 Sdn		-03/63	01/64	
4936 § **KINLET HALL**	06/29 Sdn		-01/64		
4937 **LANELAY HALL**	06/29 Sdn		-09/62	09/62	
4938 **LIDDINGTON HALL**	06/29 Sdn		-12/62	02/63	
4939 **LITTLETON HALL**	07/29 Sdn		-02/63	04/63	
4940 **LUDFORD HALL**	07/29 Sdn		-11/59	12/59	
4941 **LLANGEDWYN HALL**	07/29 Sdn		-10/62	06/64	
4942 § **MAINDY HALL**	07/29 Sdn		-12/63		
4943 **MARRINGTON HALL**	07/29 Sdn		-12/63	03/64	
4944 **MIDDLETON HALL**	07/29 Sdn		-09/62	01/64	
4945 **MILLIGAN HALL**	08/29 Sdn		-11/61	12/61	
4946 **MOSELEY HALL**	08/29 Sdn		-06/63	04/64	
4947 **NANHORAN HALL**	08/29 Sdn		-09/62	03/64	
4948 **NORTHWICK HALL**	08/29 Sdn	09/48 3902	-09/62	04/64	
4949 **PACKWOOD HALL**	08/29 Sdn		-09/64	01/65	
4950 **PATSHULL HALL**	08/29 Sdn		-05/64	08/64	
4951 **PENDEFORD HALL**	07/29 Sdn		-06/64	12/64	
4952 **PEPLOW HALL**	08/29 Sdn		-09/62	01/64	
4953 § **PITCHFORD HALL**	08/29 Sdn		-04/63		
4954 **PLAISH HALL**	08/29 Sdn		-11/64	12/64	
4955 **PLASPOWER HALL**	08/29 Sdn		-10/63	04/64	
4956 **PLOWDEN HALL**	09/29 Sdn		-07/63	06/64	
4957 **POSTLIP HALL**	09/29 Sdn		-03/62	06/62	
4958 **PRIORY HALL**	09/29 Sdn		-09/64	01/65	
4959 **PURLEY HALL**	09/29 Sdn		-12/64	04/65	
4960 **PYLE HALL**	09/29 Sdn		-09/62	09/63	
4961 **PYRLAND HALL**	11/29 Sdn		-12/62	02/63	
4962 **RAGLEY HALL**	11/29 Sdn		-10/65 ⊠11/63-12/63	03/66	
4963 **RIGNALL HALL**	11/29 Sdn		-06/62	09/62	
4964 **RODWELL HALL**	11/29 Sdn		-10/63	08/64	

4965 § 11/29 Sdn -03/62
ROOD ASHTON HALL
4966 11/29 Sdn -11/63 04/64
SHAKENHURST HALL
4967 12/29 Sdn -09/62 11/63
SHIRENEWTON HALL
4968 12/29 Sdn 03/49 3900 -07/62 11/62
SHOTTON HALL
4969 12/29 Sdn -09/62 09/62
SHRUGBOROUGH HALL
4970 12/29 Sdn -07/63 01/64
SKETTY HALL
4971 01/30 Sdn 04/49 3901 -08/62 01/64
STANWAY HALL
4972 01/30 Sdn 10/48 3904 -02/64 07/64
SAINT BRIDES HALL
4973 01/30 Sdn -07/62 11/62
SWEENEY HALL
4974 01/30 Sdn -04/62 09/62
TALGARTH HALL
4975 01/30 Sdn -09/63 07/64
UMBERSLADE HALL
4976 01/30 Sdn -05/64 08/65
WARFIELD HALL
4977 01/30 Sdn -05/62 06/62
WATCOMBE HALL
4978 02/30 Sdn -09/64 12/64
WESTWOOD HALL
4979 § 02/30 Sdn -12/63
WOOTTON HALL
4980 02/30 Sdn -07/63 06/64
WROTTESLEY HALL
4981 12/30 Sdn -10/63 07/64
ABBERLEY HALL
4982 01/31 Sdn -05/62 07/62
ACTON HALL
4983 01/31 Sdn -12/63 04/62?
ALBERT HALL
4984 01/31 Sdn -09/62 07/64
ALBRIGHTON HALL
4985 01/31 Sdn -09/64 01/65
ALLESLEY HALL
4986 01/31 Sdn -05/62 11/62
ASTON HALL
4987 01/31 Sdn -04/62 02/64
BROCKLEY HALL
4988 01/31 Sdn -02/64 03/64
BULWELL HALL
4989 02/31 Sdn -11/64 03/65
CHERWELL HALL
4990 02/31 Sdn -04/62 06/62
CLIFTON HALL
4991 02/31 Sdn -12/63 06/64
COBHAM HALL
4992 02/31 Sdn -04/65 08/65
CROSBY HALL
4993 02/31 Sdn -02/65 04/65
DALTON HALL
4994 02/31 Sdn -03/63 01/64
DOWNTON HALL
4995 02/31 Sdn -06/62 08/62
EASTON HALL
4996 03/31 Sdn -09/63 06/64
EDEN HALL
4997 03/31 Sdn -10/61 10/61
ELTON HALL
4998 03/31 Sdn -10/63 05/64
EYTON HALL
4999 03/31 Sdn -09/62 09/63
GOPSAL HALL

Class continued with 5900

4073 100A1, 111, 4000, 4016, 4032, 4037, 4073-4099, 5000-5099, 7000-7037
4-6-0 GWR Collett 'Castle'

Class continued from 4099

Number Built Renumbered BR Dates Scrap Notes

5000 09/26 Sdn -10/64 04/65 3
LAUNCESTON CASTLE
5001 09/26 Sdn -02/63 05/64 07/61⇨d
LLANDOVERY CASTLE
5002 09/26 Sdn -09/64 01/65
LUDLOW CASTLE
5003 05/27 Sdn -08/62 12/62
LULWORTH CASTLE
5004 06/27 Sdn -04/62 06/62
LLANSTEPHAN CASTLE
5005 06/27 Sdn -02/60 03/60
MANORBIER CASTLE
5006 06/27 Sdn -04/62 04/63
TREGENNA CASTLE
5007 06/27 Sdn -09/62 12/62 3
ROUGEMONT CASTLE
5008 06/27 Sdn -09/62 12/62 03/61⇨d
RAGLAN CASTLE
5009 06/27 Sdn -10/60 12/60
SHREWSBURY CASTLE
5010 07/27 Sdn -10/59 10/59
RESTORMEL CASTLE
5011 07/27 Sdn -09/62 12/62
TINTAGEL CASTLE
5012 07/27 Sdn -04/62 12/62
BERRY POMEROY CASTLE
5013 06/32 Sdn -07/62 08/62
ABERGAVENNY CASTLE
5014 06/32 Sdn -02/65 05/65
GOODRICH CASTLE
5015 07/32 Sdn -04/63 01/64
KINGSWEAR CASTLE
5016 07/32 Sdn -09/62 12/62 01/61⇨d
MONTGOMERY CASTLE
5017 07/32 Sdn -09/62 12/62
ST. DONATS CASTLE
04/54➲THE GLOUCESTERSHIRE REGIMENT 28TH/61ST
5018 07/32 Sdn -03/64 11/64
ST. MAWES CASTLE
5019 07/32 Sdn -09/62 09/62 02/61⇨d
TREAGO CASTLE
5020 07/32 Sdn -11/62 03/63
TREMATON CASTLE
5021 08/32 Sdn -09/62 06/63 3
WHITTINGTON CASTLE
5022 08/32 Sdn -06/63 06/64 03/59⇨d
WIGMORE CASTLE
5023 04/34 Sdn -02/63 06/63
BRECON CASTLE
5024 04/34 Sdn -05/62 12/62
CAREW CASTLE
5025 04/34 Sdn -11/63 06/64
CHIRK CASTLE
5026 04/34 Sdn -11/64 02/65 4 10/59⇨d
CRICCIETH CASTLE
5027 04/34 Sdn -11/62 09/63 03/61⇨d
FARLEIGH CASTLE
5028 05/34 Sdn -05/60 05/60
LLANTILIO CASTLE
5029 § 05/34 Sdn -12/63
NUNNEY CASTLE
5030 05/34 Sdn -09/62 10/62
SHIRBURN CASTLE
5031 05/34 Sdn -10/63 05/64 05/59⇨d
TOTNES CASTLE
5032 05/34 Sdn -09/62 11/62 05/59⇨d
USK CASTLE
5033 05/35 Sdn -09/62 11/62 4 10/60⇨d
BROUGHTON CASTLE
5034 05/35 Sdn -09/62 11/62 d 02/61⇨d
CORFE CASTLE
5035 05/35 Sdn -05/62 12/62
COITY CASTLE
5036 05/35 Sdn -09/62 11/62 4 12/60⇨d
LYONSHALL CASTLE
5037 05/35 Sdn -03/64 06/64 3
MONMOUTH CASTLE
5038 06/35 Sdn -09/63 07/64
MORLAIS CASTLE
5039 06/35 Sdn -06/64 12/64 o 09/48⇨c
RHUDDLAN CASTLE
5040 06/35 Sdn -10/63 05/64
STOKESAY CASTLE
5041 07/35 Sdn -12/63 06/64
TIVERTON CASTLE
5042 07/35 Sdn -06/65 10/65
WINCHESTER CASTLE
5043 § 03/36 Sdn -12/63 4 05/58⇨d
EARL OF MOUNT EDGCUMBE
5044 03/36 Sdn -04/62 06/62
EARL OF DUNRAVEN
5045 03/36 Sdn -09/62 09/62
EARL OF DUDLEY
5046 04/36 Sdn -09/62 03/63
EARL CAWDOR
5047 04/36 Sdn -09/62 03/63
EARL OF DARTMOUTH
5048 04/36 Sdn -08/62 08/62 3
EARL OF DEVON
5049 04/36 Sdn -03/63 06/64 4 08/59⇨d
EARL OF PLYMOUTH
5050 05/36 Sdn -08/63 05/64 3
EARL OF ST. GERMANS
5051 § 05/36 Sdn -05/63
EARL BATHURST
5052 05/36 Sdn -09/62 09/62
EARL OF RADNOR
5053 05/36 Sdn -07/62 12/62 3
EARL CAIRNS
5054 06/36 Sdn -10/64 12/64
EARL OF DUCIE
5055 06/36 Sdn -09/64 02/65 3
EARL OF ELDON
5056 06/36 Sdn -11/64 02/65 11/60⇨d
EARL OF POWIS
5057 06/36 Sdn -03/64 08/64 4 05/58⇨d
EARL WALDEGRAVE
5058 05/37 Sdn -03/63 04/63
EARL OF CLANCARTY
5059 05/37 Sdn -06/62 02/63
EARL ST. ALDWYN
5060 06/37 Sdn -04/63 12/64 08/61⇨d
EARL OF BERKELEY
5061 06/37 Sdn -09/62 12/62 4 08/58⇨d
EARL OF BIRKENHEAD
5062 06/37 Sdn -08/62 12/62
EARL OF SHAFTESBURY
5063 06/37 Sdn -02/65 06/65 3
EARL BALDWIN
5064 07/37 Sdn -09/62 12/62 4 09/58⇨d
BISHOP'S CASTLE
5065 07/37 Sdn -01/63 12/63 3
NEWPORT CASTLE
5066 07/37 Sdn -09/62 12/62 04/59⇨d
WARDOUR CASTLE
04/56➲SIR FELIX POLE
5067 07/37 Sdn -07/62 06/64
ST. FAGANS CASTLE
5068 07/38 Sdn -09/62 12/62 02/61⇨d
BEVERSTON CASTLE
5069 06/38 Sdn -02/62 05/62 12/58⇨d
ISAMBARD KINGDOM BRUNEL
5070 06/38 Sdn -03/64 08/64
SIR DANIEL GOOCH
5071 06/38 Sdn -10/63 05/64 4 05/59⇨d
SPITFIRE
5072 06/38 Sdn -10/62 04/63 3
HURRICANE
5073 06/38 Sdn -02/64 07/64 4 06/59⇨d
BLENHEIM
5074 07/38 Sdn -05/64 08/64 3 09/61⇨d
HAMPDEN
5075 08/38 Sdn -09/62 12/62 3
WELLINGTON
5076 08/38 Sdn -09/64 12/64
GLADIATOR
5077 08/38 Sdn -07/62 08/62 3
FAIREY BATTLE
5078 05/39 Sdn -11/62 04/63 3 12/61⇨d
BEAUFORT
5079 05/39 Sdn -05/60 06/60 3o 11/48⇨c
LYSANDER
5080 § 05/39 Sdn -04/63
DEFIANT
5081 05/39 Sdn -10/63 07/64 3
LOCKHEED HUDSON
5082 06/39 Sdn -07/62 12/62 3
SWORDFISH
5083 11/22 Sdn -01/59 01/59 so 11/48⇨c
BATH ABBEY
5084 12/22 Sdn -07/62 12/62 s 09/58⇨d
READING ABBEY
5085 12/22 Sdn -02/64 07/64 s
EVESHAM ABBEY
5086 12/22 Sdn -11/58 12/58 s
VISCOUNT HORNE
5087 01/23 Sdn -08/63 01/64 s
TINTERN ABBEY
5088 01/23 Sdn -09/62 03/63 s4 06/58⇨d
LLANTHONY ABBEY
5089 01/23 Sdn -11/64 02/65 s
WESTMINSTER ABBEY
5090 02/23 Sdn -05/62 12/62 s
NEATH ABBEY
5091 02/23 Sdn -10/64 11/64 so 11/48⇨c
CLEEVE ABBEY
5092 02/23 Sdn -07/63 10/64 s 10/61⇨d
TRESCO ABBEY
5093 06/39 Sdn -09/63 10/63 3
UPTON CASTLE
5094 06/39 Sdn -09/62 12/62 4 06/60⇨d
TRETOWER CASTLE
5095 06/39 Sdn -08/62 03/63 4 11/58⇨d
BARBURY CASTLE
5096 06/39 Sdn -06/64 12/64 3
BRIDGWATER CASTLE
5097 07/39 Sdn -03/63 06/65 3 07/61⇨d
SARUM CASTLE
5098 05/46 Sdn -06/64 12/64 3 01/59⇨d
CLIFFORD CASTLE
5099 05/46 Sdn -02/63 09/63 3
COMPTON CASTLE

Class continued with 7000

5101 4100-4179, 5101-5199
2-6-2T GWR Churchward & Collett 5ft 8in

Class continued from 4179

Number	Built	Renumbered	BR Dates	Scrap	Notes
5101	11/29 Sdn		-06/63	09/63	
5102	11/29 Sdn		-03/60	06/60	
5103	11/29 Sdn		-12/60	09/61	
5104	11/29 Sdn		-11/60	04/61	
5105	11/29 Sdn		-10/58	01/59	
5106	11/29 Sdn		-03/60	06/60	
5107	12/29 Sdn		-06/57	07/57	
5108	12/29 Sdn		-07/58	08/58	
5109	12/29 Sdn		-06/57	11/57	
5110	12/29 Sdn		-12/60	09/61	
5111	01/05 Sdn		-10/48	*48*	a
5112	01/05 Sdn		-10/55	*11/55*	a
5113	01/05 Sdn		-10/55	*55*	a
5114	02/05 Sdn		-09/50	10/50	a
5117	02/05 Sdn		-05/49	07/49	a
5119	03/05 Sdn		-06/48	*48*	a
5121	05/05 Sdn		-10/48	01/49	a
5122	05/05 Sdn		-09/50	10/50	a
5125	05/05 Sdn		-07/52	*08/52*	a
5127	06/05 Sdn		-05/48	*09/48*	a
5128	06/05 Sdn		-11/48	*48*	a
5129	06/05 Sdn		-07/51	*51*	a
5130	06/05 Sdn		-08/48	*48*	a
5131	01/06 Sdn		-10/48	11/48	a
5132	01/06 Sdn		-08/51	*51*	a
5134	02/06 Sdn		-04/51	*51*	a
5135	02/06 Sdn		-08/49	10/49	a
5136	02/06 Sdn		-10/51	*51*	a
5137	02/06 Sdn		-10/51	*51*	a
5138	02/06 Sdn		-11/52	*02/53*	a
5139	03/06 Sdn		-11/52	*52*	a
5140	03/06 Sdn		-06/53	*53*	a
5141	03/06 Sdn		-10/52	*52*	a
5142	03/06 Sdn		-05/52	*07/52*	a
5143	03/06 Sdn		-12/51	*12/51*	a
5144	03/06 Sdn		-01/52	09/52	a
5146	03/06 Sdn		-05/48	*06/48*	a
5147	03/06 Sdn		-01/53	05/53	a
5148	03/06 Sdn		-12/59	04/60	a
5150	02/30 Sdn		-08/60	12/60	
5151	02/30 Sdn		-08/62	11/63	
5152	02/30 Sdn		-11/63	04/64	
5153	03/30 Sdn		-11/64	06/65	
5154	02/30 Sdn		-08/63	04/64	
5155	03/30 Sdn		-01/60	01/61	
5156	03/30 Sdn		-09/58	11/58	
5157	03/30 Sdn		-07/58	09/58	
5158	03/30 Sdn		-04/61	07/61	
5159	03/30 Sdn		-04/56	*04/56*	
5160	10/30 Sdn		-11/58	05/60	
5161	11/30 Sdn		-04/57	10/57	
5162	11/30 Sdn		-07/58	11/58	
5163	11/30 Sdn		-11/59	02/60	
5164 §	11/30 Sdn		-04/63		
5165	11/30 Sdn		-02/58	03/58	
5166	11/30 Sdn		-05/61	08/61	
5167	12/30 Sdn		-01/62	05/62	
5168	12/30 Sdn		-08/58	10/58	
5169	12/30 Sdn		-09/60	02/61	
5170	12/30 Sdn		-12/59	05/60	
5171	12/30 Sdn		-07/58	08/58	
5172	12/30 Sdn		-10/58	11/58	
5173	12/30 Sdn		-08/62	09/63	
5174	12/30 Sdn		-11/61	01/62	
5175	01/31 Sdn		-04/61	06/61	
5176	01/31 Sdn		-01/61	09/61	
5177	01/31 Sdn		-05/61	09/61	
5178	01/31 Sdn		-03/60	08/60	
5179	02/31 Sdn		-07/60	11/60	
5180	02/31 Sdn		-07/62	01/63	
5181	03/31 Sdn		-08/62	11/62	
5182	03/31 Sdn		-05/62	07/64	
5183	03/31 Sdn		-05/62	09/62	
5184	03/31 Sdn		-10/64	04/65	
5185	03/31 Sdn		-03/60	06/60	
5186	03/31 Sdn		-08/59	12/59	
5187	04/31 Sdn		-05/62	10/62	
5188	04/31 Sdn		-07/62	11/62	
5189	04/31 Sdn		-08/59	09/59	
5190	10/34 Sdn		-09/62	10/63	
5191	10/34 Sdn		-07/64	10/64	
5192	10/34 Sdn		-06/63	09/63	
5193 §	10/34 Sdn		-06/62		
5194	10/34 Sdn		-04/61	06/61	
5195	10/34 Sdn		-06/61	09/61	
5196	10/34 Sdn		-12/59	04/60	
5197	10/34 Sdn		-07/60	11/60	
5198	11/34 Sdn		-06/61	11/61	
5199 §	11/34 Sdn		-03/63		

4200 4200-4299, 5200-5204
2-8-0T GWR Churchward

Class continued from 4299

Number	Built	Renumbered	BR Dates	Scrap	Notes
5200	12/22 Sdn		-04/65	07/65	
5201	12/22 Sdn		-06/63	12/63	
5202	12/22 Sdn		-06/65	06/66	
5203	02/23 Sdn		-12/63	08/64	
5204	02/23 Sdn		-12/62	11/63	

5205 5205-5264
2-8-0T GWR '4200' with enlarged cylinders

Power Classification:	8F
Introduced:	1923-1930 & 1940
Designer:	Collett
Company:	GWR
Weight:	82t 2cwt
Driving Wheel:	4' 7½"
Boiler Pressure:	200psi superheated
Cylinders:	Outside 19" x 30"
Tractive Effort:	33170lbf
Valve Gear:	Stephenson (piston valves)

This class was developed from the '4200' class with enlarged cylinders and detail alterations.

They were built with outside steam pipes and straight frames over the cylinders. Many were later rebuilt with raised framing over the cylinders.

As already mentioned many '4200' and '5205' were rebuilt as the '7200' class with an extra pair of trailing wheels and a larger bunker. These included 5255-5294 which became '7200' class engines in 1934-1936. Somewhat surprisingly ten more 2-8-0Ts were constructed in 1940 which were numbered 5255-5264 and were the second batch of engines to carry these numbers.

Year End Totals: '5205' class

'47	'48	'49	'50	'51	'52	'53	'54	'55	'56	'57	'58	'59	'60	'61	'62	'63	'64	'65	'66	'67
60	60	60	60	60	60	60	60	60	60	60	60	60	60	60	59	56	32	10		

Number	Built	Renumbered	BR Dates	Scrap	Notes
5205	06/23 Sdn		-12/63	04/64	
5206	06/23 Sdn		-05/65	08/65	
5207	07/23 Sdn		-01/61	05/61	
5208	08/23 Sdn		-06/65	05/66	
5209	08/23 Sdn		-07/65	10/65	
5210	09/23 Sdn		-09/64	12/64	
5211	09/23 Sdn		-05/64	08/64	
5212	10/23 Sdn		-05/62	09/62	
5213	10/23 Sdn		-10/64	01/65	
5214	11/23 Sdn		-09/64	11/64	
5215	03/24 Sdn		-07/64	09/64	
5216	04/24 Sdn		-10/63	01/64	
5217	04/24 Sdn		-05/63	03/64	
5218	04/24 Sdn		-09/64	12/64	
5219	04/24 Sdn		-12/62	10/63	
5220	05/24 Sdn		-12/63	03/64	
5221	05/24 Sdn		-10/63	01/64	
5222	05/24 Sdn		-05/64	03/65	
5223	05/24 Sdn		-03/65	07/65	
5224 §	05/24 Sdn		-04/63		
5225	05/24 Sdn		-08/63	04/64	
5226	05/24 Sdn		-03/65	07/65	
5227 §	06/24 Sdn		-02/63		
5228	06/24 Sdn		-04/64	07/64	
5229	06/24 Sdn		-05/63	03/64	
5230	06/24 Sdn		-07/64	12/64	
5231	06/24 Sdn		-04/64	07/64	
5232	07/24 Sdn		-01/63	11/63	
5233	07/24 Sdn		-08/63	05/64	
5234	07/24 Sdn		-06/63	05/64	
5235	07/24 Sdn		-09/65	12/65	
5236	08/24 Sdn		-10/63	05/64	
5237	08/24 Sdn		-09/64	11/64	
5238	08/24 Sdn		-01/64	07/64	
5239 §	08/24 Sdn		-04/63		
5240	08/24 Sdn		-02/64	05/64	
5241	08/24 Sdn		-06/65	05/66	
5242	08/24 Sdn		-12/64	04/65	
5243	08/24 Sdn		-11/64	02/65	
5244	09/24 Sdn		-05/64	04/65	
5245	11/25 Sdn		-10/64	12/64	
5246	12/25 Sdn		-12/63	02/64	
5247	12/25 Sdn		-02/63	06/65	
5248	12/25 Sdn		-10/63	05/64	
5249	12/25 Sdn		-10/63	05/64	
5250	12/25 Sdn		-12/63	04/65	
5251	12/25 Sdn		-01/64	03/64	
5252	12/25 Sdn		-05/65	08/65	
5253	12/25 Sdn		-04/63	06/65	
5254	12/25 Sdn		-07/64	12/64	
5255	01/40 Sdn		-05/63	04/64	
5256	02/40 Sdn		-03/65	06/65	
5257	02/40 Sdn		-10/64	12/64	
5258	02/40 Sdn		-12/62	06/64	
5259	02/40 Sdn		-03/64	05/65	
5260	02/40 Sdn		-03/63	03/64	
5261	02/40 Sdn		-03/65	08/65	
5262	03/40 Sdn		-08/63	06/64	
5263	03/40 Sdn		-12/63	01/64	
5264	03/40 Sdn		-09/64	01/65	

4300 4303-4386, 5300-5399, 6300-6399, 7300-7341
2-6-0 GWR Churchward

Class continued from 4386

Number	Built	Renumbered	BR Dates	Scrap	Notes
5300	12/16 Sdn		-01/53	*02/53*	
5302	12/16 Sdn		-05/48	*48*	
5303	12/16 Sdn		-05/51	*51*	
5305	12/16 Sdn		-06/52	*07/52*	
5306	01/17 Sdn		-06/64	12/64	
5307	01/17 Sdn		-11/56	*56*	
5309	01/17 Sdn		-01/53	*05/53*	
5310	06/17 Sdn		-07/58	11/58	
5311	06/17 Sdn		-10/60	04/61	
5312	06/17 Sdn		-10/58	08/59	
5313	06/17 Sdn		-05/58	08/58	
5314	06/17 Sdn		-07/57	08/57	
5315	07/17 Sdn		-02/59	09/59	
5316	07/17 Sdn		-06/56	*56*	
5317	07/17 Sdn		-11/56	*56*	
5318	07/17 Sdn		-09/61	10/61	
5319	08/17 Sdn		-11/59	05/60	
5320	08/17 Sdn		-09/48	*10/48*	
5321	08/17 Sdn		-08/59	12/59	
5322 §	08/17 Sdn		-04/64		
5323	09/17 Sdn		-06/58	06/58	
5324	09/17 Sdn		-09/60	12/60	
5325	09/17 Sdn		-08/57	09/57	
5326	09/17 Sdn		-03/62	04/62	
5327	09/17 Sdn		-07/56	*56*	
5328	09/17 Sdn		-07/58	07/58	
5330	09/17 Sdn		-06/64	11/64	
5331	09/17 Sdn		-11/60	04/61	
5332	11/17 Sdn		-10/61	12/61	
5333	11/17 Sdn		-05/60	05/60	
5334	11/17 Sdn		-11/57	12/57	
5335	12/17 Sdn		-10/58	01/59	
5336	12/17 Sdn		-09/64	12/64	
5337	12/17 Sdn		-10/60	04/61	
5338	01/18 Sdn		-08/58	08/58	
5339	01/18 Sdn		-11/60	04/61	
5340	01/18 Sdn		-09/48	*10/48*	
5341	02/18 Sdn		-07/59	08/59	
5343	02/18 Sdn		-07/48	*09/48*	
5344	03/18 Sdn		-09/58	09/58	
5345	03/18 Sdn		-06/59	12/59	
5346	03/18 Sdn		-05/51	*51*	
5347	03/18 Sdn		-04/58	05/58	
5348	03/18 Sdn		-01/52	*52*	
5349	04/18 Sdn		-05/48	*09/48*	
5350	07/18 Sdn		-12/59	03/60	
5351	08/18 Sdn		-06/61	08/61	
5353	08/18 Sdn		-05/60	08/60	
5355	08/18 Sdn		-04/59	10/59	
5356	08/18 Sdn		-10/59	02/60	
5357	09/18 Sdn		-09/62	05/64	
5358	09/18 Sdn		-07/62	09/62	
5359	09/18 Sdn		-10/51	11/51	
5360	01/19 Sdn		-09/58	12/59	
5361	02/19 Sdn		-01/60	02/60	
5362	02/19 Sdn		-07/58	08/58	
5364	03/19 Sdn		-07/51	*51*	
5365	04/19 Sdn		-03/51	*51*	
5367	05/19 Sdn		-09/58	01/59	
5368	06/19 Sdn		-09/58	10/58	
5369	06/19 Sdn		-11/63	03/64	
5370	06/19 Sdn		-09/60	09/60	
5371	07/19 Sdn		-07/58	07/58	
5372	07/19 Sdn		-07/58	07/58	
5373	07/19 Sdn		-06/50	08/50	
5374	07/19 Sdn		-06/48	*48*	
5375	08/19 Sdn		-10/59	10/59	
5376	08/19 Sdn		-06/62	08/62	
5377	08/19 Sdn		-09/58	01/59	
5378	08/19 Sdn		-09/59	12/59	
5379	08/19 Sdn		-05/58	06/58	
5380	04/20 Sdn		-09/63	05/64	
5381	06/20 Sdn		-09/59	12/59	
5382	06/20 Sdn		-04/59	09/59	
5384	07/20 Sdn		-10/60	02/61	

Number	Built	Renumbered	BR Dates	Scrap	Notes
5385	07/20 Sdn		-07/62	06/63	
5386	08/20 Sdn		-10/58	09/59	
5388	08/20 Sdn		-03/59	09/59	
5390	10/20 Sdn		-08/58	09/59	
5391	10/20 Sdn		-03/57	04/57	
5392	10/20 Sdn		-08/58	12/59	
5393	10/20 Sdn	09/48 8393	-10/59	02/60	
5394	10/20 Sdn		-01/59	02/59	
5395	10/20 Sdn		-10/55	*11/55*	
5396	11/20 Sdn		-05/60	02/61	
5397	11/20 Sdn		-07/58	12/59	
5398	11/20 Sdn		-02/59	04/59	
5399	11/20 Sdn		-09/62	02/64	

Class continued with 6300

5400 5400-5424
0-6-0PT GWR Collett 5ft 2in

Power Classification: 1P
Introduced: 1931-1935
Designer: Collett
Company: GWR
Weight: 46t 12cwt
Driving Wheel: 5' 2"
Boiler Pressure: 165psi
Cylinders: Inside 16½" x 24"
Tractive Effort: 14780lbf
Valve Gear: Stephenson (slide valves)

Refer to the Historical Survey of GWR Pannier Tank Engines at the end of this section for more details of this class.

The '5400', '6400' and '7400' classes were variations of the '5700' class for use on light passenger trains.

In the early 1930s there was a need to replace some elderly pannier tanks which had been fitted for auto-train working. '2021' class No. 2062 was rebuilt experimentally in 1930 with 5' 2" wheels and large splashers. It was renumbered 5400 and was the prototype for this class. In 1932 the original 5400 was scrapped and a new 5400 was built to replace it. These engines were apparently fitted with tall chimneys and domes recovered from scrapped Dean engines.

The '5400' class were all fitted for auto-train working (push-pull trains). They carried the modified cabs as found on the later members of the '5700' class. They proved very successful and a further batch was built with smaller wheels in 1932, known as the '6400' class.

Year End Totals: '5400' class

'47	'48	'49	'50	'51	'52	'53	'54	'55	'56	'57	'58	'59	'60	'61	'62	'63	'64	'65	'66	'67
25	25	25	25	25	25	25	25	25	24	17	14	9	6	5	3					

Number	Built	Renumbered	BR Dates	Scrap	Notes
5400	06/32 Sdn		-04/59	06/59	
5401	11/31 Sdn		-02/57	02/57	
5402	11/31 Sdn		-09/58	02/59	
5403	11/31 Sdn		-08/57	09/57	
5404	12/31 Sdn		-12/57	01/58	
5405	12/31 Sdn		-10/57	12/57	
5406	12/31 Sdn		-09/57	10/57	
5407	01/32 Sdn		-06/60	08/61	
5408	01/32 Sdn		-12/56	02/57	
5409	01/32 Sdn		-06/59	10/59	
5410	01/32 Sdn		-10/63	10/64	
5411	05/32 Sdn		-06/58	06/58	
5412	05/32 Sdn		-04/62	07/62	
5413	05/32 Sdn		-10/57	11/57	
5414	05/32 Sdn		-10/59	11/59	
5415	05/32 Sdn		-07/57	07/57	
5416	06/32 Sdn		-08/63	10/63	
5417	06/32 Sdn		-01/61	09/61	
5418	06/32 Sdn		-06/60	10/60	
5419	06/32 Sdn		-02/58	04/58	
5420	11/35 Sdn		-10/63	04/64	
5421	11/35 Sdn		-09/62	09/64	
5422	11/35 Sdn		-06/60	03/65	
5423	11/35 Sdn		-06/59	11/60	
5424	12/35 Sdn		-04/59	11/60	

4575 4575-4599, 5500-5574
2-6-2T GWR Modified '4500'

Class continued from 4599

Number	Built	Renumbered	BR Dates	Scrap	Notes
5500	04/27 Sdn		-10/59	02/60	
5501	05/27 Sdn		-07/58	09/58	
5502	05/27 Sdn		-07/58	04/59	
5503	05/27 Sdn		-05/61	06/61	
5504	05/27 Sdn		-10/60	03/61	
5505	10/27 Sdn		-05/57	06/57	
5506	10/27 Sdn		-05/58	08/58	
5507	10/27 Sdn		-08/58	09/58	
5508	10/27 Sdn		-12/64	04/65	
5509	10/27 Sdn		-12/61	06/62	
5510	11/27 Sdn		-10/60	04/65	
5511	11/27 Sdn		-12/61	04/62	p
5512	11/27 Sdn		-02/57	02/57	
5513	11/27 Sdn		-06/57	06/57	
5514	11/27 Sdn		-11/60	06/61	
5515	11/27 Sdn		-11/61	03/62	
5516	11/27 Sdn		-08/61	10/61	
5517	11/27 Sdn		-12/58	01/59	
5518	12/27 Sdn		-05/64	07/64	
5519	12/27 Sdn		-06/60	04/61	
5520	12/27 Sdn		-09/62	08/63	
5521 §	12/27 Sdn		-04/62		
5522	12/27 Sdn		-03/59	04/59	
5523	12/27 Sdn		-06/60	01/61	
5524	12/27 Sdn		-06/60	10/60	p
5525	05/28 Sdn		-09/62	09/63	
5526 §	05/28 Sdn		-06/62		
5527	05/28 Sdn		-06/60	01/61	
5528	05/28 Sdn		-11/59	12/59	
5529	05/28 Sdn		-08/60	01/61	p
5530	06/28 Sdn		-01/60	05/60	
5531	06/28 Sdn		-12/64	04/65	
5532 §	06/28 Sdn		-07/62		
5533	06/28 Sdn		-12/59	01/60	
5534	06/28 Sdn		-09/60	01/61	p
5535	06/28 Sdn		-06/57	06/57	
5536	07/28 Sdn		-12/60	12/60	
5537	07/28 Sdn		-08/62	11/64	
5538 §	07/28 Sdn		-10/61		
5539 §	07/28 Sdn		-04/62		
5540	07/28 Sdn		-08/60	01/61	
5541 §	08/28 Sdn		-07/62		
5542 §	07/28 Sdn		-12/61		
5543	07/28 Sdn		-07/60	08/60	
5544	08/28 Sdn		-09/62	06/64	
5545	09/28 Sdn		-11/64	02/65	p
5546	10/28 Sdn		-09/60	09/61	
5547	10/28 Sdn		-02/62	03/65	
5548	10/28 Sdn		-05/63	11/64	
5549	10/28 Sdn		-01/62	06/62	
5550	10/28 Sdn		-09/62	10/63	
5551	10/28 Sdn		-01/60	01/61	
5552 §	11/28 Sdn		-10/60		
5553 §	11/28 Sdn		-11/61		
5554	11/28 Sdn		-08/63	01/64	
5555	11/28 Sdn		-07/63	11/64	p
5556	11/28 Sdn		-12/59	03/60	
5557	11/28 Sdn		-10/60	08/65	
5558	11/28 Sdn		-10/60	08/65	
5559	11/28 Sdn		-01/60	06/60	p
5560	12/28 Sdn		-04/62	04/62	p
5561	12/28 Sdn		-07/60	08/60	
5562	12/28 Sdn		-09/62	03/64	
5563	12/28 Sdn		-09/64	01/65	
5564	12/28 Sdn		-12/64	04/65	
5565	01/29 Sdn		-09/60	01/61	
5566	01/29 Sdn		-01/59	08/59	
5567	01/29 Sdn		-01/60	03/60	
5568	01/29 Sdn		-01/63	06/64	p
5569	01/29 Sdn		-12/64	04/65	
5570	02/29 Sdn		-12/63	02/64	
5571	02/29 Sdn		-10/64	01/65	
5572 §	02/29 Sdn		-04/62		p
5573	02/29 Sdn		-01/64	03/64	
5574	02/29 Sdn		-12/58	01/59	p

5600 5600-5699, 6600-6699
0-6-2T GWR Collett

Power Classification: 5MT
Introduced: 1924-1928
Designer: Collett
Company: GWR
Weight: 68t 12cwt
a 69t 7cwt
Driving Wheel: 4' 7½"
Boiler Pressure: 200psi superheated
Cylinders: Inside 18" x 26"
Tractive Effort: 25800lbf
Valve Gear: Stephenson (piston valves)

The 0-6-2T type had been used extensively in the Welsh Valleys for working coal trains, in particular by the Rhymney, Taff Vale and Barry Railways. This class was a GWR development of the Rhymney Railway 'M' class (see No. 33), built to work the same services. They replaced many of the older miscellaneous engines acquired from the previously independent lines in South Wales, although some were to be found on other parts of the GWR.

They were extremely versatile engines with impressive power and acceleration. The exceptional front overhang of the boiler and smokebox gave them an overbalanced appearance. They were fitted with superheated Belpaire boilers and had sloping tops to the side tanks.

a 6600-6699 were introduced in 1927 with detail alterations. The last fifty of these were built by Armstrong Whitworth.

Year End Totals: '5600' class

'47	'48	'49	'50	'51	'52	'53	'54	'55	'56	'57	'58	'59	'60	'61	'62	'63	'64	'65	'66	'67
200	200	200	200	200	200	200	200	200	200	200	200	200	200	200	171	109	57	2		

Number	Built	Renumbered	BR Dates	Scrap	Notes
5600	12/24 Sdn		-07/62	10/62	
5601	12/24 Sdn		-01/65	05/65	
5602	12/24 Sdn		-09/64	01/65	
5603	12/24 Sdn		-09/64	12/64	
5604	01/25 Sdn		-12/62	10/63	
5605	01/25 Sdn		-05/66	12/66	
5606	02/25 Sdn		-11/65	04/66	
5607	02/25 Sdn		-12/63	01/64	
5608	02/25 Sdn		-08/63	04/64	
5609	02/25 Sdn		-10/64	01/65	
5610	02/25 Sdn		-12/63	07/64	
5611	02/25 Sdn		-01/63	07/63	
5612	02/25 Sdn		-04/63	04/64	
5613	02/25 Sdn		-05/65	08/65	
5614	02/25 Sdn		-08/63	01/64	
5615	03/25 Sdn		-07/63	01/64	
5616	03/25 Sdn		-09/63	05/64	
5617	03/25 Sdn		-09/62	08/63	
5618	03/25 Sdn		-03/65	04/65	
5619 §	03/25 Sdn		-06/64		
5620	06/25 Sdn		-07/63	03/64	
5621	06/25 Sdn		-06/65	10/65	
5622	06/25 Sdn		-06/63	12/63	
5623	06/25 Sdn		-02/64	05/64	
5624	06/25 Sdn		-06/64	07/64	
5625	08/25 Sdn		-10/63	05/64	
5626	08/25 Sdn		-12/63	09/64	
5627	08/25 Sdn		-04/63	12/63	
5628	08/25 Sdn		-02/63	10/63	
5629	08/25 Sdn		-05/64	07/64	
5630	08/25 Sdn		-12/62	*63*	
5631	08/25 Sdn		-09/62	10/63	
5632	09/25 Sdn		-09/64	12/64	
5633	09/25 Sdn		-05/65	08/65	
5634	09/25 Sdn		-07/64	12/64	
5635	09/25 Sdn		-07/64	07/64	
5636	09/25 Sdn		-05/62	09/62	
5637 §	09/25 Sdn		-06/64		
5638	09/25 Sdn		-02/64	03/64	
5639	09/25 Sdn		-05/62	09/62	
5640	10/25 Sdn		-07/63	12/63	
5641	10/25 Sdn		-09/64	12/64	
5642	10/25 Sdn		-09/62	09/62	
5643 §	10/25 Sdn		-07/63		
5644	11/25 Sdn		-06/63	08/63	
5645	11/25 Sdn		-04/63	02/64	
5646	11/25 Sdn		-09/62	01/64	
5647	11/25 Sdn		-03/64	06/64	
5648	11/25 Sdn		-09/64	02/65	
5649	11/25 Sdn		-03/63	05/64	
5650	01/26 Sdn		-06/63	05/64	
5651	01/26 Sdn		-12/64	05/65	
5652	01/26 Sdn		-09/62	11/62	
5653	01/26 Sdn		-01/63	06/63	
5654	01/26 Sdn		-12/63	07/64	
5655	01/26 Sdn		-06/65	10/65	
5656	02/26 Sdn		-02/64	07/64	
5657	02/26 Sdn		-07/62	10/62	
5658	02/26 Sdn		-11/65	04/66	
5659	02/26 Sdn		-11/65	02/66	
5660	02/26 Sdn		-10/64	03/65	
5661	02/26 Sdn		-07/62	09/62	
5662	02/26 Sdn		-11/64	02/65	
5663	02/26 Sdn		-08/62	10/62	
5664	02/26 Sdn		-08/62	06/63	
5665	06/26 Sdn		-06/65	08/65	
5666	06/26 Sdn		-07/63	12/63	
5667	06/26 Sdn		-07/65	10/65	
5668 §	06/26 Sdn		-09/64		
5669	06/26 Sdn		-09/64	03/65	
5670	08/26 Sdn		-10/64	12/64	
5671	08/26 Sdn		-01/64	03/64	
5672	08/26 Sdn		-09/63	04/64	
5673	08/26 Sdn		-03/65	05/65	
5674	08/26 Sdn		-04/64	11/64	
5675	09/26 Sdn		-12/64	04/65	
5676	09/26 Sdn		-11/65	05/66	
5677	09/26 Sdn		-11/65	05/66	
5678	09/26 Sdn		-01/64	05/64	
5679	09/26 Sdn		-07/63	09/63	
5680	09/26 Sdn		-12/63	03/64	
5681	10/26 Sdn		-05/65	08/65	
5682	10/26 Sdn		-05/62	09/62	

Number	Built	Renumbered	BR Dates	Scrap	Notes
5683	10/26 Sdn		-03/64	05/64	
5684	10/26 Sdn		-07/65	10/65	
5685	01/27 Sdn		-02/64	04/64	
5686	01/27 Sdn		-03/65	05/65	
5687	01/27 Sdn		-12/63	02/65	
5688	01/27 Sdn		-06/65	10/65	
5689	01/27 Sdn		-05/65	08/65	
5690	01/27 Sdn		-08/63	03/64	
5691	01/27 Sdn		-06/65	10/65	
5692	01/27 Sdn		-07/65	10/65	
5693	01/27 Sdn		-01/63	04/64	
5694	01/27 Sdn		-11/64	02/65	
5695	01/27 Sdn		-12/62	08/63	
5696	01/27 Sdn		-05/65	08/65	
5697	01/27 Sdn		-04/63	12/63	
5698	01/27 Sdn		-09/62	12/62	
5699	01/27 Sdn		-11/64	03/65	

Class continued with 6600

5700 3600-3799, 4600-4699, 5700-5799, 7700-7799, 8700-8799, 9600-9682, 9711-9799
0-6-0PT GWR Collett 4ft 7½in

Class continued from 4699

Number	Built	Renumbered	BR Dates	Scrap	Notes
5700	01/29 NB		-03/56	*56*	
5701	01/29 NB		-01/58	03/58	
5702	01/29 NB		-05/60	07/60	
5703	01/29 NB		-02/59	09/59	
5704	01/29 NB		-05/60	08/60	
5705	01/29 NB		-08/59	02/60	
5706	02/29 NB		-09/61	11/61	
5707	02/29 NB		-03/59	11/60	
5708	02/29 NB		-04/59	05/59	
5709	02/29 NB		-03/60	12/60	
5710	02/29 NB		-08/57	05/58	
5711	02/29 NB		-01/58	02/58	
5712	02/29 NB		-10/57	02/58	
5713	02/29 NB		-01/60	05/60	
5714	03/29 NB		-01/58	03/58	
5715	03/29 NB		-08/58	10/58	
5716	03/29 NB		-03/58	08/58	
5717	03/29 NB		-05/60	07/60	
5718	03/29 NB		-07/58	09/58	
5719	03/29 NB		-11/58	03/59	
5720	03/29 NB		-01/62	05/62	
5721	03/29 NB		-08/59	11/59	
5722	03/29 NB		-09/58	01/59	
5723	03/29 NB		-11/57	03/60	
5724	03/29 NB		-08/57	09/57	
5725	01/29 NB		-08/58	10/58	
5726	01/29 NB		-10/59	12/59	
5727	02/29 NB		-05/60	08/60	
5728	02/29 NB		-05/62	10/62	
5729	02/29 NB		-10/57	12/57	
5730	02/29 NB		-03/58	04/58	
5731	02/29 NB		-05/60	10/60	
5732	02/29 NB		-01/58	02/58	
5733	02/29 NB		-08/58	03/60	
5734	03/29 NB		-05/59	09/59	
5735	03/29 NB		-11/57	01/58	
5736	03/29 NB		-01/58	02/58	
5737	03/29 NB		-10/59	02/60	
5738	03/29 NB		-09/59	02/60	
5739	03/29 NB		-08/58	12/58	
5740	03/29 NB		-06/59	08/59	
5741	03/29 NB		-06/57	05/58	
5742	03/29 NB		-09/58	09/58	
5743	03/29 NB		-01/59	08/59	
5744	04/29 NB		-04/62	09/62	
5745	04/29 NB		-11/59	04/60	
5746	04/29 NB		-09/62	12/63	
5747	04/29 NB		-09/59	02/60	
5748	04/29 NB		-09/60	12/60	
5749	04/29 NB		-07/63	10/63	
5750	04/29 Sdn		-05/60	07/60	
5751	04/29 Sdn		-04/58	05/58	
5752	04/29 Sdn		-03/57	06/61	
5753	04/29 Sdn		-09/59	02/60	
5754	04/29 Sdn		-06/60	10/60	
5755	04/29 Sdn		-07/60	10/60	
5756	05/29 Sdn		-09/61	03/62	
5757	05/29 Sdn		-12/60	01/70	
5758	05/29 Sdn		-05/62	11/62	
5759	05/29 Sdn		-09/60	01/61	
5760	05/29 Sdn		-10/57	11/57	
5761	06/29 Sdn		-05/62	09/62	
5762	06/29 Sdn		-03/56	58	
5763	06/29 Sdn		-05/60	08/60	
5764 §	06/29 Sdn		-05/60		
5765	06/29 Sdn		-03/59	05/59	
5766	07/29 Sdn		-05/62	10/62	
5767	07/29 Sdn		-09/58	11/58	
5768	07/29 Sdn		-03/61	06/61	
5769	07/29 Sdn		-05/60	08/60	
5770	09/29 Sdn		-12/61	05/62	
5771	09/29 Sdn		-03/61	07/61	
5772	09/29 Sdn		-06/58	11/58	
5773	09/29 Sdn		-09/62	12/63	
5774	09/29 Sdn		-10/62	01/64	
5775 §	09/29 Sdn		-08/63		
5776	09/29 Sdn		-05/60	11/60	
5777	09/29 Sdn		-06/58	04/59	
5778	09/29 Sdn		-07/62	02/63	
5779	09/29 Sdn		-05/62	09/62	
5780	12/29 Sdn		-10/61	12/61	
5781	12/29 Sdn		-09/58	04/59	
5782	12/29 Sdn		-11/58	12/58	
5783	12/29 Sdn		-03/62	05/62	
5784	12/29 Sdn		-06/59	10/59	
5785	01/30 Sdn		-12/58	02/59	
5786 §	01/30 Sdn		-04/58		
5787	01/30 Sdn		-10/63	09/64	
5788	01/30 Sdn		-10/59	03/60	
5789	01/30 Sdn		-05/62	09/62	
5790	09/30 Sdn		-03/59	07/59	
5791	09/30 Sdn		-04/61	07/61	
5792	10/30 Sdn		-10/56	*10/56*	
5793	10/30 Sdn		-04/62	09/62	
5794	10/30 Sdn		-12/59	08/65	
5795	10/30 Sdn		-04/60	07/60	
5796	11/30 Sdn		-03/59	05/59	
5797	11/30 Sdn		-09/58	04/59	
5798	11/30 Sdn		-09/62	01/64	
5799	11/30 Sdn		-07/59	09/59	

Class continued with 7700

5800 5800-5819
0-4-2T GWR Collett (non-motor fitted version of '1400')

Power Classification:	1P
Introduced:	1932-1933
Designer:	Collett
Company:	GWR
Weight:	41t 6cwt
Driving Wheel:	5' 2"
Boiler Pressure:	165psi
Cylinders:	Inside 16" x 24"
Tractive Effort:	13900lbf
Valve Gear:	Stephenson (slide valves)

The '5800' class was a variation of the '1400' class. The only difference was that the '5800' class locomotives were not fitted for working auto-trains (push-pull trains).

Year End Totals: '5800' class

'47	'48	'49	'50	'51	'52	'53	'54	'55	'56	'57	'58	'59	'60	'61	'62	'63	'64	'65	'66	'67
20	20	20	20	20	20	20	20	20	20	9	5	1	1							

Number	Built	Renumbered	BR Dates	Scrap	Notes
5800	01/33 Sdn		-07/58	10/58	
5801	01/33 Sdn		-09/58	04/59	
5802	01/33 Sdn		-12/58	03/59	
5803	01/33 Sdn		-07/57	07/57	
5804	01/33 Sdn		-06/59	08/59	
5805	01/33 Sdn		-03/58	04/58	
5806	01/33 Sdn		-06/57	06/57	
5807	01/33 Sdn		-06/57	06/57	
5808	01/33 Sdn		-02/57	02/57	
5809	02/33 Sdn		-08/59	10/59	
5810	08/33 Sdn		-01/59	08/59	
5811	08/33 Sdn		-05/57	05/57	
5812	08/33 Sdn		-06/57	06/57	
5813	08/33 Sdn		-11/57	11/57	
5814	08/33 Sdn		-06/57	06/57	
5815	08/33 Sdn		-04/61	06/64	
5816	08/33 Sdn		-07/57	08/57	
5817	08/33 Sdn		-06/57	07/57	
5818	08/33 Sdn		-09/59	03/60	
5819	08/33 Sdn		-06/57	06/57	

4900 4900-4999, 5900-5999, 6900-6958, (3900-3955)
4-6-0 GWR Collett 'Hall'

Class continued from 4999

Number	Built	Renumbered	BR Dates	Scrap	Notes
5900 §	03/31 Sdn		-12/63		
HINDERTON HALL					
5901	05/31 Sdn		-06/64	12/64	
HAZEL HALL					
5902	05/31 Sdn		-12/62	12/62	
HOWICK HALL					
5903	05/31 Sdn		-09/63	12/64	
KEELE HALL					
5904	05/31 Sdn		-11/63	07/64	
KELHAM HALL					
5905	05/31 Sdn		-07/63	06/64	
KNOWSLEY HALL					
5906	05/31 Sdn		-05/62	11/62	
LAWTON HALL					
5907	05/31 Sdn		-11/61	11/61	
MARBLE HALL					
5908	06/31 Sdn		-07/63	07/64	
MORETON HALL					
5909	06/31 Sdn		-07/62	11/62	
NEWTON HALL					
5910	06/31 Sdn		-09/62	12/63	
PARK HALL					
5911	06/31 Sdn		-09/62	11/63	
PRESTON HALL					
5912	06/31 Sdn		-12/62	09/63	
QUEEN'S HALL					
5913	06/31 Sdn		-05/62	10/62	
RUSHTON HALL					
5914	07/31 Sdn		-01/64	06/64	
RIPON HALL					
5915	07/31 Sdn		-01/60	04/60	
TRENTHAM HALL					
5916	07/31 Sdn		-07/62	10/62	
TRINITY HALL					
5917	07/31 Sdn		-09/62	01/64	
WESTMINSTER HALL					
5918	07/31 Sdn		-09/62	01/64	
WALTON HALL					
5919	07/31 Sdn		-08/63	07/64	
WORSLEY HALL					
5920	08/31 Sdn		-01/62	01/62	
WYCLIFFE HALL					
5921	05/33 Sdn		-01/62	02/62	
BINGLEY HALL					
5922	05/33 Sdn		-01/64	02/64	
CAXTON HALL					
5923	05/33 Sdn		-12/63	05/64	
COLSTON HALL					
5924	05/33 Sdn		-12/63	05/64	
DINTON HALL					
5925	05/33 Sdn		-10/62	11/62	
EASTCOTE HALL					
5926	06/33 Sdn		-09/62	12/63	
GROTRIAN HALL					
5927	06/33 Sdn		-10/64	01/65	
GUILD HALL					
5928	06/33 Sdn		-05/62	08/62	
HADDON HALL					
5929	06/33 Sdn		-10/63	02/64	
HANHAM HALL					
5930	06/33 Sdn		-09/62	01/64	
HANNINGTON HALL					
5931	06/33 Sdn		-09/62	08/63	
HATHERLEY HALL					
5932	06/33 Sdn		-10/65	01/66	
HAYDON HALL					
5933	06/33 Sdn		-08/65	11/65	
KINGSWAY HALL					
5934	06/33 Sdn		-05/64	08/64	
KNELLER HALL					
5935	07/33 Sdn		-05/62	07/64	
NORTON HALL					
5936	07/33 Sdn		-01/65	02/65	
OAKLEY HALL					
5937	07/33 Sdn		-11/63	07/64	
STANFORD HALL					
5938	07/33 Sdn		-05/63	09/63	
STANLEY HALL					
5939	07/33 Sdn		-10/64	01/65	
TANGLEY HALL					
5940	08/33 Sdn		-09/62	09/63	
WHITBOURNE HALL					
5941	02/35 Sdn		-07/62	11/62	
CAMPION HALL					
5942	02/35 Sdn		-12/63	06/64	
DOLDOWLOD HALL					
5943	03/35 Sdn		-06/63	06/64	
ELMDON HALL					
5944	03/35 Sdn		-04/63	06/64	
ICKENHAM HALL					
5945	03/35 Sdn		-04/63	08/63	
LECKHAMPTON HALL					
5946	03/35 Sdn		-07/62	11/62	
MARWELL HALL					
5947	03/35 Sdn		-07/62	09/62	
SAINT BENET'S HALL					
5948	03/35 Sdn		-08/63	02/64	
SIDDINGTON HALL					
5949	04/35 Sdn		-05/61	09/61	
TREMATON HALL					
5950	04/35 Sdn		-11/61	12/61	
WARDLEY HALL					
5951	12/35 Sdn		-04/64	08/64	
CLYFFE HALL					

Number	Built	Renumbered	BR Dates	Scrap	Notes
5952 §	12/35 Sdn		-06/64		
COGAN HALL					
5953	12/35 Sdn		-10/62	12/62	
DUNLEY HALL					
5954	12/35 Sdn		-10/63	07/64	
FAENDRE HALL					
5955	12/35 Sdn	10/48 3950	-04/65	08/65	
GARTH HALL					
5956	12/35 Sdn		-03/63	05/63	
HORSLEY HALL					
5957	12/35 Sdn		-07/64	12/64	
HUTTON HALL					
5958	01/36 Sdn		-03/64	07/64	
KNOLTON HALL					
5959	01/36 Sdn		-09/62	11/63	
MAWLEY HALL					
5960	01/36 Sdn		-09/62	12/63	
SAINT EDMUND HALL					
5961	07/36 Sdn		-08/65	10/65	
TOYNBEE HALL					
5962	07/36 Sdn		-11/64	03/65	
WANTAGE HALL					
5963	07/36 Sdn		-06/64	12/64	
WIMPOLE HALL					
5964	07/36 Sdn		-09/62	11/62	
WOLSELEY HALL					
5965	08/36 Sdn		-07/62	09/62	
WOOLLAS HALL					
5966	03/37 Sdn		-09/62	12/63	
ASHFORD HALL					
5967 §	03/37 Sdn		-06/64		
BICKMARSH HALL					
5968	03/37 Sdn		-09/62	04/64	
CORY HALL					
5969	04/37 Sdn		-08/62	10/62	
HONINGTON HALL					
5970	04/37 Sdn		-11/63	04/64	
HENGRAVE HALL					
5971	04/37 Sdn		-12/65	06/66	
MEREVALE HALL					
5972 §	04/37 Sdn		-12/63		
OLTON HALL					
5973	05/37 Sdn		-09/62	11/62	
ROLLESTON HALL					
5974	04/37 Sdn		-12/64	03/65	
WALLSWORTH HALL					
5975	05/37 Sdn		-07/64	03/65	
WINSLOW HALL					
5976	09/38 Sdn	11/48 3951	-07/64	12/64	
ASHWICKE HALL					
5977	09/38 Sdn		-08/63	07/64	
BECKFORD HALL					
5978	09/38 Sdn		-10/63	05/64	
BODINNICK HALL					
5979	09/38 Sdn		-11/64	04/65	
CRUCKTON HALL					
5980	09/38 Sdn		-09/62	07/64	
DINGLEY HALL					
5981	10/38 Sdn		-09/62	11/63	
FRENSHAM HALL					
5982	10/38 Sdn		-09/62	04/64	
HARRINGTON HALL					
5983	10/38 Sdn		-04/65	09/65	
HENLEY HALL					
5984	10/38 Sdn		-01/65	04/65	
LINDEN HALL					
5985	10/38 Sdn		-09/63	06/64	
MOSTYN HALL					
5986	11/39 Sdn	02/50 3954	-09/63	08/65	
ARBURY HALL					
5987	11/39 Sdn		-01/64	08/64	
BROCKET HALL					
5988	11/39 Sdn		-10/65	12/65	
BOSTOCK HALL					
5989	12/39 Sdn		-07/62	02/63	
CRANSLEY HALL					
5990	12/39 Sdn		-01/65	06/65	
DORFORD HALL					
5991	12/39 Sdn		-07/64	10/64	
GRESHAM HALL					
5992	12/39 Sdn		-08/65	10/65	
HORTON HALL					
5993	12/39 Sdn		-05/63	08/63	
KIRBY HALL					
5994	12/39 Sdn		-03/63	06/65	
ROYDON HALL					
5995	01/40 Sdn		-04/63	06/63	
WICK HALL					
5996	06/40 Sdn		-08/62	10/62	
MYTTON HALL					
5997	06/40 Sdn		-07/62	10/62	
SPARKFORD HALL					
5998	06/40 Sdn		-03/64	06/64	
TREVOR HALL					
5999	06/40 Sdn		-09/62	11/62	
WOLLATON HALL					

Class continued with 6900

6000 6000-6029
4-6-0 GWR Collett 'King'

Power Classification:	7P reclassified 8P in 1951
Introduced:	1927-1930
Designer:	Collett
Company:	GWR
Weight:	Loco 89t 0cwt
	Tender 46t 14cwt
Driving Wheel:	6' 6"
Boiler Pressure:	250psi superheated
Cylinders:	Four 16¼" x 28"
Tractive Effort:	40285lbf
Valve Gear:	Inside Walschaert with rocking shafts (piston valves)

The 'Kings' were the ultimate development of the GWR four-cylinder 4-6-0 engines. At the time of their construction the GWR wanted to snatch back the honour of owning the most powerful locomotives in the UK from the Southern Railway, who had just built their 'Lord Nelson' class. The 'King' class was built up to the maximum weight allowed on the main line. In addition the boiler pressure and the cylinder diameter were increased and the wheels were reduced in size from the original design, in order to get the required power increase. This made them the most powerful locomotives in the UK when they were built, and they were well able to handle the heaviest GWR expresses. Due to the size and position of their cylinders the 'Kings' had an unusual form of leading bogie, with the front bogie wheels having outside bearings and the rear bogie wheels having inside bearings.

As a result of their weight they were restricted to working only the London to Plymouth lines and the London to Wolverhampton (via Bicester) line. Because of their limited route availability only thirty were ever built, but they worked successfully on those routes.

The whole of the class was named after Kings. The names carried by 6000-6027 were in reverse order of ascendance to the throne from King Richard I (6027) to King George V (6000). 6028 was formerly KING HENRY II and 6029 was KING STEPHEN. Their names were changed in 1936 and 1937 when Edward VIII and then George VI came to the throne.

In 1927 6000 KING GEORGE V visited the USA for the centenary of the Baltimore & Ohio Railway. The locomotive was presented with an American locomotive bell which it carried over the front buffer beam when it returned to England.

In 1936 6007 was seriously damaged in a crash at Shrivenham. The locomotive was officially written off, but a replacement 6007 was built using the boiler, frame and tender of the original. In 1935 6014 was partially streamlined. The streamlining was removed in sections from 1937 onwards, but the wedge-shaped front to the cab was retained until 1953. From 1947 onwards all the 'Kings' were fitted with four-row high temperature superheaters and mechanical lubricators.

d From 1955 onwards they were all fitted with double chimneys.

Although all the 'Kings' were withdrawn during 1962, 6018 was steamed again in April 1963 to work a Stephenson Locomotive Society special train.

Year End Totals: '6000' class

'47	'48	'49	'50	'51	'52	'53	'54	'55	'56	'57	'58	'59	'60	'61	'62	'63	'64	'65	'66	'67
30	30	30	30	30	30	30	30	30	30	30	30	30	30	30						

Number	Built	Renumbered	BR Dates	Scrap	Notes
6000 §	06/27 Sdn		-12/62		
KING GEORGE V					12/56⇨d
6001	07/27 Sdn		-09/62	01/63	
KING EDWARD VII					02/56⇨d
6002	07/27 Sdn		-09/62	02/63	
KING WILLIAM IV					03/56⇨d
6003	07/27 Sdn		-06/62	08/62	
KING GEORGE IV					04/57⇨d
6004	07/27 Sdn		-06/62	10/62	
KING GEORGE III					11/56⇨d
6005	07/27 Sdn		-11/62	08/63	
KING GEORGE II					07/56⇨d
6006	02/28 Sdn		-02/62	03/62	
KING GEORGE I					06/56⇨d
6007	03/28 Sdn		-09/62	02/63	
KING WILLIAM III					09/56⇨d
6008	03/28 Sdn		-06/62	11/62	
KING JAMES II					07/57⇨d
6009	03/28 Sdn		-09/62	12/62	
KING CHARLES II					05/56⇨d
6010	04/28 Sdn		-06/62	09/65	
KING CHARLES I					03/56⇨d
6011	04/28 Sdn		-12/62	01/64	
KING JAMES I					03/56⇨d
6012	04/28 Sdn		-09/62	10/63	
KING EDWARD VI					02/58⇨d
6013	05/28 Sdn		-06/62	11/62	
KING HENRY VIII					06/56⇨d
6014	05/28 Sdn		-09/62	03/63	
KING HENRY VII					09/57⇨d
6015	06/28 Sdn		-09/62	04/63	
KING RICHARD III					09/55⇨d
6016	06/28 Sdn		-09/62	11/63	
KING EDWARD V					01/58⇨d
6017	06/28 Sdn		-07/62	05/63	
KING EDWARD IV					12/55⇨d
6018	06/28 Sdn		-12/62	09/63	
KING HENRY VI					03/58⇨d
6019	07/28 Sdn		-09/62	12/62	
KING HENRY V					04/57⇨d
6020	05/30 Sdn		-07/62	01/63	
KING HENRY IV					08/56⇨d
6021	06/30 Sdn		-09/62	12/62	
KING RICHARD II					03/57⇨d
6022	06/30 Sdn		-09/62	06/63	
KING EDWARD III					05/56⇨d
6023 §	06/30 Sdn		-06/62		
KING EDWARD II					06/57⇨d
6024 §	06/30 Sdn		-06/62		
KING EDWARD I					03/57⇨d
6025	07/30 Sdn		-12/62	05/64	
KING HENRY III					03/57⇨d
6026	07/30 Sdn		-09/62	11/63	
KING JOHN					03/58⇨d
6027	07/30 Sdn		-09/62	07/63	
KING RICHARD I					08/56⇨d
6028	07/30 Sdn		-11/62	08/64	
KING GEORGE VI					01/57⇨d
6029	08/30 Sdn		-07/62	11/62	
KING EDWARD VIII					12/57⇨d

6100 6100-6169
2-6-2T GWR Collett

Power Classification:	4MT reclassified 5MT in 1953
Introduced:	1931-1935
Designer:	Collett
Company:	GWR
Weight:	78t 9cwt
Driving Wheel:	5' 8"
Boiler Pressure:	225psi superheated
Cylinders:	Outside 18" x 30"
Tractive Effort:	27340lbf
Valve Gear:	Stephenson (piston valves)

The '6100' class was a variation of the '5101' class built with increased boiler pressure to work on the London suburban area services.

Year End Totals: '6100' class

'47	'48	'49	'50	'51	'52	'53	'54	'55	'56	'57	'58	'59	'60	'61	'62	'63	'64	'65	'66	'67
70	70	70	70	70	70	70	70	70	70	70	69	68	65	65	53	47	31			

Number	Built	Renumbered	BR Dates	Scrap	Notes
6100	04/31 Sdn		-09/58	02/59	
6101	05/31 Sdn		-03/62	07/63	
6102	05/31 Sdn		-08/59	12/59	
6103	05/31 Sdn		-12/64	04/65	
6104	05/31 Sdn		-06/60	10/60	
6105	05/31 Sdn		-03/60	05/60	
6106 §	05/31 Sdn		-12/65		
6107	05/31 Sdn		-11/64	03/65	
6108	05/31 Sdn		-08/65	11/65	
6109	06/31 Sdn		-08/62	11/63	
6110	08/31 Sdn		-06/65	05/66	
6111	08/31 Sdn		-12/65	07/66	
6112	08/31 Sdn		-09/65	12/65	
6113	08/31 Sdn		-11/65	02/66	
6114	09/31 Sdn		-10/64	01/65	
6115	09/31 Sdn		-11/64	04/65	
6116	09/31 Sdn		-06/65	05/66	
6117	09/31 Sdn		-09/65	12/65	
6118	09/31 Sdn		-11/63	12/63	
6119	09/31 Sdn		-03/63	06/63	
6120	09/31 Sdn		-04/62	10/62	
6121	10/31 Sdn		-07/60	11/60	
6122	10/31 Sdn		-09/64	02/65	
6123	10/31 Sdn		-04/62	07/62	
6124	10/31 Sdn		-06/64	10/64	
6125	10/31 Sdn		-01/65	03/65	
6126	10/31 Sdn		-12/65	06/66	
6127	10/31 Sdn		-03/62	05/62	
6128	10/31 Sdn		-03/65	08/65	
6129	11/31 Sdn		-09/65	04/66	

GWR Collett '6000' 'King' class 4-6-0 No 6018 *King Henry VI.*

GWR Collett '6100' class 2-6-2T No 6137.

GWR Collett '5600' class 0-6-2T No 6671 in lined green livery.

GWR Collett '4073' 'Castle' class 4-6-0 No 7007 *Great Western* at Old Oak Common in August 1950.

Number	Built	Renumbered	BR Dates	Scrap	Notes
6130	09/32 Sdn		-07/64	12/64	
6131	10/32 Sdn		-09/64	02/65	
6132	10/32 Sdn		-10/65	03/66	
6133	10/32 Sdn		-12/63	11/64	
6134	10/32 Sdn		-12/65	06/66	
6135	10/32 Sdn		-12/65	03/66	
6136	10/32 Sdn		-12/65	05/66	
6137	10/32 Sdn		-11/64	03/65	
6138	11/32 Sdn		-09/63	11/63	
6139	11/32 Sdn		-11/64	03/65	
6140	11/32 Sdn		-07/64	12/64	
6141	11/32 Sdn		-12/65	07/66	
6142	11/32 Sdn		-09/64	12/64	
6143	11/32 Sdn		-11/65	03/66	
6144	11/32 Sdn		-06/64	08/65	
6145	12/32 Sdn		-12/65	02/66	
6146	12/32 Sdn		-09/62	08/64	
6147	01/33 Sdn		-12/65	07/66	
6148	01/33 Sdn		-09/64	04/65	
6149	01/33 Sdn		-06/64	12/64	
6150	02/33 Sdn		-03/65	04/65	
6151	02/33 Sdn		-11/63	02/64	
6152	02/33 Sdn		-01/62	04/62	
6153	02/33 Sdn		-01/62	04/62	
6154	03/33 Sdn		-06/65	10/65	
6155	03/33 Sdn		-10/65	01/66	
6156	03/33 Sdn		-12/65	02/66	
6157	03/33 Sdn		-05/62	09/62	
6158	03/33 Sdn		-06/64	12/64	
6159	04/33 Sdn		-06/65	01/66	
6160	10/35 Sdn		-12/65	04/66	
6161	10/35 Sdn		-10/65	03/66	
6162	10/35 Sdn		-03/62	04/62	
6163	10/35 Sdn		-10/65	02/66	
6164	10/35 Sdn		-11/63	12/63	
6165	10/35 Sdn		-12/65	04/66	
6166	10/35 Sdn		-01/62	05/62	
6167	10/35 Sdn		-10/65	12/65	
6168	11/35 Sdn		-03/62	08/62	
6169	11/35 Sdn		-11/65	02/66	

4300 4303-4386, 5300-5399, 6300-6399, 7300-7341
2-6-0 GWR Churchward

Class continued from 5399

Number	Built	Renumbered	BR Dates	Scrap	Notes
6300	11/20 Sdn		-06/60	08/60	
6301	12/20 Sdn		-10/62	06/64	
6302	12/20 Sdn		-03/62	04/63	
6303	12/20 Sdn		-04/59	05/59	
6304	12/20 Sdn		-01/64	06/64	
6305	12/20 Sdn		-09/59	10/59	
6306	12/20 Sdn		-11/61	12/61	
6307	01/21 Sdn		-07/60	07/60	
6308	01/21 Sdn		-08/59	12/59	
6309	01/21 Sdn		-09/64	12/64	
6310	01/21 Sdn		-07/62	02/63	
6311	01/21 Sdn		-01/60	02/60	
6312	01/21 Sdn		-09/62	09/63	
6313	01/21 Sdn		-11/61	12/61	
6314	01/21 Sdn		-07/63	10/63	
6316	01/21 Sdn		-07/62	02/63	
6317	01/21 Sdn		-11/63	03/64	
6318	02/21 Sdn		-01/59	08/59	
6319	02/21 Sdn		-08/63	05/64	
6320	02/21 Sdn		-11/63	07/64	o 08/49⇨c
6321	02/21 Sdn		-03/56	*56*	
6322	02/21 Sdn		-01/59	08/59	
6323	03/21 Sdn		-07/60	08/60	
6324	03/21 Sdn		-04/62	07/62	
6325	03/21 Sdn		-11/59	07/64	
6326	03/21 Sdn		-09/64	01/65	
6327	03/21 Sdn		-09/63	06/64	
6328	03/21 Sdn		-01/59	08/59	
6329	04/21 Sdn		-10/61	12/61	
6330	04/21 Sdn		-09/62	08/64	
6331	04/21 Sdn		-04/59	10/59	
6332	04/21 Sdn		-09/60	10/60	
6333	05/21 Sdn		-10/60	05/61	
6334	05/21 Sdn		-04/59	10/59	
6335	05/21 Sdn		-07/63	03/64	
6336	05/21 Sdn		-04/62	08/62	
6337	06/21 Sdn		-07/64	12/64	
6338	06/21 Sdn		-06/64	12/64	
6339	06/21 Sdn		-07/62	02/64	
6340	06/21 Sdn		-07/62	03/63	
6341	07/21 Sdn		-11/61	12/61	
6342	03/23 Sdn		-09/62	04/63	
6343	03/23 Sdn		-09/60	02/61	
6344	03/23 Sdn		-11/63	06/64	
6345	04/23 Sdn		-09/64	12/64	
6346	04/23 Sdn		-09/64	01/65	
6347	04/23 Sdn		-12/63	08/64	
6348	04/23 Sdn		-02/62	06/63	
6349	05/23 Sdn		-07/64	02/65	
6350	05/23 Sdn		-01/64	02/64	
6351	05/23 Sdn		-11/60	02/61	
6352	09/23 Sdn		-11/60	02/61	
6353	09/23 Sdn		-05/63	06/64	
6354	10/23 Sdn		-02/59	09/59	
6355	10/23 Sdn		-03/59	08/59	
6356	11/23 Sdn		-01/63	06/64	
6357	11/23 Sdn		-07/64	12/64	
6358	11/23 Sdn		-10/59	03/60	
6359	11/23 Sdn		-09/59	12/59	
6360	11/23 Sdn		-11/60	04/61	
6361	12/23 Sdn		-05/64	07/64	
6362	04/25 Sdn		-09/62	07/63	
6363	04/25 Sdn		-09/64	01/65	
6364	05/25 Sdn		-11/64	02/65	
6365	10/25 Sdn		-10/63	05/64	
6366	10/25 Sdn		-09/62	01/63	
6367	10/25 Sdn		-11/64	03/65	
6368	10/25 Sdn		-12/63	04/65	
6369	10/25 Sdn		-01/63	06/63	
6370	04/21 RS		-01/63	06/64	
6371	05/21 RS		-09/60	02/61	
6372	05/21 RS		-12/63	06/64	
6373	05/21 RS		-12/63	04/64	
6374	06/21 RS		-08/62	01/64	
6375	06/21 RS		-09/63	03/64	
6376	06/21 RS		-05/62	09/62	
6377	06/21 RS		-10/60	11/60	
6378	07/21 RS		-06/64	12/64	
6379	07/21 RS		-08/63	12/64	
6380	07/21 RS		-12/63	04/65	
6381	07/21 RS		-11/63	06/64	
6382	08/21 RS		-11/60	01/61	
6383	08/21 RS		-05/56	*56*	
6384	08/21 RS		-06/63	08/63	
6385	08/21 RS		-11/63	06/64	
6386	08/21 RS		-09/62	01/63	
6387	09/21 RS		-06/62	11/62	
6388	10/21 RS		-09/62	12/63	
6389	10/21 RS		-09/60	02/61	
6390	10/21 RS		-05/62	02/63	
6391	11/21 RS		-09/62	04/64	
6392	11/21 RS		-10/61	11/61	
6393	11/21 RS		-01/60	02/61	
6394	11/21 RS		-06/64	12/64	
6395	12/21 RS		-11/64	02/65	
6396	12/21 RS		-03/58	03/58	
6397	12/21 RS		-09/59	11/59	
6398	12/21 RS		-10/60	02/61	
6399	12/21 RS		-11/59	02/60	

Class continued with 7300

6400 6400-6439
0-6-0PT GWR Collett 4ft 7½in

Power Classification: 2P
Introduced: 1932-1937
Designer: Collett
Company: GWR
Weight: 45t 12cwt
Driving Wheel: 4' 7½"
Boiler Pressure: 180psi
Cylinders: Inside 16½" x 24"
Tractive Effort: 18010lbf
Valve Gear: Stephenson (slide valves)

Refer to the Historical Survey of GWR Pannier Tank Engines at the end of this section for more details of this class.

The '6400' class was a variation of the '5400' class with smaller wheels. They worked mostly in the hilly South Wales Valleys, with a few also based at Plymouth. They were all fitted for auto-train working (push-pull trains), and carried the modified cabs as found on the later members of the '5700' class.

Year End Totals: '6400' class

'47	'48	'49	'50	'51	'52	'53	'54	'55	'56	'57	'58	'59	'60	'61	'62	'63	'64	'65	'66	'67
40	40	40	40	40	40	40	40	40	40	40	37	28	25	20	13	7				

Number	Built	Renumbered	BR Dates	Scrap	Notes
6400	02/32 Sdn		-04/64	10/64	
6401	02/32 Sdn		-06/60	10/60	
6402	02/32 Sdn		-06/59	02/60	
6403	02/32 Sdn		-12/63	02/64	
6404	02/32 Sdn		-06/59	02/60	
6405	02/32 Sdn		-06/59	02/60	
6406	03/32 Sdn		-06/60	06/61	
6407	03/32 Sdn		-08/58	09/58	
6408	03/32 Sdn		-02/62	07/62	
6409	03/32 Sdn		-03/59	09/59	
6410	11/34 Sdn		-11/62	64	
6411	11/34 Sdn		-03/61	06/61	
6412 §	11/34 Sdn		-11/64		
6413	11/34 Sdn		-11/61	12/61	
6414	11/34 Sdn		-06/59	02/60	
6415	11/34 Sdn		-11/61	03/62	
6416	11/34 Sdn		-09/63	11/63	
6417	12/34 Sdn		-06/59	02/60	
6418	12/34 Sdn		-11/62	12/63	
6419	12/34 Sdn		-12/64	04/65	
6420	08/35 Sdn		-11/59	12/59	
6421	08/35 Sdn		-01/63	10/63	
6422	08/35 Sdn		-09/62	07/63	
6423	09/35 Sdn		-08/58	10/58	
6424	09/35 Sdn		-09/64	11/64	
6425	11/35 Sdn		-01/61	06/61	
6426	11/35 Sdn		-03/61	06/61	
6427	11/35 Sdn		-08/58	09/58	
6428	11/35 Sdn		-03/59	08/59	
6429	11/35 Sdn		-03/62	07/62	
6430 §	03/37 Sdn		-10/64		
6431	03/37 Sdn		-01/63	11/63	
6432	03/37 Sdn		-03/59	11/59	
6433	03/37 Sdn		-01/63	06/63	
6434	03/37 Sdn		-09/64	11/64	
6435 §	04/37 Sdn		-10/64		
6436	04/37 Sdn		-09/62	11/62	
6437	04/37 Sdn		-07/63	09/63	
6438	04/37 Sdn		-11/62	08/64	
6439	04/37 Sdn		-05/60	09/60	

5600 5600-5699, 6600-6699
0-6-2T GWR Collett

Class continued from 5699

Number	Built	Renumbered	BR Dates	Scrap	Notes
6600	08/27 Sdn		-08/62	12/63	a
6601	08/27 Sdn		-12/62	12/62	a
6602	08/27 Sdn		-10/64	02/65	a
6603	09/27 Sdn		-03/64	06/64	a
6604	09/27 Sdn		-10/65	01/66	a
6605	09/27 Sdn		-01/64	04/64	a
6606	09/27 Sdn		-01/65	06/65	a
6607	09/27 Sdn		-03/63	02/64	a
6608	09/27 Sdn		-06/64	12/64	a
6609	09/27 Sdn		-09/63	11/63	a
6610	09/27 Sdn		-01/63	01/64	a
6611	09/27 Sdn		-11/65	05/66	a
6612	10/27 Sdn		-05/65	08/65	a
6613	10/27 Sdn		-10/65	02/66	a
6614	10/27 Sdn		-06/65	10/65	a
6615	12/27 Sdn		-05/63	08/63	a
6616	12/27 Sdn		-09/62	11/63	a
6617	12/27 Sdn		-09/62	02/64	a
6618	12/27 Sdn		-11/63	01/64	a
6619 §	01/28 Sdn		-03/63		a
6620	01/28 Sdn		-12/63	03/64	a
6621	01/28 Sdn		-12/64	03/65	a
6622	01/28 Sdn		-12/64	04/65	a
6623	01/28 Sdn		-06/63	01/64	a
6624	01/28 Sdn		-06/64	10/64	a
6625	01/28 Sdn		-11/65	04/66	a
6626	01/28 Sdn		-11/65	04/66	a
6627	02/28 Sdn		-11/63	01/64	a
6628	02/28 Sdn		-05/65	08/65	a
6629	02/28 Sdn		-10/62	08/63	a
6630	08/28 Sdn		-09/62	06/63	a
6631	08/28 Sdn		-09/63	01/64	a
6632	08/28 Sdn		-09/63	11/63	a
6633	08/28 Sdn		-06/65	08/65	a
6634 §	08/28 Sdn		-04/64		a
6635	08/28 Sdn		-06/64	12/64	a
6636	08/28 Sdn		-06/63	05/64	a
6637	08/28 Sdn		-06/64	10/64	a
6638	09/28 Sdn		-06/64	12/64	a
6639	09/28 Sdn		-10/63	05/64	a
6640	09/28 Sdn		-09/62	11/63	a
6641	09/28 Sdn		-09/62	11/63	a
6642	09/28 Sdn		-01/63	08/63	a
6643	09/28 Sdn		-08/65	10/65	a
6644	09/28 Sdn		-07/65	01/66	a
6645	09/28 Sdn		-08/62	07/63	a
6646	09/28 Sdn		-05/64	08/64	a
6647	09/28 Sdn		-09/62	07/63	a
6648	09/28 Sdn		-05/65	08/65	a
6649	09/28 Sdn		-02/65	03/65	a
6650	08/28 AW		-05/65	08/65	a
6651	08/28 AW		-10/65	02/66	a
6652	08/28 AW		-12/63	06/64	a
6653	08/28 AW		-12/63	06/64	a
6654	08/28 AW		-06/65	10/65	a
6655	08/28 AW		-03/65	05/65	a
6656	08/28 AW		-09/65	03/66	a
6657	08/28 AW		-06/65	10/65	a
6658	08/28 AW		-04/65	09/65	a
6659	09/28 AW		-10/63	12/63	a
6660	09/28 AW		-06/64	12/64	a

Number	Built	Renumbered	BR Dates	Scrap	Notes
6661	09/28 AW		-06/65	10/65	a
6662	09/28 AW		-04/63	12/63	a
6663	09/28 AW		-06/63	11/63	a
6664	09/28 AW		-12/63	03/64	a
6665	09/28 AW		-10/65	12/65	a
6666	09/28 AW		-07/63	10/63	a
6667	09/28 AW		-11/65	05/66	a
6668	09/28 AW		-12/65	02/66	a
6669	09/28 AW		-12/62	01/64	a
6670	09/28 AW		-10/63	06/64	a
6671	09/28 AW		-10/65	05/66	a
6672	09/28 AW		-07/65	10/65	a
6673	09/28 AW		-03/63	11/63	a
6674	09/28 AW		-07/63	02/64	a
6675	09/28 AW		-06/63	05/64	a
6676	09/28 AW		-04/63	03/64	a
6677	09/28 AW		-01/63	06/63	a
6678	09/28 AW		-11/64	03/65	a
6679	09/28 AW		-09/65	03/66	a
6680	10/28 AW		-04/64	05/64	a
6681	10/28 AW		-10/65	12/65	a
6682	10/28 AW		-02/64	05/64	a
6683	10/28 AW		-10/65	02/66	a
6684	10/28 AW		-11/64	02/65	a
6685	10/28 AW		-09/64	01/65	a
6686 §	10/28 AW		-04/64		a
6687	10/28 AW		-05/62	09/62	a
6688	10/28 AW		-04/64	09/64	a
6689	10/28 AW		-06/65	10/65	a
6690	10/28 AW		-06/64	12/64	a
6691	10/28 AW		-06/65	01/66	a
6692	10/28 AW		-09/65	03/66	a
6693	10/28 AW		-01/63	06/63	a
6694	10/28 AW		-10/63	02/64	a
6695 §	10/28 AW		-07/64		a
6696	10/28 AW		-12/63	04/64	a
6697 §	10/28 AW		-05/66		a
6698	10/28 AW		-03/63	02/64	a
6699	10/28 AW		-12/63	07/64	a

6700 6700-6779
0-6-0PT GWR '5700' class without vacuum brakes

Power Classification: 4F
Introduced: 1930-1950
Designer: Collett
Company: GWR
Weight: 47t 10cwt
m 49t 0cwt
Driving Wheel: 4' 7½"
Boiler Pressure: 200psi
Cylinders: Inside 17½" x 24"
Tractive Effort: 22515lbf
Valve Gear: Stephenson (slide valves)

Refer to the Historical Survey of GWR Pannier Tank Engines at the end of this section for more details of this class.

The '6700' class was a variation of the '5700' class fitted with steam brakes only (no vacuum brakes) and no Automatic Train Control (ATC) fittings. They were designed for shunting duties only.

m As with the '5700' class the later locomotives were of a slightly modified design. They had many detail alterations including increased weight and a modified cab with angular windows on the front and back instead of the original round windows.

Year End Totals: '6700' class

'47	'48	'49	'50	'51	'52	'53	'54	'55	'56	'57	'58	'59	'60	'61	'62	'63	'64	'65	'66	'67
60	66	70	80	80	80	80	80	80	80	75	56	39	29	23	13	3				

Number	Built	Renumbered	BR Dates	Scrap	Notes
6700	02/30 WB		-06/61	01/62	
6701	02/30 WB		-06/59	10/59	
6702	03/30 WB		-07/60	10/60	
6703	03/30 WB		-01/58	02/58	
6704	03/30 WB		-03/58	04/58	
6705	04/30 WB		-01/58	02/58	
6706	04/30 WB		-01/58	02/58	
6707	04/30 WB		-06/59	11/59	
6708	05/30 WB		-12/57	04/59	
6709	05/30 WB		-01/58	03/58	
6710	06/30 WB		-08/57	11/57	
6711	06/30 WB		-06/59	11/60	
6712	06/30 WB		-07/60	10/60	
6713	06/30 WB		-09/57	11/57	
6714	06/30 WB		-12/63	06/64	
6715	07/30 WB		-05/58	06/58	
6716	07/30 WB		-02/59	01/60	
6717	07/30 WB		-02/59	02/59	
6718	08/30 WB		-05/58	07/58	
6719	08/30 WB		-07/60	10/60	
6720	09/30 WB		-07/61	10/61	
6721	09/30 WB		-02/59	08/59	
6722	09/30 WB		-01/58	03/58	
6723	10/30 WB		-02/59	11/59	
6724	10/30 WB		-11/63	01/64	
6725	03/30 YE		-10/59	01/60	
6726	03/30 YE		-07/58	08/58	
6727	04/30 YE		-04/58	09/59	
6728	04/30 YE		-06/60	12/60	
6729	04/30 YE		-06/59	08/59	
6730	05/30 YE		-09/57	02/60	
6731	05/30 YE		-05/58	06/58	
6732	05/30 YE		-07/58	10/58	
6733	05/30 YE		-05/58	06/58	
6734	07/30 YE		-02/59	10/61	
6735	07/30 YE		-06/59	12/59	
6736	07/30 YE		-02/59	11/60	
6737	08/30 YE		-07/57	08/59	
6738	08/30 YE		-10/62	10/63	
6739	09/30 YE		-06/62	09/62	
6740	10/30 YE		-01/58	05/58	
6741	10/30 YE		-12/63	02/64	
6742	11/30 YE		-12/63	02/64	
6743	11/30 YE		-04/59	11/60	
6744	11/30 YE		-07/58	12/58	
6745	12/30 YE		-06/59	08/59	
6746	12/30 YE		-08/58	11/58	
6747	12/30 YE		-07/58	08/58	
6748	12/30 YE		-01/58	04/58	
6749	01/31 YE		-10/62	10/63	
6750	06/47 Sdn		-01/60	11/60	m
6751	06/47 Sdn		-08/60	12/60	m
6752	07/47 Sdn		-01/61	04/61	m
6753	08/47 Sdn		-01/61	06/61	m
6754	08/47 Sdn		-12/62	12/62	m
6755	08/47 Sdn		-06/62	09/62	m
6756	08/47 Sdn		-07/60	12/60	m
6757	09/47 Sdn		-12/62	04/63	m
6758	09/47 Sdn		-06/62	07/62	m
6759	09/47 Sdn		-04/60	07/60	m
6760	11/48 Sdn		11/48-12/63	02/64	m
6761	11/48 Sdn		11/48-01/61	04/61	m
6762	11/48 Sdn		11/48-03/63	12/63	m
6763	11/48 Sdn		11/48-12/63	07/64	m
6764	11/48 Sdn		11/48-12/63	02/64	m
6765	12/48 Sdn		12/48-05/64	08/64	m
6766	01/49 Sdn		01/49-08/60	12/60	m
6767	01/49 Sdn		01/49-12/62	10/63	m
6768	01/49 Sdn		01/49-01/64	06/64	m
6769	01/49 Sdn		01/49-12/63	05/64	m
6770	10/50 Sdn		10/50-10/62	10/62	m
6771	10/50 Sdn		10/50-03/58	06/64	m
6772	11/50 Sdn		11/50-12/63	06/64	m
6773	11/50 Sdn		11/50-10/59	03/60	m
6774	11/50 Sdn		11/50-12/59	04/60	m
6775	11/50 Sdn		11/50-08/60	03/61	m
6776	11/50 Sdn		11/50-01/61	04/61	m
6777	12/50 Sdn		12/50-05/64	07/64	m
6778	12/50 Sdn		12/50-05/62	11/62	m
6779	12/50 Sdn		12/50-06/59	12/60	m

6800 6800-6879
4-6-0 GWR Collett 'Grange'

Power Classification: 5MT
Introduced: 1936-1939
Designer: Collett
Company: GWR
Weight: Loco 74t 0cwt
Tender 40t 0cwt
Driving Wheel: 5' 8"
Boiler Pressure: 225psi superheated
Cylinders: Outside 18½" x 30"
Tractive Effort: 28875lbf
Valve Gear: Stephenson (piston valves)

The 'Grange' class was version of the 'Hall' class with smaller wheels. They were intended to replace the '4300' class and they incorporated certain parts (such as the wheels and motion) of the withdrawn '4300' class 2-6-0s they were replacing. The 'Manor' class ('7800') was built at the same time, being a lighter version for lines with restricted route availability. It was intended to replace all the 4300 class with 'Granges' and 'Manors' (6800-6899 and 7800-7899 being planned), but the Second World War stopped the conversion programme after only eighty 'Granges' were completed.

Because the 'Granges' and the 'Manors' were lower in height than the 'Hall' class they had a raised section of running plate over the cylinders.

Year End Totals: '6800' class

'47	'48	'49	'50	'51	'52	'53	'54	'55	'56	'57	'58	'59	'60	'61	'62	'63	'64	'65	'66	'67
80	80	80	80	80	80	80	80	80	80	80	80	80	79	77	76	71	45			

Number	Built	Renumbered	BR Dates	Scrap	Notes
6800	08/36 Sdn		-06/64	11/64	
	ARLINGTON GRANGE				
6801	08/36 Sdn		-10/60	11/60	
	AYLBURTON GRANGE				
6802	09/36 Sdn		-08/61	10/61	
	BAMPTON GRANGE				
6803	09/36 Sdn		-09/65	01/66	
	BUCKLEBURY GRANGE				
6804	09/36 Sdn		-08/64	11/64	
	BROCKINGTON GRANGE				
6805	09/36 Sdn		-03/61	05/61	
	BROUGHTON GRANGE				
6806	09/36 Sdn		-10/64	11/64	
	BLACKWELL GRANGE				
6807	09/36 Sdn		-12/63	04/64	
	BIRCHWOOD GRANGE				
6808	09/36 Sdn		-08/64	11/64	
	BEENHAM GRANGE				
6809	09/36 Sdn		-07/63	08/63	
	BURGHCLERE GRANGE				
6810	11/36 Sdn		-10/64	02/65	
	BLAKEMERE GRANGE				
6811	11/36 Sdn		-07/64	09/64	
	CRANBOURNE GRANGE				
6812	11/36 Sdn		-02/65	05/65	
	CHESFORD GRANGE				
6813	12/36 Sdn		-09/65	12/65	
	EASTBURY GRANGE				
6814	12/36 Sdn		-12/63	01/64	
	ENBORNE GRANGE				
6815	12/36 Sdn		-11/65	01/66	
	FRILFORD GRANGE				
6816	12/36 Sdn		-07/65	10/65	
	FRANKTON GRANGE				
6817	12/36 Sdn		-04/65	07/65	
	GWENDDWR GRANGE				
6818	12/36 Sdn		-04/64	09/64	
	HARDWICK GRANGE				
6819	12/36 Sdn		-11/65	02/66	
	HIGHNAM GRANGE				
6820	01/37 Sdn		-07/65	10/65	
	KINGSTONE GRANGE				
6821	01/37 Sdn		-11/64	02/65	
	LEATON GRANGE				
6822	01/37 Sdn		-09/64	11/64	
	MANTON GRANGE				
6823	01/37 Sdn		-06/65	11/65	
	OAKLEY GRANGE				
6824	01/37 Sdn		-04/64	11/64	
	ASHLEY GRANGE				
6825	02/37 Sdn		-06/64	12/64	
	LLANVAIR GRANGE				
6826	02/37 Sdn		-05/65	07/65	
	NANNERTH GRANGE				
6827	02/37 Sdn		-09/65	05/66	
	LLANFRECHFA GRANGE				
6828	02/37 Sdn		-07/63	09/63	
	TRELLECH GRANGE				
6829	03/37 Sdn		-11/65	05/66	
	BURMINGTON GRANGE				
6830	08/37 Sdn		-10/65	01/66	
	BUCKENHILL GRANGE				
6831	08/37 Sdn		-10/65	04/66	
	BEARLEY GRANGE				
6832	08/37 Sdn		-01/64	05/64	
	BROCKTON GRANGE				
6833	08/37 Sdn		-10/65	04/66	
	CALCOT GRANGE				
6834	08/37 Sdn		-06/64	09/64	
	DUMMER GRANGE				
6835	09/37 Sdn		-05/63	10/63	
	EASTHAM GRANGE				
6836	09/37 Sdn		-08/65	10/65	
	ESTEVARNEY GRANGE				
6837	09/37 Sdn		-07/65	10/65	
	FORTHAMPTON GRANGE				
6838	09/37 Sdn		-11/65	02/66	
	GOODMOOR GRANGE				
6839	09/37 Sdn		-05/64	10/64	
	HEWELL GRANGE				
6840	09/37 Sdn		-02/65	04/65	
	HAZELEY GRANGE				
6841	09/37 Sdn		-06/65	10/65	
	MARLAS GRANGE				
6842	09/37 Sdn		-11/64	02/65	
	NUNHOLD GRANGE				
6843	10/37 Sdn		-02/64	06/64	
	POULTON GRANGE				
6844	10/37 Sdn		-04/64	09/64	
	PENHYDD GRANGE				
6845	10/37 Sdn		-09/64	12/64	
	PAVILAND GRANGE				
6846	10/37 Sdn		-09/64	12/64	
	RUCKLEY GRANGE				
6847	10/37 Sdn		-12/65	04/66	
	TIDMARSH GRANGE				

Number	Built	Name	BR Dates	Scrap
6848	10/37 Sdn	**TODDINGTON GRANGE**	-12/65	04/66
6849	10/37 Sdn	**WALTON GRANGE**	-12/65	05/66
6850	10/37 Sdn	**CLEEVE GRANGE**	-12/64	03/65
6851	10/37 Sdn	**HURST GRANGE**	-08/65	01/66
6852	11/37 Sdn	**HEADBOURNE GRANGE**	-01/64	03/64
6853	11/37 Sdn	**MOREHAMPTON GRANGE**	-10/65	03/66
6854	11/37 Sdn	**ROUNDHILL GRANGE**	-09/65	02/66
6855	11/37 Sdn	**SAIGHTON GRANGE**	-10/65	03/66
6856	11/37 Sdn	**STOWE GRANGE**	-11/65	01/67
6857	11/37 Sdn	**TUDOR GRANGE**	-10/65	02/66
6858	12/37 Sdn	**WOOLSTON GRANGE**	-10/65	02/66
6859	12/37 Sdn	**YIEWSLEY GRANGE**	-11/65	02/66
6860	02/39 Sdn	**ABERPORTH GRANGE**	-02/65	03/65
6861	02/39 Sdn	**CRYNANT GRANGE**	-10/65	03/66
6862	02/39 Sdn	**DERWENT GRANGE**	-06/65	11/65
6863	02/39 Sdn	**DOLHYWEL GRANGE**	-11/64	02/65
6864	02/39 Sdn	**DYMOCK GRANGE**	-10/65	01/66
6865	03/39 Sdn	**HOPTON GRANGE**	-05/62	06/62
6866	03/39 Sdn	**MORFA GRANGE**	-05/65	08/65
6867	03/39 Sdn	**PETERSTON GRANGE**	-08/64	11/64
6868	03/39 Sdn	**PENRHOS GRANGE**	-10/65	04/66
6869	03/39 Sdn	**RESOLVEN GRANGE**	-07/65	10/65
6870	03/39 Sdn	**BODICOTE GRANGE**	-09/65	01/66
6871	03/39 Sdn	**BOURTON GRANGE**	-10/65	03/66
6872	03/39 Sdn	**CRAWLEY GRANGE**	-12/65	05/66
6873	04/39 Sdn	**CARADOC GRANGE**	-06/64	02/65
6874	04/39 Sdn	**HAUGHTON GRANGE**	-09/65	12/65
6875	04/39 Sdn	**HINDFORD GRANGE**	-03/64	07/64
6876	04/39 Sdn	**KINGSLAND GRANGE**	-11/65	02/66
6877	04/39 Sdn	**LLANFAIR GRANGE**	-03/65	04/65
6878	05/39 Sdn	**LONGFORD GRANGE**	-11/64	02/65
6879	05/39 Sdn	**OVERTON GRANGE**	-10/65	03/66

4900 4900-4999, 5900-5999, 6900-6958, (3900-3955)
4-6-0 GWR Collett 'Hall'

Class continued from 5999

Number	Built	Renumbered	Name	BR Dates	Scrap	Notes
6900	06/40 Sdn		**ABNEY HALL**	-10/64	02/65	
6901	07/40 Sdn		**ARLEY HALL**	-06/64	10/64	
6902	07/40 Sdn		**BUTLERS HALL**	-05/61	05/61	
6903	07/40 Sdn		**BELMONT HALL**	-09/65	01/66	
6904	07/40 Sdn		**CHARFIELD HALL**	-02/65	05/65	
6905	07/40 Sdn		**CLAUGHTON HALL**	-06/64	10/64	
6906	11/40 Sdn		**CHICHELEY HALL**	-04/65	06/65	
6907	11/40 Sdn		**DAVENHAM HALL**	-02/65	05/65	
6908	11/40 Sdn		**DOWNHAM HALL**	-07/65	10/65	
6909	11/40 Sdn		**FREWIN HALL**	-06/64	12/64	
6910	12/40 Sdn		**GOSSINGTON HALL**	-10/65	02/66	
6911	01/41 Sdn		**HOLKER HALL**	-04/65	02/66	
6912	01/41 Sdn		**HELMSTER HALL**	-02/64	07/64	
6913	02/41 Sdn		**LEVENS HALL**	-06/64	12/64	
6914	02/41 Sdn		**LANGTON HALL**	-04/64	07/64	
6915	02/41 Sdn		**MURSLEY HALL**	-02/65	06/65	
6916	06/41 Sdn		**MISTERTON HALL**	-08/65	02/66	
6917	06/41 Sdn		**OLDLANDS HALL**	-09/65	01/66	
6918	06/41 Sdn		**SANDON HALL**	-09/65	12/65	
6919	06/41 Sdn		**TYLNEY HALL**	-08/63	10/63	
6920	07/41 Sdn		**BARNINGHAM HALL**	-12/63	02/64	
6921	07/41 Sdn		**BORWICK HALL**	-10/65	02/66	
6922	07/41 Sdn		**BURTON HALL**	-04/65	02/66	
6923	07/41 Sdn		**CROXTETH HALL**	-12/65	05/66	
6924	08/41 Sdn		**GRANTLEY HALL**	-10/65	02/66	
6925	08/41 Sdn		**HACKNESS HALL**	-11/64	02/65	
6926	11/41 Sdn		**HOLKHAM HALL**	-06/65	09/65	
6927	11/41 Sdn		**LILFORD HALL**	-10/65	02/66	
6928	11/41 Sdn		**UNDERLEY HALL**	-06/65	10/65	
6929	11/41 Sdn		**WHORLTON HALL**	-10/63	05/64	
6930	11/41 Sdn		**ALDERSEY HALL**	-10/65	02/66	
6931	11/41 Sdn		**ALDBOROUGH HALL**	-10/65	02/66	
6932	12/41 Sdn		**BURWARTON HALL**	-12/65	06/66	
6933	12/41 Sdn		**BIRTLES HALL**	-11/64	12/64	
6934	12/41 Sdn		**BEACHAMWELL HALL**	-10/65	01/66	
6935	12/41 Sdn		**BROWSHOLME HALL**	-02/65	04/65	
6936	12/41 Sdn		**BRECCLES HALL**	-11/64	02/65	
6937	12/41 Sdn		**CONYNGHAM HALL**	-12/65	04/66	
6938	07/42 Sdn		**CORNDEAN HALL**	-03/65	11/65	
6939	07/42 Sdn		**CALVELEY HALL**	-10/63	03/64	
6940	08/42 Sdn		**DIDLINGTON HALL**	-05/64	07/64	
6941	08/42 Sdn		**FILLONGLEY HALL**	-04/64	09/64	
6942	08/42 Sdn		**ESHTON HALL**	-12/64	04/65	
6943	08/42 Sdn		**FARNLEY HALL**	-12/63	06/64	
6944	09/42 Sdn		**FLEDBOROUGH HALL**	-12/65	02/66	
6945	09/42 Sdn		**GLASFRYN HALL**	-09/64	11/64	
6946	12/42 Sdn		**HEATHERDEN HALL**	-06/64	10/64	
6947	12/42 Sdn		**HELMINGHAM HALL**	-10/65	04/66	
6948	12/42 Sdn		**HOLBROOKE HALL**	-12/63	06/64	
6949	12/42 Sdn	04/49 3955	**HABERFIELD HALL**	-05/61	06/61	
6950	12/42 Sdn		**KINGSTHORPE HALL**	-06/64	12/64	
6951	02/43 Sdn		**IMPNEY HALL**	-12/65	04/66	
6952	02/43 Sdn		**KIMBERLEY HALL**	-12/65	04/66	
6953	02/43 Sdn	09/48 3953	**LEIGHTON HALL**	-12/65	05/66	
6954	03/43 Sdn		**LOTHERTON HALL**	-05/64	11/64	
6955	03/43 Sdn		**LYDCOTT HALL**	-02/65	02/65	
6956	03/43 Sdn		**MOTTRAM HALL**	-12/65	06/66	
6957	03/43 Sdn	03/50 3952	**NORCLIFFE HALL**	-10/65	02/66	
6958	04/43 Sdn		**OXBURGH HALL**	-06/65	10/65	

6959 6959-6999, 7900-7929
4-6-0 GWR Hawksworth 'Modified Hall'

Power Classification:	5MT
Introduced:	1944-1950
Designer:	Hawksworth
Company:	GWR
Weight:	Loco 75t 16cwt Tender 46t 14cwt
Driving Wheel:	6' 0"
Boiler Pressure:	225psi superheated
Cylinders:	Outside 18½" x 30"
Tractive Effort:	27275lbf
Valve Gear:	Stephenson (piston valves)

This was Hawksworth's development of the '4900' 'Hall' class. The frames were entirely built up of welded plate as were the bogie frames. They had a new pattern of individually cast cylinders with longer outside steam pipes and a redesigned boiler with a three row superheater giving an increased superheating surface.

w 6959-6970 were built during the Second World War. They were built without cabside windows to assist with blackout regulations and they ran without names for two or three years. The cabside windows were fitted in 1945-1948.

Year End Totals: '6959' class

'47	'48	'49	'50	'51	'52	'53	'54	'55	'56	'57	'58	'59	'60	'61	'62	'63	'64	'65	'66	'67
22	37	48	71	71	71	71	71	71	71	71	71	71	71	71	71	65	43			

Number	Built	Renumbered	Name	BR Dates	Scrap	Notes
6959	03/44 Sdn		**PEATLING HALL**	-12/65	06/66	w
6960 §	03/44 Sdn		**RAVENINGHAM HALL**	-06/64		w
6961	03/44 Sdn		**STEDHAM HALL**	-09/65	12/65	w
6962	04/44 Sdn		**SOUGHTON HALL**	-01/63	05/63	w
6963	04/44 Sdn		**THROWLEY HALL**	-07/65	10/65	w
6964	05/44 Sdn		**THORNBRIDGE HALL**	-09/65	01/66	w
6965	07/44 Sdn		**THIRLESTAINE HALL**	-10/65	03/66	w
6966	05/44 Sdn		**WITCHINGHAM HALL**	-09/64	02/65	w
6967	08/44 Sdn		**WILLESLEY HALL**	-12/65	05/66	w
6968	09/44 Sdn		**WOODCOCK HALL**	-09/63	08/64	w
6969	09/44 Sdn		**WRAYSBURY HALL**	-02/65	05/65	w
6970	09/44 Sdn		**WHADDON HALL**	-06/64	11/64	w
6971	10/47 Sdn		**ATHELHAMPTON HALL**	-10/64	01/65	
6972	10/47 Sdn		**BENINGBROUGH HALL**	-03/64	07/64	
6973	10/47 Sdn		**BRICKLEHAMPTON HALL**	-08/65	11/65	
6974	10/47 Sdn		**BRYNGWYN HALL**	-05/65	08/65	
6975	10/47 Sdn		**CAPESTHORNE HALL**	-12/63	09/64	
6976	10/47 Sdn		**GRAYTHWAITE HALL**	-10/65	02/66	
6977	11/47 Sdn		**GRUNDISBURGH HALL**	-12/63	06/64	
6978	11/47 Sdn		**HAROLDSTONE HALL**	-07/65	10/65	
6979	11/47 Sdn		**HELPERLY HALL**	-02/65	07/65	
6980	11/47 Sdn		**LLANRUMNEY HALL**	-10/65	12/65	
6981	02/48 Sdn		**MARBURY HALL**	02/48-03/64	07/64	
6982	01/48 Sdn		**MELMERBY HALL**	01/48-08/64	11/64	
6983	02/48 Sdn		**OTTERINGTON HALL**	02/48-08/65	12/65	
6984 §	02/48 Sdn		**OWSDEN HALL**	02/48-12/65		
6985	02/48 Sdn		**PARWICK HALL**	02/48-09/64	01/65	
6986	03/48 Sdn		**RYDAL HALL**	03/48-04/65	08/65	
6987	03/48 Sdn		**SHERVINGTON HALL**	03/48-09/64	11/64	
6988	03/48 Sdn		**SWITHLAND HALL**	03/48-09/64	12/64	
6989 §	03/48 Sdn		**WIGHTWICK HALL**	03/48-06/64		

Number	Built	Renumbered	BR Dates	Scrap	Notes
6990 §	04/48 Sdn		04/48-12/65		
	WITHERSLACK HALL				
6991	11/48 Sdn		11/48-12/65	05/66	
	ACTON BURNELL HALL				
6992	11/48 Sdn		11/48-06/64	12/64	
	ARBORFIELD HALL				
6993	12/48 Sdn		12/48-12/65	06/66	
	ARTHOG HALL				
6994	12/48 Sdn		12/48-11/64	02/65	
	BAGGRAVE HALL				
6995	12/48 Sdn		12/48-03/65	07/65	
	BENTHALL HALL				
6996	01/49 Sdn		01/49-10/64	02/65	
	BLACKWELL HALL				
6997	01/49 Sdn		01/49-11/64	02/65	
	BRYN-IVOR HALL				
6998 §	01/49 Sdn		01/49-12/65		
	BURTON AGNES HALL				
6999	02/49 Sdn		02/49-12/65	05/66	
	CAPEL DEWI HALL				

Class continued with 7900

4073 100A1, 111, 4000, 4016, 4032, 4037, 4073-4099, 5000-5099, 7000-7037

4-6-0 GWR Collett 'Castle'

Class continued from 5099

Number	Built	Renumbered	BR Dates	Scrap	Notes
7000	05/46 Sdn		-12/63	06/64	m3
	VISCOUNT PORTAL				
7001	05/46 Sdn		-09/63	04/64	m3
	DENBIGH CASTLE 01/48➲SIR JAMES MILNE				09/60⇔d
7002	06/46 Sdn		-03/64	06/64	m3
	DEVIZES CASTLE				07/61⇔d
7003	06/46 Sdn		-08/64	12/64	m3
	ELMLEY CASTLE				06/60⇔d
7004	06/46 Sdn		-01/64	02/64	m4
	EASTNOR CASTLE				02/58⇔d
7005	06/46 Sdn		-09/64	01/65	m3
	LAMPHEY CASTLE 08/57➲SIR EDWARD ELGAR				
7006	06/46 Sdn		-12/63	08/64	m3
	LYDFORD CASTLE				06/60⇔d
7007	07/46 Sdn		-02/63	01/64	m3
	OGMORE CASTLE 01/48➲GREAT WESTERN				06/61⇔d
7008	05/48 Sdn		05/48-09/64	02/65	m3
	SWANSEA CASTLE				05/59⇔d
7009	05/48 Sdn		05/48-03/63	08/65	m3
	ATHELNEY CASTLE				
7010	06/48 Sdn		06/48-03/64	07/64	m3
	AVONDALE CASTLE				11/60⇔d
7011	06/48 Sdn		06/48-02/65	05/65	m3
	BANBURY CASTLE				
7012	06/48 Sdn		06/48-11/64	02/65	m3
	BARRY CASTLE				
7013	07/48 Sdn		07/48-09/64	01/65	m4
	BRISTOL CASTLE				02/52➲4082
7013	04/24 Sdn	02/52 4082	-02/65	06/65	4
	BRISTOL CASTLE				05/58⇔d
7014	07/48 Sdn		07/48-02/65	05/65	m3
	CAERHAYS CASTLE				03/59⇔d
7015	07/48 Sdn		07/48-04/63	08/65	m3
	CARN BREA CASTLE				05/59⇔d
7016	08/48 Sdn		08/48-11/62	07/64	m3
	CHESTER CASTLE				
7017	09/48 Sdn		09/48-02/63	01/64	m3
	G. J. CHURCHWARD				
7018	05/49 Sdn		05/49-09/63	06/64	m4
	DRYSLLWYN CASTLE				05/56⇔d
7019	05/49 Sdn		05/49-02/65	05/65	m4
	FOWEY CASTLE				08/58⇔d
7020	05/49 Sdn		05/49-09/64	01/65	m3
	GLOUCESTER CASTLE				02/61⇔d
7021	06/49 Sdn		06/49-09/63	05/64	m3
	HAVERFORDWEST CASTLE				11/61⇔d
7022	06/49 Sdn		06/49-06/65	09/65	m4
	HEREFORD CASTLE				12/57⇔d
7023	06/49 Sdn		06/49-02/65	05/65	m3
	PENRICE CASTLE				05/58⇔d
7024	06/49 Sdn		06/49-02/65	06/65	m4
	POWIS CASTLE				03/59⇔d
7025	08/49 Sdn		08/49-09/64	11/64	m3
	SUDELEY CASTLE				
7026	08/49 Sdn		08/49-10/64	04/65	m3
	TENBY CASTLE				
7027 §	08/49 Sdn		08/49-12/63		m3
	THORNBURY CASTLE				
7028	05/50 Sdn		05/50-12/63	08/64	m3
	CADBURY CASTLE				10/61⇔d
7029 §	05/50 Sdn		05/50-12/65		m4
	CLUN CASTLE				10/59⇔d
7030	06/50 Sdn		06/50-02/63	12/63	m4
	CRANBROOK CASTLE				07/59⇔d
7031	06/50 Sdn		06/50-07/63	06/64	m3
	CROMWELL'S CASTLE				
7032	06/50 Sdn		06/50-09/64	02/65	m3
	DENBIGH CASTLE				09/60⇔d
7033	07/50 Sdn		07/50-01/63	06/64	m3
	HARTLEBURY CASTLE				06/59⇔d
7034	08/50 Sdn		08/50-06/65	09/65	m4
	INCE CASTLE				12/59⇔d
7035	08/50 Sdn		08/50-06/64	08/64	m3
	OGMORE CASTLE				01/60⇔d
7036	08/50 Sdn		08/50-09/63	06/64	m4
	TAUNTON CASTLE				07/59⇔d
7037	08/50 Sdn		08/50-03/63	08/65	m3
	SWINDON				

7200 7200-7253

2-8-2T GWR rebuilt from '5205' & '4200' classes

Power Classification:	8F
Introduced:	1910-1930 rebuilt as 2-8-2Ts 1934-1937
Designer:	Collett
Company:	GWR
Weight:	92t 12cwt
Driving Wheel:	4' 7½"
Boiler Pressure:	200psi superheated
Cylinders:	Outside 19" x 30"
Tractive Effort:	33170lbf
Valve Gear:	Stephenson (piston valves)

These engines were rebuilt from '4200' and '5205' class locomotives with an extra pair of trailing wheels and a larger bunker so that they could have a wider field of activity. In 1934 5275-5294 were rebuilt to 2-8-2Ts and renumbered 7200-7219. These were brand new locomotives which had been placed in store, and apart from trials had never run in service. In 1935-1936 5255-5274 were rebuilt and became 7220-7239. Finally some of the older '4200' class were rebuilt in 1937, becoming 7240-7253. Their old numbers were 4239, 4220, 4202, 4204, 4216, 4205, 4234, 4244, 4249, 4209, 4219, 4240, 4210 and 4245 respectively.

All the '7200' class were fitted with outside steam pipes and 19" diameter cylinders, but had the same variations in framing as the '4200' and '5205' classes (that is some with straight frames over the cylinders and others with raised framing over the cylinders).

Year End Totals: '7200' class

'47	'48	'49	'50	'51	'52	'53	'54	'55	'56	'57	'58	'59	'60	'61	'62	'63	'64	'65	'66	'67
54	54	54	54	54	54	54	54	54	54	54	54	54	54	54	54	52	39	10		

Number	Built	Renumbered	BR Dates	Scrap	Notes
7200 §	07/30 Sdn		-07/63		
7201	08/30 Sdn		-04/65	08/65	
7202 §	08/30 Sdn		-06/64		
7203	08/30 Sdn		-12/63	04/64	
7204	08/30 Sdn		-02/64	06/64	
7205	08/30 Sdn		-06/65	11/65	
7206	08/30 Sdn		-07/64	12/64	
7207	08/30 Sdn		-11/64	01/65	
7208	09/30 Sdn		-04/64	03/65	
7209	09/30 Sdn		-07/64	12/64	
7210	09/30 Sdn		-04/65	09/65	
7211	09/30 Sdn		-05/64	08/64	
7212	09/30 Sdn		-02/64	07/64	
7213	09/30 Sdn		-09/64	10/64	
7214	10/30 Sdn		-12/63	03/64	
7215	10/30 Sdn		-06/63	08/63	
7216	10/30 Sdn		-10/63	01/64	
7217	10/30 Sdn		-07/64	12/64	
7218	10/30 Sdn		-08/64	11/64	
7219	10/30 Sdn		-01/64	03/64	
7220	12/25 Sdn		-09/64	01/65	
7221	12/25 Sdn		-11/64	04/65	
7222	01/26 Sdn		-01/65	06/65	
7223	01/26 Sdn		-11/64	01/65	
7224	01/26 Sdn		-12/62	01/64	
7225	03/26 Sdn		-05/64	03/65	
7226	03/26 Sdn		-11/64	03/65	
7227	03/26 Sdn		-06/63	05/64	
7228	03/26 Sdn		-07/63	03/64	
7229 §	03/26 Sdn		-07/64		
7230	03/26 Sdn		-07/64	12/64	
7231	03/26 Sdn		-10/64	02/65	
7232	03/26 Sdn		-05/65	08/65	
7233	03/26 Sdn		-09/64	01/65	
7234	03/26 Sdn		-10/63	05/64	
7235	04/26 Sdn		-04/64	11/64	
7236	04/26 Sdn		-11/63	06/64	
7237	04/26 Sdn		-06/63	08/63	
7238	04/26 Sdn		-04/64	01/65	
7239	04/26 Sdn		-10/63	06/64	
7240	10/14 Sdn		-09/64	01/65	
7241	12/12 Sdn		-12/62	12/62	
7242	01/12 Sdn		-06/64	12/64	
7243	02/12 Sdn		-07/64	12/64	
7244	11/12 Sdn		-02/65	03/65	
7245	02/12 Sdn		-09/64	11/64	
7246	09/14 Sdn		-09/63	05/64	
7247	02/16 Sdn		-03/63	06/65	
7248	04/16 Sdn		-06/65	05/66	
7249	02/12 Sdn		-06/65	05/66	
7250	12/12 Sdn		-09/64	11/64	
7251	10/14 Sdn		-01/64	04/64	
7252	03/12 Sdn		-06/65	05/66	
7253	03/16 Sdn		-04/65	08/65	

4300 4303-4386, 5300-5399, 6300-6399, 7300-7341

2-6-0 GWR Churchward

Class continued from 6399

Number	Built	Renumbered	BR Dates	Scrap	Notes
7300	12/21 RS		-09/62	02/63	w
7301	12/21 RS		-09/62	11/62	w
7302	12/21 RS		-08/62	07/64	w
7303	01/22 RS		-09/64	01/65	w
7304	01/22 RS		-11/63	06/64	w
7305	11/21 Sdn		-09/62	08/64	
7306	11/21 Sdn		-09/64	11/64	
7307	11/21 Sdn		-05/64	07/64	
7308	11/21 Sdn		-06/64	02/65	
7309	11/21 Sdn		-09/62	01/64	
7310	12/21 Sdn		-06/64	12/64	
7311	12/21 Sdn		-09/62	10/63	
7312	12/21 Sdn		-12/63	04/64	
7313	12/21 Sdn		-07/62	10/62	
7314	12/21 Sdn		-02/63	06/63	
7315	12/21 Sdn		-12/63	06/64	
7316	12/21 Sdn		-09/62	06/64	
7317	12/21 Sdn		-12/63	06/64	
7318	12/21 Sdn		-11/64	02/65	
7319	01/22 Sdn		-10/64	04/65	
7320	04/25 Sdn		-11/64	06/65	
7321	04/25 Sdn		-09/62	10/63	
7322	02/32 Sdn	04/57 9300	-11/61	12/61	s
7323	02/32 Sdn	09/56 9301	-08/62	10/62	s
7324	02/32 Sdn	02/57 9302	-10/62	11/63	s
7325 §	02/32 Sdn	06/58 9303	-04/64		s
7326	02/32 Sdn	06/58 9304	-09/63	06/64	s
7327	02/32 Sdn	01/59 9305	-11/64	12/64	s
7328	03/32 Sdn	05/58 9306	-04/62	07/62	s
7329	03/32 Sdn	12/56 9307	-01/63	01/64	s
7330	03/32 Sdn	06/57 9308	-09/62	02/63	s
7331	03/32 Sdn	05/59 9309	-09/62	02/63	s
7332	03/32 Sdn	09/58 9310	-04/64	07/64	s
7333	03/32 Sdn	06/57 9311	-10/63	06/64	s
7334	03/32 Sdn	01/59 9312	-04/62	06/63	s
7335	03/32 Sdn	08/58 9313	-09/63	05/64	s
7336	03/32 Sdn	06/58 9314	-09/62	01/64	s
7337	03/32 Sdn	05/59 9315	-09/64	12/64	s
7338	04/32 Sdn	03/58 9316	-08/62	09/62	s
7339	04/32 Sdn	09/56 9317	-06/64	02/65	s
7340	04/32 Sdn	12/57 9318	-06/64	11/64	s
7341	04/32 Sdn	06/57 9319	-09/62	09/62	s

7400 7400-7449

0-6-0PT GWR Non motor fitted version of '6400'

Power Classification:	2F
Introduced:	1936-1950
Designer:	Collett
Company:	GWR
Weight:	45t 9cwt
Driving Wheel:	4' 7½"
Boiler Pressure:	180psi
Cylinders:	Inside 16½" x 24"
Tractive Effort:	18010lbf
Valve Gear:	Stephenson (slide valves)

Refer to the Historical Survey of GWR Pannier Tank Engines at the end of this section for more details of this class.

The '7400' class was a variation of the '6400' class. The only difference was that they were not fitted for auto-train working (push-pull trains). They carried the modified cabs as found on the later members of the '5700' class.

Year End Totals: '7400' class

'47	'48	'49	'50	'51	'52	'53	'54	'55	'56	'57	'58	'59	'60	'61	'62	'63	'64	'65	'66	'67
30	40	40	50	50	50	50	50	50	50	50	50	43	41	35	27	18	2			

Number	Built	Renumbered	BR Dates	Scrap	Notes
7400	07/36 Sdn		-06/60	10/60	
7401	08/36 Sdn		-08/59	02/60	
7402	08/36 Sdn		-07/62	01/63	
7403	08/36 Sdn		-01/64	03/64	
7404	08/36 Sdn		-06/64	12/64	
7405	08/36 Sdn		-12/63	03/64	
7406	08/36 Sdn		-03/62	06/62	
7407	08/36 Sdn		-12/63	03/64	
7408	08/36 Sdn		-08/62	01/65	
7409	08/36 Sdn		-08/61	11/61	
7410	12/36 Sdn		-01/61	06/61	
7411	12/36 Sdn		-05/59	11/60	
7412	12/36 Sdn		-07/63	08/63	
7413	12/36 Sdn		-09/64	11/64	
7414	12/36 Sdn		-09/64	11/64	
7415	12/36 Sdn		-02/59	02/63	
7416	12/36 Sdn		-01/59	10/59	
7417	01/37 Sdn		-09/61	03/62	
7418	01/37 Sdn		-08/64	11/64	
7419	01/37 Sdn		-07/60	12/60	
7420	05/37 Sdn		-07/59	09/59	
7421	05/37 Sdn		-11/61	07/62	
7422	05/37 Sdn		-03/62	07/62	
7423	05/37 Sdn		-07/64	12/64	
7424	05/37 Sdn		-09/64	11/64	
7425	06/37 Sdn		-06/62	09/62	
7426	06/37 Sdn		-07/63	08/63	
7427	06/37 Sdn		-06/64	12/64	
7428	06/37 Sdn		-10/62	06/64	
7429	06/37 Sdn		-02/61	06/61	
7430	08/48 Sdn		08/48-12/63	06/64	
7431	08/48 Sdn		08/48-09/64	11/64	
7432	08/48 Sdn		08/48-09/64	11/64	
7433	08/48 Sdn		08/48-02/61	06/61	
7434	08/48 Sdn		08/48-10/62	06/64	
7435	09/48 Sdn		09/48-07/64	12/64	
7436	09/48 Sdn		09/48-06/64	08/64	
7437	09/48 Sdn		09/48-03/65	05/65	
7438	10/48 Sdn		10/48-02/59	12/60	
7439	10/48 Sdn		10/48-04/65	08/65	
7440	01/50 Sdn		01/50-10/62	09/63	
7441	01/50 Sdn		01/50-12/63	06/64	
7442	02/50 Sdn		02/50-12/63	02/64	
7443	02/50 Sdn		02/50-09/64	11/64	
7444	02/50 Sdn		02/50-07/64	12/64	
7445	03/50 Sdn		03/50-03/64	08/64	
7446	03/50 Sdn		03/50-07/64	12/64	
7447	03/50 Sdn		03/50-04/59	09/59	
7448	04/50 Sdn		04/50-04/63	03/64	
7449	04/50 Sdn		04/50-06/63	09/63	

5700 3600-3799, 4600-4699, 5700-5799, 7700-7799, 8700-8799, 9600-9682, 9711-9799

0-6-0PT GWR Collett 4ft 7½in

Class continued from 5799

Number	Built	Renumbered	BR Dates	Scrap	Notes
7700	02/30 KS		-05/61	09/61	
7701	03/30 KS		-02/60	05/60	
7702	03/30 KS		-09/60	06/61	
7703	03/30 KS		-03/60	05/60	
7704	03/30 KS		-12/60	04/61	
7705	03/30 KS		-08/59	02/60	
7706	03/30 KS		-03/60	11/60	
7707	03/30 KS		-11/60	04/61	
7708	03/30 KS		-06/60	12/60	
7709	03/30 KS		-08/60	12/60	
7710	03/30 KS		-09/58	10/58	
7711	04/30 KS		-12/56	01/62	
7712	04/30 KS		-07/60	06/61	
7713	04/30 KS		-08/62	09/62	
7714 §	04/30 KS		-01/59		
7715 §	05/30 KS		-06/63		
7716	05/30 KS		-12/59	05/60	
7717	05/30 KS		-03/60	05/60	
7718	05/30 KS		-04/62	06/62	
7719	06/30 KS		-09/60	01/61	
7720	06/30 KS		-05/62	10/62	
7721	06/30 KS		-07/62	09/62	
7722	06/30 KS		-11/60	08/65	
7723	06/30 KS		-08/60	03/65	
7724	07/30 KS		-09/62	12/62	
7725	12/29 NB		-08/60	06/61	
7726	12/29 NB		-08/60	10/60	
7727	12/29 NB		-01/60	04/60	
7728	12/29 NB		-05/60	11/60	
7729	12/29 NB		-07/62	11/62	
7730	12/29 NB		-03/59	05/59	
7731	12/29 NB		-04/59	01/60	
7732	12/29 NB		-10/62	10/62	
7733	12/29 NB		-05/60	09/60	
7734	12/29 NB		-04/59	10/65	
7735	12/29 NB		-05/59	11/60	
7736	12/29 NB		-05/62	11/62	
7737	01/30 NB		-03/60	05/60	
7738	01/30 NB		-02/59	11/59	
7739	01/30 NB		-12/62	01/70	
7740	01/30 NB		-12/60	04/61	
7741	02/30 NB		-12/61	09/67	
7742	02/30 NB		-07/59	09/59	
7743	02/30 NB		-08/59	01/60	
7744	02/30 NB		-09/62	09/62	
7745	03/30 NB		-03/61	10/61	
7746	03/30 NB		-10/59	12/59	
7747	03/30 NB		-02/61	06/61	
7748	03/30 NB		-04/61	07/61	
7749	03/30 NB		-12/62	01/70	
7750	11/30 NB		-01/59	04/59	
7751	11/30 NB		-10/59	02/60	
7752 §	11/30 NB		-12/59		
7753	11/30 NB		-04/62	08/62	
7754 §	12/30 NB		-01/59		
7755	12/30 NB		-05/62	09/62	
7756	12/30 NB		-06/61	02/62	
7757	12/30 NB		-09/60	01/61	
7758	12/30 NB		-06/60	02/62	
7759	12/30 NB		-03/60	09/60	
7760 §	12/30 NB		-12/61		
7761	12/30 NB		-01/61	09/61	
7762	01/31 NB		-05/62	09/62	
7763	01/31 NB		-11/59	04/60	
7764	01/31 NB		-05/62	12/62	
7765	01/31 NB		-07/62	07/62	
7766	02/31 NB		-11/60	03/61	
7767	02/31 NB		-03/60	07/60	
7768	02/31 NB		-11/59	05/60	
7769	02/31 NB		-08/59	03/60	
7770	02/31 NB		-04/59	06/59	
7771	03/31 NB		-11/61	04/62	
7772	03/31 NB		-11/61	04/62	
7773	03/31 NB		-12/59	04/60	
7774	03/31 NB		-11/59	02/60	
7775	11/30 AW		-11/60	12/61	
7776	11/30 AW		-01/61	07/61	
7777	11/30 AW		-11/60	03/61	
7778	11/30 AW		-12/59	05/60	
7779	11/30 AW		-10/58	09/68	
7780	11/30 AW		-07/63	06/64	
7781	11/30 AW		-07/60	10/60	
7782	11/30 AW		-10/64	01/65	
7783	11/30 AW		-09/62	01/63	
7784	11/30 AW		-03/62	04/62	
7785	12/30 AW		-05/62	02/63	
7786	12/30 AW		-05/62	10/62	
7787	12/30 AW		-06/61	12/61	
7788	12/30 AW		-07/62	09/62	
7789	12/30 AW		-11/59	02/60	
7790	12/30 AW		-12/62	12/63	
7791	12/30 AW		-12/59	02/60	
7792	12/30 AW		-11/57	01/58	
7793	12/30 AW		-04/60	08/60	
7794	12/30 AW		-11/60	04/61	
7795	12/30 AW		-02/58	03/58	
7796	12/30 AW		-02/62	07/62	
7797	12/30 AW		-10/59	03/60	
7798	12/30 AW		-05/61	11/61	
7799	12/30 AW		-05/62	12/62	

Class continued with 8700

7800 7800-7829

4-6-0 GWR Collett 'Manor'

Power Classification:	5MT
Introduced:	1938-39, 1950
Designer:	Collett
Company:	GWR
Weight:	Loco 68t 18cwt Tender 40t 0cwt
Driving Wheel:	5' 8"
Boiler Pressure:	225psi superheated
Cylinders:	Outside 18" x 30"
Tractive Effort:	27340lbf
Valve Gear:	Stephenson (piston valves)

The 'Manor' class was built as a lighter version of the 'Grange' class ('6800') for lines with restricted route availability, such as the Midland & South Western Junction and the Cambrian main lines. They were intended to replace the '4300' class and they incorporated certain parts (such as the wheels and motion) of the withdrawn '4300' class 2-6-0s they were replacing. It was intended to replace all the '4300' class with 'Granges' and 'Manors' (6800-6899 and 7800-7899 being planned), but the Second World War stopped the conversion programme after only twenty 'Manors' were completed. However, ten more (7820-7829) did appear in 1950.

The 'Manors' were used extensively in Cornwall and on the Cambrian lines.

Year End Totals: '7800' class

'47	'48	'49	'50	'51	'52	'53	'54	'55	'56	'57	'58	'59	'60	'61	'62	'63	'64	'65	'66	'67
20	20	20	30	30	30	30	30	30	30	30	30	30	30	30	30	29	19			

Number	Built	Renumbered	BR Dates	Scrap	Notes
7800 **TORQUAY MANOR**	01/38 Sdn		-08/64	10/64	
7801 **ANTHONY MANOR**	01/38 Sdn		-07/65	01/66	
7802 § **BRADLEY MANOR**	01/38 Sdn		-11/65		
7803 **BARCOTE MANOR**	01/38 Sdn		-04/65	08/65	
7804 **BAYDON MANOR**	02/38 Sdn		-09/65	12/65	
7805 **BROOME MANOR**	03/38 Sdn		-12/64	04/65	
7806 **COCKINGTON MANOR**	03/38 Sdn		-11/64	02/65	
7807 **COMPTON MANOR**	03/38 Sdn		-11/64	02/65	
7808 § **COOKHAM MANOR**	03/38 Sdn		-12/65		
7809 **CHILDREY MANOR**	04/38 Sdn		-04/63	05/63	
7810 **DRAYCOTT MANOR**	12/38 Sdn		-09/64	01/65	
7811 **DUNLEY MANOR**	12/38 Sdn		-07/65	10/65	
7812 § **ERLESTOKE MANOR**	01/39 Sdn		-11/65		
7813 **FRESHFORD MANOR**	01/39 Sdn		-05/65	07/65	
7814 **FRINGFORD MANOR**	01/39 Sdn		-09/65	12/65	
7815 **FRITWELL MANOR**	01/39 Sdn		-10/64	02/65	
7816 **FRILSHAM MANOR**	01/39 Sdn		-11/65	02/66	
7817 **GARSINGTON MANOR**	01/39 Sdn		-06/64	02/65	
7818 **GRANVILLE MANOR**	01/39 Sdn		-01/65	04/65	
7819 § **HINTON MANOR**	02/39 Sdn		-11/65		
7820 § **DINMORE MANOR**	11/50 Sdn		11/50-11/65		
7821 § **DITCHEAT MANOR**	11/50 Sdn		11/50-11/65		
7822 § **FOXCOTE MANOR**	12/50 Sdn		12/50-11/65		
7823 **HOOK NORTON MANOR**	12/50 Sdn		12/50-07/64	10/64	
7824 **IFORD MANOR**	12/50 Sdn		12/50-11/64	02/65	
7825 **LECHLADE MANOR**	12/50 Sdn		12/50-05/64	02/65	
7826 **LONGWORTH MANOR**	12/50 Sdn		12/50-04/65	07/65	
7827 § **LYDHAM MANOR**	12/50 Sdn		12/50-10/65		
7828 § **ODNEY MANOR**	12/50 Sdn		12/50-10/65		
7829 **RAMSBURY MANOR**	12/50 Sdn		12/50-12/65	01/67	

6959 6959-6999, 7900-7929

4-6-0 GWR Hawksworth 'Modified Hall'

Class continued from 6999

Number	Built	Renumbered	BR Dates	Scrap	Notes
7900 **SAINT PETER'S HALL**	04/49 Sdn		04/49-12/64	04/65	
7901 **DODINGTON HALL**	03/49 Sdn		03/49-02/64	06/64	
7902 **EATON MASCOT HALL**	03/49 Sdn		03/49-06/64	09/64	
7903 § **FOREMARKE HALL**	04/49 Sdn		04/49-06/64		
7904 **FOUNTAINS HALL**	04/49 Sdn		04/49-12/65	06/66	
7905 **FOWEY HALL**	04/49 Sdn		04/49-05/64	08/64	
7906 **FRON HALL**	12/49 Sdn		12/49-03/65	05/65	
7907 **HART HALL**	01/50 Sdn		01/50-12/65	07/66	
7908 **HENSHALL HALL**	01/50 Sdn		01/50-10/65	12/65	
7909 **HEVENINGHAM HALL**	01/50 Sdn		01/50-11/65	04/66	

Number	Built	BR Dates	Scrap
7910	01/50 Sdn	01/50-02/65	05/65
HOWN HALL			
7911	02/50 Sdn	02/50-12/63	02/65
LADY MARGARET HALL			
7912	03/50 Sdn	03/50-10/65	01/66
LITTLE LINFORD HALL			
7913	03/50 Sdn	03/50-03/65	07/65
LITTLE WYRLEY HALL			
7914	03/50 Sdn	03/50-12/65	05/66
LLEWENI HALL			
7915	03/50 Sdn	03/50-10/65	01/66
MERE HALL			
7916	04/50 Sdn	04/50-12/64	02/65
MOBBERLEY HALL			
7917	04/50 Sdn	04/50-08/65	10/65
NORTH ASTON HALL			
7918	04/50 Sdn	05/50-02/65	05/65
RHOSE WOOD HALL			
7919	05/50 Sdn	05/50-12/65	05/66
RUNTER HALL			
7920	09/50 Sdn	09/50-06/65	09/65
CONEY HALL			
7921	09/50 Sdn	09/50-12/63	08/64
EDSTONE HALL			
7922	09/50 Sdn	09/50-12/65	07/66
SALFORD HALL			
7923	09/50 Sdn	09/50-06/65	10/65
SPEKE HALL			
7924	09/50 Sdn	09/50-12/65	05/66
THORNYCROFT HALL			
7925	10/50 Sdn	10/50-12/65	03/66
WESTOL HALL			
7926	10/50 Sdn	10/50-12/64	06/65
WILLEY HALL			
7927 §	10/50 Sdn	10/50-12/65	
WILLINGTON HALL			
7928	10/50 Sdn	10/50-03/65	04/65
WOLF HALL			
7929	11/50 Sdn	11/50-08/65	10/65
WYKE HALL			

8100 8100-8109
2-6-2T GWR Collett '5100' rebuilds 5ft 6in

Power Classification:	4MT reclassified 5MT in 1953
Introduced:	1906-1908 Rebuilt by Collett 1938-1939
Designer:	Churchward
Company:	GWR
Weight:	76t 11cwt
Driving Wheel:	5' 6"
Boiler Pressure:	225psi superheated
Cylinders:	Outside 18" x 30"
Tractive Effort:	28165lbf
Valve Gear:	Stephenson (piston valves)

The '8100' class was the last of the large Prairie tanks to be built by the GWR. They were rebuilds from '5100' class locomotives. They used the '5100' class frames, but they were fitted with higher pressure boilers and slightly smaller wheels. They were rebuilt from 5100, 5123, 5118, 5145, 5124, 5126, 5120, 5116, 5133 and 5115 respectively. (8100 contained the frames of the original prototype Prairie tank, No. 99 built in 1903, renumbered to 3100, rebuilt to 5100 and then finally rebuilt to 8100.)

These locomotives were very similar to the '3100' class rebuilds, except for the slightly larger wheels. It was originally planned to convert all the old '3100' class (see '5101' class) and '3150' class to '8100' class and new '3100' class locomotives. Fifty of the '8100' class were on order, but the Second World War put a stop to the conversion programme after only ten had been built.

The '8100' class were fast powerful locomotives with excellent acceleration.

Year End Totals: '8100' class

'47	'48	'49	'50	'51	'52	'53	'54	'55	'56	'57	'58	'59	'60	'61	'62	'63	'64	'65	'66	'67
10	10	10	10	10	10	10	10	10	10	9	9	9	8	7	5	3	1			

Number	*Built*	*Renumbered*	*BR Dates*	*Scrap*	*Notes*
8100	09/03 Sdn		-10/62	10/62	
8101	05/05 Sdn		-03/61	06/61	
8102	02/05 Sdn		-05/64	08/64	
8103	03/06 Sdn		-11/63	01/64	
8104	05/05 Sdn		-12/64	04/65	
8105	06/05 Sdn		-06/57	07/57	
8106	05/05 Sdn		-12/63	03/64	
8107	02/05 Sdn		-05/62	06/62	
8108	01/06 Sdn		-11/60	12/60	
8109	02/05 Sdn		-06/65	12/65	

8300 8393
2-6-0 GWR '4300' with ballast weights

Power Classification:	4MT
Introduced:	1911 onwards, Rebuilt by Collett 1928
Designer:	Churchward
Company:	GWR
Weight:	Loco 65t 6cwt Tender 40t 0cwt
Driving Wheel:	5' 8"
Boiler Pressure:	200psi superheated
Cylinders:	Outside 18½" x 30"
Tractive Effort:	25670lbf
Valve Gear:	Stephenson (piston valves)

The '8300' class was a variation of the '4300' with altered weight distribution. Sixty-five engines of the '5300' series had 30cwt castings fixed behind the front buffer beams and they were given corresponding numbers in the 8300 series. From 1944 onwards these gradually had the ballast weights removed and they reverted to their 5300 numbers. 8393 was the last one to be reconverted in September 1948.

Year End Totals: '8300' class

'47	'48	'49	'50	'51	'52	'53	'54	'55	'56	'57	'58	'59	'60	'61	'62	'63	'64	'65	'66	'67
1																				

Number	*Built*	*Renumbered*	*BR Dates*	*Scrap*	*Notes*
8393	10/20 Sdn		-10/59	02/60 09/48➲5393	

9400 3400-3409, 8400-8499, 9400-9499
0-6-0PT GWR Hawksworth 4ft 7½in

Class continued from 3409

Number	*Built*	*Renumbered*	*BR Dates*	*Scrap*	*Notes*
8400	08/49 WB		08/49-09/64	12/64	
8401	08/49 WB		08/49-09/64	01/65	
8402	09/49 WB		09/49-11/64	03/65	
8403	09/49 WB		09/49-06/65	10/65	
8404	09/49 WB		09/49-11/61	03/62	
8405	12/49 WB		12/49-09/64	10/65	
8406	12/49 WB		12/49-01/61	04/61	
8407	12/49 WB		12/49-10/62	12/63	
8408	01/50 WB		01/50-09/59	08/64	
8409	01/50 WB		01/50-08/64	03/65	
8410	01/50 WB		01/50-01/60	12/60	
8411	01/50 WB		01/50-06/60	12/60	
8412	01/50 WB		01/50-07/59	12/60	
8413	01/50 WB		01/50-01/61	02/61	
8414	01/50 WB		01/50-04/64	08/64	
8415	03/50 WB		03/50-06/65	10/65	
8416	03/50 WB		03/50-10/62	06/64	
8417	03/50 WB		03/50-03/59	04/65	
8418	03/50 WB		03/50-08/64	01/65	
8419	04/50 WB		04/50-01/60	03/65	
8420	07/50 WB		07/50-06/65	10/65	
8421	07/50 WB		07/50-12/59	12/60	
8422	10/50 WB		10/50-07/62	10/62	
8423	10/50 WB		10/50-12/59	12/60	
8424	12/50 WB		12/50-01/61	06/61	
8425	02/51 WB		02/51-11/63	02/64	
8426	01/51 WB		01/51-11/63	01/64	
8427	02/51 WB		02/51-09/60	08/61	
8428	02/51 WB		02/51-10/62	11/63	
8429	03/51 WB		03/51-01/60	10/61	
8430	01/53 WB		01/53-05/63	01/64	
8431	01/53 WB		01/53-08/64	10/64	
8432	02/53 WB		02/53-07/59	12/60	
8433	03/53 WB		03/53-06/65	10/65	
8434	02/53 WB		02/53-06/59	12/60	
8435	04/53 WB		04/53-02/62	05/62	
8436	05/53 WB		05/53-06/65	10/65	
8437	05/53 WB		05/53-11/64	02/65	
8438	06/53 WB		06/53-10/62	10/62	
8439	06/53 WB		06/53-10/62	11/63	
8440	03/54 WB		03/54-07/62	09/62	
8441	04/54 WB		04/54-12/61	04/62	
8442	03/54 WB		03/54-06/59	12/60	
8443	03/54 WB		03/54-06/59	12/60	
8444	04/54 WB		04/54-07/63	10/63	
8445	06/54 WB		06/54-09/62	12/62	
8446	06/54 WB		06/54-09/64	11/64	
8447	06/54 WB		06/54-06/59	12/60	
8448	06/54 WB		06/54-08/59	12/60	
8449	06/54 WB		06/54-09/62	02/64	
8450	08/49 YE		08/49-06/59	12/60	
8451	09/49 YE		09/49-11/61	04/62	
8452	10/49 YE		10/49-04/64	08/64	
8453	11/49 YE		11/49-10/62	10/62	
8454	12/49 YE		12/49-01/61	06/61	
8455	01/50 YE		01/50-01/60	12/60	
8456	02/50 YE		02/50-10/63	01/64	
8457	03/50 YE		03/50-01/61	07/61	
8458	04/50 YE		04/50-08/63	10/63	
8459	05/50 YE		05/50-06/65	01/66	
8460	06/50 YE		06/50-01/61	04/61	
8461	06/50 YE		06/50-11/63	01/64	
8462	07/50 YE		07/50-08/59	12/60	
8463	09/50 YE		09/50-01/60	12/60	
8464	10/50 YE		10/50-12/63	02/64	
8465	11/50 YE		11/50-11/63	01/64	
8466	11/50 YE		11/50-07/64	08/68	
8467	02/51 YE		02/51-02/62	07/62	
8468	02/51 YE		02/51-05/60	05/60	
8469	03/51 YE		03/51-11/64	02/65	
8470	05/51 YE		05/51-01/62	05/62	
8471	05/51 YE		05/51-06/65	10/65	
8472	07/51 YE		07/51-03/63	07/63	
8473	08/51 YE		08/51-01/61	08/61	
8474	10/51 YE		10/51-05/65	08/65	
8475	11/51 YE		11/51-09/64	01/65	
8476	03/52 YE		03/52-01/61	04/61	
8477	03/52 YE		03/52-07/62	10/62	
8478	05/52 YE		05/52-01/63	02/63	
8479	06/52 YE		06/52-10/64	03/65	
8480	03/52 RSH		03/52-07/64	10/64	
8481	03/52 RSH		03/52-06/65	10/65	
8482	04/52 RSH		04/52-09/62	07/64	
8483	05/52 RSH		05/52-02/62	05/62	
8484	05/52 RSH		05/52-06/65	10/65	
8485	06/52 RSH		06/52-06/59	12/60	
8486	06/52 RSH		06/52-06/65	10/65	
8487	07/52 RSH		07/52-11/63	01/64	
8488	07/52 RSH		07/52-05/65	08/65	
8489	07/52 RSH		07/52-02/62	04/62	
8490	07/52 RSH		07/52-10/62	11/63	
8491	08/52 RSH		08/52-07/63	01/64	
8492	08/52 RSH		08/52-06/59	12/60	
8493	09/52 RSH		09/52-11/64	02/65	
8494	09/52 RSH		09/52-01/62	07/62	
8495	10/52 RSH		10/52-11/64	02/65	
8496	10/52 RSH		10/52-07/63	09/63	
8497	11/52 RSH		11/52-07/64	06/68	
8498	11/52 RSH		11/52-06/65	10/65	
8499	11/52 RSH		11/52-06/62	09/62	

Class continued with 9400

5700 3600-3799, 4600-4699, 5700-5799, 7700-7799, 8700-8799, 9600-9682, 9711-9799
0-6-0PT GWR Collett 4ft 7½in

Class continued from 7799

Number	*Built*	*Renumbered*	*BR Dates*	*Scrap*	*Notes*
8700	03/34 Sdn		-02/62	05/62	m
8701	02/31 BP		-03/63	07/64	
8702	02/31 BP		-05/64	06/64	
8703	02/31 BP		-01/58	05/58	
8704	02/31 BP		-02/60	07/60	
8705	02/31 BP		-04/61	09/61	
8706	03/31 BP		-07/61	12/61	
8707	02/31 BP		-07/64	08/64	
8708	03/31 BP		-05/60	07/60	
8709	02/31 BP		-09/62	12/62	
8710	03/31 BP		-03/63	05/63	
8711	03/31 BP		-03/62	05/62	
8712	03/31 BP		-01/63	12/63	
8713	03/31 BP		-03/62	07/62	
8714	03/31 BP		-11/64	04/65	
8715	03/31 BP		-04/62	10/62	
8716	03/31 BP		-04/64	08/64	
8717	03/31 BP		-07/64	12/64	
8718	03/31 BP		-07/66	11/66	
8719	03/31 BP		-05/62	11/62	
8720	03/31 BP		-09/64	12/64	
8721	03/31 BP		-07/61	05/62	
8722	04/31 BP		-04/61	09/61	
8723	04/31 BP		-07/64	11/64	
8724	04/31 BP		-07/62	02/63	
8725	12/30 WB		-10/62	10/62	
8726	12/30 WB		-04/61	07/61	
8727	12/30 WB		-04/62	09/62	
8728	12/30 WB		-07/63	03/64	
8729	01/31 WB		-12/62	08/63	
8730	02/31 WB		-07/62	11/62	
8731	02/31 WB		-07/62	12/62	
8732	02/31 WB		-04/64	06/64	
8733	03/31 WB		-02/62	04/62	
8734	03/31 WB		-03/62	04/62	
8735	03/31 WB		-01/62	03/62	
8736	04/31 WB		-03/62	05/62	
8737	04/31 WB		-12/62	05/63	

Number	Built	Renumbered	BR Dates	Scrap	Notes
8738	04/31 WB		-03/63	04/64	
8739	04/31 WB		-11/64	03/65	
8740	05/31 WB		-02/61	11/61	
8741	05/31 WB		-05/62	09/62	
8742	06/31 WB		-09/62	02/63	
8743	06/31 WB		-06/64	08/64	
8744	06/31 WB		-10/62	07/64	
8745	07/31 WB		-08/65	12/65	
8746	07/31 WB		-12/62	12/63	
8747	07/31 WB		-05/64	08/64	
8748	07/31 WB		-09/62	09/62	
8749	07/31 WB		-10/64	03/65	
8750	09/33 Sdn		-05/62	09/62	m
8751	10/33 Sdn		-12/62	01/63	m
8752	10/33 Sdn		-01/63	03/64	m
8753	10/33 Sdn		-02/62	07/62	m
8754	10/33 Sdn		-11/60	12/60	m
8755	10/33 Sdn		-12/57	01/58	m
8756	10/33 Sdn		-10/62	12/63	m
8757	10/33 Sdn		-09/62	01/64	m
8758	10/33 Sdn		-01/59	07/59	m
8759	10/33 Sdn		-01/63	12/63	m
8760	10/33 Sdn		-01/62	04/62	m
8761	10/33 Sdn		-05/62	09/62	m
8762	10/33 Sdn		-08/61	04/62	m
8763	10/33 Sdn		-08/62	12/63	m
8764	10/33 Sdn		-05/62	01/63	m
8765	12/33 Sdn		-09/62	01/64	m
8766	12/33 Sdn		-07/63	10/63	m
8767	12/33 Sdn		-07/66	11/66	m
8768	12/33 Sdn		-09/64	04/65	m
8769	12/33 Sdn		-04/61	07/61	m
8770	01/34 Sdn		-12/62	07/63	m
8771	01/34 Sdn		-07/62	12/62	m
8772	01/34 Sdn		-08/61	12/61	m
8773	01/34 Sdn		-10/62	06/63	m
8774	01/34 Sdn		-08/61	11/61	m
8775	01/34 Sdn		-12/61	04/62	m
8776	01/34 Sdn		-12/62	05/63	m
8777	01/34 Sdn		-04/61	10/61	m
8778	01/34 Sdn		-08/60	12/60	m
8779	01/34 Sdn		-02/62	04/62	m
8780	01/34 Sdn		-07/62	06/63	m
8781	01/34 Sdn		-12/62	12/62	m
8782	01/34 Sdn		-11/61	02/62	m
8783	01/34 Sdn		-06/63	09/63	m
8784	01/34 Sdn		-04/62	09/62	m
8785	01/34 Sdn		-12/63	03/64	m
8786	01/34 Sdn		-07/63	10/63	m
8787	01/34 Sdn		-08/61	01/62	m
8788	01/34 Sdn		-05/62	09/62	m
8789	01/34 Sdn		-06/61	10/61	m
8790	02/34 Sdn		-05/62	09/62	m
8791	02/34 Sdn		-03/63	12/63	m
8792	02/34 Sdn		-02/62	05/62	m
8793	03/34 Sdn		-12/64	04/65	m
8794	03/34 Sdn		-07/63	10/63	m
8795	03/34 Sdn		-07/65	10/65	m
8796	03/34 Sdn		-04/61	09/61	m
8797	03/34 Sdn		-04/62	08/62	m
8798	03/34 Sdn		-06/61	08/61	m
8799	06/34 Sdn		-11/62	12/62	m

Class continued with 9600

9000 9000-9028
4-4-0 GWR 'Dukedog' or 'Earl'

Power Classification: 2P/2MT
Introduced: 1936-1939 embodying parts of earlier Dean engines
Designer: Collett
Company: GWR
Weight: Loco 49t 0cwt
Tender 40t 0cwt or 36t 15cwt
Driving Wheel: 5' 8"
Boiler Pressure: 180psi some superheated
Cylinders: Inside 18" x 26"
Tractive Effort: 18955lbf
Valve Gear: Stephenson (slide valves)

Although nominally built as new engines in 1936-1939, these were in fact reconstructions using the boilers of withdrawn 'Duke' type engines (see '3252' class below) and the outside frames of 'Bulldog' class ('3300') locomotives. Some of them received newer domed superheated boilers. They were rebuilt from the frames of 3422 ABERYSTWYTH, 3412 JOHN G. GRIFFITHS, 3416 JOHN W. WILSON, 3424, 3439 WESTON-SUPER-MARE, 3413 JAMES MASON, 3428, 3410 COLUMBIA, 3403 TRINIDAD, 3392 NEW ZEALAND, 3402 JAMAICA, 3415 GEORGE A. WILLS, 3405 EMPIRE OF INDIA, 3374 WALTER LONG, 3434 JOSEPH SHAW, 3420, 3404 BARBADOS, 3425, 3380 RIVER YELM, 3427, 3414 SIR EDWARD ELGAR / A.H.MILLS, 3411 STANLEY BALDWIN, 3436, 3423, 3409 QUEENSLAND, 3437, 3390 WOLVERHAMPTON WORKS, 3433 and 3429 respectively.

The remainder of the 'Duke' class were due to be converted but the outbreak of the Second World War prevented this from happening. A prototype (3265) was constructed in 1929 but it was not included in this class, and officially remained a 'Duke' class locomotive, later becoming 9065.

When they were built the class was numbered 3200-3228 and 3200-19 were allocated the names of Earls (the first twelve actually carrying their names for a short time). Some complaints were received from the noble Earls concerned because their names were being applied to such antiquated looking locomotives. Because of this the names were quickly transferred to the much more modern looking 'Castle' class locomotives (5043 onwards, in the same order).

The engines were generally known as 'Dukedogs' because of their ancestry. In 1946 they were all renumbered in the 9000-9028 series. They spent most of their lives on the Cambrian lines in Wales, and they also worked on the Didcot-Newbury and Southampton line until this was upgraded to allow heavier engines during the war.

Year End Totals: '9000' class

'47	'48	'49	'50	'51	'52	'53	'54	'55	'56	'57	'58	'59	'60	'61	'62	'63	'64	'65	'66	'67
29	26	26	26	26	26	26	24	22	22	8	6	5								

Number	*Built*	*Renumbered*	*BR Dates*	*Scrap*	*Notes*
9000	06/06 Sdn		-03/55	*55*	
9001	04/06 Sdn		-04/54	*54*	
9002	06/06 Sdn		-05/54	*06/54*	
9003	07/06 Sdn		-10/55	*55*	
9004	09/06 Sdn		-06/60	08/60	
9005	04/06 Sdn		-07/59	10/59	
9006	07/06 Sdn		-08/48	*09/48*	
9007	04/04 Sdn		-07/48	*48*	
9008	03/04 Sdn		-07/57	07/57	
9009	01/04 Sdn		-07/57	07/57	
9010	03/04 Sdn		-07/57	08/57	
9011	05/06 Sdn		-07/57	07/57	
9012	03/04 Sdn		-07/57	07/57	
9013	05/03 Sdn		-12/58	12/58	
9014	08/06 Sdn		-10/60	12/60	
9015	06/06 Sdn		-06/60	11/60	
9016	03/04 Sdn		-07/57	08/57	
9017 §	07/06 Sdn		-10/60		
9018	05/03 Sdn		-06/60	08/60	
9019	07/06 Sdn		-11/48	01/49	
9020	05/06 Sdn		-07/57	08/57	
9021	04/06 Sdn		-12/58	02/59	
9022	08/06 Sdn		-08/57	08/57	
9023	06/06 Sdn		-07/57	07/57	
9024	04/04 Sdn		-08/57	08/58	
9025	09/06 Sdn		-08/57	08/57	
9026	10/03 Sdn		-08/57	08/57	
9027	08/06 Sdn		-08/57	08/57	
9028	01/06 Sdn		-08/57	09/57	

3252 9054-9091
4-4-0 GWR Dean 'Duke'

Power Classification: 2MT
Introduced: 1895-1899
Designer: Dean
Company: GWR
Weight: Loco 47t 6cwt
Tender 34t 5cwt
Driving Wheel: 5' 8"
Boiler Pressure: 180psi some superheated
Cylinders: Inside 18" x 26"
Tractive Effort: 18955lbf
Valve Gear: Stephenson (slide valves)

These were the survivors of the sixty 'Duke' class locomotives, named after the original engine 3252 DUKE OF CORNWALL. They were built to work the steeply graded lines in Cornwall, but finished their days on the former Cambrian Railways lines in Wales. Until 1946 they were numbered 3254-3291.

They were built with double curved frames. Some of the class were fitted with new superheated boilers. Twenty of the class were rebuilt in 1902-1909 to become 'Bulldog' class locomotives 3300-3319.

Twenty-nine members of the class were withdrawn in 1936-1939 and their boilers and other parts were used in the construction of new '9000' class locomotives. The rest would have been similarly converted but the Second World War stopped the conversion programme.

The class mostly carried names connected with the West Country. 9072 was formerly named FOWEY, 9076 was ST. AGNES and 9089 was ST. AUSTELL.

s 9065 was rebuilt in 1929 with the straight frames from 'Bulldog' number 3365 CHARLES GREY MOTT (built in January 1903) As such it was the prototype for the 9000 class, but it was never officially included in that class.

Year End Totals: '3252' class

'47	'48	'49	'50	'51	'52	'53	'54	'55	'56	'57	'58	'59	'60	'61	'62	'63	'64	'65	'66	'67
11	11	4	2																	

Number	*Built*	*Renumbered*	*BR Dates*	*Scrap*	*Notes*
9054	07/95 Sdn		-06/50	08/50	
CORNUBIA					
9064	06/96 Sdn		-12/49	*03/50*	
TREVITHICK					
9065	07/96 Sdn		-12/49	*03/50*	s
TRE POL AND PEN					
9072	01/97 Sdn		-06/49	08/49	
9073	12/97 Sdn		-12/49	02/50	
MOUNTS BAY					
9076	03/97 Sdn		-11/49	01/50	
9083	03/99 Sdn		-12/50	*51*	
COMET					
9084	03/99 Sdn		-04/51	*05/51*	
ISLE OF JERSEY					
9087	04/99 Sdn		-07/49	09/49	
MERCURY					
9089	07/99 Sdn		-07/51	*51*	
9091	07/99 Sdn		-02/49	04/49	
THAMES					

9300 9300-9319
2-6-0 GWR '4300' with ballast weights and side window cabs

Power Classification: 4MT
Introduced: 1932
Designer: Churchward
Company: GWR
Weight: Loco 65t 6cwt
Tender 40t 0cwt
Driving Wheel: 5' 8"
Boiler Pressure: 200psi superheated
Cylinders: Outside 18½" x 30"
Tractive Effort: 25670lbf
Valve Gear: Stephenson (piston valves)

These locomotives were a variation of the '4300' class with altered weight distribution and side window cabs.

The '9300' class was built new with the same weight modifications as the '8300' class and in addition they had side window cabs and outside steam pipes. Between 1956 and 1959 they had their ballast weights removed and they were renumbered 7322-7341.

Year End Totals: '9300' class

'47	'48	'49	'50	'51	'52	'53	'54	'55	'56	'57	'58	'59	'60	'61	'62	'63	'64	'65	'66	'67
20	20	20	20	20	20	20	20	20	17	11	4									

Number	*Built*	*Renumbered*	*BR Dates*	*Scrap*	*Notes*
9300	02/32 Sdn	04/57➲7322	-11/61	12/61	
9301	02/32 Sdn	09/56➲7323	-08/62	10/62	
9302	02/32 Sdn	02/57➲7324	-10/62	11/63	
9303 §	02/32 Sdn	06/58➲7325	-04/64		
9304	02/32 Sdn	06/58➲7326	-09/63	06/64	
9305	02/32 Sdn	01/59➲7327	-11/64	12/64	
9306	03/32 Sdn	05/58➲7328	-04/62	07/62	
9307	03/32 Sdn	12/56➲7329	-01/63	01/64	
9308	03/32 Sdn	06/57➲7330	-09/62	02/63	
9309	03/32 Sdn	05/59➲7331	-09/62	02/63	
9310	03/32 Sdn	09/58➲7332	-04/64	07/64	
9311	03/32 Sdn	06/57➲7333	-10/63	06/64	
9312	03/32 Sdn	01/59➲7334	-04/62	06/63	
9313	03/32 Sdn	08/58➲7335	-09/63	05/64	
9314	03/32 Sdn	06/58➲7336	-09/62	01/64	
9315	03/32 Sdn	05/59➲7337	-09/64	12/64	

Number	Built	Renumbered	BR Dates	Scrap	Notes
9316	04/32 Sdn	03/58➲7338	-08/62	09/62	
9317	04/32 Sdn	09/56➲7339	-06/64	02/65	
9318	04/32 Sdn	12/57➲7340	-06/64	11/64	
9319	04/32 Sdn	06/57➲7341	-09/62	09/62	

9400 3400-3409, 8400-8499, 9400-9499

0-6-0PT GWR Hawksworth 4ft 7½in

Class continued from 8499

Number	Built	Renumbered	BR Dates	Scrap	Notes
9400 §	02/47 Sdn		-12/59		s
9401	02/47 Sdn		-07/63	01/64	s
9402	01/47 Sdn		-08/59	12/60	s
9403	03/47 Sdn		-06/59	12/60	s
9404	04/47 Sdn		-06/65	10/65	s
9405	05/47 Sdn		-06/65	10/65	s
9406	05/47 Sdn		-09/64	12/64	s
9407	05/47 Sdn		-07/62	12/62	s
9408	05/47 Sdn		-05/63	10/63	s
9409	05/47 Sdn		-05/62	09/62	s
9410	02/50 RSH		02/50-07/62	12/62	
9411	02/50 RSH		02/50-06/65	10/65	
9412	03/50 RSH		03/50-03/63	11/63	
9413	03/50 RSH		03/50-11/63	01/64	
9414	04/50 RSH		04/50-08/60	08/61	
9415	05/50 RSH		05/50-06/65	10/65	
9416	05/50 RSH		05/50-01/62	03/62	
9417	05/50 RSH		05/50-06/59	12/60	
9418	05/50 RSH		05/50-06/65	10/65	
9419	06/50 RSH		06/50-03/63	01/64	
9420	06/50 RSH		06/50-03/64	08/64	
9421	07/50 RSH		07/50-02/62	07/62	
9422	07/50 RSH		07/50-12/63	02/64	
9423	07/50 RSH		07/50-02/63	01/64	
9424	08/50 RSH		08/50-12/62	66	
9425	09/50 RSH		09/50-11/63	10/65	
9426	09/50 RSH		09/50-05/65	08/65	
9427	09/50 RSH		09/50-06/59	12/60	
9428	09/50 RSH		09/50-06/60	12/60	
9429	10/50 RSH		10/50-12/63	04/64	
9430	10/50 RSH		10/50-06/65	10/65	
9431	11/50 RSH		11/50-04/64	07/64	
9432	11/50 RSH		11/50-11/59	12/60	
9433	12/50 RSH		12/50-07/62	11/62	
9434	01/51 RSH		01/51-06/60	12/60	
9435	01/51 RSH		01/51-09/64	01/65	
9436	01/51 RSH		01/51-07/60	06/61	
9437	01/51 RSH		01/51-06/65	10/65	
9438	02/51 RSH		02/51-06/59	06/61	
9439	02/51 RSH		02/51-06/59	06/61	
9440	02/51 RSH		02/51-07/63	11/63	
9441	03/51 RSH		03/51-11/63	02/64	
9442	03/51 RSH		03/51-07/64	12/64	
9443	03/51 RSH		03/51-06/59	06/61	
9444	04/51 RSH		04/51-03/63	02/64	
9445	04/51 RSH		04/51-01/60	01/65	
9446	05/51 RSH		05/51-05/65	08/65	
9447	05/51 RSH		05/51-01/61	04/61	
9448	05/51 RSH		05/51-07/62	10/62	
9449	06/51 RSH		06/51-06/60	01/65	
9450	06/51 RSH		06/51-06/64	08/64	
9451	07/51 RSH		07/51-07/62	10/62	
9452	07/51 RSH		07/51-05/65	08/65	
9453	07/51 RSH		07/51-11/64	03/65	
9454	09/51 RSH		09/51-01/62	04/62	
9455	09/51 RSH		09/51-04/63	01/64	
9456	09/51 RSH		09/51-04/64	10/64	
9457	10/51 RSH		10/51-07/64	11/65	
9458	10/51 RSH		10/51-01/61	04/61	
9459	11/51 RSH		11/51-09/59	06/61	
9460	11/51 RSH		11/51-02/62	05/62	
9461	12/51 RSH		12/51-05/65	08/65	
9462	12/51 RSH		12/51-11/60	05/65	
9463	01/52 RSH		01/52-06/65	10/65	
9464	01/52 RSH		01/52-06/65	10/65	
9465	01/52 RSH		01/52-02/62	07/62	
9466 §	02/52 RSH		02/52-07/64		
9467	02/52 RSH		02/52-05/62	10/62	
9468	02/52 RSH		02/52-08/60	08/65	
9469	03/52 RSH		03/52-03/62	06/62	
9470	03/52 RSH		03/52-09/64	12/64	
9471	04/52 RSH		04/52-09/64	12/64	
9472	04/52 RSH		04/52-05/65	08/65	
9473	05/52 RSH		05/52-07/64	12/64	
9474	05/52 RSH		05/52-11/61	05/62	
9475	06/52 RSH		06/52-05/65	08/65	
9476	06/52 RSH		06/52-06/62	08/62	
9477	07/52 RSH		07/52-06/65	10/65	
9478	07/52 RSH		07/52-07/62	10/62	
9479	07/52 RSH		07/52-07/63	09/63	
9480	08/52 RSH		08/52-04/65	08/66	
9481	08/52 RSH		08/52-01/61	06/61	
9482	09/52 RSH		09/52-11/63	02/64	
9483	10/52 RSH		10/52-07/63	09/63	
9484	10/52 RSH		10/52-04/64	01/65	
9485	10/52 RSH		10/52-07/64	12/64	
9486	11/52 RSH		11/52-07/62	10/62	
9487	11/52 RSH		11/52-07/62	11/62	
9488	12/52 RSH		12/52-04/65	07/65	
9489	01/53 RSH		01/53-04/64	07/64	
9490	02/54 YE		02/54-12/64	04/65	
9491	03/54 YE		03/54-06/59	03/65	
9492	05/54 YE		05/54-06/59	02/62	
9493	06/54 YE		06/54-09/64	10/65	
9494	08/54 YE		08/54-11/64	02/65	
9495	10/54 YE		10/54-06/65	10/65	
9496	10/54 YE		10/54-12/59	06/61	
9497	12/54 YE		12/54-05/62	10/62	
9498	03/55 YE		03/55-09/64	12/64	
9499	07/55 YE		07/55-09/59	03/65	

5700 3600-3799, 4600-4699, 5700-5799, 7700-7799, 8700-8799, 9600-9682, 9711-9799

0-6-0PT GWR Collett 4ft 7½in

Class continued from 8799

Number	Built	Renumbered	BR Dates	Scrap	Notes
9600 §	02/45 Sdn		-09/65		m
9601	04/45 Sdn		-12/64	10/65	m
9602	05/45 Sdn		-03/65	07/65	m
9603	05/45 Sdn		-12/63	09/64	m
9604	05/45 Sdn		-12/62	01/64	m
9605	05/45 Sdn		-09/65	12/65	m
9606	06/45 Sdn		-11/64	12/64	m
9607	06/45 Sdn		-04/64	01/65	m
9608	06/45 Sdn		-07/66	11/66	m
9609	06/45 Sdn		-10/65	02/67	m
9610	07/45 Sdn		-09/66	01/67	m
9611	08/45 Sdn		-04/65	08/65	m
9612	08/45 Sdn		-12/63	06/64	m
9613	09/45 Sdn		-10/65	01/66	m
9614	09/45 Sdn		-07/66	11/66	m
9615	09/45 Sdn		-07/65	10/65	m
9616	09/45 Sdn		-08/65	12/65	m
9617	10/45 Sdn		-06/65	10/65	m
9618	10/45 Sdn		-12/63	03/64	m
9619	10/45 Sdn		-07/65	10/65	m
9620	10/45 Sdn		-07/64	12/64	m
9621	10/45 Sdn		-10/64	02/65	m
9622	11/45 Sdn		-07/65	10/65	m
9623	11/45 Sdn		-07/65	10/65	m
9624	11/45 Sdn		-01/65	03/65	m
9625	11/45 Sdn		-06/65	10/65	m
9626	11/45 Sdn		-12/65	06/66	m
9627	11/45 Sdn		-07/62	02/63	m
9628	12/45 Sdn		-03/63	12/64	m
9629 §	12/45 Sdn		-10/64		m
9630	12/45 Sdn		-09/66	12/66	m
9631	12/45 Sdn		-06/65	10/65	m
9632	12/45 Sdn		-11/64	02/65	m
9633	01/46 Sdn		-10/63	12/63	m
9634	01/46 Sdn		-05/64	08/64	m
9635	01/46 Sdn		-06/64	12/64	m
9636	02/46 Sdn		-10/63	11/63	m
9637	02/46 Sdn		-09/64	12/64	m
9638	02/46 Sdn		-12/63	06/64	m
9639	02/46 Sdn		-09/65	11/65	m
9640	03/46 Sdn		-07/66	11/66	m
9641	03/46 Sdn		-10/66	05/67	m
9642 §	04/46 Sdn		-11/64		m
9643	04/46 Sdn		-05/62	10/62	m
9644	04/46 Sdn		-06/65	10/65	m
9645	04/46 Sdn		-10/63	02/64	m
9646	05/46 Sdn		-05/65	08/65	m
9647	05/46 Sdn		-06/65	10/65	m
9648	05/46 Sdn		-07/64	12/64	m
9649	06/46 Sdn		-07/65	08/65	m
9650	06/46 Sdn		-12/64	06/65	m
9651	06/46 Sdn		-07/65	10/65	m
9652	11/46 Sdn		-01/63	07/63	m
9653	11/46 Sdn		-07/65	10/65	m
9654	11/46 Sdn		-10/64	02/65	m
9655	11/46 Sdn		-05/64	12/64	m
9656	11/46 Sdn		-11/65	02/66	m
9657	11/46 Sdn		-04/66	07/66	m
9658	11/46 Sdn		-10/66	04/67	m
9659	11/46 Sdn		-06/65	10/65	m
9660	12/46 Sdn		-11/64	01/65	m
9661	12/46 Sdn		-11/64	03/65	m
9662	04/48 Sdn		04/48-09/65	12/65	m
9663	04/48 Sdn		04/48-09/64	04/65	m
9664	04/48 Sdn		04/48-05/64	09/64	m
9665	04/48 Sdn		04/48-02/63	06/64	m
9666	04/48 Sdn		04/48-09/65	12/65	m
9667	05/48 Sdn		05/48-06/65	10/65	m
9668	05/48 Sdn		05/48-12/63	07/64	m
9669	05/48 Sdn		05/48-01/66	04/66	m
9670	05/48 Sdn		05/48-06/65	10/65	m
9671	06/48 Sdn		06/48-03/65	07/65	m
9672	06/48 Sdn		06/48-12/65	04/66	m
9673	02/49 Sdn		02/49-05/60	09/60	m
9674	03/49 Sdn		03/49-04/64	06/64	m
9675	03/49 Sdn		03/49-10/65	12/65	m
9676	03/49 Sdn		03/49-06/65	10/65	m
9677	03/49 Sdn		03/49-11/64	01/65	m
9678	04/49 Sdn		04/49-06/65	10/65	m
9679	04/49 Sdn		04/49-11/64	02/65	m
9680	04/49 Sdn		04/49-12/65	06/66	m
9681 §	05/49 Sdn		05/49-08/65		m
9682 §	05/49 Sdn		05/49-08/65		m

Class continued with 9711

9700 9700-9710

0-6-0PT GWR '5700' class with condensing apparatus

Power Classification:	4F
Introduced:	1933-1934
Designer:	Collett
Company:	GWR
Weight:	50t 15cwt
Driving Wheel:	4' 7½"
Boiler Pressure:	200psi
Cylinders:	Inside 17½" x 24"
Tractive Effort:	22515lbf
Valve Gear:	Stephenson (slide valves)

Refer to the Historical Survey of GWR Pannier Tank Engines at the end of this section for more details of this class.

In 1932 '5700' class locomotive number 8700 was rebuilt with condensing apparatus, a Weir feed pump and shorter pannier tanks. This was to allow the locomotive to work over the London Transport Metropolitan Line to Smithfield.

After trials with 8700, 9701-9710 were built in 1933 to a slightly modified design. It had been found that 8700s shortened pannier tanks did not carry sufficient water so the new locomotives had the pannier tanks extended at the rear down to the running plate. 8700 was converted to the new design and renumbered 9700 in 1934. (A new number 8700 was built to replace it).

The '9700' class carried the modified cabs as found on the later members of the '5700' class. The only other GWR locomotives where the pannier tanks did not flank the sides of the smokebox were the '1500' and '9400' classes.

Year End Totals: '9700' class

'47	'48	'49	'50	'51	'52	'53	'54	'55	'56	'57	'58	'59	'60	'61	'62	'63	'64	'65	'66	'67
11	11	11	11	11	11	11	11	11	11	11	11	11	10	10	7	5	3			

Number	Built	Renumbered	BR Dates	Scrap	Notes
9700	02/31 BP		-10/63	12/63	
9701	09/33 Sdn		-01/61	04/61	
9702	09/33 Sdn		-05/62	11/62	
9703	09/33 Sdn		-12/61	07/62	
9704	10/33 Sdn		-11/63	06/64	
9705	10/33 Sdn		-10/61	01/62	
9706	12/33 Sdn		-11/64	02/65	
9707	11/33 Sdn		-09/64	12/64	
9708	12/33 Sdn		-01/59	07/59	
9709	12/33 Sdn		-05/62	09/62	
9710	12/33 Sdn		-10/64	01/65	

5700 3600-3799, 4600-4699, 5700-5799, 7700-7799, 8700-8799, 9600-9682, 9711-9799

0-6-0PT GWR Collett 4ft 7½in

Class continued from 9682

Number	Built	Renumbered	BR Dates	Scrap	Notes
9711	06/34 Sdn		-07/65	10/65	m
9712	06/34 Sdn		-09/62	12/62	m
9713	06/34 Sdn		-07/63	09/63	m
9714	06/34 Sdn		-11/61	03/62	m
9715	06/34 Sdn		-07/63	10/63	m
9716	06/34 Sdn		-06/65	10/65	m
9717	06/34 Sdn		-12/62	12/62	m
9718	06/34 Sdn		-05/62	02/63	m
9719	07/34 Sdn		-07/62	10/62	m
9720	11/34 Sdn		-11/61	04/62	m

9721	11/34 Sdn	-06/62	09/62 m	
9722	12/34 Sdn	-07/62	12/62 m	
9723	12/34 Sdn	-07/62	10/62 m	
9724	12/34 Sdn	-01/66	04/66 m	
9725	12/34 Sdn	-12/62	06/63 m	
9726	12/34 Sdn	-06/65	10/65 m	⊠12/64-01/65
9727	12/34 Sdn	-12/62	03/63 m	
9728	12/34 Sdn	-05/62	09/62 m	
9729	12/34 Sdn	-10/64	04/65 m	
9730	01/35 Sdn	-05/64	12/64 m	
9731	01/35 Sdn	-05/63	11/63 m	
9732	01/35 Sdn	-04/64	06/64 m	
9733	01/35 Sdn	-09/65	11/65 m	
9734	01/35 Sdn	-07/64	12/64 m	
9735	01/35 Sdn	-03/61	11/61 m	
9736	01/35 Sdn	-06/61	10/61 m	
9737	01/35 Sdn	-12/60	03/61 m	
9738	01/35 Sdn	-01/62	07/62 m	
9739	01/35 Sdn	-07/61	02/62 m	
9740	01/35 Sdn	-02/62	07/62 m	
9741	01/35 Sdn	-08/62	11/63 m	
9742	01/35 Sdn	-09/64	10/64 m	
9743	01/35 Sdn	-05/64	10/64 m	
9744	01/35 Sdn	-01/63	04/63 m	
9745	02/35 Sdn	-06/61	01/62 m	
9746	02/35 Sdn	-04/64	01/65 m	
9747	02/35 Sdn	-01/63	06/63 m	
9748	02/35 Sdn	-01/64	03/64 m	
9749	02/35 Sdn	-11/60	01/62 m	
9750	05/35 Sdn	-05/62	10/62 m	
9751	05/35 Sdn	-06/61	09/61 m	
9752	05/35 Sdn	-12/63	08/65 m	
9753	05/35 Sdn	-05/65	10/65 m	
9754	06/35 Sdn	-06/65	10/65 m	
9755	06/35 Sdn	-05/63	01/64 m	
9756	06/35 Sdn	-09/62	01/63 m	
9757	06/35 Sdn	-08/62	10/63 m	
9758	06/35 Sdn	-05/62	09/62 m	
9759	06/35 Sdn	-10/62	06/63 m	
9760	08/35 Sdn	-12/63	02/64 m	
9761	09/35 Sdn	-10/62	10/62 m	
9762	09/35 Sdn	-05/61	08/61 m	
9763	09/35 Sdn	-09/63	11/63 m	
9764	09/35 Sdn	-08/63	12/63 m	
9765	09/35 Sdn	-12/61	04/62 m	
9766	10/35 Sdn	-07/64	12/64 m	
9767	10/35 Sdn	-06/61	10/61 m	
9768	10/35 Sdn	-12/64	03/65 m	
9769	10/35 Sdn	-03/63	06/64 m	
9770	03/36 Sdn	-12/63	05/64 m	
9771	03/36 Sdn	-05/61	09/61 m	
9772	03/36 Sdn	-01/59	02/59 m	
9773	03/36 Sdn	-12/65	06/66 m	
9774	03/36 Sdn	-11/66	04/67 m	
9775	03/36 Sdn	-12/62	06/63 m	
9776	03/36 Sdn	-04/66	06/66 m	
9777	03/36 Sdn	-05/64	07/64 m	
9778	04/36 Sdn	-11/64	03/65 m	
9779	04/36 Sdn	-02/64	07/64 m	
9780	06/36 Sdn	-07/65	10/65 m	
9781	06/36 Sdn	-05/61	09/61 m	
9782	07/36 Sdn	-11/64	01/65 m	
9783	07/36 Sdn	-05/62	10/62 m	
9784	07/36 Sdn	-05/63	01/64 m	
9785	05/36 Sdn	-09/62	10/62 m	
9786	05/36 Sdn	-05/64	07/64 m	
9787	05/36 Sdn	-09/64	11/64 m	
9788	05/36 Sdn	-04/64	10/64 m	
9789	05/36 Sdn	-12/65	04/66 m	
9790	05/36 Sdn	-09/65	01/66 m	
9791	05/36 Sdn	-01/64	03/64 m	
9792	05/36 Sdn	-04/64	04/73 m	
9793	06/36 Sdn	-08/63	11/63 m	
9794	06/36 Sdn	-09/64	11/64 m	
9795	09/36 Sdn	-11/60	04/61 m	
9796	09/36 Sdn	-02/65	03/65 m	
9797	09/36 Sdn	-09/62	10/62 m	
9798	09/36 Sdn	-10/64	12/64 m	
9799	09/36 Sdn	-10/63	12/63 m	

Preserved Locomotives

Preserved locomotives which ran in service on BR.

City 3440
4-4-0 GWR 'City' Class Preserved

Power Classification:	Not classified
Introduced:	1903
Designer:	Churchward
Company:	GWR
Weight:	Loco 55t 6cwt Tender 36t 15cwt
Driving Wheel:	6' 8½"
Boiler Pressure:	200psi superheated
Cylinders:	Inside 18" x 26"
Tractive Effort:	17790lbf
Valve Gear:	Stephenson (slide valves)

There were originally twenty locomotives in this class, ten (including 3440) being built in 1903 and ten others being converted from the 'Atbara' class in 1902 onwards. They were double framed locomotives with straight frames and they were all named after Cities. They were subsequently superheated.

3440 was the 2000th locomotive to be built at Swindon, but its main claim to fame was that it was the first locomotive to have been officially recorded as reaching a speed of over 100mph. On 9th May 1904 CITY OF TRURO achieved a speed of 102.3mph on the descent of Wellington Bank, and completed the journey mechanically sound and with cool bearings.

In 1912 the locomotive was renumbered 3717 and it was eventually withdrawn from service in 1931 (the others of the class being withdrawn between 1927 and 1931). On withdrawal it was placed in York Museum for static preservation where it remained until 1957.

Early in 1957 3717 was removed from York museum and overhauled at Swindon. It was repainted in the old 1903 GWR livery style and was renumbered 3440. As such it spent the period until 1961 working enthusiasts specials. When not working special trains 3440 could be seen working ordinary service trains from Didcot Shed, over the Didcot, Newbury & Southampton line.

In 1961 3440 was once again withdrawn and it was retired to Swindon Museum.

Number	Built	Renumbered	BR Dates	Scrap	Notes
3440 § **CITY OF TRURO**	05/03 Sdn	02/57 3717	02/57-05/61		

Miscellaneous Locomotives

Locomotives not allocated a BR number.

S&M 1
0-4-2WT Shropshire & Montgomery

Power Classification:	Not classified
Introduced:	1893
Designer:	Dodman, Lynn
Company:	Shropshire & Montgomery Railway
Weight:	5t 6cwt
Driving Wheel:	2' 0"
Boiler Pressure:	60psi
Cylinders:	Inside 4' x 9"
Tractive Effort:	305lbf
Valve Gear:	

This small engine was originally built as a 2-2-2WT in 1893. It was rebuilt as 0-4-2WT in 1911.

During the Second World War the Shropshire & Montgomery Railway was taken over by the War Department because of the number of armaments factories which it served. In 1950 the entire stock of the S&M Railway (consisting of GAZELLE and three ex-LNWR 'Coal Engines') was taken over by the Western Region of BR and all the locomotives were promptly withdrawn, without being renumbered.

After withdrawal this locomotive was saved and it was sent to the Transportation Centre of the Royal Engineers at Longmoor in Hampshire in 1950, where it was placed on display on the edge of the parade ground.

Number	Built	Renumbered	BR Dates	Scrap	Notes
1 § **GAZELLE**	93 DL		05/50-07/50		

Historical Surveys

Historical Survey of GWR Pannier Tank Engines.

The GWR was a large scale user of small saddle tank engines and later pannier tank engines. They maintained a stock of about 1000 such engines from 1900 onwards. The pannier tanks were as much a part of the day-to-day scene on the Western Region of British Railways as were the larger engines.

Most of the early engines built before grouping started life as saddle tanks. The majority of these were later rebuilt with angular pannier tanks. This also applied to a small number of engines from some of the absorbed South Wales lines.

A list of the main GWR varieties is given below.

The '655', '1501', '1813', '1854' and '2721' classes were all very similar, being originally built as saddle tanks with 4' 7½" wheels and then rebuilt as pannier tanks. The locomotives carried a variety of different cabs and bunkers, including some engines retaining open backed cabs.

The '1901', '2021' and '2181' classes differed from the above classes by having 4' 1½" wheels. They were also originally built as saddle tanks before being rebuilt as pannier tanks, and they also carried a variety of different cabs and bunkers.

The '1361' and '1366' classes were updated versions of old engines which were built for the Cornwall Minerals Railway. They differed from the GWR engines as they were smaller and had outside cylinders. The '1361' class engines were fitted with round-topped boilers and saddle tanks throughout their lives while the '1366' class engines were fitted with Belpaire boilers and pannier tanks.

The '5700' class was the GWR standard type of pannier tank locomotive. There were several different varieties, such as the '6700' class (with steam brakes only for shunting duties) and the '9700' class (fitted with condensing apparatus). Later engines (the '8750' and '6750' classes) were fitted with a modified form of cab.

The '5400', '6400' and '7400' classes were variations of the '5700' class for use on light passenger trains.

The '9400' class was designed for heavy shunting. Developed from the '5700' class, they were in fact a tank engine version of the '2251' class.

Two pannier tank designs were ordered by the GWR but did not in fact appear until BR days. These were the '1500' and '1600' classes. The '1500' class was a short wheelbase heavy shunting design, similar to the '9400' class, but with outside cylinders and Walschaert valve gear. The '1600' class were much smaller engines, being direct descendants of the '1901' and '2021' classes. They were designed for shunting and light branch work and were built to replace the older locomotives.

GWR Collett '7800' 'Manor' class 4-6-0 No 7827 *Lydham Manor* at Ruabon in April 1963.

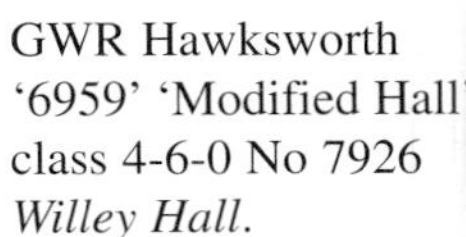
GWR Hawksworth '6959' 'Modified Hall' class 4-6-0 No 7926 *Willey Hall*.

GWR Hawksworth '9400' class 0-6-0PT No 8480 at Worcester in April 1954.

GWR Collett '9000' class 4-4-0 No 9021.

GWR Collett '5700' ('8750') class 0-6-0PT No 9659.

GWR Collett '9700' class 0-6-0PT No 9701 at Old Oak Common in March 1952.

Part 2
Southern Railway Group

Locomotive Origins

The Southern Railway was formed out of three main Railway Companies in 1923. These were:

LBSCR	London, Brighton & South Coast Railway
LSWR	London & South Western Railway
SECR	South Eastern & Chatham Railway (formed from the South Eastern Railway SER, and the London, Chatham & Dover Railway LCD in 1899)

In addition there were some locomotives remaining in BR days from the Plymouth, Devonport & South Western Junction Railway (PDSWR) and the Southampton Dock Company. The East Kent Light Railway (EKR) and the Kent & East Sussex Light Railway (KESR) became part of BR in 1948 and their locomotives became part of the Southern group (although KESR number 4 was withdrawn early in 1948 without being allocated a BR number).

Locomotive Numbering

At grouping the Southern Railway did not at first change the numbers of the locomotives they inherited, simply adding the prefix E (Eastleigh) for LSWR engines, A (Ashford) for SECR engines, and B (Brighton) for LBSCR engines. These prefixes were later abandoned and the numbers were altered by the addition of 1000 to the Ashford engines and 2000 to the Brighton engines. This meant that in BR days all LSWR locomotives carried numbers in the 30000 series, SECR locomotives in the 31000 series and LBSCR locomotives in the 32000 series. Most of the locomotives had been allocated numbers in a haphazard sequence, without locomotives of the same class being numbered together. SR built locomotives filled in some of the gaps in these number series.

As explained in the introduction to this book, each of the main sections (30xxx, 31xxx and 32xxx) starts with a numerical list and following this the classes are grouped together in alphabetical class order.

Bulleid had introduced an unusual number series for his locomotives in which the locomotive number was preceded by a code based on the continental system for showing wheel arrangement. These locomotives were renumbered by BR in the series 33000, 34000 and 35000. Bulleid was constructing a series of unusual locomotives which did not appear until 1949, the Leader class, numbered in the 36000 series. Only one locomotive was actually finished and ran trials. Unfortunately, this experiment was a failure, the remaining locomotives were scrapped without being completed and none of the class officially came into BR stock.

Service locomotives had a separate number series, originally suffixed with an S but later prefixed DS. Isle of Wight locomotives also had a separate series prefixed with a W.

Locomotive Classification

The Southern Railway locomotives were classified according to the pre-grouping classifications. This meant that in some situations two different classes had the same classification, for example the SECR and the LBSCR class 'D1'. In this book the classes are given a numerical suffix to differentiate them when cross-referencing with the appendices. Some SR-built classes had only one class name, but in fact consisted of several sub-classes with differing dimensions (for example the 'N15' 'King Arthurs').

Notes

Locomotives were built after nationalisation to SR designs in the 'BB', 'MN', 'WC' and 'Leader' classes. Many locomotives of classes 'BB', 'MN' and 'WC' were later rebuilt with modified valve gear and the air-smoothed casing removed. Details are shown in the lists.

'T9' number 30120 was restored in 1962 as LSWR 120 to run on special trains. It is listed at the end of the section under Preserved Locomotives.

LSWR Drummond 'M7' class 0-4-4T No 49 (later No 30049).

'USA' class 0-6-0T No 30069 at Southampton Docks in May 1953.

LSWR Adams 'B4' class 0-4-0T No 30094 seen fitted with a spark arrestor at Plymouth Friary in May 1952.

Numerical List 30001-30957

Number	Built	Renumbered	BR Dates	Scrap	Class
30001	04/94 9Elm	1	-07/49	09/49	T1
30002	05/94 9Elm	2	-03/49	03/49	T1
30003	05/94 9Elm	3	-10/48	11/48	T1
30005	06/94 9Elm	5	-01/50	02/50	T1
30007	07/94 9Elm	7	-06/51	06/51	T1
30008	08/94 9Elm	8	-05/49	06/49	T1
30009	08/94 9Elm	9	-07/48	10/48	T1
30010	08/94 9Elm	10	-08/48	10/48	T1
30013	06/95 9Elm	13	-03/49	03/49	T1
30020	11/95 9Elm	20	-06/51	06/51	T1
30021	01/04 9Elm	06/49 21	-03/64	07/64	M7
30022	01/99 9Elm	08/49 22	-05/58	05/58	M7
30023	01/99 9Elm	12/49 23	-10/61	11/61	M7
30024	01/99 9Elm	11/50 24	-03/63	05/63	M7
30025	02/99 9Elm	12/49 25	-05/64	10/64	M7
30026	02/99 9Elm	05/49 26	-04/59	07/59	M7
30027	01/04 9Elm	10/49 27	-11/59	12/59	M7
30028	01/04 9Elm	04/49 28	-09/62	10/62	M7
30029	02/04 9Elm	11/48 29	-05/64	10/64	M7
30030	02/04 9Elm	04/49 30	-10/59	11/59	M7
30031	03/98 9Elm	01/49 31	-01/60	02/61	M7
				01/60➲30128	
30031	11/11 Elh	01/60 30128	-05/63	05/63	M7
30032	03/98 9Elm	04/49 32	-07/63	06/64	M7
30033	04/98 9Elm	01/50 33	-12/62	04/63	M7
30034	04/98 9Elm	07/51 34	-02/63	05/63	M7
30035	04/98 9Elm	12/48 35	-02/63	06/64	M7
30036	05/98 9Elm	09/48 36	-01/64	08/64	M7
30037	05/98 9Elm	03/49 37	-05/58	06/58	M7
30038	05/98 9Elm	08/48 38	-02/58	03/58	M7
30039	05/98 9Elm	09/48 39	-02/63	05/63	M7
30040	06/98 9Elm	03/50 40	-06/61	06/61	M7
30041	03/99 9Elm	08/49 41	-08/57	09/57	M7
30042	03/99 9Elm	52 42	-06/57	06/57	M7
30043	03/99 9Elm	10/49 43	-05/61	07/61	M7
30044	03/99 9Elm	11/50 44	-09/61	10/61	M7
30045	05/05 9Elm	05/49 45	-12/62	03/63	M7
30046	05/05 9Elm	06/49 46	-02/59	04/59	M7
30047	05/05 9Elm	08/50 47	-02/60	02/60	M7
30048	05/05 9Elm	10/49 48	-01/64	07/64	M7
30049	05/05 9Elm	04/51 49	-05/62	06/62	M7
30050	06/05 9Elm	12/50 50	-01/62	02/62	M7
30051	11/05 9Elm	05/49 51	-09/62	11/62	M7
30052	12/05 9Elm	08/49 52	-05/64	10/64	M7
30053 §	12/05 9Elm	11/49 53	-05/64		M7
30054	12/05 9Elm	05/50 54	-01/59	02/59	M7
30055	12/05 9Elm	12/48 55	-09/63	02/64	M7
30056	01/06 9Elm	07/48 56	-12/63	12/63	M7
30057	01/06 9Elm	08/49 57	-06/63	07/63	M7
30058	03/06 9Elm	12/50 58	-09/60	10/60	M7
30059	03/06 9Elm	07/48 59	-02/61	05/62	M7
30060	03/06 9Elm	11/48 60	-07/61	09/61	M7
30061	42 HKP	05/51 61	-11/62	07/67	USA
				10/62➲DS233	
30062	42 V	08/48 62	-11/62	01/68	USA
				12/62➲DS234	
30063	42 V	01/51 63	-05/62	06/62	USA
30064 §	43 V	51 64	-07/67		USA
30065 §	43 V	05/48 65	-10/62		USA
				11/63➲DS237	
30066	42 V	05/48 66	-12/62	08/65	USA
				03/63➲DS235	
30067	42 V	07/48 67	-07/67	02/68	USA
30068	43 V	06/51 68	-03/64	04/64	USA
30069	43 V	08/51 69	-07/67	03/68	USA
30070 §	43 V	08/51 70	-10/62		USA
				08/63➲DS238	
30071	43 V	11/51 71	-07/67	03/68	USA
30072 §	43 V	07/48 72	-07/67		USA
30073	43 V	12/51 73	-01/67	06/67	USA
30074	43 V	11/48 74	-03/63	08/65	USA
				04/63➲DS236	
30081	11/93 9Elm	81	-02/49	62	B4[1]
JERSEY					
30082	06/08 9Elm	05/51 82	-07/57	09/57	B4[1]
30083	06/08 9Elm	05/49 83	-10/59	11/59	B4[1]
30084	06/08 9Elm	08/51 84	-08/59	02/60	B4[1]
30085	10/91 9Elm	85	-02/49	07/49	B4[1]
ALDERNEY					
30086	12/91 9Elm	07/48 86	-02/59	03/59	B4[1]
HAVRE					
30087	12/91 9Elm	52 87	-12/58	01/59	B4[1]
30088	10/92 9Elm	52 88	-07/59	08/59	B4[1]
30089	11/92 9Elm	01/50 89	-03/63	05/64	B4[1]
TROUVILLE					
30090	11/92 9Elm	90	-05/48	02/50	B4[1]
CAEN					
30091	11/92 9Elm	91	-08/48	10/48	B4[1]
30092	12/92 9Elm	92	-04/49	06/61	B4[1]
30093	12/92 9Elm	52 93	-04/60	04/60	B4[1]
ST. MALO					
30094	12/92 9Elm	05/50 94	-03/57	04/57	B4[1]
30095	11/93 9Elm	95	-04/49	10/57	B4[1]
HONFLEUR					
30096 §	11/93 9Elm	12/50 96	-10/63		B4[1]
NORMANDY					
30097	11/93 9Elm	97	-03/49	08/58	B4[1]
BRITTANY					
30098	11/93 9Elm	98	-02/49	08/58	B4[1]
CHERBOURG					
30099	12/93 9Elm	99	-02/49	08/58	B4[1]
30100	12/93 9Elm	100	-02/49	08/58	B4[1]
30101	04/08 9Elm	101	-11/48	01/54	B4[1]
DINAN					
30102 §	12/93 9Elm	12/50 102	-09/63		B4[1]
GRANVILLE					
30103	12/93 9Elm	103	-04/49	08/53	B4[1]
30104	03/05 9Elm	07/48 104	-05/61	06/61	M7
30105	03/05 9Elm	07/48 105	-05/63	06/63	M7
30106	03/05 9Elm	12/48 106	-11/60	10/64	M7
				02/61➲30667	
30107	04/05 9Elm	05/48 107	-05/64	10/64	M7
30108	03/04 9Elm	08/50 108	-05/64	10/64	M7
30109	03/04 9Elm	05/49 109	-06/61	08/61	M7
30110	03/04 9Elm	10/49 110	-05/63	05/63	M7
30111	03/04 9Elm	11/50 111	-01/64	10/64	M7
30112	07/00 9Elm	11/49 112	-02/63	04/63	M7
30113	06/99 9Elm	113	-05/51	03/52	T9
30114	06/99 9Elm	114	-05/51	05/51	T9
30115	07/99 9Elm	05/48 115	-05/51	05/51	T9
30116	07/99 9Elm	116	-05/51	05/51	T9
30117	07/99 9Elm	08/49 117	-07/61	08/61	T9
30118	07/99 9Elm	118	-05/51	05/51	T9
30119	08/99 9Elm	05/48 119	-12/52	02/53	T9
30120 §	08/99 9Elm	01/49 120	-07/63		T9
				03/62➲120	
30121	08/99 9Elm	05/48 121	-04/51	04/51	T9
30122	09/99 9Elm	01/49 122	-04/51	04/51	T9
30123	02/03 9Elm	03/49 123	-06/59	08/59	M7
30124	02/03 9Elm	05/49 124	-05/61	06/61	M7
30125	08/11 Elh	07/49 125	-12/62	02/64	M7
30127	10/11 Elh	02/51 127	-11/63	11/63	M7
30128	11/11 Elh	04/49 128	-01/60	05/63	M7
				01/60➲30031	
30128	03/98 9Elm	01/60 30031	-01/61	02/61	M7
30129	11/11 Elh	11/49 129	-11/63	12/63	M7
30130	02/03 9Elm	08/49 130	-12/59	12/59	M7
30131	11/11 Elh	06/50 131	-11/62	12/62	M7
30132	03/03 9Elm	07/48 132	-11/62	12/62	M7
30133	03/03 9Elm	03/50 133	-03/64	11/65	M7
30134	04/04 9Elm	12/48 134	-03/51	03/51	L11
30135	08/02 9Elm	135	-03/49	03/49	K10
30137	09/02 9Elm	137	-08/49	11/49	K10
30139	10/02 9Elm	139	-09/48	11/48	K10
30140	10/02 9Elm	140	-10/50	06/50	K10
30141	10/02 9Elm	141	-10/49	11/49	K10
30142	11/02 9Elm	142	-01/50	02/50	K10
30143	11/02 9Elm	143	-09/48	11/48	K10
30144	11/02 9Elm	144	-07/49	10/49	K10
30145	12/02 9Elm	145	-10/48	01/49	K10
30146	12/02 9Elm	146	-02/48	48	K10
30147	04/08 9Elm	147	-02/49	08/58	B4[1]
DINARD					
30148	04/04 9Elm	148	-03/52	03/52	L11
30150	12/02 9Elm	150	-02/48	06/48	K10
30151	12/02 9Elm	151	-02/50	03/50	K10
30152	12/02 9Elm	152	-02/49	02/49	K10
30153	12/02 9Elm	153	-03/49	03/49	K10
30154	05/03 9Elm	154	-04/51	04/51	L11
30155	05/03 9Elm	155	-04/51	04/51	L11
30156	06/03 9Elm	07/48 156	-05/51	05/51	L11
30157	06/03 9Elm	157	-03/52	03/52	L11
30158	06/03 9Elm	158	-12/50	12/50	L11
30159	07/03 9Elm	05/48 159	-03/51	03/51	L11
30160	03/00 9Elm	05/48 160	-04/59	05/59	G6
30161	08/03 9Elm	161	-02/50	06/50	L11
30162	04/00 9Elm	52 162	-03/58	03/58	G6
30163	09/03 9Elm	11/49 163	-12/51	12/51	L11
30164	10/03 9Elm	10/49 164	-10/51	10/51	L11
30165	10/03 9Elm	165	-04/51	04/51	L11
30166	04/04 9Elm	07/48 166	-07/50	08/50	L11
30167	05/04 9Elm	167	-09/49	12/49	L11
30168	05/04 9Elm	168	-02/50	03/50	L11
30169	08/04 9Elm	169	-07/49	09/49	L11
30170	08/04 9Elm	170	-06/52	06/52	L11
30171	09/04 9Elm	05/49 171	-09/51	09/51	L11
30172	09/04 9Elm	172	-06/52	06/52	L11
30173	09/04 9Elm	05/48 173	-05/51	05/51	L11
30174	04/06 9Elm	01/51 174	-09/51	09/51	L11
30175	04/06 9Elm	12/48 175	-12/51	12/51	L11
30176	10/93 9Elm	176	-06/48	02/61	B4[1]
GUERNSEY					
30177	12/89 9Elm	05/48 177	-09/59	10/59	O2
30179	03/90 9Elm	05/48 179	-12/59	01/60	O2
30181	05/90 9Elm	181	-04/49	05/67	O2
				04/49➲W35	
30182	05/90 9Elm	12/49 182	-01/60	01/60	O2
30183	05/90 9Elm	07/48 183	-09/61	11/61	O2
30192	11/90 9Elm	11/50 192	-08/61	09/61	O2
30193	11/90 9Elm	07/48 193	-04/62	10/62	O2
30197	06/91 9Elm	07/49 197	-02/53	03/53	O2
30198	04/91 9Elm	198	-04/49	10/65	O2
				04/49➲W36	
30199	06/91 9Elm	10/49 199	-12/62	12/63	O2
30200	07/91 9Elm	05/48 200	-08/62	08/62	O2
30203	08/91 9Elm	03/51 203	-12/55	01/56	O2
30204	09/91 9Elm	11/50 204	-02/53	03/53	O2
30207	12/91 9Elm	08/49 207	-06/57	09/57	O2
30212	05/92 9Elm	07/51 212	-11/59	12/59	O2
30213	05/92 9Elm	05/48 213	-02/53	03/53	O2
30216	06/92 9Elm	01/50 216	-11/57	12/57	O2
30221	09/92 9Elm	07/48 221	-08/53	53	O2
30223	10/92 9Elm	51 223	-10/61	12/61	O2
30224	10/92 9Elm	04/53 224	-02/58	02/58	O2
30225	11/92 9Elm	03/49 225	-12/62	05/63	O2
30229	12/94 9Elm	01/51 229	-03/61	04/61	O2
30230	12/94 9Elm	08/50 230	-08/56	09/56	O2
30231	12/94 9Elm	09/48 231	-03/53	53	O2
30232	01/95 9Elm	08/48 232	-09/59	10/59	O2
30233	01/95 9Elm	06/49 233	-02/58	02/58	O2
30236	03/95 9Elm	10/49 236	-01/60	02/60	O2
30237	09/98 9Elm	237	-03/49	09/60	G6
30238	09/98 9Elm	07/51 238	-11/60	05/63	G6
				11/60➲DS682	
30239	09/98 9Elm	239	-10/48	12/48	G6
30240	10/98 9Elm	240	-03/49	02/50	G6
30241	05/99 9Elm	07/48 241	-07/63	10/63	M7
30242	03/97 9Elm	05/50 242	-06/58	06/58	M7
30243	03/97 9Elm	07/48 243	-09/58	09/58	M7
30244	03/97 9Elm	09/48 244	-10/57	11/57	M7
30245 §	04/97 9Elm	08/49 245	-11/62		M7
30246	04/97 9Elm	08/51 246	-10/61	11/61	M7
30247	04/97 9Elm	10/49 247	-10/61	11/61	M7
30248	05/97 9Elm	12/48 248	-07/61	08/61	M7
30249	05/97 9Elm	08/50 249	-07/63	04/64	M7
30250	05/97 9Elm	06/51 250	-08/57	01/58	M7
30251	06/97 9Elm	03/51 251	-07/63	08/63	M7
30252	06/97 9Elm	01/50 252	-02/59	03/59	M7
30253	06/97 9Elm	51 253	-10/61	12/61	M7
30254	08/97 9Elm	07/48 254	-05/64	10/64	M7
30255	08/97 9Elm	06/51 255	-09/60	10/60	M7
30256	08/97 9Elm	02/51 256	-05/59	07/59	M7
30257	06/94 9Elm	257	-02/49	08/49	G6
30258	08/94 9Elm	06/50 258	-07/61	09/61	G6
30259	09/94 9Elm	259	-12/50	02/51	G6
30260	09/94 9Elm	07/48 260	-11/58	11/58	G6
30261	09/94 9Elm	261	-11/48	12/48	G6
30262	09/94 9Elm	262	-11/49	12/49	G6
30263	10/94 9Elm	263	-09/49	11/49	G6
30264	10/94 9Elm	264	-02/49	02/49	G6
30265	10/94 9Elm	265	-08/49	11/49	G6
30266	10/94 9Elm	04/49 266	-06/60	08/60	G6
30267	10/96 9Elm	267	-02/49	02/49	G6
30268	10/96 9Elm	268	-12/50	02/51	G6
30269	10/96 9Elm	269	-10/49	10/49	G6
30270	11/96 9Elm	07/48 270	-01/59	02/59	G6
30271	12/97 9Elm	271	-09/48	12/49	G6
30272	02/98 9Elm	272	-06/50	60	G6
				06/50➲DS3152	
30273	02/98 9Elm	273	-03/49	12/49	G6
30274	02/98 9Elm	07/48 274	-10/60	11/60	G6
30275	02/98 9Elm	275	-12/49	01/50	G6
30276	03/98 9Elm	08/48 276	-10/49	11/49	G6
30277	04/00 9Elm	04/49 277	-11/61	11/61	G6
30278	05/00 9Elm	278	-12/48	01/49	G6
30279	11/98 9Elm	279	-12/48	01/49	G6
30280	10/99 9Elm	280	-05/51	05/51	T9
30281	11/99 9Elm	04/49 281	-12/51	12/51	T9
30282	11/99 9Elm	12/51 282	-03/54	07/54	T9
30283	12/99 9Elm	03/49 283	-12/57	01/58	T9
30284	12/99 9Elm	07/48 284	-04/58	05/58	T9
30285	01/00 9Elm	12/50 285	-06/58	06/58	T9
30286	01/00 9Elm	05/48 286	-04/51	04/51	T9
30287	01/00 9Elm	01/49 287	-09/61	11/61	T9
30288	02/00 9Elm	07/49 288	-12/60	05/61	T9
30289	02/00 9Elm	03/49 289	-11/59	11/59	T9
30300	12/00 9Elm	01/50 300	-03/61	04/61	T9
30301	12/00 9Elm	10/49 301	-08/59	10/59	T9
30302	12/00 9Elm	01/49 302	-10/52	05/53	T9
30303	12/00 9Elm	303	-05/51	06/51	T9
30304	12/00 9Elm	09/51 304	-09/57	11/57	T9
30305	02/01 9Elm	305	-05/51	05/51	T9
30306	05/01 D	04/49 306	-04/62	05/62	700
30307	02/01 9Elm	11/49 307	-12/52	05/53	T9
30308	05/97 D	01/51 308	-09/61	10/61	700
30309	05/01 D	11/49 309	-12/62	07/63	700
30310	04/01 9Elm	11/48 310	-05/59	07/59	T9
30311	04/01 9Elm	09/51 311	-08/52	52	T9
30312	05/01 9Elm	08/49 312	-03/52	52	T9
30313	09/01 9Elm	06/49 313	-07/61	09/61	T9
30314	09/01 9Elm	314	-05/51	06/51	T9
30315	05/97 D	11/48 315	-12/62	07/63	700
30316	08/97 D	12/48 316	-12/62	05/63	700
30317	05/97 D	08/48 317	-07/61	08/61	700
30318	08/00 9Elm	08/50 318	-12/59	01/60	M7
30319	08/00 9Elm	10/49 319	-01/60	02/60	M7
30320	08/00 9Elm	05/48 320	-02/63	04/64	M7
30321	08/00 9Elm	06/49 321	-09/62	11/62	M7

30322 08/00 9Elm 11/49 322 -11/58 12/58 M7
30323 10/00 9Elm 10/49 323 -12/59 12/59 M7
30324 10/00 9Elm 05/50 324 -09/59 10/59 M7
30325 06/97 D 12/50 325 -12/62 03/63 700
30326 06/97 D 07/49 326 -02/62 02/62 700
30327 06/97 D 09/48 327 -05/61 06/61 700
30328 11/11 Elh 03/50 328 -03/63 06/63 M7
30329 12/01 9Elm 329 -04/50 04/50 K10
30330 09/05 Elh 08/48 330 -05/57 06/57 H15
30331 09/05 Elh 04/49 331 -03/61 05/61 H15
30332 10/05 Elh 05/49 332 -11/56 03/57 H15
30333 10/05 Elh 11/48 333 -10/58 11/58 H15
30334 11/05 Elh 07/48 334 -06/58 07/58 H15
30335 07 Elh 12/48 335 -06/59 09/59 H15
30336 10/01 9Elm 05/50 336 -02/53 05/53 T9
30337 10/01 9Elm 03/49 337 -11/58 01/59 T9
30338 10/01 9Elm 11/50 338 -04/61 06/61 T9
30339 06/97 D 09/48 339 -05/62 05/62 700
30340 12/01 9Elm 340 -06/48 10/48 K10
30341 12/01 9Elm 341 -12/49 01/50 K10
30343 12/01 9Elm 343 -02/48 10/48 K10
30345 01/02 9Elm 345 -09/49 11/49 K10
30346 08/97 D 11/49 346 -11/62 10/63 700
30348 06/00 9Elm 348 -08/48 11/48 G6
30349 06/00 9Elm 11/49 349 -07/61 08/61 G6
30350 08/97 D 05/48 350 -03/62 03/62 700
30351 06/00 9Elm 351 -03/49 03/49 G6
30352 08/97 D 05/50 352 -06/59 07/59 700
30353 06/00 9Elm 353 -03/51 03/51 G6
30354 06/00 9Elm 354 -11/49 12/49 G6
30355 08/97 D 11/50 355 -02/61 04/61 700
30356 10/00 9Elm 05/51 356 -12/58 12/58 M7
30357 10/00 9Elm 12/48 357 -04/61 06/61 M7
30361 06/96 9Elm 361 -02/49 02/49 T1
30363 07/96 9Elm 363 -06/48 10/48 T1
30366 07/96 9Elm 366 -10/48 12/48 T1
30367 07/96 9Elm 367 -06/51 06/51 T1
30368 08/97 D 10/49 368 -12/62 12/63 700
30374 04/03 9Elm 12/48 374 -10/59 10/59 M7
30375 05/03 9Elm 12/48 375 -09/62 10/62 M7
30376 05/03 9Elm 06/49 376 -01/59 03/59 M7
30377 05/03 9Elm 08/48 377 -08/62 09/62 M7
30378 05/03 9Elm 07/49 378 -12/62 04/63 M7
30379 06/04 9Elm 08/50 379 -10/63 11/63 M7
30380 04/02 9Elm 380 -06/49 10/49 K10
30382 04/02 9Elm 05/48 382 -08/50 09/50 K10
30383 04/02 9Elm 383 -05/49 09/49 K10
30384 04/02 9Elm 384 -06/51 08/51 K10
30385 05/02 9Elm 385 -02/49 02/49 K10
30386 05/02 9Elm 386 -08/49 12/49 K10
30389 06/02 9Elm 389 -07/51 08/51 K10
30390 06/02 9Elm 390 -11/50 11/50 K10
30391 07/02 9Elm 391 -10/49 10/49 K10
30392 07/02 9Elm 392 -10/48 01/49 K10
30393 02/02 9Elm 393 -02/49 02/49 K10
30394 03/02 9Elm 394 -05/49 06/49 K10
30395 06/03 9Elm 395 -10/51 10/51 S11
30396 06/03 9Elm 11/48 396 -11/51 11/51 S11
30397 07/03 9Elm 06/49 397 -12/51 12/51 S11
30398 07/03 9Elm 05/49 398 -12/51 12/51 S11
30399 08/03 9Elm 07/48 399 -12/51 12/51 S11
30400 09/03 9Elm 07/48 400 -11/54 03/55 S11
30401 11/03 9Elm 401 -09/51 09/51 S11
30402 11/03 9Elm 11/50 402 -03/51 03/51 S11
30403 12/03 9Elm 06/49 403 -10/51 10/51 S11
30404 12/03 9Elm 08/50 404 -10/51 10/51 S11
30405 09/06 9Elm 03/49 405 -02/51 03/51 L11
30406 09/06 9Elm 11/48 406 -06/51 06/51 L11
30407 05/06 9Elm 05/48 407 -11/50 11/50 L11
30408 05/06 9Elm 408 -03/51 04/51 L11
30409 06/06 9Elm 03/49 409 -06/51 06/51 L11
30410 06/06 9Elm 410 -12/49 02/50 L11
30411 06/06 9Elm 411 -06/52 06/52 L11
30412 07/06 9Elm 412 -12/50 12/50 L11
30413 07/06 9Elm 413 -03/51 03/51 L11
30414 07/06 9Elm 414 -05/51 05/51 L11
30415 06/04 9Elm 01/50 415 -02/53 02/53 L12
30416 06/04 9Elm 05/49 416 -06/51 07/51 L12
30417 06/04 9Elm 07/48 417 -12/51 *52* L12
30418 07/04 9Elm 10/49 418 -06/51 07/51 L12
30419 07/04 9Elm 11/48 419 -12/51 *52* L12
30420 09/04 9Elm 07/48 420 -09/51 09/51 L12
30421 09/04 9Elm 06/49 421 -09/51 09/51 L12
30422 10/04 9Elm 11/50 422 -09/51 09/51 L12
30423 10/04 9Elm 12/48 423 -07/51 08/51 L12
30424 11/04 9Elm 08/50 424 -07/51 08/51 L12
30425 11/04 9Elm 08/48 425 -09/51 09/51 L12
30426 12/04 9Elm 10/49 426 -11/51 11/51 L12
30427 12/04 9Elm 10/49 427 -11/51 11/51 L12
30428 01/05 9Elm 09/48 428 -04/51 *51* L12
30429 01/05 9Elm 07/48 429 -10/51 10/51 L12
30430 02/05 9Elm 430 -03/51 04/51 L12
30431 02/05 9Elm 05/48 431 -10/51 10/51 L12
30432 02/05 9Elm 05/48 432 -10/51 *10/51* L12
30433 03/05 9Elm 11/50 433 -12/51 12/51 L12
30434 03/05 9Elm 12/48 434 -03/55 08/55 L12
30435 10/06 9Elm 435 -12/49 12/49 L11
30436 11/06 9Elm 436 -07/51 08/51 L11
30437 12/06 9Elm 437 -06/52 06/52 L11
30438 03/07 9Elm 12/48 438 -10/51 10/51 L11
30439 03/07 9Elm 439 -05/49 08/49 L11
30440 04/07 9Elm 440 -05/49 08/49 L11
30441 05/07 9Elm 441 -04/51 05/51 L11
30442 05/07 9Elm 09/48 442 -12/51 12/51 L11
30443 04/11 Elh 443 -05/49 11/49 T14
30444 05/11 Elh 444 -02/50 03/50 T14
30445 06/11 Elh 445 -11/48 01/49 T14
30446 07/11 Elh 08/48 446 -05/51 05/51 T14
30447 07/11 Elh 11/49 447 -12/49 12/49 T14
30448 05/25 Elh 07/48 448 -08/60 09/60 N15
SIR TRISTRAM
30449 06/25 Elh 10/49 449 -12/59 12/59 N15
SIR TORRE
30450 06/25 Elh 10/49 450 -09/60 09/60 N15
SIR KAY
30451 06/25 Elh 07/48 451 -06/62 06/62 N15
SIR LAMORAK
30452 07/25 Elh 05/48 452 -08/59 10/59 N15
SIR MELIAGRANCE
30453 02/25 Elh 02/50 453 -07/61 10/61 N15
KING ARTHUR
30454 03/25 Elh 04/49 454 -10/58 11/58 N15
QUEEN GUINEVERE
30455 03/25 Elh 05/48 455 -04/59 05/59 N15
SIR LAUNCELOT
30456 04/25 Elh 11/48 456 -05/60 05/60 N15
SIR GALAHAD
30457 04/25 Elh 08/49 457 -05/61 07/61 N1
SIR BEDIVERE
30458 07/90 HL 10/49 3458 -06/54 09/54 0458
IRONSIDE
30459 05/12 Elh 459 -11/48 01/49 T14
30460 02/12 Elh 460 -11/48 01/49 T14
30461 04/12 Elh 05/48 461 -06/51 06/51 T14
30462 05/12 Elh 462 -02/50 03/50 T14
30463 02/12 Elh 463 -12/51 12/51 D15
30464 05/12 Elh 05/50 464 -11/54 *03/55* D15
30465 06/12 Elh 06/50 465 -01/56 *02/56* D15
30466 07/12 Elh 08/49 466 -10/52 02/53 D15
30467 07/12 Elh 05/49 467 -09/55 *10/55* D15
30468 09/12 Elh 05/48 468 -03/52 *04/52* D15
30469 10/12 Elh 05/48 469 -12/51 *01/52* D15
30470 11/12 Elh 07/48 470 -12/52 01/53 D15
30471 11/12 Elh 12/48 471 -03/54 08/54 D15
30472 12/12 Elh 12/48 472 -03/52 *03/52* D15
30473 02/24 Elh 01/50 473 -07/59 08/59 H15
30474 02/24 Elh 03/49 474 -04/60 06/60 H15
30475 03/24 Elh 11/48 475 -12/61 03/62 H15
30476 04/24 Elh 07/48 476 -12/61 03/62 H15
30477 05/24 Elh 09/48 477 -07/59 08/59 H15
30478 06/24 Elh 12/48 478 -04/59 04/59 H15
30479 11/11 Elh 04/49 479 -04/61 05/61 M7
30480 11/11 Elh 12/48 480 -05/64 10/64 M7
30481 11/11 Elh 11/50 481 -05/59 06/59 M7
30482 03/14 Elh 11/50 482 -05/59 08/59 H15
30483 04/14 Elh 08/50 483 -06/57 06/57 H15
30484 05/14 Elh 11/48 484 -05/59 07/59 H15
30485 06/14 Elh 07/48 485 -04/55 07/55 H15
30486 01/14 Elh 08/48 486 -07/59 09/59 H15
30487 02/14 Elh 07/48 487 -11/57 12/57 H15
30488 04/14 Elh 03/49 488 -04/59 05/59 H15
30489 06/14 Elh 05/48 489 -01/61 03/61 H15
30490 07/14 Elh 12/48 490 -07/55 08/55 H15
30491 07/14 Elh 04/49 491 -01/61 03/61 H15
30492 07/21 Elh 12/48 492 -02/59 02/59 G16
30493 07/21 Elh 09/48 493 -12/59 01/60 G16
30494 08/21 Elh 11/50 494 -12/62 03/63 G16
30495 08/21 Elh 05/48 495 -12/62 01/63 G16
30496 05/21 Elh 12/48 496 -06/63 08/63 S15
30497 03/20 Elh 12/48 497 -07/63 03/64 S15
30498 04/20 Elh *51* 498 -06/63 08/63 S15
30499 § 05/20 Elh 01/49 499 -01/64 S15
30500 05/20 Elh 09/48 500 -06/63 10/63 S15
30501 06/20 Elh 12/48 501 -06/63 08/63 S15
30502 07/20 Elh 08/50 502 -11/62 03/63 S15
30503 08/20 Elh 01/50 503 -06/63 10/63 S15
30504 09/20 Elh 11/48 504 -11/62 01/63 S15
30505 10/20 Elh 08/48 505 -11/62 12/62 S15
30506 § 10/20 Elh 08/49 506 -01/64 S15
30507 11/20 Elh 03/50 507 -12/63 03/64 S15
30508 12/20 Elh 07/49 508 -12/63 01/64 S15
30509 12/20 Elh 05/48 509 -07/63 03/64 S15
30510 01/21 Elh 04/49 510 -06/63 09/63 S15
30511 01/21 Elh 06/49 511 -07/63 01/64 S15
30512 02/21 Elh 05/49 512 -03/64 01/65 S15
30513 03/21 Elh 11/49 513 -03/63 06/63 S15
30514 03/21 Elh 09/48 514 -07/63 03/64 S15
30515 04/21 Elh 12/48 515 -07/63 01/64 S15
30516 11/21 Elh 10/49 516 -11/62 10/63 H16
30517 11/21 Elh 07/48 517 -11/62 06/63 H16
30518 12/21 Elh 11/50 518 -11/62 04/64 H16
30519 01/22 Elh 04/49 519 -11/62 10/63 H16
30520 02/22 Elh 12/48 520 -11/62 10/63 H16
30521 07/24 Elh 07/48 521 -12/61 01/62 H15
30522 07/24 Elh 01/49 522 -10/61 11/61 H15
30523 09/24 Elh 07/48 523 -09/61 02/62 H15
30524 09/24 Elh 01/49 524 -02/61 06/61 H15
30530 01/38 Elh 09/48 530 -12/64 05/65 Q
30531 06/38 Elh 01/49 531 -07/64 12/64 Q
30532 06/38 Elh 12/50 532 -01/64 12/64 Q
30533 07/38 Elh 08/49 533 -03/63 05/63 Q
30534 09/38 Elh 07/48 534 -12/62 05/64 Q
30535 09/38 Elh 12/48 535 -04/65 01/66 Q
30536 10/38 Elh 08/50 536 -01/64 07/64 Q
30537 10/38 Elh 11/48 537 -12/62 05/64 Q
30538 11/38 Elh 12/48 538 -07/63 11/64 Q
30539 12/38 Elh 12/48 539 -01/63 06/63 Q
30540 01/39 Elh 04/49 540 -11/62 05/64 Q
30541 § 01/39 Elh 09/48 541 -11/64 Q
30542 03/39 Elh 05/48 542 -12/64 05/65 Q
30543 03/39 Elh 05/48 543 -12/64 05/65 Q
30544 04/39 Elh 06/49 544 -01/64 07/64 Q
30545 06/39 Elh 04/49 545 -04/65 09/65 Q
30546 06/39 Elh 01/50 546 -05/64 09/64 Q
30547 07/39 Elh 08/49 547 -01/64 07/64 Q
30548 08/39 Elh 05/49 548 -03/65 07/65 Q
30549 09/39 Elh 04/49 549 -07/63 04/64 Q
30564 11/85 N 08/51 3029 -04/58 04/58 0395
30565 11/85 N 11/48 3083 -02/53 11/53 0395
30566 12/85 N 03/49 3101 -02/59 04/59 0395
30567 03/83 N 08/48 3154 -09/59 10/59 0395
30568 03/83 N 11/49 3155 -04/58 04/58 0395
30569 05/83 N 10/49 3163 -06/56 *56* 0395
30570 05/83 N 07/48 3167 -12/56 *02/57* 0395
30571 12/81 N 07/48 3397 -07/53 11/53 0395
30572 01/82 N 11/48 3400 -01/57 03/57 0395
30573 04/83 N 11/50 3433 -11/56 *01/57* 0395
30574 04/83 N 11/50 3436 -01/57 03/57 0395
30575 05/83 N 01/50 3439 -12/58 01/59 0395
30576 05/83 N 05/48 3440 -12/50 *01/51* 0395
30577 05/83 N 05/51 3441 -02/56 *02/56* 0395
30578 05/83 N 07/49 3442 -08/57 10/57 0395
30579 10/85 N 01/49 3496 -01/56 *01/56* 0395
30580 12/85 N 07/48 3506 -06/57 06/57 0395
30581 12/85 N 12/48 3509 -03/53 05/53 0395
30582 09/85 RS 04/49 3125 -07/61 03/62 0415
30583 § 03/85 N 10/49 3488 -07/61 0415
30584 12/85 D 05/48 3520 -02/61 12/61 0415
30585 § 05/74 BP 12/48 3314 -12/62 0298
30586 11/75 BP 05/48 3329 -12/62 03/64 0298
30587 § 06/74 BP 07/48 3298 -12/62 0298
30588 11/06 9Elm 12/50 3741 -12/57 01/58 C14
30589 01/07 9Elm 08/48 3744 -06/57 *08/57* C14
30618 12/92 N 618 -02/48 06/48 A12
30627 01/93 N 627 -12/48 01/49 A12
30629 01/93 N 629 -12/48 01/49 A12
30636 02/93 N 636 -10/48 12/48 A12
30667 09/97 9Elm 11/50 667 -02/61 02/61 M7
30667 03/05 9Elm 02/61 30106 -05/64 10/64 M7
30668 09/97 9Elm 11/49 668 -09/61 12/61 M7
30669 09/97 9Elm 02/50 669 -07/61 09/61 M7
30670 10/97 9Elm 03/51 670 -03/63 05/63 M7
30671 10/97 9Elm 08/49 671 -07/59 08/59 M7
30672 10/97 9Elm 672 -05/48 05/48 M7
30673 11/97 9Elm 01/49 673 -08/60 08/60 M7
30674 11/97 9Elm 03/49 674 -08/61 10/61 M7
30675 11/97 9Elm 08/49 675 -03/58 03/58 M7
30676 11/97 9Elm *49* 676 -07/61 08/61 M7
30687 03/97 D 08/48 687 -09/60 10/60 700
30688 03/97 D 07/48 688 -09/57 10/57 700
30689 03/97 D 11/48 689 -11/62 02/64 700
30690 03/97 D 08/50 690 -12/62 02/63 700
30691 03/97 D 12/51 691 -07/61 09/61 700
30692 03/97 D 07/48 692 -01/62 03/62 700
30693 03/97 D *51* 693 -07/61 07/61 700
30694 03/97 D 08/48 694 -06/61 07/61 700
30695 03/97 D 08/49 695 -12/62 05/63 700
30696 03/97 D 07/48 696 -08/61 09/61 700
30697 04/97 D 11/50 697 -11/62 03/64 700
30698 04/97 D 04/51 698 -05/62 05/62 700
30699 05/97 D 11/50 699 -07/61 12/61 700
30700 05/97 D 05/48 700 -11/62 04/64 700
30701 05/97 D 02/50 701 -07/61 10/61 700
30702 01/99 D 08/48 702 -10/59 10/59 T9
30703 01/99 D 07/49 703 -10/52 *12/52* T9
30704 01/99 D 03/50 704 -10/51 10/51 T9
30705 01/99 D 05/49 705 -01/58 02/58 T9
30706 01/99 D 08/49 706 -05/59 07/59 T9
30707 06/99 D 05/48 707 -03/61 05/61 T9
30708 06/99 D 07/48 708 -12/57 01/58 T9
30709 06/99 D 05/49 709 -07/61 09/61 T9
30710 06/99 D 08/49 710 -03/59 04/59 T9
30711 06/99 D 05/49 711 -08/59 09/59 T9
30712 06/99 D 07/49 712 -11/58 12/58 T9
30713 06/99 D 713 -04/51 04/51 T9
30714 06/99 D 04/49 714 -04/51 04/51 T9
30715 06/99 D *49* 715 -07/61 08/61 T9
30716 06/99 D 04/49 716 -10/51 10/51 T9
30717 09/99 D 04/49 717 -07/61 08/61 T9
30718 09/99 D 05/48 718 -03/61 04/61 T9
30719 09/99 D 06/49 719 -03/61 04/61 T9
30721 09/99 D 07/49 721 -01/58 01/58 T9
30722 09/99 D 722 -04/51 *08/54* T9
30723 09/99 D 723 -06/51 06/51 T9

30724	09/99	D	07/49	724	-05/59	06/59	T9	
30725	10/99	D	09/48	725	-12/52	01/53	T9	
30726	10/99	D	04/49	726	-08/59	11/59	T9	
30727	10/99	D	02/50	727	-09/58	10/58	T9	
30728	12/99	D	12/50	728	-10/56	10/56	T9	
30729	12/99	D	12/48	729	-03/61	04/61	T9	
30730	12/99	D	08/49	730	-08/57	10/57	T9	
30731	12/99	D		731	-05/51	06/51	T9	
30732	12/99	D	07/48	732	-10/59	10/59	T9	
30733	11/01	D	07/49	733	-06/52	52	T9	
30736	09/18	Elh	03/49	736	-10/56	56	N15	EXCALIBUR
30737	10/18	Elh	07/49	737	-08/56	08/56	N15	KING UTHER
30738	12/19	Elh	05/49	738	-03/58	03/58	N15	KING PELLINORE
30739	02/19	Elh	03/49	739	-05/57	05/57	N15	KING LEODEGRANCE
30740	04/19	Elh	11/48	740	-12/55	05/56	N15	MERLIN
30741	05/19	Elh	12/48	741	-02/56	02/56	N15	JOYOUS GARD
30742	06/19	Elh	11/48	742	-02/57	02/57	N15	CAMELOT
30743	08/19	Elh	06/49	743	-10/55	11/55	N15	LYONNESSE
30744	09/19	Elh	05/48	744	-01/56	01/56	N15	MAID OF ASTOLAT
30745	11/19	Elh	12/48	745	-02/56	02/56	N15	TINTAGEL
30746	06/22	Elh	11/50	746	-11/55	11/55	N15	PENDRAGON
30747	07/22	Elh	05/50	747	-10/56	02/57	N15	ELAINE
30748	08/22	Elh	12/48	748	-09/57	10/57	N15	VIVIEN
30749	09/22	Elh	12/48	749	-06/57	07/57	N15	ISEULT
30750	10/22	Elh	12/48	750	-07/57	08/57	N15	MORGAN LE FAY
30751	11/22	Elh	07/48	751	-06/57	07/57	N15	ETARRE
30752	12/22	Elh	09/48	752	-12/55	01/56	N15	LINETTE
30753	01/23	Elh	05/48	753	-03/57	03/57	N15	MELISANDE
30754	02/23	Elh	07/48	754	-02/53	02/53	N15	THE GREEN KNIGHT
30755	03/23	Elh	49	755	-05/57	05/57	N15	THE RED KNIGHT
30756	07	HL		756	-11/51	11/51	756	A. S. HARRIS
30757	07	HL	04/49	757	-12/57	12/57	757	EARL OF MOUNT EDGCUMBE
30758	07	HL	11/50	758	-12/56	02/57	757	LORD ST. LEVAN
30763	05/25	NB	08/50	763	-09/60	10/60	N15	SIR BORS DE GANIS
30764	05/25	NB	03/49	764	-07/61	08/61	N15	SIR GAWAIN
30765	05/25	NB	04/49	765	-09/62	11/62	N15	SIR GARETH
30766	05/25	NB	01/49	766	-12/58	01/59	N15	SIR GERAINT
30767	06/25	NB	12/48	767	-06/59	09/59	N15	SIR VALENCE
30768	06/25	NB	11/48	768	-10/61	01/62	N15	SIR BALIN
30769	06/25	NB	04/51	769	-02/60	02/60	N15	SIR BALAN
30770	06/25	NB	07/51	770	-11/62	02/63	N15	SIR PRIANIUS
30771	06/25	NB	06/50	771	-03/61	05/61	N15	SIR SAGRAMORE
30772	06/25	NB	05/48	772	-09/61	12/61	N15	SIR PERCIVALE
30773	06/25	NB	07/48	773	-02/62	04/62	N15	SIR LAVAINE
30774	06/25	NB	04/49	774	-01/60	01/60	N15	SIR GAHERIS
30775	06/25	NB	10/49	775	-02/60	02/60	N15	SIR AGRAVAINE
30776	06/25	NB	07/49	776	-01/59	02/59	N15	SIR GALAGARS
30777 §	06/25	NB	05/48	777	-10/61		N15	SIR LAMIEL
30778	06/25	NB	11/49	778	-05/59	09/59	N15	SIR PELLEAS
30779	07/25	NB	11/48	779	-07/59	09/59	N15	SIR COLGREVANCE
30780	07/25	NB	01/50	780	-07/59	09/59	N15	SIR PERSANT
30781	07/25	NB	04/49	781	-05/62	05/62	N15	SIR AGLOVALE
30782	07/25	NB	05/48	782	-09/62	09/62	N15	SIR BRIAN
30783	08/25	NB	05/48	783	-02/61	06/61	N15	SIR GILLEMERE
30784	08/25	NB	05/48	784	-10/59	11/59	N15	SIR NEROVENS
30785	08/25	NB	08/48	785	-10/59	11/59	N15	SIR MADOR DE LA PORTE
30786	08/25	NB	09/48	786	-08/59	10/59	N15	SIR LIONEL
30787	09/25	NB	04/49	787	-02/59	05/59	N15	SIR MENADEUKE
30788	09/25	NB	11/48	788	-02/62	02/62	N15	SIR URRE OF THE MOUNT
30789	09/25	NB	08/48	789	-12/59	01/60	N15	SIR GUY
30790	09/25	NB	09/48	790	-10/61	01/62	N15	SIR VILLIARS
30791	09/25	NB	12/48	791	-05/60	05/60	N15	SIR UWAINE
30792	10/25	NB	03/50	792	-02/59	03/59	N15	SIR HERVIS DE REVEL
30793	03/26	Elh	11/48	793	-08/62	09/62	N15	SIR ONTZLAKE
30794	03/26	Elh	01/49	794	-08/60	09/60	N15	SIR ECTOR DE MARIS
30795	04/26	Elh	04/49	795	-07/62	08/62	N15	SIR DINADAN
30796	05/26	Elh	02/50	796	-02/62	04/62	N15	SIR DODINAS LE SAVAGE
30797	06/26	Elh	01/49	797	-06/59	06/59	N15	SIR BLAMOR DE GANIS
30798	06/26	Elh	11/49	798	-06/62	07/62	N15	SIR HECTIMERE
30799	07/26	Elh	05/48	799	-02/61	04/61	N15	SIR IRONSIDE
30800	09/26	Elh	10/49	800	-08/61	09/61	N15	SIR MELEAUS DE LILE
30801	10/26	Elh	07/49	801	-04/59	06/59	N15	SIR MELIOT DE LOGRES
30802	10/26	Elh	07/48	802	-07/61	08/61	N15	SIR DURNORE
30803	11/26	Elh	07/48	803	-08/61	09/61	N15	SIR HARRY LE FISE LAKE
30804	12/26	Elh	12/48	804	-02/62	03/62	N15	SIR CADOR OF CORNWALL
30805	01/27	Elh	09/48	805	-11/59	12/59	N15	SIR CONSTANTINE
30806	01/27	Elh	09/48	806	-04/61	06/61	N15	SIR GALLERON
30823	03/27	Elh	09/48	823	-11/64	02/65	S15	
30824	03/27	Elh	01/50	824	-09/65	12/65	S15	
30825 §	04/27	Elh	05/48	825	-01/64		S15	
30826	05/27	Elh	05/49	826	-11/62	01/64	S15	
30827	06/27	Elh	04/49	827	-01/64	02/64	S15	
30828 §	07/27	Elh	11/49	828	-01/64		S15	
30829	07/27	Elh	12/48	829	-11/63	01/64	S15	
30830 §	08/27	Elh	03/50	830	-07/64		S15	
30831	09/27	Elh	04/49	831	-11/63	12/63	S15	
30832	10/27	Elh	09/48	832	-01/64	02/64	S15	
30833	11/27	Elh	12/48	833	-05/65	04/66	S15	
30834	11/27	Elh	03/49	834	-11/64	03/65	S15	
30835	12/27	Elh	09/48	835	-11/64	03/65	S15	
30836	12/27	Elh	10/49	836	-06/64	10/64	S15	
30837	01/28	Elh	05/48	837	-09/65	09/66	S15	
30838	05/36	Elh	08/49	838	-09/65	05/66	S15	
30839	05/36	Elh	11/48	839	-09/65	05/66	S15	
30840	06/36	Elh	08/49	840	-09/64	11/64	S15	
30841 §	07/36	Elh	09/48	841	-01/64		S15	
30842	08/36	Elh	08/49	842	-09/65	11/65	S15	
30843	09/36	Elh	07/48	843	-09/64	11/64	S15	
30844	10/36	Elh	08/50	844	-06/64	01/65	S15	
30845	10/36	Elh	05/48	845	-07/63	09/63	S15	
30846	11/36	Elh	05/48	846	-01/63	02/63	S15	
30847 §	12/36	Elh	08/48	847	-01/64		S15	
30850 §	08/26	Elh	12/48	850	-08/62		LN	LORD NELSON
30851	06/28	Elh	03/49	851	-12/61	05/62	LN	SIR FRANCIS DRAKE
30852	07/28	Elh	04/49	852	-02/62	03/62	LN	SIR WALTER RALEIGH
30853	09/28	Elh	12/48	853	-02/62	04/62	LN	SIR RICHARD GRENVILLE
30854	10/28	Elh	06/49	854	-09/61	10/61	LN	HOWARD OF EFFINGHAM
30855	11/28	Elh	03/49	855	-09/61	02/62	LN	ROBERT BLAKE
30856	11/28	Elh	05/48	856	-09/62	11/62	LN	LORD ST. VINCENT
30857	12/28	Elh	11/49	857	-09/62	10/62	LN	LORD HOWE
30858	01/29	Elh	07/48	858	-08/61	11/61	LN	LORD DUNCAN
30859	03/29	Elh	03/49	859	-12/61	12/61	LN	LORD HOOD
30860	04/29	Elh	12/48	860	-08/62	08/62	LN	LORD HAWKE
30861	09/29	Elh	05/48	861	-10/62	11/62	LN	LORD ANSON
30862	10/29	Elh	07/48	862	-10/62	11/62	LN	LORD COLLINGWOOD
30863	10/29	Elh	51	863	-02/62	03/62	LN	LORD RODNEY
30864	11/29	Elh	05/48	864	-01/62	03/62	LN	SIR MARTIN FROBISHER
30865	11/29	Elh	07/48	865	-05/61	08/61	LN	SIR JOHN HAWKINS
30900	03/30	Elh	05/48	900	-02/62	03/62	V	ETON
30901	03/30	Elh	11/48	901	-12/62	08/63	V	WINCHESTER
30902	04/30	Elh	01/49	902	-12/62	04/64	V	WELLINGTON
30903	04/30	Elh	05/48	903	-12/62	02/64	V	CHARTERHOUSE
30904	05/30	Elh	07/48	904	-07/61	09/61	V	LANCING
30905	05/30	Elh	10/49	905	-12/61	02/62	V	TONBRIDGE
30906	06/30	Elh	11/49	906	-12/62	04/63	V	SHERBORNE
30907	07/30	Elh	08/48	907	-09/61	09/61	V	DULWICH
30908	07/30	Elh	04/49	908	-09/61	10/61	V	WESTMINSTER
30909	07/30	Elh	01/49	909	-02/62	03/62	V	ST. PAUL'S
30910	11/32	Elh	12/48	910	-11/61	01/62	V	MERCHANT TAYLORS
30911	12/32	Elh	08/49	911	-12/62	09/63	V	DOVER
30912	12/32	Elh	04/49	912	-11/62	01/63	V	DOWNSIDE
30913	12/32	Elh	09/48	913	-01/62	02/62	V	CHRIST'S HOSPITAL
30914	12/32	Elh	05/50	914	-07/61	09/61	V	EASTBOURNE
30915	05/33	Elh	03/49	915	-12/62	11/63	V	BRIGHTON
30916	12/33	Elh	12/48	916	-12/62	09/63	V	WHITGIFT
30917	06/33	Elh	05/48	917	-11/62	04/63	V	ARDINGLY
30918	06/33	Elh	10/49	918	-10/61	11/61	V	HURSTPIERPOINT
30919	06/33	Elh	07/48	919	-02/61	03/61	V	HARROW
30920	10/33	Elh	11/48	920	-11/61	01/62	V	RUGBY
30921	11/33	Elh	03/50	921	-12/62	05/64	V	SHREWSBURY
30922	12/33	Elh	01/49	922	-11/61	01/62	V	MARLBOROUGH
30923	12/33	Elh	09/48	923	-12/62	08/63	V	BRADFIELD
30924	12/33	Elh	01/49	924	-01/62	01/62	V	HAILEYBURY
30925 §	04/34	Elh	05/50	925	-12/62		V	CHELTENHAM
30926 §	05/34	Elh	05/48	926	-12/62		V	REPTON
30927	06/34	Elh	11/49	927	-01/62	03/62	V	CLIFTON
30928 §	06/34	Elh	07/48	928	-11/62		V	STOWE
30929	07/34	Elh	01/49	929	-12/62	03/63	V	MALVERN
30930	12/34	Elh	07/48	930	-12/62	04/64	V	RADLEY
30931	12/34	Elh	11/48	931	-09/61	10/61	V	KING'S-WIMBLEDON
30932	02/35	Elh	07/48	932	-02/61	08/61	V	BLUNDELL'S
30933	02/35	Elh	07/48	933	-11/61	12/61	V	KING'S-CANTERBURY
30934	03/35	Elh	08/48	934	-12/62	08/63	V	ST. LAWRENCE
30935	05/35	Elh	12/48	935	-12/62	05/64	V	SEVENOAKS
30936	06/35	Elh	07/48	936	-12/62	10/63	V	CRANLEIGH
30937	06/35	Elh	09/48	937	-12/62	06/63	V	EPSOM
30938	07/35	Elh	04/49	938	-07/61	09/61	V	ST. OLAVE'S
30939	07/35	Elh	05/48	939	-06/61	09/61	V	LEATHERHEAD
30948	08/17	KS		EKR 4	-02/49	02/49	EKR	
30949	05/05	HL		949	-03/50	03/50	KESR	HECATE
30950	04/29	Bton	07/48	950	-11/62	12/62	Z	
30951	05/29	Bton	11/48	951	-11/62	03/64	Z	
30952	05/29	Bton	06/49	952	-11/62	01/65	Z	
30953	06/29	Bton	02/50	953	-12/62	01/63	Z	
30954	09/29	Bton	04/49	954	-12/62	02/63	Z	
30955	07/29	Bton	04/49	955	-12/62	04/63	Z	
30956	03/29	Bton	07/48	956	-12/62	01/63	Z	
30957	08/29	Bton	05/50	957	-11/62	12/62	Z	

A12 30618-30636, DS3191
0-4-2 LSWR Adams

Power Classification:	1MT
Introduced:	1887-1895
Designer:	Adams
Company:	LSWR
Weight:	Loco 42t 7cwt Tender 33t 4cwt
Driving Wheel:	6' 0"
Boiler Pressure:	160psi
Cylinders:	Inside 18" x 26"
Tractive Effort:	15910lbf
Valve Gear:	Stephenson (slide valves)

The London & South Western Railway was the largest user of 0-4-2 tender engines apart from the Glasgow & South Western Railway. In 1887 Adams introduced his 'A12' 'Jubilee' class. Ninety engines were built and they were to be found over all the system on all kinds of trains, sometimes with a considerable turn of speed. They were withdrawn gradually from 1928. Only four survived nationalisation, but they were withdrawn in 1948 without being renumbered.

No. 612, which had been withdrawn in June 1946, was retained at Eastleigh to supply steam when pacific boilers were being tested during welding repairs. It was renumbered DS3191 in 1951.

Year End Totals: 'A12' class

'47	'48	'49	'50	'51	'52	'53	'54	'55	'56	'57	'58	'59	'60	'61	'62	'63	'64	'65	'66	'67
4																				

Number	*Built*	*Renumbered*	*BR Dates*	*Scrap*	*Notes*
30618	12/92 N	618	-02/48	06/48	
30627	01/93 N	627	-12/48	01/49	
30629	01/93 N	629	-12/48	01/49	
30636	02/93 N	636	-10/48	12/48	

Class continued with DS3191 (Service Locomotives)

B4 [1] 30081-30103, 30147, 30176
0-4-0T LSWR Adams/Drummond

Power Classification:	0F reclassified 1F in 1953
Introduced:	a 1891-1893 d 1908
Designer:	a Adams d Drummond
Company:	LSWR
Weight:	a 33t 9cwt d 32t 18cwt
Driving Wheel:	3' 9¾"
Boiler Pressure:	140psi
Cylinders:	Outside 16" x 22"
Tractive Effort:	14650lbf
Valve Gear:	Stephenson (slide valves)

These dock shunting engines were designed by Adams in 1891 and twenty were built up to 1893. Dugald Drummond built a further five engines in 1908 which had 'lock-up' safety valves on the domes and smaller diameter boilers. These were classified 'K14', but they were later re-classified as 'B4'. Over time the boilers of the surviving locomotives were interchanged (for example 30088 later carried a Drummond boiler).

The fourteen named locomotives worked at Southampton Docks until replaced from 1947 by the 'USA' tanks. As they were transferred away from Southampton their names were removed.

A large number of these engines were sold for further industrial use after withdrawal, namely 81, 92, 95, 30096, 97, 98, 99, 100, 101, 103, 147 and 176.

a Adams built locomotives ('B4' class).

d Drummond built locomotives (originally 'K14' class).

Year End Totals: 'B4 [1]' class

'47	'48	'49	'50	'51	'52	'53	'54	'55	'56	'57	'58	'59	'60	'61	'62	'63	'64	'65	'66	'67
25	21	11	11	11	11	11	11	11	11	9	8	4	3	3	3					

Number	*Built*	*Renumbered*	*BR Dates*	*Scrap*	*Notes*
30081	11/93 9Elm	81	-02/49	62	a
JERSEY					
30082	06/08 9Elm	05/51 82	-07/57	09/57	d
30083	06/08 9Elm	05/49 83	-10/59	11/59	d
30084	06/08 9Elm	08/51 84	-08/59	02/60	d
30085	10/91 9Elm	85	-02/49	07/49	a
ALDERNEY					
30086	12/91 9Elm	07/48 86	-02/59	03/59	a
HAVRE					
30087	12/91 9Elm	*52* 87	-12/58	01/59	a
30088	10/92 9Elm	*52* 88	-07/59	08/59	a
30089	11/92 9Elm	01/50 89	-03/63	05/64	a
TROUVILLE					
30090	11/92 9Elm	90	-05/48	02/50	a
CAEN					
30091	11/92 9Elm	91	-08/48	10/48	a
30092	12/92 9Elm	92	-04/49	06/61	a
30093	12/92 9Elm	*52* 93	-04/60	04/60	a
ST. MALO					
30094	12/92 9Elm	05/50 94	-03/57	04/57	a
30095	11/93 9Elm	95	-04/49	10/57	a
HONFLEUR					
30096 §	11/93 9Elm	12/50 96	-10/63		a
NORMANDY					
30097	11/93 9Elm	97	-03/49	08/58	a
BRITTANY					
30098	11/93 9Elm	98	-02/49	08/58	a
CHERBOURG					
30099	12/93 9Elm	99	-02/49	08/58	a
30100	12/93 9Elm	100	-02/49	08/58	a
30101	04/08 9Elm	101	-11/48	01/54	d
DINAN					
30102 §	12/93 9Elm	12/50 102	-09/63		a
GRANVILLE					
30103	12/93 9Elm	103	-04/49	08/53	a
30147	04/08 9Elm	147	-02/49	08/58	d
DINARD					
30176	10/93 9Elm	176	-06/48	02/61	a
GUERNSEY					

C14 30588-30589, 77S
0-4-0T LSWR Drummond

Power Classification:	0F reclassified 0P in 1952
Introduced:	1906-1907 rebuilt by Urie 1913-1923
Designer:	Drummond
Company:	LSWR
Weight:	25t 15cwt
Driving Wheel:	3' 0"
Boiler Pressure:	150psi
Cylinders:	Outside 14" x 14"
Tractive Effort:	9720lbf
Valve Gear:	Walschaert (slide valves)

There were originally ten locomotives in this class which were built in 1906-1907 as 2-2-0T motor train locomotives, working with saloon trailers. Seven of the class were sold to the Government during the First World War (1916) and they were not returned. The others were rebuilt in 1913-1923 by Urie to 0-4-0Ts. In this form they worked for many years as shunting locomotives. 30588 and 30589 were based at Southampton Docks, and 77S was transferred to the Service Department in 1927 to work at Redbridge sleeper depot.

Year End Totals: 'C14' class

'47	'48	'49	'50	'51	'52	'53	'54	'55	'56	'57	'58	'59	'60	'61	'62	'63	'64	'65	'66	'67
2	2	2	2	2	2	2	2	2	2											

Year End Totals: 'C14' (service) class

'47	'48	'49	'50	'51	'52	'53	'54	'55	'56	'57	'58	'59	'60	'61	'62	'63	'64	'65	'66	'67
1	1	1	1	1	1	1	1	1	1	1	1									

Number	*Built*	*Renumbered*	*BR Dates*	*Scrap*	*Notes*
30588	11/06 9Elm	12/50 3741	-12/57	01/58	
30589	01/07 9Elm	08/48 3744	-06/57	*08/57*	

Class continued with 77S (Service Locomotives)

D15 30463-30472
4-4-0 LSWR Drummond

Power Classification:	3P
Introduced:	1912 Rebuilt by Urie in 1915-1916
Designer:	Drummond
Company:	LSWR
Weight:	Loco 61t 11cwt Tender 39t 12cwt
Driving Wheel:	6' 7"
Boiler Pressure:	180psi superheated
Cylinders:	Inside 20" x 26"
Tractive Effort:	20140lbf
Valve Gear:	Walschaert (piston valves)

This was Drummond's final design of 6' 7" 4-4-0 locomotives, being an enlarged version of the 'L12' class. Ten engines of the class were built in 1912. They were all rebuilt by Urie in 1915-1916 with superheaters. They were originally fitted with eight-wheel tenders, but these were changed for six-wheel tenders in 1926.

o 30463 was converted to oil burning during the coal crisis after the Second World War. It was scrapped without being converted back to coal burning.

Year End Totals: 'D15' class

'47	'48	'49	'50	'51	'52	'53	'54	'55	'56	'57	'58	'59	'60	'61	'62	'63	'64	'65	'66	'67
10	10	10	10	8	4	4	2	1												

Number	*Built*	*Renumbered*	*BR Dates*	*Scrap*	*Notes*
30463	02/12 Elh	463	-12/51	12/51	o
30464	05/12 Elh	05/50 464	-11/54	*03/55*	
30465	06/12 Elh	06/50 465	-01/56	*02/56*	
30466	07/12 Elh	08/49 466	-10/52	02/53	
30467	07/12 Elh	05/49 467	-09/55	*10/55*	
30468	09/12 Elh	05/48 468	-03/52	*04/52*	
30469	10/12 Elh	05/48 469	-12/51	*01/52*	
30470	11/12 Elh	07/48 470	-12/52	01/53	
30471	11/12 Elh	12/48 471	-03/54	08/54	
30472	12/12 Elh	12/48 472	-03/52	*03/52*	

EKR 30948
0-6-0T EKR

Power Classification:	1F
Introduced:	1917
Designer:	Kerr Stuart
Company:	East Kent Railway
Weight:	40t 0cwt
Driving Wheel:	5' 7"
Boiler Pressure:	160psi
Cylinders:	Outside 17" x 24"
Tractive Effort:	14080lbf
Valve Gear:	Stephenson (slide valves)

This locomotive was built by Kerr Stuart for the East Kent Railway in 1917. The line was taken over by BR at nationalisation in 1948 when the locomotive came into BR stock, but it was scrapped in 1949 without receiving its new number.

Year End Totals: 'EKR' class

'47	'48	'49	'50	'51	'52	'53	'54	'55	'56	'57	'58	'59	'60	'61	'62	'63	'64	'65	'66	'67
1	1																			

Number	*Built*	*Renumbered*	*BR Dates*	*Scrap*	*Notes*
30948	08/17 KS	EKR 4	-02/49	02/49	

G6 between 30160 & 30240, 30257-30279, between 30348 & 30354, DS682, DS3152
0-6-0T LSWR Adams

Power Classification:	2F
Introduced:	1894-1900
Designer:	Adams
Company:	LSWR
Weight:	47t 13cwt
Driving Wheel:	4' 10"
Boiler Pressure:	160psi
Cylinders:	Inside 17½" x 24"
Tractive Effort:	17235lbf
Valve Gear:	Stephenson (slide valves)

Adams introduced this class in 1894 as an 0-6-0T version of his class 'O2' 0-4-2T. The boilers, cylinders and coupled wheels were identical to the 'O2' class. They were designed for freight and shunting work. Dugald Drummond added ten more to the class using Adams boilers which had originally been intended for fitting to Beattie '0298' class 2-4-0WTs (these were originally classified 'M9' but were later included in the 'G6' class).

DS3152 worked as a service locomotive at Meldon Quarry until replaced by DS682 in 1960.

30237 was sold for further service in industry, where it survived until September 1960.

d In 1925 and 1928 two Drummond boilers (with safety valves on the dome) were fitted to engines of this class. They were exchanged from time to time among different engines, but during the BR period they could be seen fitted to 30160, 30259 and 30274. The boilers finished their lives on 30160 and 30274.

Year End Totals: 'G6' class

'47	'48	'49	'50	'51	'52	'53	'54	'55	'56	'57	'58	'59	'60	'61	'62	'63	'64	'65	'66	'67
34	28	14	11	10	10	10	10	10	10	10	8	6	3							

Year End Totals: 'G6' (service) class

'47	'48	'49	'50	'51	'52	'53	'54	'55	'56	'57	'58	'59	'60	'61	'62	'63	'64	'65	'66	'67
			1	1	1	1	1	1	1	1	1	1	1	1						

Number	Built		Renumbered		BR Dates	Scrap	Notes
30160	03/00	9Elm	05/48	160	-04/59	05/59	⇨d
30162	04/00	9Elm	*52*	162	-03/58	03/58	
30237	09/98	9Elm		237	-03/49	09/60	
30238	09/98	9Elm	07/51	238	-11/60	05/63	
						11/60➲DS682	
30239	09/98	9Elm		239	-10/48	12/48	
30240	10/98	9Elm		240	-03/49	02/50	
30257	06/94	9Elm		257	-02/49	08/49	
30258	08/94	9Elm	06/50	258	-07/61	09/61	
30259	09/94	9Elm		259	-12/50	02/51	d
30260	09/94	9Elm	07/48	260	-11/58	11/58	
30261	09/94	9Elm		261	-11/48	12/48	
30262	09/94	9Elm		262	-11/49	12/49	
30263	10/94	9Elm		263	-09/49	11/49	
30264	10/94	9Elm		264	-02/49	02/49	
30265	10/94	9Elm		265	-08/49	11/49	
30266	10/94	9Elm	04/49	266	-06/60	08/60	
30267	10/96	9Elm		267	-02/49	02/49	
30268	10/96	9Elm		268	-12/50	02/51	
30269	10/96	9Elm		269	-10/49	10/49	
30270	11/96	9Elm	07/48	270	-01/59	02/59	
30271	12/97	9Elm		271	-09/48	*11/48*	
30272	02/98	9Elm		272	-06/50	*60*	
						06/50➲DS3152	
30273	02/98	9Elm		273	-03/49	*49*	
30274	02/98	9Elm	07/48	274	-10/60	11/60	d
30275	02/98	9Elm		275	-12/49	01/50	
30276	03/98	9Elm	08/48	276	-10/49	11/49	
30277	04/00	9Elm	04/49	277	-11/61	11/61	
30278	05/00	9Elm		278	-12/48	01/49	
30279	11/98	9Elm		279	-12/48	01/49	
30348	06/00	9Elm		348	-08/48	11/48	
30349	06/00	9Elm	11/49	349	-07/61	08/61	
30351	06/00	9Elm		351	-03/49	03/49	
30353	06/00	9Elm		353	-03/51	03/51	
30354	06/00	9Elm		354	-11/49	12/49	

Class continued with DS682 (Service Locomotives)

G16 30492-30495
4-8-0T LSWR Urie

Power Classification: 7F reclassified 8F in 1953
Introduced: 1921
Designer: Urie
Company: LSWR
Weight: 95t 2cwt
Driving Wheel: 5' 1"
Boiler Pressure: 180psi superheated
Cylinders: Outside 22" x 28"
Tractive Effort: 33990lbf
Valve Gear: Walschaert (piston valves)

This class was designed for working in the newly constructed Feltham hump shunting yard. The boilers were identical with the 'H16' class and the cylinders and motion were interchangeable with the 'H16' and the Urie 'N15' classes.

They were very unusual looking engines with high pitched boilers and massive smoke-boxes. They had larger side tanks than the 'H16's and they had sloping tops towards the front end to improve visibility from the footplate while shunting in the yard. The footplate was raised over the cylinders and valve gear.

Year End Totals: 'G16' class

'47	'48	'49	'50	'51	'52	'53	'54	'55	'56	'57	'58	'59	'60	'61	'62	'63	'64	'65	'66	'67
4	4	4	4	4	4	4	4	4	4	4	4	2	2	2						

Number	Built		Renumbered		BR Dates	Scrap	Notes
30492	07/21	Elh	12/48	492	-02/59	02/59	
30493	07/21	Elh	09/48	493	-12/59	01/60	
30494	08/21	Elh	11/50	494	-12/62	03/63	
30495	08/21	Elh	05/48	495	-12/62	01/63	

H15 30330-30335, 30473-30478, 30482-30491, 30521-30524
4-6-0 LSWR Urie & SR Maunsell

Power Classification: 4MT reclassified 4P5F in 1953
Introduced: 1914-1925
Designer: Urie & Maunsell
Company: LSWR & SR
Weight: a Loco 81t 5cwt
b Loco 82t 1cwt
c Loco 79t 19cwt
d Loco 80t 11cwt
e Loco 79t 19cwt
a Tender 57t 14cwt
b Tender 48t 12cwt
c Tender 57t 11cwt
d Tender 49t 3cwt
e Tender 57t 14cwt
Driving Wheel: 6' 0"
Boiler Pressure: ace 180psi superheated
bd 175psi superheated
Cylinders: Outside 21" x 28"
Tractive Effort: ace 26240lbf
bd 25510lbf
Valve Gear: Walschaert (piston valves)

When Urie succeeded Drummond in 1912 he soon got down to the job of producing a range of 4-6-0 locomotives which were very different to his predecessor's designs. Three classes were built, the 'H15' mixed traffic engines, the 'N15' express passenger engines and the 'S15' goods engines. Each of these classes incorporated a lot of variety (including some locomotives rebuilt from earlier engines), and the designs were continued by Urie's successor, Maunsell. They were the first large wheeled engines to have the running plate raised to a sufficient height as to be able to dispense almost entirely with splashers. As such they were the forerunners of a new fashion which gradually spread to other railways and eventually appeared in its most extreme form on the BR standard types.

The 'H15' class was composed of four different groups of engines which actually had little more in common than the size of their cylinders and coupled wheels. Their history is summarised below.

a 30482-30491. This was Urie's LSWR design introduced in 1914. Two engines were built without superheaters and the remaining eight were fitted with Urie's design of superheater. They were all rebuilt from 1927 with Maunsell-type superheaters.

b 30335 was rebuilt by Urie from Drummond's 'E14' class four-cylinder 4-6-0. This was Drummond's second design of 4-6-0. Only one engine was built in 1907 and it was converted to 'H15' in 1915. The rebuilt engine retained the original boiler which was re-tubed and fitted with a superheater.

c 30473-30478 and 30521-30524. This was Maunsell's own version of the 'H15' class, which had straight footplating above the cylinders and an 'N15' type boiler. Ten engines were built in 1924.

d 30330-30334. Drummond's first class of 4-6-0s were built as four-cylinder engines in 1905 and were classified 'F13'. They were rebuilt by Maunsell in 1924-1925 in a similar fashion to 30335 but with detail differences.

e In 1927 Maunsell rebuilt one of the original Urie engines (No. 30491) with an 'N15' type boiler.

These locomotives were all fitted with eight-wheel tenders.

Year End Totals: 'H15' class

'47	'48	'49	'50	'51	'52	'53	'54	'55	'56	'57	'58	'59	'60	'61	'62	'63	'64	'65	'66	'67
26	26	26	26	26	26	26	26	24	23	20	18	10	9							

Number	Built		Renumbered		BR Dates	Scrap	Notes
30330	09/05	Elh	08/48	330	-05/57	06/57	d
30331	09/05	Elh	04/49	331	-03/61	05/61	d
30332	10/05	Elh	05/49	332	-11/56	03/57	d
30333	10/05	Elh	11/48	333	-10/58	11/58	d
30334	11/05	Elh	07/48	334	-06/58	07/58	d
30335	07	Elh	12/48	335	-06/59	09/59	b
30473	02/24	Elh	01/50	473	-07/59	08/59	c
30474	02/24	Elh	03/49	474	-04/60	06/60	c
30475	03/24	Elh	11/48	475	-12/61	03/62	c
30476	04/24	Elh	07/48	476	-12/61	03/62	c
30477	05/24	Elh	09/48	477	-07/59	08/59	c
30478	06/24	Elh	12/48	478	-04/59	04/59	c
30482	03/14	Elh	11/50	482	-05/59	06/59	a
30483	04/14	Elh	08/50	483	-06/57	06/57	a
30484	05/14	Elh	11/48	484	-05/59	07/59	a
30485	06/14	Elh	07/48	485	-04/55	07/55	a
30486	01/14	Elh	08/48	486	-07/59	09/59	a
30487	02/14	Elh	07/48	487	-11/57	12/57	a
30488	04/14	Elh	03/49	488	-04/59	05/59	a
30489	06/14	Elh	05/48	489	-01/61	03/61	a
30490	07/14	Elh	12/48	490	-07/55	08/55	a
30491	07/14	Elh	04/49	491	-01/61	03/61	e
30521	07/24	Elh	07/48	521	-12/61	01/62	c
30522	07/24	Elh	01/49	522	-10/61	11/61	c
30523	09/24	Elh	07/48	523	-09/61	02/62	c
30524	09/24	Elh	01/49	524	-02/61	06/61	c

H16 30516-30520
4-6-2T LSWR Urie

Power Classification: 5F reclassified 6F in 1953
Introduced: 1921-1922
Designer: Urie
Company: LSWR
Weight: 96t 8cwt
Driving Wheel: 5' 7"
Boiler Pressure: 180psi superheated
Cylinders: Outside 21" x 28"
Tractive Effort: 28200lbf
Valve Gear: Walschaert (piston valves)

These locomotives were built immediately after the 'G16' class (with identical boilers, cylinders and motion). They were very similar to the 'G16' class, but did not have the same sloping tops to the tanks, and they had larger coupled wheels.

They were designed specifically for working transfer freight between the Feltham Hump yard and Brent and Willesden. However in later years they could be seen on other workings such as Ascot race specials and Waterloo-Clapham Junction empty stock workings.

Year End Totals: 'H16' class

'47	'48	'49	'50	'51	'52	'53	'54	'55	'56	'57	'58	'59	'60	'61	'62	'63	'64	'65	'66	'67
5	5	5	5	5	5	5	5	5	5	5	5	5	5	5						

Number	Built		Renumbered		BR Dates	Scrap	Notes
30516	11/21	Elh	10/49	516	-11/62	10/63	
30517	11/21	Elh	07/48	517	-11/62	06/63	
30518	12/21	Elh	11/50	518	-11/62	04/64	
30519	01/22	Elh	04/49	519	-11/62	10/63	
30520	02/22	Elh	12/48	520	-11/62	10/63	

K10 between 30135 & 30153, 30329 & 30345, 30380-30394
4-4-0 LSWR Drummond

Power Classification: 1MT
Introduced: 1901-1902
Designer: Drummond
Company: LSWR
Weight: Loco 46t 14cwt
x Tender 39t 12cwt
y Tender 40t 14cwt
z Tender 44t 17cwt
Driving Wheel: 5' 7"
Boiler Pressure: 175psi
Cylinders: Inside 18½" x 26"
Tractive Effort: 19755lbf
Valve Gear: Stephenson (slide valves)

These were the survivors of forty locomotives built in 1901-1902 for mixed traffic on the LSWR. They were developed from the extinct 'C8' class. The first was withdrawn in 1947. The 'L11' class was a further development of this class.

In 1948 tenders were attached as shown below.

x Six-wheel tenders.

y Shorter (but heavier) six-wheel tenders.

z Eight-wheel tenders.

Year End Totals: 'K10' class

'47	'48	'49	'50	'51	'52	'53	'54	'55	'56	'57	'58	'59	'60	'61	'62	'63	'64	'65	'66	'67
31	23	8	2																	

Number	Built		Renumbered		BR Dates	Scrap	Notes
30135	08/02	9Elm		135	-03/49	03/49	z
30137	09/02	9Elm		137	-08/49	11/49	x
30139	10/02	9Elm		139	-09/48	11/48	z
30140	10/02	9Elm		140	-01/50	06/50	x
30141	10/02	9Elm		141	-10/49	11/49	x
30142	11/02	9Elm		142	-01/50	02/50	y
30143	11/02	9Elm		143	-09/48	11/48	z
30144	11/02	9Elm		144	-07/49	10/49	z
30145	12/02	9Elm		145	-10/48	01/49	y
30146	12/02	9Elm		146	-02/48	*48*	z
30150	12/02	9Elm		150	-02/48	06/48	z
30151	12/02	9Elm		151	-02/50	03/50	y
30152	12/02	9Elm		152	-02/49	02/49	y
30153	12/02	9Elm		153	-03/49	03/49	y
30329	12/01	9Elm		329	-04/50	04/50	y
30340	12/01	9Elm		340	-06/48	10/48	z
30341	12/01	9Elm		341	-12/49	01/50	y
30343	12/01	9Elm		343	-02/48	10/48	z
30345	01/02	9Elm		345	-09/49	11/49	x
30380	04/02	9Elm		380	-06/49	10/49	z
30382	04/02	9Elm	05/48	382	-08/50	09/50	z

LSWR Adams 'O2' class 0-4-4T No 30224.

LSWR Drummond 'L12' class 4-4-0 No 30431 in September 1950.

LSWR Drummond 'D15' class 4-4-0 No 30472 on Salisbury shed in October 1949.

LSWR Maunsell 'H15' class 4-6-0 No 30477 at Nine Elms in April 1959.

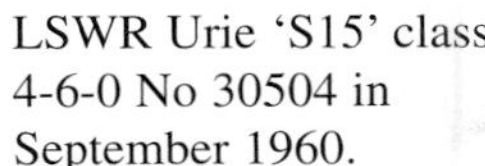

LSWR Urie 'S15' class 4-6-0 No 30504 in September 1960.

SR Maunsell 'Q' class 0-6-0 No 30542.

Number	Built	Renumbered	BR Dates	Scrap	Notes
30383	04/02 9Elm	383	-05/49	09/49	y
30384	04/02 9Elm	384	-06/51	08/51	x
30385	05/02 9Elm	385	-02/49	02/49	y
30386	05/02 9Elm	386	-08/49	12/49	z
30389	06/02 9Elm	389	-07/51	08/51	y
30390	06/02 9Elm	390	-11/50	11/50	y
30391	07/02 9Elm	391	-10/49	10/49	z
30392	07/02 9Elm	392	-10/48	01/49	z
30393	02/02 9Elm	393	-02/49	07/49	x
30394	03/02 9Elm	394	-05/49	06/49	x

KESR 30949
0-8-0T KESR

Power Classification: 2F
Introduced: 1905
Designer: Hawthorn Leslie
Company: Kent & East Sussex Railway
Weight: 47t 10cwt
Driving Wheel: 4' 3"
Boiler Pressure: 160psi
Cylinders: Outside 16" x 24"
Tractive Effort: 16385lbf
Valve Gear: Stephenson (slide valves)

This locomotive was built in 1905 for the Kent & East Sussex Railway. It was built for the proposed extension of the line to Maidstone, but this never materialised. It was too heavy for the line and did little work until 1932 when it was exchanged for an '0330' class 0-6-0ST with the Southern Railway (see '0330' class KESR No. 4). The SR rebuilt the locomotive with a LBSCR boiler, but retained the original name HECATE. It shunted for several years in Clapham Junction yard before being scrapped in 1950.

Year End Totals: 'KESR' class

'47	'48	'49	'50	'51	'52	'53	'54	'55	'56	'57	'58	'59	'60	'61	'62	'63	'64	'65	'66	'67
1	1	1																		

Number	Built	Renumbered	BR Dates	Scrap	Notes
30949 HECATE	05/05 HL	949	-03/50	03/50	

L11 between 30134 & 30175, 30405-30414, 30435-30442
4-4-0 LSWR Drummond

Power Classification: 1MT
Introduced: 1903-1907
Designer: Drummond
Company: LSWR
Weight: Loco 50t 11cwt
x Tender 39t 12cwt
y Tender 44t 17cwt
z Tender 49t 0cwt
Driving Wheel: 5' 7"
Boiler Pressure: 175psi
Cylinders: Inside 18½" x 26"
Tractive Effort: 19755lbf
Valve Gear: Stephenson (slide valves)

These mixed traffic 4-4-0s were built by Drummond as a slightly larger version of the 'K10' class and they were fitted with 'T9' type boilers and larger fireboxes. Forty engines were built in 1903-1907.

o These locomotives were converted to oil burning during the coal crisis after the Second World War. They were all scrapped without being converted back to coal burning.

In 1948 tenders were attached as shown below.

x Six-wheel tenders.

y Eight-wheel tenders.

z Larger eight-wheel tenders.

Year End Totals: 'L11' class

'47	'48	'49	'50	'51	'52	'53	'54	'55	'56	'57	'58	'59	'60	'61	'62	'63	'64	'65	'66	'67
40	40	34	28	6																

Number	Built	Renumbered	BR Dates	Scrap	Notes
30134	04/04 9Elm	12/48 134	-03/51	03/51	y
30148	04/04 9Elm	148	-03/52	03/52	yo
30154	05/03 9Elm	154	-04/51	*04/51*	yo
30155	05/03 9Elm	155	-04/51	04/51	yo
30156	06/03 9Elm	07/48 156	-05/51	05/51	y
30157	06/03 9Elm	157	-03/52	03/52	yo
30158	06/03 9Elm	158	-12/50	12/50	y
30159	07/03 9Elm	05/48 159	-03/51	03/51	y
30161	08/03 9Elm	161	-02/50	06/50	y
30163	09/03 9Elm	11/49 163	-12/51	*12/51*	y
30164	10/03 9Elm	10/49 164	-10/51	10/51	y
30165	10/03 9Elm	165	-04/51	04/51	y
30166	04/04 9Elm	07/48 166	-07/50	08/50	z
30167	05/04 9Elm	167	-09/49	12/49	y
30168	05/04 9Elm	168	-02/50	03/50	y
30169	08/04 9Elm	169	-07/49	09/49	y
30170	08/04 9Elm	170	-06/52	*06/52*	yo
30171	09/04 9Elm	05/49 171	-09/51	09/51	y
30172	09/04 9Elm	172	-06/52	*06/52*	yo
30173	09/04 9Elm	05/48 173	-05/51	05/51	y
30174	04/06 9Elm	01/51 174	-09/51	09/51	y
30175	04/06 9Elm	12/48 175	-12/51	12/51	y
30405	09/06 9Elm	03/49 405	-02/51	03/51	z
30406	09/06 9Elm	11/48 406	-06/51	06/51	y
30407	05/06 9Elm	05/48 407	-11/50	11/50	y
30408	05/06 9Elm	408	-03/51	04/51	y
30409	06/06 9Elm	03/49 409	-06/51	06/51	y
30410	06/06 9Elm	410	-12/49	02/50	y
30411	06/06 9Elm	411	-06/52	06/52	yo
30412	07/06 9Elm	412	-12/50	12/50	y
30413	07/06 9Elm	413	-03/51	03/51	y
30414	07/06 9Elm	414	-05/51	05/51	y
30435	10/06 9Elm	435	-12/49	12/49	z
30436	11/06 9Elm	436	-07/51	08/51	y
30437	12/06 9Elm	437	-06/52	06/52	yo
30438	03/07 9Elm	12/48 438	-10/51	10/51	y
30439	03/07 9Elm	439	-05/49	08/49	z
30440	04/07 9Elm	440	-05/49	08/49	x
30441	05/07 9Elm	441	-04/51	05/51	x
30442	05/07 9Elm	09/48 442	-12/51	12/51	y

L12 30415-30434
4-4-0 LSWR Drummond

Power Classification: 2P
Introduced: 1904-1905
rebuilt by Urie 1915-1922
Designer: Drummond
Company: LSWR
Weight: Loco 55t 5cwt
y Tender 44t 17cwt
z Tender 39t 12cwt
Driving Wheel: 6' 7"
Boiler Pressure: 175psi superheated
Cylinders: Inside 19" x 26"
Tractive Effort: 17675lbf
Valve Gear: Stephenson (slide valves)

This was another development of the 'T9' class with a larger boiler (see also the 'S11' class). Twenty engines were built in 1904-1905. They were fitted with superheaters by Urie in 1915-1922. Although they were successors to the 'T9' class neither the 'L12's or the 'S11's achieved the fame of the earlier 'T9' class.

y All the locomotives were all originally fitted with large eight-wheel tenders.

z Some locomotives were later fitted with smaller six-wheel tenders. The list shows the tenders attached in 1948.

Year End Totals: 'L12' class

'47	'48	'49	'50	'51	'52	'53	'54	'55	'56	'57	'58	'59	'60	'61	'62	'63	'64	'65	'66	'67
20	20	20	20	2	2	1	1													

Number	Built	Renumbered	BR Dates	Scrap	Notes
30415	06/04 9Elm	01/50 415	-02/53	02/53	y
30416	06/04 9Elm	05/49 416	-06/51	07/51	z
30417	06/04 9Elm	07/48 417	-12/51	*52*	z
30418	07/04 9Elm	10/49 418	-06/51	07/51	y
30419	07/04 9Elm	11/48 419	-12/51	*52*	z
30420	09/04 9Elm	07/48 420	-09/51	09/51	y
30421	09/04 9Elm	06/49 421	-09/51	09/51	z
30422	10/04 9Elm	11/50 422	-09/51	09/51	z
30423	10/04 9Elm	12/48 423	-07/51	08/51	y
30424	11/04 9Elm	08/50 424	-07/51	08/51	z
30425	11/04 9Elm	08/48 425	-09/51	09/51	z
30426	12/04 9Elm	10/49 426	-11/51	11/51	y
30427	12/04 9Elm	10/49 427	-11/51	11/51	y
30428	01/05 9Elm	09/48 428	-04/51	*51*	y
30429	01/05 9Elm	07/48 429	-10/51	10/51	y
30430	02/05 9Elm	430	-03/51	04/51	z
30431	02/05 9Elm	05/48 431	-10/51	10/51	z
30432	02/05 9Elm	05/48 432	-10/51	*10/51*	y
30433	03/05 9Elm	11/50 433	-12/51	12/51	z
30434	03/05 9Elm	12/48 434	-03/55	08/55	y

LN 30850-30865
4-6-0 SR Maunsell 'Lord Nelson'

Power Classification: 6P reclassified 7P in 1951
Introduced: 1926-1929
Designer: Maunsell
Company: SR
Weight: Loco 83t 10cwt
b Loco 84t 16cwt
Tender 57t 19cwt
Driving Wheel: 6' 7"
s 6' 3"
Boiler Pressure: 220psi superheated
Cylinders: Four 16½" x 26"
Tractive Effort: 33510lbf
s 35300lbf
Valve Gear: Walschaert (piston valves)

The 'Lord Nelsons' were designed to haul the heaviest and fastest expresses on the Southern Railway. 30850 was built in 1926 and the others followed in 1928-1929. They were all named after Naval Commanders of great renown. They were considered by some to rank among the most handsome 4-6-0s ever to run in this country. The engines were unusual in that the cranks were set at 135 degrees to give eight exhausts for each revolution of the driving wheels instead of the more normal four.

The 'Lord Nelsons' took the title of the most powerful locomotives running in the country from the GWR when they were built. This caused the GWR to retaliate by building the '6000' 'King' class to snatch the title back.

From 1938 onwards the cylinders and the eight-wheel tenders were modified by Bulleid and the locomotives were fitted with multiple-jet blast pipes and large diameter chimneys. They were also fitted with smoke deflectors.

From 1959 onwards the entire class was based at Eastleigh where they finished their days working the Waterloo-Southampton boat trains and the Waterloo-Bournemouth services.

b 30860 was fitted experimentally with a longer boiler in 1929.

c 30865 had the cranks adjusted to give the normal four exhausts per revolution of the driving wheels.

s 30859 was fitted experimentally with smaller driving wheels in 1929.

Year End Totals: 'LN' class

'47	'48	'49	'50	'51	'52	'53	'54	'55	'56	'57	'58	'59	'60	'61	'62	'63	'64	'65	'66	'67
16	16	16	16	16	16	16	16	16	16	16	16	16	16	10						

Number	Built	Renumbered	BR Dates	Scrap	Notes
30850 § LORD NELSON	08/26 Elh	12/48 850	-08/62		
30851 SIR FRANCIS DRAKE	06/28 Elh	03/49 851	-12/61	05/62	
30852 SIR WALTER RALEIGH	07/28 Elh	04/49 852	-02/62	03/62	
30853 SIR RICHARD GRENVILLE	09/28 Elh	12/48 853	-02/62	04/62	
30854 HOWARD OF EFFINGHAM	10/28 Elh	06/49 854	-09/61	10/61	
30855 ROBERT BLAKE	11/28 Elh	03/49 855	-09/61	02/62	
30856 LORD ST. VINCENT	11/28 Elh	05/48 856	-09/62	11/62	
30857 LORD HOWE	12/28 Elh	11/49 857	-09/62	10/62	
30858 LORD DUNCAN	01/29 Elh	07/48 858	-08/61	11/61	
30859 LORD HOOD	03/29 Elh	03/49 859	-12/61	12/61	s
30860 LORD HAWKE	04/29 Elh	12/48 860	-08/62	08/62	b
30861 LORD ANSON	09/29 Elh	05/48 861	-10/62	11/62	
30862 LORD COLLINGWOOD	10/29 Elh	07/48 862	-10/62	11/62	
30863 LORD RODNEY	10/29 Elh	*51* 863	-02/62	03/62	
30864 SIR MARTIN FROBISHER	11/29 Elh	05/48 864	-01/62	03/62	
30865 SIR JOHN HAWKINS	11/29 Elh	07/48 865	-05/61	08/61	c

M7 30021-30060, between 30104 & 30481, 30667-30676
0-4-4T LSWR Drummond

Power Classification: 2P
Introduced: 1897-1911
Designer: Drummond
Company: LSWR

Weight:	m 60t 4cwt
	x 60t 3cwt
	p 62t 0cwt
Driving Wheel:	5' 7"
Boiler Pressure:	175psi
Cylinders:	Inside 18½" x 26"
Tractive Effort:	19755lbf
Valve Gear:	Stephenson (slide valves)

Dugald Drummond constructed 105 of these engines from 1897 onwards as the 'M7' and 'X14' classes. They were developed from Adams' 'T1' and 'O2' classes with modified boilers and an increase in boiler pressure and cylinder size.

The 'M7's were initially tried out on express trains between Exeter and Plymouth, but after a derailment at speed they were relegated to suburban trains in the London area. After the spread of electrification most of them migrated to country districts. They were also a familiar sight at Waterloo, where for years they worked as station pilots.

The class remained in virtually original condition throughout their existence. No. 126 was superheated in 1921 with a '700' class boiler, but this resulted in an ungainly locomotive with a reputation for instability and it was scrapped in 1937. The next locomotive to be withdrawn was 672 which fell down the lift shaft to the Waterloo and City line at Waterloo in 1948. It was cut up on the spot.

Most engines had the sandboxes combined with the front splashers, but some were built with the sandboxes below the running plates.

In 1960 30128 and 30031 swapped numbers. 30106 was withdrawn in 1960 and was reinstated in 1961 as 30667, the original 30667 having been withdrawn.

m Drummond 'M7' class built in 1897-1900 (fifty-five in all).

x Drummond 'X14' class. These fifty engines were built in 1903-1911 with slightly longer frames, giving a longer overhang at the front. They were fitted with steam reversing gear and other detail alterations. They were all later classed as 'M7'.

p Some of the 'X14' class were fitted for push-pull working at intervals from 1925 onwards.

Year End Totals: 'M7' class

'47	'48	'49	'50	'51	'52	'53	'54	'55	'56	'57	'58	'59	'60	'61	'62	'63	'64	'65	'66	'67
104	103	103	103	103	103	103	103	103	103	99	91	75	69	49	35	14				

Number	Built	Renumbered	BR Dates	Scrap	Notes
30021	01/04 9Elm	06/49 21	-03/64	07/64	xp
30022	01/99 9Elm	08/49 22	-05/58	05/58	m
30023	01/99 9Elm	12/49 23	-10/61	11/61	m
30024	01/99 9Elm	11/50 24	-03/63	05/63	m
30025	02/99 9Elm	12/49 25	-05/64	10/64	m
30026	02/99 9Elm	05/49 26	-04/59	07/59	m
30027	01/04 9Elm	10/49 27	-11/59	12/59	xp
30028	01/04 9Elm	04/49 28	-09/62	10/62	xp
30029	02/04 9Elm	11/48 29	-05/64	10/64	xp
30030	02/04 9Elm	04/49 30	-10/59	11/59	x
30031	03/98 9Elm	01/49 31	-01/60	02/61	m
				01/60➲30128	
30031	11/11 Elh	01/60 30128	-05/63	05/63	x
				02/61⇨p	
30032	03/98 9Elm	04/49 32	-07/63	06/64	m
30033	04/98 9Elm	01/50 33	-12/62	04/63	m
30034	04/98 9Elm	07/51 34	-02/63	05/63	m
30035	04/98 9Elm	12/48 35	-02/63	06/64	m
30036	05/98 9Elm	09/48 36	-01/64	08/64	m
30037	05/98 9Elm	03/49 37	-05/58	06/58	m
30038	05/98 9Elm	08/48 38	-02/58	03/58	m
30039	05/98 9Elm	09/48 39	-02/63	05/63	m
30040	06/98 9Elm	03/50 40	-06/61	06/61	m
30041	03/99 9Elm	08/49 41	-08/57	09/57	m
30042	03/99 9Elm	52 42	-06/57	06/57	m
30043	03/99 9Elm	10/49 43	-05/61	07/61	m
30044	03/99 9Elm	11/50 44	-09/61	10/61	m
30045	05/05 9Elm	05/49 45	-12/62	03/63	xp
30046	05/05 9Elm	06/49 46	-02/59	04/59	xp
30047	05/05 9Elm	08/50 47	-02/60	02/60	xp
30048	05/05 9Elm	10/49 48	-01/64	07/64	x
				04/63⇨p	
30049	05/05 9Elm	04/51 49	-05/62	06/62	xp
30050	06/05 9Elm	12/50 50	-01/62	02/62	xp
30051	11/05 9Elm	05/49 51	-09/62	11/62	xp
30052	12/05 9Elm	08/49 52	-05/64	10/64	x
				04/63⇨p	
30053 §	12/05 9Elm	11/49 53	-05/64		xp
30054	12/05 9Elm	05/50 54	-01/59	02/59	xp
30055	12/05 9Elm	12/48 55	-09/63	02/64	xp
30056	01/06 9Elm	07/48 56	-12/63	12/63	xp
30057	01/06 9Elm	08/49 57	-06/63	07/63	xp
30058	03/06 9Elm	12/50 58	-09/60	10/60	xp
30059	03/06 9Elm	07/48 59	-02/61	05/62	xp
30060	03/06 9Elm	11/48 60	-07/61	09/61	xp
30104	03/05 9Elm	07/48 104	-05/61	06/61	xp
30105	03/05 9Elm	07/48 105	-05/63	06/63	xp
30106	03/05 9Elm	12/48 106	-11/60	10/64	xp
				02/61➲30667	
30107	04/05 9Elm	05/48 107	-05/64	10/64	xp
30108	03/04 9Elm	08/50 108	-05/64	10/64	xp
30109	03/04 9Elm	05/49 109	-06/61	08/61	xp
30110	03/04 9Elm	10/49 110	-05/63	05/63	xp
30111	03/04 9Elm	11/50 111	-01/64	10/64	xp
30112	07/00 9Elm	11/49 112	-02/63	04/63	m
30123	02/03 9Elm	03/49 123	-06/59	08/59	x
30124	02/03 9Elm	05/49 124	-05/61	06/61	x
30125	08/11 Elh	07/49 125	-12/62	02/64	xp
30127	10/11 Elh	02/51 127	-11/63	11/63	x
30128	11/11 Elh	04/49 128	-01/60	05/63	xp
				01/60➲30031	
30128	03/98 9Elm	01/60 30031	-01/61	02/61	m
30129	11/11 Elh	11/49 129	-11/63	12/63	x
				04/63⇨p	
30130	02/03 9Elm	08/49 130	-12/59	12/59	x
30131	11/11 Elh	06/50 131	-11/62	12/62	xp
30132	03/03 9Elm	07/48 132	-11/62	12/62	x
30133	03/03 9Elm	03/50 133	-03/64	11/65	x
				04/60⇨p	
30241	05/99 9Elm	07/48 241	-07/63	10/63	m
30242	03/97 9Elm	05/50 242	-06/58	06/58	m
30243	03/97 9Elm	07/48 243	-09/58	09/58	m
30244	03/97 9Elm	09/48 244	-10/57	11/57	m
30245 §	04/97 9Elm	08/49 245	-11/62		m
30246	04/97 9Elm	08/51 246	-10/61	11/61	m
30247	04/97 9Elm	10/49 247	-10/61	11/61	m
30248	05/97 9Elm	12/48 248	-07/61	08/61	m
30249	05/97 9Elm	08/50 249	-07/63	04/64	m
30250	05/97 9Elm	06/51 250	-08/57	01/58	m
30251	06/97 9Elm	03/51 251	-07/63	08/63	m
30252	06/97 9Elm	01/50 252	-02/59	03/59	m
30253	06/97 9Elm	*51* 253	-10/61	12/61	m
30254	08/97 9Elm	07/48 254	-05/64	10/64	m
30255	08/97 9Elm	06/51 255	-09/60	10/60	m
30256	08/97 9Elm	02/51 256	-05/59	07/59	m
30318	08/00 9Elm	08/50 318	-12/59	01/60	m
30319	08/00 9Elm	10/49 319	-01/60	02/60	m
30320	08/00 9Elm	05/48 320	-02/63	04/64	m
30321	08/00 9Elm	06/49 321	-09/62	11/62	m
30322	08/00 9Elm	11/49 322	-11/58	12/58	m
30323	10/00 9Elm	10/49 323	-12/59	12/59	m
30324	10/00 9Elm	05/50 324	-09/59	10/59	m
30328	11/11 Elh	03/50 328	-03/63	06/63	xp
30356	10/00 9Elm	05/51 356	-12/58	12/58	m
30357	10/00 9Elm	12/48 357	-04/61	06/61	m
30374	04/03 9Elm	12/48 374	-10/59	10/59	x
30375	05/03 9Elm	12/48 375	-09/62	10/62	x
30376	05/03 9Elm	06/49 376	-01/59	03/59	x
30377	05/03 9Elm	08/48 377	-08/62	09/62	x
30378	05/03 9Elm	07/49 378	-12/62	04/63	x
				03/62⇨p	
30379	06/04 9Elm	08/50 379	-10/63	11/63	xp
30479	11/11 Elh	04/49 479	-04/61	05/61	x
30480	11/11 Elh	12/48 480	-05/64	10/64	xp
30481	11/11 Elh	11/50 481	-05/59	06/59	xp
30667	09/97 9Elm	11/50 667	-02/61	02/61	m
30667	03/05 9Elm	02/61 30106	-05/64	10/64	x
				04/63⇨p	
30668	09/97 9Elm	11/49 668	-09/61	12/61	m
30669	09/97 9Elm	02/50 669	-07/61	09/61	m
30670	10/97 9Elm	03/51 670	-03/63	05/63	m
30671	10/97 9Elm	08/49 671	-07/59	08/59	m
30672	10/97 9Elm	672	-05/48	05/48	m
30673	11/97 9Elm	01/49 673	-08/60	08/60	m
30674	11/97 9Elm	03/49 674	-08/61	10/61	m
30675	11/97 9Elm	08/49 675	-03/58	03/58	m
30676	11/97 9Elm	*49* 676	-07/61	08/61	m

N15 30448-30457, 30736-30755, 30763-30806

4-6-0 LSWR Urie & SR Maunsell 'King Arthur'

Power Classification:	5P
Introduced:	1918-1927
Designer:	Urie & Maunsell
Company:	LSWR & SR
Weight:	ab Loco 80t 7cwt
	d Loco 79t 18cwt
	e Loco 80t 19cwt
	f Loco 80t 19cwt
	g Loco 81t 17cwt
	ab Tender 57t 16cwt
	d Tender 49t 3cwt
	e Tender 49t 3cwt
	f Tender 57t 11cwt
	g Tender 41t 5cwt
Driving Wheel:	6' 7"
Boiler Pressure:	ab 180psi superheated
	defg 200psi superheated
Cylinders:	a Outside 22" x 28"
	b Outside 21" x 28"
	defg Outside 20½" x 28"
Tractive Effort:	a 26245lbf
	b 23915lbf
	defg 25320lbf
Valve Gear:	Walschaert (piston valves)

The 'N15's were Urie's new express passenger engines (see the 'H15' class for more details of Urie's range of 4-6-0s). The history of the class is summarised below.

a 30736 to 30755 were Urie's original 'N15' design for the LSWR, built 1918-1923. The original engines were very poor steamers and in 1924 they were altered with improved draughting arrangements. As such they were able to take their place within the new 'King Arthur' class. However, they never quite matched the excellence of the later Maunsell engines. It was said that Maunsell was indignant when the SR directors decided to include them as part of the 'King Arthur' class, saying that 'names would not improve their performance'. They were fitted with eight-wheel tenders. They could be distinguished from other members of the class by their inside steam pipes and Drummond/Urie safety valves.

b In 1928 30736 to 30754 were further modified with new cylinders of reduced diameter.

d Maunsell's development of Urie's design was introduced in 1925 (30453-30457). Originally intended to be rebuilds of Drummond's 4-6-0 engines of the 'G14' class, they were in fact built as replacements, although they took the same numbers and were fitted with the eight-wheel tenders of the 'G14' engines. They had long-travel valves, higher pressure boilers and smaller fireboxes. At the time of the appearance of the first of the class the Southern Railway had just appointed the country's first Public Relations Officer to improve the company's public standing. He specified that the new class should have names connected with the legend of King Arthur and the Knights of the Round Table, and hence the class became known as the 'King Arthur' class. They proved to be versatile engines and different variations were produced to enable them to work all over the SR system.

e 30448-30452 were built in 1925. They also carried the numbers of 'G14' engines and received their tenders. They were built at Eastleigh to the LSWR loading gauge which always restricted them to working on the Western Section. They were known as 'Eastleigh Arthurs'. 30449 took part in the Darlington Railway Centenary celebrations in 1925.

f Introduced in 1925, 30763-30792 were ordered from the North British Locomotive Company in Glasgow (becoming known as the 'Scotch Arthurs'). They were fitted with modified cabs to fit the Eastern Section loading gauge, and they were attached to eight-wheeled bogie tenders.

g 30793-30806 were introduced in 1926 and built at Eastleigh for the Central (Brighton) Section, but they were transferred elsewhere on electrification. They had detail alterations and six-wheeled tenders.

m These locomotives were modified from 1938 onwards with a multiple jet blastpipe and large chimney.

o These locomotives were converted to oil burning during the coal crisis after the Second World War. They were later converted back to coal burning (c).

Year End Totals: 'N15' class

'47	'48	'49	'50	'51	'52	'53	'54	'55	'56	'57	'58	'59	'60	'61	'62	'63	'64	'65	'66	'67
74	74	74	74	74	74	73	73	69	63	55	52	35	26	12						

Number	Built	Renumbered	BR Dates	Scrap	Notes
30448	05/25 Elh	07/48 448	-08/60	09/60	e
SIR TRISTRAM					
30449	06/25 Elh	10/49 449	-12/59	12/59	e
SIR TORRE					
30450	06/25 Elh	10/49 450	-09/60	09/60	e
SIR KAY					
30451	06/25 Elh	07/48 451	-06/62	06/62	e
SIR LAMORAK					

Number	Built	Renumbered	BR Dates	Scrap	Notes
30452 SIR MELIAGRANCE	07/25 Elh	05/48 452	-08/59	10/59	e
30453 KING ARTHUR	02/25 Elh	02/50 453	-07/61	10/61	d
30454 QUEEN GUINEVERE	03/25 Elh	04/49 454	-10/58	11/58	d
30455 SIR LAUNCELOT	03/25 Elh	05/48 455	-04/59	05/59	d
30456 SIR GALAHAD	04/25 Elh	11/48 456	-05/60	05/60	d
30457 SIR BEDIVERE	04/25 Elh	08/49 457	-05/61	07/61	d
30736 EXCALIBUR	09/18 Elh	03/49 736	-10/56	*56*	bm
30737 KING UTHER	10/18 Elh	07/49 737	-08/56	*08/56*	bm
30738 KING PELLINORE	12/19 Elh	05/49 738	-03/58	03/58	b
30739 KING LEODEGRANCE	02/19 Elh	03/49 739	-05/57	05/57	b
30740 MERLIN	04/19 Elh	11/48 740	-12/55	*05/56*	bo 09/48⇨c
30741 JOYOUS GARD	05/19 Elh	12/48 741	-02/56	*02/56*	bm
30742 CAMELOT	06/19 Elh	11/48 742	-02/57	02/57	b
30743 LYONNESSE	08/19 Elh	06/49 743	-10/55	11/55	b
30744 MAID OF ASTOLAT	09/19 Elh	05/48 744	-01/56	*01/56*	b
30745 TINTAGEL	11/19 Elh	12/48 745	-02/56	*02/56*	bo 09/48⇨c
30746 PENDRAGON	06/22 Elh	11/50 746	-11/55	11/55	b
30747 ELAINE	07/22 Elh	05/50 747	-10/56	*02/57*	b
30748 VIVIEN	08/22 Elh	12/48 748	-09/57	10/57	bo 09/48⇨c
30749 ISEULT	09/22 Elh	12/48 749	-06/57	07/57	bo 09/48⇨c
30750 MORGAN LE FAY	10/22 Elh	12/48 750	-07/57	08/57	b
30751 ETARRE	11/22 Elh	07/48 751	-06/57	07/57	b
30752 LINETTE	12/22 Elh	09/48 752	-12/55	*01/56*	bmo 09/48⇨c
30753 MELISANDE	01/23 Elh	05/48 753	-03/57	03/57	b
30754 THE GREEN KNIGHT	02/23 Elh	07/48 754	-02/53	02/53	b
30755 THE RED KNIGHT	03/23 Elh	*49* 755	-05/57	05/57	am
30763 SIR BORS DE GANIS	05/25 NB	08/50 763	-09/60	10/60	f
30764 SIR GAWAIN	05/25 NB	03/49 764	-07/61	08/61	f
30765 SIR GARETH	05/25 NB	04/49 765	-09/62	11/62	f
30766 SIR GERAINT	05/25 NB	01/49 766	-12/58	01/59	f
30767 SIR VALENCE	06/25 NB	12/48 767	-06/59	09/59	f
30768 SIR BALIN	06/25 NB	11/48 768	-10/61	01/62	f
30769 SIR BALAN	06/25 NB	04/51 769	-02/60	02/60	f
30770 SIR PRIANIUS	06/25 NB	07/51 770	-11/62	02/63	f
30771 SIR SAGRAMORE	06/25 NB	06/50 771	-03/61	05/61	f
30772 SIR PERCIVALE	06/25 NB	05/48 772	-09/61	12/61	f
30773 SIR LAVAINE	06/25 NB	07/48 773	-02/62	04/62	f
30774 SIR GAHERIS	06/25 NB	04/49 774	-01/60	01/60	f
30775 SIR AGRAVAINE	06/25 NB	10/49 775	-02/60	02/60	f
30776 SIR GALAGARS	06/25 NB	07/49 776	-01/59	02/59	f
30777 § SIR LAMIEL	06/25 NB	05/48 777	-10/61		f
30778 SIR PELLEAS	06/25 NB	11/49 778	-05/59	09/59	f
30779 SIR COLGREVANCE	07/25 NB	11/48 779	-07/59	09/59	f
30780 SIR PERSANT	07/25 NB	01/50 780	-07/59	09/59	f
30781 SIR AGLOVALE	07/25 NB	04/49 781	-05/62	05/62	f
30782 SIR BRIAN	07/25 NB	05/48 782	-09/62	09/62	f
30783 SIR GILLEMERE	08/25 NB	05/48 783	-02/61	06/61	f
30784 SIR NEROVENS	08/25 NB	05/48 784	-10/59	11/59	f
30785 SIR MADOR DE LA PORTE	08/25 NB	08/48 785	-10/59	11/59	f
30786 SIR LIONEL	08/25 NB	09/48 786	-08/59	10/59	f
30787 SIR MENADEUKE	09/25 NB	04/49 787	-02/59	05/59	f
30788 SIR URRE OF THE MOUNT	09/25 NB	11/48 788	-02/62	02/62	f
30789 SIR GUY	09/25 NB	08/48 789	-12/59	01/60	f
30790 SIR VILLIARS	09/25 NB	09/48 790	-10/61	01/62	f
30791 SIR UWAINE	09/25 NB	12/48 791	-05/60	05/60	f
30792 SIR HERVIS DE REVEL	10/25 NB	03/50 792	-02/59	03/59	f
30793 SIR ONTZLAKE	03/26 Elh	11/48 793	-08/62	09/62	g
30794 SIR ECTOR DE MARIS	03/26 Elh	01/49 794	-08/60	09/60	g
30795 SIR DINADAN	04/26 Elh	04/49 795	-07/62	08/62	g
30796 SIR DODINAS LE SAVAGE	05/26 Elh	02/50 796	-02/62	04/62	g
30797 SIR BLAMOR DE GANIS	06/26 Elh	01/49 797	-06/59	06/59	g
30798 SIR HECTIMERE	06/26 Elh	11/49 798	-06/62	07/62	g
30799 SIR IRONSIDE	07/26 Elh	05/48 799	-02/61	04/61	g
30800 SIR MELEAUS DE LILE	09/26 Elh	10/49 800	-08/61	09/61	g
30801 SIR MELIOT DE LOGRES	10/26 Elh	07/49 801	-04/59	06/59	g
30802 SIR DURNORE	10/26 Elh	07/48 802	-07/61	08/61	g
30803 SIR HARRY LE FISE LAKE	11/26 Elh	07/48 803	-08/61	09/61	g
30804 SIR CADOR OF CORNWALL	12/26 Elh	12/48 804	-02/62	03/62	g
30805 SIR CONSTANTINE	01/27 Elh	09/48 805	-11/59	12/59	g
30806 SIR GALLERON	01/27 Elh	09/48 806	-04/61	06/61	g

O2 30177-30236, W14-W36
0-4-4T LSWR Adams

Power Classification:	1P reclassified 0P in 1953
Introduced:	1889-1895
Designer:	Adams
Company:	LSWR
Weight:	46t 18cwt w 48t 8cwt
Driving Wheel:	4' 10"
Boiler Pressure:	160psi
Cylinders:	Inside 17½" x 24"
Tractive Effort:	17235lbf
Valve Gear:	Stephenson (slide valves)

Adams built sixty of these engines in 1889-1895. They were originally numbered 177-236 and the first was withdrawn in 1933. They were designed to replace Beattie's well tanks ('0298' class) on branch line work and general shunting duties. They were a smaller version of the 'T1' class. Until the 1930s some of them could always be seen marshalling carriage stock in Clapham Junction sidings. The 'M7' class was developed from the 'O2' class.

d Some locomotives were fitted with Drummond type boilers with Ross 'pop' safety valves on the top of the dome. This was not in general found to be an improvement and many retained the original Adams boilers. The locomotives marked did not necessarily carry the Drummond boiler throughout their lives as there was some swapping of boilers.

p These locomotives were motor fitted for working push-pull services.

w In 1923 two locomotives were sent over to the Isle of Wight for trials and they were so successful that eventually twenty-three were transferred (the last two in 1949). They eventually took over all working on the island. They were renumbered in the Isle of Wight number series and all received local names. The Isle of Wight locomotives were fitted with larger bunkers from 1932 onwards and had Westinghouse brakes.

Year End Totals: 'O2' class

'47	'48	'49	'50	'51	'52	'53	'54	'55	'56	'57	'58	'59	'60	'61	'62	'63	'64	'65	'66	'67
48	48	48	48	48	48	43	43	39	37	35	33	29	27	23	18	18	16	14	10	

Number	Built	Renumbered	BR Dates	Scrap	Notes
30177	12/89 9Elm	05/48 177	-09/59	10/59	
30179	03/90 9Elm	05/48 179	-12/59	01/60	
30181	05/90 9Elm	181	-04/49	05/67	04/49➲W35
30182	05/90 9Elm	12/49 182	-01/60	01/60	dp
30183	05/90 9Elm	07/48 183	-09/61	11/61	dp
30192	11/90 9Elm	11/50 192	-08/61	09/61	
30193	11/90 9Elm	07/48 193	-04/62	10/62	
30197	06/91 9Elm	07/49 197	-02/53	03/53	
30198	04/91 9Elm	198	-04/49	10/65	04/49➲W36
30199	06/91 9Elm	10/49 199	-12/62	12/63	
30200	07/91 9Elm	05/48 200	-08/62	08/62	
30203	08/91 9Elm	03/51 203	-12/55	*01/56*	d
30204	09/91 9Elm	11/50 204	-02/53	03/53	d
30207	12/91 9Elm	08/49 207	-06/57	09/57	dp
30212	05/92 9Elm	07/51 212	-11/59	12/59	
30213	05/92 9Elm	05/48 213	-02/53	03/53	d
30216	06/92 9Elm	01/50 216	-11/57	12/57	
30221	09/92 9Elm	07/48 221	-08/53	*53*	d
30223	10/92 9Elm	*51* 223	-10/61	12/61	d
30224	10/92 9Elm	04/53 224	-02/58	02/58	
30225	11/92 9Elm	03/49 225	-12/62	05/63	dp
30229	12/94 9Elm	01/51 229	-03/61	04/61	
30230	12/94 9Elm	08/50 230	-08/56	*09/56*	
30231	12/94 9Elm	09/48 231	-03/53	*53*	
30232	01/95 9Elm	08/48 232	-09/59	10/59	
30233	01/95 9Elm	06/49 233	-02/58	02/58	d
30236	03/95 9Elm	10/49 236	-01/60	02/60	

Class continued with W14 (Isle of Wight Locomotives)

Q 30530-30549
0-6-0 SR Maunsell

Power Classification:	4F
Introduced:	1938-1939
Designer:	Maunsell
Company:	SR
Weight:	Loco 49t 10cwt Tender 40t 10cwt
Driving Wheel:	5' 1"
Boiler Pressure:	200psi superheated
Cylinders:	Inside 19" x 26"
Tractive Effort:	26160lbf
Valve Gear:	Stephenson (piston valves)

The 'Q' class was Maunsell's last design and twenty engines were built in 1938-1939. The locomotives were designed to meet the need for lightweight engines to replace older classes on branch line and secondary workings. They utilised a large number of standard parts already in use for existing classes. They were one of the final new designs of 0-6-0 tender locomotives to be built in this country, and did not appear until Bulleid was in office. Although designed primarily for freight duties, they were also fitted for steam heating passenger trains when required.

The locomotives were originally built with single chimneys. However they were very poor steamers until Bulleid fitted them all with multiple-jet blastpipes and large diameter chimneys. Unfortunately these suffered a lot from corrosion and a solution was found by fitting some of the engines with BR standard chimneys as used on the BR '80000' class.

s 30549 was modified in 1955 with a single stovepipe chimney and later with a BR standard single chimney.

b Some locomotives were later fitted with BR standard single chimneys.

Year End Totals: 'Q' class

'47	'48	'49	'50	'51	'52	'53	'54	'55	'56	'57	'58	'59	'60	'61	'62	'63	'64	'65	'66	'67
20	20	20	20	20	20	20	20	20	20	20	20	20	20	20	17	13	3			

Number	Built	Renumbered	BR Dates	Scrap	Notes
30530	01/38 Elh	09/48 530	-12/64	05/65	10/61⇨b
30531	06/38 Elh	01/49 531	-07/64	12/64	
30532	06/38 Elh	12/50 532	-01/64	12/64	
30533	07/38 Elh	08/49 533	-03/63	05/63	
30534	09/38 Elh	07/48 534	-12/62	05/64	
30535	09/38 Elh	12/48 535	-04/65	01/66	
30536	10/38 Elh	08/50 536	-01/64	07/64	07/61⇨b
30537	10/38 Elh	11/48 537	-12/62	05/64	
30538	11/38 Elh	12/48 538	-07/63	11/64	10/61⇨b
30539	12/38 Elh	12/48 539	-01/63	06/63	
30540	01/39 Elh	04/49 540	-11/62	05/64	
30541 §	01/39 Elh	09/48 541	-11/64		
30542	03/39 Elh	05/48 542	-12/64	05/65	
30543	03/39 Elh	05/48 543	-12/64	05/65	11/61⇨b
30544	04/39 Elh	06/49 544	-01/64	07/64	

Number	Built	Renumbered	BR Dates	Scrap	Notes
30545	06/39 Elh	04/49 545	-04/65	09/65	04/58⇨b
30546	06/39 Elh	01/50 546	-05/64	09/64	
30547	07/39 Elh	08/49 547	-01/64	07/64	10/61⇨b
30548	08/39 Elh	05/49 548	-03/65	07/65	
30549	09/39 Elh	04/49 549	-07/63	04/64	08/55⇨s⇨b

S11 30395-30404
4-4-0 LSWR Drummond

Power Classification: 2P
Introduced: 1903-1904
rebuilt by Urie 1920-1922
Designer: Drummond
Company: LSWR
Weight: Loco 53t 15cwt
y Tender 44t 17cwt
z Tender 39t 12cwt
Driving Wheel: 6' 0"
Boiler Pressure: 175psi superheated
Cylinders: Inside 19" x 26"
Tractive Effort: 19390lbf
Valve Gear: Stephenson (slide valves)

This was Drummond's development of the 'T9' class with a larger boiler and smaller wheels. They were designed for service in the West of England and ten engines were built in 1903-1904. They were fitted with superheaters in 1920-1922.

y All the locomotives were all originally fitted with large eight-wheel tenders.

z Some locomotives were later fitted with smaller six-wheel tenders. The list shows the tenders attached in 1948.

Year End Totals: 'S11' class

'47	'48	'49	'50	'51	'52	'53	'54	'55	'56	'57	'58	'59	'60	'61	'62	'63	'64	'65	'66	'67
10	10	10	10	1	1	1														

Number	*Built*	*Renumbered*	*BR Dates*	*Scrap*	*Notes*
30395	06/03 9Elm	395	-10/51	10/51	z
30396	06/03 9Elm	11/48 396	-11/51	11/51	y
30397	07/03 9Elm	06/49 397	-12/51	12/51	z
30398	07/03 9Elm	05/49 398	-12/51	12/51	y
30399	08/03 9Elm	07/48 399	-12/51	12/51	y
30400	09/03 9Elm	07/48 400	-11/54	03/55	y
30401	11/03 9Elm	401	-09/51	09/51	y
30402	11/03 9Elm	11/50 402	-03/51	03/51	y
30403	12/03 9Elm	06/49 403	-10/51	10/51	y
30404	12/03 9Elm	08/50 404	-10/51	10/51	y

S15 30496-30515, 30823-30847
4-6-0 LSWR Urie & SR Maunsell

Power Classification: 6F
Introduced: 1920-1936
Designer: Urie and Maunsell
Company: LSWR and SR
Weight: a Loco 79t 16cwt
bc Loco 80t 14cwt
d Loco 79t 5cwt
a Tender 57t 16cwt
bd Tender 56t 8cwt
c Tender 42t 8cwt
z Tender 44t 17cwt
Driving Wheel: 5' 7"
Boiler Pressure: a 180psi superheated
bcd 200psi superheated
Cylinders: a Outside 21" x 28"
bcd Outside 20½" x 28"
Tractive Effort: a 28200lbf
bcd 29855lbf
Valve Gear: Walschaert (piston valves)

The 'S15's were Urie's new 4-6-0 goods engines (see the 'H15' class for more details of Urie's range of 4-6-0s). The history of the class is summarised below.

a 30496-30515 were Urie's original design, built in 1920-1921. They were developed from the 'N15' class for goods and mixed traffic work. They could be distinguished from the later locomotives by having the footplating raised over the cylinders, and were fitted with eight-wheel tenders. They were used primarily for hauling express goods trains from Feltham Yard, but were also used on passenger trains at up to 70mph at peak times. 30496-30499 were loaned to the GWR during the Second World War.

b 30823-30832 were built in 1927 to Maunsell's design which was a development of Urie's with higher boiler pressure, reduced diameter cylinders, smaller grates and modified footplating and cabs. They were fitted with eight-wheel tenders.

c 30833-30837, built in 1927, were fitted with smaller six-wheel tenders for working on the Central Section.

d 30838-30847 were introduced in 1936. They were later locomotives with detail differences, reduced weight and a modified tender design. They were fitted with eight-wheel tenders.

z 30504-30510 were fitted with smaller eight-wheel tenders.

Year End Totals: 'S15' class

'47	'48	'49	'50	'51	'52	'53	'54	'55	'56	'57	'58	'59	'60	'61	'62	'63	'64	'65	'66	'67
45	45	45	45	45	45	45	45	45	45	45	45	45	45	45	41	23	6			

Number	*Built*	*Renumbered*	*BR Dates*	*Scrap*	*Notes*
30496	05/21 Elh	12/48 496	-06/63	08/63	a
30497	03/20 Elh	12/48 497	-07/63	03/64	a
30498	04/20 Elh	*51* 498	-06/63	08/63	a
30499 §	05/20 Elh	01/49 499	-01/64		a
30500	05/20 Elh	09/48 500	-06/63	10/63	a
30501	06/20 Elh	12/48 501	-06/63	08/63	a
30502	07/20 Elh	08/50 502	-11/62	03/63	a
30503	08/20 Elh	01/50 503	-06/63	10/63	a
30504	09/20 Elh	11/48 504	-11/62	01/63	az
30505	10/20 Elh	08/48 505	-11/62	12/62	az
30506 §	10/20 Elh	08/49 506	-01/64		az
30507	11/20 Elh	03/50 507	-12/63	03/64	az
30508	12/20 Elh	07/49 508	-12/63	01/64	az
30509	12/20 Elh	05/48 509	-07/63	03/64	az
30510	01/21 Elh	04/49 510	-06/63	09/63	az
30511	01/21 Elh	06/49 511	-07/63	01/64	a
30512	02/21 Elh	05/49 512	-03/64	01/65	a
30513	03/21 Elh	11/49 513	-03/63	06/63	a
30514	03/21 Elh	09/48 514	-07/63	03/64	a
30515	04/21 Elh	12/48 515	-07/63	01/64	a
30823	03/27 Elh	09/48 823	-11/64	02/65	b
30824	03/27 Elh	01/50 824	-09/65	12/65	b
30825 §	04/27 Elh	05/48 825	-01/64		b
30826	05/27 Elh	05/49 826	-11/62	01/64	b
30827	06/27 Elh	04/49 827	-01/64	02/64	b
30828 §	07/27 Elh	11/49 828	-01/64		b
30829	07/27 Elh	12/48 829	-11/63	01/64	b
30830 §	08/27 Elh	03/50 830	-07/64		b
30831	09/27 Elh	04/49 831	-11/63	12/63	b
30832	10/27 Elh	09/48 832	-01/64	02/64	b
30833	11/27 Elh	12/48 833	-05/65	04/66	c
30834	11/27 Elh	03/49 834	-11/64	03/65	c
30835	12/27 Elh	09/48 835	-11/64	03/65	c
30836	12/27 Elh	10/49 836	-06/64	10/64	c
30837	01/28 Elh	05/48 837	-09/65	09/66	c
30838	05/36 Elh	08/49 838	-09/65	05/66	d
30839	05/36 Elh	11/48 839	-09/65	05/66	d
30840	06/36 Elh	08/49 840	-09/64	11/64	d
30841 §	07/36 Elh	09/48 841	-01/64		d
30842	08/36 Elh	08/49 842	-09/65	11/65	d
30843	09/36 Elh	07/48 843	-09/64	11/64	d
30844	10/36 Elh	08/50 844	-06/64	01/65	d
30845	10/36 Elh	05/48 845	-07/63	09/63	d
30846	11/36 Elh	05/48 846	-01/63	02/63	d
30847 §	12/36 Elh	08/48 847	-01/64		d

T1 30001-30020, 30361-30367
0-4-4T LSWR Adams

Power Classification: 1P
Introduced: 1894-1896
Designer: Adams
Company: LSWR
Weight: 57t 2cwt
Driving Wheel: 5' 7"
Boiler Pressure: 160psi
Cylinders: Inside 18" x 26"
Tractive Effort: 17100lbf
Valve Gear: Stephenson (slide valves)

There were originally fifty engines in this class, numbered from 1-20, 61-80 and 358-367. The first locomotive was withdrawn in 1931. They were built by Adams for suburban work. These fourteen surviving locomotives were originally classed 'F6' but they were later included in the 'T1' class (61-80) which was introduced in 1888. Most of the locomotives survived in practically their original form until withdrawal, one or two being rebuilt with Drummond type boilers. The 'O2' class was developed as a smaller version of this class.

Year End Totals: 'T1' class

'47	'48	'49	'50	'51	'52	'53	'54	'55	'56	'57	'58	'59	'60	'61	'62	'63	'64	'65	'66	'67
14	9	4	3																	

Number	*Built*	*Renumbered*	*BR Dates*	*Scrap*	*Notes*
30001	04/94 9Elm	1	-07/49	09/49	
30002	05/94 9Elm	2	-03/49	03/49	
30003	05/94 9Elm	3	-10/48	11/48	
30005	06/94 9Elm	5	-01/50	02/50	
30007	07/94 9Elm	7	-06/51	06/51	
30008	08/94 9Elm	8	-05/49	06/49	
30009	08/94 9Elm	9	-07/48	10/48	
30010	08/94 9Elm	10	-08/48	10/48	
30013	06/95 9Elm	13	-03/49	03/49	
30020	11/95 9Elm	20	-06/51	06/51	
30361	06/96 9Elm	361	-02/49	02/49	
30363	07/96 9Elm	363	-06/48	10/48	
30366	07/96 9Elm	366	-10/48	12/48	
30367	07/96 9Elm	367	-06/51	06/51	

T9 30113-30122, between 30280 & 30338, 30702-30733, 120
4-4-0 LSWR Drummond

Power Classification: 2P reclassified 3P in 1953
Introduced: 1899-1901
Rebuilt 1922-1929 by Urie
Designer: Drummond
Company: LSWR
Weight: Loco 51t 18cwt
f Loco 51t 16cwt
w Loco 51t 7cwt
Tender 44t 17cwt
z Tender 39t 12cwt
Driving Wheel: 6' 7"
Boiler Pressure: 175psi superheated
Cylinders: Inside 19" x 26"
Tractive Effort: 17675lbf
Valve Gear: Stephenson (slide valves)

These locomotives were the famous LSWR 'Greyhound' class consisting of sixty-six engines built in 1899-1901. They were known as the 'Greyhounds' because of their sleek lines and speedy qualities. In the early years of the 20th Century they were in the front line in the LSWR's competition against the GWR for the West of England passenger traffic. Between 1922 and 1929 Urie rebuilt them with superheaters, larger diameter cylinders and higher pressure boilers. The rebuilt engines were found to be even more successful and they were often to be found working the expresses over the heavily graded line between Salisbury and Exeter in preference to the larger engines which should have replaced them.

30119 was for many years the locomotive used for working Royal trains on the Southern over lines which could not take heavier engines. As such it retained its immaculate green livery until it was withdrawn in 1952.

30120 was the last surviving locomotive of the class and in 1962 it was restored to LSWR livery as No. 120 for working special passenger trains and has since been preserved.

f These locomotives had detail differences and were originally fitted with Drummond's patented firebox water tubes, which were later removed by Urie.

o These locomotives were converted to oil burning during the coal crisis after the Second World War. They were all scrapped without being converted back to coal burning.

w The later built locomotives were fitted with wider cabs and splashers (without coupling-rod splashers) and they were originally fitted with firebox water tubes.

All the locomotives were all originally fitted with large eight-wheel tenders.

z Some locomotives were later fitted with smaller six-wheel tenders. The list shows the tenders attached in 1948.

Year End Totals: 'T9' class

'47	'48	'49	'50	'51	'52	'53	'54	'55	'56	'57	'58	'59	'60	'61	'62	'63	'64	'65	'66	'67
66	66	66	66	46	38	37	36	36	35	31	24	14	13	1	1					

Number	*Built*	*Renumbered*	*BR Dates*	*Scrap*	*Notes*
30113	06/99 9Elm	113	-05/51	*03/52*	o
30114	06/99 9Elm	114	-05/51	05/51	o
30115	07/99 9Elm	05/48 115	-05/51	05/51	o
30116	07/99 9Elm	116	-05/51	05/51	

30117	07/99 9Elm	08/49 117	-07/61	08/61	
30118	07/99 9Elm	118	-05/51	05/51	o
30119	08/99 9Elm	05/48 119	-12/52	02/53	
30120 §	08/99 9Elm	01/49 120	-07/63		
				03/62➲120	
30121	08/99 9Elm	05/48 121	-04/51	04/51	o
30122	09/99 9Elm	01/49 122	-04/51	04/51	
30280	10/99 9Elm	280	-05/51	05/51	o
30281	11/99 9Elm	04/49 281	-12/51	12/51	z
30282	11/99 9Elm	12/51 282	-03/54	*07/54*	z
30283	12/99 9Elm	03/49 283	-12/57	01/58	
30284	12/99 9Elm	07/48 284	-04/58	05/58	
30285	01/00 9Elm	12/50 285	-06/58	06/58	
30286	01/00 9Elm	05/48 286	-04/51	04/51	o
30287	01/00 9Elm	01/49 287	-09/61	11/61	
30288	02/00 9Elm	07/49 288	-12/60	05/61	
30289	02/00 9Elm	03/49 289	-11/59	11/59	
30300	12/00 9Elm	01/50 300	-03/61	04/61	wz
30301	12/00 9Elm	10/49 301	-08/59	10/59	wz
30302	12/00 9Elm	01/49 302	-10/52	*05/53*	w
30303	12/00 9Elm	303	-05/51	06/51	wo
30304	12/00 9Elm	09/51 304	-09/57	11/57	wz
30305	02/01 9Elm	305	-05/51	05/51	wo
30307	02/01 9Elm	11/49 307	-12/52	*05/53*	wz
30310	04/01 9Elm	11/48 310	-05/59	07/59	wz
30311	04/01 9Elm	09/51 311	-08/52	52	wz
30312	05/01 9Elm	08/49 312	-03/52	52	wz
30313	09/01 9Elm	06/49 313	-07/61	09/61	wz
30314	09/01 9Elm	314	-05/51	06/51	wo
30336	10/01 9Elm	05/50 336	-02/53	05/53	wz
30337	10/01 9Elm	03/49 337	-11/58	01/59	w
30338	10/01 9Elm	11/50 338	-04/61	06/61	w
30702	01/99 D	08/48 702	-10/59	10/59	f
30703	01/99 D	07/49 703	-10/52	*12/52*	f
30704	01/99 D	03/50 704	-10/51	10/51	fz
30705	01/99 D	05/49 705	-01/58	02/58	f
30706	01/99 D	08/49 706	-05/59	07/59	f
30707	06/99 D	05/48 707	-03/61	05/61	f
30708	06/99 D	07/48 708	-12/57	01/58	f
30709	06/99 D	05/49 709	-07/61	09/61	f
30710	06/99 D	08/49 710	-03/59	04/59	f
30711	06/99 D	05/49 711	-08/59	09/59	f
30712	06/99 D	07/49 712	-11/58	12/58	f
30713	06/99 D	713	-04/51	04/51	fo
30714	06/99 D	04/49 714	-04/51	04/51	f
30715	06/99 D	*49* 715	-07/61	08/61	f
30716	06/99 D	04/49 716	-10/51	10/51	f
30717	09/99 D	04/49 717	-07/61	08/61	f
30718	09/99 D	05/48 718	-03/61	04/61	f
30719	09/99 D	06/49 719	-03/61	04/61	f
30721	09/99 D	07/49 721	-01/58	01/58	f
30722	09/99 D	722	-04/51	*05/54*	fo
30723	09/99 D	723	-06/51	06/51	f
30724	09/99 D	07/49 724	-05/59	06/59	f
30725	10/99 D	09/48 725	-12/52	*01/53*	f
30726	10/99 D	04/49 726	-08/59	11/59	fz
30727	10/99 D	02/50 727	-09/58	10/58	f
30728	12/99 D	12/50 728	-10/56	*10/56*	f
30729	12/99 D	12/48 729	-03/61	04/61	fz
30730	12/99 D	08/49 730	-08/57	10/57	f
30731	12/99 D	731	-05/51	06/51	fo
30732	12/99 D	07/48 732	-10/59	10/59	f
30733	11/01 D	07/49 733	-06/52	52	f

Class continued with 120 (Preserved Locomotives)

T14 30443-30447, 30459-30462
4-6-0 LSWR Drummond

Power Classification: 4P
Introduced: 1911-1912
Designer: Drummond, rebuilt in 1915-1918 by Urie and again in 1930-1931 by Maunsell
Company: LSWR
Weight: Loco 76t 10cwt
Tender 60t 8cwt
Driving Wheel: 6' 7"
Boiler Pressure: 175psi superheated
Cylinders: Four 15" x 26"
Tractive Effort: 22030lbf
Valve Gear: Walschaert with rocking arms (slide valves)

Drummond did not achieve the same degree of success with his 4-6-0 engines as he did with his 4-4-0s. The first batch of four-cylinder 4-6-0 engines was the 'F13' class of 1905. They were numbered 330-334, and they were all rebuilt as two-cylinder engines of the 'H15' class by Maunsell in 1924-1925.

The second class consisted of one engine, number 335 of the 'E14' class. Built in 1907, this engine had an even shorter life. It was rebuilt with two cylinders as an 'H15' engine in 1915.

The next class was the 'G14' class of 1908. These five engines were numbered 453-457. There was a plan to rebuild them as 'N15's in 1925. In the event, the 'N15's were built new as replacements, although they did take the older engines' numbers and received their eight-wheeled tenders. The 'G14's were all scrapped in 1925.

The ten engines of this class (the 'T14's) were Drummond's last design of 4-6-0. They were designed for express passenger working and they were the most successful of his 4-6-0s. They were nicknamed 'Paddleboxes' because they were originally fitted with heavy and cumbersome splashers which incorporated a circular 'porthole' for access. They were four-cylinder engines and the cylinder casing was combined with the smokebox, giving the front end of these engines a cumbersome appearance.

The engines were originally fitted with firebox watertubes which were removed in 1915 to 1918 when superheaters were fitted by Urie. The heavy splashers were removed and replaced with a higher running plate by Maunsell in 1930-1931. The only locomotive which did not survive until 1948 was 458 which was destroyed in an air raid in 1940.

All the engines in this class were fitted with large eight-wheel tenders (they were the heaviest tender fitted to any of the ex-SR engines).

Year End Totals: 'T14' class

'47	'48	'49	'50	'51	'52	'53	'54	'55	'56	'57	'58	'59	'60	'61	'62	'63	'64	'65	'66	'67
9	6	4	2																	

Number	*Built*	*Renumbered*	*BR Dates*	*Scrap*	*Notes*
30443	04/11 Elh	443	-05/49	11/49	
30444	05/11 Elh	444	-02/50	03/50	
30445	06/11 Elh	445	-11/48	01/49	
30446	07/11 Elh	08/48 446	-05/51	05/51	
30447	07/11 Elh	11/49 447	-12/49	12/49	
30459	05/12 Elh	459	-11/48	01/49	
30460	02/12 Elh	460	-11/48	01/49	
30461	04/12 Elh	05/48 461	-06/51	06/51	
30462	05/12 Elh	462	-02/50	03/50	

USA 30061-74, DS233-DS238
0-6-0T SR War Department

Power Classification: 3F
Introduced: 1942-1943
Designer: Vulcan Ironworks (USA)
H K Porter (USA)
Company: US Army Transportation Corps.
Weight: 46t 10cwt
Driving Wheel: 4' 6"
Boiler Pressure: 210psi
Cylinders: Outside 16½" x 24"
Tractive Effort: 21600lbf
Valve Gear: Walschaert (piston valves)

During the Second World War, three American builders (H K Porter, Davenport and Vulcan) supplied 514 bar framed 0-6-0T engines to the US Army Transportation Corps. They were typical American 'Switcher' or shunting engines, carrying a stove-pipe chimney and three domes. They had a short wheelbase of only 10ft.

They were useful and sturdy engines which worked in many theatres of war. At the end of the war most of them were taken over by different European countries where they continued to work for many years. The SR purchased fourteen engines in 1946 and they were fitted with modified cabs, bunkers and brakes. The very wide cabs necessitated special warning notices to shunters riding on the steps.

The former US Army numbers were 1264, 1277, 1284, 1959, 1968, 1279, 1282, 1971, 1952, 1960, 1966, 1973, 1974 and 4326. 30074 retained the number 4326 until it received its BR number. An additional engine, No. 1261 survived at Eastleigh Works until September 1954 as a source of spare parts, but it was never taken into stock.

The engines worked at Southampton docks where they replaced fourteen Adams 'B4' tanks in 1947. In turn they were later replaced in 1963 by the fourteen class '07' diesels on dock duties and six locomotives were transferred to departmental duties as DS233-DS238. DS237 and DS238 worked as shunters at Ashford Works and were named. DS233 worked at Redbridge Sleeper Works, DS234 at Meldon Quarry and DS235 and DS236 at Lancing Carriage Works.

Year End Totals: 'USA' class

'47	'48	'49	'50	'51	'52	'53	'54	'55	'56	'57	'58	'59	'60	'61	'62	'63	'64	'65	'66	'67
14	14	14	14	14	14	14	14	14	14	14	14	14	14	14	8	7	6	6	6	

Year End Totals: 'USA' (service) class

'47	'48	'49	'50	'51	'52	'53	'54	'55	'56	'57	'58	'59	'60	'61	'62	'63	'64	'65	'66	'67
															3	6	6	4	4	

Number	*Built*	*Renumbered*	*BR Dates*	*Scrap*	*Notes*
30061	42 HKP	05/51 61	-11/62	07/67	
				10/62➲DS233	
30062	42 V	08/48 62	-11/62	01/68	
				12/62➲DS234	
30063	42 V	01/51 63	-05/62	06/62	
30064 §	43 V	*51* 64	-07/67		
30065 §	43 V	05/48 65	-10/62		
				11/63➲DS237	
30066	42 V	05/48 66	-12/62	08/65	
				03/63➲DS235	
30067	42 V	07/48 67	-07/67	02/68	
30068	43 V	06/51 68	-03/64	04/64	
30069	43 V	08/51 69	-07/67	03/68	
30070 §	43 V	08/51 70	-10/62		
				08/63➲DS238	
30071	43 V	*11/51* 71	-07/67	03/68	
30072 §	43 V	07/48 72	-07/67		
30073	43 V	*12/51* 73	-01/67	06/67	
30074	43 V	11/48 *74*	-03/63	08/65	
				04/63➲DS236	

Class continued with DS233 (Service Locomotives)

V 30900-30939
4-4-0 SR Maunsell 'Schools'

Power Classification: 5P
Introduced: 1930-1935
Designer: Maunsell
Company: SR
Weight: Loco 67t 2cwt
Tender 42t 8cwt
t Tender 43t 0cwt
n Tender 57t 19cwt
Driving Wheel: 6' 7"
Boiler Pressure: 220psi superheated
Cylinders: Three 16½" x 26"
Tractive Effort: 25135lbf
Valve Gear: Walschaert (piston valves)

The 'Schools' class was the last design of 4-4-0 locomotive to appear in this country. At the time they were built the 4-4-0 type was almost universally regarded as obsolete, but Maunsell managed to produce one of the most outstanding designs to be built in this country as well as the most powerful locomotive of that type in Europe.

They were built to replace the 'L' class locomotives on the increasingly heavy trains on the Hastings line. They were designed to have approximately the same haulage power as the 'King Arthur' class, but with a much greater route availability. In some ways they were 4-4-0 versions of the 'Lord Nelsons', but they had three perfectly balanced cylinders instead of four, and they had a round topped firebox instead of a Belpaire. The cab sides sloped inwards to provide the necessary clearance to work on the Hastings line.

The whole class was named after public schools and the engines originally worked on the South Eastern section of the Southern Railway. Later they were displaced by electrification and they worked heavy expresses over the Waterloo to Bournemouth route, and also the Portsmouth line (before that line was electrified).

30923 was named UPPINGHAM before August 1934.

m Twenty-one of the class were fitted with Lemaître multiple-jet blast pipes with wide chimneys in order to improve their draughting. The 'big-chimney Schools' had the reputation for free running but the advantages were not enough for the whole class to be rebuilt.

t 30932 was fitted for a while with a high-sided self-trimming tender. It was transferred to 30905 in 1958.

n 30912 and 30921 were later fitted with ex-'Lord Nelson' bogie tenders.

Year End Totals: 'V' class

'47	'48	'49	'50	'51	'52	'53	'54	'55	'56	'57	'58	'59	'60	'61	'62	'63	'64	'65	'66	'67
40	40	40	40	40	40	40	40	40	40	40	40	40	40	25						

Number	Built	Renumbered	BR Dates	Scrap	Notes
30900 ETON	03/30 Elh	05/48 900	-02/62	03/62	m
30901 WINCHESTER	03/30 Elh	11/48 901	-12/62	08/63	m
30902 WELLINGTON	04/30 Elh	01/49 902	-12/62	04/64	
30903 CHARTERHOUSE	04/30 Elh	05/48 903	-12/62	02/64	
30904 LANCING	05/30 Elh	07/48 904	-07/61	09/61	
30905 TONBRIDGE	05/30 Elh	10/49 905	-12/61	02/62	58⇨t
30906 SHERBORNE	06/30 Elh	11/49 906	-12/62	04/63	
30907 DULWICH	07/30 Elh	08/48 907	-09/61	09/61	m
30908 WESTMINSTER	07/30 Elh	04/49 908	-09/61	10/61	
30909 ST. PAUL'S	07/30 Elh	01/49 909	-02/62	03/62	m
30910 MERCHANT TAYLORS	11/32 Elh	12/48 910	-11/61	01/62	
30911 DOVER	12/32 Elh	08/49 911	-12/62	09/63	
30912 DOWNSIDE	12/32 Elh	04/49 912	-11/62	01/63	⇨n
30913 CHRIST'S HOSPITAL	12/32 Elh	09/48 913	-01/62	02/62	m
30914 EASTBOURNE	12/32 Elh	05/50 914	-07/61	09/61	m
30915 BRIGHTON	05/33 Elh	03/49 915	-12/62	11/63	m
30916 WHITGIFT	12/33 Elh	12/48 916	-12/62	09/63	
30917 ARDINGLY	06/33 Elh	05/48 917	-11/62	04/63	m
30918 HURSTPIERPOINT	06/33 Elh	10/49 918	-10/61	11/61	m
30919 HARROW	06/33 Elh	07/48 919	-02/61	03/61	m
30920 RUGBY	10/33 Elh	11/48 920	-11/61	01/62	m
30921 SHREWSBURY	11/33 Elh	03/50 921	-12/62	05/64	m⇨n
30922 MARLBOROUGH	12/33 Elh	01/49 922	-11/61	01/62	
30923 BRADFIELD	12/33 Elh	09/48 923	-12/62	08/63	
30924 HAILEYBURY	12/33 Elh	01/49 924	-01/62	01/62	m
30925 § CHELTENHAM	04/34 Elh	05/50 925	-12/62		
30926 § REPTON	05/34 Elh	05/48 926	-12/62		
30927 CLIFTON	06/34 Elh	11/49 927	-01/62	03/62	
30928 § STOWE	06/34 Elh	07/48 928	-11/62		
30929 MALVERN	07/34 Elh	01/49 929	-12/62	03/63	m
30930 RADLEY	12/34 Elh	07/48 930	-12/62	04/64	m
30931 KING'S-WIMBLEDON	12/34 Elh	11/48 931	-09/61	10/61	m
30932 BLUNDELL'S	02/35 Elh	07/48 932	-02/61	08/61	t
30933 KING'S-CANTERBURY	02/35 Elh	07/48 933	-11/61	12/61	m
30934 ST. LAWRENCE	03/35 Elh	08/48 934	-12/62	08/63	m
30935 SEVENOAKS	05/35 Elh	12/48 935	-12/62	05/64	
30936 CRANLEIGH	06/35 Elh	07/48 936	-12/62	10/63	
30937 EPSOM	06/35 Elh	09/48 937	-12/62	06/63	m
30938 ST. OLAVE'S	07/35 Elh	04/49 938	-07/61	09/61	m
30939 LEATHERHEAD	07/35 Elh	05/48 939	-06/61	09/61	m

Z 30950-30957
0-8-0T SR Maunsell

Power Classification:	7F reclassified 6F in 1953
Introduced:	1929
Designer:	Maunsell
Company:	SR
Weight:	71t 12cwt
Driving Wheel:	4' 8"
Boiler Pressure:	180psi
Cylinders:	Three 16" x 28"
Tractive Effort:	29375lbf
Valve Gear:	Walschaert (piston valves)

Maunsell built these eight locomotives at Brighton Works in 1929. They were designed for heavy yard shunting and were not superheated. Amongst their other duties they were also employed as bankers on trains up the 1 in 37 gradient between Exeter St. Davids and Queen Street. One was generally used at Dover to marshal the Wagon Lits sleeping cars onto the Dunkirk ferry boats. They were all withdrawn at the end of 1962.

They could be recognised by the footplate being raised over the cylinders and ending in a very deep front buffer beam. The short side tanks had a sloping top towards the front end to improve visibility while shunting.

Year End Totals: 'Z' class

'47	'48	'49	'50	'51	'52	'53	'54	'55	'56	'57	'58	'59	'60	'61	'62	'63	'64	'65	'66	'67
8	8	8	8	8	8	8	8	8	8	8	8	8	8	8						

Number	Built	Renumbered	BR Dates	Scrap	Notes
30950	04/29 Bton	07/48 950	-11/62	12/62	
30951	05/29 Bton	11/48 951	-11/62	03/64	
30952	05/29 Bton	06/49 952	-11/62	01/65	
30953	06/29 Bton	02/50 953	-12/62	01/63	
30954	09/29 Bton	04/49 954	-12/62	02/63	
30955	07/29 Bton	04/49 955	-12/62	04/63	
30956	03/29 Bton	07/48 956	-12/62	01/63	
30957	08/29 Bton	05/50 957	-11/62	12/62	

0298 30585-30587
2-4-0WT LSWR Beattie

Power Classification:	0F reclassified 0P in 1952
Introduced:	1874-1875
Designer:	Beattie
Company:	LSWR
Weight:	37t 16cwt
Driving Wheel:	5' 7"
Boiler Pressure:	160psi
Cylinders:	Outside 16½" x 20"
Tractive Effort:	11050lbf
Valve Gear:	Stephenson (slide valves)

Beattie built many 2-4-0Ts for the London area suburban work, and the '0298' class was the final class of twelve locomotives of this type to be built in 1874-1875. These three locomotives were the survivors of the class (the others being withdrawn between 1888 and 1898). They were rebuilt by Adams in 1884-1892, Urie in 1921-1922 and Maunsell in 1931-1935.

The reason for their remarkable longevity was that they were retained for working the Wadebridge-Wenford Bridge mineral line in Cornwall, where they were found to be the only suitable engines. They worked here for 64 years until displaced by GWR 1366 class locomotives.

After withdrawal they were all scheduled for preservation, but in fact only two of them survived.

r 30586 differed from the other two locomotives by having rectangular splashers instead of curved splashers.

Year End Totals: '0298' class

'47	'48	'49	'50	'51	'52	'53	'54	'55	'56	'57	'58	'59	'60	'61	'62	'63	'64	'65	'66	'67
3	3	3	3	3	3	3	3	3	3	3	3	3	3	3						

Number	Built	Renumbered	BR Dates	Scrap	Notes
30585 §	05/74 BP	12/48 3314	-12/62		
30586	11/75 BP	05/48 3329	-12/62	03/64	r
30587 §	06/74 BP	07/48 3298	-12/62		

0395 30564-30581
0-6-0 LSWR Adams

Power Classification:	1F reclassified 2F in 1953
Introduced:	1881-1886
Designer:	Adams
Company:	LSWR
Weight:	a Loco 37t 12cwt b Loco 38t 14cwt Tender 28t 13cwt t Tender 33t 4cwt
Driving Wheel:	5' 1"
Boiler Pressure:	a 140psi b 150psi
Cylinders:	Inside 17½" x 26"
Tractive Effort:	a 15535lbf b 16645lbf
Valve Gear:	Stephenson (slide valves)

This was Adams' 0-6-0 goods engine class. There were originally seventy locomotives in the class, built in 1881-1886. Fifty of the engines were sold to the Government in 1916, and were sent to the Middle East in the First World War, where they served in Palestine and Mesopotamia. They were never returned, some having been lost when the steamship 'Arabic' was torpedoed. Two more were withdrawn before 1948, leaving eighteen to come into BR stock, where they continued work on light goods trains and on yard duties.

a Adams original '395' class introduced in 1881

b Adams later '496' class, introduced in 1885. Similar to the '395' class but with increased front overhang.

d Two locomotives were subsequently fitted with Drummond type boilers. The boilers were interchanged but they were carried at different times by the locomotives marked.

s Three or four locomotives were modified from 1928 onwards with SECR 'M3' class boilers. The boilers were interchanged but they were carried at different times by the locomotives marked.

t Some of the class were fitted with larger six-wheel tenders.

Year End Totals: '0395' class

'47	'48	'49	'50	'51	'52	'53	'54	'55	'56	'57	'58	'59	'60	'61	'62	'63	'64	'65	'66	'67
18	18	18	17	17	17	14	14	14	9	5	2									

Number	Built	Renumbered	BR Dates	Scrap	Notes
30564	11/85 N	08/51 3029	-04/58	04/58	bd
30565	11/85 N	11/48 3083	-02/53	11/53	bs
30566	12/85 N	03/49 3101	-02/59	04/59	b
30567	03/83 N	08/48 3154	-09/59	10/59	adt
30568	03/83 N	11/49 3155	-04/58	04/58	a
30569	05/83 N	10/49 3163	-06/56	56	a
30570	05/83 N	07/48 3167	-12/56	*02/57*	ad
30571	12/81 N	07/48 3397	-07/53	11/53	a
30572	01/82 N	11/48 3400	-01/57	03/57	at
30573	04/83 N	11/50 3433	-11/56	*01/57*	as
30574	04/83 N	11/50 3436	-01/57	03/57	a
30575	05/83 N	01/50 3439	-12/58	01/59	a
30576	05/83 N	05/48 3440	-12/50	*01/51*	as
30577	05/83 N	05/51 3441	-02/56	*02/56*	a
30578	05/83 N	07/49 3442	-08/57	10/57	a
30579	10/85 N	01/49 3496	-01/56	*01/56*	b
30580	12/85 N	07/48 3506	-06/57	06/57	bst
30581	12/85 N	12/48 3509	-03/53	05/53	b

0415 30582-30584
4-4-2T LSWR Adams

Power Classification:	1P
Introduced:	1882-1885
Designer:	Adams
Company:	LSWR
Weight:	55t 2cwt
Driving Wheel:	5' 7"
Boiler Pressure:	160psi
Cylinders:	Outside 17½" x 24"
Tractive Effort:	14920lbf
Valve Gear:	Stephenson (slide valves)

These were the last three survivors of a class of seventy-one locomotives built in 1882-1885. The earliest was withdrawn in 1916. They were constructed for suburban work in the London area. The later locomotives (which included all three survivors) were fitted with very small side tanks, most of the water being carried in a well tank between the wheels, and in the bunker below the coal. Large numbers were taken out of service in 1916 when the LSWR suburban electrification started, but due to the war conditions they were not broken up and remained in Eastleigh yard in various stages of decay for several years. One of these, No. 0488 was sold first to the Ministry of Munitions in 1917 and then to the East Kent Railway in 1919, where it became EKR No 5.

By 1928 only two remained on the Southern Railway (0125 and 0520) and they were retained specially for working the Lyme Regis branch. These were found to be the most suitable engines for this highly curved branch line, due to their flexible wheelbase. Over a period of time it was found that two engines were not adequate for maintaining the service - if one engine was in the works, only one engine was available to work the service, with no cover in case of a breakdown. In 1946 the EKR engine was re-purchased by the SR. It was renumbered 3488 and the three engines continued to work the branch until 1961.

LSWR Adams '0395' class 0-6-0 No 30566 in May 1953.

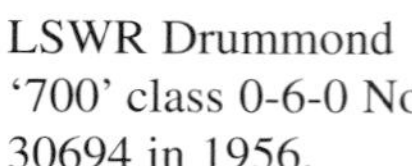

LSWR Drummond '700' class 0-6-0 No 30694 in 1956.

LSWR Drummond 'T9' class 4-4-0 No 30712, fitted with a stove-pipe chimney and an eight-wheel tender.

LSWR Maunsell 'N15' 'King Arthur' 4-6-0 No 30783 *Sir Gillemere* in July 1950.

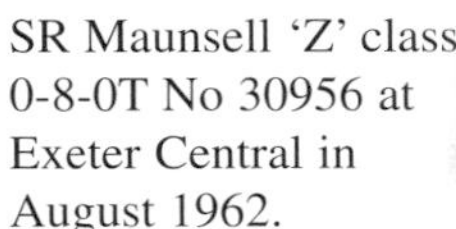
SR Maunsell 'Z' class 0-8-0T No 30956 at Exeter Central in August 1962.

SECR Wainwright 'C' class 0-6-0 No 31086.

The engines took turns to work the Lyme Regis Branch, one week at a time, with the other two being kept spare at Exmouth Junction Shed. The line was then taken over by the Western Region in 1961 and the locomotives were replaced by Ivatt '2MT' 2-6-2Ts until the line was closed.

Year End Totals: '0415' class

'47	'48	'49	'50	'51	'52	'53	'54	'55	'56	'57	'58	'59	'60	'61	'62	'63	'64	'65	'66	'67
3	3	3	3	3	3	3	3	3	3	3	3	3	3							

Number	Built	Renumbered	BR Dates	Scrap	Notes
30582	09/85 RS	04/49 3125	-07/61	03/62	
30583 §	03/85 N	10/49 3488	-07/61		
30584	12/85 D	05/48 3520	-02/61	12/61	

0458 30458
0-4-0ST Southampton Dock Company

Power Classification: 0F
Introduced: 1890
Designer: Hawthorn Leslie
Company: Southampton Dock Company
Weight: 21t 2cwt
Driving Wheel: 3' 2"
Boiler Pressure: 120psi
Cylinders: Outside 12" x 20"
Tractive Effort: 7730lbf
Valve Gear: Stephenson (slide valves)

Two locomotives were built by Hawthorn Leslie for the Southampton Dock Company (which was absorbed by the LSWR in 1892). They were numbered 457 (later 734) CLAUSENTUM and 458 (later 3458) IRONSIDE. 734 was withdrawn in 1945. Theoretically 3458 should have been renumbered in the 30564 series, but by coincidence the number 30458 was available due to a war casualty in the 'T14' class.

Year End Totals: '0458' class

'47	'48	'49	'50	'51	'52	'53	'54	'55	'56	'57	'58	'59	'60	'61	'62	'63	'64	'65	'66	'67
1	1	1	1	1	1	1														

Number	Built	Renumbered	BR Dates	Scrap	Notes
30458 IRONSIDE	07/90 HL	10/49 3458	-06/54	09/54	

700 between 30306 & 30368, 30687-30701
0-6-0 LSWR Drummond

Power Classification: 4F reclassified 3F in 1953
Introduced: 1897
Rebuilt by Urie in 1920-1929
Designer: Drummond
Company: LSWR
Weight: Loco 46t 14cwt
Tender 39t 12cwt
Driving Wheel: 5' 1"
Boiler Pressure: 180psi superheated
Cylinders: Inside 19" x 26"
Tractive Effort: 23540lbf
Valve Gear: Stephenson (slide valves)

Between 1876 and 1883 Dugald Drummond built 133 0-6-0s for the North British Railway followed by 244 very similar engines for the Caledonian Railway (which became the LMS 2F class 57230-57473). The '700' class were almost identical locomotives and thirty were built in 1897 by Dübs & Co. in Glasgow for freight work.

As built, the boilers were identical with those on the 'M7' class with which they were contemporary.

Urie rebuilt the whole class between 1921 and 1929 with superheaters and the boiler pressure and cylinder diameter was increased. The smokebox was extended and the frames were increased by 18" at the front end to accommodate it.

These locomotives were known as 'Black Motors' and they were all fitted with six-wheel tenders.

Year End Totals: '700' class

'47	'48	'49	'50	'51	'52	'53	'54	'55	'56	'57	'58	'59	'60	'61	'62	'63	'64	'65	'66	'67
30	30	30	30	30	30	30	30	30	30	29	29	28	27	17						

Number	Built	Renumbered	BR Dates	Scrap	Notes
30306	05/97 D	04/49 306	-04/62	05/62	
30308	05/97 D	01/51 308	-09/61	10/61	
30309	05/97 D	11/49 309	-12/62	07/63	
30315	05/97 D	11/48 315	-12/62	07/63	
30316	08/97 D	12/48 316	-12/62	05/63	
30317	05/97 D	08/48 317	-07/61	08/61	
30325	06/97 D	12/50 325	-12/62	03/63	
30326	06/97 D	07/49 326	-02/62	02/62	
30327	06/97 D	09/48 327	-05/61	06/61	
30339	06/97 D	09/48 339	-05/62	05/62	
30346	08/97 D	11/49 346	-11/62	10/63	
30350	08/97 D	05/48 350	-03/62	03/62	
30352	08/97 D	05/50 352	-06/59	07/59	
30355	08/97 D	11/50 355	-02/61	04/61	
30368	08/97 D	10/49 368	-12/62	12/63	
30687	03/97 D	08/48 687	-09/60	10/60	
30688	03/97 D	07/48 688	-09/57	10/57	
30689	03/97 D	11/48 689	-11/62	02/64	
30690	03/97 D	08/50 690	-12/62	02/63	
30691	03/97 D	12/51 691	-07/61	09/61	
30692	03/97 D	07/48 692	-01/62	03/62	
30693	03/97 D	*51* 693	-07/61	07/61	
30694	03/97 D	08/48 694	-06/61	07/61	
30695	03/97 D	08/49 695	-12/62	05/63	
30696	03/97 D	07/48 696	-08/61	09/61	
30697	04/97 D	11/50 697	-11/62	03/64	
30698	04/97 D	04/51 698	-05/62	05/62	
30699	05/97 D	11/50 699	-07/61	12/61	
30700	05/97 D	05/48 700	-11/62	04/64	
30701	05/97 D	02/50 701	-07/61	10/61	

756 30756
0-6-0T Plymouth Devonport & South Western Junction Railway

Power Classification: 1F
Introduced: 1907
Designer: Hawthorn Leslie
Company: PDSWJ
Weight: 35t 15cwt
Driving Wheel: 3' 10"
Boiler Pressure: 170psi
Cylinders: Outside 14" x 22"
Tractive Effort: 13545lbf
Valve Gear: Stephenson (slide valves)

This locomotive was designed for the Plymouth Devonport and South Western Junction Railway by Hawthorn Leslie. It was acquired by the LSWR in 1922 when it became No. 756.

Year End Totals: '756' class

'47	'48	'49	'50	'51	'52	'53	'54	'55	'56	'57	'58	'59	'60	'61	'62	'63	'64	'65	'66	'67
1	1	1	1																	

Number	Built	Renumbered	BR Dates	Scrap	Notes
30756 A. S. HARRIS	07 HL	756	-11/51	11/51	

757 30757-30758
0-6-2T Plymouth Devonport & South Western Junction Railway

Power Classification: 1MT reclassified 1P2F in 1953
Introduced: 1907
Designer: Hawthorn Leslie
Company: PDSWJ
Weight: 49t 19cwt
Driving Wheel: 4' 0"
Boiler Pressure: 170psi
Cylinders: Outside 16" x 24"
Tractive Effort: 18495lbf
Valve Gear: Stephenson (slide valves)

These locomotives were designed for the Plymouth Devonport and South Western Junction Railway by Hawthorn Leslie. They were acquired by the LSWR in 1922 when they became Nos. 757 and 758. The SR intended to buy more engines of this design for service in the West of England, but the rebuilding of the 'E1' class to produce the 'E1R' class provided a better and cheaper way of producing the necessary locomotives with an axle load of only 14¼ tons.

Year End Totals: '757' class

'47	'48	'49	'50	'51	'52	'53	'54	'55	'56	'57	'58	'59	'60	'61	'62	'63	'64	'65	'66	'67
2	2	2	2	2	2	2	2	2	1											

Number	Built	Renumbered	BR Dates	Scrap	Notes
30757 EARL OF MOUNT EDGCUMBE	07 HL	04/49 757	-12/57	12/57	
30758 LORD ST. LEVAN	07 HL	11/50 758	-12/56	02/57	

Numerical List 31002-31925

Number	Built	Renumbered	BR Dates	Scrap	Class
31002	11/86 Asfd	1002	-06/48	06/48	F1
31003	05/96 Asfd	1003	-01/49	*49*	O1
31004	07/01 Asfd	05/48 1004	-11/61	11/61	C
31005	05/07 Asfd	12/48 1005	-09/63	05/64	H
31007	08/99 Asfd	1007	-05/49	*49*	O1
31010	12/90 Asfd	08/48 1010	-08/59	09/59	R1 [1]
31013	10/98 Asfd	1013	-09/48	*48*	B1
31014	06/93 Asfd	1014	-06/48	*06/48*	O1
31016	07/15 Asfd	06/49 1016	-07/51	*51*	H
31018	10/00 Asfd	05/48 1018	-01/59	01/59	C
31019	07/08 Asfd	11/48 1019	-04/61	06/61	E1 [1]
31027 §	02/10 Asfd	07/48 1027	-03/61		P
31028	12/89 Asfd	1028	-05/48	05/48	F1
31031	09/94 Asfd	1031	-05/48	05/48	F1
31033	10/00 Asfd	02/50 1033	-03/60	03/60	C
31036	12/08 Asfd	03/49 1036	-03/51	03/51	E
31037	03/01 Asfd	12/48 1037	-02/61	03/61	C
31038	07/01 Asfd	07/48 1038	-03/54	*54*	C
31039	06/97 Asfd	1039	-08/49	*49*	O1
31041	06/93 Asfd	1041	-05/51	*51*	O1
31042	03/96 Asfd	1042	-02/48	*48*	F1
31044	12/98 Asfd	1044	-06/51	*51*	O1
31046	06/94 Asfd	1046	-10/48	*48*	O1
31047	08/95 Asfd	04/49 1047	-03/60	04/60	R1 [1]
31048	12/93 Asfd	03/50 1048	-10/60	10/60	O1
31051	12/98 Asfd	1051	-08/48	09/48	O1
31054	03/01 Asfd	10/49 1054	-08/60	10/60	C
31057	06/02 Asfd	08/49 1057	-04/51	*04/51*	D
31059	11/02 Asfd	04/49 1059	-02/58	03/58	C
31061	07/01 Asfd	12/49 1061	-07/61	10/61	C
31063	07/00 Asfd	12/48 1063	-04/56	*04/56*	C
31064	11/96 Asfd	*52* 1064	-05/58	05/58	O1
31065 §	09/96 Asfd	*52* 1065	-06/61		O1
31066	06/97 Asfd	1066	-06/51	*06/51*	O1
31067	08/08 Asfd	09/48 1067	-11/61	12/61	E1 [1]
31068	01/03 Asfd	07/48 1068	-10/61	11/61	C
31069	06/98 Asfd	05/48 1069	-06/58	06/58	R1 [1]
31071	07/01 Asfd	12/50 1071	-09/59	12/59	C
31075	03/03 D	01/50 1075	-12/56	12/56	D
31078	12/86 Asfd	1078	-03/49	*49*	F1
31080	06/97 Asfd	1080	-08/49	*49*	O1
31086	09/00 Asfd	11/50 1086	-10/60	11/60	C
31090	01/03 Asfd	04/49 1090	-08/53	10/53	C
31092	03/03 D	04/49 1092	-06/51	*51*	D
31093	11/97 Asfd	1093	-05/51	*05/51*	O1
31102	09/00 Asfd	05/50 1102	-05/60	06/60	C
31105	03/96 Asfd	1105	-02/49	*49*	F1
31106	05/94 Asfd	1106	-01/49	*49*	O1
31107	06/98 Asfd	04/51 1107	-08/59	02/60	R1 [1]
31108	06/97 Asfd	1108	-07/51	*51*	O1
31109	05/96 Asfd	1109	-01/49	*49*	O1
31112	09/00 Asfd	11/50 1112	-04/62	05/62	C
31113	03/02 Asfd	02/50 1113	-07/61	08/61	C
31123	05/96 Asfd	1123	-01/50	04/50	O1
31127	08/95 Asfd	1127	-01/49	*49*	R1 [1]
31128	10/92 Asfd	10/49 1128	-08/59	01/60	R1 [1]
31145	04/03 D	11/49 1145	-10/61	12/61	D1 [1]
31147	11/90 Asfd	07/51 1147	-09/58	12/58	R1 [1]
31150	11/02 Asfd	01/51 1150	-10/61	11/61	C
31151	10/99 Asfd	07/48 1151	-03/49	*49*	F1
31154	07/92 Asfd	05/48 1154	-09/55	*10/55*	R1 [1]
31157	12/07 Asfd	1157	-03/51	04/51	E
31158	12/09 Asfd	08/50 1158	-04/55	*55*	H
31159	11/08 Asfd	03/49 1159	-12/51	*52*	E
31160	07/07 Asfd	01/49 1160	-02/51	04/51	E1 [1]
31161	06/09 Asfd	07/48 1161	-11/61	12/61	H
31162	03/09 Asfd	12/50 1162	-07/61	08/61	H
31163	04/09 Asfd	1163	-05/49	*49*	E1 [1]
31164	02/09 Asfd	07/49 1164	-10/59	10/59	H
31165	12/07 Asfd	05/49 1165	-05/59	05/59	E1 [1]
31166	07/07 Asfd	06/48 1166	-05/55	*55*	E
31174	10/92 Asfd	04/51 1174	-08/59	*59*	R1 [1]
31175	08/08 Asfd	1175	-10/51	*51*	E
31176	12/07 Asfd	03/49 1176	-10/51	*51*	E
31177	03/09 Asfd	11/48 1177	-10/61	10/61	H
31178 §	02/10 Asfd	05/51 1178	-06/58		P
31179	11/08 Asfd	03/49 1179	-10/50	03/51	E1 [1]
31182	06/09 Asfd	06/49 1182	-07/51	*51*	H
31184	04/15 Asfd	02/50 1184	-03/58	03/58	H
31191	07/00 Asfd	*52* 1191	-09/59	10/59	C
31193	12/09 Asfd	08/50 1193	-03/61	05/61	H
31215	10/91 Asfd	1215	-05/48	05/48	F1
31217	10/98 Asfd	1217	-06/50	*50*	B1
31218	12/00 Asfd	11/48 1218	-04/62	04/62	C
31219	12/00 Asfd	10/49 1219	-10/59	10/59	C
31221	03/01 Asfd	10/49 1221	-08/59	08/59	C
31223	03/01 Asfd	11/50 1223	-05/60	05/60	C
31225	12/00 Asfd	03/50 1225	-06/55	*55*	C
31227	12/00 Asfd	08/50 1227	-10/59	11/59	C
31229	01/00 Asfd	02/52 1229	-10/61	11/61	C
31231	10/93 Asfd	1231	-03/49	07/51	F1
31234	04/01 Asfd	05/49 1234	-08/53	*53*	C
31238	06/93 Asfd	1238	-07/49	*49*	O1

31239 11/09 Asfd 03/49 1239 -01/60 01/60 H
31242 04/02 Asfd 07/49 1242 -09/61 09/61 C
31243 04/02 Asfd 04/49 1243 -10/59 10/59 C
31244 04/02 Asfd 11/50 1244 -10/61 10/61 C
31245 12/02 Asfd 04/51 1245 -08/59 11/59 C
31246 06/02 Asfd 05/48 1246 -03/61 05/61 D1[1]
31247 04/03 Asfd 04/49 1247 -07/61 09/61 D1[1]
31248 05/96 Asfd 1248 -06/51 51 O1
31252 12/02 Asfd 03/51 1252 -07/59 01/60 C
31253 01/03 Asfd 05/49 1253 -10/59 12/59 C
31255 06/00 Asfd 12/48 1255 -09/61 09/61 C
31256 06/00 Asfd 06/50 1256 -07/61 08/61 C
31257 06/00 Asfd 1257 -08/49 49 C
31258 05/94 Asfd 12/49 1258 -02/61 02/61 O1
31259 11/05 Asfd 05/48 1259 -11/59 01/60 H
31260 08/04 Asfd 08/50 1260 -05/53 53 C
31261 11/05 Asfd 08/50 1261 -10/61 10/61 H
31263 § 05/05 Asfd 10/49 1263 -01/64 H
31265 05/05 Asfd 03/49 1265 -08/60 09/60 H
31266 05/05 Asfd 01/50 1266 -10/60 12/60 H
31267 01/04 Asfd 01/50 1267 -06/62 07/62 C
31268 02/04 Asfd 05/48 1268 -04/62 05/62 C
31269 11/05 Asfd 10/49 1269 -12/59 12/59 H
31270 06/04 Asfd 08/48 1270 -06/59 06/59 C
31271 12/04 Asfd 06/51 1271 -07/63 12/67 C
07/63➲DS240
31272 02/04 Asfd 03/49 1272 -08/59 01/60 C
31273 02/06 Asfd 10/49 1273 -12/51 12/51 E
31274 06/05 Asfd 04/51 1274 -11/57 11/57 H
31275 02/06 Asfd 05/49 1275 -03/51 04/51 E
31276 06/05 Asfd 52 1276 -02/61 05/61 H
31277 02/04 Asfd 05/49 1277 -09/55 55 C
31278 07/05 Asfd 10/49 1278 -10/62 11/62 H
31279 11/09 Asfd 07/48 1279 -09/59 10/59 H
31280 02/08 Asfd 10/49 1280 -07/63 12/63 C
31287 05/08 Asfd 10/49 1287 -10/60 11/60 C
31291 02/08 Asfd 05/51 1291 -05/53 05/53 C
31293 06/08 Asfd 01/50 1293 -04/62 05/62 C
31294 06/08 Asfd 10/49 1294 -10/55 10/55 C
31295 12/09 Asfd 08/50 1295 -05/59 05/59 H
31297 06/08 Asfd 07/48 1297 -09/59 09/59 C
31298 03/08 Asfd 12/48 1298 -11/60 01/61 C
31302 04/81 N 1302 -07/49 07/49 1302
31305 05/06 Asfd 03/49 1305 -11/62 07/64 H
31306 05/06 Asfd 05/48 1306 -12/61 01/62 H
31307 12/06 Asfd 05/49 1307 -08/61 09/61 H
31308 06/06 Asfd 01/49 1308 -12/62 11/63 H
31309 06/06 Asfd 01/50 1309 -06/55 55 H
31310 06/06 Asfd 05/49 1310 -05/60 06/60 H
31311 05/07 Asfd 08/49 1311 -12/54 55 H
31315 04/09 Asfd 07/48 1315 -03/54 10/54 E
31316 09/82 Asfd 1316 -06/49 49 O1
31317 03/08 Asfd 04/49 1317 -02/62 03/62 C
31319 12/09 Asfd 08/50 1319 -01/60 02/60 H
31320 05/07 Asfd 07/48 1320 -12/55 56 H
31321 12/06 Asfd 51 1321 -11/57 11/57 H
31322 06/09 Asfd 02/50 1322 -04/61 06/61 H
31323 § 07/10 Asfd 03/49 1323 -07/60 P
31324 05/07 Asfd 01/50 1324 -07/62 08/62 H
31325 07/10 Asfd 01/49 1325 -03/60 03/60 P
31326 12/06 Asfd 07/48 1326 -10/61 11/61 H
31327 06/07 Asfd 04/49 1327 -11/59 11/59 H
31328 12/06 Asfd 04/49 1328 -02/61 04/61 H
31329 12/06 Asfd 07/48 1329 -11/59 11/59 H
31335 06/88 Asfd 05/51 1335 -07/55 55 R1[1]
31337 06/88 Asfd 51 1337 -02/60 05/60 R1[1]
31339 02/89 Asfd 05/51 1339 -06/58 06/58 R1[1]
31340 03/89 Asfd 09/48 1340 -02/59 03/59 R1[1]
31369 08/91 SS 1369 -09/51 51 O1
31370 08/91 SS 03/50 1370 -02/60 04/60 O1
31371 08/91 SS EKR 1371 -01/49 49 O1
31372 08/91 SS EKR 6 -02/49 49 O1
31373 09/91 SS 1373 -07/51 51 O1
31374 09/91 SS 1374 -09/49 49 O1
31377 09/91 SS 1377 -01/50 05/50 O1
31378 09/91 SS 05/48 1378 -11/48 48 O1
31379 09/93 SS 1379 -05/51 05/51 O1
31380 09/93 SS 1380 -11/49 49 O1
31381 09/93 SS 1381 -05/51 51 O1
31383 09/93 SS 10/49 EKR 2 -04/51 04/51 O1
31384 09/93 SS 1384 -12/49 50 O1
31385 09/93 SS 1385 -09/49 49 O1
31386 10/93 SS 1386 -10/48 48 O1
31388 10/93 SS 1388 -07/48 07/48 O1
31389 10/93 SS 1389 -02/49 49 O1
31390 10/93 SS 1390 -05/51 51 O1
31391 10/93 SS 1391 -06/51 06/51 O1
31395 11/93 SS 1395 -06/51 06/51 O1
31396 12/93 SS 1396 -08/48 08/48 O1
31397 12/93 SS 1397 -06/48 07/48 O1
31398 12/93 SS 1398 -05/49 49 O1
31400 07/32 Asfd 07/48 1400 -06/64 12/64 N
31401 08/32 Asfd 09/48 1401 -07/65 10/65 N
31402 08/32 Asfd 06/49 1402 -08/63 07/64 N
31403 08/32 Asfd 06/49 1403 -06/63 10/63 N
31404 10/32 Asfd 05/48 1404 -12/63 01/64 N
31405 11/32 Asfd 11/49 1405 -06/66 09/66 N
31406 01/33 Asfd 10/49 1406 -09/64 12/64 N
31407 08/32 Asfd 08/49 1407 -07/63 10/64 N
31408 09/33 Asfd 07/49 1408 -06/66 09/66 N
31409 10/33 Asfd 01/49 1409 -10/62 02/64 N
31410 11/33 Asfd 12/49 1410 -11/64 03/65 N
31411 11/33 Asfd 11/48 1411 -04/66 09/66 N
31412 12/33 Asfd 12/48 1412 -08/64 12/64 N
31413 01/34 Asfd 10/49 1413 -06/64 12/64 N
31414 01/34 Asfd 05/50 1414 -11/62 02/63 N
31425 08/97 SS 04/49 1425 -08/59 11/59 O1
31426 08/97 SS 1426 -08/48 09/48 O1
31428 09/97 SS 1428 -03/49 49 O1
31429 09/97 SS 1429 -09/49 49 O1
31430 09/97 SS 03/50 1430 -05/59 06/59 O1
31432 09/97 SS 1432 -06/51 06/51 O1
31434 09/97 SS 03/50 1434 -08/59 08/59 O1
31437 10/97 SS 1437 -10/48 48 O1
31438 10/97 SS 1438 -11/48 48 O1
31439 10/97 SS 1439 -05/49 49 O1
31440 07/98 NR 1440 -11/48 48 B1
31443 07/98 NR 1443 -03/51 04/51 B1
31445 07/98 NR 1445 -02/48 48 B1
31446 08/98 NR 07/48 1446 -07/49 09/49 B1
31448 08/98 NR 1448 -08/49 49 B1
31449 08/98 NR 1449 -03/49 49 B1
31450 08/98 NR 1450 -04/48 48 B1
31451 08/98 NR 1451 -12/49 50 B1
31452 08/98 NR 1452 -04/50 50 B1
31453 08/98 NR 1453 -10/48 10/48 B1
31454 08/98 NR 1454 -11/48 48 B1
31455 09/98 NR 1455 -06/49 07/49 B1
31457 09/98 NR 1457 -02/49 49 B1
31459 09/98 NR 1459 -02/48 48 B1
31460 10/02 Lngh 1460 -02/49 49 C
31461 12/02 Lngh 09/48 1461 -08/58 08/58 C
31470 08/06 Asfd 05/48 1470 -06/59 09/59 D1[1]
31477 03/07 Asfd 12/48 1477 -02/51 04/51 D
31480 01/04 Lngh 01/52 1480 -07/61 07/61 C
31481 04/04 Lngh 05/48 1481 -11/61 12/61 C
31486 12/02 Lngh 07/48 1486 -05/53 05/53 C
31487 07/02 Asfd 05/48 1487 -02/61 04/61 D1[1]
31488 07/02 Asfd 05/48 1488 -02/56 02/56 D
31489 04/03 D 11/48 1489 -11/61 12/61 D1[1]
31490 08/02 Asfd 05/48 1490 -09/51 51 D
31491 07/07 Asfd 1491 -02/53 05/53 E
31492 04/03 D 01/49 1492 -01/60 02/60 D1[1]
31493 03/03 D 1493 -02/54 10/54 D
31494 04/03 D 04/49 1494 -08/60 09/60 D1[1]
31495 06/04 Asfd 05/48 1495 -03/61 04/61 C
31496 03/07 Asfd 03/49 1496 -09/55 55 D
31497 09/07 Asfd 01/50 1497 -10/60 11/60 E1[1]
31498 06/04 Asfd 08/49 1498 -07/61 10/61 C
31500 11/05 Asfd 07/48 1500 -06/61 06/61 H
31501 04/03 D 05/50 1501 -05/53 05/53 D
31502 05/03 D 05/48 1502 -03/51 04/51 D1[1]
31503 12/05 Asfd 11/48 1503 -08/59 11/59 H
31504 12/05 Asfd 01/49 1504 -02/58 03/58 E1[1]
31505 02/07 Asfd 05/49 1505 -09/61 11/61 D1[1]
31506 12/05 Asfd 05/49 1506 -09/58 10/58 E1[1]
31507 09/08 Asfd 12/48 1507 -07/61 08/61 E1[1]
31508 07/04 Asfd 11/50 1508 -09/57 10/57 C
31509 09/06 Asfd 01/49 1509 -05/60 05/60 D1[1]
31510 07/04 Asfd 04/49 1510 -06/62 07/62 C
31511 12/05 Asfd 07/48 1511 -12/50 02/51 E1[1]
31512 01/09 Asfd 07/48 1512 -06/61 08/61 H
31513 06/08 Asfd 12/51 1513 -03/55 55 C
31514 12/07 Asfd 10/49 1514 -12/51 52 E
31515 09/07 Asfd 03/49 1515 -07/51 51 E
31516 04/08 Asfd 04/49 1516 -10/51 51 E
31517 01/09 Asfd 11/49 1517 -05/61 07/61 H
31518 07/09 Asfd 09/48 1518 -01/64 11/64 H
31519 07/09 Asfd 03/51 1519 -02/61 06/61 H
31520 08/09 Asfd 07/48 1520 -08/60 09/60 H
31521 08/09 Asfd 08/48 1521 -05/62 06/62 H
31522 08/09 Asfd 04/49 1522 -01/63 02/63 H
31523 09/09 Asfd 07/49 1523 -01/59 01/59 H
31530 07/05 Asfd 05/48 1530 -03/62 03/62 H
31531 07/05 Asfd 06/49 1531 -04/55 55 H
31532 07/05 Asfd 07/49 1532 -03/51 04/51 H
31533 07/05 Asfd 04/49 1533 -09/62 09/62 H
31540 11/04 Asfd 03/50 1540 -02/60 04/60 H
31541 11/04 Asfd 05/48 1541 -04/51 04/51 H
31542 11/04 Asfd 06/51 1542 -11/62 07/64 H
31543 01/09 Asfd 12/50 1543 -07/63 03/64 H
31544 11/04 Asfd 04/51 1544 -09/63 12/63 H
31545 09/06 Asfd 12/48 1545 -03/61 05/61 D1[1]
31546 11/04 Asfd 04/49 1546 -02/51 03/51 H
31547 09/08 Asfd 1547 -02/51 04/51 E
31548 12/04 Asfd 04/49 1548 -08/59 09/59 H
31549 09/06 Asfd 04/49 1549 -10/56 56 D
31550 11/04 Asfd 05/48 1550 -02/61 03/61 H
31551 01/05 Asfd 11/49 1551 -01/64 07/64 H
31552 01/05 Asfd 11/50 1552 -11/61 12/61 H
31553 02/05 Asfd 01/50 1553 -06/61 07/61 H
31554 12/09 Asfd 01/49 1554 -05/59 06/59 H
31555 06/10 Asfd 05/48 1555 -02/55 03/55 P
31556 § 02/09 Asfd 03/50 1556 -06/61 P
31557 02/09 Asfd 05/49 1557 -09/57 09/57 P
31558 06/10 Asfd 52 1558 -02/60 02/60 P
31572 09/03 Asfd 11/50 1572 -03/54 54 C
31573 09/03 Asfd 06/49 1573 -11/61 12/61 C
31574 02/07 Asfd 52 1574 -10/56 01/57 D
31575 09/03 Asfd 08/49 1575 -07/61 07/61 C
31576 05/03 Asfd 04/49 1576 -11/59 11/59 C
31577 09/06 Asfd 09/51 1577 -12/56 57 D
31578 10/03 Asfd 07/49 1578 -06/61 07/61 C
31579 10/03 Asfd 12/49 1579 -10/61 10/61 C
31580 06/03 Lngh 07/48 1580 -08/53 53 C
31581 05/03 Asfd 07/49 1581 -03/60 03/60 C
31582 06/03 Asfd 08/48 1582 -06/58 06/58 C
31583 06/03 Lngh 05/48 1583 -07/61 08/61 C
31584 06/03 Asfd 05/49 1584 -02/62 03/62 C
31585 06/03 Asfd 07/48 1585 -02/59 05/59 C
31586 02/07 Asfd 05/48 1586 -09/55 55 D
31587 02/07 Asfd 10/49 1587 -07/51 51 E
31588 03/08 Asfd 05/50 1588 -06/62 07/62 C
31589 03/08 Asfd 11/49 1589 -11/61 12/61 C
31590 07/08 Asfd 11/50 1590 -02/61 03/61 C
31591 03/07 Asfd 07/48 1591 -06/55 55 D
31592 § 02/02 Lngh 12/48 1592 -07/63 C
07/63➲DS239
31593 05/02 Lngh 12/48 1593 -02/58 04/58 C
31595 10/13 Asfd 12/48 1595 -05/51 07/51 J
31596 10/13 Asfd 04/49 1596 -10/51 10/51 J
31597 11/13 Asfd 07/48 1597 -11/50 01/51 J
31598 11/13 Asfd 06/49 1598 -12/50 04/51 J
31599 12/13 Asfd 08/48 1599 -10/49 05/50 J
31602 06/93 Lngh 1602 -07/51 07/51 T
31604 03/91 Lngh 05/50 1604 -12/50 01/51 T
31610 08/28 Bton 07/48 1610 -12/62 09/63 U
31611 08/28 Bton 02/51 1611 -10/63 01/64 U
31612 07/28 Bton 04/49 1612 -05/63 08/63 U
31613 06/28 Bton 01/50 1613 -01/64 07/64 U
31614 07/28 Bton 49 1614 -11/63 01/64 U
31615 08/28 Bton 12/48 1615 -10/63 11/63 U
31616 09/28 Bton 08/48 1616 -06/64 11/64 U
31617 10/28 Bton 11/49 1617 -01/64 07/64 U
31618 § 10/28 Bton 05/48 1618 -01/64 U
31619 12/28 Bton 05/49 1619 -12/65 03/66 U
31620 11/28 Asfd 09/48 1620 -04/65 08/65 U
31621 12/28 Asfd 10/49 1621 -06/64 11/64 U
31622 01/29 Asfd 12/48 1622 -01/64 02/64 U
31623 01/29 Asfd 51 1623 -12/63 12/63 U
31624 02/29 Asfd 08/48 1624 -06/64 11/64 U
31625 § 03/29 Asfd 12/48 1625 -01/64 U
31626 03/29 Asfd 04/49 1626 -01/64 12/64 U
31627 04/29 Asfd 04/49 1627 -10/65 02/66 U
31628 04/29 Asfd 11/48 1628 -06/64 12/64 U
31629 12/29 Asfd 06/49 1629 -01/64 12/64 U
31630 02/31 Asfd 12/48 1630 -11/62 12/62 U
31631 03/31 Asfd 10/49 1631 -09/63 11/63 U
31632 03/31 Asfd 07/48 1632 -09/64 12/64 U
31633 03/31 Asfd 07/49 1633 -12/63 02/64 U
31634 04/31 Asfd 09/48 1634 -12/63 02/64 U
31635 04/31 Asfd 08/50 1635 -12/63 01/64 U
31636 04/31 Asfd 09/48 1636 -06/63 08/63 U
31637 05/31 Asfd 12/48 1637 -09/63 09/63 U
31638 § 05/31 Asfd 11/48 1638 -01/64 U
31639 05/31 Asfd 12/48 1639 -06/66 09/66 U
31658 09/91 SS 01/49 1658 -12/52 12/52 R
31659 09/91 SS 11/49 1659 -09/51 51 R
31660 09/91 SS 03/49 1660 -12/53 04/54 R
31661 10/91 SS 03/49 1661 -09/55 55 R
31662 10/91 SS 08/49 1662 -10/53 10/53 R
31663 10/91 SS 05/50 1663 -07/53 53 R
31665 10/91 SS 06/50 1665 -10/52 52 R
31666 11/91 SS 07/48 1666 -12/55 01/56 R
31667 11/91 SS 09/48 1667 -04/51 04/51 R
31670 11/91 SS 12/48 1670 -04/51 51 R
31671 11/91 SS 11/49 1671 -11/54 03/55 R
31672 11/91 SS 1672 -12/49 50 R
31673 11/91 SS 1673 -10/52 02/53 R
31674 12/91 SS 03/49 1674 -06/52 52 R
31675 12/91 SS 08/49 1675 -12/52 12/52 R
31681 06/00 NR 11/49 1681 -02/59 03/59 C
31682 06/00 NR 05/49 1682 -10/61 10/61 C
31683 06/00 NR 11/50 1683 -06/59 06/59 C
31684 06/00 NR 04/49 1684 -10/61 10/61 C
31685 06/00 NR 1685 -10/51 10/51 S
31686 07/00 NR 12/48 1686 -04/62 05/62 C
31687 07/00 NR 07/48 1687 -04/55 55 C
31688 07/00 NR 12/48 1688 -02/60 02/60 C
31689 07/00 NR 11/48 1689 -03/62 04/62 C
31690 07/00 NR 03/50 1690 -06/62 07/62 C
31691 07/00 NR 05/50 1691 -10/61 10/61 C
31692 07/00 NR 07/48 1692 -04/60 05/60 C
31693 07/00 NR 09/50 1693 -06/61 06/61 C
31694 07/00 NR 02/50 1694 -03/61 06/61 C
31695 07/00 NR 04/49 1695 -06/61 07/61 C
31696 11/00 Asfd 04/49 1696 -03/51 03/51 R1[2]
31697 11/00 Asfd 12/48 1697 -03/53 03/53 R1[2]
31698 11/00 Asfd 10/49 1698 -10/55 11/55 R1[2]
31699 11/00 Asfd 1699 -01/50 05/50 R1[2]
31700 11/00 Asfd 07/48 1700 -10/52 52 R1[2]
31703 11/00 Asfd 03/49 1703 -03/54 54 R1[2]
31704 11/00 Asfd 07/48 1704 -04/56 05/56 R1[2]
31705 11/00 Asfd 03/49 1705 -06/51 51 R1[2]

Number	Built	Renumbered	BR Dates	Scrap	Notes
31706	12/00 Asfd	08/48 1706	-12/52	*12/52*	R1[2]
31707	12/00 Asfd	1707	-02/49	*49*	R1[2]
31708	12/00 Asfd	1708	-10/52	02/53	R1[2]
31709	12/00 Asfd	1709	-10/49	*49*	R1[2]
31710	12/00 Asfd	07/48 1710	-06/51	07/51	R1[2]
31711	12/00 SS	*52* 1711	-01/57	03/57	C
31712	12/00 SS	01/51 1712	-02/57	04/57	C
31713	12/00 SS	03/50 1713	-04/55	*55*	C
31714	12/00 SS	02/51 1714	-07/61	08/61	C
31715	12/00 SS	05/48 1715	-11/61	11/61	C
31716	01/01 SS	04/49 1716	-10/61	11/61	C
31717	01/01 SS	12/48 1717	-02/62	03/62	C
31718	01/01 SS	*52* 1718	-09/55	*10/55*	C
31719	01/01 SS	12/48 1719	-05/62	06/62	C
31720	01/01 SS	04/49 1720	-10/61	10/61	C
31721	01/01 SS	11/50 1721	-03/62	04/62	C
31722	01/01 SS	11/48 1722	-04/62	05/62	C
31723	01/01 SS	03/50 1723	-01/62	02/62	C
31724	01/01 SS	11/50 1724	-04/62	05/62	C
31725	01/01 SS	01/50 1725	-08/60	09/61	C
31727	01/01 SS	08/50 1727	-03/61	05/61	D1[1]
31728	03/01 SS	01/49 1728	-05/53	*05/53*	D
31729	03/01 SS	09/48 1729	-05/54	*07/54*	D
31730	03/01 SS	1730	-03/51	04/51	D
31731	04/01 SS	07/48 1731	-06/51	06/51	D
31732	04/01 SS	1732	-09/51	*51*	D
31733	04/01 SS	05/48 1733	-12/53	*54*	D
31734	04/01 SS	12/48 1734	-11/55	*55*	D
31735	11/01 SS	01/51 1735	-04/61	07/61	D1[1]
31736	12/01 Asfd	04/49 1736	-12/50	*51*	D1[1]
31737 §	11/01 Asfd	09/48 1737	-10/56		D
31738	12/01 Asfd	12/48 1738	-10/50	*50*	D
31739	01/02 Asfd	*49* 1739	-11/61	12/61	D1[1]
31740	12/01 Asfd	1740	-03/51	*51*	D
31741	03/03 RS	04/49 1741	-09/59	01/60	D1[1]
31743	04/03 RS	07/48 1743	-02/60	04/60	D1[1]
31744	03/03 RS	10/49 1744	-05/53	*05/53*	D
31745	06/03 RS	01/49 1745	-03/51	04/51	D1[1]
31746	07/03 VF	12/48 1746	-12/54	*55*	D
31748	08/03 VF	1748	-03/51	*03/51*	D
31749	10/03 VF	05/48 1749	-11/61	01/62	D1[1]
31750	09/03 VF	05/49 1750	-02/53	*10/53*	D
31753	03/26 NB	12/48 1753	-10/61	10/61	L1
31754	03/26 NB	11/50 1754	-11/61	11/61	L1
31755	03/26 NB	12/51 1755	-08/59	09/59	L1
31756	03/26 NB	05/48 1756	-10/61	12/61	L1
31757	03/26 NB	06/50 1757	-12/61	03/63	L1
31758	03/26 NB	*51* 1758	-10/59	11/59	L1
31759	04/26 NB	08/49 1759	-11/61	01/62	L1
31760	08/14 BP	12/48 1760	-06/61	07/61	L
31761	08/14 BP	05/48 1761	-12/56	*57*	L
31762	08/14 BP	07/48 1762	-02/60	02/60	L
31763	08/14 BP	11/48 1763	-04/60	04/60	L
31764	08/14 BP	07/49 1764	-02/61	04/61	L
31765	08/14 BP	12/48 1765	-02/61	04/61	L
31766	09/14 BP	06/49 1766	-02/61	04/61	L
31767	09/14 BP	07/48 1767	-10/58	11/58	L
31768	09/14 BP	12/48 1768	-12/61	12/61	L
31769	09/14 BP	05/48 1769	-04/56	*56*	L
31770	09/14 BP	12/50 1770	-11/59	11/59	L
31771	10/14 BP	03/49 1771	-12/61	12/61	L
31772	06/14 B	11/49 1772	-02/59	02/59	L
31773	06/14 B	08/48 1773	-08/59	09/59	L
31774	06/14 B	12/48 1774	-12/58	01/59	L
31775	06/14 B	05/48 1775	-08/59	11/59	L
31776	06/14 B	10/49 1776	-02/61	04/61	L
31777	06/14 B	04/49 1777	-09/59	09/59	L
31778	06/14 B	*51* 1778	-08/59	08/59	L
31779	07/14 B	08/48 1779	-07/59	09/59	L
31780	07/14 B	07/48 1780	-07/61	08/61	L
31781	07/14 B	11/48 1781	-06/59	06/59	L
31782	04/26 NB	07/48 1782	-02/61	05/61	L1
31783	04/26 NB	01/50 1783	-11/61	02/62	L1
31784	04/26 NB	09/48 1784	-02/60	05/60	L1
31785	04/26 NB	04/49 1785	-01/60	06/60	L1
31786	04/26 NB	07/48 1786	-02/62	02/62	L1
31787	04/26 NB	07/48 1787	-01/61	04/61	L1
31788	04/26 NB	01/49 1788	-01/60	06/60	L1
31789	04/26 NB	07/49 1789	-11/61	12/61	L1
31790	06/17 Elh	04/49 1790	-05/65	08/65	U
31791	06/28 Elh	03/49 1791	-06/66	09/66	U
31792	07/28 Elh	12/50 1792	-09/64	12/64	U
31793	07/28 Elh	01/50 1793	-05/64	12/64	U
31794	06/28 Elh	11/49 1794	-06/63	10/63	U
31795	06/28 Elh	12/48 1795	-06/63	09/63	U
31796	07/28 Elh	08/49 1796	-01/64	07/64	U
31797	07/28 Asfd	12/48 1797	-01/64	12/64	U
31798	08/28 Asfd	05/49 1798	-09/64	12/64	U
31799	07/28 Asfd	06/49 1799	-02/65	05/65	U
31800	12/28 Asfd	05/48 1800	-10/65	02/66	U
31801	07/28 Asfd	05/48 1801	-06/64	12/64	U
31802	07/28 Asfd	07/48 1802	-09/64	12/64	U
31803	06/28 Bton	10/49 1803	-03/66	07/66	U
31804	06/28 Bton	12/48 1804	-06/64	12/64	U
31805	03/28 Asfd	08/49 1805	-08/63	10/63	U
31806 §	06/28 Bton	04/49 1806	-01/64		U
31807	06/28 Bton	01/50 1807	-01/64	04/64	U
31808	07/28 Bton	11/49 1808	-01/64	03/64	U
31809	02/28 Bton	*51* 1809	-01/66	03/66	U
31810	06/17 Asfd	11/48 1810	-03/64	07/64	N
31811	06/20 Asfd	12/49 1811	-07/65	11/65	N
31812	08/20 Asfd	01/49 1812	-07/64	12/64	N
31813	09/20 Asfd	08/50 1813	-10/63	12/63	N
31814	11/20 Asfd	06/49 1814	-07/64	12/64	N
31815	12/20 Asfd	04/49 1815	-05/63	07/63	N
31816	01/22 Asfd	01/49 1816	-01/66	04/66	N
31817	01/22 Asfd	04/49 1817	-01/64	02/64	N
31818	03/22 Asfd	05/48 1818	-09/63	09/63	N
31819	05/22 Asfd	05/49 1819	-01/64	07/64	N
31820	08/22 Asfd	04/49 1820	-09/63	12/63	N
31821	10/22 Asfd	12/48 1821	-05/64	10/64	N
31822	05/23 Asfd	04/49 1822	-11/62	05/64	N1
31823	08/23 Asfd	01/49 1823	-09/63	01/64	N
31824	12/23 Asfd	08/49 1824	-10/63	01/64	N
31825	06/24 Asfd	03/51 1825	-09/63	01/64	N
31826	05/24 Asfd	12/48 1826	-09/63	01/64	N
31827	06/24 Asfd	05/48 1827	-06/64	12/64	N
31828	07/24 Asfd	08/49 1828	-09/64	11/64	N
31829	06/24 Asfd	07/48 1829	-01/64	04/64	N
31830	06/24 Asfd	12/48 1830	-01/64	04/64	N
31831	07/24 Asfd	12/48 1831	-04/65	08/65	N
31832	07/24 Asfd	07/49 1832	-01/64	04/64	N
31833	07/24 Asfd	12/48 1833	-02/64	04/64	N
31834	07/24 Asfd	01/49 1834	-09/64	12/64	N
31835	07/24 Asfd	11/48 1835	-09/64	12/64	N
31836	07/24 Asfd	12/48 1836	-12/63	04/64	N
31837	07/24 Asfd	10/49 1837	-09/64	11/64	N
31838	07/24 Asfd	12/49 1838	-02/64	03/64	N
31839	08/24 Asfd	05/48 1839	-12/63	04/64	N
31840	08/24 Asfd	09/48 1840	-09/64	12/64	N
31841	08/24 Asfd	11/49 1841	-03/64	10/64	N
31842	08/24 Asfd	01/49 1842	-09/65	11/65	N
31843	08/24 Asfd	01/49 1843	-09/64	11/64	N
31844	08/24 Asfd	03/49 1844	-12/63	04/64	N
31845	09/24 Asfd	06/49 1845	-09/64	01/65	N
31846	09/24 Asfd	05/48 1846	-09/64	12/64	N
31847	01/25 Asfd	07/48 1847	-10/63	11/63	N
31848	02/25 Asfd	08/48 1848	-02/64	02/64	N
31849	02/25 Asfd	08/49 1849	-07/64	12/64	N
31850	02/25 Asfd	12/48 1850	-01/64	07/64	N
31851	02/25 Asfd	08/48 1851	-09/63	05/64	N
31852	03/25 Asfd	11/50 1852	-09/63	12/63	N
31853	04/25 Asfd	04/49 1853	-09/64	12/64	N
31854	03/25 Asfd	05/48 1854	-06/64	12/64	N
31855	03/25 Asfd	04/49 1855	-09/64	12/64	N
31856	03/25 Asfd	06/49 1856	-07/64	12/64	N
31857	04/25 Asfd	07/48 1857	-01/64	02/64	N
31858	05/25 Asfd	08/50 1858	-12/65	05/66	N
31859	04/25 Asfd	05/49 1859	-09/64	12/64	N
31860	04/25 Asfd	05/50 1860	-11/63	02/64	N
31861	06/25 Asfd	07/48 1861	-05/63	06/63	N
31862	05/25 Asfd	05/48 1862	-04/65	07/65	N
31863	05/25 Asfd	05/48 1863	-07/63	03/64	N
31864	06/25 Asfd	02/50 1864	-01/64	12/64	N
31865	06/25 Asfd	*49* 1865	-09/63	03/64	N
31866	05/25 Asfd	01/49 1866	-01/66	03/66	N
31867	06/25 Asfd	12/48 1867	-07/63	02/64	N
31868	07/25 Asfd	12/48 1868	-01/64	02/65	N
31869	07/25 Asfd	05/48 1869	-08/64	12/64	N
31870	07/25 Asfd	05/48 1870	-04/64	11/64	N
31871	07/25 Asfd	07/48 1871	-11/63	01/64	N
31872	08/25 Asfd	07/49 1872	-05/63	08/63	N
31873	09/25 Asfd	05/48 1873	-01/66	04/66	N
31874 §	09/25 Asfd	09/48 1874	-03/64		N
31875	08/25 Asfd	05/49 1875	-08/64	12/64	N
31876	03/23 Asfd	09/48 1876	-11/62	10/63	N1
31877	04/30 Asfd	06/49 1877	-10/62	08/63	N1
31878	04/30 Asfd	01/49 1878	-10/62	08/63	N1
31879	04/30 Asfd	01/49 1879	-10/62	12/63	N1
31880	11/30 Asfd	09/48 1880	-11/62	11/63	N1
31890	06/28 Asfd	11/48 1890	-06/63	10/63	U1
31891	06/31 Elh	05/48 1891	-03/63	06/63	U1
31892	01/31 Elh	09/48 1892	-11/62	03/63	U1
31893	02/31 Elh	08/48 1893	-12/62	05/64	U1
31894	02/31 Elh	04/49 1894	-12/62	05/64	U1
31895	03/31 Elh	03/50 1895	-12/62	08/63	U1
31896	03/31 Elh	07/48 1896	-12/62	05/64	U1
31897	03/31 Elh	07/48 1897	-10/62	12/62	U1
31898	04/31 Elh	04/49 1898	-12/62	10/63	U1
31899	04/31 Elh	12/48 1899	-12/62	11/63	U1
31900	05/31 Elh	11/48 1900	-12/62	09/63	U1
31901	06/31 Elh	10/49 1901	-06/63	08/63	U1
31902	07/31 Elh	09/48 1902	-11/62	01/63	U1
31903	07/31 Elh	04/49 1903	-12/62	10/63	U1
31904	07/31 Elh	08/49 1904	-11/62	01/63	U1
31905	08/31 Elh	12/48 1905	-12/62	10/63	U1
31906	09/31 Elh	08/49 1906	-12/62	11/63	U1
31907	09/31 Elh	04/49 1907	-12/62	12/63	U1
31908	10/31 Elh	05/48 1908	-12/62	09/63	U1
31909	10/31 Elh	04/49 1909	-12/62	07/63	U1
31910	11/31 Elh	05/48 1910	-07/63	10/63	U1
31911	01/32 Elh	04/49 1911	-10/63	04/64	W
31912	01/32 Elh	10/49 1912	-08/64	11/64	W
31913	01/32 Elh	08/49 1913	-03/64	12/64	W
31914	01/32 Elh	10/49 1914	-08/64	11/64	W
31915	02/32 Elh	10/49 1915	-10/63	11/63	W
31916	04/35 Asfd	05/48 1916	-07/63	10/63	W
31917	04/35 Asfd	11/49 1917	-01/64	08/64	W
31918	06/35 Asfd	05/48 1918	-08/63	02/64	W
31919	07/35 Asfd	12/48 1919	-11/63	11/63	W
31920	08/35 Asfd	09/48 1920	-07/63	02/64	W
31921	10/35 Asfd	12/48 1921	-06/63	10/63	W
31922	11/35 Asfd	05/48 1922	-08/63	06/64	W
31923	01/36 Asfd	09/48 1923	-01/63	09/63	W
31924	02/36 Asfd	07/48 1924	-07/64	11/64	W
31925	04/36 Asfd	07/48 1925	-11/63	01/64	W

B1 between 31013 & 31459
4-4-0 SECR Stirling

Power Classification: 1P
Introduced: 1898-1899, rebuilt by Wainwright in 1910-1927
Designer: Stirling
Company: SER
Weight: Loco 45t 2cwt
Tender 34t 2cwt
Driving Wheel: 7' 0"
Boiler Pressure: 170psi
Cylinders: Inside 18" x 26"
Tractive Effort: 14490lbf
Valve Gear: Stephenson (slide valves)

Stirling originally built twenty-nine locomotives of his 'B' class for the South Eastern Railway in 1898-1899. They had domeless boilers and were an enlarged version of the 'F' class (see 'F1' class). Twenty-seven of the class were rebuilt with domed boilers by Wainwright and they all later received extended smokeboxes. They became the 'B1' class. Only sixteen locomotives came into BR stock, the first having been withdrawn in 1930.

Year End Totals: 'B1' class

'47	'48	'49	'50	'51	'52	'53	'54	'55	'56	'57	'58	'59	'60	'61	'62	'63	'64	'65	'66	'67
16	9	3	1																	

Number	Built	Renumbered	BR Dates	Scrap	Notes
31013	10/98 Asfd	1013	-09/48	*48*	
31217	10/98 Asfd	1217	-06/50	*50*	
31440	07/98 NR	1440	-11/48	*48*	
31443	07/98 NR	1443	-03/51	04/51	
31445	07/98 NR	1445	-02/48	*48*	
31446	08/98 NR	07/48 1446	-07/49	09/49	
31448	08/98 NR	1448	-08/49	*49*	
31449	08/98 NR	1449	-03/49	*49*	
31450	08/98 NR	1450	-04/48	*48*	
31451	08/98 NR	1451	-12/49	*50*	
31452	08/98 NR	1452	-04/50	*50*	
31453	08/98 NR	1453	-10/48	10/48	
31454	08/98 NR	1454	-11/48	*48*	
31455	09/98 NR	1455	-06/49	*07/49*	
31457	09/98 NR	1457	-02/49	*49*	
31459	09/98 NR	1459	-02/48	*48*	

C between 31004 & 31725, DS239-DS240
0-6-0 SECR Wainwright

Power Classification: 3F reclassified 2F in 1953
Introduced: 1900-1908
Designer: Wainwright
Company: SECR
Weight: Loco 43t 16cwt
Tender 38t 5cwt
Driving Wheel: 5' 2"
Boiler Pressure: 160psi
Cylinders: Inside 18½" x 26"
Tractive Effort: 19520lbf
Valve Gear: Stephenson (slide valves)

When the South Eastern and London Chatham & Dover Railways joined together in 1899 to form the SECR, Wainwright became the new locomotive engineer. He introduced three new classes of simple, robust and straightforward engines. They were the 4-4-0 'D' class for express passenger work, the 0-6-0 'C' class for freight and miscellaneous duties, and the 0-4-4T 'H' class for suburban services.

One hundred and nine engines of the 'C' class were built, and apart from two which were withdrawn in 1947, and one which was converted to a saddle tank in 1917 ('S' class 31685) all the class were taken into BR stock in 1948.

They were capable of hard work over all the difficult lines of the SECR and were also able to work main line passenger trains at up to 70mph when called upon to do so.

The last two engines in service were transferred to departmental stock at Ashford in 1963 and were renumbered DS239 and DS240.

Year End Totals: 'C' class

'47	'48	'49	'50	'51	'52	'53	'54	'55	'56	'57	'58	'59	'60	'61	'62	'63	'64	'65	'66	'67
106	106	104	104	104	104	98	96	89	88	85	81	64	53	21	3					

Year End Totals: 'C' (service) class

'47	'48	'49	'50	'51	'52	'53	'54	'55	'56	'57	'58	'59	'60	'61	'62	'63	'64	'65	'66	'67
																2	2	2		

Number	*Built*	*Renumbered*	*BR Dates*	*Scrap*	*Notes*
31004	07/01 Asfd	05/48 1004	-11/61	11/61	
31018	10/00 Asfd	05/48 1018	-01/59	01/59	
31033	10/00 Asfd	02/50 1033	-03/60	03/60	
31037	03/01 Asfd	12/48 1037	-02/61	03/61	
31038	07/01 Asfd	07/48 1038	-03/54	*54*	
31054	03/01 Asfd	10/49 1054	-08/60	10/60	
31059	11/02 Asfd	04/49 1059	-02/58	03/58	
31061	07/01 Asfd	12/49 1061	-07/61	10/61	
31063	07/00 Asfd	12/48 1063	-04/56	*04/56*	
31068	01/03 Asfd	07/48 1068	-10/61	11/61	
31071	07/01 Asfd	12/50 1071	-09/59	12/59	
31086	09/00 Asfd	11/50 1086	-10/60	11/60	
31090	01/03 Asfd	04/49 1090	-08/53	10/53	
31102	09/00 Asfd	05/50 1102	-05/60	06/60	
31112	09/00 Asfd	11/50 1112	-04/62	05/62	
31113	03/02 Asfd	02/50 1113	-07/61	08/61	
31150	11/02 Asfd	01/51 1150	-10/61	11/61	
31191	07/00 Asfd	52 1191	-09/59	10/59	
31218	12/00 Asfd	11/48 1218	-04/62	04/62	
31219	12/00 Asfd	10/49 1219	-10/59	10/59	
31221	03/01 Asfd	10/49 1221	-08/59	08/59	
31223	03/01 Asfd	11/50 1223	-05/60	05/60	
31225	12/00 Asfd	03/50 1225	-06/55	*55*	
31227	12/00 Asfd	08/50 1227	-10/59	11/59	
31229	01/00 Asfd	02/52 1229	-10/61	11/61	
31234	04/01 Asfd	05/49 1234	-08/53	*53*	
31242	04/02 Asfd	07/49 1242	-09/61	09/61	
31243	04/02 Asfd	04/49 1243	-10/59	10/59	
31244	04/02 Asfd	11/50 1244	-10/61	10/61	
31245	12/02 Asfd	04/51 1245	-08/59	11/59	
31252	12/02 Asfd	03/51 1252	-07/59	01/60	
31253	01/03 Asfd	05/49 1253	-10/59	12/59	
31255	06/00 Asfd	12/48 1255	-09/61	09/61	
31256	06/00 Asfd	06/50 1256	-07/61	08/61	
31257	06/00 Asfd	1257	-08/49	*49*	
31260	08/04 Asfd	08/50 1260	-05/53	*53*	
31267	01/04 Asfd	01/50 1267	-06/62	07/62	
31268	02/04 Asfd	05/48 1268	-04/62	05/62	
31270	06/04 Asfd	08/48 1270	-06/59	06/59	
31271	12/04 Asfd	06/51 1271	-07/63	12/67	
					07/63➲DS240
31272	02/04 Asfd	03/49 1272	-08/59	01/60	
31277	02/04 Asfd	05/49 1277	-09/55	*55*	
31280	02/08 Asfd	10/49 1280	-07/63	12/63	
31287	05/08 Asfd	10/49 1287	-10/60	11/60	
31291	02/08 Asfd	05/51 1291	-05/53	*05/53*	
31293	06/08 Asfd	01/50 1293	-04/62	05/62	
31294	06/08 Asfd	10/49 1294	-10/55	*10/55*	
31297	06/08 Asfd	07/48 1297	-09/59	09/59	
31298	03/08 Asfd	12/48 1298	-11/60	01/61	
31317	03/08 Asfd	04/49 1317	-02/62	03/62	
31460	10/02 Lngh	1460	-02/49	*49*	
31461	12/02 Lngh	09/48 1461	-08/58	08/58	
31480	01/04 Lngh	01/52 1480	-07/61	07/61	
31481	04/04 Lngh	05/48 1481	-11/61	12/61	
31486	12/02 Lngh	07/48 1486	-05/53	05/53	
31495	06/04 Asfd	05/48 1495	-03/61	04/61	
31498	06/04 Asfd	08/49 1498	-07/61	10/61	
31508	07/04 Asfd	11/50 1508	-09/57	10/57	
31510	07/04 Asfd	04/49 1510	-06/62	07/62	
31513	06/08 Asfd	12/51 1513	-03/55	*55*	
31572	09/03 Asfd	11/50 1572	-03/54	*54*	
31573	09/03 Asfd	06/49 1573	-11/61	12/61	
31575	09/03 Asfd	08/49 1575	-07/61	07/61	
31576	05/03 Asfd	04/49 1576	-11/59	11/59	
31578	10/03 Asfd	07/49 1578	-06/61	07/61	
31579	10/03 Asfd	12/49 1579	-10/61	10/61	
31580	06/03 Lngh	07/48 1580	-08/53	*53*	
31581	05/03 Asfd	07/49 1581	-03/60	03/60	
31582	06/03 Asfd	08/48 1582	-06/58	06/58	
31583	06/03 Lngh	05/48 1583	-07/61	08/61	
31584	06/03 Asfd	05/49 1584	-02/62	03/62	
31585	06/03 Asfd	07/48 1585	-02/59	05/59	
31588	03/08 Asfd	05/50 1588	-06/62	07/62	
31589	03/08 Asfd	11/49 1589	-11/61	12/61	
31590	07/08 Asfd	11/50 1590	-02/61	03/61	
31592 §	02/02 Lngh	12/48 1592	-07/63		
					07/63➲DS239
31593	05/02 Lngh	12/48 1593	-02/58	04/58	
31681	06/00 NR	11/49 1681	-02/59	03/59	
31682	06/00 NR	05/49 1682	-10/61	10/61	
31683	06/00 NR	11/50 1683	-06/59	06/59	
31684	06/00 NR	04/49 1684	-10/61	10/61	
31686	07/00 NR	12/48 1686	-04/62	05/62	
31687	07/00 NR	07/48 1687	-04/55	*55*	
31688	07/00 NR	12/48 1688	-02/60	02/60	
31689	07/00 NR	11/48 1689	-03/62	04/62	
31690	07/00 NR	03/50 1690	-06/62	07/62	
31691	07/00 NR	05/50 1691	-10/61	10/61	
31692	07/00 NR	07/48 1692	-04/60	05/60	
31693	07/00 NR	09/50 1693	-06/61	06/61	
31694	07/00 NR	02/50 1694	-03/61	06/61	
31695	07/00 NR	04/49 1695	-06/61	07/61	
31711	12/00 SS	52 1711	-01/57	03/57	
31712	12/00 SS	01/51 1712	-02/57	04/57	
31713	12/00 SS	03/50 1713	-04/55	*55*	
31714	12/00 SS	02/51 1714	-07/61	08/61	
31715	12/00 SS	05/48 1715	-11/61	11/61	
31716	01/01 SS	04/49 1716	-10/61	11/61	
31717	01/01 SS	12/48 1717	-02/62	03/62	
31718	01/01 SS	52 1718	-09/55	*10/55*	
31719	01/01 SS	12/48 1719	-05/62	06/62	
31720	01/01 SS	04/49 1720	-10/61	10/61	
31721	01/01 SS	11/50 1721	-03/62	04/62	
31722	01/01 SS	11/48 1722	-04/62	05/62	
31723	01/01 SS	03/50 1723	-01/62	02/62	
31724	01/01 SS	11/50 1724	-04/62	05/62	
31725	01/01 SS	01/50 1725	-08/60	09/61	

Class continued with DS239 (Service Locomotives)

D between 31057 & 31750
4-4-0 SECR Wainwright

Power Classification:	1P
Introduced:	1901-1907
Designer:	Wainwright
Company:	SECR
Weight:	Loco 50t 0cwt
	Tender 39t 2cwt
Driving Wheel:	6' 8"
Boiler Pressure:	175psi
Cylinders:	Inside 19" x 26"
Tractive Effort:	17450lbf
Valve Gear:	Stephenson (slide valves)

The 'D' class was one of Wainwright's three standard classes (the others being the 'C' and 'H' classes). Fifty-one engines were built in 1901-1907. Twenty-one of these were rebuilt into the 'D1' class in 1921-1927. The first one of the un-rebuilt engines (1742) was withdrawn in 1944, one other (1726) in 1947 and the other twenty-eight came into BR stock.

These were among some of the most elegant locomotives in the country and, when built, they were beautifully finished with burnished brass dome covers and they were known as 'Coppertops'.

Year End Totals: 'D' class

'47	'48	'49	'50	'51	'52	'53	'54	'55	'56	'57	'58	'59	'60	'61	'62	'63	'64	'65	'66	'67
28	28	28	27	18	18	13	10	6												

Number	*Built*	*Renumbered*	*BR Dates*	*Scrap*	*Notes*
31057	06/02 Asfd	08/49 1057	-04/51	*04/51*	
31075	03/03 D	01/50 1075	-12/56	12/56	
31092	03/03 D	04/49 1092	-06/51	*51*	
31477	03/07 Asfd	12/48 1477	-02/51	*04/51*	
31488	07/02 Asfd	05/48 1488	-02/56	*02/56*	
31490	08/02 Asfd	05/48 1490	-09/51	*51*	
31493	03/03 D	1493	-02/54	*10/54*	
31496	03/07 Asfd	03/49 1496	-09/55	*55*	
31501	04/03 D	05/50 1501	-05/53	*05/53*	
31549	09/06 Asfd	04/49 1549	-10/56	*56*	
31574	02/07 Asfd	52 1574	-10/56	*01/57*	
31577	09/06 Asfd	09/51 1577	-12/56	*57*	
31586	02/07 Asfd	05/48 1586	-09/55	*55*	
31591	03/07 Asfd	07/48 1591	-06/55	*55*	
31728	03/01 SS	01/49 1728	-05/53	*05/53*	
31729	03/01 SS	09/48 1729	-05/54	*07/54*	
31730	03/01 SS	1730	-03/51	04/51	
31731	04/01 SS	07/48 1731	-06/51	*06/51*	
31732	04/01 SS	1732	-09/51	*51*	
31733	04/01 SS	05/48 1733	-12/53	*54*	
31734	04/01 SS	12/48 1734	-11/55	*55*	
31737 §	11/01 Asfd	09/48 1737	-10/56		
31738	12/01 Asfd	12/48 1738	-10/50	*50*	
31740	12/01 Asfd	1740	-03/51	*51*	
31744	03/03 RS	10/49 1744	-05/53	*05/53*	
31746	07/03 VF	12/48 1746	-12/54	*55*	
31748	08/03 VF	1748	-03/51	*03/51*	
31750	09/03 VF	05/49 1750	-02/53	*10/53*	

D1[1] between 31145 & 31749
4-4-0 SECR Rebuilt class 'D'

Power Classification:	2P reclassified 3P in 1953
Introduced:	1901-1907
	Rebuilt 1921-1927 by Maunsell
Designer:	Wainwright
Company:	SECR
Weight:	Loco 52t 4cwt
	Tender 39t 0cwt
Driving Wheel:	6' 8"
Boiler Pressure:	180psi superheated
Cylinders:	Inside 19" x 26"
Tractive Effort:	17950lbf
Valve Gear:	Stephenson (piston valves)

After the successful rebuilding of the 'E1' class engines, twenty-one locomotives of the 'D' class were rebuilt in 1921-1927 in a similar manner and they become class 'D1'. The two classes thus became almost identical but they could always be differentiated as the 'D1' class had plain coupling rods while those on the 'E1' class were fluted.

One engine (1747) was withdrawn in 1944, but the rest came into BR stock in 1948.

Year End Totals: 'D1 1' class

'47	'48	'49	'50	'51	'52	'53	'54	'55	'56	'57	'58	'59	'60	'61	'62	'63	'64	'65	'66	'67
20	20	20	19	17	17	17	17	17	17	17	17	15	11							

Number	*Built*	*Renumbered*	*BR Dates*	*Scrap*	*Notes*
31145	04/03 D	11/49 1145	-10/61	12/61	
31246	06/02 Asfd	05/48 1246	-03/61	05/61	
31247	04/03 Asfd	04/49 1247	-07/61	09/61	
31470	08/06 Asfd	05/48 1470	-06/59	09/59	
31487	07/02 Asfd	05/48 1487	-02/61	04/61	
31489	04/03 D	11/48 1489	-11/61	12/61	
31492	04/03 D	01/49 1492	-01/60	02/60	
31494	04/03 D	04/49 1494	-08/60	09/60	
31502	05/03 D	05/48 1502	-03/51	*04/51*	
31505	02/07 Asfd	05/49 1505	-09/61	11/61	
31509	09/06 Asfd	01/49 1509	-05/60	05/60	
31545	09/06 Asfd	12/48 1545	-03/61	05/61	
31727	01/01 SS	08/50 1727	-03/61	05/61	
31735	11/01 SS	01/51 1735	-04/61	07/61	
31736	12/01 Asfd	04/49 1736	-12/50	*51*	
31739	01/02 Asfd	49 1739	-11/61	12/61	
31741	03/03 RS	04/49 1741	-09/59	01/60	
31743	04/03 RS	07/48 1743	-02/60	04/60	
31745	06/03 RS	01/49 1745	-03/51	04/51	
31749	10/03 VF	05/48 1749	-11/61	01/62	

E between 31036 & 31587
4-4-0 SECR Wainwright

Power Classification:	1P
Introduced:	1905-1909
Designer:	Wainwright
Company:	SECR
Weight:	Loco 52t 5cwt
	s Loco 53t 10cwt
	Tender 39t 2cwt
Driving Wheel:	6' 6"
Boiler Pressure:	180psi
	s 160psi superheated
Cylinders:	Inside 19" x 26"
	s Inside 20½" x 26"
Tractive Effort:	18410lbf
	s 19050lbf
Valve Gear:	Stephenson (slide valves)

Wainwright introduced his 'E' class 4-4-0s in 1905-1909. They were a version of the 'D' class with Belpaire boilers, extended smokeboxes and fluted coupling rods. They were more powerful than the 'D' class because of a slightly higher boiler pressure and slightly smaller wheels. Eleven of the original twenty-six locomotives were later rebuilt by Maunsell into the 'E1' class.

s 31036 and 31275 were superheated but retained their original boilers and were unaltered in external appearance.

Year End Totals: 'E' class

'47	'48	'49	'50	'51	'52	'53	'54	'55	'56	'57	'58	'59	'60	'61	'62	'63	'64	'65	'66	'67
15	15	15	15	3	3	2	1													

Number	*Built*	*Renumbered*	*BR Dates*	*Scrap*	*Notes*
31036	12/08 Asfd	03/49 1036	-03/51	03/51	s
31157	12/07 Asfd	1157	-03/51	04/51	
31159	11/08 Asfd	03/49 1159	-12/51	*52*	
31166	07/07 Asfd	06/48 1166	-05/55	*55*	
31175	08/08 Asfd	1175	-10/51	*51*	
31176	12/07 Asfd	03/49 1176	-10/51	*51*	
31273	02/06 Asfd	10/49 1273	-12/51	12/51	
31275	02/06 Asfd	05/49 1275	-03/51	04/51	s
31315	04/09 Asfd	07/48 1315	-03/54	*10/54*	
31491	07/07 Asfd	1491	-02/53	*05/53*	
31514	12/07 Asfd	10/49 1514	-12/51	*52*	
31515	09/07 Asfd	03/49 1515	-07/51	*04/51*	s
31516	04/08 Asfd	04/49 1516	-10/51	*51*	
31547	09/08 Asfd	1547	-02/51	04/51	
31587	02/07 Asfd	10/49 1587	-07/51	*51*	

E1[1] between 31019 & 31511
4-4-0 SECR Rebuilt class 'E'

Power Classification:	2P reclassified 3P in 1953
Introduced:	1905-1909, rebuilt by Maunsell in 1919-1921
Designer:	Wainwright
Company:	SECR
Weight:	Loco 53t 9cwt Tender 39t 0cwt
Driving Wheel:	6' 6"
Boiler Pressure:	180psi superheated
Cylinders:	Inside 19" x 26"
Tractive Effort:	18410lbf
Valve Gear:	Stephenson (piston valves)

After the First World War the SECR was very short of money and did not have any suitable locomotives to work the increasingly heavy boat expresses from Victoria. Maunsell solved the problem by rebuilding 'E' class locomotive 31179 in 1919 with a superheated Belpaire boiler and new cylinders with piston valves. This became known as the 'E1' class. As this proved to be a successful solution to the problem, ten further engines were converted by Beyer Peacock in 1920-1921.

Twenty-one locomotives of Class 'D' were similarly rebuilt in 1921-1927 to become class 'D1' and both classes closely resembled the Midland Fowler 'Class 2's (LMS '40332' class).

Year End Totals: 'E1 [1]' class

'47	'48	'49	'50	'51	'52	'53	'54	'55	'56	'57	'58	'59	'60	'61	'62	'63	'64	'65	'66	'67
11	11	10	8	7	7	7	7	7	7	7	5	4	3							

Number	*Built*	*Renumbered*	*BR Dates*	*Scrap*	*Notes*
31019	07/08 Asfd	11/48 1019	-04/61	06/61	
31067	08/08 Asfd	09/48 1067	-11/61	12/61	
31160	07/07 Asfd	01/49 1160	-02/51	04/51	
31163	04/09 Asfd	1163	-05/49	*49*	
31165	12/07 Asfd	05/49 1165	-05/59	05/59	
31179	11/08 Asfd	03/49 1179	-10/50	03/51	
31497	09/07 Asfd	01/50 1497	-10/60	11/60	
31504	12/05 Asfd	01/49 1504	-02/58	03/58	
31506	12/05 Asfd	05/49 1506	-09/58	10/58	
31507	09/08 Asfd	12/48 1507	-07/61	08/61	
31511	12/05 Asfd	07/48 1511	-12/50	02/51	

F1 between 31002 & 31231
4-4-0 SECR Stirling

Power Classification:	1P
Introduced:	1883-1898, rebuilt by Wainwright in 1903-1919
Designer:	Stirling
Company:	SER
Weight:	Loco 45t 2cwt Tender 30t 10cwt
Driving Wheel:	7' 0"
Boiler Pressure:	170psi
Cylinders:	Inside 18" x 26"
Tractive Effort:	14490lbf
Valve Gear:	Stephenson (slide valves)

Stirling originally built eighty-eight locomotives of his 'F' class for the South Eastern Railway in 1883-1898. They had domeless boilers and rounded cabs. Seventy-six of the class were rebuilt with domed boilers and new cabs by Wainwright between 1903 and 1919 becoming the 'F1' class. Most of these also later received extended smokeboxes. Only nine locomotives came into BR stock, the first having been withdrawn in 1920.

Year End Totals: 'F1' class

'47	'48	'49	'50	'51	'52	'53	'54	'55	'56	'57	'58	'59	'60	'61	'62	'63	'64	'65	'66	'67
9	4																			

Number	*Built*	*Renumbered*	*BR Dates*	*Scrap*	*Notes*
31002	11/86 Asfd	1002	-06/48	06/48	
31028	12/89 Asfd	1028	-05/48	05/48	
31031	09/94 Asfd	1031	-05/48	05/48	
31042	03/96 Asfd	1042	-02/48	*48*	
31078	12/86 Asfd	1078	-03/49	*49*	
31105	03/96 Asfd	1105	-02/49	*49*	
31151	10/99 Asfd	07/48 1151	-03/49	*49*	
31215	10/91 Asfd	1215	-05/48	05/48	
31231	10/93 Asfd	1231	-03/49	07/51	

H between 31005 & 31554
0-4-4T SECR Wainwright

Power Classification:	1P
Introduced:	1904-1915
Designer:	Wainwright
Company:	SECR
Weight:	54t 8cwt
Driving Wheel:	5' 6"
Boiler Pressure:	160psi
Cylinders:	Inside 18" x 26"
Tractive Effort:	17360lbf
Valve Gear:	Stephenson (slide valves)

The 'H' class was one of Wainwright's three standard classes (the others being the 'C' and 'D' classes).

Sixty-six engines of the 'H' class were built, sixty-four of which were taken into BR stock (the first being withdrawn in 1944). The last two engines were not built until 1915 when Maunsell discovered only sixty-four of the sixty-six on order had actually been built. They were built to replace the old SECR 'Q' class passenger tanks and they had to cope with the continually increasing suburban passenger traffic in the days before electrification.

The locomotives carried a distinctive 'pagoda' type cab, where the cab roof overhung both sides of the cab.

p These engines were fitted for push-pull work from 1949 onwards.

Year End Totals: 'H' class

'47	'48	'49	'50	'51	'52	'53	'54	'55	'56	'57	'58	'59	'60	'61	'62	'63	'64	'65	'66	'67
64	64	64	64	59	59	59	58	54	54	52	51	40	33	15	7	3				

Number	*Built*	*Renumbered*	*BR Dates*	*Scrap*	*Notes*
31005	05/07 Asfd	12/48 1005	-09/63	05/64	01/60⇨p
31016	07/15 Asfd	06/49 1016	-07/51	*51*	06/49⇨p
31158	12/09 Asfd	08/50 1158	-04/55	*55*	09/50⇨p
31161	06/09 Asfd	07/48 1161	-11/61	12/61	05/50⇨p
31162	03/09 Asfd	12/50 1162	-07/61	08/61	02/53⇨p
31164	02/09 Asfd	07/49 1164	-10/59	10/59	07/49⇨p
31177	03/09 Asfd	11/48 1177	-10/61	10/61	05/53⇨p
31182	06/09 Asfd	06/49 1182	-07/51	*51*	06/49⇨p
31184	04/15 Asfd	02/50 1184	-03/58	03/58	08/52⇨p
31193	12/09 Asfd	08/50 1193	-03/61	05/61	03/53⇨p
31239	11/09 Asfd	03/49 1239	-01/60	01/60	08/52⇨p
31259	11/05 Asfd	05/48 1259	-11/59	01/60	
31261	11/05 Asfd	08/50 1261	-10/61	10/61	
31263 §	05/05 Asfd	10/49 1263	-01/64		04/60⇨p
31265	05/05 Asfd	03/49 1265	-08/60	09/60	
31266	05/05 Asfd	01/50 1266	-10/60	12/60	05/58⇨p
31269	11/05 Asfd	10/49 1269	-12/59	12/59	11/53⇨p
31274	06/05 Asfd	04/51 1274	-11/57	11/57	07/53⇨p
31276	06/05 Asfd	*52* 1276	-02/61	05/61	09/53⇨p
31278	07/05 Asfd	10/49 1278	-10/62	11/62	04/56⇨p
31279	11/09 Asfd	07/48 1279	-09/59	10/59	03/53⇨p
31295	12/09 Asfd	08/50 1295	-05/59	05/59	06/52⇨p
31305	05/06 Asfd	03/49 1305	-11/62	07/64	
31306	05/06 Asfd	05/48 1306	-12/61	01/62	60⇨p
31307	12/06 Asfd	05/49 1307	-08/61	09/61	
31308	06/06 Asfd	01/49 1308	-12/62	11/63	12/53⇨p
31309	06/06 Asfd	01/50 1309	-06/55	*55*	
31310	06/06 Asfd	05/49 1310	-05/60	06/60	09/53⇨p
31311	05/07 Asfd	08/49 1311	-12/54	*55*	
31319	12/09 Asfd	08/50 1319	-01/60	02/60	06/50⇨p
31320	05/07 Asfd	07/48 1320	-12/55	*56*	11/53⇨p
31321	12/06 Asfd	*51* 1321	-11/57	11/57	
31322	06/09 Asfd	02/50 1322	-04/61	06/61	02/50⇨p
31324	05/07 Asfd	01/50 1324	-07/62	08/62	02/61⇨p
31326	12/06 Asfd	07/48 1326	-10/61	11/61	
31327	06/07 Asfd	04/49 1327	-11/59	11/59	08/53⇨p
31328	12/06 Asfd	04/49 1328	-02/61	04/61	
31329	12/06 Asfd	07/48 1329	-11/59	11/59	04/56⇨p
31500	11/05 Asfd	07/48 1500	-06/61	06/61	60⇨p
31503	12/05 Asfd	11/48 1503	-08/59	11/59	
31512	01/09 Asfd	07/48 1512	-06/61	08/61	12/51⇨p
31517	01/09 Asfd	11/49 1517	-05/61	07/61	12/49⇨p
31518	07/09 Asfd	09/48 1518	-01/64	11/64	03/52⇨p
31519	07/09 Asfd	03/51 1519	-02/61	06/61	12/52⇨p
31520	08/09 Asfd	07/48 1520	-08/60	09/60	06/49⇨p
31521	08/09 Asfd	08/48 1521	-05/62	06/62	05/53⇨p
31522	08/09 Asfd	04/49 1522	-01/63	02/63	06/52⇨p
31523	09/09 Asfd	07/49 1523	-01/59	01/59	07/49⇨p
31530	07/05 Asfd	05/48 1530	-03/62	03/62	07/53⇨p
31531	07/05 Asfd	06/49 1531	-04/55	*55*	
31532	07/05 Asfd	07/49 1532	-03/51	04/51	
31533	07/05 Asfd	04/49 1533	-09/62	09/62	04/60⇨p
31540	11/04 Asfd	03/50 1540	-02/60	04/60	
31541	11/04 Asfd	05/48 1541	-04/51	*04/51*	
31542	11/04 Asfd	06/51 1542	-11/62	07/64	
31543	01/09 Asfd	12/50 1543	-07/63	03/64	11/53⇨p
31544	11/04 Asfd	04/51 1544	-09/63	12/63	06/54⇨p
31546	11/04 Asfd	04/49 1546	-02/51	03/51	
31548	12/04 Asfd	04/49 1548	-08/59	09/59	11/49⇨p
31550	11/04 Asfd	05/48 1550	-02/61	03/61	
31551	01/05 Asfd	11/49 1551	-01/64	07/64	60⇨p
31552	01/05 Asfd	11/50 1552	-11/61	12/61	09/53⇨p
31553	02/05 Asfd	01/50 1553	-06/61	07/61	01/60⇨p
31554	12/09 Asfd	01/49 1554	-05/59	06/59	06/52⇨p

J 31595-31599
0-6-4T SECR Wainwright

Power Classification:	3MT
Introduced:	1913
Designer:	Wainwright
Company:	SECR
Weight:	70t 14cwt
Driving Wheel:	5' 6"
Boiler Pressure:	160psi superheated
Cylinders:	Inside 19½" x 26"
Tractive Effort:	20370lbf
Valve Gear:	Stephenson (piston valves)

The 'J' class was Wainwright's last design for the SECR. They were built for heavy outer-suburban work. Soon after the five engines were built Wainwright's ill health forced him into premature retirement. The engines did not conform to the ideas of his successor Maunsell, and no more engines of this class were built. The engines were based at Ashford for many years.

Year End Totals: 'J' class

'47	'48	'49	'50	'51	'52	'53	'54	'55	'56	'57	'58	'59	'60	'61	'62	'63	'64	'65	'66	'67
5	5	4	2																	

Number	*Built*	*Renumbered*	*BR Dates*	*Scrap*	*Notes*
31595	10/13 Asfd	12/48 1595	-05/51	07/51	
31596	10/13 Asfd	04/49 1596	-10/51	10/51	
31597	11/13 Asfd	07/48 1597	-11/50	*01/51*	
31598	11/13 Asfd	06/49 1598	-12/50	04/51	
31599	12/13 Asfd	08/48 1599	-10/49	05/50	

L 31760-31781
4-4-0 SECR Wainwright

Power Classification:	2P reclassified 3P in 1953
Introduced:	1914
Designer:	Wainwright/Maunsell
Company:	SECR

Weight:	Loco 57t 9cwt
	Tender 40t 6cwt
Driving Wheel:	6' 8"
Boiler Pressure:	180psi superheated
Cylinders:	Inside 19½" x 26"
Tractive Effort:	18910lbf
Valve Gear:	Stephenson (piston valves)

Before Wainwright retired in 1913 he prepared the drawings for an enlarged version of his 'D' class 4-4-0 to provide adequate power for the increasingly heavy boat expresses and for the Folkestone and Hastings business trains from Charing Cross.

Maunsell made some slight alterations to the design (such as the substitution of black beading for the brass on the splashers) and the class was built in 1914.

Twelve engines (31760-31771) were built by Beyer Peacock. The other ten engines were built by A. Borsig of Berlin. They arrived in Britain just before the outbreak of the First World War and Bosig's fitters supervised their erection at Ashford. This was one of the very rare occasions of a British Railway Company buying locomotives from overseas. The engines were subsequently nicknamed 'Germans'.

During the 1926 general strike 31763 carried the unofficial name BETTY BALDWIN which was applied by volunteers. It was soon removed as being against official policy at the time.

The 'L1' class was developed from this class by Maunsell in 1926.

Year End Totals: 'L' class

'47	'48	'49	'50	'51	'52	'53	'54	'55	'56	'57	'58	'59	'60	'61	'62	'63	'64	'65	'66	'67
22	22	22	22	22	22	22	22	22	20	20	18	10	8							

Number	Built	Renumbered	BR Dates	Scrap	Notes
31760	08/14 BP	12/48 1760	-06/61	07/61	
31761	08/14 BP	05/48 1761	-12/56	57	
31762	08/14 BP	07/48 1762	-02/60	02/60	
31763	08/14 BP	11/48 1763	-04/60	04/60	
31764	08/14 BP	07/49 1764	-02/61	04/61	
31765	08/14 BP	12/48 1765	-02/61	04/61	
31766	09/14 BP	06/49 1766	-02/61	04/61	
31767	09/14 BP	07/48 1767	-10/58	11/58	
31768	09/14 BP	12/48 1768	-12/61	12/61	
31769	09/14 BP	05/48 1769	-04/56	*56*	
31770	09/14 BP	12/50 1770	-11/59	11/59	
31771	10/14 BP	03/49 1771	-12/61	12/61	
31772	06/14 B	11/49 1772	-02/59	02/59	
31773	06/14 B	08/48 1773	-08/59	09/59	
31774	06/14 B	12/48 1774	-12/58	01/59	
31775	06/14 B	05/48 1775	-08/59	11/59	
31776	06/14 B	10/49 1776	-02/61	04/61	
31777	06/14 B	04/49 1777	-09/59	09/59	
31778	06/14 B	*51* 1778	-08/59	08/59	
31779	07/14 B	08/48 1779	-07/59	09/59	
31780	07/14 B	07/48 1780	-07/61	08/61	
31781	07/14 B	11/48 1781	-06/59	06/59	

L1 31753-31759, 31782-31789
4-4-0 SR Maunsell

Power Classification:	2P reclassified 3P in 1953
Introduced:	1926
Designer:	Maunsell
Company:	SR
Weight:	Loco 57t 16cwt
	Tender 40t 10cwt
Driving Wheel:	6' 8"
Boiler Pressure:	180psi superheated
Cylinders:	Inside 19½" x 26"
Tractive Effort:	18910lbf
Valve Gear:	Stephenson (piston valves)

The 'L1' class was a development by the SR of the SECR 'L' class. They were built in response to the need for even more powerful locomotives which would stay within the then axle load limit of 18½ tons. They initially differed from the 'L' class in having smaller cylinders with a higher working pressure, but the 'L' class engines were altered to match. They were fitted with long-travel valves and had side window cabs.

The engines were built by the North British Locomotive Company in Glasgow, and they very much resembled a slightly enlarged version of the 'D1' and 'E1' class engines.

Year End Totals: 'L1' class

'47	'48	'49	'50	'51	'52	'53	'54	'55	'56	'57	'58	'59	'60	'61	'62	'63	'64	'65	'66	'67
15	15	15	15	15	15	15	15	15	15	15	15	13	10	1						

Number	Built	Renumbered	BR Dates	Scrap	Notes
31753	03/26 NB	12/48 1753	-10/61	10/61	
31754	03/26 NB	11/50 1754	-11/61	11/61	
31755	03/26 NB	12/51 1755	-08/59	09/59	
31756	03/26 NB	05/48 1756	-10/61	12/61	
31757	03/26 NB	06/50 1757	-12/61	03/63	
31758	03/26 NB	*51* 1758	-10/59	11/59	
31759	04/26 NB	08/49 1759	-11/61	01/62	
31782	04/26 NB	07/48 1782	-02/61	05/61	
31783	04/26 NB	01/50 1783	-11/61	02/62	
31784	04/26 NB	09/48 1784	-02/60	05/60	
31785	04/26 NB	04/49 1785	-01/60	06/60	
31786	04/26 NB	07/48 1786	-02/62	02/62	
31787	04/26 NB	07/48 1787	-01/61	04/61	
31788	04/26 NB	01/49 1788	-01/60	06/60	
31789	04/26 NB	07/49 1789	-11/61	12/61	

N 31400-31414, 31810-31821, 31823-31875
2-6-0 SECR/SR Maunsell

Power Classification:	4MT reclassified 4P5F in 1953
Introduced:	1917-1934
Designer:	Maunsell
Company:	SECR
Weight:	Loco 61t 4cwt
	Tender 39t 5cwt
	s Tender 42t 8cwt
Driving Wheel:	5' 6"
Boiler Pressure:	200psi superheated
Cylinders:	Outside 19" x 28"
Tractive Effort:	26035lbf
Valve Gear:	Walschaert (piston valves)

In 1917 Maunsell produced his first new designs since he took over from Wainwright in 1913. He built a 2-6-0 tender engine No. 810 ('N' class) and a corresponding 2-6-4T engine No. 790 ('K' class - see under 'U' class). They employed some GWR features such as taper boilers with high working pressure and long travel piston valves. As such the 'N' class locomotive bore some similarities to the GWR '4300' class. They also had a few Midland design features, such as the cabs and the tenders. The engines were nicknamed 'Mongolipers' or 'Woolworths'.

The history of the class can be summarised as follows:

a Original engine (31810), built in 1917.

b After extensive trials with 31810, fifteen more engines were built in 1920-1922 (Nos. 31811-31825). One of these (31822) was fitted with three cylinders and it was known as the 'N1' class.

w In the 1920s the Government was seeking to avoid unemployment at Woolwich Arsenal resulting from the decline of arms manufacture. They ordered one-hundred complete sets of parts for 'N' class locomotives (the boilers being built by the North British Locomotive Company and the remainder at Woolwich) in 1924-1925. It was hoped that other railways would purchase these to replenish their locomotive stocks, but unfortunately there were no takers. After grouping in 1925 the Southern Railway purchased parts for fifty locomotives at a very cheap price and they were built as 31826-31875 at Ashford. Twenty-six sets of parts went to the Great Southern Railway of Ireland and six went to the Metropolitan Railway who built them as 2-6-4T engines (see LNER class 'L2').

s Fifteen more engines (31400-31414) were built by the SR at Ashford in 1932-1934 with a larger 4000 gallon tender.

The locomotives proved to be invaluable as reliable mixed traffic locomotives. Smoke deflectors were fitted to the class from 1933 onwards. From 1955 the class was renewed with new cylinders and outside steam pipes. About half of the class was converted before they were withdrawn.

Maunsell's 2-6-0 'U' class was very similar to the 'N' class, the main difference being that they were rebuilt from 'K' class 2-6-4Ts and had larger driving wheels.

l The final eight of the Ashford built engines (1407-1414) had left-hand drive, compared to right-hand drive for all the others.

e In 1930 1819 was taken into Eastleigh Works and underwent extensive experiments as a condensing engine. It was eventually reconverted to standard.

o 31831 was converted to oil burning during the coal crisis after the Second World War. It was later converted back to coal burning (c).

Year End Totals: 'N' class

'47	'48	'49	'50	'51	'52	'53	'54	'55	'56	'57	'58	'59	'60	'61	'62	'63	'64	'65	'66	'67
80	80	80	80	80	80	80	80	80	80	80	80	80	80	80	78	53	12	6		

Number	Built	Renumbered	BR Dates	Scrap	Notes
31400	07/32 Asfd	07/48 1400	-06/64	12/64	s
31401	08/32 Asfd	09/48 1401	-07/65	10/65	s
31402	08/32 Asfd	06/49 1402	-08/63	07/64	s
31403	08/32 Asfd	06/49 1403	-06/63	10/63	s
31404	10/32 Asfd	05/48 1404	-12/63	01/64	s
31405	11/32 Asfd	11/49 1405	-06/66	09/66	s
31406	01/33 Asfd	10/49 1406	-09/64	12/64	s
31407	08/32 Asfd	08/49 1407	-07/63	10/64	sl
31408	09/33 Asfd	07/49 1408	-06/66	09/66	sl
31409	10/33 Asfd	01/49 1409	-10/62	02/64	sl
31410	11/33 Asfd	12/49 1410	-11/64	03/65	sl
31411	11/33 Asfd	11/48 1411	-04/66	09/66	sl
31412	12/33 Asfd	12/48 1412	-08/64	12/64	sl
31413	01/34 Asfd	10/49 1413	-06/64	12/64	sl
31414	01/34 Asfd	05/50 1414	-11/62	02/63	sl
31810	06/17 Asfd	11/48 1810	-03/64	07/64	a
31811	06/20 Asfd	12/49 1811	-07/65	11/65	b
31812	08/20 Asfd	01/49 1812	-07/64	12/64	b
31813	09/20 Asfd	08/50 1813	-10/63	12/63	b
31814	11/20 Asfd	06/49 1814	-07/64	12/64	b
31815	12/20 Asfd	04/49 1815	-05/63	07/63	b
31816	01/22 Asfd	01/49 1816	-01/66	04/66	b
31817	01/22 Asfd	04/49 1817	-01/64	02/64	b
31818	03/22 Asfd	05/48 1818	-09/63	09/63	b
31819	05/22 Asfd	05/49 1819	-01/64	07/64	be
31820	08/22 Asfd	04/49 1820	-09/63	12/63	b
31821	10/22 Asfd	12/48 1821	-05/64	10/64	b
31823	08/23 Asfd	01/49 1823	-09/63	01/64	b
31824	12/23 Asfd	08/49 1824	-10/63	01/64	b
31825	06/24 Asfd	03/51 1825	-09/63	01/64	b
31826	05/24 Asfd	12/48 1826	-09/63	01/64	w
31827	06/24 Asfd	05/48 1827	-06/64	12/64	w
31828	07/24 Asfd	08/49 1828	-09/64	11/64	w
31829	06/24 Asfd	07/48 1829	-01/64	04/64	w
31830	06/24 Asfd	12/48 1830	-01/64	04/64	w
31831	07/24 Asfd	12/48 1831	-04/65	08/65	wo 48⇨c
31832	07/24 Asfd	07/49 1832	-01/64	04/64	w
31833	07/24 Asfd	12/48 1833	-02/64	04/64	w
31834	07/24 Asfd	01/49 1834	-09/64	12/64	w
31835	07/24 Asfd	11/48 1835	-09/64	12/64	w
31836	07/24 Asfd	12/48 1836	-12/63	04/64	w
31837	07/24 Asfd	10/49 1837	-09/64	11/64	w
31838	07/24 Asfd	12/49 1838	-02/64	03/64	w
31839	08/24 Asfd	05/48 1839	-12/63	04/64	w
31840	08/24 Asfd	09/48 1840	-09/64	12/64	w
31841	08/24 Asfd	11/49 1841	-03/64	10/64	w
31842	08/24 Asfd	01/49 1842	-09/65	11/65	w
31843	08/24 Asfd	01/49 1843	-09/64	11/64	w
31844	08/24 Asfd	03/49 1844	-12/63	04/64	w
31845	09/24 Asfd	06/49 1845	-09/64	01/65	w
31846	09/24 Asfd	05/48 1846	-09/64	12/64	w
31847	01/25 Asfd	07/48 1847	-10/63	11/63	w
31848	02/25 Asfd	08/48 1848	-02/64	02/64	w
31849	02/25 Asfd	08/49 1849	-07/64	12/64	w
31850	02/25 Asfd	12/48 1850	-01/64	07/64	w
31851	02/25 Asfd	08/48 1851	-09/63	05/64	w
31852	03/25 Asfd	11/50 1852	-09/63	12/63	w
31853	04/25 Asfd	04/49 1853	-09/64	12/64	w
31854	03/25 Asfd	05/48 1854	-06/64	12/64	w
31855	03/25 Asfd	04/49 1855	-09/64	12/64	w
31856	03/25 Asfd	06/49 1856	-07/64	12/64	w
31857	04/25 Asfd	07/48 1857	-01/64	02/64	w
31858	05/25 Asfd	08/50 1858	-12/65	05/66	w
31859	04/25 Asfd	05/49 1859	-09/64	12/64	w
31860	04/25 Asfd	05/50 1860	-11/63	02/64	w
31861	06/25 Asfd	07/48 1861	-05/63	06/63	w
31862	05/25 Asfd	05/48 1862	-04/65	07/65	w
31863	05/25 Asfd	05/48 1863	-07/63	03/64	w
31864	06/25 Asfd	02/50 1864	-01/64	12/64	w
31865	06/25 Asfd	*49* 1865	-09/63	03/64	w
31866	05/25 Asfd	01/49 1866	-01/66	03/66	w
31867	06/25 Asfd	12/48 1867	-07/63	02/64	w
31868	07/25 Asfd	12/48 1868	-01/64	02/65	w
31869	07/25 Asfd	05/48 1869	-08/64	12/64	w
31870	07/25 Asfd	05/48 1870	-04/64	11/64	w
31871	07/25 Asfd	07/48 1871	-11/63	01/64	w
31872	08/25 Asfd	07/49 1872	-05/63	08/63	w
31873	09/25 Asfd	05/48 1873	-01/66	04/66	w
31874 §	09/25 Asfd	09/48 1874	-03/64		w
31875	08/25 Asfd	05/49 1875	-08/64	12/64	w

SECR Wainwright 'E' class 4-4-0 No 31159.

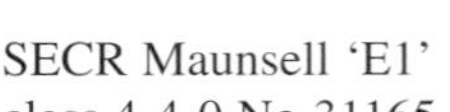

SECR Maunsell 'E1' class 4-4-0 No 31165.

SECR Wainwright 'H' class 0-4-4T No 31269.

SECR Wainwright ‘P’ class 0-6-0T No 31325 in 1956.

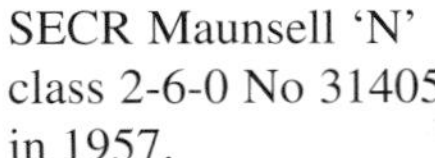
SECR Maunsell ‘N’ class 2-6-0 No 31405 in 1957.

SECR Wainwright ‘J’ class 0-6-4T No 31595.

N1 31822, 31876-31880
2-6-0 SECR Maunsell 3-cylinder version of 'N' class

Power Classification:	4MT reclassified 4P5F in 1953
Introduced:	1922-1930
Designer:	Maunsell
Company:	SECR
Weight:	Loco 64t 5cwt Tender 42t 8cwt t Tender 39t 5cwt
Driving Wheel:	5' 6"
Boiler Pressure:	200psi superheated
Cylinders:	Three 16" x 28"
Tractive Effort:	27695lbf
Valve Gear:	Walschaert (piston valves)

When the 'N' class engines were being built by the SECR in 1922, one engine (31822) was built with three cylinders instead of two, and it was classified 'N1'. It was fitted with Holcroft's valve gear. 31876-31880 were added in 1930 by the SR. These later engines were fitted with three sets of Walschaert valve gear, and 31822 was converted to this design in 1931.

The locomotives were specially built for working the Tonbridge to Hastings route over which the two-cylinder 'N' class could not work because of restricted clearances.

t 31822 was fitted with a smaller tender.

Year End Totals: 'N1' class

'47	'48	'49	'50	'51	'52	'53	'54	'55	'56	'57	'58	'59	'60	'61	'62	'63	'64	'65	'66	'67
6	6	6	6	6	6	6	6	6	6	6	6	6	6	6						

Number	Built	Renumbered	BR Dates	Scrap	Notes
31822	05/23 Asfd	04/49 1822	-11/62	05/64	t
31876	03/23 Asfd	09/48 1876	-11/62	10/63	
31877	04/30 Asfd	06/49 1877	-10/62	08/63	
31878	04/30 Asfd	01/49 1878	-10/62	08/63	
31879	04/30 Asfd	01/49 1879	-10/62	12/63	
31880	11/30 Asfd	09/48 1880	-11/62	11/63	

O1 between 31003 & 31439
0-6-0 SECR Stirling

Power Classification:	1F
Introduced:	1878-1899, rebuilt by Wainwright 1903-1927
Designer:	Stirling
Company:	SER
Weight:	Loco 41t 1cwt Tender 28t 5cwt Some fitted with eight-wheel tenders weighing on average 31t 0cwt
Driving Wheel:	5' 2" s 5' 1"
Boiler Pressure:	150psi
Cylinders:	Inside 18" x 26"
Tractive Effort:	17325lbf s 17610lbf
Valve Gear:	Stephenson (slide valves)

Stirling's first design for the South Eastern Railway was the 'O' class, built between 1878 and 1899. They had his usual domeless boilers and rounded cabs and 122 were built. Fifty-eight of these were rebuilt by Wainwright between 1903 and 1927 with domed boilers and new cabs, becoming the 'O1' class. The last 'O' class engine was withdrawn in 1932, the first of the 'O1' class going in 1912. Fifty-five engines came into BR stock.

c 31372 (one of the EKR engines) retained its original Stirling round cab roof and smoke-box wing-plates allied to the front sandboxes above the running plate as originally built.

e Three locomotives (31371, 31372 and 31383) had been sold to the East Kent Railway and were re-acquired on nationalisation.

s Two locomotives (31041 and 31048) were rebuilt with smaller wheels in 1903.

Year End Totals: 'O1' class

'47	'48	'49	'50	'51	'52	'53	'54	'55	'56	'57	'58	'59	'60	'61	'62	'63	'64	'65	'66	'67
55	44	25	23	8	8	8	8	8	8	8	7	4	2							

Number	Built	Renumbered	BR Dates	Scrap	Notes
31003	05/96 Asfd	1003	-01/49	49	
31007	08/99 Asfd	1007	-05/49	49	
31014	06/93 Asfd	1014	-06/48	06/48	
31039	06/97 Asfd	1039	-08/49	49	
31041	06/93 Asfd	1041	-05/51	51	s
31044	12/98 Asfd	1044	-06/51	51	
31046	06/94 Asfd	1046	-10/48	48	
31048	12/93 Asfd	03/50 1048	-10/60	10/60	s
31051	12/98 Asfd	1051	-08/48	09/48	
31064	11/96 Asfd	52 1064	-05/58	05/58	
31065 §	09/96 Asfd	52 1065	-06/61		
31066	06/97 Asfd	1066	-06/51	06/51	
31080	06/97 Asfd	1080	-08/49	49	
31093	11/97 Asfd	1093	-05/51	05/51	
31106	05/94 Asfd	1106	-01/49	49	
31108	06/97 Asfd	1108	-07/51	51	
31109	05/96 Asfd	1109	-01/49	49	
31123	05/96 Asfd	1123	-01/50	04/50	
31238	06/93 Asfd	1238	-07/49	49	
31248	05/96 Asfd	1248	-06/51	51	
31258	05/94 Asfd	12/49 1258	-02/61	02/61	
31316	09/82 Asfd	1316	-06/49	49	
31369	08/91 SS	1369	-09/51	51	
31370	08/91 SS	03/50 1370	-02/60	04/60	
31371	08/91 SS	EKR 1371	-01/49	49	e
31372	08/91 SS	EKR 6	-02/49	49	ec
31373	09/91 SS	1373	-07/51	51	
31374	09/91 SS	1374	-09/49	49	
31377	09/91 SS	1377	-01/50	05/50	
31378	09/91 SS	05/48 1378	-11/48	48	
31379	09/93 SS	1379	-05/51	05/51	
31380	09/93 SS	1380	-11/49	49	
31381	09/93 SS	1381	-05/51	51	
31383	09/93 SS	10/49 EKR 2	-04/51	04/51	e
31384	09/93 SS	1384	-12/49	50	
31385	09/93 SS	1385	-09/49	49	
31386	10/93 SS	1386	-10/48	48	
31388	10/93 SS	1388	-07/48	07/48	
31389	10/93 SS	1389	-02/49	49	
31390	10/93 SS	1390	-05/51	51	
31391	10/93 SS	1391	-06/51	06/51	
31395	11/93 SS	1395	-06/51	06/51	
31396	12/93 SS	1396	-08/48	08/48	
31397	12/93 SS	1397	-06/48	07/48	
31398	12/93 SS	1398	-05/49	49	
31425	08/97 SS	04/49 1425	-08/59	11/59	
31426	08/97 SS	1426	-08/48	09/48	
31428	09/97 SS	1428	-03/49	49	
31429	09/97 SS	1429	-09/49	49	
31430	09/97 SS	03/50 1430	-05/59	06/59	
31432	09/97 SS	1432	-06/51	06/51	
31434	09/97 SS	03/50 1434	-08/59	08/59	
31437	10/97 SS	1437	-10/48	48	
31438	10/97 SS	1438	-11/48	48	
31439	10/97 SS	1439	-05/49	49	

P between 31027 & 31558
0-6-0T SECR Wainwright

Power Classification:	0F
Introduced:	1909-1910
Designer:	Wainwright
Company:	SECR
Weight:	28t 10cwt
Driving Wheel:	3' 9"
Boiler Pressure:	160psi
Cylinders:	Inside 12" x 18"
Tractive Effort:	7835lbf
Valve Gear:	Stephenson (slide valves)

Wainwright designed these eight small 0-6-0Ts for rail motor work on branch lines. They were built at Ashford and could be described as a modernised version of Stroudley's LBSCR 'Terriers' ('A1' and 'A1X' classes). They were found to be too small for working the push pull trains for which they were designed, and in their later days they could be seen all over the system on light shunting work and as shed pilots. Some were also used in the docks at Dover.

They were very small engines and they were fitted with 'pagoda' type cabs, in which the roof overhung the cab sides. Four of the eight members of the class have been preserved. 31178 was sold for further service in industry before it was finally preserved.

Year End Totals: 'P' class

'47	'48	'49	'50	'51	'52	'53	'54	'55	'56	'57	'58	'59	'60	'61	'62	'63	'64	'65	'66	'67
8	8	8	8	8	8	8	8	8	7	7	6	5	5	2						

Number	Built	Renumbered	BR Dates	Scrap	Notes
31027 §	02/10 Asfd	07/48 1027	-03/61		
31178 §	02/10 Asfd	05/51 1178	-06/58		
31323 §	07/10 Asfd	03/49 1323	-07/60		
31325	07/10 Asfd	01/49 1325	-03/60	03/60	
31555	06/10 Asfd	05/48 1555	-02/55	03/55	
31556 §	02/09 Asfd	03/50 1556	-06/61		
31557	02/09 Asfd	05/49 1557	-09/57	09/57	
31558	06/10 Asfd	52 1558	-02/60	02/60	

R 31658-31675
0-4-4T LCDR (SECR) Kirtley

Power Classification:	1P
Introduced:	1891-1892
Designer:	Kirtley
Company:	LCDR
Weight:	48t 15cwt
Driving Wheel:	5' 6"
Boiler Pressure:	160psi
Cylinders:	Inside 17½" x 24"
Tractive Effort:	15145lbf
Valve Gear:	Stephenson (slide valves)

The 'R' class originally consisted of eighteen engines designed by Kirtley for local passenger services on the London Chatham & Dover Railway. They were built by Sharp Stewart in 1891-1892. They were subsequently rebuilt with 'H' class boilers. The first was withdrawn in 1929. Fifteen more engines were built to virtually the same design by the SECR in 1900, and these were known as the 'R1' class.

p Most of the later survivors were fitted for push-pull working.

Year End Totals: 'R' class

'47	'48	'49	'50	'51	'52	'53	'54	'55	'56	'57	'58	'59	'60	'61	'62	'63	'64	'65	'66	'67
15	15	14	14	11	6	3	2													

Number	Built	Renumbered	BR Dates	Scrap	Notes
31658	09/91 SS	01/49 1658	-12/52	12/52	p
31659	09/91 SS	11/49 1659	-09/51	51	p
31660	09/91 SS	03/49 1660	-12/53	04/54	p
31661	10/91 SS	03/49 1661	-09/55	55	
31662	10/91 SS	08/49 1662	-10/53	10/53	p
31663	10/91 SS	05/50 1663	-07/53	53	p
31665	10/91 SS	06/50 1665	-10/52	52	p
31666	11/91 SS	07/48 1666	-12/55	01/56	p
31667	11/91 SS	09/48 1667	-04/51	04/51	10/48⇨p
31670	11/91 SS	12/48 1670	-04/51	51	p
31671	11/91 SS	11/49 1671	-11/54	03/55	
31672	11/91 SS	1672	-12/49	50	p
31673	11/91 SS	1673	-10/52	02/53	
31674	12/91 SS	03/49 1674	-06/52	52	
31675	12/91 SS	08/49 1675	-12/52	12/52	p

R1[1] between 31010 & 31340
0-6-0T SECR Stirling

Power Classification:	2F
Introduced:	1888-1898, rebuilt 1910-1922 by Wainwright
Designer:	Stirling
Company:	SER
Weight:	46t 15cwt c 46t 8cwt
Driving Wheel:	5' 2" c 5' 1"
Boiler Pressure:	160psi
Cylinders:	Inside 18" x 26"
Tractive Effort:	18480lbf c 18780lbf
Valve Gear:	Stephenson (slide valves)

Stirling built twenty-five 'R' class 0-6-0T locomotives for the SER at Ashford between 1888 and 1898. They were based on the 'O' class standard goods engines (see 'O1' class) and had domeless boilers and rounded cab roofs.

Between 1910 and 1922 thirteen of these engines were rebuilt with domed boilers and higher pressure boilers. They were reclassified 'R1'. Most of them were also rebuilt with Pagoda type cabs as on the 'H' class.

Many of these engines had extra sandboxes in front of the leading wheels for working the 1 in 30 incline between Folkestone Harbour and Folkestone Junction. Sometimes as many as three engines could be seen at the head of these trains with a fourth banking. They were replaced on these duties by GWR 0-6-0PT engines in 1959.

c Four engines (31010, 31069, 31147 and 31339) were modified by Bulleid in 1938-1942 with cut down boiler mountings for working on the Canterbury and Whitstable branch. They retained the original Stirling round cab roofs and had truncated domes and Urie type short stovepipe chimneys.

31069 was rebuilt again in 1952 with normal boiler mountings, but retaining the original cab.

Year End Totals: 'R1 [1]' class

'47	'48	'49	'50	'51	'52	'53	'54	'55	'56	'57	'58	'59	'60	'61	'62	'63	'64	'65	'66	'67
13	13	12	12	12	12	12	12	10	10	10	7	2								

Number	Built	Renumbered	BR Dates	Scrap	Notes
31010	12/90 Asfd	08/48 1010	-08/59	09/59	c
31047	08/95 Asfd	04/49 1047	-03/60	04/60	
31069	06/98 Asfd	05/48 1069	-06/58	06/58	c
31107	06/98 Asfd	04/51 1107	-08/59	02/60	
31127	08/95 Asfd	1127	-01/49	*49*	
31128	10/92 Asfd	10/49 1128	-08/59	01/60	
31147	11/90 Asfd	07/51 1147	-09/58	12/58	c
31154	07/92 Asfd	05/48 1154	-09/55	*10/55*	
31174	10/92 Asfd	04/51 1174	-08/59	*59*	
31335	06/88 Asfd	05/51 1335	-07/55	*55*	
31337	06/88 Asfd	*51* 1337	-02/60	05/60	
31339	02/89 Asfd	05/51 1339	-06/58	06/58	c
31340	03/89 Asfd	09/48 1340	-02/59	03/59	

R1 [2] 31696-31710
0-4-4T SECR Kirtley

Power Classification: 1P
Introduced: 1900
Designer: Kirtley design modified by Wainwright
Company: SECR
Weight: 52t 3cwt
Driving Wheel: 5' 6"
Boiler Pressure: 160psi
Cylinders: Inside 17½" x 24"
Tractive Effort: 15145lbf
Valve Gear: Stephenson (slide valves)

The fifteen locomotives in this class were built in 1900 by the SECR to Kirtley's original design for the LCDR 'R' class of 1891. They had larger boilers than the original locomotives. They were subsequently fitted with 'H' class boilers.

p Most of the later survivors were fitted for push-pull working.

Year End Totals: 'R1 [2]' class

'47	'48	'49	'50	'51	'52	'53	'54	'55	'56	'57	'58	'59	'60	'61	'62	'63	'64	'65	'66	'67
13	13	11	10	7	4	3	2	1												

Number	Built	Renumbered	BR Dates	Scrap	Notes
31696	11/00 Asfd	04/49 1696	-03/51	03/51	
31697	11/00 Asfd	12/48 1697	-03/53	*03/53*	p
31698	11/00 Asfd	10/49 1698	-10/55	*11/55*	
31699	11/00 Asfd	1699	-01/50	05/50	
31700	11/00 Asfd	07/48 1700	-10/52	*52*	p
31703	11/00 Asfd	03/49 1703	-03/54	*54*	p
31704	11/00 Asfd	07/48 1704	-04/56	*05/56*	06/52⇨p
31705	11/00 Asfd	03/49 1705	-06/51	*51*	
31706	12/00 Asfd	08/48 1706	-12/52	*12/52*	p
31707	12/00 Asfd	1707	-02/49	*49*	p
31708	12/00 Asfd	1708	-10/52	02/53	
31709	12/00 Asfd	1709	-10/49	*49*	
31710	12/00 Asfd	07/48 1710	-06/51	07/51	p

S 31685
0-6-0ST SECR rebuilt from class 'C'

Power Classification: 2F
Introduced: 1900-1908
Rebuilt in 1917 by Maunsell
Designer: Wainwright
Company: SECR
Weight: 53t 10cwt
Driving Wheel: 5' 2"
Boiler Pressure: 160psi
Cylinders: Inside 18½" x 26"
Tractive Effort: 19520lbf
Valve Gear: Stephenson (slide valves)

The only 'S' class locomotive was rebuilt from a Wainwright 'C' class 0-6-0 tender engine with a saddle tank in 1917. It was converted for shunting work at Bricklayers Arms.

Year End Totals: 'S' class

'47	'48	'49	'50	'51	'52	'53	'54	'55	'56	'57	'58	'59	'60	'61	'62	'63	'64	'65	'66	'67
1	1	1	1																	

Number	Built	Renumbered	BR Dates	Scrap	Notes
31685	06/00 NR	1685	-10/51	10/51	

T 31602-31604, 500S
0-6-0T LCDR (SECR) Kirtley

Power Classification: 2F
Introduced: 1879-1893
Designer: Kirtley
Company: LCDR
Weight: 40t 15cwt
Driving Wheel: 4' 6"
Boiler Pressure: 160psi
Cylinders: Inside 17½" x 24"
Tractive Effort: 18510lbf
Valve Gear: Stephenson (slide valves)

The ten locomotives of the 'T' class were built by the London Chatham & Dover Railway between 1879 and 1893. They were inherited by the SECR in 1900 and were numbered 600-609 and then 1600-1609 on the SR. The first of the class was withdrawn in 1932. 1607 was transferred to the Service Department and was employed at Meldon Quarry as 500S. 1600 was sold out of service before 1948 and worked for the National Coal Board at Haydock Colliery in Lancashire until 1958.

Year End Totals: 'T' class

'47	'48	'49	'50	'51	'52	'53	'54	'55	'56	'57	'58	'59	'60	'61	'62	'63	'64	'65	'66	'67
2	2	2	1																	

Year End Totals: 'T' (service) class

'47	'48	'49	'50	'51	'52	'53	'54	'55	'56	'57	'58	'59	'60	'61	'62	'63	'64	'65	'66	'67
1	1																			

Number	Built	Renumbered	BR Dates	Scrap	Notes
31602	06/93 Lngh	1602	-07/51	*07/51*	
31604	03/91 Lngh	05/50 1604	-12/50	*01/51*	

Class continued with 500S (Service Locomotives)

U 31610-31639, 31790-31809
2-6-0 SR Maunsell

Power Classification: 4MT reclassified 4P3F in 1954
Introduced: k 1917-1925, rebuilt 1928
n 1928-1934
Designer: Maunsell
Company: SECR/SR
Weight: k Loco 63t 0cwt
n Loco 62t 6cwt
k Tender 40t 10cwt
n Tender 42t 8cwt
Driving Wheel: 6' 0"
Boiler Pressure: 200psi superheated
Cylinders: Outside 19" x 28"
Tractive Effort: 23865lbf
Valve Gear: Walschaert (piston valves)

When Maunsell produced his first 2-6-0 tender engine No. 810 ('N' class) in 1917, he also built a corresponding 2-6-4T engine No. 790 ('K' class). The 2-6-4T was intended for express duties on the SECR main line. After the War another nineteen appeared in 1925 and an additional engine (890) was fitted with three cylinders and was known as the 'K1' class. The whole class was named after Rivers, and were thus known as the 'River' class.

On 27th August 1927 No. 800 RIVER CRAY was derailed at speed at Sevenoaks, with disastrous results. Immediately all the engines were taken out of service pending an enquiry. Although the enquiry found that the fault lay in the track and ballast, rather than in the design of the locomotives, it was decided to rebuild the whole class as 2-6-0 tender engines. As such they became the 'U' class and they were very similar to the 'N' class, except for the larger wheel diameter. They were used on intermediate passenger duties such as semi-fast and cross-country workings.

k 31790-31809 were rebuilt from 'K' class 2-6-4Ts. They all formerly carried River names as follows: 31790 RIVER AVON, 31791 RIVER ADUR, 31792 RIVER ARUN, 31793 RIVER OUSE, 31794 RIVER ROTHER, 31795 RIVER MEDWAY, 31796 RIVER STOUR, 31797 RIVER MOLE, 31798 RIVER WEY, 31799 RIVER TEST, 31800 RIVER CRAY, 31801 RIVER DARENTH, 31802 RIVER CUCKMERE, 31803 RIVER ITCHEN, 31804 RIVER TAMAR, 31805 RIVER CAMEL, 31806 RIVER TORRIDGE, 31807 RIVER AXE, 31808 RIVER CHAR and 31809 RIVER DART.

n 31610-31639 were built new to the design of the converted engines, with a few detail alterations. They had originally been ordered as 2-6-4Ts and work had begun on the first ten of these, but they were all delivered as 2-6-0s. They had smaller splashers and minor differences when compared with the rebuilt engines.

o Two locomotives (31625 and 31797) were converted to oil burning during the coal crisis after the Second World War. They were later converted back to coal burning (c).

Year End Totals: 'U' class

'47	'48	'49	'50	'51	'52	'53	'54	'55	'56	'57	'58	'59	'60	'61	'62	'63	'64	'65	'66	'67
50	50	50	50	50	50	50	50	50	50	50	50	50	50	50	48	34	10	4		

Number	Built	Renumbered	BR Dates	Scrap	Notes
31610	08/28 Bton	07/48 1610	-12/62	09/63	n
31611	08/28 Bton	02/51 1611	-10/63	01/64	n
31612	07/28 Bton	04/49 1612	-05/63	08/63	n
31613	06/28 Bton	01/50 1613	-01/64	07/64	n
31614	07/28 Bton	*49* 1614	-11/63	01/64	n
31615	08/28 Bton	12/48 1615	-10/63	11/63	n
31616	09/28 Bton	08/48 1616	-06/64	11/64	n
31617	10/28 Bton	11/49 1617	-01/64	07/64	n
31618 §	10/28 Bton	05/48 1618	-01/64		n
31619	12/28 Bton	05/49 1619	-12/65	03/66	n
31620	11/28 Asfd	09/48 1620	-04/65	08/65	n
31621	12/28 Asfd	10/49 1621	-06/64	11/64	n
31622	01/29 Asfd	12/48 1622	-01/64	02/64	n
31623	01/29 Asfd	*51* 1623	-12/63	12/63	n
31624	02/29 Asfd	08/48 1624	-06/64	11/64	n
31625 §	03/29 Asfd	12/48 1625	-01/64		no 48⇨c
31626	03/29 Asfd	04/49 1626	-01/64	12/64	n
31627	04/29 Asfd	04/49 1627	-10/65	02/66	n
31628	04/29 Asfd	11/48 1628	-06/64	12/64	n
31629	12/29 Asfd	06/49 1629	-01/64	12/64	n
31630	02/31 Asfd	12/48 1630	-11/62	12/62	n
31631	03/31 Asfd	10/49 1631	-09/63	11/63	n
31632	03/31 Asfd	07/48 1632	-09/64	12/64	n
31633	03/31 Asfd	07/49 1633	-12/63	02/64	n
31634	04/31 Asfd	09/48 1634	-12/63	02/64	n
31635	04/31 Asfd	08/50 1635	-12/63	01/64	n
31636	04/31 Asfd	09/48 1636	-06/63	08/63	n
31637	05/31 Asfd	12/48 1637	-09/63	09/63	n
31638 §	05/31 Asfd	11/48 1638	-01/64		n
31639	05/31 Asfd	12/48 1639	-06/66	09/66	n
31790	06/17 Elh	04/49 1790	-05/65	08/65	k
31791	06/28 Elh	03/49 1791	-06/66	09/66	k
31792	07/28 Elh	12/50 1792	-09/64	12/64	k
31793	07/28 Elh	01/50 1793	-05/64	12/64	k
31794	06/28 Elh	11/49 1794	-06/63	10/63	k
31795	06/28 Elh	12/48 1795	-06/63	09/63	k
31796	07/28 Elh	08/49 1796	-01/64	07/64	k
31797	07/28 Asfd	12/48 1797	-01/64	12/64	ko 48⇨c
31798	08/28 Asfd	05/49 1798	-09/64	12/64	k
31799	07/28 Asfd	06/49 1799	-02/65	05/65	k
31800	12/28 Asfd	05/48 1800	-10/65	02/66	k
31801	07/28 Asfd	05/48 1801	-06/64	12/64	k
31802	07/28 Asfd	07/48 1802	-09/64	12/64	k
31803	06/28 Bton	10/49 1803	-03/66	07/66	k
31804	06/28 Bton	12/48 1804	-06/64	12/64	k
31805	03/28 Asfd	08/49 1805	-08/63	10/63	k
31806 §	06/28 Bton	04/49 1806	-01/64		k
31807	06/28 Bton	01/50 1807	-01/64	04/64	k
31808	07/28 Bton	11/49 1808	-01/64	03/64	k
31809	02/28 Bton	*51* 1809	-01/66	03/66	k

U1 31890-31910
2-6-0 SR Maunsell 3-cylinder version of 'U' class

Power Classification: 4MT reclassified 4P3F in 1954
Introduced: k 1925, rebuilt 1928
1928-1931
Designer: Maunsell
Company: SECR/SR
Weight: Loco 65t 6cwt
Tender 42t 8cwt
k Tender 40t 10cwt
Driving Wheel: 6' 0"
Boiler Pressure: 200psi superheated
Cylinders: Three 16" x 28"
Tractive Effort: 25385lbf
Valve Gear: Walschaert (piston valves)

In the same way that one of the 'N' class locomotives was built with three cylinders and Holcroft's conjugated valve gear, one of the 'River' class ('K' class) 2-6-4Ts (31890) was similarly built as a 'K1' class engine. After the Sevenoaks crash which caused to the 'Rivers' to be rebuilt, 31890 was also rebuilt in 1928 as a 'U1' class engine. 31891-31910 were built by the SR in 1931-1932 to the design of the rebuilt engine. They were fitted with three sets of Walschaert valve gear, and 31890 was converted to this design in 1932.

The 'U1' class was very similar to the 'N1' class, except for the larger diameter driving wheels. The locomotives were specially built for working the Tonbridge to Hastings route over which the two-cylinder 'U' class could not work because of restricted clearances.

k 31890 was a rebuilt three-cylinder 'K1' 'River' class 2-6-4T and was originally named RIVER FROME.

Year End Totals: 'U1' class

'47	'48	'49	'50	'51	'52	'53	'54	'55	'56	'57	'58	'59	'60	'61	'62	'63	'64	'65	'66	'67
21	21	21	21	21	21	21	21	21	21	21	21	21	21	21	4					

Number	Built	Renumbered	BR Dates	Scrap	Notes
31890	06/28 Asfd	11/48 1890	-06/63	10/63	k
31891	06/31 Elh	05/48 1891	-03/63	06/63	
31892	01/31 Elh	09/48 1892	-11/62	03/63	
31893	02/31 Elh	08/48 1893	-12/62	05/64	
31894	02/31 Elh	04/49 1894	-12/62	05/64	
31895	03/31 Elh	03/50 1895	-12/62	08/63	
31896	03/31 Elh	07/48 1896	-12/62	05/64	
31897	03/31 Elh	07/48 1897	-10/62	12/62	
31898	04/31 Elh	04/49 1898	-12/62	10/63	
31899	04/31 Elh	12/48 1899	-12/62	11/63	
31900	05/31 Elh	11/48 1900	-12/62	09/63	
31901	06/31 Elh	10/49 1901	-06/63	08/63	
31902	07/31 Elh	09/48 1902	-11/62	01/63	
31903	07/31 Elh	04/49 1903	-12/62	10/63	
31904	07/31 Elh	08/49 1904	-11/62	01/63	
31905	08/31 Elh	12/48 1905	-12/62	10/63	
31906	09/31 Elh	08/49 1906	-12/62	11/63	
31907	09/31 Elh	04/49 1907	-12/62	12/63	
31908	10/31 Elh	05/48 1908	-12/62	09/63	
31909	10/31 Elh	04/49 1909	-12/62	07/63	
31910	11/31 Elh	05/48 1910	-07/63	10/63	

W 31911-31925
2-6-4T SR Maunsell

Power Classification: 5F reclassified 6F in 1953
Introduced: 1931-1936
Designer: Maunsell
Company: SR
Weight: 90t 14cwt
Driving Wheel: 5' 6"
Boiler Pressure: 200psi superheated
Cylinders: Three 16½" x 28"
Tractive Effort: 29450lbf
Valve Gear: Walschaert (piston valves)

After the Sevenoaks crash of 1927 the Southern Railway stopped using 2-6-4T locomotives on passenger trains. This caused all of the 'River' class ('K' class) 2-6-4Ts to be rebuilt as 'U' class 2-6-0 tender locomotives.

In 1931-1932 Maunsell constructed this class of fifteen new 2-6-4T engines which were confined entirely to freight work. The first five were built at Eastleigh, and the remainder at Ashford. They incorporated the side tanks and other parts of the old 'River' class engines. They had three cylinders, and the cylinders and motion were interchangeable with those of the 'N1' and 'U1' classes. They were basically tank engine versions of the 'N1' class.

The locomotives were mainly used on transfer freight in the London area, but some finished up as bankers working between Exeter (St. David's) and Exeter (Central).

Year End Totals: 'W' class

'47	'48	'49	'50	'51	'52	'53	'54	'55	'56	'57	'58	'59	'60	'61	'62	'63	'64	'65	'66	'67
15	15	15	15	15	15	15	15	15	15	15	15	15	15	15	15	5				

Number	Built	Renumbered	BR Dates	Scrap	Notes
31911	01/32 Elh	04/49 1911	-10/63	04/64	
31912	01/32 Elh	10/49 1912	-08/64	11/64	
31913	01/32 Elh	08/49 1913	-03/64	12/64	
31914	01/32 Elh	10/49 1914	-08/64	11/64	
31915	02/32 Elh	10/49 1915	-10/63	11/63	
31916	04/35 Asfd	05/48 1916	-07/63	10/63	
31917	04/35 Asfd	11/49 1917	-01/64	08/64	
31918	06/35 Asfd	05/48 1918	-08/63	02/64	
31919	07/35 Asfd	12/48 1919	-11/63	11/63	
31920	08/35 Asfd	09/48 1920	-07/63	02/64	
31921	10/35 Asfd	12/48 1921	-06/63	10/63	
31922	11/35 Asfd	05/48 1922	-08/63	06/64	
31923	01/36 Asfd	09/48 1923	-01/63	09/63	
31924	02/36 Asfd	07/48 1924	-07/64	11/64	
31925	04/36 Asfd	07/48 1925	-11/63	01/64	

1302 31302
0-4-0CT SECR Crane Engine

Power Classification: 0F
Introduced: 1881
Designer: James Stirling, built by Neilson
Company: LCDR
Weight: 17t 17cwt
Driving Wheel: 3' 3"
Boiler Pressure: 120psi
Cylinders: Inside 11" x 20"
Tractive Effort: 6330lbf
Valve Gear: Stephenson (slide valves)

This crane engine was built in 1881 by the London, Chatham and Dover Railway to work at Folkestone Harbour. It was transferred to Ashford Works in 1905. In 1925 it was transferred to Lancing Carriage Works and was renumbered 234S.

In 1938 the engine was fitted with an enclosed cab and was renumbered 1302. It finished its days shunting in the milk dock at Stewarts Lane with the crane jib out of use.

Another very similar engine (No. 409) was built in 1896 and was scrapped in 1935 as 235S.

Year End Totals: '1302' class

'47	'48	'49	'50	'51	'52	'53	'54	'55	'56	'57	'58	'59	'60	'61	'62	'63	'64	'65	'66	'67
1	1																			

Number	Built	Renumbered	BR Dates	Scrap	Notes
31302	04/81 N	1302	-07/49	*07/49*	

Numerical List 32001-32699

Number	Built	Renumbered	BR Dates	Scrap	Class
32001	06/07 Bton	2001	-07/48	11/48	I1X
32002	07/07 Bton	2002	-07/51	08/51	I1X
32003	07/07 Bton	2003	-07/48	09/48	I1X
32004	08/07 Bton	2004	-11/48	01/49	I1X
32005	09/07 Bton	05/48 2005	-06/51	*06/51*	I1X
32006	10/07 Bton	2006	-07/48	11/48	I1X
32007	10/07 Bton	2007	-09/48	11/48	I1X
32008	11/07 Bton	2008	-06/51	07/51	I1X
32009	12/07 Bton	2009	-05/51	*05/51*	I1X
32010	12/07 Bton	2010	-07/48	11/48	I1X
32021	10/07 Bton	*49* 2021	-10/51	*12/51*	I3
32022	03/08 Bton	01/49 2022	-05/51	*05/51*	I3
32023	02/09 Bton	05/49 2023	-07/51	08/51	I3
32025	03/09 Bton	2025	-01/50	02/50	I3
32026	03/09 Bton	10/49 2026	-09/51	09/51	I3
32027	05/09 Bton	03/49 2027	-02/51	02/51	I3
32028	12/09 Bton	03/49 2028	-10/51	10/51	I3
32029	12/09 Bton	01/49 2029	-03/51	03/51	I3
32030	03/10 Bton	04/49 2030	-09/51	*09/51*	I3
32037	12/05 K	04/49 2037	-07/51	09/51	H1
SELSEY BILL					
32038	12/05 K	07/49 2038	-07/51	09/51	H1
PORTLAND BILL					
32039	01/06 K	08/49 2039	-03/51	03/51	H1
HARTLAND POINT					
32043	06/03 Bton	09/48 2043	-12/51	*52*	B4X
32044	06/00 Bton	2044	-09/48	11/48	B4[2]
32045	06/02 Bton	2045	-12/51	*52*	B4X
32050	07/01 SS	2050	-10/51	10/51	B4X
32051	07/01 SS	2051	-03/49	03/49	B4[2]
32052	12/99 Bton	2052	-12/51	12/51	B4X
32054	05/00 Bton	2054	-06/51	*06/51*	B4[2]
32055	07/01 SS	2055	-12/51	12/51	B4X
32056	07/01 SS	2056	-11/51	11/51	B4X
32060	08/01 SS	2060	-12/51	12/51	B4X
32062	08/01 SS	2062	-05/51	*05/51*	B4[2]
32063	08/01 SS	2063	-06/51	06/51	B4[2]
32067	09/01 SS	2067	-10/51	11/51	B4X
32068	09/01 SS	2068	-06/51	*06/51*	B4[2]
32070	09/01 SS	2070	-09/51	09/51	B4X
32071	09/01 SS	07/48 2071	-12/51	12/51	B4X
32072	09/01 SS	02/50 2072	-12/51	12/51	B4X
32073	10/01 SS	2073	-09/51	09/51	B4X
32074	10/01 SS	2074	-02/50	03/50	B4[2]
32075	03/10 Bton	*51* 2075	-12/51	12/51	I3
32076	03/10 Bton	04/49 2076	-12/50	02/51	I3
32077	10/10 Bton	07/48 2077	-03/51	*03/51*	I3
32078	11/10 Bton	05/49 2078	-02/51	03/51	I3
32079	11/10 Bton	01/49 2079	-11/50	11/50	I3
32080	12/10 Bton	2080	-03/50	04/50	I3
32081	12/10 Bton	12/48 2081	-09/51	09/51	I3
32082	08/12 Bton	09/48 2082	-06/51	07/51	I3
32083	08/12 Bton	06/49 2083	-06/51	06/51	I3
32084	08/12 Bton	08/48 2084	-03/51	03/51	I3
32085	08/12 Bton	03/49 2085	-06/50	07/50	I3
32086	09/12 Bton	05/48 2086	-10/51	10/51	I3
32087	11/12 Bton	05/48 2087	-11/50	*50*	I3
32088	11/12 Bton	07/49 2088	-11/50	11/50	I3
32089	12/12 Bton	04/49 2089	-04/51	04/51	I3
32090	03/13 Bton	07/48 2090	-12/50	12/50	I3
32091	03/13 Bton	*51* 2091	-06/52	*05/53*	I3
32094	11/83 Bton	12/48 2094	-05/55	05/55	E1R
32095	11/83 Bton	07/48 2095	-11/56	*56*	E1R
32096	12/83 Bton	08/48 2096	-11/56	12/56	E1R
32097	12/83 Bton	2097	-12/49	01/50	E1[2]
32100	06/13 Bton	12/49 2100	-11/61	01/62	E2
32101	08/13 Bton	06/51 2101	-09/62	09/62	E2
32102	10/13 Bton	08/48 2102	-10/61	10/61	E2
32103	12/13 Bton	05/50 2103	-10/62	10/62	E2
32104	01/14 Bton	02/51 2104	-04/63	05/63	E2
32105	06/15 Bton	03/50 2105	-09/62	10/62	E2
32106	09/15 Bton	02/50 2106	-10/62	10/62	E2
32107	03/16 Bton	10/49 2107	-02/61	03/61	E2
32108	07/16 Bton	05/49 2108	-06/61	07/61	E2
32109	10/16 Bton	11/50 2109	-04/63	04/63	E2
32112	04/77 Bton	2112	-12/49	02/50	E1[2]
32113	05/77 Bton	04/49 2113	-09/58	10/58	E1[2]
32122	08/78 Bton	2122	-05/48	09/48	E1[2]
32124	08/78 Bton	05/48 2124	-01/59	03/59	E1R
32127	10/78 Bton	2127	-12/49	01/50	E1[2]
32128	10/78 Bton	08/48 2128	-03/52	*04/52*	E1[2]
32129	10/78 Bton	08/48 2129	-06/51	06/51	E1[2]
32133	12/78 Bton	2133	-12/52	*12/52*	E1[2]
32135	01/79 Bton	05/48 2135	-02/59	04/59	E1R
32138	01/79 Bton	05/51 2138	-11/56	12/56	E1[2]
32139	03/79 Bton	05/48 2139	-01/59	01/59	E1[2]
32141	03/79 Bton	2141	-10/49	10/49	E1[2]
32142	03/79 Bton	05/48 2142	-11/50	*50*	E1[2]
32145	10/79 Bton	07/48 2145	-06/51	06/51	E1[2]
32147	10/79 Bton	07/48 2147	-12/51	10/52	E1[2]
32151	12/80 Bton	01/49 2151	-01/60	02/60	E1[2]
32153	03/81 Bton	2153	-05/49	10/49	E1[2]
32156	03/81 Bton	2156	-05/51	05/51	E1[2]
32160	07/91 Bton	2160	-12/51	12/51	E1[2]
32162	11/91 Bton	2162	-11/49	12/49	E1[2]
32164	12/91 Bton	2164	-06/48	10/48	E1[2]
32165	11/94 Bton	07/48 2165	-11/59	11/59	E3
32166	11/94 Bton	07/48 2166	-09/59	10/59	E3
32167	12/94 Bton	04/49 2167	-10/55	*03/56*	E3
32168	12/94 Bton	01/51 2168	-01/56	*03/56*	E3
32169	12/94 Bton	07/49 2169	-08/55	*55*	E3
32170	12/94 Bton	01/49 2170	-07/57	08/57	E3
32215	05/75 Bton	2215	-02/50	03/50	D1/M
32234	10/81 N	2234	-02/50	03/50	D1/M
32235	11/81 N	2235	-05/49	02/51	D1/M
32239	01/82 N	2239	-03/48	05/48	D1/M
32252	01/82 N	2252	-09/50	11/50	D1/M
32253	03/82 N	2253	-09/49	10/49	D1/M
32259	03/82 N	2259	-03/48	04/48	D1/M
32269	05/80 Bton	2269	-07/48	09/48	D1/M
32274	12/79 Bton	2274	-02/50	03/50	D1/M
32283	10/79 Bton	2283	-11/48	12/48	D1/M
32286	07/79 Bton	2286	-07/48	10/48	D1[2]
32289	07/79 Bton	2289	-07/48	10/48	D1/M
32299	01/74 Bton	2299	-05/49	09/49	D1/M
32300	03/06 Bton	07/48 2300	-07/51	09/51	C3
32301	06/06 Bton	08/48 2301	-03/51	04/51	C3
32302	06/06 Bton	12/48 2302	-01/52	*52*	C3
32303	06/06 Bton	07/48 2303	-10/51	11/51	C3
32306	08/06 Bton	2306	-12/51	*52*	C3
32307	08/06 Bton	2307	-05/49	*49*	C3
32308	11/06 Bton	2308	-11/48	*48*	C3
32309	09/06 Bton	2309	-01/49	*49*	C3
32325	12/10 Bton	03/49 2325	-06/51	07/51	J1
32326	03/12 Bton	05/48 2326	-06/51	07/51	J2
32327	04/14 Bton	07/48 2327	-01/56	*56*	N15X
TREVITHICK					
32328	09/14 Bton	10/48 2328	-02/55	05/55	N15X
HACKWORTH					
32329	10/21 Bton	12/48 2329	-08/56	*09/56*	N15X
STEPHENSON					
32330	12/21 Bton	08/48 2330	-08/55	09/55	N15X
CUDWORTH					
32331	12/21 Bton	05/49 2331	-07/57	09/57	N15X
BEATTIE					
32332	09/22 Bton	05/48 2332	-01/56	*01/56*	N15X
STROUDLEY					
32333	04/22 Bton	05/48 2333	-04/56	*07/56*	N15X
REMEMBRANCE					
32337	09/13 Bton	09/48 2337	-12/62	05/64	K
32338	12/13 Bton	11/48 2338	-12/62	09/63	K
32339	03/14 Bton	03/49 2339	-11/62	12/62	K
32340	06/14 Bton	10/49 2340	-12/62	05/64	K
32341	11/14 Bton	10/49 2341	-12/62	08/63	K
32342	10/16 Bton	01/51 2342	-12/62	07/63	K
32343	11/16 Bton	05/49 2343	-12/62	10/64	K
32344	12/16 Bton	07/48 2344	-11/62	01/63	K
32345	12/16 Bton	10/49 2345	-12/62	11/63	K
32346	12/16 Bton	*49* 2346	-11/62	02/63	K
32347	12/20 Bton	04/49 2347	-12/62	09/63	K
32348	12/20 Bton	05/48 2348	-11/62	12/62	K
32349	12/20 Bton	08/48 2349	-11/62	04/63	K
32350	12/20 Bton	03/50 2350	-11/62	02/63	K
32351	01/21 Bton	01/49 2351	-11/62	04/63	K

32352 02/21 Bton 01/49 2352 -11/62 03/63 K
32353 03/21 Bton 01/50 2353 -12/62 12/63 K
32358 11/86 Bton 2358 -11/48 12/48 D1/M
32359 12/86 Bton 2359 -07/51 08/51 D1[2]
32361 01/87 Bton 2361 -03/48 04/48 D1/M
32364 06/92 Bton 08/48 2364 -10/52 52 D3
32365 06/92 Bton 05/48 2365 -12/52 02/53 D3
32366 07/92 Bton 2366 -03/49 49 D3
32367 07/92 Bton 2367 -02/49 49 D3
32368 08/92 Bton 05/50 2368 -03/53 05/53 D3
32370 10/92 Bton 2370 -09/48 09/48 D3
32371 12/92 Bton 2371 -10/48 48 D3
32372 12/92 Bton 05/48 2372 -05/53 05/53 D3
32373 12/92 Bton 2373 -11/48 48 D3
32374 12/92 Bton 2374 -02/49 49 D3
32376 04/93 Bton 01/49 2376 -05/53 05/53 D3
32377 05/93 Bton 2377 -09/48 09/48 D3
32378 05/93 Bton 08/50 2378 -08/52 52 D3
32379 07/93 Bton 07/48 2379 -12/52 01/53 D3
32380 07/93 Bton 09/48 2380 -05/53 05/53 D3
32383 12/93 Bton 2383 -12/48 49 D3
32384 12/93 Bton 05/50 2384 -11/53 53 D3
32385 12/93 Bton 11/50 2385 -07/53 10/53 D3
32386 12/93 Bton 01/50 2386 -06/52 52 D3
32387 04/94 Bton 2387 -03/49 49 D3
32388 05/94 Bton 12/49 2388 -12/51 52 D3
32389 05/94 Bton 05/48 2389 -03/49 49 D3
32390 05/94 Bton 08/50 2390 -10/55 11/55 D3
32391 06/94 Bton 06/51 2391 -12/52 12/52 D3
32393 04/96 Bton 08/49 2393 -10/51 11/51 D3
32394 04/96 Bton 10/49 2394 -12/51 52 D3
32395 05/96 Bton 05/48 2395 -06/49 07/49 D3
32397 11/96 Bton 2397 -07/48 08/48 D3X
32398 11/96 Bton 05/48 2398 -03/49 03/49 D3
32399 06/04 Bton 10/49 2399 -07/53 10/53 E5
32400 06/04 Bton 10/49 2400 -12/51 52 E5
32401 06/04 Bton 08/49 2401 -08/54 03/55 E5X
32402 09/04 Bton 07/49 2402 -03/51 04/51 E5
32404 10/04 Bton 02/50 2404 -12/51 52 E5
32405 11/04 Bton 06/49 2405 -12/51 52 E5
32406 11/04 Bton 08/49 2406 -09/51 51 E5
32407 12/04 Bton 51 2407 -11/57 02/58 E6X
32408 12/04 Bton 03/52 2408 -12/62 02/63 E6
32409 12/04 Bton 08/50 2409 -01/58 03/58 E6
32410 03/05 Bton 04/49 2410 -06/61 08/61 E6
32411 05/05 Bton 10/49 2411 -02/59 04/59 E6X
32412 07/05 Bton 05/48 2412 -09/57 09/57 E6
32413 07/05 Bton 01/49 2413 -02/58 02/59 E6
32414 10/05 Bton 06/49 2414 -06/58 06/58 E6
32415 10/05 Bton 07/48 2415 -09/61 11/61 E6
32416 11/05 Bton 11/48 2416 -02/62 03/62 E6
32417 12/05 Bton 12/48 2417 -12/62 10/63 E6
32418 12/05 Bton 52 2418 -12/62 07/63 E6
32421 06/11 Bton 05/49 2421 -08/56 12/56 H2
SOUTH FORELAND
32422 07/11 Bton 05/48 2422 -10/56 02/57 H2
NORTH FORELAND
32423 09/11 Bton 2423 -05/49 06/49 H2
THE NEEDLES
32424 09/11 Bton 12/48 2424 -04/58 05/58 H2
BEACHY HEAD
32425 12/11 Bton 11/50 2425 -10/56 08/57 H2
TREVOSE HEAD
32426 01/12 Bton 08/50 2426 -08/56 02/57 H2
ST. ALBAN'S HEAD
32434 03/93 VF 08/49 2434 -03/57 03/57 C2X
32435 03/93 VF 2435 -05/48 06/48 C2
32436 03/93 VF 2436 -01/50 05/50 C2
32437 04/93 VF 11/48 2437 -06/59 06/59 C2X
32438 04/93 VF 08/50 2438 -12/61 01/62 C2X
32440 05/93 VF 05/48 2440 -10/58 10/58 C2X
32441 05/93 VF 04/49 2441 -10/61 11/61 C2X
32442 05/93 VF 07/49 2442 -03/60 03/60 C2X
32443 06/93 VF 07/48 2443 -09/60 10/60 C2X
32444 06/93 VF 07/48 2444 -03/60 04/60 C2X
32445 07/94 VF 05/48 2445 -11/61 11/61 C2X
32446 07/94 VF 05/49 2446 -11/60 12/60 C2X
32447 08/94 VF 03/51 2447 -02/60 03/60 C2X
32448 08/94 VF 05/48 2448 -10/61 10/61 C2X
32449 10/94 VF 03/49 2449 -06/61 06/61 C2X
32450 10/94 VF 08/48 2450 -10/61 11/61 C2X
32451 10/94 VF 12/48 2451 -11/61 11/61 C2X
32453 04/95 Bton 12/48 2453 -08/55 55 E3
32454 05/95 Bton 03/50 2454 -03/58 05/58 E3
32455 05/95 Bton 08/50 2455 -02/58 03/58 E3
32456 05/95 Bton 06/49 2456 -08/59 10/59 E3
32457 12/95 Bton 2457 -05/49 05/49 E3
32458 12/95 Bton 08/49 2458 -03/57 05/57 E3
32459 12/95 Bton 07/49 2459 -06/56 07/56 E3
32460 12/95 Bton 04/49 2460 -04/56 04/56 E3
32461 12/95 Bton 12/48 2461 -04/57 05/57 E3
32462 12/95 Bton 03/50 2462 -05/57 06/57 E3
32463 12/97 Bton 11/49 2463 -09/59 10/59 E4
32464 12/97 Bton 08/48 2464 -02/56 56 E4
32465 04/98 Bton 12/49 2465 -04/55 55 E4
32466 04/98 Bton 03/50 2466 -12/58 03/59 E4X
32467 05/98 Bton 03/49 2467 -04/58 04/58 E4
32468 05/98 Bton 08/49 2468 -01/63 08/63 E4
32469 06/98 Bton 07/49 2469 -10/61 10/61 E4
32470 06/98 Bton 07/49 2470 -06/62 07/62 E4
32471 06/98 Bton 10/49 2471 -09/59 01/60 E4
32472 06/98 Bton 12/50 2472 -06/62 07/62 E4
32473 § 06/98 Bton 04/51 2473 -11/62 E4
32474 08/98 Bton 10/49 2474 -05/63 06/63 E4
32475 10/98 Bton 11/50 2475 -06/61 07/61 E4
32476 10/98 Bton 04/49 2476 -04/57 05/57 E4
32477 10/98 Bton 08/48 2477 -01/59 02/59 E4X
32478 11/98 Bton 05/50 2478 -08/56 08/56 E4X
32479 12/98 Bton 05/48 2479 -06/63 07/63 E4
32480 12/98 Bton 03/50 2480 -11/59 11/59 E4
32481 12/98 Bton 10/49 2481 -04/58 04/58 E4
32482 12/98 Bton 05/49 2482 -11/55 11/55 E4
32484 05/99 Bton 03/50 2484 -09/60 10/60 E4
32485 05/99 Bton 02/53 2485 -12/57 01/58 E4
32486 05/99 Bton 05/49 2486 -01/59 02/59 E4
32487 06/99 Bton 03/51 2487 -12/62 08/63 E4
32488 06/99 Bton 05/49 2488 -06/57 08/57 E4
32489 06/99 Bton 03/49 2489 -05/55 55 E4X
32490 06/99 Bton 02/50 2490 -12/55 56 E4
32491 09/99 Bton 01/50 2491 -01/61 02/61 E4
32492 10/99 Bton 07/48 2492 -05/57 06/57 E4
32493 11/99 Bton 07/48 2493 -02/58 03/58 E4
32494 11/99 Bton 04/49 2494 -09/59 09/59 E4
32495 11/99 Bton 05/48 2495 -09/60 09/60 E4
32496 12/99 Bton 12/48 2496 -11/55 55 E4
32497 05/00 Bton 06/49 2497 -11/59 11/59 E4
32498 05/00 Bton 11/49 2498 -11/61 01/62 E4
32499 06/00 Bton 04/49 2499 -06/57 06/57 E4
32500 06/00 Bton 05/50 2500 -01/62 01/62 E4
32501 06/00 Bton 12/48 2501 -08/55 11/55 E4
32502 06/00 Bton 05/48 2502 -02/58 03/58 E4
32503 08/00 Bton 11/49 2503 -04/63 06/63 E4
32504 09/00 Bton 05/48 2504 -11/61 12/61 E4
32505 10/00 Bton 08/50 2505 -03/61 05/61 E4
32506 10/00 Bton 05/48 2506 -06/61 07/61 E4
32507 12/00 Bton 05/48 2507 -04/59 06/59 E4
32508 12/00 Bton 03/50 2508 -01/60 02/60 E4
32509 12/00 Bton 08/50 2509 -03/62 04/62 E4
32510 12/00 Bton 08/49 2510 -09/62 10/62 E4
32511 02/01 Bton 10/49 2511 -10/56 10/56 E4
32512 02/01 Bton 12/48 2512 -05/61 07/61 E4
32513 03/01 Bton 02/50 2513 -01/56 56 E4
32514 03/01 Bton 03/49 2514 -10/56 10/56 E4
32515 04/01 Bton 10/49 2515 -05/61 07/61 E4
32516 04/01 Bton 05/48 2516 -10/55 10/55 E4
32517 06/01 Bton 12/50 2517 -06/59 06/59 E4
32518 06/01 Bton 04/49 2518 -06/55 55 E4
32519 06/01 Bton 03/50 2519 -09/59 01/60 E4
32520 06/01 Bton 12/48 2520 -01/57 03/57 E4
32521 08/00 VF 08/48 2521 -12/61 12/61 C2X
32522 08/00 VF 11/50 2522 -10/61 11/61 C2X
32523 08/00 VF 05/48 2523 -02/62 02/62 C2X
32524 09/00 VF 10/49 2524 -02/58 02/58 C2X
32525 09/00 VF 04/49 2525 -01/62 02/62 C2X
32526 09/00 VF 10/49 2526 -02/60 03/60 C2X
32527 09/00 VF 06/49 2527 -11/60 12/60 C2X
32528 11/00 VF 12/49 2528 -03/61 03/61 C2X
32529 10/00 VF 08/48 2529 -10/59 12/59 C2X
32532 10/00 VF 05/48 2532 -06/60 06/60 C2X
32533 10/00 VF 2533 -02/50 50 C2
32534 10/00 VF 06/49 2534 -10/61 10/61 C2X
32535 11/00 VF 05/48 2535 -02/62 02/62 C2X
32536 11/00 VF 06/49 2536 -03/61 03/61 C2X
32537 11/00 VF 11/48 2537 -04/57 05/57 C2X
32538 11/00 VF 09/48 2538 -12/61 01/62 C2X
32539 11/00 VF 05/48 2539 -11/61 12/61 C2X
32540 11/00 VF 11/49 2540 -03/58 04/58 C2X
32541 12/01 VF 03/50 2541 -02/61 02/61 C2X
32543 12/01 VF 08/48 2543 -09/60 02/61 C2X
32544 12/01 VF 09/48 2544 -11/61 01/62 C2X
32545 12/01 VF 03/50 2545 -12/61 01/62 C2X
32546 01/02 VF 05/48 2546 -04/61 06/61 C2X
32547 01/02 VF 07/48 2547 -11/61 11/61 C2X
32548 01/02 VF 10/49 2548 -11/61 11/61 C2X
32549 01/02 VF 07/48 2549 -11/61 01/62 C2X
32550 01/02 VF 12/48 2550 -12/61 01/62 C2X
32551 02/02 VF 03/50 2551 -02/60 02/60 C2X
32552 02/02 VF 03/50 2552 -06/61 07/61 C2X
32553 02/02 VF 11/48 2553 -08/61 09/62 C2X
32554 02/02 VF 05/50 2554 -02/60 03/60 C2X
32556 01/01 Bton 11/50 2556 -09/61 10/61 E4
32557 09/01 Bton 05/49 2557 -12/62 10/63 E4
32558 10/01 Bton 05/48 2558 -11/56 56 E4
32559 10/01 Bton 07/48 2559 -06/60 07/60 E4
32560 11/01 Bton 52 2560 -08/58 08/58 E4
32561 11/01 Bton 06/50 2561 -06/56 56 E4
32562 12/01 Bton 05/48 2562 -08/60 10/60 E4
32563 12/01 Bton 12/48 2563 -08/61 08/61 E4
32564 12/01 Bton 06/50 2564 -09/61 10/61 E4
32565 05/02 Bton 12/48 2565 -06/61 08/61 E4
32566 06/02 Bton 04/49 2566 -04/59 05/59 E4
32567 10/02 Bton 2567 -11/49 49 E5
32568 10/02 Bton 07/48 2568 -02/55 03/55 E5
32570 11/02 Bton 03/51 2570 -01/56 02/56 E5X
32571 12/02 Bton 08/48 2571 -01/56 02/56 E5
32572 12/02 Bton 2572 -03/49 03/49 E5
32573 02/03 Bton 10/52 2573 -08/53 10/53 E5
32574 02/03 Bton 07/48 2574 -06/51 07/51 E5
32575 03/03 Bton 07/49 2575 -12/51 52 E5
32576 03/03 Bton 07/48 2576 -07/55 11/55 E5X
32577 06/03 Bton 06/49 2577 -10/59 01/60 E4
32578 06/03 Bton 01/49 2578 -04/61 06/61 E4
32579 07/03 Bton 11/49 2579 -11/59 12/59 E4
32580 07/03 Bton 09/48 2580 -04/62 04/62 E4
32581 09/03 Bton 10/49 2581 -04/62 04/62 E4
32582 09/03 Bton 07/49 2582 -10/56 56 E4
32583 11/03 Bton 11/48 2583 -01/56 01/56 E5
32584 11/03 Bton 05/48 2584 -02/51 04/51 E5
32585 12/03 Bton 12/48 2585 -06/54 01/55 E5
32586 12/03 Bton 05/48 2586 -04/55 55 E5X
32587 12/03 Bton 03/50 2587 -11/54 11/54 E5
32588 12/03 Bton 11/48 2588 -12/53 54 E5
32589 03/04 Bton 2589 -01/49 49 E5
32590 04/04 Bton 05/49 2590 -09/51 11/51 E5
32591 04/04 Bton 05/48 2591 -12/54 03/55 E5
32592 04/04 Bton 11/50 2592 -05/53 05/53 E5
32593 05/04 Bton 01/50 2593 -01/56 01/56 E5
32594 06/04 Bton 12/49 2594 -03/51 04/51 E5
32595 09/06 Bton 2595 -06/51 07/51 I1X
32596 11/06 Bton 2596 -06/51 08/51 I1X
32598 12/06 Bton 2598 -07/48 11/48 I1X
32599 01/07 Bton 2599 -09/48 11/48 I1X
32601 03/07 Bton 2601 -02/48 10/48 I1X
32602 04/07 Bton 2602 -06/51 07/51 I1X
32603 06/07 Bton 2603 -04/51 04/51 I1X
32604 04/07 Bton 2604 -09/48 11/48 I1X
32605 01/74 Bton 2605 -11/48 12/48 D1/M
32606 10/76 Bton 05/48 2606 -08/56 56 E1[2]
32608 11/76 Bton 05/51 2608 -05/57 06/57 E1R
32609 03/77 Bton 2609 -06/48 11/48 E1[2]
32610 12/74 Bton 01/49 2610 -04/56 04/56 E1R
32635 06/78 Bton 01/59 DS377 01/59-03/63 09/63 A1X
32636 § 09/72 Bton 08/50 2636 -11/63 A1X
32640 § 03/78 Bton 03/51 2640 -09/63 A1X
32644 06/77 Bton 07/48 2644 -04/51 04/51 A1X
32646 § 01/77 Bton 09/49 W8 09/49-11/63 A1X
32647 12/76 Bton 2647 -10/51 10/51 A1X
32650 § 12/76 Bton 08/53 DS515 11/53-11/63 A1X
32655 § 12/75 Bton 12/49 2655 -05/60 A1X
32659 10/75 Bton 03/50 2659 -08/53 06/63 A1X
08/53➲DS681
32661 10/75 Bton 05/51 2661 -04/63 08/63 A1X
32662 § 10/75 Bton 10/49 2662 -11/63 A1X
32670 § 12/72 Bton 10/49 KESR 3 -11/63 A1X
32677 07/80 Bton 09/49 W13 09/49-09/59 05/60 A1X
32678 § 07/80 Bton 08/48 2678 -10/63 A1X
32689 05/83 Bton 06/50 2689 -02/60 05/60 E1[2]
32690 05/83 Bton 2690 -01/50 02/50 E1[2]
32691 10/83 Bton 2691 -12/51 52 E1[2]
32694 03/75 Bton 02/51 2694 -07/61 08/61 E1[2]
32695 09/76 Bton 05/51 2695 -04/57 04/57 E1R
32696 10/76 Bton 01/49 2696 -01/56 01/57 E1R
32697 09/76 Bton 07/51 2697 -11/59 01/60 E1R
32699 06/78 Bton 2699 -02/48 48 D1/M

A1X 32635-32678, W8, W13, DS377, DS515, DS681

0-6-0T LBSCR Stroudley 'Terrier' (Rebuilt)

Power Classification:	0P
Introduced:	1872-1880
	Rebuilt by Marsh 1911-1947
Designer:	Stroudley
Company:	LBSCR
Weight:	28t 5cwt
Driving Wheel:	4' 0"
Boiler Pressure:	150psi
Cylinders:	Inside 12" x 20"
	b Inside 14 $^{3}/_{16}$" x 20"
Tractive Effort:	7650lbf
	b 10695lbf
Valve Gear:	Stephenson (slide valves)

Between 1872 and 1880, Stroudley built fifty engines of his famous 'A1' or 'Terrier' class. They were designed specifically for working the East London Line between New Cross and Liverpool Street, the South London Line between Victoria and London Bridge, and also on short country branches. They were extremely small engines, with tall chimneys, and they were very powerful for their small size.

In 1911 Marsh decided to bring these small engines up to date, and seventeen of them were rebuilt with new boilers and extended smokeboxes. These were then known as the 'A1X' class. The first of these was withdrawn in 1919.

The last survivors of the class were withdrawn in November 1963 on the closure of the Hayling Island

SECR Maunsell 'D1' class 4-4-0 No 31741.

SR Maunsell 'U' class 2-6-0 No 31790 at Yeovil Town Shed in October 1957.

SR Maunsell 'W' class 2-6-4T No 31911 in 1950.

LBSCR Billinton 'B4X' class 4-4-0 No 32043.

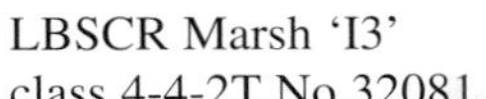
LBSCR Marsh 'I3' class 4-4-2T No 32081.

LBSCR Billinton 'K' class 2-6-0 No 32344.

Branch, which was their last regular duty. At that time they were the oldest locomotives on British Railways, and the last LBSCR engines still at work.

They had a very interesting and varied history, details for individual engines being listed below.

a 32635 was built in 1878 as 35 MORDEN. Later it became 635, then 2635. In 1946 it was transferred to the service list as the Brighton Works Shunter. Numbered 377S and later DS377, it carried the original LBSCR yellow livery which it retained even after it was transferred back to capital stock as 32635 in 1959.

b 32636 was built in 1872 as 72 FENCHURCH. It was sold to the Newhaven Harbour Company in 1898 and returned to the Southern Railway in 1925 numbered 636. Later it became 2636, then 32636. This engine had larger cylinders than the other engines of the class. It has since been preserved.

c 32640 was built in 1878 as 40 BRIGHTON. It was sold to the Isle of Wight Central Railway in 1902 as No. 11. It became W11 NEWPORT in Southern Railway days, then returned to the mainland as 2640 in 1947, later becoming 32640. It has since been preserved.

d 32644 was built in 1877 as 44 FULHAM. Later it became 644, then 2644, then 32644.

e 32646 was built in 1877 as 46 NEWINGTON. Later it became 646, before being sold to the LSWR in 1903 where it became No. 734. Later it was transferred to the Isle of Wight as W2 and later W8 FRESHWATER. It returned to the mainland in 1949 as 32646. It has since been preserved.

f 32647 was built in 1876 as 47 CHEAPSIDE. Later it became 647, then 2647. It never carried its BR number 32647, being withdrawn in 1951.

g 32650 was built in 1876 as 50 WHITECHAPEL. Later it became 650, then it was transferred to the Isle of Wight in 1930 as W9 FISHBOURNE. It returned to the mainland in 1937 when it was renumbered 515S and became the Lancing Works shunter with 680S (see 'A1' class). It later became DS515 and was returned to capital stock in 1953 as 32650. It has since been preserved.

h 32655 was built in 1875 as 55 STEPNEY. Later it became 655. It was withdrawn in 1925 then reinstated in 1927. It later became 2655, then 32655. It has since been preserved.

i 32659 was built in 1875 as 59 CHEAM. Later it became 659, then 2659, then 32659. In 1953 it replaced DS515 as the Lancing Works shunter and was renumbered DS681. It worked in Lancing Works alongside 'A1' class DS680.

j 32661 was built in 1875 as 61 SUTTON. Later it became 661, then 2661, then 32661.

k 32662 was built in 1875 as 62 MARTELLO. Later it became 662, then 2662, then 32662. It has since been preserved.

l 32670 was built in 1872 as 70 POPLAR. Later it became 670. In 1901 it was sold to the Kent & East Sussex Railway where it became KESR No. 3. In 1948 it returned to British Railways as 32670. It has since been preserved.

m 32677 was built in 1880 as 77 WONERSH. Later it became 677, and it was withdrawn in 1925. In 1927 it was reinstated and sent to the Isle of Wight as No. 3, later W13 CARISBROOKE. It returned to the mainland in 1949 and became 32677.

n 32678 was built in 1880 as 78 KNOWLE. Later it became 678, and it was withdrawn in 1925. In 1929 it was reinstated and sent to the Isle of Wight as No. 4, later W14 BEMBRIDGE. It returned to the mainland in 1946 and became 2678 and later 32678. It has since been preserved.

In addition to the above, two other Terriers came into BR stock. 43 (later 643) GIPSYHILL was built in 1877 and 53 (later 653 and 2653) ASHTEAD was built in 1875. They were sold in 1925 and 1937 respectively to the Weston, Clevedon & Portishead Railway, where they became No. 2 PORTISHEAD and No. 4. They were later renumbered 5 and 6 by the GWR, and they are listed under those numbers in the GWR group.

Year End Totals: 'A1X' class

'47	'48	'49	'50	'51	'52	'53	'54	'55	'56	'57	'58	'59	'60	'61	'62	'63	'64	'65	'66	'67
12	12	12	12	10	10	10	10	10	10	10	10	10	9	9	9					

Year End Totals: 'A1X' (service) class

'47	'48	'49	'50	'51	'52	'53	'54	'55	'56	'57	'58	'59	'60	'61	'62	'63	'64	'65	'66	'67
2	2	2	2	2	2	2	2	2	2	2	2	1	1	1	1					

Number	*Built*	*Renumbered*	*BR Dates*	*Scrap*	*Notes*
32635	06/78 Bton	01/59 DS377	01/59-03/63	09/63	a
32636 §	09/72 Bton	08/50 2636	-11/63		b
32640 §	03/78 Bton	03/51 2640	-09/63		c
32644	06/77 Bton	07/48 2644	-04/51	*04*/51	d
32646 §	01/77 Bton	09/49 W8	09/49-11/63		e
32647	12/76 Bton	2647	-10/51	10/51	f
32650 §	12/76 Bton	08/53 DS515	11/53-11/63		g
32655 §	12/75 Bton	12/49 2655	-05/60		h
32659	10/75 Bton	03/50 2659	-08/53	06/63	i
				08/53➲DS681	
32661	10/75 Bton	05/51 2661	-04/63	08/63	j
32662 §	10/75 Bton	10/49 2662	-11/63		k
32670 §	12/72 Bton	10/49 KESR 3	-11/63		l
32677	07/80 Bton	09/49 W13	09/49-09/59	05/60	m
32678 §	07/80 Bton	08/48 2678	-10/63		n

Class continued with W8 (Isle of Wight Locomotives)

B4[2] between 32044 & 32074
4-4-0 LBSCR Billinton

Power Classification: 1P
Introduced: 1899-1902
Designer: R Billinton
Company: LBSCR
Weight: Loco 51t 10cwt
Tender 35t 5cwt
Driving Wheel: 6' 9"
Boiler Pressure: 180psi
s 180psi superheated
Cylinders: Inside 19" x 26"
s Inside 20" x 26"
Tractive Effort: 17730lbf
s 19645lbf
Valve Gear: Stephenson (slide valves)
s Stephenson (piston valves)

Billinton built the 'B4' class between 1899 and 1902 as a more powerful version of his 'B2' and 'B3' classes. They were designed to haul the heaviest passenger trains of the day. Thirty-three were built, twelve of which were rebuilt to the 'B4X' class between 1922 and 1924. The first was withdrawn in 1934.

The former names of the class were as follows: 32044 CECIL RHODES, 32051 WOLFERTON, 32054 PRINCESS ROYAL (previously named EMPRESS until 1906 and LA FRANCE for a while in 1905), 32062 MAFEKING, 32063 PRETORIA, 32068 MARLBOROUGH and 32074 CORNWALL.

32074 was withdrawn in October 1937, but it was reinstated two years later due to wartime conditions.

r 32068 was fitted with a modified running plate. In 1935 2059 and 2068 were dismantled at Eastleigh. However, as the company was short of motive power, parts of both engines were reassembled to form a new 2068.

s 32044 was superheated and fitted with 20" diameter cylinders and piston valves in 1922.

Year End Totals: 'B4[2]' class

'47	'48	'49	'50	'51	'52	'53	'54	'55	'56	'57	'58	'59	'60	'61	'62	'63	'64	'65	'66	'67
7	6	5	4																	

Number	*Built*	*Renumbered*	*BR Dates*	*Scrap*	*Notes*
32044	06/00 Bton	2044	-09/48	11/48	s
32051	07/01 SS	2051	-03/49	03/49	
32054	05/00 Bton	2054	-06/51	*06/51*	
32062	08/01 SS	2062	-05/51	*05/51*	
32063	08/01 SS	2063	-06/51	06/51	
32068	09/01 SS	2068	-06/51	*06/51*	r
32074	10/01 SS	2074	-02/50	03/50	

B4X between 32043 & 32073
4-4-0 LBSCR rebuilt from 'B4'

Power Classification: 3P
Introduced: 1922-1924
Rebuilt from L Billinton B4 class engines dating from 1899-1902
Designer: R Billinton
Company: LBSCR
Weight: Loco 58t 1cwt
Tender 39t 5cwt
Driving Wheel: 6' 9"
Boiler Pressure: 180psi superheated
Cylinders: Inside 20" x 26"
Tractive Effort: 19645lbf
Valve Gear: Stephenson (piston valves)

These twelve engines were designed by Billinton as powerful express engines. They were officially regarded as rebuilds of the 'B4' class but in fact they were new engines apart from the bogies and a few minor details. They also retained the original tenders.

Their names before rebuilding as 'B4X' were as follows: 32043 DUCHESS OF FIFE, 32045 BESSBOROUGH, 32050 TASMANIA, 32052 SIEMENS then SUSSEX, 32055 EMPEROR, 32056 ROBERTS, 32060 KIMBERLEY, 32067 OSBORNE, 32070 HOLYROOD then DEVONSHIRE, 32071 GOODWOOD, 32072 SUSSEX and 32073 WESTMINSTER. After rebuilding 32052 carried the name SUSSEX for a short while.

These were the last engines to be designed and built by the LBSCR, the last ten appearing after grouping.

Year End Totals: 'B4X' class

'47	'48	'49	'50	'51	'52	'53	'54	'55	'56	'57	'58	'59	'60	'61	'62	'63	'64	'65	'66	'67
12	12	12	12																	

Number	*Built*	*Renumbered*	*BR Dates*	*Scrap*	*Notes*
32043	06/03 Bton	09/48 2043	-12/51	*52*	
32045	06/02 Bton	2045	-12/51	*52*	
32050	07/01 SS	2050	-10/51	10/51	
32052	12/99 Bton	2052	-12/51	12/51	
32055	07/01 SS	2055	-12/51	12/51	
32056	07/01 SS	2056	-11/51	11/51	
32060	08/01 SS	2060	-12/51	12/51	
32067	09/01 SS	2067	-10/51	11/51	
32070	09/01 SS	2070	-09/51	09/51	
32071	09/01 SS	07/48 2071	-12/51	12/51	
32072	09/01 SS	02/50 2072	-12/51	12/51	
32073	10/01 SS	2073	-09/51	09/51	

C2 32435-32436, 32533
0-6-0 LBSCR Billinton 'Vulcan'

Power Classification: 2F
Introduced: 1893-1902
Designer: R Billinton
Company: LBSCR
Weight: Loco 39t 10cwt
Tender 33t 10cwt
Driving Wheel: 5' 0"
Boiler Pressure: 160psi
Cylinders: Inside 17½" x 26"
Tractive Effort: 18050lbf
Valve Gear: Stephenson (slide valves)

Billinton built fifty-five locomotives of his 'C2' class in 1893-1902 for working goods trains. They were all built at the Vulcan Foundry in Newton-le-Willows and were thus commonly known as the Vulcans.

Forty-five engines were rebuilt with new boilers between 1908 and 1940. These became known as the 'C2X' class. Of the remaining engines, seven were withdrawn between 1935 and 1937, leaving three to come into BR stock.

Year End Totals: 'C2' class

'47	'48	'49	'50	'51	'52	'53	'54	'55	'56	'57	'58	'59	'60	'61	'62	'63	'64	'65	'66	'67
3	2	2																		

Number	*Built*	*Renumbered*	*BR Dates*	*Scrap*	*Notes*
32435	03/93 VF	2435	-05/48	06/48	
32436	03/93 VF	2436	-01/50	05/50	
32533	10/00 VF	2533	-02/50	*50*	

C2X between 32434 & 32451, 32521 & 32554
0-6-0 LBSCR Rebuilt 'C2'

Power Classification: 3F reclassified 2F in 1953
Introduced: 1893-1902
Rebuilt by Marsh 1908-1940
Designer: R Billinton
Company: LBSCR
Weight: Loco 45t 5cwt
Tender 33t 10cwt
Driving Wheel: 5' 0"
Boiler Pressure: 170psi
Cylinders: Inside 17½" x 26"

Tractive Effort: 19175lbf
Valve Gear: Stephenson (slide valves)

The 'C2X' class consisted of forty-five engines rebuilt from the 'C2' class with increased boiler capacity (the boilers being increased from 4' 3" diameter to 5' 0" diameter) and extended smokeboxes. This was to cope with the increased loads and the speeding up of freight trains. They were fitted with 'C3' type boilers and they were converted between 1908 and 1940.

The cabs were also altered to give them increased route availability over the Southern Railway after grouping.

b Six of the boilers fitted to the rebuilds carried two domes, the second of which carried top-feed apparatus. This was dispensed with from 1930 onwards, but the boilers retained two domes. These boilers were transferred between different engines from time to time but the locomotives marked in the lists are known to have carried them at some time.

Year End Totals: 'C2X' class

'47	'48	'49	'50	'51	'52	'53	'54	'55	'56	'57	'58	'59	'60	'61	'62	'63	'64	'65	'66	'67
45	45	45	45	45	45	45	45	45	45	43	40	38	27	3						

Number	Built	Renumbered	BR Dates	Scrap	Notes
32434	03/93 VF	08/49 2434	-03/57	03/57	
32437	04/93 VF	11/48 2437	-06/59	06/59	
32438	04/93 VF	08/50 2438	-12/61	01/62	b
32440	05/93 VF	05/48 2440	-10/58	10/58	b
32441	05/93 VF	04/49 2441	-10/61	11/61	
32442	05/93 VF	07/49 2442	-03/60	03/60	
32443	06/93 VF	07/48 2443	-09/60	10/60	
32444	06/93 VF	07/48 2444	-03/60	04/60	b
32445	07/94 VF	05/48 2445	-11/61	11/61	
32446	07/94 VF	05/49 2446	-11/60	12/60	
32447	08/94 VF	03/51 2447	-02/60	03/60	
32448	08/94 VF	05/48 2448	-10/61	10/61	b
32449	10/94 VF	03/49 2449	-06/61	06/61	
32450	10/94 VF	08/48 2450	-10/61	11/61	
32451	10/94 VF	12/48 2451	-11/61	11/61	b
32521	08/00 VF	08/48 2521	-12/61	12/61	
32522	08/00 VF	11/50 2522	-10/61	11/61	
32523	08/00 VF	05/48 2523	-02/62	02/62	b
32524	09/00 VF	10/49 2524	-02/58	02/58	
32525	09/00 VF	04/49 2525	-01/62	02/62	b
32526	09/00 VF	10/49 2526	-02/60	03/60	
32527	09/00 VF	06/49 2527	-11/60	12/60	b
32528	11/00 VF	12/49 2528	-03/61	03/61	
32529	10/00 VF	08/48 2529	-10/59	12/59	
32532	10/00 VF	05/48 2532	-06/60	06/60	
32534	10/00 VF	06/49 2534	-10/61	10/61	b
32535	11/00 VF	05/48 2535	-02/62	02/62	b
32536	11/00 VF	06/49 2536	-03/61	03/61	
32537	11/00 VF	11/48 2537	-04/57	05/57	
32538	11/00 VF	09/48 2538	-12/61	01/62	
32539	11/00 VF	05/48 2539	-11/61	12/61	b
32540	11/00 VF	11/49 2540	-03/58	04/58	
32541	12/01 VF	03/50 2541	-02/61	02/61	
32543	12/01 VF	08/48 2543	-09/60	02/61	
32544	12/01 VF	09/48 2544	-11/61	01/62	
32545	12/01 VF	03/50 2545	-12/61	01/62	
32546	01/02 VF	05/48 2546	-04/61	06/61	b
32547	01/02 VF	07/48 2547	-11/61	11/61	
32548	01/02 VF	10/49 2548	-11/61	11/61	b
32549	01/02 VF	07/48 2549	-11/61	01/62	
32550	01/02 VF	12/48 2550	-12/61	01/62	
32551	02/02 VF	03/50 2551	-02/60	02/60	b
32552	02/02 VF	03/50 2552	-06/61	07/61	
32553	02/02 VF	11/48 2553	-08/61	09/62	b
32554	02/02 VF	05/50 2554	-02/60	03/60	

C3 32300-32309
0-6-0 LBSCR Marsh

Power Classification: 3F
Introduced: 1906
Designer: Marsh
Company: LBSCR
Weight: Loco 47t 10cwt
Tender 35t 15cwt or 37t 5cwt
Driving Wheel: 5' 0"
Boiler Pressure: 170psi
Cylinders: Inside 17½ x 26"
Tractive Effort: 19175lbf
Valve Gear: Stephenson (slide valves)

This was the only class of six-coupled goods engines to be built by Marsh. Ten engines were built at Brighton between March and September 1906. The first was withdrawn in 1936.

These engines were intended to replace the 'C2' class. However they turned out to be poor performers and most of their work was later taken over by the rebuilt 'C2X' class.

Year End Totals: 'C3' class

'47	'48	'49	'50	'51	'52	'53	'54	'55	'56	'57	'58	'59	'60	'61	'62	'63	'64	'65	'66	'67
8	7	5	5	1																

Number	Built	Renumbered	BR Dates	Scrap	Notes
32300	03/06 Bton	07/48 2300	-07/51	09/51	
32301	06/06 Bton	08/48 2301	-03/51	04/51	
32302	06/06 Bton	12/48 2302	-01/52	52	
32303	06/06 Bton	07/48 2303	-10/51	11/51	
32306	08/06 Bton	2306	-12/51	52	
32307	08/06 Bton	2307	-05/49	49	
32308	11/06 Bton	2308	-11/48	48	
32309	09/06 Bton	2309	-01/49	49	

D1[2] & D1/M between 32215 & 32299, 32358 & 32361, 32605, 32699, 700-701S
0-4-2T LBSCR Stroudley

Power Classification: 1P
Introduced: 1873-1887
Designer: Stroudley
Company: LBSCR
Weight: 43t 10cwt
Driving Wheel: 5' 6"
Boiler Pressure: 170psi
Cylinders: Inside 17" x 24"
Tractive Effort: 15185lbf
Valve Gear: Stephenson (slide valves)

The 'D1' class was one of Stroudley's finest designs for the LBSCR and 125 engines were built between 1873 and 1887. They were built for general local working on the London suburban services and the country branches. They bore the brunt of the suburban traffic until replaced by Billinton's larger engines in the 1890s, but they continued to work for many years in the country areas. The first was withdrawn in 1903, most of the class were taken out of service between 1923 and 1947, and only a handful came into BR stock in 1948.

Their former names were as follows: 32215 STOCKWELL, 32234 ROTTINGDEAN, 32235 BROADWATER, 32239 PATCHAM, 32252 BUCKHURST, 32253 PELHAM, 32259 TELFORD then BARNHAM, 32269 CRAWLEY, 32274 GUILDFORD, 32283 ALDGATE, 32286 RANMORE, 32289 HOLMBURY, 32299 WIMBLEDON, 32358 HENFIELD, 32359 EGMONT, 32361 UPPERTON, 32605 STREATHAM, 32699 NEW CROSS, 700S (ex-2244) HASSOCKS and 701S (ex-2284) ASHBURNHAM.

One engine (216) was rebuilt with an enlarged boiler in 1910 and became a 'D1X' engine. It was scrapped in 1934.

During the Second World War some of the engines worked far away from home in Scotland. 32605 worked at Ayr, 32699 at Wick and 32358 at Inverness.

f Several of the class were converted for fire fighting during the Second World War. They had a powerful steam pump fitted over the rear buffer beam and were able to throw four powerful jets of water. They were withdrawn without being reconverted.

m These were motor fitted versions (for push-pull working) of Stroudley's 'D1' class and they were known as the 'D1/M' class.

o 700S and 701S were modified in 1947 as oil pumping locomotives. They fitted with oil pumping apparatus for fuelling the locomotives which were fitted for oil burning in the 1946-1949 period. They were based at Eastleigh and Fratton respectively.

Year End Totals: 'D1 2' class

'47	'48	'49	'50	'51	'52	'53	'54	'55	'56	'57	'58	'59	'60	'61	'62	'63	'64	'65	'66	'67
2	1	1	1																	

Year End Totals: 'D1/M' class

'47	'48	'49	'50	'51	'52	'53	'54	'55	'56	'57	'58	'59	'60	'61	'62	'63	'64	'65	'66	'67
16	7	4																		

Year End Totals: 'D1/M' (service) class

'47	'48	'49	'50	'51	'52	'53	'54	'55	'56	'57	'58	'59	'60	'61	'62	'63	'64	'65	'66	'67
2	2	1	1																	

Number	Built	Renumbered	BR Dates	Scrap	Notes
32215	05/75 Bton	2215	-02/50	03/50	mf
32234	10/81 N	2234	-02/50	03/50	m
32235	11/81 N	2235	-05/49	02/51	m
32239	01/82 N	2239	-03/48	05/48	mf
32252	01/82 N	2252	-09/50	11/50	mf
32253	03/82 N	2253	-09/49	10/49	mf
32259	03/82 N	2259	-03/48	04/48	m
32269	05/80 Bton	2269	-07/48	09/48	m
32274	12/79 Bton	2274	-02/50	03/50	m
32283	10/79 Bton	2283	-11/48	12/48	m
32286	07/79 Bton	2286	-07/48	10/48	
32289	07/79 Bton	2289	-07/48	10/48	m
32299	01/74 Bton	2299	-05/49	09/49	m
32358	11/86 Bton	2358	-11/48	12/48	m
32359	12/86 Bton	2359	-07/51	08/51	
32361	01/87 Bton	2361	-03/48	04/48	m
32605	01/74 Bton	2605	-11/48	12/48	m
32699	06/78 Bton	2699	-02/48	48	m

Class continued with 700S (Service Locomotives)

D3 between 32364 & 32398
0-4-4T LBSCR Billinton

Power Classification: 1P
Introduced: 1892-1896
Designer: R Billinton
Company: LBSCR
Weight: 52t 0cwt
Driving Wheel: 5' 6"
Boiler Pressure: 170psi
Cylinders: Inside 17½" x 26"
Tractive Effort: 17435lbf
Valve Gear: Stephenson (slide valves)

In 1892-1896 Billinton built thirty-six 'D3' engines. They were the first of his bogie tank engines for the LBSCR and they worked on outer suburban workings.

Two engines were converted to the 'D3X' class in 1909; apart from these the first of the class was withdrawn in 1933. All the engines were reboilered by Marsh and they were fitted with push-pull gear from 1933 onwards.

The 'D3' engines formerly carried the following names: 32364 TRUSCOTT, 32365 VICTORIA, 32366 CRYSTAL PALACE, 32367 NORWOOD, 32368 NEWPORT, 32370 HAYWARDS HEATH, 32371 ANGMERING, 32372 AMBERLEY, 32373 BILLINGSHURST, 32374 PULBOROUGH, 32376 FOLKINGTON, 32377 HURSTPIERPOINT, 32378 HORSTED KEYNES, 32379 SANDERSTEAD, 32380 THORNTON HEATH, 32383 THREE BRIDGES, 32384 COOKSBRIDGE, 32385 PORTSMOUTH, 32386 CHICHESTER, 32387 STEYNING, 32388 EMSWORTH, 32389 SHOREHAM, 32390 ST. LEONARDS, 32391 DRAYTON, 32393 WOODSIDE, 32394 COWFOLD, 32395 GATWICK and 32398 HASLEMERE.

On 28th November 1942 32365 gained fame by being the only locomotive ever to bring down an enemy aircraft. The engine was running on a coastal section of track between Brighton and Chichester, when a German plane attacked with machine guns blazing. Bullets hit the engine, but the plane came in so low that it touched the dome of the engine. An explosion of steam surrounded the plane and it crashed in a nearby field, killing the pilot. Neither the driver nor the fireman were seriously hurt, and the engine was repaired and returned to service soon afterwards.

Year End Totals: 'D3' class

'47	'48	'49	'50	'51	'52	'53	'54	'55	'56	'57	'58	'59	'60	'61	'62	'63	'64	'65	'66	'67
28	23	16	16	13	7	1	1													

Number	Built	Renumbered	BR Dates	Scrap	Notes
32364	06/92 Bton	08/48 2364	-10/52	52	
32365	06/92 Bton	05/48 2365	-12/52	02/53	
32366	07/92 Bton	2366	-03/49	49	
32367	07/92 Bton	2367	-02/49	49	
32368	08/92 Bton	05/50 2368	-03/53	05/53	
32370	10/92 Bton	2370	-09/48	09/48	
32371	12/92 Bton	2371	-10/48	48	
32372	12/92 Bton	05/48 2372	-05/53	05/53	
32373	12/92 Bton	2373	-11/48	48	
32374	12/92 Bton	2374	-02/49	49	
32376	04/93 Bton	01/49 2376	-05/53	05/53	
32377	05/93 Bton	2377	-09/48	09/48	
32378	05/93 Bton	08/50 2378	-08/52	52	
32379	07/93 Bton	07/48 2379	-12/52	01/53	
32380	07/93 Bton	09/48 2380	-05/53	05/53	
32383	12/93 Bton	2383	-12/48	49	
32384	12/93 Bton	05/50 2384	-11/53	53	
32385	12/93 Bton	11/50 2385	-07/53	10/53	
32386	12/93 Bton	01/50 2386	-06/52	52	
32387	04/94 Bton	2387	-03/49	49	
32388	05/94 Bton	12/49 2388	-12/51	52	
32389	05/94 Bton	05/48 2389	-03/49	49	

Number	Built	Renumbered	BR Dates	Scrap	Notes
32390	05/94 Bton	08/50 2390	-10/55	*11/55*	
32391	06/94 Bton	06/51 2391	-12/52	*12/52*	
32393	04/96 Bton	08/49 2393	-10/51	11/51	
32394	04/96 Bton	10/49 2394	-12/51	*52*	
32395	05/96 Bton	05/48 2395	-06/49	*07/49*	
32398	11/96 Bton	05/48 2398	-03/49	03/49	

D3X 32397
0-4-4T LBSCR Rebuilt 'D3'

Power Classification: Not classified
Introduced: 1896, rebuilt by Marsh in 1909
Designer: R Billinton
Company: LBSCR
Weight: 53t 0cwt
Driving Wheel: 5' 6"
Boiler Pressure: 170psi
Cylinders: Inside 17½" x 26"
Tractive Effort: 17435lbf
Valve Gear: Stephenson (slide valves)

In 1909 'D3' engines 396 CLAYTON and 397 BEXHILL were fitted with 'I2' type boilers. This resulted in increased boiler power, but no further engines of the class were converted. No. 2396 was withdrawn in 1937 leaving only 32397 to come into BR stock and it was withdrawn in 1948 without receiving its new number.

Year End Totals: 'D3X' class

'47	'48	'49	'50	'51	'52	'53	'54	'55	'56	'57	'58	'59	'60	'61	'62	'63	'64	'65	'66	'67
1																				

Number	Built	Renumbered	BR Dates	Scrap	Notes
32397	11/96 Bton	2397	-07/48	08/48	

E1 [2] between 32097 & 32164, 32606 & 32609, 32689-32694, W1-W4
0-6-0T LBSCR Stroudley

Power Classification: 2F
Introduced: 1874-1891
Designer: Stroudley
Company: LBSCR
Weight: 44t 3cwt
Driving Wheel: 4' 6"
Boiler Pressure: 170psi
Cylinders: Inside 17" x 24"
Tractive Effort: 18560lbf
Valve Gear: Stephenson (slide valves)

Stroudley's 'E1' class consisted of seventy-three engines built between 1874 and 1884 and six more which were built with some slight modifications by Billinton. Most of them were reboilered by Marsh. The first of the class was withdrawn in 1908.

They were designed as goods tank engines and were of the same mechanical design as Stroudley's 'D' class tanks.

The original names of the engines were as follows: 32097 HONFLEUR, 32112 VERSAILLES, 32113 GRANVILLE then DURDANS, 32122 LEGHORN, 32127 POITIERS, 32128 AVIGNON, 32129 ALENÇON, 32133 PICARDY, 32138 MACON, 32139 LOMBARDY, 32141 MENTONE, 32142 TOULON, 32145 FRANCE, 32147 DANUBE, 32151 HELVETIA, 32153 AUSTRIA, 32156 MUNICH, 32160 PORTSLADE, 32162 SOUTHWATER, 32164 SPITHEAD, 32606 GUERNSEY, 32609 STRASBOURG, 32689 BREST, 32690 BERNE, 32691 FISHBOURNE, 32694 SHORWELL, W1 (ex 136) BRINDISI, W2 (ex 152) HUNGARY, W3 (ex 154) MADRID and W4 (ex 131) GOURNAY.

Ten engines were rebuilt as 'E1R' class 0-6-2Ts by Maunsell in 1927-1929.

b 32160, 32162 and 32164 were the last three survivors of the Billinton built engines.

s 32609 still retained its original Stroudley boiler.

w Four engines were transferred to the Isle of Wight in 1932-1933 and were named. They were fitted with LSWR Drummond type chimneys and Westinghouse brakes.

x 32689 was rebuilt in 1911 as an 'E1X' class engine, with a new larger boiler similar to the 'D1X' class. It was also fitted with new side tanks boiler and cab. In 1930 the boiler needed replacing, but no new boiler of the type was available. The frames were utilised, with a second-hand boiler and various parts from previously withdrawn locomotives to rebuild it as an 'E1' engine again.

Year End Totals: 'E1 [2]' class

'47	'48	'49	'50	'51	'52	'53	'54	'55	'56	'57	'58	'59	'60	'61	'62	'63	'64	'65	'66	'67
30	27	21	19	13	11	11	11	11	8	7	6	4	1							

Number	Built	Renumbered	BR Dates	Scrap	Notes
32097	12/83 Bton	2097	-12/49	01/50	
32112	04/77 Bton	2112	-12/49	02/50	
32113	05/77 Bton	04/49 2113	-09/58	10/58	
32122	08/78 Bton	2122	-05/48	09/48	
32127	10/78 Bton	2127	-12/49	01/50	
32128	10/78 Bton	08/48 2128	-03/52	*04/52*	
32129	10/78 Bton	08/48 2129	-06/51	06/51	
32133	12/78 Bton	2133	-12/52	*12/52*	
32138	01/79 Bton	05/51 2138	-11/56	12/56	
32139	03/79 Bton	05/48 2139	-01/59	01/59	
32141	03/79 Bton	2141	-10/49	10/49	
32142	03/79 Bton	05/48 2142	-11/50	*50*	
32145	10/79 Bton	07/48 2145	-06/51	06/51	
32147	10/79 Bton	07/48 2147	-12/51	10/52	
32151	12/80 Bton	01/49 2151	-01/60	02/60	
32153	03/81 Bton	2153	-05/49	10/49	
32156	03/81 Bton	2156	-05/51	05/51	
32160	07/91 Bton	2160	-12/51	12/51	b
32162	11/91 Bton	2162	-11/49	12/49	b
32164	12/91 Bton	2164	-06/48	10/48	b
32606	10/76 Bton	05/48 2606	-08/56	*56*	
32609	03/77 Bton	2609	-06/48	11/48	s
32689	05/83 Bton	06/50 2689	-02/60	05/60	x
32690	05/83 Bton	2690	-01/50	02/50	
32691	10/83 Bton	2691	-12/51	*52*	
32694	03/75 Bton	02/51 2694	-07/61	08/61	

Class continued with W1 (Isle of Wight Locomotives)

E1R between 32094 & 32135, 32608 & 32610, 32695-32697
0-6-2T LBSCR rebuilt from 'E1'

Power Classification: 2MT reclassified 1P2F in 1953
Introduced: 1874-1891
Rebuilt 1927-1929 by Maunsell
Designer: Stroudley
Company: LBSCR
Weight: 50t 5cwt
Driving Wheel: 4' 6"
Boiler Pressure: 170psi
Cylinders: Inside 17" x 24"
Tractive Effort: 18560lbf
Valve Gear: Stephenson (slide valves)

Maunsell rebuilt ten of Stroudley's 'E1' class in 1927-1929 with trailing radial wheels and larger bunkers for passenger service in the West Country. They were also used for banking trains between Exeter St. David's and Central.

The names carried before they were rebuilt were as follows: 32094 SHORWELL, 32095 LUCCOMBE, 32096 SALZBERG, 32124 BAYONNE, 32135 FOLIGNO, 32608 STRASBOURG, 32610 BORDEAUX, 32695 NORMANDY, 32696 BRITTANY and 32697 MORLAIX.

Year End Totals: 'E1R' class

'47	'48	'49	'50	'51	'52	'53	'54	'55	'56	'57	'58	'59	'60	'61	'62	'63	'64	'65	'66	'67
10	10	10	10	10	10	10	10	9	5	3	3									

Number	Built	Renumbered	BR Dates	Scrap	Notes
32094	11/83 Bton	12/48 2094	-05/55	05/55	
32095	11/83 Bton	07/48 2095	-11/56	*56*	
32096	12/83 Bton	08/48 2096	-11/56	12/56	
32124	08/78 Bton	05/48 2124	-01/59	03/59	
32135	01/79 Bton	05/48 2135	-02/59	04/59	
32608	11/76 Bton	05/51 2608	-05/57	06/57	
32610	12/74 Bton	01/49 2610	-04/56	*04/56*	
32695	09/76 Bton	05/51 2695	-04/57	04/57	
32696	10/76 Bton	01/49 2696	-01/56	*01/57*	
32697	09/76 Bton	07/51 2697	-11/59	01/60	

E2 32100-32109
0-6-0T LBSCR Billinton

Power Classification: 3F
Introduced: 1913-1916
Designer: L Billinton
Company: LBSCR
Weight: 52t 15cwt
t 53t 10cwt
Driving Wheel: 4' 6"
Boiler Pressure: 170psi
Cylinders: Inside 17½" x 26"
Tractive Effort: 21305lbf
Valve Gear: Stephenson (slide valves)

The 'E2' class was built by L B Billinton to replace older engines of the 'E1' class. They were designed for goods traffic and shunting work. They were originally condensing engines and were fitted with Weir feed water pumps.

t 32105-32109 were built in 1915-1916 with larger water tanks. The top of the tank was extended forward at the front increasing the water capacity from 1090 gallons to 1256 gallons.

Year End Totals: 'E2' class

'47	'48	'49	'50	'51	'52	'53	'54	'55	'56	'57	'58	'59	'60	'61	'62	'63	'64	'65	'66	'67
10	10	10	10	10	10	10	10	10	10	10	10	10	10	6	2					

Number	Built	Renumbered	BR Dates	Scrap	Notes
32100	06/13 Bton	12/49 2100	-11/61	01/62	
32101	08/13 Bton	06/51 2101	-09/62	09/62	
32102	10/13 Bton	08/48 2102	-10/61	10/61	
32103	12/13 Bton	05/50 2103	-10/62	10/62	
32104	01/14 Bton	02/51 2104	-04/63	05/63	
32105	06/15 Bton	03/50 2105	-09/62	10/62	t
32106	09/15 Bton	02/50 2106	-10/62	10/62	t
32107	03/16 Bton	10/49 2107	-02/61	03/61	t
32108	07/16 Bton	05/49 2108	-06/61	07/61	t
32109	10/16 Bton	11/50 2109	-04/63	04/63	t

E3 32165-32170, 32453-32462
0-6-2T LBSCR Billinton

Power Classification: 3F reclassified 2F in 1953
Introduced: 1894-1895
Designer: R Billinton
Company: LBSCR
Weight: 56t 10cwt
Driving Wheel: 4' 6"
Boiler Pressure: 160psi
p 170psi
Cylinders: Inside 17½" x 26"
Tractive Effort: 20055lbf
p 21305lbf
Valve Gear: Stephenson (slide valves)

Between 1891 and 1905 R J Billinton built 134 six-coupled radial tank engines of four main varieties, the 'E3' and 'E6' classes for goods work fitted with 4' 6" driving wheels and the 'E4' (5' 0") and 'E5' (5' 6") classes for passenger work.

The first 'E3' was actually designed by Stroudley in 1891. It was numbered 158 (later 2158) and was named WEST BRIGHTON. It was withdrawn in 1935. The rest of the class (sixteen engines) came out in R J Billinton's period of office from 1894-1895. They were known as 'Billinton's small radials'.

From 1918 onwards the engines were reboilered and fitted with extended smokeboxes. The cylinder diameter was reduced from 18" to 17½" by the Southern Railway.

The former names of the 'E3' class were as follows: 32165 BLATCHINGTON, 32166 CLIFTONVILLE, 32167 SADDLESCOMBE, 32168 SOUTHBOROUGH, 32169 BEDHAMPTON, 32170 BISHOPSTONE, 32453 BROADBRIDGE, 32454 STORRINGTON, 32455 BROCKHURST, 32456 ALDINGBOURNE, 32457 WATERSFIELD, 32458 CHALVINGTON, 32459 WARLINGHAM, 32460 WARMINGHURST, 32461 STAPLEFIELD and 32462 WASHINGTON.

p 32453-32462 were fitted with higher pressure boilers.

Year End Totals: 'E3' class

'47	'48	'49	'50	'51	'52	'53	'54	'55	'56	'57	'58	'59	'60	'61	'62	'63	'64	'65	'66	'67
16	16	15	15	15	15	15	15	12	9	5	3									

Number	Built	Renumbered	BR Dates	Scrap	Notes
32165	11/94 Bton	07/48 2165	-11/59	11/59	
32166	11/94 Bton	07/48 2166	-09/59	10/59	
32167	12/94 Bton	04/49 2167	-10/55	*10/55*	
32168	12/94 Bton	01/51 2168	-01/56	*03/56*	
32169	12/94 Bton	07/49 2169	-08/55	*03/56*	
32170	12/94 Bton	01/49 2170	-07/57	08/57	
32453	04/95 Bton	12/48 2453	-08/55	*55*	p
32454	05/95 Bton	03/50 2454	-03/58	05/58	p
32455	05/95 Bton	08/50 2455	-02/58	03/58	p
32456	05/95 Bton	06/49 2456	-08/59	10/59	p
32457	12/95 Bton	2457	-05/49	05/49	p
32458	12/95 Bton	08/49 2458	-03/57	05/57	p
32459	12/95 Bton	07/49 2459	-06/56	*07/56*	p
32460	12/95 Bton	04/49 2460	-04/56	*04/56*	p

Number	Built	Renumbered	BR Dates	Scrap	Notes
32461	12/95 Bton	12/48 2461	-04/57	05/57	p
32462	12/95 Bton	03/50 2462	-05/57	06/57	p

E4 between 32463 & 32520, 32556-32566, 32577-32582
0-6-2T LBSCR Billinton

Power Classification: 2MT
Introduced: 1897-1903
Designer: R Billinton
Company: LBSCR
Weight: 57t 10cwt
Driving Wheel: 5' 0"
Boiler Pressure: 170psi
Cylinders: Inside 17½" x 26"
Tractive Effort: 19175lbf
Valve Gear: Stephenson (slide valves)

This class was a development of the 'E3' class with larger wheels. They were known as 'Billinton's radials' and they were built in 1897-1903. There were originally seventy-five engines in the class. Four were converted to the 'E4X' class between 1909 and 1911.

The engines were all rebuilt with Marsh boilers and extended smokeboxes from 1910 onwards (the last being 32468 in 1949). The cylinder diameter was reduced from 18" by the Southern Railway. No. 2483 was withdrawn in 1944, the rest coming into BR stock in 1948.

The former names of the 'E4' class were as follows: 32463 WIVELSFIELD, 32464 WOODMANCOTE, 32465 HURST GREEN, 32467 BERWICK, 32468 MIDHURST, 32469 BEACHY HEAD, 32470 EAST HOATHLY, 32471 FOREST HILL, 32472 FAY GATE, 32473 BIRCH GROVE, 32474 BLETCHINGLY, 32475 PARTRIDGE GREEN, 32476 BEEDING, 32479 BEVENDEAN, 32480 FLETCHING, 32481 ITCHINGFIELD, 32482 NEWTIMBER, 32484 HACKBRIDGE, 32485 ASHINGTON, 32486 GODALMING, 32487 FISHERGATE, 32488 OAKWOOD, 32490 BOHEMIA, 32491 HANGLETON, 32492 JEVINGTON, 32493 TELSCOMBE, 32494 WOODGATE, 32495 CHESSINGTON, 32496 CHIDDINGFOLD, 32497 DENNINGTON then DONNINGTON, 32498 STRETTINGTON, 32499 WOODENDEAN, 32500 PUTTENHAM, 32501 STOAT'S NEST, 32502 RIDGEWOOD, 32503 BUCKLAND, 32504 CHILWORTH, 32505 ANNINGTON, 32506 CATHERINGTON, 32507 HORLEY, 32508 BOGNOR, 32509 SOUTHOVER, 32510 TWINEHAM, 32511 LINGFIELD, 32512 KINGSWOOD, 32513 DENSWORTH, 32514 BARCOMBE, 32515 SWANMORE, 32516 RUSTINGTON, 32517 LIMPSFIELD, 32518 PORCHESTER, 32519 PORTFIELD, 32520 WESTBOURNE, 32556 TADWORTH, 32557 NORTHLANDS, 32558 CHILTINGTON, 32559 FRAMFIELD, 32560 PEMBURY, 32561 WALBERTON, 32562 LAUGHTON, 32563 WINEHAM, 32564 NETTLESTONE, 32565 LITTLETON, 32566 DURRINGTON, 32577 BLACKSTONE, 32578 HORSEBRIDGE, 32579 ROEHAMPTON, 32580 SHERMANBURY, 32581 WARNINGCAMP and 32582 HORNDEAN.

32470, 32481, 32498, 32504, 32506, 32516, 32518, 32562, 32563, 32564, 32565 and 32580 were loaned to the Railway Operating Division in 1917 and worked in France until 1919.

32510 was sent to the Isle of Wight in February 1947 for trials on the island. It was not a success and it returned to the mainland in April 1949. It never received a number in the Isle of Wight series.

Year End Totals: 'E4' class

'47	'48	'49	'50	'51	'52	'53	'54	'55	'56	'57	'58	'59	'60	'61	'62	'63	'64	'65	'66	'67
70	70	70	70	70	70	70	70	63	56	50	45	33	28	14	4					

Number	Built	Renumbered	BR Dates	Scrap	Notes
32463	12/97 Bton	11/49 2463	-09/59	10/59	
32464	12/97 Bton	08/48 2464	-02/56	56	
32465	04/98 Bton	12/49 2465	-04/55	55	
32467	05/98 Bton	03/49 2467	-04/58	04/58	
32468	05/98 Bton	08/49 2468	-01/63	08/63	
32469	06/98 Bton	07/49 2469	-10/61	10/61	
32470	06/98 Bton	07/49 2470	-06/62	07/62	
32471	06/98 Bton	10/49 2471	-09/59	01/60	
32472	06/98 Bton	12/50 2472	-06/62	07/62	
32473 §	06/98 Bton	04/51 2473	-11/62		
32474	08/98 Bton	10/49 2474	-05/63	06/63	
32475	10/98 Bton	11/50 2475	-06/61	07/61	
32476	10/98 Bton	04/49 2476	-04/57	05/57	
32479	12/98 Bton	05/48 2479	-06/63	07/63	
32480	12/98 Bton	03/50 2480	-11/59	11/59	
32481	12/98 Bton	10/49 2481	-04/58	04/58	
32482	12/98 Bton	05/49 2482	-11/55	11/55	
32484	05/99 Bton	03/50 2484	-09/60	10/60	
32485	05/99 Bton	02/53 2485	-12/57	01/58	
32486	05/99 Bton	05/49 2486	-01/59	02/59	
32487	06/99 Bton	03/51 2487	-12/62	08/63	
32488	06/99 Bton	05/49 2488	-06/57	08/57	
32490	06/99 Bton	02/50 2490	-12/55	56	
32491	09/99 Bton	01/50 2491	-01/61	02/61	
32492	10/99 Bton	07/48 2492	-05/57	06/57	
32493	11/99 Bton	07/48 2493	-02/58	03/58	
32494	11/99 Bton	04/49 2494	-09/59	09/59	
32495	11/99 Bton	05/48 2495	-09/60	09/60	
32496	12/99 Bton	12/48 2496	-11/55	55	
32497	05/00 Bton	06/49 2497	-11/59	11/59	
32498	05/00 Bton	11/49 2498	-11/61	01/62	
32499	06/00 Bton	04/49 2499	-06/57	06/57	
32500	06/00 Bton	05/50 2500	-01/62	01/62	
32501	06/00 Bton	12/48 2501	-08/55	11/55	
32502	06/00 Bton	05/48 2502	-02/58	03/58	
32503	08/00 Bton	11/49 2503	-04/63	06/63	
32504	09/00 Bton	05/48 2504	-11/61	12/61	
32505	10/00 Bton	08/50 2505	-03/61	05/61	
32506	10/00 Bton	05/48 2506	-06/61	07/61	
32507	12/00 Bton	05/48 2507	-04/59	06/59	
32508	12/00 Bton	03/50 2508	-01/60	02/60	
32509	12/00 Bton	08/50 2509	-03/62	04/62	
32510	12/00 Bton	08/49 2510	-09/62	10/62	
32511	02/01 Bton	10/49 2511	-10/56	10/56	
32512	02/01 Bton	12/48 2512	-05/61	07/61	
32513	03/01 Bton	02/50 2513	-01/56	56	
32514	03/01 Bton	03/49 2514	-10/56	10/56	
32515	04/01 Bton	10/49 2515	-05/61	07/61	
32516	04/01 Bton	05/48 2516	-10/55	10/55	
32517	06/01 Bton	12/50 2517	-06/59	06/59	
32518	06/01 Bton	04/49 2518	-06/55	55	
32519	06/01 Bton	03/50 2519	-09/59	01/60	
32520	06/01 Bton	12/48 2520	-01/57	03/57	
32556	01/01 Bton	11/50 2556	-09/61	10/61	
32557	09/01 Bton	05/49 2557	-12/62	10/63	
32558	10/01 Bton	05/48 2558	-11/56	56	
32559	10/01 Bton	07/48 2559	-06/60	07/60	
32560	11/01 Bton	52 2560	-08/58	08/58	
32561	11/01 Bton	06/50 2561	-06/56	56	
32562	12/01 Bton	05/48 2562	-08/60	10/60	
32563	12/01 Bton	12/48 2563	-08/61	08/61	
32564	12/01 Bton	06/50 2564	-09/61	10/61	
32565	05/02 Bton	12/48 2565	-06/61	08/61	
32566	06/02 Bton	04/49 2566	-04/59	05/59	
32577	06/03 Bton	06/49 2577	-10/59	01/60	
32578	06/03 Bton	01/49 2578	-04/61	06/61	
32579	07/03 Bton	11/49 2579	-11/59	12/59	
32580	07/03 Bton	09/48 2580	-04/62	04/62	
32581	09/03 Bton	10/49 2581	-04/62	04/62	
32582	09/03 Bton	07/49 2582	-10/56	56	

E4X between 32466 & 32489
0-6-2T LBSCR rebuilt from 'E4'

Power Classification: 3F
Introduced: 1897-1903
Rebuilt 1909-1911 by Marsh
Designer: R Billinton
Company: LBSCR
Weight: 59t 5cwt
Driving Wheel: 5' 0"
Boiler Pressure: 170psi
Cylinders: Inside 17½" x 26"
Tractive Effort: 19175lbf
Valve Gear: Stephenson (slide valves)

Marsh rebuilt a few engines of the 'E4', 'E5' and 'E6' classes with much larger boilers and extended smokeboxes. Four 'E4' engines were rebuilt as 'E4X' by fitting boilers from the 'I2' 4-4-2T engines in 1909-1911.

The former names of the engines before they were rebuilt as the 'E4X' class were as follows: 32466 HONOR OAK, 32477 POYNINGS, 32478 NEWICK and 32489 BOXGROVE.

Year End Totals: 'E4X' class

'47	'48	'49	'50	'51	'52	'53	'54	'55	'56	'57	'58	'59	'60	'61	'62	'63	'64	'65	'66	'67
4	4	4	4	4	4	4	4	3	2	2	1									

Number	Built	Renumbered	BR Dates	Scrap	Notes
32466	04/98 Bton	03/50 2466	-12/58	03/59	
32477	10/98 Bton	08/48 2477	-01/59	02/59	
32478	11/98 Bton	05/50 2478	-08/56	08/56	
32489	06/99 Bton	03/49 2489	-05/55	55	

E5 between 32399 & 32406, 32567 & 32594
0-6-2T LBSCR Billinton

Power Classification: 2MT
Introduced: 1902-1904
Designer: R Billinton
Company: LBSCR
Weight: 60t 0cwt
Driving Wheel: 5' 6"
Boiler Pressure: 160psi
p 175psi
Cylinders: Inside 17½" x 26"
Tractive Effort: 16410lbf
p 17945lbf
Valve Gear: Stephenson (slide valves)

The 'E5' class was a development of the 'E4' class with larger wheels and fireboxes for fast passenger work. They were known as 'Billinton's large radials' and were built in 1902-1904. The cylinder diameter was reduced from 18" by the Southern Railway. There were originally thirty engines in the class. Four were converted to the 'E5X' class in 1911 and the first of the unrebuilt engines was withdrawn in 1936.

The engines were fast runners and were often used on semi-main line duties. Some ran as 2-4-2Ts for a while in the early 1900s by simply removing the front coupling rods.

The former names of the 'E5' class were as follows: 32399 MIDDLETON, 32400 WINCHELSEA, 32402 WANBOROUGH, 32404 HARDHAM, 32405 FERNHURST, 32406 COLWORTH, 32567 FRESHWATER, 32568 CARISBROOKE, 32571 HICKSTEAD, 32572 FARNCOMBE, 32573 NUTBOURNE, 32574 COPTHORNE, 32575 WESTERGATE, 32583 HANDCOMBE, 32584 LORDINGTON, 32585 CROWBOROUGH, 32587 BRIGHTON, 32588 HAWKENBURY, 32589 AMBERSHAM, 32590 LODSWORTH, 32591 TILLINGTON, 32592 EASTERGATE, 32593 HOLLINGTON and 32594 SHORTBRIDGE.

p Some of the class had higher pressure boilers.

Year End Totals: 'E5' class

'47	'48	'49	'50	'51	'52	'53	'54	'55	'56	'57	'58	'59	'60	'61	'62	'63	'64	'65	'66	'67
24	24	21	21	11	11	7	4	3												

Number	Built	Renumbered	BR Dates	Scrap	Notes
32399	06/04 Bton	10/49 2399	-07/53	10/53	
32400	06/04 Bton	10/49 2400	-12/51	52	
32402	09/04 Bton	07/49 2402	-03/51	04/51	
32404	10/04 Bton	02/50 2404	-12/51	52	
32405	11/04 Bton	06/49 2405	-12/51	52	
32406	11/04 Bton	08/49 2406	-09/51	51	
32567	10/02 Bton	2567	-11/49	49	
32568	10/02 Bton	07/48 2568	-02/55	03/55	
32571	12/02 Bton	08/48 2571	-01/56	02/56	
32572	12/02 Bton	2572	-03/49	03/49	
32573	02/03 Bton	10/52 2573	-08/53	10/53	
32574	02/03 Bton	07/48 2574	-06/51	07/51	
32575	03/03 Bton	07/49 2575	-12/51	52	
32583	11/03 Bton	11/48 2583	-01/56	01/56	
32584	11/03 Bton	05/48 2584	-02/51	04/51	
32585	12/03 Bton	12/48 2585	-06/54	01/55	
32587	12/03 Bton	03/50 2587	-11/54	11/54	
32588	12/03 Bton	11/48 2588	-12/53	54	
32589	03/04 Bton	2589	-01/49	49	
32590	04/04 Bton	05/49 2590	-09/51	11/51	
32591	04/04 Bton	05/48 2591	-12/54	03/55	
32592	04/04 Bton	11/50 2592	-05/53	05/53	
32593	05/04 Bton	01/50 2593	-01/56	01/56	
32594	06/04 Bton	12/49 2594	-03/51	04/51	

E5X 32401, between 32570 & 32586
0-6-2T LBSCR rebuilt from 'E5'

Power Classification: 2MT
Introduced: 1902-1904
Rebuilt in 1911 by Marsh
Designer: R Billinton
Company: LBSCR
Weight: 64t 5cwt
Driving Wheel: 5' 6"
Boiler Pressure: 170psi
Cylinders: Inside 17½" x 26"
Tractive Effort: 17435lbf
Valve Gear: Stephenson (slide valves)

Marsh rebuilt a few engines of the 'E4', 'E5' and 'E6' classes with much larger boilers and extended smokeboxes. Four 'E5' engines were rebuilt as 'E5X'

LBSCR Billinton 'D3' class 0-4-4T No 32368.

LBSCR Billinton 'E6' class 0-6-2T No 32410 in 1956.

LBSCR Billinton ‘E4’ class 0-6-2T No 32499.

LBSCR Marsh ‘C2X’ class 0-6-0 No 32529 in 1957.

by fitting boilers from 'C3' 0-6-0 freight engines in 1911.

The former names of the engines before they were rebuilt as the 'E5X' class were as follows: 32401 WOLDINGHAM, 32570 ARMINGTON, 32576 BRENCHLEY and 32586 MAPLEHURST.

d 32401 for a while carried a boiler with a second dome which had formerly carried the top feed apparatus. The boiler had previously been carried by 'E6X' 32407.

Year End Totals: 'E5X' class

'47	'48	'49	'50	'51	'52	'53	'54	'55	'56	'57	'58	'59	'60	'61	'62	'63	'64	'65	'66	'67
4	4	4	4	4	4	4	3	1												

Number	Built	Renumbered	BR Dates	Scrap	Notes
32401	06/04 Bton	08/49 2401	-08/54	*03/55*	d
32570	11/02 Bton	03/51 2570	-01/56	*02/56*	
32576	03/03 Bton	07/48 2576	-07/55	*11/55*	
32586	12/03 Bton	05/48 2586	-04/55	*55*	

E6 between 32408 & 32418
0-6-2T LBSCR Billinton

Power Classification:	4F reclassified 3F in 1953
Introduced:	1904-1905
Designer:	R Billinton
Company:	LBSCR
Weight:	61t 0cwt
Driving Wheel:	4' 6"
Boiler Pressure:	160psi p 175psi
Cylinders:	Inside 18" x 26"
Tractive Effort:	21215lbf p 23205lbf
Valve Gear:	Stephenson (slide valves)

The 'E6' class was developed from the 'E5' class with smaller wheels, and they were intended for freight duties. Some of the class had a higher boiler pressure. There were originally twelve engines in the class. Two were converted to the 'E6X' class in 1911.

The former names of the 'E6' class were as follows: 32408 BINDERTON, 32409 GRAFFHAM, 32410 CHILGROVE, 32412 TANDRIDGE, 32413 FEN-CHURCH and 32414 PICCADILLY. The other four were never named.

p Some of the class had higher pressure boilers.

Year End Totals: 'E6' class

'47	'48	'49	'50	'51	'52	'53	'54	'55	'56	'57	'58	'59	'60	'61	'62	'63	'64	'65	'66	'67
10	10	10	10	10	10	10	10	10	10	9	6	6	6	4						

Number	Built	Renumbered	BR Dates	Scrap	Notes
32408	12/04 Bton	03/52 2408	-12/62	02/63	
32409	12/04 Bton	08/50 2409	-01/58	03/58	
32410	03/05 Bton	04/49 2410	-06/61	08/61	
32412	07/05 Bton	05/48 2412	-09/57	09/57	
32413	07/05 Bton	01/49 2413	-02/58	02/59	
32414	10/05 Bton	06/49 2414	-06/58	06/58	
32415	10/05 Bton	07/48 2415	-09/61	11/61	
32416	11/05 Bton	11/48 2416	-02/62	03/62	
32417	12/05 Bton	12/48 2417	-12/62	10/63	
32418	12/05 Bton	*52* 2418	-12/62	07/63	

E6X 32407, 32411
0-6-2T LBSCR rebuilt from 'E6'

Power Classification:	4F reclassified 3F in 1953
Introduced:	1904-1905 Rebuilt 1911 by Marsh
Designer:	R Billinton
Company:	LBSCR
Weight:	63t 0cwt
Driving Wheel:	4' 6"
Boiler Pressure:	170psi
Cylinders:	Inside 18" x 26"
Tractive Effort:	22540lbf
Valve Gear:	Stephenson (slide valves)

Marsh rebuilt a few engines of the 'E4', 'E5' and 'E6' classes with much larger boilers and extended smokeboxes. Two 'E6' engines were rebuilt as 'E6X' by fitting boilers from the 'C3' 0-6-0 freight engines in 1911.

The former names of the engines before they were rebuilt as the 'E6X' class were as follows: 32407 WORPLESDON and 32411 BLACKHEATH.

d 32407 for a while carried a boiler with a second dome which formerly carried the top feed apparatus. The boiler was later carried by 'E5X' 32401.

Year End Totals: 'E6X' class

'47	'48	'49	'50	'51	'52	'53	'54	'55	'56	'57	'58	'59	'60	'61	'62	'63	'64	'65	'66	'67
2	2	2	2	2	2	2	2	2	2	1	1									

Number	Built	Renumbered	BR Dates	Scrap	Notes
32407	12/04 Bton	*51* 2407	-11/57	02/58	d
32411	05/05 Bton	10/49 2411	-02/59	04/59	

H1 32037-32039
4-4-2 LBSCR Marsh Atlantics

Power Classification:	3P
Introduced:	1905-1906
Designer:	Marsh
Company:	LBSCR
Weight:	Loco 68t 5cwt Tender 39t 5cwt
Driving Wheel:	6' 7½"
Boiler Pressure:	200psi superheated
Cylinders:	Outside 19" x 26"
Tractive Effort:	20070lbf
Valve Gear:	Stephenson (slide valves) e Bulleid (sleeve valves)

D E Marsh worked at Doncaster under Ivatt before he took up office with the LBSCR in 1905. When he left he took with him a set of drawings for Ivatt's large boilered Atlantics (LNER class 'C1') and constructed his own engines to the same design. The appropriate modifications were marked on the drawings in red ink. The main differences were longer piston stroke and increased boiler pressure.

Five engines were built, and they were subsequently superheated and recylindered. The first two to be withdrawn were 2040 and 2041 in 1944.

The 'H2' class Atlantics were developed from this class.

From 1913 to 1925 32039 was named LA FRANCE after hauling the French President from Portsmouth to London.

e 32039 was used for experimental purposes by Bulleid in preparation for his 'Leader' class. It was fitted with sleeve valves in 1947, but it never ran in ordinary traffic in its converted state.

Year End Totals: 'H1' class

'47	'48	'49	'50	'51	'52	'53	'54	'55	'56	'57	'58	'59	'60	'61	'62	'63	'64	'65	'66	'67
3	3	3																		

Number	Built	Renumbered	BR Dates	Scrap	Notes
32037 SELSEY BILL	12/05 K	04/49 2037	-07/51	09/51	
32038 PORTLAND BILL	12/05 K	07/49 2038	-07/51	09/51	
32039 HARTLAND POINT	01/06 K	08/49 2039	-03/51	03/51	e

H2 32421-32426
4-4-2 LBSCR Later Marsh Atlantics

Power Classification:	4P
Introduced:	1911-1912
Designer:	Marsh, modified by L Billinton
Company:	LBSCR
Weight:	Loco 68t 5cwt Tender 39t 5cwt
Driving Wheel:	6' 7½"
Boiler Pressure:	200psi superheated
Cylinders:	Outside 21" x 26"
Tractive Effort:	24520lbf
Valve Gear:	Stephenson (piston valves)

These six 'Atlantic' engines were developed from Marsh's earlier 'H1' class. They differed in appearance from the 'H1' class in the curvature of the framing at the front end. In addition they were superheated and had larger cylinders than the 'H1' class.

These were Marsh's last engines to be built, the last one appearing after L Billinton came into office.

32424 was the last 'Atlantic' locomotive to run in service on British Railways.

Year End Totals: 'H2' class

'47	'48	'49	'50	'51	'52	'53	'54	'55	'56	'57	'58	'59	'60	'61	'62	'63	'64	'65	'66	'67
6	6	5	5	5	5	5	5	5	1	1										

Number	Built	Renumbered	BR Dates	Scrap	Notes
32421 SOUTH FORELAND	06/11 Bton	05/49 2421	-08/56	12/56	
32422 NORTH FORELAND	07/11 Bton	05/48 2422	-10/56	*02/57*	
32423 THE NEEDLES	09/11 Bton	2423	-05/49	06/49	
32424 BEACHY HEAD	09/11 Bton	12/48 2424	-04/58	05/58	
32425 TREVOSE HEAD	12/11 Bton	11/50 2425	-10/56	08/57	
32426 ST. ALBAN'S HEAD	01/12 Bton	08/50 2426	-08/56	02/57	

I1X 32001-32010, 32595-32604
4-4-2T LBSCR Marsh

Power Classification:	2P
Introduced:	1906-1907 Rebuilt 1925-1932 by Maunsell
Designer:	Marsh
Company:	LBSCR
Weight:	71t 18cwt
Driving Wheel:	5' 6"
Boiler Pressure:	180psi
Cylinders:	Inside 17½" x 26"
Tractive Effort:	18460lbf
Valve Gear:	Stephenson (slide valves)

The 'I1' class was constructed in 1906-1907 by Marsh for suburban traffic. Twenty engines were built of two different types. 32001-32010 were shorter and had a shorter wheelbase than 32594-32604 as they incorporated the wheels, coupling-rods and parts of the motion from older 'D1' and 'D2' engines which had been taken out of service. The engines were never very popular with the drivers as they were very poor steamers.

Maunsell reboilered the whole class between 1925 and 1932 with boilers taken from 'B4' class engines when they were converted to 'B4X', and from 'I3' class engines when they were superheated. They became the 'I1X' class and were a great improvement over the 'I1' class. 2600 was the first to be withdrawn in 1944 and eighteen came into BR stock in 1948.

s Engines with a shorter wheelbase.

Year End Totals: 'I1X' class

'47	'48	'49	'50	'51	'52	'53	'54	'55	'56	'57	'58	'59	'60	'61	'62	'63	'64	'65	'66	'67
18	8	8	8																	

Number	Built	Renumbered	BR Dates	Scrap	Notes
32001	06/07 Bton	2001	-07/48	11/48	s
32002	07/07 Bton	2002	-07/51	08/51	s
32003	07/07 Bton	2003	-07/48	09/48	s
32004	08/07 Bton	2004	-11/48	01/49	s
32005	09/07 Bton	05/48 2005	-06/51	*06/51*	s
32006	10/07 Bton	2006	-07/48	11/48	s
32007	10/07 Bton	2007	-09/48	11/48	s
32008	11/07 Bton	2008	-06/51	07/51	s
32009	12/07 Bton	2009	-05/51	*05/51*	s
32010	12/07 Bton	2010	-07/48	11/48	s
32595	09/06 Bton	2595	-06/51	07/51	
32596	11/06 Bton	2596	-06/51	08/51	
32598	12/06 Bton	2598	-07/48	*11/48*	
32599	01/07 Bton	2599	-09/48	11/48	
32601	03/07 Bton	2601	-02/48	*10/48*	
32602	04/07 Bton	2602	-06/51	07/51	
32603	06/07 Bton	2603	-04/51	*04/51*	
32604	04/07 Bton	2604	-09/48	11/48	

I3 32021-32030, 32075-32091
4-4-2T LBSCR Marsh

Power Classification:	3P
Introduced:	1907-1913
Designer:	Marsh c Modified by L Billinton
Company:	LBSCR
Weight:	a 75t 10cwt bc 76t 0cwt
Driving Wheel:	a 6' 9" bc 6' 7½"
Boiler Pressure:	180psi superheated
Cylinders:	a Inside 19" x 26" b Inside 20" x 26" c Inside 21" x 26"

Tractive Effort:	a 17730lbf b 20015lbf c 22065lbf
Valve Gear:	a Stephenson (slide valves) bc Stephenson (piston valves)

The 'I3' class was built by Marsh in 1907-1913 for express passenger working. Twenty-seven engines were built, the first (2024) being scrapped in 1944. They were among the first locomotives in the country to be fitted with superheaters.

a The first engine (32021) was built in 1907 as the prototype for the class. It was rebuilt with a superheater and an extended smokebox in 1919.

b 32022-32030 and 32075-32081 were built with slightly smaller wheels and were fitted with piston valves. Some of the earlier engines were built with saturated boilers, but they were all later superheated.

c Billinton built the last ten engines (32082-32091) in 1912-1913. They were developed from Marsh's design and were fitted with superheaters and larger cylinders.

Year End Totals: 'I3' class

'47	'48	'49	'50	'51	'52	'53	'54	'55	'56	'57	'58	'59	'60	'61	'62	'63	'64	'65	'66	'67
26	26	26	18	1																

Number	Built	Renumbered	BR Dates	Scrap	Notes
32021	10/07 Bton	*49* 2021	-10/51	*12/51*	a
32022	03/08 Bton	01/49 2022	-05/51	*05/51*	b
32023	02/09 Bton	05/49 2023	-07/51	08/51	b
32025	03/09 Bton	2025	-01/50	02/50	b
32026	03/09 Bton	10/49 2026	-09/51	09/51	b
32027	05/09 Bton	03/49 2027	-02/51	02/51	b
32028	12/09 Bton	03/49 2028	-10/51	10/51	b
32029	12/09 Bton	01/49 2029	-03/51	03/51	b
32030	03/10 Bton	04/49 2030	-09/51	*09/51*	b
32075	03/10 Bton	*51* 2075	-12/51	12/51	b
32076	03/10 Bton	04/49 2076	-12/50	02/51	b
32077	10/10 Bton	07/48 2077	-03/51	*03/51*	b
32078	11/10 Bton	05/49 2078	-02/51	03/51	b
32079	11/10 Bton	01/49 2079	-11/50	11/50	b
32080	12/10 Bton	2080	-03/50	04/50	b
32081	12/10 Bton	12/48 2081	-09/51	09/51	b
32082	08/12 Bton	09/48 2082	-06/51	07/51	c
32083	08/12 Bton	06/49 2083	-06/51	06/51	c
32084	08/12 Bton	08/48 2084	-03/51	03/51	c
32085	08/12 Bton	03/49 2085	-06/50	07/50	c
32086	09/12 Bton	05/48 2086	-10/51	10/51	c
32087	11/12 Bton	05/48 2087	-11/50	*50*	c
32088	11/12 Bton	07/49 2088	-11/50	11/50	c
32089	12/12 Bton	04/49 2089	-04/51	04/51	c
32090	03/13 Bton	07/48 2090	-12/50	12/50	c
32091	03/13 Bton	*51* 2091	-06/52	*05/53*	c

J1 32325
4-6-2T LBSCR Marsh

Power Classification:	4P
Introduced:	1910
Designer:	Marsh
Company:	LBSCR
Weight:	89t 0cwt
Driving Wheel:	6' 7½"
Boiler Pressure:	170psi superheated
Cylinders:	Outside 21" x 26"
Tractive Effort:	20840lbf
Valve Gear:	Stephenson (piston valves)

At the end of Marsh's period of office he designed two 4-6-2T engines, the 'J1' and the 'J2' classes.

32325, the 'J1' class engine was built at Brighton in 1910. It was the first 4-6-2 express tank engine to be built in the country, and it was originally named ABERGAVENNY.

In their early years, the 'J1' and 'J2' engines worked fast express trains on the Brighton Line, but after electrification, they ended their days at Tunbridge Wells.

Year End Totals: 'J1' class

'47	'48	'49	'50	'51	'52	'53	'54	'55	'56	'57	'58	'59	'60	'61	'62	'63	'64	'65	'66	'67
1	1	1	1																	

Number	Built	Renumbered	BR Dates	Scrap	Notes
32325	12/10 Bton	03/49 2325	-06/51	07/51	

J2 32326
4-6-2T LBSCR Marsh

Power Classification:	4P
Introduced:	1912
Designer:	Marsh, modified by L Billinton
Company:	LBSCR
Weight:	89t 0cwt
Driving Wheel:	6' 7½"
Boiler Pressure:	170psi superheated
Cylinders:	Outside 21" x 26"
Tractive Effort:	20840lbf
Valve Gear:	Walschaert (piston valves)

This was the second of Marsh's two 4-6-2T engines. 32326 was built at Brighton in 1912. It appeared during Billinton's period of office and it differed from 32325 in having Walschaert valve gear, and other detail differences. It was originally named BESSBOROUGH.

Year End Totals: 'J2' class

'47	'48	'49	'50	'51	'52	'53	'54	'55	'56	'57	'58	'59	'60	'61	'62	'63	'64	'65	'66	'67
1	1	1	1																	

Number	Built	Renumbered	BR Dates	Scrap	Notes
32326	03/12 Bton	05/48 2326	-06/51	07/51	

K 32337-32353
2-6-0 LBSCR Billinton

Power Classification:	4MT reclassified 4P5F in 1953
Introduced:	1913-1921
Designer:	L Billinton
Company:	LBSCR
Weight:	Loco 63t 15cwt Tender 41t 10cwt
Driving Wheel:	5' 6"
Boiler Pressure:	180psi superheated
Cylinders:	Outside 21" x 26"
Tractive Effort:	26580lbf
Valve Gear:	Stephenson (piston valves)

The seventeen 'K' class engines were by far the most powerful engines on the LBSCR when they were built in 1913-1921. They were intended for freight traffic, but they also worked on passenger trains at times. A design was prepared for a 2-6-2T version of this class, but more of the 'K' class were built instead.

These were the first LBSCR locomotives to carry Belpaire boilers. The cabs, domes and chimneys were modified by the Southern Railway to increase their route availability.

The locomotives did very good work right up until the end of their lives. The whole class was withdrawn en-bloc at the end of 1962. It was decreed (without warning) that the whole class should be withdrawn by 31st December of that year for purely accounting purposes. Many of the class had only recently received major repairs and were in excellent condition. This was only one of the many wasteful exercises carried out during that period in the rush to replace steam.

Year End Totals: 'K' class

'47	'48	'49	'50	'51	'52	'53	'54	'55	'56	'57	'58	'59	'60	'61	'62	'63	'64	'65	'66	'67
17	17	17	17	17	17	17	17	17	17	17	17	17	17	17						

Number	Built	Renumbered	BR Dates	Scrap	Notes
32337	09/13 Bton	09/48 2337	-12/62	05/64	
32338	12/13 Bton	11/48 2338	-12/62	09/63	
32339	03/14 Bton	03/49 2339	-11/62	12/62	
32340	06/14 Bton	10/49 2340	-12/62	05/64	
32341	11/14 Bton	10/49 2341	-12/62	08/63	
32342	10/16 Bton	01/51 2342	-12/62	07/63	
32343	11/16 Bton	05/49 2343	-12/62	10/64	
32344	12/16 Bton	07/48 2344	-11/62	01/63	
32345	12/16 Bton	10/49 2345	-12/62	11/63	
32346	12/16 Bton	*49* 2346	-11/62	02/63	
32347	12/20 Bton	04/49 2347	-12/62	09/63	
32348	12/20 Bton	05/48 2348	-11/62	12/62	
32349	12/20 Bton	08/48 2349	-11/62	04/63	
32350	12/20 Bton	03/50 2350	-11/62	02/63	
32351	01/21 Bton	01/49 2351	-11/62	04/63	
32352	02/21 Bton	01/49 2352	-11/62	03/63	
32353	03/21 Bton	01/50 2353	-12/62	12/63	

N15X 32327-32333
4-6-0 LBSCR 'Rememberance'

Power Classification:	4P
Introduced:	1914-1922 (as 4-6-4T) Rebuilt as 4-6-0 by Maunsell in 1934-1936
Designer:	L Billinton
Company:	LBSCR
Weight:	Loco 73t 2cwt Tender 57t 11cwt
Driving Wheel:	6' 9"
Boiler Pressure:	180psi superheated
Cylinders:	Outside 21" x 28"
Tractive Effort:	23325lbf
Valve Gear:	Walschaert (piston valves)

In 1914 Billinton brought out the 'L' class 4-6-4T engine for express passenger working. This was a unique wheel arrangement for any railway south of the Thames.

In this form 327 was named CHARLES C MACRAE, 329 was named STEPHENSON and 333 was named REMEMBRANCE in memory of the men of the LBSCR who lost their lives in the First World War.

When the Brighton and the Eastbourne lines were electrified the engines became redundant. They were rebuilt as 4-6-0 tender engines with eight-wheeled tenders in 1934-1936 by Maunsell and they were transferred to the Western Section at Nine Elms. During the Second World War all except 32330 and 32333 were loaned to the GWR. All the engines of this class were based at Basingstoke for their BR careers and they were mainly used on secondary duties.

Apart from REMEMBRANCE, they were all named after locomotive engineers of the past.

Year End Totals: 'N15X' class

'47	'48	'49	'50	'51	'52	'53	'54	'55	'56	'57	'58	'59	'60	'61	'62	'63	'64	'65	'66	'67
7	7	7	7	7	7	7	7	5	1											

Number	Built	Renumbered	BR Dates	Scrap	Notes
32327 TREVITHICK	04/14 Bton	07/48 2327	-01/56	*56*	
32328 HACKWORTH	09/14 Bton	10/48 2328	-02/55	05/55	
32329 STEPHENSON	10/21 Bton	12/48 2329	-08/56	*09/56*	
32330 CUDWORTH	12/21 Bton	08/48 2330	-08/55	09/55	
32331 BEATTIE	12/21 Bton	05/49 2331	-07/57	09/57	
32332 STROUDLEY	09/22 Bton	05/48 2332	-01/56	*01/56*	
32333 REMEMBRANCE	04/22 Bton	05/48 2333	-04/56	*07/56*	

Q1 33001-33040
0-6-0 SR Bulleid 'Austerity'

Power Classification:	5F
Introduced:	1942
Designer:	Bulleid
Company:	SR
Weight:	Loco 51t 5cwt Tender 38t 0cwt
Driving Wheel:	5' 1"
Boiler Pressure:	230psi superheated
Cylinders:	Inside 19" x 26"
Tractive Effort:	30080lbf
Valve Gear:	Stephenson (piston valves)

The 'Q1' class was built in 1942 in response to an urgent wartime requirement for a powerful locomotive which could work over all the system. They were the most powerful 0-6-0 locomotives ever to run in Britain. They also had the dubious reputation of being just about the ugliest locomotive ever to run in the country.

They were designed as 'Austerity' locomotives and were shorn of all non-essentials, such as running plates, splashers and conventional boiler cladding, in order to save metal and other materials for the war effort. They were fitted with five-jet Lemaître blastpipes and wide chimneys. They also had BFB 'Boxpok' cast steel wheels with holes and recesses on their discs (as on the 'Merchant Navy', 'Battle of Britain' and 'West Country' classes).

They were excellent machines, despite their unconventional appearance. Forty engines were built at Brighton and Ashford, and they carried Bulleid's continental system of numbering when first built, being numbered C1-C40.

Year End Totals: 'Q1' class

'47	'48	'49	'50	'51	'52	'53	'54	'55	'56	'57	'58	'59	'60	'61	'62	'63	'64	'65	'66	'67
40	40	40	40	40	40	40	40	40	40	40	40	40	40	40	40	27	7	3		

Number	*Built*	*Renumbered*	*BR Dates*	*Scrap*	*Notes*
33001 §	03/42 Bton	11/50 C1	-05/64		
33002	05/42 Bton	12/48 C2	-07/63	06/64	
33003	05/42 Bton	05/51 C3	-06/64	12/64	
33004	06/42 Bton	11/48 C4	-01/65	05/65	
33005	06/42 Bton	12/48 C5	-06/63	08/63	
33006	06/42 Bton	05/50 C6	-01/66	08/66	
33007	07/42 Bton	06/50 C7	-01/64	12/64	
33008	07/42 Bton	08/50 C8	-08/63	06/64	
33009	07/42 Bton	05/50 C9	-09/65	02/66	
33010	08/42 Bton	11/49 C10	-01/64	08/64	
33011	09/42 Bton	12/50 C11	-08/63	10/63	
33012	09/42 Bton	01/50 C12	-11/64	05/65	
33013	10/42 Bton	08/50 C13	-07/63	06/64	
33014	10/42 Bton	04/49 C14	-01/64	10/64	
33015	11/42 Bton	03/50 C15	-11/64	02/65	
33016	11/42 Bton	03/50 C16	-08/63	04/64	
33017	05/42 Asfd	12/49 C17	-01/64	02/64	
33018	04/42 Asfd	06/49 C18	-07/65	12/65	
33019	05/42 Asfd	05/48 C19	-12/63	01/64	
33020	05/42 Asfd	05/50 C20	-01/66	09/66	
33021	05/42 Asfd	11/50 C21	-08/63	10/63	
33022	06/42 Asfd	02/50 C22	-01/64	10/64	
33023	06/42 Asfd	12/48 C23	-06/64	12/64	
33024	06/42 Asfd	04/49 C24	-08/63	06/64	
33025	07/42 Asfd	05/48 C25	-07/63	02/64	
33026	07/42 Asfd	04/49 C26	-09/65	12/65	
33027	07/42 Asfd	07/48 C27	-01/66	09/66	
33028	08/42 Asfd	12/48 C28	-02/63	04/63	
33029	09/42 Asfd	03/50 C29	-01/64	10/64	
33030	09/42 Asfd	08/48 C30	-06/64	12/64	
33031	10/42 Asfd	07/49 C31	-09/63	07/64	
33032	10/42 Asfd	01/49 C32	-01/64	03/64	
33033	11/42 Asfd	07/48 C33	-06/64	12/64	
33034	11/42 Asfd	04/49 C34	-01/64	07/64	
33035	11/42 Asfd	05/48 C35	-06/64	10/64	
33036	12/42 Asfd	11/48 C36	-06/64	10/64	
33037	11/42 Bton	08/48 C37	-10/63	10/63	
33038	12/42 Bton	12/48 C38	-01/64	01/64	
33039	12/42 Bton	12/48 C39	-06/64	12/64	
33040	12/42 Bton	07/48 C40	-06/64	11/64	

BB & WC 34001-34110

4-6-2 SR Bulleid 'Battle of Britain' & 'West Country' Pacifics

BB & WC 34001-34109

4-6-2 SR Bulleid Rebuilt 'Battle of Britain' & 'West Country' Pacifics

Power Classification:	6MT reclassified 7P5F in 1953 r Reclassified 7P6F in 1961
Introduced:	1945-1951
Designer:	Bulleid
Company:	SR
Weight:	Loco 86t 0cwt r Loco 90t 1cwt x Tender 42t 12cwt y Tender 47t 5cwt z Tender 50t 0cwt
Driving Wheel:	6' 2"
Boiler Pressure:	280psi superheated Later reduced to 250psi superheated
Cylinders:	Three 16⅜" x 24"
Tractive Effort:	31050lbf Later reduced to 27715lbf
Valve Gear:	Bulleid (piston valves) r Walschaert (piston valves)

The 'Merchant Navy' Pacifics were restricted in their route availability and the 'West Country' and 'Battle of Britain' classes were designed as a lighter version with wider route availability.

The engines carried Bulleid's continental type numbers and were numbered from 21C101 upwards. They were fitted with the same novel features as the 'MN' class, that is Bulleid's valve gear which was driven by a chain and was completely enclosed in an oil bath, steam/hydraulic reversers, BFB 'Boxpok' cast steel wheels and powerful boilers fitted with welded steel fireboxes and thermic syphons. As on the 'MN' class the boiler pressure was originally 280psi, but it was later reduced to 250psi. Multiple-jet blastpipes were fitted, and the locomotives were covered in an air-smoothed casing.

WC The first batch of engines to be built were named after West Country holiday resorts, and they were known as the 'West Country' class. 34025 carried the name ROUGH TOR for a few days in 1948.

BB The later engines built from 1946 onwards were intended for service on the Eastern Section. They carried names with wartime connections, mainly being named after the RAF Squadrons which played such a key part in the Battle of Britain. They were therefore known as the 'Battle of Britain' class although they were identical with the 'West Country' class. 34071 carried the name 615 SQUADRON for a short while in 1948 when it was first built.

r In common with the 'MN' class the engines had problems with the enclosed valve gear, and oil leaks caused slipping and the occasional fire. From 1957 onwards sixty of the class were rebuilt with three sets of valve gear, with no oil bath. At the same time the air-smoothed casing was removed. The excellent boiler remained unaltered. The rebuilt 'WC's and 'BB's were good looking and reliable engines.

g 34064 was fitted with a Giesl ejector and chimney in 1962.

o 34019 and 34036 were converted to oil burning in 1947. They were later reconverted to coal burning (c).

x Fitted with a 4500 gallon tender.

y Fitted with a 5500 gallon tender.

z Fitted with a 6000 gallon tender.

Many tenders later were cut down to remove the raves at the top.

Year End Totals: 'BB & WC' class

'47	'48	'49	'50	'51	'52	'53	'54	'55	'56	'57	'58	'59	'60	'61	'62	'63	'64	'65	'66	'67
70	89	100	109	110	110	110	110	110	110	101	86	80	59	50	50	40	20	14	7	

Year End Totals: 'BB & WC Rebuilt' class

'47	'48	'49	'50	'51	'52	'53	'54	'55	'56	'57	'58	'59	'60	'61	'62	'63	'64	'65	'66	'67
										9	24	30	51	60	60	60	50	40	29	

Number	*Built*	*Renumbered*	*BR Dates*	*Scrap*	*Notes*
34001 EXETER	06/45 Bton	04/49 21C101	-07/67	10/67	WCx 11/57⇨r
34002 SALISBURY	06/45 Bton	12/48 21C102	-04/67	10/67	WCx
34003 PLYMOUTH	06/45 Bton	05/48 21C103	-09/64	12/64	WCx 09/57⇨r
34004 YEOVIL	06/45 Bton	05/48 21C104	-07/67	12/67	WCx 02/58⇨r
34005 BARNSTAPLE	07/45 Bton	05/48 21C105	-10/66	10/67	WCx 06/57⇨r
34006 BUDE	08/45 Bton	05/48 21C106	-03/67	09/67	WCx
34007 § WADEBRIDGE	09/45 Bton	04/49 21C107	-10/65		WCx
34008 PADSTOW	09/45 Bton	04/49 21C108	-06/67	09/68	WCx 06/60⇨r
34009 LYME REGIS	09/45 Bton	04/49 21C109	-10/66	11/67	WCx 01/61⇨r
34010 § SIDMOUTH	09/45 Bton	01/50 21C110	-03/65		WCx 02/59⇨r
34011 TAVISTOCK	10/45 Bton	05/48 21C111	-11/63	04/64	WCx
34012 LAUNCESTON	10/45 Bton	07/48 21C112	-12/66	06/67	WCx 01/58⇨r
34013 OKEHAMPTON	10/45 Bton	07/48 21C113	-07/67	11/67	WCx 10/57⇨r
34014 BUDLEIGH SALTERTON	11/45 Bton	10/49 21C114	-03/65	01/66	WCx 03/58⇨r
34015 EXMOUTH	11/45 Bton	05/48 21C115	-04/67	09/67	WCx
34016 § BODMIN	11/45 Bton	07/48 21C116	-06/64		WCx 04/58⇨r
34017 ILFRACOMBE	12/45 Bton	05/48 21C117	-10/66	12/68	WCx 11/57⇨r
34018 AXMINSTER	12/45 Bton	07/48 21C118	-07/67	04/68	WCx 09/58⇨r
34019 BIDEFORD	12/45 Bton	05/48 21C119	-03/67	09/67	WCx o 09/48⇨c
34020 SEATON	12/45 Bton	05/48 21C120	-09/64	12/64	WCx
34021 DARTMOOR	01/46 Bton	07/48 21C121	-07/67	03/68	WCx 12/57⇨r
34022 EXMOOR	01/46 Bton	07/48 21C122	-04/65	08/65	WCx 12/57⇨r
34023 § BLACKMOOR VALE *48*⇨BLACKMORE VALE	02/46 Bton	05/48 21C123	-07/67		WCx
34024 TAMAR VALLEY	02/46 Bton	07/48 21C124	-07/67	09/68	WCx 02/61⇨r
34025 WHIMPLE	03/46 Bton	09/48 21C125	-07/67	03/68	WCx 10/57⇨r
34026 YES TOR	04/46 Bton	05/49 21C126	-09/66	10/67	WCx 03/58⇨r
34027 § TAW VALLEY	04/46 Bton	07/48 21C127	-08/64		WCx 09/57⇨r
34028 § EDDYSTONE	05/46 Bton	12/48 21C128	-05/64		WCx 08/58⇨r
34029 LUNDY	05/46 Bton	03/49 21C129	-09/64	02/65	WCx 12/58⇨r
34030 WATERSMEET	05/46 Bton	12/48 21C130	-09/64	12/64	WCx
34031 TORRINGTON	06/46 Bton	01/49 21C131	-02/65	05/65	WCx 12/58⇨r
34032 CAMELFORD	06/46 Bton	05/48 21C132	-10/66	10/67	WCx 10/60⇨r
34033 CHARD	06/46 Bton	12/48 21C133	-12/65	09/66	WCx
34034 HONITON	07/46 Bton	07/48 21C134	-07/67	04/68	WCx 08/60⇨r
34035 SHAFTESBURY	07/46 Bton	01/49 21C135	-06/63	01/64	WCx
34036 WESTWARD HO	07/46 Bton	05/48 21C136	-07/67	03/68	WCx o 09/48⇨c 08/60⇨r
34037 CLOVELLY	08/46 Bton	04/49 21C137	-07/67	03/68	WCx 03/58⇨r
34038 LYNTON	09/46 Bton	03/49 21C138	-06/66	09/66	WCx
34039 § BOSCASTLE	09/46 Bton	07/48 21C139	-05/65		WCx 01/59⇨r
34040 CREWKERNE	09/46 Bton	11/48 21C140	-07/67	03/68	WCx 10/60⇨r
34041 WILTON	09/46 Bton	01/49 21C141	-01/66	05/66	WCx
34042 DORCHESTER	10/46 Bton	05/48 21C142	-10/65	09/66	WCx 01/59⇨r
34043 COMBE MARTIN	10/46 Bton	09/48 21C143	-06/63	06/63	WCx
34044 WOOLACOMBE	10/46 Bton	12/48 21C144	-05/67	09/67	WCx 05/60⇨r
34045 OTTERY ST. MARY	10/46 Bton	12/48 21C145	-06/64	05/65	WCx 10/58⇨r
34046 § BRAUNTON	11/46 Bton	01/49 21C146	-10/65		WCx 02/59⇨r
34047 CALLINGTON	11/46 Bton	01/49 21C147	-06/67	09/68	WCx 11/58⇨r
34048 CREDITON	11/46 Bton	08/48 21C148	-03/66	09/66	WCx 03/59⇨r
34049 ANTI-AIRCRAFT COMMAND	12/46 Bton	04/49 21C149	-11/63	06/64	BB x
34050 ROYAL OBSERVER CORPS	12/46 Bton	01/49 21C150	-08/65	12/65	BB x 08/58⇨r
34051 § WINSTON CHURCHILL	12/46 Bton	11/48 21C151	-09/65		BB x
34052 LORD DOWDING	12/46 Bton	03/49 21C152	-07/67	03/68	BB x 09/58⇨r
34053 § SIR KEITH PARK	01/47 Bton	06/49 21C153	-10/65		BB x 11/58⇨r
34054 LORD BEAVERBROOK	01/47 Bton	04/49 21C154	-09/64	03/65	BB x
34055 FIGHTER PILOT	02/47 Bton	07/49 21C155	-06/63	05/64	BB x
34056 CROYDON	02/47 Bton	05/48 21C156	-05/67	10/67	BB x 12/60⇨r
34057 BIGGIN HILL	03/47 Bton	06/49 21C157	-05/67	12/67	BB x
34058 § SIR FREDERICK PILE	04/47 Bton	12/48 21C158	-10/64		BB x 11/60⇨r
34059 § SIR ARCHIBALD SINCLAIR	04/47 Bton	04/49 21C159	-05/66		BB x 03/60⇨r
34060 25 SQUADRON	04/47 Bton	09/48 21C160	-07/67	09/68	BB x 11/60⇨r
34061 73 SQUADRON	04/47 Bton	02/49 21C161	-08/64	03/65	BB x
34062 17 SQUADRON	05/47 Bton	11/48 21C162	-06/64	06/66	BB x 04/59⇨r
34063 229 SQUADRON	05/47 Bton	01/49 21C163	-08/65	05/66	BB x
34064 FIGHTER COMMAND	07/47 Bton	05/48 21C164	-05/66	11/66	BB x 62⇨g
34065 HURRICANE	07/47 Bton	07/48 21C165	-04/64	11/64	BB x
34066 SPITFIRE	09/47 Bton	03/49 21C166	-09/66	09/67	BB x
34067 § TANGMERE	09/47 Bton	09/49 21C167	-11/63		BB x
34068 KENLEY	10/47 Bton	11/48 21C168	-12/63	03/64	BB x
34069 HAWKINGE	10/47 Bton	07/48 21C169	-11/63	05/64	BB x
34070 § MANSTON	10/47 Bton	04/49 21C170	-08/64		BB x

Number	Built	BR Dates	Scrap	Notes
34071	04/48 Bton	04/48-04/67	09/67	BB y
601 SQUADRON				05/60⇨r
34072 §	04/48 Bton	04/48-10/64		BB y
257 SQUADRON				
34073 §	05/48 Bton	05/48-06/64		BB y
249 SQUADRON				
34074	05/48 Bton	05/48-06/63	06/64	BB y
46 SQUADRON				
34075	06/48 Bton	06/48-04/64	06/66	BB y
264 SQUADRON				
34076	06/48 Bton	06/48-01/66	11/66	BB y
41 SQUADRON				
34077	07/48 Bton	07/48-03/67	09/67	BB y
603 SQUADRON				07/60⇨r
34078	07/48 Bton	07/48-09/64	12/64	BB y
222 SQUADRON				
34079	07/48 Bton	07/48-02/66	09/66	BB y
141 SQUADRON				
34080	08/48 Bton	08/48-09/64	12/64	BB y
74 SQUADRON				
34081 §	09/48 Bton	09/48-08/64		BB y
92 SQUADRON				
34082	09/48 Bton	09/48-04/66	10/66	BB y
615 SQUADRON				04/60⇨r
34083	10/48 Bton	10/48-07/64	06/66	BB y
605 SQUADRON				
34084	11/48 Bton	11/48-10/65	03/66	BB y
253 SQUADRON				
34085	11/48 Bton	11/48-09/65	04/66	BB y
501 SQUADRON				06/60⇨r
34086	12/48 Bton	12/48-06/66	11/66	BB y
219 SQUADRON				
34087	12/48 Bton	12/48-07/67	09/68	BB y
145 SQUADRON				12/60⇨r
34088	12/48 Bton	12/48-03/67	03/68	BB y
213 SQUADRON				04/60⇨r
34089	12/48 Bton	12/48-07/67	09/68	BB y
602 SQUADRON				11/60⇨r
34090	01/49 Bton	01/49-07/67	03/68	BB y
SIR EUSTACE MISSENDEN, SOUTHERN RAILWAY				08/60⇨r
34091	09/49 Bton	09/49-09/64	02/65	WCz
WEYMOUTH				
34092 §	09/49 Bton	09/49-11/64		WCz
WELLS 03/50➲CITY OF WELLS				
34093	10/49 Bton	10/49-07/67	03/68	WCz
SAUNTON				05/60⇨r
34094	10/49 Bton	10/49-08/64	11/64	WCz
MORTEHOE				
34095	10/49 Elh	10/49-07/67	04/68	WCz
BRENTOR				01/61⇨r
34096	11/49 Bton	11/49-09/64	03/65	WCz
TREVONE				04/61⇨r
34097	11/49 Elh	11/49-04/66	09/66	WCz
HOLSWORTHY				03/61⇨r
34098	12/49 Bton	12/49-06/67	09/68	WCz
TEMPLECOMBE				02/61⇨r
34099	12/49 Elh	12/49-11/64	03/65	WCz
LYNMOUTH				
34100	12/49 Bton	12/49-07/67	11/67	WCz
APPLEDORE				09/60⇨r
34101 §	02/50 Elh	02/50-07/66		WCz
HARTLAND				09/60⇨r
34102	03/50 Elh	03/50-07/67	09/68	WCz
LAPFORD				
34103	02/50 Bton	02/50-09/65	04/66	WCz
CALSTOCK				
34104	04/50 Elh	04/50-06/67	10/68	WCz
BERE ALSTON				05/61⇨r
34105 §	03/50 Bton	03/50-10/64		WCz
SWANAGE				
34106	03/50 Bton	03/50-09/64	02/65	WCz
LYDFORD				
34107	04/50 Bton	04/50-09/64	02/65	WCz
BLANDFORD 10/52➲BLANDFORD FORUM				
34108	04/50 Bton	04/50-06/67	10/68	WCz
WINCANTON				04/61⇨r
34109	05/50 Bton	05/50-09/64	01/65	BB z
SIR TRAFFORD LEIGH-MALLORY				03/61⇨r
34110	01/51 Bton	01/51-11/63	03/64	BB z
66 SQUADRON				

MN 35001-35030
4-6-2 SR Bulleid 'Merchant Navy' Pacifics

MN 35001-35030
4-6-2 SR Bulleid Rebuilt 'Merchant Navy' Pacifics

Power Classification: 7P reclassified 8P in 1951
Introduced: 1941-1949
Designer: Bulleid
Company: SR
Weight: Loco 94t 15cwt
r Loco 97t 18cwt
x Tender 47t 16cwt
y Tender 49t 7cwt
z Tender 52t 7cwt
Driving Wheel: 6' 2"
Boiler Pressure: 280psi superheated
Later reduced to 250psi superheated
Cylinders: Three 18" x 24"
Tractive Effort: 37515lbf
Later reduced to 33495lbf
Valve Gear: Bulleid (piston valves)
r Walschaert (piston valves)

The first 4-6-2 Pacific type locomotive to run on the Southern Railway was the 'Merchant Navy' class, which was introduced under conditions of some secrecy during the War in 1941. At one point Bulleid was called to account by the Ministry of Labour who accused him of wasting valuable resources during the war by building streamlined express passenger locomotives. Bulleid managed to convince the authorities that they were mixed traffic engines with their 6' 2" wheels (even though the engines were later classed 8P by BR). Bulleid never referred to the engines as streamlined, but preferred to call them 'airsmoothed'.

When the first engine appeared in 1941 with its continental type number 21C1, it contained a host of novel features. Bulleid fitted a modified type of Walschaert valve gear which was driven by a chain and was completely enclosed in an oil bath. A steam/hydraulic reverser was fitted. The engine was fitted with BFB 'Boxpok' cast steel wheels with holes and recesses on their discs (as also used on the 'Q1', 'Battle of Britain' and 'West Country' classes).

A modern, powerful boiler was fitted with a welded steel firebox and two thermic syphons. The boiler pressure was originally 280psi, but it was later reduced to 250psi. A multiple-jet blastpipe was fitted, and an air-smoothed casing enclosed the boilers and the cylinders.

All the engines carried the names of famous shipping lines, and they were known as the 'Merchant Navy' class. Because of their air-smoothed casing they were irreverently known as 'Spam Cans'.

The 'Merchant Navys' were restricted in their route availability and the 'West Country' and 'Battle of Britain' classes were designed as a lighter version with wider route availability.

35019 was unique in that it was the only BR steam locomotive which carried a name which was in upper and lower case, and also in a script style. This was because the nameplate was made in the house style of the shipping company that it was named after.

35013 was formerly named BLUE FUNNEL LINE.

r In service the engines had problems with the enclosed valve gear and oil leaks caused slipping, and the occasional fire. From 1956 onwards the whole class was rebuilt with three sets of valve gear, with no oil bath. At the same time the air-smoothed casing was removed. The excellent boiler remained unaltered. The rebuilt 'Merchant Navys' were good looking and reliable engines.

x Fitted with a 5000 gallon tender.

y Fitted with a 5100 gallon tender.

z Fitted with a 6000 gallon tender.

Many tenders later were cut down to remove the raves at the top.

Year End Totals: 'MN' class

'47	'48	'49	'50	'51	'52	'53	'54	'55	'56	'57	'58	'59	'60	'61	'62	'63	'64	'65	'66	'67
20	28	30	30	30	30	30	30	30	24	15	10									

Year End Totals: 'MN Rebuilt' class

'47	'48	'49	'50	'51	'52	'53	'54	'55	'56	'57	'58	'59	'60	'61	'62	'63	'64	'65	'66	'67
									6	15	20	30	30	30	30	30	23	16	10	

Number	Built	Renumbered	BR Dates	Scrap	Notes
35001	02/41 Elh	10/49 21C1	-11/64	05/65	x
CHANNEL PACKET					08/59⇨r
35002	06/41 Elh	01/50 21C2	-02/64	12/64	x
UNION CASTLE					05/58⇨r
35003	09/41 Elh	05/48 21C3	-07/67	12/67	x
ROYAL MAIL					09/59⇨r
35004	12/41 Elh	05/48 21C4	-10/65	02/66	x
CUNARD WHITE STAR					07/58⇨r
35005 §	01/42 Elh	05/48 21C5	-10/65		x
CANADIAN PACIFIC					06/59⇨r
35006 §	01/42 Elh	12/48 21C6	-08/64		x
PENINSULAR & ORIENTAL S. N. CO.					10/59⇨r
35007	06/42 Elh	12/48 21C7	-07/67	04/68	x
ABERDEEN COMMONWEALTH					06/58⇨r
35008	06/42 Elh	07/49 21C8	-07/67	10/68	x
ORIENT LINE					06/57⇨r
35009 §	06/42 Elh	08/49 21C9	-09/64		x
SHAW SAVILL					03/57⇨r
35010 §	07/42 Elh	12/48 21C10	-09/66		x
BLUE STAR					01/57⇨r
35011 §	12/44 Elh	12/48 21C11	-02/66		y
GENERAL STEAM NAVIGATION					07/59⇨r
35012	01/45 Elh	04/49 21C12	-04/67	09/68	y
UNITED STATES LINE					03/57⇨r
35013	02/45 Elh	07/48 21C13	-07/67	03/68	y
BLUE FUNNEL CERTUM PETE FINUM					05/56⇨r
35014	02/45 Elh	05/49 21C14	-03/67	09/67	y
NEDERLAND LINE					07/56⇨r
35015	03/45 Elh	06/49 21C15	-02/64	12/64	y
ROTTERDAM LLOYD					06/58⇨r
35016	03/45 Elh	11/48 21C16	-08/65	12/65	y
ELDERS FYFFES					04/57⇨r
35017	04/45 Elh	05/48 21C17	-07/66	09/66	y
BELGIAN MARINE					04/57⇨r
35018 §	05/45 Elh	05/48 21C18	-08/64		y
BRITISH INDIA LINE					02/56⇨r
35019	06/45 Elh	05/48 21C19	-09/65	02/66	y
French Line C.G.T.					05/59⇨r
35020	06/45 Elh	05/48 21C20	-02/65	03/65	y
BIBBY LINE					04/56⇨r
35021	09/48 Elh		09/48-08/65	12/65	z
NEW ZEALAND LINE					06/59⇨r
35022 §	10/48 Elh		10/48-05/66		z
HOLLAND AMERICA LINE					06/56⇨r
35023	11/48 Elh		11/48-07/67	04/68	z
HOLLAND-AFRIKA LINE					02/57⇨r
35024	11/48 Elh		11/48-01/65	02/65	z
EAST ASIATIC COMPANY					05/59⇨r
35025 §	11/48 Elh		11/48-09/64		z
BROCKLEBANK LINE					12/56⇨r
35026	12/48 Elh		12/48-03/67	09/67	z
LAMPORT & HOLT LINE					01/57⇨r
35027 §	12/48 Elh		12/48-09/66		z
PORT LINE					05/57⇨r
35028 §	12/48 Elh		12/48-07/67		z
CLAN LINE					11/59⇨r
35029 §	02/49 Elh		02/49-09/66		z
ELLERMAN LINES					09/59⇨r
35030	04/49 Elh		04/49-07/67	11/68	z
ELDER-DEMPSTER LINES					04/58⇨r

Leader 36001-36004
0-6-6-0T BR(SR) Bulleid 'Leader'

Power Classification: Not classified
Introduced: 1949
Designer: Bulleid
Company: BR (SR)
Weight: 100t 0cwt
Driving Wheel: 5' 1"
Boiler Pressure: 280psi superheated
Cylinders: Six 12¼" x 15"
Tractive Effort: 26350lbf
Valve Gear: Modified Bulleid (sleeve valves). Chain driven on each six-wheel bogie.

Bulleid was a steam locomotive designer who was always experimenting and seeking to introduce new ideas. His 'Leader' class was one of the most revolutionary designs of steam locomotive to appear for many years.

The engines were basically 0-6-6-0 single boiler articulated units which were enclosed in an overall casing. They had cabs at both ends with duplicated controls and the fireman worked in the middle of the engine alongside the boiler, which was slightly offset to one side of the engine. The engines were fitted with sleeve type valves and the two six-wheeled power units were each driven by a three-cylinder engine with chain transmission instead of coupling rods.

Five engines were ordered and 36001 did not appear until after nationalisation in 1949. The design had some major defects, not the least important being that the fireman was forced to work in conditions of almost impossible heat. It would have probably been more satisfactory if the engine had been designed as an oil-burner.

Unfortunately Bulleid was no longer around to provide the enthusiasm to proceed with the experiment and iron out the problems, and the project slowly died. Only 36001 was ever steamed, and it never ran in service. 36002 was completed and 36003 almost so, but they were never steamed. These three engines, together with the half-built 36004 were

LBSCR Rebuilt Stroudley 'Terrier' ('A1X' class) 0-6-0T No 32678 in 1952.

LBSCR Maunsell 'E1R' class 0-6-2T No 32697 in May 1959.

SR Bulleid 'Q1' Austerity class 0-6-0 No 33010 in August 1950.

SR Bulleid 'West Country' Pacific No 34021 *Dartmoor* next to the wheel hoist at Plymouth Friary shed in October 1949. Although it has received its BR number it still also carries its Southern number 21C121 with an early BR 'S' prefix.

Rebuilt 'West Country' Pacific No 34093 *Saunton*.

Rebuilt 'Merchant Navy' Pacific No 35017 *Belgian Marine* in 1965.

quietly broken up in 1951. None of the engines ever officially came into BR stock.

Bulleid later built a similar locomotive for the Coras Iompair Eireann railway in Ireland, where he became the Chief Mechanical Engineer. This engine was designed to burn turf, or peat, but nothing ever came of this engine either as the Irish Railways were moving towards complete replacement of steam by diesel even before BR.

Number	Built	Renumbered	BR Dates	Scrap	Notes
36001	06/49 Bton		06/49-11/50	05/51	
36002	06/49 Bton			*07/51*	
36003	49 Bton			05/51	
36004	49 Bton			05/51	

Miscellaneous Locomotives

Locomotive not allocated a new number as it was withdrawn early in 1948.

0330 KESR 4
0-6-0ST KESR ex-LSWR

Power Classification:	1F
Introduced:	1876-1882
Designer:	Beattie
Company:	LSWR then sold to KESR
Weight:	34t 19½cwt
Driving Wheel:	4' 3"
Boiler Pressure:	130psi
Cylinders:	Inside 17" x 24"
Tractive Effort:	15028lbf
Valve Gear:	Stephenson (slide valves)

Between 1876 and 1882 Beattie built twenty 0-6-0STs of his '0330' class. They were all built by Beyer Peacock. They were long-lived engines; amongst their other duties they could been seen shunting in Nine Elms yard right through to the 1920s.

The whole class was withdrawn from service between 1924 and 1933. In 1932 No. 0335 was sent to the Kent & East Sussex Railway in exchange for 0-8-0T No. 30949. It was still in serviceable condition on that line (although not actually at work) at the beginning of 1948, when it was taken over by BR. It was scrapped later that year without being allocated a BR number.

Year End Totals: '0330' class

'47	'48	'49	'50	'51	'52	'53	'54	'55	'56	'57	'58	'59	'60	'61	'62	'63	'64	'65	'66	'67
1																				

Number	Built	Renumbered	BR Dates	Scrap	Notes
KESR 4	BP		-05/48	08/48	

Isle of Wight Locomotives

The Isle of Wight locomotives were numbered in their own series from 1 to 36. The W prefix was not carried on the side of the locomotives, but each locomotive also had a numberplate on the rear of the bunker which did have the W prefix.

E1 [2] between 32097 & 32164, 32606 & 32609, 32689-32694, W1-W4
0-6-0T LBSCR Stroudley

Class continued from 32694

Number	Built	Renumbered	BR Dates	Scrap	Notes
W1 **MEDINA**	01/79 Bton		-04/57	*57*	w
W2 **YARMOUTH**	10/80 Bton		-10/56	*56*	w
W3 **RYDE**	03/81 Bton		-07/59	*59*	w
W4 **WROXALL**	11/78 Bton		-11/60	*60*	w

A1X 32635-32678, W8, W13, DS377, DS515, DS681
0-6-0T LBSCR Stroudley 'Terrier' (Rebuilt)

Class continued from 32678

Number	Built	Renumbered	BR Dates	Scrap	Notes
W8 § **FRESHWATER**	01/77 Bton		-09/49 09/49➲32646		e
W13 **CARISBROOKE**	07/80 Bton		-09/49 09/49➲32677	05/60	m

Class continued with DS377 (Service Locomotives)

O2 30177-30236, W14-W36
0-4-4T LSWR Adams

Class continued from 30236

Number	Built	Renumbered	BR Dates	Scrap	Notes
W14 **FISHBOURNE**	07/90 9Elm		-01/67	05/67	w
W15 **COWES**	12/90 9Elm		-06/56	*56*	w
W16 **VENTNOR**	06/92 9Elm		-01/67	05/67	w
W17 **SEAVIEW**	12/91 9Elm		-01/67	05/67	w
W18 **NINGWOOD**	09/92 9Elm		-12/65	01/67	w
W19 **OSBORNE**	09/91 9Elm		-12/55	*56*	w
W20 **SHANKLIN**	03/92 9Elm		-01/67	05/67	w
W21 **SANDOWN**	09/91 9Elm		-05/66	05/67	w
W22 **BRADING**	06/92 9Elm		-01/67	05/67	w
W23 **TOTLAND**	10/90 9Elm		-09/55	*55*	w
W24 § **CALBOURNE**	12/91 9Elm		-03/67		w
W25 **GODSHILL**	11/90 9Elm		-12/62	01/63	w
W26 **WHITWELL**	12/91 9Elm		-05/66	08/66	w
W27 **MERSTONE**	06/90 9Elm		-01/67	05/67	w
W28 **ASHEY**	07/90 9Elm		-01/67	05/67	w
W29 **ALVERSTONE**	08/91 9Elm		-05/66	05/67	w
W30 **SHORWELL**	09/92 9Elm		-09/65	11/67	w
W31 **CHALE**	04/90 9Elm		-03/67	09/67	w
W32 **BONCHURCH**	11/92 9Elm		-10/64	10/65	w
W33 **BEMBRIDGE**	08/92 9Elm		-01/67	05/67	w
W34 **NEWPORT**	07/91 9Elm		-09/55	*55*	w
W35 **FRESHWATER**	05/90 9Elm	04/49 *30181*	04/49-10/66	05/67	wp
W36 **CARISBROOKE**	04/91 9Elm	04/49 *30198*	04/49-06/64	10/65	wp

Service Locomotives

The Departmental (Service) locomotives inherited from the Southern Railway carried an S suffix. Most of these were renumbered with a DS prefix from July 1949 onwards. Those shown in the list with an S suffix (for example 77S) were not renumbered.

C14 30588-30589, 77S
0-4-0T LSWR Drummond

Class continued from 30589

Number	Built	Renumbered	BR Dates	Scrap	Notes
77S	01/07 9Elm		-04/59	*59*	

USA 30061-74, DS233-DS238
0-6-0T SR War Department

Class continued from 30074

Number	Built	Renumbered	BR Dates	Scrap	Notes
DS233	42 HKP	10/62 30061	10/62-03/67	07/67	p
DS234	42 V	12/62 30062	12/62-03/67	01/68	
DS235	42 V	03/63 30066	03/63-08/65	08/65	
DS236	43 V	04/63 30074	04/63-08/65	08/65	
DS237 § **MAUNSELL**	43 V	11/63 30065	11/63-09/67		
DS238 § **WAINWRIGHT**	43 V	08/63 30070	08/63-09/67		

C between 31004 & 31725, DS239-DS240
0-6-0 SECR Wainwright

Class continued from 31725

Number	Built	Renumbered	BR Dates	Scrap	Notes
DS239 §	02/02 Lngh	07/63 31592	07/63- 66		
DS240	12/04 Asfd	07/63 31271	07/63- 66	12/67	

A1X 32635-32678, W8, W13, DS377, DS515, DS681
0-6-0T LBSCR Stroudley 'Terrier' (Rebuilt)

Class continued from W13

Number	Built	Renumbered	BR Dates	Scrap	Notes
DS377	06/78 Bton	02/58 377S	-03/59 03/59➲32635	09/63	a
DS515 §	12/76 Bton	02/52 515S	-11/53 11/53➲32650		g
DS681	10/75 Bton	08/53 32659	08/53-06/63	06/63	i

T 31602-31604, 500S
0-6-0T LCDR (SECR) Kirtley

Class continued from 31604

Number	Built	Renumbered	BR Dates	Scrap	Notes
500S	12/90 Lngh		-11/49	01/50	

A1 DS680
0-6-0T LBSCR Stroudley 'Terrier'

Power Classification:	0P
Introduced:	1872-1880
Designer:	Stroudley
Company:	LBSCR
Weight:	27t 10cwt
Driving Wheel:	4' 0"
Boiler Pressure:	150psi
Cylinders:	Inside 12" x 20"
Tractive Effort:	7650lbf
Valve Gear:	Stephenson (slide valves)

Between 1872 and 1880, Stroudley built fifty engines of his famous 'A1' or 'Terrier' class. Seventeen of them were rebuilt with new boilers and extended smokeboxes. These were then known as the 'A1X' class (see above).

Only one of the original 'A1' engines came into BR stock. DS680 was built in 1876 as 54 WADDON. It later became 654 then it was sold to the SECR in 1904 as No. 751. It was fitted with a new boiler in 1910. After grouping it became Southern Railway No. 680S in 1932 and later DS680, and it worked as the Lancing Carriage Works shunter. It was fitted with an A1X boiler, but it retained the 'A1' class smokebox, with a Drummond chimney, and therefore retained its 'A1' classification. It has since been preserved in Canada.

One other 'A1' engine remains in existence. 82 BOXHILL was built in 1880, later becoming 682. It later became the Brighton Works shunter, being numbered B and then 380S. It was withdrawn in 1946, and thus never came into BR stock, but it was preserved by BR and is now based at the National Railway Museum in York.

Year End Totals: 'A1' (service) class

'47	'48	'49	'50	'51	'52	'53	'54	'55	'56	'57	'58	'59	'60	'61	'62	'63	'64	'65	'66	'67
1	1	1	1	1	1	1	1	1	1	1	1	1	1	1						

Number	Built	Renumbered	BR Dates	Scrap	Notes
DS680 §	02/76 Bton	11/50 680S	-06/62		

G6 between 30160 & 30240, 30257-30279, between 30348 & 30354, DS682, DS3152
0-6-0T LSWR Adams

Class continued from 30354

Number	Built	Renumbered	BR Dates	Scrap	Notes
DS682	09/98 9Elm	11/60 30238	11/60-12/62	05/63	
DS3152	02/98 9Elm	06/50 *30272*	06/50-08/60	*60*	

D1[2] & D1/M between 32215 & 32299, 32358 & 32361, 32605, 32699, 700-701S
0-4-2T LBSCR Stroudley

Class continued from 32699

Number	Built	Renumbered	BR Dates	Scrap	Notes
700S	12/81 N		-05/49	*08/49*	mo
701S	09/79 Bton		-12/51	12/51	mo

A12 30618-30636, DS3191
0-4-2 LSWR Adams

Class continued from 30636

Number	Built	Renumbered	BR Dates	Scrap	Notes
DS3191	12/92 N	04/51 612	-11/51	11/51	

Preserved Locomotives

Preserved locomotives which ran in service on BR.

T9 30113-30122, between 30280 & 30338, 30702-30733, 120
4-4-0 LSWR Drummond

Class continued from 30733

Number	Built	Renumbered	BR Dates	Scrap	Notes
120 §	08/99 9Elm	03/62 30120	03/62-07/63		

LSWR Adams 'O2' class 0-4-4T No W30 *Shorwell* in April 1957.

LSWR Drummond 'C14' class 0-4-0T No 77s.

LSWR Adams 'G6' class 0-6-0T No DS3152 in August 1953.

Part 3
London, Midland & Scottish Railway Group

Locomotive Origins

Locomotives of the following pre-grouping companies were still running in 1948.

CR	Caledonian Railway
FR	Furness Railway
GSWR	Glasgow & South Western Railway
HR	Highland Railway
LNWR	London & North Western Railway
LTSR	London, Tilbury & Southend Railway
LYR	Lancashire & Yorkshire Railway
MR	Midland Railway
NLR	North London Railway
SDJR	Somerset & Dorset Joint Railway (locomotives supplied by the Midland Railway and taken into LMS stock in 1930)
Wirral	Wirral Railway

Locomotive Numbering

Out of the four railway groups, the LMS had the most logical system of locomotive numbering. All classes were numbered in groups, and locomotives of different pre-grouping companies tended to be numbered together. Older locomotives were sometimes renumbered in the 20000 series to make space for newer build locomotives (these locomotives were renumbered in the 58000 series by BR).

Service locomotives retained a variety of numbers, including pre-nationalisation and even pre-grouping numbers. In addition some locomotives in the main number series were used as service locomotives (for example 41509). Miscellaneous locomotives included two narrow gauge locomotives and one steam rail-motor numbered in the coaching stock number series.

Locomotive Classification

The LMS had a system for locomotive classification based on the power of the locomotive (from 0 up to 9 for the most powerful). This number had the suffix F for freight locos, P for passenger locomotives and MT for mixed traffic locomotives. In addition there were other varieties such as '5XP' for a class between '5' and '6' (later superseded), and combinations such as '6P5F' where locomotives fitted into different classes for freight and passenger working. In some cases locomotives were reclassified, and the most recent classification is always used in this book. This method of Power Classification was extremely useful to BR and it was ultimately applied to all BR locomotives. However it was not helpful for specifying particular classes of locomotives, and to accurately specify an LMS locomotive class it was necessary to use a long-winded title such as 'ex-Midland Railway Johnson five foot three inch 0-6-0' or 'London & North Western Webb Coal Engine', or a shortened nickname such as 'Cauliflower'. In this section, a numerical suffix is given to the Power Classification to differentiate between different classes of engines when cross-referencing with the appendices, and locomotive classes are often referred to by the number of the first engine in the class.

Notes

New locomotives were built to LMS designs in the following classes: '41200', '42050', '43000', '44658', '46220', '46400' and '47000'.

In 1950, three ex-LNWR 'Coal Engines' ('58320' class) returned to BR stock, only to be withdrawn straight away. These locomotives are listed in their correct order in this section even though they were actually assigned to Western Region stock and were cut up at Swindon.

Four locomotives were restored during the 1950s to work special trains. They are listed under Preserved Locomotives.

LMS Fowler '3MT' 2-6-2T No 40061 at Doncaster Works in November 1954.

LMS Stanier '3MT' 2-6-2T No 40088 at Trafford Park in Manchester.

LMS Fowler '2P' 4-4-0 No 40604 at Corkerhill in Glasgow in August 1952.

3MT[1] 40001-40070
2-6-2T LMS Fowler

Power Classification:	3P reclassified 3MT in 1948
Introduced:	1930-1932
Designer:	Fowler
Company:	LMS
Weight:	70t 10cwt c 71t 16cwt
Driving Wheel:	5' 3"
Boiler Pressure:	200psi superheated
Cylinders:	Outside 17½" x 26"
Tractive Effort:	21485lbf
Valve Gear:	Walschaert (piston valves)

After putting into service his successful '4MT' ('42300') class of 2-6-4T in 1927, Fowler followed it with what turned out to be one of his most unsuccessful classes, these seventy 2-6-2Ts, in 1930.

Originally numbered 15500-15569, they were designed for general suburban and branch line work. However, they proved to be under-boilered for this work and were regarded as very poor machines.

They could be distinguished from other 2-6-2T engines by their parallel boilers. Some engines were later fitted with new cylinders and outside steam pipes.

Stanier later built his own version of the class, the '40071' class.

c 40022-40040 were built for working the St. Pancras suburban services. They were fitted with condensing apparatus for working though the Metropolitan Widened Lines tunnels to Moorgate. (40021 was also originally fitted with condensing apparatus but this was later removed.)

m Fitted with vacuum control gear for working motor trains.

Year End Totals: '3MT[1]' class

'47	'48	'49	'50	'51	'52	'53	'54	'55	'56	'57	'58	'59	'60	'61	'62	'63	'64	'65	'66	'67
70	70	70	70	70	70	70	70	70	70	70	70	38	29	7						

Number	Built	Renumbered	BR Dates	Scrap	Notes
40001	03/30 Der	09/48 1	-01/61	03/61	
40002	03/30 Der	06/49 2	-11/59	06/61	
40003	03/30 Der	08/48 3	-02/61	08/61	
40004	03/30 Der	10/48 4	-11/59	08/61	
40005	04/30 Der	11/49 5	-02/59	03/59	
40006	04/30 Der	05/50 6	-10/62	12/62	
40007	04/30 Der	10/48 7	-08/61	10/61	
40008	04/30 Der	12/49 8	-11/59	02/60	
40009	04/30 Der	02/49 9	-05/62	11/62	
40010	05/30 Der	09/48 10	-08/61	08/62	m
40011	05/30 Der	06/49 11	-08/60	09/60	
40012	05/30 Der	07/48 12	-11/60	12/60	m
40013	05/30 Der	06/49 13	-12/59	03/60	
40014	05/30 Der	04/50 14	-05/60	06/60	
40015	06/30 Der	02/50 15	-03/61	11/61	
40016	11/30 Der	12/48 16	-07/61	10/61	
40017	11/30 Der	10/49 17	-11/59	10/61	
					12/54⇨m
40018	12/30 Der	11/48 18	-08/61	06/62	
40019	12/30 Der	01/49 19	-12/59	05/60	
40020	12/30 Der	07/48 20	-07/61	02/63	m
40021	12/30 Der	08/50 21	-09/59	08/60	
40022	01/31 Der	07/49 22	-12/62	03/63	c
40023	01/31 Der	05/50 23	-11/59	05/60	c
40024	01/31 Der	07/48 24	-02/62	05/62	c
40025	01/31 Der	06/50 25	-12/59	02/60	c
40026	02/31 Der	10/48 26	-11/62	03/63	c
40027	02/31 Der	06/48 27	-11/59	05/60	c
40028	02/31 Der	11/49 28	-11/60	12/61	c
40029	02/31 Der	02/50 29	-08/61	11/61	c
40030	03/31 Der	05/50 30	-08/59	02/61	c
40031	03/31 Der	05/51 31	-11/62	02/63	c
40032	03/31 Der	12/50 32	-08/61	11/61	c
40033	03/31 Der	06/48 33	-09/61	11/61	c
40034	04/31 Der	08/48 34	-08/61	11/61	c
40035	04/31 Der	12/48 35	-08/61	11/61	c
40036	04/31 Der	07/48 36	-06/60	06/60	c
40037	05/31 Der	04/48 37	-08/61	11/61	c
40038	05/31 Der	03/51 38	-08/61	12/61	c
40039	05/31 Der	05/49 39	-12/59	04/60	c
40040	05/31 Der	04/50 40	-12/59	04/60	c
40041	05/31 Der	07/49 41	-09/60	11/60	
40042	06/31 Der	04/50 42	-08/61	06/62	
40043	06/31 Der	09/49 43	-11/59	05/60	m
40044	06/31 Der	03/49 44	-11/59	05/60	
40045	07/31 Der	03/49 45	-11/59	05/60	
					12/54⇨m
40046	07/31 Der	04/49 46	-11/59	05/60	
40047	07/31 Der	06/48 47	-11/59	01/60	
40048	07/31 Der	06/48 48	-11/59	10/60	
40049	08/31 Der	02/50 49	-08/61	09/62	
40050	08/31 Der	11/50 50	-06/61	06/61	
40051	08/31 Der	11/48 51	-04/61	06/61	
40052	08/31 Der	06/49 52	-09/59	08/60	
40053	09/31 Der	04/48 53	-08/61	11/62	
40054	09/31 Der	09/48 54	-02/61	02/62	
40055	09/31 Der	04/49 55	-11/59	08/61	
40056	10/31 Der	03/50 56	-11/59	08/61	m
40057	10/31 Der	06/50 57	-03/60	05/60	m
40058	10/31 Der	09/49 58	-11/59	03/60	
40059	10/31 Der	01/50 59	-11/59	10/61	m
40060	11/31 Der	07/50 60	-12/59	03/60	m
40061	09/32 Der	03/49 61	-12/59	06/60	m
40062	10/32 Der	02/49 62	-11/60	01/61	
40063	10/32 Der	05/48 63	-08/62	10/62	
40064	10/32 Der	04/48 64	-08/61	12/61	
40065	10/32 Der	06/48 65	-11/59	05/61	
40066	10/32 Der	04/50 66	-11/59	06/60	
40067	10/32 Der	05/50 67	-12/59	03/60	
40068	11/32 Der	01/49 68	-12/59	07/60	
40069	11/32 Der	11/49 69	-12/59	06/60	
40070	11/32 Der	10/48 70	-03/60	05/60	

3MT[2] 40071-40209
2-6-2T LMS Stanier

Power Classification:	3P reclassified 3MT in 1948
Introduced:	1935-1938
Designer:	Stanier
Company:	LMS
Weight:	71t 5cwt b 72t 10cwt
Driving Wheel:	5' 3"
Boiler Pressure:	200psi superheated
Cylinders:	Outside 17½" x 26"
Tractive Effort:	21485lbf
Valve Gear:	Walschaert (piston valves)

This was William Stanier's version of Fowler's '3MT' ('40001') class. One hundred and thirty-nine engines were built with generally similar dimensions, but they were fitted with taper boilers. They were intended to be an improvement on Fowler's engines, but they were also underboilered and in some ways proved inferior to their predecessors.

b In attempt to improve these engines, four of the class (40148, 40163, 40169 and 40203) were fitted with larger boilers in 1941. Two more (40167 and 40142) were converted in 1956.

d 40071-40144 were fitted with domeless boilers.

Year End Totals: '3MT[2]' class

'47	'48	'49	'50	'51	'52	'53	'54	'55	'56	'57	'58	'59	'60	'61	'62	'63	'64	'65	'66	'67
139	139	139	139	139	139	139	139	139	139	139	139	129	128	72						

Number	Built	Renumbered	BR Dates	Scrap	Notes
40071	02/35 Der	02/49 71	-12/61	11/62	d
40072	02/35 Der	01/49 72	-08/62	05/63	d
40073	02/35 Der	05/49 73	-08/62	04/63	d
40074	03/35 Der	09/49 74	-11/61	12/61	d
40075	03/35 Der	10/48 75	-07/61	10/61	d
40076	03/35 Der	12/50 76	-10/61	01/62	d
40077	03/35 Der	02/49 77	-07/61	10/61	d
40078	03/35 Der	09/49 78	-11/62	01/63	d
40079	03/35 Der	03/50 79	-10/61	06/62	d
40080	03/35 Der	05/50 80	-08/62	12/62	d
40081	03/35 Der	06/49 81	-10/61	09/62	d
40082	03/35 Der	05/48 82	-03/62	05/62	d
40083	03/35 Der	10/48 83	-11/62	04/63	d
40084	04/35 Der	06/48 84	-11/59	06/61	d
40085	04/35 Der	03/50 85	-07/62	05/63	d
40086	04/35 Der	12/48 86	-11/62	05/63	d
40087	04/35 Der	08/48 87	-11/62	08/63	d
40088	04/35 Der	04/50 88	-07/62	11/62	d
40089	04/35 Der	05/48 89	-08/62	05/63	d
40090	04/35 Der	06/49 90	-07/62	06/63	d
40091	05/35 Der	11/48 91	-10/61	01/63	d
40092	05/35 Der	09/48 92	-05/61	07/61	d
40093	05/35 Der	02/49 93	-01/62	05/63	d
40094	05/35 Der	10/49 94	-10/61	06/63	d
40095	05/35 Der	07/50 95	-10/61	06/62	d
40096	05/35 Der	03/49 96	-11/59	09/60	d
40097	05/35 Der	04/49 97	-08/61	10/61	d
40098	06/35 Der	11/48 98	-11/62	02/63	d
40099	06/35 Der	08/48 99	-10/62	05/63	d
40100	06/35 Der	03/49 100	-08/62	02/63	d
40101	06/35 Der	10/48 101	-10/61	03/62	d
40102	06/35 Der	06/49 102	-10/61	03/62	d
40103	06/35 Der	06/49 103	-10/61	02/63	d
40104	06/35 Der	08/49 104	-09/62	04/63	d
40105	06/35 Der	09/48 105	-07/62	06/63	d
40106	06/35 Der	06/50 106	-11/62	02/63	d
40107	06/35 Der	02/49 107	-08/61	11/61	d
40108	07/35 Der	12/49 108	-11/61	02/62	d
40109	07/35 Der	11/48 109	-07/62	05/63	d
40110	07/35 Der	08/48 110	-05/62	06/62	d
40111	07/35 Der	03/49 111	-10/61	02/63	d
40112	08/35 Der	01/49 112	-12/62	09/63	d
40113	08/35 Der	04/49 113	-07/62	06/63	d
40114	08/35 Der	11/48 114	-12/62	05/63	d
40115	08/35 Der	07/48 115	-10/61	05/63	d
40116	08/35 Der	04/49 116	-11/62	01/63	d
40117	08/35 Der	08/49 117	-12/62	01/64	d
40118	08/35 Der	02/49 118	-09/61	10/61	d
40119	08/35 Der	07/50 119	-09/62	03/63	d
40120	08/35 Der	05/49 120	-10/62	05/63	d
40121	08/35 Der	08/49 121	-10/61	03/62	d
40122	08/35 Der	09/49 122	-06/62	05/63	d
40123	09/35 Der	10/48 123	-10/61	07/62	d
40124	09/35 Der	10/49 124	-09/61	09/63	d
40125	09/35 Der	06/48 125	-11/59	08/62	d
40126	09/35 Der	02/50 126	-05/61	06/61	d
40127	09/35 Der	12/48 127	-11/59	09/61	d
40128	09/35 Der	03/50 128	-07/62	11/62	d
40129	09/35 Der	08/50 129	-10/61	07/62	d
40130	09/35 Der	06/48 130	-10/61	07/62	d
40131	09/35 Der	05/48 131	-10/61	03/62	d
40132	09/35 Der	08/48 132	-10/61	03/62	d
40133	10/35 Der	04/48 133	-10/61	07/62	d
40134	10/35 Der	12/48 134	-10/61	11/62	d
40135	10/35 Der	08/48 135	-11/62	08/63	d
40136	10/35 Der	06/49 136	-10/61	04/62	d
40137	10/35 Der	09/49 137	-11/62	02/63	d
40138	10/35 Der	11/48 138	-09/62	05/63	d
40139	10/35 Der	10/48 139	-11/59	12/59	d
40140	10/35 Der	05/49 140	-11/61	11/61	d
40141	11/35 Der	08/49 141	-10/61	06/62	d
40142	11/35 Der	06/50 142	-08/61	02/62	d
					06/56⇨b
40143	11/35 Der	11/48 143	-10/61	02/63	d
40144	11/35 Der	02/49 144	-12/61	09/62	d
40145	07/37 Der	06/49 145	-09/62	06/63	
40146	08/37 Der	06/49 146	-08/62	04/63	
40147	08/37 Der	03/49 147	-12/62	02/64	
40148	08/37 Der	03/49 148	-09/62	03/64	b
40149	08/37 Der	04/48 149	-10/61	03/63	
40150	09/37 Der	10/48 150	-12/62	09/63	
40151	09/37 Der	01/49 151	-12/62	12/63	
40152	09/37 Der	04/49 152	-01/62	06/63	
40153	09/37 Der	05/50 153	-12/62	12/63	
40154	09/37 Der	04/48 154	-01/62	10/63	
40155	10/37 Der	09/48 155	-05/61	07/61	
40156	10/37 Der	06/48 156	-10/61	09/63	
40157	10/37 Der	08/49 157	-11/62	04/63	
40158	10/37 Der	06/48 158	-01/62	04/63	
40159	10/37 Der	11/48 159	-12/62	11/63	
40160	10/37 Der	02/49 160	-11/59	05/60	
40161	11/37 Der	09/49 161	-12/60	01/61	
40162	11/37 Der	10/48 162	-10/61	01/62	
40163	11/37 Der	12/49 163	-11/59	01/63	b
40164	11/37 Der	10/49 164	-10/62	04/63	
40165	11/37 Der	06/48 165	-10/61	05/63	
40166	12/37 Der	08/50 166	-10/61	01/63	
40167	12/37 Der	05/48 167	-10/61	07/62	
					06/56⇨b
40168	12/37 Der	09/48 168	-10/61	01/64	
40169	12/37 Der	09/49 169	-11/59	03/60	b
40170	12/37 Der	09/48 170	-01/62	11/62	
40171	12/37 Der	01/50 171	-05/61	06/61	
40172	12/37 Der	07/48 172	-11/59	05/60	
40173	01/38 Der	07/48 173	-07/62	05/63	
40174	01/38 Der	12/48 174	-06/62	12/62	
40175	03/38 Der	05/49 175	-10/61	09/63	
40176	03/38 Der	05/48 176	-12/62	11/63	
40177	04/38 Der	06/49 177	-12/62	11/63	
40178	04/38 Der	04/50 178	-10/61	03/62	
40179	04/38 Der	04/49 179	-03/62	04/62	
40180	04/38 Der	06/48 180	-01/62	03/62	
40181	04/38 Der	05/48 181	-04/62	01/64	
40182	05/38 Der	04/48 182	-10/61	04/63	
40183	05/38 Der	09/49 183	-10/61	07/62	
40184	05/38 Der	12/48 184	-10/61	06/63	
40185	10/37 Crw	11/48 185	-02/62	01/63	
40186	10/37 Crw	11/48 186	-12/62	12/63	
40187	10/37 Crw	10/48 187	-12/62	10/63	
40188	10/37 Crw	10/48 188	-12/62	11/63	
40189	11/37 Crw	04/48 189	-12/62	11/63	
40190	11/37 Crw	12/49 190	-12/62	02/64	
40191	12/37 Crw	05/49 191	-09/62	06/63	
40192	12/37 Crw	07/49 192	-12/61	10/62	
40193	12/37 Crw	04/50 193	-09/62	11/63	
40194	12/37 Crw	06/48 194	-10/61	01/63	
40195	12/37 Crw	12/49 195	-11/61	09/63	
40196	01/38 Crw	04/49 196	-12/62	02/63	
40197	01/38 Crw	07/48 197	-07/62	10/62	
40198	01/38 Crw	09/48 198	-07/62	06/63	
40199	01/38 Crw	09/48 199	-10/61	01/63	
40200	01/38 Crw	12/48 200	-12/62	11/63	
40201	02/38 Crw	06/50 201	-07/62	12/62	
40202	02/38 Crw	05/48 202	-09/62	05/63	
40203	02/38 Crw	01/49 203	-07/62	02/63	b

Number	Built	Renumbered	BR Dates	Scrap	Notes
40204	03/38 Crw	09/49 204	-11/59	05/61	
40205	03/38 Crw	04/48 205	-11/62	01/63	
40206	03/38 Crw	10/49 206	-02/62	09/62	
40207	04/38 Crw	10/49 207	-02/62	11/62	
40208	04/38 Crw	12/48 208	-10/61	11/62	
40209	04/38 Crw	07/48 209	-10/61	05/62	

2P [1] 40322-40326
4-4-0 SDJR Fowler

Power Classification: 2P
Introduced: 1914-1921
Designer: Fowler
Company: SDJR
Weight: Loco 53t 7cwt
Driving Wheel: 7' 0½"
Boiler Pressure: 160psi superheated
Cylinders: Inside 20½" x 26"
Tractive Effort: 17585lbf
Valve Gear: Stephenson (piston valves)

This class was designed by Johnson for the Somerset & Dorset Joint Railway. They were identical with the '40332' class. They were rebuilt by Fowler in 1921 and were taken into LMS stock in 1930.

Year End Totals: '2P [1]' class

'47	'48	'49	'50	'51	'52	'53	'54	'55	'56	'57	'58	'59	'60	'61	'62	'63	'64	'65	'66	'67
5	5	5	5	4	4	2	2	2												

Number	Built	Renumbered	BR Dates	Scrap	Notes
40322	05/14 Der	07/48 322	-02/53	53	
40323	04/14 Der	07/48 323	-09/56	56	
40324	04/21 Der	11/48 324	-01/53	53	
40325	04/21 Der	08/49 325	-10/51	10/51	
40326	04/21 Der	02/51 326	-05/56	56	

2P [2] 40332-40562
4-4-0 MR Johnson/Fowler

Power Classification: 2P
Introduced: 1882-1901, rebuilt 1904 onwards by Deeley
Rebuilt 1912-1923 by Fowler
Designer: Johnson
Company: MR
Weight: Loco 53t 7cwt
u Loco 51t 2cwt
Driving Wheel: 7' 0½"
u 6' 6½"
Boiler Pressure: 160psi superheated
u 160psi
Cylinders: Inside 20½" x 26"
u Inside 18" x 26"
Tractive Effort: 17585lbf
u 14595lbf
Valve Gear: Stephenson (piston valves)
u Stephenson (slide valves)

During his time on the Midland Railway, Johnson pursued a process of standardisation, concentrating on a few standard types which he built in large numbers. His first 4-4-0s came out in 1876-1877, ten having 6' 6" driving wheels and twenty having 7' 0" driving wheels. Over the years up to 1901 more engines of both varieties were built, and there was eventually a total of 265 engines. (An additional forty were also built for the Midland & Great Northern Joint Railway.)

Two engines were withdrawn before 1907 and the rest were numbered 300-562. The original thirty engines were never rebuilt, but the rest (which had been built between 1882 and 1901) were rebuilt by Deeley from 1904 onwards, with or without extended smokeboxes and Belpaire fireboxes.

Between 1912 and 1923 most of Johnson's engines (which had already been rebuilt by Deeley) were rebuilt again by Fowler with superheaters and new frames, becoming virtually new engines. This design was adopted as the LMS standard 'Class 2' after grouping and the '40563' class was built new to this design.

The engines were fitted with short-travel piston valves, and made a most powerful and impressive noise. They ran well with light passenger trains and were extensively used for double heading.

u Between 1901 and 1912 Deeley rebuilt fifteen engines without a superheater. The first of these was withdrawn in 1925, but three of the saturated engines survived into BR stock.

Year End Totals: '2P [2]' class

'47	'48	'49	'50	'51	'52	'53	'54	'55	'56	'57	'58	'59	'60	'61	'62	'63	'64	'65	'66	67
160	156	138	125	113	98	86	77	69	59	41	34	22	16	3						

Number	Built	Renumbered	BR Dates	Scrap	Notes
40332	10/82 Der	07/48 332	-09/59	02/60	
40337	11/82 Der	05/49 337	-04/58	06/58	
40351	10/83 Der	09/48 351	-12/53	54	
40353	10/83 Der	03/49 353	-07/53	53	
40356	11/83 Der	10/48 356	-08/57	08/57	
40359	11/85 Der	09/49 359	-02/54	54	
40362	12/85 Der	08/48 362	-12/56	57	
40364	01/86 Der	12/51 364	-06/56	56	
40370	06/86 Der	11/48 370	-01/51	01/51	
40377	12/86 Der	05/50 377	-09/55	55	
40383	06/88 Der	08/48 383	-07/52	09/52	u
40385	06/88 Der	385	-08/49	49	u
40391	09/88 Der	391	-08/49	49	u
40394	06/91 Der	394	-03/49	49	
40395	06/91 Der	09/49 395	-09/54	09/54	
40396	06/91 Der	12/48 396	-02/61	04/62	
40397	06/91 Der	02/49 397	-03/51	51	
40400	06/91 Der	400	-01/49	49	
40401	08/91 Der	08/48 401	-08/53	53	
40402	08/91 Der	11/49 402	-09/60	10/60	
40403	04/92 SS	403	-06/50	50	
40404	04/92 SS	10/51 404	-07/57	07/57	
40405	04/92 SS	06/48 405	-03/55	55	
40406	04/92 SS	406	-01/51	51	
40407	05/92 SS	10/52 407	-06/58	09/58	
40408	05/92 SS	408	-12/48	49	
40409	05/92 SS	06/50 409	-07/57	07/57	
40410	05/92 SS	10/48 410	-02/53	03/53	
40411	05/92 SS	11/48 411	-02/61	08/61	
40412	05/92 SS	04/49 412	-05/59	60	
40413	09/92 SS	08/50 413	-01/59	60	
40414	05/92 SS	09/50 414	-01/57	01/57	
40415	05/92 SS	06/49 415	-06/52	52	
40416	05/92 SS	06/49 416	-05/59	07/59	
40417	05/92 SS	09/48 417	-02/52	04/52	
40418	07/92 SS	10/48 418	-01/57	01/57	
40419	07/92 SS	08/49 419	-09/55	09/55	
40420	07/92 SS	01/49 420	-11/58	08/60	
40421	07/92 SS	09/48 421	-01/61	08/61	
40422	07/92 SS	02/49 422	-10/53	53	
40423	08/96 Der	06/49 423	-12/52	53	
40424	08/96 Der	05/48 424	-04/51	51	
40425	08/96 Der	09/50 425	-12/53	54	
40426	09/96 Der	09/50 426	-11/57	11/57	
40427	09/96 Der	11/48 427	-05/50	50	
40430	02/93 SS	12/49 430	-04/52	04/52	
40432	02/93 SS	06/49 432	-10/53	53	
40433	02/93 SS	12/48 433	-11/57	11/57	
40434	02/93 SS	08/48 434	-11/56	56	
40436	03/93 SS	02/50 436	-09/54	09/54	
40437	03/93 SS	437	-05/49	49	
40438	03/93 SS	06/48 438	-08/54	54	
40439	03/93 SS	04/49 439	-01/61	10/61	
40443	02/94 Der	09/48 443	-01/61	10/61	
40444	02/94 Der	04/48 444	-07/53	53	
40446	03/94 Der	446	-06/50	50	
40447	03/94 Der	07/48 447	-05/58	05/58	
40448	04/94 Der	05/49 448	-11/55	11/55	
40450	04/94 Der	09/48 450	-03/57	03/57	
40452	05/94 Der	09/49 452	-01/61	08/61	
40453	06/94 Der	03/50 453	-10/62	05/63	
40454	06/94 Der	11/48 454	-09/60	09/60	
40455	06/94 Der	09/49 455	-07/54	54	
40456	06/94 Der	456	-10/49	12/49	
40458	08/94 Der	11/48 458	-02/57	03/57	
40459	08/94 Der	06/48 459	-12/49	01/50	
40461	09/94 Der	03/49 461	-02/59	04/59	
40462	09/94 Der	01/49 462	-04/51	51	
40463	08/95 Der	04/48 463	-07/56	56	
40464	09/95 Der	08/49 464	-03/58	03/58	
40466	10/95 Der	466	-03/49	49	
40468	11/95 Der	468	-05/50	50	
40470	11/95 Der	04/49 470	-05/51	05/51	
40471	12/95 Der	09/48 471	-01/52	01/52	
40472	12/95 Der	11/48 472	-09/55	09/55	
40477	03/00 BP	03/49 477	-02/51	51	
40478	04/00 BP	10/48 478	-10/50	50	
40479	04/00 BP	479	-11/49	12/49	
40480	04/00 BP	05/49 480	-02/54	54	
40482	05/00 BP	09/48 482	-07/57	07/57	
40483	12/96 Der	483	-08/49	49	
40484	12/96 Der	11/48 484	-08/53	53	
40485	09/98 Der	12/49 485	-08/57	08/57	
40486	04/01 Der	12/48 486	-02/57	02/57	
40487	10/98 Der	05/51 487	-01/61	06/61	
40488	10/96 Der	11/48 488	-12/50	51	
40489	05/01 Der	11/49 489	-08/60	10/60	
40490	06/01 Der	490	-01/50	01/50	
40491	10/98 Der	03/49 491	-10/60	11/60	
40492	06/01 Der	492	-12/48	49	
40493	09/97 Der	03/52 493	-07/59	07/60	
40494	09/97 Der	494	-12/48	49	
40495	10/97 Der	03/49 495	-07/57	07/57	
40496	10/97 Der	496	-02/49	49	
40497	10/97 Der	05/48 497	-10/51	10/51	
40498	11/97 Der	08/48 498	-08/50	10/50	
40499	11/97 Der	04/49 499	-08/52	52	
40500	12/97 Der	04/48 500	-07/49	49	
40501	12/97 Der	04/51 501	-08/60	11/60	
40502	12/97 Der	03/50 502	-02/61	06/61	
40503	10/99 SS	02/49 503	-10/52	52	
40504	10/99 SS	06/49 504	-01/61	08/61	
40505	10/99 SS	08/48 505	-10/53	53	
40506	10/99 SS	506	-11/49	49	
40507	10/99 SS	09/49 507	-07/52	52	
40508	11/99 SS	11/48 508	-07/51	51	
40509	11/99 SS	01/51 509	-06/57	06/57	
40510	11/99 SS	510	-05/49	49	
40511	11/99 SS	10/49 511	-01/61	10/61	
40512	11/99 SS	512	-01/50	01/50	
40513	12/99 SS	05/48 513	-10/59	10/61	
40514	12/99 SS	01/49 514	-01/52	52	
40515	12/99 SS	05/48 515	-08/50	10/50	
40516	12/99 SS	05/48 516	-03/50	06/50	
40517	12/99 SS	517	-06/49	49	
40518	12/99 SS	07/49 518	-08/56	56	
40519	12/99 SS	08/49 519	-12/57	01/61	
40520	12/99 SS	05/49 520	-10/57	11/57	
40521	12/99 SS	08/49 521	-03/56	56	
40522	12/99 SS	10/48 522	-10/55	55	
40523	06/98 Der	09/49 523	-10/52	52	
40524	07/98 Der	12/50 524	-07/54	54	
40525	08/98 Der	03/50 525	-05/57	05/57	
40526	08/98 Der	05/50 526	-07/56	56	
40527	09/98 Der	09/50 527	-01/56	56	
40528	10/98 Der	03/50 528	-12/52	53	
40529	10/98 Der	06/49 529	-05/54	54	
40530	11/98 Der	530	-01/51	02/51	
40531	10/98 Der	11/50 531	-08/56	56	
40532	10/98 Der	04/48 532	-01/52	01/52	
40533	06/99 Der	04/48 533	-01/50	02/50	
40534	07/99 Der	11/49 534	-07/59	07/60	
40535	07/99 Der	06/48 535	-09/55	55	
40536	08/99 Der	01/51 536	-05/59	60	
40537	08/99 Der	08/48 537	-09/62	09/62	
40538	09/99 Der	01/50 538	-05/59	10/60	
40539	10/99 Der	01/52 539	-08/54	54	
40540	10/99 Der	02/50 540	-02/62	03/62	
40541	10/99 Der	08/48 541	-03/58	03/58	
40542	10/99 Der	09/49 542	-08/59	02/60	
40543	03/01 Der	12/49 543	-01/61	05/62	
40544	04/01 Der	544	-10/49	49	
40545	04/01 Der	545	-12/48	49	
40546	05/01 Der	05/48 546	-06/51	51	
40547	05/01 Der	01/51 547	-01/53	53	
40548	06/01 Der	08/49 548	-01/61	11/61	
40549	06/01 Der	549	-05/51	51	
40550	06/01 Der	05/49 550	-06/59	01/60	
40551	07/01 Der	12/49 551	-10/53	53	
40552	07/01 Der	03/49 552	-06/60	07/60	
40553	05/01 N	07/48 553	-11/58	01/60	
40554	05/01 N	554	-08/49	49	
40555	05/01 N	555	-04/49	49	
40556	05/01 N	07/48 556	-04/56	56	
40557	05/01 N	04/50 557	-03/61	08/61	
40558	05/01 N	03/49 558	-03/52	03/52	
40559	06/01 N	08/48 559	-12/57	01/58	
40560	06/01 N	06/50 560	-12/52	53	
40561	06/01 N	561	-03/50	04/50	
40562	06/01 N	07/48 562	-11/55	12/55	

2P [3] 40563-40700
4-4-0 LMS & SDJR Fowler

Power Classification: 2P
Introduced: 1928-1932
Designer: Fowler
Company: LMS and SDJR
Weight: Loco 54t 1cwt
Tender 41t 4cwt
Driving Wheel: 6' 9"
Boiler Pressure: 180psi superheated
Cylinders: Inside 19" x 26"
Tractive Effort: 17730lbf
Valve Gear: Stephenson (piston valves)

After grouping the rebuilt '2P' ('40332') class was adopted as the LMS standard class 2. 138 new engines were built by Fowler for the LMS, with slightly smaller driving wheels (6' 9" compared with 7' 0" for the Fowler rebuilds). They were also fitted with raised boiler pressure and reduced diameter cylinders. The boiler mountings were reduced to enable them to work all over the LMS.

These engines were frequently used for double heading. They were also to be found in large numbers on the former lines of the Glasgow & South Western Railway, where they very quickly displaced that company's own 4-4-0s.

Two engines (591 and 639) were scrapped in 1934 after being involved in an accident at Port Eglinton near Glasgow. Apart from these two, the remainder all came into BR stock.

601 and 572 were built out of order as 601 was fitted experimentally with an Owen's double beat regulator in the dome.

s Three engines were built for the Somerset & Dorset Joint Railway. They were originally built as 575, 576 and 580, and then were sold to the SDJR in 1928, numbered 44-46. New engines took their original numbers, and when the LMS absorbed the SDJR stock in 1930 they were given the numbers 633-635.

d 40633 and 40653 were experimentally fitted with Dabeg feed water heaters in 1933.

Year End Totals: '2P [3]' class

'47	'48	'49	'50	'51	'52	'53	'54	'55	'56	'57	'58	'59	'60	'61	'62	'63	'64	'65	'66	'67
136	136	136	136	136	136	136	135	135	135	134	134	91	81	15						

Number	Built	Renumbered	BR Dates	Scrap	Notes
40563	03/28 Der	08/49 563	-05/62	07/62	
40564	04/28 Der	05/49 564	-02/62	02/62	
40565	04/28 Der	12/49 565	-11/59	04/62	
40566	04/28 Der	06/51 566	-09/61	10/62	
40567	04/28 Der	12/48 567	-08/59	02/60	
40568	04/28 Der	05/51 568	-11/59	12/59	
40569	05/28 Der	05/51 569	-11/61	12/61	
40570	05/28 Der	04/48 570	-08/61	12/61	
40571	05/28 Der	03/49 571	-07/61	10/61	
40572	11/28 Der	03/50 572	-07/61	09/61	
40573	05/28 Der	08/48 573	-05/59	09/59	
40574	06/28 Der	09/48 574	-04/61	05/61	
40575	10/29 Der	08/49 575	-08/61	11/61	
40576	10/29 Der	05/49 576	-11/59	01/60	
40577	06/28 Der	03/49 577	-07/61	08/61	
40578	07/28 Der	10/48 578	-11/61	09/63	
40579	07/28 Der	09/49 579	-07/61	11/61	
40580	10/29 Der	02/51 580	-02/61	08/61	
40581	07/28 Der	09/49 581	-10/60	10/60	
40582	07/28 Der	10/48 582	-12/59	04/60	
40583	07/28 Der	06/48 583	-09/60	09/60	
40584	08/28 Der	06/48 584	-11/60	11/60	
40585	08/28 Der	07/48 585	-02/61	08/61	
40586	08/28 Der	06/50 586	-04/61	01/62	
40587	08/28 Der	07/48 587	-08/59	02/60	
40588	08/28 Der	10/48 588	-10/60	12/60	
40589	08/28 Der	12/48 589	-11/59	05/61	
40590	09/28 Der	12/49 590	-05/59	10/59	
40592	09/28 Der	11/50 592	-12/61	07/63	
40593	09/28 Der	04/48 593	-08/61	10/61	
40594	09/28 Der	11/49 594	-11/59	01/60	
40595	09/28 Der	03/50 595	-06/61	11/61	
40596	09/28 Der	11/48 596	-09/61	10/61	
40597	10/28 Der	09/49 597	-08/61	11/61	
40598	10/28 Der	10/48 598	-11/59	02/60	
40599	11/28 Der	02/49 599	-05/59	08/59	
40600	11/28 Der	09/49 600	-04/59	03/60	
40601	05/28 Der	10/48 601	-12/59	01/61	
40602	11/28 Der	12/48 602	-10/61	08/63	
40603	11/28 Der	08/49 603	-07/61	09/61	
40604	11/28 Der	09/48 604	-06/61	08/61	
40605	11/28 Der	06/49 605	-10/59	02/60	
40606	11/28 Der	02/49 606	-05/59	08/59	
40607	11/28 Der	01/50 607	-07/59	07/60	
40608	11/28 Der	06/48 608	-09/59	02/60	
40609	11/28 Der	02/49 609	-10/61	10/61	
40610	12/28 Der	03/49 610	-05/59	08/59	
40611	12/28 Der	07/48 611	-09/59	04/61	
40612	12/28 Der	04/50 612	-10/61	01/62	
40613	10/29 Der	05/48 613	-10/61	06/63	
40614	10/29 Der	06/49 614	-10/61	06/62	
40615	11/29 Der	05/50 615	-10/61	09/63	
40616	11/29 Der	05/49 616	-07/59	02/60	
40617	11/29 Der	12/49 617	-11/59	02/60	
40618	11/29 Der	10/48 618	-09/61	11/61	
40619	11/29 Der	06/51 619	-10/61	02/62	
40620	11/29 Der	05/48 620	-10/61	07/63	
40621	11/29 Der	04/48 621	-10/61	07/63	
40622	11/29 Der	03/51 622	-05/61	05/61	
40623	12/29 Der	10/48 623	-08/61	11/61	
40624	12/29 Der	04/48 624	-08/61	10/62	
40625	12/29 Der	06/49 625	-10/61	09/63	
40626	12/29 Der	12/49 626	-10/61	11/61	
40627	12/29 Der	10/49 627	-01/61	05/61	
40628	12/29 Der	03/50 628	-01/61	04/62	
40629	01/30 Der	08/49 629	-04/61	05/61	
40630	01/30 Der	08/49 630	-10/60	11/60	
40631	01/30 Der	06/50 631	-09/60	10/60	
40632	01/30 Der	09/48 632	-02/61	04/61	
40633	06/28 Der	06/48 633	-11/59	05/60	sd
40634	06/28 Der	01/50 634	-05/62	08/62	s
40635	07/28 Der	11/49 635	-02/61	06/63	s
40636	08/31 Crw	07/48 636	-11/59	02/60	
40637	08/31 Crw	02/50 637	-09/61	11/61	
40638	08/31 Crw	04/49 638	-05/62	06/63	
40640	08/31 Crw	07/49 640	-09/61	07/63	
40641	08/31 Crw	04/48 641	-10/61	01/62	
40642	08/31 Crw	02/50 642	-10/61	06/63	
40643	08/31 Crw	12/48 643	-10/61	02/62	
40644	08/31 Crw	05/49 644	-11/59	12/59	
40645	08/31 Crw	09/49 645	-10/61	04/62	
40646	09/31 Crw	06/48 646	-05/62	09/62	
40647	09/31 Crw	08/48 647	-10/61	04/62	
40648	09/31 Crw	02/49 648	-09/61	11/61	
40649	09/31 Crw	11/48 649	-11/59	02/60	
40650	09/31 Crw	10/48 650	-09/61	02/62	
40651	09/31 Crw	07/48 651	-11/61	07/63	
40652	09/31 Crw	05/49 652	-05/60	07/60	
40653	09/31 Crw	06/48 653	-11/59	07/61	d
40654	10/31 Crw	06/49 654	-12/59	02/60	
40655	10/31 Crw	05/48 655	-11/59	07/61	
40656	10/31 Crw	07/50 656	-11/59	11/60	
40657	10/31 Crw	12/48 657	-10/62	12/62	
40658	10/31 Crw	05/48 658	-11/59	06/61	
40659	10/31 Crw	03/50 659	-08/61	09/61	
40660	12/31 Crw	03/49 660	-11/59	07/61	
40661	12/31 Der	12/49 661	-11/61	07/63	
40662	12/31 Der	03/49 662	-09/54	*54*	
40663	12/31 Der	06/48 663	-09/61	04/62	
40664	12/31 Der	04/48 664	-09/62	05/63	
40665	12/31 Der	07/48 665	-06/62	05/63	
40666	01/32 Der	08/51 666	-07/59	02/60	
40667	01/32 Der	09/48 667	-11/59	12/59	
40668	01/32 Der	04/48 668	-10/61	09/63	
40669	01/32 Der	12/49 669	-09/61	09/63	
40670	01/32 Der	05/48 670	-12/62	02/64	
40671	01/32 Der	12/49 671	-11/60	01/61	
40672	02/32 Der	05/48 672	-10/62	12/62	
40673	02/32 Der	09/49 673	-11/59	04/60	
40674	02/32 Der	12/48 674	-11/59	01/62	
40675	02/32 Der	12/48 675	-08/59	02/60	
40676	02/32 Der	04/51 676	-08/57	08/57	
40677	02/32 Der	11/51 677	-11/59	04/62	
40678	03/32 Der	03/49 678	-07/61	09/61	
40679	03/32 Der	06/48 679	-11/59	07/61	
40680	03/32 Der	06/50 680	-11/59	60	
40681	04/32 Der	08/51 681	-08/62	06/63	
40682	04/32 Der	04/54 682	-02/61	08/61	
40683	04/32 Der	02/49 683	-03/61	09/61	
40684	04/32 Der	09/50 684	-07/61	10/61	
40685	04/32 Der	12/50 685	-07/61	12/62	
40686	10/32 Crw	02/49 686	-10/61	01/62	
40687	10/32 Crw	01/50 687	-10/61	07/63	
40688	10/32 Crw	03/49 688	-07/59	04/61	
40689	10/32 Crw	05/48 689	-10/61	07/63	
40690	11/32 Crw	12/49 690	-10/60	11/60	
40691	11/32 Crw	06/51 691	-02/61	06/61	
40692	11/32 Crw	07/48 692	-08/61	09/61	
40693	11/32 Crw	04/48 693	-07/59	10/61	
40694	11/32 Crw	06/48 694	-11/62	07/63	
40695	11/32 Crw	05/48 695	-03/61	06/61	
40696	11/32 Crw	06/48 696	-06/62	08/62	
40697	11/32 Crw	05/48 697	-02/62	03/62	
40698	11/32 Crw	01/50 698	-08/60	10/60	
40699	12/32 Crw	10/49 699	-12/59	08/60	
40700	12/32 Crw	06/50 700	-09/62	12/62	

3P [1] 40711-40762
4-4-0 MR Johnson

Power Classification:	3P
Introduced:	1900-1905 Rebuilt by Fowler 1913-1925
Designer:	Johnson
Company:	MR
Weight:	Loco 55t 7cwt
Driving Wheel:	6' 9"
Boiler Pressure:	175psi superheated
Cylinders:	Inside 20½" x 26"
Tractive Effort:	20065lbf
Valve Gear:	Stephenson (piston valves)

In 1900 an entirely new class of 4-4-0 appeared on the Midland Railway. They were larger than Johnson's other 4-4-0s and they were fitted with larger Belpaire boilers. Eighty engines were built between 1900 and 1905 and they were numbered 700-779. (Another ten similar engines were built for the Settle and Carlisle line in 1907 with 6' 6" wheels, but they were all withdrawn in the late 1920s.)

Seventy-three engines were rebuilt between 1913 and 1925 with superheaters and larger cylinders (the unrebuilt engines being withdrawn from 1925 onwards).

The engines did very good work all over the Midland main lines alongside the compounds. In many ways they were superior to the Fowler 'Class 2's ('40332' class), but they were inclined to be heavy on coal, and this probably explains why they were not adopted as the LMS standard type.

Twenty-two of the class survived to come in to BR stock, the last engine being withdrawn in September 1952.

Year End Totals: '3P [1]' class

'47	'48	'49	'50	'51	'52	'53	'54	'55	'56	'57	'58	'59	'60	'61	'62	'63	'64	'65	'66	'67
22	17	10	8	3																

Number	Built	Renumbered	BR Dates	Scrap	Notes
40711	01/02 Der	711	-03/49	*49*	
40715	02/02 Der	715	-01/48	*48*	
40720	10/02 Der	720	-07/49	*49*	
40726	12/02 Der	09/48 726	-09/52	*09/52*	
40727	12/02 Der	727	-05/50	*06/50*	
40728	12/02 Der	06/48 728	-07/52	*09/52*	
40729	12/02 Der	729	-06/51	06/51	
40731	05/03 Der	731	-12/48	*49*	
40734	06/03 Der	734	-10/49	*49*	
40735	06/03 Der	735	-02/49	*49*	
40736	06/03 Der	736	-01/48	*48*	
40739	09/03 Der	739	-11/49	11/49	
40740	12/03 Der	05/48 740	-11/49	12/49	
40741	12/03 Der	08/48 741	-09/51	*11/51*	
40743	12/03 Der	01/49 743	-07/52	*10/52*	
40745	01/04 Der	06/48 745	-03/50	03/50	
40747	02/04 Der	03/49 747	-06/51	06/51	
40748	02/04 Der	748	-06/48	*48*	
40756	10/04 Der	756	-05/49	*49*	
40757	11/04 Der	757	-05/48	*48*	
40758	11/04 Der	08/48 758	-03/51	*03/51*	
40762	03/05 Der	762	-02/51	02/51	

4P [1] 40900-40939, 41045-41199
4-4-0 LMS Fowler Compound

Power Classification:	4P
Introduced:	1924-1932
Designer:	Fowler
Company:	LMS
Weight:	Loco 61t 14cwt Tender 42t 14cwt
Driving Wheel:	6' 9"
Boiler Pressure:	200psi superheated
Cylinders:	One inside high pressure cylinder (19" x 26") and two outside low pressure cylinders (21" x 26")
Tractive Effort:	22650lbf (TE of low pressure cylinders at 80% of boiler pressure)
Valve Gear:	Stephenson (slide valves on low pressure cylinders and piston valves on high pressure cylinder)

These engines were based on the Midland Railway compounds ('41000' class). The design was adopted as a standard design by the LMS and no fewer than 190 engines were turned out between 1924 and 1927, numbered 1045-1199, and 900-934. These had 6' 9" driving wheels in place of the 7' 0" wheels of the original engines, and 200psi boiler pressure. The final five engines (935-939) were built in 1932 and still more engines (940-959) were on order, but the order was cancelled when Stanier appeared on the scene as he had very different ideas on the subject of locomotive power.

In 1928 No. 1054 made history by running non-stop from Euston to Edinburgh (a distance of 400 miles) with a specially adapted tender. This was the LMS's quiet answer to the LNER's announcement that the Flying Scotsman would be running non-stop from London to Edinburgh with a corridor tender to allow the crew to change over en-route.

l 41085 onwards were fitted for left-hand drive. (The Midland Railway had always been a right-hand drive railway - the LMS being left-hand drive).

Year End Totals: '4P [1]' class

'47	'48	'49	'50	'51	'52	'53	'54	'55	'56	'57	'58	'59	'60	'61	'62	'63	'64	'65	'66	'67
195	195	195	195	195	189	176	153	116	89	55	19	6	2							

Number	Built	Renumbered	BR Dates	Scrap	Notes
40900	04/27 VF	10/48 900	-04/56	*56*	l
40901	04/27 VF	05/49 901	-06/54	*08/54*	l
40902	04/27 VF	06/49 902	-07/56	*08/56*	l
40903	04/27 VF	03/49 903	-08/55	*55*	l
40904	04/27 VF	09/49 904	-03/57	06/57	l
40905	04/27 VF	08/48 905	-11/53	12/53	l
40906	04/27 VF	01/49 906	-01/55	01/55	l
40907	04/27 VF	06/49 907	-10/60	10/60	l
40908	05/27 VF	08/48 908	-07/55	*01/56*	l

Number	Built	Renumbered	BR Dates	Scrap	Notes
40909	05/27 VF	10/49 909	-07/56	*08/56*	l
40910	06/27 VF	04/48 910	-06/56	*56*	l
40911	06/27 VF	12/48 911	-12/52	06/53	l
40912	06/27 VF	12/49 912	-04/55	*55*	l
40913	06/27 VF	09/48 913	-08/55	*08/55*	l
40914	06/27 VF	05/48 914	-09/54	*10/54*	l
40915	06/27 VF	01/49 915	-12/55	*01/56*	l
40916	06/27 VF	03/49 916	-07/55	*08/55*	l
40917	06/27 VF	12/49 917	-12/56	*57*	l
40918	06/27 VF	02/49 918	-12/52	*01/53*	l
40919	07/27 VF	04/48 919	-01/54	*54*	l
40920	07/27 VF	06/48 920	-05/58	07/58	l
40921	07/27 VF	06/48 921	-11/55	*55*	l
40922	07/27 VF	12/49 922	-12/52	*06/53*	l
40923	07/27 VF	03/49 923	-10/54	*54*	l
40924	07/27 VF	08/48 924	-03/55	*04/55*	l
40925	05/27 VF	05/49 925	-11/59	01/60	l
40926	05/27 VF	09/49 926	-08/57	08/57	l
40927	05/27 VF	08/48 927	-07/57	08/57	l
40928	06/27 VF	12/49 928	-03/58	03/58	l
40929	05/27 VF	09/48 929	-07/56	*56*	l
40930	05/27 VF	04/50 930	-04/57	04/57	l
40931	05/27 VF	08/48 931	-10/58	06/59	l
40932	05/27 VF	09/49 932	-08/56	*56*	l
40933	06/27 VF	07/48 933	-04/58	05/58	l
40934	06/27 VF	03/49 934	-03/57	03/57	l
40935	08/32 Der	10/49 935	-04/58	04/58	l
40936	08/32 Der	06/48 936	-01/61	09/61	l
40937	08/32 Der	05/48 937	-04/58	05/58	l
40938	09/32 Der	07/48 938	-07/56	*08/56*	l
40939	09/32 Der	11/49 939	-12/56	*57*	l

Class continued with 41045

4P ^{2} 41000-41044, 1000
4-4-0 MR Deeley Compound

Power Classification:	4P
Introduced:	1905-1909 j 1902-1903 rebuilt by Deeley 1914-1919
Designer:	Deeley j Johnson
Company:	MR
Weight:	Loco 61t 14cwt Tender 42t 14cwt
Driving Wheel:	7' 0"
Boiler Pressure:	200psi superheated
Cylinders:	One inside high pressure cylinder (19" x 26") and two outside low pressure cylinders (21" x 26")
Tractive Effort:	21840lbf (TE of low pressure cylinders at 80% of boiler pressure)
Valve Gear:	Stephenson (slide valves on low pressure cylinders and piston valves on high pressure cylinder)

These well known engines are considered by some to have been the only really successful compound engines ever to work in this country.

Compound engines use the steam produced by the boiler twice, firstly in high-pressure cylinders, and secondly in low-pressure cylinders. Several railways had experimented with compound engines in the latter part of the 19th century, but with somewhat indifferent results.

Johnson based his compounds on a system invented by the chief draughtsman of the North Eastern Railway, Mr. William Smith. One inside high-pressure cylinder and two outside low-pressure cylinders were used. A second regulator was fitted to allow live steam to be admitted directly to the low-pressure cylinders which was a great help when starting. Five engines were built in 1902-1903 and they were numbered 2631-2635. They put up some fine work on the mountainous Settle and Carlisle line.

When Deeley succeeded Johnson, he decided to build more engines of the same basic design, but with some important differences. The Smith type valve was done away with and replaced with a simpler system. The engines always started as non-compound engines, with live steam in the low-pressure cylinders, and as the regulator was opened further, the engines automatically switched over to compound working. There were also some differences in external appearance, with the running plate being raised clear of the coupling rods and the rectangular rear splasher being replaced with a quarter circle, which merged into the cab side sheet. The boiler pressure was also raised to 220psi, although it was later reduced to 200psi.

Thirty of Deeley's new engines were built in 1905-1906, numbered 1000-1029. In the 1907 Midland Railway re-numbering scheme, these became 1005-1034, and the original Johnson engines became 1000-1004. A further ten engines numbered 1035-1044 came out in 1908-1909.

Between 1914 and 1919 1000-1004 were rebuilt in line with the Deeley engines, and at the same time they were superheated. 1040 was superheated in 1913, and the rest of the class was superheated from 1919 onwards.

No more engines of the class were built by the Midland, but the design was adopted as a standard design by the LMS and 195 engines were turned out between 1924 and 1932, numbered 1045-1199, and 900-939 (see the '40900' class). These had 6' 9" driving wheels in place of the 7' 0" wheels of the original engines, and 200psi boiler pressure. They were superheated from new.

Both classes did magnificent work, not only on the Midland Railway, but also on the Caledonian and Glasgow & South Western main lines. They also worked well on the former London & North Western Railway, where they worked the Birmingham two-hour expresses, for which they were ideally suited. However, they were always viewed with some suspicion on LNWR lines, due to a mistrust of compound engines in general dating back to the unsuccessful experiments with compounds in Webb days.

Lowering standards of maintenance during and after the Second World War took a toll on these engines and they later fell into disrepute. They were gradually put to work on local trains, duties for which they were unsuitable, and in consequence they got a poor reputation. This was through no fault of their own as they were magnificent engines when kept in proper trim and well handled.

The original engine, number 1000 was fortunately kept in store at Crewe for a number of years, and in 1959 it was fully restored and rebuilt to its 1914 condition, in Midland Railway colours. It worked special trains for a number of years before being transferred to Clapham Museum, and later to the National Railway Museum in York.

j Original Johnson built engines.

Year End Totals: '4P ^{2}' class

'47	'48	'49	'50	'51	'52	'53	'54	'55	'56	'57	'58	'59	'60	'61	'62	'63	'64	'65	'66	'67
45	37	32	28	11	1															

Number	Built	Renumbered	BR Dates	Scrap	Notes
41000 §	01/02 Der	05/49 1000	-09/51 06/59➲1000		j
41001	01/02 Der	12/48 1001	-10/51	*10/51*	j
41002	07/03 Der	1002	-06/48	07/48	j
41003	09/03 Der	08/48 1003	-03/51	*51*	j
41004	11/03 Der	04/49 1004	-02/52	*03/52*	j
41005	10/05 Der	10/49 1005	-06/51	*06/51*	
41006	11/05 Der	09/49 1006	-05/51	*05/51*	
41007	11/05 Der	11/48 1007	-05/52	*05/52*	
41008	11/05 Der	1008	-06/49	*49*	
41009	12/05 Der	12/48 1009	-11/51	*51*	
41010	12/05 Der	1010	-07/49	08/49	
41011	12/05 Der	04/49 1011	-02/51	*02/51*	
41012	12/05 Der	03/49 1012	-01/51	02/51	
41013	12/05 Der	1013	-06/49	*49*	
41014	12/05 Der	08/48 1014	-05/52	05/52	
41015	03/06 Der	08/49 1015	-10/51	*01/52*	
41016	03/06 Der	03/49 1016	-10/51	*51*	
41017	03/06 Der	11/48 1017	-08/50	*10/50*	
41018	04/06 Der	1018	-07/48	*10/48*	
41019	04/06 Der	05/48 1019	-10/51	*03/52*	
41020	04/06 Der	08/49 1020	-05/51	*05/51*	
41021	04/06 Der	09/48 1021	-09/52	*09/52*	
41022	05/06 Der	01/49 1022	-04/50	*50*	
41023	05/06 Der	05/48 1023	-08/51	08/51	
41024	05/06 Der	1024	-10/48	*48*	
41025	05/06 Der	01/49 1025	-01/53	*01/53*	
41026	06/06 Der	1026	-08/48	*48*	
41027	06/06 Der	1027	-09/48	*48*	
41028	06/06 Der	06/49 1028	-09/52	*09/52*	
41029	07/06 Der	1029	-06/48	*07/48*	
41030	09/06 Der	02/49 1030	-08/51	*10/51*	
41031	09/06 Der	1031	-11/49	*49*	
41032	10/06 Der	01/49 1032	-03/52	*03/52*	
41033	10/06 Der	1033	-08/48	*48*	
41034	12/06 Der	10/48 1034	-04/50	08/50	
41035	11/08 Der	09/48 1035	-05/52	05/52	
41036	11/08 Der	1036	-09/48	*10/48*	
41037	12/08 Der	05/48 1037	-03/51	*03/51*	
41038	12/08 Der	01/49 1038	-08/52	*52*	
41039	12/08 Der	09/48 1039	-06/50	*06/50*	
41040	01/09 Der	08/49 1040	-05/52	*52*	
41041	01/09 Der	02/49 1041	-11/51	*03/52*	
41042	02/09 Der	1042	-05/49	*49*	
41043	03/09 Der	01/50 1043	-12/51	*01/52*	
41044	03/09 Der	03/49 1044	-09/52	*10/52*	

Class continued with 1000 (Preserved Locomotives)

4P ^{1} 40900-40939, 41045-41199
4-4-0 LMS Fowler Compound

Class continued from 40939

Number	Built	Renumbered	BR Dates	Scrap	Notes
41045	02/24 Der	04/49 1045	-06/57	06/57	
41046	02/24 Der	07/48 1046	-01/53	*01/53*	
41047	02/24 Der	10/48 1047	-02/54	*02/54*	
41048	03/24 Der	12/48 1048	-10/57	11/57	
41049	03/24 Der	05/48 1049	-03/59	04/59	
41050	03/24 Der	12/48 1050	-06/56	*56*	
41051	03/24 Der	12/48 1051	-10/54	11/54	
41052	04/24 Der	09/48 1052	-04/53	*53*	
41053	04/24 Der	06/48 1053	-06/56	*06/56*	
41054	04/24 Der	07/49 1054	-09/54	09/54	
41055	04/24 Der	10/48 1055	-02/53	*03/53*	
41056	05/24 Der	11/48 1056	-10/53	*53*	
41057	05/24 Der	03/49 1057	-05/53	*53*	
41058	05/24 Der	11/49 1058	-02/54	*02/54*	
41059	06/24 Der	12/48 1059	-11/55	11/55	
41060	06/24 Der	08/48 1060	-03/58	03/58	
41061	06/24 Der	02/49 1061	-06/55	06/55	
41062	06/24 Der	11/48 1062	-05/59	10/60	
41063	07/24 Der	10/48 1063	-10/60	10/60	
41064	07/24 Der	03/49 1064	-01/57	01/57	
41065	07/24 Der	05/48 1065	-03/56	*56*	
41066	08/24 Der	07/49 1066	-05/58	05/58	
41067	08/24 Der	01/49 1067	-02/55	*55*	
41068	08/24 Der	12/48 1068	-12/58	06/59	
41069	09/24 Der	10/49 1069	-11/55	11/55	
41070	09/24 Der	08/48 1070	-11/55	11/55	
41071	09/24 Der	02/49 1071	-03/58	04/58	
41072	09/24 Der	05/48 1072	-10/55	*55*	
41073	10/24 Der	07/48 1073	-08/57	08/57	
41074	10/24 Der	07/48 1074	-08/54	*54*	
41075	10/24 Der	05/49 1075	-04/57	04/57	
41076	11/24 Der	09/48 1076	-05/55	*55*	
41077	11/24 Der	07/48 1077	-04/57	04/57	
41078	11/24 Der	01/49 1078	-09/58	02/60	
41079	11/24 Der	06/50 1079	-10/56	11/56	
41080	11/24 Der	06/49 1080	-01/54	*54*	
41081	11/24 Der	07/48 1081	-11/55	11/55	
41082	11/24 Der	06/48 1082	-04/54	*54*	
41083	12/24 Der	04/48 1083	-12/58	02/60	
41084	12/24 Der	05/48 1084	-06/54	*54*	
41085	05/25 Der	05/50 1085	-01/57	01/57	l
41086	05/25 Der	10/48 1086	-05/58	06/58	l
41087	06/25 Der	05/48 1087	-10/54	10/54	l
41088	06/25 Der	01/49 1088	-12/56	*12/56*	l
41089	06/25 Der	06/48 1089	-07/57	07/57	l
41090	07/25 Der	10/48 1090	-12/58	06/60	l
41091	07/25 Der	05/48 1091	-04/55	*55*	l
41092	07/25 Der	05/48 1092	-07/53	08/53	l
41093	07/25 Der	02/49 1093	-06/58	09/58	l
41094	07/25 Der	10/48 1094	-01/59	01/59	l
41095	08/25 Der	11/48 1095	-02/58	03/58	l
41096	08/25 Der	06/48 1096	-05/54	*54*	l
41097	08/25 Der	08/48 1097	-05/56	*56*	l
41098	08/25 Der	12/48 1098	-06/57	06/57	l
41099	09/25 Der	12/48 1099	-11/53	*11/53*	l
41100	09/25 Der	02/49 1100	-03/59	04/59	l
41101	09/25 Der	05/48 1101	-08/59	10/59	l
41102	10/25 Der	05/49 1102	-12/58	06/60	l
41103	10/25 Der	12/48 1103	-11/57	11/57	l
41104	10/25 Der	03/49 1104	-07/55	08/55	l
41105	11/25 Der	06/49 1105	-09/57	09/57	l
41106	11/25 Der	06/48 1106	-07/58	08/59	l
41107	11/25 Der	05/49 1107	-09/55	*09/55*	l
41108	11/25 Der	11/49 1108	-01/57	01/57	l
41109	11/25 Der	06/49 1109	-12/52	*03/53*	l
41110	11/25 Der	01/50 1110	-08/54	*54*	l
41111	11/25 Der	10/48 1111	-05/58	05/58	l
41112	11/25 Der	02/50 1112	-11/57	11/57	l
41113	11/25 Der	06/48 1113	-12/58	02/60	l
41114	12/25 Der	10/48 1114	-05/58	09/58	l
41115	06/25 Hor	09/48 1115	-05/54	*54*	l
41116	07/25 Hor	06/48 1116	-11/57	12/57	l
41117	08/25 Hor	12/48 1117	-05/55	05/55	l
41118	08/25 Hor	08/49 1118	-01/58	02/58	l
41119	09/25 Hor	02/49 1119	-12/58	06/59	l
41120	10/25 Hor	12/49 1120	-06/59	08/60	l
41121	10/25 Hor	06/48 1121	-02/59	08/60	l
41122	11/25 Hor	11/48 1122	-12/58	02/60	l
41123	11/25 Hor	04/49 1123	-12/59	02/61	l
41124	11/25 Hor	06/49 1124	-01/55	*55*	l

Number	Built	Renumbered	BR Dates	Scrap	Notes
41125	12/25 Hor	07/49 1125	-01/53	53	l
41126	12/25 Hor	12/48 1126	-12/56	57	l
41127	12/25 Hor	06/49 1127	-08/55	08/55	l
41128	12/25 Hor	11/48 1128	-03/56	56	l
41129	12/25 Hor	12/49 1129	-05/55	06/55	l
41130	01/26 Hor	08/49 1130	-08/55	12/55	l
41131	01/26 Hor	07/50 1131	-04/56	08/56	l
41132	02/26 Hor	05/48 1132	-10/56	56	l
41133	02/26 Hor	11/48 1133	-09/54	10/54	l
41134	02/26 Hor	12/49 1134	-09/54	10/54	l
41135	06/25 NB	03/49 1135	-08/55	55	l
41136	06/25 NB	08/48 1136	-09/55	55	l
41137	07/25 NB	04/48 1137	-04/56	56	l
41138	07/25 NB	08/49 1138	-12/54	55	l
41139	07/25 NB	10/49 1139	-09/54	54	l
41140	07/25 NB	04/51 1140	-05/57	05/57	l
41141	07/25 NB	12/49 1141	-09/54	10/54	l
41142	07/25 NB	11/48 1142	-07/56	07/56	l
41143	07/25 NB	11/48 1143	-03/59	04/59	l
41144	07/25 NB	10/48 1144	-03/58	03/58	l
41145	07/25 NB	04/48 1145	-09/53	11/53	l
41146	07/25 NB	07/48 1146	-10/54	54	l
41147	08/25 NB	06/48 1147	-03/56	56	l
41148	08/25 NB	05/50 1148	-03/53	53	l
41149	08/25 NB	06/48 1149	-08/55	08/55	l
41150	08/25 NB	05/49 1150	-09/57	09/57	l
41151	08/25 NB	11/48 1151	-01/57	01/57	l
41152	09/25 NB	11/48 1152	-03/58	03/58	l
41153	09/25 NB	05/49 1153	-11/57	11/57	l
41154	09/25 NB	09/48 1154	-07/55	08/55	l
41155	09/25 NB	09/49 1155	-02/57	03/57	l
41156	09/25 NB	12/48 1156	-09/58	07/59	l
41157	09/25 NB	06/48 1157	-05/60	11/60	l
41158	09/25 NB	04/50 1158	-08/59	08/60	l
41159	10/25 NB	12/48 1159	-04/58	09/58	l
41160	09/25 VF	02/49 1160	-09/56	56	l
41161	09/25 VF	03/49 1161	-11/55	11/55	l
41162	09/25 VF	11/48 1162	-06/60	08/60	l
41163	09/25 VF	02/49 1163	-11/58	06/59	l
41164	09/25 VF	09/48 1164	-11/58	06/59	l
41165	09/25 VF	03/49 1165	-03/59	10/60	l
41166	09/25 VF	06/48 1166	-09/56	56	l
41167	10/25 VF	06/48 1167	-10/58	06/59	l
41168	10/25 VF	10/48 1168	-07/61	05/62	l
41169	10/25 VF	10/48 1169	-07/55	07/55	l
41170	11/25 VF	05/48 1170	-04/56	56	l
41171	11/25 VF	02/50 1171	-12/52	53	l
41172	11/25 VF	02/49 1172	-08/57	08/57	l
41173	11/25 VF	08/49 1173	-02/59	08/61	l
41174	11/25 VF	06/48 1174	-02/54	54	l
41175	11/25 VF	01/49 1175	-04/55	55	l
41176	11/25 VF	05/48 1176	-01/55	02/55	l
41177	11/25 VF	06/48 1177	-11/55	01/56	l
41178	11/25 VF	09/48 1178	-12/53	02/54	l
41179	11/25 VF	02/50 1179	-11/57	11/57	l
41180	11/25 VF	04/48 1180	-03/57	03/57	l
41181	11/25 VF	05/48 1181	-11/57	11/57	l
41182	11/25 VF	12/49 1182	-12/52	03/53	l
41183	11/25 VF	07/48 1183	-02/55	55	l
41184	12/25 VF	11/49 1184	-06/53	06/53	l
41185	02/27 VF	08/51 1185	-11/57	11/57	l
41186	02/27 VF	11/50 1186	-09/57	10/57	l
41187	02/27 VF	12/48 1187	-07/56	56	l
41188	03/27 VF	05/48 1188	-11/55	11/55	l
41189	03/27 VF	10/49 1189	-07/58	09/58	l
41190	03/27 VF	06/49 1190	-01/58	02/58	l
41191	03/27 VF	08/49 1191	-03/56	56	l
41192	03/27 VF	11/48 1192	-06/57	07/57	l
41193	03/27 VF	04/48 1193	-11/58	06/59	l
41194	03/27 VF	06/48 1194	-09/57	09/57	l
41195	03/27 VF	12/48 1195	-11/57	11/57	l
41196	03/27 VF	07/48 1196	-07/58	07/58	l
41197	03/27 VF	05/48 1197	-05/57	05/57	l
41198	03/27 VF	12/49 1198	-11/55	11/55	l
41199	04/27 VF	09/48 1199	-01/58	02/58	l

2MT[1] 41200-41329
2-6-2T LMS Ivatt

Power Classification:	2P reclassified 2MT in 1948
Introduced:	1946-1952
Designer:	Ivatt
Company:	LMS
Weight:	63t 5cwt
Driving Wheel:	5' 0"
Boiler Pressure:	200psi superheated
Cylinders:	Outside 16" x 24" c Outside 16½" x 24"
Tractive Effort:	17410lbf c 18510lbf
Valve Gear:	Walschaert (piston valves)

In 1946, two years before nationalisation, Ivatt introduced two new lightweight designs for cross country and branch line working. The tender engine was the '46400' class and the tank engine version was the '41200' class.

These 2-6-2T engines were completely different from previous 2-6-2Ts on the LMS (the '40071' and '40001' classes), being smaller and more compact. One hundred and thirty engines were built, only ten of which appeared before nationalisation. The design was later adopted as a BR standard design, appearing as the '84000' class in 1953. Most of this class was based on the London Midland Region, but some were on the Southern Region.

Some of these engines were fitted with tall narrow tapered chimneys. These were considered ugly and later engines reverted to the traditional wide type of chimney.

41272 was the 7000th locomotive to be built at Crewe in 1950.

c The later engines (41290-41329) were fitted with slightly larger cylinders.

m 41210-41229 and 41270-41289 were motor fitted for working push-pull trains.

Year End Totals: '2MT [1]' class

'47	'48	'49	'50	'51	'52	'53	'54	'55	'56	'57	'58	'59	'60	'61	'62	'63	'64	'65	'66	'67
10	30	60	90	100	130	130	130	130	130	130	130	130	130	130	109	91	65	39	8	

Number	Built	Renumbered	BR Dates	Scrap	Notes
41200	12/46 Crw	03/49 1200	-07/65	10/65	
41201	12/46 Crw	01/49 1201	-07/65	10/65	
41202	12/46 Crw	11/48 1202	-11/66	04/67	
41203	12/46 Crw	12/48 1203	-10/63	09/64	
41204	12/46 Crw	01/49 1204	-11/66	04/67	
41205	12/46 Crw	01/51 1205	-03/64	05/65	
41206	12/46 Crw	12/50 1206	-03/66	07/66	
41207	12/46 Crw	01/49 1207	-11/66	03/67	
41208	12/46 Crw	06/50 1208	-07/65	10/65	
41209	12/46 Crw	10/50 1209	-07/65	10/65	
41210	08/48 Crw		08/48-05/64	12/64	m
41211	08/48 Crw		08/48-09/66	02/67	m
41212	08/48 Crw		08/48-11/65	01/66	m
41213	09/48 Crw		09/48-12/63	09/64	m
41214	09/48 Crw		09/48-07/65	10/65	m
41215	09/48 Crw		09/48-01/65	05/65	m
41216	09/48 Crw		09/48-03/66	07/66	m
41217	09/48 Crw		09/48-12/66	09/67	m
41218	09/48 Crw		09/48-07/65	10/65	m
41219	09/48 Crw		09/48-10/65	01/66	m
41220	09/48 Crw		09/48-11/66	06/67	m
41221	09/48 Crw		09/48-07/65	12/65	m
41222	09/48 Crw		09/48-12/66	09/67	m
41223	10/48 Crw		10/48-03/66	07/66	m
41224	10/48 Crw		10/48-07/67	12/67	m
41225	10/48 Crw		10/48-09/64	12/64	m
41226	10/48 Crw		10/48-09/64	01/65	m
41227	10/48 Crw		10/48-09/64	12/64	m
41228	10/48 Crw		10/48-07/64	11/64	m
41229	10/48 Crw		10/48-11/66	04/67	m
41230	08/49 Crw		08/49-04/67	09/67	
41231	08/49 Crw		08/49-05/64	08/64	
41232	08/49 Crw		08/49-08/65	12/65	
41233	08/49 Crw		08/49-11/66	07/67	
41234	08/49 Crw		08/49-11/66	04/67	
41235	08/49 Crw		08/49-11/62	02/63	
41236	09/49 Crw		09/49-10/62	01/63	
41237	09/49 Crw		09/49-09/64	02/65	
41238	09/49 Crw		09/49-05/65	10/65	
41239	09/49 Crw		09/49-06/64	11/64	
41240	09/49 Crw		09/49-10/63	08/64	
41241 §	09/49 Crw		09/49-12/66		
41242	09/49 Crw		09/49-05/65	08/65	
41243	10/49 Crw		10/49-07/65	10/65	
41244	10/49 Crw		10/49-11/66	03/67	
41245	10/49 Crw		10/49-12/63	05/64	
41246	10/49 Crw		10/49-09/62	10/63	
41247	10/49 Crw		10/49-10/62	05/63	
41248	11/49 Crw		11/49-11/64	03/65	
41249	11/49 Crw		11/49-03/66	07/66	
41250	11/49 Crw		11/49-11/63	03/64	
41251	11/49 Crw		11/49-11/66	03/67	
41252	11/49 Crw		11/49-12/62	06/63	
41253	11/49 Crw		11/49-05/64	08/64	
41254	11/49 Crw		11/49-12/62	06/63	
41255	11/49 Crw		11/49-07/62	08/62	
41256	12/49 Crw		12/49-07/62	08/62	
41257	12/49 Crw		12/49-07/62	08/62	
41258	12/49 Crw		12/49-10/62	11/62	
41259	12/49 Crw		12/49-07/62	08/62	
41260	06/50 Crw		06/50-09/64	11/64	
41261	07/50 Crw		07/50-07/65	11/65	
41262	07/50 Crw		07/50-01/64	02/64	
41263	07/50 Crw		07/50-12/62	09/63	
41264	07/50 Crw		07/50-12/66	01/68	
41265	08/50 Crw		08/50-12/62	09/63	
41266	08/50 Crw		08/50-10/62	06/63	
41267	08/50 Crw		08/50-12/62	06/63	
41268	08/50 Crw		08/50-07/64	10/64	
41269	08/50 Crw		08/50-12/62	01/63	
41270	09/50 Crw		09/50-05/65	02/66	m
41271	09/50 Crw		09/50-10/62	03/63	m
41272	09/50 Crw		09/50-11/65	01/66	m
41273	09/50 Crw		09/50-12/63	03/64	m
41274	09/50 Crw		09/50-02/63	09/63	m
41275	10/50 Crw		10/50-10/65	01/66	m
41276	10/50 Crw		10/50-12/63	05/64	m
41277	10/50 Crw		10/50-11/62	03/63	m
41278	10/50 Crw		10/50-11/62	02/63	m
41279	10/50 Crw		10/50-12/63	03/64	m
41280	10/50 Crw		10/50-12/62	02/63	m
41281	10/50 Crw		10/50-11/63	01/64	m
41282	10/50 Crw		10/50-11/63	01/64	m
41283	11/50 Crw		11/50-03/66	07/66	m
41284	11/50 Crw		11/50-03/67	09/67	m
41285	11/50 Crw		11/50-12/66	05/67	m
41286	11/50 Crw		11/50-11/66	04/67	m
41287	11/50 Crw		11/50-07/66	11/66	m
41288	12/50 Crw		12/50-10/62	03/63	m
41289	12/50 Crw		12/50-01/63	03/63	m
			⊠12/62-12/62		
41290	09/51 Crw		09/51-03/66	07/66	c
41291	09/51 Crw		09/51-02/66	04/66	c
41292	09/51 Crw		09/51-10/63	02/64	c
41293	10/51 Crw		10/51-03/65	02/66	c
41294	10/51 Crw		10/51-09/66	02/67	c
41295	10/51 Crw		10/51-04/67	09/67	c
41296	10/51 Crw		10/51-03/66	07/66	c
41297	10/51 Crw		10/51-10/63	03/64	c
41298 §	10/51 Crw		10/51-07/67		c
41299	11/51 Crw		11/51-10/66	03/67	c
41300	03/52 Crw		03/52-10/64	03/65	c
41301	03/52 Crw		03/52-10/66	03/67	c
41302	03/52 Crw		03/52-11/63	12/63	c
41303	03/52 Crw		03/52-10/64	03/65	c
41304	03/52 Crw		03/52-11/66	03/67	c
41305	04/52 Crw		04/52-06/65	01/66	c
41306	04/52 Crw		04/52-12/63	02/64	c
41307	04/52 Crw		04/52-03/66	07/66	c
41308	04/52 Crw		04/52-02/65	04/65	c
41309	05/52 Crw		05/52-12/63	01/64	c
41310	05/52 Crw		05/52-10/64	03/65	c
41311	05/52 Crw		05/52-01/64	01/64	c
41312 §	05/52 Crw		05/52-07/67		c
41313 §	05/52 Crw		05/52-11/65		c
41314	05/52 Crw		05/52-07/65	03/66	c
41315	05/52 Crw		05/52-07/64	12/64	c
41316	06/52 Crw		06/52-10/66	03/67	c
41317	06/52 Crw		06/52-12/64	04/65	c
41318	06/52 Crw		06/52-10/63	02/64	c
41319	06/52 Crw		06/52-07/67	04/68	c
41320	01/52 Der		01/52-07/67	12/67	c
41321	02/52 Der		02/52-07/65	10/65	c
41322	02/52 Der		02/52-07/64	12/64	c
41323	03/52 Der		03/52-07/64	12/64	c
41324	03/52 Der		03/52-10/65	11/65	c
41325	03/52 Der		03/52-06/65	01/66	c
41326	04/52 Der		04/52-05/64	08/64	c
41327	04/52 Der		04/52-05/64	08/64	c
41328	05/52 Der		05/52-07/64	12/64	c
41329	05/52 Der		05/52-07/64	12/64	c

0F[1] 41509-41523
0-4-0ST MR Johnson

Power Classification:	0F
Introduced:	1883-1903
Designer:	Johnson
Company:	MR
Weight:	23t 3cwt l 32t 3cwt
Driving Wheel:	3' 10"
Boiler Pressure:	140psi p 150psi
Cylinders:	Inside 13" x 20" l Inside 15" x 20"
Tractive Effort:	8745lbf l 11640lbf p 12475lbf
Valve Gear:	Stephenson (slide valves)

The Midland Railway built thirty of these small 0-4-0STs in batches of five between 1883 and 1903 for shunting in docks, brewery yards and so on They were unusual in that this type of engine was usually fitted with outside cylinders, but the Midland Railway was strictly an inside cylinder railway and built them as such. They were almost the only saddle tanks that the Midland Railway ever owned. They were built with open backed cabs; most of them were later rebuilt with backs to the cabs.

The first of the class was withdrawn in 1905, and most of them had disappeared by 1930. Amongst their various duties, there were always a number of them to be seen shunting through the streets of Burton-on-Trent to the breweries of that town.

o 41516 retained its original open backed cab.

l The last group of engines, introduced in July 1897, were larger with a longer wheelbase, larger cylinders and increased water capacity.

s 41509 worked as a service engine at Derby and never carried its BR number. It was originally numbered 1506, but it was renumbered in 1930 to make way for absorbed SDJR engines.

p 41523 had a higher pressure boiler.

Year End Totals: '0F [1]' class

'47	'48	'49	'50	'51	'52	'53	'54	'55	'56	'57	'58	'59	'60	'61	'62	'63	'64	'65	'66	'67
3	3	3	3	3	3	3	3	1	1	1										

Year End Totals: '0F [1]' (service) class

'47	'48	'49	'50	'51	'52	'53	'54	'55	'56	'57	'58	'59	'60	'61	'62	'63	'64	'65	'66	'67
1	1																			

Number	*Built*	*Renumbered*	*BR Dates*	*Scrap*	*Notes*
41509	03/90 Der	1509	-10/49	11/49	s
41516	03/97 Der	09/48 1516	-10/55	*11/55*	o
41518	07/97 Der	03/49 1518	-02/58	*58*	l
41523	11/03 Der	04/49 1523	-03/55	*55*	lp

0F [2] 41528-41537
0-4-0T MR Deeley

Power Classification: 0F
Introduced: 1907-1922
Designer: Deeley
Company: MR
Weight: 32t 16cwt
Driving Wheel: 3' 9¾"
Boiler Pressure: 160psi
Cylinders: Outside 15" x 22"
Tractive Effort: 14715lbf
Valve Gear: Walschaert (slide valves)

These engines were built by Deeley in two batches. The first five were built in 1907 and the second five in 1921-1922. They were built for working in brewery yards, docks and other places where sharp curves were to be found. They were intended to replace the '41509' class.

They were large proportioned 0-4-0T engines and they were fitted with stove-pipe chimneys. Unusually for the Midland Railway they were fitted with outside cylinders, and they also had Walschaert valve gear. (The only other Midland engine to carry these two features was the 0-10-0 'Lickey Banker' 58100).

All the engines came into BR stock, and the last survivors lasted until 1966.

Year End Totals: '0F [2]' class

'47	'48	'49	'50	'51	'52	'53	'54	'55	'56	'57	'58	'59	'60	'61	'62	'63	'64	'65	'66	'67
10	10	10	10	10	10	10	10	10	10	8	8	8	8	5	5	3	2	2		

Number	*Built*	*Renumbered*	*BR Dates*	*Scrap*	*Notes*
41528	08/07 Der	03/49 1528	-12/66	04/67	
41529	09/07 Der	07/48 1529	-04/61	07/61	
41530	10/07 Der	04/48 1530	-05/57	05/57	
41531	11/07 Der	02/50 1531	-06/63	06/63	
41532	12/07 Der	06/48 1532	-03/61	08/61	
41533	07/21 Der	01/50 1533	-12/66	04/67	
41534	08/21 Der	10/48 1534	-06/57	06/57	
41535	02/22 Der	07/48 1535	-10/64	11/64	
41536	03/22 Der	04/48 1536	-03/61	05/61	
41537	05/22 Der	05/48 1537	-10/63	10/63	

1F [1] 41660-41895
0-6-0T MR Johnson

Power Classification: 1F
Introduced: 1878-1899
Designer: Johnson
Company: MR
Weight: 39t 11cwt
Driving Wheel: 4' 7"
Boiler Pressure: 140psi
b 150psi
Cylinders: Inside 17" x 24"
Tractive Effort: 15005lbf
b 16080lbf
Valve Gear: Stephenson (slide valves)

This was Johnson's first design after coming to the Midland Railway in 1873. Between 1874 and 1876 forty engines were built and then between 1878 and 1899 this class of 240 engines was built at Derby and by outside contractors. In 1907 they were renumbered in the series 1620-1899. A further sixty engines were built by Vulcan Foundry to a slightly enlarged design in 1899-1902. These were numbered 1900-1959, and they later became 47200-47259.

Some engines in the class were fitted with totally enclosed cabs, others were fitted with open backed half cabs (even after rebuilding).

This class was the standard Midland Railway shunting engine, and they were a familiar sight all over that system for 90 years. Of the 280 engines built, the first was withdrawn in 1920 and ninety-five came into BR stock. Of the seven engines still in service at the beginning of 1964, 41708 was the oldest engine still running on BR. It has since been preserved. It was a half cab fitted engine, and in preservation it has been fitted with a removable cab back, to provide extra protection in winter.

One engine of the class (number 1831) was completely rebuilt in 1932 as a diesel shunter. As such it was the direct forerunner of the standard 0-6-0 diesel shunters which were built by the LMS and BR.

b One hundred and twenty two engines were rebuilt from 1919 onwards with Belpaire boilers and pop-safety valves. The boiler pressure was increased to 150psi. 41835 was the last engine in service to retain its original round topped boiler.

w Engines from 41846 onwards had a slightly longer wheelbase.

Year End Totals: '1F [1]' class

'47	'48	'49	'50	'51	'52	'53	'54	'55	'56	'57	'58	'59	'60	'61	'62	'63	'64	'65	'66	'67
95	85	80	78	69	64	55	50	41	32	24	22	15	11	11	9	7	5	5		

Number	*Built*	*Renumbered*	*BR Dates*	*Scrap*	*Notes*
41660	05/78 Der	10/49 1660	-05/53	*53*	b
41661	06/78 Der	02/51 1661	-07/59	10/60	b
41664	07/78 Der	07/49 1664	-11/53	*53*	b
41666	07/78 Der	09/49 1666	-06/53	*53*	
41668	07/78 Der	1668	-02/48	*48*	
41671	10/78 Der	12/49 1671	-11/55	*55*	12/49⇨b
41672	11/78 Der	08/50 1672	-12/55	*56*	b
41674	11/78 Der	1674	-05/48	*48*	b
41676	12/78 Der	1676	-03/49	*49*	b
41682	02/79 Der	01/50 1682	-01/55	*55*	b
41686	02/79 Der	01/50 1686	-09/56	*56*	09/52⇨b
41690	10/79 Der	1690	-05/51	*51*	
41695	12/79 Der	02/49 1695	-04/53	*53*	b
41699	12/79 Der	05/50 1699	-02/57	02/57	b
41702	06/80 Der	09/51 1702	-06/62	02/63	b
41706	06/80 Der	05/49 1706	-04/57	07/57	b
41708 §	06/80 Der	10/49 1708	-12/66		b
41710	04/82 Der	07/48 1710	-07/57	07/57	b
41711	05/82 Der	01/50 1711	-10/54	10/54	b
41712	05/82 Der	01/50 1712	-10/64	12/64	b
41713	05/82 Der	08/48 1713	-08/55	*08/55*	
41714	05/82 Der	1714	-05/48	*48*	
41718	06/82 Der	1718	-08/48	*48*	
41720	04/83 Der	02/50 1720	-11/56	*11/56*	b
41724	06/83 Der	04/48 1724	-06/58	08/59	b
41725	06/83 Der	10/49 1725	-08/55	*08/55*	b
41726	06/83 Der	02/50 1726	-07/59	08/60	01/50⇨b
41727	06/83 Der	04/50 1727	-03/52	*52*	b
41734	10/84 Der	05/50 1734	-12/66	04/67	b
41739	11/84 Der	04/48 1739	-06/63	06/63	b
41745	12/84 Der	10/48 1745	-04/51	*51*	b
41747	12/84 Der	02/50 1747	-12/54	12/54	02/50⇨b
41748	12/84 Der	08/50 1748	-09/57	10/57	01/53⇨b
41749	12/84 Der	06/51 1749	-07/55	*55*	b
41752	12/84 Der	12/48 1752	-01/58	01/58	b
41753	12/84 Der	11/49 1753	-02/57	02/57	b
41754	12/84 Der	11/49 1754	-12/59	01/60	b
41756	01/85 Der	1756	-05/49	*49*	
41759	01/85 Der	1759	-01/48	*48*	b
41762	12/89 Der	1762	-09/48	*48*	
41763	12/89 Der	05/48 1763	-12/66	04/67	b
41767	03/90 Der	01/49 1767	-09/51	*09/51*	
41768	03/90 Der	1768	-12/49	01/50	
41769	03/90 Der	11/48 1769	-03/62	03/62	b
41770	04/90 Der	03/49 1770	-07/53	*07/53*	b
41773	04/90 Der	05/50 1773	-07/60	07/60	b
41777	06/90 Der	04/49 1777	-03/56	*56*	
41779	05/90 Der	06/50 1779	-07/57	08/57	
41780	07/90 Der	05/50 1780	-02/53	*03/53*	b
41781	07/90 Der	1781	-07/51	*51*	
41788	07/90 Der	1788	-04/49	*49*	b
41793	10/90 Der	12/48 1793	-10/51	*51*	
41794	10/90 Der	11/48 1794	-05/52	*05/52*	b
41795	10/90 Der	02/49 1795	-05/59	05/60	03/52⇨b
41797	10/90 Der	04/49 1797	-09/59	07/60	b
41803	12/90 Der	12/48 1803	-11/57	11/57	b
41804	12/90 Der	09/48 1804	-12/66	04/67	b
41805	09/91 Der	10/49 1805	-04/56	*56*	
41811	10/91 Der	10/51 1811	-09/54	09/54	b
41813	10/91 Der	08/49 1813	-05/54	*54*	b
41814	10/91 Der	05/50 1814	-03/56	*56*	b
41818	11/91 Der	1818	-06/48	*48*	b
41820	12/91 Der	03/50 1820	-08/52	*52*	b
41824	12/91 Der	05/49 1824	-02/51	02/51	
41826	07/92 VF	06/49 1826	-06/56	06/56	b
41829	09/92 VF	12/48 1829	-01/52	*52*	b
41833	10/92 VF	10/50 1833	-12/53	*54*	b
41835	10/92 VF	02/50 1835	-12/66	04/67	09/61⇨b
41838	10/92 VF	09/49 1838	-05/56	*56*	b
41839	11/92 VF	07/49 1839	-06/56	*56*	b
41842	11/92 VF	1842	-05/48	*48*	b
41844	12/92 VF	04/49 1844	-05/64	11/64	b
41846	03/95 Der	11/50 1846	-10/53	*53*	wb
41847	04/95 Der	12/49 1847	-03/60	04/60	wb
41852	06/95 Der	05/48 1852	-04/51	*51*	wb
41853	07/95 Der	05/48 1853	-10/54	*54*	w
41854	07/95 Der	07/48 1854	-04/51	*51*	w
41855	04/95 SS	03/50 1855	-05/60	06/60	wb
41856	04/95 SS	1856	-06/51	07/51	w
41857	04/95 SS	06/49 1857	-05/59	11/60	w 01/55⇨b
41859	05/95 SS	01/50 1859	-12/55	*12/55*	wb
41860	05/99 RS	05/50 1860	-03/57	03/57	wb
41865	06/99 RS	04/49 1865	-06/55	*55*	w
41869	07/99 RS	04/49 1869	-01/53	*53*	w
41870	07/99 RS	1870	-04/48	*48*	wb
41873	08/99 RS	08/48 1873	-01/50	*50*	w
41874	08/99 RS	1874	-02/49	*49*	w
41875	08/99 RS	06/49 1875	-07/63	07/63	wb
41878	09/99 RS	03/52 1878	-05/59	60	wb
41879	09/99 RS	06/49 1879	-03/60	05/60	wb
41885	10/99 RS	04/49 1885	-10/56	*10/56*	w
41889	11/99 RS	08/50 1889	-04/55	04/55	wb
41890	11/99 RS	04/49 1890	-03/52	*04/52*	wb
41893	12/99 RS	1893	-09/48	*48*	wb
41895	12/99 RS	1895	-03/50	03/50	wb

2P [4] 41900-41909
0-4-4T LMS Stanier

Power Classification: 2P
Introduced: 1932
Designer: Stanier
Company: LMS
Weight: 58t 1cwt
Driving Wheel: 5' 7"
Boiler Pressure: 160psi
Cylinders: Inside 18" x 26"
Tractive Effort: 17100lbf
Valve Gear: Stephenson (slide valves)

This was Stanier's first design when he came to the LMS in 1932 from Swindon. The ten engines (numbered 6400-6409 until 1946) were modernised and slightly enlarged versions of the '58030' class engines, which were fifty years old or more and in need of replacement.

When built they were fitted with stove-pipe chimneys. This was apparently due to an oversight by Stanier; the drawings showed stove-pipe chimneys as the design of chimney for future LMS engines had not been finalised. They were later fitted with Stanier chimneys.

The whole class was eventually push-pull fitted. 41901-41910 were withdrawn en-bloc in November 1959, leaving number 41900 in service until 1962.

m Fitted with vacuum control gear for working motor trains.

Year End Totals: '2P [4]' class

'47	'48	'49	'50	'51	'52	'53	'54	'55	'56	'57	'58	'59	'60	'61	'62	'63	'64	'65	'66	'67
10	10	10	10	10	10	10	10	10	10	10	10	1	1	1						

Number	*Built*	*Renumbered*	*BR Dates*	*Scrap*	*Notes*
41900	12/32 Der	10/49 1900	-03/62	04/62	09/50⇨m
41901	12/32 Der	12/48 1901	-11/59	06/60	02/51⇨m
41902	12/32 Der	06/48 1902	-11/59	04/62	09/50⇨m

Number	Built	Renumbered	BR Dates	Scrap	Notes
41903	12/32 Der	11/48 1903	-11/59	10/61 09/50⇨	m
41904	12/32 Der	05/48 1904	-11/59	10/61 09/50⇨	m
41905	12/32 Der	08/48 1905	-11/59	06/62 01/51⇨	m
41906	12/32 Der	07/49 1906	-11/59	06/62 03/57⇨	m
41907	12/32 Der	08/49 1907	-11/59	03/61 04/51⇨	m
41908	12/32 Der	05/49 1908	-11/59	03/61	m
41909	01/33 Der	08/48 1909	-11/59	04/62	m

2P [5] 41910-41926
4-4-2T LTSR Whitelegg 'Intermediate'

Power Classification: 2P
Introduced: 1900-1903
Designer: Whitelegg
Company: LTSR
Weight: 67t 15cwt
Driving Wheel: 6' 6"
Boiler Pressure: 170psi
Cylinders: Outside 19" x 26"
Tractive Effort: 17390lbf
Valve Gear: Stephenson (slide valves)

The London, Tilbury & Southend Railway made extensive use of the outside cylinder 4-4-2T type for its heavy outer suburban services. Three successive designs were produced by T Whitelegg until 1910, and his son R H Whitelegg thereafter. When the LTSR was taken over by the Midland Railway in 1912, the Derby imprint was placed on all the locomotives and they lost their names and distinctive green livery. However the 4-4-2Ts continued to work the line, and although the Midland Railway built no more engines, thirty-five further examples were constructed by the LMS in 1923-1930.

The first class to be built was the LTSR '1' class which consisted of forty-eight engines (numbered 1-48) being built between 1880 and 1898. Apart from twelve of these which were rebuilt (see the '41928' class below) they were all withdrawn by 1935.

This class was the second series, and they were known as the 'Intermediates' or '51' class. Eighteen engines were built in 1900. They were an enlarged version of the '1' class. One engine (2105 formerly named CHARING CROSS) was withdrawn in 1947, the rest coming into BR stock.

The original names of the engines were as follows: 41910 PURFLEET, 41911 WENNINGTON, 41912 STEPNEY GREEN, 41913 MILE END, 41914 BOW ROAD, 41915 HARRINGAY, 41916 CROUCH HILL, 41917 HORNSEY, 41918 HOLLOWAY, 41919 HIGHGATE, 41920 KENTISH TOWN, 41921 CAMDEN, 41922 MANSION HOUSE, 41923 VICTORIA, 41924 EARL'S COURT, 41925 WESTMINSTER and 41926 MARK LANE. The engines were originally numbered 51-68 on the LTSR, becoming 2158-2175 on the LMS and then renumbered 2092-2109 in 1930.

All the LTSR engines were fitted with Westinghouse brakes. Most of this class later acquired extended smokeboxes.

Year End Totals: '2P [5]' class

'47	'48	'49	'50	'51	'52	'53	'54	'55	'56	'57	'58	'59	'60	'61	'62	'63	'64	'65	'66	'67
17	16	10	9	3	2															

Number	Built	Renumbered	BR Dates	Scrap	Notes
41910	09/00 SS	2092	-09/48	*48*	
41911	09/00 SS	2093	-03/53	*53*	
41912	09/00 SS	2094	-08/49	09/49	
41913	10/00 SS	2095	-06/49	09/49	
41914	10/00 SS	2096	-05/50	06/50	
41915	10/00 SS	2097	-04/51	*04/51*	
41916	10/00 SS	2098	-03/51	*04/51*	
41917	10/00 SS	2099	-03/51	*04/51*	
41918	10/00 SS	2100	-12/49	01/50	
41919	10/00 SS	2101	-03/51	*04/51*	
41920	10/00 SS	2102	-06/49	*49*	
41921	10/00 SS	2103	-03/51	*04/51*	
41922	06/03 NB	05/49 2104	-03/53	*53*	
41923	06/03 NB	05/49 2106	-12/49	12/49	
41924	06/03 NB	2107	-12/49	12/49	
41925	06/03 NB	05/49 2108	-05/52	*05/52*	
41926	06/03 NB	2109	-03/51	*04/51*	

3P [2] 41928-41978, 80
4-4-2T LTSR Whitelegg

Power Classification: 3P
Introduced: 1909-1930
a 1897-1898, rebuilt 1905-1911
Designer: Whitelegg
Company: ab LTSR
c LMS
Weight: 71t 10cwt
a 70t 15cwt
Driving Wheel: 6' 6"
Boiler Pressure: 170psi
Cylinders: Outside 19" x 26"
Tractive Effort: 17390lbf
Valve Gear: Stephenson (slide valves)

In 1905-1911 the last twelve of the LTSR '1' class engines were rebuilt with much larger boilers and they became the basis of this class. (Apart from these twelve rebuilds all of the '1' class were withdrawn by 1935.) They were known as the 'Tilbury Tanks'.

These engines could be distinguished from the '41910' class by their rounded cabs. All the LTSR engines were fitted with Westinghouse brakes. All of this class later acquired extended smokeboxes.

a 41953-41964 were rebuilt from the '1' class in 1905-1911 and they were known as the '37' class. They were originally numbered 37-48 and their previous names were as follows: 41953 WOODGRANGE, 41954 WESTCLIFF, 41955 FOREST GATE, 41956 BENFLEET, 41957 LEYTONSTONE, 41958 EAST HORNDON, 41959 GREAT ILFORD, 41960 PRITTLEWELL, 41961 SHOEBURYNESS, 41962 SOUTHCHURCH, 41963 STRATFORD and 41964 LITTLE ILFORD. In 1912 they were renumbered 2146-2157 by the Midland Railway. In 1930 they were again renumbered 2135-2146.

b 41965-41968 were built new by the LTSR in 1909 and were known as the '79' class. They were originally numbered 79-82 and their previous names were as follows: 41965 RIPPLESIDE, 41966 THUNDERSLEY, 41967 AVELEY and 41968 CROWSTONE. In 1912 they were renumbered 2176-2179 by the Midland Railway. In 1930 they were again renumbered to 2147-2150. 41966 was restored to its LTSR livery as 80 THUNDERSLEY in 1956.

c The remainder of the class were built new by the LMS to the original design between 1923 and 1930.

Year End Totals: '3P [2]' class

'47	'48	'49	'50	'51	'52	'53	'54	'55	'56	'57	'58	'59	'60	'61	'62	'63	'64	'65	'66	'67
51	51	51	51	32	28	28	28	23	14	14	13	3								

Number	Built	Renumbered	BR Dates	Scrap	Notes
41928	05/23 Der	06/48 2110	-02/59	11/59	c
41929	06/23 Der	06/49 2111	-09/51	*51*	c
41930	06/23 Der	07/48 2112	-08/52	*52*	c
41931	07/23 Der	11/48 2113	-03/51	*51*	c
41932	07/23 Der	02/49 2114	-09/51	*09/51*	c
41933	07/23 Der	11/48 2115	-08/51	*08/51*	c
41934	07/23 Der	11/48 2116	-09/51	*09/51*	c
41935	08/23 Der	01/49 2117	-09/51	*51*	c
41936	08/23 Der	08/48 2118	-09/58	08/59	c
41937	08/23 Der	03/49 2119	-03/52	*04/52*	c
41938	08/25 NW	12/49 2120	-02/55	06/55	c
41939	08/25 NW	12/49 2121	-02/59	12/59	c
41940	08/25 NW	07/48 2122	-04/56	*56*	c
41941	08/25 NW	03/49 2123	-02/59	12/59	c
41942	08/25 NW	03/49 2124	-12/56	*12/56*	c
41943	05/27 Der	04/48 2125	-02/56	*56*	c
41944	05/27 Der	03/49 2126	-12/56	*57*	c
41945	06/27 Der	06/49 2127	-02/59	11/59	c
41946	06/27 Der	01/49 2128	-02/59	02/60	c
41947	06/27 Der	03/49 2129	-11/60	12/60	c
41948	06/27 Der	05/49 2130	-02/59	02/60	c
41949	06/27 Der	09/48 2131	-04/60	04/60	c
41950	07/27 Der	03/49 2132	-02/59	02/60	c
41951	07/27 Der	03/49 2133	-12/56	*57*	c
41952	07/27 Der	01/49 2134	-12/56	*57*	c
41953	03/97 SS	11/48 2135	-08/51	*09/51*	a
41954	04/97 SS	01/49 2136	-08/51	*08/51*	a
41955	04/97 SS	06/48 2137	-02/51	*02/51*	a
41956	04/97 SS	05/48 2138	-09/51	*10/51*	a
41957	04/97 SS	07/48 2139	-09/51	*10/51*	a
41958	04/97 SS	06/48 2140	-12/51	01/52	a
41959	12/98 D	10/48 2141	-09/51	*51*	a
41960	12/98 D	07/48 2142	-02/51	*02/51*	a
41961	12/98 D	08/48 2143	-10/52	*10/52*	a
41962	12/98 D	07/48 2144	-02/51	02/51	a
41963	01/99 D	12/48 2145	-02/51	03/51	a
41964	01/99 D	05/48 2146	-02/51	03/51	a
41965	05/09 RS	04/48 2147	-02/51	03/51	b
41966 §	05/09 RS	05/48 2148	-06/56 03/56➲80		b
41967	06/09 RS	04/48 2149	-11/52	*52*	b
41968	07/09 RS	05/48 2150	-02/51	*02/51*	b
41969	01/30 Der	04/48 2151	-04/60	04/60	c
41970	01/30 Der	04/48 2152	-12/56	*57*	c
41971	02/30 Der	05/48 2153	-02/55	02/55	c
41972	02/30 Der	05/48 2154	-02/55	02/55	c
41973	02/30 Der	05/48 2155	-02/55	02/55	c
41974	02/30 Der	05/48 2156	-02/55	02/55	c
41975	02/30 Der	06/48 2157	-11/59	02/60	c
41976	02/30 Der	05/48 2158	-12/56	*57*	c
41977	03/30 Der	04/48 2159	-02/59	02/60	c
41978	03/30 Der	05/48 2160	-02/59	02/60	c

Class continued with 80 (Preserved Locomotives)

3F [1] 41980-41993
0-6-2T LTSR Whitelegg

Power Classification: 3F
Introduced: 1903-1912
Designer: Whitelegg
Company: LTSR
Weight: 64t 13cwt
Driving Wheel: 5' 3"
Boiler Pressure: 170psi
Cylinders: Inside 18" x 26"
Tractive Effort: 19320lbf
Valve Gear: Stephenson (slide valves)

Thomas Whitelegg designed these 0-6-2T engines for freight working on the London, Tilbury & Southend Railway. They were known as the 'Corringham' or the '69' class.

The first six were built by the North British Locomotive Company in 1903, followed by four more in 1908. These were numbered 69-78. Their former names were as follows: 41980 CORRINGHAM, 41981 BASILDON, 41982 WAKERING, 41983 HADLEIGH, 41984 CRANHAM, 41985 ORSETT, 41986 CANVEY ISLAND, 41987 DUNTON, 41988 FOBBING and 41989 DAGENHAM DOCK.

The last four engines were built by Beyer Peacock in 1912. They were delivered after the London, Tilbury & Southend Railway was taken over by the Midland Railway and they were numbered 2190-2193 with no names. At the same time the other engines were renumbered 2180-2189 and they had their names removed.

The whole class was renumbered 2220-2233 by the LMS, but they later reverted to their former Midland numbers (2180-2193) in 1939. They were renumbered again in 1947 to 1980-1993, finally becoming 41980-41993 after 1948.

These engines were the last surviving LTSR engines on British Railways.

Year End Totals: '3F [1]' class

'47	'48	'49	'50	'51	'52	'53	'54	'55	'56	'57	'58	'59	'60	'61	'62	'63	'64	'65	'66	'67
14	14	14	14	14	14	14	14	14	14	14	11	1	1	1						

Number	Built	Renumbered	BR Dates	Scrap	Notes
41980	06/03 NB	04/49 1980	-05/58	05/58	
41981	06/03 NB	05/48 1981	-06/62	09/62	
41982	06/03 NB	02/49 1982	-02/59	02/60	
41983	06/03 NB	07/48 1983	-02/59	02/60	
41984	07/03 NB	02/49 1984	-02/59	02/60	
41985	07/03 NB	04/48 1985	-02/59	02/60	
41986	08/08 NB	05/48 1986	-02/59	02/60	
41987	08/08 NB	09/50 1987	-02/59	02/60	
41988	08/08 NB	10/48 1988	-04/58	05/58	
41989	09/08 NB	03/49 1989	-04/58	04/58	
41990	11/12 BP	02/51 1990	-02/59	02/60	
41991	11/12 BP	10/48 1991	-02/59	02/60	
41992	11/12 BP	02/51 1992	-02/59	02/60	
41993	11/12 BP	07/48 1993	-02/59	02/60	

4MT [1] 42050-42299, 42673-42699
2-6-4T LMS Fairburn

Power Classification: 4P reclassified 4MT in 1948
Introduced: 1945-1951
Designer: Fairburn
Company: LMS
Weight: 85t 5cwt
Driving Wheel: 5' 9"
Boiler Pressure: 200psi superheated
Cylinders: Outside 19⅝" x 26"

LMS Fowler 'Compound' 4-4-0 No 41146 at Ardrossan in July 1954.

LMS Ivatt '2MT' 2-6-2T No 41310 in September 1952.

Midland Railway Johnson '0F' 0-4-0ST No 41518 at Toton in August 1956.

Midland Railway Deeley '0F' 0-4-0T No 41537 inside Gloucester shed in April 1954.

Tractive Effort:	24670lbf
Valve Gear:	Walschaert (piston valves)

Refer to the Historical Survey of LMS 2-6-4T Engines at the end of this section for more details of this class.

This class was developed from Stanier's classes by Fairburn. They had a shorter wheelbase and other minor modifications. They could be distinguished from Stanier's engines by the gap in the running plate ahead of the cylinders.

The class continued to be built by BR until June 1951, the last few batches of engines (42066-42106) being built at Brighton. The class could be seen spread over all the BR regions.

Year End Totals: '4MT [1]' class

'47	'48	'49	'50	'51	'52	'53	'54	'55	'56	'57	'58	'59	'60	'61	'62	'63	'64	'65	'66	'67
130	176	206	260	277	277	277	277	277	277	277	277	277	277	277	274	231	201	144	90	42

Number	*Built*	*Renumbered*	*BR Dates*	*Scrap*	*Notes*
42050	09/50 Der		09/50-04/65	09/65	
42051	09/50 Der		09/50-07/65	12/65	
42052	09/50 Der		09/50-05/67	10/67	
42053	10/50 Der		10/50-06/65	10/65	
42054	10/50 Der		10/50-07/64	07/64	
42055	10/50 Der		10/50-07/67	11/67	
42056	11/50 Der		11/50-10/64	01/65	
42057	11/50 Der		11/50-07/64	11/64	
42058	11/50 Der		11/50-08/66	12/66	
42059	11/50 Der		11/50-06/64	09/64	
42060	12/50 Der		12/50-04/65	07/65	
42061	12/50 Der		12/50-09/65	12/65	
42062	12/50 Der		12/50-05/65	09/65	
42063	12/50 Der		12/50-10/63	12/63	
42064	12/50 Der		12/50-06/65	10/65	
42065	12/50 Der		12/50-07/65	01/66	
42066	10/50 Bton		10/50-09/67	02/68	
42067	10/50 Bton		10/50-02/63	06/63	
42068	10/50 Bton		10/50-12/63	01/64	
42069	10/50 Bton		10/50-11/66	06/67	
42070	11/50 Bton		11/50-07/65	09/65	
42071	11/50 Bton		11/50-03/67	09/67	
42072	11/50 Bton		11/50-10/67	03/68	
42073 §	11/50 Bton		11/50-10/67		
42074	11/50 Bton		11/50-09/66	12/66	
42075	11/50 Bton		11/50-05/65	09/65	
42076	12/50 Bton		12/50-03/67	11/67	
42077	12/50 Bton		12/50-06/64	04/65	
42078	12/50 Bton		12/50-06/66	09/66	
42079	01/51 Bton		01/51-05/67	10/67	
42080	01/51 Bton		01/51-01/67	05/67	
42081	01/51 Bton		01/51-05/67	11/67	
42082	01/51 Bton		01/51-06/65	09/65	
42083	02/51 Bton		02/51-10/67	11/67	
42084	02/51 Bton		02/51-12/64	07/65	
42085 §	02/51 Bton		02/51-10/67		
42086	03/51 Bton		03/51-04/67	10/67	
42087	03/51 Bton		03/51-10/66	01/67	
42088	03/51 Bton		03/51-10/62	11/62	
42089	04/51 Bton		04/51-10/64	11/64	
42090	04/51 Bton		04/51-06/64	08/64	
42091	04/51 Bton		04/51-10/63	10/63	
42092	05/51 Bton		05/51-08/64	09/64	
42093	05/51 Bton		05/51-10/67	04/68	
42094	05/51 Bton		05/51-10/62	09/63	
42095	06/51 Bton		06/51-06/66	08/66	
42096	07/50 Bton		07/50-12/66	05/67	
42097	07/50 Bton		07/50-12/62	02/63	
42098	07/50 Bton		07/50-02/63	06/63	
42099	08/50 Bton		08/50-12/64	01/65	
42100	08/50 Bton		08/50-03/63	06/63	
42101	09/50 Bton		09/50-02/63	03/63	
42102	09/50 Bton		09/50-12/66	06/67	
42103	09/50 Bton		09/50-05/65	10/65	
42104	09/50 Bton		09/50-09/65	01/66	
42105	09/50 Bton		09/50-12/66	04/67	
42106	10/50 Bton		10/50-05/65	10/65	
42107	03/49 Der		03/49-03/66	06/66	
42108	03/49 Der		03/49-12/66	03/67	
42109	04/49 Der		04/49-07/65	09/65	
42110	05/49 Der		05/49-06/66	10/66	
42111	06/49 Der		06/49-12/62	05/63	
42112	06/49 Der		06/49-07/65	12/65	
42113	06/49 Der		06/49-07/65	12/65	
42114	06/49 Der		06/49-06/65	10/65	
42115	07/49 Der		07/49-11/66	05/67	
42116	07/49 Der		07/49-06/67	03/68	
42117	08/49 Der		08/49-12/62	06/63	
42118	08/49 Der		08/49-09/65	12/65	
42119	08/49 Der		08/49-08/65	02/66	
42120	08/49 Der		08/49-10/63	12/63	
42121	09/49 Der		09/49-07/66	10/66	
42122	09/49 Der		09/49-11/62	09/63	
42123	10/49 Der		10/49-02/64	02/64	
42124	10/49 Der		10/49-01/64	02/64	
42125	10/49 Der		10/49-12/66	04/67	
42126	11/49 Der		11/49-10/64	02/65	
42127	11/49 Der		11/49-10/64	01/65	
42128	11/49 Der		11/49-11/66	02/67	
42129	12/49 Der		12/49-09/65	01/66	
42130	12/49 Der		12/49-12/62	11/63	
42131	12/49 Der		12/49-08/65	10/65	
42132	12/49 Der		12/49-06/66	09/66	
42133	01/50 Der		01/50-04/67	10/67	
42134	01/50 Der		01/50-04/67	12/67	
42135	01/50 Der		01/50-02/64	06/64	
42136	02/50 Der		02/50-01/63	03/63	
42137	02/50 Der		02/50-01/64	03/64	
42138	03/50 Der		03/50-09/67	05/68	
42139	03/50 Der		03/50-12/65	03/66	
42140	04/50 Der		04/50-07/63	07/63	
42141	04/50 Der		04/50-10/67	02/68	
42142	05/50 Der		05/50-06/66	10/66	
42143	05/50 Der		05/50-10/64	01/65	
42144	06/50 Der		06/50-12/62	03/64	
42145	06/50 Der		06/50-09/67	02/68	
42146	08/50 Der		08/50-10/62	12/62	
42147	04/48 Der		04/48-05/65	08/65	
42148	05/48 Der		05/48-12/64	04/68	
42149	05/48 Der		05/48-07/67	11/67	
42150	05/48 Der		05/48-12/66	03/67	
42151	05/48 Der		05/48-09/63	09/63	
42152	05/48 Der		05/48-10/67	03/68	
42153	06/48 Der		06/48-08/64	01/65	
42154	06/48 Der		06/48-01/67	06/67	
42155	06/48 Der		06/48-05/65	08/65	
42156	06/48 Der		06/48-02/66	05/66	
42157	06/48 Der		06/48-07/63	11/63	
42158	07/48 Der		07/48-04/65	08/65	
42159	07/48 Der		07/48-07/66	10/66	
42160	07/48 Der		07/48-05/65	08/65	
42161	08/48 Der		08/48-12/66	03/67	
42162	08/48 Der		08/48-12/62	09/63	
42163	08/48 Der		08/48-06/64	09/64	
42164	08/48 Der		08/48-12/62	12/63	
42165	09/48 Der		09/48-02/65	06/66	
42166	09/48 Der		09/48-10/63	03/64	
42167	09/48 Der		09/48-06/64	09/64	
42168	09/48 Der		09/48-03/64	07/64	
42169	09/48 Der		09/48-02/66	*66*	
42170	10/48 Der		10/48-10/65	02/66	
42171	10/48 Der		10/48-06/64	09/64	
42172	10/48 Der		10/48-12/62	09/63	
42173	10/48 Der		10/48-12/62	09/63	
42174	10/48 Der		10/48-08/65	07/66	
42175	11/48 Der		11/48-12/62	03/64	
42176	11/48 Der		11/48-06/66	09/66	
42177	11/48 Der		11/48-12/66	03/67	
42178	11/48 Der		11/48-07/63	09/63	
42179	12/48 Der		12/48-03/65	11/66	
42180	12/48 Der		12/48-11/63	02/64	
42181	12/48 Der		12/48-10/66	04/67	
42182	12/48 Der		12/48-04/63	05/63	
42183	01/49 Der		01/49-09/66	02/67	
42184	01/49 Der		01/49-12/66	04/67	
42185	02/49 Der		02/49-05/64	06/64	
42186	02/49 Der		02/49-06/64	09/64	
42187	12/47 Der	06/50 2187	-05/67	09/67	
42188	12/47 Der	04/50 2188	-05/63	06/63	
42189	12/47 Der	11/50 2189	-09/67	05/68	
42190	01/48 Der	05/50 2190	01/48-06/64	09/64	
42191	01/48 Der	01/50 2191	01/48-12/62	09/63	
42192	01/48 Der	02/50 2192	01/48-05/64	09/64	
42193	01/48 Der	09/50 2193	01/48-12/62	09/63	
42194	02/48 Der	03/50 2194	02/48-08/65	10/65	
42195	02/48 Der	11/49 2195	02/48-04/66	09/66	
42196	02/48 Der	*50* 2196	02/48-05/67	10/67	
42197	03/48 Der	09/49 2197	03/48-05/66	09/66	
42198	03/48 Der	04/48 2198	03/48-05/65	07/65	
42199	03/48 Der	04/48 2199	03/48-09/65	01/66	
42200	10/45 Der	06/50 2200	-06/64	09/64	
42201	11/45 Der	04/48 2201	-07/64	11/64	
42202	11/45 Der	10/50 2202	-05/65	07/65	
42203	11/45 Der	07/48 2203	-12/62	09/63	
42204	11/45 Der	07/48 2204	-12/66	04/67	
42205	11/45 Der	10/48 2205	-12/62	11/63	
42206	11/45 Der	03/48 2206	-04/63	05/63	
42207	11/45 Der	03/50 2207	-12/62	12/62	
42208	12/45 Der	04/48 2208	-07/64	11/64	
42209	12/45 Der	11/48 2209	-02/65	10/65	
42210	12/45 Der	05/49 2210	-05/67	12/67	
42211	12/45 Der	01/49 2211	-12/62	06/63	
42212	12/45 Der	12/48 2212	-08/65	12/65	
42213	12/45 Der	05/48 2213	-01/66	04/66	
42214	12/45 Der	04/48 2214	-02/65	05/65	
42215	12/45 Der	07/48 2215	-12/62	11/63	
42216	12/45 Der	01/49 2216	-07/66	12/66	
42217	12/45 Der	03/49 2217	-10/61	12/61	
42218	01/46 Der	05/49 2218	-10/64	11/64	
42219	01/46 Der	04/49 2219	-06/62	10/62	
42220	02/46 Der	10/48 2220	-12/61	01/62	
42221	02/46 Der	04/48 2221	-10/64	11/64	
42222	03/46 Der	06/49 2222	-05/65	10/65	
42223	04/46 Der	11/49 2223	-06/62	09/62	
42224	04/46 Der	04/48 2224	-01/67	09/67	
42225	04/46 Der	04/48 2225	-06/66	10/66	
42226	05/46 Der	03/49 2226	-06/64	09/64	
42227	05/46 Der	09/48 2227	-10/62	03/63	
42228	05/46 Der	12/48 2228	-10/63	10/63	
42229	05/46 Der	05/48 2229	-01/64	02/64	
42230	06/46 Der	08/48 2230	-08/65	04/66	
42231	06/46 Der	09/48 2231	-07/63	09/63	
42232	06/46 Der	11/48 2232	-01/66	05/66	
42233	06/46 Der	10/48 2233	-05/67	10/67	
42234	07/46 Der	02/49 2234	-02/64	11/64	
42235	07/46 Der	09/48 2235	-07/67	03/68	
42236	07/46 Der	02/49 2236	-05/67	10/67	
42237	08/46 Der	08/48 2237	-12/62	01/63	
42238	08/46 Der	12/48 2238	-10/63	10/63	
42239	09/46 Der	03/49 2239	-06/64	08/64	
42240	09/46 Der	12/48 2240	-04/66	07/66	
42241	09/46 Der	05/49 2241	-11/65	02/66	
42242	09/46 Der	07/49 2242	-07/64	11/64	
42243	09/46 Der	10/48 2243	-08/65	11/65	
42244	09/46 Der	02/49 2244	-06/64	09/64	
42245	10/46 Der	06/49 2245	-10/64	12/64	
42246	10/46 Der	08/49 2246	-06/64	09/64	
42247	10/46 Der	04/49 2247	-08/65	07/66	
42248	10/46 Der	05/48 2248	-12/62	02/63	
42249	10/46 Der	05/48 2249	-07/66	11/66	
42250	10/46 Der	05/48 2250	-12/64	04/65	
42251	10/46 Der	07/48 2251	-10/67	04/68	
42252	11/46 Der	04/48 2252	-10/67	04/68	
42253	11/46 Der	07/48 2253	-07/63	08/63	
42254	11/46 Der	05/48 2254	-06/62	10/62	
42255	11/46 Der	06/48 2255	-06/62	10/62	
42256	11/46 Der	08/48 2256	-06/64	10/64	
42257	11/46 Der	09/48 2257	-06/62	10/62	
42258	11/46 Der	09/49 2258	-12/62	09/63	
42259	12/46 Der	10/49 2259	-10/65	02/66	
42260	12/46 Der	07/48 2260	-05/66	09/66	
42261	12/46 Der	06/49 2261	-02/64	02/64	
42262	12/46 Der	12/48 2262	-10/64	12/64	
42263	12/46 Der	03/49 2263	-07/64	11/64	
42264	12/46 Der	02/50 2264	-07/66	10/66	
42265	01/47 Der	06/49 2265	-10/65	03/66	
42266	01/47 Der	04/49 2266	-03/66	06/66	
42267	01/47 Der	12/48 2267	-05/67	04/68	
42268	01/47 Der	06/49 2268	-12/62	03/64	
42269	02/47 Der	04/49 2269	-07/67	01/68	
42270	02/47 Der	06/49 2270	-01/63	04/63	
42271	02/47 Der	03/49 2271	-12/66	03/67	
42272	03/47 Der	02/49 2272	-12/62	09/63	
42273	05/47 Der	06/49 2273	-09/66	01/67	
42274	06/47 Der	09/49 2274	-05/67	09/67	
42275	06/47 Der	03/49 2275	-06/64	09/64	
42276	07/47 Der	08/50 2276	-12/62	03/64	
42277	07/47 Der	10/49 2277	-08/66	12/66	
42278	07/47 Der	06/50 2278	-05/64	06/64	
42279	08/47 Der	05/49 2279	-07/63	10/63	
42280	08/47 Der	06/50 2280	-03/64	04/65	
42281	08/47 Der	05/49 2281	-05/63	07/63	
42282	08/47 Der	05/50 2282	-09/64	11/64	
42283	09/47 Der	04/50 2283	-09/67	02/68	
42284	09/47 Der	06/50 2284	-12/64	07/65	
42285	09/47 Der	09/50 2285	-09/65	10/65	
42286	09/47 Der	05/50 2286	-12/64	08/65	
42287	10/47 Der	01/50 2287	-07/67	01/68	
42288	10/47 Der	07/50 2288	-10/63	11/63	
42289	10/47 Der	07/50 2289	-05/65	10/65	
42290	10/47 Der	09/50 2290	-12/62	06/63	
42291	10/47 Der	08/50 2291	-12/64	07/65	
42292	11/47 Der	03/50 2292	-05/64	07/64	
42293	11/47 Der	04/50 2293	-04/63	06/63	
42294	11/47 Der	04/50 2294	-05/63	06/63	
42295	11/47 Der	10/49 2295	-10/65	01/66	
42296	11/47 Der	09/50 2296	-07/65	11/65	
42297	12/47 Der	02/51 2297	-05/67	09/67	
42298	12/47 Der	08/50 2298	-11/62	02/63	
42299	12/47 Der	01/51 2299	-03/65	07/65	

Class continued with 42673

4MT [2] 42300-42424
2-6-4T LMS Fowler

Power Classification:	4P reclassified 4MT in 1948
Introduced:	1927-1934
Designer:	Fowler
Company:	LMS
Weight:	86t 5cwt
Driving Wheel:	5' 9"
Boiler Pressure:	200psi superheated
Cylinders:	Outside 19" x 26"
Tractive Effort:	23125lbf
Valve Gear:	Walschaert (piston valves)

Refer to the Historical Survey of LMS 2-6-4T Engines at the end of this section for more details of this class.

This was Fowler's original class of 1927. They could be distinguished from the other classes as they were fitted with parallel boilers, while all the others had taper boilers. They also had straight tops to the tanks.

The class was originally built with inside steam pipes, but most of them later received new cylinders with outside steam pipes.

42313 was originally named THE PRINCE, but the name was removed in 1933.

c 42395 onwards (introduced 1933) were fitted with side windows to the cabs.

Year End Totals: '4MT [2]' class

'47	'48	'49	'50	'51	'52	'53	'54	'55	'56	'57	'58	'59	'60	'61	'62	'63	'64	'65	'66	'67
125	125	125	125	125	125	125	125	125	125	125	125	120	109	87	50	34	14	2		

Number	Built	Renumbered	BR Dates	Scrap	Notes
42300	11/27 Der	06/48 2300	-11/60	04/61	
42301	12/27 Der	11/48 2301	-10/63	03/64	
42302	12/27 Der	07/48 2302	-10/61	04/63	
42303	12/27 Der	10/48 2303	-10/62	11/63	
42304	01/28 Der	12/48 2304	-08/62	05/63	
42305	01/28 Der	05/48 2305	-09/62	09/62	
42306	01/28 Der	02/50 2306	-12/62	02/63	
42307	01/28 Der	10/48 2307	-08/61	10/61	
42308	01/28 Der	11/49 2308	-08/59	01/60	
42309	02/28 Der	07/49 2309	-09/64	01/65	
42310	02/28 Der	02/49 2310	-03/63	01/64	
42311	02/28 Der	04/48 2311	-04/64	07/64	
42312	02/28 Der	10/48 2312	-12/59	03/60	
42313	03/28 Der	11/49 2313	-11/63	02/64	
42314	03/28 Der	04/48 2314	-12/62	02/63	
42315	03/28 Der	10/48 2315	-12/62	07/63	
42316	03/28 Der	11/48 2316	-02/63	08/63	
42317	03/28 Der	01/49 2317	-09/65	11/65	
42318	04/28 Der	11/48 2318	-08/62	04/63	
42319	04/28 Der	06/49 2319	-10/63	11/63	
42320	04/28 Der	05/48 2320	-11/62	06/63	
42321	05/28 Der	09/49 2321	-11/59	08/60	
42322	05/28 Der	05/48 2322	-07/65	12/65	
42323	06/28 Der	08/49 2323	-06/62	04/63	
42324	06/28 Der	10/48 2324	-10/62	09/63	
42325	01/29 Der	05/49 2325	-10/61	04/62	
42326	02/29 Der	10/48 2326	-07/60	08/60	
42327	02/29 Der	01/49 2327	-08/65	11/65	
42328	02/29 Der	09/48 2328	-09/61	02/62	
42329	02/29 Der	12/48 2329	-10/61	04/63	
42330	02/29 Der	06/49 2330	-12/61	02/62	
42331	03/29 Der	06/48 2331	-08/62	05/63	
42332	03/29 Der	04/49 2332	-10/61	08/62	
42333	03/29 Der	02/49 2333	-05/63	05/63	
42334	03/29 Der	09/48 2334	-12/65	04/66	
42335	03/29 Der	10/48 2335	-05/64	06/64	
42336	04/29 Der	11/49 2336	-10/62	06/63	
42337	03/29 Der	01/49 2337	-12/63	02/64	
42338	04/29 Der	01/49 2338	-01/64	03/64	
42339	04/29 Der	07/48 2339	-10/63	12/63	
42340	04/29 Der	10/48 2340	-06/62	04/63	
42341	04/29 Der	01/50 2341	-10/59	10/60	
42342	04/29 Der	02/49 2342	-06/62	07/62	
42343	04/29 Der	01/49 2343	-10/65	01/66	
42344	05/29 Der	04/48 2344	-06/61	09/61	
42345	05/29 Der	09/48 2345	-05/60	11/60	
42346	05/29 Der	07/48 2346	-09/60	09/60	
42347	05/29 Der	07/48 2347	-09/62	04/63	
42348	05/29 Der	03/49 2348	-10/61	12/61	
42349	06/29 Der	12/48 2349	-08/61	12/61	
42350	06/29 Der	10/48 2350	-02/65	05/65	
42351	06/29 Der	02/49 2351	-08/62	05/63	
42352	06/29 Der	12/48 2352	-05/62	08/62	
42353	06/29 Der	06/49 2353	-06/64	09/64	
42354	06/29 Der	11/49 2354	-11/59	60	
42355	06/29 Der	08/49 2355	-11/63	12/63	
42356	07/29 Der	09/49 2356	-10/61	03/62	
42357	07/29 Der	02/49 2357	-03/63	08/63	
42358	07/29 Der	06/48 2358	-10/62	12/62	
42359	07/29 Der	01/50 2359	-10/64	03/65	
42360	07/29 Der	08/48 2360	-09/61	10/61	
42361	07/29 Der	09/49 2361	-02/64	03/64	
42362	08/29 Der	04/49 2362	-06/62	04/63	
42363	08/29 Der	05/48 2363	-12/61	04/62	
42364	08/29 Der	09/48 2364	-10/61	03/63	
42365	08/29 Der	02/50 2365	-09/60	11/60	
42366	08/29 Der	05/50 2366	-04/64	06/64	
42367	09/29 Der	03/50 2367	-08/62	09/62	
42368	09/29 Der	11/49 2368	-06/65	11/65	
42369	09/29 Der	05/49 2369	-05/65	08/65	
42370	09/29 Der	05/48 2370	-06/62	05/63	
42371	09/29 Der	10/48 2371	-05/62	07/62	
42372	09/29 Der	11/49 2372	-12/62	09/63	
42373	10/29 Der	05/49 2373	-11/60	02/61	
42374	10/29 Der	08/48 2374	-09/65	01/66	
42375	05/32 Der	02/49 2375	-02/62	04/62	
42376	05/32 Der	04/49 2376	-11/62	01/63	
42377	05/32 Der	03/49 2377	-05/61	08/61	
42378	06/32 Der	10/49 2378	-04/64	08/64	
42379	06/32 Der	09/49 2379	-08/64	12/64	
42380	06/32 Der	01/50 2380	-12/60	12/60	
42381	06/32 Der	09/48 2381	-05/65	10/65	
42382	07/32 Der	03/49 2382	-10/61	12/61	
42383	07/32 Der	04/48 2383	-10/61	03/63	
42384	07/32 Der	05/48 2384	-08/63	12/63	
42385	05/33 Der	08/49 2385	-08/62	09/62	
42386	05/33 Der	05/48 2386	-10/61	11/62	
42387	05/33 Der	06/49 2387	-04/62	04/62	
42388	05/33 Der	11/48 2388	-10/62	12/62	
42389	06/33 Der	08/48 2389	-03/63	07/63	
42390	06/33 Der	02/49 2390	-09/60	11/60	
42391	06/33 Der	05/49 2391	-03/63	04/63	
42392	06/33 Der	05/48 2392	-02/63	03/63	
42393	06/33 Der	02/49 2393	-06/62	06/62	
42394	06/33 Der	06/49 2394	-06/66	10/66	
42395	09/33 Der	09/48 2395	-11/61	04/62	c
42396	09/33 Der	06/49 2396	-07/62	09/62	c
42397	09/33 Der	09/48 2397	-01/61	02/61	c
42398	09/33 Der	11/48 2398	-11/60	01/61	c
42399	09/33 Der	12/48 2399	-09/60	11/60	c
42400	09/33 Der	10/48 2400	-01/65	04/65	c
42401	09/33 Der	10/49 2401	-07/63	04/64	c
42402	09/33 Der	01/49 2402	-10/62	04/63	c
42403	09/33 Der	03/49 2403	-12/62	07/63	c
42404	09/33 Der	09/48 2404	-10/61	02/62	c
42405	10/33 Der	07/48 2405	-10/64	01/65	c
42406	10/33 Der	12/48 2406	-09/65	11/65	c
42407	10/33 Der	04/50 2407	-10/62	03/64	c
42408	10/33 Der	12/49 2408	-04/64	07/64	c
42409	10/33 Der	06/49 2409	-01/64	02/64	c
42410	10/33 Der	09/48 2410	-09/66	12/66	c
42411	10/33 Der	10/49 2411	-08/64	11/64	c
42412	11/33 Der	08/48 2412	-01/62	01/62	c
42413	11/33 Der	02/49 2413	-06/64	10/64	c
42414	11/33 Der	09/48 2414	-10/64	04/65	c
42415	11/33 Der	04/48 2415	-12/62	07/63	c
42416	11/33 Der	07/48 2416	-06/64	09/64	c
42417	11/33 Der	05/48 2417	-04/64	05/64	c
42418	11/33 Der	03/48 2418	-04/60	04/60	c
42419	12/33 Der	09/48 2419	-11/63	08/64	c
42420	12/33 Der	05/49 2420	-05/62	05/62	c
42421	12/33 Der	08/48 2421	-09/64	10/64	c
42422	12/33 Der	12/48 2422	-12/62	03/63	c
42423	12/33 Der	03/49 2423	-10/61	09/62	c
42424	01/34 Der	10/49 2424	-09/64	04/65	c

4MT [3] 42425-42494, 42537-42672
2-6-4T LMS Stanier 2-Cylinder

Power Classification:	4P reclassified 4MT in 1948
Introduced:	1935-1943
Designer:	Stanier
Company:	LMS
Weight:	87t 17cwt
Driving Wheel:	5' 9"
Boiler Pressure:	200psi superheated
Cylinders:	Outside 19⅝" x 26"
Tractive Effort:	24670lbf
Valve Gear:	Walschaert (piston valves)

Refer to the Historical Survey of LMS 2-6-4T Engines at the end of this section for more details of this class.

This class was Stanier's development of Fowler's engines. They were fitted with taper boilers and had sloping tops to the tanks and slightly larger cylinders.

Year End Totals: '4MT [3]' class

'47	'48	'49	'50	'51	'52	'53	'54	'55	'56	'57	'58	'59	'60	'61	'62	'63	'64	'65	'66	'67
206	206	206	206	206	206	206	206	206	206	206	206	206	204	187	144	115	64	26	15	

Number	Built	Renumbered	BR Dates	Scrap	Notes
42425	02/36 Der	04/48 2425	-09/63	07/64	
42426	02/36 Der	10/49 2426	-12/65	03/66	
42427	02/36 Der	03/49 2427	-10/61	09/62	
42428	02/36 Der	02/49 2428	-10/61	08/62	
42429	02/36 Der	11/48 2429	-10/62	05/63	
42430	03/36 Der	03/49 2430	-03/65	06/65	
42431	03/36 Der	05/48 2431	-05/66	08/66	
42432	03/36 Der	03/49 2432	-08/65	02/66	
42433	03/36 Der	11/49 2433	-05/62	08/62	
42434	03/36 Der	05/48 2434	-04/64	05/64	
42435	03/36 Der	09/48 2435	-04/65	08/65	
42436	04/36 Der	09/48 2436	-06/66	07/67	
42437	04/36 Der	06/48 2437	-06/64	12/64	
42438	04/36 Der	01/49 2438	-02/61	03/61	
42439	04/36 Der	05/48 2439	-08/65	06/68	
42440	05/36 Der	05/49 2440	-10/63	05/64	
42441	05/36 Der	10/48 2441	-01/64	01/64	
42442	05/36 Der	12/49 2442	-08/65	11/65	
42443	05/36 Der	12/48 2443	-11/62	12/62	
42444	05/36 Der	03/49 2444	-05/64	06/64	
42445	05/36 Der	11/48 2445	-10/64	03/65	
42446	06/36 Der	02/49 2446	-05/64	12/64	
42447	06/36 Der	02/50 2447	-03/65	05/65	
42448	06/36 Der	08/48 2448	-01/62	04/62	
42449	06/36 Der	03/49 2449	-11/64	12/64	
42450	07/36 Der	08/48 2450	-06/60	06/60	
42451	07/36 Der	01/49 2451	-10/64	02/65	
42452	07/36 Der	03/49 2452	-03/62	03/62	
42453	08/36 Der	02/49 2453	-05/64	09/64	
42454	08/36 Der	03/49 2454	-12/62	01/63	
42455	08/36 Der	05/48 2455	-04/66	07/66	
42456	08/36 Der	09/48 2456	-04/65	10/65	
42457	08/36 Der	11/49 2457	-11/62	07/63	
42458	09/36 Der	05/48 2458	-10/63	05/64	
42459	09/36 Der	12/48 2459	-01/65	06/65	
42460	09/36 Der	04/48 2460	-08/65	11/65	
42461	09/36 Der	01/49 2461	-04/64	05/64	
42462	10/36 Der	07/48 2462	-05/66	08/66	
42463	10/36 Der	07/48 2463	-01/64	02/64	
42464	10/36 Der	11/48 2464	-08/65	11/65	
42465	10/36 Der	11/48 2465	-02/65	06/65	
42466	10/36 Der	06/49 2466	-01/63	05/63	
42467	11/36 Der	10/48 2467	-10/61	12/61	
42468	11/36 Der	01/50 2468	-09/65	02/66	
42469	11/36 Der	08/49 2469	-05/63	06/63	
42470	11/36 Der	05/49 2470	-10/62	02/63	
42471	12/36 Der	08/48 2471	-10/61	01/62	
42472	12/36 Der	10/48 2472	-10/62	10/63	
42473	12/36 Der	03/49 2473	-10/62	10/63	
42474	12/36 Der	02/49 2474	-10/64	02/65	
42475	12/36 Der	11/48 2475	-10/61	03/62	
42476	01/37 Der	06/48 2476	-10/62	05/63	
42477	01/37 Der	01/49 2477	-07/65	09/65	
42478	01/37 Der	07/48 2478	-02/65	06/65	
42479	01/37 Der	05/48 2479	-10/61	10/62	
42480	02/37 Der	04/49 2480	-01/63	05/63	
42481	02/37 Der	03/49 2481	-09/64	04/65	
42482	02/37 Der	01/49 2482	-04/65	09/65	
42483	02/37 Der	06/49 2483	-10/62	05/63	
42484	03/37 Der	06/48 2484	-01/66	05/66	
42485	03/37 Der	06/49 2485	-06/63	06/63	
42486	03/37 Der	12/48 2486	-09/63	10/63	
42487	03/37 Der	06/48 2487	-09/63	10/63	
42488	04/37 Der	07/49 2488	-02/65	05/65	
42489	04/37 Der	11/48 2489	-11/64	12/64	
42490	04/37 Der	05/49 2490	-05/60	06/60	
42491	04/37 Der	10/49 2491	-10/63	03/64	
42492	05/37 Der	05/49 2492	-06/65	10/65	
42493	05/37 Der	06/49 2493	-05/64	06/64	
42494	05/37 Der	11/49 2494	-05/65	08/65	

Class continued with 42537

4MT [4] 42500-42536
2-6-4T LMS Stanier 3-Cylinder

Power Classification:	4P reclassified 4MT in 1948
Introduced:	1934
Designer:	Stanier
Company:	LMS
Weight:	92t 5cwt
Driving Wheel:	5' 9"
Boiler Pressure:	200psi superheated
Cylinders:	Three 16" x 26"
Tractive Effort:	24600lbf
Valve Gear:	Walschaert (piston valves)

Refer to the Historical Survey of LMS 2-6-4T Engines at the end of this section for more details of this class.

This class was designed by Stanier and built at Derby for working on the London, Tilbury & Southend section. They were developed from Fowler's engines and they were fitted with taper boilers and had sloping tops to the tanks.

The engines differed from the other classes in that they had three cylinders with three independent sets of Walschaert valve gear. The outside cylinders were noticeably smaller than the other classes and they had shorter smokeboxes and domeless boilers.

The engines spent their whole lives on the LTS section until they were replaced by electric multiple units. They were consistently good performers, and they were well liked by their crews.

Year End Totals: '4MT [4]' class

'47	'48	'49	'50	'51	'52	'53	'54	'55	'56	'57	'58	'59	'60	'61	'62	'63	'64	'65	'66	'67
37	37	37	37	37	37	37	37	37	37	37	37	37	36	29						

Number	Built	Renumbered	BR Dates	Scrap	Notes
42500 §	04/34 Der	11/48 2500	-06/62		
42501	04/34 Der	10/48 2501	-06/62	03/63	
42502	04/34 Der	05/48 2502	-06/62	11/62	
42503	04/34 Der	07/48 2503	-06/62	10/62	
42504	04/34 Der	03/49 2504	-06/62	03/63	
42505	06/34 Der	05/48 2505	-06/62	08/62	
42506	06/34 Der	12/48 2506	-09/61	10/61	
42507	06/34 Der	07/48 2507	-05/61	08/61	

Number	Built	Renumbered	BR Dates	Scrap	Notes
42508	06/34 Der	12/48 2508	-06/62	02/63	
42509	06/34 Der	08/48 2509	-06/62	02/63	
42510	06/34 Der	05/48 2510	-09/61	12/61	
42511	06/34 Der	02/49 2511	-06/62	07/62	
42512	07/34 Der	04/48 2512	-12/60	12/60	
42513	07/34 Der	12/48 2513	-06/62	09/62	
42514	07/34 Der	07/48 2514	-04/62	04/62	
42515	08/34 Der	11/48 2515	-06/62	08/62	
42516	08/34 Der	05/48 2516	-06/62	02/63	
42517	08/34 Der	11/48 2517	-06/62	10/62	
42518	08/34 Der	05/48 2518	-06/62	03/63	
42519	09/34 Der	08/48 2519	-06/62	07/62	
42520	09/34 Der	01/49 2520	-06/62	07/62	
42521	09/34 Der	09/48 2521	-11/61	01/62	
42522	09/34 Der	12/48 2522	-06/62	02/63	
42523	09/34 Der	09/48 2523	-06/62	09/62	
42524	09/34 Der	09/48 2524	-09/61	12/61	
42525	09/34 Der	06/48 2525	-06/62	03/63	
42526	10/34 Der	09/48 2526	-06/62	04/63	
42527	10/34 Der	12/48 2527	-06/62	10/62	
42528	10/34 Der	07/48 2528	-06/62	08/62	
42529	10/34 Der	10/48 2529	-06/62	10/62	
42530	11/34 Der	08/48 2530	-06/62	05/63	
42531	11/34 Der	09/48 2531	-09/61	10/61	
42532	11/34 Der	04/48 2532	-06/62	02/63	
42533	11/34 Der	04/48 2533	-06/62	02/63	
42534	11/34 Der	07/48 2534	-12/61	12/61	
42535	11/34 Der	11/48 2535	-06/62	03/63	
42536	12/34 Der	10/48 2536	-06/62	03/63	

4MT[3] 42425-42494, 42537-42672
2-6-4T LMS Stanier 2-Cylinder

Class continued from 42494

Number	Built	Renumbered	BR Dates	Scrap	Notes
42537	12/35 Der	10/48 2537	-09/62	06/63	
42538	12/35 Der	01/49 2538	-06/62	11/62	
42539	12/35 Der	03/50 2539	-02/61	08/61	
42540	12/35 Der	04/48 2540	-10/62	03/63	
42541	12/35 Der	04/49 2541	-12/62	05/63	
42542	12/35 Der	06/49 2542	-07/65	10/65	
42543	12/35 Der	05/49 2543	-05/63	06/63	
42544	12/35 Der	06/48 2544	-11/62	05/63	
42545	06/36 NB	07/48 2545	-10/61	11/61	
42546	06/36 NB	06/48 2546	-04/67	12/67	
42547	07/36 NB	08/48 2547	-05/63	08/63	
42548	07/36 NB	12/48 2548	-02/67	05/67	
42549	07/36 NB	10/48 2549	-11/61	12/61	
42550	07/36 NB	07/48 2550	-04/64	10/64	
42551	07/36 NB	06/49 2551	-12/64	07/65	
42552	07/36 NB	10/48 2552	-10/61	12/61	
42553	07/36 NB	09/48 2553	-10/62	12/62	
42554	07/36 NB	02/49 2554	-04/65	07/65	
42555	07/36 NB	11/48 2555	-05/65	08/65	
42556	07/36 NB	09/49 2556	-07/63	10/63	
42557	08/36 NB	09/49 2557	-10/63	07/64	
42558	08/36 NB	05/48 2558	-04/65	09/65	
42559	08/36 NB	12/48 2559	-09/64	11/64	
42560	08/36 NB	01/49 2560	-04/64	08/64	
42561	08/36 NB	05/48 2561	-11/63	10/64	
42562	08/36 NB	02/49 2562	-01/64	03/64	
42563	08/36 NB	04/49 2563	-11/63	12/63	
42564	08/36 NB	11/49 2564	-05/65	10/65	
42565	08/36 NB	07/48 2565	-11/64	10/65	
42566	08/36 NB	05/49 2566	-05/65	10/65	
42567	08/36 NB	12/49 2567	-03/65	08/65	
42568	09/36 NB	10/48 2568	-12/62	02/63	
42569	09/36 NB	12/48 2569	-01/64	02/65	
42570	09/36 NB	08/49 2570	-10/61	11/62	
42571	09/36 NB	09/48 2571	-11/63	12/63	
42572	09/36 NB	06/48 2572	-01/64	08/64	
42573	09/36 NB	11/49 2573	-11/64	01/65	
42574	09/36 NB	11/48 2574	-10/67	05/68	
42575	09/36 NB	09/48 2575	-10/62	01/63	
42576	09/36 NB	12/48 2576	-06/62	09/62	
42577	09/36 NB	05/48 2577	-01/67	06/67	
42578	09/36 NB	07/48 2578	-10/62	02/63	
42579	09/36 NB	02/49 2579	-06/62	12/62	
42580	10/36 NB	07/48 2580	-11/62	07/63	
42581	10/36 NB	12/48 2581	-03/66	06/66	
42582	10/36 NB	10/48 2582	-05/63	08/63	
42583	10/36 NB	08/48 2583	-10/66	02/67	
42584	10/36 NB	04/49 2584	-08/64	11/64	
42585	10/36 NB	04/48 2585	-11/62	04/63	
42586	10/36 NB	01/49 2586	-11/64	01/65	
42587	10/36 NB	04/49 2587	-06/67	01/68	
42588	10/36 NB	10/48 2588	-10/64	12/64	
42589	10/36 NB	04/48 2589	-09/64	01/65	
42590	10/36 NB	04/48 2590	-02/65	07/65	
42591	10/36 NB	03/49 2591	-10/62	04/63	
42592	10/36 NB	05/48 2592	-05/63	05/63	
42593	10/36 NB	10/48 2593	-06/62	12/62	
42594	11/36 NB	09/48 2594	-05/64	05/64	
42595	11/36 NB	04/48 2595	-10/63	01/64	
42596	11/36 NB	08/48 2596	-08/62	06/63	
42597	11/36 NB	10/49 2597	-10/65	01/66	
42598	11/36 NB	02/49 2598	-11/63	06/64	
42599	11/36 NB	01/49 2599	-10/62	04/63	
42600	11/36 NB	11/49 2600	-11/62	12/62	
42601	11/36 NB	04/49 2601	-04/65	09/65	
42602	11/36 NB	04/48 2602	-12/64	06/65	
42603	12/36 NB	03/49 2603	-05/63	09/63	
42604	12/36 NB	05/49 2604	-05/65	09/65	
42605	12/36 NB	06/48 2605	-12/64	07/65	
42606	12/36 NB	06/49 2606	-10/66	04/67	
42607	12/36 NB	11/48 2607	-02/64	06/64	
42608	12/36 NB	08/48 2608	-09/64	09/64	
42609	12/36 NB	07/48 2609	-02/65	05/65	
42610	01/37 NB	06/48 2610	-04/66	07/66	
42611	01/37 NB	04/49 2611	-05/67	09/67	
42612	01/37 NB	03/49 2612	-01/64	07/64	
42613	01/37 NB	04/49 2613	-04/67	10/67	
42614	01/37 NB	01/49 2614	-05/64	08/64	
42615	02/37 NB	06/49 2615	-10/62	11/62	
42616	02/37 NB	09/48 2616	-10/67	03/68	
42617	02/37 NB	12/48 2617	-11/63	04/64	
42618	06/38 Der	12/48 2618	-07/65	11/65	
42619	06/38 Der	09/48 2619	-06/64	09/64	
42620	07/38 Der	08/48 2620	-09/64	12/64	
42621	07/38 Der	10/48 2621	-10/62	10/63	
42622	07/38 Der	08/48 2622	-02/67	07/67	
42623	07/38 Der	05/48 2623	-02/64	04/64	
42624	07/38 Der	02/49 2624	-11/62	03/63	
42625	08/38 Der	11/49 2625	-05/66	08/66	
42626	08/38 Der	06/49 2626	-07/65	07/66	
42627	08/38 Der	03/50 2627	-10/61	10/62	
42628	09/38 Der	01/49 2628	-01/64	03/64	
42629	09/38 Der	09/49 2629	-10/64	02/65	
42630	09/38 Der	07/49 2630	-09/64	01/65	
42631	09/38 Der	06/48 2631	-09/64	01/65	
42632	09/38 Der	06/48 2632	-06/63	07/63	
42633	09/38 Der	06/48 2633	-01/64	07/64	
42634	09/38 Der	08/48 2634	-01/65	05/65	
42635	09/38 Der	04/49 2635	-10/61	02/62	
42636	10/38 Der	06/48 2636	-05/63	06/63	
42637	10/38 Der	11/49 2637	-10/61	02/62	
42638	10/38 Der	04/48 2638	-12/62	02/63	
42639	11/38 Der	03/49 2639	-09/64	01/65	
42640	11/38 Der	12/49 2640	-09/64	05/65	
42641	11/38 Der	02/50 2641	-10/62	10/63	
42642	11/38 Der	03/49 2642	-10/62	10/63	
42643	11/38 Der	04/48 2643	-12/63	04/64	
42644	11/38 Der	01/49 2644	-03/67	10/67	
42645	12/38 Der	06/48 2645	-09/65	11/65	
42646	12/38 Der	05/48 2646	-10/62	06/63	
42647	12/38 Der	04/48 2647	-05/67	11/67	
42648	12/38 Der	12/48 2648	-10/61	09/62	
42649	12/38 Der	10/49 2649	-02/65	10/65	
42650	12/38 Der	*50* 2650	-06/67	01/68	
42651	12/38 Der	08/49 2651	-09/64	10/64	
42652	01/39 Der	02/49 2652	-05/64	06/64	
42653	12/40 Der	09/49 2653	-10/62	05/63	
42654	01/41 Der	08/49 2654	-11/64	07/65	
42655	02/41 Der	09/49 2655	-01/63	04/63	
42656	02/41 Der	09/48 2656	-05/67	11/67	
42657	02/41 Der	04/49 2657	-11/64	12/64	
42658	02/41 Der	09/48 2658	-10/62	05/63	
42659	03/41 Der	04/48 2659	-04/63	05/63	
42660	04/41 Der	04/49 2660	-04/65	08/65	
42661	05/41 Der	05/48 2661	-10/62	05/63	
42662	06/41 Der	06/49 2662	-12/64	06/65	
42663	06/42 Der	05/48 2663	-03/67	10/67	
42664	07/42 Der	10/48 2664	-12/66	03/67	
42665	08/42 Der	10/49 2665	-06/67	01/68	
42666	08/42 Der	11/48 2666	-10/62	05/63	
42667	10/42 Der	11/49 2667	-02/65	05/65	
42668	11/42 Der	12/48 2668	-09/63	11/63	
42669	12/42 Der	05/49 2669	-10/61	04/62	
42670	12/42 Der	06/49 2670	-12/64	11/65	
42671	01/43 Der	07/48 2671	-12/62	02/63	
42672	02/43 Der	06/49 2672	-06/62	01/63	

4MT[1] 42050-42299, 42673-42699
2-6-4T LMS Fairburn

Class continued from 42299

Number	Built	Renumbered	BR Dates	Scrap	Notes
42673	03/45 Der	04/49 2673	-08/65	02/66	
42674	04/45 Der	01/49 2674	-11/62	01/63	
42675	04/45 Der	01/49 2675	-09/65	03/66	
42676	04/45 Der	04/48 2676	-06/66	08/66	
42677	05/45 Der	12/48 2677	-06/62	08/62	
42678	05/45 Der	06/48 2678	-06/62	08/62	
42679	05/45 Der	10/48 2679	-06/62	03/63	
42680	05/45 Der	03/49 2680	-03/65	08/65	
42681	06/45 Der	10/48 2681	-07/63	09/63	
42682	06/45 Der	01/49 2682	-08/64	09/64	
42683	06/45 Der	09/49 2683	-10/61	11/61	
42684	06/45 Der	11/48 2684	-06/62	07/62	
42685	07/45 Der	01/49 2685	-10/62	01/63	
42686	07/45 Der	02/49 2686	-05/64	08/64	
42687	07/45 Der	05/48 2687	-06/62	11/62	
42688	08/45 Der	10/49 2688	-05/65	07/65	
42689	08/45 Der	09/48 2689	-10/67	01/68	
42690	08/45 Der	02/51 2690	-12/66	05/67	
42691	08/45 Der	12/49 2691	-09/66	12/66	
42692	09/45 Der	03/49 2692	-12/62	03/64	
42693	09/45 Der	06/48 2693	-10/66	01/67	
42694	09/45 Der	11/49 2694	-12/66	04/67	
42695	10/45 Der	10/49 2695	-06/64	09/64	
42696	10/45 Der	07/49 2696	-09/64	04/65	
42697	10/45 Der	02/49 2697	-01/67	05/67	
42698	10/45 Der	05/48 2698	-10/63	12/63	
42699	10/45 Der	06/48 2699	-05/67	10/67	

5MT[1] 42700-42944
2-6-0 LMS Hughes/Fowler Horwich 'Crab'

Power Classification:	5F reclassified 5MT/6P5F in 1948
Introduced:	1926-1932
Designer:	Hughes/Fowler
Company:	LMS
Weight:	Loco 66t 0cwt Tender 42t 4cwt
Driving Wheel:	5' 6"
Boiler Pressure:	180psi superheated
Cylinders:	Outside 21" x 26"
Tractive Effort:	26580lbf
Valve Gear:	Walschaert (piston valves) v Lenz rotary cam poppet r Reidinger poppet

In 1923 Hughes (from the LYR) became the first Chief Mechanical Engineer of the LMS and he designed this class of engines which were built at Horwich in 1926. By the time they were under construction, Hughes had left and the 245 engines were built under the supervision of Fowler. They were excellent modern mixed traffic engines, and were originally numbered 13000-13244 until 1934.

The very high running plate was unusual at the time, but it was destined to become common practice in future locomotive design. The cylinders were set very high and at a sharp angle to the footplate. This was necessary to keep the dimensions within the Midland loading gauge. The height of the cylinders earned the engines the nickname of 'Spiders', but they later became more generally known as 'Crabs'.

Stanier produced a modified version of these engines with taper boilers in 1933 (see the '42945' class).

v Five of these engines were rebuilt with new cylinders and Lenz rotary cam poppet valve gear in 1931. This proved to be no advantage over the piston valve fitted engines.

r In 1952-54 these engines were again rebuilt with Reidinger poppet valve gear. This proved to be inferior to both other forms of steam distribution.

Year End Totals: '5MT [1]' class

'47	'48	'49	'50	'51	'52	'53	'54	'55	'56	'57	'58	'59	'60	'61	'62	'63	'64	'65	'66	'67
245	245	245	245	245	245	245	245	245	245	245	245	245	245	242	181	129	75	27	2	

Number	Built	Renumbered	BR Dates	Scrap	Notes
42700 §	05/26 Hor	09/48 2700	-03/66		
42701	07/26 Hor	04/48 2701	-12/64	03/65	
42702	09/26 Hor	02/50 2702	-01/66	04/68	
42703	10/26 Hor	01/49 2703	-09/64	02/65	
42704	10/26 Hor	07/49 2704	-10/63	11/63	
42705	12/26 Hor	09/49 2705	-12/64	03/65	
42706	12/26 Hor	09/48 2706	-11/63	12/63	
42707	01/27 Hor	07/48 2707	-09/64	12/64	
42708	02/27 Hor	10/48 2708	-07/64	09/64	
42709	02/27 Hor	10/49 2709	-04/64	11/64	
42710	02/27 Hor	12/49 2710	-08/65	12/65	
42711	03/27 Hor	06/48 2711	-09/63	12/63	
42712	03/27 Hor	05/48 2712	-02/66	06/66	
42713	03/27 Hor	06/49 2713	-12/62	08/63	
42714	03/27 Hor	12/49 2714	-10/62	11/62	
42715	04/27 Hor	03/49 2715	-02/66	06/66	
42716	05/27 Hor	01/49 2716	-04/65	09/65	
42717	05/27 Hor	03/49 2717	-10/64	03/65	
42718	05/27 Hor	11/48 2718	-07/63	07/63	
42719	06/27 Hor	08/48 2719	-02/64	08/64	
42720	06/27 Hor	10/48 2720	-12/62	10/63	
42721	08/27 Hor	11/49 2721	-11/63	12/63	
42722	08/27 Hor	06/48 2722	-01/65	05/65	
42723	09/27 Hor	06/48 2723	-09/63	11/63	
42724	10/27 Hor	12/49 2724	-09/62	10/62	
42725	10/27 Hor	12/49 2725	-10/64	02/65	
42726	11/27 Hor	07/49 2726	-10/62	02/63	

Number	Built		Renumbered		BR Dates	Scrap	Notes
42727	11/27	Hor	12/49	2727	-01/67	06/67	
42728	11/27	Hor	11/49	2728	-02/63	05/63	
42729	12/27	Hor	07/49	2729	-11/63	03/65	
42730	12/26	Crw	06/48	2730	-07/65	10/65	
42731	12/26	Crw	02/49	2731	-02/64	03/64	
42732	12/26	Crw	03/49	2732	-06/65	10/65	
42733	12/26	Crw	08/48	2733	-02/65	06/65	
42734	12/26	Crw	08/48	2734	-03/66	06/66	
42735	12/26	Crw	01/49	2735	-11/63	05/64	
42736	02/27	Crw	12/49	2736	-12/66	04/67	
42737	01/27	Crw	10/49	2737	-12/66	04/67	
42738	02/27	Crw	03/49	2738	-06/64	08/64	
42739	02/27	Crw	07/49	2739	-12/66	04/67	
42740	03/27	Crw	02/49	2740	-01/66	05/66	
42741	03/27	Crw	03/49	2741	-05/65	10/65	
42742	03/27	Crw	01/49	2742	-09/62	03/64	
42743	06/27	Crw	01/49	2743	-12/62	09/63	
42744	04/27	Crw	03/49	2744	-12/62	09/63	
42745	05/27	Crw	08/48	2745	-12/62	09/63	
42746	05/27	Crw	10/48	2746	-11/63	05/64	
42747	05/27	Crw	08/49	2747	-03/63	04/63	
42748	05/27	Crw	12/48	2748	-10/64	03/65	
42749	06/27	Crw	12/48	2749	-07/62	11/62	
42750	06/27	Crw	04/49	2750	-09/63	05/64	
42751	06/27	Crw	05/48	2751	-04/65	08/65	
42752	06/27	Crw	11/48	2752	-12/62	12/63	
42753	06/27	Crw	12/49	2753	-08/65	12/65	
42754	06/27	Crw	04/50	2754	-11/64	02/65	
42755	06/27	Crw	06/48	2755	-10/64	02/65	
42756	06/27	Crw	01/50	2756	-06/64	07/64	
42757	07/27	Crw	11/48	2757	-06/64	10/64	
42758	08/27	Crw	03/50	2758	-11/63	07/64	
42759	06/27	Crw	08/48	2759	-01/63	06/63	
42760	06/27	Crw	03/49	2760	-09/64	09/64	
42761	06/27	Crw	06/49	2761	-06/64	10/64	
42762	06/27	Crw	05/49	2762	-11/63	12/63	
42763	07/27	Crw	02/49	2763	-06/64	07/64	
42764	07/27	Crw	03/50	2764	-12/62	04/62	
42765 §	08/27	Crw	10/48	2765	-12/66		
42766	07/27	Crw	11/48	2766	-12/62	09/63	
42767	07/27	Crw	11/49	2767	-03/63	05/63	
42768	07/27	Crw	12/49	2768	-12/63	02/64	
42769	07/27	Crw	06/49	2769	-02/64	10/64	
42770	07/27	Crw	03/49	2770	-10/63	01/64	
42771	07/27	Crw	07/48	2771	-10/63	12/63	
42772	08/27	Crw	05/50	2772	-05/65	10/65	
42773	08/27	Crw	08/48	2773	-11/62	02/63	
42774	08/27	Crw	09/49	2774	-10/63	02/64	
42775	09/27	Crw	11/49	2775	-10/62	11/62	
42776	09/27	Crw	04/49	2776	-07/64	11/64	
42777	08/27	Crw	01/50	2777	-08/65	03/66	
42778	09/27	Crw	02/49	2778	-04/65	10/65	
42779	09/27	Crw	05/50	2779	-05/62	05/62	
42780	09/27	Crw	05/48	2780	-10/65	01/66	
42781	09/27	Crw	09/50	2781	-11/62	01/63	
42782	09/27	Crw	04/48	2782	-12/66	04/67	
42783	09/27	Crw	04/49	2783	-08/65	03/66	
42784	09/27	Crw	07/48	2784	-12/62	03/63	
42785	10/27	Crw	10/49	2785	-11/63	12/63	
42786	10/27	Crw	05/48	2786	-10/62	02/63	
42787	10/27	Crw	06/50	2787	-04/65	08/65	
42788	10/27	Crw	08/48	2788	-09/64	11/64	
42789	10/27	Crw	12/49	2789	-12/66	07/67	
42790	10/27	Crw	01/49	2790	-07/63	05/64	
42791	10/27	Crw	08/49	2791	-01/65	04/65	
42792	10/27	Crw	04/48	2792	-11/63	08/64	
42793	10/27	Crw	09/49	2793	-12/64	03/65	
42794	11/27	Crw	10/48	2794	-11/63	12/63	
42795	11/27	Crw	08/49	2795	-12/66	04/67	
42796	11/27	Crw	05/48	2796	-11/63	01/64	
42797	11/27	Crw	06/48	2797	-03/62	12/62	
42798	12/27	Crw	04/49	2798	-10/63	12/63	
42799	12/27	Crw	04/49	2799	-01/65	05/65	
42800	12/28	Crw	10/49	2800	-10/65	02/66	
42801	12/28	Crw	01/50	2801	-07/66	10/67	
42802	12/28	Crw	05/48	2802	-06/64	09/64	
42803	12/28	Crw	10/48	2803	-12/66	04/67	
42804	12/28	Crw	04/49	2804	-12/62	12/63	
42805	12/28	Crw	06/48	2805	-11/63	03/64	
42806	12/28	Crw	09/49	2806	-12/63	05/64	
42807	12/28	Crw	11/48	2807	-12/62	09/63	
42808	01/29	Crw	01/49	2808	-12/62	09/63	
42809	01/29	Crw	05/48	2809	-12/62	09/63	
42810	04/29	Hor	07/48	2810	-12/63	01/64	
42811	05/29	Hor	09/48	2811	-07/62	05/63	
42812	05/29	Hor	10/49	2812	-07/66	11/66	
42813	06/29	Hor	01/50	2813	-11/63	02/64	
42814	06/29	Hor	10/48	2814	-08/65	01/66	
42815	06/29	Hor	11/48	2815	-09/64	03/65	
42816	06/29	Hor	11/49	2816	-09/64	03/65	
42817	07/29	Hor	01/50	2817	-04/65	10/65	
42818	07/29	Hor	04/48	2818	-05/62	05/62	v 11/53⇨r
42819	08/29	Hor	05/49	2819	-09/65	12/65	
42820	08/29	Hor	05/49	2820	-04/64	09/64	
42821	08/29	Hor	01/49	2821	-03/63	05/63	
42822	09/29	Hor	01/49	2822	-06/62	06/62	v 04/53⇨r
42823	10/29	Hor	07/48	2823	-02/64	09/64	
42824	10/29	Hor	03/49	2824	-07/62	11/62	v 01/54⇨r
42825	10/29	Hor	02/49	2825	-06/62	10/62	v 11/52⇨r
42826	11/29	Hor	12/48	2826	-09/64	01/65	
42827	11/29	Hor	01/50	2827	-08/65	01/66	
42828	11/29	Hor	06/49	2828	-11/65	02/66	
42829	12/29	Hor	11/48	2829	-06/62	11/62	v 06/53⇨r
42830	05/30	Hor	04/48	2830	-11/62	03/64	
42831	05/30	Hor	12/49	2831	-12/65	03/66	
42832	05/30	Hor	11/48	2832	-03/65	06/65	
42833	05/30	Hor	07/48	2833	-12/62	11/63	
42834	06/30	Hor	04/48	2834	-12/62	11/63	
42835	06/30	Hor	*51*	2835	-12/62	11/63	
42836	07/30	Hor	10/48	2836	-12/62	11/63	
42837	07/30	Hor	05/48	2837	-12/62	11/63	
42838	08/30	Hor	08/49	2838	-05/63	06/63	
42839	08/30	Hor	11/48	2839	-06/64	07/64	
42840	08/30	Hor	02/49	2840	-09/64	01/65	
42841	09/30	Hor	05/48	2841	-03/65	06/65	
42842	09/30	Hor	10/49	2842	-06/64	12/64	
42843	10/30	Hor	01/49	2843	-05/63	05/63	
42844	10/30	Hor	05/49	2844	-08/65	10/65	
42845	10/30	Hor	09/49	2845	-09/64	12/64	
42846	11/30	Hor	10/48	2846	-09/64	02/65	
42847	11/30	Hor	05/48	2847	-06/62	11/62	
42848	11/30	Hor	07/48	2848	-03/65	06/65	
42849	12/30	Hor	12/48	2849	-07/65	03/66	
42850	02/30	Crw	11/49	2850	-07/62	01/63	
42851	02/30	Crw	09/48	2851	-07/64	01/65	
42852	03/30	Crw	11/48	2852	-07/63	07/63	
42853	03/30	Crw	06/50	2853	-06/63	10/63	
42854	03/30	Crw	06/48	2854	-11/63	12/63	
42855	03/30	Crw	02/50	2855	-09/64	05/65	
42856	03/30	Crw	03/49	2856	-11/64	04/65	
42857	03/30	Crw	08/49	2857	-12/62	02/63	
42858	03/30	Crw	12/48	2858	-05/64	04/65	
42859 §	03/30	Crw	12/48	2859	-12/66		
42860	03/30	Crw	09/48	2860	-09/64	12/64	
42861	03/30	Crw	06/48	2861	-07/66	10/67	
42862	04/30	Crw	08/49	2862	-12/62	01/64	
42863	04/30	Crw	06/49	2863	-08/66	10/67	
42864	04/30	Crw	07/49	2864	-08/61	10/61	
42865	04/30	Crw	09/48	2865	-10/63	01/64	
42866	04/30	Crw	07/49	2866	-11/62	01/63	
42867	04/30	Crw	10/49	2867	-06/64	02/65	
42868	04/30	Crw	07/48	2868	-06/62	07/62	
42869	05/30	Crw	07/49	2869	-07/65	11/65	
42870	05/30	Crw	06/48	2870	-03/63	04/63	
42871	05/30	Crw	10/48	2871	-10/63	09/64	
42872	05/30	Crw	02/49	2872	-12/63	03/64	
42873	05/30	Crw	11/48	2873	-09/63	09/64	
42874	05/30	Crw	12/48	2874	-10/62	10/62	
42875	05/30	Crw	08/49	2875	-12/62	11/63	
42876	05/30	Crw	04/48	2876	-12/62	11/63	
42877	05/30	Crw	08/48	2877	-12/62	09/63	
42878	06/30	Crw	09/48	2878	-09/65	12/65	
42879	06/30	Crw	11/48	2879	-09/65	01/66	
42880	06/30	Crw	04/48	2880	-11/64	12/64	
42881	06/30	Crw	09/49	2881	-11/62	12/62	
42882	06/30	Crw	04/49	2882	-12/62	11/63	
42883	06/30	Crw	04/49	2883	-12/62	11/63	
42884	06/30	Crw	06/48	2884	-12/62	11/63	
42885	07/30	Crw	03/50	2885	-12/63	01/64	
42886	07/30	Crw	07/49	2886	-04/65	08/65	
42887	07/30	Crw	05/49	2887	-10/62	12/62	
42888	07/30	Crw	09/49	2888	-02/64	08/64	
42889	07/30	Crw	11/49	2889	-05/62	05/62	
42890	07/30	Crw	04/49	2890	-04/63	01/64	
42891	08/30	Crw	12/48	2891	-10/62	12/62	
42892	08/30	Crw	05/48	2892	-05/65	08/65	
42893	08/30	Crw	09/48	2893	-08/61	12/61	
42894	08/30	Crw	03/49	2894	-12/64	03/65	
42895	08/30	Crw	10/48	2895	-01/63	04/63	
42896	08/30	Crw	09/49	2896	-03/65	04/65	
42897	08/30	Crw	08/48	2897	-04/64	05/64	
42898	08/30	Crw	06/48	2898	-09/65	01/66	
42899	08/30	Crw	01/51	2899	-12/62	11/63	
42900	08/30	Crw	04/49	2900	-10/65	02/66	
42901	08/30	Crw	11/49	2901	-05/65	08/65	
42902	09/30	Crw	06/48	2902	-03/64	11/64	
42903	09/30	Crw	02/49	2903	-09/62	10/62	
42904	09/30	Crw	08/49	2904	-05/65	08/65	
42905	09/30	Crw	04/49	2905	-07/65	02/66	
42906	09/30	Crw	01/49	2906	-12/62	10/63	
42907	09/30	Crw	10/48	2907	-10/64	03/65	
42908	09/30	Crw	06/48	2908	-08/66	11/66	
42909	09/30	Crw	01/49	2909	-01/66	10/67	
42910	10/30	Crw	12/48	2910	-11/63	05/64	
42911	10/30	Crw	10/49	2911	-11/63	05/64	
42912	10/30	Crw	07/48	2912	-09/65	01/66	
42913	10/30	Crw	02/49	2913	-07/66	10/66	
42914	10/30	Crw	05/48	2914	-12/63	05/64	
42915	10/30	Crw	08/48	2915	-12/62	09/63	
42916	10/30	Crw	02/49	2916	-06/65	10/65	
42917	10/30	Crw	04/49	2917	-08/66	10/67	
42918	11/30	Crw	09/48	2918	-12/62	09/63	
42919	11/30	Crw	06/49	2919	-11/66	04/67	
42920	11/30	Crw	03/49	2920	-12/64	03/65	
42921	11/30	Crw	08/49	2921	-03/63	09/64	
42922	11/30	Crw	08/48	2922	-04/64	05/64	
42923	11/30	Crw	01/50	2923	-01/64	08/64	
42924	12/30	Crw	05/49	2924	-02/66	06/66	
42925	05/31	Crw	06/48	2925	-11/64	04/65	
42926	05/31	Crw	09/48	2926	-10/64	02/65	
42927	05/31	Crw	10/48	2927	-07/62	03/64	
42928	05/31	Crw	06/48	2928	-02/63	03/63	
42929	05/31	Crw	10/48	2929	-08/62	10/62	
42930	05/31	Crw	11/49	2930	-08/61	09/61	
42931	06/31	Crw	04/49	2931	-09/64	12/64	
42932	06/31	Crw	03/50	2932	-05/65	10/65	
42933	06/31	Crw	05/48	2933	-05/63	05/63	
42934	06/31	Crw	02/49	2934	-10/64	04/65	
42935	12/32	Crw	08/48	2935	-01/63	04/63	
42936	12/32	Crw	03/49	2936	-07/65	11/65	
42937	12/32	Crw	03/49	2937	-05/65	08/65	
42938	12/32	Crw	11/49	2938	-09/65	12/65	
42939	12/32	Crw	01/50	2939	-06/62	08/62	
42940	12/32	Crw	10/48	2940	-09/65	12/65	
42941	12/32	Crw	09/49	2941	-05/65	10/65	
42942	12/32	Crw	01/49	2942	-01/67	10/67	
42943	12/32	Crw	11/49	2943	-05/64	02/65	
42944	12/32	Crw	08/48	2944	-04/63	06/63	

5MT [2] 42945-42984
2-6-0 LMS Stanier

Power Classification:	5F reclassified 5MT/6P5F in 1948
Introduced:	1933-1934
Designer:	Stanier
Company:	LMS
Weight:	Loco 69t 2cwt Tender 42t 4cwt
Driving Wheel:	5' 6"
Boiler Pressure:	225psi superheated
Cylinders:	Outside 18" x 28"
Tractive Effort:	26290lbf
Valve Gear:	Walschaert (piston valves)

This was Stanier's first design of main line engine for the LMS after he came from the GWR in 1932. They were a modified version of Hughes' 'Crabs' with a taper boiler (see the '42700' class). It was found possible to give the engines horizontal cylinders by increasing the boiler pressure, while decreasing the cylinder diameter. This allowed these engines to have approximately the same tractive effort as the Hughes engines. The engines were originally allocated the numbers 13245-13284 until renumbered in 1934.

The first engine appeared with a GWR type of cover to the top feed. This was promptly removed and replaced by the normal LMS type of dome cover. The engines originally had small superheaters, but were later fitted with 21 element superheaters.

These engines were regularly used on heavy excursion trains in addition to fast heavy freight trains. Only forty were built as they were superseded by Stanier's 'Black Fives' ('44658' class).

Year End Totals: '5MT [2]' class

'47	'48	'49	'50	'51	'52	'53	'54	'55	'56	'57	'58	'59	'60	'61	'62	'63	'64	'65	'66	'67
40	40	40	40	40	40	40	40	40	40	40	40	40	40	40	40	36	27	16	1	

Number	*Built*		*Renumbered*		*BR Dates*	*Scrap*	*Notes*
42945	10/33	Crw	09/49	2945	-03/66	06/66	
42946	11/33	Crw	12/48	2946	-11/65	02/66	
42947	11/33	Crw	10/48	2947	-12/65	02/66	
42948	11/33	Crw	10/48	2948	-11/65	01/66	
42949	12/33	Crw	11/49	2949	-11/63	12/63	
42950	12/33	Crw	02/49	2950	-11/65	01/66	
42951	11/33	Crw	07/50	2951	-03/66	06/66	
42952	12/33	Crw	01/49	2952	-09/64	10/65	
42953	12/33	Crw	03/49	2953	-01/66	06/66	
42954	12/33	Crw	05/48	2954	-02/67	08/67	
42955	12/33	Crw	02/49	2955	-04/66	07/66	
42956	12/33	Crw	01/49	2956	-09/64	12/64	
42957	12/33	Crw	02/49	2957	-01/66	04/66	
42958	01/34	Crw	04/48	2958	-11/65	06/66	
42959	01/34	Crw	06/49	2959	-12/65	06/66	
42960	12/33	Crw	12/49	2960	-01/66	04/66	
42961	01/34	Crw	09/48	2961	-08/65	11/65	
42962	01/34	Crw	08/48	2962	-02/64	04/64	
42963	12/33	Crw	10/49	2963	-07/66	01/67	
42964	01/34	Crw	05/48	2964	-11/65	06/66	
42965	01/34	Crw	05/49	2965	-08/64	11/64	
42966	01/34	Crw	03/49	2966	-08/64	11/64	
42967	01/34	Crw	07/48	2967	-05/66	11/66	
42968 §	01/34	Crw	12/48	2968	-12/66		
42969	01/34	Crw	09/49	2969	-11/64	03/65	

Number	Built	Renumbered	BR Dates	Scrap	Notes
42970	01/34 Crw	12/50 2970	-10/64	02/65	
42971	01/34 Crw	12/49 2971	-12/64	03/65	
42972	01/34 Crw	04/49 2972	-04/65	08/65	
42973	01/34 Crw	06/48 2973	-11/63	12/63	
42974	01/34 Crw	06/50 2974	-09/65	12/65	
42975	01/34 Crw	06/48 2975	-03/66	06/66	
42976	01/34 Crw	03/49 2976	-07/63	09/63	
42977	01/34 Crw	10/48 2977	-06/66	09/66	
42978	01/34 Crw	11/48 2978	-05/66	08/66	
42979	02/34 Crw	12/48 2979	-12/64	05/65	
42980	02/34 Crw	10/49 2980	-01/66	04/66	
42981	02/34 Crw	08/49 2981	-05/66	08/66	
42982	02/34 Crw	10/48 2982	-11/65	06/66	
42983	03/34 Crw	09/48 2983	-01/66	04/66	
42984	03/34 Crw	10/48 2984	-10/63	12/63	

4MT [5] 43000-43161
2-6-0 LMS Ivatt 'Mogul'

Power Classification:	4F reclassified 4MT in 1948
Introduced:	1947-1952
Designer:	Ivatt
Company:	LMS
Weight:	Loco 59t 2cwt
Driving Wheel:	5' 3"
Boiler Pressure:	225psi superheated
Cylinders:	Outside 17½" x 26"
Tractive Effort:	24170lbf
Valve Gear:	Walschaert (piston valves)

These engines were designed by Ivatt in 1947 and although originally classed as '4F', they were essentially mixed traffic engines. Only the first three came out as LMS engines in December 1947, the rest being built by BR.

The engines had the cylinders, motion and pipe-work well exposed and they were fitted with extremely high running plates. Together with the double chimneys originally fitted, these features made the engines just about the ugliest ever to appear on the LMS.

The double chimneys did nothing to help the engines' steaming capacity. After much testing the engines were fitted with single blastpipes and single chimneys which more than doubled the steam production of the boilers. The later engines were built new with single blast-pipes and chimneys.

Riddles' BR standard '76000' class was based closely on this design.

d 43000-43049 were originally fitted with double chimneys, later with single chimneys.

s 43027 was experimentally fitted with a stove pipe chimney in 1950.

Year End Totals: '4MT [5]' class

'47	'48	'49	'50	'51	'52	'53	'54	'55	'56	'57	'58	'59	'60	'61	'62	'63	'64	'65	'66	'67
3	23	50	97	155	162	162	162	162	162	162	162	162	162	162	162	156	141	99	65	6

Number	Built	Renumbered	BR Dates	Scrap	Notes
43000	12/47 Hor	10/50 3000	-09/67	11/67	d
43001	12/47 Hor	08/48 3001	-09/67	12/67	d
43002	12/47 Hor	06/50 3002	-12/67	04/68	d
43003	01/48 Hor	11/50 3003	01/48-09/67	12/67	d
43004	01/48 Hor	12/50 3004	01/48-09/67	04/68	d
43005	01/48 Hor	09/50 3005	01/48-11/65	02/66	d
43006	01/48 Hor	11/50 3006	01/48-03/68	05/68	d
43007	01/48 Hor	10/50 3007	01/48-09/67	12/67	d
43008	01/48 Hor	10/50 3008	01/48-03/68	06/68	d
43009	03/48 Hor	09/50 3009	03/48-12/66	04/67	d
43010	03/48 Hor	03/51 3010	03/48-12/67	04/68	d
43011	03/48 Hor		03/48-02/67	08/67	d
43012	04/48 Hor		04/48-05/67	08/67	d
43013	04/48 Hor		04/48-11/65	01/66	d
43014	04/48 Hor		04/48-04/66	06/66	d
43015	05/48 Hor		05/48-07/67	11/67	d
43016	05/48 Hor		05/48-02/66	05/66	d
43017	05/48 Hor		05/48-11/67	02/68	d
43018	05/48 Hor		05/48-11/66	04/67	d
43019	06/48 Hor		06/48-05/68	09/68	d
43020	12/48 Hor		12/48-10/66	01/67	d
43021	12/48 Hor		12/48-09/67	12/67	d
43022	12/48 Hor		12/48-12/66	05/67	d
43023	01/49 Hor		01/49-12/67	04/68	d
43024	01/49 Hor		01/49-06/67	10/67	d
43025	01/49 Hor		01/49-09/65	01/66	d
43026	02/49 Hor		02/49-09/66	01/67	d
43027	02/49 Hor		02/49-05/68	09/68	s
43028	03/49 Hor		03/49-11/67	02/68	d
43029	03/49 Hor		03/49-09/67	02/68	d
43030	03/49 Hor		03/49-11/66	01/67	d
43031	04/49 Hor		04/49-03/66	06/66	d
43032	04/49 Hor		04/49-01/65	04/65	d
43033	05/49 Hor		05/49-03/68	05/68	d
43034	05/49 Hor		05/49-06/67	11/67	d
43035	05/49 Hor		05/49-11/65	02/66	d
43036	06/49 Hor		06/49-05/66	10/66	d
43037	06/49 Hor		06/49-04/65	07/65	d
43038	06/49 Hor		06/49-05/64	09/64	d
43039	07/49 Hor		07/49-12/66	03/67	d
43040	07/49 Hor		07/49-12/66	03/67	d
43041	08/49 Hor		08/49-08/67	12/67	d
43042	08/49 Hor		08/49-02/66	06/66	d
43043	09/49 Hor		09/49-10/67	12/67	d
43044	09/49 Hor		09/49-09/67	04/68	d
43045	10/49 Hor		10/49-09/66	01/67	d
43046	10/49 Hor		10/49-11/67	02/68	d
43047	11/49 Hor		11/49-12/67	02/68	d
43048	11/49 Hor		11/49-05/67	11/67	d
43049	11/49 Hor		11/49-08/67	12/67	d
43050	07/50 Don		07/50-09/67	11/67	
43051	08/50 Don		08/50-01/67	04/67	
43052	08/50 Don		08/50-10/66	02/67	
43053	08/50 Don		08/50-04/64	08/64	
43054	08/50 Don		08/50-12/66	03/67	
43055	09/50 Don		09/50-07/67	11/67	
43056	09/50 Don		09/50-12/66	03/67	
43057	09/50 Don		09/50-12/66	03/67	
43058	09/50 Don		09/50-12/64	04/65	
43059	09/50 Don		09/50-01/65	03/65	
43060	09/50 Don		09/50-12/64	04/65	
43061	09/50 Don		09/50-01/64	06/64	
43062	11/50 Don		11/50-06/65	09/65	
43063	11/50 Don		11/50-09/67	10/67	
43064	11/50 Don		11/50-06/65	09/65	
43065	11/50 Don		11/50-01/65	04/65	
43066	12/50 Don		12/50-01/67	05/67	
43067	12/50 Don		12/50-04/65	07/65	
43068	12/50 Don		12/50-01/64	06/64	
43069	12/50 Don		12/50-09/66	12/66	
43070	08/50 Dar		08/50-09/67	11/67	
43071	09/50 Dar		09/50-03/67	11/67	
43072	09/50 Dar		09/50-12/64	12/64	
43073	09/50 Dar		09/50-08/67	12/67	
43074	09/50 Dar		09/50-07/66	10/66	
43075	09/50 Dar		09/50-05/65	08/65	
43076	10/50 Dar		10/50-09/67	02/68	
43077	10/50 Dar		10/50-05/67	08/67	
43078	10/50 Dar		10/50-12/66	03/67	
43079	10/50 Dar		10/50-12/66	04/67	
43080	10/50 Dar		10/50-06/65	09/65	
43081	10/50 Dar		10/50-01/65	04/65	
43082	11/50 Dar		11/50-11/65	01/66	
43083	11/50 Dar		11/50-12/63	05/64	
43084	11/50 Dar		11/50-09/67	02/68	
43085	11/50 Dar		11/50-01/65	04/65	
43086	11/50 Dar		11/50-12/64	04/65	
43087	11/50 Dar		11/50-12/64	04/65	
43088	12/50 Dar		12/50-12/67	04/68	
43089	12/50 Dar		12/50-11/65	04/66	
43090	12/50 Dar		12/50-04/65	07/65	
43091	12/50 Dar		12/50-06/65	07/65	
43092	12/50 Dar		12/50-04/65	07/65	
43093	12/50 Dar		12/50-01/65	04/65	
43094	12/50 Dar		12/50-01/64	05/64	
43095	12/50 Dar		12/50-12/66	04/67	
43096	12/50 Dar		12/50-03/67	11/67	
43097	01/51 Dar		01/51-01/67	07/67	
43098	02/51 Dar		02/51-06/67	08/67	
43099	02/51 Dar		02/51-12/66	03/67	
43100	02/51 Dar		02/51-02/67	03/67	
43101	02/51 Dar		02/51-04/67	11/67	
43102	03/51 Dar		03/51-12/66	03/67	
43103	03/51 Dar		03/51-12/66	03/67	
43104	03/51 Dar		03/51-01/64	04/64	
43105	03/51 Dar		03/51-06/67	11/67	
43106 §	04/51 Dar		04/51-06/68		
43107	05/51 Don		05/51-12/63	06/64	
43108	05/51 Don		05/51-11/65	04/66	
43109	06/51 Don		06/51-11/65	01/66	
43110	06/51 Don		06/51-12/63	10/64	
43111	07/51 Don		07/51-06/65	10/65	
43112	03/51 Hor		03/51-09/67	11/67	
43113	04/51 Hor		04/51-09/66	12/66	
43114	05/51 Hor		05/51-11/63	01/64	
43115	05/51 Hor		05/51-06/67	10/67	
43116	06/51 Hor		06/51-06/66	08/66	
43117	06/51 Hor		06/51-07/67	11/67	
43118	06/51 Hor		06/51-11/67	03/68	
43119	06/51 Hor		06/51-08/67	01/68	
43120	07/51 Hor		07/51-08/67	12/67	
43121	08/51 Hor		08/51-11/67	02/68	
43122	08/51 Hor		08/51-03/67	01/68	
43123	08/51 Hor		08/51-07/67	11/67	
43124	09/51 Hor		09/51-12/66	03/67	
43125	09/51 Hor		09/51-09/67	04/68	
43126	09/51 Hor		09/51-04/66	07/66	
43127	10/51 Hor		10/51-01/65	03/65	
43128	10/51 Hor		10/51-07/65	10/65	
43129	11/51 Hor		11/51-07/67	02/68	
43130	11/51 Hor		11/51-07/67	02/68	
43131	11/51 Hor		11/51-12/63	01/64	
43132	12/51 Hor		12/51-12/66	04/67	
43133	12/51 Hor		12/51-12/66	04/67	
43134	12/51 Hor		12/51-02/65	05/65	
43135	12/51 Hor		12/51-11/66	01/67	
43136	01/52 Hor		01/52-07/64	11/64	
43137	07/51 Don		07/51-09/67	11/67	
43138	07/51 Don		07/51-04/67	11/67	
43139	07/51 Don		07/51-09/67	02/68	
43140	08/51 Don		08/51-06/67	11/67	
43141	08/51 Don		08/51-11/66	01/67	
43142	08/51 Don		08/51-10/63	06/64	
43143	08/51 Don		08/51-06/65	10/65	
43144	09/51 Don		09/51-04/65	07/65	
43145	09/51 Don		09/51-01/65	04/65	
43146	09/51 Don		09/51-01/65	04/65	
43147	10/51 Don		10/51-12/64	01/66	
43148	10/51 Don		10/51-04/65	07/65	
43149	10/51 Don		10/51-11/65	02/66	
43150	11/51 Don		11/51-01/65	03/65	
43151	11/51 Don		11/51-02/67	08/67	
43152	11/51 Don		11/51-01/64	06/64	
43153	12/51 Don		12/51-06/65	09/65	
43154	12/51 Don		12/51-12/64	04/65	
43155	12/51 Don		12/51-01/65	02/65	
43156	01/52 Don		01/52-01/65	04/65	
43157	07/52 Don		07/52-01/65	03/65	
43158	07/52 Don		07/52-01/65	03/65	
43159	08/52 Don		08/52-06/65	10/65	
43160	08/52 Don		08/52-01/65	04/65	
43161	09/52 Don		09/52-06/65	08/65	

3F [2] (43137), 43174-43189, 43750
0-6-0 MR Johnson 4ft 11in

Power Classification:	3F
Introduced:	1875-1902 (these rebuilt engines 1885-1888) Rebuilt by Fowler 1916 onwards
Designer:	Johnson
Company:	MR
Weight:	Loco 43t 17cwt
Driving Wheel:	4' 11"
Boiler Pressure:	175psi
Cylinders:	Inside 18" x 26"
Tractive Effort:	21240lbf
Valve Gear:	Stephenson (slide valves)

Refer to the Historical Survey of Midland 0-6-0 Engines at the end of this section for more details of this class.

These '3F' engines were rebuilt from the '2F' '58114' class with larger boilers from 1916 onwards. They were later all rebuilt with Belpaire fireboxes and Deeley cabs by Fowler from 1920 onwards.

They retained their original numbers when they were rebuilt, and it was not until BR numbered the '2F's in the 58000 series that the two classes were numerically separated. The '2F's could always be distinguished from the '3F's by the square side sheet to the cabs. On the '3F's this was replaced by a small splasher merging with the cab.

43137 was renumbered 43750 in 1952 to make space for the '43000' class engines which were being built.

Year End Totals: '3F [2]' class

'47	'48	'49	'50	'51	'52	'53	'54	'55	'56	'57	'58	'59	'60	'61	'62	'63	'64	'65	'66	'67
11	11	11	11	11	11	11	11	11	11	10	10	6	1							

Number	Built	Renumbered	BR Dates	Scrap	Notes
43137	85 Der	3137	-10/59	11/59	
				01/52➲43750	
43174	10/87 Der	03/49 3174	-02/60	11/60	
43178	87 Der	03/50 3178	-03/60	05/60	
43180	87 Der	02/50 3180	-01/59	01/61	
43181	87 Der	11/49 3181	-04/57	05/57	
43183	87 Der	04/49 3183	-07/59	02/60	
43185	87 Der	10/48 3185	-09/61	06/62	
43186	87 Der	04/51 3186	-01/59	*60*	
43187	87 Der	03/50 3187	-09/60	10/60	
43188	87 Der	03/49 3188	-04/60	08/60	
43189	87 Der	05/48 3189	-11/60	01/61	

Class continued with 43750

3F [3] 43191-43763
0-6-0 MR & SDJR Johnson 5ft 3in

Power Classification:	3F
Introduced:	1875-1902 (these rebuilt engines 1888-1902) Rebuilt by Deeley from 1903 onwards and by Fowler from 1916 onwards
Designer:	Johnson
Company:	MR s SDJR
Weight:	Loco 43t 17cwt
Driving Wheel:	5' 3"
Boiler Pressure:	175psi s 175psi superheated
Cylinders:	Inside 18" x 26"
Tractive Effort:	19890lbf
Valve Gear:	Stephenson (slide valves)

Refer to the Historical Survey of Midland 0-6-0 Engines at the end of this section for more details of this class.

These engines were the 5' 3" diameter wheeled version of the '43137' class described above. They were rebuilt from the '2F' '58188' class with larger boilers from 1903 onwards. They were later all rebuilt with Belpaire fireboxes and Deeley cabs by Fowler from 1916 onwards.

They retained their original numbers when they were rebuilt, and it was not until BR numbered the '2F's in the 58000 series that the two classes were numerically separated. The '2F's could always be distinguished from the '3F's by the square side sheet to the cabs. On the '3F's this was replaced by a small splasher merging with the cab.

s These engines were built for the Somerset & Dorset Joint Railway. They were acquired by the LMS in 1930 and they took the numbers of previously withdrawn engines. These engines were all superheated.

w Three engines (43326, 43333 and 43387) were rebuilt with 6' 0" diameter wheels in 1906. They all reverted to 5' 3" wheels by 1924.

Year End Totals: '3F [3]' class

'47	'48	'49	'50	'51	'52	'53	'54	'55	'56	'57	'58	'59	'60	'61	'62	'63	'64	'65	'66	'67
324	319	317	314	312	309	302	295	275	259	240	218	145	100	54	7	3				

Number	Built	Renumbered	BR Dates	Scrap	Notes
43191	09/88 Der	01/49 3191	-05/54	*54*	
43192	09/88 Der	12/49 3192	-08/59	03/60	
43193	10/88 Der	10/48 3193	-03/58	05/58	
43194	01/96 Der	12/49 3194	-12/60	03/61	s
43200	90 N	06/48 3200	-05/61	05/61	
43201	02/96 Der	10/49 3201	-04/57	05/57	s
43203	90 N	05/48 3203	-10/60	10/60	
43204	02/96 Der	12/49 3204	-09/56	*56*	s
43205	90 N	09/48 3205	-12/59	08/61	
43207	90 N	03/49 3207	-05/60	05/60	
43208	90 N	11/51 3208	-08/58	07/59	
43210	90 N	09/49 3210	-08/59	09/60	
43211	03/96 Der	06/48 3211	-07/61	06/62	s
43212	90 N	04/48 3212	-07/60	08/60	
43213	90 N	10/49 3213	-05/62	05/63	
43214	90 N	07/48 3214	-06/61	09/61	
43216	09/02 N	07/48 3216	-09/62	09/62	s
43218	09/02 N	01/49 3218	-05/60	07/60	s
43219	90 N	10/48 3219	-11/59	07/60	
43222	90 N	07/49 3222	-07/59	01/60	
43223	90 N	02/50 3223	-06/59	07/60	
43224	90 N	09/48 3224	-11/57	12/57	
43225	90 N	08/48 3225	-05/61	06/61	
43226	90 N	07/48 3226	-09/56	*09/56*	
43228	09/02 N	01/50 3228	-10/52	*52*	s
43231	90 N	09/49 3231	-10/58	06/59	
43232	90 N	12/48 3232	-08/56	*56*	
43233	90 N	03/50 3233	-11/59	10/60	
43234	90 N	02/49 3234	-01/61	03/61	
43235	90 N	06/48 3235	-09/60	10/60	
43237	90 N	04/48 3237	-06/59	10/60	
43239	90 N	06/49 3239	-12/57	01/58	
43240	90 N	02/49 3240	-10/62	09/63	
43241	90 N	09/49 3241	-07/59	07/60	
43242	90 N	05/48 3242	-08/62	10/62	
43243	90 N	10/48 3243	-08/60	08/60	
43244	90 N	01/50 3244	-01/59	02/61	
43245	90 N	07/49 3245	-04/61	02/62	
43246	90 N	06/48 3246	-10/56	*56*	
43247	90 N	02/49 3247	-11/59	07/60	
43248	09/02 N	08/49 3248	-08/59	03/60	s
43249	90 N	08/49 3249	-12/59	12/62	
43250	90 N	05/49 3250	-05/61	02/62	
43251	90 N	12/48 3251	-12/59	08/61	
43252	90 N	10/50 3252	-06/55	*55*	
43253	90 N	01/53 3253	-05/59	11/60	
43254	90 N	03/50 3254	-08/62	08/62	
43256	90 N	04/50 3256	-02/60	03/60	
43257	90 N	03/51 3257	-10/62	10/63	
43258	12/90 Der	12/48 3258	-08/59	10/60	
43259	12/90 Der	09/48 3259	-02/57	03/57	
43260	09/02 N	3260	-10/49	*10/49*	s
43261	91 N	08/48 3261	-12/62	01/63	
43263	91 N	04/48 3263	-06/62	06/62	
43265	91 N	3265	-05/48	*48*	
43266	91 N	09/49 3266	-03/61	10/61	
43267	91 N	05/48 3267	-04/61	04/61	
43268	91 N	11/49 3268	-06/61	07/61	
43269	91 N	3269	-05/48	*48*	
43271	91 N	08/50 3271	-12/59	06/61	
43273	91 N	04/48 3273	-10/55	*55*	
43274	91 N	11/50 3274	-01/59	02/61	
43275	91 N	08/48 3275	-01/56	*56*	
43277	91 N	12/48 3277	-07/61	02/62	
43278	91 N	02/49 3278	-12/59	06/62	
43281	91 N	01/49 3281	-12/56	*57*	
43282	91 N	06/51 3282	-10/62	10/63	
43283	91 N	08/48 3283	-08/53	*53*	
43284	91 N	03/49 3284	-06/61	09/61	
43286	91 N	09/49 3286	-09/57	09/57	
43287	91 N	06/49 3287	-12/59	08/60	
43290	91 N	03/49 3290	-12/57	03/58	
43292	91 N	08/49 3292	-03/59	02/60	
43293	91 N	01/49 3293	-12/53	*54*	
43294	91 N	10/48 3294	-11/59	06/60	
43295	91 N	08/48 3295	-10/61	02/62	
43296	91 N	05/49 3296	-03/54	*54*	
43297	91 N	06/48 3297	-06/50	*10/50*	
43298	91 N	06/48 3298	-11/55	12/55	
43299	91 N	10/48 3299	-08/54	*54*	
43300	10/91 K	09/49 3300	-12/58	02/60	
43301	10/91 K	07/52 3301	-11/58	06/59	
43305	12/91 K	05/50 3305	-04/60	06/60	
43306	12/91 K	10/49 3306	-03/61	06/61	
43307	12/91 K	12/50 3307	-08/60	08/60	
43308	01/92 K	03/49 3308	-10/59	10/60	
43309	01/92 K	05/48 3309	-04/61	07/61	
43310	01/92 K	04/48 3310	-12/55	*56*	
43312	01/92 K	05/49 3312	-01/58	01/58	
43313	01/92 K	05/50 3313	-04/56	*56*	
43314	02/92 K	03/49 3314	-04/60	06/60	
43315	02/92 K	05/49 3315	-08/59	03/60	
43317	02/92 K	11/49 3317	-10/55	*55*	
43318	02/92 K	01/49 3318	-08/59	03/60	
43319	02/92 K	05/48 3319	-12/50	*51*	
43321	03/92 K	10/50 3321	-02/61	06/61	
43323	03/92 K	01/50 3323	-06/58	09/58	
43324	03/92 K	03/49 3324	-04/59	09/60	
43325	03/92 K	04/49 3325	-02/61	10/61	
43326	03/92 K	12/48 3326	-08/60	08/60	w
43327	03/92 K	04/49 3327	-12/59	12/60	
43329	04/92 K	06/49 3329	-06/60	07/60	
43330	04/92 K	04/48 3330	-09/61	02/62	
43331	05/92 K	01/49 3331	-11/55	*11/55*	
43332	05/92 K	09/52 3332	-05/58	05/58	
43333	05/92 K	05/50 3333	-01/61	03/61	w
43334	05/92 K	03/51 3334	-03/56	*56*	
43335	05/92 K	09/49 3335	-08/59	08/60	
43336	05/92 K	01/50 3336	-08/52	*52*	
43337	06/92 K	11/48 3337	-02/60	03/60	
43338	06/92 K	3338	-03/48	*48*	
43339	06/92 K	01/49 3339	-08/59	08/60	
43340	91 D	09/48 3340	-10/60	11/60	
43341	91 D	11/48 3341	-10/57	11/57	
43342	91 D	04/50 3342	-09/63	11/63	
43344	91 D	06/48 3344	-05/60	06/60	
43351	91 D	07/51 3351	-12/55	12/55	
43355	91 D	01/49 3355	-05/59	10/60	
43356	91 D	04/48 3356	-07/58	06/59	
43357	91 D	03/50 3357	-02/59	02/61	
43359	91 D	10/49 3359	-09/60	10/60	
43361	91 D	07/50 3361	-11/60	11/60	
43364	91 D	01/50 3364	-12/53	*54*	
43367	91 D	05/49 3367	-01/58	03/58	
43368	91 D	11/50 3368	-11/61	02/62	
43369	91 D	09/49 3369	-08/59	08/60	
43370	92 SS	02/50 3370	-11/59	01/60	
43371	92 SS	12/48 3371	-09/61	09/61	
43373	92 SS	03/49 3373	-08/60	11/60	
43374	92 SS	10/48 3374	-07/61	07/61	
43378	92 SS	06/49 3378	-12/59	11/60	
43379	92 SS	03/50 3379	-11/59	07/60	
43381	92 SS	11/49 3381	-07/59	10/60	
43386	92 SS	02/49 3386	-04/61	07/61	
43387	92 SS	04/48 3387	-12/59	09/61	w
43388	92 SS	03/50 3388	-09/59	08/60	
43389	92 SS	03/50 3389	-08/62	10/62	
43392	92 SS	01/51 3392	-01/58	02/58	
43394	92 SS	05/50 3394	-07/60	08/60	
43395	92 SS	10/48 3395	-03/61	04/61	
43396	92 SS	12/48 3396	-08/57	08/57	
43398	92 SS	09/49 3398	-12/59	08/60	
43399	92 SS	07/50 3399	-09/60	12/60	
43400	93 SS	06/48 3400	-03/62	06/63	
43401	93 SS	04/50 3401	-05/57	06/57	
43402	93 SS	01/49 3402	-04/57	05/57	
43405	93 SS	02/50 3405	-02/61	08/61	
43406	93 SS	08/49 3406	-02/60	05/60	
43408	93 SS	3408	-04/50	04/50	
43410	92 D	08/49 3410	-03/62	05/62	
43411	92 D	05/48 3411	-06/61	07/61	
43419	92 D	06/49 3419	-09/58	07/59	
43427	92 D	12/49 3427	-07/61	08/61	
43428	92 D	08/48 3428	-12/62	01/63	
43429	92 D	02/50 3429	-04/60	07/60	
43431	93 D	01/50 3431	-02/60	05/60	
43433	93 D	10/50 3433	-12/59	07/60	
43435	93 D	03/49 3435	-04/62	05/62	
43436	93 D	09/52 3436	-06/62	11/62	
43439	93 D	3439	-06/48	*48*	
43440	93 D	09/48 3440	-12/59	08/60	
43441	93 D	11/49 3441	-11/58	06/59	
43443	93 D	02/49 3443	-12/57	01/58	
43444	93 D	07/49 3444	-12/60	04/61	
43446	93 D	06/48 3446	-04/62	06/62	
43448	93 D	05/48 3448	-01/54	*54*	
43449	93 D	03/51 3449	-09/62	12/62	
43453	93 D	01/50 3453	-03/63	05/63	
43454	93 D	06/48 3454	-02/55	*55*	
43456	93 D	10/49 3456	-04/60	07/60	
43457	93 D	05/50 3457	-06/60	07/60	
43458	93 D	3458	-04/49	*49*	
43459	93 D	11/48 3459	-04/61	06/61	
43462	94 Der	06/50 3462	-04/56	*56*	
43463	94 Der	09/51 3463	-02/57	03/57	
43464	94 Der	09/48 3464	-04/62	07/62	
43468	94 Der	07/49 3468	-06/61	09/61	
43469	94 Der	05/48 3469	-03/57	04/57	
43474	96 N	03/49 3474	-03/61	11/62	
43476	96 N	05/50 3476	-05/57	05/57	
43482	96 N	06/48 3482	-04/61	04/61	
43484	96 N	09/50 3484	-07/60	07/60	
43490	96 N	06/50 3490	-12/59	05/60	
43491	96 N	03/49 3491	-02/58	03/58	
43494	96 N	02/50 3494	-11/55	12/55	
43496	96 N	09/49 3496	-08/62	11/62	
43497	96 N	12/48 3497	-11/55	12/55	
43499	96 N	11/48 3499	-08/62	02/63	
43502	96 N	02/49 3502	-12/59	09/62	
43506	97 N	09/48 3506	-05/59	11/60	
43507	97 N	03/50 3507	-09/61	01/62	
43509	97 N	01/50 3509	-03/60	05/60	
43510	97 N	03/49 3510	-05/62	06/62	
43514	97 N	07/52 3514	-10/62	05/63	
43515	97 N	09/49 3515	-03/61	05/61	
43520	97 N	05/49 3520	-12/59	09/60	
43521	97 N	05/48 3521	-07/63	07/63	
43522	97 N	04/50 3522	-10/58	06/59	
43523	97 N	03/49 3523	-09/60	09/60	
43524	97 N	07/48 3524	-10/55	*55*	
43529	97 N	12/49 3529	-09/61	01/62	
43531	97 N	10/48 3531	-10/59	02/60	
43538	97 N	08/48 3538	-12/59	05/60	
43540	97 N	06/50 3540	-02/53	*03/53*	
43544	97 N	01/50 3544	-11/55	12/55	
43546	97 SS	11/48 3546	-11/56	*56*	
43548	97 SS	08/49 3548	-03/61	04/61	
43550	97 SS	04/50 3550	-12/56	*57*	
43553	97 SS	09/48 3553	-02/59	08/60	
43558	97 SS	01/49 3558	-08/59	08/60	
43562	97 SS	03/49 3562	-02/61	03/61	
43565	97 SS	09/48 3565	-06/62	09/62	
43568	97 SS	08/48 3568	-05/55	05/55	
43570	08/99 K	06/49 3570	-06/60	07/60	
43572	08/99 K	05/49 3572	-11/60	04/61	
43573	08/99 K	3573	-01/48	*48*	
43574	08/99 K	08/50 3574	-11/60	06/61	
43575	09/99 K	08/49 3575	-05/58	09/58	
43578	09/99 K	04/49 3578	-02/59	02/61	
43579	09/99 K	08/50 3579	-12/60	12/60	
43580	10/99 K	09/49 3580	-04/61	06/62	
43581	10/99 K	02/49 3581	-07/55	*55*	
43582	10/99 K	06/49 3582	-05/51	*51*	
43583	10/99 K	01/49 3583	-08/62	05/63	
43584	10/99 K	05/49 3584	-06/59	07/60	
43585	10/99 K	10/48 3585	-09/62	11/62	
43586	10/99 K	08/48 3586	-08/62	12/62	
43587	11/99 K	07/49 3587	-10/59	09/60	
43593	01/00 K	03/49 3593	-10/62	06/63	
43594	01/00 K	01/50 3594	-11/60	02/61	
43595	01/00 K	04/50 3595	-03/57	07/57	
43596	01/00 K	12/49 3596	-05/57	07/57	
43598	01/00 K	04/50 3598	-08/56	*09/56*	
43599	02/00 K	05/48 3599	-12/62	09/63	
43600	99 NR	10/48 3600	-05/55	*55*	
43604	99 NR	11/49 3604	-12/53	*12/53*	
43605	99 NR	02/50 3605	-05/61	06/61	
43607	99 NR	03/50 3607	-06/56	*56*	
43608	99 NR	06/49 3608	-08/62	10/62	

Midland Railway Johnson '1F' 0-6-0T No 1661 (later No 41661), fitted with an open cab, inside Kentish Town shed in September 1950.

London, Tilbury & Southend Railway Whitelegg '3P' 4-4-2T No 41977 at Shoeburyness in April 1958.

Brighton-built Fairburn '4MT' 2-6-4T No 42070 at Ramsgate shed in September 1952.

LMS Stanier three-cylinder '4MT' 2-6-4T No 42501 at Shoeburyness in April 1958.

Number	Built	Renumbered	BR Dates	Scrap	Notes
43612	99 NR	01/49 3612	-01/59	02/61	
43615	99 NR	01/49 3615	-10/62	10/63	
43618	99 NR	12/49 3618	-03/62	06/63	
43619	99 NR	10/49 3619	-08/59	08/60	
43620	99 NR	01/50 3620	-02/64	03/64	
43621	99 NR	12/48 3621	-04/62	06/62	
43622	99 NR	04/52 3622	-12/59	11/62	
43623	99 NR	01/50 3623	-08/59	08/60	
43624	99 NR	11/48 3624	-05/61	02/62	
43627	99 NR	06/48 3627	-06/60	07/60	
43629	99 NR	06/48 3629	-04/59	10/60	
43630	00 D	09/48 3630	-09/59	08/60	
43631	00 D	03/49 3631	-08/58	07/59	
43633	00 D	11/48 3633	-05/56	*56*	
43634	00 D	01/49 3634	-11/60	01/61	
43636	00 D	09/48 3636	-11/55	*55*	
43637	00 D	08/49 3637	-02/64	03/64	
43638	00 D	06/48 3638	-12/59	03/60	
43639	00 D	03/50 3639	-09/60	10/60	
43644	00 D	06/48 3644	-10/60	11/60	
43645	00 D	10/49 3645	-10/62	06/63	
43650	00 VF	10/50 3650	-10/60	02/61	
43651	00 VF	11/49 3651	-08/59	09/60	
43652	00 VF	03/50 3652	-09/60	10/60	
43653	00 VF	05/49 3653	-07/53	*53*	
43656	00 VF	03/51 3656	-04/58	05/58	
43657	00 VF	05/48 3657	-10/62	06/63	
43658	00 VF	01/50 3658	-10/63	12/63	
43660	00 VF	02/50 3660	-12/59	07/60	
43661	00 VF	03/49 3661	-11/54	*54*	
43662	00 VF	3662	-07/53	*53*	
43664	00 VF	09/49 3664	-03/60	04/60	
43665	00 VF	10/48 3665	-11/59	04/60	
43667	00 VF	10/48 3667	-04/54	*54*	
43668	00 VF	04/49 3668	-08/62	10/62	
43669	00 VF	04/51 3669	-02/64	03/64	
43673	04/01 K	09/49 3673	-09/61	01/62	
43674	04/01 K	01/50 3674	-08/59	08/60	
43675	04/01 K	07/49 3675	-12/59	05/60	
43676	04/01 K	10/48 3676	-10/55	*55*	
43678	05/01 K	11/48 3678	-12/59	02/60	
43679	05/01 K	02/51 3679	-01/62	02/62	
43680	05/01 K	10/49 3680	-08/62	05/63	
43681	05/01 K	11/48 3681	-10/61	08/62	
43682	05/01 K	05/50 3682	-09/62	09/62	
43683	05/01 K	12/48 3683	-10/54	11/54	
43684	05/01 K	01/49 3684	-06/57	08/57	
43686	05/01 K	08/49 3686	-11/55	*11/55*	
43687	06/01 K	04/49 3687	-08/62	05/63	
43690	01 SS	08/50 3690	-08/57	10/57	
43693	01 SS	01/49 3693	-12/59	07/60	
43698	01 SS	08/49 3698	-08/56	*56*	
43705	01 SS	04/49 3705	-12/60	12/60	
43709	01 SS	08/49 3709	-08/62	10/62	
43710	01 NR	04/49 3710	-03/58	03/58	
43711	01 NR	10/49 3711	-12/59	08/60	
43712	01 NR	03/49 3712	-01/59	02/61	
43714	01 NR	02/50 3714	-01/62	02/62	
43715	01 NR	04/49 3715	-02/61	03/61	
43717	01 NR	06/49 3717	-06/57	08/57	
43721	01 NR	11/49 3721	-03/62	06/63	
43723	01 NR	01/50 3723	-09/55	*55*	
43724	01 NR	01/50 3724	-12/52	*53*	
43727	01 NR	11/48 3727	-07/59	02/60	
43728	01 NR	10/49 3728	-12/59	07/60	
43729	01 NR	01/49 3729	-05/61	05/61	
43731	01 NR	*52* 3731	-06/59	02/60	
43734	01 NR	03/49 3734	-09/62	05/63	
43735	01 NR	04/49 3735	-09/60	10/60	
43737	01 NR	12/49 3737	-02/61	02/61	
43742	02 NR	01/49 3742	-08/58	07/59	
43745	02 NR	03/49 3745	-11/58	07/59	
43747	02 NR	3747	-11/51	*51*	
43748	02 NR	11/50 3748	-10/56	11/56	
43749	02 NR	08/53 3749	-03/60	06/60	

Class continued with 43751

3F [2] (43137), 43174-43189, 43750
0-6-0 MR Johnson 4ft 11in

Class continued from 43189

Number	Built	Renumbered	BR Dates	Scrap	Notes
43750	85 Der	01/52 *43137*	-10/59	11/59	

3F [3] 43191-43763
0-6-0 MR & SDJR Johnson 5ft 3in

Class continued from 43749

Number	Built	Renumbered	BR Dates	Scrap	Notes
43751	02 NR	12/48 3751	-09/61	09/61	
43753	02 NR	08/48 3753	-12/59	07/60	
43754	02 NR	06/48 3754	-10/62	06/63	
43755	02 NR	09/49 3755	-11/55	*11/55*	
43756	02 NR	05/49 3756	-09/62	11/62	
43757	02 NR	06/48 3757	-07/58	07/58	
43759	02 NR	09/50 3759	-11/59	04/60	
43760	02 NR	09/50 3760	-04/62	04/62	
43762	02 NR	05/48 3762	-03/61	04/61	
43763	02 NR	10/48 3763	-03/62	06/63	

3F [4] 43765-43833
0-6-0 MR Deeley

Power Classification:	3F
Introduced:	1903-1908
Designer:	Deeley
Company:	MR
Weight:	Loco 46t 3cwt
Driving Wheel:	5' 3"
Boiler Pressure:	175psi
Cylinders:	Inside 18½" x 26"
Tractive Effort:	21010lbf
Valve Gear:	Stephenson (slide valves)

Refer to the Historical Survey of Midland 0-6-0 Engines at the end of this section for more details of this class.

This class was built new by Deeley to the design of the rebuilt '3F' class (see '43191' class above). They were built between 1903-1908, and were later fitted with Belpaire boilers by Fowler from 1916 onwards.

Year End Totals: '3F [4]' class

'47	'48	'49	'50	'51	'52	'53	'54	'55	'56	'57	'58	'59	'60	'61	'62	'63	'64	'65	'66	'67
63	60	59	52	47	44	40	36	30	28	24	21	16	12	6						

Number	Built	Renumbered	BR Dates	Scrap	Notes
43765	01/03 Der	05/48 3765	-05/51	*51*	
43766	01/03 Der	09/48 3766	-08/62	11/62	
43767	02/03 Der	08/49 3767	-09/53	*53*	
43769	03/03 Der	3769	-06/48	*48*	
43770	03/03 Der	11/49 3770	-02/56	*56*	
43771	04/03 Der	08/49 3771	-02/59	02/61	
43772	04/03 Der	3772	-03/50	03/50	
43773	05/03 Der	03/50 3773	-05/60	06/60	
43775	07/03 Der	06/49 3775	-11/55	*55*	
43776	08/03 Der	04/51 3776	-11/57	12/57	
43777	08/03 Der	09/49 3777	-09/51	*51*	
43778	09/03 Der	10/50 3778	-03/61	04/61	
43779	09/03 Der	10/49 3779	-03/54	*54*	
43781	10/03 Der	09/49 3781	-11/55	*11/55*	
43782	11/03 Der	01/49 3782	-01/54	*54*	
43783	11/03 Der	3783	-02/49	*49*	
43784	12/03 Der	06/48 3784	-10/60	09/61	
43785	02/04 Der	02/49 3785	-11/59	06/61	
43786	02/04 Der	10/48 3786	-11/57	12/57	
43787	03/04 Der	11/48 3787	-01/59	02/61	
43789	03/04 Der	04/49 3789	-06/62	10/63	
43790	04/04 Der	04/49 3790	-06/56	*56*	
43791	04/04 Der	03/50 3791	-11/55	*11/55*	
43792	05/04 Der	02/49 3792	-05/53	*53*	
43793	05/04 Der	02/49 3793	-03/62	06/63	
43795	06/04 Der	09/48 3795	-04/57	06/57	
43796	06/04 Der	3796	-09/48	*48*	
43797	06/04 Der	11/49 3797	-06/53	*53*	
43798	07/04 Der	12/49 3798	-07/58	09/58	
43799	07/04 Der	12/51 3799	-12/59	08/61	
43800	08/04 Der	05/48 3800	-01/61	01/62	
43801	08/04 Der	11/48 3801	-09/51	*51*	
43802	08/04 Der	3802	-11/50	*11/50*	
43803	09/04 Der	04/49 3803	-09/55	*55*	
43804	09/04 Der	02/50 3804	-12/52	*53*	
43805	01/06 Der	3805	-06/50	06/50	
43806	01/06 Der	09/48 3806	-11/57	11/57	
43807	01/06 Der	06/49 3807	-09/52	*52*	
43808	02/06 Der	07/50 3808	-09/62	12/62	
43809	02/06 Der	11/49 3809	-04/61	05/61	
43810	02/06 Der	04/50 3810	-04/55	*55*	
43811	12/06 Der	01/49 3811	-02/51	02/51	
43812	12/06 Der	10/49 3812	-06/61	09/61	
43813	01/07 Der	3813	-01/50	01/50	
43814	01/07 Der	06/49 3814	-11/60	11/60	
43815	01/08 Der	08/49 3815	-09/58	06/59	
43817	01/08 Der	02/49 3817	-09/55	*09/55*	
43818	01/08 Der	09/48 3818	-05/50	*10/50*	
43819	02/08 Der	06/48 3819	-02/54	*54*	
43820	02/08 Der	3820	-07/52	*52*	
43821	02/08 Der	04/49 3821	-04/54	*54*	
43822	02/08 Der	01/49 3822	-08/62	07/63	
43823	03/08 Der	07/49 3823	-03/58	04/58	
43824	03/08 Der	04/49 3824	-08/51	*09/51*	
43825	03/08 Der	04/49 3825	-04/62	05/62	
43826	03/08 Der	11/49 3826	-11/61	01/62	
43827	04/08 Der	3827	-12/50	*51*	
43828	04/08 Der	08/49 3828	-01/60	02/60	
43829	04/08 Der	05/51 3829	-11/59	09/60	
43830	04/08 Der	3830	-01/50	01/50	
43831	05/08 Der	3831	-05/48	*48*	
43832	05/08 Der	04/50 3832	-11/61	01/62	
43833	05/08 Der	04/50 3833	-08/53	*53*	

4F [1] 43835-44026
0-6-0 MR Fowler

Power Classification:	4F
Introduced:	1911-1922
Designer:	Fowler
Company:	MR
Weight:	Loco 48t 15cwt
	Tender 41t 4cwt
Driving Wheel:	5' 3"
Boiler Pressure:	175psi superheated
Cylinders:	Inside 20" x 26"
Tractive Effort:	24555lbf
Valve Gear:	Stephenson (piston valves)

Refer to the Historical Survey of Midland 0-6-0 Engines at the end of this section for more details of this class.

These engines were Fowler's final development of the Midland's 0-6-0 engines. The first two engines were built as prototypes in 1911 and the rest followed from 1917 onwards. They were superheated and fitted with Belpaire boilers. They had a slightly higher pitched boiler, in order to clear the piston valves. They were later adopted as an LMS standard type (see '44027' class below).

Year End Totals: '4F [1]' class

'47	'48	'49	'50	'51	'52	'53	'54	'55	'56	'57	'58	'59	'60	'61	'62	'63	'64	'65	'66	'67
192	192	192	192	192	192	192	191	186	178	159	156	120	112	97	77	56	21			

Number	Built	Renumbered	BR Dates	Scrap	Notes
43835	10/11 Der	05/49 3835	-10/55	10/55	
43836	11/11 Der	06/48 3836	-07/59	07/59	
43837	05/17 Der	08/49 3837	-10/57	10/57	
43838	17 Der	04/48 3838	-07/56	*07/56*	
43839	17 Der	03/49 3839	-03/60	12/60	
43840	17 Der	07/51 3840	-09/60	10/60	
43841	17 Der	04/48 3841	-11/59	07/60	
43842	17 Der	11/48 3842	-11/59	03/60	
43843	17 Der	08/49 3843	-05/60	12/60	
43844	17 Der	05/50 3844	-06/62	06/62	
43845	17 Der	09/48 3845	-07/63	09/63	
43846	17 Der	11/48 3846	-07/61	09/61	
43847	17 Der	01/50 3847	-06/57	06/57	
43848	17 Der	06/49 3848	-06/62	10/62	
43849	17 Der	06/48 3849	-02/62	11/62	
43850	17 Der	06/48 3850	-12/64	04/65	
43851	17 Der	06/49 3851	-08/57	08/57	
43852	18 Der	03/50 3852	-05/57	05/57	
43853	18 Der	10/49 3853	-06/63	07/63	
43854	18 Der	01/49 3854	-06/64	09/64	
43855	18 Der	03/51 3855	-02/63	08/63	
43856	18 Der	01/49 3856	-09/64	04/65	
43857	18 Der	06/48 3857	-04/57	04/57	
43858	18 Der	08/48 3858	-12/59	06/60	
43859	18 Der	05/49 3859	-03/62	03/62	
43860	18 Der	11/48 3860	-09/59	02/60	
43861	18 Der	06/48 3861	-05/63	06/63	
43862	18 Der	01/49 3862	-08/54	*54*	
43863	18 Der	02/50 3863	-09/61	09/61	
43864	18 Der	06/49 3864	-11/59	05/61	
43865	18 Der	08/48 3865	-05/65	10/65	
43866	18 Der	06/49 3866	-12/59	03/60	
43867	18 Der	02/50 3867	-10/55	*55*	
43868	18 Der	07/50 3868	-11/60	02/61	
43869	18 Der	08/48 3869	-06/62	08/62	
43870	18 Der	04/49 3870	-10/63	11/63	
43871	18 Der	06/49 3871	-12/64	02/65	
43872	18 Der	02/49 3872	-09/61	09/61	
43873	18 Der	12/49 3873	-06/59	10/61	
43874	18 Der	03/49 3874	-03/56	*56*	
43875	18 Der	06/49 3875	-05/56	*56*	
43876	18 Der	12/48 3876	-12/62	01/63	
43877	18 Der	11/48 3877	-09/59	10/59	
43878	18 Der	10/49 3878	-12/59	09/60	
43879	12/18 Der	02/49 3879	-04/58	05/58	
43880	19 Der	11/49 3880	-05/64	12/64	
43881	19 Der	03/49 3881	-12/59	08/60	
43882	19 Der	05/49 3882	-07/63	07/63	
43883	19 Der	10/48 3883	-09/61	11/61	
43884	19 Der	07/48 3884	-12/61	06/62	
43885	19 Der	06/49 3885	-02/64	09/64	
43886	19 Der	12/49 3886	-11/59	06/60	
43887	19 Der	10/49 3887	-02/65	04/65	
43888	19 Der	10/48 3888	-09/64	03/65	
43889	19 Der	02/49 3889	-03/57	*03/57*	
43890	19 Der	06/51 3890	-02/59	08/60	
43891	19 Der	09/48 3891	-01/57	02/57	
43892	19 Der	05/49 3892	-02/58	02/58	

Number	Built	Renumbered	BR Dates	Scrap	Notes
43893	19 Der	07/49 3893	-05/65	10/65	
43894	19 Der	12/48 3894	-09/55	*55*	
43895	19 Der	04/49 3895	-07/56	*56*	
43896	19 Der	04/48 3896	-11/59	02/60	
43897	19 Der	01/49 3897	-01/60	01/62	
43898	19 Der	04/48 3898	-07/57	07/57	
43899	19 Der	12/48 3899	-10/62	11/63	
43900	19 Der	02/49 3900	-07/61	08/61	
43901	19 Der	09/49 3901	-09/57	09/57	
43902	20 Der	05/48 3902	-06/62	06/63	
43903	20 Der	05/49 3903	-05/64	12/64	
43904	20 Der	01/52 3904	-07/59	07/62	
43905	20 Der	09/49 3905	-08/61	12/61	
43906	20 Der	05/49 3906	-11/65	02/66	
43907	20 Der	07/49 3907	-12/59	12/59	
43908	20 Der	12/48 3908	-11/64	03/65	
43909	20 Der	06/48 3909	-08/55	*08/55*	
43910	20 Der	04/48 3910	-12/59	07/61	
43911	20 Der	10/48 3911	-06/61	06/61	
43912	20 Der	05/48 3912	-02/57	02/57	
43913	20 Der	11/48 3913	-04/65	09/65	
43914	20 Der	10/50 3914	-09/62	01/64	
43915	20 Der	06/49 3915	-02/63	04/63	
43916	20 Der	08/48 3916	-11/57	12/57	
43917	20 Der	09/48 3917	-08/64	11/64	
43918	20 Der	07/49 3918	-02/65	07/65	
43919	20 Der	06/49 3919	-12/59	08/61	
43920	20 Der	06/49 3920	-08/61	09/61	
43921	20 Der	08/48 3921	-06/61	06/61	
43922	20 Der	10/49 3922	-07/61	08/61	
43923	20 Der	11/49 3923	-02/64	02/64	
43924 §	10/20 Der	02/49 3924	-06/65		
43925	20 Der	02/49 3925	-06/64	10/64	
43926	20 Der	01/50 3926	-08/59	10/60	
43927	20 Der	06/48 3927	-11/57	11/57	
43928	20 Der	12/48 3928	-09/64	11/64	
43929	20 Der	05/48 3929	-11/64	02/65	
43930	20 Der	10/49 3930	-12/59	11/60	
43931	20 Der	03/50 3931	-08/64	11/64	
43932	20 Der	11/50 3932	-09/62	05/63	
43933	20 Der	10/48 3933	-11/62	01/63	
43934	12/20 Der	07/49 3934	-11/59	01/60	
43935	01/21 Der	11/49 3935	-10/63	10/64	
43936	01/21 Der	04/49 3936	-02/56	*56*	
43937	21 AW	01/49 3937	-07/63	10/63	
43938	21 AW	10/48 3938	-04/62	05/62	
43939	21 AW	10/49 3939	-06/59	09/60	
43940	21 AW	06/49 3940	-10/64	12/64	
43941	21 AW	10/49 3941	-09/57	10/57	
43942	21 AW	05/51 3942	-12/63	02/64	
43943	21 AW	08/48 3943	-09/56	*56*	
43944	21 AW	01/50 3944	-04/61	06/61	
43945	21 AW	08/49 3945	-04/63	05/63	
43946	21 AW	05/50 3946	-02/59	08/60	
43947	21 AW	06/49 3947	-10/64	02/65	
43948	21 AW	03/50 3948	-04/61	05/61	
43949	21 AW	01/49 3949	-12/64	03/65	
43950	21 AW	01/50 3950	-01/65	05/65	
43951	21 AW	02/50 3951	-09/64	10/64	
43952	21 AW	08/48 3952	-03/65	07/65	
43953	21 AW	12/48 3953	-11/65	01/66	
43954	21 AW	03/50 3954	-11/64	04/65	
43955	21 AW	12/48 3955	-01/64	03/64	
43956	21 AW	03/49 3956	-05/56	*56*	
43957	21 AW	09/48 3957	-05/64	05/64	
43958	21 AW	10/48 3958	-09/64	01/65	
43959	21 AW	06/49 3959	-01/57	02/57	
43960	21 AW	06/48 3960	-11/64	04/65	
43961	21 AW	07/50 3961	-12/59	06/61	
43962	21 AW	04/50 3962	-05/61	07/61	
43963	21 AW	08/49 3963	-11/64	03/65	
43964	21 AW	05/48 3964	-09/65	07/66	
43965	21 AW	04/49 3965	-12/59	09/60	
43966	12/21 AW	06/49 3966	-12/59	12/60	
43967	01/22 AW	05/50 3967	-08/65	12/65	
43968	22 AW	05/49 3968	-11/65	01/66	
43969	22 AW	12/48 3969	-10/63	11/63	
43970	22 AW	03/49 3970	-02/59	10/60	
43971	22 AW	12/49 3971	-04/64	05/64	
43972	22 AW	08/49 3972	-03/64	04/64	
43973	22 AW	11/48 3973	-07/60	10/60	
43974	22 AW	09/49 3974	-07/56	*07/56*	
43975	22 AW	10/49 3975	-01/65	05/65	
43976	22 AW	12/48 3976	-04/64	09/64	
43977	22 AW	06/49 3977	-11/63	12/63	
43978	22 AW	06/50 3978	-01/58	02/58	
43979	22 AW	12/48 3979	-11/64	02/65	
43980	22 AW	12/49 3980	-07/57	08/57	
43981	22 AW	10/48 3981	-08/65	02/66	
43982	22 AW	09/49 3982	-07/65	09/65	
43983	22 AW	04/49 3983	-08/65	11/65	
43984	22 AW	02/49 3984	-01/59	06/60	
43985	22 AW	07/50 3985	-04/62	05/62	
43986	22 AW	11/49 3986	-02/64	03/64	
43987	21 Der	02/49 3987	-07/63	03/64	
43988	21 Der	12/48 3988	-10/64	12/64	
43989	21 Der	08/49 3989	-04/60	07/60	
43990	21 Der	07/48 3990	-12/59	07/61	
43991	21 Der	04/51 3991	-05/65	10/65	
43992	21 Der	11/48 3992	-02/57	03/57	
43993	21 Der	10/49 3993	-07/57	07/57	
43994	21 Der	05/50 3994	-03/65	07/65	
43995	21 Der	02/49 3995	-06/63	09/63	
43996	21 Der	11/48 3996	-02/62	11/62	
43997	21 Der	07/48 3997	-12/59	09/60	
43998	21 Der	03/49 3998	-11/59	02/60	
43999	21 Der	11/48 3999	-05/65	09/65	
44000	21 Der	08/48 4000	-12/59	04/62	
44001	21 Der	01/50 4001	-03/62	11/62	
44002	21 Der	08/49 4002	-09/61	09/61	
44003	21 Der	03/52 4003	-05/65	08/65	
44004	21 Der	06/49 4004	-12/62	03/63	
44005	21 Der	07/48 4005	-12/59	02/61	
44006	21 Der	02/49 4006	-10/55	*55*	
44007	21 Der	07/50 4007	-07/64	11/64	
44008	21 Der	07/48 4008	-09/62	11/62	
44009	21 Der	09/49 4009	-06/64	12/64	
44010	21 Der	09/50 4010	-10/63	12/63	
44011	21 Der	06/49 4011	-10/62	12/62	
44012	21 Der	03/50 4012	-11/63	02/64	
44013	12/21 Der	10/48 4013	-10/63	10/63	
44014	01/22 Der	11/49 4014	-12/59	07/61	
44015	22 Der	10/48 4015	-09/63	12/63	
44016	22 Der	07/48 4016	-07/62	08/62	
44017	22 Der	05/48 4017	-08/57	10/57	
44018	22 Der	09/50 4018	-12/59	12/60	
44019	22 Der	03/49 4019	-06/60	*60*	
44020	22 Der	05/48 4020	-09/62	09/62	
44021	22 Der	11/49 4021	-12/59	10/60	
44022	22 Der	05/48 4022	-11/63	01/64	
44023	22 Der	04/49 4023	-12/64	02/65	
44024	22 Der	06/48 4024	-01/57	02/57	
44025	22 Der	08/48 4025	-11/64	04/65	
44026	22 Der	03/49 4026	-07/63	03/64	

4F ^{2} 44027-44606
0-6-0 LMS & SDJR Fowler

Power Classification: 4F
Introduced: 1924-1940
s 1922
Designer: Fowler
Company: LMS
s SDJR
Weight: Loco 48t 15cwt
Tender 41t 4cwt
Driving Wheel: 5' 3"
Boiler Pressure: 175psi superheated
Cylinders: Inside 20" x 26"
Tractive Effort: 24555lbf
Valve Gear: Stephenson (piston valves)

Refer to the Historical Survey of Midland 0-6-0 Engines at the end of this section for more details of this class.

After grouping in 1923, the LMS accepted the Midland '4F' '43835' class as a standard freight engine, and 580 more engines were built up to 1940 (making a total of 772 engines of both classes). The only difference was a reduction in size of the boiler mountings to allow the engines to be used all over the LMS system, and a change from right hand drive to left hand drive. Although officially freight engines, they were often used for passenger train working.

The engines were built at Derby, Crewe, St. Rollox and Horwich, as well as at a number of outside contractors (North British, Kerr Stuart and Andrew Barclay). They were built in 1924-1928 and 1937-1940. Some of the class were later used as departmental engines.

s 44557-44561 were built in 1922 by the Midland Railway for the Somerset & Dorset Joint Railway where they were numbered 57-61. They became part of LMS stock in 1930.

o These locomotives were converted to oil burning during the coal crisis after the Second World War. They were later converted back to coal burning (c).

Year End Totals: '4F ^{2}' class

'47	'48	'49	'50	'51	'52	'53	'54	'55	'56	'57	'58	'59	'60	'61	'62	'63	'64	'65	'66	'67
580	580	580	580	580	580	580	580	580	580	580	580	536	495	472	396	261	107	11		

Number	*Built*	*Renumbered*	*BR Dates*	*Scrap*	*Notes*
44027 §	11/24 Der	05/49 4027	-11/64		
44028	11/24 Der	04/49 4028	-11/65	01/66	
44029	12/24 Der	03/49 4029	-07/60	08/60	
44030	12/24 Der	11/48 4030	-04/64	08/64	
44031	12/24 Der	11/49 4031	-05/60	05/60	
44032	12/24 Der	11/51 4032	-11/59	02/60	
44033	12/24 Der	05/50 4033	-10/61	12/61	
44034	12/24 Der	03/50 4034	-07/63	10/63	
44035	01/25 Der	03/50 4035	-02/65	05/65	
44036	01/25 Der	10/48 4036	-06/62	08/62	
44037	01/25 Der	03/50 4037	-09/61	09/61	
44038	01/25 Der	02/50 4038	-04/64	04/64	
44039	01/25 Der	12/48 4039	-06/64	07/64	
44040	01/25 Der	04/49 4040	-11/64	03/65	
44041	02/25 Der	06/49 4041	-06/64	09/64	
44042	02/25 Der	10/49 4042	-10/64	01/65	
44043	02/25 Der	06/48 4043	-07/65	10/65	
44044	02/25 Der	10/49 4044	-07/65	10/65	
44045	03/25 Der	01/49 4045	-11/64	03/65	
44046	03/25 Der	05/50 4046	-09/63	10/63	
44047	03/25 Der	04/49 4047	-10/63	04/64	
44048	03/25 Der	09/48 4048	-08/64	01/65	
44049	03/25 Der	11/49 4049	-12/64	04/65	
44050	03/25 Der	11/48 4050	-11/59	05/60	
44051	04/25 Der	02/50 4051	-12/64	07/65	
44052	04/25 Der	03/49 4052	-06/60	06/60	
44053	04/25 Der	06/48 4053	-03/63	04/63	
44054	05/25 Der	01/50 4054	-12/64	04/65	
44055	05/25 Der	06/49 4055	-11/63	02/64	
44056	05/25 Der	09/49 4056	-11/65	01/66	
44057	08/25 NB	10/48 4057	-11/65	12/65	
44058	08/25 NB	07/48 4058	-11/59	06/60	
44059	09/25 NB	04/50 4059	-08/64	01/65	
44060	09/25 NB	04/48 4060	-03/64	04/64	
44061	09/25 NB	12/48 4061	-06/65	10/65	
44062	09/25 NB	02/49 4062	-09/62	03/64	
44063	09/25 NB	11/48 4063	-06/65	10/65	
44064	10/25 NB	11/49 4064	-11/59	07/61	
44065	10/25 NB	05/50 4065	-01/65	04/65	
44066	10/25 NB	05/50 4066	-10/63	12/63	
44067	10/25 NB	02/49 4067	-04/61	05/61	
44068	10/25 NB	01/49 4068	-10/63	02/64	
44069	10/25 NB	12/49 4069	-10/63	07/64	
44070	11/25 NB	10/49 4070	-07/62	08/62	
44071	11/25 NB	03/49 4071	-05/63	06/63	
44072	11/25 NB	10/48 4072	-11/59	05/61	
44073	11/25 NB	02/49 4073	-11/59	10/60	
44074	11/25 NB	11/48 4074	-09/63	02/64	
44075	11/25 NB	08/50 4075	-11/65	01/66	
44076	11/25 NB	04/48 4076	-07/65	03/66	
44077	11/25 NB	07/49 4077	-03/60	06/60	
44078	11/25 NB	05/49 4078	-04/64	05/64	
44079	11/25 NB	06/48 4079	-11/64	03/65	
44080	11/25 NB	12/48 4080	-07/64	01/65	
44081	11/25 NB	02/50 4081	-09/65	01/66	
44082	09/25 KS	11/49 4082	-09/61	09/61	
44083	09/25 KS	01/49 4083	-12/63	01/64	
44084	10/25 KS	02/49 4084	-12/59	05/60	
44085	10/25 KS	02/49 4085	-10/63	01/64	
44086	11/25 KS	08/48 4086	-11/65	04/66	
44087	11/25 KS	10/49 4087	-03/62	03/62	
44088	11/25 KS	12/48 4088	-12/61	01/62	
44089	11/25 KS	10/48 4089	-12/63	04/64	
44090	11/25 KS	09/49 4090	-10/61	11/62	
44091	11/25 KS	03/51 4091	-02/64	03/64	
44092	11/25 KS	04/50 4092	-09/64	12/64	
44093	11/25 KS	03/49 4093	-03/60	07/61	
44094	11/25 KS	01/49 4094	-05/63	09/63	
44095	11/25 KS	12/48 4095	-12/59	10/60	
44096	11/25 KS	07/49 4096	-10/64	02/65	
44097	11/25 KS	10/48 4097	-06/63	02/64	
44098	11/25 KS	11/51 4098	-12/63	02/64	
44099	12/25 KS	05/49 4099	-02/65	05/65	
44100	12/25 KS	09/48 4100	-04/63	04/63	
44101	12/25 KS	08/48 4101	-05/63	09/63	
44102	12/25 KS	12/48 4102	-09/64	04/65	
44103	12/25 KS	11/48 4103	-12/59	01/60	
44104	12/25 KS	02/50 4104	-06/62	08/62	
44105	12/25 KS	02/50 4105	-10/61	11/62	
44106	01/26 KS	01/50 4106	-02/64	09/64	
44107	12/24 Crw	10/49 4107	-09/61	10/61	
44108	01/25 Crw	10/48 4108	-12/59	09/60	
44109	02/25 Crw	12/49 4109	-05/64	08/64	
44110	03/25 Crw	01/50 4110	-04/64	09/64	
44111	03/25 Crw	11/49 4111	-09/61	11/61	
44112	03/25 Crw	06/49 4112	-01/63	03/63	
44113	05/25 Crw	06/49 4113	-01/66	05/66	
44114	05/25 Crw	03/49 4114	-05/63	10/63	
44115	05/25 Crw	08/49 4115	-07/65	10/65	
44116	05/25 Crw	12/49 4116	-11/59	06/60	
44117	06/25 Crw	04/49 4117	-09/64	01/65	
44118	06/25 Crw	10/48 4118	-05/65	10/65	
44119	06/25 Crw	09/48 4119	-12/63	06/65	
44120	07/25 Crw	03/49 4120	-11/59	02/61	
44121	07/25 Crw	04/49 4121	-01/65	05/65	
44122	07/25 Crw	11/48 4122	-09/62	09/62	
44123 §	07/25 Crw	05/49 4123	-06/65		
44124	07/25 Crw	05/49 4124	-05/64	12/64	
44125	08/25 Crw	11/48 4125	-03/65	10/65	
44126	08/25 Crw	08/48 4126	-09/63	12/63	
44127	08/25 Crw	08/48 4127	-01/65	03/65	
44128	08/25 Crw	05/49 4128	-12/62	06/63	
44129	08/25 Crw	05/48 4129	-09/62	06/63	
44130	09/25 Crw	11/48 4130	-12/64	04/65	
44131	09/25 Crw	11/48 4131	-11/64	03/65	

44132	09/25 Crw	06/50 4132	-08/63 10/63	
44133	09/25 Crw	12/49 4133	-11/63 02/64	
44134	09/25 Crw	12/49 4134	-11/64 07/65	
44135	09/25 Crw	10/49 4135	-04/65 06/65	
44136	10/25 Crw	11/48 4136	-12/59 10/60	
44137	10/25 Crw	08/48 4137	-02/65 11/65	
44138	10/25 Crw	07/48 4138	-07/62 07/62	
44139	10/25 Crw	07/49 4139	-08/65 11/65	
44140	10/25 Crw	03/49 4140	-12/59 01/60	
44141	11/25 Crw	12/48 4141	-07/61 10/61	
44142	11/25 Crw	10/49 4142	-12/59 06/60	
44143	11/25 Crw	02/51 4143	-10/62 10/62	
44144	11/25 Crw	09/49 4144	-08/59 09/59	
44145	11/25 Crw	02/49 4145	-02/59 03/59	
44146	11/25 Crw	11/48 4146	-11/64 04/65	
44147	11/25 Crw	06/48 4147	-09/61 09/61	
44148	11/25 Crw	09/49 4148	-05/61 08/61	
44149	11/25 Crw	03/49 4149	-11/64 04/65	
44150	11/25 Crw	11/49 4150	-01/63 03/63	
44151	12/25 Crw	10/49 4151	-12/63 02/64	
44152	12/25 Crw	06/49 4152	-09/61 03/62	
44153	12/25 Crw	04/50 4153	-04/63 09/63	
44154	12/25 Crw	02/49 4154	-04/62 04/62	
44155	12/25 Crw	06/48 4155	-10/65 11/65	
44156	12/25 Crw	08/48 4156	-02/64 11/64	
44157	12/25 Crw	03/50 4157	-07/65 11/65	
44158	12/25 Crw	12/48 4158	-07/62 08/62	
44159	02/26 Crw	01/49 4159	-10/62 11/63	
44160	02/26 Crw	08/49 4160	-12/65 03/66	
44161	02/26 Crw	09/49 4161	-12/59 11/60	
44162	02/26 Crw	11/49 4162	-12/63 01/65	
44163	02/26 Crw	10/48 4163	-07/60 08/60	
44164	02/26 Crw	02/49 4164	-07/63 11/63	
44165	02/26 Crw	05/49 4165	-08/64 01/65	
44166	02/26 Crw	04/49 4166	-01/62 03/62	
44167	03/26 Crw	02/49 4167	-01/64 07/64	
44168	03/26 Crw	01/49 4168	-10/63 11/63	
44169	03/26 Crw	03/50 4169	-08/65 12/65	
44170	03/26 Crw	02/49 4170	-11/65 01/66	
44171	03/26 Crw	05/49 4171	-05/64 08/64	
44172	03/26 Crw	04/49 4172	-05/64 12/64	
44173	04/26 Crw	04/49 4173	-12/59 10/61	
44174	04/26 Crw	11/48 4174	-12/63 05/64	
44175	04/26 Crw	09/48 4175	-12/59 08/61	
44176	04/26 Crw	06/49 4176	-07/63 11/63	
44177	12/24 SRlx	10/48 4177	-11/64 02/65	
44178	12/24 SRlx	09/49 4178	-11/64 03/65	
44179	01/25 SRlx	07/50 4179	-12/64 01/65	
44180	02/25 SRlx	01/49 4180	-04/64 06/64	
44181	02/25 SRlx	04/50 4181	-08/65 01/66	
44182	02/25 SRlx	01/49 4182	-09/64 03/65	
44183	03/25 SRlx	04/50 4183	-10/63 03/64	
44184	03/25 SRlx	11/49 4184	-10/63 03/64	
44185	03/25 SRlx	04/48 4185	-11/64 02/65	
44186	03/25 SRlx	12/48 4186	-10/63 04/65	
44187	04/25 SRlx	11/49 4187	-07/62 08/62	
44188	04/25 SRlx	06/49 4188	-11/65 02/66	
44189	04/25 SRlx	12/49 4189	-12/62 11/63	
44190	05/25 SRlx	07/48 4190	-09/63 12/63	
44191	05/25 SRlx	10/49 4191	-08/64 10/64	
44192	06/25 SRlx	01/49 4192	-04/65 08/65	
44193	06/25 SRlx	02/49 4193	-10/62 09/63	
44194	06/25 SRlx	10/49 4194	-12/62 05/63	
44195	07/25 SRlx	08/49 4195	-03/65 05/65	
44196	07/25 SRlx	03/49 4196	-01/62 06/62	
44197	10/25 SRlx	12/48 4197	-09/64 01/65	
44198	10/25 SRlx	07/49 4198	-05/63 02/64	⊠12/62-02/63
44199	10/25 SRlx	05/49 4199	-12/62 11/63	
44200	10/25 SRlx	07/50 4200	-07/65 01/66	
44201	10/25 SRlx	09/49 4201	-09/59 10/59	
44202	10/25 SRlx	02/49 4202	-09/63 11/63	
44203	11/25 SRlx	03/51 4203	-03/66 06/66	
44204	11/25 SRlx	10/49 4204	-12/59 10/60	
44205	11/25 SRlx	05/49 4205	-03/63 05/63	
44206	11/25 SRlx	09/49 4206	-06/61 06/61	
44207	11/25 Der	12/50 4207	-11/63 01/64	
44208	11/25 Der	10/50 4208	-10/63 12/63	
44209	11/25 Der	10/48 4209	-06/63 08/63	
44210	11/25 Der	01/50 4210	-10/65 12/65	
44211	12/25 Der	01/49 4211	-03/65 10/65	
44212	12/25 Der	06/50 4212	-12/63 05/64	
44213	12/25 Der	12/49 4213	-06/64 12/64	
44214	12/25 Der	11/48 4214	-12/64 04/65	
44215	12/25 Der	12/50 4215	-02/65 05/65	
44216	12/25 Der	09/48 4216	-09/62 02/64	
44217	01/26 Der	10/48 4217	-12/59 10/60	
44218	01/26 Der	03/49 4218	-03/66 06/66	
44219	01/26 Der	02/49 4219	-11/63 02/64	
44220	01/26 Der	04/48 4220	-09/64 02/65	
44221	01/26 Der	06/49 4221	-05/64 11/64	
44222	01/26 Der	03/49 4222	-11/64 04/65	
44223	01/26 Der	02/49 4223	-11/63 03/64	
44224	01/26 Der	03/51 4224	-02/62 03/62	
44225	02/26 Der	08/48 4225	-11/59 06/61	
44226	02/26 Der	05/48 4226	-09/64 01/65	
44227	02/26 Der	12/49 4227	-12/59 06/60	
44228	02/26 Der	08/48 4228	-12/62 03/63	
44229	02/26 Der	12/48 4229	-11/64 03/65	
44230	02/26 Der	08/48 4230	-12/59 02/61	
44231	02/26 Der	06/49 4231	-06/63 12/63	
44232	03/26 Der	04/51 4232	-11/63 01/64	
44233	03/26 Der	06/48 4233	-11/64 03/65	
44234	03/26 Der	08/48 4234	-10/62 10/63	
44235	03/26 Der	06/48 4235	-12/64 04/65	
44236	03/26 Der	04/51 4236	-10/64 05/65	
44237	03/26 Der	06/49 4237	-10/63 04/64	
44238	03/26 Der	05/49 4238	-12/63 02/64	
44239	04/26 Der	03/50 4239	-10/63 07/64	
44240	04/26 Der	08/49 4240	-09/64 12/64	
44241	04/26 Der	06/48 4241	-07/63 11/63	
44242	04/26 Der	10/48 4242	-05/64 04/65	
44243	04/26 Der	02/49 4243	-09/65 12/65	
44244	04/26 Der	03/49 4244	-10/64 12/64	
44245	04/26 Der	05/52 4245	-05/62 05/62	
44246	05/26 Der	12/49 4246	-12/64 07/66	
44247	05/26 Der	10/48 4247	-12/65 02/66	
44248	05/26 Der	11/51 4248	-09/64 03/65	
44249	06/26 Der	02/50 4249	-12/61 01/62	
44250	06/26 Der	03/49 4250	-05/65 08/65	
44251	06/26 Der	06/49 4251	-10/62 12/62	
44252	07/26 Der	01/50 4252	-05/63 05/63	
44253	07/26 Der	03/48 4253	-10/62 10/62	
44254	07/26 Der	12/49 4254	-10/62 11/62	
44255	07/26 Der	09/49 4255	-12/62 11/63	
44256	07/26 Der	*50* 4256	-04/62 05/63	
44257	07/26 Der	04/50 4257	-10/62 07/63	
44258	08/26 Der	03/49 4258	-05/62 06/62	
44259	08/26 Der	06/49 4259	-08/64 10/64	
44260	08/26 Der	05/48 4260	-10/64 12/64	
44261	09/26 Der	11/48 4261	-10/63 10/63	
44262	09/26 Der	04/49 4262	-09/63 10/63	
44263	10/26 Der	11/49 4263	-03/65 10/65	
44264	10/26 Der	11/49 4264	-11/65 02/66	
44265	10/26 Der	06/48 4265	-12/63 05/64	
44266	10/26 Der	10/48 4266	-03/65 10/65	
44267	10/26 Der	11/50 4267	-06/62 08/62	
44268	10/26 Der	05/49 4268	-03/63 04/63	
44269	10/26 Der	05/49 4269	-12/65 03/66	
44270	11/26 Der	09/49 4270	-11/63 02/64	
44271	11/26 Der	01/49 4271	-12/65 04/66	
44272	11/26 Der	08/49 4272	-06/63 09/63	
44273	11/26 Der	04/50 4273	-09/62 09/63	
44274	11/26 Der	03/49 4274	-12/63 01/64	
44275	11/26 Der	04/48 4275	-10/64 02/65	
44276	12/26 Der	11/50 4276	-05/65 09/65	
44277	12/26 Der	07/48 4277	-05/65 09/65	
44278	12/26 Der	08/50 4278	-01/66 05/66	
44279	12/26 Der	05/51 4279	-01/64 01/65	
44280	12/26 Der	11/49 4280	-12/63 02/64	
44281	12/26 Der	08/48 4281	-12/62 11/63	
44282	12/26 Der	11/48 4282	-07/63 05/64	
44283	12/26 Der	07/48 4283	-07/63 02/64	⊠12/62-02/63
44284	12/26 Der	10/50 4284	-08/64 12/64	
44285	12/26 Der	06/49 4285	-12/59 12/60	
44286	12/26 Der	03/50 4286	-05/64 12/64	
44287	12/26 Der	12/48 4287	-12/63 05/64	
44288	01/27 Der	04/50 4288	-04/64 07/64	
44289	01/27 Der	03/50 4289	-06/64 09/64	
44290	01/27 Der	08/49 4290	-06/64 08/64	
44291	01/27 Der	03/50 4291	-11/59 07/61	
44292	01/27 Der	05/50 4292	-08/63 07/64	
44293	01/27 Der	10/48 4293	-12/59 07/61	
44294	02/27 Der	12/50 4294	-11/65 07/66	
44295	02/27 Der	04/50 4295	-02/64 02/64	
44296	02/27 Der	11/49 4296	-01/64 07/64	
44297	02/27 Der	02/49 4297	-09/63 11/63	
44298	02/27 Der	05/48 4298	-12/59 05/60	
44299	02/27 Der	08/49 4299	-05/63 06/63	
44300	02/27 Der	04/48 4300	-12/65 02/66	
44301	03/27 Der	09/48 4301	-04/64 05/64	
44302	10/26 Crw	02/49 4302	-03/64 04/64	
44303	10/26 Crw	11/49 4303	-09/63 10/63	
44304	10/26 Crw	09/48 4304	-05/64 12/64	
44305	10/26 Crw	09/48 4305	-04/65 07/65	
44306	10/26 Crw	06/49 4306	-11/59 02/60	
44307	10/26 Crw	04/48 4307	-10/62 05/63	
44308	09/26 Crw	12/48 4308	-10/63 12/63	
44309	10/26 Crw	09/48 4309	-07/63 11/63	
44310	10/26 Crw	08/49 4310	-02/66 05/66	
44311	10/26 Crw	06/49 4311	-07/66 10/66	
44312	11/27 SRlx	06/49 4312	-10/62 10/63	
44313	11/27 SRlx	05/50 4313	-12/59 10/60	
44314	12/27 SRlx	11/48 4314	-08/62 12/62	
44315	12/27 SRlx	02/49 4315	-05/64 10/64	
44316	12/27 SRlx	05/48 4316	-12/59 12/60	
44317	12/27 SRlx	05/49 4317	-12/59 01/61	
44318	01/28 SRlx	03/49 4318	-10/62 12/62	
44319	01/28 SRlx	09/49 4319	-11/61 01/62	
44320	01/28 SRlx	03/49 4320	-10/62 09/63	
44321	01/28 SRlx	03/49 4321	-04/64 11/64	
44322	01/28 SRlx	03/49 4322	-07/63 03/64	⊠12/62-02/63
44323	01/28 SRlx	03/50 4323	-10/62 10/63	
44324	01/28 SRlx	11/49 4324	-11/61 03/62	
44325	02/28 SRlx	03/48 4325	-10/62 11/63	
44326	02/28 SRlx	10/48 4326	-12/59 12/59	
44327	02/28 SRlx	12/49 4327	-05/64 12/64	
44328	02/28 SRlx	07/49 4328	-12/62 10/63	
44329	03/28 SRlx	12/49 4329	-08/62 05/63	
44330	03/28 SRlx	04/48 4330	-10/62 10/63	
44331	03/28 SRlx	03/49 4331	-05/63 02/64	⊠12/62-02/63
44332	10/26 KS	10/49 4332	-09/64 01/65	
44333	10/26 KS	12/48 4333	-05/64 12/64	
44334	10/26 KS	03/51 4334	-06/65 10/65	
44335	10/26 KS	01/52 4335	-03/63 09/63	
44336	10/26 KS	03/49 4336	-12/63 02/64	
44337	10/26 KS	05/49 4337	-05/64 07/64	
44338	10/26 KS	06/50 4338	-09/62 01/64	
44339	10/26 KS	04/49 4339	-12/65 04/66	
44340	10/26 KS	11/48 4340	-12/62 02/65	
44341	12/26 KS	06/49 4341	-02/63 05/63	
44342	12/26 KS	10/49 4342	-10/63 04/64	
44343	01/27 KS	08/49 4343	-03/60 07/60	
44344	01/27 KS	11/48 4344	-12/64 04/65	
44345	01/27 KS	10/49 4345	-12/63 11/64	
44346	01/27 KS	04/49 4346	-11/65 01/66	
44347	03/27 KS	11/48 4347	-03/65 10/65	
44348	04/27 KS	05/49 4348	-08/64 01/65	
44349	04/27 KS	06/48 4349	-07/65 10/65	
44350	04/27 KS	06/48 4350	-12/65 04/66	
44351	05/27 KS	01/50 4351	-04/63 06/64	
44352	05/27 KS	02/50 4352	-10/63 04/64	
44353	05/27 KS	05/49 4353	-02/65 05/65	
44354	05/27 KS	03/49 4354	-10/63 02/64	
44355	06/27 KS	08/48 4355	-09/65 12/65	
44356	06/27 KS	01/49 4356	-11/65 01/66	
44357	01/27 AB	02/49 4357	-11/59 05/61	
44358	01/27 AB	08/48 4358	-01/65 07/65	
44359	01/27 AB	05/50 4359	-07/63 12/63	
44360	02/27 AB	06/49 4360	-03/60 01/61	
44361	02/27 AB	09/49 4361	-11/59 01/62	
44362	04/27 AB	06/48 4362	-09/64 04/65	
44363	04/27 AB	11/48 4363	-10/63 01/64	
44364	04/27 AB	09/49 4364	-01/64 12/65	
44365	05/27 AB	06/49 4365	-11/59 01/61	
44366	05/27 AB	08/48 4366	-03/60 11/60	
44367	06/27 AB	04/49 4367	-09/64 02/65	
44368	07/27 AB	04/48 4368	-09/62 09/63	
44369	07/27 AB	09/49 4369	-12/59 09/60	
44370	07/27 AB	05/49 4370	-09/63 03/64	
44371	08/27 AB	05/49 4371	-06/61 06/61	
44372	09/27 AB	04/50 4372	-11/59 06/60	
44373	10/27 AB	03/49 4373	-12/64 05/65	
44374	10/27 AB	09/48 4374	-03/63 05/63	
44375	11/27 AB	09/49 4375	-10/60 10/60	
44376	11/27 AB	03/50 4376	-12/64 03/65	
44377	12/27 AB	01/49 4377	-10/66 02/67	
44378	12/27 AB	06/49 4378	-04/63 05/63	
44379	12/27 AB	10/48 4379	-09/64 03/65	
44380	01/28 AB	06/48 4380	-08/64 10/64	
44381	01/28 AB	05/48 4381	-09/64 02/65	
44382	09/26 NB	12/49 4382	-11/59 03/60	
44383	09/26 NB	05/49 4383	-11/59 01/60	
44384	09/26 NB	11/48 4384	-10/64 03/65	
44385	10/26 NB	09/48 4385	-08/59 08/59	
44386	10/26 NB	12/48 4386	-05/65 10/65	
44387	10/26 NB	07/48 4387	-10/63 04/64	
44388	10/26 NB	07/48 4388	-12/62 02/63	
44389	10/26 NB	10/48 4389	-07/65 11/65	
44390	10/26 NB	04/48 4390	-11/65 01/66	
44391	10/26 NB	08/48 4391	-03/60 05/60	
44392	10/26 NB	03/49 4392	-06/64 01/65	
44393	10/26 NB	08/48 4393	-10/62 03/63	
44394	10/26 NB	05/48 4394	-07/66 10/66	
44395	10/26 NB	05/49 4395	-12/63 12/64	
44396	10/26 NB	05/49 4396	-06/64 01/65	
44397	12/26 NB	06/49 4397	-04/62 04/62	
44398	12/26 NB	11/48 4398	-07/63 08/63	
44399	12/26 NB	05/50 4399	-02/64 04/65	
44400	01/27 NB	10/48 4400	-11/65 01/66	
44401	01/27 NB	10/51 4401	-06/65 10/65	
44402	01/27 NB	07/48 4402	-01/65 04/65	
44403	01/27 NB	07/48 4403	-06/64 10/64	
44404	01/27 NB	06/51 4404	-12/62 05/63	
44405	01/27 NB	04/49 4405	-06/66 10/66	
44406	01/27 NB	08/49 4406	-03/60 06/60	
44407	08/27 Der	01/49 4407	-09/62 09/62	
44408	08/27 Der	02/49 4408	-11/65 01/66	
44409	08/27 Der	03/51 4409	-12/61 03/62	
44410	08/27 Der	05/49 4410	-03/60 10/60	
44411	09/27 Der	05/49 4411	-10/63 04/64	
44412	09/27 Der	02/49 4412	-03/60 10/60	
44413	09/27 Der	11/49 4413	-03/63 07/63	
44414	09/27 Der	08/50 4414	-05/65 08/65	
44415	09/27 Der	06/49 4415	-03/60 08/60	
44416	09/27 Der	09/48 4416	-07/63 10/63	
44417	09/27 Der	02/49 4417	-10/62 05/63	
44418	09/27 Der	10/49 4418	-10/63 09/64	
44419	09/27 Der	09/49 4419	-09/63 10/64	
44420	10/27 Der	02/50 4420	-09/65 01/66	
44421	10/27 Der	02/50 4421	-12/64 04/65	

44422 §	10/27	Der	06/50	4422	-06/65	
44423	10/27	Der	01/50	4423	-11/59	60
44424	10/27	Der	07/49	4424	-10/63	04/64
44425	10/27	Der	06/48	4425	-02/65	05/65
44426	10/27	Der	07/49	4426	-12/63	04/64
44427	10/27	Der	09/49	4427	-03/60	11/60
44428	10/27	Der	09/49	4428	-02/64	08/64
44429	10/27	Der	08/48	4429	-05/65	08/65
44430	11/27	Der	07/48	4430	-03/60	12/60
44431	11/27	Der	03/49	4431	-09/64	02/65
44432	11/27	Der	05/50	4432	-10/63	01/65
44433	11/27	Der	02/49	4433	-12/64	04/65
44434	11/27	Der	04/50	4434	-09/63	10/63
44435	12/27	Der	06/51	4435	-10/62	11/62
44436	12/27	Der	02/53	4436	-04/64	09/64
44437	11/27	Crw	08/49	4437	-12/63	05/64
44438	12/27	Crw	10/48	4438	-03/60	09/61
44439	12/27	Crw	10/48	4439	-04/64	12/64
44440	12/27	Crw	03/49	4440	-04/64	04/64
44441	12/27	Crw	01/49	4441	-09/64	11/64
44442	12/27	Crw	05/48	4442	-07/63	10/63
44443	12/27	Crw	05/50	4443	-08/65	12/65
44444	12/27	Crw	12/48	4444	-09/63	10/63
44445	12/27	Crw	10/49	4445	-06/63	08/64
44446	12/27	Crw	04/48	4446	-11/65	12/65
44447	01/28	Crw	10/49	4447	-07/63	12/63
44448	01/28	Crw	11/48	4448	-11/63	12/63
44449	01/28	Crw	06/50	4449	-08/65	12/65
44450	02/28	Crw	02/49	4450	-05/65	09/65
44451	02/28	Crw	01/49	4451	-12/65	03/66
44452	02/28	Crw	05/49	4452	-06/64	12/64
44453	02/28	Crw	01/50	4453	-03/60	09/60
44454	02/28	Crw	10/48	4454	-10/63	11/63
44455	02/28	Crw	04/49	4455	-03/63	08/63
44456	02/28	Crw	07/49	4456	-03/65	08/65
44457	03/28	Hor	02/52	4457	-12/63	02/64
44458	03/28	Hor	12/49	4458	-11/65	01/66
44459	04/28	Hor	03/50	4459	-03/60	11/60
44460	05/28	Hor	06/50	4460	-10/64	02/65
44461	05/28	Hor	12/48	4461	-09/64	01/65
44462	05/28	Hor	12/48	4462	-11/65	02/66
44463	05/28	Hor	11/48	4463	-09/64	02/65
44464	05/28	Hor	08/48	4464	-05/64	08/64
44465	06/28	Hor	05/49	4465	-07/63	09/63
44466	07/28	Hor	11/48	4466	-05/65	08/65 o
						11/48⇔c
44467	05/28	SRlx	04/49	4467	-04/64	11/64
44468	05/28	SRlx	02/50	4468	-09/64	12/64
44469	05/28	SRlx	12/48	4469	-04/63	07/63
44470	05/28	SRlx	06/49	4470	-06/63	10/63
44471	06/28	SRlx	12/48	4471	-03/60	07/61
44472	06/28	SRlx	06/48	4472	-05/63	07/63
44473	07/28	SRlx	08/48	4473	-03/60	05/61
44474	07/28	SRlx	12/49	4474	-12/61	03/63
44475	08/28	SRlx	07/48	4475	-02/63	06/63
44476	08/28	SRlx	04/49	4476	-05/63	07/63
44477	12/27	NB	12/49	4477	-07/61	08/61
44478	12/27	NB	12/48	4478	-11/64	03/65
44479	12/27	NB	04/50	4479	-05/64	10/64
44480	11/27	NB	01/49	4480	-03/60	05/61
44481	12/27	NB	09/48	4481	-11/64	02/65
44482	12/27	NB	04/48	4482	-05/62	05/62
44483	12/27	NB	07/48	4483	-03/60	07/62
44484	12/27	NB	08/48	4484	-11/64	03/65
44485	12/27	NB	09/50	4485	-04/63	09/63
44486	12/27	NB	02/49	4486	-01/65	04/65
44487	12/27	NB	03/49	4487	-04/62	08/62
44488	12/27	NB	03/49	4488	-03/60	11/60
44489	12/27	NB	10/49	4489	-08/65	11/65
44490	12/27	NB	08/48	4490	-08/65	12/65
44491	12/27	NB	07/48	4491	-10/62	12/62
44492	10/27	NB	03/49	4492	-05/64	08/64
44493	11/27	NB	01/49	4493	-10/63	07/64
44494	11/27	NB	11/49	4494	-07/63	09/63
44495	11/27	NB	04/49	4495	-03/60	07/60
44496	11/27	NB	05/49	4496	-03/60	08/60
44497	11/27	NB	05/48	4497	-11/64	04/65
44498	11/27	NB	05/49	4498	-03/60	09/60
44499	11/27	NB	05/48	4499	-09/64	01/65
44500	11/27	NB	04/49	4500	-07/66	11/66
44501	11/27	NB	05/48	4501	-12/64	07/65
44502	11/27	NB	01/49	4502	-03/60	11/60
44503	11/27	NB	06/48	4503	-03/60	09/60
44504	11/27	NB	08/49	4504	-10/63	12/63
44505	11/27	NB	04/50	4505	-09/65	12/65
44506	12/27	NB	02/50	4506	-03/60	06/61
44507	06/28	Crw	06/49	4507	-03/60	10/60
44508	06/28	Crw	03/50	4508	-09/62	09/62
44509	06/28	Crw	11/48	4509	-09/62	04/63
44510	06/28	Crw	06/49	4510	-02/60	03/60
44511	06/28	Crw	06/49	4511	-03/60	11/60
44512	06/28	Crw	08/50	4512	-02/64	11/64
44513	06/28	Crw	05/49	4513	-03/60	07/61
44514	06/28	Crw	08/49	4514	-09/64	03/65
44515	06/28	Crw	03/49	4515	-03/60	07/60
44516	06/28	Crw	06/49	4516	-09/64	01/65
44517	07/28	Crw	05/48	4517	-10/63	01/64
44518	07/28	Crw	10/48	4518	-09/62	09/62

44519	07/28	Crw	08/48	4519	-01/63	03/63
44520	07/28	Crw	12/49	4520	-01/64	08/64
44521	07/28	Crw	08/50	4521	-09/62	04/63
44522	07/28	Crw	02/50	4522	-10/65	06/66
44523	08/28	Crw	04/48	4523	-08/63	09/63
44524	08/28	Crw	05/48	4524	-01/63	06/63
44525	08/28	Crw	10/48	4525	-10/66	03/67
44526	08/28	Crw	11/49	4526	-11/63	12/63
44527	08/28	Crw	12/49	4527	-03/65	08/65
44528	08/28	Crw	06/49	4528	-05/65	10/65
44529	08/28	Crw	05/48	4529	-09/64	11/64
44530	09/28	Crw	12/48	4530	-10/63	12/63
44531	09/28	Crw	09/48	4531	-04/64	12/64
44532	09/28	Crw	03/49	4532	-05/63	07/63
44533	09/28	Crw	01/49	4533	-02/64	05/64
44534	09/28	Crw	04/49	4534	-11/64	04/65
44535	09/28	Crw	06/48	4535	-10/63	12/63
44536	09/28	Crw	12/49	4536	-08/65	12/65
44537	09/28	Crw	09/49	4537	-10/62	10/62
44538	10/28	Crw	03/50	4538	-01/64	02/64
44539	10/28	Crw	06/49	4539	-09/63	10/63
44540	10/28	Crw	01/49	4540	-05/64	08/64
44541	10/28	Crw	10/48	4541	-11/63	02/64
44542	11/28	Crw	07/49	4542	-07/63	10/63
44543	11/28	Crw	05/49	4543	-05/64	12/64
44544	11/28	Crw	10/48	4544	-04/65	10/65
44545	11/28	Crw	09/49	4545	-03/63	07/63
44546	11/28	Crw	10/49	4546	-03/60	10/60
44547	11/28	Crw	05/49	4547	-09/61	09/61
44548	11/28	Crw	04/48	4548	-01/65	05/65
44549	12/28	Crw	06/50	4549	-05/64	04/65
44550	12/28	Crw	06/48	4550	-03/62	03/62
44551	12/28	Crw	06/48	4551	-05/63	07/63
44552	12/28	Crw	10/48	4552	-09/64	01/65 o
						10/48⇔c
44553	12/28	Crw	10/49	4553	-10/62	11/62
44554	12/28	Crw	03/49	4554	-08/64	01/65
44555	12/28	Crw	04/48	4555	-03/60	10/60
44556	12/28	Crw	04/48	4556	-12/63	08/64
44557	04/22	AW	02/50	4557	-09/62	09/62 s
44558	04/22	AW	07/48	4558	-12/64	04/65 s
44559	04/22	AW	04/48	4559	-01/63	05/63 s
44560	04/22	AW	04/49	4560	-09/65	12/65 s
44561	04/22	AW	10/49	4561	-04/62	05/62 s
44562	05/37	Crw	06/49	4562	-11/63	11/63
44563	07/37	Crw	12/49	4563	-03/60	05/60
44564	07/37	Crw	03/49	4564	-09/64	02/65
44565	07/37	Crw	07/48	4565	-09/64	02/65
44566	07/37	Crw	10/48	4566	-09/64	02/65
44567	07/37	Crw	08/49	4567	-06/64	11/64
44568	08/37	Crw	11/51	4568	-11/63	01/64
44569	08/37	Crw	11/48	4569	-07/64	12/64
44570	08/37	Crw	03/49	4570	-11/65	02/66
44571	08/37	Crw	10/48	4571	-12/64	08/65
44572	09/37	Crw	10/48	4572	-09/64	11/64
44573	09/37	Crw	12/49	4573	-06/62	08/62
44574	09/37	Crw	06/49	4574	-10/63	01/64
44575	09/37	Crw	12/48	4575	-11/64	02/65
44576	10/37	Crw	12/48	4576	-06/62	06/62
44577	04/39	Der	09/48	4577	-09/64	11/64
44578	04/39	Der	04/50	4578	-02/64	09/64
44579	04/39	Der	12/48	4579	-10/62	11/62
44580	05/39	Der	01/50	4580	-11/64	03/65
44581	05/39	Der	04/48	4581	-09/64	03/65
44582	05/39	Der	10/48	4582	-11/63	12/63
44583	06/39	Der	02/49	4583	-08/64	10/64
44584	07/39	Der	06/48	4584	-11/63	01/64
44585	07/39	Der	11/48	4585	-09/60	09/60 o
						11/48⇔c
44586	09/39	Der	03/49	4586	-09/64	02/65
44587	09/39	Der	10/48	4587	-05/65	10/65
44588	09/39	Der	11/48	4588	-09/64	01/65
44589	09/39	Der	05/49	4589	-11/64	04/65
44590	09/39	Der	04/48	4590	-09/61	09/61
44591	10/39	Der	03/50	4591	-11/64	03/65
44592	10/39	Der	08/49	4592	-10/63	01/64
44593	10/39	Der	10/50	4593	-12/64	05/65
44594	10/39	Der	03/49	4594	-10/62	01/63
44595	10/39	Der	06/48	4595	-10/63	04/64
44596	11/39	Der	10/48	4596	-09/63	07/64
44597	03/40	Der	05/49	4597	-09/65	01/66
44598	03/40	Der	11/48	4598	-10/63	02/64 o
						11/48⇔c
44599	04/40	Der	10/48	4599	-11/65	01/66
44600	07/40	Der	03/49	4600	-03/60	10/60
44601	08/40	Der	01/50	4601	-11/65	04/66
44602	08/40	Der	07/48	4602	-09/64	12/64
44603	09/40	Der	05/49	4603	-10/64	01/65
44604	09/40	Der	04/49	4604	-01/64	02/64
44605	02/41	Der	04/50	4605	-09/64	01/65
44606	03/41	Der	10/48	4606	-03/62	11/62

5MT[3] 44658-45499
4-6-0 LMS Stanier 'Black Five'

Power Classification:	5MT
Introduced:	1934-1951
Designer:	Stanier
Company:	LMS
Weight:	Loco 72t 2cwt
	cC Loco 74t 0cwt
	rRstT Loco 75t 6cwt
	Tender 54t 13cwt
Driving Wheel:	6' 0"
Boiler Pressure:	225psi superheated
Cylinders:	Outside 18½" x 28"
Tractive Effort:	25455lbf
Valve Gear:	Walschaert (piston valves)
	c Caprotti (poppet valves)
	C Outside Caprotti (poppet valves)
	s Outside Stephenson (piston valves)

In the history of British steam locomotives, no locomotives have ever been as universally popular as Stanier's '5MT' class, the 'Black Fives'. They were undoubtedly the most efficient design of general purpose mixed traffic engine ever seen in Britain, suitable for almost any duty. The engines could be seen all over the LMS system from Thurso in the far north, to Bournemouth (on the SDJR) in the south.

They were introduced by Stanier in 1934 soon after he became CME of the LMS, and they quickly established themselves as a reliable design. Eventually, no fewer than 842 were built up to 1951, with Crewe building 241, Horwich 120, Derby 54, Armstrong Whitworth 327 and Vulcan Foundry 100. 5000-5471 were built between 1934 and 1938. Then there was a break due to the war, and construction continued in 1943 with 5472-5499 followed by 4800-4999 and so on, working backward in batches.

The first seventy engines had domeless boilers, and low temperature 14 element superheaters. The next three hundred and seventy seven engines were built in 1935-1937 with larger grates, more firebox heating surface and 24 element superheaters. The regulator was in the dome and the top feed on the second ring of the boiler. Engines built after 1938 had 28 element superheaters and the top feed was on the first ring of the boiler. There was much swapping of boilers between the different types in service.

Only four engines were ever named. In addition 45155 was allocated the name THE QUEENS EDINBURGH, but it is doubtful if the name was ever carried.

After nationalisation Riddles built the BR standard '5MT' ('73000') class which was a development of Stanier's design with a few modifications. These engines never proved as popular with the enginemen as their predecessors. All the Stanier 'Black Fives' remained in service until 1961, and some worked until the very last few days of steam in 1968.

There were a number of experimental modifications in the later built engines, as detailed below.

c These engines were built in 1948 with Caprotti valve gear. They were also fitted with low running plates which gave them quite a distinctive appearance.

C 44686 and 44687 were the last two engines to be built and they were fitted with outside Caprotti valve gear. They were also fitted with very high running plates which was in accordance with the new BR practice.

d These engines were fitted with double chimneys. This was found to give only marginal advantage.

f 44718-44727 were built in 1949 with steel fireboxes.

o These locomotives were converted to oil burning during the coal crisis after the Second World War. They were later converted back to coal burning (b).

r These engines were fitted with Skefko roller bearings.

R These engines were fitted with Skefko roller bearings on the driving coupled axle only.

s 44767 was built in 1947 with outside Stephenson valve gear. This engine was unique in that Stephenson valve gear was normally fitted between the frames on an engine. The last time outside Stephenson valve gear had been used was on a GWR single driver express engine in 1884.

t These engines were fitted with Timken roller bearings.

T These engines were fitted with Timken roller bearings on the driving coupled axle only.

Year End Totals: '5MT [3]' class

'47	'48	'49	'50	'51	'52	'53	'54	'55	'56	'57	'58	'59	'60	'61	'62	'63	'64	'65	'66	'67
742	782	814	840	842	842	842	842	842	842	842	842	842	842	841	820	791	724	627	456	151

Number	Built	Renumbered	BR Dates	Scrap	Notes
44658	05/49 Crw		05/49-11/67	03/68	
44659	05/49 Crw		05/49-06/67	12/67	
44660	05/49 Crw		05/49-09/64	10/64	
44661	06/49 Crw		06/49-08/67	02/68	
44662	06/49 Crw		06/49-10/67	03/68	
44663	06/49 Crw		06/49-05/68	09/68	
44664	06/49 Crw		06/49-05/68	09/68	
44665	06/49 Crw		06/49-03/68	06/68	
44666	07/49 Crw		07/49-02/67	09/67	
44667	07/49 Crw		07/49-08/67	02/68	
44668	12/49 Hor		12/49-04/66	07/66	R
44669	12/49 Hor		12/49-10/67	02/68	R
44670	01/50 Hor		01/50-01/66	04/66	R
44671	02/50 Hor		02/50-02/67	06/67	R
44672	02/50 Hor		02/50-03/68	06/68	R
44673	02/50 Hor		02/50-05/65	08/65	R
44674	03/50 Hor		03/50-12/67	03/68	R
44675	03/50 Hor		03/50-09/67	02/68	R
44676	04/50 Hor		04/50-07/64	07/64	R
44677	04/50 Hor		04/50-10/67	04/68	R
44678	05/50 Hor		05/50-11/67	06/68	r
44679	05/50 Hor		05/50-09/67	06/68	r
44680	06/50 Hor		06/50-09/67	03/68	r
44681	06/50 Hor		06/50-09/67	03/68	r
44682	06/50 Hor		06/50-11/67	04/68	r
44683	07/50 Hor		07/50-04/68	09/68	r
44684	07/50 Hor		07/50-09/67	01/68	r
44685	08/50 Hor		08/50-04/67	12/67	r
44686	04/51 Hor		04/51-11/65	01/66	Crd
44687	05/51 Hor		05/51-01/66	06/66	Crd
44688	08/50 Hor		08/50-09/66	12/66	T
44689	09/50 Hor		09/50-03/67	09/67	T
44690	10/50 Hor		10/50-08/68	12/68	T
44691	10/50 Hor		10/50-04/67	12/67	T
44692	10/50 Hor		10/50-05/66	08/66	T
44693	11/50 Hor		11/50-05/67	11/67	T
44694	12/50 Hor		12/50-10/67	02/68	T
44695	12/50 Hor		12/50-06/67	02/68	T
44696	12/50 Hor		12/50-05/67	02/68	T
44697	12/50 Hor		12/50-11/67	04/68	T
44698	07/48 Hor		07/48-07/66	10/66	
44699	07/48 Hor		07/48-05/67	09/67	
44700	07/48 Hor		07/48-07/66	10/66	
44701	08/48 Hor		08/48-05/64	10/64	
44702	08/48 Hor		08/48-06/65	08/65	
44703	08/48 Hor		08/48-12/66	04/67	
44704	09/48 Hor		09/48-09/66	01/67	
44705	09/48 Hor		09/48-09/66	12/66	
44706	09/48 Hor		09/48-12/63	06/64	
44707	09/48 Hor		09/48-01/66	05/66	
44708	10/48 Hor		10/48-01/68	01/69	
44709	10/48 Hor		10/48-08/68	11/68	
44710	10/48 Hor		10/48-12/66	07/67	
44711	10/48 Hor		10/48-05/68	07/68	
44712	10/48 Hor		10/48-11/66	06/67	
44713	11/48 Hor		11/48-08/68	03/69	
44714	11/48 Hor		11/48-11/66	05/67	
44715	11/48 Hor		11/48-01/68	04/68	
44716	11/48 Hor		11/48-07/65	04/66	
44717	12/48 Hor		12/48-08/67	03/68	
44718	03/49 Crw		03/49-11/66	04/67	f
44719	03/49 Crw		03/49-10/64	02/65	f
44720	03/49 Crw		03/49-10/66	06/67	f
44721	03/49 Crw		03/49-08/65	11/65	f
44722	04/49 Crw		04/49-04/67	09/67	f
44723	04/49 Crw		04/49-10/66	01/67	f
44724	04/49 Crw		04/49-10/66	01/67	f
44725	04/49 Crw		04/49-10/67	03/68	f
44726	05/49 Crw		05/49-10/66	05/67	f
44727	05/49 Crw		05/49-10/67	02/68	f
44728	01/49 Crw		01/49-01/68	05/68	
44729	01/49 Crw		01/49-10/66	02/67	
44730	01/49 Crw		02/49-11/67	03/68	
44731	02/49 Crw		02/49-05/66	10/66	
44732	02/49 Crw		02/49-07/67	01/68	
44733	02/49 Crw		02/49-06/67	11/67	
44734	02/49 Crw		02/49-12/67	04/68	
44735	02/49 Crw		02/49-08/68	11/68	
44736	03/49 Crw		03/49-09/67	05/68	
44737	03/49 Crw		03/49-01/67	07/67	
44738	06/48 Crw		06/48-06/64	09/64	c
44739	06/48 Crw		06/48-01/65	05/65	c
44740	05/48 Crw		05/48-04/63	05/63	c
44741	06/48 Crw		06/48-03/65	10/65	c
44742	06/48 Crw		06/48-05/64	06/64	c
44743	06/48 Crw		06/48-01/66	05/66	c
44744	07/48 Crw		07/48-11/63	01/64	c
44745	07/48 Crw		07/48-10/64	02/65	c
44746	08/48 Crw		08/48-02/64	08/64	c
44747	07/48 Crw		07/48-04/63	11/63	c
44748	02/48 Crw	06/48 4748	02/48-09/64	12/64	ct
44749	02/48 Crw	06/48 4749	02/48-09/64	12/64	ct
44750	02/48 Crw	06/49 4750	02/48-09/63	06/64	ct
44751	03/48 Crw	03/49 4751	03/48-09/64	02/65	ct
44752	03/48 Crw	01/49 4752	03/48-04/64	06/64	ct
44753	03/48 Crw	06/48 4753	03/48-07/65	01/66	ct
44754	04/48 Crw		04/48-04/64	08/64	ct
44755	04/48 Crw		04/48-11/63	02/64	ctd
44756	06/48 Crw		06/48-09/64	02/65	ctd
44757	12/48 Crw		12/48-11/65	05/66	ctd
44758	09/47 Crw	05/48 4758	-07/68	12/68	t
44759	09/47 Crw	03/50 4759	-11/67	03/68	t
44760	09/47 Crw	03/50 4760	-10/66	01/67	t
44761	10/47 Crw	03/50 4761	-04/68	09/68	t
44762	10/47 Crw	07/49 4762	-01/66	04/67	t
44763	10/47 Crw	08/49 4763	-09/65	03/66	t
44764	11/47 Crw	04/49 4764	-09/65	04/66	t
44765	12/47 Crw	09/48 4765	-09/67	03/68	td
44766	12/47 Crw	05/48 4766	-08/67	12/67	td
44767 §	12/47 Crw	04/48 4767	-12/67		tds
44768	04/47 Crw	11/48 4768	-06/67	05/68	
44769	04/47 Crw	07/48 4769	-07/65	01/66	
44770	04/47 Crw	10/48 4770	-10/67	02/68	
44771	05/47 Crw	12/48 4771	-03/67	10/67	
44772	05/47 Crw	10/48 4772	-10/67	05/68	
44773	05/47 Crw	07/48 4773	-12/67	05/68	
44774	05/47 Crw	05/49 4774	-08/67	03/68	
44775	06/47 Crw	03/49 4775	-10/67	03/68	
44776	06/47 Crw	06/49 4776	-10/67	04/68	
44777	06/47 Crw	02/49 4777	-06/68	01/69	
44778	06/47 Crw	07/49 4778	-11/67	02/68	
44779	07/47 Crw	04/49 4779	-12/66	07/67	
44780	07/47 Crw	09/49 4780	-06/68	12/68	
44781	08/47 Crw	04/49 4781	-08/68	12/68	
44782	08/47 Crw	02/49 4782	-12/66	07/67	
44783	03/47 Hor	06/49 4783	-05/64	09/64	
44784	04/47 Hor	07/49 4784	-06/64	09/64	
44785	04/47 Hor	08/49 4785	-06/64	09/64	
44786	04/47 Hor	09/49 4786	-08/66	12/66	
44787	05/47 Hor	11/48 4787	-11/65	02/66	
44788	05/47 Hor	06/49 4788	-11/66	06/67	
44789	05/47 Hor	01/50 4789	-12/64	03/65	
44790	06/47 Hor	04/49 4790	-03/67	11/67	
44791	06/47 Hor	02/49 4791	-11/66	04/67	
44792	07/47 Hor	10/49 4792	-09/67	02/68	
44793	08/47 Hor	11/48 4793	-12/64	03/65	
44794	08/47 Hor	11/49 4794	-04/67	09/67	
44795	08/47 Hor	04/48 4795	-07/67	12/67	
44796	09/47 Hor	03/50 4796	-05/67	10/67	
44797	09/47 Hor	12/48 4797	-09/66	12/66	
44798	10/47 Hor	09/49 4798	-09/66	01/67	
44799	10/47 Hor	05/48 4799	-07/65	07/65	
44800	05/44 Der	11/48 4800	-03/68	06/68	
44801	05/44 Der	05/49 4801	-05/64	09/64	
44802	06/44 Der	03/49 4802	-06/68	10/68	
44803	06/44 Der	12/48 4803	-06/68	09/68	
44804	06/44 Der	11/48 4804	-03/68	06/68	
44805	06/44 Der	07/48 4805	-09/67	01/68	
44806 §	07/44 Der	06/49 4806	-08/68		
44807	09/44 Der	07/49 4807	-03/68	06/68	
44808	09/44 Der	08/48 4808	-12/66	12/67	
44809	09/44 Der	07/48 4809	-08/68	11/68	
44810	10/44 Der	02/49 4810	-08/66	11/66	
44811	10/44 Der	06/48 4811	-10/66	02/67	
44812	10/44 Der	02/49 4812	-09/67	01/68	
44813	10/44 Der	09/48 4813	-09/66	12/66	
44814	10/44 Der	08/48 4814	-09/67	02/68	
44815	11/44 Der	10/48 4815	-02/68	06/68	
44816	11/44 Der	08/49 4816	-07/68	04/69	
44817	11/44 Der	07/48 4817	-08/67	12/67	
44818	11/44 Der	10/48 4818	-06/68	12/68	
44819	11/44 Der	04/49 4819	-11/67	03/68	
44820	12/44 Der	02/50 4820	-12/66	12/67	
44821	12/44 Der	08/49 4821	-06/67	12/67	
44822	12/44 Der	05/48 4822	-10/67	05/68	
44823	12/44 Der	02/49 4823	-11/65	03/66	
44824	12/44 Der	12/49 4824	-10/67	02/68	
44825	12/44 Der	08/48 4825	-10/67	02/68	
44826	07/44 Crw	06/48 4826	-10/67	02/68	o 07/48⇔b
44827	07/44 Crw	08/48 4827	-07/65	12/65	o 08/48⇔b
44828	07/44 Crw	09/48 4828	-09/67	05/68	
44829	08/44 Crw	10/48 4829	-05/68	07/68	o 11/48⇔b
44830	08/44 Crw	09/48 4830	-08/67	01/68	o 09/48⇔b
44831	08/44 Crw	08/49 4831	-11/67	03/68	
44832	08/44 Crw	08/48 4832	-09/67	12/67	
44833	08/44 Crw	04/48 4833	-09/67	03/68	
44834	08/44 Crw	06/48 4834	-12/67	08/68	
44835	09/44 Crw	02/50 4835	-07/67	03/68	
44836	09/44 Crw	10/49 4836	-05/68	09/68	
44837	09/44 Crw	08/48 4837	-09/67	02/68	
44838	09/44 Crw	08/48 4838	-03/68	06/68	
44839	09/44 Crw	04/48 4839	-12/66	04/67	
44840	10/44 Crw	11/50 4840	-11/67	03/68	
44841	10/44 Crw	04/50 4841	-10/66	02/67	
44842	10/44 Crw	08/49 4842	-01/68	05/68	
44843	10/44 Crw	01/49 4843	-09/67	03/68	
44844	10/44 Crw	04/48 4844	-11/67	03/68	o 10/48⇔b
44845	10/44 Crw	05/48 4845	-06/68	12/68	
44846	11/44 Crw	05/48 4846	-01/68	04/68	
44847	11/44 Crw	06/49 4847	-11/66	05/67	
44848	11/44 Crw	03/49 4848	-02/68	07/68	
44849	11/44 Crw	04/48 4849	-12/64	01/65	
44850	11/44 Crw	06/49 4850	-07/66	10/66	
44851	11/44 Crw	12/48 4851	-04/68	08/68	
44852	11/44 Crw	09/49 4852	-09/67	05/68	
44853	12/44 Crw	05/49 4853	-06/67	11/67	
44854	12/44 Crw	08/49 4854	-10/67	12/67	
44855	12/44 Crw	08/48 4855	-05/68	09/68	
44856	12/44 Crw	05/49 4856	-02/67	06/67	
44857	12/44 Crw	08/48 4857	-10/67	12/67	
44858	12/44 Crw	06/49 4858	-12/67	03/68	
44859	12/44 Crw	05/48 4859	-11/67	03/68	
44860	12/44 Crw	10/49 4860	-01/67	04/68	
44861	01/45 Crw	06/48 4861	-11/67	04/68	
44862	01/45 Crw	11/49 4862	-07/67	12/67	
44863	01/45 Crw	06/49 4863	-05/67	01/68	
44864	01/45 Crw	08/48 4864	-05/68	07/68	
44865	02/45 Crw	04/49 4865	-09/67	12/67	
44866	02/45 Crw	06/48 4866	-09/67	02/68	
44867	02/45 Crw	04/48 4867	-06/67	12/67	
44868	02/45 Crw	01/49 4868	-05/68	09/68	
44869	03/45 Crw	08/49 4869	-09/66	02/67	
44870	03/45 Crw	04/48 4870	-06/67	02/68	
44871 §	03/45 Crw	12/49 4871	-08/68		
44872	03/45 Crw	03/49 4872	-09/67	03/68	
44873	03/45 Crw	12/49 4873	-11/67	03/68	
44874	04/45 Crw	10/48 4874	-08/68	03/69	
44875	04/45 Crw	09/48 4875	-05/67	09/67	
44876	04/45 Crw	02/49 4876	-11/67	03/68	
44877	04/45 Crw	07/48 4877	-08/68	12/68	
44878	05/45 Crw	09/48 4878	-07/68	02/69	
44879	05/45 Crw	09/49 4879	-04/67	09/67	
44880	05/45 Crw	06/48 4880	-11/66	05/67	
44881	05/45 Crw	08/49 4881	-07/66	11/66	
44882	06/45 Crw	06/49 4882	-07/67	12/67	
44883	06/45 Crw	02/49 4883	-07/67	12/67	
44884	06/45 Crw	01/49 4884	-06/68	10/68	
44885	07/45 Crw	06/49 4885	-12/63	04/64	
44886	07/45 Crw	07/49 4886	-10/67	03/68	
44887	08/45 Crw	12/48 4887	-12/67	02/68	
44888	08/45 Crw	02/49 4888	-08/68	05/69	
44889	08/45 Crw	06/49 4889	-01/68	06/68	
44890	08/45 Crw	02/49 4890	-06/68	01/69	
44891	08/45 Crw	03/49 4891	-06/68	11/68	
44892	09/45 Crw	05/48 4892	-04/67	12/67	
44893	09/45 Crw	12/48 4893	-11/67	04/68	
44894	09/45 Crw	05/49 4894	-08/68	05/69	
44895	09/45 Crw	08/49 4895	-12/67	06/68	
44896	09/45 Crw	02/49 4896	-09/67	05/68	
44897	09/45 Crw	04/49 4897	-08/68	12/68	
44898	09/45 Crw	01/49 4898	-10/67	03/68	
44899	09/45 Crw	08/49 4899	-07/68	01/69	
44900	10/45 Crw	07/48 4900	-06/67	11/67	
44901 §	10/45 Crw	02/50 4901	-08/65		
44902	10/45 Crw	05/49 4902	-10/67	03/68	
44903	10/45 Crw	02/49 4903	-04/68	10/68	
44904	10/45 Crw	11/48 4904	-12/65	04/66	
44905	10/45 Crw	03/50 4905	-11/67	02/68	
44906	10/45 Crw	04/48 4906	-03/68	08/68	
44907	11/45 Crw	08/49 4907	-10/67	06/68	
44908	11/45 Crw	01/49 4908	-06/66	05/67	
44909	11/45 Crw	08/49 4909	-09/67	02/68	
44910	11/45 Crw	08/48 4910	-06/68	11/68	
44911	11/45 Crw	04/49 4911	-10/67	04/68	
44912	11/45 Crw	11/48 4912	-09/67	09/68	
44913	11/45 Crw	02/50 4913	-07/67	03/68	
44914	12/45 Crw	07/48 4914	-08/67	01/68	
44915	12/45 Crw	12/49 4915	-12/67	10/68	
44916	12/45 Crw	10/48 4916	-12/67	02/68	
44917	12/45 Crw	01/49 4917	-11/67	03/68	
44918	12/45 Crw	12/48 4918	-01/67	07/67	
44919	12/45 Crw	08/48 4919	-12/66	08/67	
44920	12/45 Crw	12/49 4920	-11/67	03/68	
44921	01/46 Crw	10/48 4921	-02/65	06/65	
44922	01/46 Crw	01/50 4922	-05/64	11/64	
44923	01/46 Crw	05/50 4923	-06/64	10/64	
44924	02/46 Crw	03/49 4924	-07/65	07/65	
44925	02/46 Crw	02/49 4925	-09/66	01/67	
44926	02/46 Crw	08/48 4926	-04/68	10/68	
44927	02/46 Crw	01/50 4927	-09/67	02/68	
44928	03/46 Crw	04/48 4928	-06/67	12/67	
44929	03/46 Crw	04/48 4929	-06/68	12/68	

44930	03/46	Crw	12/49	4930	-05/67 05/68
44931	04/46	Crw	05/48	4931	-10/65 05/66
44932 §	09/45	Hor	04/49	4932	-08/68
44933	10/45	Hor	02/49	4933	-10/67 05/68
44934	10/45	Hor	02/50	4934	-09/67 03/68
44935	10/45	Hor	07/48	4935	-10/66 04/67
44936	11/45	Hor	11/49	4936	-08/67 11/67
44937	11/45	Hor	12/48	4937	-05/67 11/67
44938	11/45	Hor	08/48	4938	-10/67 03/68
44939	11/45	Hor	03/49	4939	-12/65 04/66
44940	11/45	Hor	01/50	4940	-03/68 08/68
44941	12/45	Hor	10/49	4941	-11/66 05/67
44942	12/45	Hor	03/49	4942	-06/68 01/69
44943	12/45	Hor	08/49	4943	-10/67 02/68
44944	01/46	Hor	10/49	4944	-09/67 02/68
44945	01/46	Hor	12/48	4945	-10/66 03/67
44946	01/46	Hor	12/48	4946	-06/67 11/67
44947	02/46	Hor	05/50	4947	-06/68 10/68
44948	02/46	Hor	07/48	4948	-09/67 02/68
44949	02/46	Hor	02/49	4949	-06/68 01/69
44950	03/46	Hor	01/49	4950	-08/68 03/69
44951	03/46	Hor	05/48	4951	-12/66 04/67
44952	03/46	Hor	07/48	4952	-10/66 02/67
44953	03/46	Hor	10/48	4953	-12/66 04/67
44954	04/46	Hor	11/48	4954	-09/66 01/67
44955	04/46	Hor	10/48	4955	-08/65 11/65
44956	04/46	Hor	12/49	4956	-06/66 10/66
44957	05/46	Hor	11/49	4957	-05/64 09/64
44958	05/46	Hor	06/48	4958	-03/67 08/67
44959	05/46	Hor	04/48	4959	-07/65 11/65
44960	05/46	Hor	03/49	4960	-01/66 06/66
44961	06/46	Hor	02/50	4961	-06/64 09/64
44962	06/46	Hor	09/48	4962	-12/67 03/68
44963	06/46	Hor	03/49	4963	-07/68 12/68
44964	07/46	Hor	05/50	4964	-10/67 03/68
44965	08/46	Hor	05/48	4965	-04/68 08/68
44966	08/46	Hor	10/48	4966	-09/66 01/67
44967	04/46	Crw	02/49	4967	-05/64 09/64
44968	04/46	Crw	09/48	4968	-05/64 11/64
44969	04/46	Crw	02/50	4969	-12/63 06/64
44970	04/46	Crw	07/48	4970	-09/65 01/66
44971	04/46	Crw	07/48	4971	-08/68 02/69
44972	04/46	Crw	12/48	4972	-11/66 04/67
44973	05/46	Crw	04/48	4973	-09/65 12/65
44974	05/46	Crw	06/48	4974	-06/66 04/67
44975	05/46	Crw	04/49	4975	-09/65 01/66
44976	05/46	Crw	01/49	4976	-02/64 06/64
44977	06/46	Crw	02/49	4977	-11/66 05/67
44978	06/46	Crw	10/48	4978	-07/65 11/65
44979	06/46	Crw	09/48	4979	-07/65 07/65
44980	06/46	Crw	12/49	4980	-07/65 07/65
44981	07/46	Crw	01/49	4981	-01/67 10/67
44982	09/46	Hor	11/48	4982	-05/67 11/67
44983	09/46	Hor	06/48	4983	-10/67 02/68
44984	09/46	Hor	03/49	4984	-11/66 03/67
44985	10/46	Hor	06/48	4985	-10/67 02/68
44986	10/46	Hor	12/48	4986	-05/67 11/67
44987	11/46	Hor	06/48	4987	-10/66 02/67
44988	12/46	Hor	08/48	4988	-12/67 03/68
44989	12/46	Hor	07/48	4989	-02/67 09/67
44990	12/46	Hor	05/49	4990	-10/67 02/68
44991	12/46	Hor	05/48	4991	-05/67 09/67
44992	01/47	Hor	12/48	4992	-12/66 05/67
44993	01/47	Hor	12/48	4993	-12/67 04/68
44994	01/47	Hor	06/49	4994	-07/64 11/64
44995	02/47	Hor	02/49	4995	-11/66 06/67
44996	02/47	Hor	03/49	4996	-04/64 07/64
44997	03/47	Hor	12/48	4997	-05/67 09/67
44998	03/47	Hor	06/48	4998	-04/67 09/67
44999	03/47	Hor	06/48	4999	-09/66 11/66
45000 §	02/35	Crw	01/49	5000	-10/67
45001	03/35	Crw	03/49	5001	-03/68 06/68
45002	03/35	Crw	10/48	5002	-07/65 06/66
45003	03/35	Crw	10/48	5003	-06/67 02/68
45004	03/35	Crw	05/48	5004	-09/66 03/67
45005	03/35	Crw	09/48	5005	-01/68 08/68
45006	03/35	Crw	05/49	5006	-09/67 12/67
45007	03/35	Crw	12/48	5007	-07/64 11/64
45008	03/35	Crw	07/48	5008	-05/64 09/64
45009	03/35	Crw	05/48	5009	-11/65 02/66
45010	03/35	Crw	01/49	5010	-08/63 02/64
45011	04/35	Crw	01/49	5011	-12/65 04/66
45012	04/35	Crw	09/49	5012	-10/66 03/67
45013	04/35	Crw	04/48	5013	-05/68 09/68
45014	04/35	Crw	05/48	5014	-06/67 11/67
45015	04/35	Crw	10/48	5015	-09/67 02/68
45016	05/35	Crw	12/48	5016	-07/66 11/66
45017	05/35	Crw	10/48	5017	-08/68 05/69
45018	05/35	Crw	03/50	5018	-12/66 06/67
45019	05/35	Crw	05/48	5019	-05/67 12/67
45020	08/34	VF	06/48	5020	-12/65 03/66
45021	08/34	VF	03/49	5021	-09/67 12/67
45022	08/34	VF	07/48	5022	-09/63 02/64
45023	08/34	VF	10/48	5023	-09/63 02/64
45024	08/34	VF	01/49	5024	-05/67 02/68
45025 §	08/34	VF	02/50	5025	-08/68
45026	09/34	VF	04/48	5026	-10/65 04/66
45027	09/34	VF	11/48	5027	-05/68 10/68
45028	09/34	VF	05/49	5028	-03/67 11/67
45029	09/34	VF	12/48	5029	-10/66 02/67
45030	09/34	VF	12/49	5030	-12/62 08/63
45031	09/34	VF	11/48	5031	-06/67 11/67
45032	09/34	VF	08/49	5032	-02/64 02/64
45033	09/34	VF	11/48	5033	-12/66 09/67
45034	09/34	VF	04/48	5034	-02/68 05/68
45035	09/34	VF	07/48	5035	-11/64 12/64
45036	09/34	VF	01/49	5036	-12/62 09/63
45037	09/34	VF	05/48	5037	-11/65 05/66
45038	09/34	VF	12/48	5038	-02/68 06/68
45039	10/34	VF	08/49	5039	-08/67 03/68
45040	10/34	VF	11/48	5040	-07/67 03/69
45041	10/34	VF	01/49	5041	-12/67 04/68
45042	10/34	VF	03/49	5042	-09/67 12/67
45043	10/34	VF	09/49	5043	-11/67 03/68
45044	10/34	VF	06/48	5044	-10/66 08/67
45045	10/34	VF	04/48	5045	-10/66 02/67
45046	10/34	VF	04/49	5046	-06/68 12/68
45047	10/34	VF	08/48	5047	-07/66 11/66
45048	10/34	VF	01/50	5048	-11/67 02/68
45049	10/34	VF	04/48	5049	-08/63 10/63
45050	11/34	VF	09/49	5050	-08/67 02/68
45051	11/34	VF	06/49	5051	-11/66 05/67
45052	11/34	VF	05/48	5052	-09/67 03/68
45053	11/34	VF	06/48	5053	-11/66 02/67
45054	11/34	VF	06/48	5054	-02/68 06/68
45055	11/34	VF	01/49	5055	-08/68 02/69
45056	11/34	VF	10/48	5056	-08/67 03/68
45057	12/34	VF	05/48	5057	-08/67 07/68
45058	12/34	VF	06/49	5058	-10/66 03/67
45059	12/34	VF	01/49	5059	-07/67 01/68
45060	12/34	VF	08/48	5060	-03/67 10/67
45061	12/34	VF	04/48	5061	-11/67 03/68
45062	12/34	VF	06/49	5062	-04/67 09/67
45063	12/34	VF	06/48	5063	-11/66 01/67
45064	12/34	VF	03/50	5064	-03/67 10/67
45065	12/34	VF	10/48	5065	-05/68 09/68
45066	01/35	VF	06/48	5066	-02/64 03/64
45067	01/35	VF	11/48	5067	-10/67 12/67
45068	01/35	VF	01/49	5068	-12/65 04/66
45069	01/35	VF	04/48	5069	-06/67 12/67
45070	05/35	Crw	03/49	5070	-05/67 12/67
45071	05/35	Crw	08/48	5071	-07/67 02/69
45072	06/35	Crw	06/49	5072	-09/67 02/68
45073	06/35	Crw	08/48	5073	-08/68 03/69
45074	06/35	Crw	07/48	5074	-09/65 03/66
45075	02/35	VF	06/49	5075	-09/67 04/68
45076	03/35	VF	04/48	5076	-06/68 01/69
45077	03/35	VF	04/50	5077	-08/65 03/66
45078	03/35	VF	04/49	5078	-10/65 12/65
45079	03/35	VF	05/48	5079	-03/67 09/67
45080	03/35	VF	05/48	5080	-10/67 02/68
45081	03/35	VF	04/48	5081	-11/65 03/66
45082	03/35	VF	03/49	5082	-07/66 10/66
45083	03/35	VF	03/48	5083	-12/67 05/68
45084	03/35	VF	07/48	5084	-11/66 04/67
45085	03/35	VF	07/48	5085	-12/62 11/63
45086	03/35	VF	06/48	5086	-12/62 08/63
45087	03/35	VF	04/48	5087	-07/63 05/64
45088	03/35	VF	03/49	5088	-09/64 11/64
45089	04/35	VF	10/48	5089	-08/67 12/67
45090	04/35	VF	07/48	5090	-12/65 04/66
45091	04/35	VF	07/48	5091	-09/66 03/67
45092	04/35	VF	12/48	5092	-12/67 03/68
45093	04/35	VF	01/49	5093	-11/65 02/66
45094	04/35	VF	06/49	5094	-02/67 09/67
45095	04/35	VF	07/48	5095	-08/68 12/68
45096	04/35	VF	04/48	5096	-08/68 12/68
45097	04/35	VF	12/48	5097	-06/66 11/66
45098	04/35	VF	08/48	5098	-12/62 10/63
45099	04/35	VF	02/50	5099	-09/63 12/63
45100	05/35	VF	05/48	5100	-10/63 10/63
45101	05/35	VF	03/50	5101	-03/68 07/68
45102	05/35	VF	05/48	5102	-01/65 02/66
45103	05/35	VF	02/49	5103	-09/64 10/64
45104	05/35	VF	11/50	5104	-06/68 02/69
45105	05/35	VF	06/49	5105	-10/66 02/67
45106	05/35	VF	02/49	5106	-01/67 05/67
45107	05/35	VF	10/49	5107	-09/67 10/68
45108	05/35	VF	01/49	5108	-12/65 04/66
45109	05/35	VF	05/48	5109	-04/67 09/67
45110 §	06/35	VF	04/49	5110	-08/68
45111	06/35	VF	11/48	5111	-10/67 02/68
45112	06/35	VF	07/50	5112	-10/66 06/67
45113	06/35	VF	05/48	5113	-07/65 04/66
45114	06/35	VF	01/50	5114	-01/68 05/68
45115	06/35	VF	05/48	5115	-11/66 04/67
45116	06/35	VF	04/48	5116	-07/67 12/67
45117	06/35	VF	10/48	5117	-10/65 02/66
45118	06/35	VF	05/49	5118	-10/66 03/67
45119	06/35	VF	04/48	5119	-12/62 11/63
45120	06/35	VF	02/49	5120	-06/67 11/67
45121	06/35	VF	08/48	5121	-05/64 09/64
45122	06/35	VF	04/48	5122	-04/64 04/64
45123	07/35	VF	04/48	5123	-09/63 04/64
45124	07/35	VF	04/48	5124	-05/67 09/67
45125	05/35	AW	07/48	5125	-05/63 08/63
					⊠12/62-02/63
45126	05/35	AW	06/48	5126	-05/67 11/67
45127	05/35	AW	03/49	5127	-11/66 02/67
45128	05/35	AW	05/49	5128	-09/66 03/67
45129	05/35	AW	02/49	5129	-09/66 01/67
45130	05/35	AW	05/48	5130	-01/67 03/68
45131	05/35	AW	10/49	5131	-04/68 08/68
45132	05/35	AW	04/49	5132	-03/67 10/67
45133	05/35	AW	10/48	5133	-02/68 04/68
45134	05/35	AW	09/48	5134	-08/68 03/69
45135	05/35	AW	08/48	5135	-10/67 03/68
45136	05/35	AW	01/49	5136	-10/64 02/65
45137	06/35	AW	09/48	5137	-12/66 07/67
45138	06/35	AW	11/48	5138	-09/66 03/67
45139	06/35	AW	10/48	5139	-08/67 11/68
45140	06/35	AW	01/49	5140	-09/66 02/67
45141	06/35	AW	09/48	5141	-03/67 09/67
45142	06/35	AW	10/49	5142	-04/65 06/66
45143	06/35	AW	08/49	5143	-12/65 06/66
45144	06/35	AW	03/50	5144	-06/64 08/64
45145	06/35	AW	03/49	5145	-11/67 02/68
45146	06/35	AW	05/48	5146	-06/65 12/65
45147	06/35	AW	01/49	5147	-05/67 10/67
45148	06/35	AW	03/51	5148	-12/65 04/66
45149	06/35	AW	01/49	5149	-06/68 01/69
45150	06/35	AW	09/48	5150	-03/68 06/68
45151	06/35	AW	08/48	5151	-12/62 09/63
45152	06/35	AW	01/49	5152	-12/62 09/63
45153	06/35	AW	05/48	5153	-05/64 09/64
45154	06/35	AW	01/49	5154	-11/66 05/67
LANARKSHIRE YEOMANRY					
45155	07/35	AW	09/48	5155	-11/64 03/65
45156	07/35	AW	09/48	5156	-08/68 12/68
AYRSHIRE YEOMANRY					
45157	07/35	AW	05/48	5157	-12/62 07/63
THE GLASGOW HIGHLANDER					
45158	07/35	AW	06/48	5158	-07/64 10/64
GLASGOW YEOMANRY					
45159	07/35	AW	06/49	5159	-04/63 11/63
					⊠12/62-02/63
45160	07/35	AW	08/48	5160	-09/66 06/67
45161	07/35	AW	05/49	5161	-11/66 05/67
45162	08/35	AW	07/48	5162	-11/66 02/67
45163 §	08/35	AW	10/48	5163	-05/65
45164	08/35	AW	08/48	5164	-08/66 12/66
45165	08/35	AW	11/48	5165	-12/62 11/63
45166	08/35	AW	04/48	5166	-09/63 05/64
45167	08/35	AW	04/48	5167	-05/67 09/67
45168	08/35	AW	04/48	5168	-09/66 01/67
45169	08/35	AW	09/48	5169	-05/63 12/63
					⊠12/62-02/63
45170	08/35	AW	05/48	5170	-03/64 07/64
45171	08/35	AW	05/48	5171	-10/65 02/66
45172	08/35	AW	12/48	5172	-05/64 09/64
45173	08/35	AW	09/48	5173	-07/64 11/64
45174	08/35	AW	02/49	5174	-05/63 09/63
					⊠12/62-02/63
45175	08/35	AW	06/49	5175	-07/63 05/64
45176	08/35	AW	06/49	5176	-08/66 12/66
45177	09/35	AW	05/48	5177	-07/66 12/66
45178	09/35	AW	12/48	5178	-01/65 05/65
45179	09/35	AW	06/48	5179	-06/62 09/63
45180	09/35	AW	04/49	5180	-09/65 12/65
45181	09/35	AW	05/48	5181	-01/66 05/66
45182	09/35	AW	10/48	5182	-03/66 04/67
45183	09/35	AW	06/50	5183	-10/64 03/65
45184	09/35	AW	07/48	5184	-09/65 01/66
45185	09/35	AW	08/48	5185	-07/66 10/66
45186	09/35	AW	10/48	5186	-09/67 12/67
45187	09/35	AW	11/48	5187	-06/68 03/69
45188	09/35	AW	07/49	5188	-07/67 04/68
45189	09/35	AW	08/49	5189	-07/63 08/63
45190	10/35	AW	12/48	5190	-05/68 09/68
45191	10/35	AW	07/50	5191	-07/67 02/68
45192	10/35	AW	07/48	5192	-08/65 11/65
45193	10/35	AW	07/49	5193	-09/67 03/68
45194	10/35	AW	03/48	5194	-04/65 07/65
45195	10/35	AW	07/48	5195	-07/66 10/66
45196	10/35	AW	10/48	5196	-12/67 03/68
45197	10/35	AW	11/49	5197	-01/67 07/67
45198	10/35	AW	12/49	5198	-09/67 07/68
45199	10/35	AW	08/50	5199	-09/63 09/63
45200	10/35	AW	02/49	5200	-07/68 12/68
45201	10/35	AW	03/49	5201	-05/68 08/68
45202	10/35	AW	12/48	5202	-06/68 11/68
45203	11/35	AW	08/49	5203	-06/68 02/69
45204	11/35	AW	08/49	5204	-01/67 06/67
45205	11/35	AW	06/48	5205	-10/66 03/67
45206	11/35	AW	08/49	5206	-08/68 12/68
45207	11/35	AW	12/48	5207	-10/66 12/66
45208	11/35	AW	11/48	5208	-10/67 02/68
45209	11/35	AW	05/49	5209	-06/68 10/68
45210	11/35	AW	11/48	5210	-04/66 07/66
45211	11/35	AW	06/49	5211	-05/67 10/67
45212 §	11/35	AW	10/48	5212	-08/68
45213	11/35	AW	04/48	5213	-12/66 04/67
45214	11/35	AW	10/48	5214	-12/66 04/67

LMS Ivatt '4MT' 2-6-0 No 43136.

Midland Railway Johnson '3F' 0-6-0 No 43400 at Devons Road shed in June 1948. It has just been renumbered, but still carries 'LMS' on the tender.

LMS Fowler '4F' 0-6-0 No 44596.

LMS Fowler 'Patriot' 4-6-0 No 45504 *Royal Signals*.

45215	11/35	AW	10/48	5215	-10/67	01/68	
45216	11/35	AW	09/48	5216	-02/66	06/66	
45217	11/35	AW	05/48	5217	-11/66	06/67	
45218	11/35	AW	07/48	5218	-04/66	07/66	
45219	11/35	AW	06/48	5219	-10/67	02/68	
45220	11/35	AW	04/49	5220	-09/66	08/67	
45221	11/35	AW	05/49	5221	-12/67	03/68	
45222	12/35	AW	02/49	5222	-02/67	07/67	
45223	12/35	AW	07/48	5223	-12/66	07/67	
45224	12/35	AW	08/48	5224	-11/66	05/67	
45225	08/36	AW	05/48	5225	-10/67	07/68	
45226	08/36	AW	02/49	5226	-09/67	06/68	
45227	08/36	AW	07/49	5227	-01/68	04/68	
45228	08/36	AW	02/49	5228	-03/67	12/67	
45229	08/36	AW	05/48	5229	-09/65	12/65	
45230	08/36	AW	12/48	5230	-08/65	11/65	
45231 §	08/36	AW	06/48	5231	-08/68		
45232	08/36	AW	06/49	5232	-11/67	03/68	
45233	08/36	AW	03/49	5233	-05/66	09/66	
45234	08/36	AW	07/48	5234	-09/67	01/68	
45235	08/36	AW	09/49	5235	-01/66	04/66	
45236	08/36	AW	04/48	5236	-12/67	04/68	
45237	08/36	AW	12/49	5237	-09/65	12/65	
45238	08/36	AW	02/50	5238	-12/66	07/67	
45239	08/36	AW	02/49	5239	-09/67	06/68	
45240	08/36	AW	03/50	5240	-01/67	01/68	
45241	09/36	AW	12/48	5241	-09/67	03/68	
45242	09/36	AW	08/48	5242	-06/67	07/68	
45243	09/36	AW	08/49	5243	-09/67	12/67	
45244	09/36	AW	04/49	5244	-08/63	09/63	
45245	09/36	AW	05/48	5245	-08/65	11/65	
45246	09/36	AW	04/50	5246	-12/67	03/68	
45247	09/36	AW	03/49	5247	-04/67	10/67	
45248	09/36	AW	11/48	5248	-02/66	07/66	
45249	09/36	AW	04/48	5249	-12/66	06/67	
45250	09/36	AW	09/49	5250	-03/67	09/67	
45251	09/36	AW	04/48	5251	-12/63	06/64	
45252	09/36	AW	06/48	5252	-03/66	06/66	
45253	09/36	AW	05/48	5253	-04/68	10/68	
45254	09/36	AW	03/49	5254	-05/68	08/68	
45255	10/36	AW	05/49	5255	-06/68	02/69	
45256	10/36	AW	06/48	5256	-08/67	06/68	
45257	10/36	AW	06/49	5257	-11/65	02/66	
45258	10/36	AW	06/48	5258	-03/68	06/68	
45259	10/36	AW	06/48	5259	-12/67	04/68	
45260	10/36	AW	05/48	5260	-08/68	02/69	
45261	10/36	AW	04/48	5261	-10/67	02/68	
45262	10/36	AW	08/48	5262	-08/68	09/68	
45263	10/36	AW	08/48	5263	-10/67	06/68	
45264	10/36	AW	05/48	5264	-09/67	01/68	
45265	10/36	AW	01/49	5265	-05/62	05/62	
45266	10/36	AW	06/48	5266	-12/62	12/63	
45267	10/36	AW	11/48	5267	-10/67	03/68	
45268	10/36	AW	05/48	5268	-08/68	12/68	
45269	11/36	AW	04/49	5269	-08/68	03/69	
45270	11/36	AW	11/48	5270	-09/67	01/68	
45271	11/36	AW	10/48	5271	-09/67	09/68	
45272	11/36	AW	04/48	5272	-10/65	01/66	
45273	11/36	AW	06/49	5273	-10/67	02/68	
45274	11/36	AW	01/49	5274	-05/67	11/67	
45275	11/36	AW	10/48	5275	-10/67	02/68	
45276	11/36	AW	08/48	5276	-01/67	11/67	
45277	11/36	AW	08/48	5277	-02/67	05/67	
45278	11/36	AW	10/48	5278	-06/67	01/68	
45279	11/36	AW	08/48	5279	-03/68	12/68	
45280	11/36	AW	11/48	5280	-11/67	03/68	
45281	11/36	AW	07/49	5281	-11/67	06/68	
45282	11/36	AW	06/48	5282	-05/68	10/68	
45283	11/36	AW	07/48	5283	-01/67	05/67	
45284	12/36	AW	02/49	5284	-05/68	08/68	
45285	12/36	AW	09/48	5285	-12/67	03/68	
45286	12/36	AW	03/49	5286	-03/65	03/66	
45287	12/36	AW	09/49	5287	-08/68	02/69	
45288	12/36	AW	05/48	5288	-11/67	04/68	
45289	12/36	AW	10/48	5289	-11/66	05/67	
45290	12/36	AW	07/50	5290	-06/68	12/68	
45291	12/36	AW	08/48	5291	-11/65	01/66	
45292	12/36	AW	04/48	5292	-11/67	03/68	
45293 §	12/36	AW	01/49	5293	-08/65		
45294	12/36	AW	01/49	5294	-03/68	05/68	
45295	12/36	AW	05/49	5295	-12/67	04/68	
45296	12/36	AW	04/49	5296	-02/68	05/68	
45297	12/36	AW	03/49	5297	-09/67	01/68	
45298	12/36	AW	04/49	5298	-09/67	02/68	
45299	01/37	AW	12/48	5299	-11/67	04/68	
45300	01/37	AW	06/49	5300	-12/65	03/66	
45301	01/37	AW	09/49	5301	-07/65	12/65	
45302	01/37	AW	08/48	5302	-07/67	02/68	
45303	01/37	AW	05/48	5303	-06/67	11/67	
45304	01/37	AW	05/49	5304	-08/67	11/68	
45305 §	01/37	AW	06/48	5305	-08/68		
45306	01/37	AW	05/48	5306	-01/65	04/65	
45307	01/37	AW	10/48	5307	-10/67	03/68	
45308	01/37	AW	05/48	5308	-08/67	01/68	
45309	01/37	AW	10/48	5309	-09/66	02/67	
45310	01/37	AW	05/50	5310	-08/68	12/68	
45311	02/37	AW	12/48	5311	-10/66	05/67	
45312	02/37	AW	05/48	5312	-06/68	02/69	
45313	02/37	AW	06/49	5313	-02/65	03/65	
45314	02/37	AW	12/48	5314	-11/65	04/66	
45315	02/37	AW	06/49	5315	-09/63	10/63	
45316	02/37	AW	09/48	5316	-03/68	06/68	
45317	02/37	AW	02/49	5317	-11/63	11/63	
45318	02/37	AW	09/48	5318	-08/68	04/69	
45319	02/37	AW	05/48	5319	-05/67	09/67	
45320	02/37	AW	11/48	5320	-10/63	05/64	
45321	02/37	AW	10/48	5321	-10/67	02/68	
45322	02/37	AW	06/49	5322	-09/66	04/67	
45323	02/37	AW	07/48	5323	-09/67	03/68	
45324	02/37	AW	10/49	5324	-08/67	12/67	
45325	03/37	AW	03/50	5325	-09/66	12/66	
45326	03/37	AW	04/48	5326	-03/67	09/67	
45327	03/37	AW	11/48	5327	-01/65	07/65	
45328	03/37	AW	09/48	5328	-09/67	11/67	
45329	03/37	AW	11/48	5329	-11/66	04/67	
45330	03/37	AW	03/49	5330	-08/68	12/68	
45331	03/37	AW	07/48	5331	-11/67	05/68	
45332	03/37	AW	11/48	5332	-11/66	04/67	
45333	03/37	AW	05/48	5333	-07/66	10/66	
45334	03/37	AW	09/48	5334	-07/65	12/65	
45335	03/37	AW	10/48	5335	-07/65	12/65	
45336	03/37	AW	05/48	5336	-01/67	01/68	
45337 §	04/37	AW	11/48	5337	-02/65		
45338	04/37	AW	05/48	5338	-10/66	02/67	
45339	04/37	AW	10/49	5339	-06/67	01/68	
45340	04/37	AW	12/48	5340	-04/67	07/67	
45341	04/37	AW	04/49	5341	-01/67	05/67	
45342	04/37	AW	01/50	5342	-08/68	10/68	
45343	04/37	AW	03/49	5343	-06/67	12/67	
45344	04/37	AW	11/48	5344	-09/66	03/67	
45345	04/37	AW	12/48	5345	-06/68	09/68	
45346	04/37	AW	04/49	5346	-06/67	11/67	
45347	04/37	AW	09/48	5347	-11/67	02/68	
45348	04/37	AW	05/49	5348	-08/66	11/66	
45349	05/37	AW	08/48	5349	-11/67	03/68	
45350	05/37	AW	08/49	5350	-08/68	12/68	
45351	05/37	AW	11/48	5351	-08/65	01/66	
45352	05/37	AW	03/50	5352	-04/67	08/67	
45353	05/37	AW	02/49	5353	-07/68	02/69	
45354	05/37	AW	02/49	5354	-11/65	03/66	
45355	05/37	AW	09/48	5355	-12/62	08/63	
45356	05/37	AW	03/49	5356	-05/64	10/64	
45357	05/37	AW	04/48	5357	-12/66	04/67	
45358	05/37	AW	06/48	5358	-12/63	06/64	
45359	05/37	AW	07/48	5359	-05/67	09/67	
45360	05/37	AW	04/48	5360	-09/65	01/66	
45361	05/37	AW	08/48	5361	-02/64	06/64	
45362	05/37	AW	01/49	5362	-10/65	02/66	
45363	06/37	AW	07/48	5363	-10/67	03/68	
45364	06/37	AW	10/48	5364	-08/66	01/67	
45365	06/37	AW	03/48	5365	-12/66	04/67	
45366	06/37	AW	06/48	5366	-04/64	07/64	
45367	06/37	AW	04/48	5367	-11/63	06/64	
45368	06/37	AW	02/49	5368	-11/67	05/68	
45369	06/37	AW	12/50	5369	-03/67	10/67	
45370	06/37	AW	11/49	5370	-08/66	11/66	
45371	06/37	AW	12/48	5371	-04/67	08/67	
45372	06/37	AW	02/49	5372	-11/66	05/67	
45373	06/37	AW	09/48	5373	-09/67	10/68	
45374	06/37	AW	12/50	5374	-10/67	05/68	
45375	06/37	AW	02/49	5375	-01/68	07/68	
45376	06/37	AW	08/48	5376	-04/68	02/69	
45377	06/37	AW	05/48	5377	-12/67	04/68	
45378	07/37	AW	04/48	5378	-03/65	12/65	
45379 §	07/37	AW	05/49	5379	-07/65		
45380	07/37	AW	06/48	5380	-03/65	12/65	
45381	07/37	AW	06/49	5381	-05/68	08/68	
45382	07/37	AW	03/49	5382	-06/68	12/68	
45383	07/37	AW	01/49	5383	-02/67	09/67	
45384	07/37	AW	03/49	5384	-06/64	10/64	
45385	07/37	AW	05/48	5385	-10/66	05/67	
45386	07/37	AW	07/48	5386	-08/68	04/69	
45387	07/37	AW	01/49	5387	-03/65	10/65	
45388	07/37	AW	03/49	5388	-08/68	05/69	
45389	07/37	AW	04/48	5389	-10/65	01/66	
45390	08/37	AW	10/49	5390	-08/68	10/68	
45391	08/37	AW	05/49	5391	-02/68	06/68	
45392	08/37	AW	09/49	5392	-05/68	09/68	
45393	08/37	AW	04/49	5393	-09/66	02/67	
45394	08/37	AW	08/48	5394	-07/68	12/68	
45395	08/37	AW	06/48	5395	-03/68	07/68	
45396	08/37	AW	06/48	5396	-02/66	06/66	
45397	08/37	AW	05/48	5397	-08/68	12/68	
45398	08/37	AW	06/50	5398	-09/65	02/66	
45399	08/37	AW	10/50	5399	-12/66	06/67	
45400	08/37	AW	06/48	5400	-05/64	08/64	
45401	08/37	AW	07/48	5401	-11/61	11/61	
45402	08/37	AW	04/48	5402	-04/67	10/67	
45403	08/37	AW	05/48	5403	-09/66	01/67	
45404	08/37	AW	12/48	5404	-05/67	11/67	
45405	09/37	AW	06/49	5405	-08/67	12/67	
45406	09/37	AW	06/49	5406	-07/67	12/67	
45407 §	09/37	AW	11/48	5407	-08/68		
45408	09/37	AW	05/49	5408	-11/66	05/67	
45409	09/37	AW	11/49	5409	-08/67	12/67	
45410	09/37	AW	06/48	5410	-09/66	02/67	
45411	09/37	AW	04/48	5411	-06/68	09/68	
45412	09/37	AW	09/49	5412	-08/67	07/68	
45413	09/37	AW	03/49	5413	-09/64	10/64	
45414	10/37	AW	08/49	5414	-02/65	03/65	
45415	10/37	AW	03/49	5415	-10/67	08/68	
45416	10/37	AW	06/49	5416	-07/65	12/65	
45417	10/37	AW	12/48	5417	-07/67	06/68	
45418	10/37	AW	08/48	5418	-02/66	10/66	
45419	10/37	AW	05/48	5419	-09/66	01/67	
45420	10/37	AW	06/50	5420	-06/68	02/69	
45421	10/37	AW	09/50	5421	-02/68	06/68	
45422	10/37	AW	06/48	5422	-09/66	12/66	
45423	10/37	AW	04/48	5423	-05/67	09/67	
45424	10/37	AW	12/48	5424	-04/68	10/68	
45425	10/37	AW	09/48	5425	-10/67	02/68	
45426	10/37	AW	08/50	5426	-03/68	08/68	
45427	10/37	AW	01/49	5427	-09/66	02/67	
45428 §	10/37	AW	10/48	5428	-10/67		
45429	11/37	AW	02/49	5429	-08/65	01/66	
45430	11/37	AW	07/48	5430	-09/66	03/67	
45431	11/37	AW	06/49	5431	-11/67	05/68	
45432	11/37	AW	08/49	5432	-10/66	01/67	
45433	11/37	AW	05/48	5433	-03/66	04/66	
45434	11/37	AW	09/48	5434	-09/66	12/66	
45435	11/37	AW	02/49	5435	-06/68	10/68	
45436	11/37	AW	06/48	5436	-04/68	09/68	
45437	11/37	AW	06/49	5437	-10/67	02/68	
45438	11/37	AW	10/48	5438	-09/66	03/67	
45439	11/37	AW	08/48	5439	-11/65	01/66	
45440	11/37	AW	08/48	5440	-09/67	03/68	
45441	12/37	AW	03/50	5441	-02/67	09/67	
45442	12/37	AW	04/48	5442	-09/66	12/66	
45443	12/37	AW	09/48	5443	-08/65	11/65	
45444	12/37	AW	12/48	5444	-08/68	04/69	
45445	12/37	AW	05/50	5445	-06/68	10/68	
45446	12/37	AW	09/49	5446	-02/67	09/67	
45447	12/37	AW	11/48	5447	-08/68	12/68	
45448	12/37	AW	06/48	5448	-08/67	01/68	
45449	12/37	AW	02/49	5449	-11/67	02/68	
45450	12/37	AW	08/49	5450	-11/67	02/68	
45451	12/37	AW	11/48	5451	-11/66	03/67	
45452	09/38	Crw	11/48	5452	-06/63	09/63	☒12/62-02/63
45453	09/38	Crw	03/49	5453	-12/62	11/63	
45454	09/38	Crw	02/49	5454	-08/67	03/68	
45455	09/38	Crw	08/48	5455	-08/67	02/68	
45456	10/38	Crw	04/48	5456	-12/64	03/65	
45457	10/38	Crw	08/48	5457	-09/63	02/64	
45458	10/38	Crw	11/48	5458	-12/62	02/64	
45459	10/38	Crw	05/48	5459	-05/64	08/64	
45460	10/38	Crw	11/48	5460	-06/65	08/65	
45461	10/38	Crw	09/48	5461	-08/66	11/66	
45462	11/38	Crw	03/49	5462	-06/64	09/64	
45463	11/38	Crw	10/48	5463	-11/66	04/67	
45464	11/38	Crw	05/48	5464	-10/66	05/67	
45465	11/38	Crw	05/49	5465	-02/64	03/64	
45466	11/38	Crw	03/49	5466	-02/67	05/67	
45467	11/38	Crw	06/48	5467	-12/66	04/67	
45468	12/38	Crw	03/49	5468	-05/64	11/64	
45469	12/38	Crw	04/48	5469	-11/66	02/67	
45470	12/38	Crw	11/48	5470	-09/64	12/64	
45471	12/38	Crw	04/48	5471	-07/65	10/65	
45472	04/43	Der	06/48	5472	-09/66	12/66	
45473	05/43	Der	10/49	5473	-11/66	02/67	
45474	05/43	Der	08/48	5474	-09/66	06/67	
45475	06/43	Der	07/48	5475	-09/66	12/66	
45476	07/43	Der	10/49	5476	-01/64	06/64	
45477	07/43	Der	09/48	5477	-08/66	01/67	
45478	08/43	Der	10/48	5478	-12/66	04/67	
45479	08/43	Der	03/49	5479	-05/64	10/64	
45480	08/43	Der	12/48	5480	-08/66	01/67	
45481	09/43	Der	11/48	5481	-09/67	03/68	
45482	09/43	Der	05/48	5482	-06/64	11/64	
45483	09/43	Der	09/48	5483	-12/66	11/67	
45484	10/43	Der	11/48	5484	-02/64	03/64	
45485	10/43	Der	10/48	5485	-10/63	07/64	
45486	10/43	Der	09/48	5486	-12/65	04/68	
45487	11/43	Der	05/48	5487	-02/64	11/64	
45488	11/43	Der	01/49	5488	-11/66	04/67	
45489	11/43	Der	10/48	5489	-11/66	04/67	
45490	12/43	Der	06/48	5490	-12/66	06/67	
45491 §	12/43	Der	05/48	5491	-07/65		
45492	01/44	Der	10/48	5492	-12/66	04/67	
45493	01/44	Der	01/50	5493	-01/68	04/68	
45494	01/44	Der	01/49	5494	-09/67	02/68	
45495	02/44	Der	05/49	5495	-03/67	02/68	
45496	02/44	Der	06/49	5496	-06/64	10/64	
45497	04/44	Der	06/49	5497	-02/64	10/64	
45498	04/44	Der	06/49	5498	-06/65	10/65	
45499	04/44	Der	08/48	5499	-08/65	11/65	

6P5F [1] 45500-45551
4-6-0 LMS Fowler 'Patriot'

7P [1] between 45512 & 45545
4-6-0 LMS Fowler/Ivatt 'Rebuilt Patriot'

Power Classification:	5XP reclassified 6P5F in 1951 r 6P reclassified 7P in 1951
Introduced:	1930-1934 c 1913-1921, rebuilt 1930 r Rebuilt 1946-1949 by Ivatt
Designer:	Fowler
Company:	LMS
Weight:	Loco 80t 15cwt r Loco 82t 0cwt Tender 42t 14cwt
Driving Wheel:	6' 9"
Boiler Pressure:	200psi superheated r 250psi superheated
Cylinders:	Three 18" x 26" r Three 17" x 26"
Tractive Effort:	26520lbf r 29570lbf
Valve Gear:	Walschaert (piston valves)

In the late 1920s Fowler was trying to improve the performance of the '5XP' ('46004') 'Claughton' class. Various modifications took place, including fitting larger boilers in 1928, but they did not really solve the problems.

In 1930, the decision was taken to completely rebuild two of them with three cylinders, and three sets of Walschaert valve gear. 5971 CROXTETH and 5902 SIR FRANK REE were fitted with long travel valves and the 1928 design larger boilers. Only the driving wheels remained of the earlier engines, but they retained the same names and numbers.

These new engines were completely successful and became popularly known as the 'Baby Scots', as they were similar in outline (although smaller) to the un-rebuilt 'Royal Scot' ('46100') class. The official designation was the 'Patriot' class after 5500 was renamed PATRIOT in February 1937.

Fifty new engines were built to the new design by the LMS in 1934. The first forty of these were considered as renewals of 'Claughton' engines and carried their names and numbers. However they did not contain any parts of the engines they were supposed to be rebuilt from. In 1934 the whole class was renumbered 5500-5541, with 5542-5551 officially described as new engines.

5500 was originally named CROXTETH, 5501 was SIR FRANK REE, 5524 was SIR FREDERICK HARRISON, 5525 was E. TOOTAL BROADHURST and 5529 was SIR HERBERT WALKER K.C.B.. As can be seen from the list some of these nameplates were transferred to later engines. A number of engines remained unnamed until late in their careers; some, in fact, never received names. The nameplate of 45501 ST.DUNSTAN'S was unusual in that it took the form of a brass replica badge, rather than a more conventional nameplate.

Five more of the class (5552-5556) were on order, but these were built instead by Stanier with taper boilers and top feeds, becoming the first of the 'Jubilee' ('45552') class.

c 45500 and 45501 retained the original wheels of the 'Claughton' engines from which they were nominally rebuilt, and these could be distinguished by large centre bosses.

r As a result of the successful rebuilding of the two 'Jubilee' '7P' '45735' class engines in 1942, Ivatt rebuilt eighteen engines between 1946 and 1949 with larger taper boilers, double chimneys and new cylinders. They were reclassified '7P'. This was a similar rebuild to that of the 'rebuilt Royal Scots'. The 'rebuilt Patriots' were considered to be at least the equal of the 'rebuilt Royal Scots', and they were much better riding engines.

Year End Totals: '6P5F [1]' class

'47	'48	'49	'50	'51	'52	'53	'54	'55	'56	'57	'58	'59	'60	'61	'62	'63	'64	'65	'66	'67
44	35	34	34	34	34	34	34	34	34	34	34	34	32	24						

Year End Totals: '7P [1]' class

'47	'48	'49	'50	'51	'52	'53	'54	'55	'56	'57	'58	'59	'60	'61	'62	'63	'64	'65	'66	'67
8	17	18	18	18	18	18	18	18	18	18	18	18	18	17	16	11	3			

Number	Built	Renumbered	BR Dates	Scrap	Notes
45500	11/30 Der	04/49 5500	-03/61	04/61	c
PATRIOT					
45501	11/30 Der	03/49 5501	-09/61	09/61	c
ST. DUNSTAN'S					
45502	07/32 Crw	11/48 5502	-09/60	10/60	
ROYAL NAVAL DIVISION					
45503	07/32 Crw	05/48 5503	-08/61	09/61	
THE LEICESTERSHIRE REGIMENT					
11/48➲ THE ROYAL LEICESTERSHIRE REGIMENT					
45504	07/32 Crw	10/48 5504	-03/62	03/62	
ROYAL SIGNALS					
45505	07/32 Crw	06/48 5505	-06/62	08/62	
THE ROYAL ARMY ORDNANCE CORPS					
45506	08/32 Crw	09/48 5506	-03/62	03/62	
09/48➲THE ROYAL PIONEER CORPS					
45507	08/32 Crw	10/48 5507	-10/62	03/63	
ROYAL TANK CORPS					
45508	08/32 Crw	01/49 5508	-11/60	12/60	
45509	08/32 Crw	09/49 5509	-08/61	09/61	
51➲THE DERBYSHIRE YEOMANRY					
45510	08/32 Crw	06/48 5510	-06/62	07/62	
45511	09/32 Crw	05/49 5511	-02/61	03/61	
ISLE OF MAN					
45512	09/32 Crw	07/48 5512	-03/65	07/65	
BUNSEN					07/48⇨r
45513	09/32 Crw	06/48 5513	-09/62	10/62	
45514	09/32 Crw	05/48 5514	-05/61	06/61	r
HOLYHEAD					
45515	10/32 Crw	04/48 5515	-06/62	08/62	
CAERNARVON					
45516	10/32 Crw	02/49 5516	-08/61	09/61	
THE BEDFORDSHIRE AND HERTFORDSHIRE REGIMENT					
45517	02/33 Crw	09/49 5517	-06/62	07/62	
45518	02/33 Crw	07/48 5518	-10/62	02/63	
BRADSHAW					
45519	02/33 Crw	12/48 5519	-03/62	03/62	
LADY GODIVA					
45520	02/33 Der	07/48 5520	-05/62	06/62	
LLANDUDNO					
45521	03/33 Der	08/48 5521	-09/63	11/63	r
RHYL					
45522	03/33 Der	02/49 5522	-09/64	06/65	
PRESTATYN					01/49⇨r
45523	03/33 Crw	10/48 5523	-01/64	03/64	
BANGOR					10/48⇨r
45524	03/33 Crw	02/49 5524	-09/62	10/62	
BLACKPOOL					
45525	03/33 Der	08/48 5525	-05/63	06/63	
COLWYN BAY					08/48⇨r
45526	03/33 Der	06/49 5526	-10/64	02/65	r
MORECAMBE AND HEYSHAM					
45527	04/33 Der	09/48 5527	-12/64	04/65	
SOUTHPORT					09/48⇨r
45528	04/33 Der	03/49 5528	-01/63	03/63	r
60➲R.E.M.E.					
45529	04/33 Crw	08/48 5529	-02/64	02/64	r
49➲STEPHENSON					
45530	04/33 Crw	04/48 5530	-12/65	07/66	r
SIR FRANK REE					
45531	04/33 Crw	05/48 5531	-11/65	03/66	r
SIR FREDERICK HARRISON					
45532	04/33 Crw	07/48 5532	-02/64	01/65	
ILLUSTRIOUS					06/48⇨r
45533	04/33 Der	02/49 5533	-09/62	10/62	
LORD RATHMORE					
45534	04/33 Der	12/48 5534	-05/64	06/64	
E. TOOTAL BROADHURST					12/48⇨r
45535	05/33 Der	09/48 5535	-11/63	09/64	
SIR HERBERT WALKER, K.C.B.					09/48⇨r
45536	05/33 Crw	11/48 5536	-12/62	03/64	
PRIVATE W. WOOD V.C.					11/48⇨r
45537	07/33 Crw	05/48 5537	-06/62	09/62	
PRIVATE E. SYKES V.C.					
45538	07/33 Crw	06/48 5538	-09/62	11/62	
GIGGLESWICK					
45539	07/33 Crw	09/49 5539	-09/61	10/61	
E. C. TRENCH					
45540	08/33 Crw	05/48 5540	-04/63	07/63	r
SIR ROBERT TURNBULL					
45541	08/33 Crw	04/48 5541	-06/62	09/62	
DUKE OF SUTHERLAND					
45542	03/34 Crw	06/49 5542	-06/62	09/62	
45543	03/34 Crw	05/49 5543	-11/62	09/63	
HOME GUARD					
45544	03/34 Crw	09/48 5544	-11/61	03/62	
45545	03/34 Crw	11/48 5545	-06/64	11/64	
11/48➲PLANET					11/48⇨r
45546	03/34 Crw	01/49 5546	-06/62	08/62	
FLEETWOOD					
45547	04/34 Crw	02/49 5547	-09/62	11/62	
45548	04/34 Crw	03/49 5548	-06/62	10/62	
LYTHAM ST. ANNES					
45549	04/34 Crw	02/49 5549	-06/62	08/62	
45550	05/34 Crw	10/49 5550	-11/62	08/63	
45551	05/34 Crw	05/48 5551	-06/62	10/62	

6P5F [2] 45552-45742
4-6-0 LMS Stanier 'Jubilee'

7P [2] 45735-45736
4-6-0 LMS Stanier 'Rebuilt Jubilee'

Power Classification:	5XP reclassified 6P5F in 1951 r 6P reclassified 7P in 1951
Introduced:	1934-1936 r Rebuilt 1942
Designer:	Stanier
Company:	LMS
Weight:	Loco 79t 11cwt r Loco 82t 0cwt Tender 54t 13cwt
Driving Wheel:	6' 9"
Boiler Pressure:	225psi superheated r 250psi superheated
Cylinders:	Three 17" x 26"
Tractive Effort:	26610lbf r 29570lbf
Valve Gear:	Walschaert (piston valves)

The order for the last five of Fowler's '6P5F Patriot' '45500' class (5552-5557) were built instead by Stanier with taper boilers and top feeds, becoming the first of the 'Jubilee' class.

The engines came out concurrently with Stanier's '5MT' 'Black Five' class, and were designed for all ordinary main line work on the LMS apart from the heaviest top-link jobs, for which the '8P' ('46200' class) 'Princess' pacifics had been built. One hundred and thirteen engines were ordered without a prototype and at first they were a disappointment, often being short of steam. After extensive trials, alterations to the blast-pipe and chimney dimensions greatly improved their steaming ability. The engines worked extremely well, particularly on the lines of the former Midland Railway where they handled most of the principal express trains.

In 1935 5642 exchanged numbers with 5552 and was finished in black enamel with cast chromium-plated letters and numerals, and chromium plated dome cover and cladding bands. The new 5552 was named SILVER JUBILEE (to celebrate the Silver Jubilee of King George V), giving the name to the class. The engines carried names associated with the British Empire. Some were named after admirals, and warships, others carried names of engines from an earlier age. 5572 was originally named IRISH FREE STATE and 5633 was named TRANS-JORDAN until 1946.

45637 was the first engine of the class to be withdrawn after being involved in the Harrow accident in 1952.

d 45742 was fitted with a double chimney between 1940 and 1957. The boiler carrying the double chimney later appeared on 45596 in 1961.

r 45735 and 45736 were rebuilt in 1942 with larger boilers and double chimneys, based on the boiler fitted to 46170 BRITISH LEGION in 1935. They were reclassified '7P'. As such they were hardly distinguishable from the 'rebuilt Royal Scots'. This type of boiler was later applied to the 'rebuilt Royal Scots' and the 'rebuilt Patriots', but surprisingly, no more of the 'Jubilees' were rebuilt.

Year End Totals: '6P5F [2]' class

'47	'48	'49	'50	'51	'52	'53	'54	'55	'56	'57	'58	'59	'60	'61	'62	'63	'64	'65	'66	'67
189	189	189	189	189	188	188	188	188	188	188	188	188	187	184	143	112	48	15	8	

Year End Totals: '7P [2]' class

'47	'48	'49	'50	'51	'52	'53	'54	'55	'56	'57	'58	'59	'60	'61	'62	'63	'64	'65	'66	'67
2	2	2	2	2	2	2	2	2	2	2	2	2	2	2	2	2				

Number	Built	Renumbered	BR Dates	Scrap	Notes
45552	12/34 Crw	09/51 5552	-09/64	04/65	
SILVER JUBILEE					
45553	06/34 Crw	07/49 5553	-11/64	04/65	
CANADA					
45554	06/34 Crw	11/48 5554	-11/64	06/65	
ONTARIO					
45555	06/34 Crw	04/48 5555	-08/63	09/63	
QUEBEC					
45556	06/34 Crw	03/49 5556	-09/64	01/65	
NOVA SCOTIA					
45557	06/34 NB	05/48 5557	-09/64	12/64	
NEW BRUNSWICK					
45558	07/34 NB	09/48 5558	-09/64	11/64	
MANITOBA					
45559	07/34 NB	11/48 5559	-10/62	02/63	
BRITISH COLUMBIA					

45560 07/34 NB 08/48 5560 -11/63 01/64
PRINCE EDWARD ISLAND

45561 07/34 NB 05/48 5561 -09/64 12/64
SASKATCHEWAN

45562 08/34 NB 10/48 5562 -11/67 05/68
ALBERTA

45563 08/34 NB 06/49 5563 -11/65 03/66
AUSTRALIA

45564 08/34 NB 04/49 5564 -06/64 12/64
NEW SOUTH WALES

45565 08/34 NB 05/48 5565 -01/67 06/67
VICTORIA

45566 08/34 NB 06/48 5566 -10/62 12/62
QUEENSLAND

45567 08/34 NB 11/48 5567 -01/65 05/65
SOUTH AUSTRALIA

45568 08/34 NB 10/48 5568 -05/64 01/65
WESTERN AUSTRALIA

45569 08/34 NB 12/48 5569 -05/64 05/64
TASMANIA

45570 08/34 NB 06/48 5570 -12/62 07/63
NEW ZEALAND

45571 09/34 NB 10/48 5571 -05/64 10/64
SOUTH AFRICA

45572 09/34 NB 08/48 5572 -02/64 07/64
EIRE

45573 09/34 NB 09/48 5573 -09/65 01/66
NEWFOUNDLAND

45574 09/34 NB 06/49 5574 -03/66 08/66
INDIA

45575 09/34 NB 08/48 5575 -06/63 10/63
MADRAS

45576 09/34 NB 06/48 5576 -12/62 04/64
BOMBAY

45577 09/34 NB 04/48 5577 -09/64 02/65
BENGAL

45578 09/34 NB 12/48 5578 -06/64 11/64
UNITED PROVINCES

45579 10/34 NB 09/48 5579 -09/64 11/64
PUNJAB

45580 10/34 NB 05/49 5580 -12/64 04/65
BURMA

45581 10/34 NB 04/48 5581 -08/66 12/66
BIHAR AND ORISSA

45582 11/34 NB 02/49 5582 -12/62 08/63
CENTRAL PROVINCES

45583 11/34 NB 10/48 5583 -10/64 07/65
ASSAM

45584 12/34 NB 03/48 5584 -09/64 01/65
NORTH WEST FRONTIER

45585 12/34 NB 05/48 5585 -05/64 11/64
HYDERABAD

45586 12/34 NB 07/48 5586 -01/65 04/65
MYSORE

45587 12/34 NB 07/48 5587 -12/62 09/63
BARODA

45588 12/34 NB 06/49 5588 -05/65 08/65
KASHMIR

45589 12/34 NB 06/48 5589 -03/65 03/66
GWALIOR

45590 12/34 NB 10/48 5590 -12/65 06/66
TRAVANCORE

45591 12/34 NB 09/48 5591 -11/63 11/63
UDAIPUR

45592 12/34 NB 06/48 5592 -09/64 06/65
INDORE

45593 § 12/34 NB 12/48 5593 -10/67
KOLHAPUR

45594 01/35 NB 02/49 5594 -12/62 08/63
BHOPAL

45595 01/35 NB 09/49 5595 -01/65 05/65
SOUTHERN RHODESIA

45596 § 01/35 NB 05/48 5596 -07/66 61⇔d
BAHAMAS

45597 01/35 NB 08/48 5597 -01/65 04/65
BARBADOS

45598 02/35 NB 04/48 5598 -10/64 02/65
BASUTOLAND

45599 01/35 NB 09/48 5599 -09/64 11/64
BECHUANALAND

45600 02/35 NB 07/48 5600 -12/65 04/66
BERMUDA

45601 04/35 NB 04/49 5601 -09/64 06/65
BRITISH GUIANA

45602 04/35 NB 08/49 5602 -03/65 07/65
BRITISH HONDURAS

45603 03/35 NB 03/49 5603 -12/62 02/63
SOLOMON ISLANDS

45604 03/35 NB 04/48 5604 -07/65 10/65
CEYLON

45605 04/35 NB 07/48 5605 -03/64 03/64
CYPRUS

45606 04/35 NB 05/49 5606 -06/64 02/65
FALKLAND ISLANDS

45607 06/34 Crw 05/48 5607 -11/62 05/63
FIJI

45608 07/34 Crw 10/48 5608 -09/65 01/66
GIBRALTAR

45609 07/34 Crw 08/48 5609 -09/60 09/60
GILBERT AND ELLICE ISLANDS

45610 07/34 Crw 06/49 5610 -01/64 03/64
GOLD COAST 12/58➲GHANA

45611 07/34 Crw 11/48 5611 -09/64 01/65
HONG KONG

45612 08/34 Crw 12/48 5612 -04/64 04/64
JAMAICA

45613 08/34 Crw 08/48 5613 -09/64 04/65
KENYA

45614 08/34 Crw 04/48 5614 -01/64 04/64
LEEWARD ISLANDS

45615 08/34 Crw 04/48 5615 -12/62 02/63
MALAY STATES

45616 08/34 Crw 09/48 5616 -01/61 02/61
MALTA, G.C.

45617 09/34 Crw 06/48 5617 -11/64 04/65
MAURITIUS

45618 10/34 Crw 05/48 5618 -03/64 11/64
NEW HEBRIDES

45619 10/34 Crw 06/48 5619 -08/61 09/61
NIGERIA

45620 10/34 Crw 09/48 5620 -09/64 01/65
NORTH BORNEO

45621 10/34 Crw 10/48 5621 -12/62 11/63
NORTHERN RHODESIA

45622 10/34 Crw 06/48 5622 -09/64 12/64
NYASALAND

45623 10/34 Crw 06/48 5623 -08/64 09/65
PALESTINE

45624 10/34 Crw 09/48 5624 -11/63 04/64
ST. HELENA

45625 10/34 Crw 10/49 5625 -08/63 11/63
SARAWAK

45626 11/34 Crw 03/49 5626 -11/65 01/66
SEYCHELLES

45627 11/34 Crw 10/48 5627 -09/66 02/67
SIERRA LEONE

45628 11/34 Crw 12/48 5628 -12/62 02/63
SOMALILAND

45629 11/34 Crw 11/48 5629 -05/65 08/65
STRAITS SETTLEMENTS

45630 11/34 Crw 07/48 5630 -11/61 11/61
SWAZILAND

45631 11/34 Crw 11/48 5631 -09/64 12/64
TANGANYIKA

45632 11/34 Crw 05/49 5632 -10/65 05/66
TONGA

45633 11/34 Crw 12/48 5633 -11/65 03/66
ADEN

45634 11/34 Crw 12/49 5634 -05/63 08/63
TRINIDAD

45635 11/34 Crw 05/49 5635 -09/64 01/65
TOBAGO

45636 12/34 Crw 02/49 5636 -12/62 02/63
UGANDA

45637 12/34 Crw 09/48 5637 -12/52 12/52
WINDWARD ISLANDS

45638 12/34 Crw 07/48 5638 -03/64 04/64
ZANZIBAR

45639 12/34 Crw 07/48 5639 -10/63 01/64
RALEIGH

45640 12/34 Crw 05/48 5640 -03/64 01/65
FROBISHER

45641 12/34 Crw 09/48 5641 -09/64 01/65
SANDWICH

45642 05/34 Crw 05/48 5642 -01/65 04/65
BOSCAWEN

45643 12/34 Crw 09/48 5643 -01/66 05/66
RODNEY

45644 12/34 Crw 11/48 5644 -11/63 01/64
HOWE

45645 12/34 Crw 06/48 5645 -11/63 11/63
COLLINGWOOD

45646 12/34 Crw 12/48 5646 -12/63 03/64
NAPIER

45647 01/35 Crw 08/49 5647 -04/67 09/67
STURDEE

45648 01/35 Crw 06/48 5648 -02/63 02/63
WEMYSS

45649 01/35 Crw 08/48 5649 -09/63 10/63
HAWKINS

45650 01/35 Crw 02/49 5650 -01/63 06/63
BLAKE

45651 01/35 Crw 06/49 5651 -11/62 12/62
SHOVELL

45652 01/35 Crw 10/48 5652 -01/65 06/65
HAWKE

45653 01/35 Crw 10/48 5653 -04/65 08/65
BARHAM

45654 02/35 Crw 01/49 5654 -06/66 10/66
HOOD

45655 12/34 Der 02/49 5655 -04/65 06/66
KEITH

45656 12/34 Der 04/48 5656 -12/62 03/63
COCHRANE

45657 12/34 Der 08/48 5657 -09/64 05/65
TYRWHITT

45658 12/34 Der 05/49 5658 -10/65 12/65
KEYES

45659 12/34 Der 08/48 5659 -06/63 06/63
DRAKE

45660 12/34 Der 05/48 5660 -06/66 10/66
ROOKE

45661 12/34 Der 08/49 5661 -05/65 08/65
VERNON

45662 12/34 Der 08/48 5662 -11/62 01/63
KEMPENFELT

45663 01/35 Der 08/48 5663 -10/64 04/65
JERVIS

45664 01/35 Der 11/48 5664 -05/65 07/65
NELSON

45665 11/35 Crw 03/49 5665 -12/62 12/63
LORD RUTHERFORD OF NELSON

45666 11/35 Crw 12/48 5666 -04/65 08/65
CORNWALLIS

45667 11/35 Crw 04/49 5667 -01/65 05/65
JELLICOE

45668 12/35 Crw 04/49 5668 -12/63 01/64
MADDEN

45669 12/35 Crw 08/48 5669 -05/63 07/63
FISHER

45670 12/35 Crw 03/49 5670 -10/64 02/65
HOWARD OF EFFINGHAM

45671 12/35 Crw 04/49 5671 -11/63 01/64
PRINCE RUPERT

45672 12/35 Crw 08/48 5672 -11/64 04/65
ANSON

45673 12/35 Crw 04/48 5673 -12/62 12/63
KEPPEL

45674 12/35 Crw 06/48 5674 -10/64 03/65
DUNCAN

45675 12/35 Crw 09/48 5675 -06/67 11/67
HARDY

45676 12/35 Crw 10/48 5676 -09/64 01/65
CODRINGTON

45677 12/35 Crw 08/49 5677 -12/62 12/63
BEATTY

45678 12/35 Crw 02/49 5678 -12/62 01/64
DE ROBECK

45679 12/35 Crw 08/48 5679 -12/62 11/63
ARMADA

45680 12/35 Crw 09/48 5680 -01/63 06/63
CAMPERDOWN

45681 12/35 Crw 10/49 5681 -09/64 01/65
ABOUKIR

45682 01/36 Crw 03/49 5682 -06/64 08/64
TRAFALGAR

45683 01/36 Crw 07/48 5683 -12/62 03/64
HOGUE

45684 02/36 Crw 10/48 5684 -12/65 03/66
JUTLAND

45685 02/36 Crw 05/48 5685 -04/64 01/65
BARFLEUR

45686 02/36 Crw 09/49 5686 -11/62 08/63
ST. VINCENT

45687 02/36 Crw 10/48 5687 -12/62 12/63
NEPTUNE

45688 02/36 Crw 05/48 5688 -12/62 06/63
POLYPHEMUS

45689 02/36 Crw 11/48 5689 -12/64 05/65
AJAX

45690 § 03/36 Crw 05/48 5690 -03/64
LEANDER

45691 03/36 Crw 05/49 5691 -12/62 05/63
ORION

45692 03/36 Crw 07/48 5692 -12/62 12/63
CYCLOPS

45693 03/36 Crw 08/48 5693 -12/62 12/63
AGAMEMNON

45694 03/36 Crw 04/48 5694 -01/67 06/67
BELLEROPHON

45695 03/36 Crw 10/48 5695 -02/64 07/64
MINOTAUR

45696 04/36 Crw 10/48 5696 -08/64 01/65
ARETHUSA

45697 04/36 Crw 05/48 5697 -09/67 05/68
ACHILLES

45698 04/36 Crw 09/48 5698 -11/65 02/66
MARS

45699 § 04/36 Crw 05/48 5699 -11/64
GALATEA

45700 04/36 Crw 12/48 5700 -07/64 09/64
BRITANNIA 09/51➲AMETHYST

45701 04/36 Crw 05/48 5701 -02/63 05/63
CONQUEROR

45702 05/36 Crw 06/48 5702 -05/63 08/63
COLOSSUS

45703 05/36 Crw 04/49 5703 -11/64 04/65
THUNDERER

45704 05/36 Crw 12/48 5704 -01/65 04/65
LEVIATHAN

45705 05/36 Crw 01/49 5705 -11/65 02/66
SEAHORSE

45706 05/36 Crw 08/48 5706 -09/63 10/63
EXPRESS

Number	Built	Renumbered	BR Dates	Scrap	Notes
45707 VALIANT	05/36 Crw	08/48 5707	-12/62	12/63	
45708 RESOLUTION	06/36 Crw	08/48 5708	-03/64	04/64	
45709 IMPLACABLE	06/36 Crw	01/49 5709	-11/63	08/64	
45710 IRRESISTIBLE	06/36 Crw	02/49 5710	-06/64	02/65	
45711 COURAGEOUS	06/36 Crw	12/48 5711	-12/62	12/63	
45712 VICTORY	06/36 Crw	10/48 5712	-11/63	01/64	
45713 RENOWN	07/36 Crw	10/48 5713	-10/62	06/63	
45714 REVENGE	07/36 Crw	04/49 5714	-07/63	08/63	
45715 INVINCIBLE	07/36 Crw	04/48 5715	-12/62	04/63	
45716 SWIFTSURE	07/36 Crw	02/49 5716	-09/64	09/64	
45717 DAUNTLESS	07/36 Crw	06/49 5717	-11/63	02/64	
45718 DREADNOUGHT	08/36 Crw	02/49 5718	-10/62	12/63	
45719 GLORIOUS	08/36 Crw	02/49 5719	-03/63	06/63	
45720 INDOMITABLE	08/36 Crw	09/48 5720	-12/62	12/63	
45721 IMPREGNABLE	08/36 Crw	08/48 5721	-09/65	03/66	
45722 DEFENCE	08/36 Crw	07/48 5722	-11/62	07/63	
45723 FEARLESS	08/36 Crw	05/48 5723	-09/64	01/65	
45724 WARSPITE	09/36 Crw	08/48 5724	-10/62	06/63	
45725 REPULSE	09/36 Crw	12/48 5725	-12/62	03/64	
45726 VINDICTIVE	10/36 Crw	12/48 5726	-03/65	06/65	
45727 INFLEXIBLE	10/36 Crw	06/48 5727	-12/62	12/63	
45728 DEFIANCE	10/36 Crw	10/48 5728	-10/62	11/63	
45729 FURIOUS	10/36 Crw	06/48 5729	-10/62	09/63	
45730 OCEAN	10/36 Crw	04/48 5730	-09/63	03/65	
45731 PERSEVERANCE	10/36 Crw	12/48 5731	-10/62	11/63	
45732 SANSPAREIL	10/36 Crw	03/49 5732	-03/64	08/64	
45733 NOVELTY	11/36 Crw	09/49 5733	-09/64	01/65	
45734 METEOR	11/36 Crw	09/48 5734	-12/63	04/64	
45735 COMET	11/36 Crw	06/48 5735	-09/64	01/65	r
45736 PHOENIX	11/36 Crw	10/48 5736	-09/64	01/65	r
45737 ATLAS	11/36 Crw	11/48 5737	-06/64	11/64	
45738 SAMSON	12/36 Crw	06/49 5738	-12/63	02/64	
45739 ULSTER	12/36 Crw	07/48 5739	-01/67	06/67	
45740 MUNSTER	12/36 Crw	06/48 5740	-11/63	12/63	
45741 LEINSTER	12/36 Crw	05/48 5741	-02/64	04/64	
45742 CONNAUGHT	12/36 Crw	11/48 5742	-05/65	08/65	d

5XP 46004
4-6-0 LNWR Bowen Cooke 'Rebuilt Claughton'

Power Classification: 5XP
Introduced: 1913-1921
(survivor built 1920)
Rebuilt by Fowler 1928
Designer: Bowen Cooke
Company: LNWR
Weight: Loco 79t 9cwt
Driving Wheel: 6' 9"
Boiler Pressure: 200psi superheated
Cylinders: Four 15¾" x 26"
Tractive Effort: 27070lbf
Valve Gear: Walschaert (slide valves)

Bowen Cooke designed the 'Claughton' Class and 130 of them numbered 5900-6029 were built between 1913 and 1921. They were the final LNWR passenger design and were designed for express passenger work. Although they did good work in their early years, they never managed to outshine the older engines (such as the '4P' '58000' 'Prince of Wales' class and the '3P' '58011' 'George the Fifth' class) which they were intended to replace.

Because they were poor performers and expensive to maintain many things were tried to improve their performance. Some engines were fitted with Caprotti valves and others (including 46004) were rebuilt with larger boilers in 1928.

In 1930 two engines were rebuilt to become the prototypes of the 'Patriot' '45500' class. Forty more engines were officially rebuilt as 'Patriots', but as the new engines did not contain any parts of the engines they were supposed to have been rebuilt from, it would be better to consider them as replacements.

46004 was the last survivor of the class (the first having been withdrawn in 1929). The war extended its years and it outlived the rest of the class by eight years, before being withdrawn in 1949. It was originally named PRINCESS LOUISE, the nameplates being removed in June 1935.

Year End Totals: '5XP' class

'47	'48	'49	'50	'51	'52	'53	'54	'55	'56	'57	'58	'59	'60	'61	'62	'63	'64	'65	'66	'67
1	1																			

Number	Built	Renumbered	BR Dates	Scrap	Notes
46004	08/20 Crw	6004	-04/49	08/49	

7P [3] 46100-46170
4-6-0 LMS Fowler/Stanier 'Royal Scot'

7P [3] 46100-46170
4-6-0 LMS Fowler/Stanier 'Rebuilt Royal Scot'

Power Classification: 6P reclassified 7P in 1951
Introduced: 1927-1930
Rebuilt 1943-1955 by Stanier
Designer: Fowler
Company: LMS
Weight: Loco 84t 18cwt
r Loco 83t 0cwt
e Loco 84t 1cwt
Tender 54t 13cwt
Driving Wheel: 6' 9"
Boiler Pressure: 250psi superheated
Cylinders: Three 18" x 26"
Tractive Effort: 33150lbf
Valve Gear: Walschaert (piston valves)

In late 1920s the LMS found itself facing an urgent need for large express traffic engines for the West Coast main line. The '5XP' ('46004') 'Claughton' class had never really proved themselves and the '5P' ('50412') Hughes engines which had been imported from the LYR did not really solve the problem.

After borrowing the GWR 'Castle' class engine 5000 LAUNCESTON CASTLE for tests in 1926 Fowler approached the GWR enquiring about the possibility of buying fifty 'Castles'. The GWR refused, and would not even loan a set of 'Castle' drawings to the LMS.

Fowler then turned to the Southern Railway and Maunsell loaned a set of 'Lord Nelson' drawings to the LMS. The LMS was impressed but it was decided to go for three cylinders instead of four. Fifty engines were ordered straight off the drawing board from the North British Locomotive Company, the first being delivered in July within eight months of the order being placed, and all fifty were in service by the middle of 1927.

Considering the speed with which they were designed and constructed, they proved to be very successful engines. Twenty more were built at Derby in 1930.

In 1933 6152 swapped numbers and names with 6100 ROYAL SCOT and went on a successful visit to the Chicago World Fair in America. The engine later went on an 11,194 mile tour of North America, including crossing the Rockies. The engines never reverted to their old identities, and 46100 carried a bell commemorating its trip.

6125-6149 were originally named after old LNWR locomotives as follows: 6125 LANCASHIRE WITCH, 6126 SANSPAREIL, 6127 NOVELTY, 6128 METEOR, 6129 COMET, 6130 LIVERPOOL, 6131 PLANET, 6132 PHOENIX, 6133 VULCAN, 6134 ATLAS, 6135 SAMSON, 6136 GOLIATH, 6137 VESTA, 6138 FURY (until 1929), 6139 AJAX, 6140 HECTOR, 6141 CALEDONIAN, 6142 LION, 6143 MAIL, 6144 OSTRICH, 6145 CONDOR, 6146 JENNY LIND, 6147 COURIER, 6148 VELOCIPEDE and 6149 LADY OF THE LAKE. The brass nameplates carried etchings of the locomotives represented. In 1935-1936 these names were replaced by regimental names bringing them in line with the rest of the class. 46112 had its nameplate removed in September 1961 as a diesel took its name.

The nameplates of 46127 and 46170 were unusual in that they took the form of a brass replica badges, rather than more conventional nameplates.

e An experimental version of the design was built in 1929 with a very high boiler pressure of 900psi. It was numbered 6300 FURY and it was a three-cylinder compound, built by North British. During trials a burst tube caused the death of a travelling inspector on the footplate and the engine never entered normal service. In November 1935 it was rebuilt with three simple cylinders and a taper boiler. The boiler did not prove as successful as the boilers later fitted to the rebuilds (see below) which were shorter, but it was later fitted with a double chimney which greatly improved the steaming. It was later renumbered 6170 and renamed BRITISH LEGION.

r As a result of the successful rebuilding of the two 'Jubilee' '7P' ('45735') class engines in 1942, Stanier introduced a rebuilt version of the 'Royal Scots'. The entire class was rebuilt with larger taper boilers, double chimneys and new cylinders between 1943 and 1955. They were also later fitted with smoke deflectors from 1947 onwards. In this form they were some of the finest 4-6-0 engines ever known, although they were inclined to be rough riders.

s 46106 was fitted with straight-sided smoke deflector plates of the type used on BR standard locomotives.

Year End Totals: '7P [3]' class

'47	'48	'49	'50	'51	'52	'53	'54	'55	'56	'57	'58	'59	'60	'61	'62	'63	'64	'65	'66	'67
27	24	18	12	10	7	3	1													

Year End Totals: '7P [3] Rebuilt' class

'47	'48	'49	'50	'51	'52	'53	'54	'55	'56	'57	'58	'59	'60	'61	'62	'63	'64	'65	'66	'67
44	47	53	59	61	64	68	70	71	71	71	71	71	71	71	41	26	5			

Number	Built	Renumbered	BR Dates	Scrap	Notes
46100 § ROYAL SCOT	07/30 Der	06/48 6100	-10/62		06/50➪r
46101 ROYAL SCOTS GREY	08/27 NB	04/48 6101	-09/63	04/64	r
46102 BLACK WATCH	08/27 NB	09/48 6102	-12/62	07/64	10/49➪r
46103 ROYAL SCOTS FUSILIER	08/27 NB	10/48 6103	-12/62	09/63	r
46104 SCOTTISH BORDERER	08/27 NB	08/48 6104	-12/62	07/64	r
46105 CAMERON HIGHLANDER	08/27 NB	04/48 6105	-12/62	05/64	05/48➪r
46106 GORDON HIGHLANDER	08/27 NB	06/48 6106	-12/62	04/63	s 09/49➪r
46107 ARGYLL AND SUTHERLAND HIGHLANDER	08/27 NB	04/48 6107	-12/62	05/64	02/50➪r
46108 SEAFORTH HIGHLANDER	08/27 NB	05/48 6108	-01/63	05/63	r
46109 ROYAL ENGINEER	09/27 NB	04/48 6109	-12/62	12/63	r
46110 GRENADIER GUARDSMAN	09/27 NB	03/49 6110	-02/64	12/64	01/53➪r
46111 ROYAL FUSILIER	09/27 NB	11/48 6111	-09/63	11/63	r
46112 SHERWOOD FORESTER	09/27 NB	09/48 6112	-05/64	09/64	r
46113 CAMERONIAN	09/27 NB	05/49 6113	-12/62	06/63	12/50➪r
46114 COLDSTREAM GUARDSMAN	09/27 NB	06/48 6114	-09/63	04/64	r
46115 § SCOTS GUARDSMAN	09/27 NB	01/49 6115	-12/65		r
46116 IRISH GUARDSMAN	09/27 NB	09/48 6116	-09/63	09/63	r
46117 WELSH GUARDSMAN	10/27 NB	05/48 6117	-11/62	12/63	r
46118 ROYAL WELCH FUSILIER	10/27 NB	02/49 6118	-06/64	11/64	r
46119 LANCASHIRE FUSILIER	10/27 NB	07/48 6119	-11/63	11/63	r
46120 ROYAL INNISKILLING FUSILIER	10/27 NB	06/48 6120	-07/63	10/63	r
46121 H.L.I. 01/49➪HIGHLAND LIGHT INFANTRY, CITY OF GLASGOW REGIMENT	10/27 NB	10/48 6121	-12/62	05/64	r
46122 ROYAL ULSTER RIFLEMAN	10/27 NB	04/48 6122	-10/64	02/65	r

46123 10/27 NB 06/48 6123 -10/62 04/63 05/49➪r
ROYAL IRISH FUSILIER

46124 11/27 NB 04/48 6124 -12/62 04/63 r
LONDON SCOTTISH

46125 08/27 NB 09/48 6125 -10/64 01/65 r
3RD CARABINIER

46126 08/27 NB 12/48 6126 -09/63 11/63 r
ROYAL ARMY SERVICE CORPS

46127 08/27 NB 04/48 6127 -12/62 05/63 r
OLD CONTEMPTIBLES 1914 AUG. 5 TO NOV. 22

46128 08/27 NB 02/49 6128 -05/65 07/65 r
THE LOVAT SCOUTS

46129 08/27 NB 06/48 6129 -06/64 11/64 r
THE SCOTTISH HORSE

46130 08/27 NB 05/48 6130 -12/62 10/63 12/49➪r
THE WEST YORKSHIRE REGIMENT

46131 09/27 NB 08/48 6131 -10/62 11/62 r
THE ROYAL WARWICKSHIRE REGIMENT

46132 09/27 NB 04/48 6132 -02/64 04/65 r
THE KING'S REGIMENT, LIVERPOOL

46133 09/27 NB 01/49 6133 -02/63 05/63 r
THE GREEN HOWARDS

46134 09/27 NB 11/48 6134 -11/62 04/63 12/53➪r
THE CHESHIRE REGIMENT

46135 09/27 NB 10/48 6135 -12/62 04/63 r
THE EAST LANCASHIRE REGIMENT

46136 09/27 NB 07/48 6136 -04/64 04/64 03/50➪r
THE BORDER REGIMENT

46137 09/27 NB 05/48 6137 -10/62 05/63 03/55➪r
THE PRINCE OF WALES'S VOLUNTEERS SOUTH LANCASHIRE

46138 09/27 NB 01/49 6138 -02/63 05/63 r
THE LONDON IRISH RIFLEMAN

46139 10/27 NB 05/48 6139 -10/62 05/63 r
THE WELCH REGIMENT

46140 10/27 NB 01/49 6140 -11/65 03/66 05/52➪r
THE KING'S ROYAL RIFLE CORPS

46141 10/27 NB 07/48 6141 -04/64 07/64 10/50➪r
THE NORTH STAFFORDSHIRE REGIMENT

46142 10/27 NB 07/48 6142 -01/64 01/64 02/51➪r
THE YORK & LANCASTER REGIMENT

46143 10/27 NB 09/48 6143 -12/63 01/64 06/49➪r
THE SOUTH STAFFORDSHIRE REGIMENT

46144 10/27 NB 06/48 6144 -01/64 01/64 r
HONOURABLE ARTILLERY COMPANY

46145 10/27 NB 10/48 6145 -12/62 10/63 r
THE DUKE OF WELLINGTON'S REGT. (WEST RIDING)

46146 10/27 NB 06/48 6146 -11/62 03/63 r
THE RIFLE BRIGADE

46147 10/27 NB 01/49 6147 -11/62 03/63 r
THE NORTHAMPTONSHIRE REGIMENT

46148 11/27 NB 06/48 6148 -11/64 01/65 07/54➪r
THE MANCHESTER REGIMENT

46149 11/27 NB 04/48 6149 -09/63 11/63 r
THE MIDDLESEX REGIMENT

46150 05/30 Der 01/49 6150 -11/63 12/63 r
THE LIFE GUARDSMAN

46151 06/30 Der 10/48 6151 -12/62 08/63 04/53➪r
THE ROYAL HORSE GUARDSMAN

46152 07/27 NB 06/48 6152 -04/65 07/65 r
THE KING'S DRAGOON GUARDSMAN

46153 07/30 Der 08/49 6153 -12/62 05/63 08/49➪r
THE ROYAL DRAGOON

46154 07/30 Der 04/48 6154 -11/62 03/63 r
THE HUSSAR

46155 07/30 Der 07/48 6155 -12/64 02/65 05/50➪r
THE LANCER

46156 07/30 Der 02/49 6156 -10/64 02/65 05/54➪r
THE SOUTH WALES BORDERER

46157 08/30 Der 12/48 6157 -01/64 02/64 r
THE ROYAL ARTILLERYMAN

46158 08/30 Der 10/48 6158 -11/63 11/63 09/52➪r
THE LOYAL REGIMENT

46159 08/30 Der 09/48 6159 -11/62 02/63 r
THE ROYAL AIR FORCE

46160 08/30 Der 09/48 6160 -05/65 07/65 r
QUEEN VICTORIA'S RIFLEMAN

46161 09/30 Der 07/48 6161 -11/62 12/63 r
KING'S OWN

46162 09/30 Der 04/48 6162 -06/64 09/64 10/48➪r
QUEEN'S WESTMINSTER RIFLEMAN

46163 09/30 Der 11/48 6163 -09/64 02/65 10/53➪r
CIVIL SERVICE RIFLEMAN

46164 09/30 Der 04/48 6164 -12/62 03/63 07/51➪r
THE ARTISTS' RIFLEMAN

46165 10/30 Der 10/48 6165 -11/64 03/65 06/52➪r
THE RANGER 12TH LONDON REGT.

46166 10/30 Der 07/48 6166 -10/64 12/64 r
LONDON RIFLE BRIGADE

46167 10/30 Der 12/48 6167 -04/64 05/64 12/48➪r
THE HERTFORDSHIRE REGIMENT

46168 10/30 Der 09/48 6168 -05/64 08/64 r
THE GIRL GUIDE

46169 11/30 Der 05/48 6169 -05/63 08/63 r
THE BOY SCOUT

46170 12/29 NB 04/48 6170 -11/62 01/63 e
BRITISH LEGION

8P [1] 46200-46212
4-6-2 LMS Stanier 'Princess Royal'

Power Classification:	7P reclassified 8P in 1951
Introduced:	1933-1935
Designer:	Stanier
Company:	LMS
Weight:	Loco 104t 10cwt t Loco 110t 11cwt Tender 54t 13cwt
Driving Wheel:	6' 6"
Boiler Pressure:	250psi superheated
Cylinders:	Four 16¼" x 28" t None (turbine driven engine) r Four 16½" x 28"
Tractive Effort:	40285lbf r 41540lbf
Valve Gear:	Walschaert (piston valves) t Turbine driven w Outside Walschaert with rocking shafts (piston valves)

One of Stanier's first tasks on becoming CME of the LMS in 1932 was to set about the production of a really large main line engine for the West Coast route. His first two pacifics, 6200 and 6201 appeared in June 1933 and they included several new features to LMS practice, including the use of a taper boiler and low temperature superheater. These features came from Swindon, where Stanier had been working as assistant CME before 1932.

After trials with these two engines, the boiler was modified with a new 32 element superheater, which dramatically improved the engines.

Ten more engines numbered 6203-6212 were built in 1935, and the 'Princess Roya'l engines proved themselves to be greatly superior to anything which had been previously seen on the LNWR main line.

t 46202 was ordered as the third of the original engines, but it was built as an experimental engine which differed radically from its sisters. The boiler and wheels were identical, but in place of the cylinders and motion the engine was propelled by turbines; a large one on the left hand side for forward motion and a small one on the right hand side for reverse running. It was the only successful turbine driven locomotive to be built in this country, and it was known as *'The Turbomotive'*. Many snags were encountered and it spent a lot of time out of service undergoing modifications, but when it was in service it was a very good engine and performed work equal to that of the other members of the class. In 1952 it was rebuilt as an ordinary engine with four cylinders (r). In this form it was named PRINCESS ANNE. Unfortunately it had a tragically short life, being damaged beyond repair in the accident at Harrow on 8th October 1952, only a few weeks after appearing from Crewe. It was towed to Crewe works, where it remained until officially deleted from stock in 1954.

w 46205 was rebuilt in 1947 with two sets of Walschaert valve gear instead of the four on the other engines. The inside valves were operated by rocking shafts. It was converted back to normal in 1955.

Year End Totals: '8P [1]' class

'47	'48	'49	'50	'51	'52	'53	'54	'55	'56	'57	'58	'59	'60	'61	'62	'63	'64	'65	'66	'67
13	13	13	13	13	13	13	12	12	12	12	12	12	12	6						

Number Built Renumbered BR Dates Scrap Notes

46200 07/33 Crw 08/48 6200 -11/62 10/64
THE PRINCESS ROYAL

46201 § 11/33 Crw 08/48 6201 -10/62
PRINCESS ELIZABETH

46202 06/35 Crw 03/49 6202 -06/54 06/54 t
08/52➲ PRINCESS ANNE 08/52➪r

46203 § 07/35 Crw 05/48 6203 -10/62
PRINCESS MARGARET ROSE

46204 07/35 Crw 04/48 6204 -10/61 05/62
PRINCESS LOUISE

46205 07/35 Crw 05/48 6205 -11/61 05/62 w
PRINCESS VICTORIA

46206 08/35 Crw 11/48 6206 -10/62 11/62
PRINCESS MARIE LOUISE

46207 08/35 Crw 05/49 6207 -11/61 05/62
PRINCESS ARTHUR OF CONNAUGHT

46208 08/35 Crw 05/48 6208 -10/62 11/62
PRINCESS HELENA VICTORIA

46209 08/35 Crw 01/49 6209 -09/62 11/62
PRINCESS BEATRICE

46210 09/35 Crw 06/48 6210 -10/61 05/62
LADY PATRICIA

46211 09/35 Crw 06/48 6211 -10/61 04/62
QUEEN MAUD

46212 10/35 Crw 04/48 6212 -10/61 04/62
DUCHESS OF KENT

8P [2] 46220-46257
4-6-2 LMS Stanier 'Princess Coronation' or 'Duchess'

Power Classification:	7P reclassified 8P in 1951
Introduced:	1937-1948
Designer:	Stanier
Company:	LMS
Weight:	Loco 105t 5cwt s Loco 108t 2cwt i Loco 106t 8cwt Tender 56t 7cwt
Driving Wheel:	6' 9"
Boiler Pressure:	250psi superheated
Cylinders:	Four 16½" x 28"
Tractive Effort:	40000lbf
Valve Gear:	Outside Walschaert with rocking shafts (piston valves)

Following the success of the 'Princess Royal' ('46200') class, Stanier developed an improved design of pacific for working the newly inaugurated high speed service between London and Glasgow. In order to meet the challenge of Gresley's streamlined pacifics on the LNER these engines were also streamlined. Although impressive engines they were aesthetically very ugly with a bulbous appearance.

Known as the 'Princess Coronation' or 'Coronation' class, 6220-6224 appeared at first in blue livery with horizontal white bands matching the coaches on the new service. 6225-6229 followed them and were painted in standard LMS maroon. The next batch to be built was 6230-6234 and these engines were not streamlined and were extremely handsome engines. The unstreamlined engines were known as the 'Duchess' class. 6235-6248 appeared next with full streamlining, and then between 1944 and 1948 the final batch 6249-6257 appeared without streamlining.

In July 1937 6220 was tried out on a special train and attained a maximum speed of 114mph just south of Crewe, thus breaking the then speed record of 113mph which had been held by the LNER.

In January 1939 6229 DUCHESS OF HAMILTON was sent on exhibition to the New York World's Fair in 1939. It exchanged identities with 6220 CORONATION for the trip and it made an extended tour over the USA railways. Due to the outbreak of the Second World War it was stranded in the States. It eventually returned in 1943 when it reverted back to its original identity.

6244 was named CITY OF LEEDS until 1941.

From 1946 onwards the streamlining was removed as it was found that it was of little value at speeds below 90mph, and it was a nuisance to the maintenance staff.

The whole class was fitted with double chimneys from 1938 onwards. They were also fitted with smoke deflectors, unlike the 'Princess Royal' class which never had smoke deflectors.

They proved themselves to be magnificent engines, not only working at high speed, but also managing the heaviest expresses over the West Coast route. They were displaced by diesels on the main line in 1960-1961 and they performed relief and standby duties for the next two or three years. Eventually an accounting decision decreed that the last twenty engines must be taken out of stock by 31st December 1964, even though some of them had only recently been outshopped and were still in very good condition.

s Only three engines retained their streamlined casing at the beginning of 1948 and they were all rebuilt by 1949.

d The engines which had been de-streamlined from 1946 onwards could at first be recognised by a sloping top to the smokebox. This was later removed as the smokeboxes were replaced.

i 46256 and 46257 were built in 1947-1948 by Ivatt. They were fitted with roller bearings throughout, altered rear ends and cabs, and had various other detail alterations.

Year End Totals: '8P [2]' class

'47	'48	'49	'50	'51	'52	'53	'54	'55	'56	'57	'58	'59	'60	'61	'62	'63	'64	'65	'66	'67
37	38	38	38	38	38	38	38	38	38	38	38	38	38	38	35	22				

Number	*Built*	*Renumbered*	*BR Dates*	*Scrap*	*Notes*
46220	06/37 Crw	07/48 6220	-04/63	05/63	d
CORONATION					
46221	06/37 Crw	10/48 6221	-05/63	07/63	d
QUEEN ELIZABETH					
46222	06/37 Crw	09/48 6222	-10/63	11/63	d
QUEEN MARY					
46223	07/37 Crw	03/49 6223	-10/63	10/63	d
PRINCESS ALICE					
46224	07/37 Crw	05/48 6224	-10/63	10/63	d
PRINCESS ALEXANDRA					
46225	05/38 Crw	06/48 6225	-10/64	12/64	d
DUCHESS OF GLOUCESTER					
46226	05/38 Crw	09/48 6226	-10/64	02/65	
DUCHESS OF NORFOLK					s48⇨d
46227	06/38 Crw	05/48 6227	-12/62	11/63	d
DUCHESS OF DEVONSHIRE					
46228	06/38 Crw	07/48 6228	-10/64	12/64	d
DUCHESS OF RUTLAND					
46229 §	09/38 Crw	07/48 6229	-02/64		
DUCHESS OF HAMILTON					s48⇨d
46230	07/38 Crw	05/48 6230	-11/63	12/63	
DUCHESS OF BUCCLEUCH					
46231	07/38 Crw	05/48 6231	-12/62	11/63	
DUCHESS OF ATHOLL					
46232	07/38 Crw	05/48 6232	-12/62	11/63	
DUCHESS OF MONTROSE					
46233 §	07/38 Crw	10/48 6233	-02/64		
DUCHESS OF SUTHERLAND					
46234	08/38 Crw	10/48 6234	-01/63	06/63	
DUCHESS OF ABERCORN					
46235 §	07/39 Crw	05/48 6235	-10/64		d
CITY OF BIRMINGHAM					
46236	07/39 Crw	04/48 6236	-03/64	04/64	d
CITY OF BRADFORD					
46237	08/39 Crw	07/48 6237	-10/64	12/64	d
CITY OF BRISTOL					
46238	09/39 Crw	03/49 6238	-10/64	12/64	d
CITY OF CARLISLE					
46239	09/39 Crw	08/48 6239	-10/64	12/64	d
CITY OF CHESTER					
46240	03/40 Crw	06/48 6240	-10/64	12/64	d
CITY OF COVENTRY					
46241	04/40 Crw	05/48 6241	-09/64	02/65	d
CITY OF EDINBURGH					
46242	05/40 Crw	05/48 6242	-10/63	11/63	d
CITY OF GLASGOW					
46243	06/40 Crw	04/48 6243	-10/64	08/65	s
CITY OF LANCASTER					09/49⇨d
46244	07/40 Crw	08/48 6244	-10/64	12/64	d
KING GEORGE VI					
46245	06/43 Crw	08/48 6245	-10/64	12/64	d
CITY OF LONDON					
46246	08/43 Crw	11/48 6246	-01/63	05/63	d
CITY OF MANCHESTER					
46247	09/43 Crw	11/48 6247	-06/63	07/63	d
CITY OF LIVERPOOL					
46248	10/43 Crw	03/49 6248	-09/64	11/64	d
CITY OF LEEDS					
46249	04/44 Crw	04/48 6249	-11/63	12/63	
CITY OF SHEFFIELD					
46250	05/44 Crw	02/49 6250	-10/64	12/64	
CITY OF LICHFIELD					
46251	06/44 Crw	05/48 6251	-10/64	12/64	
CITY OF NOTTINGHAM					
46252	06/44 Crw	04/49 6252	-06/63	09/63	
CITY OF LEICESTER					
46253	09/46 Crw	09/49 6253	-01/63	05/63	
CITY OF ST. ALBANS					
46254	09/46 Crw	07/49 6254	-10/64	12/64	
CITY OF STOKE-ON-TRENT					
46255	10/46 Crw	06/49 6255	-10/64	12/64	
CITY OF HEREFORD					
46256	12/47 Crw	05/48 6256	-10/64	12/64	i
SIR WILLIAM A. STANIER, F.R.S.					
46257	05/48 Crw		05/48-10/64	01/65	i
CITY OF SALFORD					

2MT [2] 46400-46527
2-6-0 LMS Ivatt

Power Classification: 2F reclassified 2MT in 1948
Introduced: 1946-1953
Designer: Ivatt
Company: LMS
Weight: Loco 47t 2cwt
Tender 37t 3cwt
Driving Wheel: 5' 0"
Boiler Pressure: 200psi superheated
Cylinders: Outside 16" x 24"
c Outside 16½" x 24"
Tractive Effort: 17410lbf
c 18510lbf
Valve Gear: Walschaert (piston valves)

In 1946, two years before nationalisation, Ivatt introduced two new lightweight designs for cross country and branch line working. The tender engine was the '2MT' '46400' class and the tank engine version was the '2MT' '41200' class.

One hundred and twenty eight of the tender engines were built, only twenty of which appeared before nationalisation. The design was later adopted as a BR standard design, appearing as the '2MT' '78000' class in 1952. Most of this class was based on the London Midland Region, but some were based on the Western, Eastern, North Eastern and Scottish Regions.

l 46400-46464 carried short LMS type chimneys.

t 46465-46489 carried tall tapered chimneys.

p 46490-46527 carried BR tall parallel type chimneys.

s 46424 was experimentally fitted with a narrow stove pipe chimney in 1951 and it was nicknamed 'The Spout'.

c The later engines (46465-46527) were fitted with slightly larger cylinders.

b The original LMS built engines had a smaller lower pitched boiler and a lower running plate than the BR built engines.

x In 1952 46460 was transferred to work on the St. Combs Light Railway in Scotland, and it was fitted with a cow-catcher which was previously attached to the LNER 'F4' engines which had worked on the branch.

Year End Totals: '2MT [2]' class

'47	'48	'49	'50	'51	'52	'53	'54	'55	'56	'57	'58	'59	'60	'61	'62	'63	'64	'65	'66	'67
20	35	35	65	95	115	128	128	128	128	128	128	128	128	127	115	111	103	82	42	

Number	*Built*	*Renumbered*	*BR Dates*	*Scrap*	*Notes*
46400	12/46 Crw	07/50 6400	-05/67	09/67	lb
46401	12/46 Crw	03/50 6401	-05/66	08/66	lb
46402	12/46 Crw	02/50 6402	-06/67	01/68	lb
46403	12/46 Crw	12/49 6403	-06/64	11/64	lb
46404	12/46 Crw	05/49 6404	-05/65	10/65	lb
46405	12/46 Crw	06/49 6405	-12/66	04/67	lb
46406	12/46 Crw	05/49 6406	-01/67	09/67	lb
46407	12/46 Crw	05/50 6407	-12/61	02/62	lb
46408	12/46 Crw	08/50 6408	-11/62	01/64	lb
46409	12/46 Crw	09/50 6409	-07/64	11/64	lb
46410	01/47 Crw	10/50 6410	-03/66	06/66	lb
46411	01/47 Crw	09/50 6411	-01/67	03/68	lb
46412	01/47 Crw	11/50 6412	-08/66	11/66	lb
46413	02/47 Crw	06/49 6413	-10/65	02/66	lb
46414	02/47 Crw	05/51 6414	-06/66	12/66	lb
46415	02/47 Crw	03/51 6415	-10/62	02/64	lb
46416	02/47 Crw	12/49 6416	-04/66	07/66	lb
46417	03/47 Crw	12/50 6417	-02/67	06/67	lb
46418	03/47 Crw	02/51 6418	-01/67	09/67	lb
46419	03/47 Crw	12/50 6419	-09/66	12/66	lb
46420	11/48 Crw		11/48-01/65	03/65	l
46421	11/48 Crw		11/48-10/66	02/67	l
46422	11/48 Crw		11/48-12/66	05/67	l
46423	11/48 Crw		11/48-01/65	05/65	l
46424	11/48 Crw		11/48-12/66	05/67	ls
46425	11/48 Crw		11/48-09/65	01/66	l
46426	12/48 Crw		12/48-09/66	06/67	l
46427	12/48 Crw		12/48-10/66	02/67	l
46428 §	12/48 Crw		12/48-12/66		l
46429	12/48 Crw		12/48-07/66	10/66	l
46430	12/48 Crw		12/48-10/65	12/65	l
46431	12/48 Crw		12/48-03/67	12/67	l
46432	12/48 Crw		12/48-05/67	11/67	l
46433	12/48 Crw		12/48-05/67	09/67	l
46434	12/48 Crw		12/48-09/66	01/67	l
46435	01/50 Crw		01/50-07/64	11/64	l
46436	01/50 Crw		01/50-05/67	10/67	l
46437	01/50 Crw		01/50-05/67	10/67	l
46438	01/50 Crw		01/50-02/63	01/64	l
46439	01/50 Crw		01/50-03/67	09/67	l
46440	02/50 Crw		02/50-03/67	09/67	l
46441 §	02/50 Crw		02/50-04/67		l
46442	02/50 Crw		02/50-10/66	01/67	l
46443 §	02/50 Crw		02/50-03/67		l
46444	02/50 Crw		02/50-07/65	10/65	l
46445	02/50 Crw		02/50-07/66	10/66	l
46446	03/50 Crw		03/50-12/66	09/67	l
46447 §	03/50 Crw		03/50-12/66		l
46448	03/50 Crw		03/50-05/67	10/67	l
46449	03/50 Crw		03/50-05/67	10/67	l
46450	04/50 Crw		04/50-01/66	04/68	l
46451	04/50 Crw		04/50-12/66	05/67	l
46452	04/50 Crw		04/50-05/67	11/67	l
46453	04/50 Crw		04/50-04/62	09/62	l
46454	04/50 Crw		04/50-10/66	03/67	l
46455	04/50 Crw		04/50-05/67	10/67	l
46456	05/50 Crw		05/50-09/65	11/65	l
46457	05/50 Crw		05/50-05/67	10/67	l
46458	05/50 Crw		05/50-12/66	05/67	l
46459	05/50 Crw		05/50-09/65	12/65	l
46460	05/50 Crw		05/50-08/66	12/66	lx
46461	06/50 Crw		06/50-07/64	12/64	l
46462	06/50 Crw		06/50-08/66	11/66	l
46463	06/50 Crw		06/50-02/66	06/66	l
46464 §	06/50 Crw		06/50-09/66		l
46465	06/51 Dar		06/51-03/67	09/67	tc
46466	06/51 Dar		06/51-09/62	09/62	tc
46467	06/51 Dar		06/51-07/64	11/64	tc
46468	07/51 Dar		07/51-10/65	02/66	tc
46469	07/51 Dar		07/51-09/62	09/62	tc
46470	07/51 Dar		07/51-05/67	10/67	tc
46471	07/51 Dar		07/51-11/62	11/62	tc
46472	07/51 Dar		07/51-01/65	04/65	tc
46473	08/51 Dar		08/51-12/63	02/64	tc
46474	08/51 Dar		08/51-07/64	11/64	tc
46475	08/51 Dar		08/51-07/64	10/64	tc
46476	09/51 Dar		09/51-02/62	04/62	tc
46477	09/51 Dar		09/51-12/62	01/64	tc
46478	09/51 Dar		09/51-05/62	06/62	tc
46479	09/51 Dar		09/51-07/65	11/65	tc
46480	09/51 Dar		09/51-05/67	12/67	tc
46481	10/51 Dar		10/51-12/62	05/63	tc
46482	10/51 Dar		10/51-08/65	11/65	tc
46483	10/51 Dar		10/51-11/63	02/64	tc
46484	10/51 Dar		10/51-06/67	02/68	tc
46485	11/51 Dar		11/51-06/67	05/68	tc
46486	11/51 Dar		11/51-05/67	09/67	tc
46487	11/51 Dar		11/51-05/67	11/67	tc
46488	11/51 Dar		11/51-06/65	10/65	tc
46489	11/51 Dar		11/51-11/63	11/63	tc
46490	11/51 Dar		11/51-05/67	10/67	pc
46491	12/51 Dar		12/51-05/67	11/67	pc
46492	12/51 Dar		12/51-06/67	02/68	pc
46493	12/51 Dar		12/51-11/62	12/62	pc
46494	12/51 Dar		12/51-10/62	10/62	pc
46495	01/52 Dar		01/52-10/66	02/67	pc
46496	02/52 Dar		02/52-04/66	07/66	pc
46497	02/52 Dar		02/52-04/65	09/65	pc
46498	02/52 Dar		02/52-09/65	12/65	pc
46499	03/52 Dar		03/52-05/67	09/67	pc
46500	03/52 Dar		03/52-01/67	06/67	pc
46501	03/52 Dar		03/52-05/67	11/67	pc
46502	03/52 Dar		03/52-02/67	06/67	pc
46503	11/52 Sdn		11/52-05/67	11/67	pc
46504	11/52 Sdn		11/52-10/66	02/67	pc
46505	11/52 Sdn		11/52-06/67	11/67	pc
46506	11/52 Sdn		11/52-05/67	11/67	pc
46507	11/52 Sdn		11/52-06/65	10/65	pc
46508	12/52 Sdn		12/52-12/66	12/67	pc
46509	12/52 Sdn		12/52-10/66	01/67	pc
46510	12/52 Sdn		12/52-09/65	03/66	pc
46511	12/52 Sdn		12/52-09/65	01/66	pc
46512 §	12/52 Sdn		12/52-12/66		pc
46513	12/52 Sdn		12/52-07/66	01/67	pc
46514	12/52 Sdn		12/52-06/66	10/66	pc
46515	01/53 Sdn		01/53-05/67	12/67	pc
46516	01/53 Sdn		01/53-05/67	11/67	pc
46517	01/53 Sdn		01/53-12/66	04/67	pc
46518	01/53 Sdn		01/53-03/66	06/66	pc
46519	02/53 Sdn		02/53-10/66	02/67	pc
46520	02/53 Sdn		02/53-05/67	11/67	pc
46521 §	02/53 Sdn		02/53-10/66		pc
46522	03/53 Sdn		03/53-05/67	02/68	pc
46523	03/53 Sdn		03/53-05/67	11/67	pc
46524	03/53 Sdn		03/53-02/65	05/65	pc
46525	03/53 Sdn		03/53-12/64	05/65	pc
46526	03/53 Sdn		03/53-07/66	12/66	pc
46527	03/53 Sdn		03/53-10/65	05/66	pc

1P [1] 46601-46757
2-4-2T LNWR Webb

Power Classification: 1P
Introduced: 1890-1897
Designer: Webb
Company: LNWR
Weight: 50t 10cwt
Driving Wheel: 5' 8½"
Boiler Pressure: 150psi
Cylinders: Inside 17" x 24"
Tractive Effort: 12910lbf
Valve Gear: Allan straight link (slide valves)

Webb produced two classes of standard simple 2-4-2Ts for the LNWR. Developed from the 2-4-0T '58092' class there was a small wheeled version (180 engines, none of which survived to enter BR stock), and a class of 160 larger wheeled engines, built between 1890 and 1897.

LMS Stanier 'Jubilee' 4-6-0 No 45571 *South Africa*.

LMS Stanier Rebuilt 'Royal Scot' 4-6-0 No 46125 *3rd Carabinier*.

LMS Stanier 'Duchess' 4-6-2 No 46228 *Duchess of Rutland* at Carlisle Upperby in 1953. It still carries the sloping front to the top of the smokebox, which remained after the streamlining was removed.

LMS Ivatt '2MT' 2-6-0 No 46432 at Guide Bridge.

These were the forty-three survivors of the larger wheeled engines, the first of which had been withdrawn in 1921. The engines remained virtually unaltered throughout their whole careers (apart from painting and numbering), even retaining their vintage LNWR chimneys.

No. 6616 was transferred to the duplicate list as 26616 in 1945. This was apparently in error as no more of the class were renumbered.

m These engines were motor fitted for working push-pull trains.

Year End Totals: '1P [1]' class

'47	'48	'49	'50	'51	'52	'53	'54	'55	'56	'57	'58	'59	'60	'61	'62	'63	'64	'65	'66	'67
43	30	21	18	15	12	4	2													

Number	Built	Renumbered	BR Dates	Scrap	Notes
46601	09/90 Crw	09/48 6601	-12/53	*54*	m
46603	02/91 Crw	11/48 6603	-07/51	*51*	m
46604	01/91 Crw	11/48 6604	-08/55	*55*	
46605	01/91 Crw	6605	-05/48	06/48	m
46616	03/91 Crw	08/48 26616	-09/55	*09/55*	m
46620	04/91 Crw	12/48 6620	-02/53	*03/53*	m
46628	12/91 Crw	6628	-07/51	*51*	
46632	01/92 Crw	6632	-08/50	*50*	
46635	01/92 Crw	03/49 6635	-04/50	*04/50*	m
46637	01/92 Crw	08/48 6637	-09/49	*49*	m
46639	01/92 Crw	6639	-06/49	06/49	m
46643	12/92 Crw	09/48 6643	-01/53	*53*	
46654	06/93 Crw	12/48 6654	-09/53	*53*	
46656	06/93 Crw	01/49 6656	-02/52	04/52	
46658	06/93 Crw	08/48 6658	-12/50	*51*	
46661	06/93 Crw	6661	-06/48	*48*	
46663	06/93 Crw	6663	-06/49	06/49	m
46666	06/93 Crw	10/48 6666	-06/54	*54*	m
46669	02/94 Crw	6669	-09/49	*49*	
46673	08/93 Crw	6673	-04/48	05/48	
46676	07/93 Crw	6676	-12/49	*50*	
46679	07/93 Crw	6679	-02/48	*07/48*	
46680	07/93 Crw	08/48 6680	-01/53	*53*	m
46681	07/93 Crw	6681	-06/48	07/48	
46682	07/93 Crw	6682	-01/48	04/48	m
46683	07/93 Crw	11/51 6683	-02/53	03/53	m
46686	09/93 Crw	6686	-05/48	07/48	
46687	09/93 Crw	05/48 6687	-12/49	*50*	
46688	09/93 Crw	6688	-04/51	*51*	m
46691	04/94 Crw	6691	-03/48	09/48	
46692	04/94 Crw	6692	-03/48	*07/48*	m
46701	06/94 Crw	01/50 6701	-02/53	*53*	
46710	02/95 Crw	6710	-09/49	*49*	m
46711	02/95 Crw	6711	-05/49	*49*	m
46712	02/95 Crw	09/48 6712	-08/54	*54*	m
46718	03/95 Crw	6718	-01/48	*48*	m
46727	04/95 Crw	12/48 6727	-12/52	*01/53*	m
46738	05/97 Crw	6738	-05/48	05/48	
46740	04/97 Crw	6740	-05/48	05/48	
46742	04/97 Crw	6742	-12/49	*50*	
46747	05/97 Crw	6747	-02/48	*07/48*	
46749	05/97 Crw	11/48 6749	-02/52	*52*	
46757	07/97 Crw	05/49 6757	-02/53	*03/53*	m

2P [6] 46762
2-4-2T Wirral Railway Aspinall (ex LYR Class '5')

Power Classification: 2P
Introduced: 1889-1911 (this engine built 1890)
Designer: Aspinall
Company: LYR, sold to Wirral Railway in 1921
Weight: 55t 19cwt
Driving Wheel: 5' 8"
Boiler Pressure: 180psi
Cylinders: Inside 17½" x 26"
Tractive Effort: 17915lbf
Valve Gear: Joy (slide valves)

This was the only surviving engine from the stock of the Wirral Railway to come into BR stock. It was originally built as a LYR engine, being part of the '50621' class. It was sold to the Wirral Railway in 1921.

The LMS renumbered all Wirral engines in the number series allocated to the LNWR. A space was left in the LYR number series where the engine could have taken its rightful place and become 10638 and later 50638. However it retained its number as a Wirral engine, even though it did not stay on the Wirral and it worked amongst its LYR contemporaries in LMS and BR days.

Year End Totals: '2P [6]' class

'47	'48	'49	'50	'51	'52	'53	'54	'55	'56	'57	'58	'59	'60	'61	'62	'63	'64	'65	'66	'67
1	1	1	1	1																

Number	Built	Renumbered	BR Dates	Scrap	Notes
46762	07/90 Hor	09/49 6762	-02/52	*52*	

2P [7] 46876-46931
0-6-2T LNWR Webb

Power Classification: 2P reclassified 2MT in 1948
Introduced: 1898-1902
Designer: Webb
Company: LNWR
Weight: 52t 6cwt
Driving Wheel: 5' 2½"
Boiler Pressure: 150psi
Cylinders: Inside 18" x 24"
Tractive Effort: 15865lbf
Valve Gear: Joy (slide valves)

These engines were the passenger variety of Webb's '58880' class 'Coal Tanks'. They were built with larger 5' 2½" wheels and they were known as 'Watford Tanks' or '18 inch passenger tanks'. They were designed specifically for suburban passenger work.

Eighty engines were built between 1898 and 1902. The first was withdrawn in 1920 and fifteen came into BR stock.

Year End Totals: '2P [7]' class

'47	'48	'49	'50	'51	'52	'53	'54	'55	'56	'57	'58	'59	'60	'61	'62	'63	'64	'65	'66	'67
15	9	5	5	2	1															

Number	Built	Renumbered	BR Dates	Scrap	Notes
46876	09/98 Crw	6876	-08/49	*49*	
46878	09/98 Crw	6878	-02/48	*07/48*	
46881	08/99 Crw	6881	-07/48	11/48	
46883	08/99 Crw	6883	-05/48	06/48	
46899	08/00 Crw	6899	-07/52	*52*	
46900	08/00 Crw	04/51 6900	-02/53	*03/53*	
46906	08/00 Crw	6906	-05/51	05/51	
46909	05/01 Crw	6909	-03/48	07/48	
46912	05/01 Crw	10/48 6912	-12/51	*52*	
46917	05/01 Crw	6917	-04/49	*49*	
46920	03/02 Crw	6920	-05/48	05/48	
46922	03/02 Crw	6922	-07/51	*51*	
46924	03/02 Crw	6924	-12/49	*50*	
46926	03/02 Crw	6926	-02/48	04/48	
46931	06/02 Crw	6931	-03/49	*49*	

0F [3] 47000-47009
0-4-0ST LMS & BR Stanier

Power Classification: 0F
Introduced: 1932
b 1953-1954
Designer: Stanier, built by Kitson
b Built at Horwich
Company: LMS
b BR
Weight: 33t 0cwt
b 34t 0cwt
Driving Wheel: 3' 10"
Boiler Pressure: 160psi
Cylinders: Outside 15½" x 20"
Tractive Effort: 14205lbf
Valve Gear: Stephenson (slide valves)

47000-47004 were built in 1932 by Kitson & Co to Stanier's design. They were designed for lines with severe curvature such as docks and collieries. They were numbered 1540-1544 until 1934.

b Five similar engines were built by BR at Horwich between October 1953 and January 1954. They were the last new engines of basically LMS design to be built. They differed from the other engines in having shorter but deeper saddle tanks, but they also had short side tanks and increased coal space. The water capacity remained the same as the earlier engines at 800 gallons, but the coal space was doubled to two tons.

Year End Totals: '0F [3]' class

'47	'48	'49	'50	'51	'52	'53	'54	'55	'56	'57	'58	'59	'60	'61	'62	'63	'64	'65	'66	'67
5	5	5	5	5	5	9	10	10	10	10	10	10	10	10	10	9	4	4		

Number	Built	Renumbered	BR Dates	Scrap	Notes
47000	11/32 K	07/50 7000	-10/66	02/67	
47001	11/32 K	06/50 7001	-12/66	04/67	
47002	11/32 K	06/50 7002	-09/64	03/65	
47003	12/32 K	08/48 7003	-04/64	06/64	
47004	12/32 K	06/48 7004	-01/64	08/64	
47005	10/53 Hor		10/53-12/66	04/67	b
47006	11/53 Hor		11/53-08/66	11/66	b
47007	11/53 Hor		11/53-12/63	11/64	b
47008	12/53 Hor		12/53-09/64	03/65	b
47009	01/54 Hor		01/54-09/64	01/65	b

2F [1] 47160-47169
0-6-0T LMS Fowler Dock Tank

Power Classification: 2F
Introduced: 1928
Designer: Fowler
Company: LMS
Weight: 43t 12cwt
Driving Wheel: 3' 11"
Boiler Pressure: 160psi
Cylinders: Outside 17" x 22"
Tractive Effort: 18400lbf
Valve Gear: Walschaert (slide valves)

Fowler built these engines in 1928 specially for use in dockyards. They had short wheelbases of only 9' 6" to enable them to work round curves of very short radius.

These engines were originally numbered 11270-11279. In 1935-1937 they were renumbered 7100-7109, and then renumbered 7160-7169 in 1939.

Some of these dock tanks were used for a while as departmental locomotives by BR.

Year End Totals: '2F [1]' class

'47	'48	'49	'50	'51	'52	'53	'54	'55	'56	'57	'58	'59	'60	'61	'62	'63	'64	'65	'66	'67
10	10	10	10	10	10	10	10	10	10	10	10	8	7	7	5	2				

Number	Built	Renumbered	BR Dates	Scrap	Notes
47160	12/28 Der	11/48 7160	-10/63	05/64	
47161	12/28 Der	09/49 7161	-08/63	11/63	
47162	12/28 Der	07/49 7162	-12/59	01/60	
47163	12/28 Der	04/48 7163	-12/62	12/63	
47164	12/28 Der	04/48 7164	-09/64	01/65	
47165	12/28 Der	02/51 7165	-09/64	01/65	
47166	12/28 Der	03/49 7166	-05/63	11/63	
47167	01/29 Der	03/48 7167	-07/60	08/60	
47168	01/29 Der	07/50 7168	-10/62	11/62	
47169	01/29 Der	05/51 7169	-09/59	09/59	

Sentinel [1] 47180-47183
0-4-0T LMS Sentinel two-speed shunter

Power Classification: 0F
Introduced: 1930
Designer: Sentinel
Company: LMS
Weight: 20t 17cwt
Driving Wheel: 2' 6"
Boiler Pressure: 275psi superheated
Cylinders: Inside 6¾" x 9"
Tractive Effort: 11800lbf
Valve Gear: Geared Sentinel (poppet valves)

The Sentinel Company specialised in building small geared steam locomotives, mainly for use in industry. The LMS bought four of these chain driven engines in 1930. They were two-speed shunters and they were very similar in their box-like appearance to the LNER 'Y3' class of Sentinel two speed shunters.

These engines were numbered 7160-7163 until 1939.

Year End Totals: 'Sentinel [1]' class

'47	'48	'49	'50	'51	'52	'53	'54	'55	'56	'57	'58	'59	'60	'61	'62	'63	'64	'65	'66	'67
4	4	4	4	4	4	3	3	2												

Number	Built	Renumbered	BR Dates	Scrap	Notes
47180	06/30 S	03/51 7180	-08/53	11/53	
47181	06/30 S	09/49 7181	-11/56	*56*	
47182	06/30 S	12/48 7182	-02/56	*08/56*	
47183	06/30 S	12/48 7183	-09/55	10/55	

Sentinel [2] 47184
0-4-0T LMS Sentinel single-speed shunter

Power Classification: 0F
Introduced: 1932
Designer: Sentinel
Company: LMS

Weight: 18t 18cwt
Driving Wheel: 2' 6"
Boiler Pressure: 275psi superheated
Cylinders: Inside 6¾" x 9"
Tractive Effort: 11800lbf
Valve Gear: Geared Sentinel (poppet valves)

The LMS bought an additional Sentinel engine in 1932. This was a single speed shunter. It had a completely different outline to the other two-speed Sentinels ('47180' class) and also to the LNER 'Y1' class of Sentinel single speed shunters.

It was numbered 7164 until 1939.

Year End Totals: 'Sentinel ²' class

'47	'48	'49	'50	'51	'52	'53	'54	'55	'56	'57	'58	'59	'60	'61	'62	'63	'64	'65	'66	'67
1	1	1	1	1	1	1	1													

Number	Built	Renumbered	BR Dates	Scrap	Notes
47184	01/32 S	11/49 7184	-12/55	01/56	

Sentinel[3] 47190-47191
0-4-0T SDJR Sentinel

Power Classification: 0F
Introduced: 1929
Designer: Sentinel
Company: SDJR
Weight: 27t 15cwt
Driving Wheel: 3' 1½"
Boiler Pressure: 275psi superheated
Cylinders: Four Inside 6¾" x 9"
Tractive Effort: 15500lbf
Valve Gear: Geared Sentinel (poppet valves)

The Somerset & Dorset Joint Railway bought two Sentinel engines in 1929 to replace elderly 0-4-0Ts for shunting at Radstock. They were chain-driven 100hp engines, of a somewhat larger design than the LMS engines, and they had a highly distinctive shape.

They were numbered 101 and 102 on the SDJR and they were taken over by the LMS in 1930.

Year End Totals: 'Sentinel ³' class

'47	'48	'49	'50	'51	'52	'53	'54	'55	'56	'57	'58	'59	'60	'61	'62	'63	'64	'65	'66	'67
2	2	2	2	2	2	2	2	2	2	2	2	1	1							

Number	Built	Renumbered	BR Dates	Scrap	Notes
47190	09/29 S	04/49 7190	-03/61	04/61	
47191	09/29 S	05/52 7191	-08/59	*59*	

3F[5] 47200-47259
0-6-0T MR Johnson 'Jinty'

Power Classification: 3F
Introduced: 1899-1902
Designer: Johnson
Company: MR
Weight: 48t 15cwt
Driving Wheel: 4' 7"
Boiler Pressure: 160psi
Cylinders: Inside 18" x 26"
Tractive Effort: 20835lbf
Valve Gear: Stephenson (slide valves)

Johnson designed the '1F' ('41660') class after coming to the Midland Railway in 1873. They were the Midland's standard type of shunting engine. Between 1874 and 1899 280 engines were built at Derby and by outside contractors. In 1907 they were renumbered in the series 1620-1899.

A further sixty engines were built by Vulcan Foundry to a slightly enlarged design in 1899-1902. These were numbered 1900-1959. Many of them were fitted with condensing apparatus for working over the Metropolitan widened lines and they subsequently spent most of their working lives in the London area.

The engines were all built with round topped boilers and enclosed cabs. Between 1919 and 1942 they were all rebuilt with Belpaire boilers and a raised cab roof. They were renumbered 7200-7259 in 1934.

The rebuilt engines formed the basis for the '47260' class. Some of the class worked for a while as departmental engines on BR.

c These engines were fitted with condensing apparatus for working on the Metropolitan widened lines through London.

Year End Totals: '3F ⁵' class

'47	'48	'49	'50	'51	'52	'53	'54	'55	'56	'57	'58	'59	'60	'61	'62	'63	'64	'65	'66	'67
60	60	60	60	60	60	60	58	54	50	44	40	31	26	18	13	11	4	3		

Number	Built	Renumbered	BR Dates	Scrap	Notes
47200	12/99 VF	09/49 7200	-04/61	07/61	c
47201	12/99 VF	09/48 7201	-12/66	06/67	
47202	12/99 VF	05/50 7202	-12/66	04/67	c
47203	12/99 VF	09/50 7203	-08/60	09/60	c
47204	12/99 VF	02/50 7204	-03/61	04/61	c
47205	12/99 VF	11/50 7205	-09/59	10/59	c
47206	01/00 VF	04/48 7206	-10/57	10/57	c
47207	01/00 VF	06/48 7207	-02/64	03/64	c
47208	01/00 VF	09/50 7208	-01/59	03/59	c
47209	02/00 VF	06/48 7209	-04/61	02/62	c
47210	02/00 VF	07/48 7210	-06/59	07/60	c
47211	02/00 VF	02/51 7211	-11/64	05/65	c
47212	02/00 VF	04/50 7212	-01/61	02/61	c
47213	03/00 VF	02/50 7213	-03/62	07/62	c
47214	03/00 VF	08/50 7214	-05/59	08/60	c
47215	03/00 VF	09/50 7215	-01/56	*56*	c
47216	03/00 VF	08/50 7216	-08/59	09/60	c
47217	03/00 VF	10/48 7217	-09/62	05/63	c
47218	04/00 VF	07/48 7218	-10/61	04/62	c
47219	04/00 VF	04/48 7219	-01/59	02/59	c
47220	07/01 VF	07/48 7220	-01/56	*56*	c
47221	07/01 VF	04/50 7221	-11/61	11/61	c
47222	07/01 VF	02/49 7222	-02/58	04/58	c
47223	07/01 VF	09/49 7223	-01/64	03/64	c
47224	07/01 VF	09/48 7224	-05/62	06/62	c
47225	08/01 VF	11/48 7225	-06/63	08/63	c
47226	08/01 VF	10/50 7226	-05/59	06/60	c
47227	08/01 VF	12/50 7227	-07/57	07/57	c
47228	09/01 VF	04/48 7228	-02/64	02/65	c
47229	09/01 VF	07/49 7229	-02/60	03/60	c
47230	04/02 VF	03/50 7230	-11/64	02/65	
47231	04/02 VF	05/49 7231	-03/66	04/67	
47232	04/02 VF	07/49 7232	-04/55	04/55	
47233	04/02 VF	07/50 7233	-08/56	*56*	
47234	04/02 VF	05/50 7234	-02/58	03/58	
47235	04/02 VF	12/50 7235	-10/62	10/63	
47236	05/02 VF	01/51 7236	-08/64	12/64	
47237	05/02 VF	08/50 7237	-04/55	*55*	
47238	05/02 VF	09/51 7238	-01/60	02/60	
47239	05/02 VF	06/51 7239	-09/61	11/61	
47240	05/02 VF	05/49 7240	-03/57	05/57	c
47241	05/02 VF	01/50 7241	-10/60	12/60	c
47242	05/02 VF	09/49 7242	-09/57	10/57	c
47243	05/02 VF	05/49 7243	-10/57	11/57	c
47244	05/02 VF	10/49 7244	-12/54	01/55	c
47245	06/02 VF	10/49 7245	-12/54	12/54	c
47246	06/02 VF	02/52 7246	-02/59	08/60	
47247	06/02 VF	06/48 7247	-08/59	08/60	c
47248	06/02 VF	12/48 7248	-09/63	10/63	
47249	06/02 VF	02/50 7249	-11/58	03/60	c
47250	06/02 VF	07/49 7250	-06/65	12/65	
47251	06/02 VF	06/48 7251	-08/58	10/58	c
47252	07/02 VF	03/50 7252	-01/55	*55*	
47253	07/02 VF	02/50 7253	-06/55	06/55	
47254	07/02 VF	03/49 7254	-12/60	01/61	
47255	07/02 VF	08/50 7255	-09/61	01/62	
47256	07/02 VF	07/48 7256	-09/56	*56*	
47257	08/02 VF	04/49 7257	-09/64	12/64	
47258	08/02 VF	09/49 7258	-11/57	01/58	
47259	08/02 VF	07/48 7259	-03/62	04/62	

3F[6] 47260-47681
0-6-0T LMS & SDJR Fowler 'Jinty'

Power Classification: 3F
Introduced: 1924-1931
s 1929
Designer: Fowler
Company: LMS
s SDJR
Weight: 49t 10cwt
s 46t 3cwt
Driving Wheel: 4' 7"
Boiler Pressure: 160psi
Cylinders: Inside 18" x 26"
Tractive Effort: 20835lbf
Valve Gear: Stephenson (slide valves)

After the '47200' class engines were rebuilt with Belpaire boilers the design was adopted by the LMS after grouping as a standard shunting design. The engines were known as 'Jinties' and they differed from the preceding class in having larger smokeboxes and increased capacity tanks and bunkers.

Four hundred and fifteen engines were built between 1924 and 1931, plus another seven for the SDJR. They were built by a number of outside contractors and they were intended to replace the large number of varied shunting engines inherited by the LMS.

The engines were numbered 7100-7156 and 16400-16764 until 1934. Apart from the War Department locomotives mentioned below, and two engines which were sold to the NCC in Northern Ireland in 1944 (and re-gauged to the 5' 3" gauge), all the engines came into BR stock.

Several of the class were later used as departmental engines by BR. Apart from shunting, some engines were used on North London passenger services, and others were based at Bromsgrove for banking on the Lickey Incline.

47445 was sold for further service in industry, before being preserved.

m These engines were motor fitted for working push-pull trains, and they were based on the Western Region.

s 47310-47316 were built in 1929 for the Somerset & Dorset Joint Railway. They were numbered 19-25 and they became part of LMS stock in 1930.

w Eight engines were transferred to the War Department in 1940 for overseas service. Five of these engines returned to Britain from France in 1948, complete with bullet holes in the tanks! 47659 had carried the name CORSAIR while in France. 47589 was carrying a chimney from a GWR Dean Goods 0-6-0 when it returned.

Year End Totals: '3F ⁶' class

'47	'48	'49	'50	'51	'52	'53	'54	'55	'56	'57	'58	'59	'60	'61	'62	'63	'64	'65	'66	'67
412	417	417	417	417	417	417	417	417	417	417	417	392	344	310	235	195	146	83	4	

Number	Built	Renumbered	BR Dates	Scrap	Notes
47260	07/24 VF	10/49 7260	-07/60	07/60	
47261	07/24 VF	05/51 7261	-06/62	10/62	
47262	07/24 VF	03/50 7262	-12/60	02/61	
47263	07/24 VF	04/48 7263	-11/61	11/61	
47264	07/24 VF	06/50 7264	-05/63	06/63	
47265	07/24 VF	04/48 7265	-09/60	10/60	
47266	07/24 VF	12/49 7266	-09/66	02/67	
47267	07/24 VF	10/49 7267	-11/63	01/64	
47268	07/24 VF	10/48 7268	-08/61	12/61	
47269	07/24 VF	05/50 7269	-09/62	12/62	
47270	08/24 VF	03/50 7270	-09/62	05/63	
47271	08/24 VF	01/49 7271	-12/60	03/61	
47272	08/24 VF	05/49 7272	-06/66	12/66	
47273	08/24 VF	06/49 7273	-12/66	05/67	
47274	08/24 VF	08/48 7274	-12/59	60	
47275	08/24 VF	09/49 7275	-03/62	04/62	
47276	08/24 VF	09/49 7276	-03/66	07/66	
47277	08/24 VF	11/49 7277	-05/61	08/61	
47278	08/24 VF	02/49 7278	-06/63	09/63	
47279 §	08/24 VF	09/49 7279	-12/66		
47280	08/24 NB	08/50 7280	-04/66	07/66	
47281	08/24 NB	09/49 7281	-03/63	01/64	
47282	09/24 NB	04/48 7282	-12/60	06/61	
47283	09/24 NB	11/49 7283	-04/63	04/63	
47284	09/24 NB	01/49 7284	-09/64	02/65	
47285	09/24 NB	05/50 7285	-08/65	12/65	
47286	09/24 NB	03/51 7286	-08/65	11/65	
47287	10/24 NB	08/48 7287	-10/63	04/64	
47288	10/24 NB	03/49 7288	-11/64	03/65	
47289	10/24 NB	03/50 7289	-10/67	03/68	
				☒12/66-02/67	
47290	10/24 NB	04/51 7290	-06/62	01/63	
47291	10/24 NB	01/49 7291	-12/59	11/61	
47292	10/24 NB	06/50 7292	-12/62	07/63	
47293	10/24 NB	08/48 7293	-12/66	02/68	
47294	10/24 NB	09/49 7294	-10/63	04/64	
47295	10/24 HE	02/51 7295	-04/65	07/65	
47296	10/24 HE	12/49 7296	-12/59	02/60	
47297	10/24 HE	12/48 7297	-06/64	09/64	
47298 §	10/24 HE	08/48 7298	-12/66		
47299	11/24 HE	01/49 7299	-11/59	61	
47300	12/24 HE	12/50 7300	-08/63	04/64	
47301	12/24 HE	08/48 7301	-12/59	07/61	
47302	01/25 HE	03/50 7302	-09/62	02/63	
47303	01/25 HE	03/49 7303	-09/60	09/60	
47304	01/25 HE	10/48 7304	-06/62	03/63	
47305	02/25 HE	10/48 7305	-02/65	04/68	
47306	02/25 HE	02/49 7306	-12/64	01/65	
47307	03/25 HE	04/50 7307	-09/66	12/66	
47308	03/25 HE	08/48 7308	-08/64	12/64	
47309	03/25 HE	12/48 7309	-11/59	60	
47310	12/28 WB	05/48 7310	-04/62	05/62	s
47311	01/29 WB	03/49 7311	-12/60	06/61	s
47312	01/29 WB	08/49 7312	-03/61	04/61	s
47313	01/29 WB	12/48 7313	-06/67	11/67	s
47314	01/29 WB	04/50 7314	-12/66	04/67	s
47315	02/29 WB	05/49 7315	-08/59	09/59	s
47316	02/29 WB	12/50 7316	-10/62	10/62	s
47317	06/26 NB	10/48 7317	-04/66	07/66	
47318	06/26 NB	12/49 7318	-10/66	01/67	
47319	06/26 NB	01/50 7319	-09/62	10/62	
47320	06/26 NB	03/49 7320	-05/64	12/64	

No.			
47321	06/26 NB	11/49 7321	-11/65 02/66
47322	06/26 NB	06/48 7322	-07/63 09/63
47323	06/26 NB	09/48 7323	-03/60 12/60
47324 §	06/26 NB	09/50 7324	-12/66
47325	06/26 NB	07/49 7325	-09/65 05/66
47326	07/26 NB	08/48 7326	-12/66 09/67
47327 §	07/26 NB	11/48 7327	-12/66
47328	07/26 NB	07/48 7328	-06/62 11/62
47329	07/26 NB	05/49 7329	-05/59 06/59
47330	07/26 NB	07/49 7330	-08/65 01/66
47331	07/26 NB	02/51 7331	-04/59 05/59
47332	07/26 NB	12/49 7332	-05/62 08/62
47333	07/26 NB	12/49 7333	-11/64 01/65
47334	07/26 NB	04/51 7334	-09/61 02/62
47335	07/26 NB	08/49 7335	-12/60 01/61
47336	07/26 NB	02/50 7336	-06/66 08/66
47337	08/26 NB	04/48 7337	-12/59 08/61
47338	08/26 NB	06/49 7338	-10/65 01/66
47339	08/26 NB	02/51 7339	-12/59 12/60
47340	08/26 NB	10/50 7340	-03/62 05/62
47341	08/26 NB	03/50 7341	-07/66 11/66
47342	08/26 NB	08/50 7342	-05/62 04/63
47343	08/26 NB	06/49 7343	-09/64 10/64
47344	08/26 NB	07/48 7344	-09/64 04/65
47345	09/26 NB	04/50 7345	-09/64 12/64
47346	09/26 NB	08/48 7346	-12/59 03/60
47347	07/26 NB	10/49 7347	-11/60 06/61
47348	07/26 NB	03/49 7348	-09/62 12/62
47349	07/26 NB	01/49 7349	-08/64 10/64
47350	07/26 NB	01/49 7350	-12/65 02/66
47351	07/26 NB	02/51 7351	-06/62 10/62
47352	07/26 NB	03/49 7352	-03/60 10/61
47353	07/26 NB	11/48 7353	-02/62 03/62
47354	07/26 NB	02/49 7354	-10/64 01/65
47355	07/26 NB	10/50 7355	-09/64 12/64
47356	07/26 NB	02/50 7356	-09/62 12/62
47357 §	07/26 NB	09/51 7357	-12/66
47358	07/26 NB	03/49 7358	-12/62 06/63
47359	07/26 NB	09/49 7359	-07/65 10/65
47360	07/26 NB	04/49 7360	-07/63 01/64
47361	07/26 NB	07/48 7361	-05/65 08/65
47362	08/26 NB	05/48 7362	-11/65 01/66
47363	08/26 NB	01/49 7363	-12/59 08/61
47364	07/26 NB	02/49 7364	-12/59 08/62
47365	07/26 NB	06/48 7365	-12/64 04/65
47366	07/26 NB	11/49 7366	-05/62 07/62
47367	08/26 NB	04/50 7367	-12/66 04/67
47368	08/26 NB	05/48 7368	-02/64 08/64
47369	09/26 NB	09/49 7369	-02/61 02/61
47370	09/26 NB	08/49 7370	-10/59 12/61
47371	09/26 NB	01/51 7371	-09/65 01/66
47372	09/26 NB	10/49 7372	-09/64 09/64
47373	09/26 NB	09/48 7373	-12/66 09/67
47374	09/26 NB	01/49 7374	-03/60 06/61
47375	09/26 NB	09/49 7375	-08/64 10/64
47376	09/26 NB	10/49 7376	-12/62 03/63
47377	09/26 VF	09/53 7377	-10/66 03/67
47378	10/26 VF	06/49 7378	-11/65 02/66
47379	10/26 VF	05/49 7379	-11/63 02/64
47380	10/26 VF	03/49 7380	-05/64 05/64
47381	10/26 VF	03/52 7381	-09/62 04/63
47382	10/26 VF	07/49 7382	-12/59 04/60
47383 §	10/26 VF	09/49 7383	-10/67
			☒12/66-02/67
47384	10/26 VF	11/48 7384	-10/66 02/67
47385	10/26 VF	03/50 7385	-04/64 10/64
47386	10/26 VF	12/49 7386	-05/63 07/63
47387	11/26 VF	11/48 7387	-12/59 10/61
47388	11/26 VF	01/49 7388	-12/66 04/67
47389	11/26 VF	06/50 7389	-07/66 10/66
47390	11/26 VF	07/49 7390	-09/64 01/65
47391	11/26 VF	03/51 7391	-10/66 05/67
47392	11/26 VF	11/49 7392	-08/62 10/63
47393	11/26 VF	05/49 7393	-02/66 05/66
47394	11/26 VF	04/50 7394	-12/59 10/60
47395	11/26 VF	09/49 7395	-04/65 09/65
47396	11/26 VF	05/50 7396	-10/66 06/67
47397	11/26 VF	03/49 7397	-09/66 02/67
47398	11/26 VF	02/50 7398	-05/61 05/61
47399	11/26 VF	05/49 7399	-08/65 01/66
47400	11/26 VF	04/50 7400	-08/65 01/66
47401	11/26 VF	11/48 7401	-11/60 04/61
47402	12/26 VF	02/50 7402	-12/62 04/63
47403	12/26 VF	09/50 7403	-09/61 01/62
47404	12/26 VF	11/49 7404	-02/62 03/62
47405	12/26 VF	08/50 7405	-09/61 01/62
47406 §	12/26 VF	05/50 7406	-12/66
47407	12/26 VF	03/53 7407	-12/59 03/60
47408	12/26 VF	10/49 7408	-11/65 02/66
47409	12/26 VF	01/50 7409	-12/59 12/60
47410	12/26 VF	10/49 7410	-09/66 04/67
47411	12/26 VF	04/49 7411	-12/59 03/60
47412	12/26 VF	07/51 7412	-10/63 04/64
47413	12/26 VF	10/48 7413	-05/63 06/63
47414	12/26 VF	06/49 7414	-05/62 08/62
47415	12/26 VF	04/49 7415	-04/66 05/66
47416	12/26 VF	01/49 7416	-07/66 10/66
47417	12/26 VF	09/50 7417	-10/62 06/63
47418	12/26 VF	05/48 7418	-06/61 07/61
47419	12/26 VF	11/52 7419	-12/63 03/64
47420	12/26 VF	06/51 7420	-09/61 01/62
47421	12/26 VF	01/50 7421	-09/61 10/61
47422	12/26 VF	02/49 7422	-08/62 08/62
47423	12/26 VF	12/53 7423	-07/65 11/65
47424	12/26 VF	04/48 7424	-06/62 08/62
47425	12/26 VF	02/49 7425	-05/62 08/62
47426	12/26 VF	08/48 7426	-09/62 09/62
47427	10/26 HE	06/49 7427	-09/66 02/67
47428	10/26 HE	11/49 7428	-10/65 01/66
47429	10/26 HE	12/49 7429	-12/65 02/66
47430	10/26 HE	10/49 7430	-01/64 11/64
47431	10/26 HE	06/50 7431	-10/62 12/62
47432	10/26 HE	06/50 7432	-08/65 02/66
47433	10/26 HE	06/49 7433	-09/62 11/62
47434	11/26 HE	01/49 7434	-05/64 06/64
47435	11/26 HE	01/49 7435	-10/66 06/67
47436	04/27 HE	03/50 7436	-12/60 12/60
47437	04/27 HE	10/50 7437	-08/66 04/67
47438	04/27 HE	01/50 7438	-09/61 10/61
47439	05/27 HE	05/49 7439	-09/65 03/66
47440	05/27 HE	05/49 7440	-12/59 09/61
47441	05/27 HE	11/50 7441	-12/63 04/64
47442	05/27 HE	05/49 7442	-03/65 07/65
47443	05/27 HE	10/48 7443	-12/60 01/61
47444	05/27 HE	02/49 7444	-11/66 04/67
47445 §	05/27 HE	12/49 7445	-04/66
47446	06/27 HE	12/48 7446	-12/60 01/61
47447	06/27 HE	10/49 7447	-12/66 05/67
47448	06/27 HE	04/50 7448	-09/61 11/61
47449	07/27 HE	07/48 7449	-04/63 05/63
47450	07/27 HE	11/50 7450	-04/66 09/66
47451	07/27 HE	09/50 7451	-09/65 12/65
47452	10/26 WB	09/49 7452	-03/65 07/65
47453	10/26 WB	08/48 7453	-04/66 08/66
47454	10/26 WB	03/50 7454	-07/65 12/65
47455	10/26 WB	03/49 7455	-06/62 06/62
47457	11/26 WB	03/49 7457	-09/62 10/62
47458	11/26 WB	10/48 7458	-08/63 09/63
47459	12/26 WB	08/49 7459	-01/63 04/63
47460	12/26 WB	04/49 7460	-05/63 05/63
47461	04/27 WB	10/49 7461	-09/64 12/64
47462	04/27 WB	02/50 7462	-09/61 10/61
47463	04/27 WB	09/49 7463	-12/60 12/60
47464	05/27 WB	08/49 7464	-09/65 12/65
47465	05/27 WB	09/49 7465	-06/63 06/63
47466	06/27 WB	04/50 7466	-09/62 10/63
47467	01/28 VF	02/49 7467	-09/64 12/64
47468	01/28 VF	04/50 7468	-01/65 05/65
47469	01/28 VF	11/50 7469	-01/64 01/64
47470	01/28 VF	08/48 7470	-06/62 12/62
47471	01/28 VF	06/49 7471	-12/66 09/67
47472	12/27 VF	06/49 7472	-11/66 04/67
47473	12/27 VF	10/48 7473	-02/62 02/62
47474	12/27 VF	01/50 7474	-09/62 07/63
47475	12/27 VF	09/49 7475	-02/62 03/62
47476	12/27 VF	08/49 7476	-05/64 03/65
47477	12/27 VF	08/49 7477	-12/59 07/61 m
47478	01/28 VF	10/48 7478	-04/64 07/64 m
47479	01/28 VF	01/49 7479	-08/62 04/63 m
47480	01/28 VF	12/49 7480	-09/65 01/66 m
47481	01/28 VF	10/50 7481	-04/63 07/63 m
47482	01/28 VF	11/49 7482	-10/66 02/67
47483	01/28 VF	08/50 7483	-03/62 03/62
47484	01/28 VF	03/49 7484	-02/61 04/61
47485	01/28 VF	04/49 7485	-01/65 05/65
47486	01/28 VF	04/48 7486	-03/60 06/60
47487	01/28 VF	03/49 7487	-08/65 12/65
47488	01/28 VF	02/50 7488	-11/62 09/63
47489	01/28 VF	01/49 7489	-12/59 01/60
47490	02/28 VF	01/50 7490	-07/63 07/63
47491	02/28 VF	01/52 7491	-12/62 02/63
47492	02/28 VF	02/50 7492	-08/64 01/65
47493 §	02/28 VF	11/48 7493	-12/66
47494	02/28 VF	09/48 7494	-10/66 02/67
47495	02/28 VF	12/48 7495	-09/65 01/66
47496	02/28 VF	09/52 7496	-11/63 12/63
47497	04/28 VF	02/49 7497	-09/62 05/63
47498	04/28 VF	04/49 7498	-03/60 07/60
47499	04/28 VF	08/49 7499	-08/65 10/65
47500	04/28 VF	09/48 7500	-07/65 10/65
47501	04/28 VF	06/49 7501	-09/64 02/65
47502	04/28 VF	01/51 7502	-08/63 12/63
47503	04/28 VF	01/51 7503	-03/64 06/64
47504	04/28 VF	10/48 7504	-04/62 07/62
47505	04/28 VF	07/51 7505	-08/65 01/66
47506	04/28 VF	05/48 7506	-03/66 06/66
47507	04/28 VF	08/50 7507	-09/66 12/66
47508	04/28 VF	03/51 7508	-09/61 02/62
47509	04/28 VF	10/50 7509	-12/60 01/61
47510	05/28 VF	09/49 7510	-11/60 01/61
47511	05/28 VF	03/50 7511	-04/64 05/64
47512	05/28 VF	08/49 7512	-05/65 09/65
47513	05/28 VF	06/48 7513	-05/61 06/61
47514	05/28 VF	01/49 7514	-05/62 12/62
47515	05/28 VF	10/48 7515	-07/64 01/65
47516	05/28 VF	06/48 7516	-02/62 03/62
47517	02/28 BM	11/48 7517	-06/64 10/64
47518	02/28 BM	10/49 7518	-10/63 08/64
47519	02/28 BM	10/49 7519	-09/65 12/65
47520	02/28 BM	08/48 7520	-11/65 02/66
47521	02/28 BM	08/48 7521	-10/66 02/67
47522	02/28 BM	02/49 7522	-08/62 02/63
47523	02/28 BM	06/50 7523	-11/60 11/60
47524	03/28 BM	03/50 7524	-09/64 03/65
47525	03/28 BM	03/50 7525	-03/60 07/60
47526	03/28 BM	06/49 7526	-11/62 12/62
47527	03/28 BM	09/48 7527	-03/60 06/61
47528	03/28 BM	06/48 7528	-03/60 11/61
47529	03/28 BM	08/48 7529	-10/61 12/61
47530	03/28 BM	02/49 7530	-10/66 02/67
47531	03/28 BM	11/51 7531	-02/67 03/67
47532	04/28 BM	03/50 7532	-04/63 07/63
47533	04/28 BM	04/48 7533	-11/66 04/67
47534	04/28 BM	04/49 7534	-03/67 09/67
47535	04/28 BM	03/49 7535	-01/66 05/66
47536	04/28 BM	06/48 7536	-06/62 11/62
47537	04/28 BM	03/49 7537	-09/60 09/60
47538	04/28 BM	11/49 7538	-06/59 07/59
47539	04/28 BM	01/50 7539	-02/63 01/66
47540	04/28 BM	08/48 7540	-04/61 05/61
47541	04/28 BM	08/50 7541	-06/60 07/60
47542	11/27 HE	09/50 7542	-06/62 06/62
47543	12/27 HE	12/48 7543	-11/65 01/66
47544	12/27 HE	06/49 7544	-12/65 03/66
47545	12/27 HE	05/48 7545	-08/62 08/62
47546	12/27 HE	02/49 7546	-07/62 11/62
47547	12/27 HE	09/48 7547	-12/63 02/64
47548	12/27 HE	09/49 7548	-08/62 08/62
47549	12/27 HE	11/50 7549	-08/64 04/65
47550	01/28 HE	10/51 7550	-03/64 07/65
47551	01/28 HE	07/48 7551	-02/63 04/63
47552	01/28 HE	10/49 7552	-10/62 07/64
47554	02/28 HE	12/49 7554	-09/62 10/62
47555	02/28 HE	03/51 7555	-06/62 08/62
47556	02/28 HE	12/49 7556	-12/62 01/64
47557	03/28 HE	02/50 7557	-02/64 04/64
47558	03/28 HE	10/49 7558	-03/64 04/64
47559	03/28 HE	07/48 7559	-05/61 05/61
47560	03/28 HE	01/49 7560	-07/60 08/60
47561	04/28 HE	07/49 7561	-08/60 09/60
47562	04/28 HE	11/49 7562	-11/62 02/63
47563	04/28 HE	06/50 7563	-03/60 03/60
47564 §	04/28 HE	07/48 7564	-03/65
47565	05/28 HE	11/48 7565	-04/66 09/66
47566	05/28 HE	12/49 7566	-10/66 03/67
47567	09/28 HE	09/48 7567	-11/60 12/60
47568	10/28 HE	09/49 7568	-12/60 01/61
47569	10/28 HE	08/49 7569	-12/60 12/60
47570	10/28 HE	08/49 7570	-09/61 01/62
47571	10/28 HE	06/49 7571	-05/61 06/61
47572	10/28 HE	05/48 7572	-05/62 06/63
47573	10/28 HE	09/49 7573	-12/60 02/61
47574	10/28 HE	10/48 7574	-12/62 02/63
47575	10/28 HE	05/49 7575	-03/60 06/61
47576	10/28 HE	12/48 7576	-09/60 10/60
47577	10/28 HE	08/48 7577	-03/65 08/65
47578	10/28 HE	07/49 7578	-03/65 05/65
47579	11/28 HE	07/49 7579	-07/64 08/64
47580	11/28 HE	12/49 7580	-09/61 02/62
47581	11/28 HE	09/50 7581	-02/63 09/63
47582	11/28 HE	09/49 7582	-08/63 04/64
47583	11/28 HE	12/50 7583	-03/63 05/63
47584	12/28 HE	09/48 7584	-08/64 05/65
47585	12/28 HE	01/49 7585	-03/60 04/62
47586	12/28 HE	04/50 7586	-03/60 11/61
47587	01/29 HE	06/48 7587	-11/64 03/65
47588	01/29 HE	04/48 7588	-10/62 11/62
47589	01/29 HE	10/48 030T027	10/48-12/63 03/64 w
47590	02/29 HE	08/48 7590	-11/66 05/67
47591	02/29 HE	08/48 7591	-03/60 06/62
47592	08/28 WB	09/48 7592	-03/66 11/66
47593	08/28 WB	05/50 7593	-09/62 01/63
47594	09/28 WB	09/50 7594	-07/64 10/64
47595	09/28 WB	12/49 7595	-03/60 09/60
47596	09/28 WB	06/49 7596	-07/65 10/65
47597	10/28 WB	04/52 7597	-11/65 01/66
47598	11/28 WB	09/49 7598	-07/66 10/67
47599	11/28 WB	06/48 7599	-12/66 09/67
47600	11/28 WB	08/48 7600	-03/60 08/61
47601	11/28 WB	03/50 7601	-03/62 04/62
47602	09/28 BM	10/48 7602	-01/66 04/66
47603	09/28 BM	08/51 7603	-11/66 04/67
47604	09/28 BM	12/49 7604	-08/62 01/63
47605	10/28 BM	08/48 7605	-05/61 07/61
47606	10/28 BM	07/48 7606	-06/65 11/65
47607	10/28 BM	11/48 030T043	11/48-01/61 04/61 w
47608	10/28 BM	12/49 7608	-11/62 12/62
47609	10/28 BM	02/49 7609	-01/64 03/64
47610	10/28 BM	06/48 7610	-08/62 02/63
47611	10/28 BM	10/48 030T042	10/48-05/66 08/66 w
47612	10/28 BM	03/49 7612	-12/66 12/67
47614	11/28 BM	10/49 7614	-07/65 10/65
47615	11/28 BM	10/48 7615	-10/66 02/67
47616	11/28 BM	12/49 7616	-01/65 04/65

47618	11/28 BM	11/49 7618	-10/63	10/63	
47619	11/28 BM	05/49 7619	-03/61	05/61	
47620	11/28 BM	07/49 7620	-09/61	09/61	
47621	11/28 BM	01/49 7621	-05/62	06/63	
47622	11/28 BM	06/48 7622	-07/64	10/64	
47623	11/28 BM	01/50 7623	-04/64	04/64	
47624	11/28 BM	06/51 7624	-09/61	09/61	
47625	11/28 BM	09/52 7625	-05/61	06/61	
47626	11/28 BM	08/48 7626	-05/61	06/61	
47627	11/28 BM	02/50 7627	-04/66	06/66	
47628	12/28 BM	11/49 7628	-08/64	01/65	
47629	12/28 BM	08/49 7629	-10/67	02/68	
47630	12/28 BM	02/50 7630	-08/62	09/62	
47631	12/28 BM	01/50 7631	-06/66	02/67	
47632	12/28 BM	09/49 7632	-09/61	02/62	
47633	12/28 BM	06/49 7633	-09/62	05/63	
47634	12/28 BM	12/49 7634	-09/61	10/61	
47635	12/28 BM	09/50 7635	-12/60	01/61	
47636	12/28 BM	08/50 7636	-03/60	03/60	
47637	12/28 BM	04/49 7637	-05/61	05/61	
47638	12/28 BM	04/48 7638	-07/63	02/64	
47639	12/28 BM	11/48 7639	-03/60	11/61	
47640	12/28 BM	05/48 7640	-09/64	01/65	
47641	01/29 BM	06/49 7641	-12/66	02/68	
47642	01/29 BM	12/49 7642	-05/62	11/62	
47643	01/29 BM	08/48 7643	-10/66	06/67	
47644	01/29 BM	01/50 7644	-11/62	12/62	
47645	02/29 BM	02/51 7645	-04/65	08/65	
47646	02/29 BM	04/50 7646	-08/65	12/65	
47647	02/29 BM	07/50 7647	-05/65	09/65	
47648	02/29 BM	08/49 7648	-04/64	06/64	
47649	02/29 BM	06/49 7649	-10/66	02/67	
47650	02/29 BM	04/48 7650	-03/60	07/61	
47651	02/29 BM	05/50 7651	-12/63	01/64	
47652	03/29 BM	11/48 7652	-07/60	08/60	
47653	03/29 BM	11/50 7653	-10/64	02/65	
47654	03/29 BM	03/50 7654	-02/63	09/63	
47655	03/29 BM	06/49 7655	-11/65	03/66	
47656	03/29 BM	09/49 7656	-12/65	04/66	
47657	03/29 BM	03/49 7657	-10/63	04/64	
47658	03/29 BM	10/49 7658	-10/66	02/67	
47659	03/29 BM	11/48 030T026	11/48-11/66	04/67	w
47660	03/29 BM	10/48 030T044	10/48-12/65	04/66	w
47661	03/29 BM	09/49 7661	-10/66	02/67	
47662	03/29 BM	04/48 7662	-01/66	04/66	
47664	04/29 BM	04/49 7664	-01/65	04/65	
47665	04/29 BM	09/48 7665	-07/65	10/65	
47666	04/29 BM	04/49 7666	-09/65	01/66	
47667	04/31 Hor	07/48 7667	-11/66	03/67	
47668	05/31 Hor	10/49 7668	-10/66	04/67	
47669	05/31 Hor	09/50 7669	-02/65	05/65	
47670	05/31 Hor	11/49 7670	-10/60	12/60	
47671	06/31 Hor	12/49 7671	-11/66	04/67	
47672	06/31 Hor	06/50 7672	-03/60	03/61	
47673	07/31 Hor	10/48 7673	-11/66	06/67	
47674	07/31 Hor	10/50 7674	-12/66	05/67	
47675	08/31 Hor	02/49 7675	-04/66	03/67	
47676	08/31 Hor	02/51 7676	-08/65	11/65	
47677	08/31 Hor	08/48 7677	-11/65	05/66	
47678	09/31 Hor	06/51 7678	-01/62	02/62	
47679	09/31 Hor	02/49 7679	-08/63	10/63	
47680	10/31 Hor	02/50 7680	-07/65	10/65	
47681	10/31 Hor	12/50 7681	-08/65	12/65	

1F [2] 47862-47865
0-4-2PT LNWR Webb 'Bissel Truck'

Power Classification: 1F
Introduced: 1896-1901 (survivors built 1901)
Designer: Webb
Company: LNWR
Weight: 34t 17cwt
Driving Wheel: 4' 5½"
Boiler Pressure: 150psi
Cylinders: Inside 17" x 24"
Tractive Effort: 16530lbf
Valve Gear: Stephenson (slide valves)

These engines were the last two survivors of Webb's twenty 'square saddle, Bissel truck' tank engines, also known as 'box tanks'.

They were designed for use in such places as works sidings and docks, where an 0-6-0T would be too large, but an 0-4-0T would be lacking in power.

The first engine of the class was withdrawn in 1929, and these last two engines survived as works shunters in Crewe Works.

Year End Totals: '1F [2]' class

'47	'48	'49	'50	'51	'52	'53	'54	'55	'56	'57	'58	'59	'60	'61	'62	'63	'64	'65	'66	'67
2	2	2	2	2	2	1	1	1												

Number	*Built*	*Renumbered*	*BR Dates*	*Scrap*	*Notes*
47862	10/01 Crw	03/49 7862	-10/56	*56*	
47865	11/01 Crw	09/48 7865	-11/53	11/53	

6F [1] 47875-47896
0-8-2T LNWR Bowen Cooke

Power Classification: 6F
Introduced: 1911-1917
Designer: Bowen Cooke
Company: LNWR
Weight: 72t 10cwt
Driving Wheel: 4' 5½"
Boiler Pressure: 170psi
Cylinders: Inside 20½" x 24"
Tractive Effort: 27240lbf
Valve Gear: Joy (slide valves)

Bowen Cooke designed this class as a tank version of the '48892' 'G1' class. Thirty engines were built between 1911 and 1917 and they were designed for shunting in large yards, although on occasions they were pressed into main line use.

The first of the class was withdrawn in 1934 and they retained their round-topped fireboxes throughout their lives.

Year End Totals: '6F [1]' class

'47	'48	'49	'50	'51	'52	'53	'54	'55	'56	'57	'58	'59	'60	'61	'62	'63	'64	'65	'66	'67
9	5	5	3	1	1															

Number	*Built*	*Renumbered*	*BR Dates*	*Scrap*	*Notes*
47875	01/12 Crw	7875	-08/48	*48*	
47877	01/12 Crw	05/48 7877	-02/53	03/53	
47881	08/15 Crw	09/48 7881	-07/51	*51*	
47884	09/15 Crw	10/48 7884	-06/51	*51*	
47885	09/15 Crw	7885	-03/50	*04/50*	
47887	09/15 Crw	7887	-08/48	*48*	
47888	09/15 Crw	7888	-12/48	*49*	
47892	01/17 Crw	7892	-02/48	06/48	
47896	01/17 Crw	06/48 7896	-11/50	*11/50*	

7F [1] 47930-47959
0-8-4T LNWR Beames

Power Classification: 7F
Introduced: 1923-1924
Designer: Beames
Company: LNWR/LMS
Weight: 88t 0cwt
Driving Wheel: 4' 5½"
Boiler Pressure: 185psi superheated
Cylinders: Inside 20½" x 24"
Tractive Effort: 29645lbf
Valve Gear: Joy (piston valves)

Beames built thirty engines of this class which did not appear until after grouping in 1923. They were similar in design to Bowen Cooke's '47875' class with the exception of an additional pair of trailing wheels to allow for larger bunkers. They were essentially tank versions of the '7F' '49395' 'G2' class.

They were built specifically to work on the Abergavenny-Merthyr line in South Wales with its steep gradients. The first of the class was withdrawn in 1944.

Year End Totals: '7F [1]' class

'47	'48	'49	'50	'51	'52	'53	'54	'55	'56	'57	'58	'59	'60	'61	'62	'63	'64	'65	'66	'67
14	7	4	1																	

Number	*Built*	*Renumbered*	*BR Dates*	*Scrap*	*Notes*
47930	02/23 Crw	7930	-08/48	*48*	
47931	02/23 Crw	11/48 7931	-12/51	01/52	
47932	02/23 Crw	7932	-09/49	*49*	
47933	02/23 Crw	7933	-06/50	07/50	
47936	04/23 Crw	7936	-06/49	06/49	
47937	04/23 Crw	02/49 7937	-10/50	*50*	
47938	04/23 Crw	7938	-02/48	*06/48*	
47939	04/23 Crw	7939	-12/50	*12/50*	
47948	09/23 Crw	7948	-07/48	08/48	
47951	10/23 Crw	7951	-01/49	*49*	
47954	10/23 Crw	7954	-10/48	10/48	
47956	11/23 Crw	7956	-11/48	*48*	
47958	11/23 Crw	7958	-12/48	*49*	
47959	01/24 Crw	7959	-06/48	08/48	

Garratt 47967-47999
2-6-6-2T LMS Fowler & Beyer Peacock

Power Classification: Not classified
Introduced: 1927-1930
Designer: Fowler and Beyer Peacock
Company: LMS
Weight: 155t 10cwt
c 148t 15cwt
Driving Wheel: 5' 3"
Boiler Pressure: 190psi superheated
Cylinders: Four Outside 18½" x 26"
Tractive Effort: 45620lbf
Valve Gear: Walschaert (piston valves)

The 'Garratt' type of engine was of an unmistakable design. They were in effect two engines in one, employing a single large boiler, and they were a patent of the Beyer Peacock Company in Manchester. The type achieved great success abroad, particularly in South Africa, but only two classes were built for working in Britain, the solitary LNER 'U1' class engine, and these 'Garratt' engines on the LMS.

Three 'Garratt' engines were purchased by the LMS in 1927 to overcome the need for double heading on the Toton to Brent coal trains. They were numbered 4997-4999 and they were fitted with fixed coal bunkers. The boiler and cab were mounted centrally between the large rectangular tank at the front and the coal bunker at the back.

4967-4996 appeared in 1930 and they had increased coal capacity. In 1931 these engines and 4997 were fitted with revolving coal bunkers. These were conical in shape and they could be revolved or oscillated by a small two-cylinder steam engine. Not only were they self-trimming, but they also prevented coal dust blowing into the cab.

The engines were later renumbered 7967-7999 in the same order. They were employed on heavy coal trains right up to the 1950s but they were always heavy on coal and maintenance.

c 47998 and 47999 always retained their fixed coal bunkers.

Year End Totals: 'Garratt' class

'47	'48	'49	'50	'51	'52	'53	'54	'55	'56	'57	'58	'59	'60	'61	'62	'63	'64	'65	'66	'67
33	33	33	33	33	33	33	33	26	13	1										

Number	*Built*	*Renumbered*	*BR Dates*	*Scrap*	*Notes*
47967	08/30 BP	12/48 7967	-11/57	12/57	
47968	08/30 BP	11/48 7968	-09/57	10/57	
47969	08/30 BP	08/48 7969	-08/57	08/57	
47970	08/30 BP	05/49 7970	-07/55	*07/55*	
47971	08/30 BP	10/48 7971	-11/56	*56*	
47972	09/30 BP	06/48 7972	-04/57	04/57	
47973	09/30 BP	02/49 7973	-04/57	04/57	
47974	09/30 BP	09/48 7974	-06/56	07/56	
47975	09/30 BP	06/48 7975	-07/55	08/55	
47976	09/30 BP	11/48 7976	-04/56	05/56	
47977	09/30 BP	09/48 7977	-06/56	07/56	
47978	09/30 BP	11/48 7978	-03/57	04/57	
47979	09/30 BP	06/48 7979	-02/57	03/57	
47980	10/30 BP	10/48 7980	-02/57	03/57	
47981	10/30 BP	02/49 7981	-10/56	*01/57*	
47982	10/30 BP	09/48 7982	-12/57	12/57	
47983	10/30 BP	10/48 7983	-01/56	03/56	
47984	10/30 BP	06/48 7984	-02/56	*02/56*	
47985	10/30 BP	05/48 7985	-06/55	06/55	
47986	11/30 BP	09/48 7986	-07/57	08/57	
47987	10/30 BP	01/49 7987	-05/57	06/57	
47988	10/30 BP	12/48 7988	-08/56	*56*	
47989	10/30 BP	06/49 7989	-11/55	05/56	
47990	11/30 BP	04/48 7990	-06/55	*55*	
47991	11/30 BP	08/48 7991	-12/55	*01/56*	
47992	11/30 BP	06/48 7992	-03/56	05/56	
47993	11/30 BP	04/48 7993	-12/55	*01/56*	
47994	11/30 BP	04/49 7994	-04/58	04/58	
47995	11/30 BP	04/49 7995	-07/57	07/57	
47996	12/30 BP	06/49 7996	-06/56	07/56	
47997	04/27 BP	05/48 7997	-02/56	04/56	
47998	04/27 BP	03/49 7998	-08/56	*10/56*	c
47999	04/27 BP	01/49 7999	-01/56	03/56	c

8F 48000-48775
2-8-0 LMS & War Department Stanier

Power Classification: 8F
Introduced: 1935-1945
Designer: Stanier

Company:	LMS and WD
Weight:	Loco 72t 2cwt
	Tender 54t 13cwt
Driving Wheel:	4' 8½"
Boiler Pressure:	225psi superheated
Cylinders:	Outside 18½" x 28"
Tractive Effort:	32440lbf
Valve Gear:	Walschaert (piston valves)

Following Stanier's new designs of express and mixed traffic engines for the LMS he turned his attention to the need for a heavy standard freight engine. The '8F' class was introduced in 1935 and the design was a success straight off the drawing board, proving itself far superior to the 0-8-0s which had been inherited from the LYR and LNWR.

Production continued steadily from 1935-1942, by which time 8000-8225 had been built. 8000-8011 originally had domeless boilers.

In 1939 the type was adopted for war-time use, just as Robinson's GCR 2-8-0s had been 25 years earlier (see GWR 'ROD' and LNER 'O4' classes). 240 engines were ordered from North British, Beyer Peacock and the Vulcan Foundry. They were allocated War Department numbers 300-539 (later 70300-70539). Some of these ran for a while carrying LMS numbers 8226 upwards before transfer to WD stock. All the WD engines went overseas to the Middle East, together with some of the earlier LMS engines numbered between 8012 and 8094, many of them never to return.

In addition to the engines already mentioned, many more engines were built for home use during the war. It gave rise to a unique situation in 1944 when engines of purely LMS design were being built in the workshops of each of the four (still independent) Railway Companies, as well as by outside firms.

A total of 849 engines were built as follows: North British Locomotive Company (208), Crewe (136), Brighton (93), Swindon (80), Horwich (75), Vulcan Foundry (67), Darlington (53), Doncaster (50), Beyer Peacock (50), Eastleigh (23) and Ashford (14). A total of 666 engines eventually came into BR stock. Another eighty engines were ordered from North British, but the order was changed to eighty 'Austerity' class engines (see BR WD '90000' class). The Austerity class was developed from this class by Riddles.

The history of 48773 is often quoted to show the complexity of this class. Built by North British in 1940 (with works number 24607) it became LMS 8233. In 1941 it was transferred to the War Department as WD 307 and it was sent overseas, where it became Iran State Railways No. 41-109. In 1952 it was returned to this country as WD 70307, and after overhaul at Derby it was transferred to the Longmoor Military Railway as WD 500, later working at Bicester. In 1957 it was reabsorbed into BR stock, at first being allocated the number 90733 (following the WD 'Austerities', with which it was confused), but quickly being altered to 48773 at the end of the LMS '8F's. This engine has now been preserved.

This class was one of the last to remain in considerable numbers during the last days of BR steam, some being in active service right through to the end.

e LNER built engines, built in 1943-1945. They were transferred to the LMS in 1946.

g GWR built engines, built in 1943-1945. They were transferred to the LMS in 1946.

m Engines which were built for the LMS.

s SR built engine, built in 1942-1944.

w War Department engines, built by Vulcan Foundry, North British and Beyer Peacock from 1940 onwards. Those engines marked as entering stock in 1949 were returned from overseas service in 1948, and after a period in storage at Crewe Carriage shed, they were overhauled and returned to service. Three engines (48773-48775) were based on the Longmoor Military Railway as WD 500, 501 and 512 before being sold to BR in 1957. At first they were allocated the numbers 90733-90735 following on from the 'Austerity' 2-8-0s. 48774 was at first numbered 90743 in error which was immediately corrected to 90734. Then it was realised that the engines did not belong to the 'Austerity' class and the number was again altered to 48773 before it entered service.

l 48705-48772 were the LNER owned 'O6' class before nationalisation. 48705-48729 were built for the LNER at Brighton by the SR in 1944 and they were temporarily numbered 7651-7675. They were later renumbered 3100-3124, and the remainder were built as 3125-3167 by the LNER. In 1947 the entire sequence was renumbered 3500-3567, and then they returned to the LMS on loan in 1947 receiving the LMS numbers 8705-8772. No. 3554 was not returned to the LMS until early 1948, becoming 8759 and therefore it is also included in the LNER section of this book. Finally the engines were renumbered in 1948 onwards with 40000 added to their numbers. It can be seen that 48705-48729 carried five different numbers in the period 1944-1948 (for example 7651, 3100, 3500, 8705 and 48705).

o Several engines were converted to oil burning as a result of the coal crisis after the end of the Second World War. They were reconverted to coal burning (c) in 1948-1949.

Year End Totals: '8F' class

'47	'48	'49	'50	'51	'52	'53	'54	'55	'56	'57	'58	'59	'60	'61	'62	'63	'64	'65	'66	'67
556	624	663	663	663	663	663	663	663	663	666	666	666	665	665	661	663	638	543	381	150

Number	Built	Renumbered	BR Dates	Scrap	Notes
48000	06/35 Crw	07/48 8000	-03/67	09/67	m
48001	06/35 Crw	01/49 8001	-01/65	10/65	m
48002	07/35 Crw	12/48 8002	-09/66	02/67	m
48003	06/35 Crw	05/48 8003	-03/66	06/66	m
48004	06/35 Crw	04/48 8004	-11/65	01/66	m
48005	06/35 Crw	12/48 8005	-03/66	06/66	m
48006	09/35 Crw	05/49 8006	-01/65	05/65	m
48007	09/35 Crw	03/49 8007	-01/65	05/65	m
48008	10/35 Crw	07/48 8008	-05/64	07/64	m
48009	10/35 Crw	05/48 8009	-12/62	05/63	m
48010	10/35 Crw	09/49 8010	-01/68	05/68	m
48011	10/35 Crw	05/49 8011	-06/67	11/67	m
48012	12/36 Crw	12/49 70577	12/49-04/68	07/68	m
48016	01/37 Crw	10/49 70591	10/49-11/65	02/66	m
48017	01/37 Crw	05/48 8017	-10/67	07/68	m
48018	02/37 Crw	12/49 70582	12/49-10/67	02/68	m
48020	02/37 Crw	12/49 70579	12/49-08/65	02/66	m
48024	03/37 Crw	02/49 8024	-11/67	03/68	m
48026	04/37 Crw	04/49 8026	-06/68	09/68	m
48027	07/36 VF	06/49 8027	-03/65	10/65	m
48029	08/36 VF	07/48 8029	-02/67	08/67	m
48033	08/36 VF	05/48 8033	-06/68	12/68	m
48035	08/36 VF	06/48 8035	-03/67	09/67	m
48036	08/36 VF	02/50 8036	-03/68	07/68	m
48037	09/36 VF	04/48 8037	-12/65	04/66	m
48039	09/36 VF	10/49 70588	10/49-07/65	12/65	m
48045	09/36 VF	07/49 70573	07/49-05/68	08/68	m
48046	09/36 VF	08/49 70599	08/49-01/68	04/68	m
48050	10/36 VF	05/48 8050	-03/66	07/66	m
48053	10/36 VF	05/48 8053	-03/67	03/68	m
48054	10/36 VF	06/49 8054	-09/67	03/68	m
48055	10/36 VF	11/48 8055	-11/67	04/68	m
48056	10/36 VF	10/49 8056	-05/68	08/68	m
48057	10/36 VF	08/49 8057	-05/67	11/67	m
48060	10/36 VF	04/49 8060	-04/68	08/68	m
48061	11/36 VF	09/49 70614	09/49-09/67	10/68	m
48062	11/36 VF	01/49 8062	-08/68	12/68	m
48063	11/36 VF	12/48 8063	-03/68	07/68	m
48064	11/36 VF	10/48 8064	-05/66	08/66	mo 10/48⇨c
48065	11/36 VF	12/49 8065	-02/66	05/66	m
48067	11/36 VF	11/49 8067	-10/67	02/68	m
48069	11/36 VF	11/48 8069	-11/64	11/64	m
48070	11/36 VF	12/49 8070	-11/67	04/68	m
48073	12/36 VF	09/48 8073	-04/67	09/67	m
48074	12/36 VF	02/50 8074	-11/67	04/68	m
48075	12/36 VF	03/49 8075	-05/67	09/67	m
48076	12/36 VF	08/48 8076	-11/67	04/68	m
48077	12/36 VF	12/49 70611	12/49-03/68	06/68	m
48078	12/36 VF	08/48 8078	-08/65	12/65	m
48079	12/36 VF	08/48 8079	-12/66	06/67	mo 08/48⇨c
48080	12/36 VF	02/49 8080	-11/66	01/67	m
48081	01/37 VF	05/49 8081	-03/68	06/68	m
48082	01/37 VF	06/48 8082	-04/67	11/67	m
48083	01/37 VF	07/48 8083	-11/66	05/67	m
48084	01/37 VF	06/49 8084	-11/67	04/68	m
48085	01/37 VF	04/48 8085	-08/67	11/67	m
48088	01/37 VF	08/49 8088	-12/66	04/67	m
48089	01/37 VF	08/49 8089	-02/66	06/66	m
48090	01/37 VF	04/50 8090	-04/68	07/68	m
48092	02/37 VF	12/48 8092	-05/66	12/66	m
48093	02/37 VF	02/49 8093	-11/67	04/68	m
48094	02/37 VF	12/49 70606	12/49-09/65	12/65	m
48095	02/37 VF	06/49 8095	-02/65	07/65	m
48096	12/38 Crw	02/49 8096	-11/65	01/66	m
48097	12/38 Crw	02/49 8097	-07/65	11/65	m
48098	01/39 Crw	01/49 8098	-03/67	09/67	m
48099	01/39 Crw	04/48 8099	-07/65	12/65	m
48100	01/39 Crw	11/48 8100	-09/67	07/68	m
48101	01/39 Crw	06/48 8101	-09/66	10/66	m
48102	01/39 Crw	01/50 8102	-08/65	02/66	m
48103	02/39 Crw	06/49 8103	-10/66	02/67	m
48104	02/39 Crw	01/50 8104	-07/67	11/67	m
48105	02/39 Crw	01/50 8105	-03/67	07/67	m
48106	02/39 Crw	03/50 8106	-06/67	11/67	m
48107	02/39 Crw	11/49 8107	-04/68	07/68	m
48108	02/39 Crw	09/48 8108	-08/67	02/68	m
48109	02/39 Crw	06/49 8109	-01/66	06/66	m
48110	02/39 Crw	08/48 8110	-06/67	10/67	m
48111	03/39 Crw	06/48 8111	-03/68	07/68	m
48112	03/39 Crw	04/49 8112	-11/65	06/66	m
48113	03/39 Crw	09/49 8113	-10/67	02/68	m
48114	03/39 Crw	04/48 8114	-04/67	09/67	m
48115	04/39 Crw	12/48 8115	-07/68	10/68	m
48116	04/39 Crw	09/48 8116	-06/65	12/65	m
48117	04/39 Crw	07/48 8117	-03/68	08/68	m
48118	04/39 Crw	07/49 8118	-06/66	09/66	m
48119	05/39 Crw	10/48 8119	-11/67	04/68	m
48120	05/39 Crw	07/50 8120	-01/66	09/66	m
48121	05/39 Crw	04/48 8121	-04/67	12/67	m
48122	05/39 Crw	05/49 8122	-02/67	08/67	m
48123	06/39 Crw	07/48 8123	-03/67	08/67	m
48124	06/39 Crw	50 8124	-05/68	10/68	m
48125	06/39 Crw	06/48 8125	-10/67	08/68	m
48126	01/41 Crw	10/49 8126	-05/67	09/67	m
48127	01/41 Crw	12/49 8127	-10/66	01/67	m
48128	01/41 Crw	02/50 8128	-06/67	10/67	m
48129	01/41 Crw	10/48 8129	-03/66	06/66	m
48130	02/41 Crw	05/49 8130	-02/67	06/67	m
48131	03/41 Crw	05/48 8131	-06/67	10/67	m
48132	03/41 Crw	03/49 8132	-06/68	11/68	m
48133	04/41 Crw	04/48 8133	-11/66	07/67	m
48134	04/41 Crw	04/50 8134	-01/66	04/66	m
48135	05/41 Crw	09/48 8135	-09/65	12/65	m
48136	08/41 Crw	09/49 8136	-03/67	07/67	m
48137	09/41 Crw	12/49 8137	-10/66	01/67	m
48138	09/41 Crw	10/49 8138	-11/65	03/66	m
48139	12/41 Crw	06/48 8139	-11/66	04/67	m
48140	01/42 Crw	07/48 8140	-04/64	05/64	m
48141	01/42 Crw	04/49 8141	-05/67	09/67	m
48142	02/42 Crw	08/49 8142	-11/66	05/67	m
48143	03/42 Crw	01/49 8143	-11/66	05/67	m
48144	04/42 Crw	04/48 8144	-01/64	05/64	m
48145	04/42 Crw	06/48 8145	-06/65	09/65	m
48146	07/42 Crw	06/48 8146	-01/67	06/67	m
48147	07/42 Crw	08/49 8147	-07/66	11/66	m
48148	07/42 Crw	03/49 8148	-06/65	11/65	m
48149	08/42 Crw	06/49 8149	-01/67	01/68	m
48150	08/42 Crw	03/49 8150	-01/64	11/64	m
48151 §	09/42 Crw	04/49 8151	-01/68		m
48152	09/42 Crw	09/49 8152	-03/67	09/67	m
48153	09/42 Crw	05/48 8153	-03/68	09/68	m
48154	10/42 Crw	12/48 8154	-07/67	12/67	m
48155	10/42 Crw	06/48 8155	-09/66	02/67	m
48156	11/42 Crw	08/49 8156	-08/65	02/66	m
48157	12/42 Crw	12/49 8157	-05/67	11/67	m
48158	01/43 Crw	10/49 8158	-09/67	03/68	m
48159	01/43 Crw	11/49 8159	-03/67	09/67	m
48160	02/43 Crw	08/49 8160	-08/67	02/68	m
48161	02/43 Crw	04/49 8161	-09/67	03/68	m
48162	02/43 Crw	08/49 8162	-07/67	11/67	m
48163	03/43 Crw	08/48 8163	-06/67	11/67	m
48164	03/43 Crw	06/48 8164	-10/67	02/68	m
48165	03/43 Crw	06/48 8165	-03/67	09/67	m
48166	04/43 Crw	09/49 8166	-10/67	04/68	m
48167	04/43 Crw	06/48 8167	-08/68	12/68	m
48168	04/43 Crw	05/48 8168	-06/68	09/68	m
48169	04/43 Crw	05/49 8169	-11/67	05/68	m
48170	05/43 Crw	09/48 8170	-06/68	12/68	m
48171	05/43 Crw	08/48 8171	-09/67	06/68	m
48172	06/43 Crw	11/48 8172	-05/64	08/64	m
48173 §	06/43 Crw	02/50 8173	-07/65		m
48174	07/43 Crw	11/48 8174	-05/67	11/67	m
48175	08/43 Crw	09/49 8175	-02/66	06/66	m
48176	03/42 NB	09/48 8176	-08/67	11/67	m
48177	03/42 NB	01/49 8177	-03/67	07/67	m
48178	03/42 NB	06/48 8178	-11/66	06/67	m
48179	03/42 NB	04/50 8179	-11/64	11/64	m
48180	03/42 NB	10/48 8180	-03/67	07/67	m
48181	04/42 NB	10/50 8181	-02/66	06/66	m
48182	04/42 NB	11/48 8182	-05/68	10/68	m
48183	04/42 NB	04/48 8183	-07/65	11/65	m
48184	04/42 NB	03/48 8184	-07/65	11/65	m
48185	04/42 NB	05/49 8185	-02/67	08/67	m
48186	04/42 NB	06/49 8186	-10/66	01/67	m
48187	04/42 NB	08/48 8187	-01/67	05/67	m
48188	04/42 NB	05/48 8188	-05/66	08/66	m
48189	05/42 NB	06/48 8189	-07/65	03/66	m
48190	05/42 NB	11/48 8190	-12/67	03/68	m
48191	05/42 NB	11/48 8191	-08/68	12/68	mo 11/48⇨c
48192	05/42 NB	07/48 8192	-04/68	08/68	m
48193	05/42 NB	05/49 8193	-01/68	05/68	m
48194	06/42 NB	12/48 8194	-08/67	12/67	m
48195	06/42 NB	09/48 8195	-04/66	07/66	m

48196 06/42 NB 03/50 8196 -10/66 02/67 m
48197 06/42 NB 12/48 8197 -04/68 08/68 m
48198 06/42 NB 08/48 8198 -09/65 12/65 m
48199 06/42 NB 01/49 8199 -02/67 07/67 m
48200 06/42 NB 01/49 8200 -01/68 04/68 m
48201 06/42 NB 10/48 8201 -03/68 07/68 m
48202 07/42 NB 09/50 8202 -07/67 11/67 m
48203 07/42 NB 11/48 8203 -04/66 07/66 m
48204 07/42 NB 07/48 8204 -08/67 06/68 m
48205 07/42 NB 10/49 8205 -12/67 03/68 m
48206 07/42 NB 04/49 8206 -05/68 08/68 m
48207 07/42 NB 03/49 8207 -01/66 04/66 m
48208 08/42 NB 09/49 8208 -08/67 01/68 m
48209 08/42 NB 09/48 8209 -04/64 05/64 m
48210 08/42 NB 12/48 8210 -04/64 05/64 m
48211 08/42 NB 06/49 8211 -11/67 03/68 m
48212 08/42 NB 03/49 8212 -06/68 10/68 m
48213 08/42 NB 08/48 8213 -09/66 02/67 m
48214 08/42 NB 08/48 8214 -11/67 03/68 m
48215 08/42 NB 08/48 8215 -07/66 11/66 m
48216 08/42 NB 11/49 8216 -01/64 05/64 m
48217 09/42 NB 08/49 8217 -02/65 02/66 m
48218 09/42 NB 08/48 8218 -09/67 02/68 m
48219 09/42 NB 05/49 8219 -12/66 06/67 m
48220 09/42 NB 01/49 8220 -08/67 02/68 m
48221 09/42 NB 06/50 8221 -02/67 08/67 m
48222 09/42 NB 11/48 8222 -11/67 04/68 m
48223 09/42 NB 04/48 8223 -11/66 06/67 m
48224 09/42 NB 09/49 8224 -03/68 09/68 m
48225 09/42 NB 02/49 8225 -10/66 02/67 m
48246 05/40 NB 12/49 70300 12/49-01/66 04/66 w
48247 06/40 NB 09/49 70301 09/49-08/68 12/68 w
48248 07/40 NB 11/49 70311 11/49-12/65 04/66 w
48249 07/40 NB 11/49 70314 11/49-12/66 10/68 w
48250 08/40 NB 10/49 70318 10/49-04/66 07/66 w
48251 09/40 NB 12/49 70332 12/49-10/66 02/67 w
48252 12/41 NB 11/49 70363 11/49-05/68 09/68 w
48253 07/41 NB 10/49 70376 10/49-08/68 01/69 w
48254 07/41 NB 12/49 70378 12/49-09/66 11/66 w
48255 08/41 NB 12/49 70384 12/49-11/66 08/67 w
48256 09/41 NB 10/49 70394 10/49-05/67 11/67 w
48257 08/41 NB 09/49 70395 09/49-07/68 10/68 w
48258 10/41 NB 09/49 70398 09/49-08/67 01/68 w
48259 10/41 NB 12/49 70504 12/49-07/65 10/65 w
48260 11/41 NB 10/49 70518 10/49-11/65 04/66 w
48261 02/42 NB 12/49 70544 12/49-08/67 12/67 w
48262 06/41 NB 09/49 70576 09/49-11/65 02/66 w
48263 10/41 NB 09/49 70584 09/49-09/66 02/67 w
48264 05/42 NB 05/50 8264 -07/66 11/66 w
48265 05/42 NB 12/50 8265 -06/67 11/67 w
48266 05/42 NB 12/48 8266 -06/67 11/67 w
48267 05/42 NB 12/50 8267 -06/68 02/69 w
48268 05/42 NB 08/48 8268 -10/67 06/68 w
48269 05/42 NB 11/49 8269 -07/67 12/67 wo
11/48➪c
48270 06/42 NB 04/49 8270 -12/66 06/67 w
48271 06/42 NB 01/49 8271 -08/67 05/68 w
48272 06/42 NB 06/49 8272 -03/68 07/68 w
48273 06/42 NB 12/48 8273 -08/65 11/65 wo
12/48➪c
48274 06/42 NB 08/49 8274 -09/66 03/67 w
48275 06/42 NB 01/50 8275 -06/67 12/67 w
48276 07/42 NB 09/49 8276 -11/67 04/68 w
48277 07/42 NB 07/48 8277 -04/66 07/66 w
48278 07/42 NB 08/52 8278 -08/68 01/69 w
48279 08/42 NB 11/48 8279 -10/67 03/68 w
48280 08/42 NB 01/49 8280 -05/66 09/66 w
48281 08/42 NB 09/49 8281 -09/67 01/68 w
48282 08/42 NB 10/48 8282 -06/68 01/69 w
48283 08/42 NB 11/49 8283 -09/67 04/68 w
48284 08/42 NB 10/49 8284 -07/66 10/66 w
48285 09/42 NB 05/48 8285 -09/65 03/66 w
48286 07/40 BP 12/49 70401 12/49-09/66 05/67 w
48287 07/40 BP 09/49 70402 09/49-06/67 05/68 w
48288 08/40 BP 08/49 70403 08/49-02/67 07/67 w
48289 10/40 BP 11/49 70413 11/49-10/66 02/67 w
48290 06/41 BP 09/49 70438 09/49-08/65 02/66 w
48291 07/41 BP 12/49 70440 12/49-07/66 10/66 w
48292 08/41 BP 09/49 70442 09/49-04/68 08/68 w
48293 10/40 BP 06/48 8293 -06/68 01/69 w
48294 11/41 BP 11/49 70443 11/49-08/68 02/69 w
48295 12/41 BP 11/49 70446 11/49-09/65 12/65 w
48296 12/41 BP 10/49 70447 10/49-09/66 04/67 w
48297 01/42 BP 11/49 70449 11/49-07/65 12/65 w
48301 09/43 Crw 03/49 8301 -03/67 09/67 m
48302 10/43 Crw 04/49 8302 -01/66 04/66 m
48303 10/43 Crw 04/49 8303 -07/66 10/66 m
48304 10/43 Crw 05/49 8304 -03/68 07/68 m
48305 § 11/43 Crw 10/48 8305 -01/68 m
48306 11/43 Crw 07/48 8306 -07/64 10/64 m
48307 11/43 Crw 08/49 8307 -03/68 05/68 m
48308 11/43 Crw 06/48 8308 -04/68 08/68 m
48309 11/43 Crw 03/49 8309 -03/66 07/66 m
48310 12/43 Crw 02/53 8310 -12/67 05/68 m
48311 12/43 Crw 01/50 8311 -09/66 02/67 m
48312 12/43 Crw 03/49 8312 -02/65 05/65 m
48313 12/43 Crw 03/49 8313 -09/67 08/68 m
48314 12/43 Crw 08/49 8314 -12/65 02/66 m
48315 12/43 Crw 06/49 8315 -08/67 12/67 m
48316 12/43 Crw 03/49 8316 -04/67 11/67 m
48317 01/44 Crw 03/49 8317 -03/68 08/68 m
48318 01/44 Crw 05/50 8318 -10/66 02/67 m
48319 01/44 Crw 06/48 8319 -06/68 10/68 m
48320 02/44 Crw 05/48 8320 -03/67 10/67 m
48321 02/44 Crw 12/48 8321 -06/68 11/68 m
48322 02/44 Crw 05/49 8322 -05/68 09/68 m
48323 02/44 Crw 07/49 8323 -06/68 12/68 m
48324 02/44 Crw 03/49 8324 -06/67 11/67 m
48325 03/44 Crw 03/50 8325 -05/68 10/68 m
48326 03/44 Crw 09/48 8326 -07/66 11/66 m
48327 03/44 Crw 02/49 8327 -06/68 01/69 m
48328 04/44 Crw 09/49 8328 -09/65 01/66 m
48329 04/44 Crw 11/49 8329 -05/68 09/68 m
48330 05/44 Crw 06/48 8330 -09/65 02/66 m
48331 09/43 Hor 04/49 8331 -02/66 09/66 m
48332 10/43 Hor 06/48 8332 -10/67 05/68 m
48333 11/43 Hor 11/49 8333 -07/65 12/65 m
48334 11/43 Hor 08/50 8334 -01/68 05/68 m
48335 11/43 Hor 03/49 8335 -04/68 07/68 m
48336 12/43 Hor 05/49 8336 -12/67 05/68 m
48337 12/43 Hor 02/49 8337 -09/67 02/68 m
48338 01/44 Hor 02/49 8338 -06/68 11/68 m
48339 01/44 Hor 09/49 8339 -10/66 01/67 m
48340 01/44 Hor 02/50 8340 -08/68 12/68 m
48341 02/44 Hor 05/48 8341 -04/64 09/64 m
48342 02/44 Hor 12/49 8342 -09/66 12/66 m
48343 02/44 Hor 05/48 8343 -02/67 05/67 m
48344 03/44 Hor 01/49 8344 -04/68 07/68 m
48345 03/44 Hor 01/49 8345 -03/68 07/68 m
48346 03/44 Hor 08/48 8346 -07/66 11/66 m
48347 03/44 Hor 02/49 8347 -07/67 03/68 m
48348 04/44 Hor 12/48 8348 -08/68 01/69 m
48349 04/44 Hor 09/48 8349 -10/66 02/67 m
48350 04/44 Hor 04/49 8350 -09/67 08/68 m
48351 05/44 Hor 04/50 8351 -01/68 06/68 m
48352 05/44 Hor 11/48 8352 -11/67 04/68 m
48353 06/44 Hor 06/48 8353 -09/66 01/67 m
48354 06/44 Hor 04/50 8354 -11/66 05/67 m
48355 06/44 Hor 02/50 8355 -09/65 12/65 m
48356 06/44 Hor 03/50 8356 -06/68 12/68 m
48357 06/44 Hor 07/48 8357 -09/66 12/66 m
48358 07/44 Hor 11/48 8358 -09/66 12/66 m
48359 07/44 Hor 05/49 8359 -09/67 02/68 m
48360 07/44 Hor 01/50 8360 -07/65 01/66 m
48361 08/44 Hor 04/49 8361 -10/66 03/67 m
48362 08/44 Hor 05/49 8362 -12/67 03/68 m
48363 08/44 Hor 12/48 8363 -11/67 07/68 m
48364 08/44 Hor 06/48 8364 -09/67 01/68 m
48365 09/44 Hor 07/49 8365 -05/68 09/68 m
48366 09/44 Hor 09/48 8366 -11/65 01/66 m
48367 09/44 Hor 04/49 8367 -09/66 11/66 m
48368 09/44 Hor 03/49 8368 -06/68 12/68 m
48369 10/44 Hor 10/48 8369 -06/68 01/69 m
48370 10/44 Hor 11/48 8370 -11/66 05/67 mo
11/48➪c
48371 10/44 Hor 10/48 8371 -10/67 06/68 m
48372 10/44 Hor 10/49 8372 -12/66 04/67 m
48373 11/44 Hor 01/49 8373 -06/68 12/68 m
48374 11/44 Hor 12/49 8374 -06/68 01/69 m
48375 11/44 Hor 03/49 8375 -09/67 04/68 m
48376 11/44 Hor 02/50 8376 -07/67 12/67 m
48377 12/44 Hor 07/49 8377 -10/67 01/68 m
48378 12/44 Hor 06/49 8378 -08/65 02/66 m
48379 12/44 Hor 11/48 8379 -03/67 09/67 m
48380 12/44 Hor 07/49 8380 -06/68 09/68 m
48381 12/44 Hor 03/50 8381 -11/67 03/68 m
48382 01/45 Hor 10/48 8382 -10/67 02/68 m
48383 01/45 Hor 06/49 8383 -01/66 04/66 m
48384 01/45 Hor 03/49 8384 -06/68 12/68 m
48385 02/45 Hor 05/48 8385 -11/66 06/67 mo
11/48➪c
48386 02/45 Hor 12/48 8386 -08/67 11/68 mo
12/48➪c
48387 03/45 Hor 08/49 8387 -01/65 07/65 m
48388 03/45 Hor 11/49 8388 -10/66 05/67 m
48389 03/45 Hor 11/49 8389 -08/65 01/66 m
48390 03/45 Hor 05/50 8390 -05/68 08/68 m
48391 04/45 Hor 10/49 8391 -12/65 03/66 m
48392 04/45 Hor 06/48 8392 -06/68 09/68 m
48393 04/45 Hor 10/48 8393 -08/68 12/68 m
48394 05/45 Hor 11/49 8394 -07/67 11/67 m
48395 05/45 Hor 04/50 8395 -09/67 03/68 m
48396 05/45 Hor 05/50 8396 -01/64 05/64 m
48397 06/45 Hor 05/49 8397 -10/66 02/67 m
48398 06/45 Hor 03/50 8398 -04/66 07/66 m
48399 06/45 Hor 12/49 8399 -09/67 03/68 m
48400 06/43 Sdn 06/48 8400 -08/68 12/68 g
48401 07/43 Sdn 11/49 8401 -09/65 01/66 g
48402 07/43 Sdn 09/48 8402 -12/67 03/68 g
48403 07/43 Sdn 06/49 8403 -07/65 10/65 g
48404 07/43 Sdn 03/49 8404 -09/66 02/67 g
48405 08/43 Sdn 02/49 8405 -07/66 10/66 g
48406 08/43 Sdn 05/48 8406 -09/65 12/65 g
48407 08/43 Sdn 06/49 8407 -12/63 11/64 g
48408 09/43 Sdn 03/49 8408 -11/67 06/68 g
48409 09/43 Sdn 12/48 8409 -03/65 07/65 g
48410 09/43 Sdn 08/49 8410 -08/68 01/69 g
48411 09/43 Sdn 12/48 8411 -07/67 11/67 g
48412 10/43 Sdn 10/49 8412 -12/66 06/67 g
48413 10/43 Sdn 11/48 8413 -11/65 01/66 g
48414 10/43 Sdn 04/48 8414 -10/66 02/67 g
48415 10/43 Sdn 07/48 8415 -08/66 12/66 g
48416 11/43 Sdn 10/49 8416 -07/65 12/65 g
48417 11/43 Sdn 12/48 8417 -05/67 11/67 g
48418 11/43 Sdn 06/49 8418 -09/66 02/67 g
48419 11/43 Sdn 11/49 8419 -05/65 11/65 g
48420 11/43 Sdn 12/48 8420 -04/64 08/64 g
48421 12/43 Sdn 12/49 8421 -02/68 07/68 g
48422 12/43 Sdn 08/49 8422 -03/66 06/66 g
48423 12/43 Sdn 06/49 8423 -08/68 12/68 g
48424 12/43 Sdn 02/49 8424 -02/68 06/68 g
48425 12/43 Sdn 04/49 8425 -10/67 08/68 g
48426 12/43 Sdn 06/49 8426 -06/66 09/66 g
48427 01/44 Sdn 06/49 8427 -08/65 11/65 g
48428 01/44 Sdn 03/50 8428 -09/66 03/67 g
48429 01/44 Sdn 03/49 8429 -09/65 12/65 g
48430 03/44 Sdn 07/49 8430 -04/65 08/65 g
48431 § 03/44 Sdn 11/49 8431 -05/64 g
48432 03/44 Sdn 07/49 8432 -10/66 02/67 g
48433 03/44 Sdn 03/50 8433 -04/68 08/68 g
48434 03/44 Sdn 12/49 8434 -12/65 04/66 g
48435 04/44 Sdn 02/49 8435 -05/67 09/67 g
48436 04/44 Sdn 08/49 8436 -02/67 03/68 g
48437 05/44 Sdn 12/49 8437 -04/68 07/68 g
48438 05/44 Sdn 02/50 8438 -11/67 06/68 g
48439 05/44 Sdn 01/49 8439 -10/67 04/68 g
48440 06/44 Sdn 10/49 8440 -02/67 08/67 g
48441 06/44 Sdn 02/50 8441 -04/68 07/68 g
48442 06/44 Sdn 02/49 8442 -03/68 05/68 g
48443 06/44 Sdn 07/48 8443 -11/66 03/67 g
48444 06/44 Sdn 11/49 8444 -02/66 04/66 g
48445 07/44 Sdn 02/50 8445 -05/68 09/68 g
48446 07/44 Sdn 06/49 8446 -07/65 11/65 g
48447 07/44 Sdn 10/49 8447 -01/66 05/66 g
48448 07/44 Sdn 01/50 8448 -07/68 10/68 g
48449 08/44 Sdn 08/49 8449 -05/67 09/67 g
48450 08/44 Sdn 02/50 8450 -09/67 09/68 g
48451 09/44 Sdn 03/50 8451 -05/68 09/68 g
48452 09/44 Sdn 05/49 8452 -01/66 04/66 g
48453 09/44 Sdn 05/48 8453 -04/68 07/68 g
48454 09/44 Sdn 01/50 8454 -07/67 02/68 g
48455 10/44 Sdn 12/49 8455 -11/64 12/64 g
48456 10/44 Sdn 06/50 8456 -08/67 02/68 g
48457 10/44 Sdn 04/48 8457 -09/66 02/67 g
48458 11/44 Sdn 12/49 8458 -04/67 10/67 g
48459 11/44 Sdn 12/49 8459 -04/67 10/67 g
48460 12/44 Sdn 09/49 8460 -09/67 02/68 g
48461 12/44 Sdn 08/49 8461 -01/65 05/65 g
48462 12/44 Sdn 01/49 8462 -12/66 04/67 g
48463 01/45 Sdn 01/50 8463 -07/64 12/64 g
48464 01/45 Sdn 06/50 8464 -08/67 07/68 g
48465 02/45 Sdn 08/48 8465 -03/68 07/68 g
48466 02/45 Sdn 03/50 8466 -05/67 11/67 g
48467 03/45 Sdn 10/48 8467 -06/68 01/69 g
48468 03/45 Sdn 04/50 8468 -03/68 06/68 g
48469 03/45 Sdn 10/49 8469 -12/67 03/68 g
48470 04/45 Sdn 04/48 8470 -11/67 03/68 g
48471 04/45 Sdn 03/50 8471 -05/68 09/68 g
48472 05/45 Sdn 07/48 8472 -05/66 08/66 g
48473 05/45 Sdn 08/49 8473 -10/67 05/68 g
48474 05/45 Sdn 04/48 8474 -09/67 01/68 g
48475 06/45 Sdn 03/49 8475 -10/66 04/67 g
48476 06/45 Sdn 09/49 8476 -08/68 12/68 g
48477 06/45 Sdn 05/50 8477 -09/66 01/67 g
48478 06/45 Sdn 09/48 8478 -06/65 10/65 g
48479 07/45 Sdn 08/50 8479 -02/66 05/66 g
48490 06/45 Hor 11/49 8490 -09/65 12/65 m
48491 07/45 Hor 09/49 8491 -06/68 12/68 m
48492 07/45 Hor 02/50 8492 -02/68 05/68 m
48493 08/45 Hor 10/49 8493 -08/68 04/69 m
48494 08/45 Hor 07/49 8494 -04/67 09/67 m
48495 08/45 Hor 04/49 8495 -10/67 04/68 m
48500 02/44 Dar 04/48 8500 -12/65 03/66 e
48501 06/44 Dar 02/49 8501 -07/67 11/67 e
48502 08/44 Dar 12/48 8502 -11/66 08/67 e
48503 09/44 Dar 01/49 8503 -03/68 07/68 e
48504 09/44 Dar 03/50 8504 -06/68 10/68 e
48505 09/44 Dar 03/49 8505 -10/67 05/68 e
48506 10/44 Dar 08/49 8506 -09/67 02/68 e
48507 10/44 Dar 08/48 8507 -03/68 07/68 e
48508 10/44 Dar 04/48 8508 -01/64 05/64 e
48509 11/44 Dar 01/49 8509 -05/67 03/68 e
48510 06/43 Don 10/52 8510 -01/68 10/68 e
48511 03/44 Don 01/50 8511 -07/66 10/66 e
48512 04/44 Don 10/48 8512 -09/66 02/67 e
48513 04/44 Don 09/49 8513 -03/67 09/67 e
48514 05/44 Don 09/49 8514 -10/66 05/67 e
48515 06/44 Don 09/49 8515 -01/66 04/66 e
48516 07/44 Don 11/49 8516 -12/66 08/67 e
48517 07/44 Don 05/49 8517 -11/67 02/68 e
48518 § 08/44 Don 08/49 8518 -07/65 e
48519 09/44 Don 05/50 8519 -08/68 01/69 e
48520 10/44 Don 01/49 8520 -09/66 02/67 e
48521 10/44 Don 10/49 8521 -05/66 08/66 e

Motor-fitted LNWR Webb '1P' 2-4-2T No 46643 at Rhyl in September 1952.

LMS 'Sentinel' 0-4-0T No 47182.

LMS Fowler '3F' 0-6-0T No 47390 at Moor Row in March 1950.

LMS Fowler 'Garratt' 2-6-6-2T No 47998 at Toton in August 1956. It was one of only two to retain its fixed coal bunker.

Number	Built	Renumbered	BR Dates	Scrap	Notes
48522	11/44 Don	04/49 8522	-08/67	02/68	e
48523	11/44 Don	10/49 8523	-02/66	06/66	e
48524	12/44 Don	03/50 8524	-04/64	08/64	e
48525	12/44 Don	02/50 8525	-10/65	04/66	e
48526	12/44 Don	03/50 8526	-09/66	12/66	e
48527	12/44 Don	10/48 8527	-10/66	05/67	e
48528	02/45 Don	11/49 8528	-08/67	12/67	e
48529	04/45 Don	10/49 8529	-06/68	11/68	e
48530	04/45 Don	06/49 8530	-03/66	06/66	e
48531	04/45 Don	03/49 8531	-09/67	01/68	e
48532	04/45 Don	06/48 8532	-03/68	07/68	e
48533	05/45 Don	09/49 8533	-05/68	08/68	e
48534	05/45 Don	09/49 8534	-10/67	04/68	e
48535	06/45 Don	05/50 8535	-08/67	12/67	e
48536	06/45 Don	08/48 8536	-01/67	06/67	e
48537	07/45 Don	12/49 8537	-10/67	05/68	e
48538	08/45 Don	05/48 8538	-03/67	08/67	e
48539	08/45 Don	08/49 8539	-01/66	06/66	e
48540	12/44 Dar	10/49 8540	-10/67	05/68	e
48541	12/44 Dar	09/48 8541	-06/66	09/66	e
48542	12/44 Dar	11/49 8542	-07/67	02/68	e
48543	01/45 Dar	08/49 8543	-02/66	05/66	e
48544	01/45 Dar	01/50 8544	-03/68	05/68	e
48545	02/45 Dar	04/49 8545	-02/67	08/67	e
48546	02/45 Dar	04/49 8546	-07/68	11/68	e
48547	03/45 Dar	01/50 8547	-03/67	09/67	e
48548	03/45 Dar	08/49 8548	-04/67	12/67	e
48549	03/45 Dar	03/50 8549	-06/68	02/69	e
48550	04/45 Dar	06/49 8550	-09/67	02/68	e
48551	04/45 Dar	03/49 8551	-05/68	09/68	e
48552	05/45 Dar	05/49 8552	-05/67	11/67	e
48553	05/45 Dar	05/49 8553	-03/68	07/68	e
48554	06/45 Dar	11/49 8554	-08/66	11/66	e
48555	06/45 Dar	03/49 8555	-01/66	04/66	e
48556	07/45 Dar	07/49 8556	-08/67	11/68	e
48557	07/45 Dar	03/50 8557	-07/67	11/67	e
48558	08/45 Dar	01/50 8558	-10/65	03/66	e
48559	08/45 Dar	03/49 8559	-01/68	04/68	e
48600	02/43 Elh	08/48 8600	-11/66	05/67	s
48601	02/43 Elh	08/48 8601	-06/65	10/65	s
48602	04/43 Elh	04/53 8602	-07/67	12/67	s
48603	05/43 Elh	04/50 8603	-06/67	12/67	s
48604	06/43 Elh	05/48 8604	-05/67	11/67	s
48605	07/43 Elh	04/48 8605	-08/66	11/66	s
48606	09/43 Elh	12/48 8606	-09/66	11/66	so 12/48⇨c
48607	09/43 Elh	01/49 8607	-08/65	11/65	s
48608	10/43 Elh	10/48 8608	-02/66	05/66	s
48609	10/43 Elh	06/49 8609	-01/68	04/68	s
48610	04/43 Asfd	03/49 8610	-08/65	09/65	s
48611	05/43 Asfd	03/49 8611	-12/64	10/65	s
48612	07/43 Asfd	07/48 8612	-06/68	11/68	s
48613	07/43 Bton	12/48 8613	-07/67	12/67	s
48614	08/43 Bton	04/48 8614	-05/68	08/68	s
48615	09/43 Bton	08/48 8615	-02/66	01/67	s
48616	10/43 Bton	02/50 8616	-10/60	10/60	s
48617	11/43 Bton	10/48 8617	-03/68	07/68	s
48618	09/43 Asfd	04/48 8618	-09/67	03/68	s
48619	10/43 Asfd	01/50 8619	-03/66	06/66	s
48620	11/43 Asfd	02/50 8620	-06/68	11/68	s
48621	11/43 Asfd	12/48 8621	-07/66	10/66	s
48622	11/43 Asfd	05/50 8622	-10/67	04/68	s
48623	12/43 Asfd	01/50 8623	-10/66	03/67	s
48624 §	12/43 Asfd	11/48 8624	-07/65		s
48625	04/43 Bton	06/50 8625	-06/66	08/66	s
48626	05/43 Bton	11/50 8626	-01/68	07/68	s
48627	05/43 Bton	04/48 8627	-03/66	06/66	s
48628	05/43 Bton	02/49 8628	-09/66	02/67	s
48629	06/43 Bton	07/48 8629	-09/66	12/66	s
48630	06/43 Bton	06/49 8630	-07/65	11/65	s
48631	06/43 Bton	10/49 8631	-02/68	06/68	s
48632	06/43 Bton	05/49 8632	-03/68	07/68	s
48633	07/43 Bton	09/48 8633	-03/66	11/66	s
48634	08/43 Bton	01/49 8634	-08/65	11/65	s
48635	08/43 Bton	09/48 8635	-10/66	02/67	s
48636	08/43 Bton	04/48 8636	-08/67	03/68	s
48637	09/43 Bton	03/49 8637	-09/67	08/68	s
48638	09/43 Bton	12/48 8638	-01/66	04/66	s
48639	09/43 Bton	04/48 8639	-02/68	07/68	s
48640	10/43 Bton	09/48 8640	-05/67	11/67	s
48641	10/43 Bton	09/49 8641	-12/66	02/67	s
48642	10/43 Bton	05/48 8642	-04/64	05/64	s
48643	11/43 Bton	03/49 8643	-06/67	12/67	s
48644	11/43 Bton	12/48 8644	-01/66	04/66	s
48645	11/43 Bton	04/49 8645	-06/67	10/67	s
48646	11/43 Bton	06/49 8646	-06/68	12/68	s
48647	12/43 Bton	09/50 8647	-04/66	07/66	s
48648	12/43 Bton	11/48 8648	-07/67	11/67	s
48649	12/43 Bton	02/49 8649	-02/65	05/65	s
48650	10/43 Elh	02/50 8650	-08/67	12/67	s
48651	11/43 Elh	01/49 8651	-11/66	06/67	s
48652	11/43 Elh	03/50 8652	-06/68	10/68	s
48653	11/43 Elh	06/48 8653	-08/65	11/65	so 01/49⇨c
48654	11/43 Elh	05/49 8654	-09/64	10/64	s
48655	11/43 Elh	11/48 8655	-08/67	12/67	s
48656	11/43 Elh	02/49 8656	-08/65	11/65	s
48657	11/43 Elh	04/49 8657	-09/64	10/64	s
48658	11/43 Elh	12/49 8658	-07/65	12/65	s
48659	11/43 Elh	01/49 8659	-05/66	10/66	s
48660	11/43 Elh	06/48 8660	-07/65	10/65	s
48661	07/44 Elh	11/48 8661	-09/65	12/65	s
48662	07/44 Elh	06/49 8662	-11/66	05/67	s
48663	02/44 Bton	12/49 8663	-11/66	06/67	s
48664	02/44 Bton	09/48 8664	-10/67	05/68	s
48665	03/44 Bton	05/49 8665	-08/68	12/68	s
48666	04/44 Bton	12/48 8666	-08/68	12/68	s
48667	04/44 Bton	09/49 8667	-03/66	06/66	s
48668	05/44 Bton	02/49 8668	-12/66	06/67	s
48669	05/44 Bton	11/49 8669	-10/67	04/68	s
48670	07/44 Bton	06/50 8670	-10/66	12/66	s
48671	12/43 Asfd	02/50 8671	-08/67	12/67	s
48672	01/44 Asfd	05/49 8672	-11/66	05/67	s
48673	05/44 Asfd	08/49 8673	-10/67	03/68	s
48674	03/44 Asfd	07/48 8674	-12/67	04/68	s
48675	03/44 Bton	10/48 8675	-09/67	07/68	s
48676	04/44 Bton	05/48 8676	-10/67	08/68	s
48677	05/44 Bton	08/48 8677	-01/68	05/68	s
48678	06/44 Bton	05/49 8678	-06/68	11/68	s
48679	12/43 Bton	12/48 8679	-10/66	03/67	s
48680	12/43 Bton	09/48 8680	-09/66	02/67	s
48681	01/44 Bton	02/50 8681	-07/67	03/68	s
48682	01/44 Bton	12/48 8682	-09/65	12/65	s
48683	01/44 Bton	09/48 8683	-02/68	08/68	s
48684	01/44 Bton	10/49 8684	-05/68	09/68	s
48685	02/44 Bton	08/48 8685	-04/67	11/67	s
48686	02/44 Bton	02/50 8686	-11/66	06/67	s
48687	02/44 Bton	11/49 8687	-06/68	09/68	s
48688	02/44 Bton	06/48 8688	-07/65	10/65	s
48689	02/44 Bton	11/49 8689	-07/65	09/65	s
48690	03/44 Bton	12/48 8690	-03/67	08/67	s
48691	03/44 Bton	04/49 8691	-03/66	06/66	s
48692	03/44 Bton	10/48 8692	-06/68	10/68	s
48693	03/44 Bton	04/48 8693	-04/67	09/67	s
48694	04/44 Bton	12/49 8694	-03/66	07/66	s
48695	04/44 Bton	02/49 8695	-08/67	12/67	s
48696	04/44 Bton	01/49 8696	-12/67	03/68	so 01/49⇨c
48697	04/44 Bton	10/49 8697	-12/67	03/68	s
48698	05/44 Bton	02/49 8698	-04/66	07/66	s
48699	05/44 Bton	10/48 8699	-09/67	02/68	s
48700	05/44 Bton	01/49 8700	-03/68	05/68	s
48701	05/44 Bton	09/49 8701	-03/67	09/67	s
48702	05/44 Bton	11/48 8702	-05/68	08/68	s
48703	06/44 Bton	01/49 8703	-10/67	01/68	s
48704	06/44 Bton	11/49 8704	-09/65	12/65	s
48705	06/44 Bton	01/49 8705	-03/67	08/67	sl
48706	06/44 Bton	03/49 8706	-03/66	05/66	sl
48707	06/44 Bton	12/49 8707	-04/67	09/67	sl
48708	06/44 Bton	11/48 8708	-04/67	09/67	sl
48709	06/44 Bton	02/50 8709	-07/67	01/68	sl
48710	07/44 Bton	06/49 8710	-10/67	02/68	sl
48711	07/44 Bton	12/49 8711	-01/67	06/67	sl
48712	07/44 Bton	01/50 8712	-06/67	11/67	sl
48713	07/44 Bton	09/49 8713	-03/66	07/66	sl
48714	07/44 Bton	07/49 8714	-10/67	05/68	sl
48715	07/44 Bton	08/49 8715	-08/68	12/68	sl
48716	07/44 Bton	12/48 8716	-08/65	01/66	sl
48717	07/44 Bton	09/49 8717	-04/67	09/67	sl
48718	08/44 Bton	01/49 8718	-04/66	02/67	sl
48719	08/44 Bton	04/50 8719	-08/65	02/66	sl
48720	08/44 Bton	01/50 8720	-06/68	10/68	sl
48721	08/44 Bton	06/48 8721	-09/67	01/68	sl
48722	08/44 Bton	05/49 8722	-05/68	01/69	sl
48723	08/44 Bton	01/49 8723	-08/68	12/68	sl
48724	09/44 Bton	08/48 8724	-10/67	08/68	sl
48725	09/44 Bton	03/49 8725	-08/67	02/68	sl
48726	09/44 Bton	09/49 8726	-09/66	01/67	sl
48727	09/44 Bton	07/49 8727	-08/68	01/69	sl
48728	09/44 Bton	03/50 8728	-03/67	08/67	sl
48729	09/44 Bton	04/48 8729	-12/67	06/68	sl
48730	09/45 Dar	06/48 8730	-08/68	01/69	el
48731	09/45 Dar	05/50 8731	-08/67	07/68	el
48732	10/45 Dar	08/50 8732	-11/65	02/66	el
48733	10/45 Dar	10/49 8733	-06/65	08/65	el
48734	10/45 Dar	09/49 8734	-09/64	10/64	el
48735	11/45 Dar	01/50 8735	-10/67	08/68	el
48736	11/45 Dar	06/49 8736	-08/66	11/66	el
48737	11/45 Dar	03/50 8737	-05/65	08/65	el
48738	12/45 Dar	04/50 8738	-12/66	08/67	el
48739	12/45 Dar	01/50 8739	-01/67	07/67	el
48740	01/46 Dar	01/50 8740	-03/68	05/68	el
48741	02/46 Dar	11/49 8741	-10/67	02/68	el
48742	03/46 Dar	02/50 8742	-08/67	01/68	el
48743	03/46 Dar	12/49 8743	-03/67	09/67	el
48744	05/46 Dar	06/50 8744	-03/68	07/68	el
48745	04/46 Dar	08/52 8745	-05/68	09/68	el
48746	05/46 Dar	03/50 8746	-06/68	09/68	el
48747	05/46 Dar	03/49 8747	-09/66	01/67	el
48748	06/46 Dar	10/48 8748	-05/66	08/66	el
48749	08/46 Dar	04/50 8749	-04/68	07/68	el
48750	08/46 Dar	10/49 8750	-01/68	06/68	el
48751	09/46 Dar	05/48 8751	-02/67	07/67	el
48752	10/46 Dar	03/49 8752	-08/68	02/69	el
48753	10/45 Don	07/48 8753	-03/67	08/67	el
48754	10/45 Don	02/49 8754	-06/67	09/67	el
48755	10/45 Don	07/48 8755	-09/66	06/67	el
48756	11/45 Don	01/50 8756	-01/67	05/67	el
48757	11/45 Don	06/50 8757	-12/67	04/68	el
48758	12/45 Don	10/48 8758	-12/67	03/68	el
48759	12/45 Don	01/50 8759	-11/65	03/66	el ex-LNER 3554 (01/48)
48760	12/45 Don	10/48 8760	-03/66	07/66	el
48761	01/46 Don	04/48 8761	-01/65	04/65	el
48762	01/46 Don	11/48 8762	-02/66	06/66	el
48763	02/46 Don	03/51 8763	-04/68	01/69	el
48764	02/46 Don	09/50 8764	-12/67	04/68	el
48765	03/46 Don	07/48 8765	-08/68	12/68	el
48766	03/46 Don	08/48 8766	-02/67	05/67	el
48767	03/46 Don	03/49 8767	-09/67	01/68	el
48768	03/46 Don	06/48 8768	-08/67	07/68	el
48769	04/46 Don	09/48 8769	-08/65	01/66	el
48770	05/46 Don	05/48 8770	-04/67	10/67	el
48771	05/46 Don	11/50 8771	-12/65	04/66	el
48772	06/46 Don	09/48 8772	-01/64	05/64	el
48773 §	06/40 NB	09/57 500	09/57-08/68		w ⊠12/62-02/63 ⊠06/63-11/63
48774	08/40 NB	09/57 501	09/57-07/65	04/66	w ⊠12/62-02/63 ⊠06/63-11/63
48775	04/37 Crw	09/57 512	09/57-08/68	12/68	w ⊠12/62-02/63 ⊠06/63-11/63

4F 3 48801-48834
4-6-0 LNWR Whale '19in Goods'

Power Classification: 4F
Introduced: 1906-1909
Designer: Whale
Company: LNWR
Weight: Loco 63t 0cwt
Driving Wheel: 5' 2½"
Boiler Pressure: 175psi
Cylinders: Inside 19" x 26"
Tractive Effort: 22340lbf
Valve Gear: Joy (piston valves)

Built by Whale between 1906 and 1909, these '19" Goods' engines were basically a freight locomotive equivalent of the LNWR 'Experiment' class of 1905.

One hundred and seventy engines of this class were built, the first being withdrawn in 1931. Only three came into BR stock and they were all gone by 1950, none of them receiving its BR number.

b 48824 was fitted with a Belpaire boiler.

Year End Totals: '4F 3' class

'47	'48	'49	'50	'51	'52	'53	'54	'55	'56	'57	'58	'59	'60	'61	'62	'63	'64	'65	'66	'67
3	1	1																		

Number	*Built*	*Renumbered*	*BR Dates*	*Scrap*	*Notes*
48801	05/08 Crw	8801	-11/48		*48*
48824	08/08 Crw	8824	-02/50		*50* b
48834	09/08 Crw	8834	-12/48		*49*

6F 2 between 48892 & 49384
0-8-0 LNWR 'G1' Class
7F 2 between 48893 & 49394
0-8-0 LNWR 'G2A' Class

Power Classification: G1 6F
G2A 7F
Introduced: 1892 onwards
G1 Rebuilt 1912 onwards
G2A Rebuilt 1936 onwards
Designer: Webb, Whale, Bowen Cooke and Beames
Company: LNWR
Weight: G1 Loco 60t 5cwt
G2A Loco 62t 0cwt
Tender 40t 15cwt
Driving Wheel: 4' 5½"
Boiler Pressure: G1 160psi superheated
G2A 175psi superheated
Cylinders: Inside 20½" x 24"
Tractive Effort: G1 25640lbf
G2A 28045lbf
Valve Gear: Joy (piston valves)

The history of the LNWR 0-8-0s is fairly complicated, but it is summarised below. The codes shown in the class list correspond to the different stages the individual engines passed through.

p The prototype 0-8-0 engine was built by Webb in 1892. It was an 0-8-0 simple engine numbered

2524, and it later was rebuilt as a 'D' class engine; later becoming 49011.

a Webb's 'A' class was built between 1893 and 1900. These engines were three-cylinder compounds and one hundred and ten engines were built. They were all later rebuilt to 'C', 'C1' and 'D' classes.

b Between 1901 and 1904 Webb built one hundred and seventy four-cylinder compound engines. These were known as the 'B' class.

c Many of the 'A' class engines were rebuilt as two-cylinder simples by Whale between 1904 and 1906. In this form they were known as the 'C' class. They were fitted with larger boilers. Some engines (8968-9001) kept the original small boilers when they were rebuilt in 1909 and they were classified 'C1'; they were all withdrawn between 1927 and 1933.

d The 'D' class were 'A' class engines which were rebuilt by Whale in 1906-1909 as two-cylinder simples with larger saturated boilers. When these engines were later fitted with 'G1' superheated boilers (see below) they gained the nickname of 'Super Ds' - a name by which all of the LNWR 0-8-0s were later known.

e Between 1904 and 1907 twenty-six 'B' class four-cylinder compounds were rebuilt as 2-8-0 compounds by Whale. They retained their small boilers and were called the 'E' class. Some were later rebuilt as 0-8-0 simples between 1917 and 1925, the rest being scrapped as 2-8-0s.

f The 'F' class consisted of twelve 'B' class engines which were rebuilt as 2-8-0s in 1904-1907 in the same manner as the 'E' class. They were fitted with larger boilers than the 'E' class engines. Some were later rebuilt as 0-8-0 simples between 1917 and 1925, the rest being scrapped as 2-8-0s.

g The 'G' class was introduced by Whale and Bowen Cooke and was built from 1910-1912. These were two-cylinder simple engines with large 160psi non-superheated boilers.

1 In 1912 49145 was fitted with a superheated 160psi boiler and this became the first 'G1' class engine. One hundred and eighty more were built by Bowen Cooke between 1912 and 1918, and most of the earlier engines were also included in this class as they were superheated.

2 Beames introduced the 'G2' class in 1921-1922. These were fitted with 175psi boilers and were classified '7F' (see the '49395' class below). Many 'G1' engines were rebuilt with these higher pressure boilers from 1936 onwards and became known as the 'G2A' class.

Considering the complicated history of the class, the engines which came into BR stock all presented the same general appearance. In the class list below, the last column shows the classification of the engines in BR stock, either 'G1' ('6F') or 'G2A' ('7F'). The only noticeable difference was that many engines of both varieties were fitted with Belpaire fireboxes. There was some interchanging of boilers causing several 'G2A' engines to be reclassified to 'G1' (a retrograde step).

There was eventually a total of 572 engines (including the 'G2' class) of which 502 came into BR stock (the first engine was withdrawn in 1921 due to a boiler explosion). They were the LNWR's principal type of heavy freight traffic engine, and the only LNWR type to survive in any great number into BR days. They were unusual in that (along with other ex-LNWR classes) they never carried BR style number plates on the front of the smokebox.

Year End Totals: '6F [2]' class

'47	'48	'49	'50	'51	'52	'53	'54	'55	'56	'57	'58	'59	'60	'61	'62	'63	'64	'65	'66	'67
123	85	48	25	14	5	2	1													

Year End Totals: '7F [2]' class

'47	'48	'49	'50	'51	'52	'53	'54	'55	'56	'57	'58	'59	'60	'61	'62	'63	'64	'65	'66	'67
319	319	273	242	221	215	215	212	212	207	168	155	96	91	62	3	3				

Number	*Built*	*Renumbered*	*BR Dates*	*Scrap*	*Notes*	*Class*
48892	09/01 Crw		8892 -01/49	*49*	be1	G1
48893	08/02 Crw	12/49	8893 -10/54	*10/54*	be12	G2A
48894	11/02 Crw		8894 -02/49	*49*	be1	G1
48895	05/04 Crw	11/48	8895 -12/64	05/65	be12	G2A
48896	04/02 Crw		8896 -01/50	*50*	bf12	G2A
48897	05/02 Crw		8897 -10/49	*49*	bf12	G2A
48898	04/03 Crw	10/49	8898 -08/62	08/62	bf12	G2A
48899	05/04 Crw	08/49	8899 -02/56	04/56	bef12	G2A
48901	09/01 Crw	09/48	8901 -05/52	*05/52*	b12	G2A
48902	12/01 Crw	12/49	8902 -02/53	*53*	b1	G1
48903	03/02 Crw		8903 -09/49	*49*	b12	G2A
48904	04/02 Crw		8904 -10/49	*49*	b1	G1
48905	04/02 Crw	04/48	8905 -06/59	02/60	b12	G2A
48906	04/02 Crw		8906 -03/49	*49*	b1	G1
48907	05/02 Crw	08/48	8907 -10/57	11/57	b12	G2A
48908	05/02 Crw	05/48	8908 -09/50	*50*	b1	G1
48909	05/02 Crw		8909 -02/49	*49*	b12	G2A
48910	05/02 Crw		8910 -01/48	*07/48*	b1	G1
48911	05/02 Crw		8911 -12/49	*50*	b1	G1
48912	07/02 Crw		8912 -08/48	11/48	b1	G1
48913	08/02 Crw		8913 -08/48	09/48	b1	G1
48914	08/02 Crw	10/48	8914 -07/57	12/57	b12	G2A
48915	08/02 Crw	02/50	8915 -10/61	01/62	b12	G2A
48917	08/02 Crw	08/48	8917 -11/57	11/57	b12	G2A
48918	09/02 Crw		8918 -03/49	*49*	b1	G1
48920	09/02 Crw	10/48	8920 -05/51	*51*	b12	G2A
48921	10/02 Crw	09/52	8921 -04/58	04/58	b12	G2A
48922	11/02 Crw	04/48	8922 -05/59	06/59	b12	G2A
48924	12/02 Crw		8924 -12/48	*49*	b1	G1
48925	12/02 Crw	07/48	8925 -09/49	*49*	b12	G2A
48926	01/03 Crw	01/52	8926 -08/59	09/59	b12	G2A
48927	01/03 Crw	01/50	8927 -11/61	12/61	b12	G2A
48929	03/03 Crw	06/48	8929 -07/50	*50*	b1	G1
48930	04/03 Crw	05/48	8930 -12/62	01/63	b12	G2A
48931	04/03 Crw		8931 -06/49	06/49	b1	G1
48932	05/03 Crw	10/48	8932 -10/61	11/61	b12	G2A
48933	05/03 Crw		8933 -12/50	*51*	b12	G2A
48934	05/03 Crw		8934 -03/50	*50*	b12	G2A
48935	05/03 Crw		8935 -02/49	*49*	b1	G1
48936	05/03 Crw		8936 -04/51	*51*	b12	G2A
48939	07/03 Crw		8939 -11/48	*48*	b1	G1
48940	06/03 Crw	03/50	8940 -05/57	05/57	b12	G2A
48941	09/03 Crw	06/48	8941 -05/50	*50*	b12	G2A
48942	09/03 Crw	10/48	8942 -10/61	01/62	b12	G2A
48943	09/03 Crw	02/50	8943 -08/59	10/59	b12	G2A
48944	09/03 Crw	07/48	8944 -10/57	11/57	b12	G2A
48945	10/03 Crw	05/48	8945 -03/59	03/60	b12	G2A
48948	02/04 Crw		8948 -07/49	*08/49*	b12	G2A
48950	07/04 Crw	05/48	8950 -12/61	01/62	b12	G2A
48951	08/04 Crw	06/52	8951 -09/57	11/57	b12	G2A
48952	08/04 Crw	11/48	8952 -05/57	05/57	b12	G2A
48953	08/96 Crw	11/48	8953 -10/61	10/62	ac12	G2A
48954	11/94 Crw		8954 -06/49	*49*	ac12	G2A
48962	08/96 Crw		8962 -12/48	*49*	ac1	G1
48964	02/99 Crw	12/49	8964 -04/62	05/62	ac12	G2A
48966	10/98 Crw	08/48	8966 -02/50	*50*	ac12	G2A
49002	05/99 Crw	03/50	9002 -09/62	10/62	ad12	G2A
49003	10/98 Crw		9003 -03/49	*49*	ad12	G2A
49004	09/96 Crw		9004 -06/49	06/49	ad12	G2A
49005	04/98 Crw	02/51	9005 -08/57	11/57	ad12	G2A
49006	05/99 Crw	05/48	9006 -05/51	*51*	ad12	G2A
49007	05/00 Crw	04/51	9007 -10/61	02/62	ad12	G2A
49008	09/93 Crw	04/48	9008 -12/62	02/63	ad12	G2A
49009	07/98 Crw	02/51	9009 -11/59	12/59	ad12	G2A
49010	08/98 Crw	09/52	9010 -06/59	02/60	ad12	G2A
49011	10/92 Crw	11/48	9011 -12/49	*50*	pb1	G1
49012	09/96 Crw		9012 -12/48	*49*	ad1	G1
49013	12/97 Crw		9013 -05/48	05/48	ad1	G1
49014	10/97 Crw	08/48	9014 -06/51	*51*	ad12	G2A
49015	05/00 Crw		9015 -05/49	06/49	ad1	G1
49016	10/97 Crw		9016 -03/49	*49*	ad12	G2A
49017	10/97 Crw	06/48	9017 -06/52	*52*	ad1	G1
49018	05/98 Crw	10/49	9018 -08/59	10/59	ad12	G2A
49019	08/96 Crw		9019 -06/49	06/49	ad12	G2A
49020	08/96 Crw	04/51	9020 -10/61	10/61	ad12	G2A
49021	05/00 Crw	08/51	9021 -10/61	11/61	ad12	G2A
49022	10/98 Crw	11/49	9022 -04/51	*51*	ad12	G2A
49023	02/99 Crw	05/51	9023 -10/61	01/62	ad12	G2A
49024	05/00 Crw	11/49	9024 -02/57	03/57	ad12	G2A
49025	05/00 Crw	11/50	9025 -09/62	10/62	ad12	G2A
49026	02/99 Crw		9026 -09/49	*49*	ad12	G2A
49027	11/94 Crw	04/50	9027 -11/59	11/59	ad12	G2A
49028	07/98 Crw	10/48	9028 -02/56	04/56	ad12	G2A
49029	02/95 Crw	08/48	9029 -05/50	*50*	ad12	G2A
49030	04/00 Crw	01/50	9030 -06/51	*07/51*	ad1	G1
49031	08/96 Crw		9031 -06/51	*51*	ad12	G2A
49032	08/98 Crw	05/48	9032 -06/50	*50*	ad1	G1
49033	08/96 Crw	12/49	9033 -12/57	12/57	ad12	G2A
49034	12/96 Crw	05/51	9034 -09/62	10/62	ad12	G2A
49035	04/98 Crw	09/49	9035 -01/57	02/57	ad12	G2A
49036	02/99 Crw		9036 -11/49	*49*	ad12	G2A
49037	11/00 Crw	09/49	9037 -12/62	03/63	ad12	G2A
49038	07/98 Crw		9038 -04/48	05/48	ad1	G1
49039	07/98 Crw		9039 -01/50	*50*	ad12	G2A
49040	08/96 Crw		9040 -04/49	*49*	ad1	G1
49041	05/98 Crw	11/48	9041 -08/50	*50*	ad12	G2A
49042	02/99 Crw		9042 -04/49	*49*	ad12	G2A
49043	11/94 Crw		9043 -09/49	*49*	ad1	G1
49044	11/97 Crw	03/51	9044 -10/59	12/59	ad12	G2A
49045	11/97 Crw	05/49	9045 -12/62	03/63	ad12	G2A
49046	05/00 Crw	06/48	9046 -03/57	06/57	ad12	G2A
49047	10/97 Crw	11/51	9047 -01/58	02/58	ad12	G2A
49048	10/98 Crw	11/50	9048 -11/59	11/59	ad12	G2A
49049	02/95 Crw	07/51	9049 -11/62	02/63	ad12	G2A
49050	01/98 Crw		9050 -10/50	*50*	ad12	G2A
49051	11/94 Crw	12/51	9051 -01/57	03/57	ad12	G2A
49052	12/96 Crw		9052 -04/49	*49*	ad1	G1
49053	04/98 Crw		9053 -05/50	*50*	ad1	G1
49054	05/00 Crw		9054 -04/49	*49*	ad1	G1
49055	07/98 Crw		9055 -04/49	*49*	ad12	G2A
49056	05/99 Crw		9056 -08/48	*48*	ad1	G1
49057	05/99 Crw	05/48	9057 -05/57	06/57	ad12	G2A
49058	12/97 Crw		9058 -03/50	*50*	ad1	G1
49059	10/98 Crw	08/48	9059 -02/50	*50*	ad1	G1
49060	11/97 Crw		9060 -05/49	06/49	ad1	G1
49061	07/98 Crw	03/52	9061 -10/61	11/61	ad12	G2A
49062	05/99 Crw	04/49	9062 -05/51	*51*	ad12	G2A
49063	05/99 Crw	02/51	9063 -08/59	09/59	ad12	G2A
49064	04/98 Crw	08/50	9064 -06/60	06/60	ad12	G2A
49065	12/01 Crw	06/48	9065 -03/50	*50*	bg12	G2A
49066	12/01 Crw	06/49	9066 -11/57	11/57	bg12	G2A
49067	09/02 Crw		9067 -12/49	*50*	bg1	G1
49068	05/04 Crw	02/52	9068 -01/57	03/57	bg12	G2A
49069	05/04 Crw	08/48	9069 -06/50	*50*	bg12	G2A
49070	01/03 Crw	02/51	9070 -11/62	03/63	bg12	G2A
49071	05/03 Crw	08/48	9071 -01/51	*51*	bg1	G1
49072	10/02 Crw	01/49	9072 -02/49	*49*	bg12	G2A
49073	04/03 Crw	07/48	9073 -01/58	02/58	bg12	G2A
49074	10/03 Crw	03/49	9074 -12/50	*51*	bg12	G2A
49075	10/03 Crw	06/48	9075 -01/50	*50*	bg1	G1
49076	12/02 Crw		9076 -05/50	*50*	bg1	G1
49077	01/10 Crw	08/50	9077 -10/61	01/62	g12	G2A
49078	01/10 Crw	06/49	9078 -12/62	11/64	g12	G2A
49079	02/10 Crw	09/48	9079 -11/62	01/63	g12	G2A
49080	02/10 Crw		9080 -02/50	*50*	g12	G2A
49081	02/10 Crw	01/50	9081 -11/62	01/63	g12	G2A
49082	03/10 Crw	04/48	9082 -10/60	10/60	g12	G2A
49083	03/10 Crw		9083 -01/50	*50*	g121	G1
49084	03/10 Crw		9084 -09/49	*49*	g12	G2A
49085	12/01 Crw	01/49	9085 -08/50	*50*	bg121	G1
49086	02/10 Crw		9086 -04/49	*49*	g12	G2A
49087	02/10 Crw	01/50	9087 -09/62	11/62	g12	G2A
49088	02/10 Crw	12/48	9088 -11/57	01/58	g12	G2A
49089	02/10 Crw	01/50	9089 -04/54	*54*	g121	G1
49090	02/04 Crw	12/48	9090 -12/50	*51*	bg12	G2A
49091	04/10 Crw		9091 -09/49	*49*	g1	G1
49092	03/10 Crw	06/48	9092 -09/52	*52*	g1	G1
49093	03/10 Crw	08/48	9093 -11/62	03/63	g12	G2A
49094	03/10 Crw	09/48	9094 -11/62	03/63	g12	G2A
49095	03/10 Crw		9095 -06/48	07/48	g1	G1
49096	03/10 Crw	05/48	9096 -04/52	*05/52*	g12	G2A
49097	04/10 Crw		9097 -03/50	*50*	g12	G2A
49098	04/10 Crw	03/50	9098 -05/51	*51*	g1	G1
49099	05/04 Crw	09/49	9099 -07/62	08/62	bg12	G2A
49100	07/03 Crw		9100 -05/50	*50*	bg1	G1
49101	04/10 Crw	07/49	9101 -09/50	*50*	g12	G2A
49102	04/10 Crw		9102 -07/49	*49*	g1	G1
49103	04/10 Crw		9103 -06/48	07/48	g1	G1
49104	04/10 Crw	11/48	9104 -11/62	11/63	g12	G2A
49105	05/10 Crw	08/48	9105 -11/59	06/60	g12	G2A
49106	05/10 Crw	09/49	9106 -12/62	03/63	g12	G2A
49107	05/10 Crw	06/48	9107 -04/50	*50*	g1	G1
49108	05/10 Crw	11/52	9108 -11/57	01/58	g12	G2A
49109	05/10 Crw	05/50	9109 -03/59	02/60	g12	G2A
49110	05/10 Crw		9110 -03/49	*49*	g12	G2A
49111	05/10 Crw		9111 -03/49	*49*	g12	G2A
49112	06/10 Crw	09/50	9112 -11/59	02/61	g12	G2A
49113	06/10 Crw	07/48	9113 -01/59	02/60	g12	G2A
49114	06/10 Crw	04/51	9114 -11/62	02/63	g12	G2A
49115	06/10 Crw	09/48	9115 -11/59	02/60	g12	G2A
49116	06/10 Crw	11/52	9116 -11/59	04/60	g12	G2A
49117	06/10 Crw	09/50	9117 -03/59	02/60	g12	G2A
49119	06/10 Crw	07/48	9119 -10/61	02/62	g12	G2A
49120	12/02 Crw	09/51	9120 -08/59	09/59	bg12	G2A
49121	07/10 Crw	08/48	9121 -09/58	10/58	g12	G2A
49122	01/04 Crw	10/48	9122 -11/62	02/63	bg12	G2A
49123	07/10 Crw		9123 -06/49	*06/49*	g12	G2A
49124	07/10 Crw		9124 -01/50	*50*	g121	G1
49125	08/10 Crw	02/50	9125 -09/62	10/62	g12	G2A
49126	08/10 Crw	11/48	9126 -09/62	10/62	g12	G2A
49127	08/10 Crw		9127 -03/50	*50*	g12	G2A
49128	08/10 Crw		9128 -11/48	*48*	g1	G1
49129	08/10 Crw	07/52	9129 -11/62	02/63	g12	G2A
49130	08/10 Crw	10/49	9130 -11/62	02/63	g12	G2A
49131	08/10 Crw		9131 -07/48	11/48	g1	G1
49132	05/04 Crw	11/51	9132 -04/59	06/59	bg12	G2A
49133	09/02 Crw		9133 -02/50	*50*	bg1	G1
49134	08/10 Crw	05/49	9134 -04/62	04/62	g12	G2A
49135	08/10 Crw		9135 -11/49	*49*	g1	G1
49136	09/10 Crw		9136 -08/48	09/48	g1	G1
49137	09/10 Crw	12/48	9137 -10/61	05/62	g12	G2A
49138	09/10 Crw	03/50	9138 -02/52	02/52	g12	G2A
49139	09/10 Crw	12/49	9139 -09/62	10/62	g12	G2A
49140	09/10 Crw	12/50	9140 -09/55	10/55	g1	G1
49141	09/10 Crw	08/49	9141 -07/62	09/62	g12	G2A
49142	01/03 Crw	03/50	9142 -12/62	03/63	bg12	G2A
49143	09/10 Crw	05/48	9143 -10/59	11/59	g12	G2A
49144	09/10 Crw	05/50	9144 -11/62	02/63	g12	G2A
49145	04/03 Crw	07/48	9145 -01/58	02/58	bg12	G2A
49146	04/02 Crw	07/50	9146 -02/58	03/58	bg12	G2A
49147	01/03 Crw	05/49	9147 -09/62	10/62	bg12	G2A
49148	09/01 Crw	06/48	9148 -08/57	09/57	bg12	G2A
49149	06/03 Crw	09/48	9149 -11/59	03/61	bg12	G2A
49150	04/03 Crw	08/48	9150 -11/59	02/61	bg12	G2A
49151	02/04 Crw	02/50	9151 -08/52	52	bg1	G1

49152	08/02	Crw		9152	-10/48	10/48	bg1	G1
49153	10/02	Crw	08/48	9153	-11/59	04/61	bg12	G2A
49154	01/10	Crw	07/48	9154	-11/62	02/63	g12	G2A
49155	02/12	Crw	02/51	9155	-06/62	08/62	12	G2A
49156	02/12	Crw	08/49	9156	-02/51	*51*	1	G1
49157	02/12	Crw	12/48	9157	-08/59	02/60	12	G2A
49158	02/12	Crw	04/48	9158	-10/61	05/62	12	G2A
49159	02/12	Crw		9159	-05/49	*49*	1	G1
49160	03/12	Crw	05/50	9160	-11/59	08/60	12	G2A
49161	03/12	Crw	08/49	9161	-04/57	05/57	12	G2A
49162	03/12	Crw	10/50	9162	-05/53	*53*	1	G1
49163	03/12	Crw	06/48	9163	-12/51	*52*	12	G2A
49164	03/12	Crw	12/48	9164	-10/61	02/62	12	G2A
49165	03/12	Crw		9165	-09/48	*10/48*	1	G1
49166	04/12	Crw		9166	-03/49	*49*	1	G1
49167	04/12	Crw	03/50	9167	-12/57	01/58	12	G2A
49168	04/12	Crw	12/48	9168	-01/58	02/58	12	G2A
49169	04/12	Crw		9169	-12/49	*50*	12	G2A
49170	05/12	Crw		9170	-06/49	*49*	12	G2A
49171	05/12	Crw		9171	-02/52	*03/52*	1	G1
49172	04/12	Crw	06/49	9172	-08/57	09/57	12	G2A
49173	04/12	Crw	04/49	9173	-08/64	11/64	12	G2A
49174	05/12	Crw	09/48	9174	-02/58	03/58	12	G2A
49175	05/12	Crw		9175	-01/48	02/48	1	G1
49176	05/12	Crw		9176	-01/50	*50*	12	G2A
49177	05/12	Crw	06/48	9177	-02/59	02/59	12	G2A
49178	06/12	Crw	10/48	9178	-04/51	*51*	12	G2A
49179	06/12	Crw		9179	-12/48	*49*	1	G1
49180	06/12	Crw	12/48	9180	-03/59	02/60	12	G2A
49181	06/12	Crw	06/49	9181	-04/59	02/60	12	G2A
49183	07/12	Crw		9183	-06/50	07/50	1	G1
49184	07/12	Crw		9184	-01/49	*49*	121	G1
49185	10/12	Crw		9185	-04/49	*49*	12	G2A
49186	10/12	Crw	09/49	9186	-09/57	11/57	12	G2A
49187	10/12	Crw	12/50	9187	-02/52	*03/52*	1	G1
49188	10/12	Crw	08/48	9188	-09/49	*49*	12	G2A
49189	10/12	Crw	10/49	9189	-01/57	03/57	12	G2A
49190	11/12	Crw		9190	-02/50	*50*	1	G1
49191	11/12	Crw	07/48	9191	-10/61	02/62	12	G2A
49192	11/12	Crw		9192	-11/49	*49*	12	G2A
49193	12/12	Crw		9193	-11/51	*51*	1	G1
49194	12/12	Crw		9194	-10/49	*49*	1	G1
49195	12/12	Crw		9195	-03/49	*49*	1	G1
49196	12/12	Crw	02/50	9196	-10/61	06/62	12	G2A
49197	12/12	Crw		9197	-05/48	11/48	1	G1
49198	11/12	Crw	12/50	9198	-11/59	02/60	12	G2A
49199	11/12	Crw	10/52	9199	-09/62	11/62	12	G2A
49200	12/12	Crw	06/48	9200	-04/59	05/59	12	G2A
49201	01/13	Crw		9201	-06/48	07/48	1	G1
49202	01/13	Crw	07/48	9202	-10/57	11/57	12	G2A
49203	01/13	Crw	05/51	9203	-11/59	06/60	12	G2A
49204	01/13	Crw	11/49	9204	-04/51	*51*	1	G1
49205	06/13	Crw		9205	-04/51	*51*	12	G2A
49207	07/13	Crw		9207	-07/49	*49*	12	G2A
49208	07/13	Crw		9208	-02/51	*02/51*	1	G1
49209	07/13	Crw	08/48	9209	-10/61	02/62	12	G2A
49210	07/13	Crw	08/50	9210	-10/61	11/61	12	G2A
49211	07/13	Crw		9211	-09/49	*49*	121	G2A 09/48⇔G1
49212	08/13	Crw	12/49	9212	-04/56	*56*	12	G2A
49213	08/13	Crw		9213	-09/51	*51*	1	G1
49214	08/13	Crw	06/48	9214	-08/57	09/57	12	G2A
49216	08/13	Crw	07/48	9216	-11/62	05/63	12	G2A
49217	08/13	Crw		9217	-02/49	*49*	12	G2A
49218	09/13	Crw		9218	-03/51	*51*	12	G2A
49219	09/13	Crw	07/48	9219	-09/50	*50*	12	G2A
49220	09/13	Crw	05/48	9220	-02/50	*50*	12	G2A
49221	09/13	Crw		9221	-09/49	*49*	1	G1
49222	09/13	Crw	06/49	9222	-09/51	*51*	1	G1
49223	09/13	Crw	06/48	9223	-04/57	04/57	12	G2A
49224	10/13	Crw	01/49	9224	-11/62	05/63	12	G2A
49225	03/14	Crw		9225	-03/48	*48*	1	G1
49226	03/14	Crw	06/49	9226	-03/59	02/60	12	G2A
49227	03/14	Crw		9227	-02/49	*49*	12	G2A
49228	04/14	Crw	10/48	9228	-04/59	03/60	12	G2A
49229	04/14	Crw	07/48	9229	-11/60	12/60	12	G2A
49230	04/14	Crw	09/48	9230	-11/57	12/57	12	G2A
49231	03/14	Crw		9231	-02/48	04/48	1	G1
49232	04/14	Crw	04/48	9232	-06/50	*50*	1	G1
49233	04/14	Crw		9233	-05/48	06/48	1	G1
49234	04/14	Crw	02/50	9234	-07/60	08/60	12	G2A
49235	05/14	Crw	08/48	9235	-02/50	*50*	12	G2A
49236	05/14	Crw		9236	-03/48	*48*	1	G1
49237	05/14	Crw		9237	-12/49	*50*	12	G2A
49238	06/14	Crw		9238	-08/49	*49*	12	G2A
49239	05/14	Crw	06/51	9239	-10/57	11/57	12	G2A
49240	06/14	Crw	02/50	9240	-09/62	11/62	12	G2A
49241	05/14	Crw	06/48	9241	-09/52	*52*	1	G1
49242	05/14	Crw		9242	-05/49	06/49	12	G2A
49243	06/14	Crw	08/50	9243	-03/61	03/61	12	G2A
49244	06/14	Crw	05/50	9244	-04/52	*04/52*	12	G2A
49245	06/14	Crw	11/49	9245	-12/59	01/60	12	G2A
49246	07/14	Crw	09/51	9246	-01/62	01/62	12	G2A
49247	07/14	Crw	05/48	9247	-11/57	12/57	12	G2A
49248	07/14	Crw		9248	-05/49	*49*	1	G1
49249	07/14	Crw	04/50	9249	-12/59	01/60	12	G2A
49250	07/14	Crw		9250	-04/48	05/48	1	G1
49251	07/14	Crw		9251	-01/48	02/48	1	G1
49252	08/14	Crw	08/48	9252	-11/59	01/61	12	G2A
49253	08/14	Crw	09/50	9253	-03/52	*04/52*	12	G2A
49254	08/14	Crw	11/51	9254	-04/57	05/57	12	G2A
49255	05/16	Crw		9255	-03/50	*03/50*	1	G1
49256	05/16	Crw		9256	-05/49	*49*	12	G2A
49257	05/16	Crw	01/49	9257	-10/50	*11/50*	12	G2A
49258	05/16	Crw		9258	-03/51	*51*	12	G2A
49259	05/16	Crw		9259	-03/49	*49*	1	G1
49260	05/16	Crw	05/49	9260	-04/58	05/58	12	G2A
49261	05/16	Crw	11/48	9261	-03/51	*51*	1	G1
49262	06/16	Crw	05/48	9262	-12/62	04/63	12	G2A
49263	06/16	Crw		9263	-03/49	*49*	1	G1
49264	06/16	Crw	09/48	9264	-01/51	*51*	12	G2A
49265	10/03	Crw		9265	-04/52	*04/52*	b12	G2A
49266	09/01	Crw	06/48	9266	-11/59	05/60	be12	G2A
49267	09/01	Crw	05/48	9267	-11/62	02/63	be12	G2A
49268	11/17	Crw	04/49	9268	-11/59	08/60	12	G2A
49269	10/17	Crw		9269	-09/49	*49*	1	G1
49270	11/17	Crw	07/52	9270	-11/59	01/61	12	G2A
49271	11/17	Crw	10/48	9271	-11/57	12/57	12	G2A
49272	12/02	Crw		9272	-03/48	*48*	b1	G1
49273	11/03	Crw		9273	-02/48	08/48	b121	G1
49274	10/17	Crw		9274	-04/48	04/48	1	G1
49275	10/17	Crw	05/53	9275	-10/61	11/62	12	G2A
49276	11/17	Crw	11/48	9276	-12/58	03/59	12	G2A
49277	11/17	Crw	02/53	9277	-02/62	02/62	12	G2A
49278	11/17	Crw	05/48	9278	-10/59	11/59	12	G2A
49279	12/17	Crw	09/48	9279	-02/50	*50*	1	G1
49280	01/18	Crw	06/48	9280	-09/49	*49*	12	G2A
49281	01/18	Crw	10/48	9281	-12/62	04/63	12	G2A
49282	01/18	Crw	07/49	9282	-01/51	*51*	12	G2A
49283	01/18	Crw		9283	-06/49	*49*	1	G1
49284	01/18	Crw		9284	-03/50	*50*	12	G2A
49285	02/18	Crw		9285	-08/49	*49*	1	G1
49286	02/18	Crw		9286	-04/48	*48*	1	G1
49287	02/18	Crw	05/49	9287	-11/62	03/63	12	G2A
49288	02/18	Crw	06/48	9288	-10/61	05/62	12	G2A
49289	03/18	Crw	03/49	9289	-11/59	04/60	12	G2A
49290	03/18	Crw		9290	-03/49	*49*	12	G2A
49291	03/18	Crw	05/48	9291	-05/50	*50*	12	G2A
49292	09/03	Crw		9292	-03/51	*51*	b12	G2A
49293	03/18	Crw	12/48	9293	-11/62	04/63	12	G2A
49294	03/18	Crw		9294	-12/49	*50*	12	G2A
49295	04/18	Crw		9295	-08/48	11/48	1	G1
49296	04/18	Crw	04/49	9296	-06/51	*51*	12	G2A
49297	05/18	Crw		9297	-04/49	*49*	1	G1
49298	05/18	Crw	11/48	9298	-12/49	*50*	12	G2A
49299	04/18	Crw	06/48	9299	-07/49	*49*	12	G2A
49300	04/18	Crw	02/50	9300	-11/51	*51*	12	G2A
49301	04/18	Crw	05/49	9301	-03/59	04/59	12	G2A
49302	05/18	Crw		9302	-11/51	01/52	12	G2A
49303	05/18	Crw		9303	-11/48	*48*	1	G1
49304	10/02	Crw	11/51	9304	-12/59	02/60	b12	G2A
49305	05/18	Crw		9305	-04/49	*49*	1	G1
49306	06/18	Crw	09/48	9306	-11/59	10/60	12	G2A
49307	06/18	Crw	04/48	9307	-09/50	*50*	12	G2A
49308	06/18	Crw	10/48	9308	-04/59	03/60	12	G2A
49309	06/18	Crw		9309	-07/48	08/48	1	G1
49310	07/18	Crw	07/48	9310	-10/61	11/62	12	G2A
49311	07/18	Crw	03/50	9311	-10/59	11/59	12	G2A
49312	07/18	Crw		9312	-04/51	*51*	12	G2A
49313	07/18	Crw	05/48	9313	-12/61	01/62	12	G2A
49314	07/18	Crw	08/48	9314	-11/62	04/63	12	G2A
49315	08/18	Crw	08/49	9315	-07/59	09/59	12	G2A
49316	08/18	Crw	11/48	9316	-01/57	05/57	12	G2A
49317	08/18	Crw		9317	-03/50	*03/50*	12	G2A
49318	09/18	Crw	03/50	9318	-11/57	01/58	12	G2A
49319	09/01	Crw		9319	-10/50	*50*	be12	G2A
49320	09/18	Crw		9320	-12/49	*50*	1	G1
49321	09/18	Crw	01/49	9321	-07/60	08/60	12	G2A
49322	09/18	Crw	02/50	9322	-03/56	05/56	12	G2A
49323	10/18	Crw	09/48	9323	-09/62	11/62	12	G2A
49324	12/02	Crw	04/48	9324	-03/50	*50*	b1	G1
49325	11/18	Crw	06/48	9325	-11/49	*49*	12	G2A
49326	10/18	Crw	03/51	9326	-07/53	*53*	1	G1
49327	10/18	Crw	09/49	9327	-11/59	04/60	12	G2A
49328	10/18	Crw	08/49	9328	-11/62	01/63	12	G2A
49329	10/18	Crw		9329	-03/49	*49*	12	G2A
49330	11/18	Crw	12/52	9330	-03/59	03/60	12	G2A
49331	04/04	Crw	12/49	9331	-10/50	*50*	b12	G2A
49332	11/18	Crw	09/48	9332	-07/50	*50*	1	G1
49333	11/18	Crw	12/48	9333	-05/50	*50*	12	G2A
49334	12/18	Crw		9334	-12/50	*51*	1	G1
49335	07/04	Crw	07/50	9335	-10/62	05/63	b12	G2A
49337	04/02	Crw		9337	-07/49	*49*	b12	G1 01/48⇔G2A
49338	05/02	Crw		9338	-04/49	*49*	b1	G1
49339	09/03	Crw	09/48	9339	-12/54	01/55	b12	G2A
49340	11/02	Crw	04/49	9340	-08/59	08/59	be12	G2A
49341	02/04	Crw	01/50	9341	-03/57	05/57	b12	G2A
49342	10/02	Crw	10/48	9342	-10/61	10/62	b12	G2A
49343	05/03	Crw	06/48	9343	-10/61	01/62	be12	G2A
49344	09/01	Crw	07/51	9344	-11/62	03/63	b12	G2A
49345	09/01	Crw	10/50	9345	-02/58	03/58	be12	G2A
49346	04/03	Crw	05/50	9346	-05/52	*52*	b1	G1
49347	09/03	Crw		9347	-01/51	*51*	bg12	G2A
49348	12/01	Crw	12/48	9348	-11/59	04/61	bg12	G2A
49349	09/02	Crw		9349	-12/48	*49*	bef1	G1
49350	01/03	Crw	05/49	9350	-12/62	02/63	b12	G2A
49351	01/03	Crw	06/48	9351	-11/49	*49*	be12	G2A
49352	07/03	Crw	05/48	9352	-09/62	11/62	b12	G2A
49353	01/04	Crw		9353	-12/49	*50*	be1	G1
49354	10/03	Crw	11/49	9354	-03/56	04/56	b12	G2A
49355	10/02	Crw	06/49	9355	-11/59	04/60	b12	G2A
49356	11/03	Crw		9356	-04/50	*50*	b12	G2A
49357	05/04	Crw	05/48	9357	-10/61	08/63	b12	G2A
49358	04/03	Crw	03/50	9358	-04/58	05/58	b12	G2A
49359	05/04	Crw	04/51	9359	-02/52	02/52	be1	G1
49360	10/03	Crw		9360	-05/49	*49*	b12	G2A
49361	09/03	Crw	09/49	9361	-12/64	04/65	b12	G2A
49362	06/03	Crw		9362	-07/48	11/48	b1	G1
49363	01/03	Crw		9363	-03/49	*49*	be12	G2A
49364	11/03	Crw		9364	-12/50	12/50	b1	G1
49365	09/02	Crw		9365	-07/49	*49*	bf12	G2A
49366	10/03	Crw	11/49	9366	-10/59	10/59	b12	G2A
49367	10/02	Crw	11/49	9367	-11/57	12/57	bf12	G2A
49368	12/02	Crw	01/50	9368	-03/59	03/60	be12	G2A
49369	05/04	Crw		9369	-04/50	*50*	b12	G2A
49370	12/01	Crw	06/48	9370	-06/51	*51*	b1	G1
49371	08/04	Crw	08/49	9371	-01/52	02/52	b1	G1
49372	07/04	Crw		9372	-04/49	*49*	be12	G2A
49373	05/03	Crw	10/48	9373	-12/62	01/63	bf12	G2A
49375	04/02	Crw	04/50	9375	-12/62	02/65	b12	G2A
49376	11/02	Crw	01/50	9376	-03/58	04/58	b12	G2A
49377	11/02	Crw	01/51	9377	-10/62	04/63	b12	G2A
49378	01/03	Crw	10/48	9378	-11/59	04/60	b12	G2A
49379	01/04	Crw	06/48	9379	-10/49	*49*	b12	G2A
49381	06/03	Crw	04/49	9381	-11/62	04/63	b12	G2A
49382	12/01	Crw	04/48	9382	-09/62	05/63	b12	G2A
49383	01/04	Crw		9383	-05/48	06/48	b1	G1
49384	07/04	Crw		9384	-12/48	*49*	b1	G1
49385	12/01	Crw	12/52	9385	-12/57	01/58	b12	G2A
49386	05/02	Crw	01/49	9386	-11/59	12/59	bf12	G2A
49387	11/02	Crw	08/49	9387	-11/59	04/60	b12	G2A
49388	04/03	Crw		9388	-03/51	*51*	b12	G2A
49389	06/03	Crw	06/48	9389	-09/54	*54*	b12	G2A
49390	09/01	Crw	08/48	9390	-12/57	12/57	be12	G2A
49391	12/01	Crw	06/48	9391	-01/62	01/62	b12	G2A
49392	08/04	Crw	12/48	9392	-10/61	05/62	b12	G2A
49393	08/04	Crw	09/48	9393	-07/57	07/57	be12	G2A
49394	05/03	Crw	08/50	9394	-10/62	04/63	b12	G2A

7F[3] 49395-49454
0-8-0 LNWR 'G2' Class

Power Classification: 7F
Introduced: 1921-1922
Designer: Beames
Company: LNWR
Weight: Loco 62t 0cwt
Tender 40t 15cwt
Driving Wheel: 4' 5½"
Boiler Pressure: 175psi superheated
Cylinders: Inside 20½" x 24"
Tractive Effort: 28045lbf
Valve Gear: Joy (piston valves)

Beames introduced the 'G2' class in 1921-1922 as described above (see the '48893' class). They were developed from the 'G1' class and were fitted with 175psi superheated boilers, causing them to be classified '7F'. The 'G2A' engines were converted from 'G1' engines to the same design from 1936 onwards.

Many engines were later fitted with Belpaire fireboxes, replacing the original round-topped fireboxes. The 0-8-0s were the LNWR's principal type of heavy freight traffic engine, and the only LNWR type to survive in any great number into BR days. They were unusual in that (along with all the other LNWR classes) they never carried BR style number plates on the front of the smokebox.

Year End Totals: '7F[3]' class

'47	'48	'49	'50	'51	'52	'53	'54	'55	'56	'57	'58	'59	'60	'61	'62	'63	'64	'65	'66	'67
60	60	60	60	60	60	60	60	60	60	60	60	41	41	26	6	3				

Number	Built		Renumbered		BR Dates	Scrap	Notes
49395 §	11/21	Crw	09/50	9395	-11/59		
49396	11/21	Crw	09/50	9396	-11/59	10/60	
49397	11/21	Crw	11/48	9397	-11/59	11/60	
49398	11/21	Crw	10/49	9398	-11/59	10/60	
49399	11/21	Crw	05/50	9399	-10/61	05/62	
49400	11/21	Crw	06/48	9400	-11/59	08/60	
49401	11/21	Crw	05/48	9401	-10/61	12/61	
49402	11/21	Crw	06/49	9402	-11/62	04/63	
49403	11/21	Crw	10/48	9403	-06/62	09/62	
49404	11/21	Crw	03/49	9404	-05/62	06/62	
49405	01/22	Crw	04/50	9405	-10/61	05/62	
49406	01/22	Crw	12/50	9406	-06/63	10/63	
49407	01/22	Crw	08/48	9407	-12/64	03/65	
49408	02/22	Crw	09/48	9408	-11/62	10/63	
49409	02/22	Crw	08/50	9409	-06/59	02/60	

Number	Built	Renumbered	BR Dates	Scrap	Notes
49410	01/22 Crw	06/48 9410	-11/59	03/60	
49411	01/22 Crw	10/48 9411	-10/61	01/62	
49412	01/22 Crw	10/48 9412	-10/61	06/62	
49413	01/22 Crw	08/49 9413	-10/61	11/62	
49414	01/22 Crw	12/49 9414	-10/61	06/62	
49415	01/22 Crw	02/50 9415	-11/62	06/63	
49416	03/22 Crw	12/48 9416	-09/62	09/62	
49417	03/22 Crw	07/53 9417	-11/59	02/60	
49418	03/22 Crw	07/50 9418	-11/59	03/60	
49419	03/22 Crw	01/49 9419	-11/59	04/60	
49420	03/22 Crw	06/50 9420	-11/59	10/60	
49421	03/22 Crw	06/50 9421	-10/61	09/62	
49422	03/22 Crw	08/49 9422	-09/61	10/61	
49423	03/22 Crw	06/49 9423	-11/61	11/61	
49424	03/22 Crw	10/48 9424	-11/59	11/60	
49425	07/22 Crw	10/48 9425	-09/62	05/63	
49426	07/22 Crw	06/48 9426	-09/62	06/63	
49427	07/22 Crw	03/49 9427	-11/59	06/60	
49428	07/22 Crw	05/49 9428	-12/62	08/63	
49429	07/22 Crw	10/48 9429	-11/59	05/60	
49430	07/22 Crw	04/48 9430	-12/64	05/65	
49431	07/22 Crw	05/48 9431	-11/62	02/63	
49432	07/22 Crw	09/49 9432	-11/62	04/63	
49433	07/22 Crw	11/51 9433	-10/61	11/61	
49434	08/22 Crw	10/48 9434	-10/62	05/63	
49435	08/22 Crw	04/48 9435	-11/59	08/60	
49436	08/22 Crw	12/48 9436	-06/59	06/59	
49437	08/22 Crw	01/52 9437	-09/62	09/62	
49438	07/22 Crw	04/48 9438	-11/62	04/63	
49439	09/22 Crw	03/49 9439	-12/62	05/63	
49440	08/22 Crw	04/50 9440	-03/62	04/62	
49441	09/22 Crw	12/51 9441	-10/61	09/62	
49442	10/22 Crw	06/48 9442	-11/59	02/61	
49443	09/22 Crw	04/50 9443	-10/61	11/62	
49444	09/22 Crw	05/51 9444	-10/61	05/62	
49445	09/22 Crw	04/50 9445	-11/59	11/60	
49446	10/22 Crw	09/48 9446	-04/64	07/64	
49447	10/22 Crw	01/49 9447	-11/62	04/63	
49448	10/22 Crw	12/49 9448	-06/63	07/63	
49449	10/22 Crw	04/50 9449	-12/62	07/63	
49450	10/22 Crw	02/51 9450	-11/59	04/60	
49451	10/22 Crw	06/48 9451	-11/62	04/63	
49452	10/22 Crw	10/48 9452	-12/62	06/64	
49453	10/22 Crw	08/48 9453	-10/61	12/61	
49454	10/22 Crw	11/48 9454	-06/63	08/63	

7F [4] 49500-49674
0-8-0 LMS Fowler

Power Classification: 7F
Introduced: 1929-1932
Designer: Fowler
Company: LMS
Weight: Loco 60t 15cwt
Tender 41t 4cwt
Driving Wheel: 4' 8½"
Boiler Pressure: 200psi superheated
Cylinders: Inside 19½" x 26"
Tractive Effort: 29745lbf
Valve Gear: Walschaert (piston valves)

In 1929-1932 Fowler built these one hundred and seventy-five 0-8-0 engines. They were developed from the LNWR 'G2' class (see the '49395' class), carrying the same type of boiler. The Belpaire firebox and chassis however were of purely Midland Railway design, and the engines could be regarded as looking like a Midland 0-8-0 (bearing in mind the fact that the Midland never used anything larger than an 0-6-0 for its freight services).

The boiler pressure was raised to 200psi and the engines were powerful and economical. However they were not fitted with adequate bearing surfaces (as was the Derby practice), and they frequently ran hot and had problems with the motion. As a result they were withdrawn from service long before the LNWR engines they were built to replace.

o Several engines were converted to oil burning as a result of the coal crisis after the end of the Second World War. One was reconverted to coal burning (c) in 1949, the rest being scrapped in the same year without being reconverted.

Year End Totals: '7F [4]' class

'47	'48	'49	'50	'51	'52	'53	'54	'55	'56	'57	'58	'59	'60	'61	'62	'63	'64	'65	'66	'67
175	175	114	77	53	47	43	41	38	32	20	20	9	5	1						

Number	Built	Renumbered	BR Dates	Scrap	Notes
49500	03/29 Crw	12/48 9500	-06/50	50	
49501	03/29 Crw	04/48 9501	-03/50	50	
49502	04/29 Crw	07/48 9502	-06/51	51	
49503	04/29 Crw	08/49 9503	-09/54	54	
49504	04/29 Crw	9504	-04/49	49	
49505	04/29 Crw	06/48 9505	-11/60	12/60	
49506	04/29 Crw	02/50 9506	-10/52	11/52	
49507	04/29 Crw	9507	-04/49	06/49	
49508	05/29 Crw	04/48 9508	-01/62	02/62	
49509	05/29 Crw	12/48 9509	-05/59	12/61	
49510	05/29 Crw	12/49 9510	-09/51	09/51	
49511	05/29 Crw	07/49 9511	-05/59	09/61	o 07/49⇨c
49512	05/29 Crw	9512	-05/49	08/49	
49513	05/29 Crw	04/48 9513	-10/49	49	
49514	05/29 Crw	9514	-08/50	50	
49515	05/29 Crw	01/49 9515	-11/59	08/60	
49516	05/29 Crw	08/48 9516	-08/50	50	
49517	05/29 Crw	9517	-03/49	04/49	
49518	06/29 Crw	9518	-03/49	04/49	
49519	06/29 Crw	08/48 9519	-03/50	03/50	
49520	06/29 Crw	05/48 9520	-05/50	50	
49521	06/29 Crw	9521	-04/49	49	
49522	06/29 Crw	9522	-05/49	49	
49523	06/29 Crw	12/48 9523	-02/51	51	
49524	06/29 Crw	07/48 9524	-12/53	54	
49525	06/29 Crw	05/48 9525	-03/49	49	
49526	06/29 Crw	10/48 9526	-08/49	49	
49527	06/29 Crw	9527	-05/49	06/49	
49528	06/29 Crw	9528	-08/49	49	
49529	06/29 Crw	9529	-01/50	50	
49530	07/29 Crw	9530	-06/49	49	
49531	07/29 Crw	08/48 9531	-10/50	50	
49532	07/29 Crw	10/48 9532	-06/56	56	
49533	07/29 Crw	9533	-07/49	09/49	o
49534	07/29 Crw	9534	-09/49	49	
49535	07/29 Crw	12/48 9535	-11/50	11/50	
49536	07/29 Crw	06/48 9536	-10/57	10/57	
49537	07/29 Crw	04/48 9537	-05/50	50	
49538	07/29 Crw	06/48 9538	-08/57	10/57	
49539	08/29 Crw	11/48 9539	-10/49	49	
49540	08/29 Crw	07/48 9540	-05/51	51	
49541	08/29 Crw	11/48 9541	-07/50	50	
49542	08/29 Crw	9542	-03/49	49	
49543	08/29 Crw	05/49 9543	-08/50	50	
49544	08/29 Crw	07/48 9544	-02/60	02/60	
49545	08/29 Crw	05/48 9545	-07/57	08/57	
49546	08/29 Crw	9546	-10/49	12/49	
49547	08/29 Crw	01/49 9547	-05/57	05/57	
49548	08/29 Crw	06/48 9548	-01/52	52	
49549	08/29 Crw	9549	-04/49	49	
49550	09/29 Crw	9550	-08/49	11/49	
49551	09/29 Crw	12/48 9551	-03/49	04/49	
49552	09/29 Crw	04/49 9552	-08/56	56	
49553	09/29 Crw	04/49 9553	-02/50	50	
49554	09/29 Crw	10/48 9554	-09/55	09/55	
49555	09/29 Crw	06/49 9555	-04/57	05/57	
49556	09/29 Crw	10/48 9556	-04/50	50	
49557	09/29 Crw	09/49 9557	-11/55	55	
49558	09/29 Crw	09/49 9558	-04/51	51	
49559	09/29 Crw	9559	-04/49	49	
49560	09/29 Crw	06/48 9560	-12/57	12/57	
49561	09/29 Crw	09/48 9561	-06/50	50	
49562	09/29 Crw	06/48 9562	-04/49	49	
49563	10/29 Crw	09/49 9563	-06/52	52	
49564	10/29 Crw	07/48 9564	-09/49	49	
49565	10/29 Crw	9565	-03/49	04/49	
49566	10/29 Crw	09/48 9566	-08/57	11/57	
49567	10/29 Crw	03/49 9567	-02/50	50	
49568	10/29 Crw	08/48 9568	-05/51	51	
49569	10/29 Crw	09/48 9569	-01/50	01/50	
49570	10/29 Crw	04/48 9570	-09/55	10/55	
49571	10/29 Crw	12/49 9571	-06/51	51	
49572	11/29 Crw	9572	-09/49	49	
49573	11/29 Crw	9573	-12/49	01/50	
49574	11/29 Crw	10/48 9574	-08/50	50	
49575	11/29 Crw	01/49 9575	-05/50	50	
49576	11/29 Crw	9576	-10/49	49	
49577	11/29 Crw	9577	-03/49	49	
49578	11/29 Crw	03/49 9578	-05/59	05/59	
49579	11/29 Crw	01/49 9579	-06/50	50	
49580	11/29 Crw	05/49 9580	-03/51	51	
49581	11/29 Crw	06/48 9581	-06/49	11/49	
49582	11/29 Crw	01/49 9582	-05/59	09/61	
49583	11/29 Crw	08/48 9583	-08/50	50	
49584	11/29 Crw	05/48 9584	-08/49	49	
49585	11/29 Crw	08/49 9585	-02/51	02/51	
49586	11/29 Crw	05/48 9586	-08/59	09/59	
49587	11/29 Crw	06/48 9587	-06/51	07/51	
49588	12/29 Crw	9588	-12/49	01/50	
49589	12/29 Crw	06/49 9589	-06/51	07/51	
49590	12/29 Crw	08/49 9590	-05/51	05/51	
49591	12/29 Crw	09/48 9591	-12/52	53	
49592	12/29 Crw	05/48 9592	-05/59	09/61	
49593	12/29 Crw	10/48 9593	-05/51	51	
49594	12/29 Crw	08/49 9594	-09/51	51	
49595	12/29 Crw	11/49 9595	-12/51	52	
49596	12/29 Crw	07/48 9596	-04/50	50	
49597	12/29 Crw	9597	-05/49	07/49	
49598	12/29 Crw	12/48 9598	-01/59	02/59	
49599	12/29 Crw	9599	-08/49	49	
49600	12/30 Crw	10/48 9600	-08/53	53	
49601	12/30 Crw	9601	-04/49	49	
49602	12/30 Crw	12/48 9602	-02/54	54	
49603	01/31 Crw	11/49 9603	-03/56	56	
49604	01/31 Crw	9604	-06/49	49	
49605	01/31 Crw	10/48 9605	-02/50	50	
49606	01/31 Crw	9606	-06/49	09/49	
49607	01/31 Crw	05/48 9607	-07/49	49	
49608	02/31 Crw	01/49 9608	-07/53	53	
49609	02/31 Crw	04/49 9609	-10/50	50	
49610	02/31 Crw	03/49 9610	-05/51	51	
49611	02/31 Crw	08/48 9611	-08/49	49	
49612	02/31 Crw	10/48 9612	-08/53	53	
49613	03/31 Crw	9613	-07/49	02/50	o
49614	03/31 Crw	9614	-06/49	08/49	
49615	03/31 Crw	10/48 9615	-04/50	50	
49616	03/31 Crw	9616	-03/49	49	
49617	04/31 Crw	06/48 9617	-06/51	54	
49618	04/31 Crw	03/49 9618	-10/61	11/62	
49619	04/31 Crw	9619	-08/50	50	
49620	10/31 Crw	06/48 9620	-01/56	03/56	
49621	11/31 Crw	9621	-01/50	50	
49622	11/31 Crw	08/48 9622	-07/49	49	
49623	11/31 Crw	10/48 9623	-01/51	01/51	
49624	11/31 Crw	11/48 9624	-02/60	05/60	
49625	11/31 Crw	08/49 9625	-01/51	51	
49626	12/31 Crw	9626	-05/49	49	
49627	12/31 Crw	12/48 9627	-10/61	10/61	
49628	12/31 Crw	11/48 9628	-06/50	50	
49629	12/31 Crw	9629	-05/49	49	
49630	12/31 Crw	11/48 9630	-03/49	49	
49631	12/31 Crw	06/48 9631	-04/51	51	
49632	12/31 Crw	9632	-03/49	09/49	
49633	01/32 Crw	9633	-03/49	49	
49634	12/31 Crw	09/48 9634	-06/50	50	
49635	12/31 Crw	08/48 9635	-11/50	11/50	
49636	01/32 Crw	07/48 9636	-08/50	50	
49637	01/32 Crw	06/48 9637	-06/61	10/61	
49638	01/32 Crw	10/48 9638	-07/56	56	
49639	01/32 Crw	9639	-09/49	12/49	
49640	01/32 Crw	06/48 9640	-05/59	08/61	
49641	01/32 Crw	10/49 9641	-12/50	51	
49642	02/32 Crw	9642	-07/49	02/50	o
49643	02/32 Crw	02/49 9643	-12/49	50	
49644	02/32 Crw	9644	-05/49	49	
49645	02/32 Crw	9645	-12/49	50	
49646	02/32 Crw	9646	-03/49	08/49	
49647	02/32 Crw	07/48 9647	-07/49	09/49	
49648	02/32 Crw	02/50 9648	-09/57	11/57	
49649	02/32 Crw	12/48 9649	-12/50	51	
49650	03/32 Crw	11/49 9650	-05/51	51	
49651	03/32 Crw	03/49 9651	-12/50	51	
49652	03/32 Crw	9652	-09/49	49	
49653	03/32 Crw	10/48 9653	-08/50	50	
49654	03/32 Crw	9654	-12/49	50	
49655	04/32 Crw	08/48 9655	-03/50	50	
49656	04/32 Crw	9656	-09/49	49	
49657	04/32 Crw	09/48 9657	-02/57	02/57	
49658	04/32 Crw	9658	-08/49	49	
49659	04/32 Crw	06/48 9659	-03/57	04/57	
49660	04/32 Crw	02/49 9660	-03/51	04/51	
49661	04/32 Crw	05/48 9661	-01/52	52	
49662	05/32 Crw	05/50 9662	-05/59	04/62	
49663	05/32 Crw	11/48 9663	-04/51	51	
49664	05/32 Crw	11/48 9664	-02/57	02/57	
49665	06/32 Crw	08/48 9665	-08/50	50	
49666	06/32 Crw	10/48 9666	-05/56	56	
49667	06/32 Crw	01/50 9667	-05/59	09/61	
49668	06/32 Crw	08/48 9668	-11/61	08/62	
49669	06/32 Crw	9669	-04/49	08/49	
49670	06/32 Crw	9670	-07/49	09/49	o
49671	06/32 Crw	11/48 9671	-03/52	04/52	
49672	06/32 Crw	01/49 9672	-03/57	05/57	
49673	07/32 Crw	11/49 9673	-02/51	51	
49674	07/32 Crw	09/49 9674	-02/60	02/60	

5P 50412-50455
4-6-0 LYR Hughes

Power Classification: 5P
Introduced: 1908-1909 (rebuilt 1921) and 1921-1925
Designer: Hughes
Company: LYR
Weight: Loco 79t 1cwt
c Loco 77t 18cwt
Driving Wheel: 6' 3"
Boiler Pressure: 180psi superheated
Cylinders: Four 16½" x 26"
c Four 15¾" x 26"
Tractive Effort: 28880lbf
c 26315lbf
Valve Gear: Walschaert with rocking shafts (piston valves)

These 4-6-0s, known as the 'Lanky Dreadnoughts', were the largest class of passenger tender engine on the LYR.

The first twenty engines of the class were built in 1908-1909 and they were not a success. It was not until the last fifteen of these (10405-10419) were rebuilt in 1921 as more modern engines (including superheaters) that the engines performed successfully. 10420-10433 were built to the revised design in 1921. 10434-10454 were also ordered by the LYR, but they were in fact delivered new to the LMS in 1923.

There was also a 4-6-4T version of the class on the LYR (all of which disappeared by 1942). The LMS ordered twenty more of these tank engines, but while they were under construction the order was changed. The frames were cut back and they were delivered as 4-6-0s, being numbered 10455-10474.

One engine (10456) was converted to a four-cylinder compound in 1926, but it was scrapped before 1948. Seven out of the original seventy-five engines survived to come into BR stock, of which only 50455 received its new number. The unrebuilt engines (10400-10405) were withdrawn in 1925-1926, the first of the rebuilt engines going in 1934.

c Some engines of the class had their cylinder diameter reduced.

t The batch numbered 10455-10474 which were originally under construction as tank engines, had a larger wheelbase, and larger fireboxes.

Year End Totals: '5P' class

'47	'48	'49	'50	'51	'52	'53	'54	'55	'56	'57	'58	'59	'60	'61	'62	'63	'64	'65	'66	'67
7	5	2	1																	

Number	*Built*	*Renumbered*	*BR Dates*	*Scrap*	*Notes*
50412	10/08 Hor	10412	-02/49	04/49	
50423	08/21 Hor	10423	-07/48	*48*	
50429	05/22 Hor	10429	-04/48	*04/48*	
50432	12/22 Hor	10432	-03/49	04/49	c
50442	04/23 Hor	10442	-08/50	*50*	c
50448	06/23 Hor	10448	-10/49	*49*	c
50455	06/24 Hor	12/48 10455	-10/51	12/51	t

Rail Motor [1] 50617
0-4-0T LYR Hughes

Power Classification: Unclassified
Introduced: 1906-1911
Designer: Hughes
Company: LYR
Weight: Loco 32t 14cwt
Coach 14t 16cwt
Driving Wheel: 3' 7½"
Boiler Pressure: 160psi
Cylinders: Outside 12" x 16"
Tractive Effort: 7200lbf
Valve Gear: Walschaert

Between 1903 and 1911 many railways in Britain attempted to reduce their costs on branch lines with little traffic by introducing steam railcars (or 'rail motors'). These consisted of a single saloon coach, with a small engine unit (usually an 0-4-0T) forming the bogie at one end. In some designs the engine was detachable, in others the engine was completely enclosed within the body.

Steam railcars were designed to avoid the need for turning at the end of each run. A driving cab was fitted at the other end of the unit which duplicated some of the controls, and there was a bell code system by which the driver could communicate with the fireman.

Hughes built eighteen of these rail motors from 1906-1911, numbered 10600-10617. The engines were detachable from the coaches (although this was only ever done when they were being overhauled), and the coaches carried separate numbers in the coaching stock series.

10617 survived until early 1948, working on the LYR Horwich branch. It was the last rail motor to work in this country. The other members of the class had been withdrawn from 1927 onwards, although 10600 (which was withdrawn in June 1947) was still in the scrap lines at Horwich at the beginning of 1948, and was scrapped at the same time as 10617.

Year End Totals: 'Rail Motor [1]' class

'47	'48	'49	'50	'51	'52	'53	'54	'55	'56	'57	'58	'59	'60	'61	'62	'63	'64	'65	'66	'67
1																				

Number	*Built*	*Renumbered*	*BR Dates*	*Scrap*	*Notes*
50617	12/11 Hor	10617	-03/48	*04/48*	

2P [8] between 50621 & 50899, 10897
2-4-2T LYR Aspinall Class '5'

Power Classification: 2P
Introduced: 1889-1911
Designer: Aspinall
h Hughes
Company: LYR
Weight: 55t 19cwt
bhl 59t 3cwt
Driving Wheel: 5' 8"
Boiler Pressure: 180psi
Cylinders: Inside 18" x 26"
c Inside 17½" x 26"
Tractive Effort: 18955lbf
c 17915lbf
Valve Gear: Joy (slide valves)

The LYR was a very large user of the 2-4-2T type of engine. Designed by Aspinall, 330 of them were built between 1889 and 1911. The general design remained the same but it underwent a number of modifications as listed below.

a Original Aspinall design of 1889 (including 46762).

l Aspinall's second series which were fitted with longer coal bunkers, giving increased coal and water capacity.

h Hughes' development of Aspinall's design, introduced in 1905, with a longer bunker and a Belpaire boiler with an extended smokebox, but still not superheated.

b Many of the Aspinall engines were fitted from 1910 onwards with saturated Belpaire boilers with extended smokeboxes.

c Some engines were built or rebuilt with smaller cylinders.

Many engines were later fitted with superheated Belpaire boilers and as such they became part of the '3P' class (see '50835' class below). Those rebuilt before grouping in 1923 were allocated numbers in the 10900 series, but those rebuilt after 1923 retained their numbers in the 10800 series.

These 'Radial Tanks' did a tremendous amount of hard work over the steeply graded lines of the LYR, not only on local services, but also on main line services. They were fitted with a special type of water pick-up apparatus for picking up water from water troughs in either direction, as they frequently ran tender first.

The first of this class was withdrawn in 1927, and 109 engines came into BR stock. One engine was sold to the Wirral Railway in 1921 and later became 46762. Another engine (10897) was still in existence, although not officially in stock, and was used by the CME's department at Uttoxeter.

Year End Totals: '2P [8]' class

'47	'48	'49	'50	'51	'52	'53	'54	'55	'56	'57	'58	'59	'60	'61	'62	'63	'64	'65	'66	'67
109	100	88	78	70	47	39	37	29	23	20	7	4	3							

Year End Totals: '2P [8]' (misc.) class

'47	'48	'49	'50	'51	'52	'53	'54	'55	'56	'57	'58	'59	'60	'61	'62	'63	'64	'65	'66	'67
1	1	1	1	1	1	1	1	1												

Number	*Built*	*Renumbered*	*BR Dates*	*Scrap*	*Notes*
50621 §	02/89 Hor	03/49 10621	-09/54		a
50622	03/89 Hor	01/50 10622	-08/52	*52*	a
50623	03/89 Hor	11/48 10623	-07/52	07/52	a
50625	05/89 Hor	04/49 10625	-11/52	*52*	a
50630	07/89 Hor	04/48 10630	-10/50	*50*	a
50631	04/90 Hor	10631	-11/48	*48*	a
50633	05/90 Hor	10/49 10633	-07/52	07/52	ab
50634	06/90 Hor	05/49 10634	-10/52	*52*	ac
50636	06/90 Hor	03/49 10636	-08/57	08/57	a
50639	07/90 Hor	09/49 10639	-05/52	*52*	a
50640	07/90 Hor	10/48 10640	-04/52	*06/52*	a
50642	08/90 Hor	05/48 10642	-03/51	*51*	a
50643	08/90 Hor	04/50 10643	-11/58	05/59	ac
50644	08/90 Hor	11/49 10644	-11/58	11/59	a
50646	08/90 Hor	01/49 10646	-11/58	06/59	a
50647	09/90 Hor	09/49 10647	-02/59	11/59	a
50648	04/92 Hor	02/49 10648	-11/55	*55*	a
50650	05/92 Hor	05/49 10650	-09/56	*10/56*	ab
50651	05/92 Hor	03/49 10651	-12/55	*56*	ab
50652	05/92 Hor	10/48 10652	-10/56	*10/56*	abc
50653	05/92 Hor	04/49 10653	-02/56	*02/56*	ac
50654	06/92 Hor	11/48 10654	-04/51	*51*	a
50655	06/92 Hor	02/50 10655	-06/56	*56*	ab
50656	06/92 Hor	09/49 10656	-03/55	*03/55*	abc
50660	07/92 Hor	01/50 10660	-04/58	04/58	a
50665	07/92 Hor	10665	-08/49	08/49	ac
50667	08/92 Hor	10667	-03/48	*48*	ab
50670	08/92 Hor	10670	-04/49	*49*	ab
50671	08/92 Hor	06/49 10671	-03/52	*52*	ab
50675	09/92 Hor	01/49 10675	-12/49	*50*	abc
50676	09/92 Hor	10676	-03/50	*50*	ab
50678	09/92 Hor	08/48 10678	-12/53	*54*	ac
50681	10/92 Hor	02/49 10681	-07/52	*07/52*	a
50686	11/92 Hor	01/50 10686	-09/55	*09/55*	ab
50687	09/93 Hor	08/48 10687	-09/53	*53*	a
50689	09/93 Hor	02/50 10689	-08/52	*52*	a
50692	11/93 Hor	10692	-10/49	*49*	ab
50695	11/93 Hor	05/48 10695	-07/52	*07/52*	a
50696	11/93 Hor	10696	-02/49	*07/49*	a
50697	11/93 Hor	01/50 10697	-05/52	*52*	a
50703	12/93 Hor	06/50 10703	-02/53	*53*	ab
50705	02/95 Hor	01/50 10705	-11/58	05/59	a
50711	03/95 Hor	10711	-06/49	*08/49*	ab
50712	03/95 Hor	06/48 10712	-03/59	07/60	a
50714	03/95 Hor	02/50 10714	-09/53	*53*	ac
50715	03/95 Hor	11/49 10715	-02/55	*55*	ac
50720	05/95 Hor	03/49 10720	-12/51	*52*	a
50721	05/95 Hor	08/49 10721	-01/61	01/61	a
50725	03/96 Hor	12/53 10725	-10/58	07/59	a
50728	03/96 Hor	10728	-08/48	*48*	ab
50731	04/96 Hor	10/49 10731	-10/55	*55*	ab
50732	04/96 Hor	10732	-06/49	*49*	a
50735	04/96 Hor	10735	-06/52	06/52	a
50736	04/96 Hor	10736	-12/51	*52*	ab
50738	05/96 Hor	10738	-07/49	*07/49*	a
50743	06/96 Hor	10743	-06/50	*50*	a
50746	06/96 Hor	12/48 10746	-02/61	03/61	a
50748	06/96 Hor	10748	-09/50	*50*	a
50749	06/96 Hor	12/48 10749	-01/52	*52*	ab
50750	06/96 Hor	10750	-12/49	*50*	a
50752	07/96 Hor	02/49 10752	-08/57	08/57	ac
50755	08/96 Hor	10755	-07/50	*50*	a
50757	08/96 Hor	04/50 10757	-10/58	07/59	a
50762	09/96 Hor	12/48 10762	-12/53	*54*	a
50764	01/97 Hor	07/49 10764	-07/56	*56*	a
50765	01/97 Hor	12/50 10765	-06/54	*54*	a
50766	01/97 Hor	07/48 10766	-08/51	*51*	ac
50777	03/97 Hor	08/50 10777	-10/58	07/59	ab
50778	03/97 Hor	11/49 10778	-02/53	*53*	a
50781	04/97 Hor	06/49 10781	-02/60	07/60	a
50788	04/98 Hor	08/49 10788	-07/56	*56*	a
50793	05/98 Hor	10793	-02/50	*50*	a
50795	05/98 Hor	12/48 10795	-12/59	07/60	ac
50798	05/98 Hor	10798	-07/50	*50*	ab
50799	06/98 Hor	06/51 10799	-08/52	*08/52*	ac
50800	06/98 Hor	10800	-08/48	*48*	abc
50801	06/98 Hor	10801	-12/48	*49*	a
50802	06/98 Hor	08/48 10802	-07/52	*07/52*	a
50804	07/98 Hor	10804	-02/50	*50*	ac
50806	07/98 Hor	09/48 10806	-02/52	*52*	a
50807	07/98 Hor	04/52 10807	-05/55	*55*	ac
50812	08/98 Hor	11/48 10812	-05/52	*52*	a
50813	08/98 Hor	10813	-05/49	*49*	a
50815	08/98 Hor	10815	-02/51	*51*	abc
50818	09/98 Hor	07/49 10818	-10/58	07/59	a
50823	10/98 Hor	10823	-12/48	*49*	lb
50829	11/98 Hor	05/48 10829	-04/58	04/58	lb
50831	11/98 Hor	01/51 10831	-10/58	07/59	l

Class continued with 50840

3P [3] between 50835 & 50953
2-4-2T LYR Aspinall/Hughes Class '6'

Power Classification: 3P
Introduced: 1898 onwards.
Rebuilt 1912 onwards
s 1911
Designer: Aspinall and Hughes
Company: LYR
Weight: 60t 5cwt
w 66t 9cwt
Driving Wheel: 5' 8"
Boiler Pressure: 180psi superheated
Cylinders: Inside 20½" x 26"
c Inside 19½" x 26"
Tractive Effort: 24585lbf
c 22245lbf
Valve Gear: Joy (piston valves)

In 1911 Hughes built twenty engines which were developed from Aspinall's '2P' '50621' class, but which were fitted with superheated Belpaire boilers. The original engines were numbered 10900-10919 and from 1912 onwards many more engines were rebuilt from the earlier class. Those rebuilt before 1923 were renumbered 10920-10954, and several more in the 10800 series were rebuilt after 1923 without being renumbered.

Twenty engines were built new and forty-four were rebuilt. The first engine was withdrawn in 1928.

a Rebuilt from original Aspinall engines with short bunkers (nine engines, none of which came into BR stock).

l Rebuilt from Aspinall engines with longer bunkers.

h Rebuilt from Hughes engines with longer bunkers.

s Original Hughes design with long bunkers and superheated Belpaire boilers with extended smokeboxes.

c Some engines were built or rebuilt with smaller cylinders.

w 50909 was heavier than the other engines.

Year End Totals: '3P 3' class

'47	'48	'49	'50	'51	'52	'53	'54	'55	'56	'57	'58	'59	'60	'61	'62	'63	'64	'65	'66	'67
14	7	6	2	1																

Number	Built	Renumbered	BR Dates	Scrap	Notes
50835	12/98 Hor	10835	-08/48	*48*	l

Class continued with 50891

2P 8 between 50621 & 50899, 10897
2-4-2T LYR Aspinall Class '5'

Class continued from 50831

Number	Built	Renumbered	BR Dates	Scrap	Notes
50840	06/99 Hor	05/49 10840	-02/52	*52*	lb
50842	07/99 Hor	09/49 10842	-08/51	*51*	l
50844	08/99 Hor	10844	-09/50	*50*	l
50849	09/99 Hor	10849	-02/50	*50*	lb
50850	09/99 Hor	05/50 10850	-10/61	12/61	lb
50852	10/00 Hor	04/48 10852	-01/53	*53*	l
50855	11/00 Hor	06/50 10855	-10/58	07/59	lc
50859	12/00 Hor	01/49 10859	-11/53	*53*	l
50865	01/01 Hor	10/50 10865	-10/58	06/59	lc
50869	02/01 Hor	11/48 10869	-10/55	*55*	l
50872	04/05 Hor	06/48 10872	-03/52	*52*	h
50873	05/05 Hor	12/48 10873	-03/52	*52*	h
50875	05/05 Hor	10875	-05/48	*48*	h
50880	06/05 Hor	10880	-10/49	*49*	h
50886	09/05 Hor	05/48 10886	-12/51	*52*	h
50887	10/05 Hor	09/51 10887	-12/57	12/57	h
50889	01/10 Hor	10889	-10/49	*49*	h

Class continued with 50892

3P 3 between 50835 & 50953
2-4-2T LYR Aspinall/Hughes Class '6'

Class continued from 50835

Number	Built	Renumbered	BR Dates	Scrap	Notes
50891	02/10 Hor	08/48 10891	-03/50	*50*	h

Class continued with 50893

2P 8 between 50621 & 50899, 10897
2-4-2T LYR Aspinall Class '5'

Class continued from 50889

Number	Built	Renumbered	BR Dates	Scrap	Notes
50892	03/10 Hor	10892	-06/52	07/52	h

Class continued with 50896

3P 3 between 50835 & 50953
2-4-2T LYR Aspinall/Hughes Class '6'

Class continued from 50891

Number	Built	Renumbered	BR Dates	Scrap	Notes
50893	03/10 Hor	11/48 10893	-04/50	*50*	h

Class continued with 50901

2P 8 between 50621 & 50899, 10897
2-4-2T LYR Aspinall Class '5'

Class continued from 50892

Number	Built	Renumbered	BR Dates	Scrap	Notes
50896	03/10 Hor	10896	-12/48	*49*	h
50898	04/10 Hor	09/48 10898	-02/52	*52*	h
50899	04/10 Hor	10899	-10/48	*48*	h

Class continued with 10897 (Miscellaneous Locomotives)

3P 3 between 50835 & 50953
2-4-2T LYR Aspinall/Hughes Class '6'

Class continued from 50893

Number	Built	Renumbered	BR Dates	Scrap	Notes
50901	03/11 Hor	10901	-03/48	*04/48*	s
50903	03/11 Hor	10903	-02/48	*03/48*	sc
50909	05/11 Hor	02/51 10909	-03/51	*51*	sw
50925	03/10 Hor	09/48 10925	-08/52	10/52	hc
50934	02/10 Hor	10934	-08/48	*48*	h
50943	12/00 Hor	10943	-12/48	*49*	lc
50945	04/10 Hor	10945	-01/49	*49*	h
50950	12/98 Hor	10950	-08/48	*48*	lc
50951	08/99 Hor	10951	-01/50	*50*	l
50952	11/98 Hor	10952	-06/48	*48*	lc
50953	10/98 Hor	04/48 10953	-04/50	*50*	l

0F 4 51202-51253
0-4-0ST LYR Aspinall Pug Class '21'

Power Classification:	0F
Introduced:	1891-1910
Designer:	Aspinall
Company:	LYR
Weight:	21t 5cwt
Driving Wheel:	3' 0⅜"
Boiler Pressure:	160psi
Cylinders:	Outside 13" x 18"
Tractive Effort:	11335lbf
Valve Gear:	Stephenson (slide valves)

Aspinall built fifty-seven of these small saddle tanks for the LYR in batches between 1891 and 1910. They were based on a small class of three engines built by the Vulcan Foundry in 1886. Known as 'Pugs', they were designed for dock shunting work. The first engines were withdrawn in 1927, and twenty-three came into BR stock.

The engines had outside cylinders, but they were fitted with inside Stephenson valve gear. No coal bunkers were fitted, the coal being carried inside the cab side sheets. They had disc wheels, covered in slide bars, and were fitted with dumb buffers (wooden buffers).

Some engines of this class were based in Liverpool docks and they were fitted with simple spark arrestors.

In addition to 51218 which has been preserved, LYR No. 19 (LMS 11243 which was sold out of service in 1931) has also been preserved.

c 51204 retained a low cab roof and a cut down chimney which were fitted when it worked at Maryport in 1929.

Year End Totals: '0F 4' class

'47	'48	'49	'50	'51	'52	'53	'54	'55	'56	'57	'58	'59	'60	'61	'62	'63	'64	'65	'66	'67
23	23	23	23	23	23	23	23	23	22	19	16	15	13	10	4	1				

Number	Built	Renumbered	BR Dates	Scrap	Notes
51202	11/91 Hor	06/48 11202	-01/58	02/58	
51204	12/91 Hor	10/48 11204	-09/62	12/62	c
51206	12/91 Hor	06/49 11206	-09/62	11/62	
51207	12/93 Hor	09/50 11207	-03/62	07/62	
51212	01/94 Hor	08/49 11212	-08/57	10/57	
51216	12/95 Hor	12/49 11216	-12/56	*57*	
51217	12/95 Hor	04/50 11217	-11/61	11/61	
51218 §	10/01 Hor	04/49 11218	-09/64		
51221	11/01 Hor	11/50 11221	-01/60	02/60	
51222	12/01 Hor	02/50 11222	-03/62	04/62	
51227	12/01 Hor	08/50 11227	-09/60	11/60	
51229	12/05 Hor	02/50 11229	-01/61	03/61	
51230	01/06 Hor	11/48 11230	-12/58	12/58	
51231	01/06 Hor	10/49 11231	-06/59	08/59	
51232	02/06 Hor	05/49 11232	-06/63	08/63	
51234	02/06 Hor	08/49 11234	-10/57	10/57	
51235	02/06 Hor	06/49 11235	-11/58	12/58	
51237	03/06 Hor	01/49 11237	-05/63	07/63	
51240	05/10 Hor	10/48 11240	-04/57	*57*	
51241	05/10 Hor	03/51 11241	-01/62	01/62	
51244	05/10 Hor	05/51 11244	-03/62	04/62	
51246	06/10 Hor	12/48 11246	-10/61	12/61	
51253	06/10 Hor	08/50 11253	-07/63	07/63	

2F 2 51307-51530, 11304-11394
0-6-0ST LYR Aspinall Rebuilt Saddle Tank Class '23'

Power Classification:	2F
Introduced:	1876-1887 Rebuilt by Aspinall 1891-1900
Designer:	Barton Wright
Company:	LYR
Weight:	43t 17cwt
Driving Wheel:	4' 6"
Boiler Pressure:	140psi
Cylinders:	Inside 17½" x 26"
Tractive Effort:	17545lbf
Valve Gear:	Stephenson (slide valves)

These saddle tanks must rate as one of the most successful and simplest rebuildings ever.

When Aspinall became CME at Horwich, he produced his own class of 0-6-0, the '3F' '52088' class. These engines replaced the earlier Barton Wright 0-6-0s (the '2F' '52016' class). At the same time the LYR had an acute shortage of shunting engines, so Aspinall set about rebuilding his predecessor's 0-6-0s ('2F' '52016' class) as saddle tanks.

The rebuilt engines proved to be successful, and a total of 230 were rebuilt, between 1891 and 1900, leaving only fifty engines in their original form. The only visible sign of the fact that these engines had been rebuilt was the curved rear steps, which originally matched the steps on the tender.

The engines in departmental stock (11304-11394) were all based at Horwich Works. They retained their original LMS numbers and they were never renumbered. Four other engines (51429 at Horwich and 51412, 51444 and 51446 at Crewe) also later worked in the departmental stock as works shunters, but they retained their BR numbers.

Withdrawal of the class began in 1926 and ninety-six (plus the five departmental engines) came into BR stock in 1948. 11456 was sold by the LMS in 1937 to a colliery near Wigan. In 1967 it was purchased from the NCB and has now been preserved with its former LYR number, 752. 11305 (built in 1877) was the last of the class to be withdrawn and it was for a short time in 1964 the oldest engine working on BR.

Year End Totals: '2F 2' class

'47	'48	'49	'50	'51	'52	'53	'54	'55	'56	'57	'58	'59	'60	'61	'62	'63	'64	'65	'66	'67
96	90	79	79	79	79	76	70	61	45	31	25	16	10	3						

Year End Totals: '2F 2' (service) class

'47	'48	'49	'50	'51	'52	'53	'54	'55	'56	'57	'58	'59	'60	'61	'62	'63	'64	'65	'66	'67
5	5	5	5	5	5	5	5	5	5	5	5	5	4	3	3	1				

Number	Built	Renumbered	BR Dates	Scrap	Notes
51307	03/77 K	10/48 11307	-11/57	01/58	
51313	07/77 K	04/48 11313	-10/56	*56*	
51316	03/77 K	09/49 11316	-01/59	09/60	
51318	04/77 K	11318	-02/49	*49*	
51319	09/77 SS	02/49 11319	-11/59	12/59	
51320	11/77 SS	11320	-04/48	*48*	
51321	07/77 K	08/48 11321	-02/58	02/58	
51323	10/77 SS	07/48 11323	-05/56	*56*	
51325	08/77 SS	11325	-03/49	04/49	
51336	07/77 SS	09/49 11336	-11/60	11/60	
51338	10/77 SS	10/50 11338	-08/57	08/57	
51342	04/79 Mlsp	11342	-09/48	*48*	
51343	02/78 K	07/48 11343	-01/60	02/60	
51345	12/78 Mlsp	09/49 11345	-09/56	*56*	
51348	10/78 K	10/48 11348	-08/53	*53*	
51353	10/78 K	06/50 11353	-07/57	08/57	
51358	02/78 K	11/49 11358	-11/59	11/59	
51361	02/78 K	07/48 11361	-10/56	*56*	
51371	10/78 K	11/50 11371	-03/61	04/61	
51375	01/80 K	10/50 11375	-09/54	10/54	
51376	09/80 K	06/50 11376	-04/55	*55*	
51379	12/79 K	04/49 11379	-04/55	*55*	
51381	01/80 K	04/50 11381	-11/57	12/57	
51390	03/82 BP	04/50 11390	-07/56	*56*	
51396	09/81 BP	05/50 11396	-02/56	*03/56*	
51397	09/80 VF	12/49 11397	-03/59	08/60	
51400	03/83 VF	11400	-11/49	*49*	
51404	01/83 VF	11/48 11404	-03/59	08/60	
51405	09/80 K	11405	-12/48	*49*	
51408	02/80 K	03/49 11408	-02/62	09/62	
51410	06/80 Mlsp	05/48 11410	-04/54	*54*	

LMS Stanier '8F' 2-8-0 No 48774 at Polmadie depot in Glasgow in 1964.

LNWR 'G2A' class 0-8-0 No 49006 at Birkenhead shed in October 1949.

LNWR Bowen Cooke 'G2' class 0-8-0 No 49402, fitted with a tender cab, in Crewe Works in February 1950.

LYR Aspinall Class 5 2-4-2T No 50636 at Bradford Forster Square in April 1950.

Number	Built		Renumbered		BR Dates	Scrap	Notes
51412	03/81	BP	10/48	11412	-09/62	10/62	
51413	04/81	BP	09/48	11413	-08/61	11/61	
51415	08/80	Mlsp	10/49	11415	-11/58	07/60	
51419	05/80	K	11/49	11419	-09/61	12/61	
51423	03/81	VF	06/48	11423	-12/58	07/60	
51424	04/81	VF	12/49	11424	-10/58	08/59	
51425	03/80	Mlsp	04/48	11425	-07/56	*56*	
51427	09/80	VF		11427	-11/48	*48*	
51429	02/82	BP	02/49	11429	-05/61	11/61	
51432	03/81	BP	03/49	11432	-08/57	08/57	
51436	11/81	BP	10/48	11436	-03/55	04/55	
51438	09/80	K		11438	-04/49	*08/49*	
51439	12/82	VF	08/49	11439	-06/56	*56*	
51441	01/83	VF	12/48	11441	-03/61	04/61	
51443	01/82	BP		11443	-05/49	*08/49*	
51444	07/81	Mlsp	01/50	11444	-09/61	09/61	
51445	04/81	VF	03/50	11445	-06/60	08/60	
51446	03/81	BP	09/48	11446	-02/62	03/62	
51447	04/81	BP	09/48	11447	-01/57	02/57	
51453	01/83	VF	10/49	11453	-10/58	09/59	
51457	02/82	BP	12/48	11457	-03/59	08/60	
51458	06/80	Mlsp	04/50	11458	-05/59	09/61	
51460	05/81	VF	05/49	11460	-09/54	10/54	
51462	10/80	VF	05/48	11462	-10/56	*56*	
51464	10/81	BP	05/49	11464	-09/56	*10/56*	
51467	01/82	BP		11467	-11/48	*48*	
51468	06/81	BP		11468	-01/49	*49*	
51469	11/81	BP		11469	-05/49	*08/49*	
51470	05/81	VF	09/50	11470	-10/55	12/55	
51471	10/80	VF	06/49	11471	-10/54	10/54	
51472	04/81	VF	04/50	11472	-04/55	*55*	
51474	09/80	K	05/48	11474	-06/57	08/57	
51475	03/83	VF		11475	-11/49	*49*	
51477	03/85	K	07/48	11477	-08/55	*08/55*	
51479	04/85	K	01/49	11479	-09/56	*10/56*	
51481	01/81	Mlsp	07/49	11481	-11/57	11/57	
51482	03/85	K		11482	-10/49	*49*	
51484	03/82	BP	07/50	11484	-06/59	07/59	
51486	04/81	VF	12/50	11486	-09/60	10/60	
51487	12/82	VF		11487	-10/48	*48*	
51488	03/85	K	11/48	11488	-03/56	*03/56*	
51489	02/80	Mlsp	02/49	11489	-02/54	*54*	
51490	04/83	VF	09/50	11490	-08/53	*53*	
51491	04/85	K	03/50	11491	-02/57	05/57	
51492	01/82	BP		11492	-07/49	08/49	
51495	09/81	BP		11495	-04/49	08/49	
51496	03/85	K	08/50	11496	-03/61	04/61	
51497	04/81	VF	02/49	11497	-05/59	09/61	
51498	04/85	K	09/50	11498	-11/60	01/61	
51499	10/81	BP	05/48	11499	-06/57	08/57	
51500	10/80	VF	05/48	11500	-02/57	02/57	
51503	03/82	BP	05/49	11503	-04/57	05/57	
51504	05/85	K	11/48	11504	-07/56	*56*	
51506	04/85	K	07/49	11506	-05/57	05/57	
51510	04/83	VF	09/49	11510	-10/55	*55*	
51511	09/81	Mlsp	09/50	11511	-10/55	11/55	
51512	02/82	BP	07/48	11512	-07/58	08/60	
51513	05/81	BP	01/49	11513	-05/56	*56*	
51514	04/83	VF	08/50	11514	-11/53	*53*	
51516	05/85	K	07/50	11516	-10/56	*56*	
51519	03/85	K	10/50	11519	-09/54	*54*	
51521	08/80	VF	10/49	11521	-10/56	*56*	
51524	02/83	VF	04/48	11524	-09/60	01/61	
51526	09/81	BP	09/48	11526	-09/57	10/57	
51530	03/81	BP	01/50	11530	-11/55	*55*	

Class continued with 11304 (Service Locomotives)

1F [3] 51535-51546
0-6-0T LYR Aspinall Dock Tank Class '24'

Power Classification: 1F
Introduced: 1897
Designer: Aspinall
Company: LYR
Weight: 50t 0cwt
Driving Wheel: 4' 0"
Boiler Pressure: 140psi
Cylinders: Outside 17" x 24"
Tractive Effort: 17195lbf
Valve Gear: Allan straight link (slide valves)

In 1897 Aspinall built twenty engines of this class for dock shunting. They were compact looking engines and they were among the first British locomotives to be fitted with Belpaire boilers.

From 1917 onwards the engines were rebuilt with round topped boilers. The first of the class was withdrawn in 1917 and five came into BR stock in 1948. They were based at Liverpool docks and were fitted with simple spark deflectors.

11537 was the last engine in the whole LMS group to receive its BR number, not being renumbered 51537 until September 1954.

d 51535 was fitted with dumb (wooden) buffers.

Year End Totals: '1F [3]' class

'47	'48	'49	'50	'51	'52	'53	'54	'55	'56	'57	'58	'59	'60	'61	'62	'63	'64	'65	'66	'67
5	5	5	5	5	5	4	4	4	3	3	3	1	1							

Number	Built		Renumbered		BR Dates	Scrap	Notes
51535	09/97	Hor	02/50	11535	-08/56	*10/56*	d
51536	09/97	Hor	12/49	11536	-12/53	01/54	
51537	10/97	Hor	09/54	11537	-09/61	12/61	
51544	11/97	Hor	05/49	11544	-06/59	07/59	
51546	12/97	Hor	09/49	11546	-01/59	08/60	

2F [3] 52016-52064
0-6-0 LYR Barton Wright Class '25'

Power Classification: 2F
Introduced: 1876-1887
(all survivors built 1887)
Designer: Barton Wright
Company: LYR
Weight: Loco 39t 1cwt
Driving Wheel: 4' 6"
Boiler Pressure: 140psi
Cylinders: Inside 17½" x 26"
Tractive Effort: 17545lbf
Valve Gear: Stephenson (slide valves)

Barton Wright introduced his standard 0-6-0 in 1876 and a total of 280 were built up to 1887. When Aspinall built his 0-6-0s in 1889, many of these engines became surplus to requirements and all except the last fifty were rebuilt as saddle tanks (see '51307' class).

The engines were withdrawn from 1930 onwards and twenty-five of the unrebuilt fifty survived to come into BR stock.

Year End Totals: '2F [3]' class

'47	'48	'49	'50	'51	'52	'53	'54	'55	'56	'57	'58	'59	'60	'61	'62	'63	'64	'65	'66	'67
25	20	19	14	11	9	8	6	3	1	1	1									

Number	Built		Renumbered		BR Dates	Scrap	Notes
52016	08/87	VF	04/48	12016	-10/56	*10/56*	
52019	09/87	VF	04/48	12019	-09/49	*49*	
52021	09/87	VF	04/48	12021	-09/55	*09/55*	
52022	09/87	VF	04/48	12022	-09/50	*50*	
52023	10/87	VF	04/48	12023	-04/50	*50*	
52024	10/87	VF	04/48	12024	-05/54	*54*	
52030	11/87	VF	04/48	12030	-10/52	*52*	
52031	11/87	VF	04/48	12031	-12/54	*55*	
52032	11/87	VF		12032	-01/48	*48*	
52034	12/87	VF	04/48	12034	-09/51	*51*	
52036	07/87	BP	04/48	12036	-11/48	*48*	
52037	07/87	BP	04/48	12037	-08/52	*52*	
52041	08/87	BP	04/48	12041	-10/50	*50*	
52043	08/87	BP	04/48	12043	-08/53	*53*	
52044 §	08/87	BP	04/48	12044	-06/59		
52045	08/87	BP	04/48	12045	-08/55	*08/55*	
52046	08/87	BP		12046	-02/48	*48*	
52047	08/87	BP	04/48	12047	-01/50	*50*	
52049	09/87	BP	04/48	12049	-10/48	*48*	
52051	09/87	BP	04/48	12051	-02/56	03/56	
52053	09/87	BP	04/48	12053	-03/55	03/55	
52056	10/87	BP	04/48	12056	-08/51	*51*	
52059	11/87	BP	09/48	12059	-05/51	*51*	
52063	12/87	BP	04/48	12063	-09/48	*48*	
52064	12/87	BP	04/48	12064	-12/50	*51*	

3F [7] between 52088 & 52529
0-6-0 LYR Aspinall Class '27'

Power Classification: 3F
Introduced: 1889-1918
Designer: Aspinall
Company: LYR
Weight: Loco 42t 3cwt
b Loco 43t 11cwt
Driving Wheel: 5' 1"
Boiler Pressure: 180psi
Cylinders: Inside 18" x 26"
Tractive Effort: 21130lbf
Valve Gear: Joy (slide valves)

Aspinall introduced the '27' class in 1889 for freight work on the LYR. They were built over a long period until 1918, when 468 engines had been built by Aspinall and his successors Hoy and Hughes. The first engine was withdrawn in 1931 and 245 came into BR stock.

In such a large class there was inevitably a large number of variations, particularly in the boilers. These are described below.

a These engines were the original Aspinall built engines of 1889. They were originally built with round-topped, saturated boilers.

h These were Hughes built engines, constructed from 1906 onwards. 52461-52467 were built in 1917-1918, reputedly from spare parts left over after the rest of the class had been constructed.

s 52515 was rebuilt from an Aspinall engine and 52517-52529 were built new as superheated engines with round topped fireboxes and extended smokeboxes in 1909 by Hughes. The survivors were later rebuilt with saturated boilers and short smokeboxes.

b Many engines were rebuilt with Belpaire boilers and extended smokeboxes from 1911 onwards.

In 1912 Hughes introduced a superheated version of the class with Belpaire boilers and extended smokeboxes (see the '52528' class). Many of the saturated boiler engines were rebuilt from 1913 onwards, becoming 52528 and 52557-52619.

Year End Totals: '3F [7]' class

'47	'48	'49	'50	'51	'52	'53	'54	'55	'56	'57	'58	'59	'60	'61	'62	'63	'64	'65	'66	'67
245	233	221	219	191	184	166	150	136	118	89	75	58	32	16						

Number	Built		Renumbered		BR Dates	Scrap	Notes
52088	11/89	Hor	07/48	12088	-06/51	*51*	ab
52089	12/89	Hor	05/48	12089	-11/60	01/61	a
52091	01/90	Hor	03/50	12091	-07/53	*53*	ab
52092	01/90	Hor	07/48	12092	-02/51	*51*	a
52093	02/90	Hor	07/48	12093	-09/62	10/62	a
52094	02/90	Hor	02/49	12094	-05/57	05/57	ab
52095	02/90	Hor	06/48	12095	-11/59	12/59	a
52098	10/90	Hor	06/49	12098	-10/53	*53*	a
52099	10/90	Hor	09/49	12099	-01/56	02/56	a
52100	10/90	Hor	12/48	12100	-09/51	*51*	a
52102	11/90	Hor	04/50	12102	-01/53	*53*	a
52103	11/90	Hor		12103	-05/49	*08/49*	a
52104	11/90	Hor	02/49	12104	-03/56	03/56	ab
52105	11/90	Hor	12/49	12105	-05/53	*53*	a
52107	12/90	Hor	06/48	12107	-02/53	*53*	a
52108	12/90	Hor	03/49	12108	-10/59	12/59	a
52110	12/90	Hor		12110	-05/50	*50*	ab
52111	12/90	Hor	04/48	12111	-03/51	*51*	a
52112	01/91	Hor	01/49	12112	-09/51	*51*	a
52118	04/91	Hor	08/48	12118	-09/54	*54*	a
52119	04/91	Hor	01/51	12119	-10/62	05/63	a
52120	04/91	Hor	08/49	12120	-07/58	07/59	a
52121	05/91	Hor	11/50	12121	-11/62	12/62	a
52123	05/91	Hor	04/52	12123	-09/57	10/57	a
52124	05/91	Hor	11/50	12124	-01/54	*54*	a
52125	05/91	Hor	02/49	12125	-11/57	04/58	a
52126	06/91	Hor	07/48	12126	-05/51	*51*	a
52127	06/91	Hor		12127	-06/48	*48*	a
52129	06/91	Hor	04/50	12129	-09/61	10/61	a
52132	10/91	Hor	04/50	12132	-03/57	05/57	ab
52133	10/91	Hor	04/48	12133	-12/60	02/61	a
52135	10/91	Hor	08/48	12135	-11/59	11/59	ab
52136	10/91	Hor	09/48	12136	-09/57	09/57	a
52137	10/91	Hor	11/48	12137	-07/54	*54*	a
52138	11/91	Hor	11/49	12138	-03/54	*54*	a
52139	11/91	Hor	10/48	12139	-02/60	11/60	a
52140	11/91	Hor	01/50	12140	-07/60	07/60	ab
52141	11/91	Hor	01/49	12141	-05/60	06/60	a
52143	12/91	Hor	06/48	12143	-11/57	04/58	a
52150	01/92	Hor	12/49	12150	-03/55	*03/55*	a
52152	02/92	Hor		12152	-03/48	*48*	a
52154	02/92	Hor	12/48	12154	-11/60	01/61	ab
52156	03/92	Hor	03/50	12156	-02/53	*53*	a
52157	03/92	Hor	12/48	12157	-04/53	*53*	a
52159	03/92	Hor	04/50	12159	-06/58	07/58	a
52160	03/92	Hor	04/48	12160	-07/57	08/57	a
52161	04/92	Hor	03/50	12161	-10/60	10/60	ab
52162	04/92	Hor	05/51	12162	-04/60	04/60	ab
52163	04/92	Hor	08/48	12163	-09/57	07/58	a
52164	04/92	Hor	04/50	12164	-06/55	*55*	a
52165	04/92	Hor	03/49	12165	-04/57	05/57	a
52166	11/92	Hor	09/48	12166	-10/56	*56*	a
52167	12/92	Hor	04/49	12167	-03/56	*56*	a
52169	12/92	Hor	06/49	12169	-12/52	*53*	a
52170	12/92	Hor		12170	-09/48	*48*	a
52171	12/92	Hor	04/48	12171	-05/61	06/61	a
52172	01/93	Hor	09/48	12172	-11/57	12/57	a
52174	01/93	Hor	07/50	12174	-09/54	10/54	a
52175	01/93	Hor	06/48	12175	-10/57	04/58	a
52176	02/93	Hor	04/49	12176	-11/51	*51*	a
52177	02/93	Hor	10/48	12177	-12/56	*57*	a
52179	02/93	Hor	03/51	12179	-08/60	11/60	a

Number	Built	Renumbered	BR Dates	Scrap	Notes
52181	02/93 Hor	12181	-06/49	*08/49*	a
52182	02/93 Hor	06/51 12182	-05/61	06/61	a
52183	02/93 Hor	11/48 12183	-11/59	10/61	a
52184	03/93 Hor	06/48 12184	-12/49	*50*	a
52186	03/93 Hor	06/49 12186	-08/57	08/57	a
52189	03/93 Hor	08/48 12189	-09/54	*54*	a
52191	04/93 Hor	05/48 12191	-12/51	*12/51*	ab
52192	04/93 Hor	12192	-11/49	*49*	ab
52194	04/93 Hor	08/49 12194	-08/55	*08/55*	a
52196	05/93 Hor	04/50 12196	-01/57	03/57	a
52197	05/93 Hor	05/50 12197	-09/56	*10/56*	ab
52201	05/93 Hor	08/48 12201	-02/61	03/61	ab
52203	06/93 Hor	05/52 12203	-03/57	04/57	a
52207	07/93 Hor	07/48 12207	-05/61	05/61	a
52208	07/93 Hor	12208	-11/50	*50*	a
52212	07/93 Hor	02/49 12212	-09/58	03/59	a
52215	08/93 Hor	03/51 12215	-03/55	03/55	a
52216	09/93 Hor	08/48 12216	-12/58	11/59	a
52217	08/93 Hor	06/49 12217	-07/57	08/57	a
52218	09/93 Hor	11/48 12218	-05/62	06/62	a
52219	09/93 Hor	12219	-04/51	*51*	a
52220	04/94 Hor	03/50 12220	-02/55	03/55	a
52225	05/94 Hor	12/48 12225	-12/60	12/60	a
52229	06/94 Hor	12229	-07/49	*08/49*	a
52230	06/94 Hor	11/48 12230	-04/61	04/61	a
52231	06/94 Hor	02/49 12231	-10/52	*01/53*	a
52232	06/94 Hor	06/50 12232	-09/59	10/59	a
52233	06/94 Hor	11/48 12233	-11/51	*51*	a
52235	07/94 Hor	07/50 12235	-08/57	08/57	a
52236	07/94 Hor	09/50 12236	-09/57	04/58	a
52237	07/94 Hor	12/48 12237	-03/59	11/59	a
52238	07/94 Hor	08/48 12238	-07/51	*51*	a
52239	07/94 Hor	03/50 12239	-02/56	*10/56*	a
52240	07/94 Hor	05/48 12240	-04/61	06/61	a
52243	08/94 Hor	02/49 12243	-06/53	*53*	a
52244	08/94 Hor	06/48 12244	-11/60	03/61	a
52245	08/94 Hor	04/50 12245	-11/54	*54*	a
52246	08/94 Hor	08/49 12246	-02/53	*53*	ab
52248	09/94 Hor	10/49 12248	-03/62	11/62	a
52250	09/94 Hor	03/49 12250	-11/51	*51*	ab
52252	09/94 Hor	03/49 12252	-11/60	01/61	a
52253	10/94 Hor	12253	-06/48	*48*	ab
52255	10/94 Hor	04/49 12255	-08/53	*53*	a
52256	10/94 Hor	12256	-02/48	*04/48*	ab
52258	10/94 Hor	03/50 12258	-08/54	*54*	a
52260	11/94 Hor	11/49 12260	-04/61	06/61	a
52262	11/94 Hor	06/50 12262	-01/53	*53*	a
52266	11/94 Hor	02/50 12266	-12/52	*01/53*	ab
52268	12/94 Hor	04/48 12268	-03/59	11/59	a
52269	12/94 Hor	02/53 12269	-11/59	10/61	a
52270	12/94 Hor	10/48 12270	-01/61	03/61	a
52271	12/94 Hor	10/49 12271	-08/61	11/61	a
52272	01/95 Hor	12/48 12272	-04/55	*55*	a
52273	01/95 Hor	02/49 12273	-10/56	*56*	ab
52275	01/95 Hor	11/50 12275	-10/62	05/63	a
52278	06/95 Hor	09/50 12278	-08/59	08/59	a
52279	06/95 Hor	01/50 12279	-04/53	*53*	a
52280	06/95 Hor	01/49 12280	-03/51	*51*	a
52284	07/95 Hor	02/49 12284	-09/51	*51*	a
52285	07/95 Hor	06/49 12285	-12/52	*53*	a
52288	07/95 Hor	07/48 12288	-10/51	*51*	a
52289	07/95 Hor	11/50 12289	-10/59	10/59	a
52290	07/95 Hor	12/49 12290	-11/60	11/60	a
52293	08/95 Hor	05/52 12293	-09/57	04/58	ab
52294	08/95 Hor	12294	-08/49	*49*	a
52296	08/95 Hor	07/48 12296	-06/51	*51*	a
52299	09/95 Hor	01/51 12299	-09/54	*54*	a
52300	09/95 Hor	05/48 12300	-01/56	02/56	a
52304	09/95 Hor	08/50 12304	-01/53	*53*	a
52305	10/95 Hor	07/49 12305	-11/60	01/61	a
52309	10/95 Hor	12/50 12309	-01/54	*54*	a
52311	11/95 Hor	06/48 12311	-03/62	03/62	a
52312	11/95 Hor	05/48 12312	-09/62	10/62	ab
52317	12/95 Hor	05/50 12317	-06/55	*55*	a
52319	12/95 Hor	11/50 12319	-11/60	12/60	a
52321	12/95 Hor	01/49 12321	-02/54	*54*	a
52322 §	12/95 Hor	07/50 12322	-08/60		a
52326	01/96 Hor	12326	-12/49	*50*	a
52328	02/96 Hor	12/49 12328	-11/57	01/58	a
52330	02/96 Hor	12/48 12330	-12/51	*52*	a
52331	09/96 Hor	10/48 12331	-09/55	*55*	a
52333	09/96 Hor	12/49 12333	-04/53	*53*	a
52334	10/96 Hor	06/48 12334	-12/54	*55*	a
52336	10/96 Hor	08/49 12336	-03/57	05/57	a
52337	10/96 Hor	12337	-03/48	*48*	a
52338	10/96 Hor	01/49 12338	-06/57	08/57	a
52341	11/96 Hor	09/50 12341	-11/60	11/60	a
52343	11/96 Hor	04/48 12343	-07/56	*56*	a
52345	12/96 Hor	07/48 12345	-09/62	05/63	a
52348	12/96 Hor	06/50 12348	-08/59	10/59	a
52349	05/97 Hor	03/49 12349	-09/54	10/54	a
52350	05/97 Hor	09/50 12350	-12/58	01/59	a
52351	05/97 Hor	08/49 12351	-09/60	09/60	a
52353	05/97 Hor	12353	-12/51	*52*	a
52355	05/97 Hor	11/50 12355	-02/61	03/61	a
52356	05/97 Hor	02/49 12356	-04/58	05/58	a
52357	06/97 Hor	01/50 12357	-08/52	*52*	a
52358	06/97 Hor	10/48 12358	-12/56	*57*	a
52360	06/97 Hor	05/49 12360	-11/58	07/59	ab
52362	07/97 Hor	09/48 12362	-11/52	*52*	a
52363	07/97 Hor	10/48 12363	-11/51	*51*	a
52365	08/97 Hor	05/50 12365	-02/54	*54*	a
52366	08/97 Hor	04/49 12366	-04/58	04/58	a
52368	01/98 Hor	08/48 12368	-08/57	08/57	a
52369	01/98 Hor	03/49 12369	-06/56	*56*	a
52374	01/98 Hor	12374	-09/48	*48*	a
52376	01/98 Hor	01/51 12376	-04/57	09/57	a
52378	02/98 Hor	03/50 12378	-11/60	11/60	a
52379	02/98 Hor	09/48 12379	-04/57	05/57	a
52381	02/98 Hor	04/49 12381	-02/56	03/56	a
52382	03/98 Hor	03/50 12382	-05/53	*53*	a
52386	11/99 Hor	08/48 12386	-12/52	*53*	a
52387	11/99 Hor	02/50 12387	-05/58	06/59	a
52388	11/99 Hor	02/50 12388	-03/58	04/58	a
52389	11/99 Hor	08/48 12389	-11/59	09/61	a
52390	12/99 Hor	09/48 12390	-08/56	*56*	ab
52393	12/99 Hor	12/48 12393	-06/61	06/61	a
52397	01/00 Hor	05/48 12397	-07/55	08/55	a
52399	02/00 Hor	04/48 12399	-05/58	06/59	a
52400	02/00 Hor	05/48 12400	-11/60	12/60	a
52401	02/00 Hor	12401	-01/48	*48*	a
52403	02/00 Hor	12403	-12/49	*50*	a
52404	02/00 Hor	05/48 12404	-05/53	*53*	a
52405	03/00 Hor	08/48 12405	-12/56	*57*	ab
52407	03/00 Hor	10/48 12407	-01/51	*51*	a
52408	03/00 Hor	08/48 12408	-09/55	*09/55*	a
52410	04/00 Hor	06/48 12410	-01/60	01/60	a
52411	04/00 Hor	04/48 12411	-11/60	01/61	a
52412	09/00 Hor	06/50 12412	-03/57	05/57	a
52413	09/00 Hor	10/48 12413	-11/62	12/62	ab
52414	09/00 Hor	08/49 12414	-12/51	*12/51*	a
52415	09/00 Hor	02/50 12415	-03/61	04/61	a
52416	10/00 Hor	04/49 12416	-07/55	08/55	a
52417	10/00 Hor	12417	-02/48	*48*	a
52418	02/01 Hor	03/50 12418	-01/57	02/57	a
52422	03/01 Hor	12422	-03/48	*04/48*	a
52427	04/01 Hor	09/48 12427	-06/58	05/59	a
52428	04/01 Hor	05/49 12428	-09/51	*51*	ab
52429	04/01 Hor	10/49 12429	-10/60	11/60	a
52430	05/01 Hor	07/48 12430	-12/51	*52*	a
52431	05/01 Hor	02/50 12431	-11/59	03/62	ab
52432	05/01 Hor	10/50 12432	-11/58	05/59	a
52433	05/01 Hor	10/48 12433	-09/51	*51*	a
52435	05/01 Hor	03/50 12435	-07/54	*54*	a
52437	05/06 Hor	11/50 12437	-05/56	*56*	h
52438	05/06 Hor	05/48 12438	-04/62	06/62	h
52439	06/06 Hor	12439	-08/49	*49*	h
52440	06/06 Hor	05/50 12440	-01/53	*53*	h
52441	07/06 Hor	09/48 12441	-09/62	10/62	h
52442	07/06 Hor	12442	-09/49	*49*	h
52443	07/06 Hor	05/50 12443	-11/59	08/61	h
52444	08/06 Hor	08/48 12444	-03/51	*51*	hb
52445	08/06 Hor	10/49 12445	-11/60	01/61	hb
52446	08/06 Hor	07/48 12446	-07/51	*51*	h
52447	08/06 Hor	04/49 12447	-12/55	*56*	h
52448	08/06 Hor	11/48 12448	-11/51	*51*	hb
52449	09/06 Hor	09/48 12449	-11/57	12/57	h
52450	05/09 Hor	04/50 12450	-03/56	*56*	h
52452	06/09 Hor	09/48 12452	-06/60	12/60	h
52453	08/09 Hor	05/49 12453	-01/56	*56*	h
52454	08/09 Hor	12454	-08/49	*49*	h
52455	09/09 Hor	04/49 12455	-11/59	05/61	h
52456	10/09 Hor	08/48 12456	-10/62	05/63	h
52457	11/09 Hor	12457	-05/48	*48*	h
52458	11/09 Hor	04/51 12458	-09/59	10/59	h
52459	11/09 Hor	10/48 12459	-12/61	01/62	h
52460	12/09 Hor	01/49 12460	-06/51	*51*	h
52461	08/17 Hor	11/48 12461	-10/62	12/62	h
52464	11/17 Hor	04/49 12464	-04/61	06/61	h
52465	09/18 Hor	02/49 12465	-07/55	*55*	h
52466	10/18 Hor	11/49 12466	-10/60	11/60	h
52467	12/18 Hor	12467	-05/48	*48*	h

Class continued with 52515

3F 8 52494-52510
0-6-0 FR Pettigrew

Power Classification:	3F
Introduced:	1913-1920
Designer:	Pettigrew
Company:	Furness Railway
Weight:	Loco 42t 13cwt
Driving Wheel:	4' 7½"
Boiler Pressure:	180psi f 170psi
Cylinders:	Inside 18" x 26"
Tractive Effort:	23225lbf f 21935lbf
Valve Gear:	Joy (slide valves)

The Furness Railway was one of Britain's smaller railways, and these engines were the only engines from that railway to come into BR stock. Nineteen engines were built between 1913 and 1920 by North British and Kitsons, and the first was withdrawn in 1930. Six engines survived to come into BR stock.

Most of the class were rebuilt by the LMS with LYR boilers with Belpaire fireboxes and extended smokeboxes.

f One Furness type of round topped boiler remained in use on engines of this class. It was fitted to 52508, and later was fitted to 52494, which retained it until withdrawal.

Year End Totals: '3F 8' class

'47	'48	'49	'50	'51	'52	'53	'54	'55	'56	'57	'58	'59	'60	'61	'62	'63	'64	'65	'66	'67
6	6	6	5	5	5	5	5	5	3											

Number	Built	Renumbered	BR Dates	Scrap	Notes
52494	13 NB	03/50 12494	-05/56	05/56	➪f
52499	13 NB	02/49 12499	-02/57	02/57	
52501	18 K	08/50 12501	-07/57	07/57	
52508	20 NB	12/48 12508	-09/50	*50*	f
52509	20 NB	08/48 12509	-12/56	02/57	
52510	20 NB	09/48 12510	-08/57	08/58	

3F 7 between 52088 & 52529
0-6-0 LYR Aspinall Class '27'

Class continued from 52467

Number	Built	Renumbered	BR Dates	Scrap	Notes
52515	11/06 Hor	01/51 12515	-12/62	05/63	s
52517	04/09 Hor	10/49 12517	-05/58	06/59	s
52518	04/09 Hor	12518	-02/49	04/49	s
52521	05/09 Hor	05/50 12521	-05/57	08/57	s
52522	06/09 Hor	05/48 12522	-03/55	04/55	s
52523	07/09 Hor	09/49 12523	-09/62	05/63	s
52524	07/09 Hor	02/51 12524	-08/54	*54*	s
52525	07/09 Hor	03/49 12525	-04/53	*53*	s
52526	07/09 Hor	04/50 12526	-03/61	06/61	s
52527	08/09 Hor	03/50 12527	-08/59	10/59	s

Class continued with 52529

3F 9 between 52528 & 52619
0-6-0 LYR Hughes Class '28'

Power Classification:	3F
Introduced:	1912 r 1889-1909, rebuilt 1913-1922
Designer:	Hughes
Company:	LYR
Weight:	Loco 46t 10cwt
Driving Wheel:	5' 1"
Boiler Pressure:	180psi superheated
Cylinders:	Inside 20½" x 26"
Tractive Effort:	27405lbf
Valve Gear:	Joy (piston valves)

In 1912 Hughes introduced a superheated version of the '52088' class with Belpaire boilers. Twenty were built new and sixty-three were rebuilds. The first engines were withdrawn in 1935 and thirty-seven came into BR stock.

r These engines were the survivors of sixty-three engines which were converted from the '52088' class by Hughes between 1913 and 1922. 52528 was converted after grouping and retained its original number.

Year End Totals: '3F 9' class

'47	'48	'49	'50	'51	'52	'53	'54	'55	'56	'57	'58	'59	'60	'61	'62	'63	'64	'65	'66	'67
37	31	26	25	22	17	11	7	2	2											

Number	Built	Renumbered	BR Dates	Scrap	Notes
52528	09/09 Hor	12528	-11/48	*48*	r

Class continued with 52541

3F 7 between 52088 & 52529
0-6-0 LYR Aspinall Class '27'

Class continued from 52527

Number	Built	Renumbered	BR Dates	Scrap	Notes
52529	09/09 Hor	12/48 12529	-03/57	07/57	s

3F [9] between 52528 & 52619
0-6-0 LYR Hughes Class '28'

Class continued from 52528

Number	Built	Renumbered	BR Dates	Scrap	Notes
52541	04/12 Hor	10/48 12541	-07/49	49	
52542	04/12 Hor	12542	-03/50	50	
52545	05/12 Hor	12545	-11/48	48	
52549	06/12 Hor	07/48 12549	-10/54	54	
52551	06/12 Hor	03/50 12551	-03/57	57	
52554	08/12 Hor	10/50 12554	-10/52	52	
52557	09/96 Hor	12/48 12557	-09/51	51	r
52558	11/91 Hor	09/50 12558	-07/54	54	r
52559	03/01 Hor	03/50 12559	-01/53	53	r
52561	09/90 Hor	04/50 12561	-02/55	55	r
52568	11/09 Hor	12568	-03/48	48	r
52569	07/97 Hor	12/48 12569	-04/55	55	r
52572	03/01 Hor	02/50 12572	-08/53	53	r
52574	03/00 Hor	12574	-10/48	48	r
52575	02/96 Hor	05/48 12575	-12/55	02/56	r
52576	07/06 Hor	02/50 12576	-02/57	57	r
52578	01/91 Hor	12578	-08/49	49	r
52579	11/96 Hor	12/49 12579	-10/52	52	r
52580	10/89 Hor	11/49 12580	-02/54	54	r
52581	08/93 Hor	06/50 12581	-04/53	53	r
52582	09/93 Hor	05/48 12582	-06/55	55	r
52583	06/95 Hor	10/48 12583	-08/51	51	r
52586	01/90 Hor	12586	-04/49	49	r
52587	10/00 Hor	03/49 12587	-11/52	52	r
52588	10/89 Hor	10/49 12588	-09/52	52	r
52590	10/00 Hor	12590	-06/51	51	r
52592	12/99 Hor	06/48 12592	-08/54	54	r
52598	10/17 Hor	05/49 12598	-08/52	52	r
52602	05/09 Hor	12602	-11/48	48	r
52607	03/06 Hor	12607	-10/49	49	r
52608	03/00 Hor	08/49 12608	-02/55	55	r
52609	06/97 Hor	07/48 12609	-12/49	50	r
52615	12/94 Hor	05/48 12615	-07/53	53	r
52616	09/06 Hor	04/49 12616	-11/53	53	r
52618	01/92 Hor	12618	-05/48	48	r
52619	08/09 Hor	01/49 12619	-12/53	54	r

6F [3] 52727-52839
0-8-0 LYR Aspinall Class '30'

Power Classification: 6F
Introduced: 1900-1918
Designer: a Aspinall
h Hughes
Company: LYR
Weight: a Loco 53t 16cwt
h Loco 63t 0cwt
Driving Wheel: 4' 6"
Boiler Pressure: 180psi
Cylinders: Inside 20" x 26"
Tractive Effort: 29465lbf
Valve Gear: Joy (slide valves)

Aspinall introduced a series of 0-8-0 engines in 1900 for working heavy goods trains. The history of the engines is summarised below.

a Between 1900 and 1908 Aspinall built 130 engines which were fitted with small boilers. Seventy of these were later rebuilt with large saturated or superheated boilers. The sixty remaining engines were renumbered 12700-12759 by the LMS and withdrawal started in 1926 leaving only 52727 to come into BR stock.

c One of Aspinall's small boilered engines was rebuilt in 1904 as a four-cylinder compound engine. Ten more were built in 1907, but they were all withdrawn in 1926-1927. They were numbered 12760-12770 by the LMS.

h Between 1910 and 1918 Hughes built a larger saturated boiler version of the 0-8-0s. These were numbered 12771-12839 by the LMS and 12771-12800 were rebuilds of the smaller boilered engines. They were withdrawn from 1927 onwards.

s Between 1912 and 1920 Hughes built a superheated version of his large boilered engines, numbered 12840-12994. These are listed under the '7F' '52841' class below.

w Some engines were rebuilt with side window cabs, but none of these survived to come into BR stock.

Year End Totals: '6F [3]' class

'47	'48	'49	'50	'51	'52	'53	'54	'55	'56	'57	'58	'59	'60	'61	'62	'63	'64	'65	'66	'67
12	11	5	1																	

Number	Built	Renumbered	BR Dates	Scrap	Notes
52727	02/03 Hor	04/48 12727	-10/50	50	a
52782	03/03 Hor	11/48 12782	-03/50	50	h
52806	09/10 Hor	12806	-06/49	08/49	h
52821	12/17 Hor	05/48 12821	-03/49	49	h
52822	01/18 Hor	08/49 12822	-10/50	50	h
52825	03/18 Hor	09/48 12825	-03/50	50	h
52827	04/18 Hor	12827	-08/49	08/49	h
52828	04/18 Hor	12828	-05/49	08/49	h
52831	07/18 Hor	05/48 12831	-02/51	07/51	h
52834	09/18 Hor	12834	-03/49	04/49	h
52837	11/18 Hor	12837	-04/48	04/48	h
52839	12/18 Hor	05/48 12839	-10/49	49	h

7F [5] 52841-52971
0-8-0 LYR Hughes Class '31'

Power Classification: 7F
Introduced: 1912-1920
Designer: Hughes
Company: LYR
Weight: Loco 66t 4cwt
Driving Wheel: 4' 6"
Boiler Pressure: 180psi superheated
Cylinders: Inside 21½" x 26"
Tractive Effort: 34055lbf
Valve Gear: Joy (piston valves)

Between 1912 and 1920 Hughes built a superheated version of his large boilered engines (see '6F' '52727' class above) and they were numbered 12840-12994 by the LMS. There were originally 115 engines in the class of which thirty-five were rebuilds from the '52727' class. (52971 was the only survivor of the rebuilds to come into BR stock). Withdrawal started in 1926.

w Some engines were rebuilt with side window cabs.

Year End Totals: '7F [5]' class

'47	'48	'49	'50	'51	'52	'53	'54	'55	'56	'57	'58	'59	'60	'61	'62	'63	'64	'65	'66	'67
17	13	10	3																	

Number	Built	Renumbered	BR Dates	Scrap	Notes
52841	12/12 Hor	12841	-03/48	48	w
52856	05/13 Hor	10/48 12856	-05/50	50	
52857	06/13 Hor	12/48 12857	-12/51	05/52	w
52870	11/13 Hor	04/48 12870	-09/51	51	
52873	12/13 Hor	12873	-05/48	48	
52877	01/14 Hor	12877	-10/48	48	
52886	08/14 Hor	12/48 12886	-07/49	08/49	
52906	04/17 Hor	03/49 12906	-09/50	50	
52910	04/17 Hor	01/49 12910	-09/50	50	
52913	06/17 Hor	12913	-02/50	50	
52916	08/17 Hor	03/49 12916	-11/50	50	
52935	07/19 Hor	12935	-06/48	48	
52945	12/19 Hor	03/49 12945	-05/51	51	
52952	05/20 Hor	12952	-04/49	49	
52956	07/20 Hor	12956	-01/50	50	
52962	09/20 Hor	08/48 12962	-06/50	50	
52971	08/00 Hor	12971	-07/49	49	w

7F [6] 53800-53810
2-8-0 SDJR Fowler

Power Classification: 7F
Introduced: 1914
b 1925
Designer: Fowler
Company: SDJR
Weight: Loco 64t 15cwt
b Loco 68t 11cwt, later 64t 15cwt
Tender 42t 13cwt
Driving Wheel: 4' 8½"
Boiler Pressure: 190psi superheated
Cylinders: Outside 21" x 28"
Tractive Effort: 35295lbf
Valve Gear: Walschaert (piston valves)

This class was unusual in that it was the only class of large engines that the Midland Railway had built, even though they were not built for themselves.

The Somerset and Dorset Joint Railway (which was jointly owned by the Midland and the London & South Western Railways) depended on the Midland Railway for all its motive power requirements. The SDJR acquired a stock of standard MR type engines, but it was realised in 1914 that something more powerful was needed to work the steeply graded Bath-Bournemouth line. The Midland Railway never owned anything larger than 0-6-0 engines throughout its existence (apart from the single 0-10-0 'Lickey Banker').

Fowler designed and built the first six of these engines at Derby in 1914. They were fitted with 4' 9" diameter Belpaire boilers and they were numbered 80-85. The engines were pure Midland in their design. They were very distinctive in having a straight footplate which was raised with square corners over the cylinders which were set at a slight angle to the horizontal.

In 1925 a further five engines (numbered 86-90) were built by Robert Stephenson and they were fitted with larger (5' 3") diameter boilers and left hand drive. They were later all fitted with the smaller diameter boilers.

The engines were at first numbered 9670-9680 when they came into LMS stock in 1930, but they were renumbered 13800-13810 in 1932.

They spent the whole of their lives working freight traffic over the SDJR line. For a few months in 1918 No. 85 was lent to the Midland Railway and it was tested on coal trains between Wellingborough and Brent. This was with a view to the Midland building some of these engines for themselves, but nothing ever came of it.

b 53806-53810 were the batch of engines built by Robert Stephenson in 1925 and fitted with larger diameter boilers and left hand drive. They were later all fitted with the smaller diameter boilers, 53806-53808 retaining their large boilers until 1953-1955.

Year End Totals: '7F [6]' class

'47	'48	'49	'50	'51	'52	'53	'54	'55	'56	'57	'58	'59	'60	'61	'62	'63	'64	'65	'66	'67
11	11	11	11	11	11	11	11	11	11	11	11	10	9	7	5	4				

Number	Built	Renumbered	BR Dates	Scrap	Notes
53800	02/14 Der	05/49 13800	-07/59	10/59	
53801	03/14 Der	07/49 13801	-07/61	09/61	
53802	03/14 Der	06/48 13802	-03/60	04/60	
53803	04/14 Der	04/49 13803	-02/62	02/62	
53804	04/14 Der	10/48 13804	-02/62	02/62	
53805	08/14 Der	11/49 13805	-03/61	04/61	
53806	07/25 RS	01/50 13806	-01/64	07/64	b
53807	07/25 RS	04/50 13807	-10/64	04/65	b
53808 §	07/25 RS	08/49 13808	-03/64		b
53809 §	07/25 RS	09/49 13809	-06/64		b
53810	08/25 RS	04/49 13810	-12/63	02/64	b

2P [9] 54363
4-4-0 CR McIntosh 'Dunalastair IV'

Power Classification: 2P
Introduced: 1904-1910
Designer: McIntosh
Company: CR
Weight: Loco 56t 10cwt
Driving Wheel: 6' 6"
Boiler Pressure: 180psi
Cylinders: Inside 19" x 26"
Tractive Effort: 18410lbf
Valve Gear: Stephenson (piston valves)

Refer to the Historical Survey of Caledonian 4-4-0 Engines at the end of this section for more details of this class.

This engine was the last survivor of the saturated boiler engines of the 'Dunalastair IV' class.

Year End Totals: '2P [9]' class

'47	'48	'49	'50	'51	'52	'53	'54	'55	'56	'57	'58	'59	'60	'61	'62	'63	'64	'65	'66	'67
1																				

Number	Built	Renumbered	BR Dates	Scrap	Notes
54363	06/10 SRIx	14363	-10/48	06/49	

2P [10] 54379-54385
4-4-0 HR Jones 'Loch'

Power Classification: 2P
Introduced: 1896-1917
Designer: Jones
Company: HR
Weight: Loco 54t 10cwt
Driving Wheel: 6' 3½"
Boiler Pressure: 180psi
Cylinders: Outside 19" x 24"
Tractive Effort: 17560lbf
Valve Gear: Stephenson (slide valves)

This class was Jones' last design for the Highland Railway. The engines were designed for working main line passenger trains and they were amongst the most powerful passenger locomotives in the country when they were built by Dübs & Co. All the class of eighteen engines were built in 1896 except for the last three (later LMS 14394-14396) which were built in 1917. The engines were originally fitted with piston valves, but were later rebuilt with slide valves.

The engines were withdrawn from 1930 onwards and most of the class (including the last two survivors) were rebuilt with larger Caledonian boilers by the LMS.

Year End Totals: '2P [10]' class

'47	'48	'49	'50	'51	'52	'53	'54	'55	'56	'57	'58	'59	'60	'61	'62	'63	'64	'65	'66	'67
2	1	1																		

Number	Built	Renumbered	BR Dates	Scrap	Notes
54379 LOCH INSH	07/96 D	14379	-03/48	05/48	
54385 LOCH TAY	08/96 D	14385	-04/50	*50*	

2P [11] 54397-54416
4-4-0 HR Drummond 'Small Ben'

Power Classification: 2P
Introduced: 1898-1906
Designer: P Drummond
Company: HR
Weight: Loco 46t 17cwt
Driving Wheel: 6' 0"
Boiler Pressure: 180psi
Cylinders: Inside 18¼" x 26"
Tractive Effort: 18400lbf
Valve Gear: Stephenson (slide valves)

When Drummond succeeded Jones in 1896 he built his own design of inside cylinder 4-4-0s. These were the 'Small Ben' class built in 1898-1906, and the 'Large Ben' class (built in 1908-1909 and all withdrawn between 1932 and 1937).

The 'Small Bens' were Peter Drummond's first design for the Highland Railway and they were very similar in design to his brother Dugald Drummond's 'T9' class which was being built at the same time on the LSWR. They were the first Highland tender engines to be fitted with inside cylinders.

The first of the 'Small Bens' was withdrawn in 1931 but half of the class of twenty survived to come into BR stock. They were all rebuilt with Caledonian type boilers by the LMS.

54398 BEN ALDER was the last of the class to remain in service and it was stored for many years after withdrawal with hopes of preservation. However, these hopes did not materialise and it was cut up in 1966.

s 54399 was latterly fitted with a stovepipe chimney.

Year End Totals: '2P [11]' class

'47	'48	'49	'50	'51	'52	'53	'54	'55	'56	'57	'58	'59	'60	'61	'62	'63	'64	'65	'66	'67
10	7	4	2	2	1															

Number	Built	Renumbered	BR Dates	Scrap	Notes
54397 BEN-Y-GLOE	07/98 D	14397	-02/49	05/49	
54398 BEN ALDER	07/98 D	11/50 14398	-02/53	04/66	
54399 BEN WYVIS	07/98 D	01/51 14399	-05/52	52	s
54401 BEN VRACKIE	02/99 D	14401	-10/48	07/49	
54403 BEN ATTOW	02/99 D	14403	-02/49	05/49	
54404 BEN CLEBRIG	02/99 D	10/48 14404	-10/50	*50*	
54409 BEN ALISKY	06/00 Lchg	14409	-03/50	*50*	
54410 BEN DEARG	08/00 Lchg	14410	-12/49	*50*	
54415 BEN BHACH ARD	07/06 NB	14415	-05/48	10/48	
54416 BEN A'BHUIRD	07/06 NB	14416	-08/48	*10/48*	

3P [4] 54434
4-4-0 CR McIntosh 'Dunalastair III' Superheated

Power Classification: 3P
Introduced: 1899-1900, rebuilt 1914-1918
Designer: McIntosh
Company: CR
Weight: Loco 51t 14cwt
Driving Wheel: 6' 6"
Boiler Pressure: 180psi superheated
Cylinders: Inside 19½" x 26"
Tractive Effort: 19395lbf
Valve Gear: Stephenson (piston valves)

Refer to the Historical Survey of Caledonian 4-4-0 Engines at the end of this section for more details of this class.

This engine was the last survivor of the superheated rebuilds of the 'Dunalastair III' class.

Year End Totals: '3P [4]' class

'47	'48	'49	'50	'51	'52	'53	'54	'55	'56	'57	'58	'59	'60	'61	'62	'63	'64	'65	'66	'67
1																				

Number	Built	Renumbered	BR Dates	Scrap	Notes
54434	06/00 SRlx	14434	-04/48	*06/48*	

3P [5] 54438-54460
4-4-0 CR McIntosh 'Dunalastair IV' Superheated

Power Classification: 3P
Introduced: 1910-1914
r 1904-1910, rebuilt 1915-1917
Designer: McIntosh
Company: CR
Weight: Loco 61t 5cwt
Driving Wheel: 6' 6"
Boiler Pressure: 180psi superheated
Cylinders: Inside 20¼" x 26"
Tractive Effort: 20915lbf
Valve Gear: Stephenson (piston valves)

Refer to the Historical Survey of Caledonian 4-4-0 Engines at the end of this section for more details of this class.

This class was the superheated version of the 'Dunalastair IV' class.

r 54438 (rebuilt in 1917) and 54439 (rebuilt in 1915) were originally saturated boiler engines.

Year End Totals: '3P [5]' class

'47	'48	'49	'50	'51	'52	'53	'54	'55	'56	'57	'58	'59	'60	'61	'62	'63	'64	'65	'66	'67
22	22	22	22	22	21	18	16	7	7	1										

Number	Built	Renumbered	BR Dates	Scrap	Notes
54438	12/07 SRlx	04/48 14438	-05/55	09/55	r
54439	01/08 SRlx	08/49 14439	-08/58	*58*	r
54440	07/10 SRlx	08/48 14440	-01/57	*57*	
54441	04/11 SRlx	02/50 14441	-08/57	*57*	
54443	05/11 SRlx	04/50 14443	-10/55	*55*	
54444	05/11 SRlx	04/48 14444	-10/53	*12/53*	
54445	05/12 SRlx	05/48 14445	-12/52	*05/53*	
54446	05/12 SRlx	09/48 14446	-08/55	12/55	
54447	06/12 SRlx	07/50 14447	-06/53	*53*	
54448	06/12 SRlx	08/48 14448	-02/55	04/55	
54449	07/12 SRlx	06/50 14449	-11/53	12/53	
54450	05/13 SRlx	12/49 14450	-10/55	*10/55*	
54451	05/13 SRlx	09/49 14451	-09/55	*55*	
54452	05/13 SRlx	06/49 14452	-08/57	*57*	
54453	06/13 SRlx	09/48 14453	-08/57	*57*	
54454	06/13 SRlx	10/51 14454	-10/55	*10/55*	
54455	06/13 SRlx	05/48 14455	-07/54	10/54	
54456	04/14 SRlx	06/48 14456	-02/57	*57*	
54457	04/14 SRlx	11/48 14457	-02/55	09/55	
54458	04/14 SRlx	12/48 14458	-12/57	*58*	
54459	04/14 SRlx	04/49 14459	-12/54	*55*	
54460	05/14 SRlx	06/48 14460	-10/55	*55*	

3P [6] 54461-54508
4-4-0 CR Pickersgill Classes '113', '918' & '72'

Power Classification: 3P
Introduced: 1916-1922
Designer: Pickersgill
Company: CR
Weight: Loco 61t 5cwt
Driving Wheel: 6' 6"
Boiler Pressure: 180psi superheated
Cylinders: Inside 20" x 26"
c Inside 20½" x 26"
Tractive Effort: 20400lbf
c 21435lbf
Valve Gear: Stephenson (piston valves)

Refer to the Historical Survey of Caledonian 4-4-0 Engines at the end of this section for more details of this class.

This class was Pickersgill's version of the 'Dunalastairs'. They were known as the '113' and '918' classes and the '72' class.

54481 was the first of the class to be withdrawn after the Gollanfield collision of 1953.

c The '72' class engines (introduced in 1920) were fitted with slightly larger cylinders.

Year End Totals: '3P [6]' class

'47	'48	'49	'50	'51	'52	'53	'54	'55	'56	'57	'58	'59	'60	'61	'62	'63	'64	'65	'66	'67
48	48	48	48	48	48	47	47	47	47	47	47	31	23	8						

Number	Built	Renumbered	BR Dates	Scrap	Notes
54461	02/16 SRlx	08/50 14461	-05/59	02/60	
54462	03/16 SRlx	11/48 14462	-05/60	08/60	
54463	04/16 SRlx	06/48 14463	-12/62	12/64	
54464	04/16 SRlx	08/48 14464	-10/61	02/62	
54465	02/16 SRlx	09/48 14465	-10/62	11/63	
54466	05/16 SRlx	07/48 14466	-02/62	11/63	
54467	03/16 NB	02/51 14467	-10/59	02/60	
54468	04/16 NB	01/50 14468	-10/59	02/60	
54469	04/16 NB	01/49 14469	-11/59	12/59	
54470	05/16 NB	09/48 14470	-12/59	03/60	
54471	05/16 NB	05/48 14471	-10/59	02/60	
54472	05/16 NB	11/49 14472	-10/59	02/60	
54473	06/16 NB	08/48 14473	-10/59	02/60	
54474	06/16 NB	11/48 14474	-10/59	02/60	
54475	06/16 NB	03/49 14475	-06/61	01/62	
54476	06/16 NB	10/50 14476	-03/60	07/60	
54477	05/20 SRlx	04/49 14477	-05/60	09/60	c
54478	05/20 SRlx	02/49 14478	-07/61	10/61	c
54479	06/20 SRlx	04/48 14479	-10/59	02/60	c
54480	07/20 SRlx	10/48 14480	-08/60	11/60	c
54481	07/20 SRlx	02/49 14481	-06/53	07/53	c
54482	07/20 SRlx	06/50 14482	-02/62	11/63	c
54483	08/20 SRlx	10/49 14483	-06/61	01/62	c
54484	09/20 SRlx	09/48 14484	-11/59	12/59	c
54485	09/20 SRlx	04/48 14485	-10/61	09/62	c
54486	09/20 SRlx	07/50 14486	-02/62	11/63	c
54487	02/21 AW	02/51 14487	-03/61	04/61	c
54488	03/21 AW	07/48 14488	-02/61	04/61	c
54489	03/21 AW	04/50 14489	-12/61	11/63	c
54490	04/21 AW	06/49 14490	-05/60	09/60	c
54491	04/21 AW	06/48 14491	-12/61	01/62	c
54492	04/21 AW	04/49 14492	-11/61	09/62	c
54493	05/21 AW	02/50 14493	-11/61	01/62	c
54494	05/21 AW	09/50 14494	-08/60	08/60	c
54495	06/21 AW	12/49 14495	-02/62	06/63	c
54496	06/21 AW	10/48 14496	-10/59	02/60	c
54497	11/22 NB	10/48 14497	-10/59	12/59	c
54498	11/22 NB	06/49 14498	-05/60	08/60	c
54499	11/22 NB	05/48 14499	-05/60	08/60	c
54500	12/22 NB	12/49 14500	-02/62	06/63	c
54501	12/22 NB	12/49 14501	-12/61	09/63	c
54502	12/22 NB	04/49 14502	-10/62	09/63	c
54503	12/22 NB	10/49 14503	-10/59	02/60	c
54504	12/22 NB	04/48 14504	-10/59	02/60	c
54505	12/22 NB	10/48 14505	-04/61	05/61	c
54506	12/22 NB	07/48 14506	-11/61	06/63	c
54507	12/22 NB	01/50 14507	-11/61	06/63	c
54508	12/22 NB	01/49 14508	-12/59	07/64	c

4P [3] 54630-54654
4-6-0 CR & LMS Pickersgill Class '60'

Power Classification: 4P reclassified 3MT in 1948
then reclassified 4MT in 1949
Introduced: 1916-1926
Designer: Pickersgill
Company: LMS
c CR
Weight: Loco 74t 15cwt
c Loco 75t 0cwt
Driving Wheel: 6' 1"
Boiler Pressure: 180psi superheated
Cylinders: Outside 20½" x 26"
c Outside 20" x 26"
Tractive Effort: 22900lbf
c 21795lbf
Valve Gear: Stephenson (piston valves)

Between 1902 and 1922 McIntosh and Pickersgill of the Caledonian built nine widely differing varieties of 4-6-0 engines. This class was the only one to survive to BR days and it was Pickersgill's third class of outside cylinder 4-6-0 engines.

The '55350' class engines were basically a tank version of this class, although they were slightly smaller.

The first six engines (54650-54654 and LMS 14655) were built by the Caledonian Railway in 1916-1917 and the remainder were built by the LMS in 1925-1926. Three engines were withdrawn before 1948 (the earliest in 1944) and twenty-three survived to come into BR stock.

c The Caledonian built engines had slightly smaller cylinders, and were heavier.

Year End Totals: '4P [3]' class

'47	'48	'49	'50	'51	'52	'53	'54	'55	'56	'57	'58	'59	'60	'61	'62	'63	'64	'65	'66	'67
23	17	14	12	7	3															

Number	Built		Renumbered		BR Dates	Scrap	Notes
54630	07/25	SRlx	08/49	14630	-12/51	52	
54631	11/25	SRlx		14631	-05/48	06/48	
54634	05/26	SRlx	07/49	14634	-11/52	52	
54635	06/26	SRlx	03/49	14635	-01/52	52	
54636	06/26	SRlx	06/48	14636	-02/53	53	
54637	07/26	SRlx		14637	-03/48	04/48	
54638	07/26	SRlx	04/48	14638	-05/51	51	
54639	08/26	SRlx	08/48	14639	-12/53	54	
54640	08/26	SRlx	06/49	14640	-10/52	52	
54641	09/26	SRlx		14641	-11/48	02/49	
54642	09/26	SRlx	05/48	14642	-10/49	49	
54643	10/26	SRlx		14643	-02/48	04/48	
54644	10/26	SRlx		14644	-04/48	07/48	
54645	11/26	SRlx		14645	-07/50	50	
54646	11/26	SRlx		14646	-03/49	49	
54647	11/26	SRlx	04/48	14647	-03/51	51	
54648	12/26	SRlx	02/49	14648	-11/51	51	
54649	12/26	SRlx	09/48	14649	-10/51	51	
54650	11/16	SRlx	12/48	14650	-09/53	53	c
54651	12/16	SRlx	06/49	14651	-03/50	50	c
54652	01/17	SRlx		14652	-11/48	48	c
54653	02/17	SRlx		14653	-07/49	49	c
54654	03/17	SRlx	01/49	14654	-01/52	52	c

4P [4] 54764-54767
4-6-0 HR Cumming 'Clan'

Power Classification: 4P reclassified 4MT in 1948
Introduced: 1919-1921
Designer: Cumming
Company: HR
Weight: Loco 62t 5cwt
Driving Wheel: 6' 0"
Boiler Pressure: 175psi superheated
Cylinders: Outside 21" x 26"
Tractive Effort: 23690lbf
Valve Gear: Walschaert (piston valves)

The Highland Railway 'Clan' class consisted of eight engines built in 1918-1921. They were a six-foot passenger version of the '57950' 'Clan Goods' class and they were designed for express passenger work.

They were originally built as a replacement for the 'River' class engines. The 'Rivers' were ordered by the Highland Railway in 1915, but on delivery they were found to be too heavy to run on that railway. The resulting argument between the Chief Mechanical Engineer (F. G. Smith) and the Civil Engineer led to Smith being sacked, and the 'River' class engines were sold to the Caledonian Railway where they worked successfully until 1945.

The first 'Clan' was withdrawn in 1944 and two engines came into BR stock in 1948.

Year End Totals: '4P [4]' class

'47	'48	'49	'50	'51	'52	'53	'54	'55	'56	'57	'58	'59	'60	'61	'62	'63	'64	'65	'66	'67
2	1	1																		

Number	Built		Renumbered		BR Dates	Scrap	Notes
54764 CLAN MUNRO	04/19	HL		14764	-02/48	48	
54767 CLAN MACKINNON	07/21	HL	08/48	14767	-01/50	02/50	

0P 55051-55053
0-4-4T HR Drummond

Power Classification: 0P
Introduced: 1905-1906
Designer: P Drummond
Company: HR
Weight: 35t 15cwt
Driving Wheel: 4' 6"
Boiler Pressure: 150psi
Cylinders: Inside 14" x 20"
Tractive Effort: 9255lbf
Valve Gear: Stephenson (slide valves)

The Highland Railway built four engines of the 'W' class for branch line working in 1905-1906. They were the last locomotives to be built at the Lochgorm works of the Highland Railway in Inverness.

The first of these engines was withdrawn in 1930 and the last two engines survived for many years working the branch line between The Mound and Dornoch. They were the last Highland engines to remain in ordinary service and they remained in virtually original condition throughout their whole lives. 55051 was named STRATHPEFFER until 1920.

When they were finally withdrawn from service, they were replaced on the Dornoch branch by two GWR designed pannier tanks, Nos. 1646 and 1649.

Year End Totals: '0P' class

'47	'48	'49	'50	'51	'52	'53	'54	'55	'56	'57	'58	'59	'60	'61	'62	'63	'64	'65	'66	'67
2	2	2	2	2	2	2	2	2	1											

Number	Built		Renumbered		BR Dates	Scrap	Notes
55051	03/05	Lchg	04/49	15051	-07/56	56	
55053	12/05	Lchg	01/49	15053	-01/57	02/58	

2P [12] 55116-55146
0-4-4T CR McIntosh Class '19' & '92'

Power Classification: 2P
Introduced: 1895-1900
Designer: McIntosh
Company: CR
Weight: 53t 16cwt
l 53t 19cwt
Driving Wheel: 5' 9"
Boiler Pressure: 180psi
Cylinders: Inside 18" x 26"
Tractive Effort: 18680lbf
Valve Gear: Stephenson (slide valves)

This class was the original Caledonian McIntosh design of 0-4-4T, built for suburban and branch line work. They were very successful engines and further enlarged engines were built of the '55159', '55237' and '55260' classes.

Thirty-two engines were built in total and the first of the class was withdrawn in 1946. They were all originally fitted with condensing apparatus for working over the Glasgow Central low level lines but this was later removed from most of the engines. A number of engines were later fitted with stovepipe chimneys.

The first ten engines were fitted with smaller tanks and they were known as the '19' class.

l The remainder were known as the '92' class and they were a later development (built 1897-1900) with larger tanks and a high sided coal bunker.

Year End Totals: '2P [12]' class

'47	'48	'49	'50	'51	'52	'53	'54	'55	'56	'57	'58	'59	'60	'61	'62	'63	'64	'65	'66	'67
26	22	22	19	16	9	6	5	4	4	3	2	2	2							

Number	Built		Renumbered		BR Dates	Scrap	Notes
55116	04/95	SRlx		15116	-05/48	05/48	
55117	04/95	SRlx		15117	-06/48	07/48	
55119	04/95	SRlx	01/49	15119	-08/53	03/54	
55121	05/95	SRlx	12/48	15121	-06/52	52	
55122	05/95	SRlx	03/51	15122	-01/52	52	
55123	05/95	SRlx	01/49	15123	-01/50	50	
55124	05/95	SRlx	10/48	15124	-10/61	09/63	
55125	05/97	SRlx	10/48	15125	-01/57	06/57	l
55126	05/97	SRlx	07/48	15126	-07/61	08/61	l
55127	06/97	SRlx		15127	-03/50	50	l
55129	06/97	SRlx	04/48	15129	-08/50	50	l
55130	06/97	SRlx		15130	-09/48	48	l
55132	07/97	SRlx	06/49	15132	-10/51	51	l
55133	07/97	SRlx		15133	-12/48	02/49	l
55134	07/97	SRlx	03/49	15134	-04/51	51	l
55135	07/97	SRlx	08/49	15135	-07/53	53	l
55136	07/97	SRlx	12/49	15136	-09/52	52	l
55138	01/00	SRlx	04/48	15138	-08/51	08/51	l
55139	02/00	SRlx	10/49	15139	-08/52	52	l
55140	02/00	SRlx	11/49	15140	-09/52	52	l
55141	02/00	SRlx	08/49	15141	-07/58	07/58	l
55142	02/00	SRlx	05/49	15142	-12/52	53	l
55143	02/00	SRlx	09/49	15143	-04/53	53	l
55144	02/00	SRlx	02/50	15144	-07/52	52	l
55145	03/00	SRlx	11/48	15145	-04/55	55	l
55146	03/00	SRlx	04/49	15146	-06/54	54	l

2P [13] 55159-55236
0-4-4T CR McIntosh Class '439'

Power Classification: 2P
Introduced: 1900-1922
Designer: McIntosh
p Pickersgill
Company: CR
Weight: 53t 19cwt
p 57t 12cwt
Driving Wheel: 5' 9"
Boiler Pressure: 180psi
Cylinders: Inside 18" x 26"
Tractive Effort: 18680lbf
Valve Gear: Stephenson (slide valves)

These engines were developed from the '55116' class and they were known as the '439' or 'Standard Passenger' class. They were a direct development from the '92' class, but they were not fitted with condensing apparatus.

Seventy-eight engines were built, the first being withdrawn in 1946. A number of engines were later fitted with stovepipe chimneys.

p The last ten engines (55227-55236) were built in 1915-1922 by Pickersgill and had detail differences.

Year End Totals: '2P [13]' class

'47	'48	'49	'50	'51	'52	'53	'54	'55	'56	'57	'58	'59	'60	'61	'62	'63	'64	'65	'66	'67
76	74	72	69	66	63	59	58	53	51	50	44	43	42	6						

Number	Built		Renumbered		BR Dates	Scrap	Notes
55159	03/00	SRlx	09/48	15159	-12/49	50	
55160	03/00	SRlx	12/49	15160	-10/58	01/59	
55161	03/00	SRlx	11/48	15161	-10/53	11/53	
55162	04/00	SRlx	04/49	15162	-04/56	07/56	
55164	09/00	SRlx	02/51	15164	-02/59	06/59	
55165	10/00	SRlx	12/48	15165	-10/61	03/62	
55166	10/00	SRlx	09/48	15166	-09/53	11/53	
55167	10/00	SRlx	08/49	15167	-07/61	08/61	
55168	10/00	SRlx	05/50	15168	-05/57	09/57	
55169	10/00	SRlx	02/51	15169	-05/61	08/61	
55170	11/00	SRlx	08/50	15170	-10/52	52	
55171	11/00	SRlx	03/50	15171	-11/51	51	
55172	11/00	SRlx	02/50	15172	-11/52	06/53	
55173	11/00	SRlx	06/48	15173	-01/62	07/62	
55174	12/00	SRlx	11/51	15174	-02/56	05/56	
55175	12/00	SRlx	10/50	15175	-02/53	03/53	
55176	03/06	SRlx	50	15176	-10/58	12/58	
55177	03/06	SRlx	05/49	15177	-06/55	08/55	
55178	03/06	SRlx	06/48	15178	-12/58	01/59	
55179	12/06	SRlx	05/49	15179	-09/53	53	
55180	04/06	SRlx	05/48	15180	-08/48	48	
55181	01/07	SRlx	12/48	15181	-11/51	51	
55182	04/06	SRlx	07/51	15182	-05/58	10/58	
55183	01/07	SRlx	11/48	15183	-07/50	08/50	
55184	01/07	SRlx		15184	-11/49	49	
55185	01/07	SRlx	01/49	15185	-07/61	07/61	
55186	04/06	SRlx	06/49	15186	-01/52	52	
55187	02/07	SRlx	01/49	15187	-02/55	04/55	
55188	11/07	SRlx		15188	-03/51	51	
55189 §	11/07	SRlx	07/49	15189	-12/62		
55190	11/07	SRlx		15190	-06/48	48	
55191	11/07	SRlx	06/48	15191	-11/50	50	
55192	11/07	SRlx		15192	-10/50	50	
55193	10/09	SRlx	06/49	15193	-04/55	06/55	
55194	10/09	SRlx	09/49	15194	-03/55	55	
55195	11/09	SRlx	02/51	15195	-06/61	09/61	
55196	11/09	SRlx	07/48	15196	-12/55	56	
55197	11/09	SRlx	07/48	15197	-11/54	54	
55198	11/09	SRlx	05/50	15198	-05/61	01/62	
55199	12/09	SRlx	01/50	15199	-07/61	08/61	
55200	12/09	SRlx	09/49	15200	-08/61	11/61	
55201	12/09	SRlx	09/48	15201	-10/61	03/63	
55202	12/09	SRlx	11/48	15202	-08/61	11/61	
55203	04/10	SRlx	12/49	15203	-12/61	09/63	
55204	04/10	SRlx	11/48	15204	-12/62	12/64	
55206	01/11	SRlx	01/49	15206	-09/61	09/63	
55207	03/11	SRlx	12/48	15207	-09/61	01/62	
55208	03/11	SRlx	02/49	15208	-10/61	02/62	
55209	04/11	SRlx	01/49	15209	-06/61	08/61	

55210	05/11	SRlx	05/48	15210	-07/61	08/61	
55211	06/11	SRlx	07/49	15211	-09/61	01/62	
55212	06/11	SRlx	09/48	15212	-12/58	01/59	
55213	04/12	SRlx	11/49	15213	-05/58	06/58	
55214	04/12	SRlx	03/50	15214	-09/61	02/62	
55215	07/12	SRlx	12/49	15215	-10/61	01/62	
55216	07/12	SRlx	03/51	15216	-10/61	01/62	
55217	06/13	SRlx	03/49	15217	-08/62	09/62	
55218	06/13	SRlx	01/50	15218	-01/60	04/60	
55219	06/13	SRlx	08/48	15219	-05/61	09/61	
55220	06/13	SRlx	07/48	15220	-10/61	05/62	
55221	08/14	SRlx	08/48	15221	-10/61	09/63	
55222	08/14	SRlx	02/50	15222	-09/61	02/62	
55223	08/14	SRlx	10/48	15223	-09/61	03/62	
55224	09/14	SRlx	01/50	15224	-10/61	02/62	
55225	10/14	SRlx	05/49	15225	-01/62	09/63	
55226	10/14	SRlx	02/49	15226	-09/61	02/62	
55227	07/15	SRlx	12/49	15227	-12/61	02/62	p
55228	08/15	SRlx	07/48	15228	-09/61	01/62	p
55229	09/15	SRlx	12/49	15229	-09/61	04/62	p
55230	10/15	SRlx	04/51	15230	-09/61	01/62	p
55231	08/22	SRlx	12/48	15231	-06/61	08/61	p
55232	07/22	SRlx	06/48	15232	-09/61	06/62	p
55233	07/22	SRlx	10/48	15233	-02/61	02/62	p
55234	08/22	SRlx	09/51	15234	-12/62	12/63	p
55235	10/22	SRlx	07/50	15235	-05/61	08/61	p
55236	11/22	SRlx	12/51	15236	-09/61	11/61	p

2P [14] 55237-55240
0-4-4T CR Pickersgill Class '431'

Power Classification: 2P
Introduced: 1922
Designer: Pickersgill
Company: CR
Weight: 57t 17cwt
Driving Wheel: 5' 9"
Boiler Pressure: 180psi
Cylinders: Inside 18¼" x 26"
Tractive Effort: 19200lbf
Valve Gear: Stephenson (slide valves)

These engines (known as Pickersgill's '431' class) were a direct derivative of the '55159' class, but they were fitted with cast-iron buffer beams for banking purposes at Beattock.

s 55237 latterly carried a stovepipe chimney.

Year End Totals: '2P [14]' class

'47	'48	'49	'50	'51	'52	'53	'54	'55	'56	'57	'58	'59	'60	'61	'62	'63	'64	'65	'66	'67
4	4	4	4	4	4	4	4	4	4	4	4	4	4							

Number	*Built*		*Renumbered*		*BR Dates*	*Scrap*	*Notes*
55237	08/22	SRlx	08/49	15237	-07/61	08/61	s
55238	09/22	SRlx	03/49	15238	-09/61	01/62	
55239	09/22	SRlx	05/49	15239	-07/61	08/61	
55240	09/22	SRlx	07/48	15240	-11/61	10/63	

2P [15] 55260-55269
0-4-4T LMS (CR) McIntosh Class '439'

Power Classification: 2P
Introduced: 1925
Designer: McIntosh
Company: LMS
Weight: 59t 12cwt
Driving Wheel: 5' 9"
Boiler Pressure: 180psi
Cylinders: Inside 18¼" x 26"
Tractive Effort: 19200lbf
Valve Gear: Stephenson (slide valves)

These engines were a post-grouping version of the '55159' class. Built by the LMS in 1925 they were a slightly enlarged version of Pickersgill's engines.

Year End Totals: '2P [15]' class

'47	'48	'49	'50	'51	'52	'53	'54	'55	'56	'57	'58	'59	'60	'61	'62	'63	'64	'65	'66	'67
10	10	10	10	10	10	10	10	10	10	10	10	10	10	2						

Number	*Built*		*Renumbered*		*BR Dates*	*Scrap*	*Notes*
55260	05/25	NW	08/50	15260	-12/62	10/63	
55261	05/25	NW	10/50	15261	-09/61	05/62	
55262	05/25	NW	05/51	15262	-10/61	09/63	
55263	05/25	NW	07/48	15263	-11/61	11/63	
55264	06/25	NW	03/51	15264	-10/61	09/63	
55265	06/25	NW	01/49	15265	-02/61	08/62	
55266	06/25	NW	02/50	15266	-09/61	09/63	
55267	06/25	NW	12/49	15267	-10/61	01/63	
55268	06/25	NW	10/49	15268	-09/61	07/62	
55269	06/25	NW	06/50	15269	-03/62	11/63	

4P [5] 55350-55361
4-6-2T CR Pickersgill Class '944'

Power Classification: 4P
Introduced: 1917
Designer: Pickersgill
Company: CR
Weight: 91t 13cwt
Driving Wheel: 5' 9"
Boiler Pressure: 180psi superheated
Cylinders: Outside 19½" x 26"
Tractive Effort: 21920lbf
Valve Gear: Stephenson (piston valves)

Pickersgill built twelve engines of the '944' class in 1917. They were the only large passenger tank class to be built for the Caledonian Railway, and they were designed for the semi-express services out of Glasgow to the Ayrshire Coast. They were often referred to as 'Wemyss Bay Tanks'.

The engines were basically a tank version of the '54630' class, although they were slightly smaller.

The first engine of the class was withdrawn in 1946 and ten engines came into BR stock. The last engines in service in the 1950s were to be found on banking duties at Beattock.

Year End Totals: '4P [5]' class

'47	'48	'49	'50	'51	'52	'53	'54	'55	'56	'57	'58	'59	'60	'61	'62	'63	'64	'65	'66	'67
10	8	7	6	5	1															

Number	*Built*		*Renumbered*		*BR Dates*	*Scrap*	*Notes*
55350	03/17	SRlx	04/50	15350	-04/52	*52*	
55351	03/17	SRlx		15351	-12/48	*49*	
55352	01/17	SRlx	05/50	15352	-03/52	*52*	
55353	01/17	SRlx	07/49	15353	-08/51	*51*	
55354	01/17	SRlx	02/49	15354	-08/49	*49*	
55355	01/17	SRlx		15355	-01/48	*48*	
55356	01/17	SRlx	04/48	15356	-06/50	*50*	
55359	04/17	SRlx	06/48	15359	-10/53	*12/53*	
55360	05/17	SRlx	06/48	15360	-02/52	*52*	
55361	05/17	SRlx	01/50	15361	-06/52	*52*	

0F [5] 56010-56039
0-4-0ST CR Drummond 'Pugs'

Power Classification: 0F
Introduced: 1885-1908
Designer: D Drummond and McIntosh
Company: CR
Weight: 27t 7cwt
Driving Wheel: 3' 8"
Boiler Pressure: 160psi
Cylinders: Outside 14" x 20"
Tractive Effort: 12115lbf
Valve Gear: Stephenson (slide valves)

Both the Caledonian and the North British Railways in Scotland used small 0-4-0STs for dockyard shunting, and shunting in other small yards with tight curvature. Both classes were known as 'Pugs', the NBR engines becoming the LNER 'Y9' class.

Thirty-four of these Caledonian 'Pugs' were built between 1885 and 1908. They were developed from older engines built by Neilson & Co. in 1878.

The engines had open backed cabs and no coal bunkers. As they were limited by the amount of coal they could carry in the cab, many of the engines were permanently coupled to small four-wheeled wooden tenders, with an extra coal supply. They could be distinguished from the LNER 'Y9' class by their tall tapering chimneys with flared tops. One or two engines were latterly fitted with stovepipe chimneys.

The first engine was withdrawn in 1920 and fourteen came into BR stock in 1948. Several later worked as departmental engines although not renumbered. 56025 was the St. Rollox Works shunter, and 56027 and 56032 worked as Crewe Works pilots.

Year End Totals: '0F [5]' class

'47	'48	'49	'50	'51	'52	'53	'54	'55	'56	'57	'58	'59	'60	'61	'62	'63	'64	'65	'66	'67
14	14	14	12	12	12	12	12	11	11	10	9	7	3	3						

Number	*Built*		*Renumbered*		*BR Dates*	*Scrap*	*Notes*
56010	07/85	SRlx		16010	-03/50	*50*	
56011	07/85	SRlx	01/52	16011	-01/59	01/59	
56020	02/90	SRlx	04/48	16020	-03/55	*55*	
56025	05/90	SRlx	08/48	16025	-05/60	05/60	
56026	10/95	SRlx		16026	-06/50	08/50	
56027	10/95	SRlx	02/50	16027	-10/60	02/61	
56028	10/95	SRlx	01/49	16028	-05/57	07/57	
56029	11/95	SRlx	02/52	16029	-12/62	08/64	
56030	07/00	SRlx	02/51	16030	-05/58	07/58	
56031	07/00	SRlx	09/51	16031	-04/62	10/62	
56032	07/00	SRlx	07/49	16032	-10/60	02/61	
56035	08/00	SRlx	07/51	16035	-08/60	05/61	
56038	12/08	SRlx	04/48	16038	-05/59	10/59	
56039	12/08	SRlx	11/52	16039	-10/62	05/63	

2F [4] 56151-56173
0-6-0T CR McIntosh Class '498'

Power Classification: 2F
Introduced: 1912-1922
Designer: McIntosh
p Pickersgill
Company: CR
Weight: 47t 15cwt
Driving Wheel: 4' 0"
Boiler Pressure: 160psi
Cylinders: Outside 17" x 22"
Tractive Effort: 18015lbf
Valve Gear: Stephenson (slide valves)

This class (known as the 'Caledonian Dock Tank' or '498' class) was designed by McIntosh for dock shunting work. The engines had a very short coupled wheelbase of only 10ft. and were compact and powerful engines. They were the only engines to be designed by McIntosh with outside cylinders.

Mcintosh built the first two engines in 1911, and the other twenty-one were built by Pickersgill with larger bunkers in 1918. Some engines were latterly fitted with stovepipe chimneys.

p Pickersgill built engines with larger bunkers.

Year End Totals: '2F [4]' class

'47	'48	'49	'50	'51	'52	'53	'54	'55	'56	'57	'58	'59	'60	'61	'62	'63	'64	'65	'66	'67
23	23	23	23	23	23	23	23	23	23	23	19	11	8	1						

Number	*Built*		*Renumbered*		*BR Dates*	*Scrap*	*Notes*
56151	01/12	SRlx	05/49	16151	-09/61	11/61	
56152	01/12	SRlx	12/49	16152	-02/59	07/59	
56153	04/15	SRlx	05/48	16153	-06/59	10/59	p
56154	04/15	SRlx	05/50	16154	-07/59	11/59	p
56155	04/15	SRlx	09/48	16155	-09/58	11/58	p
56156	04/15	SRlx	06/49	16156	-10/59	03/60	p
56157	04/15	SRlx	02/50	16157	-12/58	03/59	p
56158	06/15	SRlx	05/49	16158	-02/61	02/61	p
56159	08/18	SRlx	03/49	16159	-04/62	10/62	p
56160	08/18	SRlx	06/48	16160	-07/59	11/59	p
56161	08/18	SRlx	02/49	16161	-12/58	02/59	p
56162	08/18	SRlx	08/49	16162	-02/59	02/60	p
56163	10/18	SRlx	10/49	16163	-06/59	10/59	p
56164	10/18	SRlx	02/52	16164	-11/58	01/59	p
56165	10/20	SRlx	11/48	16165	-01/60	04/60	p
56166	11/20	SRlx	01/50	16166	-06/59	10/59	p
56167	12/20	SRlx	05/49	16167	-04/61	04/61	p
56168	12/20	SRlx	03/49	16168	-04/61	04/61	p
56169	12/20	SRlx	10/48	16169	-03/61	08/61	p
56170	01/21	SRlx	05/48	16170	-02/60	02/60	p
56171	02/21	SRlx	09/50	16171	-03/61	03/61	p
56172	02/21	SRlx	02/51	16172	-11/60	11/60	p
56173	02/21	SRlx	10/49	16173	-05/61	05/61	p

3F [10] 56230-56376
0-6-0T CR McIntosh Class '782' & '29'

Power Classification: 3F
Introduced: 1895-1922
Designer: McIntosh
Company: CR
Weight: 47t 15cwt
Driving Wheel: 4' 6"
Boiler Pressure: 160psi
Cylinders: Inside 18" x 26"
Tractive Effort: 21215lbf
Valve Gear: Stephenson (slide valves)

These engines, known as the '782' and '29' classes, were designed by Lambie just before his death and built under McIntosh's supervision. They were the most numerous goods tank engines on the Caledonian Railway, and they were built for freight and general shunting work.

One hundred and forty seven engines were built and they all came into BR stock. Many engines were latterly fitted with stovepipe chimneys.

LYR Aspinall Class 23 0-6-0ST No 51321 at Fleetwood in March 1955.

LYR Aspinall Class 24 0-6-0T No 51535 at Bank Hall in Liverpool in May 1950. It is fitted with a simple spark arrestor for working the dock lines beneath the Liverpool Overhead Railway.

LYR Aspinall Class 27 0-6-0 No 52390, fitted with a Belpaire boiler. It is seen awaiting banking duties in the rain at Manchester Victoria.

Furness Railway Pettigrew '3F' 0-6-0 No 52510.

56250 was sold to the Wemyss Private Railway, being scrapped in 1959.

c 56231-56239 were the original '29' class (all the other engines being the '782' class). They were originally fitted with condensing apparatus for the Glasgow underground, but this was later removed in 1920-1922.

w These engines were later fitted with Westinghouse brakes.

Year End Totals: '3F [10]' class

'47	'48	'49	'50	'51	'52	'53	'54	'55	'56	'57	'58	'59	'60	'61	'62	'63	'64	'65	'66	'67
147	145	145	145	145	144	141	140	138	124	109	79	48	28	9						

Number	Built	Renumbered	BR Dates	Scrap	Notes
56230	05/05 SRlx	03/50 16230	-01/57	03/57	
56231	11/95 SRlx	02/49 16231	-03/56	03/56	cw
56232	11/95 SRlx	10/48 16232	-04/62	06/63	cw
56233	11/95 SRlx	03/50 16233	-10/56	*56*	cw
56234	11/95 SRlx	02/51 16234	-12/57	03/58	cw
56235	12/95 SRlx	02/49 16235	-11/59	03/60	cw
56236	12/95 SRlx	06/50 16236	-12/58	03/59	cw
56237	12/95 SRlx	10/48 16237	-02/53	53	cw
56238	01/96 SRlx	04/48 16238	-09/58	10/58	cw
56239	01/96 SRlx	03/49 16239	-03/61	04/61	cw
56240	12/98 SRlx	01/49 16240	-07/61	07/61	
56241	12/98 SRlx	04/50 16241	-01/60	01/60	
56242	12/98 SRlx	01/51 16242	-07/61	07/61	
56243	12/98 SRlx	11/49 16243	-02/57	04/57	
56244	12/98 SRlx	11/48 16244	-05/58	06/58	
56245	12/98 SRlx	06/48 16245	-03/59	04/59	
56246	01/99 SRlx	11/50 16246	-04/61	05/61	
56247	01/99 SRlx	07/49 16247	-01/59	04/59	
56248	01/99 SRlx	06/49 16248	-01/55	01/55	
56249	01/99 SRlx	06/48 16249	-10/56	*56*	
56250	01/99 SRlx	05/50 16250	-01/54	59	
56251	01/99 SRlx	04/50 16251	-10/58	11/58	
56252	01/99 SRlx	03/49 16252	-05/59	09/59	
56253	01/99 SRlx	05/49 16253	-11/58	03/59	
56254	06/98 SRlx	06/48 16254	-04/58	06/58	
56255	06/98 SRlx	02/51 16255	-11/58	11/58	
56256	06/98 SRlx	10/48 16256	-06/59	07/59	
56257	06/98 SRlx	09/50 16257	-02/57	03/57	
56258	07/98 SRlx	09/50 16258	-04/53	53	
56259	07/98 SRlx	12/49 16259	-07/60	09/60	
56260	07/98 SRlx	03/49 16260	-12/60	12/60	
56261	08/98 SRlx	05/48 16261	-10/56	*56*	
56262	08/98 SRlx	10/48 16262	-02/59	05/59	
56263	09/98 SRlx	03/48 16263	-12/55	*56*	
56264	09/98 SRlx	02/50 16264	-10/59	10/59	
56265	09/98 SRlx	05/50 16265	-08/58	09/58	
56266	09/98 SRlx	03/50 16266	-11/59	11/59	
56267	09/98 SRlx	06/50 16267	-07/58	07/58	
56268	09/98 SRlx	03/49 16268	-02/52	*52*	
56269	09/98 SRlx	06/48 16269	-12/59	01/60	
56270	10/98 SRlx	16270	-10/48	*48*	
56271	10/98 SRlx	03/49 16271	-04/56	*56*	
56272	10/98 SRlx	04/48 16272	-10/58	10/58	
56273	10/98 SRlx	02/49 16273	-06/56	*56*	
56274	10/98 SRlx	08/50 16274	-01/58	03/58	
56275	10/98 SRlx	08/49 16275	-03/58	03/58	
56276	10/98 SRlx	09/48 16276	-02/53	05/53	
56277	11/98 SRlx	03/48 16277	-04/58	06/58	
56278	11/98 SRlx	01/50 16278	-06/62	09/63	
56279	11/98 SRlx	06/48 16279	-11/60	11/60	
56280	11/98 SRlx	05/50 16280	-12/57	02/58	
56281	11/98 SRlx	04/48 16281	-11/58	01/59	
56282	11/98 SRlx	12/48 16282	-04/62	07/62	
56283	12/98 SRlx	04/48 16283	-08/58	10/58	
56284	01/10 SRlx	04/48 16284	-05/58	10/58	
56285	10/04 SRlx	12/49 16285	-09/59	09/59	
56286	10/04 SRlx	11/48 16286	-05/58	09/58	
56287	11/04 SRlx	04/49 16287	-04/59	06/59	
56288	11/04 SRlx	03/50 16288	-01/59	01/59	
56289	12/04 SRlx	12/48 16289	-11/60	11/60	
56290	11/04 SRlx	09/50 16290	-06/59	06/59	w
56291	11/04 SRlx	06/50 16291	-07/59	07/59	w
56292	12/04 SRlx	01/50 16292	-05/60	06/60	w
56293	12/04 SRlx	05/51 16293	-11/58	12/58	w
56294	12/04 SRlx	09/49 16294	-04/57	06/57	w
56295	03/05 SRlx	07/49 16295	-12/59	12/59	w
56296	03/05 SRlx	09/51 16296	-08/59	09/59	w
56297	04/05 SRlx	11/48 16297	-11/57	12/57	w
56298	04/05 SRlx	12/48 16298	-10/61	11/62	w
56299	04/05 SRlx	12/48 16299	-01/57	03/57	w
56300	04/05 SRlx	11/50 16300	-11/60	11/60	w
56301	05/05 SRlx	02/49 16301	-10/58	12/58	w
56302	05/05 SRlx	01/49 16302	-12/62	01/64	w
56303	05/05 SRlx	11/50 16303	-08/56	*56*	w
56304	04/07 SRlx	09/48 16304	-03/60	03/60	
56305	04/07 SRlx	05/49 16305	-12/61	01/62	
56306	04/07 SRlx	11/49 16306	-12/58	06/59	
56307	04/07 SRlx	05/50 16307	-10/56	*56*	
56308	04/07 SRlx	02/49 16308	-10/60	05/61	
56309	09/07 SRlx	07/51 16309	-01/61	10/61	
56310	09/07 SRlx	04/48 16310	-11/60	11/60	
56311	04/07 SRlx	04/49 16311	-01/59	01/59	
56312	05/07 SRlx	03/49 16312	-05/62	06/63	
56313	05/07 SRlx	11/48 16313	-01/62	01/63	
56314	10/07 SRlx	12/48 16314	-02/58	03/58	
56315	06/07 SRlx	06/48 16315	-05/58	07/58	
56316	10/07 SRlx	02/50 16316	-10/59	04/60	
56317	05/07 SRlx	03/49 16317	-06/56	*07/56*	
56318	10/07 SRlx	12/49 16318	-06/59	08/59	
56319	02/10 SRlx	11/50 16319	-06/56	*07/56*	
56320	07/10 SRlx	03/48 16320	-11/57	01/58	
56321	07/10 SRlx	06/50 16321	-09/59	10/59	
56322	07/10 SRlx	03/50 16322	-09/59	10/59	
56323	07/10 SRlx	06/49 16323	-10/58	11/58	
56324	08/10 SRlx	03/50 16324	-03/61	04/61	
56325	01/10 SRlx	04/50 16325	-12/62	12/63	
56326	07/10 SRlx	09/49 16326	-10/61	11/62	
56327	07/10 SRlx	08/48 16327	-09/59	10/59	
56328	03/10 SRlx	12/49 16328	-09/58	11/58	
56329	10/10 SRlx	07/50 16329	-08/57	11/57	
56330	09/10 SRlx	04/50 16330	-05/58	06/58	
56331	03/10 SRlx	08/50 16331	-06/60	09/60	
56332	10/10 SRlx	07/49 16332	-10/59	04/60	
56333	10/10 SRlx	01/50 16333	-10/59	11/59	
56334	10/10 SRlx	12/49 16334	-01/58	03/58	
56335	11/10 SRlx	05/48 16335	-07/60	09/60	
56336	11/10 SRlx	06/48 16336	-12/62	12/63	
56337	11/10 SRlx	08/50 16337	-06/61	08/61	
56338	04/11 SRlx	11/49 16338	-03/61	05/61	
56339	04/11 SRlx	01/49 16339	-08/56	*56*	
56340	04/11 SRlx	10/48 16340	-10/59	10/59	
56341	04/11 SRlx	06/48 16341	-03/61	08/61	
56342	10/11 SRlx	09/49 16342	-03/57	04/57	
56343	10/11 SRlx	03/50 16343	-11/60	04/61	
56344	04/11 SRlx	01/49 16344	-09/59	10/59	
56345	10/12 SRlx	01/49 16345	-10/58	11/58	
56346	12/12 SRlx	06/48 16346	-09/57	11/57	
56347	10/12 SRlx	03/50 16347	-08/62	09/63	w
56348	10/12 SRlx	03/49 16348	-05/60	07/60	w
56349	10/12 SRlx	05/49 16349	-03/60	07/60	w
56350	12/12 SRlx	11/48 16350	-07/57	08/57	w
56351	10/12 SRlx	16351	-11/48	*48*	w
56352	10/12 SRlx	11/49 16352	-05/59	06/59	
56353	09/13 SRlx	11/49 16353	-07/58	11/58	
56354	09/13 SRlx	02/51 16354	-02/58	03/58	
56355	09/13 SRlx	11/49 16355	-12/56	*57*	
56356	09/13 SRlx	09/49 16356	-12/61	11/62	
56357	09/13 SRlx	08/50 16357	-12/57	01/58	
56358	10/13 SRlx	12/50 16358	-10/56	*56*	
56359	06/16 SRlx	04/48 16359	-05/59	06/59	
56360	06/16 SRlx	08/49 16360	-08/61	10/61	
56361	06/16 SRlx	04/48 16361	-11/60	12/60	
56362	06/16 SRlx	11/50 16362	-08/61	10/61	
56363	06/16 SRlx	03/51 16363	-07/60	08/60	
56364	06/16 SRlx	02/50 16364	-12/60	12/61	
56365	09/16 SRlx	01/49 16365	-05/59	06/59	
56366	07/21 SRlx	08/49 16366	-12/56	*57*	
56367	07/21 SRlx	12/48 16367	-02/60	03/60	
56368	08/21 SRlx	10/48 16368	-12/61	06/62	
56369	08/21 SRlx	09/48 16369	-11/57	01/58	
56370	04/22 SRlx	09/49 16370	-02/61	08/61	
56371	04/22 SRlx	02/50 16371	-01/60	02/60	
56372	05/22 SRlx	10/50 16372	-05/61	08/61	
56373	05/22 SRlx	09/49 16373	-10/59	04/60	
56374	05/22 SRlx	05/49 16374	-10/59	04/60	
56375	06/22 SRlx	02/49 16375	-08/58	09/58	
56376	06/22 SRlx	03/51 16376	-03/61	08/61	

3F [11] 56905
0-6-2T GSWR Drummond

Power Classification: 3F
Introduced: 1915-1919
Designer: Drummond and Whitelegg
Company: GSWR
Weight: 66t 4cwt
Driving Wheel: 5' 0"
Boiler Pressure: 180psi
Cylinders: Inside 18¼" x 26"
Tractive Effort: 22080lbf
Valve Gear: Stephenson (slide valves)

This was the last surviving engine of the former Glasgow and South Western Railway, and the only one to come into BR stock. During the LMS period, all the workings on the GSWR section were taken over by engines of Midland design, and this engine only survived so long due to the Second World War.

Originally one of twenty-eight locomotives which were designed for working the steeply graded branches in the Ayrshire coalfield, the class was based on an 0-6-4T which had been designed by Drummond for the Highland Railway. The last ten engines to be built (including 56905) were built by Whitelegg with increased tank capacity.

Two other engines which were sold to Ashington Colliery still survived in 1948, 16904 (scrapped in March 1953) and 16908 (scrapped in June 1956).

Year End Totals: '3F [11]' class

'47	'48	'49	'50	'51	'52	'53	'54	'55	'56	'57	'58	'59	'60	'61	'62	'63	'64	'65	'66	'67
1																				

Number	Built	Renumbered	BR Dates	Scrap	Notes
56905	06/19 NB	16905	-04/48	*48*	

2F [5] 57230-57473
0-6-0 CR Drummond class '294' 'Jumbo'

Power Classification: 2F
Introduced: 1883-1897
Designer: D Drummond
Company: CR
Weight: Loco 41t 6cwt
b Loco 42t 4cwt
Driving Wheel: 5' 0"
Boiler Pressure: 180psi
Cylinders: Inside 18" x 26"
Tractive Effort: 21480lbf
Valve Gear: Stephenson (slide valves)

This was the Caledonian '294' or 'standard goods' class, more affectionately known as the 'Jumbos'. Drummond based the engines on 133 0-6-0s which he had built for the North British Railway during his term of office there from 1876 to 1883. Later when he went to the LSWR in 1897 he built thirty more almost identical engines (see the SR '700' class).

Two hundred and forty-four engines were built by Dugald Drummond, Lambie and McIntosh in the period 1883-1897, making them by far the most numerous Caledonian Railway class. Two hundred and thirty-eight of these came into BR stock, the first having been withdrawn in 1946.

McIntosh later built an enlarged version of this class, the '812' class (see the '57550' class below).

Many engines later received stovepipe chimneys.

d Drummond built engines.

l Lambie built engines.

m McIntosh built engines (1895 onwards).

b Some engines were rebuilt with LMS boilers.

c Some engines were fitted with condensing apparatus for working on the Glasgow Underground (including those marked in the list).

r Twenty-five engines saw war service with the ROD in the First World War.

w A large number of engines were fitted with Westinghouse brakes for working passenger trains.

Year End Totals: '2F [5]' class

'47	'48	'49	'50	'51	'52	'53	'54	'55	'56	'57	'58	'59	'60	'61	'62	'63	'64	'65	'66	'67
238	219	198	188	174	165	154	154	150	144	140	134	118	115	58	16					

Number	Built	Renumbered	BR Dates	Scrap	Notes
57230	11/83 N	10/49 17230	-07/56	*08/56*	d
57231	11/83 N	17231	-05/49	*49*	d
57232	11/83 N	12/48 17232	-05/61	05/61	d
57233	11/83 N	09/50 17233	-10/61	02/62	d
57234	11/83 N	06/49 17234	-02/57	03/57	d
57235	11/83 N	02/50 17235	-10/55	*55*	d
57236	12/83 N	09/48 17236	-09/61	03/62	d
57237	11/83 SRlx	05/49 17237	-10/62	11/63	d
57238	12/83 SRlx	10/48 17238	-09/61	03/62	d
57239	12/83 SRlx	06/50 17239	-11/61	06/62	d
57240	12/83 SRlx	10/49 17240	-10/62	05/63	d
57241	12/83 N	05/50 17241	-05/59	06/59	d
57242	12/83 N	01/50 17242	-08/62	11/62	d
57243	12/83 N	04/48 17243	-06/59	07/59	d
57244	12/83 N	05/50 17244	-09/61	02/62	d
57245	12/83 N	07/48 17245	-10/61	01/63	d
57246	11/83 N	11/49 17246	-10/61	02/62	d
57247	12/83 N	09/48 17247	-07/59	08/59	d
57249	11/83 N	02/49 17249	-08/62	05/64	dr
57250	01/84 SRlx	08/49 17250	-09/61	04/62	d
57251	01/84 SRlx	12/49 17251	-10/62	09/63	d
57252	03/84 N	05/49 17252	-11/62	10/63	d
57253	03/84 N	05/50 17253	-10/62	04/63	d
57254	03/84 N	10/48 17254	-08/62	11/62	d
57255	03/84 N	02/50 17255	-04/52	*52*	d
57256	03/84 N	11/48 17256	-10/61	02/62	d
57257	04/84 N	08/49 17257	-10/61	01/62	d

Number	Built	Renumbered	BR Dates	Scrap	Notes
57258	04/84 N	06/48 17258	-10/62	01/65	d
57259	04/84 N	06/49 17259	-10/62	04/63	d
57260	04/84 N	07/48 17260	-10/55	55	d
57261	04/84 N	05/48 17261	-11/63	06/64	d
57262	04/84 N	04/49 17262	-10/61	05/63	d
57263	04/84 N	09/49 17263	-10/61	05/63	d
57264	04/84 N	06/48 17264	-10/61	10/61	d
57265	04/84 N	04/50 17265	-08/62	11/62	d
57266	04/84 N	09/48 17266	-12/62	09/63	d
57267	05/84 N	08/49 17267	-04/62	04/63	d
57268	05/84 N	05/48 17268	-10/61	09/62	d
57269	03/84 N	10/50 17269	-08/63	11/63	dr
57270	03/84 N	12/49 17270	-11/63	02/64	dr
57271	04/84 N	08/48 17271	-10/61	11/62	dr
57272	12/85 SRlx	11/48 17272	-10/51	51	d
57273	12/85 SRlx	12/48 17273	-02/60	03/60	d
57274	12/85 SRlx	10/50 17274	-04/62	11/62	d
57275	12/85 SRlx	12/48 17275	-04/62	11/62	d
57276	12/85 SRlx	02/50 17276	-11/59	12/59	d
57277	12/86 SRlx	04/49 17277	-04/51	51	d
57278	12/86 SRlx	06/50 17278	-06/63	03/64	d
57279	12/86 SRlx	07/48 17279	-10/59	11/59	d
57280	12/86 SRlx	03/50 17280	-08/52	52	d
57282	12/86 SRlx	06/49 17282	-11/55	55	d
57283	09/86 SRlx	04/49 17283	-02/51	51	d
57284	09/86 SRlx	12/48 17284	-10/62	01/64	d
57285	09/86 SRlx	10/49 17285	-11/61	03/63	d
57286	09/86 SRlx	17286	-02/49	49	d
57287	09/86 SRlx	12/48 17287	-11/61	10/62	d
57288	07/86 SRlx	10/49 17288	-11/61	11/62	d
57289	07/86 SRlx	04/48 17289	-11/51	51	d
57290	09/86 SRlx	17290	-06/48	07/48	dr
57291	09/86 SRlx	05/48 17291	-08/63	03/64	dr
57292	09/86 SRlx	05/48 17292	-11/61	08/62	dr
57294	12/85 SRlx	05/48 17294	-11/49	49	dr
57295	06/87 SRlx	06/49 17295	-06/62	11/63	d
57296	06/87 SRlx	06/50 17296	-11/63	05/64	d
57298	07/87 SRlx	05/48 17298	-04/50	50	d
57299	07/87 SRlx	12/48 17299	-10/62	11/63	d
57300	08/87 SRlx	05/49 17300	-06/62	11/62	d
57301	08/87 SRlx	17301	-05/48	07/48	d
57302	08/87 SRlx	08/49 17302	-10/63	02/64	d
57303	08/87 SRlx	02/50 17303	-10/61	11/62	d
57304	02/87 SRlx	17304	-06/48	07/48	d
57305	02/87 SRlx	17305	-02/49	49	d
57306	02/87 SRlx	03/49 17306	-08/51	51	d
57307	02/87 SRlx	05/48 17307	-08/59	09/59	d
57308	03/87 SRlx	17308	-05/48	07/48	d
57309	05/87 SRlx	09/48 17309	-11/63	02/64	d
57310	05/87 SRlx	05/48 17310	-12/49	50	d
57311	06/87 SRlx	10/49 17311	-09/62	11/62	dr
57312	02/87 SRlx	09/48 17312	-09/51	51	dr
57313	11/89 SRlx	17313	-01/48	02/48	dr
57314	11/89 SRlx	04/49 17314	-02/62	12/62	d
57315	11/89 SRlx	09/48 17315	-12/55	01/56	d
57316	11/89 SRlx	07/48 17316	-10/49	49	d
57317	11/89 SRlx	04/48 17317	-11/61	08/62	d
57318	11/89 SRlx	05/49 17318	-11/51	51	d
57319	01/90 SRlx	09/48 17319	-12/61	11/62	dw
57320	01/90 SRlx	10/48 17320	-03/56	56	dw
57321	01/90 SRlx	11/48 17321	-11/61	08/62	dw
57322	02/90 SRlx	06/50 17322	-03/53	53	dw
57323	02/90 SRlx	07/48 17323	-06/51	51	dw
57324	02/90 SRlx	02/50 17324	-05/61	05/61	dw
57325	11/91 SRlx	11/48 17325	-12/61	11/62	d
57326	11/91 SRlx	07/50 17326	-04/63	12/63	d
57327	12/91 SRlx	17327	-04/48	48	d
57328	12/91 SRlx	09/49 17328	-04/63	12/63	d
57329	12/91 SRlx	09/48 17329	-10/62	11/63	d
57330	12/91 SRlx	17330	-06/48	07/48	d
57331	12/91 SRlx	12/48 17331	-09/62	11/62	d
57332	02/92 SRlx	07/48 17332	-11/52	52	d
57333	02/92 SRlx	17333	-03/48	48	d
57334	03/92 SRlx	04/49 17334	-03/51	51	d
57335	03/92 SRlx	09/48 17335	-10/61	11/62	d
57336	07/92 SRlx	05/49 17336	-09/63	11/63	d
57337	07/92 SRlx	08/48 17337	-12/52	53	d
57338	07/92 SRlx	08/48 17338	-03/62	01/63	d
57339	07/92 SRlx	11/49 17339	-06/59	07/59	d
57340	08/92 SRlx	03/49 17340	-11/62	09/63	d
57341	08/92 SRlx	01/49 17341	-08/62	10/62	d
57342	04/92 SRlx	04/48 17342	-06/50	50	dw
57343	04/92 SRlx	17343	-04/48	48	dw
57344	04/92 SRlx	10/48 17344	-12/51	52	dw
57345	04/92 SRlx	10/49 17345	-02/62	11/62	dw
57346	05/92 SRlx	03/49 17346	-08/57	09/57	dw
57347	05/92 SRlx	01/50 17347	-03/62	11/62	dw
57348	11/91 SRlx	05/49 17348	-03/63	11/63	dr
57349	08/92 SRlx	08/49 17349	-07/61	01/62	dr
57350	07/92 SRlx	09/49 17350	-11/61	11/62	dr
57351	08/92 SRlx	05/48 17351	-08/49	49	dr
57352	12/92 SRlx	12/48 17352	-10/51	51	lr
57353	10/94 SRlx	03/49 17353	-11/61	06/63	lr
57354	10/94 SRlx	01/50 17354	-12/59	04/60	lr
57355	11/94 SRlx	06/49 17355	-11/63	06/64	lr
57356	11/94 SRlx	09/49 17356	-06/61	11/61	lr
57357	08/92 SRlx	03/50 17357	-03/62	06/63	d
57358	12/92 SRlx	06/48 17358	-05/49	07/49	l
57359	12/92 SRlx	12/49 17359	-03/62	06/63	l
57360	12/92 SRlx	09/48 17360	-03/63	12/63	l
57361	12/92 SRlx	06/48 17361	-12/59	05/63	l
57362	01/93 SRlx	12/49 17362	-06/62	10/62	l
57363	01/93 SRlx	06/49 17363	-12/61	11/62	l
57364	01/93 SRlx	11/49 17364	-12/61	05/63	l
57365	01/93 SRlx	06/49 17365	-05/62	11/62	l
57366	01/93 SRlx	03/50 17366	-11/61	01/63	l
57367	06/93 SRlx	06/50 17367	-12/61	08/62	lw
57368	06/93 SRlx	10/48 17368	-06/58	10/58	lw
57369	06/93 SRlx	10/49 17369	-10/62	10/62	lw
57370	07/93 SRlx	08/48 17370	-03/62	01/63	lw
57371	07/93 SRlx	17371	-07/48	48	lw
57372	07/93 SRlx	03/49 17372	-01/52	52	lw
57373	02/94 SRlx	04/49 17373	-07/61	11/61	lw
57374	02/94 SRlx	17374	-05/48	48	lw
57375	02/94 SRlx	01/49 17375	-11/63	06/64	lw
57377	05/94 SRlx	08/48 17377	-10/61	07/62	l
57378	05/94 SRlx	03/49 17378	-09/62	11/62	l
57379	06/94 SRlx	06/49 17379	-02/51	51	l
57380	07/94 SRlx	17380	-04/48	48	l
57381	07/94 SRlx	17381	-08/49	49	l
57382	08/94 SRlx	17382	-03/49	49	l
57383	11/94 SRlx	07/49 17383	-08/62	10/62	l
57384	11/94 SRlx	02/50 17384	-01/63	11/63	l
57385	10/94 SRlx	05/48 17385	-06/62	10/62	l
57386	10/94 SRlx	02/49 17386	-05/62	01/63	l
57387	06/95 SRlx	03/48 17387	-11/52	52	mw
57388	06/95 SRlx	01/49 17388	-02/53	53	mw
57389	07/94 SRlx	05/48 17389	-11/61	11/62	lr
57390	07/94 SRlx	05/48 17390	-05/50	50	lr
57391	07/94 SRlx	06/48 17391	-10/50	50	lr
57392	08/94 SRlx	02/49 17392	-12/61	05/63	lr
57393	06/95 SRlx	17393	-04/49	49	mw
57394	06/95 SRlx	03/49 17394	-11/51	51	mw
57395	06/95 SRlx	08/50 17395	-12/53	54	mw
57396	07/95 SRlx	05/50 17396	-05/58	06/58	mw
57397	07/96 SRlx	07/48 17397	-03/53	03/53	mw
57398	07/96 SRlx	07/48 17398	-05/62	09/62	mw
57399	08/96 SRlx	17399	-09/49	49	mw
57400	08/96 SRlx	17400	-07/49	49	mw
57401	08/96 SRlx	17401	-02/50	50	mw
57402	08/96 SRlx	17402	-08/49	49	mw
57403	09/96 SRlx	17403	-10/49	49	mw
57404	09/96 SRlx	02/49 17404	-10/61	01/62	mw
57405	09/96 SRlx	03/50 17405	-09/58	09/58	mw
57406	09/96 SRlx	17406	-01/48	48	mw
57407	09/96 SRlx	09/49 17407	-05/59	08/59	mw
57408	10/96 SRlx	17408	-02/48	48	mw
57409	10/96 SRlx	04/48 17409	-01/50	50	mw
57410	10/96 SRlx	04/50 17410	-02/53	08/53	mw
57411	10/96 SRlx	07/49 17411	-09/61	04/62	mw
57412	10/96 SRlx	03/49 17412	-04/56	56	mw
57413	11/96 SRlx	09/50 17413	-10/58	10/58	mw
57414	11/96 SRlx	09/50 17414	-04/59	05/59	mw
57415	11/96 SRlx	17415	-11/49	49	mw
57416	11/96 SRlx	09/49 17416	-07/61	08/61	mw
57417	02/97 SRlx	12/48 17417	-10/62	12/62	mw
57418	03/97 SRlx	02/49 17418	-10/61	11/62	mw
57419	03/97 SRlx	04/49 17419	-05/59	07/59	mw
57420	03/97 SRlx	17420	-10/49	49	mw
57421	03/97 SRlx	17421	-10/48	48	mw
57422	03/97 SRlx	17422	-06/48	07/48	mw
57423	03/97 SRlx	12/48 17423	-03/53	53	mw
57424	04/97 SRlx	08/50 17424	-12/59	02/60	mw
57425	04/97 SRlx	04/48 17425	-11/50	50	mw
57426	04/97 SRlx	03/48 17426	-09/61	02/62	mw
57427	04/97 SRlx	17427	-07/49	49	mw
57429	09/97 SRlx	03/49 17429	-09/61	02/62	mw
57430	10/97 SRlx	06/48 17430	-09/57	10/57	mw
57431	10/97 SRlx	01/49 17431	-06/61	08/61	mw
57432	10/97 SRlx	03/48 17432	-10/61	12/61	mw
57433	05/96 SRlx	04/50 17433	-05/52	52	mw
57434	05/96 SRlx	11/48 17434	-05/61	09/61	mw
57435	05/96 SRlx	10/48 17435	-02/60	03/60	mw
57436	06/96 SRlx	10/48 17436	-10/61	09/62	mw
57437	06/96 SRlx	12/49 17437	-07/58	11/58	mw
57438	06/96 SRlx	03/48 17438	-06/53	06/53	mw
57439	06/96 SRlx	06/48 17439	-02/53	05/53	mw
57440	06/96 SRlx	17440	-05/50	07/50	mw
57441	06/96 SRlx	01/49 17441	-11/61	11/62	mw
57442	06/96 SRlx	17442	-07/48	48	mw
57443	07/96 SRlx	11/48 17443	-08/58	09/58	mw
57444	07/96 SRlx	03/50 17444	-11/59	12/59	mw
57445	11/96 SRlx	09/48 17445	-08/62	10/62	mw
57446	12/96 SRlx	04/50 17446	-10/61	01/62	mw
57447	12/96 SRlx	11/48 17447	-10/62	12/63	mw
57448	12/96 SRlx	06/50 17448	-02/60	02/60	mw
57449	12/96 SRlx	17449	-11/49	49	mw
57450	12/96 SRlx	11/49 17450	-03/53	05/53	mw
57451	12/96 SRlx	11/49 17451	-10/61	07/63	mw
57452	08/97 SRlx	17452	-07/49	49	mw
57453	08/97 SRlx	08/48 17453	-11/50	50	mw
57454	09/97 SRlx	02/50 17454	-03/53	53	mw
57455	09/97 SRlx	06/49 17455	-06/51	51	mw
57456	09/97 SRlx	50 17456	-01/56	01/56	mw
57457	10/97 SRlx	10/49 17457	-03/56	56	mw
57458	10/97 SRlx	10/50 17458	-11/52	52	mw
57459	11/97 SRlx	03/50 17459	-12/56	57	mw
57460	11/97 SRlx	01/50 17460	-01/57	01/57	mw
57461	11/97 SRlx	09/48 17461	-10/61	11/62	mw
57462	11/97 SRlx	03/50 17462	-06/59	07/59	mw
57463	11/97 SRlx	09/48 17463	-12/61	11/62	mw
57464	04/97 SRlx	05/48 17464	-02/53	05/53	mw
57465	05/97 SRlx	03/49 17465	-04/59	07/59	mw
57466	05/97 SRlx	17466	-04/49	07/49	mw
57467	06/97 SRlx	08/48 17467	-02/50	50	mw
57468	06/97 SRlx	09/48 17468	-02/52	52	mw
57469	02/97 SRlx	17469	-11/48	02/49	mwc
57470	02/97 SRlx	01/50 17470	-10/61	03/63	mwc
57471	02/97 SRlx	17471	-09/48	48	mwc
57472	02/97 SRlx	12/48 17472	-09/61	03/62	mwc
57473	02/97 SRlx	04/49 17473	-06/61	08/61	mwc

3F [12] 57550-57628
0-6-0 CR McIntosh Class '812'

Power Classification: 3F
Introduced: 1899-1900
Designer: McIntosh
Company: CR
Weight: Loco 45t 14cwt
Driving Wheel: 5' 0"
Boiler Pressure: 180psi
Cylinders: Inside 18½" x 26"
Tractive Effort: 22690lbf
Valve Gear: Stephenson (slide valves)

This class was an enlarged version of the '57230' class 'Jumbos', and they were built by McIntosh in 1899-1900. They were fitted with larger boilers and larger cylinders. Of the original seventy-nine engines, seventy-six came into BR stock.

They were fitted with 'Dunalastair I' type boilers and 'Dunalastair II' type cabs. LMS boilers were later fitted to most of them. They were originally classified as mixed traffic engines but only seventeen were built with Westinghouse brakes and five with vacuum brakes for working passenger trains.

A further seventeen engines were built in 1908-1909 with detail differences and these were the '652' class (see the '57629' class).

w 57550-57566 were built with Westinghouse brakes for passenger working, and some others were also later converted.

Year End Totals: '3F [12]' class

'47	'48	'49	'50	'51	'52	'53	'54	'55	'56	'57	'58	'59	'60	'61	'62	'63	'64	'65	'66	'67
76	71	68	68	68	68	68	68	68	67	65	63	58	53	37	10					

Number	Built	Renumbered	BR Dates	Scrap	Notes
57550	05/99 SRlx	01/50 17550	-12/62	06/64	w
57551	05/99 SRlx	17551	-07/48	48	w
57552	05/99 SRlx	09/49 17552	-12/59	02/61	w
57553	06/99 SRlx	09/49 17553	-10/59	11/59	w
57554	06/99 SRlx	06/49 17554	-05/60	07/60	w
57555	06/99 SRlx	06/49 17555	-11/62	02/64	w
57556	06/99 SRlx	05/48 17556	-04/58	06/58	w
57557	06/99 SRlx	11/48 17557	-10/61	05/62	w
57558	06/99 SRlx	06/50 17558	-09/60	12/60	w
57559	07/99 SRlx	02/49 17559	-10/61	04/62	w
57560	07/99 SRlx	11/50 17560	-10/61	04/62	w
57561	07/99 SRlx	17561	-07/49	49	w
57562	07/99 SRlx	04/48 17562	-05/62	10/62	w
57563	07/99 SRlx	10/49 17563	-12/61	09/62	w
57564	08/99 SRlx	02/49 17564	-10/61	11/62	w
57565	08/99 SRlx	12/49 17565	-12/62	08/63	w
57566 §	08/99 SRlx	07/48 17566	-08/63		w
57568	12/99 NR	12/49 17568	-11/63	12/63	
57569	12/99 NR	06/49 17569	-11/62	02/64	
57570	12/99 NR	07/48 17570	-08/61	02/62	
57571	12/99 NR	09/50 17571	-04/62	05/63	
57572	12/99 NR	06/49 17572	-06/63	02/64	
57573	12/99 NR	05/48 17573	-11/57	12/57	
57574	12/99 NR	17574	-06/48	07/48	
57575	12/99 NR	10/48 17575	-10/59	11/59	
57576	12/99 NR	09/48 17576	-10/61	03/63	
57577	04/00 NR	01/49 17577	-08/62	09/62	
57578	04/00 NR	17578	-11/48	48	
57579	04/00 NR	02/50 17579	-11/61	02/63	
57580	04/00 NR	04/49 17580	-11/61	02/63	
57581	04/00 NR	10/48 17581	-11/63	02/64	
57582	04/00 NR	07/48 17582	-09/57	10/57	
57583	04/00 NR	07/48 17583	-11/61	10/62	
57584	04/00 NR	17584	-06/49	07/49	
57585	05/00 NR	09/49 17585	-11/61	02/62	
57586	05/00 NR	06/50 17586	-06/61	02/62	
57587	08/00 SS	11/50 17587	-08/62	02/63	
57588	08/00 SS	05/48 17588	-01/58	07/58	
57589	08/00 SS	02/49 17589	-10/56	56	
57590	08/00 SS	06/50 17590	-09/63	02/64	

Number	Built	Renumbered	BR Dates	Scrap	Notes
57591	08/00 SS	11/49 17591	-06/61	09/61	
57592	08/00 SS	06/49 17592	-08/63	12/63	
57593	08/00 SS	12/49 17593	-11/61	11/62	
57594	08/00 SS	05/48 17594	-12/62	02/64	
57595	08/00 SS	01/49 17595	-11/59	04/60	
57596	08/00 SS	05/49 17596	-10/62	02/64	
57597	08/00 SS	08/49 17597	-04/62	11/62	
57599	09/00 SS	08/48 17599	-11/59	12/59	
57600	09/00 SS	06/49 17600	-11/63	05/64	
57601	09/00 SS	06/49 17601	-12/62	02/64	
57602	04/00 D	12/49 17602	-12/62	02/64	
57603	04/00 D	05/50 17603	-03/62	11/62	
57604	05/00 D	06/48 17604	-12/62	03/64	
57605	05/00 D	06/49 17605	-05/60	08/60	
57606	05/00 D	17606	-09/48	*48*	
57607	05/00 D	06/49 17607	-03/63	07/63	
57608	05/00 D	05/48 17608	-12/62	03/64	
57609	05/00 D	*50* 17609	-07/60	02/61	
57611	05/00 D	01/50 17611	-11/62	02/64	
57612	05/00 D	09/50 17612	-04/62	01/63	
57613	05/00 D	01/49 17613	-09/62	11/62	
57614	05/00 D	06/48 17614	-10/62	02/64	
57615	05/00 D	03/49 17615	-11/62	02/64	
57616	05/00 D	17616	-05/48	*48*	
57617	09/99 SRIx	03/49 17617	-10/62	03/63	
57618	09/99 SRIx	02/49 17618	-03/62	03/63	
57619	09/99 SRIx	07/48 17619	-06/61	08/61	
57620	09/99 SRIx	02/49 17620	-06/62	09/62	
57621	09/99 SRIx	08/49 17621	-04/62	10/62	
57622	10/99 SRIx	10/48 17622	-08/62	09/62	
57623	10/99 SRIx	06/49 17623	-11/61	03/63	
57624	10/99 SRIx	17624	-05/49	*49*	
57625	10/99 SRIx	08/49 17625	-06/63	10/63	
57626	10/99 SRIx	11/49 17626	-02/62	10/62	
57627	11/99 SRIx	12/50 17627	-11/63	02/64	
57628	11/99 SRIx	03/50 17628	-02/60	06/60	

3F [13] 57629-57645
0-6-0 CR McIntosh Class '652'

Power Classification: 3F
Introduced: 1908-1909
Designer: McIntosh
Company: CR
Weight: Loco 45t 14cwt
Driving Wheel: 5' 0"
Boiler Pressure: 180psi
Cylinders: Inside 18½" x 26"
Tractive Effort: 22690lbf
Valve Gear: Stephenson (slide valves)

These engines were identical to the '812' class (see the '57550' class above) except that they were fitted with 'Dunalastair III' type cabs and deeper mainframes behind the splashers.

Year End Totals: '3F [13]' class

'47	'48	'49	'50	'51	'52	'53	'54	'55	'56	'57	'58	'59	'60	'61	'62	'63	'64	'65	'66	'67
17	13	13	13	13	13	13	13	13	13	13	13	12	12	8	2					

Number	Built	Renumbered	BR Dates	Scrap	Notes
57629	03/08 SRIx	17629	-09/48	*10/48*	
57630	03/08 SRIx	06/49 17630	-11/63	05/64	
57631	03/08 SRIx	06/48 17631	-10/62	03/63	
57632	07/09 SRIx	07/48 17632	-11/61	07/62	
57633	03/08 SRIx	08/50 17633	-12/61	08/62	
57634	03/08 SRIx	*50* 17634	-08/63	11/63	
57635	06/08 SRIx	06/48 17635	-03/62	04/63	
57636	06/08 SRIx	17636	-12/48	*49*	
57637	08/08 SRIx	06/49 17637	-12/61	04/62	
57638	09/08 SRIx	11/48 17638	-10/59	11/59	
57639	09/08 SRIx	17639	-09/48	*48*	
57640	06/08 SRIx	11/49 17640	-11/61	02/63	
57641	06/09 SRIx	17641	-04/48	*48*	
57642	06/09 SRIx	12/49 17642	-08/62	05/63	
57643	06/09 SRIx	05/48 17643	-10/62	02/64	
57644	07/09 SRIx	02/49 17644	-10/62	02/64	
57645	07/09 SRIx	04/49 17645	-11/62	05/63	

3F [14] 57650-57691
0-6-0 CR Pickersgill Classes '294' & '670'

Power Classification: 3F
Introduced: 1918-1920
Designer: Pickersgill
Company: CR
Weight: Loco 50t 13cwt
Driving Wheel: 5' 0"
Boiler Pressure: 180psi superheated
Cylinders: Inside 18½" x 26"
Tractive Effort: 22690lbf
Valve Gear: Stephenson (piston valves)

In 1912 McIntosh built a class of 0-6-0s known as the '30' class. They were a superheated version of the '812' class (see the '57550' class above). Four engines were built and they were all withdrawn by 1946.

The '294' class was then introduced by Pickersgill in 1918, being a composite version of the '812' class and the '30' class. They were originally fitted with saturated boilers, but they were later superheated by the LMS. Forty-three engines were built, and twenty-nine came into BR stock, the first having been withdrawn in 1934.

a 57684-57691 were built in 1919 and were known as the '670' class.

Year End Totals: '3F [14]' class

'47	'48	'49	'50	'51	'52	'53	'54	'55	'56	'57	'58	'59	'60	'61	'62	'63	'64	'65	'66	'67
29	29	29	29	29	29	29	29	29	29	29	29	29	29	22	8					

Number	Built	Renumbered	BR Dates	Scrap	Notes
57650	06/19 SRIx	12/48 17650	-11/61	05/63	
57651	06/19 SRIx	10/48 17651	-11/61	05/63	
57652	06/19 SRIx	10/48 17652	-11/63	01/64	
57653	07/19 SRIx	11/48 17653	-01/61	05/63	
57654	07/19 SRIx	07/49 17654	-04/62	05/63	
57655	07/19 SRIx	03/50 17655	-04/62	11/62	
57658	03/18 SRIx	05/49 17658	-12/62	02/64	
57659	04/18 SRIx	06/48 17659	-11/61	06/62	
57661	05/18 SRIx	06/48 17661	-09/63	02/64	
57663	06/18 SRIx	05/50 17663	-11/61	09/62	
57665	07/18 SRIx	04/48 17665	-11/61	06/62	
57666	07/18 SRIx	03/50 17666	-08/62	03/63	
57667	08/18 SRIx	07/49 17667	-08/62	11/63	
57668	12/18 SRIx	11/49 17668	-01/63	02/64	
57669	12/18 SRIx	07/48 17669	-11/61	02/63	
57670	12/18 SRIx	05/49 17670	-03/63	03/64	
57671	01/19 SRIx	10/49 17671	-08/62	10/62	
57672	02/19 SRIx	01/50 17672	-10/62	02/64	
57673	03/19 SRIx	09/50 17673	-03/62	02/63	
57674	03/19 SRIx	03/49 17674	-11/62	02/64	
57679	06/19 SRIx	01/49 17679	-11/63	06/64	
57681	10/19 SRIx	04/48 17681	-10/62	02/64	
57682	10/19 SRIx	02/50 17682	-05/62	05/63	
57684	11/19 SRIx	02/49 17684	-11/62	10/63	a
57686	12/19 SRIx	07/48 17686	-03/62	03/63	a
57688	12/19 SRIx	08/51 17688	-11/63	05/64	a
57689	01/20 SRIx	12/48 17689	-08/63	11/63	a
57690	01/20 SRIx	06/48 17690	-08/63	02/64	a
57691	02/20 SRIx	03/50 17691	-08/62	10/62	a

3F [15] 57693-57702
0-6-0 HR Drummond 'Barney'

Power Classification: 3F
Introduced: 1900-1907
Designer: P Drummond
Company: HR
Weight: Loco 43t 10cwt
Driving Wheel: 5' 0"
Boiler Pressure: 175psi
Cylinders: Inside 18¼" x 26"
Tractive Effort: 21470lbf
Valve Gear: Stephenson (slide valves)

Peter Drummond built these twelve engines in 1900-1907 for freight work. They were known as the 'Barneys'. The first was withdrawn in 1936 and seven came into BR stock.

Most engines of the class were later fitted with Caledonian type boilers.

h 57695 and 57699 retained their Drummond Highland Railway boilers.

s 57697 was later fitted with a stovepipe chimney.

Year End Totals: '3F [15]' class

'47	'48	'49	'50	'51	'52	'53	'54	'55	'56	'57	'58	'59	'60	'61	'62	'63	'64	'65	'66	'67
7	7	4	3	1																

Number	Built	Renumbered	BR Dates	Scrap	Notes
57693	02/00 D	17693	-06/49	06/49	
57694	02/00 D	17694	-02/50	*50*	
57695	02/00 D	05/48 17695	-01/52	*52*	h
57697	02/00 D	10/48 17697	-02/51	*51*	s
57698	02/00 D	11/48 17698	-12/51	*52*	
57699	08/02 D	17699	-02/49	*49*	h
57702	08/02 D	17702	-10/49	*49*	

4F [4] 57950-57956
4-6-0 HR Cumming 'Clan Goods'

Power Classification: 4F reclassified 4MT in 1948
Introduced: 1917-1919
Designer: Cumming
Company: HR
Weight: Loco 56t 9cwt
Driving Wheel: 5' 3"
Boiler Pressure: 175psi superheated
Cylinders: Outside 20½" x 26"
Tractive Effort: 25800lbf
Valve Gear: Walschaert (piston valves)

Cumming built eight engines for working goods trains on the Highland Railway in 1917-1919. Six survived in 1948, the first having been withdrawn in 1946.

These engines were always known as the 'Clan Goods' class, even though they were built before their passenger counterpart, the 'Clan' class (see the '54764' class).

Year End Totals: '4F [4]' class

'47	'48	'49	'50	'51	'52	'53	'54	'55	'56	'57	'58	'59	'60	'61	'62	'63	'64	'65	'66	'67
6	5	5	4	3																

Number	Built	Renumbered	BR Dates	Scrap	Notes
57950	04/17 HL	06/49 17950	-07/50	*07/50*	
57951	04/17 HL	11/48 17951	-06/51	*51*	
57953	06/17 HL	17953	-09/48	*48*	
57954	10/19 HL	05/49 17954	-10/52	*52*	
57955	10/19 HL	11/48 17955	-07/52	*08/52*	
57956	11/19 HL	11/48 17956	-06/52	*52*	

4P [6] 58000-58003
4-6-0 LNWR Bowen Cooke 'Prince of Wales'

Power Classification: 4P
Introduced: 1911-1922
Designer: Bowen Cooke
Company: LNWR
Weight: Loco 66t 5cwt
Driving Wheel: 6' 3"
Boiler Pressure: 180psi superheated
Cylinders: Inside 20½" x 26"
Tractive Effort: 22290lbf
Valve Gear: Joy (piston valves)

Bowen Cooke introduced the 'Prince of Wales' class in 1911. They were a superheated version of the earlier 'Experiment' class and a six-coupled version of the 'George the Fifth' 4-4-0s (see the '58011' class).

They were designed as general purpose mixed traffic locomotives and they proved to be excellent engines. They handled the heavy main line trains on the West Coast main line when they were built. They were built with round topped fireboxes and many of them were rebuilt with Belpaire fireboxes.

246 engines were built up to 1922 and they were numbered 5600-5844. The later survivors were transferred to the duplicate list in 1934 by having 20000 added to their numbers. The first of the class was withdrawn in 1933 and only six came into BR stock. Two of these engines were withdrawn in the early months of 1948 and were never allocated BR numbers, none of the others ever carried their allocated numbers.

r 58000 retained its round topped firebox.

Year End Totals: '4P [6]' class

'47	'48	'49	'50	'51	'52	'53	'54	'55	'56	'57	'58	'59	'60	'61	'62	'63	'64	'65	'66	'67
6	2																			

Number	Built	Renumbered	BR Dates	Scrap	Notes
58000	12/15 Crw	25648	-10/48	11/48	r
QUEEN OF THE BELGIANS					
58001	03/16 Crw	25673	-01/49	02/49	
LUSITANIA					
	06/19 Crw	25722	-03/48	*04/48*	
58002	11/19 Crw	25752	-05/49	10/49	
58003	10/21 BM	25787	-05/48	06/48	
	01/22 BM	25827	-03/48	04/48	

3P [7] 58010
4-4-0 LNWR Whale ‘Precursor’

Power Classification:	3P
Introduced:	1904-1907
Designer:	Whale
Company:	LNWR
Weight:	Loco 59t 17cwt
Driving Wheel:	6' 9"
Boiler Pressure:	180psi superheated
Cylinders:	Inside 20½" x 26"
Tractive Effort:	20640lbf
Valve Gear:	Joy (piston valves)

The ‘Precursor’ class was undoubtedly the most efficient passenger engine ever owned by the LNWR. Designed by Whale, 130 were built in 1904-1907 numbered 5187-5319 by the LMS. Originally built without superheaters, most of the class (including this last survivor) were rebuilt with superheaters and Belpaire boilers.

The ‘George the Fifth’ class (see the ‘58011’ class below) was a version of this class which was built new with superheaters by Bowen Cooke in 1910.

The first engine was withdrawn in 1927 and the surviving engines were transferred to the duplicate list in 1934 by having 20000 added to their numbers. 25297 was the last survivor and the only engine to come into BR stock, but it was withdrawn without ever carrying its BR number.

Year End Totals: ‘3P [7]’ class

'47	'48	'49	'50	'51	'52	'53	'54	'55	'56	'57	'58	'59	'60	'61	'62	'63	'64	'65	'66	'67
1	1																			

Number	Built	Renumbered	BR Dates	Scrap	Notes
58010	11/04 Crw	25297	-06/49	10/49	
SIROCCO					

3P [8] 58011-58012
4-4-0 LNWR Bowen Cooke ‘George the Fifth’

Power Classification:	3P
Introduced:	1910-1915
Designer:	Bowen Cooke
Company:	LNWR
Weight:	Loco 59t 17cwt
Driving Wheel:	6' 9"
Boiler Pressure:	180psi superheated
Cylinders:	Inside 20½" x 26"
Tractive Effort:	20640lbf
Valve Gear:	Joy (piston valves)

The ‘George the Fifth’ class was a superheated version of the ‘Precursor’ class (see the ‘58010’ class above). They were built by Bowen Cooke who was Whale’s successor, and ninety were built between 1910 and 1915 numbered 5320-5409 by the LMS. Most of the class were rebuilt with Belpaire boilers.

The first engine was withdrawn in 1935 and the surviving engines were later transferred to the duplicate list by having 20000 added to their numbers. Three engines survived to come into BR stock; 25321 was withdrawn in February 1948 without being allocated a BR number, and neither of the other two survived long enough to carry their allocated BR numbers.

58011 was originally named INDIA.

Year End Totals: ‘3P [8]’ class

'47	'48	'49	'50	'51	'52	'53	'54	'55	'56	'57	'58	'59	'60	'61	'62	'63	'64	'65	'66	'67
3																				

Number	Built	Renumbered	BR Dates	Scrap	Notes
	11/10 Crw	25321	-02/48	04/48	
LORD LOCH					
58011	06/11 Crw	25350	-05/48	06/48	
58012	09/11 Crw	25373	-05/48	05/48	
PTARMIGAN					

1P [2] 58020
2-4-0 MR Johnson 6ft 3in

Power Classification:	1P
Introduced:	1876
Designer:	Johnson
Company:	MR
Weight:	Loco 40t 10cwt
Driving Wheel:	6' 3"
Boiler Pressure:	140psi
Cylinders:	Inside 18" x 24"
Tractive Effort:	12340lbf
Valve Gear:	Stephenson (slide valves)

When Johnson succeeded Kirtley as the Chief Engineer of the Midland Railway in 1873 he preferred using inside frames to the outside frames of his predecessor. He built a succession of handsome 2-4-0 designs up to 1881 when he started constructing larger 4-4-0 engines.

The 2-4-0 engines were built in four varieties with different wheel dimensions, 6ft 3in, 6ft 6in, 6ft 9in and 7ft 0in (which did not survive into BR days). See the ‘58020’, ‘58021’ and ‘58022’ classes.

This engine was the last survivor of Johnson’s ten 6ft 3in engines which were built in 1876. The first was withdrawn in 1912. Some of the class (including this engine) were rebuilt with Belpaire boilers from 1926 onwards. The engines were originally numbered 147-156, the survivors in 1934 being transferred to the duplicate list by the addition of 20000 to their numbers.

This engine worked in the service department from 1933-1936 when it was based at Abergavenny and carried the name ENGINEER SOUTH WALES. It never carried its allocated BR number.

Year End Totals: ‘1P [2]’ class

'47	'48	'49	'50	'51	'52	'53	'54	'55	'56	'57	'58	'59	'60	'61	'62	'63	'64	'65	'66	'67
1	1	1																		

Number	Built	Renumbered	BR Dates	Scrap	Notes
58020	04/76 Der	20155	-10/50	12/50	

1P [3] 58021
2-4-0 MR Johnson 6ft 6in

Power Classification:	1P
Introduced:	1876-1880
Designer:	Johnson
Company:	MR
Weight:	Loco 40t 10cwt
Driving Wheel:	6' 6½"
Boiler Pressure:	120psi
Cylinders:	Inside 18" x 28"
Tractive Effort:	11790lbf
Valve Gear:	Stephenson (slide valves)

This engine was the last survivor of Johnson’s forty 6ft 6in engines which were built in 1876-1880. The first was withdrawn in 1922. Some of the class (including this engine) were rebuilt with Belpaire boilers from 1926 onwards. The engines were originally numbered 157-191 and 217-221, the survivors in 1934 being transferred to the duplicate list by the addition of 20000 to their numbers. This engine never carried its allocated BR number.

Year End Totals: ‘1P [3]’ class

'47	'48	'49	'50	'51	'52	'53	'54	'55	'56	'57	'58	'59	'60	'61	'62	'63	'64	'65	'66	'67
1																				

Number	Built	Renumbered	BR Dates	Scrap	Notes
58021	04/76 D	20185	-08/48	*48*	

1P [4] 58022
2-4-0 MR Johnson 6ft 9in

Power Classification:	1P
Introduced:	1876-1881
Designer:	Johnson
Company:	MR
Weight:	Loco 40t 16cwt
Driving Wheel:	6' 9"
Boiler Pressure:	140psi
Cylinders:	Inside 18" x 26"
Tractive Effort:	12375lbf
Valve Gear:	Stephenson (slide valves)

This engine was the last survivor of Johnson’s sixty-five 6ft 9in engines which were built in 1876-1881 (this engine being built in 1879). The first was withdrawn in 1925. Most of the class (including this engine) were rebuilt with Belpaire boilers from 1926 onwards. The engines were originally numbered 192-196, 207-216 and 222-271, the survivors in 1934 being transferred to the duplicate list by the addition of 20000 to their numbers. This engine never carried its allocated BR number.

Year End Totals: ‘1P [4]’ class

'47	'48	'49	'50	'51	'52	'53	'54	'55	'56	'57	'58	'59	'60	'61	'62	'63	'64	'65	'66	'67
1	1																			

Number	Built	Renumbered	BR Dates	Scrap	Notes
58022	11/79 Der	20216	-11/49	12/49	

1P [5] 58030-58038
0-4-4T MR Johnson 5ft 7in

Power Classification:	1P
Introduced:	1875-1876
Designer:	Johnson
Company:	MR
Weight:	53t 4cwt
Driving Wheel:	5' 7"
Boiler Pressure:	140psi
Cylinders:	Inside 18" x 24"
Tractive Effort:	13810lbf
Valve Gear:	Stephenson (slide valves)

Refer to the Historical Survey of Midland 0-4-4T Engines at the end of this section for more details of this class.

This class was the original batch of engines with 5ft 7in wheels, originally numbered 1236-1265. Many were later rebuilt with Belpaire boilers. Of the original thirty engines nine came into BR stock.

Year End Totals: ‘1P [5]’ class

'47	'48	'49	'50	'51	'52	'53	'54	'55	'56	'57	'58	'59	'60	'61	'62	'63	'64	'65	'66	'67
9	8	5	1	1	1	1														

Number	Built	Renumbered	BR Dates	Scrap	Notes
58030	11/75 N	1239	-04/49	*49*	
58031	12/75 N	1246	-06/49	*49*	
58032	01/76 N	1247	-12/49	12/49	
58033	01/76 N	11/48 1249	-09/50	*50*	
58034	03/76 N	1251	-09/50	*50*	
58035	03/76 N	1252	-01/50	*50*	
58036	03/76 N	10/48 1255	-06/50	08/50	
58037	04/76 N	1260	-05/48	*48*	
58038	05/76 N	07/48 1261	-05/54	*54*	

1P [6] 58039-58091
0-4-4T MR Johnson 5ft 4in

Power Classification:	1P
Introduced:	1881-1900
Designer:	Johnson
Company:	MR
Weight:	53t 4cwt
Driving Wheel:	5' 4"
Boiler Pressure:	140psi b 150psi
Cylinders:	Inside 18" x 24"
Tractive Effort:	14460lbf b 15490lbf
Valve Gear:	Stephenson (slide valves)

Refer to the Historical Survey of Midland 0-4-4T Engines at the end of this section for more details of this class.

This class comprised the second and third batches of engines with 5ft 4in wheels, originally numbered 1266-1430. Of the original 165 engines fifty-six came into BR stock, including three which were withdrawn early in 1948 without being allocated BR numbers. Most of the engines were rebuilt with Belpaire boilers from 1925 onwards.

b These engines, built from 1889 onwards had higher pressure boilers.

h The last batch, built from 1895 onwards were fitted with higher pitched boilers and larger tanks.

c These engines were fitted with condensing apparatus for working through the Metropolitan tunnels on the London suburban services.

p Most of the later survivors were motor fitted for working push-pull services, including those marked in the list.

Year End Totals: ‘1P [6]’ class

'47	'48	'49	'50	'51	'52	'53	'54	'55	'56	'57	'58	'59	'60	'61	'62	'63	'64	'65	'66	'67
56	48	45	38	32	28	19	17	12	5	4	3	1								

Number	Built	Renumbered	BR Dates	Scrap	Notes
58039	10/81 Der	1272	-10/48	*10/48*	
58040	10/81 Der	12/48 1273	-03/55	*55*	
58041	11/81 Der	01/49 1275	-10/50	*50*	
58042	12/81 Der	01/49 1278	-12/51	*52*	
58043	06/83 Der	03/49 1287	-02/51	*02/51*	
58044	07/83 Der	1290	-04/48	*48*	
58045	02/84 Der	07/49 1295	-10/51	*10/51*	
58046	03/84 Der	08/49 1298	-12/51	*52*	
58047	04/84 Der	05/50 1303	-08/52	*52*	
	04/84 Der	1307	-01/48	*48*	
58048	06/85 Der	1315	-10/49	*49*	
58049	03/86 Der	1322	-03/50	04/50	c
58050	03/86 Der	1324	-02/53	*03/53*	
58051	05/86 Der	02/49 1330	-10/56	*10/56*	
58052	05/89 Der	04/49 1337	-04/51	*51*	
58053	05/89 Der	05/48 1340	-01/53	*02/53*	
58054	02/92 Der	07/50 1341	-11/55	12/55	
58055	02/92 Der	1342	-06/48	*48*	
58056	03/92 Der	03/50 1344	-09/54	09/54	
58057	03/92 Der	1348	-05/49	*49*	
58058	03/92 Der	03/49 1350	-10/52	*10/52*	
58059	02/92 D	03/49 1353	-10/50	*10/50*	b
58060	02/92 D	05/49 1357	-07/52	*52*	b
58061	02/92 D	03/49 1358	-11/50	*11/50*	b
58062	02/92 D	12/48 1360	-02/56	*56*	b
	04/92 D	1361	-02/48	*48*	b
58063	05/92 D	1365	-05/51	*51*	b
58064	05/92 D	1366	-02/50	02/50	b
58065	05/92 D	04/49 1367	-11/59	10/60	bp
58066	05/92 D	07/49 1368	-10/58	09/59	bp
58067	05/92 D	1370	-01/53	02/53	b
58068	08/93 N	11/49 1371	-10/53	*53*	bc
58069	08/93 N	03/49 1373	-05/52	*52*	bc
58070	09/93 N	06/48 1375	-02/53	*02/53*	bc
58071	09/93 N	01/51 1377	-07/56	*07/56*	bc
58072	09/93 N	08/51 1379	-10/56	*10/56*	bc
58073	04/95 D	12/48 1382	-01/56	*56*	bc
	04/95 D	1385	-01/48	*48*	bc
58074	02/95 D	1389	-10/48	*48*	bh
58075	02/95 D	06/49 1390	-09/53	*09/53*	bh
58076	03/95 D	04/51 1396	-01/53	*03/53*	bh
58077	03/95 D	08/49 1397	-09/55	10/55	bh
58078	02/98 Der	1402	-05/49	*49*	bh
58079	04/98 Der	1406	-08/50	10/50	bh
58080	06/00 D	08/48 1411	-01/56	*56*	bh
58081	06/00 D	1413	-09/48	*48*	bh
58082	07/00 D	05/48 1416	-04/50	06/50	bh
58083	07/00 D	12/49 1420	-10/57	10/57	bhp
58084	08/00 D	04/49 1421	-02/55	*55*	bh
58085	08/00 D	10/48 1422	-04/59	10/60	bhp
58086	08/00 D	12/48 1423	-08/60	10/60	bhp
58087	08/00 D	12/49 1424	-06/55	*55*	bh
58088	08/00 D	02/50 1425	-02/53	*03/53*	bh
58089	09/00 D	05/48 1426	-10/54	*54*	bh
58090	09/00 D	10/50 1429	-02/53	*03/53*	bh
58091	09/00 D	02/49 1430	-09/56	*56*	bh

1P [7] 58092
2-4-0T LNWR Webb

Power Classification:	1P
Introduced:	1876-1885
Designer:	Webb
Company:	LNWR
Weight:	38t 4cwt
Driving Wheel:	4' 8½"
Boiler Pressure:	150psi
Cylinders:	Inside 17" x 20"
Tractive Effort:	13045lbf
Valve Gear:	Allan straight link (slide valves)

Between 1876 and 1885 Webb built fifteen engines of this class of 2-4-0Ts and they were known as 'Chopper Tanks'. They were allocated the numbers 6420-6434 and the first was withdrawn in 1924. Apart from this last survivor, the whole class was withdrawn by 1936.

58092 outlasted all the others by many years and it was based on the Cromford and High Peak line in the Peak District. It was transferred to the duplicate list and renumbered 26428 in March 1948, and then later renumbered 58092.

Year End Totals: '1P [7]' class

'47	'48	'49	'50	'51	'52	'53	'54	'55	'56	'57	'58	'59	'60	'61	'62	'63	'64	'65	'66	'67
1	1	1	1	1																

Number	Built	Renumbered	BR Dates	Scrap	Notes
58092	10/77 Crw	08/49 6428	-03/52	*05/52*	
				03/48➲26428	

0-10-0 58100
0-10-0 MR Fowler 'Lickey Banker'

Power Classification:	Unclassified
Introduced:	1919
Designer:	Fowler
Company:	MR
Weight:	Loco 73t 13cwt Tender 31t 10cwt
Driving Wheel:	4' 7½"
Boiler Pressure:	180psi superheated
Cylinders:	Four 16¾" x 28"
Tractive Effort:	43315lbf
Valve Gear:	Walschaert (slide valves)

In 1919 this engine appeared from Derby works and it was the largest engine ever built for the Midland Railway, which remained a 'small engine' line throughout its existence. It was only the second ten-coupled engine to have ever been built in Britain (the other being the short lived GER three-cylinder 'Decapod' engine of 1902).

It was a four-cylinder engine which was designed specifically for banking duties on the Lickey Incline at Bromsgrove on the Birmingham to Bristol main line. This consisted of two miles of continuous 1 in 37 ascent. It was a locomotive of great power and of distinctive appearance, having steeply inclined cylinders.

The locomotive was not named, but it was always known as *'Big Bertha'* or *'Big Emma'*. It worked continuously for 36 years on the Lickey Incline, (apart from a brief vacation in 1924 for working trials on the Toton-Brent coal trains) and a spare boiler was kept for it at Derby to reduce the amount of time the engine had to spend out of service. The tender (which was fitted with a tender cab) had originally been coupled to the Paget experimental 2-6-2 engine in 1936. The engine was fitted with a powerful electric headlight in order to assist when drawing up to the rear of a train in darkness; this headlight was later fitted to BR standard 9F No. 92079 which took over 58100's duties in 1956.

Originally numbered 2290, it was renumbered 22290 in 1947 and later became 58100.

Year End Totals: '0-10-0' class

'47	'48	'49	'50	'51	'52	'53	'54	'55	'56	'57	'58	'59	'60	'61	'62	'63	'64	'65	'66	'67
1	1	1	1	1	1	1	1	1												

Number	Built	Renumbered	BR Dates	Scrap	Notes
58100	12/19 Der	01/49 22290	-05/56	04/57	

2F [6] 58110
0-6-0 MR Kirtley Double Framed

Power Classification:	2F
Introduced:	1863-1874
Designer:	Kirtley
Company:	MR
Weight:	Loco 37t 12cwt
Driving Wheel:	5' 3"
Boiler Pressure:	160psi
Cylinders:	Inside 18" x 24"
Tractive Effort:	16785lbf
Valve Gear:	Stephenson (slide valves)

Refer to the Historical Survey of Midland 0-6-0 Engines at the end of this section for more details of this class.

The first of Kirtley's double framed 0-6-0s came out in the 1850s, but what may be regarded as his standard design appeared in 1863. Several hundred were built between 1863 and 1874. They were remarkably long lived engines. Some were withdrawn before 1907, but in the Midland renumbering scheme of that year the survivors were numbered 2300-2867.

2700-2788 were lent to the Railway Operating Division during the First World War for overseas service and all returned safely.

2630 became 22630 on the duplicate list and survived to become 58110. It was still fitted with a Johnson boiler and was withdrawn in 1951 at the age of 81.

Year End Totals: '2F [6]' class

'47	'48	'49	'50	'51	'52	'53	'54	'55	'56	'57	'58	'59	'60	'61	'62	'63	'64	'65	'66	'67
1	1	1	1																	

Number	Built	Renumbered	BR Dates	Scrap	Notes
58110	70 D	12/48 22630	-11/51	*12/51*	

2F [7] 58111-58113
0-6-0 MR Kirtley Double Framed Belpaire Boilered

Power Classification:	2F
Introduced:	1863-1874
Designer:	Kirtley rebuilt by Johnson & Deeley
Company:	MR
Weight:	Loco 37t 12cwt
Driving Wheel:	5' 3"
Boiler Pressure:	160psi
Cylinders:	Inside 18" x 24"
Tractive Effort:	16785lbf
Valve Gear:	Stephenson (slide valves)

Refer to the Historical Survey of Midland 0-6-0 Engines at the end of this section for more details of this class.

These three engines were all members of the '58110' class that had been rebuilt with Belpaire boilers. They were transferred to the LMS duplicate list with 20000 added to their numbers, but none of them survived long enough to receive their allocated BR numbers.

Year End Totals: '2F [7]' class

'47	'48	'49	'50	'51	'52	'53	'54	'55	'56	'57	'58	'59	'60	'61	'62	'63	'64	'65	'66	'67
3	3	1																		

Number	Built	Renumbered	BR Dates	Scrap	Notes
58111	73 D	22846	-09/49	*49*	
58112	73 D	22853	-03/50	02/51	
58113	74 D	22863	-01/49	*49*	

2F [8] 58114-58187, 58229-58248
0-6-0 MR Johnson 4ft 11in

Power Classification:	2F
Introduced:	1875-1902
Designer:	Johnson
Company:	MR
Weight:	Loco between 37t 12cwt and 40t 3cwt
Driving Wheel:	4' 11"
Boiler Pressure:	160psi
Cylinders:	Inside 18" x 26"
Tractive Effort:	19420lbf
Valve Gear:	Stephenson (slide valves)

Refer to the Historical Survey of Midland 0-6-0 Engines at the end of this section for more details of this class.

Johnson developed his 'Class 2' engines in 1875. They were inside framed engines and as such they were the forerunners of several large classes of inside framed 0-6-0s, numbering 1763 in total (including fifty-six engines built for the SDJR and the MGNJR). This constituted the largest single basic design of engine ever built on a railway in this country.

The first 120 engines were built in 1875-1876 and they were eventually numbered 2900-3019 under the 1907 renumbering scheme. They were built with 4' 11" diameter wheels. The next batch of 110 engines were built up to 1884 with 5' 3" wheels (see the '58188' class below). 3130-3189 came next, again with 4' 11" wheels, but from then on all subsequent batches (including '3F's and '4F's) carried 5' 3" wheels.

All these engines were built with round topped boilers and small Johnson cabs. From 1917 onwards many of the engines were rebuilt with Belpaire boilers, pop safety valves and much larger Deeley cabs, resulting in a very mixed class. Some engines even received small superheated Belpaire boilers.

Many of these engines were rebuilt with much larger Belpaire boilers, becoming the '3F' '43137' class. They retained their original numbers, and it was not until BR numbered this class in the 58000 series that the two classes were numerically separated. The '2F's could always be distinguished from the '3F's by the square side sheet to the cabs. On the '3F's this was replaced by a small splasher merging with the cab.

The first of these engines was withdrawn in 1925. Some engines were renumbered in the duplicate sequence (with 20000 added to their numbers), when their number series were required for newly built engines. Some of the engines withdrawn early in 1948 were never allocated a BR number, even though they came into BR stock. 58182 was the last survivor, and when it was withdrawn in 1964 it was the oldest locomotive running on BR, having been built in 1876.

s 58161-58187 were originally built with 17½" x 26" cylinders and 4' 10" driving wheels.

r These engines still retained their round-topped Johnson fireboxes, the rest having been rebuilt with Belpaire fireboxes from 1917 onwards.

Year End Totals: '2F [8]' class

'47	'48	'49	'50	'51	'52	'53	'54	'55	'56	'57	'58	'59	'60	'61	'62	'63	'64	'65	'66	'67
96	92	91	87	84	81	76	70	60	51	43	41	34	23	12	3	1				

Number	Built	Renumbered	BR Dates	Scrap	Notes
58114	02/75 K	07/52 22900	-07/57	10/57	
58115	03/75 K	04/49 22901	-03/61	05/62	
58116	03/75 K	12/48 22902	-01/60	10/62	
58117	03/75 K	09/49 22904	-03/56	56	
58118	04/75 K	02/50 22907	-01/60	60	
58119	06/75 K	06/49 22911	-05/59	08/61	
58120	06/75 K	08/51 22912	-11/62	01/63	
58121	06/75 K	04/50 22913	-05/57	05/57	
58122	08/75 K	10/48 22915	-09/61	01/62	
58123	09/75 K	11/49 22918	-07/62	10/62	
58124	01/76 K	11/49 22920	-07/62	10/62	
58125	01/76 K	01/49 22921	-11/55	11/55	
58126	01/76 K	09/49 22924	-06/56	56	
58127	02/76 K	06/50 22926	-11/55	11/55	
58128	02/76 K	09/50 22929	-10/62	11/62	
58129	75 D	11/49 22931	-02/55	55	
58130	75 D	05/48 22932	-05/59	12/60	
58131	75 D	02/49 22933	-02/61	11/61	
58132	75 D	01/49 22934	-05/59	09/60	
58133	75 D	09/49 22935	-12/55	56	
58134	75 D	22940	-02/50	03/50	r
58135	75 D	01/51 22944	-09/61	11/61	
58136	75 D	09/50 22945	-09/57	09/57	
58137	75 D	06/48 22946	-09/61	10/62	
58138	75 D	12/48 22947	-12/62	03/63	
58139	75 D	05/51 22950	-11/56	56	
58140	75 D	08/51 22951	-07/57	10/57	
58141	75 D	22953	-09/48	48	r
58142	75 D	03/49 22954	-01/57	02/57	
58143	75 D	02/52 22955	-11/63	01/64	
58144	75 D	10/48 22958	-05/60	11/60	
58145	75 D	02/51 22959	-08/53	53	
58146	02/76 BP	05/50 22963	-01/60	03/60	
58147	03/76 BP	22965	-12/52	53	
58148	03/76 BP	08/48 22967	-12/63	09/64	
58149	03/76 BP	04/49 22968	-08/52	52	
58150	03/76 BP	22969	-08/48	48	r
58151	03/76 BP	22970	-04/51	51	
58152	03/76 BP	05/49 22971	-11/55	11/55	
58153	04/76 BP	09/48 22974	-08/60	08/60	
58154	04/76 BP	10/50 22975	-06/56	56	
58155	04/76 BP	22976	-03/50	03/50	r
58156	04/76 BP	09/48 22977	-03/57	07/57	
58157	04/76 BP	11/50 22978	-10/58	11/60	
58158	12/76 BP	01/49 22982	-05/60	10/60	
58159	12/76 BP	12/50 22983	-03/56	56	
58160	12/76 BP	02/50 22984	-09/62	04/63	
58161	12/76 BP	12/48 2987	-01/53	53	s
58162	12/76 BP	12/50 2988	-09/55	55	s
58163	12/76 BP	06/49 2989	-10/61	10/62	s
58164	76 N	04/48 2990	-04/55	05/55	s
58165	76 N	05/50 2992	-09/60	10/60	s
58166	76 N	05/50 2993	-03/62	10/62	s
58167	76 N	07/52 2994	-08/59	09/60	s
58168	76 N	12/50 2995	-07/60	09/60	s
58169	76 N	05/51 2996	-02/61	04/61	s
58170	76 N	05/49 2997	-10/60	10/60	s
58171	76 N	08/52 2998	-08/59	07/60	s
58172	76 N	03/49 2999	-05/54	54	s
58173	76 N	10/49 23000	-06/60	07/60	s
58174	76 N	05/49 23001	-12/61	01/62	s
58175	76 N	10/48 23002	-12/61	02/62	s
58176	76 N	12/49 23003	-07/56	56	s
58177	76 N	06/49 23005	-10/62	04/63	s
58178	76 N	11/50 23006	-05/59	10/60	s
58179	76 N	11/49 23007	-04/56	56	s
58180	76 N	02/49 23008	-10/53	53	s
58181	76 N	01/49 23009	-07/61	12/61	s
58182	76 N	11/50 23010	-01/64	09/64	s
58183	76 N	04/49 23011	-01/60	12/60	s
58184	76 N	12/48 23012	-10/56	11/56	s
58185	76 N	08/48 23013	-07/62	10/62	s
58186	76 N	02/49 23014	-02/61	10/61	s
	76 N	23016	-03/48	48	s
58187	76 N	07/48 23018	-07/57	07/57	s

Class continued with 58229

2F [9] 58188-58228, 58249-58310
0-6-0 MR Johnson 5ft 3in

Power Classification:	2F
Introduced:	1878-1902
Designer:	Johnson
Company:	MR
Weight:	Loco between 37t 12cwt and 40t 3cwt
Driving Wheel:	5' 3"
Boiler Pressure:	160psi
Cylinders:	Inside 18" x 26"
Tractive Effort:	18185lbf
Valve Gear:	Stephenson (slide valves)

Refer to the Historical Survey of Midland 0-6-0 Engines at the end of this section for more details of this class.

These engines were the 5' 3" version of the '58114' class described above. Many of these engines were rebuilt with much larger Belpaire boilers, becoming the '43191' class.

Forty engines of this class were loaned to the GWR during the Second World War.

s 58188-58228 were originally built with 17½" x 26" cylinders and 5' 2½" driving wheels.

r These engines still retained their round-topped Johnson fireboxes, the rest having been rebuilt with Belpaire fireboxes from 1917 onwards.

Year End Totals: '2F [9]' class

'47	'48	'49	'50	'51	'52	'53	'54	'55	'56	'57	'58	'59	'60	'61	'62	'63	'64	'65	'66	'67
109	92	84	79	70	65	62	54	48	40	33	29	19	10	3						

Number	Built	Renumbered	BR Dates	Scrap	Notes
	78 D	3021	-03/48	48	s
58188	78 D	12/48 3023	-04/57	05/57	s
58189	78 D	07/48 3027	-08/57	09/57	s
58190	78 D	08/49 3031	-11/59	06/60	s
58191	78 D	12/49 3035	-10/59	03/60	s
58192	78 D	06/49 3037	-11/58	03/60	s
58193	78 D	10/49 3038	-04/56	56	s
58194	78 D	03/49 3039	-03/56	56	s
58195	03/80 Der	08/49 3042	-09/54	54	s
58196	03/80 Der	09/49 3044	-07/58	09/59	s
58197	03/80 Der	11/49 3045	-11/60	12/60	s
58198	03/80 Der	12/49 3047	-09/59	07/60	s
58199	03/80 Der	05/48 3048	-12/59	04/60	s
58200	03/80 Der	12/49 3049	-09/54	54	s
	01/80 RS	3050	-02/48	48	s
58201	01/80 RS	08/48 3051	-08/51	51	s
58202	01/80 RS	3052	-04/50	50	s
58203	01/80 RS	08/48 3054	-01/58	03/58	s
58204	03/80 RS	11/50 3058	-05/59	08/61	s
58205	03/80 RS	3061	-06/48	48	s
58206	04/80 RS	06/53 3062	-07/57	07/57	s
58207	04/80 RS	02/49 3064	-09/55	55	s
58208	05/80 RS	3066	-08/49	49	s
58209	06/81 RS	06/49 3071	-09/60	10/60	s
58210	07/81 RS	3073	-06/48	48	s
58211	07/81 RS	05/48 3074	-06/53	53	s
58212	08/81 RS	09/49 3078	-03/56	56	s
58213	12/82 BP	11/49 3084	-08/59	09/60	s
58214	01/83 BP	04/50 3090	-02/62	02/62	s
58215	02/83 BP	03/49 3094	-03/61	07/61	s
58216	02/83 BP	10/49 3095	-05/57	05/57	s
58217	02/83 BP	11/49 3096	-10/59	03/60	s
58218	02/83 BP	08/48 3098	-07/62	10/62	s
58219	02/83 BP	09/50 3099	-02/60	60	s
58220	10/83 BP	08/50 3101	-10/60	11/60	s
58221	10/83 BP	09/49 3103	-03/61	05/61	s
58222	10/83 BP	05/48 3108	-04/49	49	s
58223	11/83 BP	3109	-05/49	49	s
58224	12/83 BP	03/49 3113	-10/56	56	s
58225	02/84 BP	10/48 3118	-12/58	11/60	s
58226	02/84 BP	05/49 3119	-01/52	01/52	s
58227	02/84 BP	3123	-05/48	48	s
58228	03/84 BP	09/49 3127	-03/62	04/62	s

Class continued with 58249

2F [8] 58114-58187, 58229-58248
0-6-0 MR Johnson 4ft 11in

Class continued from 58187

Number	Built	Renumbered	BR Dates	Scrap	Notes
58229	85 Der	10/49 3130	-11/53	53	r
58230	85 Der	10/49 3134	-11/55	11/55	
58231	85 Der	01/49 3138	-08/52	10/52	
58232	85 Der	01/50 3140	-05/54	54	
58233	85 Der	01/50 3144	-06/56	06/56	
58234	85 Der	05/50 3149	-07/54	54	
58235	86 Der	04/48 3150	-12/54	55	
58236	86 Der	03/49 3151	-10/55	55	r
	86 Der	3153	-03/48	48	
58237	86 Der	02/49 3154	-07/51	51	
58238	86 Der	05/48 3156	-11/57	12/57	
58239	86 Der	3157	-05/50	50	
58240	87 Der	04/48 3161	-05/53	53	r
58241	87 Der	06/48 3164	-06/55	55	
58242	87 Der	10/49 3166	-12/54	12/54	
58243	87 Der	3168	-06/49	49	r
58244	87 Der	10/49 3171	-05/54	54	
58245	87 Der	3173	-05/50	06/50	
58246	87 Der	04/48 3175	-07/59	08/61	r
58247	87 Der	10/48 3176	-01/58	02/58	
58248	87 Der	3177	-12/51	52	

2F [9] 58188-58228, 58249-58310
0-6-0 MR Johnson 5ft 3in

Class continued from 58228

Number	Built	Renumbered	BR Dates	Scrap	Notes
58249	09/88 Der	05/48 3190	-02/53	53	
	10/88 Der	3195	-03/48	48	r
58250	10/88 Der	3196	-08/48	48	r
58251	90 N	09/48 3229	-05/49	49	r
58252	91 N	11/48 3262	-12/51	52	
58253	91 N	3264	-12/49	12/49	r
58254	91 N	07/50 3270	-03/52	03/52	
58255	01/92 K	3311	-09/48	48	r
58256	91 D	3360	-01/49	49	r
58257	92 SS	11/49 3372	-10/55	55	
58258	92 SS	01/49 3377	-01/54	54	
58259	92 SS	04/49 3385	-11/52	52	
58260	92 D	11/48 3420	-12/60	12/60	
58261	92 D	08/49 3423	-01/60	04/60	
	92 D	3424	-03/48	04/48	r
58262	92 D	03/49 3425	-01/51	51	r
58263	93 D	3437	-04/48	48	r
58264	93 D	12/48 3445	-02/54	54	
58265	93 D	11/48 3451	-01/54	54	
58266	94 Der	3466	-05/48	48	r
	96 N	3473	-02/48	48	r
58267	96 N	3477	-03/50	03/50	r
58268	96 N	02/49 3479	-10/51	11/51	
58269	96 N	08/49 3485	-04/56	56	
58270	96 N	3489	-02/49	49	
58271	96 N	11/49 3492	-06/61	06/61	
58272	96 N	07/48 3493	-05/54	54	
58273	12/96 N	01/49 3503	-10/55	55	
58274	97 N	08/48 3508	-05/51	51	r
58275	97 N	3511	-06/50	10/50	
58276	97 N	08/49 3512	-06/56	56	
58277	97 N	06/49 3516	-11/55	11/55	
58278	97 N	09/48 3517	-09/54	09/54	
58279	97 N	09/49 3525	-07/59	07/59	
58280	97 N	04/50 3526	-12/52	53	
58281	97 N	09/49 3527	-05/59	08/60	
58282	97 N	3533	-03/50	03/50	r
58283	97 N	06/49 3536	-03/61	08/61	
58284	97 N	3537	-09/48	48	r
58285	97 N	10/49 3539	-06/51	51	
58286	97 N	05/50 3543	-10/55	55	
58287	97 SS	02/49 3545	-08/60	10/60	
58288	97 SS	07/51 3551	-10/57	10/57	
58289	97 SS	11/48 3559	-05/51	05/51	
58290	97 SS	09/49 3561	-09/54	10/54	
58291	97 SS	05/49 3564	-02/61	12/61	
58292	97 SS	3566	-04/48	48	r
58293	08/99 K	07/48 3571	-01/61	09/61	
58294	01/00 K	3592	-02/49	49	
	99 NR	3602	-01/48	48	r
58295	99 NR	10/48 3603	-11/60	12/60	
58296	99 NR	3617	-07/51	51	
58297	00 D	3632	-08/48	48	r
58298	00 D	02/49 3648	-11/60	12/60	
58299	00 VF	02/50 3655	-02/57	03/57	
58300	06/01 K	01/49 3688	-05/55	05/55	
58301	06/01 K	3689	-04/48	48	r
58302	01 SS	07/48 3691	-07/51	51	
58303	01 SS	04/50 3696	-11/53	53	
58304	01 SS	09/48 3703	-02/52	52	
58305	01 SS	06/49 3707	-06/61	08/61	
58306	01 NR	08/48 3725	-02/57	03/57	
58307	01 NR	3726	-10/50	50	
58308	01/02 NR	08/50 3738	-04/59	09/60	
58309	01/02 NR	10/49 3739	-02/56	56	
58310	02 NR	10/50 3764	-11/56	56	

Caledonian Railway Pickersgill '3P' 4-4-0 No 54465.

Caledonian Railway McIntosh Class 439 0-4-4T No 55210.

Caledonian Railway Drummond 0-4-0ST No 56032 shunting at Crewe Works in September 1949.

Caledonian Railway McIntosh '3F' 0-6-0Ts Nos 56373 and 56374. No 56374 is fitted with a stove-pipe chimney.

Caledonian Railway McIntosh Class 812 0-6-0 No 57576.

Midland Railway Johnson '1P' 0-4-4T No 58046, fitted with a Belpaire boiler.

2F [10] 58320-58361
0-6-0 LNWR Webb 'Coal Engine'

Power Classification:	2F
Introduced:	1873-1892
Designer:	Webb
Company:	LNWR
Weight:	Loco 38t 0cwt
Driving Wheel:	4' 5½"
Boiler Pressure:	150psi
Cylinders:	Inside 17" x 24"
Tractive Effort:	16530lbf
Valve Gear:	Stephenson (slide valves)

Webb built this class of 500 'Coal Engines' between 1873 and 1892. They were built purely for freight work and the first was withdrawn as long ago as 1903.

Forty-five engines were rebuilt as tanks (see the '58870' class), and an 'official' tank engine version of the class was introduced in 1882 (see the '58880' class).

227 engines were taken into LMS stock and they were numbered 8088-8314. The engines surviving in 1940 were transferred to the duplicate list with 20000 added to their numbers.

Forty-six engines came into BR stock in 1948, but four of these were withdrawn in the first few months of 1948 without being allocated BR numbers. The last few survivors were employed as Crewe Works shunters.

s In 1950 BR took over the stock of the Shropshire & Montgomery Railway from the War Department. This included three ex-LNWR 'Coal engines' still carrying their original numbers. The whole stock of the railway was immediately withdrawn from service, and these three engines were cut up at Swindon works in 1950.

Year End Totals: '2F [10]' class

'47	'48	'49	'50	'51	'52	'53	'54	'55	'56	'57	'58	'59	'60	'61	'62	'63	'64	'65	'66	'67
46	28	25	20	18	10															

Number	Built	Renumbered	BR Dates	Scrap	Notes
58320	05/73 Crw	28088	-07/48	08/48	
58321	02/73 Crw	09/48 28091	-07/53	53	
58322	06/73 Crw	01/49 28093	-01/52	52	
	05/73 Crw	28095	-01/48	48	
	05/73 Crw	28097	-02/48	08/48	
58323	04/74 Crw	08/48 28100	-05/53	53	
58324	03/74 Crw	28104	-08/48	09/48	
58325	03/74 Crw	28105	-08/48	48	
58326	01/74 Crw	11/48 28106	-05/53	53	
58327	12/74 Crw	28107	-06/52	07/52	
	12/74 Crw	8108	05/50-07/50	10/50	s
58328	06/75 Crw	08/48 28115	-02/53	53	
58329	03/77 Crw	28116	-01/50	50	
58330	09/75 Crw	28128	-02/53	53	
58331	05/75 Crw	28133	-10/48	11/48	
58332	11/76 Crw	10/48 28141	-09/53	53	
58333	03/77 Crw	28152	-01/52	02/52	
	01/78 Crw	28153	-02/48	04/48	
58334	02/78 Crw	28158	-10/49	49	
58335	01/79 Crw	28166	-03/52	03/52	
58336	04/79 Crw	10/48 28172	-07/53	53	
	12/79 Crw	8182	05/50-07/50	10/50	s
58337	07/80 Crw	28191	-06/48	48	
58338	08/80 Crw	28199	-05/50	50	
58339	12/80 Crw	28202	-05/48	48	
58340	12/80 Crw	28205	-03/52	04/52	
58341	01/81 Crw	28216	-04/50	50	
58342	01/81 Crw	28221	-01/49	49	
58343	05/81 Crw	10/48 28227	-09/53	10/53	
	05/81 Crw	28230	-01/48	07/48	
58344	05/81 Crw	28233	-03/49	49	
58345	05/81 Crw	28234	-04/48	09/48	
	06/81 Crw	8236	05/50-07/50	10/50	s
58346	06/81 Crw	28239	-03/52	03/52	
58347	10/89 Crw	09/48 28245	-02/53	03/53	
58348	07/82 Crw	28246	-03/50	50	
58349	07/82 Crw	28247	-08/51	51	
58350	11/82 Crw	28251	-05/52	05/52	
58351	07/82 Crw	11/48 28253	-01/50	50	
58352	07/82 Crw	11/49 28256	-04/51	51	
58353	10/89 Crw	28262	-10/48	10/48	
58354	01/81 Crw	10/51 28263	-03/53	03/53	
58355	12/90 Crw	28271	-12/48	49	
58356	05/92 Crw	28295	-11/48	48	
58357	05/92 Crw	28296	-07/48	48	
58358	10/92 Crw	28308	-06/48	48	
58359	10/92 Crw	28309	-09/48	48	
58360	10/92 Crw	28312	-04/52	05/52	
58361	10/92 Crw	28313	-09/48	10/48	

2F [11] 58362-58430
0-6-0 LNWR Webb '18in Goods' 'Cauliflower'

Power Classification:	2F
Introduced:	1880-1902
Designer:	Webb
Company:	LNWR
Weight:	Loco 36t 10cwt
Driving Wheel:	5' 2½"
Boiler Pressure:	150psi
Cylinders:	Inside 18" x 24"
Tractive Effort:	15865lbf
Valve Gear:	Joy (slide valves)

Between 1880 and 1902 Webb built 310 engines of his '18 inch goods' engines. They were usually known as 'Cauliflowers' because they originally carried the LNWR crest on the central splasher and this resembled a cauliflower.

These were amongst the most famous British 0-6-0 engines. They were designed for express goods workings and had larger wheels than the 'Coal Engines'. They were built as replacements for the earlier 'DX' class of 1858 and they were often used on passenger trains.

The engines were numbered 8315-8624 by the LMS. Many of the class (including most of the later survivors) were rebuilt with Belpaire boilers. The surviving engines were renumbered between 1940 and 1944 by the addition of 20000, to make way for the construction of new 8F engines.

The first of the class was withdrawn in 1922, and seventy-five engines came into BR stock in 1948. Six of these were withdrawn early in 1948 without being allocated new numbers.

Year End Totals: '2F [11]' class

'47	'48	'49	'50	'51	'52	'53	'54	'55	'56	'57	'58	'59	'60	'61	'62	'63	'64	'65	'66	'67
75	50	43	31	25	17	9	7													

Number	Built	Renumbered	BR Dates	Scrap	Notes
58362	07/92 Crw	05/50 28318	-02/53	53	
58363	06/80 Crw	10/48 28333	-04/51	51	
58364	11/82 Crw	11/49 28335	-02/51	51	
58365	11/82 Crw	03/49 28337	-05/52	05/52	
58366	11/82 Crw	28338	-07/48	11/48	
58367	11/82 Crw	28339	-01/50	50	
58368	03/87 Crw	28345	-07/51	51	
	05/87 Crw	28350	-02/48	07/48	
58369	08/95 Crw	28370	-04/50	50	
58370	09/95 Crw	28372	-07/48	11/48	
58371	10/95 Crw	28385	-03/50	03/50	
58372	10/95 Crw	28392	-12/48	49	
58373	01/96 Crw	28403	-04/50	50	
58374	02/96 Crw	28404	-08/48	10/48	
58375	02/96 Crw	01/49 28408	-02/55	02/55	
	03/96 Crw	28415	-01/48	07/48	
58376	03/96 Crw	11/50 28417	-03/55	55	
58377	02/97 Crw	08/48 28428	-07/52	09/54	
58378	02/97 Crw	02/49 28430	-07/53	07/53	
	03/97 Crw	28441	-02/48	07/48	
58379	03/97 Crw	28442	-11/49	49	
58380	03/97 Crw	28443	-12/49	50	
58381	03/98 Crw	06/50 28450	-07/52	07/52	
58382	03/98 Crw	02/49 28451	-01/54	54	
58383	11/98 Crw	07/50 28457	-01/53	02/53	
58384	11/98 Crw	28458	-03/50	50	
58385	10/98 Crw	28460	-09/48	48	
58386	11/98 Crw	28464	-10/48	48	
58387	05/99 Crw	28484	-05/48	05/48	
58388	05/99 Crw	28487	-11/50	50	
58389	05/99 Crw	03/50 28492	-01/53	53	
58390	09/99 Crw	28494	-08/48	48	
58391	10/99 Crw	28499	-09/48	48	
58392	11/99 Crw	01/49 28505	-02/51	51	
58393	11/99 Crw	07/48 28507	-06/52	07/52	
58394	12/99 Crw	05/50 28509	-08/55	55	
58395	12/99 Crw	28511	-05/48	48	
58396	02/00 Crw	06/48 28512	-08/53	53	
58397	02/00 Crw	28513	-03/50	50	
58398	02/00 Crw	04/48 28515	-02/52	03/52	
58399	03/00 Crw	28521	-09/49	49	
58400	03/00 Crw	03/50 28525	-09/51	51	
58401	03/00 Crw	28526	-10/48	10/48	
58402	03/00 Crw	28527	-11/48	48	
58403	04/00 Crw	28529	-12/48	49	
58404	05/00 Crw	28531	-01/50	01/50	
58405	05/00 Crw	28532	-07/48	11/48	
	09/00 Crw	28542	-02/48	07/48	
58406	09/00 Crw	28543	-01/50	50	
58407	09/00 Crw	28544	-05/49	49	
58408	10/00 Crw	28547	-05/48	48	
58409	10/00 Crw	10/48 28548	-12/55	01/56	
58410	10/00 Crw	28549	-11/50	50	
58411	10/00 Crw	28551	-06/50	50	
58412	10/00 Crw	01/49 28553	-12/55	12/55	
58413	11/00 Crw	10/50 28555	-01/54	54	
58414	11/00 Crw	28556	-10/48	48	
58415	11/00 Crw	09/50 28559	-11/53	53	
58416	11/00 Crw	28561	-03/49	49	
58417	01/01 Crw	28575	-09/49	49	
58418	02/01 Crw	28580	-07/52	07/52	
58419	02/01 Crw	28583	-01/53	53	
58420	02/01 Crw	28585	-11/51	11/51	
	02/01 Crw	28586	-01/48	08/48	
58421	03/01 Crw	28589	-11/52	52	
58422	03/01 Crw	28592	-03/50	50	
58423	04/01 Crw	28594	-06/48	06/48	
	04/01 Crw	28597	-01/48	07/48	
58424	05/01 Crw	28598	-06/49	06/49	
58425	07/01 Crw	28608	-09/48	10/48	
58426	07/01 Crw	01/50 28611	-10/52	11/52	
58427	07/01 Crw	50 28616	-12/55	05/56	
58428	04/02 Crw	28618	-07/48	48	
58429	05/02 Crw	03/49 28619	-02/53	53	
58430	05/02 Crw	10/49 28622	-03/55	55	

2F [12] 58850-58863
0-6-0T North London Railway (Park)

Power Classification:	2F
Introduced:	1880-1905
Designer:	Park
Company:	NLR
Weight:	45t 10cwt
Driving Wheel:	4' 4"
Boiler Pressure:	160psi
Cylinders:	Outside 17" x 24"
Tractive Effort:	18140lbf
Valve Gear:	Stephenson (slide valves)

Thirty of these engines were built for the North London Railway by Park in 1880-1905. They were rugged tank engines which provided the motive power for all the NLR freight workings. Their short wheelbase made them suitable for dock workings in the Poplar area, but they were also to be found working on the main line.

Nine engines were taken over by the LNWR in 1909 and they were joined by the remainder when taken over by the LMS in 1923. They were numbered 7503-7532 by the LMS. The first of the class was withdrawn in 1930, and the survivors in 1934 were renumbered by the addition of 20000 to their numbers. Fifteen engines were taken into BR stock in 1948, of which 27525 was withdrawn in March 1948 without being allocated a new number.

Several engines were transferred from the North London Section to the Cromford and High Peak line in the Peak District in 1931, from where the last engine was withdrawn in 1960.

Year End Totals: '2F [12]' class

'47	'48	'49	'50	'51	'52	'53	'54	'55	'56	'57	'58	'59	'60	'61	'62	'63	'64	'65	'66	'67
15	14	14	14	14	13	11	10	8	5	2	1	1								

Number	Built	Renumbered	BR Dates	Scrap	Notes
58850 §	12/80 Bow	05/49 27505	-09/60		
58851	05/87 Bow	02/50 27509	-02/55	02/55	
58852	06/87 Bow	08/50 27510	-06/55	06/55	
58853	06/88 Bow	06/48 27512	-10/54	11/54	
58854	07/88 Bow	06/50 27513	-11/56	11/56	
58855	07/89 Bow	04/50 27514	-07/56	07/56	
58856	07/89 Bow	09/48 27515	-10/57	11/57	
58857	11/89 Bow	01/50 27517	-04/58	05/58	
58858	03/92 Bow	04/49 27520	-05/53	05/53	
58859	06/94 Bow	10/48 27522	-11/57	11/57	
	04/95 Bow	27525	-03/48	48	
58860	12/00 Bow	04/48 27527	-05/57	07/57	
58861	05/01 Bow	03/49 27528	-04/53	04/53	
58862	08/01 Bow	10/48 27530	-03/56	56	
58863	06/05 Bow	12/50 27532	-12/52	53	

Crane 58865
0-4-2ST North London Railway Crane Tank

Power Classification:	0F
Introduced:	1858 Rebuilt 1872 by Park
Designer:	Sharp Stewart
Company:	NLR
Weight:	32t 6cwt
Driving Wheel:	3' 10"
Boiler Pressure:	120psi
Cylinders:	Inside 13" x 17"

Tractive Effort:	6370lbf
Valve Gear:	Allan straight link (slide valves)

This engine was the oldest engine to be inherited by BR.

It was built in 1858 as an 0-4-0ST for the North & South West Junction Railway, which was later taken over by the North London Railway. In 1872 it was rebuilt as an 0-4-2ST. It had square saddle tanks and was fitted with a crane.

It was originally NLR No. 29A, then LNWR 2896 before becoming LMS 7217. It was renumbered 27217 in 1935 and was finally renumbered to 58865 in 1949.

Year End Totals: 'Crane' class

'47	'48	'49	'50	'51	'52	'53	'54	'55	'56	'57	'58	'59	'60	'61	'62	'63	'64	'65	'66	'67
1	1	1	1																	

Number	*Built*	*Renumbered*	*BR Dates*	*Scrap*	*Notes*
58865	02/58 SS	03/49 27217	-02/51	10/52	

2F[13] 58870
0-6-0ST LNWR Webb Saddle Tank

Power Classification:	2F
Introduced:	1873-1892 Rebuilt 1905-1907 by Whale
Designer:	Webb
Company:	LNWR
Weight:	34t 10cwt
Driving Wheel:	4' 5½"
Boiler Pressure:	150psi
Cylinders:	Inside 17" x 24"
Tractive Effort:	16530lbf
Valve Gear:	Joy (slide valves)

Between 1905 and 1907 forty-five of Webb's 'Coal engines' ('58320' class) were rebuilt as saddle tanks. This was to allow the older engines, which were no longer suitable for main line work, to have an extended life as shunting engines.

They were also known as 'Box Tanks'. They were a development from the 'Special Tanks' (see the 'CD3' class), although they were more similar in looks to the '47862' class.

The engines were numbered 7458-7502 by the LMS. The first of the class was withdrawn in 1924. The survivors in 1934 were transferred to the duplicate list and were renumbered by the addition of 20000 to their numbers. 58870 (which was built in February 1891 and rebuilt in October 1906) was the only one of the class to come into BR stock, being withdrawn in 1948 without being renumbered.

Year End Totals: '2F 13' class

'47	'48	'49	'50	'51	'52	'53	'54	'55	'56	'57	'58	'59	'60	'61	'62	'63	'64	'65	'66	'67
1																				

Number	*Built*	*Renumbered*	*BR Dates*	*Scrap*	*Notes*
58870	02/91 Crw	27480	-12/48	*49*	

2F[14] 58880-58937
0-6-2T LNWR Webb 'Coal Tank'

Power Classification:	2F
Introduced:	1881-1896
Designer:	Webb
Company:	LNWR
Weight:	43t 15cwt
Driving Wheel:	4' 5½"
Boiler Pressure:	150psi
Cylinders:	Inside 17" x 24"
Tractive Effort:	16530lbf
Valve Gear:	Stephenson (slide valves)

Between 1881 and 1897 Webb built these 300 0-6-2Ts which were tank engine versions of his 'Coal Engines' (see the 58320 class) and they were known as 'Coal Tanks'. They were highly versatile engines and could be seen all over the system, often working on passenger trains (some even being fitted for push-pull working in later years).

The first engine was withdrawn in 1921 and the 291 engines which came into LMS stock were numbered 7550-7841. Some of these were renumbered by the addition of 20000 to their numbers in 1934, (27830 in 1945). Sixty-four came into BR stock in 1948 of which six were withdrawn before being allocated BR numbers.

w 58916 was fitted with widened side tanks.

Year End Totals: '2F 14' class

'47	'48	'49	'50	'51	'52	'53	'54	'55	'56	'57	'58	'59	'60	'61	'62	'63	'64	'65	'66	'67
64	41	33	26	21	16	15	5	1	1	1										

Number	*Built*	*Renumbered*	*BR Dates*	*Scrap*	*Notes*
58880	08/82 Crw	08/48 27553	-04/54	*11/54*	
58881	02/87 Crw	27561	-09/50	09/50	
58882	05/87 Crw	27562	-10/49	*49*	
58883	10/81 Crw	03/49 27580	-12/49	*50*	
58884	10/81 Crw	27585	-11/48	12/48	
58885	11/81 Crw	27586	-09/48	*48*	
58886	12/81 Crw	27591	-01/49	*49*	
58887	12/81 Crw	06/48 27596	-04/55	*55*	
58888	08/82 Crw	05/49 27602	-09/54	*11/54*	
58889	09/82 Crw	08/48 27603	-08/53	*53*	
58890	01/83 Crw	27619	-12/49	*50*	
58891	01/83 Crw	10/49 27621	-09/55	09/55	
58892	02/83 Crw	09/49 27625	-05/52	*52*	
58893	01/83 Crw	27627	-10/48	11/48	
58894	03/83 Crw	27635	-03/49	*49*	
	02/83 Crw	27648	-01/48	02/48	
58895	07/83 Crw	27654	-09/51	*51*	
58896	08/83 Crw	27669	-01/49	*49*	
58897	11/83 Crw	07/48 27674	-11/50	11/50	
58898	12/83 Crw	27681	-10/48	10/48	
58899	04/84 Crw	01/50 7692	-05/54	*54*	
58900	09/84 Crw	02/50 7699	-09/54	*09/54*	
	09/84 Crw	7700	-03/48	*07/48*	
58901	10/84 Crw	7703	-07/48	10/48	
58902	12/84 Crw	10/48 7710	-12/54	*55*	
58903	01/85 Crw	06/49 7711	-06/54	*54*	
	01/85 Crw	7715	-01/48	02/48	
58904	01/85 Crw	09/49 7720	-09/55	09/55	
58905	01/85 Crw	7721	-08/48	09/48	
58906	04/86 Crw	7730	-11/48	*48*	
58907	04/86 Crw	7733	-10/48	10/48	
58908	07/86 Crw	10/48 7737	-11/51	*51*	
58909	07/86 Crw	7740	-06/48	07/48	
58910	07/86 Crw	03/50 7741	-07/52	*08/52*	
58911	08/86 Crw	08/48 7746	-03/54	*03/54*	
58912	08/86 Crw	05/49 7751	-12/50	12/50	
58913	08/86 Crw	7752	-06/52	07/52	
58914	08/86 Crw	7756	-08/48	09/48	
58915	08/86 Crw	01/49 7757	-09/54	*10/54*	
58916	12/86 Crw	04/48 7759	-10/50	*50*	w
58917	02/87 Crw	7765	-02/50	*50*	
58918	02/87 Crw	7769	-04/48	05/48	
58919	02/87 Crw	09/49 7773	-12/52	*53*	
58920	05/87 Crw	7780	-08/48	*48*	
58921	05/87 Crw	07/48 7782	-07/54	*08/54*	
58922	05/87 Crw	7787	-07/48	09/48	
58923	06/87 Crw	7789	-01/50	*50*	
58924	06/87 Crw	05/48 7791	-09/54	*10/54*	
58925	06/87 Crw	11/48 7794	-09/55	09/55	
	07/87 Crw	7796	-02/48	*07/48*	
58926 §	09/88 Crw	09/49 7799	-11/58		
58927	09/88 Crw	7802	-10/49	*49*	
58928	09/88 Crw	01/49 7803	-01/51	*01/51*	
58929	12/88 Crw	7808	-03/50	*50*	
	12/88 Crw	7812	-01/48	*07/48*	
58930	07/92 Crw	7816	-09/48	09/48	
58931	07/92 Crw	7821	-03/48	*05/48*	
58932	07/92 Crw	7822	-06/52	*07/52*	
58933	10/96 Crw	04/49 7829	-12/51	*52*	
58934	10/96 Crw	27830	-10/49	*49*	
58935	02/97 Crw	7833	-10/51	*51*	
58936	02/97 Crw	7836	-05/48	*48*	
58937	02/97 Crw	7840	-04/48	09/48	
	02/97 Crw	7841	-02/48	*07/48*	

Service Locomotives

Most departmental or service locomotives were not specially renumbered but retained their old numbers. For example 41509 worked as a service locomotive retaining its original number 1509 until withdrawal in 1949. It is therefore listed in the main number series. Of the locomotives listed here, CD3-CD8 were renumbered to work in the carriage department, 3323 retained its original LNWR number and 11304-11394 retained their pre-nationalisation numbers right through into the 1960s. It could be argued that these last five should be listed with the main series of locomotives, but it seems to make sense to list them separately.

2F[15] CD3-CD8, 3323
0-6-0ST LNWR Webb 'Special Tank'

Power Classification:	2F
Introduced:	1870-1880
Designer:	Ramsbottom and Webb
Company:	LNWR
Weight:	34t 10cwt
Driving Wheel:	4' 5½"
Boiler Pressure:	140psi
Cylinders:	Inside 17" x 24"
Tractive Effort:	15430lbf
Valve Gear:	Stephenson (slide valves)

Between 1870 and 1880 Webb built 258 of these 'Special Tanks' for shunting work on the LNWR. They were based on a design by Ramsbottom. The first was withdrawn in 1920 and 243 were taken into LMS stock. These were numbered 7220-7457 (all of which were withdrawn by 1941) and seven departmental engines which were numbered separately.

Six engines worked in the Carriage Department, CD1, CD3, CD6 and CD7 at Wolverton, CD4 at Crewe and CD8 at Earlestown. The survivors after 1948 were all at Wolverton.

The other engine was 3323 which retained its original LNWR number and worked as a shunter at Crewe works. It was renumbered 43323 for a short time in error in 1948, was withdrawn in December 1950 and scrapped in May 1954.

(The numbers CD2 and CD5 were carried by Webb 0-4-2ST Crane tanks of 1892, which worked at Wolverton and were withdrawn by 1947.)

Year End Totals: '2F 15' (service) class

'47	'48	'49	'50	'51	'52	'53	'54	'55	'56	'57	'58	'59	'60	'61	'62	'63	'64	'65	'66	'67
5	5	5	5	5	5	5	4	4	4	3	3									

Number	*Built*	*Renumbered*	*BR Dates*	*Scrap*	*Notes*
CD3	04/80 Crw		- 59	59	
CD6	11/75 Crw		-05/59	59	
CD7	08/78 Crw		-11/59	59	
CD8 **EARLESTOWN**	Crw		-10/57	57	
3323	08/78 Crw		- 12/50	05/54	

2F[2] 51307-51530, 11304-11394
0-6-0ST LYR Aspinall Rebuilt Saddle Tank Class '23'

Class continued from 51530

Number	*Built*	*Renumbered*	*BR Dates*	*Scrap*	*Notes*
11304	08/77 SS		-12/61	*62*	
11305	06/77 SS		-09/64	*64*	
11324	06/77 SS		-10/63	*63*	
11368	05/79 Mlsp		-11/63	*63*	
11394	06/80 K		-05/60	*60*	

Miscellaneous Locomotives

These locomotives were not officially listed in stock.

NG [1] WREN
0-4-0ST Horwich Works Narrow Gauge

Power Classification:	Unclassified
Introduced:	1887-1901
Designer:	Beyer Peacock
Company:	LYR
Weight:	3t 11½cwt
Driving Wheel:	1' 4¼"
Boiler Pressure:	180psi
Cylinders:	Outside 5" x 6"
Tractive Effort:	1410lbf
Valve Gear:	Allan
Gauge:	18"

This 18" gauge shunting engine was the last survivor of the eight locomotives which worked the extensive narrow gauge system at Horwich Works. The system was used for moving components around the works and WREN was fitted with a strongbox on the tender for distributing wage packets.

The eight engines were built in 1887-1901 and they were named as follows: DOT, ROBIN, WREN, FLY, WASP, MIDGET, MOUSE and BEE. The first locomotive was withdrawn in 1930, and WREN was the only survivor in 1948 working on the truncated remains of the system. It has since been preserved at York.

Year End Totals: 'NG [1]' class

'47	'48	'49	'50	'51	'52	'53	'54	'55	'56	'57	'58	'59	'60	'61	'62	'63	'64	'65	'66	'67
1	1	1	1	1	1	1	1	1	1	1	1	1	1	1						

Number	Built	Renumbered	BR Dates	Scrap	Notes
WREN §	11/87 BP		- 62		

NG [2] 10
0-4-0ST Beeston Depot Narrow Gauge

Power Classification:	Unclassified
Introduced:	1924 Purchased by LMS in 1945
Designer:	Bagnall
Company:	
Weight:	
Driving Wheel:	2' 9"
Boiler Pressure:	
Cylinders:	Outside 10" x 15½"
Tractive Effort:	
Valve Gear:	Modified Walschaert with eccentrics on driving axle (slide valves)
Gauge:	3' 0"

This small saddle tank engine worked at Beeston Creosote Works.

Year End Totals: 'NG [2]' class

'47	'48	'49	'50	'51	'52	'53	'54	'55	'56	'57	'58	'59	'60	'61	'62	'63	'64	'65	'66	'67
1	1	1	1	1	1	1	1													

Number	Built	Renumbered	BR Dates	Scrap	Notes
10 BATLEY	24 WB		-10/55	10/55	

2P [8] between 50621 & 50899, 10897
2-4-2T LYR Aspinall Class '5'

Class continued from 50899

Number	Built	Renumbered	BR Dates	Scrap	Notes
10897	03/10 Hor		-10/56	*10/56*	h

Rail Motor [2] 29988
0-4-0T LNWR Whale

Power Classification:	Unclassified
Introduced:	1905-1906
Designer:	Whale
Company:	LNWR
Weight:	43t 8cwt
Driving Wheel:	3' 9"
Boiler Pressure:	175psi
Cylinders:	Inside 9½" x 15"
Tractive Effort:	4475lbf
Valve Gear:	Stephenson (slide valves)

Between 1903 and 1911 many railways in Britain attempted to reduce their costs on branch lines with little traffic by introducing steam railcars. These consisted of a single saloon coach, with a small engine unit (usually an 0-4-0T) forming the bogie at one end. In some designs the engine was detachable, in others the engine was completely enclosed within the body.

Steam railcars were designed to avoid the need for turning at the end of each run. A driving cab was fitted at the other end of the unit which duplicated some of the controls, and there was a bell code system by which the driver could communicate with the fireman.

The LNWR built seven of these units in 1905 with the engine contained within the bodywork. The engine part was built at Crewe and the coach part built at Wolverton. They were at first numbered 10694-10700. The class was withdrawn from 1927 onwards, and in 1933, when 10697 was the only survivor, it was renumbered 29988 in the coaching stock series. It outlived the rest of the class by fifteen years. Although not officially withdrawn until November 1948, it had not worked since February 1947 when it was damaged in a collision.

Year End Totals: 'Rail Motor [2]' class

'47	'48	'49	'50	'51	'52	'53	'54	'55	'56	'57	'58	'59	'60	'61	'62	'63	'64	'65	'66	'67
1																				

Number	Built	Renumbered	BR Dates	Scrap	Notes
29988	05 Crw		-11/48	*48*	

Preserved Locomotives

Preserved locomotives which ran in service on BR.

3P [2] 41928-41978, 80
4-4-2T LTSR Whitelegg

Class continued from 41978

Number	Built	Renumbered	BR Dates	Scrap	Notes
80 § THUNDERSLEY	05/09 RS	03/56 41966	03/56-06/56		b

Jones Goods 103
4-6-0 HR Preserved

Power Classification:	4F
Introduced:	1894
Designer:	Jones
Company:	HR
Weight:	Loco 56t 0cwt
Driving Wheel:	5' 3"
Boiler Pressure:	175psi
Cylinders:	Outside 20" x 26"
Tractive Effort:	24555lbf
Valve Gear:	Stephenson (slide valves)

This engine earned its place in history by being the first 4-6-0 to appear in Britain. Designed by Jones for the Highland Railway in 1894, fifteen engines were built by Sharp Stewart and they were the most powerful main line engines in the country at that time. They were intended principally as freight engines, but were often called upon to work passenger trains during the summer season.

The class was numbered 103-117 on the Highland Railway and then 17916-17930 by the LMS and they were all withdrawn between 1929 and 1940. 17916 was set aside for preservation in 1934 as HR 103.

In 1959 the engine was restored to working order for working special trains. It was painted in Stroudley's 'improved engine green', which was in fact a brilliant yellow colour. It hauled many enthusiasts' trains for several years before finding a permanent resting place in Glasgow Museum, the only Highland engine still in existence.

Number	Built	Renumbered	BR Dates	Scrap	Notes
103 §	09/94 SS		59-10/65		

CR Single 123
4-2-2 CR Preserved

Power Classification:	1P
Introduced:	1886
Designer:	Neilson & Co. & D Drummond
Company:	CR
Weight:	Loco 41t 7cwt
Driving Wheel:	7' 0"
Boiler Pressure:	160psi
Cylinders:	Inside 18" x 26"
Tractive Effort:	13638lbf
Valve Gear:	Stephenson (slide valves)

This engine was a one-off engine which was built by Neilson & Co. in 1886 for the Edinburgh exhibition of that year. Afterwards it was acquired by the Caledonian Railway, whose Chief Mechanical Engineer Dugald Drummond had obviously had a hand in its design, as it contained many of his characteristic features.

It was the only single wheeler ever to appear on a Scottish railway and it put in many years of useful service on main line trains, including participating in the 1888 'Race to Scotland' between the East and West coast routes.

After the First World War it was put to work hauling the directors' saloon, but in 1930 it reverted to ordinary service as 14010 working light trains between Perth and Dundee. As such it was the last express single wheeler to work in ordinary traffic anywhere in the British Isles, and probably in the world.

In 1935 it was withdrawn from service and repainted in CR blue livery for preservation in St. Rollox works. In 1958 it was given a complete overhaul and it was put to work on enthusiasts' special workings. These workings took the engine far and wide, not just in Scotland, but as far south as the Bluebell Railway in Sussex.

In 1965 the engine was again retired and placed in the Glasgow Transport Museum.

Number	Built	Renumbered	BR Dates	Scrap	Notes
123 §	86 N		03/58-10/65		

4P [2] 41000-41044, 1000
4-4-0 MR Deeley Compound

Class continued from 41044

Number	Built	Renumbered	BR Dates	Scrap	Notes
1000 §	01/02 Der	06/59 41000	06/59-	*65*	j

Historical Surveys

Historical survey of LMS 2-6-4T engines.

In 1927 Fowler introduced his 2-6-4T design for general passenger use. They were excellent and popular engines and were to become the first in a long line of engines built over a number of years as outlined below.

1. '42300' class. Original Fowler engines with parallel boilers, introduced 1927.
2. '42500' class. Stanier three-cylinder engines with taper boilers, introduced 1934.
3. '42425' class. Stanier two-cylinder engines, introduced 1935.
4. '42050' class. Fairburn two-cylinder engines, introduced 1945.
5. '80000' class. Riddles standard BR design introduced 1951.

Historical survey of Midland 0-6-0 engines.

The Midland Railway was committed to using 0-6-0 engines for freight traffic throughout its history. The development of these engines took place over a long period of time and can be summarised as follows:

1. The '2F' '58110' and '58111' classes were the last survivors of Kirtley's 0-6-0 class '1' engines. They were double framed and were built between 1850 and 1875.
2. The '2F' '58114' and '58188' classes were Johnson's class '2' engines, built between 1875 and 1902. The two classes were fitted with 4' 11" and 5' 3" diameter wheels respectively. They were inside framed engines and were the direct ancestors of all the later engines.
3. The next class was Deeley's class '3' built 1903 onwards with Belpaire boilers. The '3F' '43137' class was rebuilt from the '2F' '58114' class with 4' 11" diameter wheels and the '3F' '43191' class was rebuilt from the '2F' '58188' class with 5' 3" diameter wheels. The '43765' class was built new.
4. Class '4' was Fowler's enlarged and superheated design, built from 1911 onwards. It consisted of the '4F' '43835' class built by the Midland Railway, and the '44027' class, which was adopted as an LMS standard type in 1923 and was built up to 1940.

Historical survey of Caledonian 4-4-0 engines ('Dunalastair' classes).

When McIntosh became the locomotive superintendent of the CR in 1895, he inaugurated what became known as the 'big engine policy', later to be followed by many other railways.

McIntosh developed his 'Dunalastair' class which consisted of four variations with successive enlargements, as listed below. The engines were designed to work the main line services on the Caledonian. In their day the 'Dunalastairs' were among the most advanced engines in the country, and the superheated rebuilds were the first Scottish engines to be superheated.

1. The 'Dunalastair I' class appeared in 1896, as the first of McIntosh's inside cylinder 4-4-0s. Fifteen engines were built (renumbered 14311-14325 by the LMS and classified '2P') and they were all withdrawn between 1930 and 1935.
2. The second class was known as 'Dunalastair II'. It was an enlarged version of the 'Dunalastair I' class and the engines all appeared in 1897. Fifteen engines were built (renumbered 14326-14336 by the LMS and classified '2P') and they were all withdrawn between 1936 and 1947. Four engines (renumbered 14430-14433) were rebuilt with superheaters in 1914 becoming '3P', and they were all withdrawn in 1935-1937.
3. The 'Dunalastair III' class appeared in 1899-1900. It was an enlarged version of the 'Dunalastair II' class and sixteen engines were built (numbered 14337-14348 by the LMS and classified '2P') and they were all withdrawn between 1932 and 1947. Four engines (which became 14434-14437) were rebuilt with superheaters in 1914-1918 becoming '3P'. The engines were withdrawn from 1928 onwards but 14434 survived to come into BR stock in 1948 (see the '54434' class).
4. The final development was the 'Dunalastair IV' class which appeared in 1904-1910. It was an enlarged version of the 'Dunalastair III' class and initially nineteen saturated boiler engines were built (renumbered 14349-14365 by the LMS and classified '2P') and they were all withdrawn between 1937 and 1948. The last survivor entered BR stock and was allocated the number 54363. Two engines (later 14438-14439) which had been built in 1907 were rebuilt with superheaters in 1915-1917 becoming '3P'. Twenty-two other engines were built new in 1910-1914 with superheaters and they became 14440-14460 (see the '54438' class). All except 14442 (which was withdrawn in 1946) and CR No. 121 (which was destroyed in the Quintinshill accident in 1915) came into BR stock in 1948.
5. Pickersgill built his class of 4-4-0s in 1916-1922 (see the '54461' class). They were an enlarged version of the 'Dunalastair IV' class and were visually very similar. They could almost be regarded as the 'Dunalastair V' class, although they were never known by this name.

Historical survey of Midland 0-4-4T engines.

Between 1875 and 1900 Johnson built a total of 205 0-4-4T engines for suburban passenger work on the Midland Railway. They were to be seen all over the system, those based in the London area being fitted with condensing apparatus. There were three different varieties as follows:

1. The first batch built in 1875-1876 were fitted with 5ft 7in wheels. They had 140psi boilers and 17" x 24" cylinders (the '58030' class).
2. The second batch built from 1881 onwards were fitted with 5ft 4in wheels. They also had 140psi boilers but had larger 18" x 24" cylinders (the '58039' class).
3. The final batch built in 1889-1900 were also fitted with 5ft 4in wheels. They had 150psi boilers and 18" x 24" cylinders (also part of the '58039' class).

Midland Railway Johnson '2F' 0-6-0 No 58309 at Derby in January 1953, fitted with a Belpaire boiler.

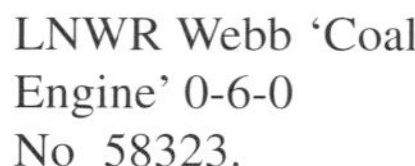

LNWR Webb 'Coal Engine' 0-6-0 No 58323.

LNWR Webb 'Coal Tank' 0-6-2T No 58928 on pilot duties at Birmingham New Street station in August 1950.

Part 3
London & North Eastern Railway Group

Locomotive Origins

Locomotives of the following pre-grouping companies were still running in 1948:

GCR	Great Central Railway
GER	Great Eastern Railway
GNoSR	Great North of Scotland Railway
GNR	Great Northern Railway
HBR	Hull & Barnsley Railway
LDECR	Lancashire, Derbyshire & East Coast Railway (taken over by the GCR in 1907)
Met.	Metropolitan Railway (some locomotives acquired in 1937)
M&GNJR	Midland & Great Northern Joint Railway (locomotives acquired in 1937)
MSLR	Manchester, Sheffield & Lincolnshire Railway (renamed GCR in 1897)
NBR	North British Railway
NER	North Eastern Railway

Two-hundred locomotives of class 'O7' were purchased from the Ministry of Supply at the end of the war. They were later renumbered in the BR Standard number series in 1949 where they joined the rest of the locomotives which BR purchased in 1948.

Sixty-eight locomotives of class 'O6' were in fact LMS designed class '8F' locomotives, even though they were constructed by the LNER during the war. At the start of 1948 they were on loan to the LMS, and all except LNER number 3554 had been renumbered as LMS locomotives.

One GER railway 'J66' locomotive had been acquired by the Mersey Railway. It became part of BR stock in 1948 and is shown under Miscellaneous Locomotives.

Locomotive Numbering

Until 1946, LNER locomotives had been numbered in a very haphazard scheme, individual locomotives taking any available number as they were built. At grouping engines of the former companies had their numbers altered as follows: NER engines unchanged, GNR engines increased by 3000, GCR engines increased by 5000, GNoSR engines increased by 6800, GER engines increased by 7000 and NBR engines increased by 9000. New LNER engines carried numbers between the NER and the GNR number series or used blank numbers in the NER series. This led to the numbers of many classes being widely distributed.

In 1946 the LNER carried out an extensive renumbering scheme, allocating a block of numbers to each class, as on the LMS. (The plan had been originally devised in 1943 but it was not carried out until after the War). This meant that at the time of nationalisation the LNER locomotives had very few gaps in their number sequences, and similar locomotive types were numbered consecutively. It also meant that as new locomotives were constructed a certain amount of renumbering had to take place to keep blocks of numbers free. This happened with classes 'B7', 'B16', 'D31' and 'L1'. (Details of the LNER renumbering scheme can be found in Appendix 9).

Until 1952 service locomotives retained their capital stock numbers. From 1952 onwards a new number series was created for service locomotives. Over the years some of these numbers were used more than once.

Locomotive Classification

The system of locomotive classification on the LNER was relatively simple if not always consistent. Each locomotive type was allocated a letter, and each class within that type was allocated a number. For example 0-6-0 locomotives were coded 'J', tender locomotive classes being from 'J1' upwards, tank locomotives from 'J50' upwards. Many classes were further subdivided into parts to indicate varieties within the class (for example 'A2', 'A2/1', 'A2/2', 'A2/3'). The parts in some classes referred to major differences (for example class 'A2') while in other classes they referred to very minor differences. Some classes which did have differences within them were not split into parts at all.

Notes

New locomotives were built to LNER designs after nationalisation in the following classes: 'A1', 'A2', 'B1', 'K1', 'L1' and 'J72' (to a 19th Century NER design!).

One steam railcar was in service at the start of 1948, numbered in the coaching stock series. This is shown under Miscellaneous Locomotives.

Two locomotives were restored and returned to service to work special trains in Scotland, and these are shown under Preserved Locomotives.

LNER Gresley streamlined 'A4' Pacific No 60027 *Merlin* on the 'Flying Scotsman' at Newcastle Central in November 1953.

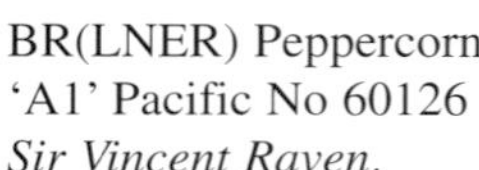

BR(LNER) Peppercorn 'A1' Pacific No 60126 *Sir Vincent Raven.*

LNER Thompson 'B1' class 4-6-0 No 61406 at Immingham in August 1965.

A4 60001-60034
4-6-2 LNER Gresley Streamlined Pacific

Power Classification:	7P reclassified 8P in 1951
Introduced:	1935-1938
Designer:	Gresley
Company:	LNER
Weight:	Loco 109t 19cwt Tender 60t 7cwt t Tender 64t 19cwt
Driving Wheel:	6' 8"
Boiler Pressure:	250psi superheated
Cylinders:	Three 18½" x 26" c Inside cylinder reduced to 17" x 26"
Tractive Effort:	35455lbf c 33616lbf
Valve Gear:	Walschaert with derived motion (piston valves)

In the early 1930s the LNER was considering providing a high speed service between London and Newcastle. At first the possibility of a diesel-electric train was considered, based on the German 'Flying Hamburger' train. It was decided instead to use conventional rolling stock with streamlined steam propulsion and Sir Nigel Gresley set about producing an engine which would cover the requirements.

The first of the new streamlined 'A4' class engines was named SILVER LINK and it appeared in 1935. It was a development of his 'A3' class, but it was greatly altered in appearance. The wedge shaped streamlined casing was startling to contemporary eyes and caused something of a furore. The first four engines (2509-2512, later 60014-60017) were painted silver and hauled the new 'Silver Jubilee' train between London and Newcastle in only four hours.

The engines proved successful and more were added in 1936-1939. They proved able to handle the fastest trains on the East Coast Main Line, and ran smoothly at speeds over 100mph.

The engines were originally fitted with valences over the driving wheels but these were removed during the war to facilitate maintenance of the motion. Four engines (later 60005, 60022, 60033 and 60034) were built with Kylchap blast-pipes and double chimneys which considerably improved the running at high speeds, the rest having single chimneys. Eventually the whole class was rebuilt by BR with double chimneys and modified middle big ends (to overcome persistent problems with the big ends over-running).

The engines were regarded as Gresley's masterpiece, and they proved it when 4468 (later 60022) MALLARD took the World speed record for steam locomotives (which still remains unbroken) of 126½mph on 7th July 1938. At the end of this high speed run MALLARD had managed to melt all the bearing metal in the middle big-end, and had to be towed back home!

Some changes of names took place before 1948. The following names were previously carried: 60001 GARGANEY, 60002 POCHARD, 60003 OSPREY, 60004 GREAT SNIPE, 60005 CAPERCAILLE then CHARLES H NEWTON, 60006 HERRING GULL, 60008 GOLDEN SHUTTLE, 60010 WOODCOCK, 60026 KESTREL, 60028 SEA EAGLE and 60030 GREAT SNIPE.

No. 4469 SIR RALPH WEDGWOOD (formerly GADWALL) was destroyed in an air raid in York in 1942. The remainder were renumbered 1-34 in 1946, but not in building date order (the build order being 14-17, 23-28, 9-13, 29, 3, 30, 8, 31, 7, 4, 18-20, 6, 21-22, (4469), 2, 1, 32, 5, 33 and 34). The main reason for this apparently haphazard numbering was to give prominent numbers to the engines named after the directors of the LNER. They came into BR stock as 60001-60034 and remained in service until replaced by diesels in the 1960s.

60010 carried a bell in front of the chimney, which was presented by the Canadian Pacific Railway in 1938. This engine has since been preserved in Canada.

c Some engines had the inside cylinder reduced to 17" x 26". Of these 60003, 60014 and 60031 were later reconverted to normal by BR.

d Double chimneys.

t Most engines of the class were fitted with corridor tenders to allow a change of crew on long non-stop runs. Changing of tenders was quite common, locomotives attached to corridor tenders for only part of the BR era are marked with an asterisk.

Year End Totals: 'A4' class

'47	'48	'49	'50	'51	'52	'53	'54	'55	'56	'57	'58	'59	'60	'61	'62	'63	'64	'65	'66	'67
34	34	34	34	34	34	34	34	34	34	34	34	34	34	34	29	19	12	6		

Number	*Built*	*Renumbered*	*BR Dates*	*Scrap*	*Notes*
60001	04/38 Don	07/48 1	-10/64	01/65	
SIR RONALD MATTHEWS					04/58⇨d
60002	04/38 Don	05/48 2	-05/64	11/64	
SIR MURROUGH WILSON					07/57⇨d
60003	08/37 Don	03/49 3	-12/62	02/63	ct*
ANDREW K. MCCOSH					07/57⇨d
60004	11/37 Don	06/48 4	-07/66	12/66	t*
WILLIAM WHITELAW					01/58⇨d
60005	06/38 Don	07/48 5	-03/64	09/64	d
SIR CHARLES NEWTON					
60006	01/38 Don	12/48 6	-09/65	01/66	t*
SIR RALPH WEDGWOOD					09/57⇨d
60007 §	11/37 Don	03/48 7	-02/66		t
SIR NIGEL GRESLEY					01/58⇨d
60008 §	09/37 Don	10/48 8	-07/63		t*
DWIGHT D. EISENHOWER					08/58⇨d
60009 §	06/37 Don	05/48 9	-06/66		t*
UNION OF SOUTH AFRICA					11/58⇨d
60010 §	05/37 Don	10/48 10	-05/65		t*
DOMINION OF CANADA					01/58⇨d
60011	06/37 Don	03/49 11	-05/64	07/64	t
EMPIRE OF INDIA					01/58⇨d
60012	06/37 Don	06/48 12	-08/64	05/65	tc
COMMONWEALTH OF AUSTRALIA					07/58⇨d
60013	06/37 Don	05/49 13	-04/63	06/63	t*
DOMINION OF NEW ZEALAND					07/58⇨d
60014	09/35 Don	06/49 14	-12/62	08/63	tc
SILVER LINK					12/58⇨d
60015	09/35 Don	12/48 15	-04/63	06/63	t
QUICKSILVER					08/57⇨d
60016	11/35 Don	06/48 16	-03/65	05/65	t*
SILVER KING					06/57⇨d
60017	12/35 Don	04/49 17	-10/63	01/64	t
SILVER FOX					05/57⇨d
60018	12/37 Don	10/48 18	-06/63	08/63	
SPARROW HAWK					01/58⇨d
60019 §	12/37 Don	10/48 19	-09/66		
BITTERN					09/57⇨d
60020	12/37 Don	10/48 20	-03/64	07/64	c
GUILLEMOT					01/58⇨d
60021	02/38 Don	03/50 21	-10/63	01/64	t*
WILD SWAN					04/58⇨d
60022 §	03/38 Don	09/49 22	-04/63		d t*
MALLARD					
60023	12/36 Don	03/48 23	-10/64	03/65	
GOLDEN EAGLE					09/58⇨d
60024	12/36 Don	06/48 24	-09/66	02/67	t*
KINGFISHER					08/58⇨d
60025	02/37 Don	01/50 25	-10/63	01/64	t
FALCON					09/58⇨d
60026	02/37 Don	09/49 26	-12/65	01/68	t*
MILES BEEVOR					08/57⇨d
60027	03/37 Don	06/48 27	-09/65	02/66	t*
MERLIN					02/58⇨d
60028	04/37 Don	06/48 28	-12/62	01/63	t*
WALTER K. WHIGHAM					01/58⇨d
60029	07/37 Don	07/48 29	-10/63	01/64	t
WOODCOCK					10/58⇨d
60030	08/37 Don	07/48 30	-12/62	02/63	t*
GOLDEN FLEECE					05/58⇨d
60031	10/37 Don	06/48 31	-11/65	02/66	tc
GOLDEN PLOVER					03/58⇨d
60032	05/38 Don	06/49 32	-10/63	01/64	t*
GANNET					11/58⇨d
60033	06/38 Don	04/48 33	-12/62	02/63	d t*
SEAGULL					
60034	07/38 Don	03/48 34	-08/66	01/67	d t*
PEREGRINE	02/48➲LORD FARINGDON				

A3 60035-60112
4-6-2 GNR & LNER Gresley Pacific

A10 60068
4-6-2 GNR Unrebuilt Gresley Pacific

Power Classification:	7P
Introduced:	1922-1925, rebuilt 1927-1948 3 1928-1934
Designer:	Gresley
Company:	GNR and LNER
Weight:	Loco 96t 5cwt A10 Loco 92t 9cwt Tender 57t 18cwt t Tender 56t 6cwt
Driving Wheel:	6' 8"
Boiler Pressure:	220psi superheated A10 180psi superheated
Cylinders:	Three 19" x 26" A10 Three 20" x 26"
Tractive Effort:	32910lbf A10 29835lbf
Valve Gear:	Walschaert with derived motion (piston valves)

In 1922 Gresley put the first of his three-cylinder pacific locomotives to work on the Great Northern Railway. Apart from the solitary GWR engine the GREAT BEAR they were the first pacifics (4-6-2 type) to be built in this country. They were designed to haul the fastest and heaviest trains on the LNER.

The first two engines appeared as GNR engines 1470 and 1471 (later 4470 and 4471 and BR 60113 and 60102) and they were originally classified 'A1'. They were a logical development from the GNR Atlantics, but nevertheless caused a sensation and great interest when they first arrived. They were excellent engines and they rode magnificently. They had large cabs and for the first time in British locomotive history the enginemen were provided with padded seats.

Gresley's pacifics had three cylinders all driving on the second coupled axle. They had two outside sets of Walschaert valve gear with the centre valve being driven by Gresley's conjugated valve gear in front of the cylinders. This led to the one Achilles Heel of all Gresley's pacifics, which was the problems they experienced with the middle valve over-running, causing middle big-end failures.

Fifty more 'A1' pacifics were built by the LNER in 1923-1925 (60103-60112 and 60044-60083). In 1925 4474 was tested against GWR 'Castle' class 4079 PENDENNIS CASTLE. The 'Castle' proved to be a superior engine and this led to all the 'A1's being rebuilt with long-travel, long-lap valves which improved their performance. The engines were fitted with corridor tenders and regularly worked long non-stop trips at high speed. Most of the class were named after famous racehorses.

In 1927 4480 was rebuilt with a larger superheater, the boiler pressure was raised from 180psi to 220psi, and it was converted to left-hand drive. This was the first 'A3' engine, and (together with 2573, 2578 and 2580 when they were rebuilt) was originally classified 'A3/1'. 2544 was similarly rebuilt with the cylinders reduced from 20" to 18¼" diameter and was originally reclassified 'A3/2'. In 1928 twenty-seven new 'A3's were built with 19" diameter cylinders and these were originally classified 'A3/3'. Later all the engines were rebuilt with 19" cylinders and were known as 'A3'.

In 1945 the original engine was completely rebuilt to form the 'A1' prototype (see 'A1/1' 60113). The surviving 'A1' engines were then reclassified 'A10'.

60054 was named MANNA until 1926, 60064 was named WILLIAM WHITELAW until 1941 and 60065 was named KNIGHT OF THE THISTLE until 1932.

2751 (later 60097) was fitted with smoke deflectors and a Kylchap blastpipe and double chimney. Between 1958 and 1960 the rest of the class were also fitted with double chimneys and Kylchap blastpipes. This gave the engines a much softer exhaust which caused problems with smoke drifting across the driver's vision. To solve this problem trough type smoke deflectors (of the German pattern) were later fitted to most members of the class.

60103 FLYING SCOTSMAN was privately preserved with its former number 4472, and has become one of the most famous of all preserved BR steam locomotives.

A10 60068 was the only 'A10' engine to come into BR stock, being converted to 'A3' in December 1948.

3 These engines were built new as 'A3' from 1928 onwards. The rest were originally 'A1' (later 'A10') engines which were rebuilt to 'A3' in 1927-1948.

t Some engines were fitted with GNR type tenders with coal rails, the rest being fitted with LNER tenders.

d Fitted with double chimney.

g Fitted with German type smoke deflectors.

s 60097 was fitted with a different pattern of smoke deflectors, and was the only engine to have a double chimney before 1958.

Year End Totals: 'A3' class

'47	'48	'49	'50	'51	'52	'53	'54	'55	'56	'57	'58	'59	'60	'61	'62	'63	'64	'65	'66	'67
77	78	78	78	78	78	78	78	78	78	78	78	77	77	71	59	26	3	1		

Year End Totals: 'A10' class

'47	'48	'49	'50	'51	'52	'53	'54	'55	'56	'57	'58	'59	'60	'61	'62	'63	'64	'65	'66	'67
1																				

Number	Name	Built	Renumbered	BR Dates	Scrap	Notes
60035	WINDSOR LAD	07/34 Don	12/48 35	-09/61	10/61	3 02/59⇨d
60036	COLOMBO	07/34 Don	07/48 36	-11/64	04/65	3 11/58⇨d 07/62⇨g
60037	HYPERION	07/34 Don	10/48 37	-12/63	07/64	3 10/58⇨d 05/62⇨g
60038	FIRDAUSSI	08/34 Don	06/48 38	-11/63	01/64	3 08/59⇨d
60039	SANDWICH	09/34 Don	07/48 39	-03/63	04/63	3 07/59⇨d 06/61⇨g
60040	CAMERONIAN	10/34 Don	09/48 40	-07/64	09/64	3 10/59⇨d 03/62⇨g
60041	SALMON TROUT	12/34 Don	12/48 41	-11/65	11/66	3 07/59⇨d 01/63⇨g
60042	SINGAPORE	12/34 Don	06/48 42	-07/64	11/64	3 09/58⇨d 09/62⇨g
60043	BROWN JACK	02/35 Don	08/48 43	-05/64	08/64	3 02/59⇨d 02/62⇨g
60044	MELTON	06/24 Don	08/49 44	-06/63	12/63	10/59⇨d 08/61⇨g
60045	LEMBERG	07/24 Don	06/48 45	-11/64	03/65	10/59⇨d 11/61⇨g
60046	DIAMOND JUBILEE	08/24 Don	08/49 46	-06/63	09/63	07/58⇨d 12/61⇨g
60047	DONOVAN	08/24 Don	05/48 47	-04/63	04/63	07/59⇨d 12/61⇨g
60048	DONCASTER	08/24 Don	11/48 48	-09/63	10/63	05/59⇨d 12/61⇨g
60049	GALTEE MORE	09/24 Don	06/48 49	-12/62	04/63	03/59⇨d 10/60⇨g
60050	PERSIMMON	10/24 Don	08/48 50	-06/63	07/63	04/59⇨d 10/61⇨g
60051	BLINK BONNY	11/24 Don	09/48 51	-11/64	02/65	08/59⇨d 03/62⇨g
60052	PRINCE PALATINE	11/24 Don	10/48 52	-01/66	09/66	11/58⇨d 10/62⇨g
60053	SANSOVINO	11/24 Don	02/49 53	-05/63	07/63	11/58⇨d 11/60⇨g
60054	PRINCE OF WALES	12/24 Don	04/48 54	-06/64	10/64	08/58⇨d 05/62⇨g
60055	WOOLWINDER	12/24 Don	06/48 55	-09/61	10/61	06/58⇨d
60056	CENTENARY	02/25 Don	05/49 56	-05/63	11/63	07/59⇨d 08/61⇨g
60057	ORMONDE	02/25 Don	06/48 57	-10/63	07/64	10/58⇨d 09/61⇨g
60058	BLAIR ATHOL	02/25 Don	03/49 58	-06/63	07/63	10/58⇨d
60059	TRACERY	03/25 Don	07/48 59	-12/62	06/63	07/58⇨d 09/61⇨g
60060	THE TETRARCH	03/25 Don	10/48 60	-09/63	11/63	03/59⇨d
60061	PRETTY POLLY	04/25 Don	11/48 61	-09/63	10/63	10/58⇨d 02/62⇨g
60062	MINORU	05/25 Don	07/49 62	-12/64	04/65	02/59⇨d 07/61⇨g
60063	ISINGLASS	06/25 Don	01/49 63	-06/64	10/64	02/59⇨d 08/61⇨g
60064	TAGALIE	07/24 NB	07/49 64	-09/61	10/61	06/59⇨d
60065	KNIGHT OF THISTLE	07/24 NB	07/48 65	-06/64	03/65	10/58⇨d 11/61⇨g
60066	MERRY HAMPTON	07/24 NB	03/48 66	-09/63	10/63	10/58⇨d 10/61⇨g
60067	LADAS	08/24 NB	08/48 67	-12/62	01/63	04/59⇨d 04/61⇨g
60068	SIR VISTO	08/24 NB	10/48 68	-08/62	09/62	A10 12/48⇨A3 04/59⇨d
60069	SCEPTRE	09/24 NB	07/48 69	-10/62	06/63	08/59⇨d
60070	GLADIATEUR	09/24 NB	08/48 70	-05/64	12/64	04/59⇨d 09/61⇨g
60071	TRANQUIL	09/24 NB	05/48 71	-10/64	01/65	06/58⇨d 11/61⇨g
60072	SUNSTAR	09/24 NB	08/48 72	-10/62	05/63	07/59⇨d
60073	ST. GATIEN	10/24 NB	03/49 73	-08/63	09/63	07/58⇨d 07/61⇨g
60074	HARVESTER	10/24 NB	05/48 74	-04/63	06/63	03/59⇨d
60075	ST. FRUSQUIN	10/24 NB	05/48 75	-01/64	04/64	09/59⇨d 04/62⇨g
60076	GALOPIN	10/24 NB	09/48 76	-10/62	05/63	06/59⇨d
60077	THE WHITE KNIGHT	10/24 NB	11/48 77	-07/64	11/64	04/59⇨d 07/61⇨g
60078	NIGHT HAWK	10/24 NB	06/48 78	-10/62	06/63	02/59⇨d 03/62⇨g
60079	BAYARDO	10/24 NB	03/48 79	-09/61	10/61	04/60⇨d
60080	DICK TURPIN	11/24 NB	03/49 80	-10/64	12/64	10/59⇨d 11/61⇨g
60081	SHOTOVER	11/24 NB	06/48 81	-10/62	11/62	10/58⇨d 08/61⇨g
60082	NEIL GOW	11/24 NB	05/48 82	-09/63	11/63	08/59⇨d 08/61⇨g
60083	SIR HUGO	12/24 NB	05/49 83	-05/64	09/64	08/59⇨d 02/62⇨g
60084	TRIGO	02/30 Don	06/48 84	-11/64	02/65	3 06/58⇨d 01/62⇨g
60085	MANNA	02/30 Don	07/48 85	-10/64	01/65	3 11/58⇨d 04/62⇨g
60086	GAINSBOROUGH	04/30 Don	09/48 86	-11/63	02/64	3 06/59⇨d
60087	BLENHEIM	04/30 Don	10/48 87	-10/63	07/64	3 07/58⇨d 02/62⇨g
60088	BOOK LAW	07/30 Don	07/48 88	-10/63	01/64	3 07/59⇨d 06/61⇨g
60089	FELSTEAD	08/28 Don	09/48 89	-10/63	03/64	3 10/59⇨d 11/61⇨g
60090	GRAND PARADE	08/28 Don	02/49 90	-10/63	01/64	3 08/58⇨d 01/63⇨g
60091	CAPTAIN CUTTLE	09/28 Don	04/48 91	-10/64	01/65	3 03/59⇨d 10/61⇨g
60092	FAIRWAY	10/28 Don	04/49 92	-10/64	01/65	3 10/59⇨d 10/61⇨g
60093	CORONACH	11/28 Don	10/48 93	-05/62	05/62	3 12/58⇨d
60094	COLORADO	12/28 Don	12/48 94	-02/64	07/64	3 08/59⇨d 08/61⇨g
60095	FLAMINGO	01/29 Don	10/48 95	-04/61	10/61	3 02/59⇨d
60096	PAPYRUS	02/29 Don	10/48 96	-09/63	07/64	3 07/58⇨d 09/61⇨g
60097	HUMORIST	03/29 Don	06/48 97	-08/63	09/63	3 s 08/57⇨d
60098	SPION KOP	04/29 Don	11/48 98	-10/63	03/64	3 07/59⇨d
60099	CALL BOY	04/30 Don	08/49 99	-10/63	07/64	3 07/58⇨d 07/61⇨g
60100	SPEARMINT	05/30 Don	04/49 100	-06/65	07/65	3 09/58⇨d 08/61⇨g
60101	CICERO	06/30 Don	08/48 101	-04/63	07/64	3 02/59⇨d
60102	SIR FREDERICK BANBURY	07/22 Don	05/49 102	-11/61	11/61	04/59⇨d
60103 §	FLYING SCOTSMAN	02/23 Don	12/48 103	-01/63		01/59⇨d 12/61⇨g
60104	SOLARIO	03/23 Don	07/48 104	-12/59	01/60	04/59⇨d
60105	VICTOR WILD	03/23 Don	08/48 105	-06/63	08/63	03/59⇨d 12/60⇨g
60106	FLYING FOX	04/23 Don	12/48 106	-12/64	04/65	04/59⇨d 10/61⇨g
60107	ROYAL LANCER	05/23 Don	04/48 107	-09/63	10/63	06/59⇨d 02/62⇨g
60108	GAY CRUSADER	06/23 Don	03/49 108	-10/63	01/64	04/59⇨d 11/61⇨g
60109	HERMIT	06/23 Don	04/48 109	-12/62	04/63	03/59⇨d 01/61⇨g
60110	ROBERT THE DEVIL	07/23 Don	03/49 110	-05/63	07/63	05/59⇨d 06/61⇨g
60111	ENTERPRISE	08/23 Don	10/49 111	-12/62	04/63	06/59⇨d 04/62⇨g
60112	ST. SIMON	09/23 Don	03/49 112	-12/64	04/65	07/58⇨d 10/62⇨g

A1 60113-60162
4-6-2 LNER and BR Thompson and Peppercorn Pacifics

Power Classification:	7P reclassified 8P in 1951
Introduced:	1948-1949 1 1922, rebuilt 1945
Designer:	Peppercorn 1 Gresley, rebuilt by Thompson
Company:	BR (LNER) 1 GNR / LNER
Weight:	Loco 104t 2cwt 1 Loco 101t 0cwt Tender 60t 7cwt
Driving Wheel:	6' 8"
Boiler Pressure:	250psi superheated
Cylinders:	Three 19" x 26"
Tractive Effort:	37400lbf
Valve Gear:	Walschaert (piston valves)

It has been said that Thompson (who succeeded Gresley) had a dislike for all things to do with Gresley. It seems, therefore, to have been no co-incidence that Gresley's prototype pacific of 1922 (number 4470 GREAT NORTHERN) was chosen by Thompson to be rebuilt as the prototype for his new class of pacifics, in which almost all of Gresley's distinctive features were totally eradicated.

This engine (BR number 60113, and classified 'A1/1') was rebuilt in September 1945 with an 'A4' type boiler, double blast-pipe and chimney, three cylinders with divided drive, three sets of Walschaert valve gear and the wheelbase extended to 38ft 5in.

Peppercorn introduced his development of the class in 1948. They were identical in layout with Peppercorn's 'A2' class but were fitted with larger 6' 8" coupled wheels and with double blast-pipes and chimneys. They were originally fitted with plain topped chimneys but these were later replaced with chimneys carrying a lipped top, which greatly improved their appearance.

The 'A1's were excellent locomotives which ran and steamed well, and they required less maintenance than any of the other major express locomotive types running on BR. The only problem they experienced was that they were rough riders.

The locomotives ran at first without names, but eventually they all carried names on the side of the smoke deflectors.

No engines of this class were preserved, but in 1995 an ambitious project was started to build a new 'A1' engine, to be known as 60163 TORNADO.

1 60113 was Thompson's prototype engine, classified 'A1/1'.

r 60153-60157 were fitted with roller bearings.

Year End Totals: 'A1' class

'47	'48	'49	'50	'51	'52	'53	'54	'55	'56	'57	'58	'59	'60	'61	'62	'63	'64	'65	'66	'67
	21	49	49	49	49	49	49	49	49	49	49	49	49	49	43	37	26	2		

Year End Totals: 'A1/1' class

'47	'48	'49	'50	'51	'52	'53	'54	'55	'56	'57	'58	'59	'60	'61	'62	'63	'64	'65	'66	'67
1	1	1	1	1	1	1	1	1	1	1	1	1	1	1						

Number	Name	Built	Renumbered	BR Dates	Scrap	Notes
60113	GREAT NORTHERN	04/22 Don	10/48 113	-12/62	02/63	1
60114	W. P. ALLEN	08/48 Don		08/48-12/64	05/65	
60115	MEG MERRILIES	09/48 Don		09/48-10/62	11/62	
60116	HAL O' THE WYND	10/48 Don		10/48-06/65	11/65	
60117	BOIS ROUSSEL	10/48 Don		10/48-06/65	10/65	
60118	ARCHIBALD STURROCK	11/48 Don		11/48-10/65	12/65	
60119	PATRICK STIRLING	11/48 Don		11/48-05/64	11/64	
60120	KITTIWAKE	12/48 Don		12/48-01/64	02/64	
60121	SILURIAN	12/48 Don		12/48-10/65	12/65	
60122	CURLEW	12/48 Don		12/48-11/62	12/62	
60123	H. A. IVATT	02/49 Don		02/49-10/62	10/62	
60124	KENILWORTH	03/49 Don		03/49-03/66	08/66	
60125	SCOTTISH UNION	04/49 Don		04/49-07/64	11/64	
60126	SIR VINCENT RAVEN	04/49 Don		04/49-01/65	05/65	
60127	WILSON WORSDELL	05/49 Don		05/49-06/65	11/65	
60128	BONGRACE	05/49 Don		05/49-01/65	04/65	
60129	GUY MANNERING	06/49 Don		06/49-10/65	01/66	
60130	KESTREL	09/48 Dar		09/48-10/65	10/65	
60131	OSPREY	10/48 Dar		10/48-10/65	11/65	
60132	MARMION	10/48 Dar		10/48-06/65	11/65	
60133	POMMERN	10/48 Dar		10/48-07/65	10/65	
60134	FOXHUNTER	11/48 Dar		11/48-10/65	12/65	
60135	MADGE WILDFIRE	11/48 Dar		11/48-10/62	05/63	
60136	ALCAZAR	11/48 Dar		11/48-05/63	05/63	
60137	REDGAUNTLET	12/48 Dar		12/48-10/62	05/63	
60138	BOSWELL	12/48 Dar		12/48-10/65	12/65	

Number	Built	BR Dates	Scrap	Notes
60139 SEA EAGLE	12/48 Dar	12/48-06/64	01/65	
60140 BALMORAL	12/48 Dar	12/48-01/65	04/65	
60141 ABBOTSFORD	12/48 Dar	12/48-10/64	12/64	
60142 EDWARD FLETCHER	02/49 Dar	02/49-06/65	11/65	
60143 SIR WALTER SCOTT	02/49 Dar	02/49-05/64	12/64	
60144 KING'S COURIER	03/49 Dar	03/49-04/63	06/63	
60145 SAINT MUNGO	03/49 Dar	03/49-06/66	09/66	
60146 PEREGRINE	04/49 Dar	04/49-10/65	03/66	
60147 NORTH EASTERN	04/49 Dar	04/49-08/64	11/64	
60148 ABOYEUR	05/49 Dar	05/49-06/65	10/65	
60149 AMADIS	05/49 Dar	05/49-06/64	01/65	
60150 WILLBROOK	06/49 Dar	06/49-10/64	12/64	
60151 MIDLOTHIAN	06/49 Dar	06/49-11/65	02/66	
60152 HOLYROOD	07/49 Dar	07/49-06/65	12/65	
60153 FLAMBOYANT	08/49 Don	08/49-10/62	04/63	r
60154 BON ACCORD	09/49 Don	09/49-10/65	12/65	r
60155 BORDERER	09/49 Don	09/49-10/65	12/65	r
60156 GREAT CENTRAL	10/49 Don	10/49-04/65	11/65	r
60157 GREAT EASTERN	11/49 Don	11/49-01/65	04/65	r
60158 ABERDONIAN	11/49 Don	11/49-12/64	04/65	
60159 BONNIE DUNDEE	11/49 Don	11/49-10/63	03/64	
60160 AULD REEKIE	12/49 Don	12/49-12/63	03/64	
60161 NORTH BRITISH	12/49 Don	12/49-10/63	02/64	
60162 SAINT JOHNSTOUN	12/49 Don	12/49-10/63	03/64	

A2 60500-60539
4-6-2 LNER Thompson and Peppercorn Pacifics

Power Classification:	23a 7MT
	1 6MT
Introduced:	1 1944-1945
	2 1934-1936, rebuilt 1943-1944
	3 1946-1947
	a 1947-1948
Designer:	13 Thompson
	2 Gresley (as 2-8-2), rebuilt by Thompson
	a Peppercorn
Company:	LNER
Weight:	a Loco 101t 0cwt
	1 Loco 98t 0cwt
	23 Loco 101t 10cwt
	Tender 60t 7cwt
	1 Tender orig. 52t 0cwt
Driving Wheel:	6' 2"
Boiler Pressure:	12 225psi superheated
	3a 250psi superheated
Cylinders:	13a Three 19" x 26"
	2 Three 20" x 26"
Tractive Effort:	1 36385lbf
	2 40320lbf
	3a 40430lbf
Valve Gear:	Walschaert (piston valves)

The 'A2' class actually consisted of four very distinct sub-classes of mixed traffic locomotives built by Thompson and Peppercorn. The different types are described below.

Edward Thompson's pacifics were designed on quite a different plan from Sir Nigel Gresley's. They all had three sets of cylinders with divided drive, the inside cylinder driving on the leading coupled axle and the outside cylinder driving on the second axle. Three independent sets of Walschaert valve gear replaced Gresley's conjugate gear. They had a coupled wheelbase about one foot longer than Gresley's pacifics and were all fitted with double chimneys (at first unlipped chimneys, but later chimneys with lips were fitted).

2 The first of Thompson's engines to appear in 1943 were in fact rebuilds of Gresley's three-cylinder 'P2' 2-8-2 engines, built in 1934-1936. These streamlined engines had been designed to work on the line from Edinburgh to Aberdeen and had a rigid coupled wheelbase of 19ft 6in. This had proved to be too long for the curves on the route and the engines were all experiencing cracked frames. As rebuilt they retained their original boilers (although they were shortened by 2ft) and they were classified 'A2/2'. They were disliked by their Scottish crews as they tended to slip badly. They differed from the other 'A2' engines in not carrying smoke deflectors.

1 The next four Thompson pacifics appeared in 1944 and they were classified 'A2/1'. They were originally ordered as 'V2' class 2-6-2s but they were redesigned as pacifics with a 'B1' bogie, 19" diameter cylinders and steam reversers. The 'V2' boiler was retained. They were originally fitted with 4200 gallon six-wheel tenders, but these were all replaced with eight-wheel tenders by 1950.

3 The 'A2/3's were Thompson's new pacific design and they had the boiler pressure increased to 250psi. Originally thirty were ordered, but only fifteen were actually built, appearing after Thompson's retirement. The other fifteen appeared as Peppercorn's 'A2' class (see below). 500 (60500) EDWARD THOMPSON was the 2000th engine to be built at Doncaster.

a The final fifteen engines of Thompson's 'A2/3' class were redesigned by his successor Peppercorn after he came to office in 1946. Classified 'A2', they retained many of Thompson's features, but had the wheelbase reduced by 2ft 7in. The cylinders were fitted further forwards between the bogie wheels and single blast-pipes and chimneys were fitted.

d Of Thompson's 'A2' engines, 60539 was built with a double chimney, and five others were rebuilt with double chimneys and multiple valve regulators.

Year End Totals: 'A2' class

'47	'48	'49	'50	'51	'52	'53	'54	'55	'56	'57	'58	'59	'60	'61	'62	'63	'64	'65	'66	'67
1	15	15	15	15	15	15	15	15	15	15	15	15	15	15	7	5	5	3		

Year End Totals: 'A2/1' class

'47	'48	'49	'50	'51	'52	'53	'54	'55	'56	'57	'58	'59	'60	'61	'62	'63	'64	'65	'66	'67
4	4	4	4	4	4	4	4	4	4	4	4	4	1							

Year End Totals: 'A2/2' class

'47	'48	'49	'50	'51	'52	'53	'54	'55	'56	'57	'58	'59	'60	'61	'62	'63	'64	'65	'66	'67
6	6	6	6	6	6	6	6	6	6	6	6	4	3							

Year End Totals: 'A2/3' class

'47	'48	'49	'50	'51	'52	'53	'54	'55	'56	'57	'58	'59	'60	'61	'62	'63	'64	'65	'66	'67
15	15	15	15	15	15	15	15	15	15	15	15	15	15	15	7	3	3			

Number	*Built*	*Renumbered*	*BR Dates*	*Scrap*	*Notes*
60500 EDWARD THOMPSON	05/46 Don	10/49 500	-06/63	08/63	3
60501 COCK O' THE NORTH	09/44 Don	05/48 501	-02/60	04/60	2
60502 EARL MARISCHAL	06/44 Don	07/48 502	-07/61	07/61	2
60503 LORD PRESIDENT	12/44 Don	09/48 503	-11/59	02/60	2
60504 MONS MEG	11/44 Don	04/48 504	-01/61	02/61	2
60505 THANE OF FIFE	01/43 Don	06/48 505	-11/59	01/60	2
60506 WOLF OF BADENOCH	05/44 Don	12/48 506	-04/61	05/61	2
60507 HIGHLAND CHIEFTAN	05/44 Dar	11/48 507	-12/60	01/61	1
60508 DUKE OF ROTHESAY	06/44 Dar	05/48 508	-02/61	04/61	1
60509 WAVERLEY	11/44 Dar	08/48 509	-08/60	08/60	1
60510 ROBERT THE BRUCE	01/45 Dar	04/48 510	-11/60	02/61	1
60511 AIRBORNE	07/46 Don	04/48 511	-10/62	05/63	3
60512 STEADY AIM	08/46 Don	03/48 512	-06/65	10/65	3
60513 DANTE	08/46 Don	11/48 513	-04/63	05/63	3
60514 CHAMOSSAIRE	09/46 Don	03/48 514	-12/62	06/63	3
60515 SUN STREAM	10/46 Don	06/48 515	-10/62	04/63	3
60516 HYCILLA	11/46 Don	10/48 516	-10/62	04/63	3
60517 OCEAN SWELL	11/46 Don	08/48 517	-10/62	05/63	3
60518 TEHRAN	12/46 Don	07/48 518	-10/62	04/63	3
60519 HONEYWAY	02/47 Don	10/48 519	-12/62	03/63	3
60520 OWEN TUDOR	03/47 Don	08/48 520	-06/63	11/63	3
60521 WATLING STREET	05/47 Don	05/48 521	-10/62	05/63	3
60522 STRAIGHT DEAL	06/47 Don	09/49 522	-06/65	10/65	3
60523 SUN CASTLE	08/47 Don	01/49 523	-06/63	08/63	3
60524 HERRINGBONE	09/47 Don	01/49 524	-02/65	05/65	3
60525 A. H. PEPPERCORN	12/47 Don	08/49 525	-03/63	06/63	a
60526 SUGAR PALM	01/48 Don	08/48 526	01/48-10/62	05/63	ad
60527 SUN CHARIOT	01/48 Don	06/48 527	01/48-04/65	07/65	a
60528 TUDOR MINSTREL	02/48 Don	06/48 528	02/48-06/66	10/66	a
60529 PEARL DIVER	02/48 Don	09/49 529	02/48-12/62	07/64	ad
60530 SAYAJIRAO	03/48 Don	11/48 530	03/48-11/66	03/67	a
60531 BAHRAM	03/48 Don	11/48 531	03/48-12/62	03/63	a
60532 § BLUE PETER	03/48 Don		03/48-12/66		ad
60533 HAPPY KNIGHT	04/48 Don		04/48-06/63	11/63	ad
60534 IRISH ELEGANCE	04/48 Don		04/48-12/62	07/64	a
60535 HORNET'S BEAUTY	05/48 Don		05/48-06/65	07/66	a
60536 TRIMBUSH	05/48 Don		05/48-12/62	03/63	a
60537 BACHELORS BUTTON	06/48 Don		06/48-12/62	07/64	a
60538 VELOCITY	06/48 Don		06/48-10/62	07/63	ad
60539 BRONZINO	08/48 Don		08/48-10/62	06/63	ad

W1 60700
4-6-4 LNER Gresley Streamlined

Power Classification:	7P reclassified 8P in 1951
Introduced:	1929, rebuilt 1937
Designer:	Gresley
Company:	LNER
Weight:	Loco 107t 17cwt
	c Tender 64t 19cwt
	n Tender 60t 7cwt
Driving Wheel:	6' 8"
Boiler Pressure:	250psi superheated
Cylinders:	Three 20" x 26"
	Later three 19" x 26"
Tractive Effort:	41435lbf
	Later 37400lbf
Valve Gear:	Walschaert with derived motion (piston valves)

At about the same time as the LMS had been experimenting with the high pressure engine FURY (see 46170), Sir Nigel Gresley of the LNER was also experimenting with similar ideas, although quite different in concept. In 1929 he turned out the only 4-6-4 tender engine ever to run in Britain and at the time it was the most powerful passenger engine in the country. It was a four-cylinder compound engine and it was built under conditions of great secrecy at Darlington, becoming known as the 'Hush-hush' engine. Numbered 10000 it carried a high pressure (450psi) marine-type Yarrow water tube boiler. It was partially streamlined and was the first engine to appear in this form, appearing five years before the 'A4's.

It ran with some success for many years, but it was a poor steamer due to the impossibility of preventing air-leaks.

In 1937 it was rebuilt as a three-cylinder simple engine with a conventional boiler, more or less in conformity with the streamlined 'A4' pacifics, but still retaining its unique 4-6-4 wheel arrangement.

In 1948 the corridor tender (c) was replaced with a non-corridor tender (n), and the cylinder diameter was reduced to 19" in 1955.

Year End Totals: 'W1' class

'47	'48	'49	'50	'51	'52	'53	'54	'55	'56	'57	'58	'59	'60	'61	'62	'63	'64	'65	'66	'67
1	1	1	1	1	1	1	1	1	1	1	1									

Number	*Built*	*Renumbered*	*BR Dates*	*Scrap*	*Notes*
60700	06/30 Dar	06/48 10000	-06/59	06/59	

V2 60800-60983
2-6-2 LNER Gresley 'Green Arrow'

Power Classification: 6MT
Introduced: 1936-1944
Designer: Gresley
Company: LNER
Weight: Loco 93t 2cwt
Tender 52t 0cwt
Driving Wheel: 6' 2"
Boiler Pressure: 220psi superheated
Cylinders: Three 18½" x 26"
Tractive Effort: 33730lbf
Valve Gear: Walschaert with derived motion (piston valves)

The first 'V2' engine (number 4771) appeared in 1936 and it was named GREEN ARROW to coincide with the introduction of a special fast freight service of the same name. The 'V2's were the first three-cylinder 2-6-2 engines to appear in this country. Designed for express mixed traffic duties, they were in fact able to hold their own alongside the pacifics on the top link duties on the LNER main line when required.

The engines proved so successful that their construction continued right through the war years at Doncaster and Darlington until 1944. They have sometimes been described as 'the engines that helped to win the war' as they were invaluable in helping to keep the extra traffic moving on the East Coast main line under the difficult wartime conditions. They put in magnificent work until supplanted by diesels in the 1960s. Some engines were later rebuilt with the original monobloc cylinder casting replaced by three separate cylinders. These engines could be recognised by their outside steam pipes.

The final four engines on order were built as 'A2/1' pacifics.

s 60813 was fitted with a stovepipe chimney which it acquired during experiments with self-cleaning smokeboxes.

d Eight engines were fitted with double chimneys in 1960-1961, but these proved to be of no great advantage.

Year End Totals: 'V2' class

'47	'48	'49	'50	'51	'52	'53	'54	'55	'56	'57	'58	'59	'60	'61	'62	'63	'64	'65	'66	'67
184	184	184	184	184	184	184	184	184	184	184	184	184	184	184	115	72	40	14		

Number	Built	Renumbered	BR Dates	Scrap	Notes
60800 §	06/36 Don	02/49 800	-08/62		
GREEN ARROW					
60801	08/36 Don	01/49 801	-10/62	05/63	
60802	10/36 Don	05/49 802	-03/64	04/64	
60803	10/36 Don	03/50 803	-06/63	12/63	
60804	11/36 Don	09/48 804	-12/63	03/64	
60805	07/37 Dar	11/48 805	-12/63	02/64	
60806	08/37 Dar	06/48 806	-09/66	01/67	
60807	08/37 Dar	10/48 807	-12/62	12/62	
60808	09/37 Dar	06/48 808	-10/64	11/64	
60809	09/37 Dar	06/48 809	-07/64	10/64	
THE SNAPPER, THE EAST YORKSHIRE REGIMENT, THE DUKE OF YORK'S OWN					
60810	09/37 Dar	10/48 810	-11/65	03/66	
60811	09/37 Dar	08/48 811	-04/62	05/62	
60812	09/37 Dar	06/49 812	-07/64	10/64	
60813	09/37 Dar	12/48 813	-11/66	01/67	s
60814	10/37 Dar	06/48 814	-04/63	06/63	
60815	10/37 Dar	07/49 815	-06/62	09/62	
60816	10/37 Dar	07/48 816	-10/65	12/65	
60817	11/37 Dar	09/48 817	-06/63	01/64	d
60818	11/37 Dar	07/48 818	-08/66	06/67	
60819	11/37 Dar	03/48 819	-12/62	10/63	
60820	11/37 Dar	04/48 820	-06/62	07/62	
60821	12/37 Dar	04/48 821	-12/62	05/63	
60822	12/37 Dar	04/48 822	-12/64	03/65	
60823	12/37 Dar	12/49 823	-05/62	05/62	
60824	12/37 Dar	07/48 824	-11/66	02/67	
60825	01/38 Dar	05/48 825	-04/64	10/64	
60826	01/38 Dar	10/48 826	-04/62	04/62	
60827	03/38 Dar	11/48 827	-12/62	10/63	
60828	03/38 Dar	09/49 828	-10/65	12/65	
60829	04/38 Dar	03/50 829	-05/62	07/62	
60830	04/38 Dar	03/49 830	-06/63	10/63	
60831	05/38 Dar	11/48 831	-12/66	06/67	
60832	07/38 Dar	03/49 832	-12/62	06/63	
60833	08/38 Dar	10/48 833	-05/64	09/64	
60834	09/38 Dar	05/48 834	-03/64	12/64	
60835	09/38 Dar	06/48 835	-10/65	02/66	
THE GREEN HOWARD, ALEXANDRA, PRINCESS OF WALES'S OWN YORKSHIRE REGIMENT					
60836	09/38 Dar	05/48 836	-12/66	09/67	
60837	10/38 Dar	12/48 837	-11/65	02/66	
60838	10/38 Dar	02/49 838	-01/64	03/64	
60839	10/38 Dar	06/48 839	-10/62	01/63	
60840	10/38 Dar	05/49 840	-12/62	10/63	
60841	11/38 Dar	06/49 841	-09/63	11/63	
60842	12/38 Dar	05/50 842	-10/62	01/63	
60843	12/38 Dar	05/50 843	-10/65	07/66	
60844	02/39 Dar	11/49 844	-11/65	02/66	
60845	02/39 Dar	09/49 845	-09/62	12/62	
60846	02/39 Dar	01/49 846	-10/65	01/66	
60847	03/39 Dar	03/49 847	-06/65	10/65	
ST. PETER'S SCHOOL, YORK, A.D. 627					
60848	03/39 Dar	06/49 848	-07/62	10/62	
60849	03/39 Dar	08/48 849	-04/62	04/62	
60850	03/39 Dar	10/48 850	-02/62	03/62	
60851	04/39 Dar	01/50 851	-12/62	09/63	
60852	03/39 Dar	06/50 852	-09/63	02/64	
60853	04/39 Dar	03/49 853	-09/63	10/63	
60854	04/39 Dar	09/48 854	-06/63	02/64	
60855	04/39 Dar	07/49 855	-04/64	08/64	
60856	05/39 Dar	11/48 856	-05/64	10/64	
60857	05/39 Dar	10/49 857	-04/62	04/62	
60858	05/39 Dar	07/49 858	-10/63	02/64	d
60859	05/39 Dar	02/49 859	-09/65	12/65	
60860	05/39 Dar	11/48 860	-10/62	05/63	
DURHAM SCHOOL					
60861	06/39 Dar	06/49 861	-08/63	09/63	
60862	06/39 Dar	01/49 862	-06/63	11/63	d
60863	06/39 Dar	03/49 863	-06/62	07/62	
60864	06/39 Dar	08/50 864	-03/64	04/64	
60865	06/39 Dar	04/50 865	-06/65	11/65	
60866	07/39 Dar	04/48 866	-12/62	06/63	
60867	07/39 Dar	04/50 867	-05/62	05/62	
60868	07/39 Dar	08/48 868	-11/66	02/67	
60869	08/39 Dar	04/48 869	-06/63	12/63	
60870	08/39 Dar	07/48 870	-07/63	07/63	
60871	08/39 Dar	03/49 871	-09/63	12/63	
60872	04/39 Don	06/50 872	-09/63	10/63	
KING'S OWN YORKSHIRE LIGHT INFANTRY					
60873	05/39 Don	06/49 873	-12/62	09/63	
COLDSTREAMER					
60874	06/39 Don	12/49 874	-08/62	08/62	
60875	07/39 Don	09/49 875	-03/62	04/62	
60876	05/40 Don	10/48 876	-10/65	01/66	
60877	06/40 Don	06/48 877	-02/66	09/66	
60878	07/40 Don	06/49 878	-10/62	02/63	
60879	08/40 Don	07/49 879	-12/62	01/63	
60880	09/40 Don	06/48 880	-09/63	11/63	d
60881	10/40 Don	05/48 881	-07/63	11/63	d
60882	09/39 Dar	05/48 882	-07/64	02/65	
60883	10/39 Dar	07/48 883	-04/63	05/63	
60884	10/39 Dar	04/48 884	-09/65	10/65	
60885	11/39 Dar	10/48 885	-09/65	10/65	
60886	11/39 Dar	11/48 886	-08/66	02/67	
60887	11/39 Dar	11/48 887	-07/64	10/64	
60888	12/39 Dar	06/49 888	-12/62	09/63	
60889	12/39 Dar	03/49 889	-06/63	06/63	
60890	12/39 Dar	07/49 890	-06/62	09/62	
60891	12/39 Dar	11/49 891	-10/64	11/64	
60892	01/40 Dar	08/48 892	-11/63	02/64	
60893	01/40 Dar	02/49 893	-09/62	12/62	
60894	02/40 Dar	09/48 894	-12/62	11/63	
60895	01/40 Dar	01/49 895	-10/65	12/65	
60896	02/40 Dar	04/49 896	-09/62	10/62	
60897	02/40 Dar	05/50 897	-06/63	09/63	
60898	02/40 Dar	09/48 898	-11/63	12/63	
60899	02/40 Dar	09/49 899	-09/63	11/63	
60900	03/40 Dar	11/49 900	-04/63	09/63	
60901	03/40 Dar	12/49 901	-06/65	09/65	
60902	03/40 Dar	12/48 902	-09/63	11/63	d
60903	03/40 Dar	03/50 903	-02/63	05/63	d
60904	04/40 Dar	12/49 904	-07/64	10/64	
60905	04/40 Dar	01/50 905	-09/63	10/63	
60906	04/40 Dar	01/50 906	-05/63	06/63	
60907	04/40 Dar	01/50 907	-05/62	06/62	
60908	04/40 Dar	11/48 908	-06/62	06/62	
60909	05/40 Dar	01/49 909	-06/62	06/62	
60910	05/40 Dar	08/48 910	-04/64	07/64	
60911	05/40 Dar	05/49 911	-12/62	03/63	
60912	05/40 Dar	06/49 912	-04/63	05/63	
60913	06/40 Dar	08/48 913	-10/64	12/64	
60914	06/40 Dar	05/48 914	-09/62	12/62	
60915	06/40 Dar	05/49 915	-12/62	01/63	
60916	07/40 Dar	08/49 916	-06/64	10/64	
60917	08/40 Dar	06/49 917	-04/62	04/62	
60918	08/41 Dar	12/48 918	-10/62	11/62	
60919	09/41 Dar	10/48 919	-09/66	01/67	
60920	10/41 Dar	08/48 920	-12/62	09/63	
60921	10/41 Dar	11/49 921	-06/63	06/63	
60922	11/41 Dar	07/48 922	-07/64	10/64	
60923	11/41 Dar	06/48 923	-10/65	02/66	
60924	11/41 Dar	01/50 924	-09/63	11/63	
60925	12/41 Dar	04/48 925	-05/64	09/64	
60926	12/41 Dar	02/49 926	-10/62	02/63	
60927	12/41 Dar	10/48 927	-12/62	12/63	
60928	06/41 Don	04/49 928	-03/62	04/62	
60929	06/41 Don	01/50 929	-06/65	11/65	
60930	07/41 Don	01/49 930	-09/62	11/62	
60931	09/41 Don	03/49 931	-09/65	10/65	
60932	10/41 Don	10/48 932	-05/64	10/64	
60933	10/41 Don	04/48 933	-12/62	09/63	
60934	01/42 Don	10/48 934	-10/62	05/63	
60935	02/42 Don	12/49 935	-06/63	06/63	
60936	03/42 Don	11/49 936	-09/62	10/62	
60937	03/42 Don	03/50 937	-12/62	10/63	
60938	01/42 Dar	10/49 938	-09/62	09/62	
60939	01/42 Dar	07/49 939	-10/64	11/64	
60940	02/42 Dar	09/48 940	-10/65	01/66	
60941	03/42 Dar	09/48 941	-07/64	10/64	
60942	03/42 Dar	09/48 942	-05/64	09/64	
60943	03/42 Dar	03/50 943	-09/62	10/62	
60944	04/42 Dar	01/49 944	-09/65	01/66	
60945	05/42 Dar	02/50 945	-07/64	10/64	
60946	05/42 Dar	12/48 946	-10/65	01/66	
60947	06/42 Dar	11/49 947	-10/62	11/62	
60948	06/42 Dar	12/48 948	-09/63	11/63	
60949	06/42 Dar	08/49 949	-12/62	06/63	
60950	06/42 Dar	01/50 950	-09/63	11/63	
60951	07/42 Dar	12/48 951	-12/62	10/63	
60952	07/42 Dar	01/49 952	-10/65	01/66	
60953	08/42 Dar	09/48 953	-05/62	06/62	
60954	09/42 Dar	04/49 954	-11/63	01/64	
60955	09/42 Dar	06/49 955	-11/66	12/66	
60956	09/42 Dar	05/48 956	-09/62	12/62	
60957	10/42 Dar	09/49 957	-12/64	03/65	
60958	10/42 Dar	03/50 958	-12/62	09/63	
60959	11/42 Dar	05/48 959	-07/63	09/63	
60960	11/42 Dar	12/48 960	-02/62	03/62	
60961	12/42 Dar	10/48 961	-04/65	07/65	
60962	12/42 Dar	10/48 962	-09/65	12/65	
60963	01/43 Dar	09/49 963	-06/65	11/65	d
60964	01/43 Dar	06/48 964	-05/64	10/64	
04/58➲THE DURHAM LIGHT INFANTRY					
60965	02/43 Dar	06/48 965	-12/62	12/63	
60966	03/43 Dar	04/48 966	-06/63	07/63	
60967	03/43 Dar	02/49 967	-02/64	03/64	
60968	04/43 Dar	07/49 968	-05/63	06/63	
60969	04/43 Dar	01/49 969	-05/64	09/64	
60970	05/43 Dar	12/48 970	-03/66	06/66	
60971	06/43 Dar	12/48 971	-12/62	12/63	
60972	07/43 Dar	05/48 972	-11/63	12/63	
60973	07/43 Dar	05/48 973	-01/66	03/66	
60974	08/43 Dar	08/48 974	-12/63	01/64	
60975	09/43 Dar	08/48 975	-05/64	10/64	
60976	10/43 Dar	01/50 976	-11/66	01/67	
60977	10/43 Dar	12/49 977	-02/62	04/62	
60978	12/43 Dar	11/49 978	-12/62	07/63	
60979	01/44 Dar	09/48 979	-10/62	02/63	
60980	03/44 Dar	09/48 980	-12/62	02/64	
60981	04/44 Dar	11/48 981	-04/63	05/63	
60982	06/44 Dar	03/48 982	-10/64	11/64	
60983	07/44 Dar	03/50 983	-09/62	12/62	

B1 61000-61409, 17-32
4-6-0 LNER Thompson 'Bongo' or 'Antelope'

Power Classification: 5MT
Introduced: 1942-1952
Designer: Thompson
Company: LNER
Weight: Loco 71t 3cwt
Tender 52t 0cwt
Driving Wheel: 6' 2"
Boiler Pressure: 225psi superheated
Cylinders: Outside 20" x 26"
Tractive Effort: 26880lbf
Valve Gear: Walschaert (piston valves)

The 'B1' class was Thompson's first new design for the LNER. They were 4-6-0 mixed traffic engines and they were designed to replace various 4-4-2, 4-6-0 and 4-4-0 engines which had been inherited from many of the LNER's constituent companies.

Due to difficult wartime conditions it took from 1942 to 1944 for the first ten engines to appear from Darlington Works, and they were originally classed as 'B'. The majority of the 410 engines which were eventually built were constructed by the North British Locomotive Company in Glasgow, but some also came from Vulcan Foundry and the LNER works at Gorton and Darlington.

The 'B1's were general mixed traffic engines and could be compared with the LMS Stanier 'Black Fives' ('44658' class) and the GWR 'Halls' ('4900' class). They were popular engines and they worked all over the former LNER system.

The first forty engines to be turned out from Darlington were named after various species of Antelopes (giving the class name). As the number of engines increased it was impossible to find enough antelope species to continue this naming policy, and, apart from some engines named after directors of the company, most of the remaining engines remained unnamed.

Apart from 61057, which was scrapped after a collision at Chelmsford in 1950, all the engines remained in service until the 1960s, being one of the last LNER classes to remain in service in large numbers. A number of engines survived for a while in departmental service as stationary boilers for carriage warming purposes. They were renumbered in the Service stock list as 17-32 and they were based at various centres in the Eastern Counties.

There were four coal-weighing tenders which circulated amongst various members of the class at different times.

61306 has been preserved with the name MAYFLOWER which was formerly carried by 61379.

Year End Totals: 'B1' class

'47	'48	'49	'50	'51	'52	'53	'54	'55	'56	'57	'58	'59	'60	'61	'62	'63	'64	'65	'66	'67
274	342	360	383	402	409	409	409	409	409	409	409	409	409	408	288	226	172	91	27	

Year End Totals: 'B1' (service) class

'47	'48	'49	'50	'51	'52	'53	'54	'55	'56	'57	'58	'59	'60	'61	'62	'63	'64	'65	'66	'67
																8	7	8	4	2

Number	*Built*	*Renumbered*	*BR Dates*	*Scrap*	*Notes*
61000	12/42 Dar	05/48 1000	-03/62	04/62	
SPRINGBOK					
61001	06/43 Dar	01/49 1001	-09/63	12/63	
ELAND					
61002	09/43 Dar	04/48 1002	-06/67	10/67	
IMPALA					
61003	11/43 Dar	12/48 1003	-12/65	02/66	
GAZELLE					
61004	12/43 Dar	10/48 1004	-12/63	02/64	
ORYX					
61005	02/44 Dar	03/49 1005	-09/62	11/62	
BONGO					
61006	03/44 Dar	01/49 1006	-09/63	01/64	
BLACKBUCK					
61007	04/44 Dar	01/49 1007	-02/64	07/64	
KLIPSPRINGER					
61008	05/44 Dar	05/48 1008	-12/66	03/67	
KUDU					
61009	04/44 Dar	09/49 1009	-09/62	06/64	
HARTEBEESTE					
61010	11/46 Dar	05/48 1010	-11/65	02/66	
WILDEBEESTE					
61011	11/46 Dar	04/48 1011	-12/62	01/63	
WATERBUCK					
61012	11/46 Dar	06/48 1012	-06/67	09/67	
PUKU					
61013	12/46 Dar	05/48 1013	-12/66	04/67	
TOPI					
61014	12/46 Dar	06/48 1014	-12/66	12/66	
ORIBI					
61015	01/47 Dar	09/48 1015	-12/62	12/62	
DUIKER					
61016	01/47 Dar	11/48 1016	-10/65	03/66	
INYALA					
61017	01/47 Dar	11/48 1017	-11/66	03/67	
BUSHBUCK					
61018	02/47 Dar	01/49 1018	-11/65	02/66	
GNU					
61019	02/47 Dar	07/48 1019	-03/67	12/67	
NILGHAI					
61020	02/47 Dar	07/48 1020	-11/62	12/62	
GEMSBOK					
61021	03/47 Dar	12/48 1021	-06/67	09/67	
REITBOK					
61022	03/47 Dar	02/49 1022	-11/66	02/67	
SASSABY					
61023	04/47 Dar	07/48 1023	-10/65	03/66	
HIROLA					
61024	04/47 Dar	12/48 1024	-05/66	08/66	
ADDAX					
61025	04/47 Dar	12/48 1025	-12/62	03/63	
PALLAH					
61026	04/47 Dar	01/49 1026	-02/66	05/66	
OUREBI					
61027	05/47 Dar	05/49 1027	-09/62	04/63	
MADOQUA					
61028	05/47 Dar	04/49 1028	-10/62	04/63	
UMSEKE					
61029	06/47 Dar	09/49 1029	-12/66	04/67	
CHAMOIS					
61030	06/47 Dar	12/49 1030	-09/67	01/68	
NYALA					
61031	07/47 Dar	12/49 1031	-11/64	04/65	
REEDBUCK					
61032	08/47 Dar	01/50 1032	-11/66	05/67	
STEMBOK					
61033	08/47 Dar	01/50 1033	-03/63	03/63	
DIBATAG					
61034	10/47 Dar	08/49 1034	-12/64	04/65	
CHIRU					
61035	10/47 Dar	05/49 1035	-12/66	05/67	
PRONGHORN					
61036	11/47 Dar	03/49 1036	-09/62	11/62	
RALPH ASSHETON					
61037	11/47 Dar	02/50 1037	-05/64	07/64	
JAIROU					
61038	12/47 Dar	11/50 1038	-05/64	09/64	
BLACKTAIL					
61039	12/47 Dar	12/49 1039	-06/65	11/65	
STEINBOK					
61040	04/46 NB	06/48 1040	-07/66	10/66	
ROEDEER					
61041	04/46 NB	04/48 1041	-04/64	04/65	
61042	05/46 NB	07/48 1042	-04/66	07/66	
61043	05/46 NB	04/48 1043	-07/62	08/62	
61044	05/46 NB	04/48 1044	-03/64	08/64	
61045	05/46 NB	09/48 1045	-09/62	11/62	
61046	05/46 NB	11/49 1046	-04/62	05/62	
61047	06/46 NB	11/48 1047	-09/62	04/63	
61048	06/46 NB	04/48 1048	-09/62	12/62	
61049	06/46 NB	03/48 1049	-11/65	03/66	
61050	06/46 NB	08/48 1050	-02/66	10/68	02/66➲30
61051	06/46 NB	03/50 1051	-02/66	05/66	02/66➲31
61052	06/46 NB	03/48 1052	-09/62	12/63	
61053	06/46 NB	07/48 1053	-01/63	04/63	
61054	07/46 NB	04/48 1054	-09/62	12/63	
61055	07/46 NB	06/49 1055	-02/66	05/66	
61056	07/46 NB	08/49 1056	-04/64	04/65	
61057	07/46 NB	04/48 1057	-04/50	04/50	
61058	07/46 NB	09/48 1058	-02/66	06/66	
61059	07/46 NB	06/48 1059	-11/63	07/66	11/63➲17
61060	08/46 NB	04/48 1060	-09/62	03/63	
61061	08/46 NB	05/49 1061	-09/65	12/65	
61062	08/46 NB	01/49 1062	-08/64	11/64	
61063	08/46 NB	03/48 1063	-04/62	10/62	
61064	08/46 NB	10/48 1064	-11/62	08/63	
61065	08/46 NB	03/48 1065	-09/64	11/64	
61066	08/46 NB	05/50 1066	-09/62	12/63	
61067	08/46 NB	11/48 1067	-12/62	02/63	
61068	08/46 NB	10/49 1068	-06/63	07/63	
61069	08/46 NB	05/48 1069	-08/63	09/63	
61070	08/46 NB	03/48 1070	-08/65	12/65	
61071	08/46 NB	04/48 1071	-02/63	02/63	
61072	09/46 NB	06/48 1072	-05/67	09/67	
61073	09/46 NB	03/49 1073	-09/63	03/64	
61074	09/46 NB	03/48 1074	-09/63	03/64	
61075	09/46 NB	05/48 1075	-09/63	04/64	
61076	09/46 NB	03/48 1076	-09/65	11/65	
61077	09/46 NB	05/48 1077	-05/62	07/62	
61078	09/46 NB	05/48 1078	-10/62	04/63	
61079	09/46 NB	04/48 1079	-06/62	07/62	
61080	09/46 NB	08/48 1080	-03/64	07/64	
61081	10/46 NB	03/48 1081	-07/64	09/64	
61082	10/46 NB	09/49 1082	-12/62	07/63	
61083	10/46 NB	07/48 1083	-09/63	04/64	
61084	10/46 NB	05/48 1084	-06/64	10/64	
61085	10/46 NB	08/48 1085	-12/61	12/61	
61086	10/46 NB	05/48 1086	-12/62	05/63	
61087	10/46 NB	11/48 1087	-12/65	06/66	
61088	10/46 NB	09/48 1088	-09/63	03/64	
61089	10/46 NB	03/48 1089	-04/66	07/66	
61090	10/46 NB	12/48 1090	-09/63	09/63	
61091	10/46 NB	01/49 1091	-09/62	11/62	
61092	10/46 NB	10/48 1092	-02/66	07/66	
61093	11/46 NB	03/49 1093	-07/65	11/65	
61094	11/46 NB	03/49 1094	-06/65	11/65	
61095	11/46 NB	03/49 1095	-12/63	03/64	
61096	11/46 NB	01/49 1096	-09/62	12/63	
61097	11/46 NB	03/49 1097	-01/65	05/65	
61098	11/46 NB	08/48 1098	-07/65	10/65	
61099	11/46 NB	04/49 1099	-09/66	12/66	
61100	11/46 NB	08/48 1100	-12/62	03/63	
61101	11/46 NB	06/48 1101	-12/66	04/67	
61102	12/46 NB	07/48 1102	-04/67	09/67	
61103	12/46 NB	08/48 1103	-07/66	11/66	
61104	12/46 NB	12/48 1104	-04/64	10/64	
61105	12/46 NB	07/49 1105	-12/64	08/66	12/64➲27
61106	12/46 NB	05/48 1106	-11/62	12/62	
61107	12/46 NB	10/48 1107	-08/65	02/66	
61108	12/46 NB	08/48 1108	-12/62	02/63	
61109	12/46 NB	10/48 1109	-07/64	10/64	
61110	12/46 NB	12/48 1110	-10/65	03/66	
61111	12/46 NB	06/48 1111	-09/62	05/63	
61112	12/46 NB	10/48 1112	-12/62	08/63	
61113	12/46 NB	05/48 1113	-09/63	10/63	
61114	01/47 NB	07/49 1114	-09/62	04/63	
61115	01/47 NB	10/48 1115	-05/67	09/67	
61116	01/47 NB	07/48 1116	-07/66	11/66	
61117	01/47 NB	06/48 1117	-02/64	03/64	
61118	01/47 NB	08/48 1118	-07/64	11/64	
61119	01/47 NB	12/48 1119	-11/63	01/64	
61120	01/47 NB	10/48 1120	-01/65	07/65	
61121	01/47 NB	11/48 1121	-04/66	08/66	
61122	01/47 NB	04/48 1122	-11/63	02/64	
61123	01/47 NB	11/48 1123	-05/67	12/67	
61124	02/47 NB	10/48 1124	-09/62	11/62	
61125	02/47 NB	11/48 1125	-12/63	01/64	
61126	02/47 NB	09/48 1126	-09/63	02/64	
61127	02/47 NB	09/48 1127	-08/65	12/65	
61128	02/47 NB	08/48 1128	-12/62	07/63	
61129	02/47 NB	03/49 1129	-09/65	12/65	
61130	02/47 NB	10/48 1130	-09/62	02/63	
61131	02/47 NB	09/48 1131	-12/66	04/67	
61132	02/47 NB	08/48 1132	-09/66	12/66	
61133	03/47 NB	04/48 1133	-09/66	12/66	
61134	03/47 NB	04/48 1134	-10/65	01/66	
61135	03/47 NB	01/49 1135	-09/63	11/63	
61136	03/47 NB	09/48 1136	-10/62	01/63	
61137	03/47 NB	12/48 1137	-05/62	09/62	
61138	03/47 NB	12/48 1138	-01/65	01/68	01/65➲26
61139	03/47 NB	02/49 1139	-09/62	04/63	
61140	04/47 VF	01/49 1140	-12/66	04/67	
61141	04/47 VF	11/48 1141	-07/65	12/65	
61142	04/47 VF	03/49 1142	-09/63	01/64	
61143	04/47 VF	01/49 1143	-01/64	04/64	
61144	04/47 VF	02/49 1144	-04/64	10/65	
61145	04/47 VF	12/48 1145	-01/66	04/66	
61146	04/47 VF	08/48 1146	-03/64	07/64	
61147	04/47 VF	11/48 1147	-12/65	03/66	
61148	04/47 VF	03/49 1148	-09/66	12/66	
61149	04/47 VF	11/48 1149	-09/62	12/63	
61150	04/47 VF	09/48 1150	-09/62	04/63	
61151	04/47 VF	10/48 1151	-09/62	04/63	
61152	05/47 VF	01/49 1152	-04/64	11/64	
61153	05/47 VF	12/48 1153	-01/65	07/65	
61154	05/47 VF	11/48 1154	-09/62	04/63	
61155	05/47 VF	12/48 1155	-03/64	01/65	
61156	05/47 VF	01/49 1156	-11/63	01/64	
61157	05/47 VF	10/48 1157	-08/65	12/65	
61158	05/47 VF	02/49 1158	-04/66	08/66	
61159	05/47 VF	09/48 1159	-09/63	02/64	
61160	05/47 VF	05/49 1160	-09/63	02/64	
61161	05/47 VF	02/49 1161	-12/66	03/67	
61162	05/47 VF	02/49 1162	-12/64	04/65	
61163	05/47 VF	05/48 1163	-09/62	04/63	
61164	05/47 VF	12/48 1164	-09/62	09/62	
61165	05/47 VF	08/49 1165	-11/64	05/65	
61166	05/47 VF	03/49 1166	-09/62	11/63	
61167	05/47 VF	05/49 1167	-12/64	04/65	
61168	06/47 VF	05/49 1168	-10/65	01/66	
61169	06/47 VF	05/48 1169	-12/63	03/64	
61170	06/47 VF	10/49 1170	-07/62	07/62	
61171	06/47 VF	03/49 1171	-09/62	12/63	
61172	06/47 VF	10/48 1172	-12/65	03/66	
61173	06/47 VF	05/49 1173	-01/67	04/67	
61174	06/47 VF	07/49 1174	-12/63	03/64	
61175	06/47 VF	01/49 1175	-12/63	02/64	
61176	06/47 VF	09/49 1176	-11/65	03/66	
61177	06/47 VF	06/49 1177	-09/63	03/64	
61178	06/47 VF	10/48 1178	-02/64	06/64	
61179	06/47 VF	03/49 1179	-01/65	06/65	
61180	06/47 VF	12/48 1180	-05/67	08/67	
61181	07/47 VF	03/49 1181	-11/63	02/66	11/63➲18
61182	07/47 VF	05/49 1182	-09/62	01/64	
61183	07/47 VF	03/49 1183	-07/62	07/62	
61184	07/47 VF	01/49 1184	-12/62	03/63	
61185	07/47 VF	03/49 1185	-10/64	01/65	
61186	07/47 VF	03/49 1186	-12/62	01/63	
61187	07/47 VF	03/49 1187	-09/62	09/62	
61188	07/47 VF	03/49 1188	-11/65	02/66	
61189	08/47 VF	12/49 1189	-05/67	12/67	
SIR WILLIAM GRAY					
61190	05/47 NB	03/49 1190	-06/65	09/65	
61191	05/47 NB	06/49 1191	-08/65	10/65	
61192	05/47 NB	04/48 1192	-10/62	03/63	
61193	05/47 NB	01/49 1193	-09/62	11/62	
61194	05/47 NB	02/49 1194	-08/65	10/66	08/65➲28
61195	05/47 NB	12/48 1195	-11/65	03/66	
61196	05/47 NB	08/49 1196	-09/65	12/65	
61197	05/47 NB	11/48 1197	-06/64	10/64	
61198	06/47 NB	10/48 1198	-04/65	06/65	
61199	06/47 NB	05/48 1199	-01/67	05/67	
61200	06/47 NB	07/49 1200	-12/62	11/64	
61201	06/47 NB	07/49 1201	-01/62	02/62	
61202	06/47 NB	03/49 1202	-09/62	03/63	
61203	06/47 NB	06/49 1203	-07/62	07/62	
61204	06/47 NB	08/48 1204	-11/63	07/66	11/63➲19
61205	06/47 NB	04/49 1205	-11/63	07/66	11/63➲20
61206	07/47 NB	11/49 1206	-09/62	09/62	
61207	07/47 NB	08/49 1207	-12/63	03/64	
61208	07/47 NB	11/49 1208	-09/65	12/65	
61209	07/47 NB	08/49 1209	-09/62	04/63	
61210	07/47 NB	09/49 1210	-02/66	06/66	
61211	07/47 NB	05/49 1211	-10/62	11/62	
61212	07/47 NB	06/49 1212	-11/64	04/65	
61213	07/47 NB	09/49 1213	-04/64	09/64	
61214	07/47 NB	04/50 1214	-05/65	08/65	

NER Raven 'B16/3' class 4-6-0 No 61449.

LNER Gresley 'B17' 'Sandringham' class 4-6-0 No 61613 *Woodbastwick Hall*.

GNR Gresley 'K2' class 2-6-0 No 61730 at New Holland Pier in June 1952.

GNR Gresley 'K3' class 2-6-0 No 61858 at Edinburgh St Margarets in June 1959, fitted with a GNR tender.

Number	Built	Renumbered	BR Dates	Scrap	Notes
61215	07/47 NB	04/49 1215	-03/65	05/65	
WILLIAM HENTON CARVER					
61216	07/47 NB	03/49 1216	-01/67	04/67	
61217	08/47 NB	10/48 1217	-03/62	07/62	
61218	08/47 NB	11/48 1218	-07/65	10/65	
61219	08/47 NB	10/48 1219	-06/64	09/64	
61220	08/47 NB	07/50 1220	-10/65	12/65	
61221	08/47 NB	07/49 1221	-03/65	05/65	
SIR ALEXANDER ERSKINE-HILL					
61222	08/47 NB	10/48 1222	-01/62	02/62	
61223	08/47 NB	12/49 1223	-01/66	06/66	
61224	08/47 NB	05/49 1224	-07/66	11/66	
61225	08/47 NB	09/49 1225	-06/65	11/65	
61226	08/47 NB	04/49 1226	-09/62	11/62	
61227	08/47 NB	02/50 1227	-09/63	03/64	
61228	08/47 NB	10/49 1228	-09/62	05/63	
61229	09/47 NB	12/49 1229	-06/64	09/64	
61230	09/47 NB	10/49 1230	-12/62	12/62	
61231	09/47 NB	01/50 1231	-07/62	08/62	
61232	09/47 NB	08/49 1232	-02/66	06/66	
61233	09/47 NB	02/49 1233	-11/63	07/66	11/63➲21
61234	09/47 NB	04/49 1234	-08/62	08/62	
61235	09/47 NB	05/49 1235	-09/62	06/64	
61236	09/47 NB	02/49 1236	-09/62	04/63	
61237	09/47 NB	02/49 1237	-12/66	03/67	
GEOFFREY H. KITSON					
61238	09/47 NB	07/48 1238	-02/67	06/67	
LESLIE RUNCIMAN					
61239	10/47 NB	12/48 1239	-08/62	01/63	
61240	10/47 NB	04/49 1240	-12/66	03/67	
HARRY HINCHLIFFE					
61241	10/47 NB	07/48 1241	-12/62	04/63	
VISCOUNT RIDLEY					
61242	10/47 NB	04/49 1242	-07/64	11/64	
ALEXANDER REITH GRAY					
61243	10/47 NB	03/49 1243	-05/64	08/64	
SIR HAROLD MITCHELL					
61244	10/47 NB	04/49 1244	-10/65	01/66	
STRANG STEEL					
61245	10/47 NB	05/48 1245	-07/65	10/65	
MURRAY OF ELIBANK					
61246	10/47 NB	11/49 1246	-12/62	03/63	
LORD BALFOUR OF BURLEIGH					
61247	10/47 NB	08/49 1247	-06/62	06/62	
LORD BURGHLEY					
61248	10/47 NB	06/50 1248	-11/65	04/66	
GEOFFREY GIBBS					
61249	10/47 NB	06/50 1249	-06/64	01/65	
FITZHERBERT WRIGHT					
61250	10/47 NB	06/50 1250	-04/66	08/66	
A. HAROLD BIBBY					
61251	11/47 NB	04/48 1251	-04/64	11/64	
OLIVER BURY					
61252	11/47 NB	06/49 1252	-11/63	07/66	11/63➲22
61253	11/47 NB	06/49 1253	-09/62	11/62	
61254	11/47 NB	05/49 1254	-09/62	01/64	
61255	11/47 NB	11/48 1255	-06/67	10/67	
61256	11/47 NB	03/49 1256	-11/65	02/66	
61257	11/47 NB	04/49 1257	-10/65	01/66	
61258	11/47 NB	02/49 1258	-01/64	04/64	
61259	11/47 NB	01/49 1259	-08/65	02/66	
61260	11/47 NB	06/49 1260	-12/62	08/63	
61261	11/47 NB	06/49 1261	-09/66	04/67	
61262	12/47 NB	06/49 1262	-04/67	04/68	
61263	12/47 NB	05/49 1263	-12/66	04/67	
61264 §	12/47 NB	10/49 1264	-12/65		12/65➲29
61265	12/47 NB	06/48 1265	-02/62	10/62	
61266	12/47 NB	05/48 1266	-09/62	06/63	
61267	12/47 NB	01/49 1267	-12/62	03/63	
61268	12/47 NB	05/50 1268	-12/64	05/65	
61269	12/47 NB	12/49 1269	-12/63	01/65	
61270	12/47 NB	09/49 1270	-09/63	11/63	
61271	12/47 NB	05/49 1271	-09/62	09/62	
61272	12/47 NB	07/49 1272	-01/65	04/66	01/65➲25
61273	12/47 NB	03/50 1273	-05/63	05/63	
61274	01/48 NB	03/50 1274	01/48-11/64	03/65	
61275	01/48 NB	05/50 1275	01/48-10/65	03/66	
61276	01/48 NB	05/50 1276	01/48-06/65	10/65	
61277	01/48 NB	05/49 1277	01/48-06/64	09/64	
61278	01/48 NB	09/49 1278	01/48-04/67	06/68	
61279	01/48 NB	10/49 1279	01/48-09/63	11/63	
61280	01/48 NB	01/50 1280	01/48-09/62	12/63	
61281	01/48 NB	12/49 1281	01/48-02/66	07/66	
61282	01/48 NB	04/49 1282	01/48-09/62	02/63	
61283	02/48 NB	11/48 1283	02/48-09/62	11/62	
61284	02/48 NB	02/50 1284	02/48-09/62	06/64	
61285	02/48 NB	03/49 1285	02/48-12/65	08/66	
61286	02/48 NB	09/49 1286	02/48-09/62	12/63	
61287	02/48 NB	06/49 1287	02/48-09/62	05/63	
61288	02/48 NB	06/50 1288	02/48-01/64	03/64	
61289	02/48 NB	11/49 1289	02/48-06/67	11/67	
61290	02/48 NB	08/49 1290	02/48-03/62	07/62	
61291	02/48 NB	06/50 1291	02/48-05/65	08/65	
61292	02/48 NB	06/48 1292	02/48-09/65	01/66	
61293	02/48 NB	12/49 1293	02/48-08/66	12/66	
61294	03/48 NB	11/49 1294	03/48-11/64	02/65	
61295	03/48 NB	06/50 1295	03/48-11/62	02/63	
61296	03/48 NB	07/50 1296	03/48-12/62	06/63	
61297	03/48 NB	03/50 1297	03/48-11/62	02/63	
61298	03/48 NB	10/48 1298	03/48-06/62	08/62	
61299	03/48 NB	12/49 1299	03/48-07/65	12/65	
61300	03/48 NB	06/49 1300	03/48-11/63	03/66	11/63➲23
61301	03/48 NB	12/49 1301	03/48-09/62	12/62	
61302	03/48 NB	08/49 1302	03/48-04/66	07/66	
61303	03/48 NB	08/50 1303	03/48-11/66	06/67	
61304	03/48 NB		03/48-10/65	03/66	
61305	04/48 NB		04/48-09/63	11/63	
61306 §	04/48 NB		04/48-09/67		
61307	04/48 NB		04/48-11/66	06/67	
61308	04/48 NB		04/48-11/66	02/67	
61309	04/48 NB		04/48-01/67	04/67	
61310	04/48 NB		04/48-04/65	06/65	
61311	04/48 NB		04/48-09/62	11/62	
61312	04/48 NB		04/48-03/64	01/65	
61313	04/48 NB		04/48-11/65	03/66	
61314	04/48 NB		04/48-12/63	02/64	
61315	04/48 NB		04/48-02/66	10/68	02/66➲32
61316	05/48 NB		05/48-12/62	08/63	
61317	05/48 NB		05/48-09/62	04/63	
61318	05/48 NB		05/48-09/63	03/64	
61319	05/48 NB		05/48-12/66	05/67	
61320	05/48 NB		05/48-08/65	02/66	
61321	05/48 NB		05/48-08/64	11/64	
61322	05/48 NB		05/48-02/66	06/66	
61323	05/48 NB		05/48-11/63	03/64	➲*24*
61324	06/48 NB		06/48-11/65	02/66	
61325	06/48 NB		06/48-09/63	02/64	
61326	06/48 NB		06/48-03/66	05/66	
61327	06/48 NB		06/48-02/65	04/65	
61328	06/48 NB		06/48-09/63	03/64	
61329	06/48 NB		06/48-04/66	08/66	
61330	06/48 NB		06/48-11/66	02/67	
61331	06/48 NB		06/48-09/63	03/64	
61332	06/48 NB		06/48-12/62	06/63	
61333	07/48 NB		07/48-12/62	09/63	
61334	07/48 NB		07/48-12/63	08/64	
61335	07/48 NB		07/48-09/62	11/62	
61336	08/48 NB		08/48-09/63	01/64	
61337	08/48 NB		08/48-09/67	12/67	
61338	08/48 NB		08/48-01/65	05/65	
61339	09/48 NB		09/48-11/62	09/63	
61340	11/48 Gor		11/48-04/67	09/67	
61341	12/48 Gor		12/48-12/63	03/64	
61342	01/49 Gor		01/49-12/66	04/67	
61343	02/49 Gor		02/49-03/66	07/66	
61344	03/49 Gor		03/49-09/66	06/67	
61345	04/49 Gor		04/49-07/66	11/66	
61346	04/49 Gor		04/49-06/64	10/64	
61347	05/49 Gor		05/49-04/67	09/67	
61348	06/49 Gor		06/49-12/65	06/66	
61349	07/49 Gor		07/49-08/66	11/66	
61350	07/49 Dar		07/49-11/66	04/67	
61351	08/49 Dar		08/49-07/64	11/64	
61352	08/49 Dar		08/49-11/62	09/63	
61353	09/49 Dar		09/49-08/65	02/66	
61354	09/49 Dar		09/49-04/67	09/67	
61355	09/49 Dar		09/49-06/64	10/64	
61356	09/49 Dar		09/49-07/64	10/64	
61357	10/49 Dar		10/49-06/65	10/65	
61358	10/49 Dar		10/49-12/63	02/64	
61359	10/49 Dar		10/49-12/63	02/64	
61360	03/50 NB		03/50-04/66	08/66	
61361	03/50 NB		03/50-12/65	03/66	
61362	03/50 NB		03/50-09/62	12/62	
61363	04/50 NB		04/50-09/62	01/64	
61364	04/50 NB		04/50-09/62	02/63	
61365	04/50 NB		04/50-07/65	10/65	
61366	04/50 NB		04/50-12/62	12/62	
61367	04/50 NB		04/50-08/65	12/65	
61368	06/50 NB		06/50-01/62	03/62	
61369	06/50 NB		06/50-12/63	02/65	
61370	10/50 NB		10/50-07/65	10/65	
61371	10/50 NB		10/50-09/62	05/63	
61372	12/50 NB		12/50-06/65	09/65	
61373	12/50 NB		12/50-09/62	01/64	
61374	02/51 NB		02/51-09/63	03/64	
61375	02/51 NB		03/51-11/63	08/66	11/63➲24
61376	04/51 NB		04/51-02/62	03/62	
61377	05/51 NB		05/51-09/62	02/63	
61378	05/51 NB		05/51-11/63	01/64	
61379	06/51 NB		06/51-08/62	08/62	
MAYFLOWER					
61380	08/51 NB		08/51-04/62	05/62	
61381	09/51 NB		09/51-10/62	03/63	
61382	09/51 NB		09/51-12/64	04/65	
61383	10/51 NB		10/51-01/63	04/63	
61384	10/51 NB		10/51-01/66	06/66	
61385	10/51 NB		10/51-10/65	02/66	
61386	10/51 NB		10/51-12/66	03/67	
61387	11/51 NB		11/51-10/65	03/66	
61388	11/51 NB		11/51-06/67	10/67	
61389	11/51 NB		11/51-11/65	03/66	
61390	12/51 NB		12/51-02/66	07/66	
61391	12/51 NB		12/51-09/62	09/62	
61392	12/51 NB		12/51-06/65	10/65	
61393	01/52 NB		01/52-09/63	09/63	
61394	01/52 NB		01/52-11/65	03/66	
61395	02/52 NB		02/52-10/62	11/62	
61396	02/52 NB		02/52-09/65	11/65	
61397	03/52 NB		03/52-06/65	09/65	
61398	04/52 NB		04/52-11/64	02/65	
61399	04/52 NB		04/52-09/63	04/64	
61400	03/50 Dar		03/50-12/64	03/65	
61401	04/50 Dar		04/50-04/64	07/64	
61402	04/50 Dar		04/50-06/64	09/64	
61403	04/50 Dar		04/50-07/66	09/66	
61404	05/50 Dar		05/50-11/65	02/66	
61405	05/50 Dar		05/50-09/62	04/63	
61406	05/50 Dar		05/50-04/66	08/66	
61407	06/50 Dar		06/50-04/67	09/67	
61408	06/50 Dar		06/50-12/62	07/63	
61409	05/50 Dar		06/50-09/63	01/64	

Class continued with 17 (Service Locomotives)

B8 61353-61358
4-6-0 GCR Robinson 'Glenalmond'

Power Classification:	5MT
Introduced:	1913-1915
Designer:	Robinson
Company:	GCR
Weight:	Loco 74t 7cwt Tender 48t 6cwt
Driving Wheel:	5' 7"
Boiler Pressure:	180psi superheated
Cylinders:	Inside 21½" x 26"
Tractive Effort:	27445lbf
Valve Gear:	Stephenson (slide valves)

Refer to the Historical Survey of Great Central 4-6-0 Engines at the end of this section for more details of this class.

The 'B8' class was a mixed express freight version of the 'B2' ('Sir Sam Fay', later 'B19') class with 5' 7" wheels. Known as the 'Glenalmond' class, eleven engines were built between 1913 and 1915, being scrapped between 1947 and 1949. None of the five which came into BR stock carried their allocated BR numbers.

Year End Totals: 'B8' class

'47	'48	'49	'50	'51	'52	'53	'54	'55	'56	'57	'58	'59	'60	'61	'62	'63	'64	'65	'66	'67
5	2																			

Number	*Built*	*Renumbered*	*BR Dates*	*Scrap*	*Notes*
61353	09/14 Gor	1353	-03/49	*49*	
61354	10/14 Gor	1354	-03/48	*48*	
61355	10/14 Gor	1355	-09/48	*09/48*	
61357	11/14 Gor	1357	-04/49	*49*	
EARL ROBERTS OF KANDAHAR					
61358	12/14 Gor	1358	-08/48	*09/48*	
EARL KITCHENER OF KHARTOUM					

B7 61360-61397, 61702-61713
4-6-0 GCR Robinson

Power Classification:	6MT
Introduced:	1921-1924
Designer:	Robinson
Company:	GCR
Weight:	Loco 79t 10cwt Tender 48t 6cwt
Driving Wheel:	5' 8"
Boiler Pressure:	180psi superheated
Cylinders:	Four 16" x 26"
Tractive Effort:	29950lbf
Valve Gear:	Stephenson (piston valves)

Refer to the Historical Survey of Great Central 4-6-0 Engines at the end of this section for more details of this class.

The 'B7' class was the most numerous of the GCR 2-6-0 engines comprising thirty-eight engines which all came into BR stock. They were four-cylinder mixed traffic engines which were developed from the 'B6' class.

Most of the engines did not carry their allocated numbers in the 61360 series. In 1949 the last survivors were allocated the numbers 61702-61713 to make way for new construction of 'B1' locomotives. The last engines were withdrawn in 1950.

1 The first twenty-eight engines were classified 'B7/1' and they were constructed by the GCR in 1921-1922.

2 The last ten engines were built by the LNER after grouping in 1923-1924. They were fitted with smaller chimneys and cabs and were classified 'B7/2'.

Year End Totals: 'B7' class

'47	'48	'49	'50	'51	'52	'53	'54	'55	'56	'57	'58	'59	'60	'61	'62	'63	'64	'65	'66	'67
38	18	4																		

Number	Built	Renumbered	BR Dates	Scrap	Notes
61360	05/21 Gor	1360	-09/48	10/48	1
61361	06/21 Gor	1361	-03/49	*49*	1
61362	07/21 Gor	1362	-04/49	*49*	1
61363	09/21 VF	1363	-06/48	*09/48*	1
61364	10/21 VF	1364	-06/48	*48*	1
61365	10/21 VF	1365	-06/49	*07/49*	1
					05/49➲61702
61366	10/21 VF	1366	-12/48	*49*	1
61367	10/21 VF	1367	-09/49	*49*	1
					05/49➲61703
61368	10/21 VF	1368	-10/48	*48*	1
61369	11/21 VF	1369	-08/48	*48*	1
61370	11/21 VF	1370	-11/48	*48*	1
61371	11/21 VF	1371	-01/49	*49*	1
61372	11/21 VF	1372	-09/48	*09/48*	1
61373	08/21 Gor	1373	-08/48	*48*	1
61374	10/21 Gor	1374	-09/48	*48*	1
61375	02/22 Gor	1375	-06/49	*06/49*	1
					04/49➲61704
61376	03/22 Gor	1376	-12/48	*49*	1
61377	04/22 Gor	1377	-02/50	*50*	1
					05/49➲61705
61378	05/22 Gor	1378	-08/48	10/48	1
61379	06/22 Gor	1379	-02/49	*03/49*	1
61380	06/22 Gor	1380	-08/48	*48*	1
61381	07/22 Gor	1381	-12/49	*50*	1
					04/49➲61706
61382	08/22 Gor	1382	-06/49	*07/49*	1
					04/49➲61707
61383	07/22 BP	1383	-05/48	*48*	1
61384	07/22 BP	1384	-08/48	*48*	1
61385	08/22 BP	1385	-01/49	*49*	1
61386	08/22 BP	1386	-06/49	*49*	1
					➲*61708*
61387	08/22 BP	1387	-01/50	*50*	1
					05/49➲61709
61388	08/23 Gor	1388	-02/50	04/50	2
					05/49➲61710
61389	08/23 Gor	1389	-02/49	*03/49*	2
61390	09/23 Gor	1390	-11/48	*48*	2
61391	10/23 Gor	01/49 1391	-07/50	*08/50*	2
					04/49➲61711
61392	11/23 Gor	1392	-06/49	*07/49*	2
					05/49➲61712
61393	11/23 Gor	1393	-08/48	*48*	2
61394	12/23 Gor	1394	-04/48	*48*	2
61395	12/23 Gor	1395	-11/48	*48*	2
61396	02/24 Gor	02/49 1396	-09/49	*49*	2
					05/49➲61713
61397	03/24 Gor	1397	-06/48	06/48	2

Class continued with 61702

B16 61410-61478, (61400-61409)
4-6-0 NER Raven

Power Classification:	1 6MT reclassified 5MT in 1953 23 6MT
Introduced:	1919-1924 2 Rebuilt 1937-1940 by Gresley 3 Rebuilt 1942-1949 by Thompson
Designer:	Raven
Company:	NER
Weight:	1 Loco 77t 14cwt 2 Loco 79t 4cwt 3 Loco 78t 19cwt Tender 46t 12cwt
Driving Wheel:	5' 8"
Boiler Pressure:	180psi superheated
Cylinders:	Three 18½" x 26"
Tractive Effort:	30030lbf
Valve Gear:	1 Stephenson (slide valves) 2 Walschaert with derived motion (piston valves) 3 Walschaert (piston valves)

Between 1919 and 1924 Vincent Raven put seventy three-cylinder mixed traffic locomotives into service on the NER. They were known as the NER 'S3' class, later becoming the LNER 'B16' class. They were developed from the 'B15' class of 1911 (none of which came into BR stock) which in turn were developed from the 'B13' class.

They were good engines in their day, equally at home on heavy fast freight trains and on Scarborough excursion traffic. Sixty-nine engines came into BR stock, one engine (No. 925) being destroyed in an air raid in June 1942.

61400-61409 were renumbered 61469-61478 in 1949 to make space for the construction of new 'B1' engines (by which time the 'B9' class was extinct).

1 The original engines were known as 'B16/1' and they were fitted with three sets of Stephenson valve gear.

2 In 1937-1940 seven engines were rebuilt to 'B16/2' by Gresley. They were fitted with outside Walschaert valve gear with derived motion for the inside cylinders, higher running plates and longer smokeboxes.

3 In 1942-1949 seventeen engines were rebuilt to 'B16/3' by Thompson. They were similar to the Gresley rebuilds, but they were fitted with three independent sets of Walschaert valve gear.

When the 'B16's were being rebuilt to 'B16/2' and 'B16/3' an extra set of frames was made. Often an engine could come out from the works with a different frame and a different boiler. Sometimes it was possible to see two engines with the same number at the same time, one going into works and one coming out.

Year End Totals: 'B16/1' class

'47	'48	'49	'50	'51	'52	'53	'54	'55	'56	'57	'58	'59	'60	'61	'62	'63	'64	'65	'66	'67
47	46	45	45	45	45	45	45	45	45	45	44	38	26							

Year End Totals: 'B16/2' class

'47	'48	'49	'50	'51	'52	'53	'54	'55	'56	'57	'58	'59	'60	'61	'62	'63	'64	'65	'66	'67
7	7	7	7	7	7	7	7	7	7	7	7	7	7	7	7	5				

Year End Totals: 'B16/3' class

'47	'48	'49	'50	'51	'52	'53	'54	'55	'56	'57	'58	'59	'60	'61	'62	'63	'64	'65	'66	'67
15	16	17	17	17	17	17	17	17	17	17	17	17	17	17	15	8				

Number	Built	Renumbered	BR Dates	Scrap	Notes
61400	12/19 Dar	02/49 1400	-11/60	11/60	1
					12/49➲61469
61401	12/19 Dar	12/48 1401	-11/59	01/60	1
					12/49➲61470
61402	12/19 Dar	10/48 1402	-09/60	09/60	1
					12/49➲61471
61403	12/19 Dar	1403	-05/64	11/64	3
					12/49➲61472
61404	12/19 Dar	10/48 1404	-09/61	09/61	1
					12/49➲61473
61405	04/20 Dar	05/49 1405	-02/58	02/58	1
					12/49➲61474
61406	03/20 Dar	09/48 1406	-04/63	05/63	2
					12/49➲61475
61407	03/20 Dar	07/49 1407	-09/63	12/63	3
					12/49➲61476
61408	04/20 Dar	1408	-02/60	02/60	1
					12/49➲61477
61409	04/20 Dar	1409	-12/60	12/60	1
					12/49➲61478
61410	06/20 Dar	05/48 1410	-10/60	10/60	1
61411	08/20 Dar	03/50 1411	-09/61	11/62	1
61412	08/20 Dar	06/50 1412	-09/61	11/63	1
61413	08/20 Dar	05/48 1413	-09/61	03/63	1
61414	09/20 Dar	10/48 1414	-09/61	11/61	1
61415	09/20 Dar	07/49 1415	-09/61	03/63	1
61416	09/20 Dar	07/50 1416	-05/61	05/61	1
61417	10/20 Dar	12/50 1417	-12/62	12/62	3
61418	11/20 Dar	08/48 1418	-06/64	10/64	3
61419	11/20 Dar	09/51 1419	-09/61	05/63	1
61420	12/20 Dar	04/48 1420	-09/63	02/64	3
61421	12/20 Dar	01/49 1421	-06/64	09/64	2
61422	12/20 Dar	03/49 1422	-09/61	12/61	1
61423	01/21 Dar	04/52 1423	-09/61	11/61	1
61424	02/21 Dar	09/49 1424	-10/60	10/60	1
61425	02/21 Dar	05/51 1425	-09/61	11/61	1
61426	03/21 Dar	02/51 1426	-09/59	10/59	1
61427	03/21 Dar	02/50 1427	-03/60	03/60	1
61428	03/21 Dar	11/48 1428	-10/60	11/60	1
61429	04/21 Dar	05/51 1429	-09/61	10/61	1
61430	04/21 Dar	09/48 1430	-10/59	10/59	1
61431	05/21 Dar	05/51 1431	-09/61	12/61	1
61432	06/21 Dar	12/48 1432	-07/61	10/61	1
61433	06/21 Dar	08/51 1433	-11/59	01/60	1
61434	11/22 Dar	05/48 1434	-06/64	09/64	1
					06/49⇨3
61435	11/22 Dar	01/49 1435	-07/64	11/64	2
61436	12/22 Dar	09/49 1436	-09/61	03/62	1
61437	01/23 Dar	01/49 1437	-06/64	10/64	2
61438	01/23 Dar	09/48 1438	-06/64	10/64	2
61439	02/23 Dar	01/49 1439	-08/62	11/62	3
61440	03/23 Dar	06/48 1440	-08/60	11/60	1
61441	03/23 Dar	12/48 1441	-10/59	11/59	1
61442	04/23 Dar	11/48 1442	-02/60	02/60	1
61443	04/23 Dar	10/48 1443	-09/61	01/63	1
61444	05/23 Dar	06/48 1444	-06/64	09/64	3
61445	05/23 Dar	09/49 1445	-07/61	08/61	1
61446	05/23 Dar	10/48 1446	-01/61	04/61	1
61447	06/23 Dar	09/48 1447	-09/61	11/61	1
61448	05/23 Dar	10/48 1448	-06/64	09/64	3
61449	07/23 Dar	04/48 1449	-07/63	09/63	3
61450	06/23 Dar	08/50 1450	-09/61	01/63	1
61451	07/23 Dar	01/49 1451	-09/61	04/63	1
61452	08/23 Dar	11/49 1452	-09/61	02/62	1
61453	08/23 Dar	10/48 1453	-06/63	07/63	3
61454	10/23 Dar	08/48 1454	-06/64	09/64	3
61455	10/23 Dar	07/48 1455	-09/63	10/63	2
61456	10/23 Dar	07/50 1456	-08/60	09/60	1
61457	10/23 Dar	06/48 1457	-06/64	09/64	2
61458	10/23 Dar	01/51 1458	-11/59	12/59	1
61459	11/23 Dar	10/48 1459	-09/61	02/62	1
61460	11/23 Dar	08/49 1460	-10/61	02/63	1
61461	11/23 Dar	08/48 1461	-09/63	12/63	1
					08/48⇨3
61462	11/23 Dar	08/49 1462	-05/61	06/61	1
61463	12/23 Dar	05/50 1463	-06/64	09/64	3
61464	12/23 Dar	02/49 1464	-09/63	12/63	3
61465	12/23 Dar	11/48 1465	-02/60	01/61	1
61466	12/23 Dar	04/50 1466	-07/61	11/61	1
61467	01/24 Dar	03/49 1467	-05/64	10/64	3
61468	01/24 Dar	08/48 1468	-09/63	02/64	3
61469	12/19 Dar	12/49 61400	-11/60	11/60	1
61470	12/19 Dar	12/49 61401	-11/59	01/60	1
61471	12/19 Dar	12/49 61402	-09/60	09/60	1
61472	12/19 Dar	12/49 *61403*	-05/64	11/64	3
61473	12/19 Dar	12/49 61404	-09/61	09/61	1
61474	04/20 Dar	12/49 61405	-02/58	02/58	1
61475	03/20 Dar	12/49 61406	-04/63	05/63	2
61476	03/20 Dar	12/49 61407	-09/63	12/63	3
61477	04/20 Dar	12/49 *61408*	-02/60	02/60	1
61478	04/20 Dar	12/49 *61409*	-12/60	12/60	1

B9 61469-61476
4-6-0 GCR Robinson

Power Classification:	5MT
Introduced:	1906
Designer:	Robinson
Company:	GCR
Weight:	Loco 65t 0cwt Tender 48t 6cwt
Driving Wheel:	5' 4"
Boiler Pressure:	180psi superheated
Cylinders:	Outside 19" x 26"
Tractive Effort:	22440lbf
Valve Gear:	Stephenson (piston valves)

Refer to the Historical Survey of Great Central 4-6-0 Engines at the end of this section for more details of this class.

Ten 'B9' class engines were built in 1906 for express freight duties and they were later superheated. They were all withdrawn in 1947-1949. Four came into BR stock and only two received their BR numbers.

Year End Totals: 'B9' class

'47	'48	'49	'50	'51	'52	'53	'54	'55	'56	'57	'58	'59	'60	'61	'62	'63	'64	'65	'66	'67
4	2																			

Number	Built	Renumbered	BR Dates	Scrap	Notes
61469	09/06 BP	02/49 1469	-04/49	*49*	
61470	09/06 BP	1470	-11/48	*48*	
61475	10/06 BP	02/49 1475	-05/49	*49*	
61476	10/06 BP	1476	-08/48	*48*	

B4 61482-61488
4-6-0 GCR Robinson 'Immingham'

Power Classification:	4P
Introduced:	1906
Designer:	Robinson
Company:	GCR
Weight:	3 Loco 71t 15cwt 4 Loco 70t 14cwt Tender 48t 6cwt
Driving Wheel:	6' 7"
Boiler Pressure:	180psi superheated
Cylinders:	3 Outside 21" x 26" 4 Outside 19" x 26"
Tractive Effort:	3 22205lbf 4 18180lbf

Valve Gear: 3 Stephenson (piston valves)
4 Stephenson (slide valves)

Refer to the Historical Survey of Great Central 4-6-0 Engines at the end of this section for more details of this class.

The 'B4' class comprised ten engines which were designed for working fast fish trains to London and the first engine was named IMMINGHAM, giving the class their name. They were built in 1906 by Beyer Peacock, and were often to be seen working passenger trains. They were all scrapped between 1944 and 1950, four engines coming into BR stock, but none receiving their allocated numbers.

The class was divided into four parts as follows:

1 'B4/1'. Engines rebuilt from 1925 with superheaters, piston valves and larger cylinders. Later all converted to 'B4/3'.

2 'B4/2'. Original engines with slide valves. Later superheated and all converted to 'B4/4'.

3 'B4/3'. 'B4/1' engines with cab and chimney reduced to LNER loading gauge.

4 'B4/4'. 'B4/2' engines with cab and chimney reduced to LNER loading gauge.

Year End Totals: 'B4' class

'47	'48	'49	'50	'51	'52	'53	'54	'55	'56	'57	'58	'59	'60	'61	'62	'63	'64	'65	'66	'67
4	3	1																		

Number	*Built*	*Renumbered*	*BR Dates*	*Scrap*	*Notes*
61482	06/06 BP	1482	-11/50	02/51	4
IMMINGHAM					
61483	06/06 BP	1483	-09/49	*49*	3
61485	06/06 BP	1485	-06/49	*49*	3
61488	07/06 BP	1488	-10/48	*48*	3

B3 61497
4-6-0 GCR Robinson 'Lord Faringdon'

Power Classification: 4P
Introduced: 1917-1920 (this engine 1920)
3 Rebuilt 1943 by Thompson
Designer: Robinson
Company: GCR
Weight: Loco 71t 7cwt
Tender 48t 6cwt
Driving Wheel: 6' 9"
Boiler Pressure: 225psi superheated
Cylinders: Outside 20" x 26"
Tractive Effort: 24555lbf
Valve Gear: Walschaert (piston valves)

Refer to the Historical Survey of Great Central 4-6-0 Engines at the end of this section for more details of this class.

The 'B3's were Robinson's largest 4-6-0 class. Six engines were built at Gorton in 1917-1920 and they were known as the 'Lord Faringdon' class. They were four-cylinder express engines.

There was a number of different parts to this class and the only engine to come into BR stock had been completely rebuilt as a two-cylinder engine with a high running plate in 1943, much resembling a Thompson 'B1'. Before rebuilding it had been named EARL HAIG. It was withdrawn in 1949, the other engines being withdrawn in 1946-1947.

1 'B3/1'. Original four-cylinder engines with Belpaire boilers.

2 'B3/2'. Four engines which were rebuilt in 1928 with Caprotti valve gear.

3 'B3/3'. 1497 was rebuilt in 1942 from a 'B3/2' engine, with a '100A' ('B1' type) boiler, Walschaert valve gear and a high running plate.

Year End Totals: 'B3' class

'47	'48	'49	'50	'51	'52	'53	'54	'55	'56	'57	'58	'59	'60	'61	'62	'63	'64	'65	'66	'67
1	1																			

Number	*Built*	*Renumbered*	*BR Dates*	*Scrap*	*Notes*
61497	08/20 Gor	04/48 1497	-04/49	*49*	3

B12 61500-61580
4-6-0 GER Holden

Power Classification: 4P
Introduced: 1911-1928
3 Rebuilt 1932-1944 by Gresley
Designer: S D Holden
Company: GER
Weight: Loco 63t 0cwt
3 Loco 69t 10cwt
Tender 39t 6cwt
Driving Wheel: 6' 6"
Boiler Pressure: 180psi superheated
Cylinders: Inside 20" x 28"
Tractive Effort: 21970lbf
Valve Gear: Stephenson (piston valves)

Holden built his 'S69' (LNER 'B12') class of 4-6-0 engines in 1911-1921. They were the successors to the 'D15' and 'D16' 'Claud Hamilton' 4-4-0s. Originally designed to handle the heavily loaded continental trains from Harwich (Parkeston Quay) to Liverpool Street, they performed very well on that difficult route. Seventy-one were built and a further ten were added in 1928.

The first seventy-one engines were originally numbered 1500-1570 on the GER and 1506 had a very short life, being damaged beyond repair in an accident in 1913. Renumbered 8500-5,7-70 by the LNER they coincidentally resumed their original numbers (1500 upwards) in the LNER re-numbering scheme of 1946.

1 'B12/1' comprised the original design fitted with a small Belpaire boiler. As originally built they had elaborate framing over the wheels but this was later removed.

2 In 1926 one engine was rebuilt with Lenz oscillating cam poppet valves. The last ten engines were built new with these and with the running plates raised over the wheels. They were classified 'B12/2' and were all rebuilt as 'B12/3' before 1948.

3 Between 1932 and 1944 Gresley rebuilt many engines with larger round topped boilers (5' 6" diameter compared with the original 5' 1" diameter boilers). They were reclassified 'B12/3'.

4 Many of the unrebuilt engines were sent to work on the old Great North of Scotland Railway during and after the Second World War. Most of these engines were rebuilt with smaller round topped boilers (the same diameter as the original boilers) and they were reclassified 'B12/4'.

Year End Totals: 'B12/1' class

'47	'48	'49	'50	'51	'52	'53	'54	'55	'56	'57	'58	'59	'60	'61	'62	'63	'64	'65	'66	'67
13	13	12	11	10	7	2														

Year End Totals: 'B12/3' class

'47	'48	'49	'50	'51	'52	'53	'54	'55	'56	'57	'58	'59	'60	'61	'62	'63	'64	'65	'66	'67
50	48	47	47	44	44	44	44	42	42	25	16	1	1							

Year End Totals: 'B12/4' class

'47	'48	'49	'50	'51	'52	'53	'54	'55	'56	'57	'58	'59	'60	'61	'62	'63	'64	'65	'66	'67
9	8	8	7	6	4															

Number	*Built*	*Renumbered*	*BR Dates*	*Scrap*	*Notes*
61500	12/11 Str	1500	-06/48	*48*	4
61501	02/12 Str	06/48 1501	-05/53	02/54	1
61502	02/12 Str	06/48 1502	-04/54	07/54	1
61503	03/12 Str	04/48 1503	-06/51	*51*	1
61504	05/12 Str	05/48 1504	-06/50	08/50	4
61505	02/13 Str	03/49 1505	-03/52	*52*	4
61507	03/13 Str	01/49 1507	-03/53	06/53	4
61508	03/13 Str	10/48 1508	-05/53	06/53	4
61509	04/13 Str	1509	-10/48	*48*	3
61510	04/13 Str	1510	-06/49	*49*	3
61511	05/13 Str	05/48 1511	-04/52	*52*	4
61512	06/13 Str	11/48 1512	-01/57	02/57	3
61513	06/13 Str	03/48 1513	-02/53	*06/53*	1
61514	06/13 Str	07/48 1514	-10/59	11/59	3
61515	11/13 Str	03/49 1515	-11/51	*51*	3
61516	11/13 Str	03/49 1516	-07/58	08/58	3
61517	11/13 Str	1517	-10/48	*48*	3
61519	12/13 Str	05/49 1519	-12/57	04/58	3
61520	04/14 Str	09/48 1520	-06/57	09/57	3
61521	04/14 Str	10/48 1521	-07/52	*52*	1
61523	05/14 Str	04/48 1523	-03/55	*55*	3
61524	05/14 Str	07/48 1524	-11/53	*12/53*	4
61525	06/14 Str	06/49 1525	-08/51	*51*	3
61526	06/14 Str	02/49 1526	-09/51	*51*	4
61528	08/14 Str	11/48 1528	-07/53	*09/53*	1
61529	09/14 Str	04/48 1529	-02/50	*50*	1
61530	11/14 Str	05/49 1530	-11/59	11/59	3
61532	12/14 Str	05/49 1532	-07/53	11/53	4
61533	12/14 Str	04/48 1533	-11/59	11/59	3
61535	03/15 Str	12/48 1535	-12/59	01/60	3
61536	05/15 Str	07/48 1536	-12/49	*50*	1
61537	07/15 Str	06/48 1537	-04/57	05/57	3
61538	07/15 Str	08/49 1538	-01/57	01/57	3
61539	06/17 Str	09/48 1539	-11/54	*11/54*	1
61540	07/17 Str	08/48 1540	-10/57	11/57	3
61541	06/20 BM	02/49 1541	-01/57	02/57	3
61542	07/20 BM	08/49 1542	-07/58	08/58	3
61543	07/20 BM	11/48 1543	-06/53	12/53	1
61545	08/20 BM	09/50 1545	-01/57	01/57	3
61546	09/20 BM	03/49 1546	-05/59	07/59	3
61547	09/20 BM	09/48 1547	-10/58	12/58	3
61549	09/20 BM	12/48 1549	-01/59	02/59	3
61550	10/20 BM	07/48 1550	-01/57	01/57	3
61552	12/20 BM	10/48 1552	-07/52	*52*	1
61553	12/20 BM	11/49 1553	-08/58	09/58	3
61554	01/21 BM	01/49 1554	-09/58	11/58	3
61555	01/21 BM	09/49 1555	-09/57	11/57	3
61556	02/21 BM	11/48 1556	-12/57	02/58	3
61557	02/21 BM	01/50 1557	-01/57	02/57	3
61558	02/21 BM	06/48 1558	-04/59	05/59	3
61559	02/21 BM	08/48 1559	-09/51	*51*	3
61560	04/21 BM	10/48 1560	-04/52	*52*	1
61561	03/20 Str	01/49 1561	-09/58	12/58	3
61562	04/20 Str	08/48 1562	-08/55	*09/55*	3
61563	04/20 Str	04/48 1563	-04/53	*06/53*	1
61564	04/20 Str	01/49 1564	-11/58	12/58	3
61565	05/20 Str	03/49 1565	-01/57	02/57	3
61566	05/20 Str	04/48 1566	-01/59	04/59	3
61567	05/20 Str	02/50 1567	-10/58	01/59	3
61568	06/20 Str	10/48 1568	-08/59	09/59	3
61569	06/20 Str	05/49 1569	-01/57	01/57	3
61570	06/20 Str	04/48 1570	-04/58	04/58	3
61571	08/28 BP	10/48 1571	-12/59	01/60	3
61572 §	08/28 BP	04/48 1572	-09/61		3
61573	08/28 BP	04/48 1573	-01/59	04/59	3
61574	08/28 BP	03/48 1574	-01/57	02/57	3
61575	09/28 BP	04/48 1575	-04/59	04/59	3
61576	08/28 BP	12/48 1576	-01/59	04/59	3
61577	09/28 BP	03/49 1577	-09/59	11/59	3
61578	09/28 BP	05/48 1578	-01/57	02/57	3
61579	09/28 BP	10/49 1579	-01/57	02/57	3
61580	10/28 BP	05/48 1580	-03/59	04/59	3

B17 61600-61672
4-6-0 LNER Gresley 'Sandringham'

B2 Between 61603 & 61671
4-6-0 LNER 'Rebuilt Sandringham'

Power Classification: 4P reclassified 5P in 1953
Introduced: 1928-1937
B2 Rebuilt 1945-1949 by Thompson
Designer: Gresley
Company: LNER
Weight: Loco 77t 5cwt
5 Loco 80t 10cwt
B2 Loco 73t 10c
Tender 39t 6cwt
46p Tender 52t 0cwt
5 Tender 52t 13cwt
n Tender 46t 12cwt
Driving Wheel: 6' 8"
Boiler Pressure: 180psi superheated
6,B2 225psi superheated
Cylinders: Three 17½" x 26"
B2 Outside 20" x 26"
Tractive Effort: 22845lbf
6 28555lbf
B2 24865lbf
Valve Gear: Walschaert with derived motion (piston valves)
B2 Walschaert (piston valves)

Between 1928 and 1937 Gresley built the seventy-three members of the three-cylinder 4-6-0 'Sandringham' class. They were designed to meet the need for a more powerful engine to replace the 'B12's on the GER main line. Later engines were built for use on other lines, in particular the GCR. They were built by North British, R Stephenson and Darlington Works.

The first batch of forty-eight engines were named after country houses, the class name SANDRINGHAM coming from the name of the first member of the class (actually the third engine to be delivered). The following twenty-five engines were named after football clubs and were nicknamed 'Footballers', although some name changes were later made.

61605 was originally named BURNHAM THORPE, 61639 was THORESBY PARK, 61658 was NEW-

CASTLE UNITED, 61659 was NORWICH CITY, 61670 was MANCHESTER CITY for sixteen days and then became TOTTENHAM HOTSPUR and 61671 was MANCHESTER CITY. 61671 was renamed ROYAL SOVEREIGN in 1946, in order to work Royal trains to and from Wolferton station for Sandringham. On its withdrawal in 1958, 61632 took over these duties and received the ROYAL SOVEREIGN nameplates.

1 The classification 'B17/1' originally covered the first forty-eight engines which were fitted with GER type tenders.

2 & 3 'B17/2' and 'B17/3' were variants of 'B17/1', but they were included in 'B17/1' before 1948.

4 The last twenty-five engines were fitted with larger LNER 4200 gallon tenders when they were introduced in 1936 and were classified 'B17/4'.

5 In 1937 two members of the class (61659 and 61670) were rebuilt with streamlining similar to the 'A4' pacifics for working the 'East Anglian' train between London and Norwich. They were given the names EAST ANGLIAN and CITY OF LONDON and were reclassified 'B17/5'. 61659 was fitted with a '100A' ('B1' type) boiler in 1949, technically making it a 'B17/6' engine, but still retaining its streamlining. Both engines had their streamlining removed in 1951, when 61670 was also converted to 'B17/6'.

6 From 1943 onwards, most of the class were rebuilt with '100A' ('B1' type) boilers, and they were reclassified 'B17/6'.

B2 From 1945 onwards Thompson rebuilt ten engines with two cylinders and '100A' ('B1' type) boilers. The footplates were also slightly modified. They were all fitted with NER tenders (n) except 61615 and 61632 which had LNER tenders from withdrawn 'P1' 2-8-2s (p) and 61671 which retained its original tender (as 'B17/4').

Year End Totals: 'B17/1, B17/4' class

'47	'48	'49	'50	'51	'52	'53	'54	'55	'56	'57	'58	'59	'60	'61	'62	'63	'64	'65	'66	'67
60	53	43	34	28	26	21	18	12	11	7	3	1								

Year End Totals: 'B17/5' class

'47	'48	'49	'50	'51	'52	'53	'54	'55	'56	'57	'58	'59	'60	'61	'62	'63	'64	'65	'66	'67
2	2	1	1																	

Year End Totals: 'B17/6' class

'47	'48	'49	'50	'51	'52	'53	'54	'55	'56	'57	'58	'59	'60	'61	'62	'63	'64	'65	'66	'67
2	9	19	28	35	36	39	42	48	49	53	38	16								

Year End Totals: 'B2' class

'47	'48	'49	'50	'51	'52	'53	'54	'55	'56	'57	'58	'59	'60	'61	'62	'63	'64	'65	'66	'67
9	9	10	10	10	10	10	10	10	10	10	7									

Number	Name	Built	Renumbered	BR Dates	Scrap	Notes
61600	SANDRINGHAM	12/28 NB	05/48 1600	-07/58	10/58	1 06/50⇨6
61601	HOLKHAM	12/28 NB	01/49 1601	-01/58	03/58	1
61602	WALSINGHAM	11/28 NB	06/49 1602	-01/58	03/58	1 08/51⇨6
61603	FRAMLINGHAM	11/28 NB	01/49 1603	-09/58	09/58	B2
61604	ELVEDEN	12/28 NB	07/48 1604	-08/53	09/53	1 11/51⇨6
61605	LINCOLNSHIRE REGIMENT	12/28 NB	03/49 1605	-05/58	07/58	1 01/48⇨6
61606	AUDLEY END	12/28 NB	03/50 1606	-09/58	01/59	1 03/50⇨6
61607	BLICKLING	12/28 NB	07/49 1607	-12/59	01/60	B2
61608	GUNTON	12/28 NB	04/48 1608	-03/60	04/60	1 10/50⇨6
61609	QUIDENHAM	12/28 NB	03/49 1609	-06/58	08/58	1 01/52⇨6
61610	HONINGHAM HALL	08/30 Dar	05/50 1610	-01/60	02/60	1 10/53⇨6
61611	RAYNHAM HALL	08/30 Dar	04/49 1611	-10/59	02/60	1 02/56⇨6
61612	HOUGHTON HALL	10/30 Dar	02/49 1612	-09/59	12/59	1 03/50⇨6
61613	WOODBASTWICK HALL	10/30 Dar	08/49 1613	-12/59	01/60	1 12/51⇨6
61614	CASTLE HEDINGHAM	10/30 Dar	12/48 1614	-06/59	11/59	B2
61615	CULFORD HALL	10/30 Dar	05/48 1615	-02/59	02/59	B2
61616	FALLODON	10/30 Dar	04/48 1616	-09/59	11/59	B2
61617	FORD CASTLE	11/30 Dar	06/48 1617	-08/58	09/58	B2
61618	WYNYARD PARK	11/30 Dar	03/49 1618	-01/60	02/60	1 04/58⇨6
61619	WELBECK ABBEY	11/30 Dar	08/48 1619	-09/58	11/58	1 01/53⇨6
61620	CLUMBER	11/30 Dar	11/48 1620	-01/60	02/60	1 12/51⇨6
61621	HATFIELD HOUSE	11/30 Dar	06/48 1621	-10/58	12/58	1 01/55⇨6
61622	ALNWICK CASTLE	01/31 Dar	05/48 1622	-09/58	01/59	6
61623	LAMBTON CASTLE	02/31 Dar	04/48 1623	-07/59	09/59	1 04/48⇨6
61624	LUMLEY CASTLE	02/31 Dar	11/48 1624	-03/53	04/53	1
61625	RABY CASTLE	02/31 Dar	02/49 1625	-12/59	01/60	1
61626	BRANCEPETH CASTLE	03/31 Dar	10/49 1626	-01/60	02/60	1 04/55⇨6
61627	ASKE HALL	03/31 Dar	11/48 1627	-07/59	08/59	1 11/48⇨6
61628	HAREWOOD HOUSE	03/31 Dar	01/49 1628	-09/52	*10/52*	1 01/49⇨6
61629	NAWORTH CASTLE	04/31 Dar	02/49 1629	-09/59	10/59	1
61630	TOTTENHAM HOTSPUR	04/31 Dar	01/49 1630	-09/58	10/58	1 01/49⇨6
61631	SERLBY HALL	05/31 Dar	10/48 1631	-04/59	05/59	1 10/57⇨6
61632	BELVOIR CASTLE 10/58➔ROYAL SOVEREIGN	05/31 Dar	06/48 1632	-02/59	03/59	B2
61633	KIMBOLTON CASTLE	05/31 Dar	08/48 1633	-09/59	10/59	1 08/48⇨6
61634	HINCHINGBROOKE	06/31 Dar	09/48 1634	-08/58	09/58	1 01/57⇨6
61635	MILTON	07/31 Dar	02/49 1635	-01/59	05/59	1 02/49⇨6
61636	HARLAXTON MANOR	07/31 Dar	05/50 1636	-10/59	02/60	1 05/50⇨6
61637	THORPE HALL	03/33 Dar	09/48 1637	-09/59	10/59	1 11/57⇨6
61638	MELTON HALL	03/33 Dar	09/49 1638	-03/58	05/58	1 01/49⇨6
61639	NORWICH CITY	05/33 Dar	05/50 1639	-05/59	07/59	B2
61640	SOMERLEYTON HALL	05/33 Dar	02/49 1640	-10/58	12/58	1 05/55⇨6
61641	GAYTON HALL	05/33 Dar	02/49 1641	-01/60	02/60	1 02/49⇨6
61642	KILVERSTONE HALL	05/33 Dar	02/49 1642	-09/58	11/58	1 01/49⇨6
61643	CHAMPION LODGE	03/35 Dar	08/48 1643	-07/58	10/58	1 10/54⇨6
61644	EARLHAM HALL	05/35 Dar	03/49 1644	-07/59	01/60	1 03/49⇨B2
61645	THE SUFFOLK REGIMENT	06/35 Dar	03/49 1645	-02/59	04/59	1 12/52⇨6
61646	GILWELL PARK	08/35 Dar	12/48 1646	-01/59	02/59	1 02/51⇨6
61647	HELMINGHAM HALL	09/35 Dar	03/49 1647	-11/59	03/60	4 02/58⇨6
61648	ARSENAL	03/36 Dar	03/49 1648	-12/58	05/59	4 10/57⇨6
61649	SHEFFIELD UNITED	03/36 Dar	06/48 1649	-02/59	03/59	4 03/54⇨6
61650	GRIMSBY TOWN	03/36 Dar	10/48 1650	-09/58	10/58	4 02/55⇨6
61651	DERBY COUNTY	03/36 Dar	01/49 1651	-08/59	09/59	4 06/53⇨6
61652	DARLINGTON	04/36 Dar	04/49 1652	-09/59	12/59	4 03/48⇨6
61653	HUDDERSFIELD TOWN	04/36 Dar	06/48 1653	-01/60	02/60	4 03/54⇨6
61654	SUNDERLAND	04/36 Dar	04/48 1654	-11/59	01/60	4 04/48⇨6
61655	MIDDLESBROUGH	04/36 Dar	10/48 1655	-04/59	05/59	4 07/50⇨6
61656	LEEDS UNITED	05/36 Dar	08/50 1656	-01/60	02/60	4 11/53⇨6
61657	DONCASTER ROVERS	05/36 Dar	07/48 1657	-06/60	06/60	4 10/50⇨6
61658	THE ESSEX REGIMENT	05/36 Dar	06/48 1658	-12/59	02/60	1 09/50⇨6
61659	EAST ANGLIAN	06/36 Dar	04/48 1659	-03/60	03/60	5 07/49, 04/51⇨6
61660	HULL CITY	06/36 Dar	02/49 1660	-06/60	06/60	4
61661	SHEFFIELD WEDNESDAY	06/36 Dar	04/48 1661	-07/59	11/59	4 08/55⇨6
61662	MANCHESTER UNITED	01/37 RS	09/49 1662	-12/59	02/60	4 03/55⇨6
61663	EVERTON	02/37 RS	11/49 1663	-02/60	03/60	4 12/51⇨6
61664	LIVERPOOL	01/37 RS	03/50 1664	-06/60	06/60	4 02/48⇨6
61665	LEICESTER CITY	01/37 RS	07/48 1665	-04/59	06/59	4 08/49⇨6
61666	NOTTINGHAM FOREST	02/37 RS	05/48 1666	-03/60	04/60	6
61667	BRADFORD	04/37 RS	09/49 1667	-06/58	07/58	4
61668	BRADFORD CITY	04/37 RS	06/49 1668	-08/60	09/60	4 06/49⇨6
61669	BARNSLEY	05/37 RS	09/49 1669	-09/58	11/58	4 09/49⇨6
61670	CITY OF LONDON	05/37 RS	08/48 1670	-04/60	04/60	5 04/51⇨6
61671	ROYAL SOVEREIGN	06/37 RS	09/48 1671	-09/58	10/58	B2
61672	WEST HAM UNITED	07/37 RS	02/49 1672	-03/60	03/60	4 09/50⇨6

B5 61680-61690
4-6-0 GCR Robinson 'Fish'

Power Classification:	3MT
Introduced:	1902-1904
Designer:	Robinson
Company:	GCR
Weight:	Loco 64t 3cwt p Loco 65t 4cwt Tender 48t 6cwt
Driving Wheel:	6' 1"
Boiler Pressure:	180psi superheated
Cylinders:	Outside 19" x 26" p Outside 21" x 26"
Tractive Effort:	19670lbf p 24030lbf
Valve Gear:	Stephenson (slide valves) p Stephenson (piston valves)

Refer to the Historical Survey of Great Central 4-6-0 Engines at the end of this section for more details of this class.

The 'B5's were the first of Robinson's 4-6-0s to appear, fourteen engines being built in 1902-1904 by Neilson and Beyer Peacock.

They were designed for working fast fish trains from Grimsby to London and they were nicknamed 'Fish engines'. In later years they were often used on passenger trains. The first of the class was withdrawn in 1939, seven came into BR stock and they were all scrapped by 1950.

p Some engines were rebuilt with piston valves and larger cylinders.

Year End Totals: 'B5' class

'47	'48	'49	'50	'51	'52	'53	'54	'55	'56	'57	'58	'59	'60	'61	'62	'63	'64	'65	'66	'67
7	3	1																		

Number	Built	Renumbered	BR Dates	Scrap	Notes
61680	12/02 NR	1680	-11/48	*48*	
61681	12/02 NR	1681	-06/48	*06/48*	
61685	01/04 BP	1685	-03/48	*48*	
61686	02/04 BP	1686	-07/50	*08/50*	p
61688	02/04 BP	1688	-11/49	*49*	p
61689	02/04 BP	1689	-10/49	*49*	
61690	03/04 BP	1690	-04/48	*48*	p

B13 61699
4-6-0 NER (Counter Pressure Test Locomotive)

Power Classification:	Not classified
Introduced:	1899-1909 (this engine built 1906)
Designer:	W Worsdell
Company:	NER
Weight:	Loco 62t 10cwt Tender 46t 12cwt
Driving Wheel:	6' 1¼"
Boiler Pressure:	160psi superheated
Cylinders:	Outside 20" x 26"
Tractive Effort:	19310lbf
Valve Gear:	Stephenson (piston valves)

This engine was the sole survivor of the NER 'S' class of forty engines which were built at Gateshead Works between 1899 and 1909. They were built for working main line passenger trains between Newcastle and Edinburgh.

The other engines of the class were withdrawn between 1928 and 1938, but 61699 was transferred to departmental stock in 1934 and it was used as a counter-pressure locomotive for testing purposes at Darlington and later at Rugby. It was scrapped in 1951 as 1699.

Year End Totals: 'B13' (service) class

'47	'48	'49	'50	'51	'52	'53	'54	'55	'56	'57	'58	'59	'60	'61	'62	'63	'64	'65	'66	'67
1	1	1	1																	

Number	Built	Renumbered	BR Dates	Scrap	Notes
61699	06/06 Ghd	1699	-05/51	05/51	

V4 61700-61701
2-6-2 LNER Gresley

Power Classification: 5MT reclassified 4MT in 1953
Introduced: 1941
Designer: Gresley
Company: LNER
Weight: Loco 70t 8cwt
Tender 42t 15cwt
Driving Wheel: 5' 8"
Boiler Pressure: 250psi superheated
Cylinders: Three 15" x 26"
Tractive Effort: 27420lbf
Valve Gear: Walschaert (piston valves)

The 'V4' class was Gresley's last new design, introduced in 1941. They were lightweight mixed traffic engines and they were intended as the prototypes of a new powerful general-purpose machine with wide route availability. However after Gresley's death in 1941 no more engines were built, and they were superseded by Thompson's 'B1' class in 1942.

After initial trials, which included one engine being tried on the Great Eastern section, both engines spent all of their lives in Scotland, mostly working on the West Highland line. 61700 was named BANTAM COCK, and although 61701 was never named it was (perhaps inevitably) always known as *'Bantam Hen'*.

Year End Totals: 'V4' class

'47	'48	'49	'50	'51	'52	'53	'54	'55	'56	'57	'58	'59	'60	'61	'62	'63	'64	'65	'66	'67
2	2	2	2	2	2	2	2	2	2											

Number	*Built*	*Renumbered*	*BR Dates*	*Scrap*	*Notes*
61700	02/41 Don	10/48 1700	-03/57	57	
BANTAM COCK					
61701	03/41 Don	04/48 1701	-10/57	57	

B7 61360-61397, 61702-61713
4-6-0 GCR Robinson

Class continued from 61397

Number	*Built*	*Renumbered*	*BR Dates*	*Scrap*	*Notes*
61702	10/21 VF	05/49 *61365*	-06/49	*07/49*	1
61703	10/21 VF	05/49 *61367*	-09/49	*49*	1
61704	02/22 Gor	04/49 *61375*	-06/49	*06/49*	1
61705	04/22 Gor	05/49 *61377*	-02/50	*50*	1
61706	07/22 Gor	04/49 *61381*	-12/49	*50*	1
61707	08/22 Gor	04/49 *61382*	-06/49	*07/49*	1
61708	08/22 BP	*61386*	-06/49	*49*	1
61709	08/22 BP	05/49 *61387*	-01/50	*50*	1
61710	08/23 Gor	05/49 *61388*	-02/50	04/50	2
61711	10/23 Gor	04/49 61391	-07/50	*08/50*	2
61712	11/23 Gor	05/49 *61392*	-06/49	*07/49*	2
61713	02/24 Gor	04/49 61396	-09/49	*49*	2

K2 61720-61794
2-6-0 GNR Gresley

Power Classification: 4MT
Introduced: 1 1912-1913, rebuilt 1931-1937
2 1914-1921
Designer: Gresley
Company: GNR
Weight: Loco 64t 8cwt
Tender 43t 2cwt
Driving Wheel: 5' 8"
Boiler Pressure: 180psi superheated
Cylinders: Outside 20" x 26"
Tractive Effort: 23400lbf
Valve Gear: Walschaert (piston valves)

In 1912 Gresley built ten mixed traffic 2-6-0s for the GNR. They had raised running plates and outside Walschaert valve gear and they were known as the 'H2' class (LNER 'K1' class). However they were only a moderate success and they were underboilered with a boiler diameter of only 4' 8".

The next batch of engines were built in 1914-1921 with larger boilers (5' 6" diameter). They became known as the 'H3' class (LNER 'K2' class), and they were an immediate success. As they were introduced during the Ragtime era they were nicknamed 'Ragtimers'.

1 The earlier 'K1' class engines were rebuilt with larger boilers in 1931-1937 and became known as 'K2/1'. They could always be distinguished from the later engines as they had inside steam pipes.

2 The engines built new as 'K2' became known as 'K2/2' when the earlier engines were rebuilt.

s After 1925 a number of the class were transferred to work on the West Highland line in Scotland. The engines were given side-window cabs (some of these being fitted in BR days) and many of them were named after Lochs.

Year End Totals: 'K2' class

'47	'48	'49	'50	'51	'52	'53	'54	'55	'56	'57	'58	'59	'60	'61	'62	'63	'64	'65	'66	'67
75	75	75	75	75	75	75	75	74	70	62	56	24	10	2						

Number	*Built*	*Renumbered*	*BR Dates*	*Scrap*	*Notes*
61720	08/12 Don	05/50 1720	-06/56	05/57	1
61721	02/13 Don	09/48 1721	-12/59	03/60	1
					06/51⇨s
61722	02/13 Don	04/49 1722	-09/55	09/55	1
61723	02/13 Don	03/49 1723	-11/59	03/60	1
61724	02/13 Don	02/50 1724	-01/58	03/58	1
61725	03/13 Don	06/50 1725	-02/58	03/58	1
61726	03/13 Don	06/49 1726	-05/57	07/57	1
61727	03/13 Don	04/48 1727	-06/56	*07/56*	1
61728	04/13 Don	09/50 1728	-12/60	12/60	1
61729	04/13 Don	09/49 1729	-06/57	06/57	1
61730	04/14 Don	12/48 1730	-08/57	10/57	2
61731	04/14 Don	08/50 1731	-06/59	01/60	2
61732	04/14 Don	09/49 1732	-04/57	08/57	2
61733	04/14 Don	09/48 1733	-10/57	01/58	2
					01/51⇨s
61734	04/14 Don	06/48 1734	-07/56	*08/56*	2
					06/51⇨s
61735	05/14 Don	04/48 1735	-01/57	04/57	2
					01/51⇨s
61736	05/14 Don	02/49 1736	-05/57	06/57	2
61737	05/14 Don	09/50 1737	-11/56	03/57	2
61738	06/14 Don	05/48 1738	-07/59	12/59	2
61739	06/14 Don	11/50 1739	-02/59	04/59	2
61740	01/16 Don	01/49 1740	-01/61	01/61	2
61741	02/16 Don	09/48 1741	-03/60	04/60	2
					01/51⇨s
61742	05/16 Don	09/49 1742	-05/62	06/62	2
61743	06/16 Don	05/48 1743	-06/59	12/59	2
61744	07/16 Don	01/50 1744	-01/57	04/57	2
61745	10/16 Don	07/48 1745	-11/60	12/60	2
61746	11/16 Don	11/49 1746	-02/59	03/59	2
61747	11/16 Don	01/49 1747	-12/60	12/60	2
61748	12/16 Don	04/48 1748	-06/59	01/60	2
61749	12/16 Don	03/49 1749	-01/59	03/59	2
61750	06/18 NB	12/48 1750	-06/59	12/59	2
61751	06/18 NB	03/50 1751	-06/59	01/60	2
61752	06/18 NB	09/50 1752	-12/59	01/60	2
61753	07/18 NB	08/49 1753	-09/59	03/60	2
61754	07/18 NB	04/48 1754	-12/59	01/60	2
61755	07/18 NB	04/48 1755	-11/59	03/60	2
					02/51⇨s
61756	07/18 NB	12/48 1756	-06/62	07/63	2
61757	08/18 NB	10/48 1757	-02/59	03/59	2
61758	08/18 NB	05/48 1758	-06/59	10/59	2
					04/51⇨s
61759	08/18 NB	09/49 1759	-01/60	01/60	2
61760	06/18 NB	05/50 1760	-12/60	12/60	2
61761	06/18 NB	03/49 1761	-01/61	02/61	2
61762	06/18 NB	07/48 1762	-06/59	01/60	2
61763	06/18 NB	01/49 1763	-02/61	02/61	2
61764	07/18 NB	01/49 1764	-08/61	12/61	2 s
LOCH ARKAIG					
61765	07/18 NB	02/49 1765	-05/58	05/58	2
61766	08/18 NB	08/49 1766	-01/61	02/61	2
61767	08/18 NB	06/48 1767	-01/61	01/61	2
61768	08/18 NB	08/48 1768	-01/59	02/59	2
61769	08/18 NB	10/48 1769	-09/60	09/60	2
					05/51⇨s
61770	06/21 K	11/48 1770	-07/59	11/59	2
					01/51⇨s
61771	06/21 K	04/48 1771	-12/60	12/60	2
61772	06/21 K	04/48 1772	-11/59	01/60	2 s
LOCH LOCHY					
61773	06/21 K	05/50 1773	-12/60	12/60	2
61774	06/21 K	06/48 1774	-04/58	07/58	2 s
LOCH GARRY					
61775	06/21 K	07/48 1775	-05/58	07/58	2 s
LOCH TREIG					
61776	06/21 K	12/49 1776	-03/59	04/59	2 s
61777	06/21 K	06/48 1777	-05/59	08/59	2
61778	07/21 K	12/50 1778	-10/59	02/60	2
61779	07/21 K	05/48 1779	-05/60	08/60	2 s
61780	07/21 K	02/50 1780	-10/59	01/60	2
61781	07/21 K	05/48 1781	-12/58	01/59	2 s
LOCH MORAR					
61782	07/21 K	01/49 1782	-06/60	08/60	2 s
LOCH EIL					
61783	07/21 K	04/48 1783	-06/59	09/59	2 s
LOCH SHEIL					
61784	07/21 K	10/48 1784	-03/61	04/61	2 s
61785	07/21 K	12/48 1785	-04/59	05/59	2 s
61786	07/21 K	04/48 1786	-12/59	03/60	2 s
61787	08/21 K	06/48 1787	-10/59	12/59	2 s
LOCH QUOICH					
61788	08/21 K	09/48 1788	-06/61	09/61	2 s
LOCH RANNOCH					
61789	08/21 K	10/48 1789	-09/59	12/59	2 s
LOCH LAIDON					
61790	08/21 K	04/48 1790	-11/59	02/60	2 s
LOCH LOMOND					
61791	08/21 K	11/48 1791	-03/60	05/60	2 s
LOCH LAGGAN					
61792	08/21 K	07/48 1792	-11/60	11/60	2 s
61793	08/21 K	06/49 1793	-02/59	11/59	2 s
61794	09/21 K	07/48 1794	-07/60	08/60	2 s
LOCH OICH					

K3 61800-61992
2-6-0 GNR Gresley 3-cylinder

K5 61863
2-6-0 LNER Thompson 2-cylinder rebuild

Power Classification: 6MT
Introduced: 1920-1937
K5 Rebuilt 1945 by Thompson
Designer: Gresley
Company: GNR
Weight: Loco 72t 12cwt
K5 Loco 71t 5cwt
Tender 52t 0cwt
g Tender 43t 2cwt
Driving Wheel: 5' 8"
Boiler Pressure: 180psi superheated
K5 225psi superheated
Cylinders: Three 18½" x 26"
K5 Outside 20" x 26"
Tractive Effort: 30030lbf
K5 29250lbf
Valve Gear: Walschaert with derived motion (piston valves)
K5 Walschaert (piston valves)

Gresley's 'K3' class (GNR 'H4' class) first appeared in 1920 being developed from the earlier 'K2' class. The first ten engines were built by the GNR and they caused a sensation in railway circles. They carried the largest diameter boilers (6ft) to have ever appeared on a British locomotive, and they were the first three-cylinder 2-6-0 design to appear. In addition they were the first engines to have Gresley's conjugated valve gear, and they had connecting rods made of high tensile nickel chrome steel, which (being highly resonant) made a characteristic ringing 'clank'. They were originally fitted with GNR tenders.

One hundred and eighty-three more engines were built by the LNER between 1923 and 1937, being constructed at Darlington, Doncaster and by Armstrong Whitworth, R Stephenson and North British. These had improved double-window cabs, and the chimneys and domes were reduced to suit the Scottish loading gauge. They were excellent mixed traffic engines, although their large size restricted their route availability.

Apart from the one engine rebuilt as 'K5' (see below) all the engines were simply classified 'K3' by 1948. Until 1947 the class was split into several parts as listed below.

1 'K3/1' consisted of the original ten engines built by the GNR. They were later rebuilt with larger cabs and reduced chimneys and domes in line with the rest of the class.

2 The LNER built engines were classified 'K3/2'.

3 'K3/3' consisted of a batch of engines fitted with Westinghouse and vacuum brakes, and shorter coupled-wheel springs. They were combined with the 'K3/2' class as 'K3' in 1947.

4, 5 & 6 'K3/4', 'K3/5' and 'K3/6' were engines which differed in details such as weights and springs. They were all modified or reclassified 'K3/2' by 1940.

g Some engines were fitted with GNR tenders.

K5 When Thompson succeeded Gresley in 1941 he was reputed to have had a strong dislike for Gresley and Gresley's designs. In particular he did not like Gresley's three-cylinder engines with their conjugated valve gear. In 1945 he rebuilt 61863 with two cylinders and it was reclassified 'K5'. This was the only engine to be converted.

Year End Totals: 'K3' class

'47	'48	'49	'50	'51	'52	'53	'54	'55	'56	'57	'58	'59	'60	'61	'62	'63	'64	'65	'66	'67
192	192	192	192	192	192	192	192	192	192	192	192	192	192	180	163	121				

Year End Totals: 'K5' class

'47	'48	'49	'50	'51	'52	'53	'54	'55	'56	'57	'58	'59	'60	'61	'62	'63	'64	'65	'66	'67
1	1	1	1	1	1	1	1	1	1	1	1	1	1							

Number	Built	Renumbered	BR Dates	Scrap	Notes
61800	03/20 Don	07/48 1800	-07/62	08/62	1
61801	06/20 Don	02/49 1801	-04/62	04/62	1
61802	09/20 Don	05/50 1802	-03/60	03/60	1
61803	10/20 Don	05/48 1803	-07/61	08/61	1
61804	12/20 Don	10/48 1804	-03/62	04/62	1
61805	12/20 Don	02/49 1805	-09/62	10/62	1
61806	04/21 Don	02/49 1806	-03/60	04/60	1
61807	05/21 Don	05/48 1807	-11/62	03/63	1
61808	07/21 Don	05/49 1808	-09/61	10/61	1
61809	08/21 Don	03/49 1809	-04/62	04/62	1
61810	08/24 Dar	12/49 1810	-08/62	08/62	2
61811	08/24 Dar	11/49 1811	-10/62	10/62	2
61812	08/24 Dar	02/49 1812	-09/62	09/62	2g
61813	09/24 Dar	10/48 1813	-04/62	04/62	2
61814	09/24 Dar	10/48 1814	-12/61	01/62	2
61815	10/24 Dar	11/48 1815	-07/60	07/60	2
61816	10/24 Dar	11/48 1816	-05/62	06/62	2
61817	10/24 Dar	11/48 1817	-09/62	12/63	2
61818	10/24 Dar	11/49 1818	-03/62	03/62	2
61819	10/24 Dar	10/48 1819	-12/62	02/63	2
61820	10/24 Dar	08/48 1820	-11/62	02/63	2
61821	10/24 Dar	04/48 1821	-09/62	03/63	2
61822	10/24 Dar	04/50 1822	-11/62	02/63	2
61823	11/24 Dar	10/49 1823	-12/59	02/60	2
61824	11/24 Dar	07/48 1824	-07/61	08/61	2
61825	11/24 Dar	04/48 1825	-09/62	10/62	2
61826	11/24 Dar	10/50 1826	-09/62	02/63	2
61827	11/24 Dar	05/48 1827	-09/62	02/63	2
61828	11/24 Dar	08/48 1828	-03/61	03/61	2
61829	12/24 Dar	03/49 1829	-03/62	03/62	2
61830	12/24 Dar	06/48 1830	-11/62	11/62	2
61831	12/24 Dar	10/48 1831	-09/62	02/63	2
61832	12/24 Dar	12/49 1832	-11/62	11/62	2
61833	12/24 Dar	04/49 1833	-09/61	10/61	2
61834	12/25 Dar	04/48 1834	-05/62	05/62	2
61835	01/25 Dar	01/50 1835	-09/62	09/62	2
61836	01/25 Dar	09/48 1836	-02/60	02/60	2
61837	01/25 Dar	08/49 1837	-04/62	04/62	2
61838	01/25 Dar	09/49 1838	-03/60	05/60	2
61839	01/25 Dar	01/50 1839	-01/62	01/62	2
61840	02/25 Dar	03/49 1840	-09/62	11/62	2
61841	02/25 Dar	09/49 1841	-03/62	04/62	2g
61842	02/25 Dar	11/48 1842	-08/61	09/61	2
61843	02/25 Dar	05/50 1843	-11/62	12/62	2
61844	02/25 Dar	12/48 1844	-06/61	06/61	2
61845	02/25 Dar	12/48 1845	-09/62	03/63	2
61846	02/25 Dar	03/48 1846	-12/62	01/63	2
61847	02/25 Dar	01/49 1847	-12/62	02/63	2
61848	03/25 Dar	03/48 1848	-09/62	03/63	2
61849	03/25 Dar	08/48 1849	-04/61	05/61	2
61850	03/25 Dar	10/48 1850	-06/61	07/61	2
61851	03/25 Dar	10/48 1851	-11/61	08/62	2
61852	03/25 Dar	03/49 1852	-07/61	07/61	2
61853	03/25 Dar	12/49 1853	-12/62	01/63	2
61854	03/25 Dar	11/48 1854	-11/62	01/63	2g
61855	03/25 Dar	05/49 1855	-07/59	11/59	2g
61856	03/25 Dar	02/50 1856	-12/62	01/63	2g
61857	04/25 Dar	09/48 1857	-12/62	02/63	2g
61858	04/25 Dar	10/48 1858	-04/61	07/61	2g
61859	04/25 Dar	11/48 1859	-11/62	02/63	2g
61860	08/25 Dar	09/49 1860	-11/61	11/61	2
61861	08/25 Dar	05/49 1861	-01/62	01/62	2
61862	08/25 Dar	01/49 1862	-01/62	02/62	2
61863	09/25 Dar	01/50 1863	-06/60	06/60	K5
61864	09/25 Dar	05/49 1864	-09/62	02/63	2
61865	09/25 Dar	12/48 1865	-06/61	07/61	2
61866	10/25 Dar	12/48 1866	-10/61	11/61	2
61867	10/25 Dar	08/48 1867	-11/62	12/62	2
61868	10/25 Dar	12/48 1868	-05/62	05/62	2
61869	12/25 Dar	10/48 1869	-12/62	02/63	2
61870	04/29 Don	06/49 1870	-07/62	07/62	3
61871	05/29 Don	02/49 1871	-12/62	02/63	3
61872	06/29 Don	07/48 1872	-12/62	01/63	3
61873	06/29 Don	06/49 1873	-05/62	05/62	3
61874	07/29 Don	12/48 1874	-05/61	06/61	3
61875	07/29 Don	04/48 1875	-12/62	01/63	3
61876	07/29 Don	11/48 1876	-09/59	09/59	3
61877	08/29 Don	07/49 1877	-07/62	08/62	3
61878	08/29 Don	10/48 1878	-08/59	03/60	3
61879	09/29 Don	08/50 1879	-06/59	08/59	3
61880	10/29 Don	06/49 1880	-09/62	07/63	3
61881	10/29 Don	06/48 1881	-04/60	05/60	3
61882	10/29 Don	09/48 1882	-05/60	06/60	3
61883	10/29 Don	01/49 1883	-12/62	02/63	3
61884	11/29 Don	12/48 1884	-07/62	08/62	3
61885	11/29 Don	07/48 1885	-11/59	01/60	3
61886	11/29 Don	09/49 1886	-09/62	07/63	3
61887	11/29 Don	09/48 1887	-03/62	03/62	3
61888	12/29 Don	06/49 1888	-09/61	10/61	3
61889	12/29 Don	10/48 1889	-11/62	02/63	3
61890	07/30 Dar	12/48 1890	-09/62	07/63	2
61891	07/30 Dar	10/49 1891	-09/61	10/61	2
61892	07/30 Dar	05/48 1892	-10/61	10/61	2
61893	07/30 Dar	12/48 1893	-12/62	03/63	2
61894	07/30 Dar	08/49 1894	-10/61	10/61	2
61895	07/30 Dar	01/49 1895	-07/62	07/62	2
61896	08/30 Dar	04/49 1896	-05/62	06/62	2
61897	08/30 Dar	10/48 1897	-12/62	02/63	2
61898	08/30 Dar	10/48 1898	-01/59	03/59	2
61899	03/31 AW	04/48 1899	-12/62	01/63	2
61900	03/31 AW	11/49 1900	-03/60	04/60	2
61901	03/31 AW	02/50 1901	-12/61	12/61	2
61902	03/31 AW	11/48 1902	-07/61	07/61	2
61903	04/31 AW	07/48 1903	-12/61	12/61	2
61904	05/31 AW	05/48 1904	-06/61	06/61	2
61905	05/31 AW	04/48 1905	-11/62	04/63	2
61906	04/31 AW	09/48 1906	-12/62	03/63	2
61907	04/31 AW	12/48 1907	-09/62	11/63	2
61908	04/31 AW	01/50 1908	-01/62	01/62	2
61909	04/31 AW	08/48 1909	-04/60	05/60	2
61910	04/31 AW	12/49 1910	-07/62	07/62	2
61911	05/31 AW	03/48 1911	-11/59	01/60	2
61912	05/31 AW	03/48 1912	-09/62	05/65	2
61913	05/31 AW	11/48 1913	-02/62	02/62	2
61914	05/31 AW	02/49 1914	-08/62	08/62	2
61915	05/31 AW	11/49 1915	-09/62	12/63	2
61916	05/31 AW	07/48 1916	-12/60	04/61	2
61917	05/31 AW	01/49 1917	-11/62	01/63	2
61918	06/31 AW	07/49 1918	-03/62	04/62	2
61919	07/34 AW	03/49 1919	-06/61	07/61	2
61920	07/34 AW	10/49 1920	-09/61	10/61	2
61921	07/34 AW	05/48 1921	-07/61	10/61	2
61922	08/34 AW	05/48 1922	-05/62	06/62	2
61923	08/34 AW	03/48 1923	-04/62	05/62	2
61924	09/34 AW	04/49 1924	-12/60	05/61	2
61925	09/34 AW	05/50 1925	-07/61	09/61	2
61926	09/34 AW	07/49 1926	-04/62	04/62	2
61927	01/35 AW	01/49 1927	-07/61	07/61	2
61928	01/35 AW	05/48 1928	-02/60	04/60	2
61929	08/34 RS	10/49 1929	-07/62	08/62	2
61930	09/34 RS	12/48 1930	-12/62	03/63	2
61931	09/34 RS	08/50 1931	-07/59	08/59	2
61932	09/34 RS	11/48 1932	-02/62	02/62	2
61933	09/34 RS	03/49 1933	-09/60	02/61	2
61934	01/35 RS	08/49 1934	-11/62	01/63	2
61935	01/35 RS	04/48 1935	-07/62	07/62	2
61936	01/35 RS	08/48 1936	-11/61	12/61	2
61937	01/35 RS	10/48 1937	-04/60	04/60	2
61938	01/35 RS	04/48 1938	-12/61	01/62	2
61939	08/35 NB	06/49 1939	-11/62	02/63	2
61940	08/35 NB	11/48 1940	-05/62	05/62	2
61941	08/35 NB	08/48 1941	-07/61	07/61	2
61942	08/35 NB	08/49 1942	-09/62	12/63	2
61943	08/35 NB	03/50 1943	-09/62	02/66	2
61944	09/35 NB	03/48 1944	-09/62	11/63	2
61945	09/35 NB	01/49 1945	-02/62	03/62	2
61946	09/35 NB	09/48 1946	-06/62	07/62	2
61947	09/35 NB	04/48 1947	-08/62	08/62	2
61948	09/35 NB	04/48 1948	-03/62	04/62	2
61949	09/35 NB	02/49 1949	-04/62	04/62	2
61950	09/35 NB	02/49 1950	-11/62	12/63	2
61951	10/35 NB	06/49 1951	-11/62	01/63	2
61952	10/35 NB	02/50 1952	-12/62	04/63	2
61953	10/35 NB	10/49 1953	-03/62	04/62	2
61954	10/35 NB	09/49 1954	-09/62	07/63	2
61955	10/35 NB	12/48 1955	-05/60	06/60	2
61956	10/35 NB	12/49 1956	-09/62	10/62	2
61957	11/35 NB	03/49 1957	-09/62	12/63	2
61958	11/35 NB	08/48 1958	-05/62	06/62	2
61959	05/36 AW	01/49 1959	-11/61	01/62	2
61960	05/36 AW	12/48 1960	-09/62	04/63	2
61961	05/36 AW	04/49 1961	-10/61	10/61	2
61962	05/36 AW	10/49 1962	-12/62	01/63	2
61963	06/36 AW	08/49 1963	-09/62	11/63	2
61964	06/36 AW	12/49 1964	-07/61	07/61	2
61965	06/36 AW	04/48 1965	-12/62	01/63	2
61966	06/36 AW	11/50 1966	-02/62	02/62	2
61967	07/36 AW	06/48 1967	-04/61	05/61	2
61968	08/36 AW	09/48 1968	-10/61	05/62	2
61969	10/36 Dar	04/48 1969	-12/62	03/63	2
61970	10/36 Dar	02/49 1970	-11/62	12/63	2
61971	10/36 Dar	03/48 1971	-03/61	04/61	2
61972	10/36 Dar	12/48 1972	-09/62	11/62	2
61973	11/36 Dar	09/48 1973	-11/62	11/62	2
61974	11/36 Dar	08/49 1974	-07/62	07/62	2
61975	11/36 Dar	04/49 1975	-09/61	09/61	2
61976	11/36 Dar	04/48 1976	-01/62	01/62	2
61977	11/36 Dar	11/48 1977	-09/62	11/63	2
61978	11/36 Dar	09/48 1978	-08/61	09/61	2
61979	12/36 Dar	01/49 1979	-10/61	11/61	2
61980	12/36 Dar	03/49 1980	-12/62	01/63	2
61981	12/36 Dar	12/49 1981	-11/62	11/63	2
61982	12/36 Dar	11/49 1982	-09/62	01/64	2
61983	12/36 Dar	06/48 1983	-07/59	08/59	2
61984	12/36 Dar	06/48 1984	-11/62	01/63	2
61985	01/37 Dar	04/48 1985	-12/62	01/63	2
61986	01/37 Dar	01/49 1986	-05/62	06/62	2
61987	01/37 Dar	12/48 1987	-03/62	04/62	2
61988	01/37 Dar	11/48 1988	-11/59	12/59	2
61989	02/37 Dar	05/49 1989	-06/62	07/62	2
61990	02/37 Dar	06/48 1990	-10/60	11/60	2
61991	02/37 Dar	06/48 1991	-05/59	08/59	2
61992	02/37 Dar	04/48 1992	-06/60	06/60	2

K4 61993-61998
2-6-0 LNER Gresley

K1/1 61997
2-6-0 LNER Thompson 'K4' rebuilt as 'K1' prototype

Power Classification:	6MT
Introduced:	1937-1939 K1/1 Rebuilt 1945 by Thompson
Designer:	Gresley
Company:	LNER
Weight:	Loco 68t 8cwt K1/1 Loco 66t 17cwt Tender 44t 4cwt
Driving Wheel:	5' 2"
Boiler Pressure:	200psi superheated K1/1 225psi superheated
Cylinders:	Three 18½" x 26" K1/1 Outside 20" x 26"
Tractive Effort:	36600lbf K1/1 32080lbf
Valve Gear:	Walschaert with derived motion (piston valves) K1/1 Walschaert (piston valves)

In 1937-1939 Gresley introduced his three-cylinder 'K4' class specifically for working the West Highland line in Scotland. Although they were nominally the most powerful of Gresley's moguls, with their small 5' 6" diameter wheels, they only had a relatively small sized boiler. This was because they only needed to use their high power for short periods at low speed on the West Highland line.

61994 was at first named MACCAILEIN MÓR (until 1938), and 61998 was named LORD OF DUNVEGAN until 1939.

K1/1 In 1945 Thompson rebuilt 61997 with two cylinders and it was reclassified 'K1' (later 'K1/1'). This was the only engine to be converted and it was the prototype for the Peppercorn 'K1' class.

Year End Totals: 'K4' class

'47	'48	'49	'50	'51	'52	'53	'54	'55	'56	'57	'58	'59	'60	'61	'62	'63	'64	'65	'66	'67
5	5	5	5	5	5	5	5	5	5	5	5	5	5							

Year End Totals: 'K1/1' class

'47	'48	'49	'50	'51	'52	'53	'54	'55	'56	'57	'58	'59	'60	'61	'62	'63	'64	'65	'66	'67
1	1	1	1	1	1	1	1	1	1	1	1	1	1							

Number	Built	Renumbered	BR Dates	Scrap	Notes
61993	01/37 Dar	05/48 1993	-10/61	03/62	
LOCH LONG					
61994 §	07/38 Dar	10/48 1994	-12/61		
THE GREAT MARQUESS					
61995	12/38 Dar	07/48 1995	-10/61	03/62	
CAMERON OF LOCHIEL					
61996	12/38 Dar	11/48 1996	-10/61	03/62	
LORD OF THE ISLES					
61997	01/39 Dar	01/49 1997	-06/61	06/61	K1/1
MACCAILIN MÓR					
61998	01/39 Dar	04/48 1998	-10/61	03/62	
MACLEOD OF MACLEOD					

D3 62000, 62116-62148
4-4-0 GNR Ivatt

Power Classification:	1P
Introduced:	1896-1899 Rebuilt by Gresley 1912-1928
Designer:	Ivatt
Company:	GNR
Weight:	Loco 45t 14cwt Tender 38t 10cwt
Driving Wheel:	6' 8"
Boiler Pressure:	175psi
Cylinders:	Inside 17½" x 26"
Tractive Effort:	14805lbf
Valve Gear:	Stephenson (slide valves)

The 'D3' class originally consisted of fifty-one engines which were built by Ivatt between 1896 and 1899. They were rebuilt with larger boilers by Gresley

Great North of Scotland Railway Johnson 'D41' class 4-4-0 No 62225 on Elgin Shed in September 1951.

NBR Reid 'Glen' 'D34' class 4-4-0 No 62471 *Glen Falloch.*

GER ‘D16/3’ ‘Rebuilt Claud’ 4-4-0 No 62613.

LNER-built ‘D11/2’ ‘Large Director’ 4-4-0 No 62678 *Luckie Mucklebackit*.

between 1912 and 1928. The first engine of the class was withdrawn in 1935.

r Several engines had raised running plates over the coupling rods and were very similar in appearance to classes 'D1' and 'D2'.

s 62131 differed from all other engines of the class by having two separate splashers over the driving wheels instead of one continuous splasher.

c 62000 was formerly LNER number 4075. It was rebuilt in September 1944 with a new side window cab for working officers' saloons. When it first emerged from Doncaster Works in workshop grey it carried the number 1, but within a few days it was repainted green and was renumbered 2000. This was the first available number in the 4-4-0 series for the proposed LNER renumbering (which was not implemented for most other engines until 1946).

Year End Totals: 'D3' class

'47	'48	'49	'50	'51	'52	'53	'54	'55	'56	'57	'58	'59	'60	'61	'62	'63	'64	'65	'66	'67
19	13	5	1																	

Number	Built	Renumbered	BR Dates	Scrap	Notes
62000	06/97 Don	01/50 2000	-09/51	*51*	c

Class continued with 62116

K1 62001-62070
2-6-0 BR (LNER) Peppercorn

Power Classification: 6MT
Introduced: 1949-1950
Designer: Peppercorn
Company: BR (LNER)
Weight: Loco 66t 17cwt
Tender 44t 4cwt
Driving Wheel: 5' 2"
Boiler Pressure: 225psi superheated
Cylinders: Outside 20" x 26"
Tractive Effort: 32080lbf
Valve Gear: Walschaert (piston valves)

After Thompson rebuilt 'K4' 61997 with two cylinders in 1945 to become the sole class 'K1/1', Peppercorn developed the design into his 'K1' class. Seventy engines were built and there were a number of minor detail alterations from the prototype, including slightly longer frames and a break in the running plate in front of the cylinders.

They worked successfully as mixed traffic engines in the East and North East, as well as in Scotland.

Year End Totals: 'K1' class

'47	'48	'49	'50	'51	'52	'53	'54	'55	'56	'57	'58	'59	'60	'61	'62	'63	'64	'65	'66	'67
		61	70	70	70	70	70	70	70	70	70	70	70	70	67	60	48	31	24	

Number	Built	Renumbered	BR Dates	Scrap	Notes
62001	05/49 NB		05/49-04/67	08/67	
62002	06/49 NB		06/49-10/66	03/67	
62003	06/49 NB		06/49-06/65	08/65	
62004	06/49 NB		06/49-12/66	03/67	
62005 §	06/49 NB		06/49-12/67		
62006	06/49 NB		06/49-09/66	01/67	
62007	06/49 NB		06/49-09/67	10/67	
62008	06/49 NB		06/49-12/66	04/67	
62009	06/49 NB		06/49-11/64	01/65	
62010	06/49 NB		06/49-10/65	04/66	
62011	06/49 NB		06/49-09/67	01/68	
62012	07/49 NB		07/49-05/67	08/67	
62013	07/49 NB		07/49-10/63	08/64	
62014	07/49 NB		07/49-06/65	10/65	
62015	07/49 NB		07/49-07/65	11/65	
62016	07/49 NB		07/49-07/63	01/64	
62017	07/49 NB		07/49-02/67	05/67	
62018	07/49 NB		07/49-02/64	08/64	
62019	07/49 NB		07/49-07/64	11/64	
62020	08/49 NB		08/49-01/65	06/65	
62021	08/49 NB		08/49-10/66	05/67	
62022	08/49 NB		08/49-09/66	12/66	
62023	08/49 NB		08/49-06/67	10/67	
62024	08/49 NB		08/49-02/67	05/67	
62025	08/49 NB		08/49-04/67	09/67	
62026	08/49 NB		08/49-07/67	11/67	
62027	08/49 NB		08/49-03/67	11/67	
62028	08/49 NB		08/49-11/66	03/67	
62029	08/49 NB		08/49-10/64	12/64	
62030	08/49 NB		08/49-08/65	01/66	
62031	08/49 NB		08/49-02/62	03/64	
62032	08/49 NB		08/49-09/63	09/64	
62033	08/49 NB		08/49-01/65	04/65	
62034	09/49 NB		09/49-02/62	02/63	
62035	09/49 NB		09/49-07/65	11/65	
62036	09/49 NB		09/49-10/63	11/63	
62037	09/49 NB		09/49-12/64	05/65	
62038	09/49 NB		09/49-10/63	09/64	
62039	09/49 NB		09/49-12/63	02/64	
62040	10/49 NB		10/49-01/65	06/65	
62041	10/49 NB		10/49-04/67	09/67	
62042	10/49 NB		10/49-07/67	11/67	
62043	10/49 NB		10/49-07/65	10/65	
62044	10/49 NB		10/49-07/67	11/67	
62045	10/49 NB		10/49-09/67	10/67	
62046	10/49 NB		10/49-02/67	06/67	
62047	10/49 NB		10/49-03/65	05/65	
62048	10/49 NB		10/49-06/67	11/67	
62049	10/49 NB		10/49-06/65	12/65	
62050	10/49 NB		10/49-09/67	10/67	
62051	11/49 NB		11/49-01/65	03/65	
62052	11/49 NB		11/49-02/62	04/64	
62053	11/49 NB		11/49-12/63	02/64	
62054	11/49 NB		11/49-12/64	04/65	
62055	11/49 NB		11/49-12/64	04/65	
62056	11/49 NB		11/49-05/65	08/65	
62057	11/49 NB		11/49-05/67	08/67	
62058	12/49 NB		12/49-08/64	11/64	
62059	12/49 NB		12/49-02/67	06/67	
62060	12/49 NB		12/49-08/67	10/67	
62061	12/49 NB		12/49-12/64	03/65	
62062	01/50 NB		01/50-05/67	08/67	
62063	01/50 NB		01/50-08/64	11/64	
62064	01/50 NB		01/50-09/65	11/65	
62065	01/50 NB		01/50-03/67	08/67	
62066	01/50 NB		01/50-01/65	05/65	
62067	02/50 NB		02/50-01/67	04/67	
62068	02/50 NB		02/50-02/64	02/64	
62069	02/50 NB		02/50-02/64	02/64	
62070	03/50 NB		03/50-01/65	05/65	

D31 62059-62072, 62281-62283
4-4-0 NBR Holmes

Power Classification: 2P
Introduced: 1884-1899
Rebuilt 1918-1924 by Reid and Chalmers
Designer: Holmes
Company: NBR
Weight: Loco 46t 8cwt
Tender 33t 9cwt
Driving Wheel: 6' 6"
Boiler Pressure: 175psi
Cylinders: Inside 18¼" x 26"
Tractive Effort: 16515lbf
Valve Gear: Stephenson (slide valves)

Holmes built forty-eight 4-4-0 engines of three different classes between 1884 and 1899 for the NBR. They were all rebuilt into one class by Reid and Chalmers between 1918 and 1924. They were known as the NBR 'M' class.

The first engine was withdrawn in 1931 and seven engines came into BR stock in 1948. The last three survivors were renumbered 62281-62283 in 1949 to make way for newly constructed 'K1' engines.

Year End Totals: 'D31' class

'47	'48	'49	'50	'51	'52	'53	'54	'55	'56	'57	'58	'59	'60	'61	'62	'63	'64	'65	'66	'67
7	4	3	2	1																

Number	Built	Renumbered	BR Dates	Scrap	Notes
62059	05/90 Cow	10/48 2059	-12/52	*01/53*	
				08/49➲62281	
62060	09/90 Cow	10/48 2060	-02/50	*05/50*	
				06/49➲62282	
62062	01/93 Cow	2062	-03/48	*05/48*	
62064	04/98 Cow	2064	-08/48	*48*	
62065	05/98 Cow	07/48 2065	-04/49	06/49	
62066	05/98 Cow	2066	-05/48	*48*	
62072	11/99 Cow	07/48 2072	-02/51	*51*	
				06/49➲62283	

Class continued with 62281

D17 62111-62112
4-4-0 NER Worsdell

Power Classification: 1P
Introduced: 1896-1897
Designer: W Worsdell
Company: NER
Weight: Loco 50t 2cwt
Tender 41t 4cwt
Driving Wheel: 7' 1¼"
Boiler Pressure: 160psi superheated
Cylinders: Inside 19" x 26"
Tractive Effort: 14975lbf
Valve Gear: Stephenson (slide valves)

These engines were the last survivors of the NER 'Q' class of thirty engines built 1896-1897. They were classified 'D17/2' and they were a lighter development of the original 'D17/1' design (twenty engines built 1892-1894 and classified 'M' on the NER).

The first engine of the class was withdrawn in 1927 and both of the two survivors were scrapped in 1948 without receiving their new BR numbers.

s 62111 retained its old North Eastern type brass column safety valve.

Year End Totals: 'D17' class

'47	'48	'49	'50	'51	'52	'53	'54	'55	'56	'57	'58	'59	'60	'61	'62	'63	'64	'65	'66	'67
2																				

Number	Built	Renumbered	BR Dates	Scrap	Notes
62111	06/96 Ghd	2111	-02/48	*02/48*	s
62112	06/97 Ghd	2112	-02/48	*02/48*	

D3 62000, 62116-62148
4-4-0 GNR Ivatt

Class continued from 62000

Number	Built	Renumbered	BR Dates	Scrap	Notes
62116	05/97 Don	2116	-10/48	*48*	
62122	10/97 Don	2122	-02/48	*48*	
62123	11/97 Don	2123	-12/49	*50*	
62124	11/97 Don	2124	-11/48	*48*	
62125	11/97 Don	2125	-08/49	*49*	
62126	12/97 Don	2126	-08/48	*10/48*	
62128	03/98 Don	2128	-12/49	*50*	
62131	04/98 Don	03/48 2131	-10/49	*49*	s
62132	05/98 Don	2132	-12/50	*51*	
62133	05/98 Don	2133	-08/49	*49*	
62135	12/98 Don	06/48 2135	-02/50	*50*	
62137	12/98 Don	2137	-01/49	01/49	
62139	12/98 Don	2139	-06/49	*49*	
62140	12/98 Don	2140	-07/50	*08/50*	
62143	11/99 Don	2143	-03/48	*48*	r
62144	11/99 Don	2144	-08/48	*48*	r
62145	12/99 Don	2145	-01/49	01/49	r
62148	12/99 Don	2148	-11/50	*50*	r

D2 62150-62199
4-4-0 GNR Ivatt

Power Classification: 1P
Introduced: 1897-1909
Designer: Ivatt
Company: GNR
Weight: Loco 47t 10cwt
Tender 40t 18cwt
Driving Wheel: 6' 8"
Boiler Pressure: 175psi
s 170psi superheated
Cylinders: Inside 17½" x 26"
Tractive Effort: 14805lbf
s 14380lbf
Valve Gear: Stephenson (slide valves)

Ivatt built seventy engines of the 'D2' class in 1897-1909. Originally built for main line working these engines were very quickly transferred to secondary duties. The first of these engines was withdrawn in 1936.

s Some engines were superheated with extended smokeboxes and resembled the slightly more powerful 'D1' class.

f Some engines had flat running plates and resembled the 'D3' class.

Year End Totals: 'D2' class

'47	'48	'49	'50	'51	'52	'53	'54	'55	'56	'57	'58	'59	'60	'61	'62	'63	'64	'65	'66	'67
31	21	6	1																	

Number	Built	Renumbered	BR Dates	Scrap	Notes
62150	11/97 Don	2150	-05/49	*49*	f
62151	06/98 Don	2151	-04/49	*49*	
62152	06/98 Don	2152	-01/49	01/49	f
62153	06/98 Don	2153	-04/49	*49*	f
62154	06/98 Don	2154	-11/50	*50*	f
62155	10/98 Don	2155	-02/48	*48*	
62156	10/98 Don	2156	-01/49	*49*	s
62157	11/98 Don	2157	-04/48	*48*	
62160	11/98 Don	2160	-10/48	*48*	s
62161	11/98 Don	2161	-07/50	*09/50*	
62163	10/99 Don	2163	-10/48	*48*	s
62165	10/99 Don	2165	-03/49	*49*	s
62167	11/99 Don	2167	-02/49	*49*	s

62169	11/99 Don	2169	-07/48	48	s
62172	10/00 Don	03/48 2172	-06/51	06/51	
62173	11/00 Don	2173	-05/50	50	
62175	11/00 Don	2175	-11/48	48	
62177	01/01 Don	2177	-10/49	49	s
62179	11/00 Don	2179	-03/49	07/49	
62180	01/01 Don	2180	-05/50	08/50	s
62181	12/00 Don	2181	-11/50	50	
62187	04/03 Don	2187	-10/48	48	s
62188	02/03 Don	2188	-10/49	49	
62189	05/03 Don	2189	-11/48	48	s
62190	03/03 Don	2190	-09/49	49	
62193	10/07 Don	2193	-06/49	49	
62194	04/09 Don	2194	-06/49	49	
62195	04/09 Don	2195	-02/48	48	
62197	05/09 Don	2197	-01/49	49	
62198	06/09 Don	2198	-08/48	10/48	
62199	06/09 Don	2199	-07/49	49	s

D1 62203-62215
4-4-0 GNR Ivatt

Power Classification: 1P
Introduced: 1911
Designer: Ivatt
Company: GNR
Weight: Loco 53t 6cwt
Tender 43t 2cwt
Driving Wheel: 6' 8"
Boiler Pressure: 170psi superheated
Cylinders: Inside 18½" x 26"
Tractive Effort: 16075lbf
Valve Gear: Stephenson (piston valves)

Ivatt's 'D1' class of 4-4-0s consisted of fifteen engines which were built in 1911. They were slightly more powerful than the 'D2' class engines from which they were developed and they had Westinghouse brakes in addition to vacuum brakes.

Originally built for main line working these engines were very quickly transferred to secondary duties. The engines were withdrawn from 1946 onwards, leaving seven to come into BR stock.

Year End Totals: 'D1' class

'47	'48	'49	'50	'51	'52	'53	'54	'55	'56	'57	'58	'59	'60	'61	'62	'63	'64	'65	'66	'67
7	5	4																		

Number	Built	Renumbered	BR Dates	Scrap	Notes
62203	04/11 Don	03/48 2203	-08/50	50	
62205	04/11 Don	2205	-11/48	11/48	
62207	05/11 Don	2207	-11/48	11/48	
62208	05/11 Don	04/48 2208	-07/50	08/50	
62209	05/11 Don	2209	-11/50	50	
62214	06/11 Don	2214	-10/49	11/49	
62215	07/11 Don	03/48 2215	-02/50	50	

D41 62225-62256
4-4-0 GNoSR Johnson

Power Classification: 2P
Introduced: 1893-1898
Designer: J Johnson
Company: GNoSR
Weight: Loco 45t 0cwt
Tender 37t 8cwt
Driving Wheel: 6' 1"
Boiler Pressure: 165psi
Cylinders: Inside 18" x 26"
Tractive Effort: 16185lbf
Valve Gear: Stephenson (slide valves)

From the 1860s onwards, the GNoSR built no tender locomotives for its services other than 4-4-0s. The 'D41's were designed by James Johnson and thirty-two engines were built in 1893-1898. They were GNoSR classes 'S' and 'T' and were very similar to the saturated boiler 'D40's.

Twenty-two of these engines came into BR stock, the first having been withdrawn in 1946.

Year End Totals: 'D41' class

'47	'48	'49	'50	'51	'52	'53	'54	'55	'56	'57	'58	'59	'60	'61	'62	'63	'64	'65	'66	'67
22	21	19	16	9	3															

Number	Built	Renumbered	BR Dates	Scrap	Notes
62225	12/93 N	12/48 2225	-02/53	06/53	
62227	12/93 N	11/48 2227	-03/51	51	
62228	12/93 N	09/48 2228	-02/52	52	
62229	12/93 N	04/48 2229	-12/51	52	
62230	12/93 N	04/49 2230	-03/52	52	
62231	02/96 N	04/48 2231	-10/52	06/53	
62232	02/96 N	09/48 2232	-09/51	51	
62234	03/96 N	04/48 2234	-11/49	49	
62235	03/96 N	2235	-05/50	50	
62238	12/95 N	03/48 2238	-08/48	48	
62240	12/95 N	04/48 2240	-10/49	49	
62241	12/95 N	04/49 2241	-03/53	04/53	
62242	12/95 N	10/48 2242	-03/53	06/53	
62243	12/95 N	08/48 2243	-01/51	51	
62246	09/97 NR	10/48 2246	-08/51	51	
62247	09/97 NR	05/48 2247	-10/50	50	
62248	09/97 NR	08/49 2248	-10/52	52	
62249	09/97 NR	05/48 2249	-10/50	50	
62251	02/98 NR	03/49 2251	-06/51	06/51	
62252	02/98 NR	11/48 2252	-11/51	51	
62255	02/98 NR	05/48 2255	-06/52	52	
62256	02/98 NR	09/49 2256	-12/52	53	

D40 62260-62279, 49
4-4-0 GNoSR Pickersgill

Power Classification: 2P reclassified 1P in 1953
Introduced: 1899-1915
s 1920-1921
Designer: Pickersgill
s Heywood
Company: GNoSR
Weight: Loco 46t 7cwt
s Loco 48t 13cwt
Tender 37t 8cwt
Driving Wheel: 6' 1"
Boiler Pressure: 165psi
s 165psi superheated
Cylinders: Inside 18" x 26"
Tractive Effort: 16185lbf
Valve Gear: Stephenson (slide valves)

The 'D40's were developed from the 'D41's by Pickersgill. The first thirteen engines (GNoSR class 'V') were introduced in 1899 and they were fitted with saturated boilers. One or two engines of this batch were later superheated.

The GNoSR found itself in financial difficulties after ordering the first ten of these engines and they could only afford to take delivery of the first five. The builders Neilson Reid sold the remaining five engines to the South Eastern & Chatham Railway were they remained at work until withdrawn by the Southern Railway in 1925-1927.

s Heywood introduced a superheated version with piston valves and extended smokeboxes in 1920 (GNoSR class 'F'). These were the first GNoSR engines to be named.

There was originally a total of twenty-one engines in the class and the first three were withdrawn in 1947.

62277 was the last survivor of this class and in 1958 it was restored to its original condition as GNoSR No. 49 GORDON HIGHLANDER. It worked on special trains for a number of years before being retired as a static exhibit in Glasgow Museum.

Year End Totals: 'D40' class

'47	'48	'49	'50	'51	'52	'53	'54	'55	'56	'57	'58	'59	'60	'61	'62	'63	'64	'65	'66	'67
18	18	18	18	18	18	15	15	6	2	1										

Number	Built	Renumbered	BR Dates	Scrap	Notes
62260	10/99 NR	12/48 2260	-08/53	09/53	
62261	10/99 NR	06/48 2261	-03/53	06/53	
62262	10/99 NR	02/49 2262	-10/55	55	
62264	10/99 NR	04/48 2264	-03/57	07/57	
62265	04/09 Inv	03/49 2265	-12/56	57	
62267	07/09 Inv	10/48 2267	-08/56	56	
62268	06/10 Inv	12/48 2268	-07/56	08/56	
62269	09/13 Inv	02/49 2269	-09/55	11/55	
62270	03/15 Inv	12/48 2270	-09/53	09/53	
62271	09/14 Inv	04/48 2271	-11/56	56	
62272	08/10 Inv	12/48 2272	-03/55	04/55	
62273	06/21 Inv	07/48 2273	-01/55	02/55	s
GEORGE DAVIDSON					
62274	09/21 Inv	05/49 2274	-08/55	11/55	s
BENACHIE					
62275	09/20 NB	07/48 2275	-12/55	56	s
SIR DAVID STEWART					
62276	10/20 NB	10/48 2276	-10/55	10/55	s
ANDREW BAIN					
62277 §	10/20 NB	11/48 2277	-06/58	06/58➲49	s
GORDON HIGHLANDER					
62278	10/20 NB	01/49 2278	-07/55	09/55	s
HATTON CASTLE					
62279	10/20 NB	12/48 2279	-05/55	07/55	s
GLEN GRANT					

Class continued with 49 (Preserved Locomotives)

D31 62059-62072, 62281-62283
4-4-0 NBR Holmes

Class continued from 62072

Number	Built	Renumbered	BR Dates	Scrap	Notes
62281	05/90 Cow	08/49 62059	-12/52	01/53	
62282	09/90 Cow	06/49 62060	-02/50	05/50	
62283	11/99 Cow	06/49 62072	-02/51	51	

D9 62300-62333
4-4-0 GCR Robinson

Power Classification: 2P
Introduced: 1901-1904
Designer: Robinson
Company: GCR
Weight: Loco 55t 14cwt
Tender 48t 6cwt
Driving Wheel: 6' 9"
Boiler Pressure: 180psi superheated
Cylinders: Inside 19" x 26"
Tractive Effort: 17730lbf
Valve Gear: Stephenson (piston valves)

In 1901-1904 Robinson built forty handsome 4-4-0 engines for the GCR. They were originally built to work the London expresses, but they were displaced from these services by Atlantics in their early years. Four of the class were originally named. They were the GCR '11B', '11C' and '11D' classes.

In later years they were fitted with larger boilers and they were superheated. The first was withdrawn in 1939. Twenty-six survivors came into BR stock and they finished their days on the fast expresses on the Cheshire Lines route between Manchester and Liverpool.

Year End Totals: 'D9' class

'47	'48	'49	'50	'51	'52	'53	'54	'55	'56	'57	'58	'59	'60	'61	'62	'63	'64	'65	'66	'67
26	26	7																		

Number	Built	Renumbered	BR Dates	Scrap	Notes
62300	10/01 SS	03/48 2300	-11/49	12/49	
62301	10/01 SS	07/48 2301	-04/50	05/50	
62302	10/01 SS	09/48 2302	-03/50	09/50	
62303	10/01 SS	03/49 2303	-08/49	49	
62304	10/01 SS	03/49 2304	-01/50	50	
62305	02/02 SS	12/48 2305	-07/50	08/50	
62306	02/02 SS	2306	-01/49	49	
62307	02/02 SS	09/48 2307	-06/50	06/50	
QUEEN MARY					
62308	02/02 SS	06/48 2308	-08/49	49	
62309	02/02 SS	03/49 2309	-11/49	12/49	
62311	03/02 SS	03/49 2311	-07/49	07/49	
62312	03/02 SS	10/48 2312	-04/50	05/50	
62313	03/02 SS	03/48 2313	-10/49	49	
62314	03/02 SS	02/49 2314	-05/49	49	
62315	03/02 SS	06/48 2315	-07/49	07/49	
62317	03/02 SS	09/48 2317	-07/49	49	
62318	03/02 SS	02/49 2318	-11/49	12/49	
62319	04/02 SS	03/49 2319	-07/49	07/49	
62321	05/02 SS	03/49 2321	-10/49	49	
62322	03/03 SS	2322	-01/49	49	
62324	03/03 SS	03/49 2324	-11/49	12/49	
62325	03/03 SS	06/48 2325	-02/50	03/50	
62329	04/04 VF	2329	-02/49	49	
62330	04/04 VF	01/49 2330	-08/49	49	
62332	05/04 VF	2332	-09/49	49	
62333	05/04 VF	08/48 2333	-12/49	12/49	

D20 62340-62397
4-4-0 NER Worsdell

Power Classification: 2P
Introduced: 1899-1907
2 Rebuilt 1936-1948 by Gresley
Designer: W Worsdell
Company: NER
Weight: Loco 54t 2cwt
2 Loco 55t 9cwt
Tender 41t 4cwt
2 Tender 43t 0cwt
Driving Wheel: 6' 10"
Boiler Pressure: 175psi superheated
Cylinders: Inside 19" x 26"
Tractive Effort: 17025lbf
Valve Gear: Stephenson (piston valves)

Between 1899 and 1907 Wilson Worsdell built sixty engines of his 'R' class (LNER 'D20' class) for working the principal expresses over the East Coast main line between York and Newcastle. The later engines were built with superheaters and the earlier ones soon received them.

They were the most successful and economical of all the NER express engines and many drivers preferred them to the later and more powerful Atlantics. The first engine of the class was withdrawn in 1943.

In 1908-1909 Worsdell built a larger version known as the 'R1' class (LNER 'D21'). These were not successful and only ten engines were built, all being scrapped by 1946.

1 'D20/1' comprised the original engines which had been built or rebuilt with superheaters.

2 'D20/2' was the classification used for engines fitted with long travel piston valves.

r 62349 was rebuilt with raised framing over the coupled wheels.

Year End Totals: 'D20' class

'47	'48	'49	'50	'51	'52	'53	'54	'55	'56	'57	'58	'59	'60	'61	'62	'63	'64	'65	'66	'67
50	48	47	47	28	28	27	17	14	7											

Number	Built	Renumbered	BR Dates	Scrap	Notes
62340	08/99 Ghd	07/48 2340	-02/51	03/51	1
62341	09/99 Ghd	11/49 2341	-03/51	03/51	1
62342	09/99 Ghd	10/48 2342	-03/51	51	1
62343	10/99 Ghd	04/49 2343	-10/56	56	1
62344	11/99 Ghd	01/49 2344	-03/51	51	1
62345	11/99 Ghd	09/49 2345	-10/56	56	1
62347	12/99 Ghd	08/48 2347	-11/54	54	1
62348	12/99 Ghd	10/49 2348	-02/51	03/51	1
62349	12/99 Ghd	09/49 2349	-02/56	05/56	2r
62351	08/00 Ghd	12/48 2351	-11/54	54	1
62352	09/00 Ghd	10/49 2352	-06/54	54	1
62353	09/00 Ghd	01/49 2353	-04/51	05/51	1
62354	09/00 Ghd	10/49 2354	-04/51	51	1
62355	10/00 Ghd	03/50 2355	-11/55	55	1
62357	11/00 Ghd	10/49 2357	-01/51	51	1
62358	12/00 Ghd	09/49 2358	-10/54	11/54	1
62359	12/00 Ghd	02/49 2359	-10/55	55	1
62360	12/00 Ghd	07/52 2360	-10/56	56	2
62361	12/00 Ghd	2361	-02/51	03/51	1
62362	12/00 Ghd	06/49 2362	-04/51	51	1
62363	02/01 Ghd	01/49 2363	-03/51	51	1
62365	03/01 Ghd	12/48 2365	-04/51	51	1
62366	03/01 Ghd	09/48 2366	-03/51	51	1
62367	04/01 Ghd	2367	-01/48	48	1
62369	05/01 Ghd	11/49 2369	-03/51	03/51	1
62370	09/06 Ghd	2370	-04/51	51	1
62371	09/06 Ghd	10/48 2371	-10/54	11/54	2
62372	10/06 Ghd	10/52 2372	-11/56	56	1
62373	10/06 Ghd	10/48 2373	-02/53	04/53	1
62374	10/06 Ghd	05/50 2374	-10/54	11/54	1
62375	11/06 Ghd	10/48 2375	-05/57	05/57	1 10/48⇨2
62376	11/06 Ghd	2376	-02/51	03/51	1
62377	11/06 Ghd	2377	-05/49	05/49	1
62378	12/06 Ghd	02/49 2378	-11/56	01/57	1
62379	12/06 Ghd	08/48 2379	-04/51	05/51	1
62380	02/07 Ghd	10/49 2380	-09/54	10/54	1
62381	03/07 Ghd	04/50 2381	-11/57	12/57	1
62382	06/07 Ghd	2382	-02/51	03/51	1
62383	06/07 Ghd	09/49 2383	-05/57	05/57	1
62384	06/07 Ghd	09/50 2384	-08/55	09/55	1
62386	08/07 Ghd	06/50 2386	-10/56	56	1
62387	04/07 Ghd	05/48 2387	-09/57	12/57	1
62388	08/07 Ghd	04/48 2388	-04/54	07/54	1
62389	05/07 Ghd	07/48 2389	-09/54	10/54	1
62390	09/07 Ghd	2390	-11/48	12/48	1
62391	05/07 Ghd	11/48 2391	-06/51	08/51	1
62392	09/07 Ghd	11/48 2392	-05/54	07/54	1
62395	06/07 Ghd	07/53 2395	-11/57	02/58	1
62396	09/07 Ghd	10/48 2396	-11/57	12/57	1
62397	09/07 Ghd	05/49 2397	-02/57	57	1

D29 62400-62413
4-4-0 NBR Reid 'Scott'

Power Classification: 3P
Introduced: 1909-1911
Designer: Reid
Company: NBR
Weight: Loco 54t 4cwt
Tender 46t 0cwt
Driving Wheel: 6' 6"
Boiler Pressure: 190psi superheated
Cylinders: Inside 19" x 26"
Tractive Effort: 19435lbf
Valve Gear: Stephenson (piston valves)

This was the famous 'Scott' class which was built for hauling passenger trains on the NBR by Reid in 1909-1911. Sixteen engines were originally built with saturated boilers, but they were later superheated. They were known as the NBR 'J' class and they were withdrawn from 1947 onwards.

They were fine strong engines and they retained their North British appearance to the end. They were all named after characters in Sir Walter Scott's novels.

Reid later built the 'D30' class as an improved version of this class.

Year End Totals: 'D29' class

'47	'48	'49	'50	'51	'52	'53	'54	'55	'56	'57	'58	'59	'60	'61	'62	'63	'64	'65	'66	'67
12	9	5	3	2																

Number	Built	Renumbered	BR Dates	Scrap	Notes
62400 ROB ROY	07/09 NB	2400	-08/48	48	
62401 DANDIE DINMONT	07/09 NB	2401	-11/49	49	
62402 REDGAUNTLET	08/09 NB	2402	-06/49	49	
62403 SIR WALTER SCOTT	08/09 NB	2403	-03/48	48	
62404 JEANIE DEANS	08/09 NB	2404	-08/49	49	
62405 THE FAIR MAID	09/09 NB	03/49 2405	-02/51	51	
62406 MEG MERRILIES	09/11 Cow	2406	-10/49	49	
62409 HELEN MACGREGOR	10/11 Cow	2409	-10/48	10/48	
62410 IVANHOE	10/11 Cow	05/49 2410	-01/52	52	
62411 LADY OF AVENEL	11/11 Cow	07/48 2411	-10/52	53	
62412 DIRK HATTERAICK	12/11 Cow	02/49 2412	-09/50	09/50	
62413 GUY MANNERING	12/11 Cow	03/49 2413	-08/50	50	

D30 62417-62442
4-4-0 NBR Reid 'Scott'

Power Classification: 3P
Introduced: 1 1912
2 1914-1920
Designer: Reid
Company: NBR
Weight: 1 Loco 57t 6cwt
2 Loco 57t 16cwt
1 Tender 46t 0cwt
2 Tender 46t 13cwt
Driving Wheel: 6' 6"
Boiler Pressure: 165psi superheated
Cylinders: Inside 20" x 26"
Tractive Effort: 18700lbf
Valve Gear: Stephenson (piston valves)

In 1912 Reid built an improved version of the earlier 'D29' 'Scott' class. They were superheated and had larger cylinders with piston valves, but lower pressure boilers.

They were all named after characters in Sir Walter Scott's novels, and were also known as the 'Scott' class. A total of twenty-seven engines were built at Cowlairs. They were known as the NBR 'J' class and two of them were scrapped before nationalisation (the first in 1945). They outlived the earlier 'D29' class by several years.

Reid also built a mixed traffic version with smaller wheels known as the 'D34' 'Glen' class.

1 The first two engines built in 1912 were classified 'D30/1'. One of these two engines was scrapped before 1948.

2 The remainder of the class, which were built in 1914-1920, had detail differences and were known as 'D30/2'.

Year End Totals: 'D30' class

'47	'48	'49	'50	'51	'52	'53	'54	'55	'56	'57	'58	'59	'60	'61	'62	'63	'64	'65	'66	'67
25	25	25	25	24	24	24	24	24	24	16	6	2								

Number	Built	Renumbered	BR Dates	Scrap	Notes
62417 HAL O' THE WYND	10/12 Cow	05/48 2417	-01/51	51	1
62418 THE PIRATE	04/14 Cow	08/48 2418	-08/59	12/60	2
62419 MEG DODS	04/14 Cow	03/49 2419	-09/57	10/57	2
62420 DOMINIE SAMPSON	04/14 Cow	10/48 2420	-05/57	05/57	2
62421 LAIRD O' MONKBARNS	04/14 Cow	05/48 2421	-06/60	08/60	2
62422 CALEB BALDERSTONE	05/14 Cow	12/49 2422	-12/58	02/60	2
62423 DUGALD DALGETTY	06/14 Cow	12/48 2423	-12/57	01/58	2
62424 CLAVERHOUSE	06/14 Cow	05/48 2424	-08/57	12/57	2
62425 ELLANGOWAN	06/14 Cow	02/49 2425	-08/58	02/60	2
62426 CUDDIE HEADRIGG	07/14 Cow	02/49 2426	-06/60	08/60	2
62427 DUMBIEDYKES	07/14 Cow	11/48 2427	-04/59	09/59	2
62428 THE TALISMAN	09/14 Cow	09/49 2428	-12/58	02/60	2
62429 THE ABBOT	10/14 Cow	01/50 2429	-09/57	09/57	2
62430 JINGLING GEORDIE	10/14 Cow	05/50 2430	-01/57	03/57	2
62431 KENILWORTH	10/14 Cow	03/50 2431	-11/58	02/60	2
62432 QUENTIN DURWARD	10/14 Cow	03/48 2432	-12/58	02/60	2
62434 KETTLEDRUMMLE	07/15 Cow	05/48 2434	-05/58	07/58	2
62435 NORNA	07/15 Cow	04/50 2435	-12/57	12/57	2
62436 LORD GLENVARLOCH	08/15 Cow	07/48 2436	-06/59	02/60	2
62437 ADAM WOODCOCK	08/15 Cow	10/50 2437	-06/58	11/58	2
62438 PETER POUNDTEXT	12/20 Cow	02/49 2438	-11/57	12/57	2
62439 FATHER AMBROSE	11/20 Cow	07/48 2439	-09/59	02/60	2
62440 WANDERING WILLIE	11/20 Cow	06/49 2440	-08/58	02/60	2
62441 BLACK DUNCAN	11/20 Cow	03/49 2441	-09/58	02/60	2
62442 SIMON GLOVER	12/20 Cow	11/48 2442	-06/58	02/60	2

D32 62443-62454
4-4-0 NBR Reid 'Intermediates'

Power Classification: 3P
Introduced: 1906
Designer: Reid
Company: NBR
Weight: Loco 53t 14cwt
Tender 40t 0cwt
Driving Wheel: 6' 0"
Boiler Pressure: 180psi superheated
Cylinders: Inside 19" x 26"
Tractive Effort: 19945lbf
Valve Gear: Stephenson (piston valves)

The 'D32' class consisted of twelve engines which were built by Reid for the NBR in 1906 as the NBR 'K' class. They were originally built with saturated boilers, later being superheated. They were almost identical in appearance to the slightly heavier 'D33' class and they were all scrapped between 1947 and 1951.

Year End Totals: 'D32' class

'47	'48	'49	'50	'51	'52	'53	'54	'55	'56	'57	'58	'59	'60	'61	'62	'63	'64	'65	'66	'67
10	2	1	1																	

Number	Built	Renumbered	BR Dates	Scrap	Notes
62443	10/06 Cow	2443	-03/48	48	
62444	11/06 Cow	2444	-09/48	48	
62445	11/06 Cow	2445	-12/49	50	
62446	12/06 Cow	2446	-09/48	10/48	
62448	12/06 Cow	2448	-09/48	48	
62449	12/06 Cow	2449	-11/48	11/48	
62450	12/06 Cow	2450	-02/48	48	
62451	01/07 Cow	02/49 2451	-03/51	51	
62453	01/07 Cow	2453	-05/48	48	
62454	01/07 Cow	2454	-09/48	10/48	

D33 62455-62466
4-4-0 NBR Reid

Power Classification: 3P
Introduced: 1909-1910
Designer: Reid
Company: NBR
Weight: Loco 54t 3cwt
Tender 44t 11cwt
Driving Wheel: 6' 0"

Boiler Pressure:	180psi superheated
Cylinders:	Inside 19" x 26"
Tractive Effort:	19945lbf
Valve Gear:	Stephenson (piston valves)

The 'D33' class was a slightly heavier version of the 'D32' class, to which they were almost identical in appearance. Twelve engines were built by Reid for the NBR in 1909-1910 as the NBR 'K' class. Originally built with saturated boilers, they were later superheated and they were all withdrawn between 1947 and 1953.

Year End Totals: 'D33' class

'47	'48	'49	'50	'51	'52	'53	'54	'55	'56	'57	'58	'59	'60	'61	'62	'63	'64	'65	'66	'67
10	9	7	7	3	1															

Number	*Built*	*Renumbered*	*BR Dates*	*Scrap*	*Notes*
62455	10/09 Cow	09/48 2455	-12/49	*50*	
62457	11/09 Cow	04/48 2457	-06/52	*03/53*	
62458	11/09 Cow	2458	-09/49	*11/49*	
62459	11/09 Cow	05/48 2459	-10/51	*51*	
62460	10/09 Cow	06/49 2460	-08/51	*51*	
62461	12/09 Cow	07/49 2461	-06/51	*51*	
62462	12/09 Cow	12/49 2462	-11/52	*12/52*	
62463	12/09 Cow	2463	-03/48	*48*	
62464	01/10 Cow	02/49 2464	-09/53	02/54	
62466	02/10 Cow	12/48 2466	-09/51	*51*	

D34 62467-62498, 256
4-4-0 NBR Reid 'Glen'

Power Classification:	3P
Introduced:	1913-1920
Designer:	Reid
Company:	NBR
Weight:	Loco 57t 4cwt Tender 46t 13cwt
Driving Wheel:	6' 0"
Boiler Pressure:	165psi superheated
Cylinders:	Inside 20" x 26"
Tractive Effort:	20260lbf
Valve Gear:	Stephenson (piston valves)

The North British 'Glen' class consisted of thirty-two engines which were built at Cowlairs in 1913-1920. They were the NBR 'K' class (later becoming LNER 'D34' class) and they were a mixed traffic version of the superheated 'Scotts' ('D30' class). Two engines were withdrawn before 1948 (the first in 1946), the rest coming into BR stock.

In April 1959 62469 was restored to working order in NBR livery as NBR 256 GLEN DOUGLAS. (It was not withdrawn from stock, but instead was officially renumbered in November 1959.) It worked rail tours for a few years before being retired to Glasgow Museum as a static exhibit.

Year End Totals: 'D34' class

'47	'48	'49	'50	'51	'52	'53	'54	'55	'56	'57	'58	'59	'60	'61	'62	'63	'64	'65	'66	'67
30	30	28	27	27	27	27	27	27	27	27	26	14	6	1						

Number	*Built*	*Renumbered*	*BR Dates*	*Scrap*	*Notes*
62467	09/13 Cow	04/48 2467	-08/60	11/60	
GLENFINNAN					
62468	09/13 Cow	11/48 2468	-09/58	10/59	
GLEN ORCHY					
62469 §	09/13 Cow	12/49 2469	-11/59	11/59➔256	
GLEN DOUGLAS					
62470	09/13 Cow	09/48 2470	-05/59	02/60	
GLEN ROY					
62471	10/13 Cow	03/49 2471	-03/60	07/60	
GLEN FALLOCH					
62472	12/13 Cow	10/49 2472	-09/59	02/60	
GLEN NEVIS					
62473	12/13 Cow	2473	-05/49	*49*	
GLEN SPEAN					
62474	12/13 Cow	03/50 2474	-05/61	07/61	
GLEN CROE					
62475	12/13 Cow	05/50 2475	-06/59	02/60	
GLEN BEASDALE					
62476	12/13 Cow	2476	-02/50	*50*	
GLEN SLOY					
62477	05/17 Cow	05/50 2477	-10/59	02/60	
GLEN DOCHART					
62478	05/17 Cow	11/48 2478	-12/59	04/60	
GLEN QUOICH					
62479	05/17 Cow	03/48 2479	-05/61	08/61	
GLEN SHEIL					
62480	06/17 Cow	12/49 2480	-09/59	03/60	
GLEN FRUIN					
62481	07/17 Cow	2481	-09/49	*11/49*	
GLEN OGLE					
62482	03/19 Cow	04/48 2482	-03/60	07/60	
GLEN MAMIE					
62483	03/19 Cow	12/48 2483	-04/59	09/59	
GLEN GARRY					
62484	04/19 Cow	11/49 2484	-11/61	05/63	
GLEN LYON					
62485	04/19 Cow	05/48 2485	-03/60	06/60	
GLEN MURRAN					
62487	05/20 Cow	12/48 2487	-09/59	02/60	
GLEN ARKLET					
62488	04/20 Cow	05/48 2488	-10/60	01/61	
GLEN ALADALE					
62489	05/20 Cow	02/50 2489	-12/59	07/60	
GLEN DESSARY					
62490	05/20 Cow	06/49 2490	-02/59	02/60	
GLEN FINTAIG					
62492	06/20 Cow	04/49 2492	-06/59	02/60	
GLEN GARVIN					
62493	06/20 Cow	08/50 2493	-06/60	10/60	
GLEN GLOY					
62494	07/20 Cow	09/48 2494	-04/59	08/59	
GLEN GOUR					
62495	07/20 Cow	12/48 2495	-04/61	05/61	
GLEN LUSS					
62496	08/20 Cow	06/48 2496	-12/61	09/62	
GLEN LOY					
62497	08/20 Cow	04/48 2497	-02/60	08/60	
GLEN MALLIE					
62498	09/20 Cow	04/48 2498	-03/60	07/60	
GLEN MOIDART					

Class continued with 256 (Preserved Locomotives)

D15 between 62501 & 62538
4-4-0 GER Holden 'Claud Hamilton'

D16 between 62510 & 62620
4-4-0 GER 'Super Claud' and 'Rebuilt Claud'

Power Classification:	2P reclassified 3P in 1953
Introduced:	1900-1911 2 Built or rebuilt 1923-1930 by Hill 3 Rebuilt 1933-1949 by Gresley
Designer:	J Holden
Company:	GER
Weight:	2 Loco 54t 18cwt 3 Loco 55t 18cwt D15 Loco 52t 4cwt Tender 39t 5cwt
Driving Wheel:	7' 0"
Boiler Pressure:	180psi superheated
Cylinders:	Inside 19" x 26"
Tractive Effort:	17095lbf
Valve Gear:	Stephenson (slide valves) pq Stephenson (piston valves)

The first engine of this famous class was built by James Holden at Stratford. It was numbered after the year of its birth (1900), named CLAUD HAMILTON, and it was exhibited at Paris. It was followed in succession by batches of ten engines which were numbered in reverse order (that is, 1890-1899, 1880-1889 down to LNER-built E1780-1789 in 1923, by which time 121 engines had been built). They were very handsome engines with decorative framing over the coupling rods, and they did fine work on the tightly timed trains on the GER main line.

The first batch of engines which were built in 1900-1903 were the GER 'S46' class (LNER 'D14'). They had 4' 9" diameter round topped boilers. Class 'D56' soon followed (LNER 'D15'), these being engines with Belpaire boilers built 1904-1911. The final batch of ten engines were built in 1923 by Hill as the GER class 'H88' (LNER 'D16'). These were engines fitted with 5' 1" diameter superheated Belpaire boilers (the 'Super Clauds').

The original engine was withdrawn as 'D16/3' No. 2500 in 1947, and its name was transferred to 62546. 117 out of the original 121 engines came into BR stock.

There was subsequently a large amount of rebuilding of the various members of the class and this is summarised below.

D15 These engines were the surviving 'D15' engines, which included the earlier 'D14's rebuilt with Belpaire boilers. Many of these engines were later rebuilt to 'D16/2' and 'D16/3'. (Originally the 'D15' class was split into three parts, 'D15' being saturated boiler engines, 'D15/1' superheated with short smokeboxes and 'D15/2' superheated with extended smokeboxes. All the remaining engines were converted to 'D15/2' and were then simply known as 'D15'.)

f 62507 was the only 'D15' engine which had the decorative framing over the coupling rods removed.

1 'D16/1' was used for the original 'D16's with short smokeboxes. They were all later rebuilt with longer smokeboxes as 'D16/2'.

2 'D16/2' (the 'Super Clauds') comprised the 1923 built engines which had been built with larger superheated Belpaire boilers, together with a number of similar rebuilds from the earlier 'D15' class. Many of these were later rebuilt to 'D16/3', including some in BR days.

3 The 'D16/3' engines (the 'Rebuilt Clauds') were introduced by Gresley in 1933. They were rebuilds of 'D14', 'D15' and 'D16/2' engines with superheated round topped boilers.

There were a number of variations in this class as shown below.

a 'D16/3's which were rebuilt from 'D15's from, 1933 onwards.

b 'D16/3's which were rebuilt from 'D16/2's, from 1938 onwards.

m Many 'D16/3's (including all those rebuilt from 'D15' engines) had modified splashers and framing, with the decorative framing over the coupling rods being removed.

p Engines fitted with 8" piston valves when converted from 'D15' to 'D16/3'.

q Engines fitted with 9½" piston valves when converted from 'D15' to 'D16/3'.

Year End Totals: 'D15' class

'47	'48	'49	'50	'51	'52	'53	'54	'55	'56	'57	'58	'59	'60	'61	'62	'63	'64	'65	'66	'67
13	12	12	10	5																

Year End Totals: 'D16/2' class

'47	'48	'49	'50	'51	'52	'53	'54	'55	'56	'57	'58	'59	'60	'61	'62	'63	'64	'65	'66	'67
16	10	4	3	1																

Year End Totals: 'D16/3' class

'47	'48	'49	'50	'51	'52	'53	'54	'55	'56	'57	'58	'59	'60	'61	'62	'63	'64	'65	'66	'67
88	89	94	94	94	92	90	90	75	67	39	17	4								

Number	*Built*	*Renumbered*	*BR Dates*	*Scrap*	*Notes*
62501	04/00 Str	08/49 2501	-06/51	*51*	D15
62502	04/00 Str	03/50 2502	-02/52	*52*	D15
62503	04/00 Str	11/48 2503	-02/51	*51*	D15
62504	05/00 Str	2504	-06/48	*48*	D15
62505	05/00 Str	10/49 2505	-11/51	*51*	D15
62506	06/00 Str	02/50 2506	-04/52	*52*	D15
62507	06/00 Str	10/49 2507	-04/52	*52*	D15f
62508	06/00 Str	11/48 2508	-10/50	*50*	D15
62509	07/00 Str	04/48 2509	-09/52	*52*	D15
62510	07/00 Str	02/49 2510	-09/57	11/57	3am
62511	04/01 Str	05/49 2511	-12/59	01/60	3am
62512	05/01 Str	05/48 2512	-08/50	*50*	D15
62513	05/01 Str	10/49 2513	-10/58	12/58	3am
62514	05/01 Str	01/49 2514	-03/57	06/57	3am
62515	05/01 Str	09/48 2515	-04/58	06/58	3am
62516	05/01 Str	02/49 2516	-08/57	09/57	3am
62517	06/01 Str	01/49 2517	-09/59	11/59	3am
62518	06/01 Str	12/48 2518	-10/58	12/58	3am
62519	06/01 Str	03/49 2519	-01/57	03/57	3am
62520	06/01 Str	12/48 2520	-09/51	*04/52*	D15
62521	03/02 Str	08/49 2521	-01/58	04/58	3am
62522	03/02 Str	03/49 2522	-08/58	10/58	3am
62523	03/02 Str	05/48 2523	-08/56	*01/57*	3am
62524	03/02 Str	12/50 2524	-03/60	05/60	3am
62525	03/02 Str	05/49 2525	-09/55	*55*	3am
62526	04/02 Str	07/48 2526	-05/57	09/57	3am
62527	04/02 Str	08/48 2527	-07/52	*52*	3am
62528	04/02 Str	10/48 2528	-06/51	*51*	D15
62529	05/02 Str	04/50 2529	-12/59	01/60	3am
62530	05/02 Str	10/48 2530	-09/58	11/58	3am
62531	05/03 Str	08/48 2531	-03/55	*55*	3am
62532	05/03 Str	07/48 2532	-11/56	*56*	3amq
62533	05/03 Str	06/49 2533	-09/57	12/57	3am
62534	06/03 Str	12/48 2534	-10/58	02/59	3am
62535	06/03 Str	08/48 2535	-11/57	01/58	3amq
62536	09/03 Str	03/48 2536	-07/55	*01/56*	3amq
62538	10/03 Str	08/48 2538	-04/52	*52*	D15
62539	10/03 Str	04/49 2539	-10/57	12/57	3am
62540	11/03 Str	11/48 2540	-08/59	09/59	3am
62541	12/03 Str	04/49 2541	-10/55	*55*	3am
62542	12/03 Str	10/48 2542	-09/56	*56*	3b
62543	12/03 Str	05/48 2543	-10/58	12/58	2 02/49➔3b
62544	12/03 Str	07/48 2544	-12/59	01/60	3b
62545	01/04 Str	02/49 2545	-09/58	12/58	3am

Number	Built	Renumbered	BR Dates	Scrap	Notes
62546	02/04 Str	10/48 2546	-06/57	09/57	3amp
CLAUD HAMILTON					
62547	03/04 Str	06/48 2547	-02/51	51	2
62548	03/04 Str	06/48 2548	-09/57	11/57	3am
62549	03/04 Str	02/49 2549	-12/55	56	3am
62551	11/06 Str	04/49 2551	-07/56	56	3am
62552	11/06 Str	02/49 2552	-10/55	55	2 01/49⇨3b
62553	11/06 Str	05/48 2553	-01/57	03/57	2 08/49⇨3b
62554	11/06 Str	06/49 2554	-11/55	55	3b
62555	11/06 Str	05/48 2555	-03/58	04/58	3am
62556	11/06 Str	05/48 2556	-01/57	02/57	3b
62557	12/06 Str	06/49 2557	-10/55	55	3b
62558	12/06 Str	09/48 2558	-05/57	07/57	2 09/48⇨3b
62559	01/07 Str	03/49 2559	-12/55	56	3am
62560	01/07 Str	2560	-09/48	48	3amp
62561	03/08 Str	02/49 2561	-02/58	04/58	3am
62562	03/08 Str	05/48 2562	-09/57	11/57	3b
62563	03/08 Str	2563	-08/48	48	3amq
62564	04/08 Str	02/50 2564	-03/58	04/58	2 01/48⇨3b
62565	04/08 Str	08/49 2565	-01/57	02/57	3b
62566	05/08 Str	10/48 2566	-12/58	12/58	3am
62567	05/08 Str	04/49 2567	-12/56	57	3am
62568	06/08 Str	04/48 2568	-04/58	07/58	3amp
62569	07/08 Str	04/48 2569	-11/56	56	2 04/48⇨3b
62570	07/08 Str	09/49 2570	-12/59	01/60	2 09/49⇨3b
62571	06/09 Str	09/48 2571	-01/59	02/59	3am
62572	06/09 Str	08/49 2572	-07/58	12/58	3am
62573	09/09 Str	04/49 2573	-10/55	55	3b
62574	11/09 Str	04/48 2574	-12/55	56	3am
62575	11/09 Str	12/48 2575	-05/57	08/57	3am
62576	11/09 Str	06/48 2576	-09/57	10/57	3amq
62577	12/09 Str	05/49 2577	-10/56	56	2 04/49⇨3b
62578	12/09 Str	04/48 2578	-09/57	11/57	3b
62579	12/09 Str	06/48 2579	-03/55	55	3am
62580	12/09 Str	04/48 2580	-06/58	07/58	2 04/48⇨3b
62581	03/10 Str	08/48 2581	-03/53	53	3amq
62582	03/10 Str	01/50 2582	-01/59	04/59	3am
62583	03/10 Str	2583	-11/48	48	3amq
62584	04/10 Str	04/50 2584	-12/57	02/58	3b
62585	04/10 Str	05/49 2585	-04/55	55	3am
62586	05/10 Str	08/50 2586	-03/58	04/58	3am
62587	06/10 Str	04/48 2587	-12/56	57	3amp
62588	06/10 Str	08/48 2588	-10/58	11/59	3amp
62589	06/10 Str	02/49 2589	-08/59	09/59	3b
62590	06/10 Str	09/49 2590	-01/52	52	2
62591	07/10 Str	04/49 2591	-04/50	50	2
62592	07/10 Str	11/49 2592	-04/58	07/58	3b
62593	08/10 Str	01/50 2593	-09/57	11/57	3am
62594	08/10 Str	2594	-03/49	49	3amq
62596	09/10 Str	04/49 2596	-10/57	11/57	3b
62597	09/10 Str	01/50 2597	-01/60	01/60	3am
62598	10/10 Str	06/49 2598	-05/52	52	3am
62599	10/10 Str	11/49 2599	-09/58	01/59	3amq
62600	11/10 Str	2600	-06/48	48	3amp
62601	02/11 Str	04/50 2601	-01/57	02/57	3b
62602	03/11 Str	2602	-09/48	48	3amq
62603	03/11 Str	04/48 2603	-09/51	51	2
62604	04/11 Str	06/48 2604	-01/60	03/60	3am
62605	05/11 Str	10/48 2605	-06/57	08/57	3b
62606	07/11 Str	06/50 2606	-09/59	11/59	3b
62607	07/11 Str	01/49 2607	-11/55	55	3b
62608	07/11 Str	08/49 2608	-01/57	02/57	3am
62609	08/11 Str	04/48 2609	-02/57	02/57	3amp
62610	08/11 Str	12/49 2610	-01/59	02/59	3am
62611	06/23 Str	12/48 2611	-01/57	02/57	3b
62612	06/23 Str	04/49 2612	-12/59	01/60	2 04/49⇨3b
62613	06/23 Str	12/48 2613	-11/60	12/60	2 12/48⇨3b
62614	07/23 Str	11/49 2614	-07/58	01/59	3bm
62615	07/23 Str	03/49 2615	-10/58	12/58	3b
62616	07/23 Str	11/48 2616	-02/53	53	3b
62617	08/23 Str	09/48 2617	-05/57	09/57	3b
62618	08/23 Str	10/49 2618	-12/59	12/59	3b
62619	09/23 Str	10/50 2619	-09/57	02/58	3b
62620	09/23 Str	52 2620	-10/55	55	2 03/48⇨3b

D10 62650-62659
4-4-0 GCR Robinson 'Director'

Power Classification: 3P
Introduced: 1913
Designer: Robinson
Company: GCR
Weight: Loco 61t 0cwt
Tender 48t 6cwt
Driving Wheel: 6' 9"
Boiler Pressure: 180psi superheated
Cylinders: Inside 20" x 26"
Tractive Effort: 19645lbf
Valve Gear: Stephenson (piston valves)

One of the most handsome British designs of 4-4-0 was the 'Director' class, consisting of ten engines built by Robinson for the GCR. They were built at Gorton in 1913 and they were GCR class '11E'. They carried the names of the Directors of the GCR, hence the class name, and they were designed for working fast passenger trains.

The engines were originally built with straight framing and coupling rod splashers, but these were later cut away to improve access to the coupling rods.

62650 was originally named SIR ALEXANDER HENDERSON until 1917 and then SIR DOUGLAS HAIG until 1920. 62658 was named CHARLES STUART HENRY until 1920.

An enlarged version of the class appeared in 1920 known as the 'Large Director' (see 'D11' class below).

Year End Totals: 'D10' class

'47	'48	'49	'50	'51	'52	'53	'54	'55	'56	'57	'58	'59	'60	'61	'62	'63	'64	'65	'66	'67
10	10	10	10	10	10	6	3													

Number	Built	Renumbered	BR Dates	Scrap	Notes
62650	08/13 Gor	03/49 2650	-02/54	54	
PRINCE HENRY					
62651	09/13 Gor	08/48 2651	-02/53	53	
PURDON VICCARS					
62652	10/13 Gor	02/49 2652	-05/54	54	
EDWIN A. BEAZLEY					
62653	10/13 Gor	11/48 2653	-09/55	11/55	
SIR EDWARD FRASER					
62654	10/13 Gor	49 2654	-08/53	53	
WALTER BURGH GAIR					
62655	11/13 Gor	03/49 2655	-08/53	53	
THE EARL OF KERRY					
62656	11/13 Gor	05/48 2656	-01/55	02/55	
SIR CLEMENT ROYDS					
62657	11/13 Gor	07/49 2657	-02/53	05/53	
SIR BERKELEY SHEFFIELD					
62658	11/13 Gor	08/48 2658	-08/55	11/55	
PRINCE GEORGE					
62659	12/13 Gor	50 2659	-11/54	02/55	
WORSLEY-TAYLOR					

D11 62660-62694
4-4-0 GCR Robinson 'Large Director'

Power Classification: 3P
Introduced: 1920-1924
Designer: Robinson
Company: GCR
Weight: Loco 61t 3cwt
Tender 48t 6cwt
Driving Wheel: 6' 9"
Boiler Pressure: 180psi superheated
Cylinders: Inside 20" x 26"
Tractive Effort: 19645lbf
Valve Gear: Stephenson (piston valves)

The 'Large' or 'Improved Director' class appeared in 1920-1924. Originally GCR class '11F' (LNER 'D11'), they were slightly heavier than the 'D10's and had deeper frames, side window cabs and a higher pitched boiler.

The engines were originally built with straight framing and coupling rod splashers, but these were later cut away to improve access to the coupling rods.

1 'D11/1' comprised the 1920-1922 batch of eleven engines built for the GCR. They had horizontal nameplates on the edge of the splashers.

2 After grouping Gresley received a request for some more 'D30' 'Scott' engines to work in Scotland. He decided that the GCR 'Directors' would be a more suitable design and another batch of twenty-four of these engines was built in 1924. They were known as 'D11/2' and they had cut down boiler mountings for the Scottish gauge. The 'Scottish Directors' were given names from the Sir Walter Scott novels, and the names were painted on the splashers in typical NBR style.

Year End Totals: 'D11' class

'47	'48	'49	'50	'51	'52	'53	'54	'55	'56	'57	'58	'59	'60	'61	'62	'63	'64	'65	'66	'67
35	35	35	35	35	35	35	35	35	35	35	33	24	14	1						

Number	Built	Renumbered	BR Dates	Scrap	Notes
62660 §	12/19 Gor	09/49 2660	-10/60		1
BUTLER-HENDERSON					
62661	02/20 Gor	12/48 2661	-11/60	12/60	1
GERARD POWYS DEWHURST					
62662	03/20 Gor	05/49 2662	-08/60	08/60	1
PRINCE OF WALES					
62663	03/20 Gor	08/49 2663	-05/60	06/60	1
PRINCE ALBERT					
62664	05/20 Gor	04/48 2664	-08/60	08/60	1
PRINCESS MARY					
62665	09/22 Gor	06/48 2665	-05/59	07/59	1
MONS					
62666	10/22 Gor	09/49 2666	-12/60	12/60	1
ZEEBRUGGE					
62667	11/22 Gor	10/49 2667	-08/60	08/60	1
SOMME					
62668	11/22 Gor	05/48 2668	-11/60	11/60	1
JUTLAND					
62669	12/22 Gor	02/49 2669	-08/60	08/60	1
YPRES					
62670	12/22 Gor	04/49 2670	-11/60	01/61	1
MARNE					
62671	07/24 K	04/48 2671	-05/61	06/61	2
BAILIE MACWHEEBLE					
62672	08/24 K	09/51 2672	-08/61	09/61	2
BARON OF BRADWARDINE					
62673	08/24 K	11/48 2673	-07/59	08/59	2
EVAN DHU					
62674	08/24 K	03/49 2674	-07/61	01/62	2
FLORA MACIVOR					
62675	08/24 K	05/49 2675	-10/59	01/60	2
COLONEL GARDINER					
62676	08/24 K	08/48 2676	-10/59	02/60	2
JONATHAN OLDBUCK					
62677	09/24 K	04/48 2677	-08/59	11/59	2
EDIE OCHILTREE					
62678	09/24 K	05/49 2678	-03/59	02/60	2
LUCKIE MUCKLEBACKIT					
62679	10/24 K	11/50 2679	-09/58	09/59	2
LORD GLENALLAN					
62680	10/24 K	02/49 2680	-08/61	09/61	2
LUCY ASHTON					
62681	10/24 K	08/49 2681	-07/61	08/61	2
CAPTAIN CRAIGENGELT					
62682	10/24 K	06/49 2682	-07/61	09/61	2
HAYSTOUN OF BUCKLAW					
62683	10/24 AW	05/48 2683	-10/58	03/59	2
HOBBIE ELLIOTT					
62684	10/24 AW	02/50 2684	-10/59	02/60	2
WIZARD OF THE MOOR					
62685	10/24 AW	05/49 2685	-01/62	07/63	2
MALCOLM GRAEME					
62686	10/24 AW	07/48 2686	-07/61	08/62	2
THE FIERY CROSS					
62687	10/24 AW	09/49 2687	-08/61	01/62	2
LORD JAMES OF DOUGLAS					
62688	11/24 AW	09/48 2688	-07/61	09/61	2
ELLEN DOUGLAS					
62689	11/24 AW	07/49 2689	-07/61	08/61	2
MAID OF LORN					
62690	11/24 AW	07/48 2690	-07/61	09/61	2
THE LADY OF THE LAKE					
62691	11/24 AW	01/50 2691	-12/61	03/63	2
LAIRD OF BALMAWHAPPLE					
62692	11/24 AW	01/49 2692	-11/59	02/60	2
ALLAN-BANE					
62693	11/24 AW	05/49 2693	-12/61	03/63	2
RODERICK DHU					
62694	11/24 AW	02/50 2694	-11/59	02/60	2
JAMES FITZJAMES					

D49 62700-62775
4-4-0 LNER Gresley 'Shire' & 'Hunt'

Power Classification: 4P
Introduced: 1 1927-1929
2 1928-1935
4 Rebuilt 1942 by Thompson
Designer: Gresley
Company: LNER
Weight: 1 Loco 66t 0cwt
2 Loco 64t 10cwt
4 Loco 62t 0cwt
l Tender 52t 0cwt
g Tender 48t 6cwt
n Tender 44t 2cwt
Driving Wheel: 6' 8"
Boiler Pressure: 180psi superheated
Cylinders: 12 Three 17" x 26"
4 Inside 20" x 26"
Tractive Effort: 12 21555lbf
4 19890lbf

Valve Gear:	1 Walschaert with derived motion (piston valves)
	2 Lenz rotary cam (poppet valves)
	4 Stephenson (piston valves)
	v Reidinger rotary valve gear

Between 1927 and 1935 Gresley built seventy-six 'D49' three-cylinder 4-4-0s at Darlington. They were intended for intermediate express work on the North Eastern and North British sections of the LNER.

1 The first thirty-six engines built in 1927-1929 were named after counties and they were known as the 'Shire' class ('D49/1'). Apart from 62726 and 62727 (see 'D49/2' below) they were fitted with Walschaert valve gear with piston valves.

2 In 1929 two engines (62726 and 62727) were fitted with Lenz rotary cam poppet valves. Further engines built in 1932-1935 were similarly equipped and these engines were named after Hunts. The two altered 'Shires' had their names changed in 1932 (originally named LEICESTERSHIRE and BUCKINGHAMSHIRE respectively) and the whole series was known as the 'D49/2' 'Hunt' class. 62751-62775 had larger valves than the others and they were originally classified 'D49/4'.

3 62720-62725 were built with Lenz oscillating cam poppet valves and were originally known as 'D49/3'. From 1938 these were all converted to piston valve engines ('D49/1').

4 62768 was rebuilt by Thompson in 1942 with two inside cylinders of the 'D11' pattern. This was the only engine to be converted and it was withdrawn prematurely in 1952 after sustaining collision damage. It was classified 'D49/4'.

v In 1949 62763 and 62764 were fitted experimentally with Reidinger rotary valve gear.

g Engines fitted with GCR 4000 gallon tenders.

n Engines fitted with NER 4125 gallon tenders.

l Engines fitted with LNER standard 4200 gallon tenders.

Year End Totals: 'D49/1' class

'47	'48	'49	'50	'51	'52	'53	'54	'55	'56	'57	'58	'59	'60	'61	'62	'63	'64	'65	'66	'67
34	34	34	34	34	34	34	34	34	34	32	22	12	9							

Year End Totals: 'D49/2' class

'47	'48	'49	'50	'51	'52	'53	'54	'55	'56	'57	'58	'59	'60	'61	'62	'63	'64	'65	'66	'67
41	41	41	41	41	41	41	41	41	41	36	16	10	5							

Year End Totals: 'D49/4' class

'47	'48	'49	'50	'51	'52	'53	'54	'55	'56	'57	'58	'59	'60	'61	'62	'63	'64	'65	'66	'67
1	1	1	1	1																

Number	*Built*	*Renumbered*	*BR Dates*	*Scrap*	*Notes*
62700 YORKSHIRE	10/27 Dar	03/49 2700	-09/58	11/58	1g
62701 DERBYSHIRE	11/28 Dar	06/48 2701	-09/59	10/59	1g
62702 OXFORDSHIRE	11/27 Dar	03/50 2702	-10/58	01/59	1g
62703 HERTFORDSHIRE	12/27 Dar	04/49 2703	-05/58	08/58	1n
62704 STIRLINGSHIRE	12/27 Dar	07/48 2704	-09/58	09/58	1g
62705 LANARKSHIRE	12/27 Dar	05/48 2705	-11/59	01/60	1g
62706 FORFARSHIRE	12/27 Dar	09/48 2706	-02/58	02/58	1g
62707 LANCASHIRE	01/28 Dar	05/48 2707	-10/59	10/59	1g
62708 ARGYLLSHIRE	01/28 Dar	03/50 2708	-05/59	05/59	1g
62709 BERWICKSHIRE	01/28 Dar	03/50 2709	-01/60	01/60	1g
62710 LINCOLNSHIRE	02/28 Dar	10/48 2710	-10/60	10/60	1g
62711 DUMBARTONSHIRE	02/28 Dar	10/48 2711	-05/61	06/61	1g
62712 § MORAYSHIRE	02/28 Dar	03/50 2712	-07/61		1g
62713 ABERDEENSHIRE	02/28 Dar	07/48 2713	-09/57	10/57	1g
62714 PERTHSHIRE	03/28 Dar	10/49 2714	-08/59	10/59	1g
62715 ROXBURGHSHIRE	03/28 Dar	02/49 2715	-06/59	07/59	1g
62716 KINCARDINESHIRE	03/28 Dar	03/50 2716	-04/61	05/61	1g
62717 BANFFSHIRE	03/28 Dar	09/50 2717	-01/61	02/61	1g
62718 KINROSS-SHIRE	05/28 Dar	01/49 2718	-04/61	05/61	1g
62719 PEEBLES-SHIRE	05/28 Dar	03/49 2719	-01/60	01/60	1g
62720 CAMBRIDGESHIRE	05/28 Dar	05/49 2720	-10/59	10/59	1n
62721 WARWICKSHIRE	05/28 Dar	03/49 2721	-09/58	09/58	1n
62722 HUNTINGDONSHIRE	07/28 Dar	05/48 2722	-10/59	12/59	1n
62723 NOTTINGHAMSHIRE	07/28 Dar	10/48 2723	-01/61	02/61	1n
62724 BEDFORDSHIRE	08/28 Dar	05/48 2724	-12/57	02/58	1n
62725 INVERNESS-SHIRE	08/28 Dar	03/50 2725	-11/58	11/58	1g
62726 THE MEYNELL	03/29 Dar	06/49 2726	-12/57	03/58	2l
62727 THE QUORN	06/29 Dar	08/50 2727	-01/61	04/61	2n
62728 CHESHIRE	02/29 Dar	05/48 2728	-10/59	11/59	1g
62729 RUTLANDSHIRE	04/29 Dar	09/48 2729	-05/61	05/61	1g
62730 BERKSHIRE	03/29 Dar	10/48 2730	-12/58	05/59	1g
62731 SELKIRKSHIRE	03/29 Dar	10/48 2731	-04/59	04/59	1g
62732 DUMFRIES-SHIRE	03/29 Dar	10/48 2732	-10/58	11/58	1g
62733 NORTHUMBERLAND	03/29 Dar	04/48 2733	-04/61	05/61	1g
62734 CUMBERLAND	05/29 Dar	10/48 2734	-03/61	03/61	1g
62735 WESTMORLAND	06/29 Dar	10/48 2735	-09/58	11/58	1g
62736 THE BRAMHAM MOOR	04/32 Dar	10/50 2736	-06/58	08/58	2l
62737 THE YORK AND AINSTY	05/32 Dar	05/48 2737	-01/58	02/58	2l
62738 THE ZETLAND	05/32 Dar	02/49 2738	-09/59	10/59	2l
62739 THE BADSWORTH	05/32 Dar	02/50 2739	-10/60	11/60	2l
62740 THE BEDALE	06/32 Dar	12/49 2740	-08/60	09/60	2l
62741 THE BLANKNEY	07/32 Dar	08/49 2741	-10/58	11/58	2l
62742 THE BRAES OF DERWENT	08/32 Dar	09/49 2742	-10/58	02/59	2l
62743 THE CLEVELAND	08/32 Dar	10/48 2743	-05/60	07/60	2l
62744 THE HOLDERNESS	10/32 Dar	10/48 2744	-12/60	04/61	2l
62745 THE HURWORTH	10/32 Dar	05/49 2745	-03/59	04/59	2l
62746 THE MIDDLETON	08/33 Dar	04/48 2746	-06/58	09/58	2l
62747 THE PERCY	08/33 Dar	04/48 2747	-03/61	04/61	2l
62748 THE SOUTHWOLD	08/33 Dar	06/49 2748	-12/57	01/58	2l
62749 THE COTTESMORE	08/33 Dar	04/48 2749	-07/58	08/58	2l
62750 THE PYTCHLEY	09/33 Dar	10/49 2750	-10/58	01/59	2l
62751 THE ALBRIGHTON	07/34 Dar	06/48 2751	-03/59	03/59	2l
62752 THE ATHERSTONE	07/34 Dar	04/48 2752	-08/58	08/58	2l
62753 THE BELVOIR	07/34 Dar	04/48 2753	-09/59	10/59	2l
62754 THE BERKELEY	07/34 Dar	01/49 2754	-10/58	02/59	2l
62755 THE BILSDALE	07/34 Dar	09/49 2755	-10/58	01/59	2l
62756 THE BROCKLESBY	08/34 Dar	06/49 2756	-05/58	08/58	2l
62757 THE BURTON	08/34 Dar	08/48 2757	-12/57	02/58	2l
62758 THE CATTISTOCK	08/34 Dar	03/48 2758	-12/57	03/58	2l
62759 THE CRAVEN	08/34 Dar	01/49 2759	-01/61	02/61	2l
62760 THE COTSWOLD	09/34 Dar	06/49 2760	-10/59	11/59	2l
62761 THE DERWENT	09/34 Dar	08/48 2761	-12/57	12/57	2l
62762 THE FERNIE	09/34 Dar	04/48 2762	-10/60	11/60	2l
62763 THE FITZWILLIAM	09/34 Dar	10/49 2763	-01/61	03/61	2l 49⇨v
62764 THE GARTH	10/34 Dar	04/48 2764	-10/58	12/58	2l 49⇨v
62765 THE GOATHLAND	10/34 Dar	07/48 2765	-01/61	04/61	2l
62766 THE GRAFTON	11/34 Dar	08/48 2766	-09/58	11/58	2l
62767 THE GROVE	11/34 Dar	04/49 2767	-10/58	10/58	2l
62768 THE MORPETH	12/34 Dar	08/48 2768	-10/52	11/52	4l
62769 THE OAKLEY	12/34 Dar	05/48 2769	-09/58	09/58	2l
62770 THE PUCKERIDGE	12/34 Dar	11/49 2770	-09/59	10/59	2l
62771 THE RUFFORD	01/35 Dar	04/48 2771	-10/58	11/58	2l
62772 THE SINNINGTON	01/35 Dar	02/49 2772	-09/58	11/58	2l
62773 THE SOUTH DURHAM	01/35 Dar	02/50 2773	-08/58	08/58	2l
62774 THE STAINTONDALE	02/35 Dar	08/48 2774	-10/58	12/58	2l
62775 THE TYNEDALE	02/35 Dar	09/48 2775	-12/58	05/59	2l

E4 62780-62797
2-4-0 GER Holden

Power Classification:	1MT
Introduced:	1891-1902
Designer:	J Holden
Company:	GER
Weight:	Loco 40t 6cwt
	Tender 30t 13cwt
Driving Wheel:	5' 8"
Boiler Pressure:	160psi
Cylinders:	Inside 17½" x 24"
Tractive Effort:	14700lbf
Valve Gear:	Stephenson (slide valves)

Between 1891 and 1902 Holden built one hundred mixed traffic 2-4-0s for the GER. Known as GER class 'T26' (LNER 'E4'), they were built to satisfy the GER's need for engines suitable for working cross country trains. Originally built with GER stovepipes chimneys, most of the survivors were fitted with lipped chimneys.

The majority of the class (eighty-two engines) were withdrawn between 1926 and 1940, leaving eighteen survivors to come into BR stock being withdrawn between 1954 and 1959. Most of the later survivors were employed on branch lines in Cambridgeshire and the Eastern Counties.

g 62780 retained its GER stovepipe chimney.

s Six engines worked for a while in the 1930s on the NER line between Darlington and Penrith. They were fitted with side-window cabs at Doncaster to make them more suitable for this exposed line.

Year End Totals: 'E4' class

'47	'48	'49	'50	'51	'52	'53	'54	'55	'56	'57	'58	'59	'60	'61	'62	'63	'64	'65	'66	'67
18	18	18	18	18	18	18	16	10	5	3	1									

Number	*Built*	*Renumbered*	*BR Dates*	*Scrap*	*Notes*
62780	04/91 Str	06/50 2780	-09/55	*55*	g
62781	11/92 Str	02/49 2781	-01/56	*56*	s
62782	12/92 Str	08/48 2782	-11/54	*54*	
62783	10/94 Str	01/52 2783	-12/54	02/55	
62784	10/94 Str	08/50 2784	-05/55	08/55	s
62785 §	01/95 Str	02/51 2785	-12/59		
62786	01/95 Str	06/48 2786	-07/56	*56*	
62787	01/95 Str	06/48 2787	-11/56	*56*	
62788	01/95 Str	10/48 2788	-03/58	*03/58*	s
62789	07/96 Str	12/49 2789	-12/57	*58*	
62790	09/96 Str	07/49 2790	-01/56	*01/56*	
62791	10/96 Str	06/49 2791	-04/55	08/55	
62792	06/02 Str	01/50 2792	-06/56	*56*	
62793	06/02 Str	10/49 2793	-02/55	08/55	s
62794	06/02 Str	03/50 2794	-08/55	*55*	
62795	06/02 Str	12/51 2795	-03/55	*55*	s
62796	07/02 Str	05/50 2796	-05/57	*57*	
62797	08/02 Str	05/49 2797	-03/58	*03/58*	s

C1 62808-62885
4-4-2 GNR Ivatt 'Large Atlantic'

Power Classification:	2P
Introduced:	1902-1910
Designer:	Ivatt
Company:	GNR
Weight:	Loco 69t 12cwt
	r Loco 69t 19cwt
	Tender 43t 2cwt
Driving Wheel:	6' 8"
Boiler Pressure:	170psi superheated
Cylinders:	Outside 20" x 24"
	s Outside 19" x 24"
	r Outside 20" x 26"

LNER Gresley 'D49/2' 'Hunt' class 4-4-0 No 62741 *The Blankney*.

GER Holden 'E4' class 2-4-0 No 62781 at Ipswich in September 1949, fitted with side-window cabs.

NER Raven 'Q6' class 0-8-0 No 63379 at Consett in June 1956.

GCR Robinson 'O4' class 2-8-0 No 63606.

Tractive Effort:	17340lbf s 15650lbf r 18785lbf
Valve Gear:	Stephenson (piston valves) s Stephenson (slide valves) r Walschaert (piston valves)

The first British Atlantics (4-4-2s) were the twenty-two engines built between 1898 and 1903 by Ivatt for the GNR (the 'C2' class). All were withdrawn between 1935 and 1946, but the original engine 990 HENRY OAKLEY has been preserved and ran on a few enthusiasts' specials in the 1950s.

A much larger version was built in 1902 (the 'C1' class), and ninety-four of these were built up to 1910. They had much larger boilers and very wide fireboxes extending over the frames. Regarded by many as the most handsome of all LNER locomotives, these 'Large Atlantics' worked all of the principal main line workings until the coming of the pacifics (4-6-2s). They were later superheated and fitted with piston valves which improved their performance.

In 1905 Douglas Earle Marsh left Doncaster (where he had been working as Ivatt's assistant) to take up office with the LBSCR. He took with him a complete set of drawings for these Atlantics and these were used as the basis for the SR 'H1' class of engines.

The original engine No. 251 (withdrawn before 1948, but numbered 2800 in the LNER 1946 renumbering scheme) has been preserved and ran on a few enthusiasts' specials in the 1950s.

The first engine was withdrawn in 1924. Of the seventeen engines which survived to come into BR stock, all were withdrawn by 1950.

s Several engines retained their original slide valves.

r In 1915 62808 was fitted with four cylinders and with Walschaert valve gear by Gresley. In this form it proved costly to maintain and in 1938 it was converted back to two cylinders. It retained the modified running plate that it was fitted with when first converted.

c Immediately after grouping 62849 was fitted with a booster (an auxiliary pair of cylinders on the trailing wheels to give assistance when starting a heavy train). It was also fitted with a pacific type cab with side windows. The booster was removed in 1935, but it retained the new cab.

Year End Totals: 'C1' class

'47	'48	'49	'50	'51	'52	'53	'54	'55	'56	'57	'58	'59	'60	'61	'62	'63	'64	'65	'66	'67
17	10	5																		

Number	Built	Renumbered	BR Dates	Scrap	Notes
62808	06/04 Don	2808	-02/48	03/48	r
62810	06/04 Don	2810	-05/49	07/49	
62817	06/04 Don	2817	-05/50	08/50	
62821	05/05 Don	2821	-07/48	08/50	
62822	04/05 Don	02/49 2822	-11/50	05/51	
62828	06/05 Don	2828	-08/49	08/49	
62829	05/05 Don	2829	-07/48	07/53	
62839	07/05 Don	2839	-01/50	01/50	
62849	05/06 Don	2849	-07/48	07/53	c
62854	04/07 Don	2854	-04/50	05/50	
62870	04/08 Don	2870	-02/48	02/48	s
62871	04/08 Don	2871	-05/48	05/48	s
62875	06/08 Don	2875	-01/49	01/49	s
62876	06/08 Don	2876	-01/48	01/48	s
62877	06/08 Don	2877	-11/49	04/52	
62881	08/08 Don	2881	-04/49	06/49	
62885	09/10 Don	05/48 2885	-01/50	05/50	

C4 62900-62925
4-4-2 GCR Robinson 'Atlantic'

Power Classification:	2P
Introduced:	1903-1906
Designer:	Robinson
Company:	GCR
Weight:	2 Loco 70t 17cwt 4 Loco 71t 18cwt Tender 48t 6cwt
Driving Wheel:	6' 9"
Boiler Pressure:	180psi superheated
Cylinders:	2 Outside 19" x 26" 4 Outside 21" x 26"
Tractive Effort:	2 17730lbf 4 21660lbf
Valve Gear:	2 Stephenson (slide valves) 4 Stephenson (piston valves)

Robinson's GCR Atlantics were built in 1903-1906 (GCR classes '8B' and '8J') to handle top main line work. Twenty-seven two-cylinder engines were built and they were some of the most handsome of all British Atlantics. Originally built with saturated boilers, they were all later superheated. The first engine was withdrawn in 1939. Twenty engines came into BR stock, but they had all been withdrawn by 1950, and none of them carried their BR numbers.

Four very similar engines were built as four-cylinder compounds. Known as the 'C5' class they were all named and were withdrawn in 1946-1947.

2 'C4/2' was the classification for those engines which retained their slide valves when they were superheated.

4 Some engines were fitted with piston valves and larger cylinders when they were superheated from 1911 onwards. They were known as 'C4/4'.

1 & 3 'C4/1' and 'C4/3' were engines of 'C4/2' and 'C4/4' before the engines were cut down to the LNER loading gauge.

Year End Totals: 'C4' class

'47	'48	'49	'50	'51	'52	'53	'54	'55	'56	'57	'58	'59	'60	'61	'62	'63	'64	'65	'66	'67
20	14	6																		

Number	Built	Renumbered	BR Dates	Scrap	Notes
62900	12/03 BP	2900	-11/50	02/51	4
62901	12/03 BP	2901	-11/50	02/51	4
62902	07/04 BP	2902	-04/49	05/49	2
62903	07/04 BP	2903	-06/49	07/49	4
62908	10/05 NB	2908	-11/50	02/51	2
62909	10/05 NB	2909	-11/50	12/50	4
62910	10/05 NB	2910	-02/49	02/49	4
62912	10/05 NB	2912	-08/49	08/49	2
62914	11/05 NB	2914	-03/48	03/48	4
62915	11/05 NB	2915	-06/49	07/49	4
62916	11/05 NB	2916	-11/48	11/48	4
62917	11/05 NB	2917	-05/49	05/49	2
62918	02/06 Gor	2918	-12/50	01/51	2
62919	03/06 Gor	2919	-11/50	01/51	4
62920	04/06 Gor	2920	-02/48	02/48	4
62921	05/06 Gor	2921	-04/48	04/48	4
62922	06/06 Gor	2922	-06/48	06/48	4
62923	07/06 Gor	2923	-02/49	02/49	4
62924	06/06 Gor	2924	-01/48	02/48	2
62925	08/06 Gor	2925	-04/49	04/49	4

C6 62933-62937
4-4-2 NER Worsdell 'Atlantic'

Power Classification:	3P
Introduced:	1903-1910
Designer:	W Worsdell
Company:	NER
Weight:	Loco 76t 4cwt Tender 46t 12cwt
Driving Wheel:	6' 10"
Boiler Pressure:	175psi superheated
Cylinders:	Outside 20" x 28"
Tractive Effort:	20315lbf
Valve Gear:	Stephenson (piston valves)

The NER had three different classes of Atlantics; twenty engines built by Worsdell in 1903 ('C6' class), two four-cylinder compounds designed by the chief draughtsman Smith in 1906, and fifty three-cylinder engines built by Raven in 1911 ('C7' class).

The first ten engines of the 'C6' class (NER class 'V') were built at Gateshead in 1903-1904 and the second ten at Darlington in 1910. They were all scrapped between 1943 and 1948. Only two engines survived to come into BR stock (both Gateshead built engines), neither of which carried its allocated BR number.

Year End Totals: 'C6' class

'47	'48	'49	'50	'51	'52	'53	'54	'55	'56	'57	'58	'59	'60	'61	'62	'63	'64	'65	'66	'67
2																				

Number	Built	Renumbered	BR Dates	Scrap	Notes
62933	06/04 Ghd	2933	-03/48	48	
62937	10/04 Ghd	2937	-03/48	48	

C7 62954-62995
4-4-2 NER Raven 'Atlantic'

Power Classification:	3P
Introduced:	1911-1918
Designer:	Raven
Company:	NER
Weight:	Loco 79t 5cwt Tender 46t 12cwt
Driving Wheel:	6' 10"
Boiler Pressure:	175psi superheated
Cylinders:	Three 16½" x 26"
Tractive Effort:	19260lbf
Valve Gear:	Stephenson (piston valves)

The 'C7's (NER class 'Z') were introduced by Raven soon after he took office, and fifty were built in 1911-1918. They were fine engines and they bore the brunt of main-line working over the NER for many years.

They were all withdrawn between 1942 and 1948, fourteen engines surviving long enough to come into BR stock, but none of them long enough to carry a BR number.

Two engines were modernised in 1931 with high running plates, and they were fitted with four wheel boosters, articulated to the tender. They were re-classified 'C9' and they were both withdrawn before 1948.

Year End Totals: 'C7' class

'47	'48	'49	'50	'51	'52	'53	'54	'55	'56	'57	'58	'59	'60	'61	'62	'63	'64	'65	'66	'67
14																				

Number	Built	Renumbered	BR Dates	Scrap	Notes
62954	07/11 NB	2954	-06/48	07/48	
62970	05/14 Dar	2970	-12/48	01/49	
62972	06/14 Dar	2972	-08/48	48	
62973	06/14 Dar	2973	-06/48	07/48	
62975	06/14 Dar	2975	-07/48	07/48	
62978	12/14 Dar	2978	-08/48	48	
62981	02/15 Dar	2981	-07/48	07/48	
62982	02/15 Dar	2982	-07/48	07/48	
62983	03/15 Dar	2983	-07/48	07/48	
62988	06/15 Dar	2988	-07/48	07/48	
62989	06/15 Dar	2989	-08/48	48	
62992	01/17 Dar	2992	-11/48	11/48	
62993	02/17 Dar	2993	-03/48	48	
62995	05/17 Dar	2995	-07/48	07/48	

O7 63000-63199
2-8-0 MOS (WD) Riddles 'Austerity'

Power Classification:	8F
Introduced:	1943-1946
Designer:	Riddles
Company:	Ministry of Supply (MOS)
Weight:	Loco 70t 5cwt Tender 55t 10cwt
Driving Wheel:	4' 8½"
Boiler Pressure:	225psi superheated
Cylinders:	Outside 19" x 28"
Tractive Effort:	34215lbf
Valve Gear:	Walschaert (piston valves)

Class 'O7' consisted of two-hundred 2-8-0 'Austerity' locomotives which were purchased from the War Department in 1947 on their return from overseas service.

Originally 934 of these Riddles designed engines were built by North British and Vulcan Foundry from 1943 onwards. Apart from these engines which were purchased by the LNER, there were another 533 engines on loan to BR at nationalisation. After these engines were purchased by BR in December 1948, the whole batch was renumbered into one series (90000-90732) in 1949.

o 63152 was converted to oil-burning after the end of the war. It was later converted back to coal burning (c) in 1948.

Year End Totals: 'O7' class

'47	'48	'49	'50	'51	'52	'53	'54	'55	'56	'57	'58	'59	'60	'61	'62	'63	'64	'65	'66	'67
200	200																			

Number	Built	Renumbered	BR Dates	Notes
63000	02/43 NB	06/48 3000	-01/49	10/50➔90000
63001	01/43 NB	04/48 3001	-01/49	04/49➔90001
63002	03/43 NB	05/48 3002	-01/49	06/50➔90002
63003	03/43 NB	10/48 3003	-01/49	12/49➔90003
63004	04/43 NB	3004	-01/49	03/49➔90004
63005	04/43 NB	3005	-01/49	04/49➔90005
63006	05/43 NB	3006	-01/49	05/49➔90006
63007	05/43 NB	10/48 3007	-01/49	09/49➔90007
63008	05/43 NB	48 3008	-01/49	03/49➔90008
63009	06/43 NB	03/48 3009	-01/49	10/50➔90009
63010	07/43 NB	05/48 3010	-01/49	07/49➔90010
63011	07/43 NB	06/48 3011	-01/49	05/51➔90011
63012	08/43 NB	04/48 3012	-01/49	03/50➔90012
63013	08/43 NB	04/48 3013	-01/49	04/49➔90013
63014	09/43 NB	3014	-01/49	12/50➔90014

Number	Built		Renumbered		BR Dates	Scrap
63015	08/43	NB	07/48	3015	-01/49	01/50➲90015
63016	08/43	NB	04/48	3016	-01/49	09/50➲90016
63017	08/43	NB	09/48	3017	-01/49	06/51➲90017
63018	08/43	NB	04/48	3018	-01/49	04/51➲90018
63019	09/43	NB	04/48	3019	-01/49	02/50➲90019
63020	09/43	NB	12/48	3020	-01/49	09/50➲90020
63021	10/43	NB		3021	-01/49	06/49➲90021
63022	10/43	NB		3022	-01/49	08/50➲90022
63023	09/43	NB	08/48	3023	-01/49	11/50➲90023
63024	09/43	NB	12/48	3024	-01/49	07/50➲90024
63025	09/43	NB		3025	-01/49	10/49➲90025
63026	10/43	NB	07/48	3026	-01/49	06/49➲90026
63027	10/43	NB		3027	-01/49	06/50➲90027
63028	11/43	NB	04/48	3028	-01/49	04/49➲90028
63029	11/43	NB	10/48	3029	-01/49	05/50➲90029
63030	11/43	NB	08/48	3030	-01/49	09/50➲90030
63031	10/43	NB		3031	-01/49	07/50➲90031
63032	11/43	NB		3032	-01/49	03/49➲90032
63033	11/43	NB	08/48	3033	-01/49	10/50➲90033
63034	12/43	NB	05/48	3034	-01/49	09/49➲90034
63035	12/43	NB	08/48	3035	-01/49	02/51➲90035
63036	01/44	NB		3036	-01/49	10/49➲90036
63037	01/44	NB	05/48	3037	-01/49	10/50➲90037
63038	01/44	NB	07/48	3038	-01/49	07/50➲90038
63039	01/44	NB		3039	-01/49	10/49➲90039
63040	02/44	NB		3040	-01/49	07/50➲90040
63041	02/44	NB	12/48	3041	-01/49	04/49➲90041
63042	02/44	NB	10/48	3042	-01/49	10/50➲90042
63043	03/44	NB	07/48	3043	-01/49	03/51➲90043
63044	03/44	NB		3044	-01/49	06/49➲90044
63045	03/44	NB	06/48	3045	-01/49	11/50➲90045
63046	04/44	NB		3046	-01/49	07/49➲90046
63047	04/44	NB	07/48	3047	-01/49	08/50➲90047
63048	04/44	NB	05/48	3048	-01/49	10/50➲90048
63049	04/44	NB		3049	-01/49	12/49➲90049
63050	04/44	NB	06/48	3050	-01/49	05/50➲90050
63051	05/44	NB	04/48	3051	-01/49	04/49➲90051
63052	05/44	NB	05/48	3052	-01/49	04/50➲90052
63053	05/44	NB	06/48	3053	-01/49	05/49➲90053
63054	05/44	NB		3054	-01/49	05/49➲90054
63055	05/44	NB	03/48	3055	-01/49	06/51➲90055
63056	05/44	NB		3056	-01/49	11/49➲90056
63057	05/44	NB	03/48	3057	-01/49	09/50➲90057
63058	05/44	NB		3058	-01/49	02/50➲90058
63059	05/44	NB		3059	-01/49	09/50➲90059
63060	06/44	NB		3060	-01/49	11/50➲90060
63061	06/44	NB	07/48	3061	-01/49	01/50➲90061
63062	06/44	NB	06/48	3062	-01/49	10/50➲90062
63063	06/44	NB	10/48	3063	-01/49	03/50➲90063
63064	06/44	NB	04/48	3064	-01/49	01/51➲90064
63065	06/44	NB	08/48	3065	-01/49	06/50➲90065
63066	07/44	NB	11/48	3066	-01/49	07/51➲90066
63067	07/44	NB	05/48	3067	-01/49	07/49➲90067
63068	07/44	NB	07/48	3068	-01/49	11/50➲90068
63069	07/44	NB		3069	-01/49	09/50➲90069
63070	07/43	NB	04/48	3070	-01/49	08/50➲90070
63071	07/44	NB	05/48	3071	-01/49	11/49➲90071
63072	08/44	NB	05/48	3072	-01/49	07/50➲90072
63073	08/44	NB	06/48	3073	-01/49	10/49➲90073
63074	09/44	NB	04/48	3074	-01/49	09/49➲90074
63075	08/43	NB	11/48	3075	-01/49	02/50➲90075
63076	08/43	NB	07/48	3076	-01/49	07/50➲90076
63077	08/43	NB	07/48	3077	-01/49	06/50➲90077
63078	08/43	NB	08/48	3078	-01/49	09/50➲90078
63079	08/44	NB	06/48	3079	-01/49	10/50➲90079
63080	08/44	NB		3080	-01/49	10/49➲90080
63081	09/44	NB	04/48	3081	-01/49	01/50➲90081
63082	09/44	NB	04/48	3082	-01/49	11/50➲90082
63083	09/44	NB	07/48	3083	-01/49	05/49➲90083
63084	09/44	NB	09/48	3084	-01/49	02/51➲90084
63085	10/44	NB		3085	-01/49	02/49➲90085
63086	10/44	NB		3086	-01/49	08/49➲90086
63087	09/44	NB	09/48	3087	-01/49	12/50➲90087
63088	10/44	NB		3088	-01/49	08/50➲90088
63089	10/44	NB	04/48	3089	-01/49	05/49➲90089
63090	10/44	NB		3090	-01/49	10/50➲90090
63091	10/44	NB		3091	-01/49	10/50➲90091
63092	10/44	NB	04/48	3092	-01/49	10/50➲90092
63093	11/44	NB	07/48	3093	-01/49	12/50➲90093
63094	11/44	NB	06/48	3094	-01/49	05/50➲90094
63095	11/44	NB		3095	-01/49	10/49➲90095
63096	12/44	NB	48	3096	-01/49	12/51➲90096
63097	12/44	NB	06/48	3097	-01/49	03/49➲90097
63098	02/45	NB		3098	-01/49	07/49➲90098
63099	02/45	NB	04/48	3099	-01/49	04/49➲90099
63100	03/45	NB	11/48	3100	-01/49	11/51➲90100
63101	08/43	VF	09/48	3101	-01/49	03/50➲90422
63102	08/43	VF	07/48	3102	-01/49	04/51➲90423
63103	09/43	VF	08/48	3103	-01/49	11/49➲90424
63104	09/43	VF	07/48	3104	-01/49	11/49➲90425
63105	10/43	VF	06/48	3105	-01/49	11/50➲90426
63106	10/43	VF	10/48	3106	-01/49	12/50➲90427
63107	10/43	VF	05/48	3107	-01/49	10/50➲90428
63108	11/43	VF	07/48	3108	-01/49	08/50➲90429
63109	11/43	VF	10/48	3109	-01/49	06/51➲90430
63110	11/43	VF	06/48	3110	-01/49	06/49➲90431
63111	12/43	VF		3111	-01/49	02/49➲90432
63112	01/44	VF		3112	-01/49	10/50➲90433
63113	01/44	VF		3113	-01/49	08/50➲90434
63114	02/44	VF	05/48	3114	-01/49	01/50➲90435
63115	02/44	VF		3115	-01/49	07/50➲90436
63116	02/44	VF	06/48	3116	-01/49	10/49➲90437
63117	02/44	VF		3117	-01/49	06/49➲90438
63118	03/44	VF	08/48	3118	-01/49	02/51➲90439
63119	03/44	VF		3119	-01/49	03/49➲90440
63120	03/44	VF	04/48	3120	-01/49	06/49➲90441
63121	03/44	VF		3121	-01/49	11/50➲90442
63122	03/44	VF	04/48	3122	-01/49	02/51➲90443
63123	03/44	VF	04/48	3123	-01/49	06/50➲90444
63124	03/44	VF		3124	-01/49	08/50➲90445
63125	03/44	VF	04/48	3125	-01/49	09/49➲90446
63126	03/44	VF	10/48	3126	-01/49	12/49➲90447
63127	03/44	VF	06/48	3127	-01/49	01/51➲90448
63128	03/44	VF		3128	-01/49	04/49➲90449
63129	04/44	VF		3129	-01/49	12/49➲90450
63130	04/44	VF	04/48	3130	-01/49	05/50➲90451
63131	04/44	VF		3131	-01/49	04/49➲90452
63132	04/44	VF		3132	-01/49	03/49➲90453
63133	04/44	VF	10/48	3133	-01/49	08/51➲90454
63134	04/44	VF		3134	-01/49	11/49➲90455
63135	04/44	VF		3135	-01/49	10/50➲90456
63136	04/44	VF		3136	-01/49	05/50➲90457
63137	04/44	VF	08/48	3137	-01/49	05/50➲90458
63138	04/44	VF		3138	-01/49	05/50➲90459
63139	05/44	VF		3139	-01/49	04/49➲90460
63140	05/44	VF	04/48	3140	-01/49	03/49➲90461
63141	05/44	VF	06/48	3141	-01/49	02/49➲90462
63142	05/44	VF	04/48	3142	-01/49	09/50➲90463
63143	05/44	VF		3143	-01/49	04/50➲90464
63144	05/44	VF	06/48	3144	-01/49	06/50➲90465
63145	05/44	VF	06/48	3145	-01/49	12/50➲90466
63146	05/44	VF	48	3146	-01/49	09/50➲90467
63147	05/44	VF		3147	-01/49	10/49➲90468
63148	05/44	VF		3148	-01/49	10/49➲90469
63149	05/44	VF	05/48	3149	-01/49	11/49➲90470
63150	05/44	VF		3150	-01/49	04/49➲90471
63151	05/44	VF	05/48	3151	-01/49	06/50➲90472
63152	05/44	VF	04/48	3152	-01/49	12/49➲90473
						o 48➪c
63153	06/44	VF		3153	-01/49	08/50➲90474
63154	06/44	VF		3154	-01/49	06/49➲90475
63155	06/44	VF	06/48	3155	-01/49	11/50➲90476
63156	06/44	VF		3156	-01/49	04/49➲90477
63157	06/44	VF		3157	-01/49	11/49➲90478
63158	06/44	VF		3158	-01/49	05/49➲90479
63159	06/44	VF	04/48	3159	-01/49	03/49➲90480
63160	07/44	VF		3160	-01/49	06/49➲90481
63161	07/44	VF		3161	-01/49	11/50➲90482
63162	07/44	VF	05/48	3162	-01/49	02/51➲90483
63163	07/44	VF	04/48	3163	-01/49	09/49➲90484
63164	07/44	VF	06/48	3164	-01/49	11/50➲90485
63165	07/44	VF	07/48	3165	-01/49	09/51➲90486
63166	07/44	VF	06/48	3166	-01/49	12/50➲90487
63167	07/44	VF	04/48	3167	-01/49	12/50➲90488
63168	07/44	VF	04/48	3168	-01/49	02/50➲90489
63169	07/44	VF	04/48	3169	-01/49	05/50➲90490
63170	08/44	VF	06/48	3170	-01/49	09/49➲90491
63171	08/44	VF		3171	-01/49	11/49➲90492
63172	08/44	VF		3172	-01/49	01/50➲90493
63173	08/44	VF	03/48	3173	-01/49	50➲90494
63174	08/44	VF	04/48	3174	-01/49	07/50➲90495
63175	08/44	VF		3175	-01/49	10/49➲90496
63176	08/44	VF	06/48	3176	-01/49	09/50➲90497
63177	08/44	VF	04/48	3177	-01/49	06/49➲90498
63178	08/44	VF	03/48	3178	-01/49	07/50➲90499
63179	09/44	VF	04/48	3179	-01/49	08/49➲90500
63180	09/44	VF		3180	-01/49	09/49➲90501
63181	09/44	VF		3181	-01/49	03/49➲90502
63182	09/44	VF	07/48	3182	-01/49	11/50➲90503
63183	09/44	VF	05/48	3183	-01/49	09/50➲90504
63184	09/44	VF		3184	-01/49	11/49➲90505
63185	10/44	VF	11/48	3185	-01/49	05/51➲90506
63186	10/44	VF		3186	-01/49	09/50➲90507
63187	11/44	VF	01/49	3187	-01/49	10/50➲90508
63188	11/44	VF	06/48	3188	-01/49	09/50➲90509
63189	12/44	VF		3189	-01/49	11/50➲90510
63190	12/44	VF	06/48	3190	-01/49	02/50➲90511
63191	12/44	VF	06/48	3191	-01/49	02/51➲90512
63192	01/45	VF	07/48	3192	-01/49	08/50➲90513
63193	01/45	VF	05/48	3193	-01/49	09/50➲90514
63194	01/45	VF	04/48	3194	-01/49	10/49➲90515
63195	01/45	VF	06/48	3195	-01/49	12/49➲90516
63196	03/45	VF	09/48	3196	-01/49	10/50➲90517
63197	03/45	VF	04/48	3197	-01/49	10/51➲90518
63198	04/45	VF	01/49	3198	-01/49	02/51➲90519
63199	04/45	VF		3199	-01/49	03/49➲90520

Q4 63200-63243
0-8-0 GCR Robinson

Power Classification: 5F
Introduced: 1902-1911
Designer: Robinson
Company: GCR
Weight: 1 Loco 62t 8cwt
s Loco 63t 0cwt
p Loco 64t 1cwt
Tender 48t 6cwt
Driving Wheel: 4' 8"
Boiler Pressure: 180psi
2 180psi superheated
Cylinders: Outside 19" x 26"
p Outside 21" x 26"
Tractive Effort: 25645lbf
p 31325lbf
Valve Gear: Stephenson (slide valves)
p Stephenson (piston valves)

Robinson built eighty-nine 0-8-0 goods engines for the GCR in 1902, known as class '8A' (LNER 'Q4'). They were originally built with saturated boilers, but some were later superheated. The later engines had a continuous splasher over the rear three sets of wheels.

The engines were superseded by Robinson's 2-8-0 'O4' class and they were all withdrawn between 1934 and 1951. Thirty-four engines came into BR stock. Thirteen engines were rebuilt to tank engines in 1942-1943, becoming 'Q1' class 0-8-0T shunting engines. As such they survived longer than the unrebuilt engines, the last few being withdrawn in 1959.

1 The original saturated boiler locomotives were known as 'Q4/1'.

2 Some engines were superheated from 1914 onwards and they were classified 'Q4/2'.

s Many of the 'Q4/2' engines retained their original slide valves.

p Some of the 'Q4/2' engines received larger cylinders with piston valves when they were rebuilt.

Year End Totals: 'Q4' class

'47	'48	'49	'50	'51	'52	'53	'54	'55	'56	'57	'58	'59	'60	'61	'62	'63	'64	'65	'66	'67
34	34	25	13																	

Number	Built		Renumbered		BR Dates	Scrap	Notes
63200	11/02	NR	10/48	3200	-09/49	49	2s
63201	11/02	NR	04/49	3201	-01/51	02/51	2s
63202	09/03	NR	12/48	3202	-09/51	09/51	1
63203	09/03	K		3203	-11/50	02/51	1
63204	10/03	K	11/48	3204	-06/51	51	1
63205	10/03	K		3205	-12/50	02/51	1
63206	10/03	K		3206	-02/49	49	2s
63207	10/03	K	03/49	3207	-08/50	06/51	2s
63210	11/03	K		3210	-10/49	49	2s
63212	12/03	K		3212	-05/49	49	2s
63213	01/04	K		3213	-07/50	08/50	2p
63214	01/04	K		3214	-05/49	49	2p
63216	03/04	K	07/48	3216	-09/49	49	2s
63217	03/04	K	04/48	3217	-03/51	05/51	2s
63219	05/04	K		3219	-12/49	03/50	2s
63220	05/05	K	11/48	3220	-03/51	05/51	2p
63221	08/05	K		3221	-12/50	01/51	2p
63223	02/07	K	04/48	3223	-06/51	51	2s
63224	02/07	K		3224	-02/49	49	1
63225	02/07	K	11/48	3225	-09/51	51	2p
63226	03/07	K		3226	-10/50	10/50	1
63227	03/07	K	11/48	3227	-05/51	51	1
63228	03/07	K		3228	-08/49	49	2s
63229	02/09	Gor		3229	-12/50	02/51	2s
63231	11/09	Gor		3231	-03/50	02/51	2s
63232	11/09	Gor	08/48	3232	-07/50	06/51	2p
63233	12/09	Gor	02/49	3233	-02/50	02/51	2s
63234	12/09	Gor	04/49	3234	-03/51	51	1
63235	12/09	Gor		3235	-05/51	09/51	2s
63236	12/09	Gor	05/48	3236	-05/51	51	2s
63238	11/10	Gor		3238	-02/50	06/51	2s
63240	07/10	Gor	02/49	3240	-06/51	06/51	2s
63241	07/10	Gor		3241	-04/50	06/51	1
63243	01/11	Gor	04/49	3243	-09/51	09/51	2s

Q5 63250-63339
0-8-0 NER Worsdell

Power Classification: 6F
Introduced: 1901-1911
2 Rebuilt 1932 onwards by Gresley
Designer: W Worsdell
Company: NER
Weight: 1 Loco 58t 8cwt
2 Loco 60t 4cwt
Tender 40t 8cwt
Driving Wheel: 4' 7¼"
Boiler Pressure: 175psi
Cylinders: Outside 20" x 26"
Tractive Effort: 28000lbf

Valve Gear:	Stephenson (slide valves) p Stephenson (piston valves)

The NER was a large user of the 0-8-0 type which it used exclusively for its heavy mineral traffic. There were three main varieties, all fitted with outside cylinders. The 'Q5' class was built by Worsdell in 1901-1911, the 'Q6' class by Raven in 1913-1921 and the 'Q7' three-cylinder engines by Raven in 1919-1924.

The 'Q5' class (NER 'T' and 'T1' classes) consisted of ninety engines built by Worsdell in 1901-1911. They were fitted with saturated boilers. The first engine was withdrawn in 1946.

1 Engines of the original Worsdell design were classified 'Q5/1'.

2 Gresley rebuilt some of these engines with larger boilers taken from withdrawn Hull & Barnsley 0-8-0s (class 'Q10'). Converted in 1932 onwards, they had modified cabs and were classified 'Q5/2'.

p Some engines were fitted with piston valves.

Year End Totals: 'Q5' class

'47	'48	'49	'50	'51	'52	'53	'54	'55	'56	'57	'58	'59	'60	'61	'62	'63	'64	'65	'66	'67
77	58	32	10																	

Number	Built		Renumbered		BR Dates	Scrap	Notes
63250	08/01	Ghd		3250	-06/48	48	1
63251	09/01	Ghd		3251	-12/50	51	1
63252	10/01	Ghd		3252	-02/48	48	1
63253	10/01	Ghd		3253	-11/48	12/48	2
63254	10/01	Ghd		3254	-06/48	06/48	1
63255	10/01	Ghd		3255	-11/49	49	1
63256	11/01	Ghd		3256	-06/50	50	1
63257	12/01	Ghd		3257	-11/50	50	1
63259	12/01	Ghd		3259	-05/51	05/51	1
63260	03/02	Ghd		3260	-06/50	50	1
63261	03/02	Ghd		3261	-10/50	50	1
63262	03/02	Ghd		3262	-08/50	50	1
63263	03/02	Ghd		3263	-11/48	48	2
63264	04/02	Ghd		3264	-06/48	48	1
63267	05/02	Ghd		3267	-06/51	06/51	1
63268	06/02	Ghd		3268	-02/48	48	1
63270	12/02	Ghd		3270	-08/51	08/51	1p
63271	12/02	Ghd		3271	-11/50	50	1p
63272	12/02	Ghd		3272	-07/50	50	1p
63273	02/03	Ghd		3273	-03/49	49	1p
63274	03/03	Ghd		3274	-09/50	50	1p
63275	06/03	Ghd		3275	-04/49	05/49	1p
63276	03/03	Ghd		3276	-02/50	50	1p
63277	04/03	Ghd		3277	-05/49	05/49	1p
63278	04/03	Ghd		3278	-08/50	50	1p
63279	05/03	Ghd		3279	-02/48	02/48	1p
63280	06/03	Ghd		3280	-10/50	50	1p
63281	06/03	Ghd		3281	-06/50	50	1p
63282	06/03	Ghd	05/48	3282	-12/50	51	1p
63283	06/03	Ghd		3283	-12/50	51	1p
63284	06/03	Ghd		3284	-06/51	06/51	1p
63285	09/03	Ghd		3285	-09/50	50	1p
63286	09/03	Ghd	05/48	3286	-04/49	49	1p
63287	10/03	Ghd		3287	-08/50	50	1p
63289	08/03	Ghd		3289	-08/50	50	1p
63290	12/03	Ghd	06/48	3290	-07/50	50	1p
63291	12/03	Ghd		3291	-02/49	02/49	1p
63292	03/04	Ghd		3292	-11/48	12/48	1p
63293	02/04	Ghd		3293	-01/50	50	1p
63294	03/04	Ghd		3294	-10/49	49	1p
63295	03/04	Ghd		3295	-11/48	12/48	1p
63296	03/04	Ghd		3296	-08/49	49	1p
63297	04/04	Ghd		3297	-02/49	02/49	1p
63298	04/04	Ghd		3298	-02/48	48	1p
63299	05/04	Ghd		3299	-02/49	02/49	1p
63300	06/07	Dar		3300	-05/49	06/49	1
63301	06/07	Dar		3301	-12/48	02/49	2
63303	08/07	Dar		3303	-04/51	05/51	1
63305	09/07	Dar		3305	-05/49	06/49	2
63306	10/07	Dar		3306	-12/48	49	2
63307	10/07	Dar		3307	-05/49	05/49	1
63308	10/07	Dar		3308	-02/49	02/49	1
63310	12/07	Dar		3310	-06/48	48	1
63311	12/07	Dar		3311	-09/51	51	1
63312	12/07	Dar		3312	-08/49	49	1
63313	12/07	Dar	12/48	3313	-11/49	09/50	1
63314	03/08	Dar		3314	-09/51	51	1
63315	03/08	Dar		3315	-03/48	04/48	1
63316	03/08	Dar		3316	-04/49	49	2
63317	04/08	Dar		3317	-02/49	02/49	1
63318	05/08	Dar		3318	-06/49	49	1
63319	05/08	Dar	04/48	3319	-04/51	05/51	1
63321	06/11	Dar		3321	-03/48	48	1
63322	06/11	Dar	11/48	3322	-02/49	02/49	2
63323	06/11	Dar		3323	-11/48	12/48	1
63326	07/11	Dar		3326	-10/51	51	1
63327	08/11	Dar		3327	-11/48	12/48	1
63328	08/11	Dar	09/48	3328	-01/51	51	1
63330	09/11	Dar		3330	-12/49	50	1
63331	09/11	Dar		3331	-02/49	49	1
63332	09/11	Dar		3332	-03/49	03/49	1
63333	09/11	Dar	09/48	3333	-12/50	51	1
63334	10/11	Dar		3334	-05/49	05/49	1
63335	10/11	Dar		3335	-08/49	49	1
63336	10/11	Dar		3336	-10/50	50	1
63338	11/11	Dar	04/48	3338	-09/49	49	1
63339	11/11	Dar		3339	-02/48	02/48	1

Q6 63340-63459
0-8-0 NER Raven 2-cylinder

Power Classification:	6F
Introduced:	1913-1921
Designer:	Raven
Company:	NER
Weight:	Loco 65t 18cwt Tender 44t 2cwt b Tender 44t 0cwt
Driving Wheel:	4' 7¼"
Boiler Pressure:	180psi superheated
Cylinders:	Outside 20" x 26"
Tractive Effort:	28800lbf
Valve Gear:	Stephenson (piston valves)

The 'Q6' class (NER 'T2') was built by Raven between 1913 and 1921. A total of 120 engines were built with superheated boilers. The first seventy were built at Darlington and the last fifty by Armstrong Whitworth. The boilers were interchangeable with those of the 'B15' 4-6-0 class. The engines remained active in the North East of England until the last days of steam, and together with some 'J27' 0-6-0s they were the last pre-grouping engines of any railway to remain in service.

They could be distinguished from the 'Q7' class, by the fact that the outside cylinders on the 'Q6's drove on the third pair of wheels, while those on the 'Q7's drove on the second pair.

b Some engines were fitted with tenders from withdrawn 'B15' engines.

Year End Totals: 'Q6' class

'47	'48	'49	'50	'51	'52	'53	'54	'55	'56	'57	'58	'59	'60	'61	'62	'63	'64	'65	'66	'67
120	120	120	120	120	120	120	120	120	120	120	120	120	119	118	118	85	62	40	17	

Number	Built		Renumbered		BR Dates	Scrap	Notes
63340	02/13	Dar	09/48	3340	-07/63	09/63	
63341	02/13	Dar	02/49	3341	-11/64	12/64	
63342	02/13	Dar	06/51	3342	-12/63	01/64	
63343	02/13	Dar	07/48	3343	-06/65	07/65	
63344	02/13	Dar	10/48	3344	-09/67	11/67	
63345	03/13	Dar	06/48	3345	-06/64	07/64	
63346	03/13	Dar	09/48	3346	-05/67	08/67	
63347	03/13	Dar	06/48	3347	-10/65	01/66	
63348	03/13	Dar	04/49	3348	-06/64	08/64	
63349	04/13	Dar	09/48	3349	-06/66	10/66	
63350	04/13	Dar	05/48	3350	-06/63	08/63	
63351	06/13	Dar	06/48	3351	-01/65	05/65	
63352	04/13	Dar	12/48	3352	-02/64	04/64	
63353	05/13	Dar	09/50	3353	-07/63	09/63	
63354	05/13	Dar	07/48	3354	-05/65	08/65	
63355	05/13	Dar	07/48	3355	-07/63	08/63	
63356	05/13	Dar	05/50	3356	-12/63	01/64	
63357	05/13	Dar	07/49	3357	-05/65	08/65	
63358	06/13	Dar	11/48	3358	-03/64	05/64	
63359	06/13	Dar	01/51	3359	-04/65	07/65	
63360	06/13	Dar	11/48	3360	-06/66	09/66	
63361	06/13	Dar	08/48	3361	-06/65	08/65	
63362	06/13	Dar	08/48	3362	-11/65	05/66	
63363	06/13	Dar	02/49	3363	-09/66	12/66	
63364	07/13	Dar	10/48	3364	-04/63	05/63	
63365	07/13	Dar	07/48	3365	-06/63	07/63	
63366	07/13	Dar	11/49	3366	-05/67	09/67	
63367	08/13	Dar	11/48	3367	-08/64	02/65	
63368	08/13	Dar	02/49	3368	-12/66	05/67	
63369	09/13	Dar	11/49	3369	-07/63	09/63	
63370	04/17	Dar	01/50	3370	-06/64	07/64	
63371	05/17	Dar	05/50	3371	-10/65	05/66	
63372	06/17	Dar	03/50	3372	-05/60	06/60	
63373	06/17	Dar	09/50	3373	-07/63	09/63	
63374	06/17	Dar	05/48	3374	-04/63	07/63	
63375	06/17	Dar	06/50	3375	-08/63	10/63	
63376	06/17	Dar	02/50	3376	-07/63	11/63	
63377	06/17	Dar	06/48	3377	-11/66	02/67	
63378	06/17	Dar	06/50	3378	-04/65	08/65	
63379	06/17	Dar	12/48	3379	-09/66	02/67	
63380	07/17	Dar	07/48	3380	-07/63	08/63	
63381	08/17	Dar	05/49	3381	-12/66	03/67	
63382	08/17	Dar	07/50	3382	-09/64	02/65	
63383	09/17	Dar	06/48	3383	-04/64	09/64	
63384	10/17	Dar	01/51	3384	-01/66	04/66	
63385	10/17	Dar	12/50	3385	-10/63	01/64	
63386	10/17	Dar	09/48	3386	-12/65	04/66	
63387	11/17	Dar	09/48	3387	-09/67	11/67	
63388	12/17	Dar	12/48	3388	-03/64	04/64	
63389	12/17	Dar	06/48	3389	-12/65	05/66	
63390	08/18	Dar	11/48	3390	-08/63	09/63	
63391	09/18	Dar	09/48	3391	-04/65	09/65	
63392	10/18	Dar	04/48	3392	-11/63	12/63	
63393	10/18	Dar	08/48	3393	-06/64	10/64	
63394	11/18	Dar	05/48	3394	-07/67	08/67	
63395 §	12/18	Dar	06/48	3395	-09/67		
63396	12/18	Dar	11/50	3396	-04/63	06/63	
63397	12/18	Dar	05/48	3397	-05/67	08/67	
63398	12/18	Dar	10/48	3398	-10/65	12/65	
63399	12/18	Dar	12/48	3399	-03/64	05/64	
63400	05/19	Dar	04/51	3400	-08/63	09/63	
63401	05/19	Dar	12/48	3401	-04/64	08/64	
63402	05/19	Dar	06/48	3402	-09/64	02/65	
63403	05/19	Dar	08/49	3403	-07/64	08/64	
63404	06/19	Dar	05/50	3404	-05/65	08/65	
63405	06/19	Dar	02/51	3405	-12/66	05/67	
63406	06/19	Dar	11/48	3406	-07/66	12/66	
63407	07/19	Dar	07/50	3407	-07/67	11/67	
63408	07/19	Dar	05/50	3408	-07/63	09/63	
63409	08/19	Dar	05/48	3409	-09/66	12/66	
63410	11/19	AW	05/48	3410	-06/66	10/66	
63411	12/19	AW	03/49	3411	-04/65	07/65	
63412	12/19	AW	09/50	3412	-07/66	05/67	
63413	02/20	AW	12/48	3413	-01/67	04/67	
63414	02/20	AW	07/50	3414	-05/65	08/65	
63415	02/20	AW	05/48	3415	-04/64	07/64	
63416	02/20	AW	10/48	3416	-07/63	08/63	
63417	02/20	AW	03/49	3417	-02/66	05/66	
63418	02/20	AW	08/48	3418	-07/63	10/63	
63419	02/20	AW	06/48	3419	-06/65	08/65	
63420	03/20	AW	12/48	3420	-02/67	05/67	
63421	03/20	AW	03/50	3421	-06/66	10/67	
63422	03/20	AW	08/49	3422	-05/64	07/64	
63423	03/20	AW	12/48	3423	-11/64	12/64	
63424	03/20	AW	06/50	3424	-01/64	02/64	
63425	03/20	AW	12/49	3425	-04/63	05/63	
63426	04/20	AW	09/48	3426	-07/67	10/67	
63427	04/20	AW	11/49	3427	-06/65	10/65	
63428	04/20	AW	10/50	3428	-04/63	05/63	
63429	05/20	AW	12/48	3429	-07/67	11/67	
63430	05/20	AW	03/49	3430	-04/63	05/63	
63431	05/20	AW	11/48	3431	-08/67	09/67	
63432	05/20	AW	08/50	3432	-05/65	08/65	
63433	05/20	AW	03/49	3433	-09/63	01/64	
63434	05/20	AW	08/48	3434	-09/63	11/63	
63435	06/20	AW	08/50	3435	-06/66	11/66	
63436	06/20	AW	01/49	3436	-04/67	09/67	
63437	06/20	AW	01/51	3437	-07/67	10/67	
63438	06/20	AW	11/48	3438	-11/64	11/64	
63439	06/20	AW	09/50	3439	-04/64	09/64	
63440	06/20	AW	05/49	3440	-12/66	03/67	
63441	07/20	AW	01/49	3441	-12/63	02/64	
63442	07/20	AW	08/49	3442	-07/63	08/63	
63443	07/20	AW	03/49	3443	-10/65	12/65	
63444	08/20	AW	10/49	3444	-05/65	07/65	
63445	09/20	AW	06/50	3445	-06/66	09/66	
63446	09/20	AW	10/50	3446	-06/66	10/66	
63447	10/20	AW	12/48	3447	-04/63	08/63	
63448	10/20	AW	07/48	3448	-11/63	01/64	
63449	10/20	AW	08/48	3449	-07/63	09/63	
63450	11/20	AW	10/48	3450	-12/66	05/67	
63451	11/20	AW	08/48	3451	-01/64	01/64	
63452	11/20	AW	10/50	3452	-04/63	06/63	
63453	12/20	AW	04/48	3453	-10/66	12/66	
63454	12/20	AW	08/48	3454	-06/66	10/66	
63455	12/20	AW	09/48	3455	-07/67	09/67	
63456	01/21	AW	01/49	3456	-11/64	01/65	
63457	01/21	AW	09/49	3457	-12/61	12/61	
63458	03/21	AW	04/50	3458	-07/67	11/67	
63459	03/21	AW	04/48	3459	-10/66	05/67	

Q7 63460-63474
0-8-0 NER Raven 3-cylinder

Power Classification:	7F reclassified 8F in 1953
Introduced:	1919-1924
Designer:	Raven
Company:	NER
Weight:	Loco 71t 12cwt Tender 44t 2cwt
Driving Wheel:	4' 7¼"
Boiler Pressure:	180psi superheated
Cylinders:	Three 18½" x 26"
Tractive Effort:	36965lbf
Valve Gear:	Stephenson (piston valves)

The 'Q7' class (NER class 'T3'), designed by Raven, consisted of fifteen three-cylinder engines. The first five engines were built in 1919 and the final ten after grouping in 1924. The boilers were interchangeable with those of the 'B16' three-cylinder 4-6-0 class. They were excellent engines and in trials held between Edinburgh and Perth in 1921, they came out very favourably when pitted against a NBR 'J37' and a GWR '2800'.

They could be distinguished from the 'Q6' class, by the fact that the outside cylinders on the 'Q6's drove on the third pair of wheels, while those on the 'Q7's drove on the second pair. The engines were all withdrawn at the end of 1962.

Year End Totals: 'Q7' class

'47	'48	'49	'50	'51	'52	'53	'54	'55	'56	'57	'58	'59	'60	'61	'62	'63	'64	'65	'66	'67
15	15	15	15	15	15	15	15	15	15	15	15	15	15	15						

Number	*Built*	*Renumbered*	*BR Dates*	*Scrap*	*Notes*
63460 §	10/19 Dar	06/51 3460	-12/62		
63461	10/19 Dar	07/50 3461	-12/62	03/63	
63462	10/19 Dar	05/48 3462	-12/62	03/63	
63463	11/19 Dar	02/49 3463	-12/62	05/63	
63464	11/19 Dar	05/50 3464	-12/62	03/63	
63465	03/24 Dar	06/48 3465	-12/62	05/63	
63466	03/24 Dar	04/48 3466	-12/62	05/63	
63467	04/24 Dar	10/50 3467	-11/62	01/63	
63468	04/24 Dar	07/48 3468	-11/62	01/63	
63469	04/24 Dar	09/48 3469	-12/62	04/63	
63470	04/24 Dar	04/50 3470	-12/62	03/63	
63471	05/24 Dar	12/49 3471	-12/62	05/63	
63472	04/24 Dar	04/50 3472	-12/62	04/63	
63473	05/24 Dar	09/49 3473	-12/62	04/63	
63474	05/24 Dar	01/49 3474	-12/62	12/62	

O3 63475-63494
2-8-0 GNR Gresley 2-cylinder

Power Classification: 8F
Introduced: 1913-1919
Designer: Gresley
Company: GNR
Weight: Loco 76t 4cwt
Tender 43t 2cwt
Driving Wheel: 4' 8"
Boiler Pressure: 180psi superheated
Cylinders: Outside 21" x 28"
Tractive Effort: 33735lbf
Valve Gear: Walschaert (piston valves)

The 'O3' class was Gresley's two-cylinder design which was built for the GNR. A total of twenty engines were built in 1913-1919. The class was withdrawn in 1947-1952 and seventeen came into BR stock. They were known as the 'O1' class until 1944.

Year End Totals: 'O3' class

'47	'48	'49	'50	'51	'52	'53	'54	'55	'56	'57	'58	'59	'60	'61	'62	'63	'64	'65	'66	'67
17	15	15	14	4																

Number	*Built*	*Renumbered*	*BR Dates*	*Scrap*	*Notes*
63475	12/13 Don	11/49 3475	-08/51	*11/51*	
63476	12/13 Don	03/48 3476	-03/52	04/52	
63477	12/13 Don	07/48 3477	-09/51	51	
63478	01/14 Don	06/48 3478	-09/51	*51*	
63479	03/14 Don	10/48 3479	-05/51	*05/51*	
63480	05/19 NB	04/49 3480	-03/51	*05/51*	
63481	05/19 NB	01/49 3481	-04/51	*05/51*	
63482	05/19 NB	06/50 3482	-01/52	*52*	
63483	05/19 NB	04/48 3483	-04/51	*05/51*	
63484	05/19 NB	10/48 3484	-12/52	*12/52*	
63485	05/19 NB	08/48 3485	-09/51	*09/51*	
63486	06/19 NB	09/48 3486	-02/51	*51*	
63488	07/19 NB	07/48 3488	-03/52	*06/53*	
63489	07/19 NB	3489	-07/48	*48*	
63491	10/19 NB	12/48 3491	-12/50	*51*	
63493	11/19 NB	07/48 3493	-02/51	52	
63494	11/19 NB	3494	-03/48	*04/48*	

O6 (63554)
2-8-0 MOS (WD) Stanier '8F'

Power Classification: 8F
Introduced: 1935-1945 (on LNER 1944)
Designer: Stanier
Company: MOS (WD)
Weight: Loco 72t 2cwt
Tender 54t 13cwt
Driving Wheel: 4' 8½"
Boiler Pressure: 225psi superheated
Cylinders: Outside 18½" x 28"
Tractive Effort: 32440lbf
Valve Gear: Walschaert (piston valves)

Stanier's heavy standard freight engine design for the LMS (the '8F' class) was introduced in 1935. The design was an immediate success and in 1939 the type was adopted for war-time use. 240 engines were ordered for the War Department, and these engines went overseas to the Middle East, many of them never to return.

In addition many more engines were built for home use during the war. It gave rise to a unique situation in 1944 when engines of purely LMS design were being built in the workshops of each of the four (still independent) Railway Companies, as well as by outside firms.

The LNER owned sixty-eight of these engines and they were known as the 'O6' class. 7651-7675 were built for the LNER at Brighton by the SR in 1944. They were later renumbered 3100-3124, and another batch was built as 3125-3167 by the LNER. In 1947 the entire sequence was renumbered 3500-3567, and then they returned to the LMS on loan in 1947 receiving the LMS numbers 8705-8772 (these are listed in the LMS section of this book as 48705-48772). However No. 3554 was not returned to the former LMS until early 1948 (becoming 8759 and later 48759) and therefore it is listed here.

Although this engine is listed here as 63554 it was never allocated this number as it was transferred early in 1948 before the renumbering scheme was finalised.

Year End Totals: 'O6' class

'47	'48	'49	'50	'51	'52	'53	'54	'55	'56	'57	'58	'59	'60	'61	'62	'63	'64	'65	'66	'67
68																				

Number	*Built*	*Renumbered*	*BR Dates*	*Notes*
(63554)	12/45 Don	3554	-01/48	01/48➲ (4)8759

O4 63570-63920
2-8-0 GCR and ROD Robinson

O1 between 63571 & 63901
2-8-0 LNER Thompson rebuild of 'O4'

Power Classification: 7F
O1 8F
Introduced: 1911-1920
4 Rebuilt 1932-1939 by Gresley
5 Rebuilt 1932 onwards by Gresley
6 1918, rebuilt 1924 onwards by Gresley
7 Rebuilt 1939-1944 by Gresley
8 Rebuilt 1944-1958 by Thompson
O1 Rebuilt 1944-1949 by Thompson
Designer: Robinson
Company: GCR and ROD
Weight: Loco 73t 4cwt
5 Loco 74t 13cwt
7 Loco 73t 17cwt
8 Loco 72t 10cwt
O1 Loco 73t 6cwt
Tender 47t 6cwt
w Tender 48t 6cwt
Driving Wheel: 4' 8"
Boiler Pressure: 180psi superheated
O1 225psi superheated
Cylinders: Outside 21" x 26"
O1 Outside 20" x 26"
Tractive Effort: 31325lbf
O1 35520lbf
Valve Gear: Stephenson (piston valves)
O1 Walschaert (piston valves)

In 1911 Robinson introduced a highly successful design of 2-8-0 on the Great Central Railway for hauling coal. Known as the '8K' class (LNER 'O4' class) 130 of these strong, but graceful engines were built between 1911 and 1920 and they soon became favourites with the men.

In 1918 eighteen more engines were built at Gorton with large 6ft diameter boilers (GCR class '8M', LNER class 'O5') and they were known as the 'Tiny's'. They were later rebuilt with 5ft diameter boilers and were incorporated in the 'O4' class.

During the First World War the class was adopted by the Railway Operating Division of the Royal Engineers as a standard type for war service. 521 locomotives were built between 1917 and 1919 by many different locomotive builders for service in France. They were almost identical with the GCR engines, but most of them were fitted with steel fireboxes. Some engines stayed in this country and eventually all returned safely to Britain.

At the end of the war the engines were disposed of by the War Department. One hundred engines were purchased by the GWR ('ROD' class), fifty by the LNWR (all withdrawn by 1933), and the LNER eventually absorbed another 273 into its stock alongside the original GCR engines. Others were sold overseas to China and Australia, where they were reported to be still at work in the late 1960s.

Again in the Second World War ninety-two of the LNER engines were commandeered for work overseas in Egypt and Palestine. Many of these were engines which had already worked overseas in 1917-1918. When the LNER renumbering scheme was drawn up the class was to be renumbered from 3500 upwards, with space left for the return of these engines. However, none of them did return after the second World War and the LNER engines eventually became 3570-3920.

By the time 329 engines came into BR ownership they had all been fitted with 'flower-pot' chimneys by Gresley, and they were provided with a variety of different boilers. Five engines were sold to the War Department in 1952.

1 'O4/1'. These were the original engines built with small GCR Belpaire boilers, steam vacuum brakes and tenders with water scoops.

2 'O4/2' were 'O4/3' engines with cab and boiler mountings reduced to fit the Scottish loading gauge. They were converted from 1925 onwards. They were reclassified 'O4/1' in 1947.

3 'O4/3'. These were ROD engines with small Belpaire boilers, steam brake only and tenders without water scoops. They were reclassified 'O4/1' in 1947.

4 'O4/4' was the classification used for engines rebuilt with 'O2' boilers. The last of these was converted to 'O4/8' in 1947.

5 'O4/5'. These were engines which were rebuilt from 1932 onwards with shortened 'O2' type boilers with round top fireboxes and the smokebox on a saddle.

6 'O4/6'. These were the original large boilered 'O5' class. They were rebuilt from 1924 onwards with smaller Belpaire boilers, but still retained the higher cabs.

7 'O4/7'. These engines were rebuilt from 1939 onwards with shortened 'O2' type boilers with round top fireboxes. As such they were similar to the 'O4/5' class, but they retained their original GCR smokeboxes.

8 'O4/8'. These engines were rebuilt from 1944 onwards with '100A' ('B1' type) boilers, retaining the original cylinders. They were fitted with side window cabs.

O1 Thompson rebuilt fifty-eight engines from 1944 onwards with '100A' ('B1' type) boilers, side window cabs, Walschaert valve gear and raised running plates. Classified 'O1', they had a much more modern appearance and looked like a 2-8-0 version of the 'B1' class.

s 63912-63920 of the 'O4/6' class had side window cabs.

w Two different types of tenders were fitted, some with a water scoop (w) and some without, but these are not noted in the lists.

Year End Totals: 'O4/1, O4/6' class

'47	'48	'49	'50	'51	'52	'53	'54	'55	'56	'57	'58	'59	'60	'61	'62	'63	'64	'65	'66	'67
213	212	209	209	209	202	197	191	179	163	145	130	96	92	83	34	20	13	1		

Year End Totals: 'O4/5' class

'47	'48	'49	'50	'51	'52	'53	'54	'55	'56	'57	'58	'59	'60	'61	'62	'63	'64	'65	'66	'67
8	7	6	6	6	6	6	6	4	4	3	2									

Year End Totals: 'O4/7' class

'47	'48	'49	'50	'51	'52	'53	'54	'55	'56	'57	'58	'59	'60	'61	'62	'63	'64	'65	'66	'67
41	41	40	40	40	40	40	40	40	39	35	34	27	24	18	7	4	3			

Year End Totals: 'O4/8' class

'47	'48	'49	'50	'51	'52	'53	'54	'55	'56	'57	'58	'59	'60	'61	'62	'63	'64	'65	'66	'67
16	16	16	16	16	18	23	29	43	60	83	99	99	99	95	75	64	41	12		

Year End Totals: 'O1' class

'47	'48	'49	'50	'51	'52	'53	'54	'55	'56	'57	'58	'59	'60	'61	'62	'63	'64	'65	'66	'67
51	53	58	58	58	58	58	58	58	58	58	58	58	58	58	30	18	10			

Number	Built	Renumbered	BR Dates	Scrap	Notes
63570	10/12 NB	01/49 3570	-12/61	02/62	7
63571	10/12 NB	08/48 3571	-12/64	04/65	1 08/49⇨O1
63572	09/11 Gor	06/49 3572	-11/59	12/59	1
63573	11/12 NB	02/50 3573	-04/61	05/61	1 04/55⇨8
63574	11/12 NB	08/48 3574	-09/62	02/64	1
63575	11/12 NB	10/48 3575	-11/62	12/62	8
63576	11/12 NB	05/50 3576	-11/63	02/64	1
63577	12/11 Gor	07/49 3577	-12/63	02/64	1
63578	11/12 NB	01/50 3578	-12/62	06/63	O1
63579	11/12 NB	03/48 3579	-12/62	09/63	5 03/48⇨O1
63580	12/11 Gor	05/48 3580	-02/52	*61*	1
63581	11/12 NB	12/49 3581	-02/59	03/59	1
63582	12/11 Gor	01/49 3582	-08/59	09/59	7
63583	11/12 NB	10/50 3583	-06/59	08/59	1
63584	11/19 NB	01/50 3584	-08/62	12/62	1
63585	10/11 Gor	10/50 3585	-12/63	03/64	1
63586	10/11 Gor	11/50 3586	-10/65	03/66	1
63587	12/12 NB	07/48 3587	-09/62	10/63	1
63588	12/12 NB	07/48 3588	-08/62	12/62	7
63589	12/12 NB	04/49 3589	-07/65	10/65	5 04/49⇨O1
63590	12/12 NB	01/49 3590	-07/65	10/65	O1
63591	12/12 NB	07/48 3591	-12/62	09/63	O1
63592	12/12 NB	07/48 3592	-07/63	09/63	O1
63593	12/12 NB	06/48 3593	-10/65	12/65	1
63594	11/11 Gor	04/49 3594	-04/64	10/64	O1
63595	12/12 NB	06/48 3595	-04/61	05/61	7
63596	12/12 NB	07/49 3596	-08/63	02/64	7 08/49⇨O1
63597	12/12 NB	05/49 3597	-05/61	06/61	1
63598	11/11 Gor	09/49 3598	-11/62	03/63	1
63599	01/13 NB	02/49 3599	-02/62	03/62	1
63600	11/11 Gor	09/49 3600	-11/62	12/62	7
63601 §	01/12 Gor	09/49 3601	-06/63		1
63602	05/13 Gor	04/50 3602	-12/62	09/63	1 03/55⇨8
63603	05/13 Gor	11/48 3603	-07/62	10/62	7
63604	06/13 Gor	04/48 3604	-05/64	10/64	1 01/54⇨8
63605	06/13 Gor	04/48 3605	-08/62	12/62	1
63606	07/13 Gor	07/48 3606	-06/65	09/65	1 06/55⇨8
63607	01/12 Gor	09/48 3607	-09/65	03/66	1
63608	02/12 Gor	12/48 3608	-05/61	06/61	1
63609	09/13 Gor	05/49 3609	-09/62	08/63	1
63610	12/13 Gor	04/49 3610	-12/62	01/63	O1
63611	01/14 Gor	02/51 3611	-03/64	07/64	1
63612	01/14 Gor	03/50 3612	-11/65	02/66	1 07/55⇨8
63613	02/14 Gor	10/48 3613	-07/65	11/65	8
63614	02/14 Gor	10/48 3614	-04/59	09/59	1
63615	02/14 Gor	10/48 3615	-09/64	05/65	7
63616	03/14 Gor	12/50 3616	-09/62	10/63	7
63617	06/12 Gor	05/50 3617	-12/62	07/63	1
63618	03/14 Gor	03/49 3618	-02/63	05/63	1
63619	04/14 Gor	08/49 3619	-10/63	07/64	O1
63620	04/14 Gor	03/50 3620	-02/59	03/59	1
63621	05/14 Gor	05/50 3621	-09/62	08/63	1
63622	05/14 Gor	10/48 3622	-05/63	06/63	1
63623	05/14 Gor	07/48 3623	-02/62	03/62	1
63624	06/14 Gor	09/50 3624	-12/62	08/63	1 05/55⇨8
63625	06/12 Gor	08/48 3625	-04/59	07/59	1
63626	06/19 Gor	05/48 3626	-06/61	07/61	1
63627	06/19 Gor	06/49 3627	-02/52	*61*	1
63628	06/19 Gor	07/48 3628	-09/65	10/65	5 02/55⇨8
63629	12/17 NW	11/49 3629	-02/59	02/61	3
63630	02/18 NW	06/48 3630	-07/65	10/65	O1
63631	06/18 NW	07/48 3631	-09/62	12/62	1 01/57⇨8
63632	07/12 Gor	11/50 3632	-01/64	03/64	1
63633	07/18 NW	02/49 3633	-08/62	11/62	8
63634	07/12 Gor	06/48 3634	-09/62	08/63	7
63635	08/12 Gor	03/49 3635	-05/62	05/64	1
63636	10/18 NW	07/48 3636	-12/64	04/65	3 12/57⇨8
63637	10/18 NW	07/49 3637	-12/62	10/63	3
63638	10/18 NW	10/48 3638	-03/59	05/59	3
63639	10/18 NW	08/49 3639	-12/65	03/66	3 12/54⇨8
63640	08/12 Gor	11/49 3640	-05/59	07/59	1
63641	09/19 NW	12/49 3641	-09/62	12/62	3 06/57⇨8
63642	09/19 NW	02/50 3642	-11/59	12/59	3
63643	08/12 Gor	10/49 3643	-11/60	01/61	7
63644	01/18 K	08/49 3644	-01/66	04/66	2 08/54⇨8
63645	02/18 K	08/48 3645	-04/64	11/64	3 09/56⇨8
63646	02/18 K	05/49 3646	-07/65	10/65	O1
63647	02/18 K	52 3647	-05/64	08/64	2 03/58⇨8
63648	02/18 K	02/51 3648	-01/62	03/62	2
63649	03/18 K	01/50 3649	-03/61	04/61	3 11/57⇨8
63650	03/18 K	09/49 3650	-06/65	10/65	O1
63651	03/18 K	01/49 3651	-07/65	12/65	8
63652	03/18 K	04/48 3652	-11/63	05/64	O1
63653	04/18 K	06/49 3653	-04/66	07/66	8
63654	09/12 Gor	03/49 3654	-06/59	09/59	1
63655	06/18 K	10/48 3655	-12/62	09/63	7 01/57⇨8
63656	06/18 K	06/48 3656	-12/62	02/64	3
63657	06/18 K	12/50 3657	-09/62	05/64	3
63658	02/12 Gor	09/48 3658	-12/62	08/63	1
63659	07/18 K	05/50 3659	-12/62	04/64	3
63660	03/12 Gor	08/49 3660	-09/59	10/59	1
63661	07/18 K	12/48 3661	-08/65	10/65	7
63662	08/18 K	05/48 3662	-05/61	06/61	7
63663	08/18 K	08/49 3663	-11/64	03/65	O1
63664	03/12 Gor	05/48 3664	-09/62	01/63	1
63665	09/18 K	01/50 3665	-12/63	04/64	3
63666	09/18 K	05/48 3666	-12/62	10/63	3
63667	09/18 K	06/50 3667	-01/59	01/59	3
63668	10/18 K	06/49 3668	-12/58	02/59	3
63669	04/12 Gor	06/49 3669	-11/60	11/60	7
63670	09/17 RS	09/48 3670	-06/64	01/65	O1
63671	05/12 Gor	11/49 3671	-06/65	08/65	1
63672	10/17 RS	08/50 3672	-12/63	04/64	3 04/57⇨8
63673	10/17 RS	06/48 3673	-04/59	09/59	7
63674	10/17 RS	04/48 3674	-01/66	04/66	2 05/57⇨8
63675	10/17 RS	08/48 3675	-01/66	04/66	7 02/57⇨8
63676	11/17 RS	04/49 3676	-12/62	12/62	O1
63677	05/12 Gor	01/49 3677	-03/62	03/62	1
63678	05/12 Gor	09/48 3678	-07/63	09/63	O1
63679	12/17 RS	06/50 3679	-05/65	08/65	3 11/57⇨8
63680	07/12 K	07/50 3680	-09/59	12/59	2
63681	12/17 RS	05/48 3681	-03/62	03/62	3
63682	12/17 RS	06/49 3682	-03/59	09/59	2
63683	07/12 K	04/51 3683	-03/65	05/65	1 08/53⇨8
63684	07/12 K	03/50 3684	-12/63	04/64	1
63685	01/18 RS	02/49 3685	-03/64	12/64	3
63686	02/18 RS	04/48 3686	-09/62	12/62	3
63687	02/18 RS	06/49 3687	-10/63	02/64	O1
63688	02/18 RS	01/49 3688	-09/65	12/65	3 11/56⇨8
63689	03/18 RS	10/49 3689	-12/62	09/63	O1
63690	07/12 K	09/49 3690	-12/62	09/63	2
63691	04/18 RS	10/48 3691	-06/65	01/66	3 03/56⇨8
63692	07/12 K	09/48 3692	-02/65	07/65	1
63693	08/12 K	02/51 3693	-12/62	03/64	1
63694	04/18 RS	01/49 3694	-10/59	01/60	3
63695	05/18 RS	05/48 3695	-12/62	07/63	3
63696	05/18 RS	03/49 3696	-04/59	07/59	3
63697	06/18 RS	01/49 3697	-08/65	10/65	3 05/58⇨8
63698	08/12 K	04/48 3698	-12/62	04/64	1
63699	06/18 RS	05/49 3699	-06/59	08/59	7
63700	08/12 K	01/49 3700	-12/60	01/61	1
63701	07/18 RS	09/50 3701	-08/65	11/65	3
63702	07/18 RS	05/48 3702	-09/64	03/65	3
63703	08/18 RS	10/50 3703	-01/65	03/65	3 01/53⇨8
63704	10/18 RS	11/50 3704	-03/63	09/63	2 12/53⇨8
63705	10/18 RS	07/49 3705	-04/63	12/63	7 07/58⇨8
63706	10/18 RS	12/48 3706	-09/65	01/66	7 11/56⇨8
63707	09/12 K	12/50 3707	-07/65	04/66	1
63708	11/18 RS	05/48 3708	-09/62	08/63	7
63709	12/18 RS	08/50 3709	-02/61	05/61	2 02/58⇨8
63710	09/12 K	10/50 3710	-07/59	09/59	1
63711	09/12 K	06/49 3711	-12/62	09/63	O1
63712	01/19 RS	02/49 3712	-11/62	12/62	O1
63713	01/19 RS	10/49 3713	-08/62	10/62	3
63714	01/19 RS	02/50 3714	-03/59	05/59	3
63715	02/19 RS	06/48 3715	-01/64	03/64	3 01/58⇨8
63716	02/19 RS	04/49 3716	-07/60	09/60	3
63717	03/19 RS	10/48 3717	-04/65	08/65	3 03/58⇨8
63718	03/19 RS	06/48 3718	-12/62	10/63	3 06/56⇨8
63719	09/12 K	11/50 3719	-08/61	09/61	1
63720	05/19 RS	10/48 3720	-03/64	12/64	3 02/57⇨8
63721	06/19 RS	08/49 3721	-11/62	12/62	3 04/54⇨8
63722	09/12 K	03/49 3722	-09/63	11/63	1
63723	10/12 K	01/49 3723	-11/59	12/59	1
63724	08/19 RS	06/49 3724	-08/62	11/62	3
63725	08/19 RS	08/49 3725	-07/65	10/65	O1
63726	10/19 RS	06/48 3726	-04/64	08/64	5 01/58⇨8
63727	10/12 K	12/49 3727	-02/64	03/64	1
63728	10/19 RS	06/48 3728	-12/64	08/65	3 02/56⇨8
63729	11/19 RS	06/48 3729	-03/59	10/59	3
63730	11/19 RS	02/49 3730	-01/66	02/66	2 03/58⇨8
63731	12/19 RS	01/49 3731	-10/63	07/64	3 09/56⇨8
63732	12/19 RS	06/48 3732	-09/65	11/65	3 07/56⇨8
63733	04/20 RS	10/50 3733	-01/60	04/60	3
63734	04/20 RS	08/48 3734	-08/65	10/65	3 56⇨8
63735	09/17 NB	12/48 3735	-12/62	06/63	3
63736	08/17 NB	10/49 3736	-08/63	10/63	1
63737	09/17 NB	04/50 3737	-12/62	07/63	3
63738	08/17 NB	05/48 3738	-08/65	10/65	8
63739	10/17 NB	03/48 3739	-10/65	01/66	3 05/58⇨8
63740	10/17 NB	04/48 3740	-12/62	09/63	O1
63741	10/17 NB	11/49 3741	-04/65	07/65	3 07/58⇨8
63742	10/17 NB	10/48 3742	-02/63	07/63	3 09/56⇨8
63743	08/17 NB	06/49 3743	-06/62	07/62	1
63744	10/17 NB	05/48 3744	-07/63	08/63	3
63745	08/17 NB	01/50 3745	-04/59	07/59	5
63746	10/17 NB	11/48 3746	-02/64	12/64	3 11/48⇨O1
63747	11/17 NB	04/48 3747	-05/61	06/61	7
63748	11/17 NB	08/48 3748	-12/62	09/63	7
63749	11/17 NB	08/48 3749	-10/59	01/60	7
63750	11/17 NB	01/50 3750	-03/64	06/64	3 10/52⇨8
63751	12/17 NB	02/49 3751	-03/59	07/59	3
63752	12/17 NB	11/48 3752	-12/62	06/63	O1
63753	12/17 NB	03/50 3753	-12/59	04/60	3
63754	12/17 NB	09/49 3754	-02/64	06/64	3 57⇨8
63755	11/17 NB	08/49 3755	-11/62	03/63	O1
63756	12/17 NB	12/48 3756	-06/59	09/59	3
63757	08/12 NB	06/48 3757	-11/61	12/61	1
63758	01/18 NB	08/48 3758	-05/62	07/62	7
63759	01/18 NB	08/48 3759	-09/62	08/63	3
63760	02/18 NB	06/49 3760	-11/62	05/63	O1
63761	08/12 NB	02/49 3761	-06/59	09/59	7
63762	08/12 NB	09/48 3762	-03/62	04/62	1
63763	03/18 NB	08/48 3763	-02/64	04/64	3 10/53⇨8
63764	03/18 NB	06/48 3764	-02/66	05/66	3
63765	03/18 NB	03/48 3765	-10/64	01/65	3 12/57⇨8
63766	03/18 NB	05/48 3766	-08/62	10/62	3
63767	03/18 NB	05/49 3767	-11/62	12/62	3
63768	03/18 NB	05/48 3768	-07/65	11/65	O1
63769	04/18 NB	06/49 3769	-03/59	07/59	3
63770	04/18 NB	10/49 3770	-12/65	03/66	7
63771	04/18 NB	12/48 3771	-12/62	10/63	3
63772	08/12 NB	11/49 3772	-03/63	04/64	7
63773	08/12 NB	04/48 3773	-10/64	02/65	O1
63774	04/18 NB	01/49 3774	-03/63	10/63	3
63775	04/18 NB	05/49 3775	-03/62	04/62	7
63776	04/18 NB	10/50 3776	-12/62	03/64	3 04/55⇨8
63777	09/12 NB	04/48 3777	-11/62	09/63	O1
63778	09/12 NB	08/49 3778	-02/52	*61*	1
63779	05/18 NB	12/49 3779	-04/62	05/62	3
63780	05/18 NB	09/48 3780	-07/63	09/63	O1
63781	05/18 NB	10/48 3781	-04/66	07/66	3 04/58⇨8
63782	05/18 NB	05/49 3782	-05/61	06/61	3
63783	05/18 NB	12/48 3783	-12/62	08/63	3
63784	05/18 NB	08/48 3784	-08/63	12/63	O1
63785	05/18 NB	02/49 3785	-03/66	06/66	8
63786	06/18 NB	02/49 3786	-09/64	01/65	O1
63787	06/18 NB	02/49 3787	-06/62	07/62	3
63788	06/18 NB	03/49 3788	-01/66	02/66	5 03/57⇨8
63789	09/12 NB	04/48 3789	-12/62	06/63	O1
63790	02/18 NB	08/49 3790	-03/59	05/59	3
63791	02/18 NB	07/48 3791	-09/65	12/65	3 10/56⇨8
63792	02/18 NB	02/49 3792	-11/62	09/63	O1
63793	02/18 NB	09/50 3793	-05/65	08/65	3 04/58⇨8
63794	02/18 NB	10/48 3794	-11/62	12/62	7 05/57⇨8
63795	02/18 NB	12/48 3795	-10/63	02/64	O1
63796	03/18 NB	12/48 3796	-11/62	09/63	O1
63797	09/12 NB	01/50 3797	-02/59	04/59	1
63798	03/18 NB	08/49 3798	-05/62	06/62	3
63799	10/12 NB	05/48 3799	-11/61	02/62	1
63800	03/18 NB	06/48 3800	-05/64	03/65	3 06/57⇨8
63801	03/18 NB	10/48 3801	-07/63	10/63	3 08/56⇨8

63802	04/18 NB	05/49 3802	-06/64	10/64	8
63803	10/12 NB	10/49 3803	-03/63	04/63	O1
63804	04/18 NB	03/49 3804	-12/59	01/60	3
63805	10/12 NB	11/49 3805	-11/62	12/62	1
					06/54⇨8
63806	05/18 NB	01/51 3806	-12/62	10/63	O1
63807	05/18 NB	09/50 3807	-09/64	01/65	3
					11/52⇨8
63808	05/18 NB	11/49 3808	-12/62	09/63	O1
63809	10/12 NB	07/49 3809	-02/52	*61*	1
63812	06/18 NB	01/49 3812	-05/59	07/59	3
63813	06/18 NB	09/50 3813	-03/65	07/65	3
63816	06/18 NB	11/48 3816	-01/66	04/66	5
					12/55⇨8
63817	07/18 NB	01/49 3817	-12/62	09/63	O1
63818	07/18 NB	09/49 3818	-04/66	07/66	8
63819	07/18 NB	02/49 3819	-11/65	03/66	8
63821	10/18 NB	01/50 3821	-12/62	08/63	3
63822	10/18 NB	04/48 3822	-03/64	07/64	3
					12/58⇨8
63823	10/18 NB	09/48 3823	-08/62	12/62	3
					11/57⇨8
63824	11/18 NB	08/50 3824	-06/63	08/63	7
63827	11/18 NB	10/49 3827	-01/64	12/64	8
63828	12/18 NB	09/48 3828	-08/65	09/65	8
63829	12/18 NB	09/48 3829	-03/64	04/64	3
					05/58⇨8
63832	02/19 NB	09/49 3832	-12/62	03/64	3
					02/58⇨8
63833	02/19 NB	03/48 3833	-01/62	02/62	3
63835	10/18 NB	09/48 3835	-02/59	04/59	3
63836	10/18 NB	11/49 3836	-04/64	10/64	8
63837	11/18 NB	12/48 3837	-12/62	05/64	3
					02/54⇨8
63838	11/18 NB	06/49 3838	-11/62	10/63	3
					06/49⇨O1
63839	12/18 NB	06/49 3839	-04/59	09/59	7
63840	01/19 NB	11/50 3840	-09/63	11/63	3
					08/57⇨8
63841	02/19 NB	02/49 3841	-03/64	07/64	3
					05/56⇨8
63842	02/19 NB	03/51 3842	-04/65	08/65	3
63843	02/19 NB	11/49 3843	-11/65	02/66	7
63845	05/19 NB	08/49 3845	-06/61	06/61	3
63846	05/19 NB	06/48 3846	-06/64	10/64	3
63847	05/19 NB	09/49 3847	-05/59	07/59	2
63848	05/19 NB	12/48 3848	-11/62	12/62	7
63849	06/19 NB	11/48 3849	-02/52	*61*	3
63850	06/19 NB	06/50 3850	-06/65	08/65	3
					10/55⇨8
63851	06/19 NB	12/48 3851	-04/59	06/59	5
63852	06/19 NB	06/50 3852	-01/64	12/64	3
					11/55⇨8
63853	06/19 NB	01/49 3853	-11/63	02/64	8
63854	06/19 NB	06/48 3854	-12/62	09/63	O1
63855	06/19 NB	09/48 3855	-03/59	06/59	3
63856	06/19 NB	10/49 3856	-11/62	05/63	3
					10/49⇨O1
63857	07/19 NB	06/49 3857	-08/62	11/62	7
63858	07/19 NB	11/48 3858	-04/66	07/66	3
					05/53⇨8
63859	07/19 NB	05/49 3859	-10/63	05/64	3
63860	07/19 NB	04/50 3860	-10/61	01/62	7
63861	07/19 NB	04/48 3861	-02/65	04/65	3
					11/57⇨8
63862	08/19 NB	03/49 3862	-11/62	12/62	3
					07/57⇨8
63863	08/19 NB	05/50 3863	-06/65	10/65	O1
63864	08/19 NB	04/49 3864	-08/62	10/62	3
					09/57⇨8
63865	08/19 NB	08/50 3865	-12/62	09/63	O1
63867	08/19 NB	10/48 3867	-12/62	08/63	O1
63868	08/19 NB	11/49 3868	-07/65	11/65	O1
63869	08/19 NB	06/48 3869	-12/62	08/63	O1
63870	09/19 NB	03/51 3870	-01/62	02/62	3
63872	05/19 NB	04/48 3872	-01/64	12/64	O1
63873	05/19 NB	12/48 3873	-01/66	04/66	3
					08/55⇨8
63874	05/19 NB	02/49 3874	-11/62	01/63	O1
63876	06/19 NB	11/48 3876	-03/59	06/59	7
63877	06/19 NB	11/49 3877	-03/65	05/65	3
					04/57⇨8
63878	06/19 NB	05/50 3878	-03/65	07/65	3
					57⇨8
63879	07/19 NB	01/49 3879	-07/65	12/65	O1
63880	07/19 NB	10/49 3880	-03/63	03/64	7
63881	07/19 NB	04/48 3881	-12/62	09/63	3
					08/58⇨8
63882	08/19 NB	01/50 3882	-05/65	06/65	8
63883	04/19 NB	03/49 3883	-12/62	04/64	3
63884	04/19 NB	02/50 3884	-06/64	11/64	7
					02/57⇨8
63885	09/19 NB	06/48 3885	-08/62	10/62	3
					10/56⇨8
63886	09/19 NB	11/48 3886	-11/62	09/63	O1
63887	09/19 NB	09/48 3887	-02/63	03/63	O1
63888	09/19 NB	07/50 3888	-04/60	07/60	3
63889	09/19 NB	09/50 3889	-12/59	01/60	3
63890	05/19 NB	06/48 3890	-03/63	04/63	O1
63891	05/19 NB	08/48 3891	-09/61	01/62	7
63893	06/19 NB	05/49 3893	-06/65	08/65	8
63894	06/19 NB	11/48 3894	-07/60	07/60	7
63895	06/19 NB	08/48 3895	-07/62	08/62	3
					02/55⇨8
63897	06/19 NB	08/49 3897	-05/63	06/63	3
					02/56⇨8
63898	07/19 NB	12/49 3898	-05/63	06/63	3
					04/56⇨8
63899	10/19 NB	12/48 3899	-05/63	06/63	3
					09/55⇨8
63900	11/19 NB	02/50 3900	-09/62	05/64	3
63901	12/19 NB	02/50 3901	-12/62	08/63	O1
63902	01/18 Gor	04/48 3902	-04/65	08/65	6
63904	04/18 Gor	11/49 3904	-11/61	12/61	6
63905	05/18 Gor	09/49 3905	-04/59	05/59	6
63906	06/18 Gor	08/50 3906	-01/65	04/65	6
63907	08/18 Gor	06/48 3907	-05/64	08/64	6
63908	09/18 Gor	12/49 3908	-10/63	02/64	6
63911	06/19 Gor	12/49 3911	-12/62	04/64	6
63912	08/19 Gor	03/49 3912	-12/62	06/63	6s
63913	08/19 Gor	*52* 3913	-06/65	11/65	6s
63914	09/19 Gor	03/49 3914	-05/64	07/64	6s
					07/55⇨8
63915	10/19 Gor	04/48 3915	-06/61	07/61	6s
					01/56⇨8
63917	12/20 Gor	05/48 3917	-06/62	07/62	6s
63920	02/21 Gor	04/49 3920	-08/62	11/62	6s

O2 63921-63987
2-8-0 GNR Gresley 3-cylinder

Power Classification:	8F
Introduced:	1921-1943 o 1918 4 Rebuilt 1943 onwards by Thompson
Designer:	Gresley
Company:	GNR
Weight:	o Loco 76t 8cwt 12 Loco 75t 16cwt 3 Loco 78t 13cwt 4 Loco 74t 2cwt g Tender 43t 2cwt l Tender 52t 0cwt
Driving Wheel:	4' 8"
Boiler Pressure:	180psi superheated
Cylinders:	Three 18½" x 26"
Tractive Effort:	36470lbf
Valve Gear:	Walschaert with derived motion (piston valves)

After building the two-cylinder 'O3' class for the GNR, Gresley followed it by building the three-cylinder 'O2' class. The first engine was built in 1918 and sixty-six more were built between 1921 and 1943.

They were fine freight engines and they made it possible to run 80-wagon coal trains between Peterborough and London.

o The original engine (63921) was classified 'O2'. It differed from the rest of the class by having inclined cylinders and original Gresley conjugated valve gear. It was withdrawn in 1948 as 3921.

1 The next batch introduced in 1921 was classified 'O2/1'. These engines had horizontal cylinders and a modified form of Gresley's conjugated valve gear. They were later rebuilt with side-window cabs and reduced boiler mountings.

2 The next batch appeared after grouping in 1924 and were known as 'O2/2'. They had some detail alterations and reduced boiler mountings.

3 The 'O2/3' class was introduced in 1932. These engines were developed from 'O2/2' with side window cabs and LNER standard 4200 gallon tenders.

4 From 1943 onwards Thompson rebuilt some engines with '100A' ('B1' type) boilers. They were known as class 'O2/4'. Engines which were rebuilt from 'O2/1' and 'O2/2' were also fitted with side window cabs.

g Engines fitted with GNR type tenders.

l Engines fitted with standard LNER tenders.

Year End Totals: 'O2' class

'47	'48	'49	'50	'51	'52	'53	'54	'55	'56	'57	'58	'59	'60	'61	'62	'63	'64	'65	'66	'67
67	66	66	66	66	66	66	66	66	66	66	66	66	62	56	40					

Number	*Built*	*Renumbered*	*BR Dates*	*Scrap*	*Notes*
63921	05/18 Don	3921	-05/48	05/48	og
63922	05/21 NB	12/49 3922	-11/62	11/62	1g
63923	05/21 NB	09/48 3923	-12/62	12/63	1g
63924	05/21 NB	11/48 3924	-10/63	01/64	4g
63925	05/21 NB	05/49 3925	-09/63	10/64	1g
					07/58⇨4
63926	05/21 NB	10/48 3926	-09/63	09/64	1g
					60⇨4
63927	05/21 NB	07/49 3927	-09/63	02/64	1g
63928	05/21 NB	08/48 3928	-09/63	02/64	1g
					60⇨4
63929	05/21 NB	11/48 3929	-07/62	07/62	1g
					07/59⇨4
63930	05/21 NB	04/48 3930	-12/62	12/63	1g
					08/59⇨4
63931	05/21 NB	11/49 3931	-09/63	10/63	1g
					60⇨4
63932	11/23 Don	06/49 3932	-09/63	02/64	4g
					06/49⇨2 04/58⇨4
63933	11/23 Don	08/48 3933	-12/62	12/63	2g
					01/58⇨4
63934	11/23 Don	07/48 3934	-07/62	07/62	2g
63935	11/23 Don	08/50 3935	-09/63	02/64	2g
					04/58⇨4
63936	12/23 Don	05/49 3936	-09/63	03/64	2g
63937	12/23 Don	12/49 3937	-09/63	02/64	2g
63938	12/23 Don	05/49 3938	-09/63	02/64	2g
					07/58⇨4
63939	12/23 Don	08/49 3939	-09/63	10/64	2g
63940	02/24 Don	05/48 3940	-09/63	02/64	2g
63941	02/24 Don	12/48 3941	-09/63	02/64	2g
63942	03/24 Don	05/48 3942	-09/63	02/64	2g
63943	03/24 Don	06/48 3943	-09/63	02/64	2g
63944	04/24 Don	04/48 3944	-04/61	04/61	2g
63945	05/24 Don	10/48 3945	-09/63	01/64	2g
					11/56⇨4
63946	06/24 Don	05/49 3946	-04/63	09/63	2g
63947	04/32 Don	05/48 3947	-04/61	05/61	4l
					08/50⇨3
63948	05/32 Don	01/49 3948	-10/62	12/63	3l
					08/59⇨4
63949	05/32 Don	05/49 3949	-09/63	10/63	3l
					08/55⇨4
63950	06/32 Don	07/49 3950	-11/60	12/60	4l
63951	07/32 Don	08/49 3951	-06/62	07/62	3l
63952	07/32 Don	02/49 3952	-04/61	05/61	3l
63953	07/32 Don	06/49 3953	-11/60	12/60	3l
63954	08/32 Don	05/48 3954	-03/61	04/61	3l
63955	11/33 Don	06/48 3955	-05/62	05/62	3l
					04/59⇨4
63956	12/33 Don	12/49 3956	-09/63	09/64	3l
63957	12/33 Don	06/48 3957	-07/61	07/61	3l
63958	12/33 Don	04/48 3958	-05/61	06/61	3l
63959	01/34 Don	02/49 3959	-10/60	12/60	3l
63960	01/34 Don	03/49 3960	-09/63	10/63	3l
					08/59⇨4
63961	02/34 Don	06/48 3961	-12/62	09/63	3l
					03/59⇨4
63962	03/34 Don	03/48 3962	-09/63	03/64	4l
					01/50⇨3
63963	05/42 Don	04/50 3963	-09/63	10/63	3l
63964	06/42 Don	05/48 3964	-09/63	03/64	3l
					60⇨4
63965	06/42 Don	11/49 3965	-10/62	11/62	3l
					09/59⇨4
63966	07/42 Don	04/49 3966	-12/62	03/64	3l
					01/58⇨4
63967	08/42 Don	11/48 3967	-12/62	12/62	3l
63968	09/42 Don	07/48 3968	-09/63	10/63	3l
					60⇨4
63969	09/42 Don	03/49 3969	-10/63	01/64	3l
63970	09/42 Don	04/50 3970	-05/60	06/60	3l
63971	10/42 Don	04/48 3971	-12/62	12/63	3l
63972	10/42 Don	12/48 3972	-05/63	01/64	3l
63973	10/42 Don	11/48 3973	-09/63	02/64	3l
63974	11/42 Don	07/48 3974	-09/63	03/64	3l
63975	11/42 Don	02/49 3975	-10/63	01/64	3l
63976	11/42 Don	05/48 3976	-09/63	10/63	3l
					60⇨4
63977	11/42 Don	02/49 3977	-09/63	02/64	3l
63978	11/42 Don	05/49 3978	-05/63	09/63	3l
63979	12/42 Don	01/49 3979	-09/62	11/62	3l
					06/59⇨4
63980	12/42 Don	04/48 3980	-09/63	10/64	3l
63981	12/42 Don	05/48 3981	-10/63	01/64	3l
63982	12/42 Don	06/48 3982	-12/62	04/63	3l
					08/57⇨4
63983	12/42 Don	11/48 3983	-07/63	08/63	3l
					07/56⇨4
63984	12/42 Don	09/48 3984	-10/63	01/64	3l
63985	01/43 Don	05/48 3985	-09/63	10/64	3l
63986	01/43 Don	07/49 3986	-06/63	08/63	3l
63987	01/43 Don	06/49 3987	-09/63	03/64	3l

GNR Ivatt 'J1' class 0-6-0 No 65014 at Colwick in July 1950.

Manchester, Sheffield & Lincolnshire Railway Parker 'J10' class 0-6-0 No 65134 at Northwich in February 1956.

NBR Holmes 'J36' class 0-6-0 No 65261 at Kittybrewster in July 1954.

GER Worsdell 'J15' class 0-6-0 No 65425 at Cambridge in July 1954.

J3 between 64105 & 64163
0-6-0 GNR & M&GNJR Stirling & Ivatt

J4 between 64109 & 64167
0-6-0 GNR & M&GNJR Stirling & Ivatt (Small Boilers)

Power Classification:	2F
Introduced:	J3 1892-1901, rebuilt 1912-1928 by Gresley J4 1896-1901
Designer:	P Stirling and Ivatt
Company:	GNR m M&GNJR
Weight:	J3 Loco 42t 12c J4 Loco 41t 5cwt J3 Tender 38t 10cwt J4 Tender 34t 18cwt
Driving Wheel:	5' 2"
Boiler Pressure:	175psi
Cylinders:	Inside 17½" x 26"
Tractive Effort:	19105lbf
Valve Gear:	Stephenson (slide valves)

Between 1873 and 1901 Stirling and Ivatt built no less than 302 0-6-0s with 5' 2" diameter wheels and 4' 4" diameter boilers. Twelve more were constructed to the same design for the M&GNJR. The Stirling engines originally had domeless boilers and round topped cabs.

J4 The 'J4' engines (originally GNR 'J5' class) were Ivatt engines built as a development of Stirling's 1892 design. They retained their original boilers. The first engine was withdrawn in 1924.

J3 The 'J3' engines (originally GNR 'J4' class) were rebuilt by Gresley in 1912-1928 with larger 4' 8" diameter boilers. Some of these were rebuilt from earlier Stirling engines dating from 1892. A total of 153 engines were rebuilt and the first of these was withdrawn in 1928.

m 64158-64167 were Midland & Great Northern Joint Railway engines. They came into LNER stock in 1937 and the M&GNJR numbers of those engines which came into BR stock were 83, 85, 87, 88 and 92 respectively.

Year End Totals: 'J3' class

'47	'48	'49	'50	'51	'52	'53	'54	'55	'56	'57	'58	'59	'60	'61	'62	'63	'64	'65	'66	'67
33	29	26	25	14	7	3														

Year End Totals: 'J4' class

'47	'48	'49	'50	'51	'52	'53	'54	'55	'56	'57	'58	'59	'60	'61	'62	'63	'64	'65	'66	'67
8	7	5	2																	

Number	Built	Renumbered	BR Dates	Scrap	Notes
64105	12/92 Don	06/48 4105	-01/52	*52*	J3
64106	06/96 D	4106	-05/49	*49*	J3
64107	06/96 D	4107	-10/48	07/49	J3
64109	07/96 D	4109	-10/49	*05/50*	J4
64110	07/96 D	4110	-05/49	*49*	J4
64112	12/96 Don	01/49 4112	-12/51	*12/51*	J4
64114	12/97 D	4114	-10/52	*10/52*	J3
64115	12/97 D	4115	-03/51	*51*	J3
64116	02/98 D	09/48 4116	-06/52	*52*	J3
64117	03/98 D	4117	-06/52	*52*	J3
64118	01/99 D	12/48 4118	-06/52	*52*	J3
64119	01/99 D	10/48 4119	-08/51	*51*	J3
64120	02/99 D	4120	-11/50	*05/51*	J4
64121	02/99 D	4121	-11/50	*50*	J4
64122	02/99 D	12/48 4122	-05/53	*06/53*	J3
64123	03/99 D	4123	-05/51	*05/51*	J3
64124	03/99 D	4124	-09/51	*51*	J3
64125	05/99 D	02/51 4125	-12/53	*54*	J3
64127	05/99 D	4127	-04/49	*49*	J3
64128	05/99 D	4128	-11/50	*50*	J3
64129	05/99 D	10/48 4129	-09/52	*52*	J3
64131	08/98 Don	10/48 4131	-06/54	*12/54*	J3
64132	09/98 Don	06/50 4132	-06/54	*54*	J3
64133	08/98 Don	11/48 4133	-01/53	*53*	J3
64135	07/99 Don	4135	-02/51	*05/51*	J3
64136	07/99 Don	4136	-03/48	*48*	J3
64137	09/99 Don	12/48 4137	-02/51	*05/51*	J3
64140	06/00 Don	08/52 4140	-12/54	*55*	J3
64141	07/00 Don	05/50 4141	-09/53	*53*	J3
64142	08/00 Don	06/49 4142	-08/51	*51*	J3
64145	04/00 K	4145	-03/48	*48*	J3
64148	06/00 K	4148	-04/51	*05/51*	J3
64150	06/00 K	4150	-06/51	*51*	J3
64151	07/00 K	4151	-03/51	*05/51*	J3
64152	07/01 D	4152	-04/48	*48*	J3
64153	08/01 D	06/48 4153	-05/52	*52*	J3
64158	10/00 D	4158	-12/51	*52*	J3m
64160	10/00 D	11/48 4160	-12/51	*12/51*	J4m
64162	10/00 D	4162	-12/50	*05/51*	J4m
64163	10/00 D	4163	-01/49	*49*	J3m
64167	10/00 D	4167	-07/48	*48*	J4m

J6 64170-64279
0-6-0 GNR Ivatt & Gresley

Power Classification:	3F
Introduced:	1911-1922
Designer:	Ivatt and Gresley
Company:	GNR
Weight:	Loco 50t 10cwt Tender 43t 2cwt
Driving Wheel:	5' 2"
Boiler Pressure:	170psi superheated
Cylinders:	Inside 19" x 26"
Tractive Effort:	21875lbf
Valve Gear:	Stephenson (piston valves)

Between 1911 and 1922 Gresley built 110 engines of the 'J6' class. The first fifteen engines were built to Ivatt's design (GNR 'J22' class) and they were a slightly heavier version of Ivatt's 'J5' class. The remainder were built by Gresley to a slightly modified design. The boilers were identical with the 'D1' 4-4-0s.

They were very versatile engines and they were much used on passenger trains and general mixed-traffic duties.

Year End Totals: 'J6' class

'47	'48	'49	'50	'51	'52	'53	'54	'55	'56	'57	'58	'59	'60	'61	'62	'63	'64	'65	'66	'67
110	110	110	110	110	110	110	110	107	107	105	75	40	23	7						

Number	Built	Renumbered	BR Dates	Scrap	Notes
64170	08/11 Don	01/50 4170	-07/61	07/61	
64171	09/11 Don	01/50 4171	-09/61	10/61	
64172	09/11 Don	11/48 4172	-02/60	03/60	
64173	10/11 Don	03/48 4173	-01/61	01/61	
64174	10/11 Don	08/51 4174	-09/61	10/61	
64175	10/11 Don	05/48 4175	-06/60	07/60	
64176	11/11 Don	10/48 4176	-03/59	05/59	
64177	11/11 Don	03/51 4177	-02/62	02/62	
64178	11/11 Don	07/50 4178	-04/60	05/60	
64179	11/11 Don	12/48 4179	-05/60	05/60	
64180	11/11 Don	01/49 4180	-03/60	04/60	
64181	11/11 Don	03/49 4181	-08/59	08/59	
64182	12/11 Don	10/50 4182	-11/60	12/60	
64183	12/11 Don	06/48 4183	-11/58	01/59	
64184	12/11 Don	01/49 4184	-11/59	12/59	
64185	11/12 Don	10/48 4185	-04/61	04/61	
64186	11/12 Don	11/48 4186	-01/58	02/58	
64187	11/12 Don	10/50 4187	-01/58	02/58	
64188	11/12 Don	02/50 4188	-10/59	10/59	
64189	11/12 Don	02/51 4189	-10/58	12/58	
64190	11/12 Don	10/48 4190	-09/59	10/59	
64191	11/12 Don	11/50 4191	-02/62	02/62	
64192	12/12 Don	03/49 4192	-04/60	05/60	
64193	12/12 Don	04/48 4193	-12/57	02/58	
64194	12/12 Don	10/48 4194	-11/55	12/55	
64195	05/13 Don	07/48 4195	-01/58	03/58	
64196	05/13 Don	04/48 4196	-09/60	10/60	
64197	05/13 Don	06/49 4197	-10/59	12/59	
64198	05/13 Don	11/49 4198	-03/59	04/59	
64199	05/13 Don	05/48 4199	-04/58	05/58	
64200	06/13 Don	02/49 4200	-02/58	03/58	
64201	06/13 Don	10/48 4201	-11/58	01/59	
64202	06/13 Don	10/48 4202	-09/58	10/58	
64203	06/13 Don	05/49 4203	-06/62	06/62	
64204	06/13 Don	12/49 4204	-12/57	02/58	
64205	06/13 Don	03/49 4205	-10/58	01/59	
64206	06/13 Don	11/49 4206	-09/60	11/60	
64207	07/13 Don	01/51 4207	-10/59	11/59	
64208	07/13 Don	07/50 4208	-05/61	05/61	
64209	07/13 Don	11/50 4209	-09/60	11/60	
64210	07/13 Don	03/49 4210	-05/59	06/59	
64211	08/13 Don	04/48 4211	-03/58	04/58	
64212	08/13 Don	03/49 4212	-12/55	12/55	
64213	08/13 Don	06/48 4213	-02/60	03/60	
64214	08/13 Don	02/51 4214	-10/59	11/59	
64215	08/13 Don	09/49 4215	-03/59	04/59	
64216	09/13 Don	07/51 4216	-12/58	01/59	
64217	09/13 Don	01/51 4217	-01/59	01/59	
64218	09/13 Don	09/50 4218	-09/58	10/58	
64219	09/13 Don	06/48 4219	-11/61	11/61	
64220	09/13 Don	04/50 4220	-06/58	10/58	
64221	09/13 Don	03/51 4221	-01/58	02/58	
64222	10/13 Don	05/48 4222	-11/60	11/60	
64223	10/13 Don	06/48 4223	-04/61	05/61	
64224	10/13 Don	01/49 4224	-05/59	06/59	
64225	07/14 Don	06/48 4225	-07/58	07/58	
64226	07/14 Don	12/49 4226	-06/62	06/62	
64227	07/14 Don	01/49 4227	-07/58	10/58	
64228	07/14 Don	02/49 4228	-08/59	09/59	
64229	07/14 Don	05/50 4229	-10/59	11/59	
64230	07/14 Don	12/48 4230	-01/58	03/58	
64231	07/14 Don	02/50 4231	-02/61	02/61	
64232	08/14 Don	04/51 4232	-01/61	02/61	
64233	08/14 Don	04/48 4233	-07/61	07/61	
64234	08/14 Don	10/49 4234	-12/59	12/59	
64235	09/14 Don	08/49 4235	-12/59	12/59	
64236	09/14 Don	07/49 4236	-04/61	05/61	
64237	10/14 Don	11/48 4237	-12/59	12/59	
64238	10/14 Don	06/50 4238	-10/59	11/59	
64239	10/14 Don	09/49 4239	-10/59	11/59	
64240	10/14 Don	04/48 4240	-08/60	08/60	
64241	11/14 Don	12/48 4241	-11/59	12/59	
64242	11/14 Don	04/48 4242	-08/55	09/55	
64243	11/14 Don	07/48 4243	-06/58	07/58	
64244	11/14 Don	12/48 4244	-05/58	07/58	
64245	10/17 Don	06/49 4245	-02/62	03/62	
64246	10/17 Don	10/49 4246	-06/59	08/59	
64247	10/17 Don	09/48 4247	-10/59	11/59	
64248	01/18 Don	08/50 4248	-03/59	05/59	
64249	01/18 Don	07/49 4249	-10/58	01/59	
64250	10/18 Don	11/50 4250	-10/59	11/59	
64251	11/18 Don	05/49 4251	-10/60	11/60	
64252	11/18 Don	08/48 4252	-07/58	07/58	
64253	02/19 Don	08/50 4253	-05/62	05/62	
64254	02/19 Don	03/49 4254	-10/59	11/59	
64255	03/19 Don	09/49 4255	-08/58	10/58	
64256	04/19 Don	05/49 4256	-05/60	06/60	
64257	04/19 Don	08/48 4257	-06/60	06/60	
64258	04/19 Don	09/48 4258	-05/59	08/59	
64259	05/19 Don	07/48 4259	-08/59	10/59	
64260	12/19 Don	04/48 4260	-03/61	03/61	
64261	12/19 Don	05/48 4261	-03/59	04/59	
64262	12/19 Don	08/49 4262	-02/59	04/59	
64263	12/19 Don	05/48 4263	-07/58	07/58	
64264	01/20 Don	05/49 4264	-01/58	04/58	
64265	02/20 Don	09/49 4265	-07/61	07/61	
64266	02/20 Don	04/50 4266	-04/59	05/59	
64267	03/20 Don	06/48 4267	-07/58	10/58	
64268	05/20 Don	02/49 4268	-01/61	02/61	
64269	05/20 Don	10/48 4269	-10/59	11/59	
64270	12/21 Don	07/50 4270	-04/60	05/60	
64271	12/21 Don	04/49 4271	-10/58	10/58	
64272	12/21 Don	07/49 4272	-09/59	10/59	
64273	03/22 Don	04/49 4273	-12/59	12/59	
64274	06/22 Don	09/48 4274	-12/58	01/59	
64275	06/22 Don	02/51 4275	-08/58	10/58	
64276	07/22 Don	06/50 4276	-10/58	01/59	
64277	08/22 Don	03/48 4277	-06/62	06/62	
64278	08/22 Don	05/50 4278	-03/61	03/61	
64279	09/22 Don	10/49 4279	-08/59	10/59	

J11 64280-64453
0-6-0 GCR Robinson

Power Classification:	3F
Introduced:	1901-1910 3 Rebuilt 1942-1953 by Thompson
Designer:	Robinson
Company:	GCR
Weight:	Loco 51t 19cwt s Loco 52t 2cwt 3 Loco 53t 6cwt y Tender 44t 3cwt z Tender 48t 6cwt
Driving Wheel:	5' 2"
Boiler Pressure:	180psi s3 180psi superheated
Cylinders:	Inside 18½" x 26"
Tractive Effort:	21960lbf
Valve Gear:	Stephenson (slide valves) 3 Stephenson (piston valves)

Between 1901 and 1911 Robinson put 174 very handsome 0-6-0 engines into service on the GCR. Known as GCR class '9J' and later LNER class 'J11' they were known as 'Pom-Poms' because of their mellow exhaust beats. In common with many of Robinson's other engines, they were later disfigured when Gresley fitted them with 'flower-pot' type chimneys.

3 Between 1942 and 1954 thirty-one engines were rebuilt with long travel piston valves, which resulted in a higher pitched boiler. It was at one time decided that these 'J11/3' engines should form a standard class on BR and a large number of new engines were scheduled. This plan was later abandoned.

The rest of the class was originally split into four parts as shown below. There were frequent exchanges between 'J11/1', 'J11/2', 'J11/4' and 'J11/5' and by 1952 they were all fitted with low boiler mountings, they were all superheated (s), and they were combined as 'J11'.

1 'J11/1'. 3250 gallon tender (y). High boiler mountings. Some superheated (s).

2 'J11/2'. 4000 gallon tender (z). High boiler mountings. Some superheated (s).

4 'J11/4'. 3250 gallon tender (y). Low boiler mountings. All superheated (s).

5 'J11/5'. 4000 gallon tender (z). Low boiler mountings. All superheated (s).

Year End Totals: 'J11' class

'47	'48	'49	'50	'51	'52	'53	'54	'55	'56	'57	'58	'59	'60	'61	'62	'63	'64	'65	'66	'67
174	174	174	174	174	174	174	171	146	136	117	100	76	56	30						

Number	*Built*	*Renumbered*	*BR Dates*	*Scrap*	*Notes*
64280	09/01 NR	01/49 4280	-06/59	09/59	
64281	09/01 NR	04/48 4281	-11/58	02/59	
64282	09/01 NR	05/50 4282	-04/55	01/57	
64283	09/01 NR	01/49 4283	-04/59	04/59	
64284	09/01 NR	03/49 4284	-07/62	12/62	3
64285	09/01 NR	10/50 4285	-08/58	02/59	
64286	09/01 NR	11/48 4286	-10/55	*55*	
64287	09/01 NR	08/48 4287	-05/59	09/59	
64288	09/01 NR	12/50 4288	-11/60	11/60	
64289	09/01 NR	12/49 4289	-06/55	*55*	
64290	10/01 NR	12/50 4290	-05/58	06/58	
64291	10/01 NR	05/50 4291	-11/55	*55*	
64292	12/01 NR	08/48 4292	-07/62	09/62	
64293	12/01 NR	04/48 4293	-12/57	01/58	
64294	12/01 NR	11/48 4294	-09/59	10/59	
64295	12/01 NR	02/49 4295	-09/57	09/57	
64296	12/01 NR	04/48 4296	-07/58	02/59	
64297	12/01 NR	08/49 4297	-06/59	09/59	
64298	12/01 NR	05/48 4298	-12/59	01/60	
64299	12/01 NR	02/49 4299	-11/55	*11/55*	
64300	12/01 NR	11/49 4300	-09/57	09/57	
64301	12/01 NR	05/50 4301	-05/55	*11/55*	
64302	01/02 NR	04/48 4302	-09/58	09/58	
64303	01/02 NR	06/48 4303	-02/57	03/57	
64304	03/02 NR	10/48 4304	-04/59	09/59	
64305	04/02 NR	03/50 4305	-07/62	09/62	
64306	04/02 NR	05/48 4306	-08/58	09/58	
64307	04/02 NR	04/49 4307	-07/55	06/56	
64308	04/02 NR	06/49 4308	-09/61	10/61	
64309	04/02 NR	05/48 4309	-08/56	*56*	
64310	04/02 NR	09/48 4310	-03/61	04/61	
64311	04/02 NR	12/48 4311	-01/61	02/61	
64312	04/02 NR	09/49 4312	-02/57	02/57	
64313	04/02 NR	06/50 4313	-05/61	06/61	
64314	04/02 NR	05/49 4314	-09/62	12/62	3
64315	04/02 NR	05/50 4315	-04/60	05/60	
64316	05/02 NR	12/49 4316	-08/61	09/61	3
64317	05/02 NR	10/48 4317	-03/61	05/61	
					10/48⇨3
64318	05/02 NR	02/49 4318	-08/62	10/62	3
64319	05/02 NR	07/50 4319	-08/59	10/59	
64320	10/02 NR	04/48 4320	-10/57	09/58	
64321	10/02 NR	04/50 4321	-07/59	09/59	
64322	10/02 NR	12/49 4322	-10/57	01/58	
64323	10/02 NR	10/50 4323	-10/55	*11/55*	
64324	10/02 NR	03/49 4324	-09/62	05/63	
					03/49⇨3
64325	10/02 NR	09/49 4325	-11/60	11/60	
64326	10/02 NR	06/50 4326	-08/55	*11/55*	
64327	11/02 NR	09/48 4327	-01/57	01/57	
64328	11/02 NR	04/50 4328	-03/59	06/59	
64329	09/03 BP	06/49 4329	-08/62	10/62	
64330	10/03 BP	07/48 4330	-02/57	02/57	
64331	10/03 BP	10/48 4331	-01/60	03/60	
64332	10/03 BP	08/49 4332	-09/62	03/63	3
64333	10/03 BP	08/48 4333	-08/62	10/62	3
64334	10/03 BP	02/49 4334	-11/55	*55*	
64335	10/03 BP	02/50 4335	-09/54	*54*	
64336	10/03 BP	04/48 4336	-07/59	07/59	
64337	11/03 BP	08/48 4337	-06/61	09/61	
64338	11/03 BP	06/49 4338	-10/58	02/59	
64339	02/04 BP	09/48 4339	-10/54	*54*	
64340	02/04 BP	09/49 4340	-08/58	09/58	
64341	02/04 BP	09/49 4341	-02/61	02/61	
64342	03/04 BP	11/48 4342	-03/55	*05/56*	
64343	03/04 BP	05/48 4343	-11/58	02/59	
64344	03/04 BP	02/51 4344	-06/58	06/58	
64345	03/04 BP	06/49 4345	-12/58	02/59	
64346	04/04 BP	04/50 4346	-09/62	12/62	3
64347	04/04 BP	04/50 4347	-03/55	*55*	
64348	04/04 BP	05/49 4348	-03/60	03/60	
64349	04/04 BP	08/49 4349	-10/57	01/58	
64350	04/04 BP	11/49 4350	-08/55	*55*	
64351	04/04 BP	10/49 4351	-10/59	11/59	
64352	04/04 BP	07/48 4352	-08/61	09/61	3
64353	04/04 BP	02/51 4353	-02/58	04/58	
64354	11/03 Gor	08/48 4354	-10/62	05/63	3
64355	12/03 Gor	02/50 4355	-07/62	11/62	
64356	12/03 Gor	06/49 4356	-08/55	*11/55*	
64357	01/04 Gor	09/48 4357	-04/60	04/60	
64358	02/04 Gor	11/48 4358	-10/55	*11/55*	
64359	02/04 Gor	06/50 4359	-04/61	06/61	3
64360	03/04 Gor	10/49 4360	-07/55	*05/56*	
64361	03/04 Gor	09/49 4361	-03/59	04/59	
64362	04/04 Gor	06/50 4362	-09/62	12/62	3
64363	05/04 Gor	01/50 4363	-02/61	04/61	
64364	07/04 Gor	04/49 4364	-07/61	09/61	3
64365	07/04 Gor	06/49 4365	-08/59	08/59	
64366	06/04 VF	04/49 4366	-12/56	*57*	
64367	06/04 VF	03/49 4367	-01/54	*54*	
64368	06/04 VF	10/50 4368	-05/60	07/60	
64369	06/04 VF	08/48 4369	-10/55	*11/55*	
64370	06/04 VF	03/49 4370	-06/55	*55*	
64371	07/04 VF	10/50 4371	-01/61	02/61	
64372	07/04 VF	11/50 4372	-10/57	11/57	
64373	07/04 VF	05/50 4373	-09/62	03/63	3
64374	07/04 VF	09/48 4374	-07/55	*05/56*	
64375	07/04 VF	11/48 4375	-09/62	12/62	3
64376	07/04 VF	01/49 4376	-11/59	11/59	
64377	07/04 VF	08/50 4377	-07/62	10/62	
64378	07/04 VF	02/51 4378	-12/56	*57*	
64379	08/04 VF	02/51 4379	-09/62	12/62	
					02/48⇨3
64380	08/04 VF	01/49 4380	-08/56	*56*	
64381	03/04 YE	06/49 4381	-03/59	05/59	
64382	03/04 YE	04/49 4382	-10/59	10/59	
64383	03/04 YE	09/48 4383	-03/60	04/60	
64384	03/04 YE	05/49 4384	-06/61	08/61	
64385	04/04 YE	08/48 4385	-10/61	10/61	
64386	08/05 YE	03/50 4386	-09/62	12/62	3
64387	08/05 YE	08/49 4387	-06/60	07/60	
64388	08/05 YE	10/48 4388	-03/59	03/59	
64389	09/05 YE	03/49 4389	-01/60	02/60	
64390	09/05 YE	11/49 4390	-05/55	*11/55*	
64391	06/06 YE	08/49 4391	-01/55	*55*	
64392	06/06 YE	08/48 4392	-12/58	12/58	
64393	07/06 YE	03/49 4393	-06/62	09/62	
					01/52⇨3
64394	08/06 YE	12/49 4394	-08/62	10/62	
					03/53⇨3
64395	08/06 YE	03/49 4395	-01/62	03/62	
					04/53⇨3
64396	12/06 Gor	06/50 4396	-02/60	02/60	
64397	12/06 Gor	04/49 4397	-05/60	05/60	
64398	01/07 Gor	06/49 4398	-11/56	*56*	
64399	02/07 Gor	09/50 4399	-10/57	10/57	
64400	02/07 Gor	01/49 4400	-11/55	*55*	
64401	02/07 Gor	10/49 4401	-10/57	12/57	
64402	03/07 Gor	06/48 4402	-07/61	08/61	3
64403	03/07 Gor	01/51 4403	-07/60	07/60	
64404	03/07 Gor	07/51 4404	-02/61	04/61	
64405	03/07 Gor	03/49 4405	-04/60	05/60	
64406	04/07 Gor	03/49 4406	-09/62	12/62	3
64407	04/07 Gor	03/48 4407	-12/59	01/60	
64408	04/07 Gor	01/49 4408	-11/56	*56*	
64409	05/07 Gor	11/50 4409	-12/58	01/59	
64410	05/07 Gor	10/48 4410	-12/56	*57*	
64411	05/07 Gor	11/50 4411	-10/57	01/58	
64412	06/07 Gor	02/49 4412	-10/57	12/57	
64413	06/07 Gor	10/48 4413	-11/55	*55*	
64414	06/07 Gor	02/49 4414	-07/57	07/57	
64415	07/07 Gor	07/48 4415	-10/55	*55*	
64416	07/07 Gor	12/48 4416	-11/58	11/58	
64417	08/07 Gor	12/48 4417	-08/61	09/61	3
64418	08/07 Gor	08/49 4418	-11/61	02/62	3
64419	08/07 Gor	12/48 4419	-08/62	10/62	
64420	09/07 Gor	03/49 4420	-06/62	07/62	
					05/49⇨3
64421	09/07 Gor	09/49 4421	-12/59	01/60	
64422	10/07 Gor	06/48 4422	-09/58	10/58	
64423	10/07 Gor	01/50 4423	-03/62	04/62	
64424	10/07 Gor	02/49 4424	-01/58	02/58	
64425	11/07 Gor	05/49 4425	-11/60	11/60	
64426	11/07 Gor	08/50 4426	-01/56	*02/56*	
64427	11/07 Gor	02/49 4427	-07/61	08/61	3
64428	11/07 Gor	01/49 4428	-04/59	04/59	
64429	11/07 Gor	06/48 4429	-12/59	01/60	
64430	12/07 Gor	02/50 4430	-05/59	05/59	
64431	12/07 Gor	09/49 4431	-09/56	*02/57*	
64432	12/07 Gor	04/50 4432	-01/57	01/57	
64433	01/08 Gor	08/48 4433	-03/60	03/60	
64434	01/08 Gor	07/49 4434	-10/60	10/60	
64435	02/08 Gor	09/49 4435	-08/61	09/61	
64436	02/08 Gor	09/49 4436	-11/55	*55*	
64437	03/08 Gor	03/50 4437	-06/62	07/62	
64438	04/08 Gor	03/50 4438	-01/60	04/60	
64439	05/08 Gor	11/49 4439	-02/61	04/61	3
64440	06/08 Gor	03/49 4440	-11/60	11/60	
64441	10/08 Gor	08/48 4441	-02/61	04/61	3
64442	10/08 Gor	09/50 4442	-09/62	12/62	3
64443	11/08 Gor	10/48 4443	-04/62	05/62	
64444	04/09 Gor	06/49 4444	-05/61	06/61	
64445	01/10 Gor	09/48 4445	-08/62	10/62	
64446	02/10 Gor	11/49 4446	-03/61	04/61	
64447	02/10 Gor	11/49 4447	-04/61	06/61	
64448	03/10 Gor	05/49 4448	-02/57	02/57	
64449	03/10 Gor	07/49 4449	-09/56	*56*	
64450	04/10 Gor	12/48 4450	-04/62	05/62	3
64451	04/10 Gor	10/48 4451	-12/59	01/60	
64452	04/10 Gor	03/48 4452	-06/60	06/60	
64453	05/10 Gor	03/49 4453	-10/57	01/58	

J35 64460-64535
0-6-0 NBR Reid

Power Classification:	3F
Introduced:	1906-1913
Designer:	Reid
Company:	NBR
Weight:	4 Loco 50t 15cwt 5 Loco 51t 0cwt 4 Tender 37t 15cwt 5 Tender 38t 1cwt
Driving Wheel:	5' 0"
Boiler Pressure:	180psi superheated
Cylinders:	Inside 18¼" x 26"
Tractive Effort:	22080lbf
Valve Gear:	4 Stephenson (slide valves) 5 Stephenson (piston valves)

Between 1906 and 1913 Reid built seventy-six 'Intermediate' 0-6-0 freight engines for the NBR (NBR class 'B', LNER class 'J35'). The design was developed from the smaller Holmes 'J36' class.

Originally built as saturated boiler engines with piston valves, they were all later rebuilt with superheated boilers, and some later engines were fitted with slide valves. The superheated boilers were identical to those fitted to the 'J37' class, although they were pitched lower. The engines were frequently used for secondary passenger duties.

Six were withdrawn before 1948 (the first going in 1946), but no more were withdrawn until 1958.

1, 2 & 3 'J35/1', 'J35/2' and 'J35/3' were variations of the class before they were all superheated.

4 'J35/4'. Engines fitted with slide valves.

5 'J35/5'. Engines fitted with piston valves.

Year End Totals: 'J35' class

'47	'48	'49	'50	'51	'52	'53	'54	'55	'56	'57	'58	'59	'60	'61	'62	'63	'64	'65	'66	'67
70	70	70	70	70	70	70	70	70	70	70	64	44	34	14						

Number	*Built*	*Renumbered*	*BR Dates*	*Scrap*	*Notes*
64460	06/06 NB	04/48 4460	-09/59	10/59	5
64461	06/06 NB	03/48 4461	-10/61	05/62	5
64462	06/06 NB	11/48 4462	-11/60	02/61	5
64463	06/06 NB	04/49 4463	-09/60	12/60	5
64464	06/06 NB	04/49 4464	-05/58	06/58	5
64466	06/06 NB	12/48 4466	-07/59	09/59	5
64468	06/06 NB	08/48 4468	-05/60	07/60	5
64470	07/06 Cow	08/49 4470	-02/62	03/63	5
64471	07/06 Cow	05/48 4471	-06/61	01/62	5
64472	07/08 Cow	04/50 4472	-03/62	11/62	5
64473	07/08 Cow	03/50 4473	-12/59	04/60	5
64474	07/08 Cow	04/48 4474	-10/61	01/62	5
64475	07/08 Cow	09/48 4475	-04/59	08/59	5
64476	08/08 Cow	10/49 4476	-05/61	06/61	5
64477	08/08 Cow	09/48 4477	-11/61	11/62	5
64478	12/08 Cow	03/48 4478	-08/62	12/62	4
64479	12/08 Cow	03/50 4479	-12/61	06/63	4
64480	12/08 Cow	04/50 4480	-09/62	10/62	4
64482	12/08 Cow	07/50 4482	-06/61	08/61	4
64483	01/09 Cow	01/50 4483	-06/60	07/60	4
64484	08/09 NB	06/49 4484	-09/59	12/59	4
64485	08/09 NB	03/48 4485	-03/59	08/59	4
64486	09/09 NB	04/50 4486	-09/58	02/60	4
64487	09/09 NB	10/49 4487	-04/60	07/60	4
64488	09/09 NB	04/49 4488	-10/61	01/62	4
64489	09/09 NB	05/48 4489	-06/61	09/61	4
64490	09/09 NB	04/49 4490	-12/59	02/60	4
64491	09/09 NB	06/48 4491	-12/62	05/63	4
64492	09/09 NB	06/48 4492	-02/59	03/59	4
64493	09/09 NB	07/48 4493	-11/60	06/61	4
64494	11/09 NB	06/48 4494	-06/61	07/61	4
64495	11/09 NB	11/50 4495	-06/58	07/58	4
64496	11/09 NB	09/48 4496	-10/59	01/60	4
64497	11/09 NB	01/49 4497	-04/62	10/63	4
64498	11/09 NB	04/48 4498	-09/59	10/59	4
64499	12/09 NB	10/48 4499	-11/62	03/63	4
64500	12/09 NB	09/49 4500	-06/61	06/62	4
64501	12/09 NB	04/48 4501	-08/59	*59*	4
64502	12/09 NB	11/48 4502	-09/60	12/60	4
64504	03/10 NB	05/48 4504	-09/60	01/61	4
64505	03/10 NB	01/50 4505	-10/61	01/62	4
64506	03/10 NB	04/48 4506	-12/59	01/60	4
64507	03/10 NB	04/48 4507	-01/62	03/63	4
64509	03/10 NB	12/49 4509	-10/59	02/60	4
64510	04/10 NB	09/48 4510	-11/62	05/63	4
64511	04/10 NB	10/48 4511	-10/59	03/60	4
64512	03/10 NB	09/48 4512	-09/60	01/61	4
64513	03/10 NB	11/49 4513	-09/59	01/60	4
64514	09/10 Cow	01/49 4514	-02/62	04/63	4
64515	09/10 Cow	12/48 4515	-11/61	01/63	4
64516	10/10 Cow	05/48 4516	-06/59	07/59	4

Number	Built	Renumbered	BR Dates	Scrap	Notes
64517	10/10 Cow	08/48 4517	-10/58	01/59	4
64518	10/10 Cow	02/49 4518	-11/61	11/62	4
64519	10/10 Cow	03/48 4519	-04/62	06/63	4
64520	11/10 Cow	07/48 4520	-09/59	12/59	4
64521	12/10 Cow	01/51 4521	-04/59	08/59	4
64522	12/10 Cow	07/48 4522	-01/59	05/59	4
64523	12/10 Cow	09/48 4523	-02/61	08/61	4
64524	12/10 Cow	06/48 4524	-03/61	04/61	4
64525	01/11 Cow	03/49 4525	-07/62	06/63	4
64526	11/12 Cow	10/48 4526	-02/58	03/58	4
64527	12/12 Cow	11/48 4527	-06/62	06/63	4
64528	11/12 Cow	01/49 4528	-09/58	10/60	4
64529	12/12 Cow	01/49 4529	-09/60	12/60	4
64530	12/12 Cow	10/48 4530	-10/59	01/60	4
64531	02/13 Cow	10/48 4531	-07/61	08/61	4
64532	02/13 Cow	08/48 4532	-11/61	03/63	4
64533	03/13 Cow	09/50 4533	-01/62	07/62	4
64534	03/13 Cow	05/48 4534	-05/61	05/61	4
64535	03/13 Cow	06/49 4535	-11/61	11/62	4

J37 64536-64639
0-6-0 NBR Reid

Power Classification: 4F reclassified 5F in 1953
Introduced: 1914-1921
Designer: Reid
Company: NBR
Weight: Loco 54t 14cwt
Tender 40t 19cwt
Driving Wheel: 5' 0"
Boiler Pressure: 180psi superheated
Cylinders: Inside 19½" x 26"
Tractive Effort: 25210lbf
Valve Gear: Stephenson (piston valves)

In 1914 Reid introduced a superheated version of the 'J35' class on the NBR. These engines (NBR class 'S', LNER class 'J37') were the most powerful 0-6-0s ever to be built for a Scottish railway. They had higher pitched boilers and shorter chimneys than the 'J35' class. A total of 104 engines were built between 1914 and 1921. When the last few engines were withdrawn in 1967 they were amongst the last survivors of the pre-grouping era.

They were excellent engines, designed for main-line freight, but also at home on passenger trains on occasion. They worked both passenger and freight trains on the West Highland Line and they were also to be found on coal trains in Fife.

Year End Totals: 'J37' class

'47	'48	'49	'50	'51	'52	'53	'54	'55	'56	'57	'58	'59	'60	'61	'62	'63	'64	'65	'66	'67
104	104	104	104	104	104	104	104	104	104	104	104	101	100	95	67	47	25	17	4	

Number	Built	Renumbered	BR Dates	Scrap	Notes
64536	12/14 Cow	11/48 4536	-05/59	08/59	
64537	12/14 Cow	06/48 4537	-06/64	11/64	
64538	12/14 Cow	04/50 4538	-12/59	01/60	
64539	01/15 Cow	08/48 4539	-08/61	09/61	
64540	01/15 Cow	02/49 4540	-12/62	12/63	
64541	04/15 Cow	07/49 4541	-07/64	11/64	
64542	04/15 Cow	08/48 4542	-10/61	03/62	
64543	04/15 Cow	05/48 4543	-12/62	05/63	
64544	04/15 Cow	05/50 4544	-12/62	02/64	
64545	05/15 Cow	08/48 4545	-06/62	09/62	
64546	11/15 Cow	09/49 4546	-05/64	09/64	
64547	11/15 Cow	08/49 4547	-12/66	04/67	
64548	11/15 Cow	12/49 4548	-11/63	02/64	
64549	11/15 Cow	08/50 4549	-07/64	11/64	
64550	12/15 Cow	07/48 4550	-12/63	05/64	
64551	05/16 Cow	02/49 4551	-09/63	10/63	
64552	05/16 Cow	02/49 4552	-10/64	01/65	
64553	06/16 Cow	01/49 4553	-03/62	03/62	
64554	06/16 Cow	04/48 4554	-01/64	05/64	
64555	06/18 Cow	03/49 4555	-10/64	01/65	
64556	06/18 NB	02/50 4556	-12/62	05/63	
64557	06/18 NB	05/48 4557	-10/63	12/63	
64558	06/18 NB	04/48 4558	-09/65	12/65	
64559	06/18 NB	05/48 4559	-11/63	04/64	
64560	07/18 NB	06/48 4560	-03/61	04/61	
64561	07/18 NB	08/50 4561	-05/64	09/64	
64562	07/18 NB	03/49 4562	-11/63	05/64	
64563	07/18 NB	11/50 4563	-10/64	01/65	
64564	07/18 NB	09/49 4564	-06/64	10/64	
64565	07/18 NB	11/49 4565	-10/61	11/61	
64566	08/18 NB	08/48 4566	-04/62	05/62	
64567	08/18 Cow	08/48 4567	-03/60	05/60	
64568	08/18 NB	01/50 4568	-08/63	09/63	
64569	08/18 Cow	08/48 4569	-12/66	04/67	
64570	08/18 Cow	07/48 4570	-11/66	02/67	
64571	08/18 NB	04/49 4571	-10/65	01/66	
64572	08/18 NB	03/49 4572	-09/64	12/64	
64573	08/18 NB	12/49 4573	-10/64	01/65	
64574	08/18 Cow	01/50 4574	-12/62	02/64	
64575	09/18 Cow	05/48 4575	-12/63	07/64	
64576	08/18 NB	12/48 4576	-04/67	09/67	
64577	09/18 NB	12/49 4577	-08/66	12/66	
64578	09/18 NB	04/49 4578	-05/62	07/62	
64579	09/18 NB	09/49 4579	-12/63	03/64	
64580	09/18 NB	05/48 4580	-10/65	02/66	
64581	10/18 NB	12/50 4581	-12/62	08/63	
64582	10/18 NB	05/48 4582	-11/63	05/64	
64583	10/18 NB	03/50 4583	-12/63	05/64	
64584	10/18 NB	04/49 4584	-07/59	08/59	
64585	11/18 NB	12/48 4585	-12/64	03/65	
64586	11/18 NB	01/50 4586	-06/64	10/64	
64587	11/18 NB	02/49 4587	-06/64	09/64	
64588	11/18 NB	03/48 4588	-06/66	09/66	
64589	11/18 NB	07/48 4589	-06/63	04/64	
64590	12/18 NB	12/49 4590	-05/62	06/62	
64591	01/19 NB	07/49 4591	-10/64	12/64	
64592	01/19 NB	12/48 4592	-07/65	11/65	
64593	01/19 NB	08/48 4593	-11/63	05/64	
64594	01/19 NB	06/49 4594	-12/62	05/63	
64595	11/19 NB	04/48 4595	-03/66	07/66	
64596	11/19 NB	06/50 4596	-04/61	05/61	
64597	11/19 NB	02/50 4597	-08/66	12/66	
64598	11/19 NB	10/49 4598	-09/62	02/63	
64599	11/19 NB	03/50 4599	-10/65	01/66	
64600	11/19 NB	07/48 4600	-07/63	10/63	
64601	11/19 NB	09/50 4601	-04/63	04/64	
					⊠12/62-02/63
64602	11/19 NB	05/48 4602	-04/67	09/67	
64603	11/19 NB	11/50 4603	-12/63	03/64	
64604	12/19 NB	04/49 4604	-08/62	10/62	
64605	12/19 NB	03/49 4605	-06/64	09/64	
64606	12/19 NB	10/50 4606	-07/66	10/66	
64607	12/19 NB	12/48 4607	-08/62	10/62	
64608	12/19 NB	04/49 4608	-08/66	12/66	
64609	01/20 NB	04/48 4609	-12/62	05/63	
64610	01/20 NB	04/48 4610	-02/66	05/66	
64611	01/20 NB	06/49 4611	-04/67	09/67	
64612	01/20 NB	03/48 4612	-06/63	02/64	
					⊠12/62-01/63
64613	01/20 NB	05/48 4613	-01/64	08/64	
64614	01/20 NB	08/48 4614	-12/64	05/65	
64615	12/20 NB	12/49 4615	-04/63	04/64	
					⊠12/62-01/63
64616	12/20 NB	11/49 4616	-12/63	09/64	
64617	12/20 NB	06/49 4617	-02/63	05/63	
					⊠12/62-01/63
64618	12/20 NB	11/48 4618	-10/66	02/67	
64619	12/20 NB	04/49 4619	-12/63	01/64	
64620	12/20 NB	08/48 4620	-04/67	09/67	
64621	01/21 NB	12/48 4621	-05/65	07/65	
64622	01/21 NB	03/49 4622	-12/62	12/63	
64623	01/21 NB	10/50 4623	-11/66	02/67	
64624	01/21 NB	06/48 4624	-01/66	04/66	
64625	01/21 NB	04/48 4625	-09/65	11/65	
64626	02/21 NB	06/49 4626	-11/63	06/64	
64627	02/21 NB	05/48 4627	-10/63	10/63	
64628	02/21 NB	05/48 4628	-03/62	04/62	
64629	02/21 NB	12/48 4629	-10/63	11/63	
64630	06/21 Cow	09/48 4630	-09/62	09/62	
64631	06/21 Cow	09/48 4631	-05/63	04/64	
					⊠12/62-01/63
64632	06/21 Cow	05/50 4632	-12/65	03/66	
64633	06/21 Cow	03/48 4633	-06/64	10/64	
64634	07/21 Cow	04/49 4634	-01/64	06/64	
64635	08/21 Cow	04/50 4635	-04/63	02/64	
					⊠12/62-01/63
64636	08/21 Cow	03/48 4636	-10/64	01/65	
64637	09/21 Cow	11/50 4637	-08/62	10/62	
64638	09/21 Cow	05/48 4638	-12/62	02/64	
64639	10/21 Cow	10/49 4639	-12/62	02/64	

J19 64640-64674
0-6-0 GER Hill

Power Classification: 4F reclassified 5F in 1953
Introduced: 1912-1920, rebuilt 1934-1939 by Gresley
Designer: Hill
Company: GER
Weight: Loco 50t 7cwt
Tender 38t 5cwt
Driving Wheel: 4' 11"
Boiler Pressure: 170psi superheated
h 180psi superheated
l 160psi superheated
Cylinders: Inside 20" x 28"
c Inside 19" x 28"
Tractive Effort: 27430lbf
h 26215lbf
l 23300lbf
Valve Gear: Stephenson (piston valves)

Hill built twenty-five large 0-6-0s for the GER in 1916-1920. They were GER class 'T77' (LNER class 'J19'), and they had superheated Belpaire boilers which were identical with the 'D15's. They were developed from the very similar 'J18' class of ten engines built to Holden's design in 1912 (GER 'E72' class). In 1934-1939 Gresley rebuilt both classes with round topped boilers as applied to 'D16/3', and they all became one class ('J19').

c Rebuilt with smaller 19" diameter cylinders.

h Rebuilt with higher pressure boilers.

l Rebuilt with lower pressure boilers.

Year End Totals: 'J19' class

'47	'48	'49	'50	'51	'52	'53	'54	'55	'56	'57	'58	'59	'60	'61	'62	'63	'64	'65	'66	'67
35	35	35	35	35	35	35	35	35	35	35	34	22	13	4						

Number	Built	Renumbered	BR Dates	Scrap	Notes
64640	11/12 Str	06/48 4640	-11/59	01/60	
64641	11/12 Str	06/48 4641	-01/60	03/60	
64642	11/12 Str	52 4642	-04/60	04/60	
64643	11/12 Str	08/48 4643	-11/61	01/62	
64644	11/12 Str	04/50 4644	-07/59	09/59	
64645	11/12 Str	12/49 4645	-12/58	02/59	
64646	11/12 Str	10/48 4646	-10/61	11/61	
64647	12/12 Str	06/48 4647	-04/60	04/60	
64648	12/12 Str	08/50 4648	-08/59	09/59	
64649	01/13 Str	07/48 4649	-01/59	03/59	
64650	08/16 Str	05/51 4650	-10/60	10/60	
64651	08/16 Str	05/49 4651	-01/59	02/59	
64652	08/16 Str	07/48 4652	-01/61	08/61	
64653	09/16 Str	01/49 4653	-01/61	06/61	
64654	10/16 Str	03/49 4654	-01/60	02/60	
64655	11/16 Str	05/49 4655	-08/61	08/61	
64656	11/16 Str	03/49 4656	-05/60	05/60	
64657	11/16 Str	04/48 4657	-09/62	03/63	
64658	12/16 Str	08/48 4658	-11/59	12/59	
64659	01/17 Str	01/50 4659	-04/60	04/60	
64660	12/17 Str	12/50 4660	-08/60	09/60	
64661	12/17 Str	02/49 4661	-08/59	09/59	
64662	01/17 Str	05/48 4662	-01/59	02/59	
64663	03/18 Str	04/49 4663	-10/60	11/60	
64664	09/18 Str	12/50 4664	-09/62	03/63	ch
64665	11/18 Str	03/49 4665	-12/59	02/60	
64666	11/18 Str	11/48 4666	-01/61	06/61	
64667	12/18 Str	09/48 4667	-09/61	10/61	
64668	01/19 Str	01/49 4668	-12/59	01/60	
64669	03/19 Str	07/48 4669	-09/61	10/61	
64670	09/20 Str	03/49 4670	-11/59	01/60	
64671	10/20 Str	03/49 4671	-02/62	04/62	ch
64672	10/20 Str	09/50 4672	-01/59	02/59	cl
64673	10/20 Str	01/49 4673	-08/62	09/62	
64674	11/20 Str	11/50 4674	-01/61	02/61	

J20 64675-64699
0-6-0 GER Hill

Power Classification: 6F reclassified 5F in 1953
Introduced: 1920-1922
1 Rebuilt 1943-1956
Designer: Hill
Company: GER
Weight: Loco 54t 15cwt
1 Loco 54t 0cwt
Tender 38t 5cwt
Driving Wheel: 4' 11"
Boiler Pressure: 180psi superheated
Cylinders: Inside 20" x 28"
Tractive Effort: 29045lbf
Valve Gear: Stephenson (piston valves)

Twenty-five of these goods engines were built by Hill for the GER at Stratford in 1920-1922. Known as the GER 'D81' class (LNER 'J20'), they had 5' 1" diameter boilers, and the boilers and cylinders were identical with the 'B12/1' class.

These were the most powerful pre-grouping 0-6-0s to be built. In fact the only 0-6-0 class ever to have a greater tractive effort was Bulleid's Q1 class of 1942 on the Southern Railway.

1 From 1943 onwards the whole class was rebuilt with 5' 6" diameter boilers with round-topped fireboxes (identical to the 'B12/3' engines) and they were known as 'J20/1'.

Year End Totals: 'J20' class

'47	'48	'49	'50	'51	'52	'53	'54	'55	'56	'57	'58	'59	'60	'61	'62	'63	'64	'65	'66	'67
25	25	25	25	25	25	25	25	25	25	25	25	22	13	5						

Number	Built	Renumbered	BR Dates	Scrap	Notes
64675	04/20 Str	11/50 4675	-12/59	01/60	1
64676	12/20 Str	08/49 4676	-09/61	10/61	
					01/56⇨1
64677	12/20 Str	05/51 4677	-09/61	10/61	1
64678	12/20 Str	04/48 4678	-09/60	11/60	1
64679	12/20 Str	06/48 4679	-01/61	06/61	1

Number	Built	Renumbered	BR Dates	Scrap	Notes
64680	09/22 Str	05/50 4680	-01/61	06/61	1
64681	09/22 Str	12/50 4681	-11/60	12/60	1
64682	09/22 Str	03/49 4682	-09/60	11/60	1
64683	09/22 Str	04/50 4683	-11/59	11/59	05/51⇔1
64684	09/22 Str	10/49 4684	-07/60	07/60	1
64685	10/22 Str	11/49 4685	-10/60	11/60	1
64686	10/22 Str	10/50 4686	-08/60	09/60	1
64687	10/22 Str	02/51 4687	-09/62	12/62	03/53⇔1
64688	11/22 Str	06/51 4688	-01/59	02/59	1
64689	11/22 Str	05/49 4689	-01/61	06/61	08/51⇔1
64690	12/22 Str	09/49 4690	-09/62	03/63	09/49⇔1
64691	12/22 Str	08/48 4691	-09/62	09/63	1
64692	12/22 Str	12/49 4692	-09/61	11/61	12/49⇔1
64693	12/22 Str	04/51 4693	-08/60	09/60	1
64694	12/22 Str	11/50 4694	-01/60	02/60	1
64695	12/22 Str	11/50 4695	-01/60	02/60	1
64696	12/22 Str	12/50 4696	-04/62	05/62	10/53⇔1
64697	01/23 Str	01/49 4697	-09/61	11/61	1
64698	01/23 Str	10/48 4698	-03/61	11/61	02/55⇔1
64699	01/23 Str	04/49 4699	-09/62	09/63	1

J39 64700-64988
0-6-0 LNER Gresley

Power Classification:	4F reclassified 5F in 1953
Introduced:	1926-1941
Designer:	Gresley
Company:	LNER
Weight:	Loco 57t 17cwt 1 Tender 44t 4cwt 2 Tender 52t 13cwt 3 Tender (various)
Driving Wheel:	5' 2"
Boiler Pressure:	180psi superheated
Cylinders:	Inside 20" x 26"
Tractive Effort:	25665lbf
Valve Gear:	Stephenson (piston valves)

Gresley designed two classes of powerful 0-6-0s to replace the many ageing 0-6-0s inherited by the LNER in 1923. The two classes were identical except for the wheel size (5' 2" in 'J39', and 4' 8" in 'J38'), and the 'J38's had 6" longer boilers.

289 'J39's were built between 1926 and 1941. They were very free running engines and they could be found all over the LNER system, working on goods and general mixed-traffic duties.

1 'J39/1' engines were fitted with LNER standard 3500 gallon tenders.

2 'J39/2' engines were fitted with LNER standard 4200 gallon tenders.

3 'J39/3' engines were fitted with various ex-NER tenders taken from withdrawn engines.

Year End Totals: 'J39' class

'47	'48	'49	'50	'51	'52	'53	'54	'55	'56	'57	'58	'59	'60	'61	'62	'63	'64	'65	'66	'67
289	289	289	289	289	289	289	289	289	289	289	289	241	178	128						

Number	*Built*	*Renumbered*	*BR Dates*	*Scrap*	*Notes*
64700	09/26 Dar	08/49 4700	-04/61	08/61	1
64701	10/26 Dar	06/48 4701	-10/62	02/63	1
64702	10/26 Dar	11/48 4702	-09/59	11/59	1
64703	10/26 Dar	09/49 4703	-03/62	02/63	1
64704	10/26 Dar	05/50 4704	-12/62	08/63	1
64705	10/26 Dar	05/49 4705	-03/62	06/62	1
64706	10/26 Dar	12/49 4706	-03/62	09/62	1
64707	10/26 Dar	05/48 4707	-08/61	10/61	1
64708	11/26 Dar	08/51 4708	-08/60	08/60	1
64709	11/26 Dar	11/48 4709	-12/62	04/63	1
64710	11/26 Dar	10/49 4710	-04/61	09/61	1
64711	11/26 Dar	11/49 4711	-05/62	10/62	1
64712	11/26 Dar	12/48 4712	-02/60	05/60	1
64713	12/26 Dar	08/48 4713	-04/62	09/62	1
64714	12/26 Dar	02/51 4714	-05/59	09/59	1
64715	12/26 Dar	03/49 4715	-05/59	09/59	1
64716	12/26 Dar	05/50 4716	-04/61	04/61	1
64717	03/27 Dar	02/49 4717	-08/60	09/60	1
64718	04/27 Dar	12/50 4718	-03/62	03/62	1
64719	04/27 Dar	03/50 4719	-12/62	06/63	1
64720	04/27 Dar	01/50 4720	-09/61	10/61	1
64721	05/27 Dar	10/50 4721	-02/60	03/60	1
64722	05/27 Dar	10/50 4722	-02/60	03/60	1
64723	05/27 Dar	01/49 4723	-03/61	04/61	1
64724	05/27 Dar	07/48 4724	-02/60	03/60	1
64725	05/27 Dar	02/49 4725	-10/61	01/62	1
64726	05/27 Dar	05/48 4726	-11/60	12/60	1
64727	05/27 Dar	10/48 4727	-11/62	09/63	1
64728	05/27 Dar	03/51 4728	-02/60	05/60	1
64729	05/27 Dar	02/49 4729	-03/61	03/61	1
64730	05/27 Dar	04/48 4730	-11/62	02/63	1
64731	05/27 Dar	07/48 4731	-07/59	09/59	1
64732	05/27 Dar	11/49 4732	-08/61	12/61	1
64733	06/27 Dar	11/48 4733	-10/61	08/62	1
64734	06/27 Dar	12/48 4734	-05/59	09/59	1
64735	06/27 Dar	07/48 4735	-08/59	09/59	1
64736	06/27 Dar	05/48 4736	-07/61	07/61	1
64737	06/27 Dar	10/50 4737	-08/59	09/59	1
64738	06/27 Dar	05/50 4738	-11/60	11/60	1
64739	06/27 Dar	06/49 4739	-11/62	09/63	1
64740	07/27 Dar	09/49 4740	-09/62	12/62	1
64741	07/27 Dar	08/49 4741	-07/60	07/60	1
64742	08/27 Dar	06/49 4742	-07/62	12/62	1
64743	09/27 Dar	12/48 4743	-01/61	03/61	1
64744	07/28 Dar	10/48 4744	-03/62	04/62	1
64745	07/28 Dar	05/48 4745	-11/61	03/62	1
64746	07/28 Dar	10/48 4746	-02/61	03/61	1
64747	08/28 Dar	08/48 4747	-12/62	12/64	1
64748	08/28 Dar	03/49 4748	-07/61	09/61	1
64749	08/28 Dar	11/50 4749	-11/62	09/63	1
64750	08/28 Dar	11/48 4750	-11/59	12/59	1
64751	08/28 Dar	08/48 4751	-12/59	12/59	1
64752	08/28 Dar	04/48 4752	-06/59	09/59	1
64753	08/28 Dar	05/48 4753	-08/59	10/59	1
64754	08/28 Dar	03/50 4754	-11/62	09/63	1
64755	08/28 Dar	05/48 4755	-08/59	09/59	1
64756	08/28 Dar	06/49 4756	-12/62	06/63	1
64757	09/28 Dar	12/49 4757	-11/62	03/63	1
64758	09/28 Dar	01/50 4758	-11/62	02/63	1
64759	09/28 Dar	01/49 4759	-03/60	03/60	1
64760	09/28 Dar	07/48 4760	-11/62	09/63	1
64761	09/28 Dar	03/50 4761	-11/59	11/59	1
64762	09/28 Dar	11/48 4762	-06/59	09/59	1
64763	09/28 Dar	02/49 4763	-06/59	09/59	1
64764	10/28 Dar	10/49 4764	-10/60	12/60	1
64765	10/28 Dar	08/49 4765	-08/60	09/60	1
64766	11/28 Dar	04/48 4766	-09/59	11/59	1
64767	11/28 Dar	07/48 4767	-01/61	06/61	1
64768	11/28 Dar	09/51 4768	-05/59	09/59	1
64769	11/28 Dar	02/49 4769	-01/60	01/60	1
64770	11/28 Dar	10/48 4770	-10/60	11/60	1
64771	11/28 Dar	10/48 4771	-02/60	03/60	1
64772	12/28 Dar	10/49 4772	-07/61	07/61	1
64773	12/28 Dar	11/51 4773	-08/59	09/59	1
64774	03/29 Dar	12/49 4774	-03/60	03/60	1
64775	04/29 Dar	05/48 4775	-08/60	10/60	1
64776	04/29 Dar	02/50 4776	-08/59	11/59	1
64777	04/29 Dar	03/49 4777	-01/60	01/60	1
64778	04/29 Dar	12/48 4778	-09/60	10/60	1
64779	04/29 Dar	08/49 4779	-09/61	10/61	1
64780	04/29 Dar	03/48 4780	-01/60	04/60	1
64781	05/29 Dar	08/48 4781	-03/60	04/60	1
64782	05/29 Dar	11/50 4782	-03/60	03/60	1
64783	05/29 Dar	02/51 4783	-11/60	12/60	1
64784	05/29 Dar	09/48 4784	-08/60	09/60	2
64785	05/29 Dar	11/50 4785	-06/59	09/59	2
64786	06/29 Dar	02/50 4786	-12/62	05/63	2
64787	06/29 Dar	10/48 4787	-06/59	09/59	2
64788	06/29 Dar	06/48 4788	-06/59	07/59	2
64789	06/29 Dar	09/48 4789	-07/60	07/60	2
64790	06/29 Dar	07/48 4790	-12/62	04/63	2
64791	07/29 Dar	07/48 4791	-11/62	08/63	2
64792	07/29 Dar	11/49 4792	-01/62	06/62	2
64793	07/29 Dar	05/48 4793	-11/59	12/59	2
64794	07/29 Dar	05/48 4794	-08/62	10/62	2
64795	07/29 Dar	11/50 4795	-12/62	05/63	2
64796	08/29 Dar	12/48 4796	-12/62	09/63	1
64797	09/29 Dar	03/48 4797	-09/59	10/59	1
64798	09/29 Dar	12/48 4798	-09/62	11/62	1
64799	09/29 Dar	06/49 4799	-07/59	09/59	1
64800	09/29 Dar	02/50 4800	-01/60	01/60	1
64801	09/29 Dar	06/51 4801	-11/62	08/63	1
64802	10/29 Dar	02/51 4802	-07/60	10/60	1
64803	10/29 Dar	06/50 4803	-09/59	09/59	1
64804	10/30 Dar	06/49 4804	-04/61	04/61	1
64805	10/30 Dar	01/51 4805	-10/59	11/59	1
64806	11/30 Dar	09/48 4806	-05/62	07/62	1
64807	11/30 Dar	12/48 4807	-04/60	04/60	1
64808	11/30 Dar	08/48 4808	-02/61	02/61	1
64809	11/30 Dar	12/49 4809	-01/62	02/62	1
64810	12/30 Dar	11/51 4810	-06/61	07/61	1
64811	12/30 Dar	11/49 4811	-03/62	04/62	1
64812	12/30 Dar	05/49 4812	-12/62	06/63	1
64813	12/30 Dar	04/49 4813	-12/62	02/63	1
64814	01/31 Dar	12/48 4814	-11/62	06/63	1
64815	01/31 Dar	01/50 4815	-08/61	08/61	1
64816	01/31 Dar	11/49 4816	-12/61	09/62	1
64817	01/31 Dar	03/50 4817	-03/62	06/62	1
64818	01/31 Dar	06/49 4818	-12/62	11/63	1
64819	01/31 Dar	01/51 4819	-09/62	10/62	1
64820	02/31 Dar	06/50 4820	-05/62	12/62	2
64821	02/31 Dar	07/48 4821	-11/62	02/63	2
64822	02/31 Dar	05/49 4822	-12/62	07/63	2
64823	09/31 Dar	03/49 4823	-01/61	01/61	1
64824	09/31 Dar	06/51 4824	-04/60	04/60	1
64825	09/31 Dar	04/49 4825	-10/61	12/61	1
64826	10/31 Dar	03/50 4826	-02/60	02/60	1
64827	12/31 Dar	07/50 4827	-02/60	03/60	1
64828	10/31 Dar	08/48 4828	-03/60	04/60	1
64829	11/31 Dar	09/48 4829	-05/59	05/59	1
64830	12/31 Dar	01/50 4830	-02/60	04/60	1
64831	12/31 Dar	03/48 4831	-06/61	06/61	1
64832	01/32 Dar	06/48 4832	-09/59	11/59	1
64833	01/32 Dar	08/49 4833	-11/62	08/63	1
64834	02/32 Dar	08/48 4834	-11/59	12/59	1
64835	02/32 Dar	10/49 4835	-12/62	02/63	1
64836	03/32 Dar	01/49 4836	-04/62	05/62	1
64837	03/32 Dar	02/49 4837	-11/61	12/61	1
64838	05/32 Dar	12/49 4838	-01/60	02/60	2
64839	06/32 Dar	04/48 4839	-10/61	12/61	2
64840	06/32 Dar	02/49 4840	-11/62	03/63	2
64841	06/32 Dar	01/51 4841	-10/59	11/59	2
64842	08/32 Dar	02/49 4842	-04/62	01/63	3
64843	10/32 Dar	03/49 4843	-03/62	03/63	3
64844	10/32 Dar	10/48 4844	-12/62	06/63	3
64845	11/32 Dar	05/48 4845	-07/61	09/61	3
64846	05/33 Dar	07/50 4846	-11/62	09/63	1
64847	05/33 Dar	09/48 4847	-11/62	07/63	1
64848	03/34 Dar	10/48 4848	-12/62	01/63	1
64849	03/34 Dar	07/48 4849	-11/62	03/63	1
64850	03/34 Dar	11/49 4850	-12/62	04/63	1
64851	03/34 Dar	06/49 4851	-12/62	02/63	1
64852	03/34 Dar	10/49 4852	-12/62	03/63	1
64853	12/34 Dar	05/48 4853	-12/62	06/63	1
64854	12/34 Dar	03/48 4854	-12/62	08/63	1
64855	10/34 Dar	05/48 4855	-08/62	07/63	3
64856	10/34 Dar	04/50 4856	-10/62	11/62	3
64857	10/34 Dar	09/50 4857	-12/62	07/63	3
64858	11/34 Dar	06/49 4858	-03/62	03/63	3
64859	12/34 Dar	03/49 4859	-12/62	07/63	3
64860	10/35 Dar	08/48 4860	-12/62	08/63	1
64861	11/35 Dar	04/48 4861	-12/62	08/63	1
64862	11/35 Dar	04/48 4862	-10/61	12/61	1
64863	11/35 Dar	05/49 4863	-01/62	12/62	1
64864	11/35 Dar	08/48 4864	-12/62	07/63	1
64865	11/35 Dar	05/50 4865	-12/62	08/63	1
64866	11/35 Dar	03/50 4866	-09/62	10/62	1
64867	12/35 Dar	10/48 4867	-02/62	08/62	1
64868	12/35 Dar	05/50 4868	-04/62	10/62	1
64869	12/35 Dar	11/48 4869	-12/62	05/63	1
64870	12/35 Dar	10/49 4870	-01/62	06/62	1
64871	12/35 Dar	02/49 4871	-10/62	12/62	1
64872	06/35 Dar	09/48 4872	-11/62	08/63	2
64873	06/35 Dar	11/48 4873	-05/59	05/59	2
64874	06/35 Dar	08/49 4874	-04/61	05/61	2
64875	06/35 Dar	10/48 4875	-11/62	09/63	2
64876	06/35 Dar	12/49 4876	-09/59	09/59	2
64877	06/35 Dar	04/48 4877	-11/62	06/63	2
64878	07/35 Dar	08/49 4878	-02/61	03/61	2
64879	07/35 Dar	09/48 4879	-11/62	09/63	2
64880	07/35 Dar	03/48 4880	-11/62	06/63	2
64881	07/35 Dar	09/49 4881	-09/59	10/59	2
64882	08/35 Dar	11/48 4882	-04/61	05/61	2
64883	08/35 Dar	07/49 4883	-03/60	03/60	2
64884	08/35 Dar	10/48 4884	-03/62	08/62	2
64885	08/35 Dar	11/48 4885	-02/61	03/61	2
64886	08/35 Dar	04/51 4886	-11/62	09/63	2
64887	09/35 Dar	07/48 4887	-01/60	01/60	2
64888	09/35 Dar	04/48 4888	-11/62	05/63	2
64889	09/35 Dar	04/49 4889	-08/60	09/60	2
64890	09/35 Dar	02/50 4890	-02/60	04/60	2
64891	09/35 Dar	06/48 4891	-02/60	02/60	2
64892	10/35 Dar	04/48 4892	-05/61	06/61	2
64893	10/35 Dar	05/48 4893	-07/60	07/60	2
64894	10/35 Dar	03/50 4894	-10/59	11/59	2
64895	10/35 Dar	10/48 4895	-11/62	06/63	2
64896	10/35 Dar	05/49 4896	-08/60	10/60	2
64897	10/35 Dar	03/49 4897	-12/62	04/63	2
64898	08/36 Dar	05/49 4898	-02/60	03/60	2
64899	08/36 Dar	04/48 4899	-11/62	05/63	2
64900	08/36 Dar	06/48 4900	-07/59	09/59	2
64901	08/36 Dar	01/49 4901	-10/61	10/61	2
64902	08/36 Dar	06/49 4902	-03/60	04/60	2
64903	08/36 Dar	09/50 4903	-04/62	04/62	2
64904	08/36 Dar	06/48 4904	-10/61	12/61	2
64905	09/36 BP	06/48 4905	-09/59	10/59	2
64906	09/36 BP	03/49 4906	-04/61	05/61	2
64907	09/36 BP	03/51 4907	-11/62	08/63	2
64908	09/36 BP	08/48 4908	-03/61	04/61	2
64909	09/36 BP	10/48 4909	-04/61	04/61	2
64910	09/36 BP	02/51 4910	-12/62	05/63	2
64911	10/36 BP	07/48 4911	-11/62	08/63	2
64912	10/36 BP	08/48 4912	-12/59	12/59	2
64913	10/36 BP	01/50 4913	-10/59	11/59	2
64914	10/36 BP	07/48 4914	-07/61	11/61	2
64915	10/36 BP	07/48 4915	-03/62	02/63	2
64916	10/36 BP	11/48 4916	-08/61	09/61	2
64917	10/36 BP	05/50 4917	-12/62	07/63	2
64918	10/36 BP	11/49 4918	-11/62	08/63	2
64919	10/36 BP	02/50 4919	-12/62	06/63	2
64920	11/36 BP	05/49 4920	-11/61	06/62	2
64921	11/36 BP	04/48 4921	-12/62	06/63	2
64922	11/36 BP	02/50 4922	-12/62	07/63	2

64923	11/36 BP	12/49 4923	-10/62	11/62	2
64924	03/37 BP	08/51 4924	-12/62	05/63	2
64925	04/37 BP	06/48 4925	-12/62	07/63	2
64926	04/37 BP	01/50 4926	-10/62	07/63	2
64927	04/37 BP	11/49 4927	-12/62	07/63	2
64928	04/37 BP	10/49 4928	-07/61	10/61	2
64929	04/37 BP	08/51 4929	-12/62	05/63	2
64930	05/37 BP	10/48 4930	-07/61	08/61	2
64931	05/37 BP	04/49 4931	-10/61	12/61	2
64932	05/37 BP	10/48 4932	-07/61	08/61	2
64933	12/37 Dar	08/50 4933	-12/62	06/63	1
64934	01/38 Dar	07/51 4934	-12/62	04/63	1
64935	02/38 Dar	06/48 4935	-12/62	04/63	1
64936	02/38 Dar	01/49 4936	-12/62	07/63	1
64937	02/38 Dar	04/48 4937	-02/60	03/60	1
64938	02/38 Dar	03/50 4938	-11/62	07/63	1
64939	03/38 Dar	04/49 4939	-04/62	03/63	1
64940	03/38 Dar	02/50 4940	-12/62	04/63	1
64941	03/38 Dar	12/49 4941	-12/62	04/63	1
64942	03/38 Dar	06/50 4942	-12/62	07/63	1
64943	04/38 Dar	06/49 4943	-12/62	07/63	1
64944	04/38 Dar	04/48 4944	-12/62	09/63	1
64945	03/38 Dar	09/49 4945	-10/62	12/62	2
64946	03/38 Dar	01/49 4946	-12/62	05/63	2
64947	04/38 Dar	04/48 4947	-05/62	09/62	2
64948	04/38 Dar	04/48 4948	-04/60	05/60	2
64949	04/38 Dar	11/48 4949	-08/62	11/62	2
64950	04/38 Dar	09/49 4950	-12/62	08/63	2
64951	04/38 Dar	07/49 4951	-03/60	03/60	2
64952	04/38 Dar	08/51 4952	-03/60	03/60	2
64953	05/38 Dar	04/48 4953	-03/60	03/60	2
64954	05/38 Dar	04/48 4954	-03/60	03/60	2
64955	05/38 Dar	08/49 4955	-07/62	12/62	2
64956	05/38 Dar	10/50 4956	-03/60	03/60	2
64957	05/38 Dar	10/48 4957	-03/60	03/60	2
64958	05/38 Dar	04/48 4958	-03/60	03/60	2
64959	05/38 Dar	10/48 4959	-01/60	01/60	2
64960	06/38 Dar	07/50 4960	-02/60	02/60	2
64961	06/38 Dar	04/50 4961	-10/59	11/59	2
64962	06/38 Dar	12/48 4962	-03/60	03/60	2
64963	06/38 Dar	06/50 4963	-01/62	05/62	2
64964	06/38 Dar	09/48 4964	-04/61	11/61	2
64965	07/38 Dar	06/49 4965	-03/60	03/60	2
64966	07/38 Dar	11/49 4966	-07/60	07/60	2
64967	07/38 Dar	07/48 4967	-02/60	03/60	2
64968	07/38 Dar	01/49 4968	-03/60	04/60	2
64969	08/38 Dar	09/50 4969	-11/62	09/63	2
64970	08/38 Dar	09/48 4970	-05/61	06/61	2
64971	02/41 Dar	50 4971	-06/62	09/62	3
64972	02/41 Dar	06/48 4972	-12/59	01/60	3
64973	02/41 Dar	01/49 4973	-11/59	12/59	3
64974	03/41 Dar	08/48 4974	-08/60	08/60	3
64975	03/41 Dar	09/48 4975	-12/62	11/63	3
64976	03/41 Dar	05/48 4976	-11/59	03/60	3
64977	04/41 Dar	06/48 4977	-02/60	05/60	3
64978	04/41 Dar	12/50 4978	-12/62	07/63	3
64979	05/41 Dar	02/51 4979	-01/62	03/62	3
64980	05/41 Dar	12/48 4980	-12/59	01/60	3
64981	05/41 Dar	06/49 4981	-02/60	03/60	3
64982	05/41 Dar	05/49 4982	-12/62	01/63	3
64983	06/41 Dar	10/48 4983	-11/59	11/59	3
64984	06/41 Dar	03/48 4984	-12/59	01/60	3
64985	07/41 Dar	10/48 4985	-12/59	01/60	3
64986	07/41 Dar	09/49 4986	-12/62	06/63	3
64987	08/41 Dar	05/48 4987	-03/61	04/61	3
64988	08/41 Dar	06/50 4988	-12/59	01/60	3

J1 65002-65014
0-6-0 GNR Ivatt

Power Classification: 2MT
Introduced: 1908
Designer: Ivatt
Company: GNR
Weight: Loco 46t 14cwt
Tender 43t 2cwt
Driving Wheel: 5' 8"
Boiler Pressure: 175psi
Cylinders: Inside 18" x 26"
Tractive Effort: 18430lbf
Valve Gear: Stephenson (slide valves)

In 1908 Ivatt introduced fifteen mixed traffic 0-6-0s on the GNR. They were GNR class 'J21' (later LNER class 'J1') and they were built at Doncaster. They had the same saturated boilers as fitted to the 'N1' class 0-6-2Ts. Four engines (including 5000, originally GNR No. 1) were scrapped in 1947, the rest coming into BR stock. In later years there was a lot of variation in the domes and boilers fitted to these engines.

The 'J5' class was identical except they were had 5' 2" wheels, compared to the 5' 8" wheels of the 'J1's.

Year End Totals: 'J1' class

'47	'48	'49	'50	'51	'52	'53	'54	'55	'56	'57	'58	'59	'60	'61	'62	'63	'64	'65	'66	'67
11	11	11	11	10	5	2														

Number	Built	Renumbered	BR Dates	Scrap	Notes
65002	09/08 Don	02/51 5002	-08/54	09/54	
65003	09/08 Don	10/48 5003	-01/53	53	
65004	09/08 Don	12/49 5004	-11/52	52	
65005	09/08 Don	02/49 5005	-05/52	52	
65006	10/08 Don	5006	-07/51	51	
65007	10/08 Don	10/49 5007	-02/52	52	
65008	10/08 Don	02/49 5008	-03/52	52	
65009	10/08 Don	09/49 5009	-03/52	52	
65010	10/08 Don	12/48 5010	-01/53	53	
65013	11/08 Don	05/50 5013	-11/54	12/54	
65014	11/08 Don	02/49 5014	-08/53	53	

J2 65015-65023
0-6-0 GNR Gresley

Power Classification: 2MT
Introduced: 1912
Designer: Gresley
Company: GNR
Weight: Loco 50t 10cwt
Tender 43t 2cwt
Driving Wheel: 5' 8"
Boiler Pressure: 170psi superheated
Cylinders: Inside 19" x 26"
Tractive Effort: 19945lbf
Valve Gear: Stephenson (piston valves)

In 1912 Gresley introduced the 'J2' class, a larger superheated version of Ivatt's 'J1' class. The engines were basically Ivatt's design, but they were built after he was succeeded by Gresley at Doncaster. Ten engines were built and nine came into BR stock (5024 having been scrapped in 1946).

Year End Totals: 'J2' class

'47	'48	'49	'50	'51	'52	'53	'54	'55	'56	'57	'58	'59	'60	'61	'62	'63	'64	'65	'66	'67
9	9	9	8	8	8	2														

Number	Built	Renumbered	BR Dates	Scrap	Notes
65015	08/12 Don	09/49 5015	-12/53	54	
65016	08/12 Don	07/48 5016	-10/53	53	
65017	08/12 Don	06/49 5017	-01/54	54	
65018	09/12 Don	05/51 5018	-11/53	53	
65019	09/12 Don	09/50 5019	-03/53	53	
65020	09/12 Don	08/48 5020	-07/54	08/54	
65021	09/12 Don	5021	-11/50	50	
65022	10/12 Don	06/51 5022	-12/53	01/54	
65023	10/12 Don	05/48 5023	-11/53	12/53	

J21 65025-65123
0-6-0 NER Worsdell

Power Classification: 2F
Introduced: 1886-1894
Designer: T W Worsdell
Company: NER
Weight: Loco 42t 1cwt
s Loco 43t 15cwt
r Loco 42t 19cwt
Tender 36t 19cwt
Driving Wheel: 5' 1¼"
Boiler Pressure: 160psi
s 160psi superheated
Cylinders: Inside 18" x 24"
sr Inside 19" x 24"
c Inside 19" x 26"
Tractive Effort: 17265lbf
sr 19240lbf
c 20840lbf
Valve Gear: Joy (slide valves)
rs Stephenson (piston valves)

Between 1886 and 1894 Worsdell built 201 of these 5' 1" 0-6-0s for the NER. Most of the class were built as two-cylinder compounds (NER class 'C'). Thirty engines (65116-65123, NER class 'C1') were originally built as simples, and the rest were converted by 1913. The whole class then became NER class 'C', and then LNER class 'J21'. The first engine was withdrawn in 1929.

The 'N8' and 'N9' classes were 0-6-2T versions of this class.

They were popular engines with the drivers (particularly on the trans-Pennine routes and for working excursion trains in the North East) and they were excellent and economical all-round machines.

s Many engines were fitted with superheaters and extended smokeboxes. They were also fitted with larger cylinders and they had piston valves, replacing the original slide valves operated by Joy valve gear.

r Some of the superheated engines later had the superheaters removed, but they still retained the piston valves and the larger cylinders.

c One engine (65043) had the cylinder piston stroke increased from 24" to 26".

Year End Totals: 'J21' class

'47	'48	'49	'50	'51	'52	'53	'54	'55	'56	'57	'58	'59	'60	'61	'62	'63	'64	'65	'66	'67
83	75	56	43	29	28	27	15	12	11	9	5	4	2	1						

Number	Built	Renumbered	BR Dates	Scrap	Notes
65025	08/86 Ghd	5025	-11/51	51	r
65026	05/87 Ghd	5026	-10/49	49	r
65027	06/87 Ghd	10/48 5027	-02/50	50	r
65028	06/87 Ghd	10/48 5028	-09/51	51	s
65029	09/87 Ghd	5029	-05/49	49	
65030	10/88 Ghd	04/48 5030	-04/51	05/51	r
65031	03/89 Ghd	5031	-06/48	06/48	s
65032	03/89 Ghd	5032	-08/48	48	r
65033 §	03/89 Ghd	12/48 5033	-04/62		s 09/56➪r
65035	05/89 Ghd	01/49 5035	-05/56	06/56	r
65036	05/89 Ghd	04/49 5036	-12/49	50	r
65037	05/89 Ghd	5037	-04/50	50	s
65038	06/89 Ghd	12/48 5038	-11/54	54	s
65039	06/89 Ghd	10/48 5039	-11/58	12/58	r
65040	06/89 Ghd	05/49 5040	-09/52	52	s
65041	06/89 Ghd	04/48 5041	-02/51	51	
65042	06/89 Ghd	12/50 5042	-07/54	07/54	r
65043	06/89 Ghd	5043	-01/51	51	rc
65044	06/89 Ghd	04/49 5044	-10/49	49	
65047	10/89 Ghd	08/48 5047	-12/54	01/55	s
65049	11/89 Ghd	5049	-06/48	48	r
65051	12/89 Ghd	5051	-07/49	49	
65052	12/89 Ghd	5052	-08/49	49	s
65056	05/90 Ghd	5056	-12/48	49	
65057	06/90 Ghd	01/49 5057	-10/50	50	s
65058	06/90 Ghd	5058	-11/49	49	r
65059	06/90 Ghd	5059	-08/49	49	r
65060	09/90 Ghd	5060	-08/49	49	r
65061	09/90 Ghd	05/48 5061	-05/58	06/58	s
65062	10/90 Ghd	12/50 5062	-12/54	01/55	s
65063	10/90 Ghd	5063	-02/48	02/48	
65064	10/90 Ghd	06/48 5064	-09/58	09/58	s
65066	11/90 Dar	06/48 5066	-11/49	49	r
65067	11/90 Dar	06/48 5067	-11/51	51	r
65068	12/90 Dar	06/49 5068	-06/54	07/54	s
65069	12/90 Dar	5069	-04/48	04/48	r
65070	01/91 Dar	11/48 5070	-09/60	09/60	r
65072	01/91 Dar	5072	-02/50	50	r
65073	01/91 Dar	5073	-02/50	50	
65075	03/91 Dar	09/48 5075	-06/54	07/54	s
65076	04/91 Dar	5076	-06/51	06/51	r
65077	04/91 Dar	08/49 5077	-08/53	53	s
65078	04/91 Dar	10/48 5078	-03/57	04/57	s
65079	05/91 Dar	5079	-11/49	49	r
65080	05/91 Dar	11/48 5080	-12/51	52	r
65081	04/91 Ghd	01/49 5081	-01/50	50	r
65082	05/91 Ghd	08/48 5082	-01/55	55	s
65083	05/91 Ghd	5083	-04/50	50	r
65084	05/91 Ghd	10/48 5084	-07/50	50	s
65086	06/91 Ghd	5086	-02/49	49	
65088	06/91 Ghd	08/48 5088	-11/55	55	s
65089	06/91 Ghd	05/49 5089	-12/54	01/55	s
65090	06/91 Ghd	11/48 5090	-12/55	56	s
65091	06/91 Ghd	03/49 5091	-10/57	11/57	s
65092	06/91 Ghd	05/48 5092	-12/54	01/55	s
65093	06/91 Ghd	5093	-09/49	49	r
65094	07/91 Dar	5094	-02/50	50	r
65095	07/91 Dar	07/49 5095	-04/51	51	s
65097	09/91 Dar	10/48 5097	-12/54	55	s
65098	09/91 Dar	02/49 5098	-12/54	01/55	s
65099	09/91 Dar	08/48 5099	-10/61	01/66	r
65100	08/91 Ghd	12/48 5100	-12/54	12/54	r
65101	01/92 Ghd	5101	-04/50	50	r
65102	01/92 Ghd	08/49 5102	-11/51	51	r
65103	02/92 Ghd	08/48 5103	-10/58	05/59	s
65104	02/92 Ghd	06/48 5104	-10/48	48	r
65105	03/92 Ghd	10/48 5105	-09/51	51	r
65107	03/92 Ghd	04/48 5107	-05/49	05/49	r
65108	04/92 Ghd	5108	-10/49	49	r
65109	10/92 Ghd	5109	-04/49	49	s
65110	11/92 Ghd	04/48 5110	-07/60	07/60	s 11/56➪r
65111	11/92 Ghd	10/49 5111	-03/51	51	r
65112	12/92 Ghd	5112	-11/49	49	
65114	12/92 Ghd	5114	-05/49	05/49	
65115	12/92 Ghd	5115	-06/48	07/48	s
65116	04/94 Ghd	5116	-02/50	50	
65117	04/94 Ghd	02/52 5117	-02/59	03/59	r
65118	05/94 Ghd	09/48 5118	-11/51	51	r
65119	06/94 Ghd	11/48 5119	-12/54	55	s

Number	Built		Renumbered		BR Dates	Scrap	Notes
65120	06/94	Ghd	11/48	5120	-02/50	*50*	
65121	06/94	Ghd		5121	-12/49	*50*	s
65122	12/94	Ghd	*50*	5122	-09/51	*51*	
65123	02/95	Ghd		5123	-02/50	*50*	s

J10 65126-65209
0-6-0 MS&LR & GCR Parker

Power Classification: 2F
Introduced: 1892-1902
Designer: Parker and Pollitt
Company: MS&LR
Weight: Loco 41t 6cwt
Tender 37t 6cwt
4 Tender 43t 0cwt
Driving Wheel: 5' 1"
Boiler Pressure: 160psi
Cylinders: Inside 18" x 26"
Tractive Effort: 18780lbf
Valve Gear: Stephenson (slide valves)

This class was originally designed by Parker and Pollitt for the Manchester, Sheffield & Lincolnshire Railway, the first engine appearing in 1892. They were tender versions of the 'N5' 0-6-2T class. Eventually 124 engines were built between 1892 and 1902 (the MS&LR becoming the GCR in 1897). 65126-65157 were built by Pollitt in 1892-1896, 65158-65171 by Parker in 1897, and 65172-65209 by Robinson in 1901-1902. The engines were known as GCR classes '9D', '9H' and '9M', differing in the size of tender attached. They were fitted with 'flower-pot' chimneys by Gresley during LNER days, in common with many other ex-GCR engines. The first engine was withdrawn in 1933.

2 'J10/2' consisted of the original Parker 1892 engines with 3080 gallon tenders (65127 and 65128 were fitted with larger tenders).

4 'J10/4' were engines introduced in 1896, fitted with larger bearings and larger 4000 gallon tenders. Some of these engines became 'J10/6' when they exchanged tenders.

6 'J10/6' engines were introduced by Robinson for the GCR in 1901. They had larger bearings and 3080 gallon tenders. Some of these engines became 'J10/4' when they exchanged tenders.

1, 3 & 5 'J10/1', 'J10/3' and 'J10/5' were variations of 'J10/2', 'J10/4' and 'J10/6' before the boiler mountings were cut down to the standard LNER loading gauge.

Year End Totals: 'J10' class

'47	'48	'49	'50	'51	'52	'53	'54	'55	'56	'57	'58	'59	'60	'61	'62	'63	'64	'65	'66	'67
78	77	77	75	75	60	53	53	53	37	35	15	4	2							

Number	Built		Renumbered		BR Dates	Scrap	Notes
65126	08/93	Gor	03/49	5126	-12/52	*53*	2
65127	08/92	K	03/49	5127	-02/50	*50*	2
65128	08/92	K	02/49	5128	-10/50	*50*	2
65130	09/92	K	07/48	5130	-08/52	*52*	2
65131	03/96	BP	03/49	5131	-03/59	04/59	4
65132	03/96	BP	02/49	5132	-05/58	06/58	4
65133	03/96	BP	04/48	5133	-12/59	04/60	6
65134	04/96	BP	03/49	5134	-12/59	02/60	4
65135	04/96	BP	02/49	5135	-04/58	05/58	4
65136	04/96	BP	03/49	5136	-02/53	*03/53*	4
65137	05/96	BP	02/49	5137	-05/52	*52*	4
65138	06/96	BP	01/49	5138	-08/59	09/59	4
65139	06/96	BP	03/49	5139	-12/56	*57*	6
65140	06/96	BP	03/49	5140	-12/59	01/60	4
65141	07/96	BP	01/49	5141	-09/52	*52*	4
65142	07/96	BP	03/49	5142	-10/58	02/59	4
65143	07/96	BP	03/49	5143	-08/56	*56*	4
65144	07/96	BP	05/48	5144	-03/58	06/58	4
65145	08/96	BP	03/49	5145	-11/58	02/59	4 ⇨6
65146	09/96	BP	03/49	5146	-12/58	02/59	4
65147	09/96	BP	03/49	5147	-03/58	04/58	4
65148	10/96	BP	02/49	5148	-12/56	*57*	4
65149	11/96	BP	03/49	5149	-02/53	*04/53*	4
65151	11/96	BP	02/49	5151	-05/52	*52*	4
65153	12/96	BP	03/49	5153	-12/56	*57*	4
65154	12/96	BP	02/49	5154	-05/53	*53*	4
65155	12/96	BP	01/49	5155	-06/52	*06/52*	4
65156	01/97	BP	03/49	5156	-02/58	03/58	4
65157	01/97	BP	09/48	5157	-08/61	09/61	4
65158	02/97	BP	03/49	5158	-12/59	06/60	6
65159	02/97	BP	02/49	5159	-12/57	01/58	6
65160	02/97	BP	05/48	5160	-06/58	07/58	4
65161	02/97	BP	04/48	5161	-09/52	*52*	4
65162	02/97	BP	02/49	5162	-12/56	01/57	4
65163	02/97	BP	03/49	5163	-12/52	*05/53*	6
65164	03/97	BP	07/48	5164	-05/53	*53*	4
65165	03/97	BP	03/49	5165	-03/56	*05/56*	4
65166	04/97	BP	03/49	5166	-12/59	02/60	4
65167	04/97	BP	03/49	5167	-09/58	02/59	4
65168	04/97	BP	01/49	5168	-12/52	*53*	4
65169	05/97	BP	10/48	5169	-02/60	04/60	4
65170	05/97	BP	08/48	5170	-06/58	02/59	6 ⇨4
65171	05/97	BP	08/48	5171	-10/56	*56*	4
65172	02/01	Gor	03/49	5172	-02/53	*03/53*	6
65173	02/01	Gor	04/48	5173	-12/56	*57*	6 ⇨4
65175	03/01	Gor	02/49	5175	-03/58	04/58	6
65176	04/01	Gor	02/49	5176	-12/56	01/57	6
65177	05/01	Gor	09/48	5177	-09/59	10/59	6
65178	05/01	Gor	06/48	5178	-10/58	02/59	4
65179	06/01	Gor	04/48	5179	-11/52	*52*	4
65180	06/01	Gor	03/49	5180	-12/56	*57*	6
65181	06/01	Gor	02/49	5181	-12/56	01/57	6
65182	07/01	Gor	03/49	5182	-11/56	*02/57*	6
65183	08/01	Gor	02/49	5183	-04/52	*52*	6
65184	08/01	Gor	02/49	5184	-09/59	10/59	4
65185	08/01	Gor	02/49	5185	-12/56	*01/57*	6 ⇨4
65186	09/01	Gor	03/49	5186	-08/57	09/57	4
65187	10/01	Gor	03/49	5187	-02/59	05/59	6 ⇨4
65188	10/01	Gor	02/49	5188	-08/52	*52*	6
65189	11/01	Gor	09/48	5189	-09/52	*52*	6
65190	12/01	Gor	03/49	5190	-02/53	*06/53*	6
65191	12/01	Gor	03/49	5191	-01/58	01/58	6
65192	01/02	Gor	03/49	5192	-05/60	07/60	6
65193	01/02	Gor	02/49	5193	-08/52	*52*	6
65194	02/02	Gor	10/48	5194	-12/59	02/60	6
65195	04/02	Gor		5195	-02/48	*02/48*	6
65196	02/02	Gor	01/49	5196	-06/58	09/58	6
65197	08/02	Gor	03/48	5197	-05/56	*06/56*	6
65198	04/02	Gor	02/49	5198	-08/61	09/61	6
65199	08/02	Gor	02/49	5199	-12/58	02/59	6
65200	09/02	Gor	02/49	5200	-04/58	05/58	6
65201	03/02	Gor	12/48	5201	-03/53	*06/53*	6
65202	03/02	Gor	03/49	5202	-03/58	04/58	6
65203	05/02	Gor	02/49	5203	-12/56	01/57	6
65204	06/02	Gor	03/49	5204	-11/52	*52*	6
65205	06/02	Gor	12/48	5205	-07/56	*56*	6
65208	06/02	Gor	02/49	5208	-12/58	01/59	6
65209	07/02	Gor	02/49	5209	-11/58	12/58	6

J36 65210-65346
0-6-0 NBR Holmes

Power Classification: 2F
Introduced: 1888-1900
Designer: Holmes
Company: NBR
Weight: Loco 41t 19cwt
Tender 33t 9cwt
Driving Wheel: 5' 0"
Boiler Pressure: 165psi
Cylinders: Inside 18¼" x 26"
Tractive Effort: 20240lbf
Valve Gear: Stephenson (slide valves)

Holmes built 168 engines of his class 'C' for the NBR in 1888-1900. They were the most numerous class on the NBR and they became LNER class 'J36'.

The class achieved some degree of fame when twenty-five engines were sent overseas in 1917-1918, and they were named after famous military leaders and places connected with the First World War when they returned. The names were painted on the middle splasher, but at nationalisation (and also at various other times during BR days) many of the engines ran nameless.

The first engine was scrapped after the Linlithgow accident of December 1925, and 123 engines came into BR stock.

c Two engines (65285 and 65287) had cut down chimneys and boiler mountings for working on the Gartsherrie/Glenbeigh branch. They were shedded at Kipps (Coatbridge).

Year End Totals: 'J36' class

'47	'48	'49	'50	'51	'52	'53	'54	'55	'56	'57	'58	'59	'60	'61	'62	'63	'64	'65	'66	'67
123	118	118	114	104	96	96	96	95	93	87	86	82	75	67	32	11	9	8	3	

Number	Built		Renumbered		BR Dates	Scrap	Notes
65210	08/88	Cow	03/49	5210	-10/62	08/63	
65211	09/89	Cow	10/48	5211	-07/62	06/63	
65213	11/89	Cow	09/52	5213	-04/57	05/57	
65214	01/90	Cow	03/48	5214	-11/63	05/64	
65215	01/90	Cow	06/48	5215	-04/50	*05/50*	
65216	01/90	Cow	10/48	5216	-04/62	04/63	
BYNG							
65217	04/90	Cow	11/48	5217	-10/62	03/63	
FRENCH							
65218	04/90	Cow	10/49	5218	-10/62	12/62	
65220	02/91	Cow		5220	-03/48	*48*	
65221	02/91	Cow	09/50	5221	-07/59	09/59	
65222	02/91	Cow	04/48	5222	-11/63	06/64	
SOMME							
65224	02/91	Cow	12/48	5224	-06/63	03/64	
MONS							
65225	04/91	Cow	07/48	5225	-10/57	11/57	
65226	04/91	Cow		5226	-04/51	*51*	
HAIG							
65227	05/91	Cow	08/50	5227	-08/61	11/61	
65228	05/91	Cow	03/48	5228	-12/62	10/63	
65229	05/91	Cow	11/49	5229	-05/60	06/60	
65230	05/91	Cow	05/48	5230	-10/62	08/63	
65231	07/91	Cow	09/48	5231	-04/52	*52*	
65232	07/91	Cow	06/49	5232	-10/61	09/62	
65233	07/91	Cow	08/48	5233	-11/60	06/61	
PLUMER							
65234	07/91	Cow	03/48	5234	-04/67	08/67	
65235	08/91	Cow	01/49	5235	-10/61	06/63	
GOUGH							
65236	08/91	Cow	03/48	5236	-04/56	*56*	
HORNE							
65237	10/91	N	07/48	5237	-12/62	03/63	
65238	10/91	N	04/49	5238	-07/51	*51*	
65239	10/91	N	10/48	5239	-01/61	05/63	
65240	11/91	N	09/48	5240	-04/52	*52*	
65241	11/91	N	04/48	5241	-10/62	08/63	
65242	11/91	N	03/48	5242	-08/57	11/57	
65243 §	12/91	N	06/48	5243	-07/66		
MAUDE							
65244	12/91	N	10/49	5244	-08/57	11/57	
65245	12/91	N	08/49	5245	-06/51	*51*	
65246	12/91	Cow	04/48	5246	-01/62	02/62	
65247	12/91	Cow	07/48	5247	-07/59	10/59	
65248	12/91	Cow	09/48	5248	-05/56	*56*	
65249	02/92	SS	03/48	5249	-10/60	12/60	
65250	02/92	SS	04/48	5250	-02/57	05/57	
65251	02/92	SS	11/49	5251	-11/63	06/64	
65252	02/92	SS	03/49	5252	-05/60	06/60	
65253	02/92	SS	09/48	5253	-06/63	10/63	
JOFFRE							
65254	02/92	SS	09/48	5254	-04/51	*51*	
65255	02/92	SS	11/49	5255	-08/51	*51*	
65256	02/92	SS		5256	-04/48	*05/48*	
65257	02/92	SS	06/49	5257	-10/62	03/63	
65258	12/92	SS	06/48	5258	-03/62	10/62	
65259	02/92	SS	09/49	5259	-07/59	07/59	
65260	03/92	SS	03/48	5260	-10/62	08/63	
65261	03/92	SS	12/49	5261	-06/63	07/63	
65264	07/92	Cow	06/50	5264	-06/52	*52*	
65265	07/92	Cow	10/48	5265	-12/63	06/64	
65266	07/92	Cow	07/48	5266	-05/62	04/63	
65267	07/92	Cow	08/48	5267	-11/66	04/67	
65268	08/92	Cow	06/48	5268	-12/62	01/63	
ALLENBY							
65270	03/93	Cow	02/51	5270	-02/58	03/58	
65271	03/93	Cow	04/50	5271	-08/52	*52*	
65273	03/93	Cow	07/48	5273	-11/63	02/64	
65274	01/93	Cow	05/48	5274	-12/50	*51*	
65275	01/93	Cow	01/51	5275	-12/62	03/64	
65276	06/96	Cow	10/49	5276	-03/61	07/61	
65277	06/96	Cow	09/48	5277	-06/63	12/63	
65278	06/96	Cow	12/48	5278	-01/52	*52*	
65279	06/96	Cow	06/48	5279	-03/51	*51*	
65280	06/96	Cow	01/50	5280	-05/62	07/62	
65281	06/96	Cow	09/48	5281	-07/61	08/61	
65282	11/96	Cow	06/50	5282	-01/66	04/66	
65283	11/96	Cow	04/48	5283	-12/52	*53*	
65285	11/96	Cow	08/49	5285	-11/63	07/64	c
65286	12/96	Cow	11/48	5286	-02/52	*52*	
65287	12/96	Cow	06/49	5287	-06/63	07/65	c
65288	04/97	Cow	02/49	5288	-06/67	11/67	
65289	04/97	Cow		5289	-03/48	*48*	
65290	04/97	Cow	12/48	5290	-08/63	03/64	
65291	05/97	Cow	06/48	5291	-11/50	*50*	
65292	05/97	Cow	12/48	5292	-02/51	*51*	
65293	06/97	Cow	10/48	5293	-12/62	02/65	
65294	07/97	Cow	04/48	5294	-03/50	*05/50*	
65295	07/97	Cow	09/48	5295	-04/61	06/61	
65296	07/97	Cow	12/50	5296	-02/62	03/62	
65297	07/97	Cow	01/53	5297	-01/66	05/66	
65298	07/97	Cow	01/49	5298	-04/51	*51*	
65300	10/98	Cow	12/48	5300	-07/62	06/63	
65303	10/98	Cow	12/48	5303	-12/62	09/63	
65304	10/98	Cow	10/48	5304	-10/62	03/63	
65305	12/98	Cow	03/48	5305	-02/62	06/63	
65306	01/99	Cow	02/49	5306	-07/62	04/63	
65307	01/99	Cow	06/49	5307	-12/63	07/64	
65308	01/99	Cow	11/48	5308	-06/51	*51*	
65309	01/99	Cow	04/48	5309	-06/64	10/64	
65310	01/99	Cow	06/49	5310	-07/62	05/63	
65311	03/99	Cow	03/50	5311	-11/63	06/64	
05/54 ➲HAIG							
65312	03/99	Cow	04/48	5312	-12/62	05/63	
65313	03/99	Cow	06/48	5313	-07/62	11/62	
65314	03/99	Cow	01/49	5314	-08/55	*55*	
65315	04/99	Cow	10/48	5315	-04/62	04/63	
65316	04/99	Cow	04/48	5316	-12/62	09/63	
65317	05/99	Cow	12/48	5317	-07/60	08/60	
65318	05/99	Cow	05/50	5318	-05/62	06/62	

LNER Gresley 'J38' class 0-6-0 No 65909 at Polmont in May 1961.

GER Holden 'F5' class 2-4-2T No 67218 at Yarmouth in September 1953, fitted with push-pull gear.

GNR Ivatt 'C12' class 4-4-2T No 67390.

LNER Thompson 'L1' class 2-6-4T No 67765.

Number	Built	Renumbered	BR Dates	Scrap	Notes
65319	05/99 Cow	10/48 5319	-11/66	12/66	
65320	05/99 Cow	10/48 5320	-04/62	09/62	
65321	05/99 Cow	10/48 5321	-12/62	05/63	
65322	06/99 Cow	50 5322	-08/51	51	
65323	01/00 Cow	06/50 5323	-12/63	06/64	
65324	01/00 Cow	07/48 5324	-02/57	04/57	
65325	01/00 Cow	12/49 5325	-11/63	03/64	
65327	01/00 Cow	05/48 5327	-11/65	09/66	
65328	01/00 Cow	5328	-03/48	48	
65329	03/00 Cow	01/50 5329	-12/63	07/64	
65330	03/00 Cow	08/48 5330	-06/62	08/62	
65331	03/00 Cow	04/52 5331	-08/63	03/64	
65333	05/00 Cow	11/48 5333	-10/59	10/59	
65334	05/00 Cow	03/49 5334	-10/62	03/63	
65335	07/00 Cow	02/49 5335	-11/63	06/64	
65337	07/00 Cow	5337	-04/48	05/48	
65338	07/00 Cow	06/49 5338	-12/63	06/64	
65339	07/00 Cow	09/51 5339	-03/61	04/61	
65340	07/00 Cow	10/48 5340	-01/52	52	
65341	12/00 Cow	07/48 5341	-07/63	10/63	
65342	12/00 Cow	06/48 5342	-02/60	04/60	
65343	12/00 Cow	03/52 5343	-02/60	05/60	
65344	12/00 Cow	04/48 5344	-10/62	06/64	
65345	12/00 Cow	09/49 5345	-06/67	11/67	
65346	12/00 Cow	09/48 5346	-06/64	10/64	

J15 65350-65479
0-6-0 GER Worsdell, Holden and Hill

Power Classification: 2F
Introduced: 1883-1913
Designer: T W Worsdell
Company: GER
Weight: Loco 37t 2cwt
Tender 30t 13cwt
Driving Wheel: 4' 11"
Boiler Pressure: 160psi
Cylinders: Inside 17½" x 24"
Tractive Effort: 16940lbf
Valve Gear: Stephenson (slide valves)

The 'J15' class of mixed traffic 0-6-0s was originally introduced on the GER by Worsdell in 1883. Originally known as GER class 'Y14' a total of 289 engines were built between 1883 and 1913 by Worsdell and his successors J Holden, S D Holden and Hill. They were all built at Stratford, apart from nineteen built by Sharp Stewart in 1884. Forty-three engines were loaned to the Government for work overseas during the First World War.

For many years the engines were an essential part of the railway scene in East Anglia and could be seen on all types of duty. The first engines were withdrawn in 1920, 272 were still in service at grouping in 1923 and 127 came into BR stock in 1948. The last survivors were withdrawn in 1962, one engine being preserved.

c Five engines were fitted with side-window cabs and tender cabs for working on the Colne Valley line.

Year End Totals: 'J15' class

'47	'48	'49	'50	'51	'52	'53	'54	'55	'56	'57	'58	'59	'60	'61	'62	'63	'64	'65	'66	'67
127	114	92	80	65	62	62	59	53	52	41	26	14	11							

Number	Built	Renumbered	BR Dates	Scrap	Notes
65350	12/86 Str	5350	-02/51	04/51	
65351	09/87 Str	5351	-05/49	49	
65352	09/87 Str	5352	-05/48	48	
65353	09/87 Str	5353	-12/49	50	
65354	10/87 Str	5354	-02/51	51	
65355	11/87 Str	5355	-04/51	05/51	
65356	01/88 Str	09/50 5356	-04/57	05/57	
65357	10/88 Str	5357	-09/49	49	
65359	10/88 Str	01/50 5359	-12/55	01/56	
65361	07/89 Str	01/50 5361	-09/62	03/63	
65362	07/89 Str	5362	-07/51	51	
65363	07/89 Str	5363	-08/49	49	
65364	07/89 Str	5364	-06/49	49	
65365	10/89 Str	5365	-07/50	50	
65366	10/89 Str	03/49 5366	-06/52	52	
65367	10/89 Str	5367	-01/50	50	
65368	10/89 Str	5368	-05/48	48	
65369	10/89 Str	5369	-02/51	04/51	
65370	10/89 Str	09/48 5370	-04/56	56	
65371	10/89 Str	5371	-12/49	50	
65372	10/89 Str	5372	-09/49	49	
65373	10/89 Str	5373	-10/50	50	
65374	11/89 Str	5374	-11/50	50	
65375	11/89 Str	5375	-11/49	49	
65376	11/89 Str	5376	-06/49	49	
65377	12/89 Str	5377	-02/51	51	
65378	12/89 Str	08/48 5378	-04/51	05/51	
65379	12/89 Str	5379	-09/49	49	
65380	12/89 Str	5380	-01/48	04/48	
65381	12/89 Str	5381	-11/48	48	
65382	08/90 Str	5382	-03/52	52	
65383	08/90 Str	5383	-02/48	03/48	
65384	08/90 Str	09/48 5384	-03/55	55	
65385	08/90 Str	5385	-12/48	49	
65386	09/90 Str	5386	-01/50	50	
65387	09/90 Str	5387	-08/49	49	
65388	09/90 Str	02/50 5388	-05/59	06/59	
65389	10/90 Str	09/48 5389	-04/60	04/60	
65390	10/90 Str	02/49 5390	-12/58	01/59	
65391	10/90 Str	03/50 5391	-12/58	01/59	c
65392	11/90 Str	5392	-05/49	07/49	
65393	11/90 Str	5393	-08/49	02/51	
65394	11/90 Str	5394	-05/48	48	
65395	09/91 Str	5395	-05/49	07/49	
65396	09/91 Str	5396	-03/51	05/51	
65397	09/91 Str	5397	-09/49	49	
65398	10/91 Str	04/48 5398	-02/52	52	
65399	10/91 Str	5399	-03/48	48	
65400	10/91 Str	5400	-02/48	03/48	
65401	10/91 Str	5401	-09/51	51	
65402	10/91 Str	5402	-10/50	50	
65404	11/91 Str	10/48 5404	-10/56	56	
65405	11/91 Str	02/49 5405	-10/58	01/59	c
65406	11/91 Str	5406	-04/51	05/51	
65407	11/91 Str	04/48 5407	-04/51	04/51	
65408	11/91 Str	12/48 5408	-12/51	52	
65409	11/91 Str	5409	-11/49	49	
65410	12/91 Str	5410	-02/48	48	
65411	12/91 Str	5411	-10/48	48	
65412	12/91 Str	08/48 5412	-11/49	49	
65413	12/91 Str	5413	-11/50	50	
65414	12/91 Str	5414	-11/49	49	
65415	12/91 Str	5415	-05/49	07/49	
65416	12/91 Str	5416	-12/49	50	
65417	12/91 Str	07/48 5417	-08/56	56	
65418	12/91 Str	5418	-03/48	48	
65419	01/92 Str	5419	-02/50	50	
65420	01/92 Str	09/48 5420	-08/62	12/62	
65421	01/92 Str	5421	-03/48	48	
65422	08/92 Str	08/48 5422	-07/55	07/55	
65423	08/92 Str	5423	-11/50	50	
65424	08/92 Str	03/49 5424	-12/59	01/60	c
65425	09/92 Str	03/49 5425	-09/56	01/57	
65426	09/92 Str	07/48 5426	-05/51	05/51	
65427	11/92 Str	5427	-10/50	50	
65428	05/99 Str	5428	-08/49	49	
65429	05/99 Str	5429	-11/50	50	
65430	05/99 Str	09/48 5430	-01/56	56	
65431	05/99 Str	04/48 5431	-03/51	51	
65432	05/99 Str	11/48 5432	-03/58	04/58	c
65433	05/99 Str	02/50 5433	-01/58	02/58	
65434	06/99 Str	01/50 5434	-11/59	01/60	
65435	06/99 Str	08/48 5435	-09/56	56	
65436	06/99 Str	5436	-12/49	50	
65437	06/99 Str	5437	-09/50	50	
65438	09/99 Str	06/49 5438	-06/58	12/58	c
65439	10/99 Str	5439	-11/51	51	
65440	07/99 Str	08/49 5440	-10/60	11/60	
65441	07/99 Str	10/49 5441	-10/58	01/59	
65442	07/99 Str	04/49 5442	-05/58	01/59	
65443	07/99 Str	08/49 5443	-12/59	01/60	
65444	07/99 Str	02/51 5444	-10/58	01/59	
65445	08/99 Str	04/49 5445	-08/62	03/63	
65446	08/99 Str	10/49 5446	-12/60	01/61	
65447	08/99 Str	07/48 5447	-04/59	05/59	
65448	09/99 Str	09/48 5448	-03/60	04/60	
65449	09/99 Str	10/48 5449	-12/59	01/60	
65450	09/06 Str	05/49 5450	-10/61	11/61	
65451	05/06 Str	06/48 5451	-09/59	10/59	
65452	06/06 Str	05/49 5452	-12/59	01/60	
65453	06/06 Str	09/49 5453	-08/62	12/62	
65454	06/06 Str	03/51 5454	-05/59	06/59	
65455	06/06 Str	06/49 5455	-03/60	04/60	
65456	06/06 Str	04/48 5456	-09/58	10/58	
65457	06/06 Str	02/49 5457	-02/62	04/62	
65458	07/06 Str	05/49 5458	-10/61	12/61	
65459	07/06 Str	06/49 5459	-02/60	03/60	
65460	02/12 Str	08/49 5460	-09/62	12/62	
65461	02/12 Str	10/48 5461	-04/60	06/60	
65462 §	03/12 Str	02/49 5462	-09/62		
65463	03/12 Str	04/48 5463	-11/59	01/60	
65464	03/12 Str	06/50 5464	-09/62	03/63	
65465	03/12 Str	08/49 5465	-09/62	01/63	
65466	04/12 Str	10/48 5466	-07/58	04/59	
65467	04/12 Str	04/48 5467	-02/59	02/59	
65468	05/12 Str	03/49 5468	-09/59	01/60	
65469	05/12 Str	11/50 5469	-08/62	03/63	
65470	06/13 Str	08/50 5470	-12/59	01/60	
65471	06/13 Str	11/49 5471	-07/60	08/60	
65472	06/13 Str	11/48 5472	-12/59	01/60	
65473	06/13 Str	06/48 5473	-03/60	04/60	
65474	07/13 Str	05/49 5474	-02/60	03/60	
65475	08/13 Str	09/50 5475	-09/59	01/60	
65476	08/13 Str	12/48 5476	-09/62	12/62	
65477	08/13 Str	05/48 5477	-02/60	03/60	
65478	09/13 Str	09/49 5478	-10/61	11/61	
65479	09/13 Str	12/48 5479	-08/60	08/60	

J5 65480-65499
0-6-0 GNR Ivatt

Power Classification: 3F
Introduced: 1909-1910
Designer: Ivatt
Company: GNR
Weight: Loco 47t 6cwt
Tender 43t 2cwt
Driving Wheel: 5' 2"
Boiler Pressure: 175psi
s 170psi superheated
Cylinders: Inside 18" x 26"
Tractive Effort: 20210lbf
s 19630lbf
Valve Gear: Stephenson (slide valves)

In 1909-1910 Ivatt introduced twenty freight 0-6-0s on the GNR. They were GNR class 'J22' (LNER class 'J5') and they were identical with the 'J1' class of 1908 except that they were fitted with 5' 2" wheels, compared to the 5' 8" wheels of the 'J1's.

In later years there was a lot of variation in the domes and boilers fitted to these engines.

s Two engines were later fitted with superheated boilers.

Year End Totals: 'J5' class

'47	'48	'49	'50	'51	'52	'53	'54	'55	'56	'57	'58	'59	'60	'61	'62	'63	'64	'65	'66	'67
20	20	20	20	20	20	10	3													

Number	Built	Renumbered	BR Dates	Scrap	Notes
65480	06/10 Don	05/49 5480	-10/54	12/54	s
65481	06/10 Don	12/48 5481	-10/53	53	
65482	06/10 Don	11/48 5482	-11/53	53	
65483	06/10 Don	10/49 5483	-12/55	02/56	
65484	06/10 Don	04/49 5484	-03/53	04/53	
65485	07/10 Don	01/49 5485	-12/54	55	
65486	06/10 Don	10/48 5486	-12/54	55	
65487	07/10 Don	08/48 5487	-06/53	53	
65488	07/10 Don	11/48 5488	-10/53	12/53	
65489	07/10 Don	04/48 5489	-12/53	12/53	s
65490	10/09 Don	07/49 5490	-10/54	12/54	
65491	11/09 Don	01/49 5491	-10/53	53	
65492	11/09 Don	01/49 5492	-09/53	53	
65493	11/09 Don	08/49 5493	-08/54	09/54	
65494	12/09 Don	02/49 5494	-01/55	55	
65495	12/09 Don	12/49 5495	-08/54	09/54	
65496	12/09 Don	04/49 5496	-02/54	54	
65497	12/09 Don	09/49 5497	-12/53	01/54	
65498	12/09 Don	12/48 5498	-12/55	02/56	
65499	01/10 Don	02/49 5499	-04/53	53	

J17 65500-65589
0-6-0 GER Holden

Power Classification: 4F
Introduced: 1900-1910
Designer: J Holden
Company: GER
Weight: Loco 45t 8cwt
l Tender 38t 5cwt
s Tender 30t 12cwt
Driving Wheel: 4' 11"
Boiler Pressure: 180psi superheated
Cylinders: Inside 19" x 26"
Tractive Effort: 24340lbf
Valve Gear: Stephenson (slide valves)

Between 1900 and 1911 ninety 0-6-0 freight engines of GER class 'G58' were built for freight working. The first batch of fifty-nine engines (introduced in 1900), had round topped boilers which were interchangeable with the early 'Claud Hamiltons' ('D14' class - see under 'D15' class). They were the GER 'F48' class and later the LNER 'J16' class.

The later engines (introduced in 1901 as the GER 'G58' class) were fitted with larger Belpaire boilers as fitted to the later 'Claud Hamiltons' ('D15' class). All the earlier 'J16' engines were later fitted with this type of boiler (becoming 'J17') and all the engines were superheated. Some were later fitted with vacuum brakes for passenger train working.

Eighty-nine of the class came into BR stock, the missing engine (8200 which would have become 65550) was destroyed by a German rocket in 1944.

r These engines were rebuilt from 'J16' engines which were introduced in 1900 with round topped boilers.

c These engines were fitted with tender cabs by BR.

l These engines had larger tenders.

s These engines were fitted with small tenders. Some were later fitted with larger tenders by BR.

Year End Totals: 'J17' class

'47	'48	'49	'50	'51	'52	'53	'54	'55	'56	'57	'58	'59	'60	'61	'62	'63	'64	'65	'66	'67
89	89	89	89	89	89	89	86	78	78	75	58	41	20	12						

Number	Built	Renumbered	BR Dates	Scrap	Notes
65500	09/00 Str	03/51 5500	-03/58	04/58	rs⇨l
65501	09/00 Str	05/49 5501	-01/58	04/58	rs⇨l
65502	09/00 Str	10/50 5502	-09/59	11/59	rs
65503	09/00 Str	03/49 5503	-08/60	09/60	rs⇨l
65504	10/00 Str	06/49 5504	-10/58	12/58	rs⇨l
65505	10/00 Str	01/49 5505	-11/59	11/59	rs⇨l
65506	10/00 Str	07/48 5506	-08/60	09/60	rs⇨l
65507	10/00 Str	07/49 5507	-09/61	12/61	rs
65508	11/00 Str	04/51 5508	-06/58	07/58	rs
65509	11/00 Str	12/49 5509	-01/58	04/58	rl
65510	11/00 Str	12/48 5510	-03/55	*55*	rs
65511	11/00 Str	03/51 5511	-11/60	12/60	rs⇨l
65512	11/00 Str	01/51 5512	-12/59	12/59	rs
65513	11/00 Str	01/51 5513	-03/61	04/61	rs⇨l
65514	12/00 Str	12/49 5514	-01/60	02/60	rs⇨l
65515	12/00 Str	01/49 5515	-09/58	10/58	rs
65516	01/01 Str	11/50 5516	-03/55	*55*	rs⇨l
65517	01/01 Str	06/49 5517	-05/55	*55*	rs⇨l
65518	01/01 Str	08/49 5518	-09/58	10/58	rs⇨lc
65519	02/01 Str	05/48 5519	-03/60	04/60	rs⇨l
65520	09/01 Str	09/48 5520	-02/61	04/61	rl⇨c
65521	09/01 Str	12/48 5521	-02/62	04/62	rl
65522	09/01 Str	03/49 5522	-09/58	10/58	rl
65523	10/01 Str	10/48 5523	-05/57	06/57	rl
65524	10/01 Str	09/49 5524	-03/55	*55*	rl
65525	10/01 Str	02/50 5525	-04/59	05/59	rl
65526	10/01 Str	01/50 5526	-08/59	11/59	rl
65527	10/01 Str	12/49 5527	-04/59	05/59	rl
65528	10/01 Str	12/50 5528	-11/61	11/61	rs
65529	10/01 Str	05/48 5529	-05/58	07/58	rl
65530	11/01 Str	11/50 5530	-01/60	01/60	rl
65531	11/01 Str	08/48 5531	-04/59	05/59	rl
65532	11/01 Str	09/48 5532	-02/62	03/62	rs⇨l
65533	11/01 Str	07/48 5533	-01/60	01/60	rl
65534	11/01 Str	09/49 5534	-05/58	05/58	rl⇨c
65535	11/01 Str	09/48 5535	-05/58	06/58	rl
65536	12/01 Str	05/48 5536	-03/60	04/60	rl
65537	12/01 Str	04/48 5537	-01/57	02/57	rl
65538	12/01 Str	05/50 5538	-04/59	05/59	rl
65539	12/01 Str	01/49 5539	-08/60	09/60	l
65540	09/02 Str	09/48 5540	-04/59	05/59	rl
65541	09/02 Str	08/51 5541	-09/62	02/64	rl
65542	09/02 Str	02/49 5542	-05/59	05/59	rl
65543	09/02 Str	10/48 5543	-05/55	08/55	rs⇨l
65544	09/02 Str	05/49 5544	-11/59	01/60	rl
65545	10/02 Str	06/48 5545	-10/59	11/59	rl
65546	10/02 Str	02/50 5546	-01/60	02/60	rl
65547	10/02 Str	08/49 5547	-09/54	10/54	rl
65548	10/02 Str	02/51 5548	-03/60	04/60	rl
65549	11/02 Str	07/51 5549	-12/60	01/61	rl
65551	12/02 Str	09/49 5551	-02/60	03/60	rl
65552	12/02 Str	05/48 5552	-01/55	*55*	rl
65553	12/02 Str	09/48 5553	-04/59	05/59	rl
65554	12/02 Str	03/52 5554	-09/61	10/61	rl
65555	01/03 Str	09/50 5555	-03/60	04/60	rl
65556	01/03 Str	11/48 5556	-03/61	05/61	rl
65557	02/03 Str	02/49 5557	-04/59	05/59	rl
65558	02/03 Str	06/48 5558	-01/60	02/60	rl
65559	02/03 Str	10/48 5559	-11/59	01/60	rl
65560	04/05 Str	06/48 5560	-06/62	09/62	l
65561	04/05 Str	12/50 5561	-12/59	01/60	l
65562	04/05 Str	06/49 5562	-08/58	10/58	l
65563	05/05 Str	09/49 5563	-01/60	02/60	l
65564	05/05 Str	05/48 5564	-08/60	09/60	l
65565	05/05 Str	52 5565	-04/60	04/60	l
65566	05/05 Str	12/48 5566	-07/60	08/60	l
65567 §	05/05 Str	09/50 5567	-08/62		l
65568	05/05 Str	06/49 5568	-09/58	01/59	l⇨c
65569	06/05 Str	10/48 5569	-02/55	*55*	l
65570	12/05 Str	06/48 5570	-04/60	06/60	l
65571	12/05 Str	11/48 5571	-02/58	03/58	s
65572	12/05 Str	03/49 5572	-12/57	12/57	l
65573	12/05 Str	01/49 5573	-10/58	12/58	l
65574	12/05 Str	08/51 5574	-04/55	*55*	l
65575	02/06 Str	07/48 5575	-02/58	03/58	l⇨c
65576	02/06 Str	08/48 5576	-09/62	02/63	l
65577	02/06 Str	06/51 5577	-02/62	05/62	l
65578	03/06 Str	03/51 5578	-03/62	05/62	l
65579	03/06 Str	04/49 5579	-11/54	*54*	l
65580	10/10 Str	10/50 5580	-11/59	01/60	l
65581	11/10 Str	02/49 5581	-04/62	09/62	l
65582	11/10 Str	09/48 5582	-09/62	09/63	l
65583	11/10 Str	09/48 5583	-02/62	04/62	l
65584	11/10 Str	05/48 5584	-02/60	03/60	l
65585	11/10 Str	07/48 5585	-11/54	*54*	l
65586	12/10 Str	05/50 5586	-04/62	09/62	l
65587	12/10 Str	10/48 5587	-12/58	12/58	l
65588	12/10 Str	02/50 5588	-05/61	06/61	l
65589	12/10 Str	05/48 5589	-01/61	01/61	l

J24 65600-65644
0-6-0 NER Worsdell

Power Classification:	3F
Introduced:	1894-1898
Designer:	W Worsdell
Company:	NER
Weight:	Loco 38t 10cwt sr Loco 39t 11cwt Tender 36t 19cwt
Driving Wheel:	4' 7¼"
Boiler Pressure:	160psi s 160psi superheated
Cylinders:	Inside 18" x 24" sr Inside 18½" x 24"
Tractive Effort:	19140lbf sr 20220lbf
Valve Gear:	Stephenson (slide valves) srp Stephenson (piston valves)

In 1890 Wilson Worsdell succeeded his older brother T W Worsdell as CME of the NER. He introduced his 'P' class (LNER 'J24' class) of 0-6-0 in 1894 for mineral working. They were originally all fitted with saturated boilers, and as they were designed purely for freight working they had no continuous brakes. The class was developed over the years up to 1906 into the 'J25', 'J26' and 'J27' classes.

Seventy engines were built between 1894 and 1898, thirty-four of which came into BR stock. The first engine was withdrawn in 1933. Some engines retained the NER type of safety valve columns in BR days although most engines had acquired pop safety valves.

65626 survived in industrial service until July 1956.

p This engine was rebuilt with piston valves, but not superheated.

s These engines were rebuilt with superheaters and piston valves.

r Some of the superheated engines had the superheaters removed. 65644 was superheated again by BR.

Year End Totals: 'J24' class

'47	'48	'49	'50	'51	'52	'53	'54	'55	'56	'57	'58	'59	'60	'61	'62	'63	'64	'65	'66	'67
34	28	21	9																	

Number	Built	Renumbered	BR Dates	Scrap	Notes
65600	12/94 Ghd	5600	-10/50	*50*	
65601	12/94 Ghd	02/49 5601	-12/51	*52*	
65602	12/94 Ghd	5602	-05/49	*05/49*	
65603	12/94 Ghd	5603	-01/50	*50*	s
65604	02/95 Ghd	5604	-12/50	*51*	
65606	04/95 Ghd	5606	-02/49	*49*	s
65607	04/95 Ghd	5607	-12/48	*49*	
65608	08/95 Ghd	5608	-08/49	*49*	
65609	08/95 Ghd	5609	-10/49	*49*	
65611	09/95 Ghd	5611	-10/50	*50*	s
65612	10/95 Ghd	5612	-02/48	*48*	
65614	12/95 Ghd	5614	-05/51	*51*	
65615	12/95 Ghd	01/49 5615	-11/51	*51*	
65617	02/96 Ghd	02/49 5617	-12/51	*01/52*	s
65619	03/96 Ghd	10/48 5619	-11/51	*51*	
65621	12/96 Ghd	5621	-09/50	*50*	s
65622	12/96 Ghd	5622	-02/51	*03/51*	
65623	12/96 Ghd	5623	-06/51	*06/51*	
65624	03/97 Ghd	5624	-09/50	*50*	s
65625	03/97 Ghd	5625	-05/48	*05/48*	
65626	12/97 Ghd	5626	-11/48	07/56	
65627	12/97 Ghd	5627	-12/50	*51*	r
65628	12/97 Ghd	03/49 5628	-11/50	*50*	p
65629	12/97 Ghd	04/48 5629	-05/49	*05/49*	r
65631	12/97 Ghd	5631	-11/50	*50*	s
65632	12/97 Dar	5632	-11/49	*49*	
65633	04/98 Dar	5633	-04/49	*49*	r
65634	05/98 Dar	10/48 5634	-04/50	*50*	
65636	05/98 Dar	5636	-12/50	*51*	s
65639	06/98 Dar	5639	-02/48	*02/48*	
65640	06/98 Dar	04/48 5640	-04/51	*51*	
65641	06/98 Dar	5641	-09/48	10/48	
65642	06/98 Dar	04/48 5642	-11/50	*50*	
65644	10/98 Dar	5644	-09/51	*51*	r⇨s

J25 65645-65728
0-6-0 NER Worsdell

Power Classification:	3F
Introduced:	1898-1902
Designer:	W Worsdell
Company:	NER
Weight:	Loco 39t 11cwt s Loco 41t 14cwt r Loco 40t 17cwt Tender 36t 19cwt
Driving Wheel:	4' 7¼"
Boiler Pressure:	160psi s 160psi superheated
Cylinders:	Inside 18½" x 26"
Tractive Effort:	21905lbf
Valve Gear:	Stephenson (slide valves) srp Stephenson (piston valves)

In 1898 Wilson Worsdell built a larger and more powerful version of his 'P' class (LNER 'J24' class) for mineral working. Known as the 'P1' class (LNER 'J25' class) they had boilers which were identical with the 'J21' class, but they were fitted with smaller wheels. They were originally all fitted with saturated boilers, and as they were designed purely for freight working they had no continuous brakes. The class was developed over the years up to 1906 into the 'J26' and 'J27' classes.

120 engines were built between 1898 and 1902 (eighty at Gateshead and forty at Darlington). Forty of these engines were loaned to the GWR in the Second World War. The first engine was withdrawn in 1933 and seventy-six engines came into BR stock. Some engines retained the NER type of safety valve columns in BR days although most engines had acquired pop safety valves.

In 1902-1903 Worsdell also built a tank version of this class, the 0-6-2T 'N10' class.

p This engine was rebuilt with piston valves, but not superheated.

s These engines were rebuilt with superheaters and piston valves.

r Some of the superheated engines had the superheaters removed. 65692 was superheated again by BR.

Year End Totals: 'J25' class

'47	'48	'49	'50	'51	'52	'53	'54	'55	'56	'57	'58	'59	'60	'61	'62	'63	'64	'65	'66	'67
76	74	66	59	54	53	52	39	38	36	34	23	15	11	8						

Number	Built	Renumbered	BR Dates	Scrap	Notes
65645	05/98 Ghd	12/50 5645	-04/62	12/62	s
65646	05/98 Ghd	10/48 5646	-04/50	*50*	s
65647	06/98 Ghd	08/48 5647	-04/56	05/56	
65648	06/98 Ghd	11/50 5648	-09/58	11/58	
65649	06/98 Ghd	5649	-03/49	*03/49*	
65650	06/98 Ghd	04/48 5650	-09/57	09/57	p
65651	06/98 Ghd	5651	-09/50	*50*	
65653	09/98 Ghd	05/49 5653	-05/51	*06/51*	
65654	10/98 Ghd	11/48 5654	-05/58	05/58	r
65655	11/98 Ghd	05/48 5655	-12/58	05/59	
65656	11/98 Ghd	03/49 5656	-08/59	09/59	
65657	11/98 Ghd	01/50 5657	-11/58	07/59	
65658	11/98 Ghd	5658	-08/50	06/55	
65659	12/98 Ghd	12/48 5659	-02/51	*03/51*	s
65660	12/98 Ghd	07/50 5660	-01/53	*53*	
65661	12/98 Ghd	04/51 5661	-10/54	*10/54*	
65662	12/98 Ghd	09/49 5662	-06/60	07/60	s
65663	12/98 Ghd	06/51 5663	-04/62	07/62	
65664	12/98 Ghd	01/50 5664	-09/52	*52*	
65665	12/98 Ghd	5665	-10/49	*49*	s
65666	12/98 Ghd	09/48 5666	-06/60	08/60	
65667	03/99 Ghd	07/51 5667	-09/54	*10/54*	
65668	03/99 Ghd	5668	-03/49	*03/49*	
65669	03/99 Ghd	09/48 5669	-04/50	*50*	s
65670	06/99 Ghd	07/48 5670	-06/62	08/62	
65671	06/99 Dar	01/49 5671	-09/54	*54*	
65672	06/99 Dar	05/48 5672	-05/51	*51*	
65673	06/99 Dar	06/48 5673	-06/58	07/58	r
65674	09/99 Dar	5674	-07/48	*48*	
65675	09/99 Dar	06/49 5675	-03/59	03/59	
65676	09/99 Dar	10/48 5676	-01/54	*54*	
65677	10/99 Dar	11/50 5677	-10/58	11/58	r
65679	11/99 Dar	02/49 5679	-05/51	*06/51*	
65680	11/99 Dar	12/49 5680	-09/57	09/57	
65681	11/99 Dar	01/49 5681	-04/50	*50*	r
65683	11/99 Dar	09/49 5683	-06/58	09/58	r
65684	12/99 Dar	04/48 5684	-04/49	*49*	r
65685	12/99 Dar	01/49 5685	-09/59	11/59	
65686	12/99 Dar	08/51 5686	-11/54	*11/54*	
65687	12/99 Dar	08/49 5687	-08/59	08/59	

Number	Built	Renumbered	BR Dates	Scrap	Notes
65688	12/99 Dar	09/48 5688	-09/54	*54*	
65689	12/99 Dar	01/49 5689	-05/54	*54*	
65690	01/00 Ghd	10/50 5690	-12/54	*55*	
65691	03/00 Ghd	06/50 5691	-10/61	11/61	
65692	03/00 Ghd	08/48 5692	-03/54	*54*	r➪s
65693	04/00 Ghd	01/49 5693	-04/62	06/63	
65694	04/00 Ghd	05/51 5694	-11/54	*54*	
65695	04/00 Ghd	09/48 5695	-06/62	06/63	
65696	05/00 Ghd	10/50 5696	-12/58	05/59	
65697	05/00 Ghd	12/48 5697	-11/58	05/59	
65698	05/00 Ghd	12/50 5698	-09/59	10/59	
65699	06/00 Ghd	10/50 5699	-03/58	03/58	
65700	06/00 Ghd	04/51 5700	-08/59	09/59	
65702	06/00 Ghd	01/51 5702	-10/59	11/59	r
65703	06/00 Ghd	5703	-04/49	*05/49*	
65704	03/00 Dar	5704	-06/48	*48*	
65705	04/00 Dar	12/50 5705	-10/54	*01/55*	
65706	05/00 Dar	11/48 5706	-12/59	12/59	s
65707	05/00 Dar	5707	-01/50	*50*	
65708	05/00 Dar	06/48 5708	-05/56	*06/56*	
65710	06/00 Dar	11/48 5710	-11/54	*11/54*	
65712	06/00 Dar	04/48 5712	-08/60	09/60	
65713	06/00 Dar	08/49 5713	-08/60	08/60	
65714	06/00 Dar	06/48 5714	-01/61	01/61	
65715	05/02 Ghd	5715	-03/49	*03/49*	
65716	06/02 Ghd	12/50 5716	-04/54	*54*	
65717	06/02 Ghd	10/48 5717	-10/58	10/58	s
65718	06/02 Ghd	03/48 5718	-05/51	*51*	
65720	08/02 Ghd	10/50 5720	-04/62	05/62	
65721	09/02 Ghd	5721	-12/49	*50*	
65723	10/02 Ghd	04/49 5723	-03/55	05/55	
65724	10/02 Ghd	05/48 5724	-11/49	*49*	
65725	11/02 Ghd	5725	-10/50	*50*	
65726	11/02 Ghd	08/50 5726	-06/62	09/62	
65727	11/02 Ghd	01/52 5727	-01/61	02/61	
65728	12/02 Dar	06/48 5728	-04/62	08/62	

J26 65730-65779
0-6-0 NER Worsdell

Power Classification:	4F reclassified 5F in 1953
Introduced:	1904-1905
Designer:	W Worsdell
Company:	NER
Weight:	Loco 46t 16cwt Tender 36t 19cwt
Driving Wheel:	4' 7¼"
Boiler Pressure:	180psi
Cylinders:	Inside 18½" x 26"
Tractive Effort:	24640lbf
Valve Gear:	Stephenson (slide valves)

After Worsdell had built the 'J25' class (an enlarged version of the 'J24' class) his next class of 0-6-0s to be built for heavy mineral working was the 'J26' class.

Fifty of these engines were built in 1904-1905. Known as the NER 'P2' class (LNER 'J26'), thirty were built at Darlington and twenty at Gateshead. They had 5' 6" boilers as against the 4' 3" boilers of the earlier classes. They were fitted with saturated boilers of 200psi pressure, but this was later reduced to 180psi. All the engines came into BR stock and they remained at the forefront of North Eastern freight power for nearly sixty years.

Year End Totals: 'J26' class

'47	'48	'49	'50	'51	'52	'53	'54	'55	'56	'57	'58	'59	'60	'61	'62	'63	'64	'65	'66	'67
50	50	50	50	50	50	50	50	50	50	50	44	25	24	14						

Number	*Built*	*Renumbered*	*BR Dates*	*Scrap*	*Notes*
65730	06/04 Dar	04/48 5730	-01/59	02/59	
65731	06/04 Dar	12/50 5731	-06/62	08/62	
65732	06/04 Dar	11/50 5732	-11/59	11/59	
65733	06/04 Dar	12/48 5733	-01/59	02/59	
65734	06/04 Dar	09/48 5734	-10/58	11/58	
65735	06/04 Dar	09/50 5735	-06/62	08/62	
65736	06/04 Dar	03/51 5736	-02/61	03/61	
65737	06/04 Dar	08/48 5737	-10/59	01/60	
65738	06/04 Dar	11/49 5738	-02/59	02/59	
65739	06/04 Dar	04/49 5739	-02/59	03/59	
65740	09/04 Dar	04/48 5740	-01/59	02/59	
65741	10/04 Dar	07/48 5741	-10/61	12/62	
65742	10/04 Dar	03/50 5742	-02/59	03/59	
65743	10/04 Dar	12/50 5743	-06/62	10/62	
65744	10/04 Dar	09/49 5744	-02/59	03/59	
65745	11/04 Dar	09/48 5745	-12/61	01/62	
65746	11/04 Dar	09/48 5746	-06/58	07/58	
65747	11/04 Dar	08/50 5747	-04/62	05/62	
65748	12/04 Dar	01/49 5748	-01/59	02/59	
65749	12/04 Dar	01/49 5749	-03/59	04/59	
65750	04/05 Ghd	05/49 5750	-02/59	03/59	
65751	04/05 Ghd	10/48 5751	-01/62	10/62	
65752	05/05 Ghd	09/48 5752	-06/58	08/58	
65753	05/05 Dar	08/50 5753	-05/61	06/61	
65754	05/05 Dar	05/48 5754	-06/58	07/58	
65755	05/05 Dar	01/51 5755	-06/62	06/62	
65756	05/05 Ghd	04/48 5756	-06/62	06/62	
65757	05/05 Ghd	12/48 5757	-04/62	08/62	
65758	06/05 Ghd	04/48 5758	-01/59	03/59	
65759	06/05 Ghd	01/49 5759	-01/59	02/59	
65760	06/05 Ghd	01/51 5760	-07/61	08/61	
65761	06/05 Ghd	10/48 5761	-06/62	08/62	
65762	06/05 Ghd	06/48 5762	-01/61	01/61	
65763	06/05 Dar	08/48 5763	-01/62	04/62	
65764	06/05 Dar	12/48 5764	-03/59	03/59	
65765	06/05 Dar	04/48 5765	-06/58	08/58	
65766	06/05 Dar	06/48 5766	-02/59	04/59	
65767	06/05 Dar	09/48 5767	-06/58	08/58	
65768	06/05 Dar	06/48 5768	-06/62	10/62	
65769	06/05 Dar	05/51 5769	-10/61	06/62	
65770	09/05 Ghd	10/50 5770	-02/59	03/59	
65771	09/05 Ghd	06/49 5771	-01/59	03/59	
65772	10/05 Ghd	02/51 5772	-06/62	08/62	
65773	10/05 Ghd	01/51 5773	-06/62	08/62	
65774	10/05 Ghd	07/48 5774	-07/61	08/61	
65775	11/05 Ghd	06/48 5775	-02/59	04/59	
65776	11/05 Ghd	10/49 5776	-06/62	08/62	
65777	11/05 Ghd	10/50 5777	-09/60	11/60	
65778	12/05 Ghd	12/50 5778	-07/61	08/61	
65779	12/05 Ghd	09/48 5779	-03/61	07/61	

J27 65780-65894
0-6-0 NER Worsdell and Raven

Power Classification:	4F reclassified 5F in 1953
Introduced:	1906-1923
Designer:	W Worsdell and Raven
Company:	NER
Weight:	Loco 47t 0cwt s Loco 49t 10cwt Tender 36t 19cwt
Driving Wheel:	4' 7¼"
Boiler Pressure:	180psi s 180psi superheated
Cylinders:	Inside 18½" x 26"
Tractive Effort:	24640lbf
Valve Gear:	Stephenson (slide valves) rs Stephenson (piston valves)

The last development of Worsdell's 'J24', 'J25' and 'J26' classes was the 'J27' class which first appeared in 1906. They were originally the NER 'P3' class and they had deeper fireboxes and they were built with a boiler pressure of 180psi.

115 engines were built between 1906 and 1923 (the last ten appearing after grouping). They all came into BR stock and they were a familiar sight in the North-East until steam was eliminated from that area in September 1967.

s The last batch of thirty-five engines was built under the direction of Vincent Raven in 1921-1923. These engines were superheated with longer smokeboxes, and they were fitted with piston valves.

r From 1943 onwards the superheaters were removed from many of the Raven engines (some by BR), but they still retained the piston valves.

Year End Totals: 'J27' class

'47	'48	'49	'50	'51	'52	'53	'54	'55	'56	'57	'58	'59	'60	'61	'62	'63	'64	'65	'66	'67
115	115	115	115	115	115	115	115	115	115	115	115	94	93	91	79	61	55	44	26	

Number	*Built*	*Renumbered*	*BR Dates*	*Scrap*	*Notes*
65780	04/06 Dar	08/48 5780	-04/59	05/59	
65781	04/06 Dar	10/50 5781	-10/59	11/59	
65782	04/06 Dar	06/48 5782	-11/61	12/61	
65783	05/06 Dar	03/49 5783	-06/59	06/59	
65784	05/06 Dar	06/49 5784	-08/59	10/59	
65785	06/06 Dar	09/48 5785	-06/59	07/59	
65786	06/06 Dar	05/48 5786	-04/62	05/62	
65787	06/06 Dar	06/49 5787	-05/62	08/62	
65788	06/06 Dar	05/48 5788	-06/66	09/66	
65789	06/06 Dar	08/48 5789	-07/67	11/67	
65790	09/06 Dar	06/49 5790	-08/66	12/66	
65791	09/06 Dar	05/48 5791	-10/64	12/64	
65792	09/06 Dar	06/48 5792	-05/65	11/65	
65793	10/06 Dar	06/49 5793	-04/59	05/59	
65794	10/06 Dar	07/48 5794	-06/65	11/65	
65795	10/06 Dar	11/48 5795	-07/67	11/67	
65796	11/06 Dar	04/51 5796	-05/66	09/66	
65797	11/06 Dar	01/49 5797	-11/62	01/63	
65798	11/06 Dar	04/48 5798	-06/59	07/59	
65799	12/06 Dar	08/48 5799	-08/62	10/62	
65800	06/08 Dar	03/49 5800	-09/62	10/62	
65801	06/08 Dar	11/48 5801	-07/66	12/66	
65802	06/08 Dar	04/51 5802	-08/66	12/66	
65803	06/08 Dar	10/48 5803	-04/59	04/59	
65804	08/08 Dar	04/48 5804	-07/67	11/67	
65805	09/08 Dar	12/50 5805	-01/66	05/66	
65806	08/08 Dar	01/49 5806	-07/59	08/59	
65807	10/08 Dar	01/49 5807	-05/62	06/62	
65808	11/08 Dar	12/48 5808	-03/65	07/65	
65809	11/08 Dar	08/48 5809	-09/66	12/66	
65810	05/08 NB	03/49 5810	-12/63	01/64	
65811	05/08 NB	05/48 5811	-09/67	11/67	
65812	05/08 NB	06/49 5812	-06/67	08/67	
65813	05/08 NB	12/48 5813	-05/67	08/67	
65814	05/08 NB	11/48 5814	-06/66	09/66	
65815	05/08 NB	04/48 5815	-11/66	03/67	
65816	05/08 NB	06/48 5816	-10/59	12/59	
65817	05/08 NB	08/49 5817	-05/67	08/67	
65818	05/08 NB	04/48 5818	-07/62	08/62	
65819	05/08 NB	11/50 5819	-10/66	02/67	
65820	06/08 NB	05/48 5820	-05/63	07/63	
65821	06/08 NB	04/49 5821	-02/66	05/66	
65822	06/08 NB	06/49 5822	-03/65	06/65	
65823	06/08 NB	11/48 5823	-03/67	07/67	
65824	06/08 NB	07/49 5824	-12/59	12/59	
65825	06/08 NB	04/48 5825	-06/66	09/66	
65826	06/08 NB	07/49 5826	-08/59	09/59	
65827	06/08 NB	01/49 5827	-07/59	08/59	
65828	06/08 NB	11/48 5828	-05/64	07/64	
65829	06/08 NB	07/50 5829	-03/59	03/59	
65830	04/09 RS	12/48 5830	-03/63	03/63	
65831	04/09 RS	05/48 5831	-02/66	05/66	
65832	05/09 RS	11/48 5832	-03/66	06/66	
65833	05/09 RS	05/48 5833	-05/67	08/67	
65834	06/09 RS	07/49 5834	-05/67	08/67	
65835	07/09 RS	07/48 5835	-01/67	03/67	
65836	07/09 RS	02/49 5836	-04/59	04/59	
65837	09/09 RS	10/49 5837	-10/62	11/62	
65838	09/09 RS	10/48 5838	-01/67	05/67	
65839	09/09 RS	11/48 5839	-01/62	02/62	
65840	07/08 BP	07/48 5840	-05/59	06/59	
65841	07/08 BP	06/48 5841	-08/65	01/66	
65842	07/08 BP	09/48 5842	-01/67	07/67	
65843	08/08 BP	09/49 5843	-04/59	04/59	
65844	08/08 BP	04/49 5844	-12/65	05/66	
65845	08/08 BP	04/48 5845	-02/65	03/65	
65846	08/08 BP	12/48 5846	-10/65	04/66	
65847	08/08 BP	04/48 5847	-02/60	02/60	
65848	08/08 BP	05/49 5848	-09/59	09/59	
65849	08/08 BP	04/48 5849	-05/63	06/63	
65850	08/08 BP	01/51 5850	-04/63	07/63	
65851	08/08 BP	04/48 5851	-12/65	05/66	
65852	08/08 BP	10/48 5852	-12/63	01/64	
65853	08/08 BP	03/49 5853	-02/67	05/67	
65854	08/08 BP	04/48 5854	-12/63	02/64	
65855	08/08 BP	01/49 5855	-09/67	11/67	
65856	08/08 BP	11/48 5856	-08/59	09/59	
65857	08/08 BP	06/49 5857	-04/63	07/63	
65858	08/08 BP	05/49 5858	-10/65	03/66	
65859	08/08 BP	06/49 5859	-09/66	12/66	
65860	11/21 Dar	02/49 5860	-07/67	10/67	r
65861	12/21 Dar	09/49 5861	-05/67	08/67	r
65862	12/21 Dar	08/48 5862	-10/65	01/66	r
65863	12/21 Dar	11/49 5863	-08/62	10/62	s 03/59➪r
65864	12/21 Dar	02/49 5864	-12/63	02/64	r
65865	12/21 Dar	09/48 5865	-02/67	07/67	r
65866	03/22 Dar	05/48 5866	-06/59	07/59	s
65867	03/22 Dar	09/48 5867	-06/62	10/62	r
65868	04/22 Dar	08/48 5868	-05/61	07/61	r
65869	04/22 Dar	12/49 5869	-02/67	05/67	s 08/56➪r
65870	05/22 Dar	04/50 5870	-10/64	01/65	r
65871	05/22 Dar	12/48 5871	-01/63	02/63	s
65872	05/22 Dar	10/48 5872	-01/67	07/67	s 01/58➪r
65873	06/22 Dar	11/48 5873	-10/66	05/67	r
65874	06/22 Dar	12/49 5874	-08/66	12/66	s 02/60➪r
65875	06/22 Dar	04/48 5875	-03/63	03/63	r
65876	06/22 Dar	03/49 5876	-03/64	04/64	r
65877	06/22 Dar	09/49 5877	-11/62	01/63	r
65878	06/22 Dar	09/49 5878	-10/64	01/65	s 07/55➪r
65879	06/22 Dar	02/49 5879	-09/67	11/67	r
65880	08/22 Dar	10/48 5880	-06/67	08/67	s
65881	08/22 Dar	03/50 5881	-02/63	02/63	s 01/61➪r
65882	08/22 Dar	06/48 5882	-09/67	11/67	r
65883	09/22 Dar	10/48 5883	-04/63	05/63	s
65884	10/22 Dar	12/49 5884	-12/63	01/64	r
65885	06/23 Dar	11/48 5885	-06/67	08/67	r
65886	06/23 Dar	02/49 5886	-08/59	10/59	s➪r
65887	06/23 Dar	02/49 5887	-05/63	07/63	s
65888	06/23 Dar	06/48 5888	-12/63	01/64	r
65889	06/23 Dar	10/48 5889	-02/64	03/64	s➪r
65890	07/23 Dar	10/51 5890	-05/63	07/63	s
65891	07/23 Dar	10/48 5891	-12/63	02/64	r
65892	08/23 Dar	09/48 5892	-08/67	12/67	s➪r
65893	09/23 Dar	12/48 5893	-07/66	12/66	s➪r
65894 §	09/23 Dar	09/51 5894	-09/67		s➪r

J38 65900-65934
0-6-0 LNER Gresley

Power Classification:	6F
Introduced:	1926
Designer:	Gresley
Company:	LNER
Weight:	Loco 58t 19cwt Tender 44t 4cwt
Driving Wheel:	4' 8"
Boiler Pressure:	180psi superheated
Cylinders:	Inside 20" x 26"
Tractive Effort:	28415lbf
Valve Gear:	Stephenson (piston valves)

Gresley designed two classes of powerful 0-6-0s to replace the many ageing 0-6-0s inherited by the LNER in 1923. The two classes were identical except for the wheel size (5' 2" in 'J39', and 4' 8" in 'J38'), and the 'J38's had six inch longer boilers (with correspondingly six inch shorter smokeboxes).

The 'J38's appeared in service a few months before the 'J39's and thirty-five engines were built in 1926. They spent their entire working lives in Scotland, mainly on the heavy coal trains on the ex-NBR lines in the Fife coalfield.

Some engines were later rebuilt with 'J39' type boilers.

Year End Totals: 'J38' class

'47	'48	'49	'50	'51	'52	'53	'54	'55	'56	'57	'58	'59	'60	'61	'62	'63	'64	'65	'66	'67
35	35	35	35	35	35	35	35	35	35	35	35	35	35	35	33	31	25	21	3	

Number	*Built*	*Renumbered*	*BR Dates*	*Scrap*	*Notes*
65900	01/26 Dar	10/49 5900	-11/63	12/63	
65901	01/26 Dar	03/50 5901	-04/67	09/67	
65902	01/26 Dar	12/49 5902	-12/63	07/64	
65903	01/26 Dar	02/50 5903	-11/66	06/67	
65904	01/26 Dar	02/49 5904	-07/64	11/64	
65905	01/26 Dar	06/48 5905	-05/66	10/66	
65906	02/26 Dar	04/50 5906	-08/65	11/65	
65907	03/26 Dar	12/48 5907	-08/66	11/66	
65908	02/26 Dar	01/50 5908	-09/64	12/64	
65909	02/26 Dar	11/49 5909	-11/66	04/67	
65910	03/26 Dar	08/48 5910	-07/66	11/66	
65911	03/26 Dar	01/49 5911	-03/67	09/67	
65912	03/26 Dar	12/49 5912	-11/66	04/67	
65913	03/26 Dar	07/48 5913	-08/64	09/64	
65914	03/26 Dar	08/48 5914	-11/66	06/67	
65915	03/26 Dar	09/48 5915	-11/66	02/67	
65916	03/26 Dar	05/49 5916	-10/65	12/65	
65917	03/26 Dar	05/48 5917	-11/66	04/67	
65918	03/26 Dar	01/49 5918	-11/66	01/67	
65919	03/26 Dar	04/50 5919	-08/64	11/64	
65920	03/26 Dar	04/50 5920	-11/66	04/67	
65921	03/26 Dar	05/49 5921	-11/66	06/67	
65922	03/26 Dar	08/50 5922	-10/66	02/67	
65923	03/26 Dar	08/48 5923	-12/62	01/63	
65924	04/26 Dar	01/50 5924	-06/64	09/64	
65925	04/26 Dar	08/49 5925	-11/66	04/67	
65926	04/26 Dar	12/49 5926	-02/65	07/65	
65927	04/26 Dar	07/50 5927	-12/64	03/65	
65928	04/26 Dar	03/50 5928	-12/62	05/63	
65929	04/26 Dar	07/48 5929	-04/67	09/67	
65930	05/26 Dar	05/48 5930	-09/66	01/67	
65931	04/26 Dar	06/49 5931	-09/66	01/67	
65932	05/26 Dar	02/49 5932	-03/66	06/66	
65933	05/26 Dar	04/48 5933	-04/65	07/65	
65934	05/26 Dar	06/50 5934	-12/66	09/67	

F7 67093-67094
2-4-2T GER Holden 'Crystal Palace Tanks'

Power Classification:	1P
Introduced:	1909
Designer:	S D Holden
Company:	GER
Weight:	45t 14cwt
Driving Wheel:	4' 10"
Boiler Pressure:	160psi
Cylinders:	Inside 15" x 22"
Tractive Effort:	11605lbf
Valve Gear:	Stephenson (slide valves)

Refer to the Historical Survey of Great Eastern 2-4-2T Engines at the end of this section for more details of this class.

The 'F7's were smaller than all the other 2-4-2Ts on the GER. Twelve were built and they were originally the GER 'Y65' class. They were designed specifically for light branch work and fitted for push-pull operation. They were known as the 'Crystal Palace Tanks' because of their large glass window cabs.

The first engine was withdrawn in 1931. Two engines came into BR stock and they were both scrapped without receiving their new BR numbers.

Year End Totals: 'F7' class

'47	'48	'49	'50	'51	'52	'53	'54	'55	'56	'57	'58	'59	'60	'61	'62	'63	'64	'65	'66	'67
2																				

Number	*Built*	*Renumbered*	*BR Dates*	*Scrap*	*Notes*
67093	12/09 Str	7093	-11/48	11/48	
67094	01/10 Str	7094	-11/48	11/48	

F1 67097-67100
2-4-2T MS&LR (GCR) Parker

Power Classification:	1P
Introduced:	1889-1892
Designer:	Parker
Company:	MS&LR
Weight:	60t 12cwt
Driving Wheel:	5' 7"
Boiler Pressure:	160psi
Cylinders:	Inside 18" x 24"
Tractive Effort:	15785lbf
Valve Gear:	Joy (slide valves)

Parker built thirty-nine of these 2-4-2Ts for the MS&LR (later GCR) in 1889-1892. They were the GCR class '3'. They were originally fitted with round-topped boilers but they were later fitted with Belpaire boilers in common with the 'F2' class. Both classes were similar in appearance. The first engine was withdrawn in 1930. Three engines came into BR stock and these had all been withdrawn by 1949.

Year End Totals: 'F1' class

'47	'48	'49	'50	'51	'52	'53	'54	'55	'56	'57	'58	'59	'60	'61	'62	'63	'64	'65	'66	'67
3	2																			

Number	*Built*	*Renumbered*	*BR Dates*	*Scrap*	*Notes*
67097	09/89 Gor	7097	-03/48	48	
67099	02/91 Gor	7099	-01/49	49	
67100	03/91 N	7100	-01/49	49	

F2 67104-67113
2-4-2T GCR Pollitt

Power Classification:	1P
Introduced:	1898
Designer:	Pollitt
Company:	GCR
Weight:	62t 6cwt
Driving Wheel:	5' 7"
Boiler Pressure:	160psi
Cylinders:	Inside 18" x 26"
Tractive Effort:	17100lbf
Valve Gear:	Stephenson (slide valves)

Pollitt built this class of ten engines in 1898 (GCR class '9G'). They were developed from Parker's 'F1' class and they were fitted with Belpaire boilers. When the 'F1's were rebuilt with Belpaire boilers, both classes were similar in appearance.

All of the engines were fitted with push-pull gear between 1936 and 1943. The first engine was withdrawn in 1947.

Year End Totals: 'F2' class

'47	'48	'49	'50	'51	'52	'53	'54	'55	'56	'57	'58	'59	'60	'61	'62	'63	'64	'65	'66	'67
9	7	2																		

Number	*Built*	*Renumbered*	*BR Dates*	*Scrap*	*Notes*
67104	03/98 BP	7104	-05/49	49	
67105	03/98 BP	7105	-08/48	48	
67106	03/98 BP	08/48 7106	-12/48	49	
67107	03/98 BP	7107	-02/49	49	
67108	04/98 BP	7108	-07/50	08/50	
67109	04/98 BP	7109	-11/49	11/49	
67111	04/98 BP	7111	-12/50	12/50	
67112	05/98 BP	7112	-05/49	49	
67113	06/98 BP	7113	-04/49	49	

F3 67114-67150
2-4-2T GER Holden

Power Classification:	1P
Introduced:	1893-1902
Designer:	J Holden
Company:	GER
Weight:	58t 12cwt
Driving Wheel:	5' 8"
Boiler Pressure:	160psi
Cylinders:	Inside 17½" x 24"
Tractive Effort:	14710lbf
Valve Gear:	Stephenson (slide valves)

Refer to the Historical Survey of Great Eastern 2-4-2T Engines at the end of this section for more details of this class.

The 'F3's were James Holden's 5' 8" version of the 2-4-2T design. Fifty were built and they were the GER 'C32' class. They were a tank engine version of the 'E4' class and they were larger than the 'F4', 'F5' and 'F6' classes. There was a lot of variation in boiler mountings (chimneys, domes and safety valves) in the class. The first engine was withdrawn in 1936.

Year End Totals: 'F3' class

'47	'48	'49	'50	'51	'52	'53	'54	'55	'56	'57	'58	'59	'60	'61	'62	'63	'64	'65	'66	'67
15	8	5	1	1	1															

Number	*Built*	*Renumbered*	*BR Dates*	*Scrap*	*Notes*
67114	05/93 Str	7114	-03/48	48	
67115	05/93 Str	7115	-05/48	48	
67117	06/93 Str	7117	-05/48	48	
67119	06/93 Str	7119	-02/48	02/48	
67124	01/94 Str	7124	-03/50	50	
67126	01/94 Str	7126	-01/50	50	
67127	01/94 Str	01/49 7127	-03/53	53	
67128	02/94 Str	06/48 7128	-12/50	51	
67134	05/95 Str	7134	-05/48	48	
67139	05/95 Str	7139	-12/50	51	
67140	05/95 Str	7140	-03/49	49	
67141	05/02 Str	7141	-05/48	48	
67143	05/02 Str	7143	-07/48	08/48	
67149	06/02 Str	11/48 7149	-07/49	49	
67150	06/02 Str	7150	-10/49	49	

F4 67151-67187
2-4-2T GER Holden

Power Classification:	1P
Introduced:	1884-1909
Designer:	J Holden
Company:	GER
Weight:	53t 19cwt
Driving Wheel:	5' 4"
Boiler Pressure:	160psi
Cylinders:	Inside 17½" x 24"
Tractive Effort:	15620lbf
Valve Gear:	Stephenson (slide valves)

Refer to the Historical Survey of Great Eastern 2-4-2T Engines at the end of this section for more details of this class.

These engines were built by James Holden in 1903-1909 as a modified version of Worsdell's original engines of 1884-1887. A total of 160 engines of both types were built and they were known as the GER 'M15' class. There was a lot of variation in boiler mountings (chimneys, domes and safety valves) in the class. The first engine was withdrawn in 1913.

Some engines of the class were fitted with condensing apparatus and had their chimneys reduced in height. This was to enable them to work the LPTB Circle line if the electricity supply was disrupted due to enemy action during the Second World War.

c 67151, 67157 and 67164 were transferred to Kittybrewster and they worked on the St. Combs branch (St. Combs to Fraserburgh). For this service they were fitted with cow-catchers. One set of cow-catchers was later transferred to LMS '4MT' 46460 in 1952.

p 67151 was fitted with push-pull control apparatus.

Year End Totals: 'F4' class

'47	'48	'49	'50	'51	'52	'53	'54	'55	'56	'57	'58	'59	'60	'61	'62	'63	'64	'65	'66	'67
37	26	26	23	12	8	4	3	1												

Number	*Built*	*Renumbered*	*BR Dates*	*Scrap*	*Notes*
67151	07/06 Str	06/48 7151	-08/51	51	cp
67152	09/06 Str	11/48 7152	-02/52	52	
67153	03/07 Str	7153	-08/51	51	
67154	03/07 Str	12/48 7154	-09/51	51	
67155	04/07 Str	04/50 7155	-08/51	51	
67156	04/07 Str	7156	-11/50	50	
67157	05/07 Str	06/50 7157	-06/56	08/56	c
67158	05/07 Str	04/49 7158	-01/53	53	
67159	06/07 Str	7159	-04/48	04/48	

Number	Built	Renumbered	BR Dates	Scrap	Notes
67160	06/07 Str	7160	-04/50	50	
67161	11/07 Str	7161	-04/48	04/48	
67162	09/07 Str	05/50 7162	-08/55	55	
67163	10/07 Str	10/48 7163	-12/51	52	
67164	11/07 Str	08/48 7164	-08/51	51	c
67165	11/07 Str	08/48 7165	-01/51	51	
67166	12/07 Str	03/49 7166	-04/51	04/51	
67167	09/08 Str	02/49 7167	-09/52	52	
67168	09/08 Str	7168	-04/48	04/48	
67169	09/08 Str	7169	-04/48	04/48	
67170	09/08 Str	7170	-04/48	04/48	
67171	10/08 Str	04/49 7171	-08/51	51	
67172	10/08 Str	7172	-04/48	04/48	
67173	10/08 Str	7173	-04/48	04/48	
67174	11/08 Str	11/49 7174	-12/54	08/55	
67175	12/08 Str	05/49 7175	-08/51	51	
67176	01/09 Str	11/48 7176	-07/53	53	
67177	01/09 Str	08/48 7177	-03/51	51	
67178	02/09 Str	10/48 7178	-08/52	52	
67179	02/09 Str	7179	-04/48	04/48	
67180	03/09 Str	7180	-04/48	04/48	
67181	03/09 Str	7181	-04/48	04/48	
67182	03/09 Str	10/48 7182	-01/53	53	
67183	04/09 Str	7183	-04/50	50	
67184	04/09 Str	05/49 7184	-12/52	53	
67185	04/09 Str	7185	-04/48	48	
67186	04/09 Str	07/48 7186	-07/53	53	
67187	05/09 Str	01/50 7187	-08/55	55	

F5 67188-67219
2-4-2T GER Holden

Power Classification: 2P reclassified 1P in 1953
Introduced: 1884-1909
Rebuilt from 1911 by S D Holden
Designer: J Holden
Company: GER
Weight: 53t 19cwt
Driving Wheel: 5' 4"
Boiler Pressure: 180psi
Cylinders: Inside 17½" x 24"
Tractive Effort: 17570lbf
Valve Gear: Stephenson (slide valves)

Refer to the Historical Survey of Great Eastern 2-4-2T Engines at the end of this section for more details of this class.

These engines were rebuilt from 1911 onwards from 'F4' class engines built in 1903-1909 at Stratford. They were fitted with higher pressure boilers. There was a lot of variation in boiler mountings (chimneys, domes and safety valves) in the class.

Some engines of the class were fitted with condensing apparatus and had their chimneys reduced in height. This was to enable them to work the LPTB Circle line if the electricity supply was disrupted due to enemy action during the Second World War.

p Seven engines were fitted with steam brakes and vacuum operated push-pull gear in 1949.

w The last two engines to be converted were fitted with side-window cabs. As such they were similar in appearance to the 'F6' class and they were mistakenly classified 'F6' by the LNER in 1923. In 1948 this mistake was rectified and the engines were correctly re-classified 'F5' which gave them a wider route availability.

Year End Totals: 'F5' class

'47	'48	'49	'50	'51	'52	'53	'54	'55	'56	'57	'58	'59	'60	'61	'62	'63	'64	'65	'66	'67
30	32	32	32	32	32	32	32	18	12	5										

Number	Built	Renumbered	BR Dates	Scrap	Notes
67188	06/03 Str	05/49 7188	-12/55	01/56	
67189	06/03 Str	01/50 7189	-12/56	01/57	
67190	06/03 Str	12/48 7190	-12/55	56	
67191	06/03 Str	04/49 7191	-12/55	56	
67192	07/03 Str	07/48 7192	-04/58	58	
67193	07/03 Str	09/48 7193	-11/57	57	09/49⇨p
67194	10/04 Str	09/49 7194	-10/56	56	
67195	11/04 Str	11/50 7195	-05/58	58	
67196	11/04 Str	05/48 7196	-03/55	55	
67197	11/04 Str	05/51 7197	-03/55	03/55	
67198	11/04 Str	11/49 7198	-08/55	55	
67199	11/04 Str	11/48 7199	-02/57	57	11/49⇨p
67200	11/04 Str	03/49 7200	-12/57	58	09/49⇨p
67201	11/04 Str	09/49 7201	-12/56	01/57	
67202	07/05 Str	03/48 7202	-12/57	58	09/49⇨p
67203	07/05 Str	04/48 7203	-12/57	58	09/49⇨p
67204	08/05 Str	08/49 7204	-09/55	55	
67205	09/05 Str	07/48 7205	-11/55	55	
67206	10/05 Str	06/50 7206	-09/55	55	
67207	11/05 Str	05/48 7207	-12/55	56	
67208	11/05 Str	09/49 7208	-01/57	01/57	
67209	01/06 Str	11/48 7209	-02/57	57	
67210	02/06 Str	01/50 7210	-07/55	08/55	
67211	01/06 Str	06/48 7211	-10/56	56	
67212	07/06 Str	11/48 7212	-05/58	58	
67213	06/07 Str	02/49 7213	-02/55	02/55	09/49⇨p
67214	07/07 Str	05/49 7214	-06/58	58	
67215	08/08 Str	11/49 7215	-09/55	55	
67216	11/08 Str	06/51 7216	-12/56	01/57	
67217	02/09 Str	08/48 7217	-11/55	55	
67218	12/04 Str	04/48 7218	-03/58	58	w F6 12/48⇨F5 11/49⇨p
67219	12/04 Str	11/49 7219	-11/56	01/57	w F6 12/48⇨F5

F6 (67218-67219), 67220-67239
2-4-2T GER Holden

Power Classification: 2P reclassified 1P in 1953
Introduced: 1911-1912
Designer: S D Holden
Company: GER
Weight: 56t 9cwt
Driving Wheel: 5' 4"
Boiler Pressure: 180psi
Cylinders: Inside 17½" x 24"
Tractive Effort: 17570lbf
Valve Gear: Stephenson (slide valves)

Refer to the Historical Survey of Great Eastern 2-4-2T Engines at the end of this section for more details of this class.

The 'F6' class was built to the same design as the rebuilt 'F5' class, with the addition of side window cabs and larger side tanks. They were the GER 'G69' class. There was a lot of variation in boiler mountings (chimneys, domes and safety valves) in the class. One or two engines later acquired stove pipe chimneys.

67218 and 67219 were included in this class until 1948.

Year End Totals: 'F6' class

'47	'48	'49	'50	'51	'52	'53	'54	'55	'56	'57	'58	'59	'60	'61	'62	'63	'64	'65	'66	'67
22	20	20	20	20	20	20	20	10	6	5										

Number	Built	Renumbered	BR Dates	Scrap	Notes
67220	04/11 Str	07/51 7220	-07/55	08/55	
67221	04/11 Str	12/49 7221	-10/57	57	
67222	04/11 Str	10/48 7222	-08/55	55	
67223	05/11 Str	05/48 7223	-12/55	56	
67224	05/11 Str	06/50 7224	-11/56	56	
67225	05/11 Str	04/49 7225	-05/56	56	
67226	05/11 Str	04/50 7226	-11/55	55	
67227	05/11 Str	09/48 7227	-05/58	58	
67228	06/11 Str	05/50 7228	-04/58	58	
67229	06/11 Str	02/49 7229	-03/58	58	
67230	10/11 Str	11/49 7230	-05/58	12/58	
67231	10/11 Str	11/49 7231	-03/58	58	
67232	11/11 Str	06/49 7232	-11/55	55	
67233	11/11 Str	10/50 7233	-12/55	56	
67234	11/11 Str	01/49 7234	-08/56	56	
67235	12/11 Str	06/49 7235	-01/56	01/56	
67236	12/11 Str	12/49 7236	-08/55	55	
67237	01/12 Str	03/48 7237	-08/55	55	
67238	01/12 Str	01/51 7238	-11/55	01/56	
67239	01/12 Str	08/50 7239	-12/55	01/56	

G5 67240-67349
0-4-4T NER Worsdell

Power Classification: 2P reclassified 1P in 1953
Introduced: 1894-1901
Designer: W Worsdell
Company: NER
Weight: 54t 4cwt
Driving Wheel: 5' 1¼"
Boiler Pressure: 160psi
Cylinders: Inside 18" x 24"
Tractive Effort: 17265lbf
Valve Gear: Stephenson (slide valves)

The 'G5' class was designed by Wilson Worsdell and 110 engines were built at Darlington between 1894 and 1901 for light passenger work on the NER. They were the NER class 'O'.

Most engines of the class were fitted with larger bunkers to increase the coal capacity, some of them with hoppers on the bunkers.

The class did a lot of hard work on the North East Coast. Some of the engines worked the Seven Sisters-Palace Gates service in the 1930s.

The entire class came into BR stock in 1948, and they had all disappeared by the end of the 1950s due to the advent of the diesel railcar.

p A number of engines were fitted with push-pull control apparatus (two of them by BR).

t 67340 was rebuilt with extended side tanks in 1938.

Year End Totals: 'G5' class

'47	'48	'49	'50	'51	'52	'53	'54	'55	'56	'57	'58	'59	'60	'61	'62	'63	'64	'65	'66	'67
110	109	109	107	102	95	88	80	59	42	22										

Number	Built	Renumbered	BR Dates	Scrap	Notes
67240	05/94 Dar	11/49 7240	-04/56	56	
67241	06/94 Dar	01/49 7241	-03/55	55	
67242	06/94 Dar	12/48 7242	-02/53	53	
67243	06/94 Dar	05/50 7243	-09/55	55	
67244	06/94 Dar	03/49 7244	-11/52	11/52	
67245	06/94 Dar	02/49 7245	-06/51	51	
67246	06/94 Dar	08/48 7246	-11/58	02/59	
67247	06/94 Dar	07/48 7247	-12/54	55	
67248	08/94 Dar	10/48 7248	-12/58	01/59	
67249	09/94 Dar	06/49 7249	-03/55	05/55	
67250	03/95 Dar	10/48 7250	-09/57	57	p
67251	03/95 Dar	09/48 7251	-03/56	56	
67252	04/95 Dar	08/48 7252	-11/52	11/52	
67253	04/95 Dar	04/48 7253	-10/58	11/58	p
67254	04/95 Dar	05/48 7254	-12/57	01/58	
67255	06/95 Dar	02/49 7255	-05/51	05/51	
67256	06/95 Dar	10/48 7256	-04/57	57	
67257	06/95 Dar	02/50 7257	-04/54	54	
67258	06/95 Dar	01/50 7258	-10/57	11/57	
67259	06/95 Dar	06/48 7259	-12/57	01/58	
67260	02/96 Dar	10/48 7260	-11/52	12/52	
67261	02/96 Dar	06/48 7261	-12/58	01/59	p
67262	02/96 Dar	03/49 7262	-12/58	59	
67263	02/96 Dar	04/48 7263	-10/58	11/58	
67264	03/96 Dar	06/48 7264	-07/51	51	
67265	03/96 Dar	05/48 7265	-02/58	02/58	
67266	03/96 Dar	09/48 7266	-12/55	56	
67267	03/96 Dar	06/49 7267	-06/54	54	
67268	03/96 Dar	03/49 7268	-04/55	55	
67269	03/96 Dar	06/49 7269	-09/56	01/57	p
67270	06/96 Dar	07/49 7270	-01/58	58	
67271	06/96 Dar	12/48 7271	-02/55	03/55	
67272	06/96 Dar	08/48 7272	-11/54	54	
67273	08/96 Dar	07/48 7273	-05/57	57	p
67274	08/96 Dar	03/50 7274	-12/58	02/59	
67275	09/96 Dar	04/48 7275	-09/52	11/52	
67276	09/96 Dar	09/50 7276	-10/52	11/52	
67277	10/96 Dar	04/49 7277	-10/57	57	04/49⇨p
67278	11/96 Dar	06/49 7278	-07/57	57	
67279	11/96 Dar	12/50 7279	-11/56	56	p
67280	12/96 Dar	04/50 7280	-12/58	01/59	p
67281	12/96 Dar	04/48 7281	-12/58	01/59	p
67282	12/96 Dar	09/48 7282	-05/57	57	p
67283	12/96 Dar	12/48 7283	-08/54	54	
67284	12/96 Dar	05/48 7284	-10/56	56	07/51⇨p
67285	12/96 Dar	7285	-06/50	50	
67286	12/96 Dar	06/50 7286	-10/56	01/57	p
67287	12/96 Dar	06/50 7287	-03/53	06/53	
67288	12/96 Dar	12/48 7288	-06/54	07/54	
67289	05/97 Dar	08/48 7289	-12/56	01/57	
67290	06/97 Dar	09/48 7290	-03/56	05/56	
67291	06/97 Dar	11/49 7291	-02/53	53	
67292	06/97 Dar	06/49 7292	-08/52	10/52	
67293	06/97 Dar	10/48 7293	-04/55	04/55	
67294	06/97 Dar	11/48 7294	-01/57	57	
67295	06/97 Dar	08/48 7295	-03/54	54	
67296	06/97 Dar	03/51 7296	-03/55	06/55	
67297	06/97 Dar	01/49 7297	-09/58	58	p
67298	06/97 Dar	07/48 7298	-12/56	57	
67299	09/97 Dar	10/48 7299	-05/50	50	
67300	09/97 Dar	11/48 7300	-11/55	55	
67301	10/97 Dar	04/48 7301	-03/55	55	
67302	10/97 Dar	09/49 7302	-04/56	56	
67303	10/97 Dar	04/50 7303	-02/53	53	
67304	11/97 Dar	10/51 7304	-02/55	04/55	
67305	11/97 Dar	07/48 7305	-12/58	12/58	p
67306	11/97 Dar	7306	-06/48	07/48	
67307	12/97 Dar	10/48 7307	-05/55	06/55	
67308	12/97 Dar	12/48 7308	-11/55	55	
67309	12/96 Dar	03/51 7309	-03/55	05/55	
67310	10/00 Dar	06/48 7310	-09/55	55	
67311	11/00 Dar	11/48 7311	-12/58	12/58	p
67312	11/00 Dar	11/48 7312	-04/56	05/56	
67313	11/00 Dar	05/48 7313	-08/51	51	

Number	Built	Renumbered	BR Dates	Scrap	Notes
67314	11/00 Dar	10/48 7314	-12/55	*56*	
67315	12/00 Dar	04/50 7315	-12/58	*01/59*	
67316	12/00 Dar	10/49 7316	-12/55	*56*	
67317	12/00 Dar	05/48 7317	-09/51	*51*	
67318	12/00 Dar	07/48 7318	-03/57	*57*	
67319	12/00 Dar	05/49 7319	-12/57	01/58	
67320	12/00 Dar	01/49 7320	-11/58	*12/58*	
67321	12/00 Dar	07/50 7321	-01/57	*01/57*	
67322	12/00 Dar	03/51 7322	-11/56	*56*	p
67323	12/00 Dar	07/50 7323	-12/58	*12/58*	p
67324	12/00 Dar	09/48 7324	-11/57	12/57	
67325	03/01 Dar	11/48 7325	-10/58	*58*	
67326	03/01 Dar	12/48 7326	-10/57	*57*	
67327	04/01 Dar	05/49 7327	-02/55	*55*	
67328	04/01 Dar	03/50 7328	-11/55	*55*	
67329	04/01 Dar	09/48 7329	-11/58	05/59	
67330	06/01 Dar	08/48 7330	-12/52	12/52	
67331	06/01 Dar	06/49 7331	-01/53	*53*	
67332	06/01 Dar	10/49 7332	-04/56	*56*	
67333	06/01 Dar	10/50 7333	-10/56	*01/57*	
67334	06/01 Dar	11/50 7334	-03/56	*56*	
67335	06/01 Dar	06/50 7335	-08/53	*53*	
67336	06/01 Dar	01/49 7336	-03/55	05/55	
67337	06/01 Dar	01/50 7337	-03/57	*57*	p
67338	09/01 Dar	05/50 7338	-08/57	*57*	p
67339	09/01 Dar	03/50 7339	-03/57	04/57	p
67340	09/01 Dar	10/49 7340	-04/58	*58*	pt
67341	10/01 Dar	11/48 7341	-11/58	*11/58*	
67342	10/01 Dar	11/48 7342	-12/58	*12/58*	
67343	10/01 Dar	08/49 7343	-11/57	11/57	
67344	10/01 Dar	09/48 7344	-02/56	*03/56*	
67345	11/01 Dar	11/48 7345	-12/55	*56*	
67346	11/01 Dar	03/49 7346	-02/57	*03/57*	
67347	11/01 Dar	01/49 7347	-03/56	05/56	
67348	11/01 Dar	12/48 7348	-01/53	*53*	
67349	12/01 Dar	03/49 7349	-04/54	*54*	

C12 67350-67399
4-4-2T GNR Ivatt

Power Classification: 2P reclassified 1P in 1953
Introduced: 1898-1907
Designer: Ivatt
Company: GNR
Weight: 62t 6cwt
Driving Wheel: 5' 8"
Boiler Pressure: 175psi
b 170psi
Cylinders: Inside 18" x 26"
Tractive Effort: 18425lbf
b 17900lbf
Valve Gear: Stephenson (slide valves)

Ivatt built sixty 4-4-2Ts between 1898 and 1907 for working the GNR London suburban services. They were built at Doncaster and they were originally the GNR 'C2' class. They were never superheated and had boilers which were interchangeable with the 'J4' 0-6-0s. There was some variation in chimneys between different members of the class.

Ten engines were withdrawn before the Second World War (the first going in 1937), and they were not included in the LNER renumbering scheme. Forty-nine engines came into BR stock and they were all withdrawn by 1958.

b Five engines had reduced boiler pressure.

c The last fifty engines to be built were originally fitted with condensing apparatus for working through the Metropolitan tunnels. When the engines were replaced on these duties by the larger 'N2' class of 0-6-2Ts this apparatus was removed and the engines were drafted to work on country branches. These engines could be distinguished from the first ten by the flared out tops to the bunkers.

p Five engines were fitted with push-pull control apparatus in 1948-1949.

Year End Totals: 'C12' class

'47	'48	'49	'50	'51	'52	'53	'54	'55	'56	'57	'58	'59	'60	'61	'62	'63	'64	'65	'66	'67
49	43	40	40	38	37	33	32	20	17	16										

Number	Built	Renumbered	BR Dates	Scrap	Notes
67350	02/98 Don	10/48 7350	-04/55	*55*	
67351	02/98 Don	7351	-12/48	*49*	
67352	05/98 Don	07/48 7352	-11/58	*58*	
67353	03/98 Don	04/51 7353	-04/55	*55*	
67354	10/98 Don	07/48 7354	-07/53	*53*	b
67355	10/98 Don	7355	-03/48	*48*	
67356	12/98 Don	01/49 7356	-10/51	*51*	
					05/49⇨p
67357	10/98 Don	02/51 7357	-05/58	*58*	
67358	02/99 Don	7358	-01/48	*48*	
67359	02/99 Don	7359	-08/49	*49*	c
67360	03/99 Don	05/48 7360	-01/55	*55*	c
67361	03/99 Don	01/50 7361	-04/55	*55*	c
67362	03/99 Don	08/50 7362	-01/58	01/58	c
67363	04/99 Don	02/49 7363	-11/58	*58*	cb
					02/49⇨p
67364	04/99 Don	09/48 7364	-05/56	06/56	c
67365	04/99 Don	06/50 7365	-05/58	*58*	c
67366	05/99 Don	04/48 7366	-04/58	*58*	c
67367	05/99 Don	02/51 7367	-08/58	*58*	c
67368	05/99 Don	03/50 7368	-10/55	11/55	c
67369	08/99 Don	01/49 7369	-07/54	*08/54*	c
67370	08/99 Don	7370	-01/48	*48*	c
67371	09/99 Don	10/48 7371	-04/55	*55*	c
67372	10/99 Don	12/50 7372	-05/53	*53*	c
67373	10/99 Don	11/48 7373	-03/51	*06/53*	c
67374	11/99 Don	02/51 7374	-04/58	*58*	cb
					01/48⇨p
67375	11/99 Don	07/48 7375	-04/55	*55*	c
67376	06/01 Don	06/50 7376	-05/58	*58*	c
67377	06/01 Don	7377	-07/49	*49*	c
67378	10/01 Don	7378	-01/48	*48*	c
67379	08/01 Don	11/49 7379	-06/58	*58*	c
67380	06/01 Don	10/48 7380	-05/58	*58*	c
67381	11/01 Don	01/49 7381	-01/52	*52*	c
67382	10/01 Don	12/49 7382	-04/55	*55*	c
67383	11/01 Don	12/49 7383	-01/55	*55*	c
67384	12/03 Don	12/48 7384	-05/56	*56*	c
67385	12/03 Don	01/51 7385	-04/55	*55*	c
67386	12/03 Don	09/48 7386	-04/58	*58*	c
					03/49⇨p
67387	12/03 Don	10/49 7387	-02/55	*55*	c
					10/49⇨p
67388	12/03 Don	7388	-07/48	*48*	c
67389	01/04 Don	10/49 7389	-04/55	*55*	c
67390	12/03 Don	08/50 7390	-06/53	*53*	c
67391	07/07 Don	04/49 7391	-01/58	01/58	c
67392	07/07 Don	05/49 7392	-09/56	*56*	c
67393	07/07 Don	01/49 7393	-05/53	*06/53*	c
67394	07/07 Don	08/48 7394	-06/58	*58*	c
67395	07/07 Don	01/49 7395	-03/57	*57*	c
67397	08/07 Don	03/50 7397	-12/58	*59*	c
67398	08/07 Don	05/48 7398	-11/58	*58*	cb
67399	08/07 Don	7399	-11/49	*49*	cb

C13 67400-67439
4-4-2T GCR Robinson

Power Classification: 2P
Introduced: 1903-1905
Designer: Robinson
Company: GCR
Weight: 66t 13cwt
Driving Wheel: 5' 7"
Boiler Pressure: 160psi superheated
Cylinders: Inside 18" x 26"
Tractive Effort: 17100lbf
Valve Gear: Stephenson (slide valves)

In 1903-1905 Robinson constructed forty 4-4-2T engines for working the GCR suburban services out of London Marylebone Station. They were 4-4-2T versions of the 0-6-2T 'N5' class. They were GCR class '9K' and they were all later superheated and fitted with ugly 'flower-pot' chimneys. The original design was further developed as the 'C14' class.

Like their contemporaries on the GNR (the 'C12' class) they were displaced from the London area when larger engines (the 'A5' 4-6-2Ts) took over their duties. Some spent the rest of their lives on country branch lines, but the majority were used for local and suburban services in Manchester, Liverpool, Sheffield and Nottingham.

All the engines came into BR stock in 1948 and the last one was withdrawn in 1960.

p A number of engines were fitted with push-pull control apparatus.

Year End Totals: 'C13' class

'47	'48	'49	'50	'51	'52	'53	'54	'55	'56	'57	'58	'59	'60	'61	'62	'63	'64	'65	'66	'67
40	40	40	40	40	39	36	29	24	16	10	1	1								

Number	Built	Renumbered	BR Dates	Scrap	Notes
67400	03/03 VF	03/49 7400	-12/56	*57*	
67401	03/03 VF	04/48 7401	-11/55	*02/56*	
67402	04/03 VF	10/49 7402	-08/54	*09/54*	
67403	04/03 VF	06/49 7403	-04/55	*55*	
67404	05/03 VF	06/48 7404	-02/53	*53*	
67405	05/03 VF	11/48 7405	-05/55	*55*	
67406	05/03 VF	08/50 7406	-03/53	*08/53*	
67407	06/03 VF	05/48 7407	-09/56	*56*	
67408	06/03 VF	10/48 7408	-05/54	*08/54*	
67409	06/03 VF	04/49 7409	-12/56	*57*	
67410	06/03 VF	07/48 7410	-03/53	*04/53*	
67411	06/03 VF	05/48 7411	-05/55	*55*	
67412	05/03 Gor	06/49 7412	-06/54	*08/54*	
67413	05/03 Gor	03/48 7413	-12/57	09/58	
67414	06/03 Gor	03/49 7414	-06/55	*55*	
67415	07/03 Gor	11/48 7415	-02/56	*56*	
67416	08/03 Gor	05/48 7416	-12/58	02/59	p
67417	08/03 Gor	04/48 7417	-01/60	02/60	p
67418	09/03 Gor	05/49 7418	-12/58	02/59	p
67419	09/03 Gor	10/48 7419	-06/57	07/57	
67420	08/04 Gor	05/49 7420	-12/58	02/59	p
67421	08/04 Gor	11/49 7421	-12/58	02/59	p
67422	09/04 Gor	07/50 7422	-09/54	*54*	
67423	10/04 Gor	06/49 7423	-10/57	12/57	
67424	10/04 Gor	09/48 7424	-11/58	02/59	
67425	11/04 Gor	05/48 7425	-08/56	10/56	
67426	11/04 Gor	03/49 7426	-12/54	01/55	
67427	12/04 Gor	08/49 7427	-01/58	02/59	
67428	12/04 Gor	06/48 7428	-11/57	01/58	
67429	12/04 Gor	03/49 7429	-12/54	01/55	
67430	01/05 Gor	03/48 7430	-04/56	*56*	
67431	02/05 Gor	06/48 7431	-09/56	*02/57*	
67432	02/05 Gor	05/49 7432	-12/54	*55*	
67433	03/05 Gor	04/48 7433	-01/58	02/59	p
67434	04/05 Gor	04/49 7434	-10/57	12/57	
67435	04/05 Gor	05/49 7435	-12/52	*53*	
67436	04/05 Gor	02/49 7436	-02/56	*05/56*	p
67437	05/05 Gor	04/48 7437	-08/57	08/57	
67438	07/05 Gor	05/48 7438	-01/58	09/58	p
67439	08/05 Gor	06/49 7439	-11/58	12/58	

C14 67440-67451
4-4-2T GCR Robinson

Power Classification: 2P
Introduced: 1907
Designer: Robinson
Company: GCR
Weight: 71t 0cwt
Driving Wheel: 5' 7"
Boiler Pressure: 160psi superheated
Cylinders: Inside 18" x 26"
Tractive Effort: 17100lbf
Valve Gear: Stephenson (slide valves)

In 1907 Robinson built an enlarged version of the 'C13' class at Gorton. They were GCR class '9L' (LNER 'C14' class) and they were all later superheated and fitted with 'flower-pot' chimneys. They had larger tanks and bigger bunkers than the 'C13' class.

All the engines came into BR stock in 1948 and the last one was withdrawn in 1960.

Year End Totals: 'C14' class

'47	'48	'49	'50	'51	'52	'53	'54	'55	'56	'57	'58	'59	'60	'61	'62	'63	'64	'65	'66	'67
12	12	12	12	12	12	12	12	12	12	4	3	1								

Number	Built	Renumbered	BR Dates	Scrap	Notes
67440	05/07 BP	11/49 7440	-07/57	08/57	
67441	05/07 BP	04/49 7441	-08/57	09/57	
67442	05/07 BP	03/49 7442	-11/57	01/58	
67443	05/07 BP	04/48 7443	-06/57	07/57	
67444	05/07 BP	09/49 7444	-07/57	07/57	
67445	05/07 BP	10/48 7445	-12/59	01/60	
67446	05/07 BP	08/48 7446	-05/57	06/57	
67447	06/07 BP	08/48 7447	-03/58	04/59	
67448	06/07 BP	08/50 7448	-06/59	09/59	
67449	06/07 BP	06/49 7449	-12/57	01/58	
67450	06/07 BP	03/49 7450	-01/60	02/60	
67451	06/07 BP	02/49 7451	-01/57	01/57	

C15 67452-67481
4-4-2T NBR Reid

Power Classification: 2P
Introduced: 1911-1913
Designer: Reid
Company: NBR
Weight: 68t 15cwt
Driving Wheel: 5' 9"
Boiler Pressure: 175psi
Cylinders: Inside 18" x 26"
Tractive Effort: 18160lbf
Valve Gear: Stephenson (slide valves)

The 'C15' class was built in 1911-1913 by Reid for working passenger trains on the NBR. They were originally known as the NBR 'M' class, and thirty engines were built.

The 'C15' and 'C16' classes were the standard passenger tank engines on the NBR from 1911 onwards. The two classes were very similar in

WD 'J94' class 0-6-0ST No 68025.

NBR Holmes 'Y9' class 0-4-0ST No 68101 at Dunfermline Lower in July 1957.

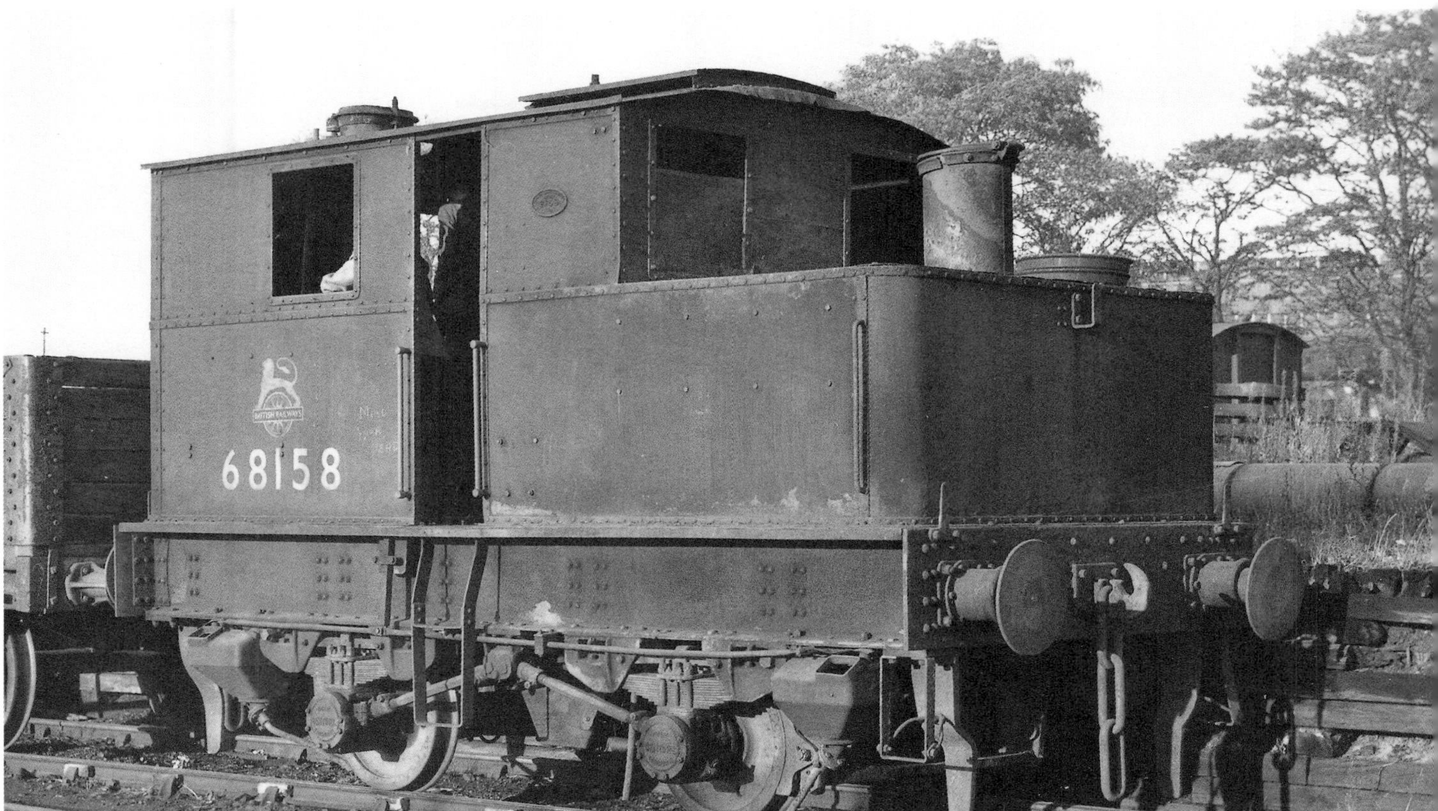

LNER 'Y3' class Sentinel 0-4-0T No 68158.

GER Holden 'J70' class tram engine 0-6-0T No 68222 at Colchester in September 1953.

appearance, but the 'C15's had longer chimneys and domes than the 'C16's.

p Three engines were fitted with push-pull control apparatus (two of them by BR), and two of these engines outlived the others of the class by several years.

Year End Totals: 'C15' class

'47	'48	'49	'50	'51	'52	'53	'54	'55	'56	'57	'58	'59	'60	'61	'62	'63	'64	'65	'66	'67
30	30	30	30	30	29	27	14	9	2	2	2	2								

Number	Built	Renumbered	BR Dates	Scrap	Notes
67452	12/11 YE	08/48 7452	-02/56	*56*	
67453	12/12 YE	02/50 7453	-01/54	*02/54*	
67454	01/12 YE	02/49 7454	-06/54	02/55	
67455	03/12 YE	04/48 7455	-02/55	07/55	
67456	04/12 YE	06/51 7456	-09/54	*10/54*	
67457	05/12 YE	05/51 7457	-06/55	09/55	
67458	06/12 YE	10/48 7458	-03/56	*56*	
67459	07/12 YE	09/50 7459	-10/55	01/56	
67460	08/12 YE	06/48 7460	-04/60	05/60	p
67461	09/12 YE	7461	-12/54	*55*	
67462	10/12 YE	06/50 7462	-06/54	09/55	
67463	11/12 YE	07/48 7463	-09/55	01/56	
67464	01/13 YE	12/48 7464	-08/53	*53*	
67465	02/13 YE	7465	-11/54	02/55	
67466	02/13 YE	10/49 7466	-04/56	*05/56*	
67467	03/13 YE	03/49 7467	-03/55	*55*	
67468	03/13 YE	04/50 7468	-10/53	*11/53*	
67469	04/13 YE	05/50 7469	-09/54	10/54	
67470	04/13 YE	7470	-11/54	*54*	
67471	05/13 YE	7471	-12/52	02/53	
67472	07/13 YE	11/48 7472	-04/56	*56*	
67473	07/13 YE	07/50 7473	-12/54	*55*	
67474	08/13 YE	10/48 7474	-04/60	05/60	09/54⇨p
67475	08/13 YE	10/48 7475	-04/54	*54*	10/50⇨p
67476	10/13 YE	02/49 7476	-09/54	*54*	
67477	10/13 YE	12/49 7477	-09/54	*10/54*	
67478	11/13 YE	02/49 7478	-02/56	*03/56*	
67479	11/13 YE	02/49 7479	-01/54	02/54	
67480	12/13 YE	01/50 7480	-02/56	*03/56*	
67481	12/13 YE	10/48 7481	-02/56	*56*	

C16 67482-67502
4-4-2T NBR Reid

Power Classification: 2P
Introduced: 1915-1921
Designer: Reid
Company: NBR
Weight: 72t 10cwt
Driving Wheel: 5' 9"
Boiler Pressure: 165psi superheated
r 165psi
Cylinders: Inside 19" x 26"
Tractive Effort: 19080lbf
Valve Gear: Stephenson (piston valves)

In 1915-1921 Reid built twenty-one engines which were a superheated version of the 'C15' class. They were fitted with larger cylinders and piston valves, and the boiler was slightly higher pitched.

The 'C15' and 'C16' classes were the standard passenger tank engines on the NBR from 1911 onwards. The two classes were very similar in appearance, but the 'C15's had longer chimneys and domes than the 'C16's.

r 67483 later had its superheater removed.

Year End Totals: 'C16' class

'47	'48	'49	'50	'51	'52	'53	'54	'55	'56	'57	'58	'59	'60	'61	'62	'63	'64	'65	'66	'67
21	21	21	21	21	21	21	21	19	16	16	16	11	3							

Number	Built	Renumbered	BR Dates	Scrap	Notes
67482	12/15 NB	05/49 7482	-10/59	02/60	
67483	12/15 NB	03/49 7483	-04/56	*05/56*	r
67484	12/15 NB	10/49 7484	-04/60	05/60	
67485	12/15 NB	09/48 7485	-04/61	05/61	
67486	12/15 NB	11/48 7486	-04/60	06/60	
67487	01/16 NB	05/48 7487	-10/59	02/60	
67488	02/16 NB	06/52 7488	-10/59	03/60	
67489	02/16 NB	02/49 7489	-02/61	03/61	
67490	02/16 NB	03/48 7490	-04/60	06/60	
67491	03/16 NB	06/49 7491	-03/60	04/60	
67492	04/16 NB	06/48 7492	-03/60	03/60	
67493	04/16 NB	05/49 7493	-04/56	*05/56*	
67494	04/16 NB	11/51 7494	-02/61	04/61	
67495	04/16 NB	11/49 7495	-05/56	*05/56*	
67496	05/16 NB	01/49 7496	-03/60	04/60	
67497	02/21 NB	04/50 7497	-10/59	02/60	
67498	02/21 NB	09/48 7498	-07/55	*01/56*	
67499	02/21 NB	09/48 7499	-11/55	01/56	
67500	03/21 NB	01/53 7500	-10/59	02/60	
67501	03/21 NB	01/49 7501	-04/60	06/60	
67502	03/21 NB	11/48 7502	-04/60	06/60	

V1 between 67600 & 67681
2-6-2T LNER Gresley

V3 between 67600 & 67691
2-6-2T LNER Gresley

Power Classification: V1 4MT
reclassified 3MT in 1953
V3 4MT
Introduced: V1 1930-1939
V3 1939-1961
(including rebuilds)
Designer: Gresley
Company: LNER
Weight: V1 84t 0cwt
V3 86t 16cwt
Driving Wheel: 5' 8"
Boiler Pressure: V1 180psi superheated
V3 200psi superheated
Cylinders: Three 16" x 26"
Tractive Effort: V1 22465lbf
V3 24960lbf
Valve Gear: Walschaert with derived motion (piston valves)

The first of Gresley's 'V1' class three-cylinder 2-6-2Ts appeared in 1930. Originally they were intended for the Metropolitan widened lines and the GNR suburban services, but they were never used on these duties and they spent virtually the whole of their lives on suburban services in the Newcastle, Glasgow and Edinburgh districts.

A total of ninety-two engines were built up to 1940, but the last ten engines (built in 1939-1940) were fitted with higher pressure boilers and they were classified 'V3'. They were externally indistinguishable from the 'V1' engines.

The LNER made a start on converting some of the earlier engines to 'V3' by increasing the boiler pressure from 180psi to 200psi, and during BR days most of the class was converted (making a total of seventy-three 'V3's, as shown in the list below).

Year End Totals: 'V1' class

'47	'48	'49	'50	'51	'52	'53	'54	'55	'56	'57	'58	'59	'60	'61	'62	'63	'64	'65	'66	'67
78	78	78	78	78	72	62	59	57	48	42	34	28	20	16						

Year End Totals: 'V3' class

'47	'48	'49	'50	'51	'52	'53	'54	'55	'56	'57	'58	'59	'60	'61	'62	'63	'64	'65	'66	'67
14	14	14	14	14	20	30	33	35	44	50	58	64	70	66	26	13				

Number	Built	Renumbered	BR Dates	Scrap	Notes
67600	09/30 Don	08/50 7600	-12/62	10/63	03/56⇨V3
67601	10/30 Don	09/49 7601	-01/62	09/62	
67602	10/30 Don	10/48 7602	-05/62	12/62	
67603	10/30 Don	08/48 7603	-03/62	01/63	
67604	11/30 Don	10/50 7604	-12/62	07/63	11/52⇨V3
67605	11/30 Don	07/48 7605	-12/62	08/63	10/53⇨V3
67606	12/30 Don	52 7606	-12/62	08/63	12/52⇨V3
67607	12/30 Don	06/50 7607	-12/62	11/63	10/58⇨V3
67608	12/30 Don	04/48 7608	-12/62	07/63	02/61⇨V3
67609	02/31 Don	07/49 7609	-02/62	04/62	10/53⇨V3
67610	04/31 Don	09/48 7610	-06/61	07/61	
67611	04/31 Don	12/49 7611	-12/62	10/63	07/53⇨V3
67612	04/31 Don	08/49 7612	-01/61	04/61	09/53⇨V3
67613	05/31 Don	07/48 7613	-01/62	01/63	04/56⇨V3
67614	06/31 Don	05/48 7614	-07/62	08/62	09/58⇨V3
67615	06/31 Don	06/48 7615	-12/62	08/63	12/53⇨V3
67616	06/31 Don	07/48 7616	-12/62	10/63	60⇨V3
67617	08/31 Don	03/50 7617	-08/62	09/63	10/57⇨V3
67618	08/31 Don	10/48 7618	-12/62	11/63	09/58⇨V3
67619	08/31 Don	06/49 7619	-12/62	10/63	02/57⇨V3
67620	10/31 Don	07/49 7620	-11/64	08/65	07/53⇨V3
67621	10/31 Don	10/49 7621	-12/62	10/63	12/59⇨V3
67622	10/31 Don	06/48 7622	-03/62	03/63	
67623	11/31 Don	03/49 7623	-01/62	09/63	05/59⇨V3
67624	11/31 Don	08/48 7624	-09/60	11/60	11/52⇨V3
67625	12/31 Don	11/49 7625	-12/62	11/63	09/53⇨V3
67626	12/31 Don	12/48 7626	-12/62	10/63	05/53⇨V3
67627	12/31 Don	01/49 7627	-08/61	09/61	09/53⇨V3
67628	12/34 Don	09/48 7628	-11/64	02/65	01/57⇨V3
67629	02/35 Don	07/48 7629	-05/62	10/62	
67630	03/35 Don	07/48 7630	-12/62	11/63	
67631	03/35 Don	05/48 7631	-03/62	02/63	
67632	03/35 Don	04/48 7632	-12/62	11/63	05/57⇨V3
67633	04/35 Don	10/48 7633	-12/62	10/63	02/60⇨V3
67634	04/35 Don	11/48 7634	-04/62	06/62	V3
67635	04/35 Don	08/48 7635	-09/63	11/63	10/60⇨V3
67636	05/35 Don	12/48 7636	-11/64	12/65	11/52⇨V3
67637	05/35 Don	06/48 7637	-05/62	04/63	
67638	05/35 Don	08/48 7638	-11/64	02/65	01/55⇨V3
67639	06/35 Don	12/48 7639	-10/62	11/62	
67640	06/35 Don	10/48 7640	-11/64	02/65	12/60⇨V3
67641	06/35 Don	10/49 7641	-10/62	02/63	
67642	07/35 Don	01/49 7642	-06/64	08/64	04/60⇨V3
67643	07/35 Don	12/48 7643	-11/64	02/65	05/56⇨V3
67644	08/35 Don	03/50 7644	-05/62	01/63	07/58⇨V3
67645	08/35 Don	09/49 7645	-09/63	10/63	11/59⇨V3
67646	10/35 Don	11/49 7646	-11/64	02/65	05/56⇨V3
67647	11/35 Don	01/49 7647	-01/63	06/63	12/59⇨V3
67648	12/35 Don	05/49 7648	-02/62	02/63	59⇨V3
67649	12/35 Don	05/48 7649	-06/62	08/63	
67650	01/36 Don	09/48 7650	-08/61	10/63	09/58⇨V3
67651	01/36 Don	01/49 7651	-05/64	09/64	05/56⇨V3
67652	01/36 Don	01/50 7652	-12/63	01/64	10/52⇨V3
67653	02/36 Don	05/50 7653	-09/63	12/63	09/54⇨V3
67654	03/36 Don	03/49 7654	-09/63	11/63	10/54⇨V3
67655	03/36 Don	01/49 7655	-03/62	11/62	
67656	03/36 Don	06/50 7656	-12/63	02/64	07/52⇨V3
67657	04/36 Don	03/50 7657	-12/62	05/63	56⇨V3
67658	04/36 Don	09/49 7658	-09/63	02/64	01/60⇨V3
67659	05/36 Don	09/48 7659	-02/62	03/62	
67660	07/36 Don	06/49 7660	-02/62	07/62	05/56⇨V3
67661	10/36 Don	08/48 7661	-02/62	04/62	02/59⇨V3
67662	07/38 Don	11/48 7662	-01/63	07/63	02/55⇨V3
67663	07/38 Don	12/48 7663	-09/63	12/63	56⇨V3
67664	07/38 Don	03/50 7664	-12/62	10/63	
67665	08/38 Don	06/48 7665	-06/61	08/61	
67666	08/38 Don	03/50 7666	-02/62	08/62	01/61⇨V3
67667	09/38 Don	09/49 7667	-08/62	12/63	08/58⇨V3
67668	10/38 Don	12/48 7668	-12/62	03/63	05/54⇨V3
67669	10/38 Don	08/49 7669	-09/61	03/62	V3
67670	10/38 Don	09/49 7670	-08/61	09/61	06/56⇨V3
67671	10/38 Don	06/49 7671	-06/60	08/60	
67672	11/38 Don	04/48 7672	-12/62	12/63	V3
67673	11/38 Don	01/50 7673	-10/62	04/63	
67674	11/38 Don	09/49 7674	-12/62	08/63	08/57⇨V3
67675	12/38 Don	06/49 7675	-12/62	10/63	V3
67676	12/38 Don	11/48 7676	-07/62	09/63	09/60⇨V3
67677	01/39 Don	06/48 7677	-10/62	11/62	09/58⇨V3
67678	02/39 Don	07/48 7678	-11/64	02/65	10/58⇨V3

Number	Built	Renumbered	BR Dates	Scrap	Notes
67679	02/39 Don	03/49 7679	-01/62	03/63	10/53⇨V3
67680	02/39 Don	03/50 7680	-12/62	10/63	
67681	02/39 Don	03/49 7681	-11/61	04/62	11/57⇨V3
67682	09/39 Don	09/49 7682	-09/63	11/63	V3
67683	10/39 Don	04/50 7683	-09/63	12/63	V3
67684	10/39 Don	04/48 7684	-11/64	08/65	V3
67685	12/39 Don	06/49 7685	-12/62	04/63	V3
67686	12/39 Don	02/49 7686	-09/63	12/63	V3
67687	12/39 Don	12/48 7687	-12/62	06/63	V3
67688	02/40 Don	05/48 7688	-12/62	06/63	V3
67689	02/40 Don	03/49 7689	-12/62	09/63	V3
67690	03/40 Don	07/48 7690	-11/64	02/65	V3
67691	04/40 Don	06/48 7691	-11/64	02/65	V3

L1 67701-67800, (69000-69015)
2-6-4T LNER Thompson

Power Classification:	4MT
Introduced:	1945-1950
Designer:	Thompson
Company:	LNER
Weight:	89t 9cwt
Driving Wheel:	5' 2"
Boiler Pressure:	225psi superheated b 200psi superheated
Cylinders:	Outside 20" x 26" c Outside 18¾" x 26"
Tractive Effort:	32080lbf b 28515lbf c 28195lbf
Valve Gear:	Walschaert (piston valves)

In 1945 Thompson introduced the 'L1' class two-cylinder 2-6-4T. The first engine was numbered 9000 and it was painted in LNER green when it appeared from Doncaster works. It was the prototype engine designed principally for working the King's Cross and Marylebone suburban services.

A total of one-hundred engines were eventually built, but apart from the first engine they all were built in BR days. Twenty-nine engines were built at Darlington and the first of these appeared early in 1948 as 9001-9003, E9004-E9012 and 69013-69015. It was then decided that they would be renumbered to prevent clashes with other classes which were numbered from 69050 onwards and the whole series was renumbered from 67701 upwards.

The remaining seventy engines (67731 upwards) were built between 1948 and 1950 by North British and Robert Stephenson & Hawthorn. They were distinguishable from the earlier engines as they had the running plate cut away in front of the piston valves.

They were the most powerful 2-6-4Ts to run on BR and, apart from the London services which they were designed for, they could also be seen in Yorkshire. They were all withdrawn by the end of 1962 with the mass introduction of diesel multiple units on local passenger services.

b Some engines had reduced boiler pressure for a period from 1954 onwards.

c Some engines were modified from 1954 onwards with reduced diameter cylinders.

Year End Totals: 'L1' class

'47	'48	'49	'50	'51	'52	'53	'54	'55	'56	'57	'58	'59	'60	'61	'62	'63	'64	'65	'66	'67
1	60	75	100	100	100	100	100	100	100	100	100	100	88	64						

Number	*Built*	*Renumbered*	*BR Dates*	*Scrap*	*Notes*
67701	45 Don	05/48 *69000*	-12/60	09/61	
67702	01/48 Dar	05/48 *69001*	01/48-10/60	11/60	
67703	02/48 Dar	05/48 *69002*	01/48-09/62	11/62	
67704	02/48 Dar	04/48 *69003*	02/48-11/60	02/61	
67705	02/48 Dar	04/48 *69004*	02/48-12/60	01/61	
67706	02/48 Dar	04/48 *69005*	02/48-12/60	09/61	
67707	02/48 Dar	04/48 *69006*	02/48-07/61	11/62	
67708	03/48 Dar	05/48 *69007*	03/48-12/60	10/61	
67709	03/48 Dar	05/48 *69008*	03/48-12/60	10/61	
67710	03/48 Dar	05/48 *69009*	03/48-11/62	12/62	
67711	03/48 Dar	04/48 *69010*	03/48-12/60	04/61	
67712	04/48 Dar	07/48 *69011*	03/48-10/61	11/61	
67713	04/48 Dar	04/48 *69012*	04/48-10/61	01/62	
67714	04/48 Dar	05/48 69013	04/48-12/60	01/61	
67715	04/48 Dar	05/48 69014	04/48-02/62	09/62	
67716	04/48 Dar	05/48 69015	04/48-09/62	12/62	
67717	04/48 Dar		04/48-07/61	11/61	
67718	05/48 Dar		05/48-11/61	01/62	
67719	05/48 Dar		05/48-07/61	07/61	
67720	05/48 Dar		05/48-02/62	06/62	
67721	05/48 Dar		05/48-11/62	05/63	
67722	06/48 Dar		06/48-10/61	02/62	
67723	06/48 Dar		06/48-09/62	01/63	
67724	06/48 Dar		06/48-09/62	11/62	
67725	06/48 Dar		06/48-12/60	12/60	
67726	07/48 Dar		07/48-11/60	09/61	
67727	07/48 Dar		07/48-01/62	02/62	
67728	07/48 Dar		07/48-09/61	10/61	
67729	07/48 Dar		07/48-09/62	11/62	
67730	08/48 Dar		08/48-08/62	10/62	
67731	10/48 NB		10/48-09/62	11/62	
67732	10/48 NB		10/48-07/61	08/61	
67733	11/48 NB		11/48-11/62	12/62	
67734	11/48 NB		11/48-09/62	12/62	
67735	11/48 NB		11/48-09/62	11/62	
67736	11/48 NB		11/48-12/60	10/61	
67737	11/48 NB		11/48-08/62	11/62	
67738	11/48 NB		11/48-07/61	07/61	
67739	11/48 NB		11/48-11/61	06/62	
67740	11/48 NB		11/48-07/61	10/61	
67741	11/48 NB		11/48-12/62	01/63	
67742	11/48 NB		11/48-12/62	06/63	
67743	11/48 NB		11/48-02/62	03/62	
67744	11/48 NB		11/48-12/62	02/63	
67745	11/48 NB		11/48-12/62	03/63	
67746	12/48 NB		12/48-07/62	10/62	
67747	12/48 NB		12/48-07/62	07/62	⇨b
67748	12/48 NB		12/48-11/61	12/61	
67749	12/48 NB		12/48-12/62	02/63	
67750	12/48 NB		12/48-01/61	11/62	
67751	12/48 NB		12/48-03/62	05/62	
67752	12/48 NB		12/48-03/62	05/62	
67753	12/48 NB		12/48-02/62	09/62	⇨b
67754	12/48 NB		12/48-11/62	06/63	
67755	12/48 NB		12/48-12/62	09/63	
67756	12/48 NB		12/48-03/62	05/62	
67757	12/48 NB		12/48-07/62	11/62	
67758	12/48 NB		12/48-09/61	10/61	
67759	12/48 NB		12/48-10/62	03/63	
67760	12/48 NB		12/48-08/61	09/61	
67761	01/49 NB		01/49-11/62	05/63	⇨b
67762	01/49 NB		01/49-10/61	11/61	
67763	01/49 NB		01/49-11/62	06/63	
67764	02/49 NB		02/49-08/62	10/62	
67765	02/49 NB		02/49-11/62	07/63	
67766	09/49 RSH		09/49-12/62	06/63	
67767	09/49 RSH		09/49-12/62	03/63	
67768	10/49 RSH		10/49-02/61	03/61	
67769	10/49 RSH		10/49-09/61	09/61	
67770	11/49 RSH		11/49-12/62	05/63	⇨c
67771	11/49 RSH		11/49-11/62	03/63	⇨c
67772	11/49 RSH		11/49-11/61	01/62	⇨c
67773	12/49 RSH		12/49-12/62	08/63	
67774	12/49 RSH		12/49-01/62	06/62	
67775	12/49 RSH		12/49-09/61	12/62	
67776	01/50 RSH		01/50-12/62	06/63	⇨c
67777	01/50 RSH		01/50-12/62	06/63	
67778	02/50 RSH		02/50-05/62	07/62	
67779	02/50 RSH		02/50-12/62	01/63	⇨c
67780	02/50 RSH		02/50-12/62	03/63	
67781	03/50 RSH		03/50-11/62	12/62	
67782	03/50 RSH		03/50-11/61	11/62	
67783	03/50 RSH		03/50-12/62	03/63	
67784	03/50 RSH		03/50-11/62	04/63	
67785	04/50 RSH		04/50-12/62	01/63	
67786	04/50 RSH		04/50-12/62	03/63	
67787	04/50 RSH		04/50-12/62	03/63	
67788	05/50 RSH		05/50-05/62	09/62	
67789	05/50 RSH		05/50-11/62	03/63	
67790	05/50 RSH		05/50-02/61	03/61	
67791	06/50 RSH		06/50-12/62	12/62	
67792	06/50 RSH		06/50-12/62	04/63	
67793	06/50 RSH		06/50-09/62	10/62	
67794	07/50 RSH		07/50-10/61	12/61	
67795	07/50 RSH		07/50-05/62	11/62	⇨b
67796	08/50 RSH		08/50-11/62	12/62	
67797	08/50 RSH		08/50-10/62	11/62	
67798	08/50 RSH		08/50-12/62	04/63	⇨b
67799	09/50 RSH		09/50-03/62	04/62	
67800	09/50 RSH		09/50-12/62	03/63	

Class continued with 69000

J94 68006-68080
0-6-0ST MOS (War Department)

Power Classification:	4F
Introduced:	1943-1946
Designer:	Riddles and Hunslet Engine Company
Company:	MOS (purchased by LNER in 1946)
Weight:	48t 5cwt
Driving Wheel:	4' 3"
Boiler Pressure:	170psi
Cylinders:	Inside 18" x 26"
Tractive Effort:	23870lbf
Valve Gear:	Stephenson (slide valves)

During the Second World War there was a need for a powerful shunting engine for war work. The Hunslet Engine Company designed the engines to the specification of Riddles in the Ministry of Supply. Between 1943 and 1946 several hundred of these powerful and useful engines were built by a number of private builders (Hudswell-Clarke, Bagnall, Stephenson & Hawthorn, Hunslet, Barclay and Vulcan Foundry).

At the end of the war many of the engines were sold out of service to collieries and other industrial concerns, and seventy-five were purchased by the LNER. These were classified 'J94'.

Some slightly more powerful engines were built in 1950-1953 with 4' 0" wheels and with the boiler pressure increased to 180psi. These could be found at work at industrial premises all over the country.

All the 'J94's came into BR stock in 1948, and the last two engines (68006 and 68012) survived until 1967, when they were withdrawn on the closure of the Cromford and High Peak railway. Many of the class later acquired hopper type bunkers.

A number of the class were sold out of service for further use in industry. These were: 68020 (scrapped March 1970), 68050 (February 1966), 68067 (June 1972), 68070 (September 1969), 68077 and 68078 (both preserved).

The design proved ideal for use on preserved lines. Apart from the two ex-BR engines which have been preserved, a total of about fifty engines are now working on preserved lines in this country. This makes them by far the largest class in preservation.

Year End Totals: 'J94' class

'47	'48	'49	'50	'51	'52	'53	'54	'55	'56	'57	'58	'59	'60	'61	'62	'63	'64	'65	'66	'67
75	75	75	75	75	75	75	75	75	75	75	75	75	69	66	45	24	13	3	2	

Number	*Built*	*Renumbered*	*BR Dates*	*Scrap*	*Notes*
68006	01/44 HC	06/49 8006	-05/67	10/67	
68007	02/44 HC	11/49 8007	-10/62	11/62	
68008	02/44 HE	09/49 8008	-12/63	02/64	
68009	03/44 HE	06/48 8009	-07/62	07/62	
68010	05/44 HE	01/49 8010	-05/65	10/65	
68011	05/44 HE	10/49 8011	-05/65	10/65	
68012	06/44 HE	05/51 8012	-10/67	02/68	
68013	06/44 HE	11/50 8013	-09/64	11/64	
68014	09/44 HE	10/48 8014	-10/64	01/65	
68015	10/44 HE	11/48 8015	-08/63	09/63	
68016	12/44 HE	12/48 8016	-05/64	09/64	
68017	12/44 HE	07/49 8017	-11/62	12/62	
68018	05/44 WB	11/48 8018	-08/62	09/62	
68019	06/44 WB	09/49 8019	-10/64	01/65	
68020	09/44 WB	10/48 8020	-07/63	03/70	
68021	04/44 RSH	10/49 8021	-10/63	01/64	
68022	04/44 RSH	10/48 8022	-09/60	09/60	
68023	06/44 RSH	07/49 8023	-05/65	10/65	
68024	09/44 RSH	11/49 8024	-01/64	02/64	
68025	11/44 HC	11/49 8025	-10/63	01/64	
68026	04/45 HC	09/48 8026	-03/61	05/61	
68027	02/45 HE	04/49 8027	-12/60	04/61	
68028	04/45 HE	01/49 8028	-09/60	11/60	
68029	05/45 HE	11/49 8029	-09/63	10/63	
68030	05/45 HE	11/48 8030	-04/62	10/62	
68031	02/45 RSH	01/50 8031	-02/63	05/63	
68032	04/45 RSH	11/49 8032	-05/64	09/64	
68033	06/45 VF	09/48 8033	-10/60	04/61	
68034	06/45 VF	06/48 8034	-11/62	06/63	
68035	07/45 VF	03/49 8035	-10/63	01/64	
68036	07/45 VF	06/49 8036	-05/64	09/64	
68037	07/45 VF	01/49 8037	-05/65	10/65	
68038	07/45 VF	05/49 8038	-11/63	02/64	
68039	07/45 VF	02/49 8039	-10/63	03/64	
68040	07/45 VF	01/50 8040	-10/63	10/63	
68041	07/45 VF	02/50 8041	-10/63	01/64	
68042	07/45 VF	09/49 8042	-12/63	02/64	
68043	07/45 VF	05/49 8043	-05/65	10/65	
68044	08/45 VF	09/49 8044	-11/62	05/63	
68045	08/45 VF	10/49 8045	-09/63	10/63	
68046	08/45 VF	12/49 8046	-06/64	09/64	
68047	07/45 WB	09/49 8047	-05/65	10/65	
68048	07/45 WB	12/49 8048	-10/62	05/63	
68049	08/45 WB	03/50 8049	-09/63	10/63	
68050	08/45 WB	09/49 8050	-12/64	02/66	
68051	09/45 WB	09/48 8051	-06/64	09/64	
68052	09/45 WB	10/49 8052	-06/62	07/62	
68053	10/45 WB	12/49 8053	-05/65	10/65	
68054	11/45 WB	03/50 8054	-06/64	09/64	
68055	12/45 WB	05/50 8055	-07/62	05/63	
68056	12/45 WB	01/50 8056	-10/62	05/63	
68057	12/45 WB	12/49 8057	-06/62	10/62	
68058	02/46 WB	04/49 8058	-11/62	05/63	

Number	Built		Renumbered		BR Dates	Scrap	Notes
68059	02/46	WB	10/49	8059	-12/63	02/64	
68060	09/45	HC	12/49	8060	-05/65	10/65	
68061	10/45	HC	06/49	8061	-12/63	02/64	
68062	10/45	HC	09/49	8062	-05/65	10/65	
68063	10/45	HC	06/49	8063	-01/62	05/62	
68064	11/45	HC	07/48	8064	-02/62	04/62	
68065	12/45	HC	06/49	8065	-12/62	08/63	
68066	12/45	HC	02/50	8066	-12/62	08/63	
68067	01/46	HC	01/49	8067	-02/63	06/72	
68068	02/46	HC	03/48	8068	-06/65	04/66	
68069	02/46	HC	12/48	8069	-09/62	12/62	
68070	09/45	RSH	05/48	8070	-03/63	09/69	
68071	06/45	AB	02/49	8071	-08/63	08/63	
68072	07/45	AB	03/49	8072	-09/60	03/61	
68073	10/45	AB	07/48	8073	-08/61	10/61	
68074	12/45	AB	07/50	8074	-10/62	11/62	
68075	03/46	AB	08/48	8075	-12/62	05/63	
68076	04/46	AB	01/49	8076	-09/60	09/60	
68077 §	01/47	AB	08/49	8077	-12/62		
68078 §	07/46	AB	08/49	8078	-03/63		
68079	09/46	AB	10/50	8079	-10/66	02/67	
68080	11/46	AB	03/49	8080	-04/61	06/61	

Y5 68081
0-4-0ST GER

Power Classification: Not classified
Introduced: 1874-1903
Designer: Neilson & Co.
Company: GER
Weight: 21t 4cwt
Driving Wheel: 3' 7"
Boiler Pressure: 140psi
Cylinders: Outside 12" x 20"
Tractive Effort: 7970lbf
Valve Gear: Stephenson (slide valves)

This engine was the last survivor of eight engines built in 1874-1903 for the GER as the GER '209' class. The other engines were withdrawn in 1911-1931, but No. 7230, one of the 1903 engines, was retained for departmental duties at Stratford works.

The engine had an unusual 'ogee'-shaped saddle tank, and the coal bunker straddled the boiler behind the saddle tank, instead of in the more usual position behind the cab. It was scrapped in 1948 as 8081.

Another member of the class, GER No. 229 was sold to the Admiralty in 1917. After a period in industrial service it has been preserved.

Year End Totals: 'Y5' (service) class

'47	'48	'49	'50	'51	'52	'53	'54	'55	'56	'57	'58	'59	'60	'61	'62	'63	'64	'65	'66	'67
1																				

Number	Built		Renumbered		BR Dates	Scrap	Notes
68081	03/03	Str		8081	-04/48	*48*	

Y6 68082-68083
0-4-0T GER Tram

Power Classification: 0F
Introduced: 1883-1897
Designer: T W Worsdell
Company: GER
Weight: 21t 5cwt
Driving Wheel: 3' 1"
Boiler Pressure: 140psi
Cylinders: Inside 11" x 15"
Tractive Effort: 5835lbf
Valve Gear: Stephenson (slide valves)

Roadside tramways like the Wisbech & Upwell Tramway usually had special engines for working their services. They were totally enclosed by a canopy which gave them the appearance of brake vans, and they were fitted with side shields covering the wheels to avoid frightening horses. The GER had three classes of tram engines on its books, the 'Y6' 0-4-0T, the 'J70' 0-6-0T and the slightly different 'Y10' double-ended super-Sentinel class.

The 'Y6' class originally consisted of ten engines built in 1883-1897 for the Wisbech & Upwell Tramway. They were known as the GER class 'G15' and the first engine was withdrawn in 1907. Two engines came into BR stock and they had both gone by 1952.

Year End Totals: 'Y6' class

'47	'48	'49	'50	'51	'52	'53	'54	'55	'56	'57	'58	'59	'60	'61	'62	'63	'64	'65	'66	'67
2	2	2	2	1																

Number	Built		Renumbered		BR Dates	Scrap	Notes
68082	08/97	Str	07/48	8082	-05/51	05/51	
68083	08/97	Str	03/50	8083	-11/52	*10/53*	

Y7 68088-68089, 34
0-4-0T NER Worsdell

Power Classification: 0F
Introduced: 1888-1923
Designer: T W Worsdell
Company: NER
Weight: 22t 14cwt
Driving Wheel: 3' 6¼"
Boiler Pressure: 140psi
Cylinders: Inside 14" x 20"
Tractive Effort: 11040lbf
Valve Gear: Stephenson (slide valves)

Worsdell built nineteen of these small tank engines for the NER in 1888 and 1897, and a further five engines were added to the class in 1923. They had fully enclosed cabs and the cab roof overhung the back of the engine. They were the NER class 'H'.

The first engine was withdrawn in 1929 and two engines came into BR stock in 1948. 68088 was a departmental engine at Stratford Works (allocated the number 34 in 1952, but withdrawn without being renumbered). 68089 worked the last passenger trains on the North Sunderland Railway.

Both engines were sold out of service in 1952. 68089 was sold to a firm of contractors for constructional work on Morecambe promenade. It was finally scrapped in December 1955. 68088 has now been preserved. In addition NER no. 1310 (which was sold out of service in 1931) has also been preserved.

Year End Totals: 'Y7' class

'47	'48	'49	'50	'51	'52	'53	'54	'55	'56	'57	'58	'59	'60	'61	'62	'63	'64	'65	'66	'67
2	1	1	1	1																

Year End Totals: 'Y7' (service) class

'47	'48	'49	'50	'51	'52	'53	'54	'55	'56	'57	'58	'59	'60	'61	'62	'63	'64	'65	'66	'67
	1	1	1	1																

Number	Built		Renumbered		BR Dates	Scrap	Notes
68088 §	10/23	Dar	10/48	8088	-12/52		➲*34*
68089	10/23	Dar	11/48	8089	-01/52	12/55	

Class continued with 34 (Service Locomotives)

Y8 68090-68091, 55
0-4-0T NER Worsdell

Power Classification: 0F reclassified Dock Tank in 1953
Introduced: 1890
Designer: T W Worsdell
Company: NER
Weight: 15t 10cwt
Driving Wheel: 3' 0"
Boiler Pressure: 140psi
Cylinders: Inside 11" x 15"
Tractive Effort: 6000lbf
Valve Gear: Stephenson (slide valves)

Worsdell introduced these dock tanks on the NER in 1890 as a smaller version of the 'Y7' class. They had smaller open backed cabs and marine type boilers. They were the NER class 'K'.

Five engines were built and the first was withdrawn in 1936. Two engines survived to come into BR stock.

68091 was later transferred to departmental stock as No. 55, and it worked as the shed pilot at York.

Year End Totals: 'Y8' class

'47	'48	'49	'50	'51	'52	'53	'54	'55	'56	'57	'58	'59	'60	'61	'62	'63	'64	'65	'66	'67
2	1	1	1	1	1	1														

Year End Totals: 'Y8' (service) class

'47	'48	'49	'50	'51	'52	'53	'54	'55	'56	'57	'58	'59	'60	'61	'62	'63	'64	'65	'66	'67
							1	1												

Number	Built		Renumbered		BR Dates	Scrap	Notes
68090	06/90	Ghd		8090	-11/48	*12/48*	
68091	06/90	Ghd		8091	-07/54	*11/56*	
							07/54➲55

Class continued with 55 (Service Locomotives)

Y9 68092-68124
0-4-0ST NBR Holmes

Power Classification: 0F
Introduced: 1882-1899
Designer: Holmes
Company: NBR
Weight: Loco 27t 16cwt
t Tender 6t 0cwt
Driving Wheel: 3' 8"
Boiler Pressure: 130psi
Cylinders: Outside 14" x 20"
Tractive Effort: 9845lbf
Valve Gear: Stephenson (slide valves)

Both the Caledonian and the North British Railways in Scotland used small 0-4-0STs for dockyard shunting, and shunting in other small yards with tight curvature. Both classes were known as 'Pugs'. The NBR engines were the 'G' class later becoming the LNER 'Y9' class, and the Caledonian engines were the LMS '0F' ('56010') class.

Thirty-eight of these NBR 'Pugs' were built between 1882 and 1899. They could be distinguished from the LMS Pugs by their stovepipe chimneys.

The first engine was withdrawn in 1913. Thirty-three engines came into BR stock in 1948. They were a familiar sight in the docks of the East Coast of Scotland.

t The engines were fitted with open backed cabs and no coal bunkers. As they were limited by the amount of coal they could carry in the cab, these engines were permanently coupled to small four-wheeled wooden tenders (which were converted from ancient wagons), with an extra coal supply.

Year End Totals: 'Y9' class

'47	'48	'49	'50	'51	'52	'53	'54	'55	'56	'57	'58	'59	'60	'61	'62	'63	'64	'65	'66	'67
33	33	33	33	33	33	30	26	19	18	16	11	9	6	4						

Number	Built		Renumbered		BR Dates	Scrap	Notes
68092	82	N	02/49	8092	-03/53	*53*	
68093	82	N	05/48	8093	-05/55	07/55	t
68094	87	Cow	10/48	8094	-04/55	*55*	t
68095 §	87	Cow	08/48	8095	-12/62		
68096	87	Cow		8096	-05/54	*54*	
68097	87	Cow	05/48	8097	-10/58	09/59	
68098	87	Cow	09/51	8098	-12/54	*55*	
68099	89	Cow	11/50	8099	-11/56	*56*	t
68100	89	Cow	06/48	8100	-05/60	*60*	t
68101	89	Cow	01/49	8101	-10/62	03/63	
68102	11/89	Cow	11/51	8102	-12/58	07/59	
68103	12/90	Cow		8103	-06/54	10/54	t
68104	11/90	Cow	06/49	8104	-10/62	09/63	
68105	11/90	Cow	05/48	8105	-04/55	07/55	
68106	11/90	Cow	12/50	8106	-08/57	09/57	t
68107	12/90	Cow	11/50	8107	-12/53	01/54	t
68108	12/90	Cow	11/52	8108	-11/59	02/60	t
68109	06/91	Cow		8109	-04/54	*54*	t
68110	06/91	Cow	*52*	8110	-08/61	11/61	
68111	01/91	Cow	03/48	8111	-03/53	*06/53*	
68112	01/91	Cow	11/51	8112	-01/55	02/55	t
68113	11/97	Cow	11/48	8113	-01/58	03/58	
68114	11/97	Cow	11/48	8114	-09/60	11/60	t
68115	11/97	Cow	03/51	8115	-07/57	09/57	
68116	11/97	Cow	01/49	8116	-02/58	04/58	t
68117	12/97	Cow	04/48	8117	-07/62	10/62	t
68118	12/97	Cow	07/48	8118	-10/58	09/59	t
68119	06/99	Cow	01/51	8119	-10/61	03/63	t
68120	07/99	Cow	07/49	8120	-08/55	*08/55*	t
68121	07/99	Cow	12/43	8121	-07/55	*55*	t
68122	08/99	Cow	04/51	8122	-08/55	09/55	t
68123	08/99	Cow	03/50	8123	-08/60	04/61	
68124	09/99	Cow	02/54	8124	-09/59	11/59	

Y4 68125-68129, 33
0-4-0T GER Hill

Power Classification: 0F
Introduced: 1913-1921
Designer: Hill
Company: GER
Weight: 38t 0cwt
Driving Wheel: 3' 10"
Boiler Pressure: 180psi
Cylinders: Outside 17" x 20"
Tractive Effort: 19225lbf
Valve Gear: Walschaert (slide valves)

Hill built these five squat little dock tanks at Stratford in two batches in 1913 and 1921. They were the GER 'B74'/'B77' class and later the LNER 'Y4' class.

The engines had Belpaire boilers and Walschaert valve gear. They latterly had shorter chimneys and coal rails fitted on top of the tanks in front of the cab (no coal bunkers being fitted behind the cab).

68129 worked as a departmental engine at Stratford Works. It was renumbered 33 in the departmental list in 1952 and outlived the rest of the class by several years. It latterly acquired a GNR type chimney.

Year End Totals: 'Y4' class

'47	'48	'49	'50	'51	'52	'53	'54	'55	'56	'57	'58	'59	'60	'61	'62	'63	'64	'65	'66	'67
4	4	4	4	4	4	4	4	3	1											

Year End Totals: 'Y4' (service) class

'47	'48	'49	'50	'51	'52	'53	'54	'55	'56	'57	'58	'59	'60	'61	'62	'63	'64	'65	'66	'67
1	1	1	1	1	1	1	1	1	1	1	1	1	1	1	1					

Number	Built	Renumbered	BR Dates	Scrap	Notes
68125	11/13 Str	11/49 8125	-09/55	*55*	
68126	10/14 Str	06/49 8126	-10/57	*57*	
68127	09/14 Str	05/49 8127	-04/56	*56*	
68128	01/21 Str	12/49 8128	-09/56	*01/57*	
68129	01/21 Str	01/49 8129	-09/52	*64*	
					09/52➔33

Class continued with 33 (Service Locomotives)

Y1 68130-68153, 4, 6, 37, 39, 51-54
0-4-0T LNER Sentinel Single-speed gearbox

Power Classification:	Unclassified
Introduced:	1925-1933
Designer:	Sentinel Co.
Company:	LNER
Weight:	1 20t 17cwt 2 19t 16cwt 3 14t 0cwt 4 19t 7cwt
Driving Wheel:	2' 6"
Boiler Pressure:	275psi superheated
Cylinders:	Inside 6¾" x 9"
Tractive Effort:	7260lbf g 8870lbf
Valve Gear:	Sentinel (poppet valves)

The Sentinel Company specialised in building small geared steam locomotives, mainly for use in industry. The engines used high pressure boilers with chain or geared transmission to the wheels.

The 'Y1' class was first introduced by the LNER in 1925, with the first engines intended for use in Lowestoft Harbour. They were fitted with single-speed gears compared to the 'Y3' class which had two-speed gears. They were very similar in their box-like appearance to the 'Y3' class and the LMS Sentinel ('47180') class of Sentinel shunters.

Many engines were used as service locomotives at various locations (including 68134 and 68135 which were never renumbered into service stock). Their small size made them ideal for this type of duty. 68131 retained its original number 7773 until August 1951 when it was renumbered 8131.

The class was split into several parts which differed in such details as the size of the boilers and the fuel capacity.

1 'Y1/1' class built 1925-1933.

2 'Y1/2' class built 1927-1929.

3 'Y1/3' class built 1926.

4 'Y1/4' class built 1927.

g These engines had a sprocket gear ratio of 9:25. The remainder had a ratio of 11:25.

The body section of 68149 remained in use as a hut in Darlington scrapyard until the 1960s.

Year End Totals: 'Y1' class

'47	'48	'49	'50	'51	'52	'53	'54	'55	'56	'57	'58	'59	'60	'61	'62	'63	'64	'65	'66	'67
15	15	15	15	14	12	11	6	5	5	3	2									

Year End Totals: 'Y1' (service) class

'47	'48	'49	'50	'51	'52	'53	'54	'55	'56	'57	'58	'59	'60	'61	'62	'63	'64	'65	'66	'67
9	7	7	7	7	7	7	7	6	4	4	4	2	2	1	1					

Number	Built	Renumbered	BR Dates	Scrap	Notes
68130	09/25 S	8130	-05/53	*56*	1
					05/53➔37
68131	12/26 S	7773/8131	-08/53	*63*	1
					08/53➔39
68132	10/26 S	05/48 8132	-12/52	*59*	1
					12/52➔4
68133	10/26 S	06/48 8133	-03/53	*55*	1
					03/53➔6
68134	10/26 S	8134	-02/48	04/48	1
68135	08/27 S	8135	-09/48	09/48	1
68136	08/27 S	11/52 8136	-11/52	*56*	4
					11/52➔51
68137	12/27 S	8137	-12/53	01/54	2
68138	12/27 S	09/52 8138	-01/59	*01/59*	2
68139	01/29 S	8139	-09/51	*51*	3
68140	07/29 S	05/48 8140	-05/54	*06/54*	2
68141	07/29 S	10/48 8141	-02/52	*52*	2
68142	07/29 S	05/52 8142	-05/57	*57*	2
68143	07/29 S	8143	-05/54	*54*	2g
68144	07/29 S	11/51 8144	-11/54	*54*	2g
68145	07/29 S	07/52 8145	-01/57	*57*	2g
68146	07/29 S	04/48 8146	-04/54	*54*	2g
68147	08/29 S	8147	-02/52	*52*	2g
68148	08/29 S	08/51 8148	-12/55	*56*	2g
68149	08/29 S	08/53 8149	-01/58	*01/58*	2g
68150	08/29 S	07/48 8150	-05/59	*59*	2g
68151	08/29 S	05/51 8151	-11/54	*54*	2g
68152	09/30 S	05/51 8152	-04/54	03/59	1
					04/54➔53
68153 §	12/33 S	05/51 8153	-10/54		2
					10/54➔54

Class continued with 4 (Service Locomotives)

Y3 68154-68185, 3, 5, 7-8, 21, 38, 40-42, 57
0-4-0T LNER Sentinel Two-speed gearbox

Power Classification:	Unclassified
Introduced:	1927-1931
Designer:	Sentinel Co.
Company:	LNER
Weight:	20t 16cwt
Driving Wheel:	2' 6"
Boiler Pressure:	275psi superheated
Cylinders:	Inside 6¾" x 9"
Tractive Effort:	High Gear 4705lbf, Low Gear 12600lbf g High Gear 5960lbf, Low Gear 15960lbf
Valve Gear:	Sentinel (poppet valves)

The 'Y3' Sentinel class was first introduced by the LNER in 1927, designed for light dock shunting. They were fitted with two speed gears allowing top speeds of 10mph and 27mph. They were very similar in their box-like appearance to the 'Y1' class and the LMS Sentinel ('47180') class of Sentinel shunters.

Many engines (including 68167 which was never renumbered into service stock) were used as service locomotives at various places on the LNER system (including several based at Lowestoft). Their small size made them ideal for this type of duty.

g These engines had a sprocket gear ratio of 15:19. The remainder had a ratio of 19:19.

68159 and 68179 were sold for further industrial use. They were scrapped in 1962 and May 1956 respectively.

The body section of 68180 remained in use as a hut in Darlington scrapyard until the 1960s.

Year End Totals: 'Y3' class

'47	'48	'49	'50	'51	'52	'53	'54	'55	'56	'57	'58	'59	'60	'61	'62	'63	'64	'65	'66	'67
28	26	25	24	18	17	13	11	6	3	1										

Year End Totals: 'Y3' (service) class

'47	'48	'49	'50	'51	'52	'53	'54	'55	'56	'57	'58	'59	'60	'61	'62	'63	'64	'65	'66	'67
3	5	5	6	7	7	7	7	8	10	10	9	6	4	3	3	2				

Number	Built	Renumbered	BR Dates	Scrap	Notes
68154	12/27 S	8154	-10/53	*53*	
68155	12/27 S	01/49 8155	-08/55	09/55	
68156	08/29 S	06/49 8156	-06/54	*54*	
68157	08/29 S	8157	-12/52	*53*	
68158	08/29 S	03/52 8158	-09/55	*55*	
68159	08/29 S	07/49 8159	-03/57	62	
68160	08/29 S	02/49 8160	-11/56	*61*	
					11/56➔57
68161	08/29 S	8161	-08/53	*53*	
68162	09/30 S	01/50 8162	-01/56	*60*	
					01/56➔21
68163	09/30 S	06/49 8163	-05/51	*51*	
68164	09/30 S	06/49 8164	-09/57	*57*	
68165	09/30 S	05/48 8165	-03/53	*58*	
					03/53➔5
68166	09/30 S	08/48 8166	-03/53	*64*	
					03/53➔7
68167	09/30 S	8167	-11/49	*49*	
68168	09/30 S	8168	-05/53	*59*	
					05/53➔38
68169	09/30 S	09/49 8169	-07/55	*55*	
68171	09/30 S	04/48 8171	-11/51	*51*	
68172	10/30 S	8172	-12/51	*52*	
68173	10/30 S	8173	-05/53	*64*	
					05/53➔40
68174	10/30 S	03/52 8174	-03/53	*53*	
68175	10/30 S	8175	-08/51	*51*	
68176	10/30 S	8176	-08/53	*53*	
68177	10/30 S	8177	-05/53	*63*	
					05/53➔41
68178	10/30 S	8178	-03/53	*60*	
					03/53➔42
68179	10/30 S	12/48 8179	-12/51	05/56	
68180	04/31 S	04/49 8180	-05/56	*06/56*	g
68181	04/31 S	06/51 8181	-12/52	*59*	g
					12/52➔3
68182	04/31 S	08/49 8182	-01/58	*58*	g
68183	05/31 S	09/51 8183	-09/55	*59*	g
					09/55➔8
68184	05/31 S	01/49 8184	-11/54	*54*	
68185	12/31 S	01/51 8185	-04/55	*55*	

Class continued with 3 (Service Locomotives)

Y10 68186-68187
0-4-0T LNER Sentinel Tram

Power Classification:	Unclassified
Introduced:	1930
Designer:	Sentinel Co.
Company:	LNER
Weight:	23t 19cwt
Driving Wheel:	3' 2"
Boiler Pressure:	275psi superheated
Cylinders:	Inside 6¾" x 9"
Tractive Effort:	High Gear 7965lbf, Low Gear 11435lbf
Valve Gear:	Sentinel (poppet valves)

In 1930 the LNER purchased two double-ended super-Sentinel engines to work on the Wisbech and Upwell Tramway. They were fitted with two-speed gear boxes. They were designed as tram locomotives with the wheels and motion covered in. They were of a completely different outline to the 'Y1' and 'Y3' classes and they had a cab at each end.

The engines later worked on the Yarmouth quayside lines. Neither of these engines received its BR number. However a photograph does exist of 68186 in which the BR number was carefully chalked on the engine by the photographer!

Year End Totals: 'Y10' class

'47	'48	'49	'50	'51	'52	'53	'54	'55	'56	'57	'58	'59	'60	'61	'62	'63	'64	'65	'66	'67
2	1	1	1	1																

Number	Built	Renumbered	BR Dates	Scrap	Notes
68186	06/30 S	8186	-02/52	*52*	
68187	06/30 S	8187	-08/48	*48*	

Y11 68188-68189
0-4-0P LNER Petrol Shunter

These petrol locomotives are only included in the lists because they carried numbers in the main steam locomotive number series. They were both renumbered into the correct series in 1949.

Number	Built	Renumbered	BR Dates	Notes
68188		8188	-02/49	02/49➔15098
68189		12/48 8189	-02/49	05/49➔15099

Z4 68190-68191
0-4-2T GNoSR Aberdeen Harbour shunters

Power Classification:	0F
Introduced:	1915
Designer:	Manning Wardle
Company:	GNoSR
Weight:	25t 17cwt
Driving Wheel:	3' 6"
Boiler Pressure:	160psi
Cylinders:	Outside 13" x 20"
Tractive Effort:	10945lbf
Valve Gear:	Stephenson (slide valves)

The GNoSR bought four 0-4-2T engines from Manning Wardle (to Heywood's design) in 1915 for shunting duties at Aberdeen Docks. Two engines were classified 'X' (LNER 'Z4') and two classified 'Y' (LNER 'Z5').

The 'Z4's were smaller engines with 3' 6" wheels and 13" x 20" cylinders.

Year End Totals: 'Z4' class

'47	'48	'49	'50	'51	'52	'53	'54	'55	'56	'57	'58	'59	'60	'61	'62	'63	'64	'65	'66	'67
2	2	2	2	2	2	2	2	2	2	2	2	1								

Number	*Built*	*Renumbered*	*BR Dates*	*Scrap*	*Notes*
68190	08/15 MW	06/48 8190	-05/60	*60*	
68191	08/15 MW	08/48 8191	-03/59	*59*	

Z5 68192-68193
0-4-2T GNoSR Aberdeen Harbour Shunters

Power Classification: 0F
Introduced: 1915
Designer: Manning Wardle
Company: GNoSR
Weight: 30t 18cwt
Driving Wheel: 4' 0"
Boiler Pressure: 160psi
Cylinders: Outside 14" x 20"
Tractive Effort: 11105lbf
Valve Gear: Stephenson (slide valves)

The 'Z5's were the larger of the Aberdeen Docks engines with 4' 0" wheels and 14" x 20" cylinders.

Year End Totals: 'Z5' class

'47	'48	'49	'50	'51	'52	'53	'54	'55	'56	'57	'58	'59	'60	'61	'62	'63	'64	'65	'66	'67
2	2	2	2	2	2	2	2	2	1	1	1	1								

Number	*Built*	*Renumbered*	*BR Dates*	*Scrap*	*Notes*
68192	01/15 MW	11/48 8192	-05/60	*60*	
68193	01/15 MW	04/49 8193	-04/56	*56*	

J62 68200-68203
0-6-0ST GCR Pollitt

Power Classification: 0F
Introduced: 1897
Designer: Pollitt
Company: GCR
Weight: 30t 17cwt
Driving Wheel: 3' 6"
Boiler Pressure: 150psi
Cylinders: Outside 13" x 20"
Tractive Effort: 10260lbf
Valve Gear: Stephenson (slide valves)

Pollitt built twelve of these 0-6-0ST engines in 1897 for the GCR as the GCR class '5'. The first engine was withdrawn in 1935. Three engines came into BR stock in 1948, and they had all been withdrawn by 1951. The 'J63' class was developed in 1906 as a side tank version of this class.

Year End Totals: 'J62' class

'47	'48	'49	'50	'51	'52	'53	'54	'55	'56	'57	'58	'59	'60	'61	'62	'63	'64	'65	'66	'67
3	3	1	1																	

Number	*Built*	*Renumbered*	*BR Dates*	*Scrap*	*Notes*
68200	02/97 Gor	06/49 8200	-11/51	*11/51*	
68201	03/97 Gor	8201	-01/49	*49*	
68203	07/97 Gor	8203	-02/49	*49*	

J63 68204-68210
0-6-0T GCR Robinson

Power Classification: 0F
Introduced: 1906-1914
Designer: Robinson
Company: GCR
Weight: 37t 9cwt
Driving Wheel: 3' 6"
Boiler Pressure: 150psi
Cylinders: Outside 13" x 20"
Tractive Effort: 10260lbf
Valve Gear: Stephenson (slide valves)

Robinson built seven engines of this class of 0-6-0Ts in 1906-1914 for shunting in Immingham docks. They were a side tank version of the 'J62' 0-6-0STs, and were GCR class '5A'. The first two engines were originally fitted with condensing apparatus, but this was later removed.

Year End Totals: 'J63' class

'47	'48	'49	'50	'51	'52	'53	'54	'55	'56	'57	'58	'59	'60	'61	'62	'63	'64	'65	'66	'67
7	7	7	7	7	7	6	6	4	1											

Number	*Built*	*Renumbered*	*BR Dates*	*Scrap*	*Notes*
68204	08/06 Gor	11/48 8204	-04/56	*56*	
68205	08/06 Gor	06/48 8205	-04/56	*56*	
68206	10/06 Gor	07/48 8206	-03/55	*55*	
68207	10/06 Gor	10/49 8207	-04/56	*56*	
68208	11/06 Gor	10/48 8208	-09/53	*53*	
68209	11/06 Gor	04/49 8209	-01/55	*02/55*	
68210	06/14 Gor	12/49 8210	-02/57	*57*	

J65 68211-68215
0-6-0T GER Holden

Power Classification: 0F
Introduced: 1889-1893
Designer: J Holden
Company: GER
Weight: 36t 11cwt
Driving Wheel: 4' 0"
Boiler Pressure: 160psi
Cylinders: Inside 14" x 20"
Tractive Effort: 11105lbf
Valve Gear: Stephenson (slide valves)

Refer to the Historical Survey of Great Eastern 0-6-0T Engines at the end of this section for more details of this class.

The 'J65's were the smallest variety of GER 0-6-0s. Twenty engines were built in 1889-1893 as the GER class 'E22'. The first engine was withdrawn in 1930 and four came into BR stock in 1948.

Year End Totals: 'J65' class

'47	'48	'49	'50	'51	'52	'53	'54	'55	'56	'57	'58	'59	'60	'61	'62	'63	'64	'65	'66	'67
4	3	2	2	2	2	1	1	1												

Number	*Built*	*Renumbered*	*BR Dates*	*Scrap*	*Notes*
68211	02/89 Str	02/51 8211	-11/53	*53*	
68213	02/93 Str	8213	-02/48	*48*	
68214	03/93 Str	08/51 8214	-08/56	*01/57*	
68215	04/93 Str	8215	-05/49	07/49	

J70 68216-68226
0-6-0T GER Tram

Power Classification: 0F
Introduced: 1903-1921
Designer: J Holden
Company: GER
Weight: 27t 1cwt
Driving Wheel: 3' 1"
Boiler Pressure: 180psi
Cylinders: Outside 12" x 15"
Tractive Effort: 8930lbf
Valve Gear: Walschaert (slide valves)

The 'J70's were 0-6-0T tram engines with outside cylinders. They were the GER 'C53' class. Twelve were built in 1903-1921 for the Wisbech & Upwell Tramway and for Yarmouth and Ipswich quayside duties. The engines on the Wisbech & Upwell Tramway were fitted with cow-catchers and side shields over the wheels. They were similar in appearance to the smaller 'Y6' 0-4-0T tram engines.

One engine was scrapped in 1942, the rest came into BR stock in 1948.

Year End Totals: 'J70' class

'47	'48	'49	'50	'51	'52	'53	'54	'55	'56	'57	'58	'59	'60	'61	'62	'63	'64	'65	'66	'67
11	11	10	10	9	8	4	4													

Number	*Built*	*Renumbered*	*BR Dates*	*Scrap*	*Notes*
68216	10/03 Str	02/49 8216	-11/53	*53*	
68217	11/03 Str	09/49 8217	-03/53	*53*	
68218	09/08 Str	8218	-09/49	*10/49*	
68219	10/08 Str	11/50 8219	-08/53	*10/53*	
68220	04/10 Str	06/50 8220	-02/53	53	
68221	06/14 Str	08/48 8221	-05/51	05/51	
68222	06/14 Str	03/49 8222	-01/55	*55*	
68223	06/14 Str	08/49 8223	-07/55	08/55	
68224	03/21 Str	03/50 8224	-03/52	06/52	
68225	03/21 Str	05/50 8225	-03/55	*55*	
68226	03/21 Str	05/48 8226	-08/55	08/55	

J71 68230-68316
0-6-0T NER Worsdell

Power Classification: 0F changed to Unclassified in 1953
Introduced: 1886-1895
Designer: T W Worsdell
Company: NER
Weight: 37t 12cwt
Driving Wheel: 4' 7¼"
Boiler Pressure: 140psi
Cylinders: Inside 16" x 22"
b Inside 18" x 22"
c Inside 16¾" x 22"
Tractive Effort: 12130lbf
b 15355lbf
c 13300lbf
Valve Gear: Stephenson (slide valves)

Worsdell built this class of 120 0-6-0T engines for the NER in 1886-1895. Known as NER class 'E' they were built for light freight and for station shunting (for which some engines were fitted with Westinghouse brakes, and later dual fitted).

The 'J72' class was developed from the 'J71' class in 1898 with smaller wheels.

The first engine was withdrawn in 1933. Eighty-one engines survived to come into BR stock and some of them lasted until 1961.

bc Alterations were made to the cylinder dimensions on some engines of this class.

Year End Totals: 'J71' class

'47	'48	'49	'50	'51	'52	'53	'54	'55	'56	'57	'58	'59	'60	'61	'62	'63	'64	'65	'66	'67
81	80	80	76	71	67	64	58	49	39	30	23	14	4							

Number	*Built*	*Renumbered*	*BR Dates*	*Scrap*	*Notes*
68230	11/86 Dar	10/51 8230	-01/60	02/60	c
68231	12/86 Dar	8231	-07/51	*51*	
68232	01/87 Dar	05/49 8232	-02/57	03/57	
68233	02/87 Dar	09/48 8233	-03/61	03/61	
68234	02/87 Dar	10/50 8234	-08/54	*08/54*	c
68235	04/87 Dar	04/48 8235	-11/60	11/60	
68236	04/87 Dar	03/50 8236	-11/55	*55*	
68238	05/87 Dar	06/50 8238	-09/55	09/55	
68239	06/87 Dar	03/52 8239	-11/56	*01/57*	
68240	06/87 Dar	06/48 8240	-09/56	10/56	
68242	05/88 Dar	11/49 8242	-08/58	08/58	
68243	05/88 Dar	09/49 8243	-03/50	*50*	
68244	06/88 Dar	01/51 8244	-04/58	04/58	
68245	06/88 Dar	11/48 8245	-04/59	05/59	
68246	07/89 Dar	04/49 8246	-11/58	11/58	c
68247	07/89 Dar	8247	-08/51	*51*	
68248	08/89 Dar	04/48 8248	-06/51	*51*	
68249	08/89 Dar	8249	-01/53	*53*	
68250	09/89 Dar	04/48 8250	-04/59	04/59	c
68251	09/89 Dar	11/51 8251	-01/59	04/59	
68252	05/90 Dar	12/50 8252	-04/57	04/57	c
68253	05/90 Dar	08/50 8253	-09/57	10/57	c
68254	06/90 Dar	10/51 8254	-11/60	11/60	
68255	06/90 Dar	01/49 8255	-08/52	*52*	
68256	06/90 Dar	06/48 8256	-07/54	*07/54*	
68258	07/90 Dar	05/51 8258	-11/54	*11/54*	c
68259	07/90 Dar	12/49 8259	-09/55	*55*	c
68260	07/90 Dar	02/49 8260	-03/60	03/60	
68262	09/90 Dar	07/48 8262	-01/60	02/60	
68263	09/90 Dar	06/49 8263	-05/59	07/59	
68264	09/90 Dar	12/48 8264	-01/60	02/60	
68265	09/90 Dar	03/49 8265	-08/59	09/59	
68266	09/90 Dar	11/49 8266	-02/57	03/57	
68267	09/90 Dar	09/50 8267	-11/57	01/58	
68268	10/90 Dar	08/49 8268	-05/52	*52*	
68269	10/90 Dar	09/50 8269	-10/60	10/60	
68270	11/91 Dar	03/50 8270	-11/55	*55*	
68271	11/91 Dar	10/48 8271	-05/54	*54*	
68272	11/91 Dar	12/51 8272	-02/61	03/61	
68273	11/91 Dar	09/50 8273	-11/57	01/58	
68275	01/92 Dar	12/48 8275	-01/61	03/61	
68276	01/92 Dar	09/48 8276	-11/56	*01/57*	
68277	01/92 Dar	8277	-11/50	*50*	
68278	02/92 Dar	04/48 8278	-01/61	03/61	
68279	02/92 Dar	03/51 8279	-06/57	06/57	
68280	02/92 Dar	02/50 8280	-05/57	05/57	c
68281	02/92 Dar	07/50 8281	-11/53	12/53	
68282	02/92 Dar	11/50 8282	-10/53	*53*	
68283	03/92 Dar	09/48 8283	-07/59	08/59	
68284	03/92 Dar	08/50 8284	-10/55	*55*	
68285	03/92 Dar	8285	-10/48	10/48	
68286	07/92 Dar	01/50 8286	-06/52	*07/52*	c
68287	07/92 Dar	01/50 8287	-11/56	*01/57*	c
68288	07/92 Dar	8288	-11/50	*50*	
68289	07/92 Dar	10/50 8289	-06/55	*55*	c
68290	07/92 Dar	04/48 8290	-01/59	02/59	
68291	08/92 Dar	07/48 8291	-04/56	05/56	

68292	08/92 Dar	01/49 8292	-10/54	10/54	
68293	11/92 Dar	06/49 8293	-09/56	10/56	c
68294	11/92 Dar	06/49 8294	-11/56	01/57	
68295	11/92 Dar	11/48 8295	-02/59	03/59	
68296	11/92 Dar	08/49 8296	-06/58	07/58	
68297	01/93 Dar	09/50 8297	-05/56	06/56	
68298	01/93 Dar	08/51 8298	-03/57	57	
68299	01/93 Dar	10/49 8299	-12/52	12/52	
68300	01/93 Dar	09/49 8300	-03/55	55	
68301	01/93 Dar	03/49 8301	-11/56	01/57	
68302	11/94 Dar	10/48 8302	-09/51	51	c
68303	11/94 Dar	12/49 8303	-06/55	55	c
68304	12/94 Dar	10/51 8304	-10/54	11/54	c
68305	12/94 Dar	08/48 8305	-11/58	12/58	c
68306	12/94 Dar	12/50 8306	-07/58	08/58	c
68307	12/94 Dar	06/48 8307	-06/55	55	c
68308	12/94 Dar	09/50 8308	-05/58	06/58	c
68309	12/94 Dar	09/48 8309	-05/60	05/60	c
68310	08/95 Dar	8310	-11/50	50	c
68311	09/95 Dar	8311	-08/51	51	c
68312	10/95 Dar	06/51 8312	-02/59	02/59	b
68313	10/95 Dar	11/48 8313	-09/56	10/56	c
68314	10/95 Dar	09/50 8314	-05/60	05/60	
68316	11/95 Dar	02/51 8316	-10/60	10/60	c

J55 68317-68319
0-6-0ST GNR Stirling

Power Classification: 3F
Introduced: 1874-1892
Rebuilt 1912 onwards (these two 1928 and 1934) by Gresley
Designer: P Stirling
Company: GNR
Weight: 45t 16cwt
Driving Wheel: 4' 8"
Boiler Pressure: 175psi
b 160psi
Cylinders: Inside 17½" x 26"
Tractive Effort: 21150lbf
b 19340lbf
Valve Gear: Stephenson (slide valves)

Stirling built 105 0-6-0STs for the GNR between 1874 and 1892, originally with domeless boilers. They were the GNR 'J15' and 'J17' classes (later LNER 'J54' and 'J56' classes). The first engine was withdrawn in 1925.

Most of these engines were rebuilt by Gresley with domed boilers from 1912 onwards. They were the GNR 'J16' class (LNER 'J55' class). The two survivors which came into BR stock were 1891 engines which were rebuilt in 1928 and 1934.

b 68319 was fitted with a lower pressure boiler. It was used as a departmental locomotive at Doncaster Works, but it was withdrawn in 1950 before it could be allocated a number in the service stock number series. It was cut up before it was officially withdrawn.

Year End Totals: 'J55' class

'47	'48	'49	'50	'51	'52	'53	'54	'55	'56	'57	'58	'59	'60	'61	'62	'63	'64	'65	'66	'67
1																				

Year End Totals: 'J55' (service) class

'47	'48	'49	'50	'51	'52	'53	'54	'55	'56	'57	'58	'59	'60	'61	'62	'63	'64	'65	'66	'67
1	1	1																		

Number	Built	Renumbered	BR Dates	Scrap	Notes
68317	03/92 Don	8317	-12/48	49	
68319	12/91 Don	07/48 8319	-12/50	08/50	b

J88 68320-68354
0-6-0T NBR Reid

Power Classification: 0F
Introduced: 1904-1919
Designer: Reid
Company: NBR
Weight: 38t 14cwt
Driving Wheel: 3' 9"
Boiler Pressure: 130psi
Cylinders: Outside 15" x 22"
Tractive Effort: 12155lbf
Valve Gear: Stephenson (slide valves)

Thirty-five of these small 0-6-0Ts were built by Reid for light freight work on the NBR in 1904-1919. They were the NBR class 'F'. They had a short wheelbase of only 11ft and wooden block buffers to prevent the buffers locking. This made them ideal for working in sidings with sharp curves, such as in dockyards.

Some engines were fitted with Drummond boilers with the safety valves on the dome.

s 68345 was later fitted with a stove-pipe chimney.

Year End Totals: 'J88' class

'47	'48	'49	'50	'51	'52	'53	'54	'55	'56	'57	'58	'59	'60	'61	'62	'63	'64	'65	'66	'67
35	35	35	35	35	35	35	34	33	32	31	20	16	10	7						

Number	Built	Renumbered	BR Dates	Scrap	Notes
68320	12/04 Cow	03/50 8320	-06/60	11/60	
68321	12/04 Cow	09/49 8321	-06/58	03/59	
68322	12/04 Cow	04/48 8322	-12/58	02/60	
68323	12/04 Cow	01/50 8323	-10/56	56	
68324	01/05 Cow	06/48 8324	-07/58	03/59	
68325	01/05 Cow	12/50 8325	-05/61	08/61	
68326	09/05 Cow	03/51 8326	-10/59	02/60	
68327	09/05 Cow	07/51 8327	-07/58	08/58	
68328	09/05 Cow	01/52 8328	-03/58	05/58	
68329	10/05 Cow	05/49 8329	-02/59	02/60	
68330	10/05 Cow	04/49 8330	-08/58	09/58	
68331	10/05 Cow	01/49 8331	-03/59	02/60	
68332	03/09 Cow	11/49 8332	-08/60	06/63	
68333	03/09 Cow	05/48 8333	-03/58	05/58	
68334	03/09 Cow	04/49 8334	-06/59	02/60	
68335	03/09 Cow	06/50 8335	-10/62	04/63	
68336	04/09 Cow	03/49 8336	-05/62	09/63	
68337	04/09 Cow	09/51 8337	-11/55	55	
68338	04/12 Cow	07/49 8338	-09/61	03/62	
68339	04/12 Cow	09/51 8339	-10/58	02/60	
68340	05/12 Cow	06/49 8340	-02/58	05/58	
68341	05/12 Cow	03/51 8341	-11/54	54	
68342	05/12 Cow	06/50 8342	-02/62	10/62	
68343	06/12 Cow	09/49 8343	-09/60	12/60	
68344	06/12 Cow	02/50 8344	-01/61	01/62	
68345	07/12 Cow	07/51 8345	-12/62	07/63	s
68346	07/12 Cow	09/48 8346	-10/62	06/63	
68347	07/12 Cow	08/50 8347	-08/58	09/58	
68348	09/19 Cow	11/49 8348	-08/58	02/59	
68349	10/19 Cow	10/50 8349	-08/60	09/60	
68350	11/19 Cow	07/48 8350	-07/62	09/63	
68351	11/19 Cow	02/51 8351	-01/57	02/57	
68352	11/19 Cow	06/48 8352	-06/60	12/60	
68353	10/19 Cow	07/48 8353	-02/62	09/63	
68354	10/19 Cow	03/51 8354	-09/60	11/60	

J73 68355-68364
0-6-0T NER Worsdell

Power Classification: 3F
Introduced: 1891-1892
Designer: W Worsdell
Company: NER
Weight: 46t 15cwt
Driving Wheel: 4' 7¼"
Boiler Pressure: 160psi
Cylinders: Inside 19" x 24"
Tractive Effort: 21320lbf
Valve Gear: Stephenson (slide valves)

Worsdell built ten of these 0-6-0Ts for the NER in 1891-1892 as the NER 'L' class. They were a larger version of the 'J71' class. They were all withdrawn between 1955 and 1960.

Year End Totals: 'J73' class

'47	'48	'49	'50	'51	'52	'53	'54	'55	'56	'57	'58	'59	'60	'61	'62	'63	'64	'65	'66	'67
10	10	10	10	10	10	10	10	9	9	8	5	3								

Number	Built	Renumbered	BR Dates	Scrap	Notes
68355	12/91 Ghd	02/51 8355	-12/58	01/59	
68356	12/91 Ghd	09/48 8356	-08/58	09/58	
68357	03/92 Ghd	08/48 8357	-01/58	02/58	
68358	04/92 Ghd	06/48 8358	-03/55	04/55	
68359	04/92 Ghd	05/49 8359	-12/59	01/60	
68360	05/92 Ghd	07/48 8360	-02/60	03/60	
68361	06/92 Ghd	12/49 8361	-11/60	11/60	
68362	06/92 Ghd	12/50 8362	-09/57	10/57	
68363	06/92 Ghd	09/50 8363	-10/59	11/59	
68364	06/92 Ghd	10/48 8364	-05/60	05/60	

J75 68365
0-6-0T H&BR

Power Classification: 3F
Introduced: 1901-1908
(survivor built 1908)
Designer: M Stirling
Company: H&BR
Weight: 47t 7cwt
Driving Wheel: 4' 6"
Boiler Pressure: 175psi
Cylinders: Inside 18" x 26"
Tractive Effort: 23205lbf
Valve Gear: Stephenson (slide valves)

Stirling built sixteen of these 0-6-0Ts for the Hull & Barnsley Railway in 1901-1908. They were the H&BR class 'G3'. They were originally fitted with domeless boilers, but were later rebuilt with domed boilers. The first engine was withdrawn in 1937. This was the last survivor of the class. In 1948 it was based at Walton-on-the-Hill in Liverpool and it was scrapped in 1949 as 8365.

Year End Totals: 'J75' class

'47	'48	'49	'50	'51	'52	'53	'54	'55	'56	'57	'58	'59	'60	'61	'62	'63	'64	'65	'66	'67
1	1																			

Number	Built	Renumbered	BR Dates	Scrap	Notes
68365	03/08 K	8365	-01/49	49	

J60 68366-68368
0-6-0T Lancashire, Derbyshire & East Coast Railway (GCR)

Power Classification: 1F
Introduced: 1897
Designer: Kitson & Co.
Company: LD&ECR
Weight: 46t 16cwt
Driving Wheel: 4' 7"
Boiler Pressure: 160psi
Cylinders: Inside 17" x 24"
Tractive Effort: 17150lbf
Valve Gear: Stephenson (slide valves)

These two engines were the survivors of four engines built and designed by Kitson & Company in 1897 (the other two engines were withdrawn in 1947). They were built for the Lancashire, Derbyshire & East Coast Railway which was absorbed by the GCR in 1907. They were the GCR class 'B'. Both engines were withdrawn from Wrexham shed and scrapped in 1948 without being renumbered.

Year End Totals: 'J60' class

'47	'48	'49	'50	'51	'52	'53	'54	'55	'56	'57	'58	'59	'60	'61	'62	'63	'64	'65	'66	'67
2																				

Number	Built	Renumbered	BR Dates	Scrap	Notes
68366	02/97 K	8366	-03/48	48	
68368	02/97 K	8368	-08/48	09/48	

J66 68370-68388, Mersey Railway No 3, 31, 32, 36
0-6-0T GER Holden

Power Classification: 2F
Introduced: 1886-1888
Designer: J Holden
Company: GER
Weight: 40t 6cwt
Driving Wheel: 4' 0"
Boiler Pressure: 160psi
Cylinders: Inside 16½" x 22"
Tractive Effort: 16970lbf
Valve Gear: Stephenson (slide valves)

Refer to the Historical Survey of Great Eastern 0-6-0T Engines at the end of this section for more details of this class.

Fifty engines of the 'J66' class were built by Holden in 1886-1888. They were the GER 'T18' class. The first engine was withdrawn in 1936. Twenty engines came into BR stock in 1948, two of which (68370 and Mersey Railway No. 3) were departmental engines. Some engines carried the old type of stove-pipe chimney.

Later on three engines were renumbered into service stock, all working at Stratford Works.

Mersey Railway No. 3 was the only engine on the stock of the Mersey Railway at the time of nationalisation in 1948. It was formerly LNER number 7297 and it was sold to the Mersey Railway in 1939.

Year End Totals: 'J66' class

'47	'48	'49	'50	'51	'52	'53	'54	'55	'56	'57	'58	'59	'60	'61	'62	'63	'64	'65	'66	'67
18	18	18	14	9	3	3	1													

Year End Totals: 'J66' (service) class

'47	'48	'49	'50	'51	'52	'53	'54	'55	'56	'57	'58	'59	'60	'61	'62	'63	'64	'65	'66	'67
2	2	2	1	1	3	3	3	3	3	3	3	1	1	1						

NER Worsdell 'J73' class 0-6-0T No 68361at Darlington in June 1956.

NER Worsdell 'J77' class 0-6-0T No 68429 inside the shed at Hull Springhead in April 1950. The rounded sides to the cab roof indicate that this engine was rebuilt at York.

NBR Holmes 'J83' class 0-6-0T No 68480.

NER Worsdell 'J72' class 0-6-0T No 68736 painted in lined green NER livery, seen at Newcastle in April 1963.

Number	Built	Renumbered	BR Dates	Scrap	Notes
68370	06/86 Str	01/49 8370	-10/52	*62*	
				10/52➲32	
68371	03/87 Str	08/49 8371	-04/54	*54*	
68372	03/87 Str	04/48 8372	-02/51	*51*	
68373	04/87 Str	02/49 8373	-01/52	*52*	
68374	05/87 Str	12/48 8374	-06/54	*54*	
68375	10/87 Str	04/50 8375	-11/52	*52*	
68376	06/87 Str	8376	-07/51	*51*	
68377	09/87 Str	8377	-05/51	05/51	
68378	06/88 Str	07/49 8378	-11/52	*59*	
				11/52➲36	
68379	06/88 Str	09/48 8379	-10/50	*50*	
68380	07/88 Str	8380	-03/52	*52*	
68381	07/88 Str	8381	-10/50	*50*	
68382	08/88 Str	05/49 8382	-08/52	01/59	
				08/52➲31	
68383	11/88 Str	11/51 8383	-10/55	*10/55*	
68384	11/88 Str	8384	-04/50	*50*	
68385	11/88 Str	05/48 8385	-06/51	*51*	
68386	12/88 Str	8386	-04/50	*50*	
68387	12/88 Str	8387	-02/51	*02/51*	
68388	12/88 Str	01/49 8388	-04/52	*52*	

Class continued with Mersey Railway No 3

J77 68390-68441
0-6-0T NER Rebuilt from 'Fletcher Well Tanks'

Power Classification: 2F
Introduced: 1874-1884
Rebuilt 1899-1921 by W Worsdell and Raven
Designer: Fletcher
Company: NER
Weight: 43t 0cwt
Driving Wheel: 4' 1¼"
Boiler Pressure: 160psi
Cylinders: Inside 17" x 22"
Tractive Effort: 17560lbf
Valve Gear: Stephenson (slide valves)

Between 1874 and 1883 Fletcher built 130 0-4-4WT engines for the NER. These well tanks were classified 'B.T.P.' (Bogie Tank Passenger) on the NER.

Between 1899 and 1921 a total of sixty of these engines were rebuilt as 0-6-0Ts for light freight and shunting duties. The rebuilt engines were known as the NER 290 class. Forty-six of these came into BR stock in 1948, the first engine having been withdrawn in 1933.

68396 and 68416 were sold for further industrial use. They were scrapped in 1955 and 1960 respectively.

y These engines were rebuilt at York in 1899-1904. They retained their original rounded cab roofs.

d The remainder were converted at Darlington in 1907-1921 and these were given Worsdell type cabs with square cornered roofs.

Year End Totals: 'J77' class

'47	'48	'49	'50	'51	'52	'53	'54	'55	'56	'57	'58	'59	'60	'61	'62	'63	'64	'65	'66	'67
46	43	42	40	38	38	37	32	28	21	16	7	5	1							

Number	Built	Renumbered	BR Dates	Scrap	Notes
68390	04/74 N	8390	-09/48	*48*	y
68391	08/74 N	05/48 8391	-07/57	08/57	y
68392	08/74 N	05/48 8392	-05/60	07/60	d
68393	08/74 N	08/48 8393	-07/55	07/55	d
68395	05/75 H	10/48 8395	-06/56	*56*	d
68396	05/75 H	8396	-04/50	55	y
68397	05/75 H	06/51 8397	-01/58	04/58	d
68398	06/75 H	09/49 8398	-01/53	*53*	y
68399	06/75 H	09/48 8399	-04/58	05/58	y
68400	06/75 H	8400	-10/48	10/48	y
68401	06/75 H	09/48 8401	-07/54	*07/54*	y
68402	06/75 H	12/50 8402	-05/58	06/58	y
68404	09/75 H	8404	-04/51	05/51	d
68405	09/75 H	05/52 8405	-12/58	01/59	d
68406	09/75 H	04/48 8406	-11/59	12/59	y
68407	10/75 H	01/50 8407	-02/56	*56*	y
68408	11/75 H	09/49 8408	-02/61	03/61	y
68409	06/77 Dar	03/49 8409	-11/59	12/59	y
68410	05/77 Ghd	12/49 8410	-10/60	10/60	y
68412	07/77 Ghd	01/49 8412	-02/57	03/57	d
68413	07/77 Ghd	10/50 8413	-05/54	*54*	y
68414	09/77 Ghd	03/49 8414	-12/58	01/59	y
68415	10/77 Ghd	8415	-10/49	*49*	y
68416	11/77 Ghd	8416	-04/50	60	y
68417	11/77 Ghd	02/51 8417	-09/56	10/56	y
68420	04/78 Ghd	12/49 8420	-04/55	05/55	d
68421	07/78 Ghd	01/50 8421	-05/54	*54*	y
68422	09/78 Dar	03/49 8422	-06/54	*07/54*	y
68423	10/78 Ghd	07/48 8423	-11/57	12/57	y
68424	03/79 Ghd	09/48 8424	-06/58	07/58	y
68425	04/79 Dar	03/49 8425	-01/60	01/60	y
68426	06/79 Dar	11/48 8426	-08/57	09/57	y
68427	06/79 Dar	04/48 8427	-01/58	02/58	y
68428	06/79 Ghd	07/50 8428	-02/55	*55*	y
68429	07/79 Ghd	03/50 8429	-01/56	*56*	y
68430	12/79 Ghd	04/49 8430	-06/56	*56*	y
68431	12/79 Ghd	08/50 8431	-02/60	03/60	y
68432	12/79 Ghd	03/49 8432	-05/55	06/55	d
68433	06/80 Ghd	8433	-05/51	06/51	y
68434	07/80 Ghd	07/48 8434	-01/57	01/57	y
68435	08/80 Ghd	09/50 8435	-10/58	11/58	y
68436	10/80 Ghd	12/48 8436	-06/56	*56*	y
68437	11/80 Dar	10/48 8437	-01/56	*56*	y
68438	06/82 Ghd	12/51 8438	-02/58	03/58	y
68440	12/84 Yrk	02/50 8440	-08/54	*54*	d
68441	12/84 Yrk	8441	-06/48	*06/48*	d

J83 68442-68481
0-6-0T NBR Holmes

Power Classification: 2F
Introduced: 1900-1901
Designer: Holmes
Company: NBR
Weight: 45t 5cwt
Driving Wheel: 4' 6"
Boiler Pressure: 150psi
Cylinders: Inside 17" x 26"
Tractive Effort: 17745lbf
Valve Gear: Stephenson (slide valves)

Holmes built forty 0-6-0Ts for shunting and transfer freight duties on the NBR. They were known as NBR class 'D'. They were the largest and most powerful of the NBR 0-6-0Ts. One engine (8462) was withdrawn in 1947, but the rest came into BR stock, and no others were withdrawn until 1956.

A number of these engines were fitted with Westinghouse and steam brakes and they were always noisily in evidence as station pilots at some of the larger Scottish stations, such as Edinburgh (Waverley) and Glasgow (Queen Street). The engines working at Edinburgh (Waverley) were repainted in light green livery for their station pilot duties by the LNER in 1947.

Year End Totals: 'J83' class

'47	'48	'49	'50	'51	'52	'53	'54	'55	'56	'57	'58	'59	'60	'61	'62	'63	'64	'65	'66	'67
39	39	39	39	39	39	39	39	39	34	32	21	18	16	11						

Number	Built	Renumbered	BR Dates	Scrap	Notes
68442	08/00 NR	06/50 8442	-01/62	06/63	
68443	09/00 NR	12/50 8443	-02/61	06/61	
68444	09/00 NR	05/51 8444	-01/60	04/60	
68445	09/00 NR	12/49 8445	-10/62	07/63	
68446	09/00 NR	11/48 8446	-03/56	*56*	
68447	09/00 NR	08/48 8447	-02/61	07/61	
68448	09/00 NR	04/50 8448	-10/62	02/63	
68449	09/00 NR	08/48 8449	-09/58	02/60	
68450	09/00 NR	08/50 8450	-12/57	03/58	
68451	09/00 NR	09/49 8451	-02/58	03/58	
68452	04/01 NR	03/50 8452	-06/58	05/59	
68453	04/01 NR	01/50 8453	-10/62	03/63	
68454	04/01 NR	09/50 8454	-02/62	08/62	
68455	04/01 NR	04/48 8455	-05/56	*56*	
68456	04/01 NR	04/48 8456	-01/61	05/61	
68457	04/01 NR	09/48 8457	-03/60	04/60	
68458	04/01 NR	05/50 8458	-01/62	04/63	
68459	04/01 NR	08/50 8459	-05/61	02/62	
68460	04/01 NR	07/50 8460	-11/58	02/60	
68461	04/01 NR	05/48 8461	-06/58	02/60	
68463	04/01 SS	06/50 8463	-11/58	02/60	
68464	04/01 SS	07/48 8464	-03/58	04/58	
68465	04/01 SS	05/48 8465	-08/57	10/57	
68466	04/01 SS	09/48 8466	-12/58	02/59	
68467	04/01 SS	05/48 8467	-09/59	02/60	
68468	04/01 SS	07/50 8468	-06/59	02/60	
68469	04/01 SS	12/48 8469	-10/56	*56*	
68470	04/01 SS	10/49 8470	-10/62	01/63	
68471	04/01 SS	10/50 8471	-08/61	11/61	
68472	04/01 SS	05/48 8472	-02/62	08/62	
68473	04/01 SS	04/50 8473	-05/56	*56*	
68474	04/01 SS	07/50 8474	-04/58	07/58	
68475	05/01 SS	07/50 8475	-03/58	07/58	
68476	05/01 SS	04/48 8476	-03/56	*56*	
68477	05/01 SS	08/49 8477	-12/62	07/64	
68478	05/01 SS	10/49 8478	-11/58	02/60	
68479	05/01 SS	06/50 8479	-10/62	06/63	
68480	05/01 SS	05/51 8480	-03/59	02/60	
68481	05/01 SS	05/48 8481	-02/62	06/63	

J93 68484-68489
0-6-0T M&GNJR

Power Classification: 2F
Introduced: 1897-1905
Designer: Marriott
Company: M&GNJR
Weight: 37t 14cwt
Driving Wheel: 3' 7"
Boiler Pressure: 150psi
Cylinders: Outside 16" x 20"
Tractive Effort: 15180lbf
Valve Gear: Stephenson (slide valves)

Nine 0-6-0Ts were acquired by the LNER from the Midland & Great Northern Joint Railway in 1937. Some of these had been built at the M&GNJR's workshops at Melton Constable between 1897 and 1905, while others were partly rebuilds of Cornwall Mineral Railway engines which had been built in 1873-1874.

These last three survivors (originally M&GNJR Nos. 96, 94 and 16) were all withdrawn in 1948/1949 without receiving their new BR numbers.

s 68484 carried a stove-pipe chimney.

Year End Totals: 'J93' class

'47	'48	'49	'50	'51	'52	'53	'54	'55	'56	'57	'58	'59	'60	'61	'62	'63	'64	'65	'66	'67
3	1																			

Number	Built	Renumbered	BR Dates	Scrap	Notes
68484	04/99 Mel	8484	-05/48	*48*	s
68488	01/04 Mel	8488	-01/48	05/48	
68489	05/05 Mel	8489	-08/49	*49*	

J67 between 68490 & 68628
0-6-0T GER Holden

J69 between 68490 & 68636, 43-45
0-6-0T GER Holden

Power Classification: J67 2F
J69 3F reclassified 2F in 1953
Introduced: J67 1890-1901
J69 1902-1904
Designer: J Holden
Company: GER
Weight: J67/1 40t 0cwt
J67/2 41t 8cwt
J69 40t 9cwt
Driving Wheel: 4' 0"
Boiler Pressure: J67 160psi
J69 180psi
Cylinders: Inside 16½" x 22"
Tractive Effort: J67 16970lbf
J69 19090lbf
Valve Gear: Stephenson (slide valves)

Refer to the Historical Survey of Great Eastern 0-6-0T Engines at the end of this section for more details of this class.

The 'J67' and 'J69' classes (originally GER 'R24' and 'S56' classes) consisted of 160 engines which were built at Stratford in 1890-1904. The two classes were very similar in appearance with the 'J67's originally designed for freight work and the 'J69's for London suburban passenger work. Fifty-one engines were originally built as 'J67' but there was some rebuilding between the classes (sometimes more than once). The main visual difference between the two classes was in the larger tanks of the 'J69's. The differences between the different parts are shown below. The first 'J67' engine was withdrawn in 1937 and the first of the 'J69's in 1940.

A total of 134 engines came into BR stock in 1948. Some engines still retained the original stove-pipe chimneys, but most engines were later rebuilt with lipped chimneys. 68619 was repainted in GER dark blue livery in 1959 and it was kept in immaculate condition for station pilot duties at Liverpool Street. Three engines were later transferred to departmental stock at Stratford Works.

J67/1 This was Holden's original design of 1890.

J67/2 These engines were rebuilt from 1937 onwards from 'J69' engines with lower pressure boilers and smaller fireboxes.

J69/1 These were originally 'J69', but they were reclassified 'J69/1' in 1950 by BR. Introduced in 1902, they were a development of the 'J67's with a higher boiler pressure, larger tanks and firebox. Some were rebuilt from 'J67's.

J69/2 These were engines which were rebuilt from 'J67/1' (from 1950 to 1953) with higher boiler pressure and a larger firebox.

t 68492 was permanently coupled to a 'J36' tender and 68511 to a 'J37' tender. They were based at Galashiels. Because of weight restrictions on the Lauder branch and on other branches in the Borders area they ran with the side tanks empty to reduce their axle-load.

Year End Totals: 'J67' class

'47	'48	'49	'50	'51	'52	'53	'54	'55	'56	'57	'58	'59	'60	'61	'62	'63	'64	'65	'66	'67
45	44	44	39	36	34	34	30	20	11	7										

Year End Totals: 'J69' class

'47	'48	'49	'50	'51	'52	'53	'54	'55	'56	'57	'58	'59	'60	'61	'62	'63	'64	'65	'66	'67
89	90	90	95	98	100	96	96	95	92	87	62	43	29	11						

Year End Totals: 'J69' (service) class

'47	'48	'49	'50	'51	'52	'53	'54	'55	'56	'57	'58	'59	'60	'61	'62	'63	'64	'65	'66	'67
												2	2	2						

Number	Built	Renumbered	BR Dates	Scrap	Notes
68490	03/90 Str	05/50 8490	-05/58	06/58	J67/1
					05/50⇨J69/2
68491	03/90 Str	04/48 8491	-06/58	08/58	J69/1
68492	03/90 Str	06/50 8492	-05/56	*08/56*	J67/1 t
68493	03/90 Str	10/48 8493	-10/54	08/55	J67/1
68494	03/90 Str	*52* 8494	-04/58	08/58	J69/1
68495	04/90 Str	12/50 8495	-05/58	08/58	J69/1
68496	04/90 Str	02/49 8496	-05/56	*56*	J67/1
68497	04/90 Str	12/50 8497	-10/60	10/60	J69/1
68498	04/90 Str	08/48 8498	-08/59	09/62	J67/1
					08/51⇨J69/2 08/59➡44
68499	04/90 Str	10/48 8499	-09/62	01/63	J69/1
68500	05/90 Str	03/51 8500	-01/61	06/61	J69/1
68501	05/90 Str	12/48 8501	-08/60	08/60	J69/1
68502	05/90 Str	05/50 8502	-02/61	02/61	J69/1
68503	05/90 Str	12/49 8503	-01/57	*57*	J69/1
68504	05/90 Str	05/52 8504	-01/56	*56*	J69/1
68505	05/90 Str	02/51 8505	-11/53	*53*	J69/1
68507	05/90 Str	12/48 8507	-06/60	06/60	J69/1
68508	05/90 Str	01/50 8508	-02/61	02/61	J69/1
68509	11/90 Str	06/51 8509	-03/54	*54*	J67/1
68510	11/90 Str	03/50 8510	-09/59	10/59	J67/1
					03/50⇨J69/2
68511	11/90 Str	05/49 8511	-12/56	*12/56*	J67/1 t
68512	11/90 Str	02/51 8512	-04/57	05/57	J67/1
					02/51⇨J69/2
68513	11/90 Str	06/49 8513	-10/60	06/61	J67/1
					06/52⇨J69/2
68514	12/90 Str	07/52 8514	-07/55	*55*	J67/1
68515	12/90 Str	06/49 8515	-01/57	*01/57*	J67/1
68516	12/90 Str	01/49 8516	-05/57	06/57	J67/1
68517	12/90 Str	02/51 8517	-03/56	*03/56*	J67/1
					02/51⇨J69/2 09/53⇨J67/1
68518	12/90 Str	08/48 8518	-02/58	03/58	J67/1
68519	01/91 Str	04/50 8519	-08/58	09/58	J67/1
					04/50⇨J69/2
68520	01/91 Str	12/48 8520	-08/59	09/59	J67/1
					02/50⇨J69/2
68521	01/91 Str	10/49 8521	-08/56	*56*	J67/1
68522	01/91 Str	03/50 8522	-03/61	04/61	J67/1
					04/50⇨J69/2
68523	01/91 Str	05/49 8523	-12/55	*56*	J67/1
68524	02/92 Str	09/48 8524	-06/59	09/59	J69/1
68525	02/92 Str	8525	-12/53	*54*	J69/1
68526	03/92 Str	10/48 8526	-10/60	12/60	J69/1
68527	03/92 Str	02/50 8527	-06/58	08/58	J69/1
68528	03/92 Str	10/51 8528	-10/59	11/59	J69/1
68529	03/92 Str	03/48 8529	-08/58	02/59	J67/2
					05/54⇨J69/1
68530	03/92 Str	01/50 8530	-02/61	02/61	J69/1
68531	03/92 Str	06/49 8531	-10/55	*55*	J67/2
68532	03/92 Str	11/50 8532	-12/58	11/59	J69/1
					12/58➡43
68533	03/92 Str	05/49 8533	-07/53	*53*	J69/1
68534	04/92 Str	04/51 8534	-08/54	09/54	J69/1
68535	04/92 Str	10/48 8535	-08/59	01/60	J69/1
68536	04/92 Str	06/49 8536	-02/58	04/58	J67/2
68537	04/92 Str	04/48 8537	-06/58	08/58	J69/1
68538	04/92 Str	10/49 8538	-09/61	10/61	J69/1
68540	05/92 Str	02/49 8540	-01/56	*01/56*	J67/2
68541	05/92 Str	12/48 8541	-08/58	02/59	J69/1
68542	05/92 Str	11/48 8542	-09/62	12/62	J69/1
68543	04/94 Str	06/49 8543	-11/59	09/62	J69/1
					11/59➡45
68544	04/94 Str	08/49 8544	-02/55	*55*	J69/1
68545	04/94 Str	11/48 8545	-02/61	02/61	J69/1
68546	05/94 Str	11/51 8546	-05/58	08/58	J69/1
68547	05/94 Str	03/49 8547	-04/56	*56*	J67/2
68548	05/94 Str	12/49 8548	-11/53	*53*	J69/1
68549	05/94 Str	*50* 8549	-02/62	02/62	J69/1
68550	06/94 Str	05/50 8550	-07/61	07/61	J69/1
68551	06/94 Str	06/49 8551	-06/57	07/57	J69/1
68552	06/94 Str	06/48 8552	-09/61	10/61	J69/1
68553	10/95 Str	10/49 8553	-12/58	01/59	J69/1
68554	10/95 Str	09/50 8554	-07/61	07/61	J69/1
68555	10/95 Str	11/50 8555	-05/58	08/58	J69/1
68556	10/95 Str	10/49 8556	-09/62	12/62	J69/1
68557	10/95 Str	12/48 8557	-10/59	11/59	J69/1
68558	11/95 Str	04/49 8558	-01/61	01/61	J69/1
68559	11/95 Str	03/49 8559	-04/56	06/56	J69/1
68560	11/95 Str	08/49 8560	-01/61	01/61	J69/1
68561	11/95 Str	03/50 8561	-07/58	12/58	J69/1
68562	12/95 Str	10/51 8562	-08/56	*56*	J69/1
68563	12/95 Str	*50* 8563	-10/60	11/60	J69/1
68565	12/95 Str	11/48 8565	-08/62	09/62	J69/1
68566	12/95 Str	10/50 8566	-09/62	01/63	J69/1
68567	01/96 Str	06/48 8567	-08/57	09/57	J69/1
68568	01/96 Str	04/56 8568	-05/58	06/58	J69/1
68569	01/96 Str	01/49 8569	-06/60	07/60	J69/1
68570	01/96 Str	02/50 8570	-09/61	09/61	J69/1
68571	02/96 Str	12/49 8571	-12/60	06/61	J69/1
68572	02/96 Str	12/48 8572	-11/54	07/55	J67/2
68573	04/96 Str	10/48 8573	-08/60	10/60	J69/1
68574	04/96 Str	07/51 8574	-01/59	04/59	J69/1
68575	04/96 Str	05/51 8575	-10/60	10/60	J69/1
68576	04/96 Str	09/49 8576	-03/58	04/58	J69/1
68577	05/96 Str	03/49 8577	-11/60	11/60	J69/1
68578	05/96 Str	07/49 8578	-01/61	06/61	J69/1
68579	05/96 Str	01/52 8579	-01/60	02/60	J69/1
68581	06/96 Str	10/48 8581	-09/59	10/59	J69/1
68583	03/99 Str	05/49 8583	-04/58	05/58	J67/1
68584	03/99 Str	03/49 8584	-08/55	*55*	J67/1
68585	03/99 Str	03/49 8585	-06/58	06/58	J69/1
68586	03/99 Str	07/50 8586	-05/56	*56*	J67/1
68587	04/99 Str	08/49 8587	-10/59	11/59	J69/1
68588	04/99 Str	12/50 8588	-05/58	06/58	J67/1
					08/53⇨J69/2
68589	04/99 Str	03/49 8589	-01/56	*01/56*	J67/1
68590	04/99 Str	10/48 8590	-09/55	*55*	J67/1
68591	12/99 Str	11/48 8591	-01/60	07/61	J67/1
					11/48⇨J69/2
68592	12/99 Str	03/49 8592	-07/55	*55*	J67/1
68593	12/99 Str	11/50 8593	-01/58	04/58	J67/1
68594	01/00 Str	11/48 8594	-11/55	*55*	J67/1
68595	01/00 Str	11/48 8595	-01/57	*57*	J67/1
68596	06/00 Str	05/49 8596	-11/59	11/59	J69/1
68597	07/00 Str	08/49 8597	-10/55	*55*	J67/2
68598	07/00 Str	06/48 8598	-05/57	06/57	J69/1
68599	07/00 Str	09/49 8599	-11/59	11/59	J69/1
68600	07/00 Str	11/48 8600	-09/62	12/62	J69/1
68601	07/00 Str	12/50 8601	-10/59	11/59	J69/1
68602	07/00 Str	05/48 8602	-10/59	11/59	J69/1
68603	08/00 Str	07/48 8603	-03/58	04/58	J69/1
68605	08/00 Str	10/48 8605	-07/58	01/59	J69/1
68606	12/00 Str	07/48 8606	-03/55	07/55	J67/1
68607	06/01 Str	12/48 8607	-05/58	08/58	J69/1
68608	06/01 Str	09/49 8608	-10/58	11/58	J67/1
68609	06/01 Str	11/48 8609	-09/62	10/62	J67/2
					06/52⇨J69/1
68610	06/01 Str	04/51 8610	-01/57	02/57	J67/2
68611	06/01 Str	08/48 8611	-07/55	08/55	J67/1
68612	07/01 Str	06/49 8612	-06/61	06/61	J69/1
68613	07/01 Str	05/48 8613	-09/61	10/61	J69/1
68616	08/01 Str	11/49 8616	-12/58	01/59	J67/1
68617	05/04 Str	12/49 8617	-07/58	12/58	J69/1
68618	05/04 Str	11/48 8618	-08/58	02/59	J69/1
68619	05/04 Str	06/53 8619	-10/61	10/61	J69/1
68621	05/04 Str	10/48 8621	-09/62	01/63	J69/1
68623	06/04 Str	04/51 8623	-02/61	02/61	J69/1
68625	06/04 Str	02/50 8625	-01/59	02/59	J69/1
68626	06/04 Str	01/50 8626	-05/62	06/62	J69/1
68628	08/04 Str	09/50 8628	-02/58	03/58	J67/2
68629	08/04 Str	10/49 8629	-11/59	12/59	J69/1
68630	08/04 Str	06/49 8630	-01/59	02/59	J69/1
68631	08/04 Str	11/48 8631	-07/58	08/58	J69/1
68632	09/04 Str	07/51 8632	-05/58	12/58	J69/1
68633 §	09/04 Str	01/49 8633	-12/60		J69/1
68635	09/04 Str	07/48 8635	-09/62	01/63	J69/1
68636	09/04 Str	11/50 8636	-01/59	02/59	J69/1

Class continued with 43 (Service Locomotives)

J68 68638-68666
0-6-0T GER Hill

Power Classification:	3F reclassified 2F in 1953
Introduced:	1912-1923
Designer:	Hill
Company:	GER
Weight:	42t 9cwt
Driving Wheel:	4' 0"
Boiler Pressure:	180psi
Cylinders:	Inside 16½" x 22"
Tractive Effort:	19090lbf
Valve Gear:	Stephenson (slide valves)

Refer to the Historical Survey of Great Eastern 0-6-0T Engines at the end of this section for more details of this class.

The 'J68's were built in 1912-1923 by Hill and they were the last of the GER 0-6-0Ts to be built. They were the GER 'C72' class and they were developed from the 'J69's. They had the large tanks of the 'J69's but they were also fitted with side-window cabs.

Thirty engines were built, but the first engine of the class (GER 41) was sold to the War Department in 1940, becoming WD 70085. This left twenty-nine engines to come into BR stock. The first ten engines had been built for working passenger trains in the London area, and the last twenty were fitted with steam brakes only for shunting duties.

Year End Totals: 'J68' class

'47	'48	'49	'50	'51	'52	'53	'54	'55	'56	'57	'58	'59	'60	'61	'62	'63	'64	'65	'66	'67
29	29	29	29	29	29	29	29	29	29	29	22	10	3							

Number	Built	Renumbered	BR Dates	Scrap	Notes
68638	06/12 Str	09/50 8638	-03/59	04/59	
68639	06/12 Str	09/49 8639	-04/59	04/59	
68640	07/12 Str	02/49 8640	-04/59	12/59	
68641	07/12 Str	09/48 8641	-11/59	02/60	
68642	08/12 Str	02/50 8642	-09/61	10/61	
68643	08/12 Str	10/48 8643	-11/59	01/60	
68644	09/12 Str	12/49 8644	-11/60	01/61	
68645	09/12 Str	07/51 8645	-11/59	11/59	
68646	09/12 Str	04/49 8646	-09/61	09/61	
68647	12/13 Str	04/50 8647	-12/60	06/61	
68648	12/13 Str	06/48 8648	-08/59	09/59	
68649	12/13 Str	06/50 8649	-09/61	10/61	
68650	12/13 Str	08/51 8650	-10/60	11/60	
68651	12/13 Str	03/50 8651	-05/58	06/58	
68652	12/13 Str	06/49 8652	-10/59	10/59	
68653	12/13 Str	12/49 8653	-07/58	02/59	
68654	01/14 Str	10/51 8654	-03/60	04/60	
68655	01/14 Str	01/49 8655	-11/59	01/60	
68656	02/14 Str	04/49 8656	-04/60	04/60	
68657	10/23 Str	02/50 8657	-08/58	02/59	
68658	10/23 Str	04/51 8658	-04/59	04/59	
68659	10/23 Str	10/50 8659	-08/58	02/59	
68660	10/23 Str	03/49 8660	-12/60	06/61	
68661	10/23 Str	12/49 8661	-12/59	01/60	
68662	11/23 Str	04/48 8662	-08/58	02/59	
68663	11/23 Str	01/49 8663	-10/60	11/60	
68664	11/23 Str	*52* 8664	-09/58	10/58	
68665	11/23 Str	03/51 8665	-12/59	01/60	
68666	11/23 Str	04/48 8666	-08/58	02/59	

J92 68667-68669, 35
0-6-0CT GER Stratford Works Crane Tanks

Power Classification:	0F
Introduced:	1868, rebuilt 1891-1894 by J Holden
Designer:	Ruston & Proctor
Company:	GER
Weight:	40t 8cwt
Driving Wheel:	4' 0"
Boiler Pressure:	140psi
Cylinders:	Inside 16" x 22"
Tractive Effort:	13960lbf
Valve Gear:	Stephenson (slide valves)

Five engines were originally built in 1868 by Ruston & Proctor as 0-6-0Ts. Two engines were withdrawn in 1889 and 1892 and Holden rebuilt the three other engines in 1891-1894 when the cranes were added. They were used as departmental engines at Stratford Works, and from the 1890s until 1946 they were simply known as 'B', 'C', and 'D'. They were the GER class '204'.

They were all scrapped between 1950 and 1952. 68668 survived long enough to be renumbered 35 in the service stock in 1952, but it was withdrawn from service later that year.

Year End Totals: 'J92' (service) class

'47	'48	'49	'50	'51	'52	'53	'54	'55	'56	'57	'58	'59	'60	'61	'62	'63	'64	'65	'66	'67
3	3	3	2	2																

Number	Built	Renumbered	BR Dates	Scrap	Notes
68667	05/68 RP	03/49 8667	-05/52	*52*	
68668	07/68 RP	02/50 8668	-09/52	*52*	
					09/52➡35
68669	09/68 RP	09/50 8669	-10/50	*50*	

Class continued with 35 (Service Locomotives)

J72 68670-68754, 69001-69028, 58-59
0-6-0T NER and BR Worsdell

Power Classification:	2F
Introduced:	1898-1925, 1949-1951
Designer:	W Worsdell
Company:	NER
Weight:	38t 12cwt
Driving Wheel:	4' 1¼"
Boiler Pressure:	140psi
Cylinders:	Inside 17" x 24" c Inside 18" x 24"
Tractive Effort:	16760lbf c 18790lbf
Valve Gear:	Stephenson (slide valves)

This design of small 0-6-0T is unique in that the engines were constructed over a span of fifty-three years, by three different Railway Companies and during the regimes of four different locomotive superintendents.

Wilson Worsdell originated the design on the NER in 1893. Known as the NER 'E1' class, they were based on T W Worsdell's 'J71' class (NER 'E' class), but they were fitted with smaller wheels.

The first twenty engines were built at Darlington in 1898-1899. No more appeared until twenty were built in 1914 by Sir Vincent Raven. These had very slight modifications to the original design and ten more appeared in 1920, followed by another twenty-five in 1922. After grouping Gresley built another ten at Doncaster in 1925 for the LNER. This brought the total up to eighty-five engines and it might have been considered the end of the story.

However, a further twenty-eight engines were built for BR in 1949-1951. They were ordered by Peppercorn who was the temporary CME of the Eastern and North Eastern regions of British Railways in 1948-1949. These last engines were similar in practically every respect to the original 1898 design. They did not even have such modern features as pop safety valves which might have been expected. As no provision had been made in the numbering system for further engines, the BR-built engines were numbered in a separate series, 69001-69028.

68723 and 68736 were latterly painted in the old NER light green livery for station pilot work at Newcastle. They carried the NER crest and the new British Railways emblem on the side tanks.

Two engines of the BR-built batch were later transferred to service stock numbered 58 and 59. They were based initially at Gateshead but later at North Blyth and Heaton, where they were used for de-icing.

c 68685 had larger cylinders.

s 68709 worked in Scotland for some years and it acquired a stove-pipe chimney at Cowlairs.

Year End Totals: 'J72' class

'47	'48	'49	'50	'51	'52	'53	'54	'55	'56	'57	'58	'59	'60	'61	'62	'63	'64	'65	'66	'67
85	85	100	105	113	113	113	113	113	113	113	108	100	78	34	18	4				

Year End Totals: 'J72' (service) class

'47	'48	'49	'50	'51	'52	'53	'54	'55	'56	'57	'58	'59	'60	'61	'62	'63	'64	'65	'66	'67
																	2	2	1	

Number	Built	Renumbered	BR Dates	Scrap	Notes
68670	12/98 Dar	02/50 8670	-01/60	04/60	
68671	12/98 Dar	05/48 8671	-03/60	03/60	
68672	12/98 Dar	09/51 8672	-10/61	03/62	
68673	12/98 Dar	04/48 8673	-05/61	06/61	
68674	12/98 Dar	04/48 8674	-10/61	02/62	
68675	12/98 Dar	09/48 8675	-10/61	11/61	
68676	12/98 Dar	12/48 8676	-09/60	11/60	
68677	12/98 Dar	04/48 8677	-10/61	11/61	
68678	12/98 Dar	10/48 8678	-02/61	04/61	
68679	12/98 Dar	05/50 8679	-06/60	07/60	
68680	03/99 Dar	10/49 8680	-10/61	05/62	
68681	03/99 Dar	09/51 8681	-11/60	01/61	
68682	03/99 Dar	08/50 8682	-12/59	12/59	
68683	03/99 Dar	07/48 8683	-03/61	04/61	
68684	03/99 Dar	08/50 8684	-03/61	04/61	
68685	03/99 Dar	11/50 8685	-10/60	10/60	c
68686	04/99 Dar	10/48 8686	-08/61	09/61	
68687	04/99 Dar	10/48 8687	-09/61	11/61	
68688	04/99 Dar	06/48 8688	-10/61	05/62	
68689	04/99 Dar	04/48 8689	-10/61	05/62	
68690	08/14 Dar	01/50 8690	-02/61	04/61	
68691	09/14 Dar	04/48 8691	-12/60	01/61	
68692	09/14 Dar	03/48 8692	-10/61	12/61	
68693	09/14 Dar	10/48 8693	-08/61	09/61	
68694	09/14 Dar	12/49 8694	-12/59	12/59	
68695	09/14 Dar	05/49 8695	-04/62	05/62	
68696	09/14 Dar	12/48 8696	-02/61	03/61	
68697	09/14 Dar	06/50 8697	-02/60	02/60	
68698	09/14 Dar	11/48 8698	-10/61	03/62	
68699	10/14 Dar	11/48 8699	-12/58	02/59	
68700	10/14 Dar	06/48 8700	-12/58	03/59	
68701	10/14 Dar	06/49 8701	-10/60	10/60	
68702	10/14 Dar	04/48 8702	-08/61	10/61	
68703	10/14 Dar	09/50 8703	-10/61	05/62	
68704	10/14 Dar	10/48 8704	-10/61	11/63	
68705	11/14 Dar	04/49 8705	-11/60	11/60	
68706	11/14 Dar	06/48 8706	-10/60	11/60	
68707	11/14 Dar	05/51 8707	-04/62	07/62	
68708	11/14 Dar	03/49 8708	-08/61	08/61	
68709	11/14 Dar	05/48 8709	-02/62	09/62	
					06/49⇨s
68710	10/20 Dar	04/48 8710	-03/59	08/59	
68711	10/20 Dar	05/48 8711	-08/61	09/61	
68712	10/20 Dar	08/48 8712	-01/59	02/59	
68713	10/20 Dar	03/49 8713	-10/61	04/62	
68714	11/20 Dar	06/49 8714	-04/60	01/61	
68715	11/20 Dar	02/50 8715	-07/61	08/61	
68716	11/20 Dar	06/48 8716	-02/61	03/61	
68717	11/20 Dar	12/48 8717	-11/61	07/62	
68718	12/20 Dar	11/50 8718	-06/58	08/58	
68719	12/20 Dar	02/49 8719	-01/61	02/61	
68720	04/22 AW	02/50 8720	-09/61	10/61	
68721	04/22 AW	10/49 8721	-08/61	09/61	
68722	04/22 AW	09/48 8722	-02/60	03/60	
68723	04/22 AW	10/48 8723	-09/63	10/63	
68724	04/22 AW	05/48 8724	-12/60	01/61	
68725	04/22 AW	04/48 8725	-04/60	05/60	
68726	04/22 AW	10/49 8726	-06/61	06/61	
68727	04/22 AW	06/49 8727	-02/60	03/60	
68728	04/22 AW	08/48 8728	-10/61	10/61	
68729	04/22 AW	01/51 8729	-10/61	05/62	
68730	05/22 AW	12/50 8730	-11/60	11/60	
68731	05/22 AW	06/50 8731	-05/60	05/60	
68732	05/22 AW	09/48 8732	-10/61	03/62	
68733	05/22 AW	12/50 8733	-07/62	09/62	
68734	05/22 AW	11/50 8734	-10/61	05/62	
68735	05/22 AW	04/48 8735	-10/58	10/58	
68736	06/22 AW	08/50 8736	-10/63	11/63	
68737	06/22 AW	05/50 8737	-08/61	09/61	
68738	06/22 AW	02/49 8738	-11/60	01/61	
68739	06/22 AW	08/49 8739	-08/59	09/59	
68740	06/22 AW	10/50 8740	-07/61	09/61	
68741	08/22 AW	06/50 8741	-07/59	07/59	
68742	08/22 AW	05/50 8742	-10/61	11/61	
68743	09/22 AW	05/48 8743	-10/61	06/62	
68744	10/22 AW	09/48 8744	-09/61	10/61	
68745	11/25 Don	11/48 8745	-09/61	10/61	
68746	11/25 Don	09/50 8746	-12/58	02/59	
68747	11/25 Don	05/48 8747	-10/61	06/62	
68748	11/25 Don	07/51 8748	-01/59	02/59	
68749	12/25 Don	08/50 8749	-08/60	11/60	
68750	12/25 Don	05/49 8750	-12/62	02/64	
68751	12/25 Don	04/50 8751	-05/59	06/59	
68752	12/25 Don	01/50 8752	-02/60	02/60	
68753	12/25 Don	05/48 8753	-08/60	05/61	
68754	12/25 Don	09/49 8754	-04/62	05/62	

Class continued with 69001

J52 68757-68889, 1-2, 9
0-6-0ST GNR Stirling and Ivatt

Power Classification:	3F
Introduced:	1 1892-1897 rebuilt 1922-1932 by Gresley 2 1897-1909
Designer:	1 P Stirling 2 Ivatt
Company:	GNR
Weight:	51t 14cwt
Driving Wheel:	4' 8"
Boiler Pressure:	170psi b 175psi
Cylinders:	Inside 18" x 26"
Tractive Effort:	21735lbf b 22370lbf
Valve Gear:	Stephenson (slide valves)

Both Stirling and Ivatt adopted the 0-6-0ST as the standard shunting engine on the GNR. A total of 264 of these engines were built between 1868 and 1909, all being to the same general design, but with increasing dimensions.

Ivatt built his engines with domed boilers, compared to his predecessor's domeless engines. Eighty-eight were built between 1897 and 1909, and they were the GNR 'J13' class (LNER 'J52' class).

Forty-nine of Stirling's engines of 1892-1897 (GNR 'J14' class and LNER 'J53' class) were rebuilt with domed boilers from 1922 onwards. They became part of the 'J52' class with which they were now virtually indistinguishable. Some of these were fitted with condensing apparatus when rebuilt. Some engines later acquired stove-pipe chimneys. The first engine was withdrawn in 1936.

68782 worked as departmental engine at Doncaster works, but it was withdrawn without being renumbered into service stock. It was actually scrapped four months before it was officially withdrawn. Several other engines later were renumbered into service stock also for working at Doncaster Works. Two different engines carried the number 2, first 68816 then 68858 after the other engine was withdrawn.

1 'J52/1' consisted of the former Stirling domeless saddle tanks ('J53'), which had been rebuilt to 'J52'.

2 'J52/2' were the Ivatt engines. There were a few small detailed differences (such as the flared top to the bunker) which could be used to distinguish these engines.

b These three engines had the boiler pressure increased.

c Some of Stirling's engines were fitted with condensing apparatus when they were converted to 'J52/1'. This could be recognised by side pipes between the smoke-box and the tank on the left side, and by a small casing on the saddle tank between the chimney and the dome. It was fitted to enable the engines to work through the Metropolitan line tunnels.

Year End Totals: 'J52' class

'47	'48	'49	'50	'51	'52	'53	'54	'55	'56	'57	'58	'59	'60	'61	'62	'63	'64	'65	'66	'67
132	132	132	127	126	122	113	97	65	45	27	7	3	2							

Year End Totals: 'J52' (service) class

'47	'48	'49	'50	'51	'52	'53	'54	'55	'56	'57	'58	'59	'60	'61	'62	'63	'64	'65	'66	'67
1	1	1	2	2	2	2	2	2	2	2	2	2	2							

Number	Built	Renumbered	BR Dates	Scrap	Notes
68757	12/92 Don	11/50 8757	-11/54	*54*	1c
68758	02/93 Don	09/48 8758	-11/55	*55*	1c
68759	03/93 Don	05/51 8759	-07/56	*56*	1c
68760	03/93 Don	03/51 8760	-11/54	*54*	1c
68761	04/93 Don	10/49 8761	-05/57	07/57	1c
68762	06/93 Don	12/48 8762	-08/51	*51*	1
68763	06/93 Don	8763	-10/50	*50*	1
68764	07/93 Don	04/51 8764	-11/54	*54*	1
68765	08/93 Don	01/50 8765	-12/55	*02/56*	1
68766	08/93 Don	04/48 8766	-01/52	*52*	1
68767	11/93 Don	03/48 8767	-11/50	*50*	1
68768	12/93 Don	01/49 8768	-10/57	12/57	1
68769	12/93 Don	05/48 8769	-09/55	12/55	1
68770	01/94 Don	01/50 8770	-08/53	*53*	1
68771	02/94 Don	05/49 8771	-10/55	12/55	1
68772	03/94 Don	05/50 8772	-09/54	*54*	1
68773	08/94 Don	07/49 8773	-04/53	*53*	1c
68774	09/94 Don	12/49 8774	-07/53	*53*	1c
68775	10/94 Don	02/49 8775	-06/52	*52*	1
68776	11/94 Don	12/49 8776	-10/53	*53*	1c
68777	12/94 Don	08/48 8777	-11/54	12/54	1c
68778	12/94 Don	02/49 8778	-07/57	07/57	1c
68779	05/95 Don	05/50 8779	-04/53	*53*	1
68780	06/95 Don	08/50 8780	-01/54	*54*	1
68781	08/95 Don	10/48 8781	-12/54	*55*	1c
68782	10/95 Don	07/48 8782	-12/50	*08/50*	1
68783	07/96 N	06/48 8783	-12/55	*12/55*	1c
68784	07/96 N	03/49 8784	-11/57	12/57	1c
68785	07/96 N	07/49 8785	-01/58	02/58	1c
68786	07/96 N	10/50 8786	-11/53	*53*	1
68787	07/96 N	09/50 8787	-10/55	12/55	1c
68788	07/96 N	05/52 8788	-12/54	*55*	1c
68789	07/96 N	07/49 8789	-04/52	*52*	1
68790	07/96 N	04/49 8790	-07/55	*55*	1
68791	07/96 N	02/49 8791	-11/54	12/54	1c
68792	07/96 N	12/49 8792	-06/52	*52*	1
68793	07/96 N	11/51 8793	-05/56	06/56	1c
68794	07/96 N	02/49 8794	-12/53	*54*	1c
68795	07/96 N	02/52 8795	-11/55	*55*	1c
68796	07/96 N	05/48 8796	-11/55	12/55	1c
68797	07/97 N	07/48 8797	-11/55	12/55	1
68798	06/97 N	11/50 8798	-11/54	12/54	1
68799	06/97 N	06/48 8799	-10/54	12/54	1
68800	06/97 N	09/50 8800	-07/58	07/58	1
68801	06/97 N	8801	-11/50	*50*	1
68802	08/97 N	06/48 8802	-11/54	*54*	1
68803	08/97 Don	07/50 8803	-08/53	*53*	1
68804	08/97 Don	04/49 8804	-10/55	*10/55*	1
68805	08/97 Don	11/49 8805	-10/55	12/55	2
68806	08/97 Don	07/49 8806	-11/55	*55*	2
68807	09/97 Don	08/48 8807	-09/55	*10/55*	2

Number	Built	Renumbered	BR Dates	Scrap	Notes
68808	09/97 Don	12/51 8808	-04/57	05/57	2
68809	09/97 Don	08/48 8809	-09/56	*56*	2
68810	10/97 Don	09/50 8810	-11/55	*55*	2
68811	10/97 Don	03/49 8811	-05/57	06/57	2
68812	10/97 Don	12/49 8812	-09/55	*55*	2
68813	10/97 Don	06/48 8813	-09/56	*56*	2
68814	10/97 Don	04/50 8814	-11/55	*55*	2
68815	12/98 RS	11/48 8815	-05/58	07/58	2
68816	01/99 RS	05/51 8816	-12/52	*56*	2
					12/52➲2
68817	02/99 RS	10/48 8817	-04/58	04/58	2
68818	02/99 RS	12/49 8818	-11/55	*55*	2
68819	02/99 RS	11/50 8819	-06/56	*56*	2
68820	03/99 RS	05/50 8820	-12/55	*02/56*	2
68821	03/99 RS	09/50 8821	-03/56	*56*	2
68822	04/99 RS	06/50 8822	-09/56	*56*	2
68823	04/99 RS	02/51 8823	-06/57	07/57	2
68824	04/99 RS	03/49 8824	-06/59	07/59	2
68825	04/99 SS	02/49 8825	-08/53	*53*	2
68826	04/99 SS	08/48 8826	-03/57	04/57	2
68827	04/99 SS	09/49 8827	-01/56	*02/56*	2
68828	04/99 SS	12/50 8828	-02/58	03/58	2
68829	04/99 SS	09/51 8829	-02/58	03/58	2
68830	04/99 SS	11/48 8830	-07/56	*56*	2
68831	04/99 SS	11/48 8831	-01/59	02/59	2
68832	04/99 SS	07/48 8832	-10/57	12/57	2
68833	04/99 SS	01/49 8833	-02/56	*56*	2
68834	04/99 SS	01/50 8834	-02/60	02/60	2
68835	04/99 SS	12/48 8835	-02/58	03/58	2
68836	04/99 SS	04/48 8836	-09/56	*56*	2
68837	04/99 SS	08/48 8837	-02/59	03/59	2
68838	04/99 SS	09/50 8838	-08/56	*56*	2
68839	04/99 SS	09/49 8839	-04/58	05/58	2
68840	05/99 SS	04/48 8840	-02/58	04/61	2b
					02/58➲9
68841	05/99 SS	03/49 8841	-04/57	04/57	2
68842	05/99 SS	12/48 8842	-07/58	10/58	2
68843	05/99 SS	04/48 8843	-04/57	05/57	2
68844	05/99 SS	12/48 8844	-10/54	*54*	2
68845	05/99 SS	8845	-12/52	*58*	2
					12/52➲1
68846 §	05/99 SS	12/48 8846	-05/59		2
68847	05/99 SS	05/48 8847	-08/58	10/58	2
68848	05/99 SS	02/51 8848	-10/58	10/58	2
68849	05/99 SS	07/48 8849	-12/57	01/58	2
68850	12/01 Don	02/49 8850	-10/54	12/54	2
68851	12/01 Don	11/49 8851	-05/57	06/57	2
68852	12/01 Don	02/50 8852	-12/55	*56*	2
68853	12/01 Don	09/48 8853	-07/56	*56*	2
68854	12/01 Don	05/48 8854	-07/54	*08/54*	2
68855	12/01 Don	10/50 8855	-11/56	*56*	2
68856	12/01 Don	10/51 8856	-11/55	*55*	2
68857	12/01 Don	12/50 8857	-04/58	05/58	2
68858	12/01 Don	06/48 8858	-11/55	*61*	2
					03/56➲2
68859	02/02 Don	07/49 8859	-08/54	*08/54*	2
68860	01/02 Don	06/49 8860	-12/57	03/58	2b
68861	02/02 Don	11/49 8861	-10/55	11/55	2
68862	02/02 Don	07/48 8862	-10/58	10/58	2
68863	03/02 Don	06/49 8863	-05/58	06/58	2
68864	03/02 Don	06/50 8864	-12/55	12/55	2
68865	03/02 Don	03/48 8865	-10/55	12/55	2
68866	03/02 Don	11/49 8866	-09/58	10/58	2
68867	04/02 Don	08/48 8867	-02/58	03/58	2
68868	03/02 Don	08/50 8868	-10/55	12/55	2
68869	03/02 Don	11/48 8869	-03/61	03/61	2
68870	10/05 Don	02/51 8870	-03/58	04/58	2
68871	10/05 Don	05/51 8871	-02/58	03/58	2
68872	10/05 Don	08/48 8872	-08/56	*56*	2
68873	10/05 Don	11/48 8873	-09/55	12/55	2
68874	11/05 Don	05/50 8874	-10/57	11/57	2
68875	11/05 Don	07/48 8875	-04/61	04/61	2
68876	11/05 Don	03/50 8876	-03/56	*56*	2b
68877	11/05 Don	02/49 8877	-11/56	*56*	2
68878	11/05 Don	05/50 8878	-05/56	06/56	2
68879	12/05 Don	04/48 8879	-09/55	*10/55*	2
68880	12/08 Don	05/50 8880	-08/56	*56*	2
68881	12/08 Don	05/50 8881	-11/55	*02/56*	2
68882	12/08 Don	03/49 8882	-01/58	03/58	2
68883	12/08 Don	12/48 8883	-09/55	*10/55*	2
68884	01/09 Don	06/48 8884	-09/55	*55*	2
68885	02/09 Don	06/49 8885	-09/56	*56*	2
68886	02/09 Don	09/48 8886	-11/57	12/57	2
68887	02/09 Don	09/48 8887	-09/57	10/57	2
68888	02/09 Don	08/50 8888	-10/57	12/57	2
68889	03/09 Don	11/48 8889	-05/55	*55*	2

Class continued with 1 (Service Locomotives)

J50 68890-68991, 10-16
0-6-0T GNR and LNER Gresley

Power Classification: 4F
Introduced: 1913-1939
Designer: Gresley
Company: GNR and LNER
Weight: 1 56t 6cwt
2 57t 0cwt
34 58t 3cwt
Driving Wheel: 4' 8"
Boiler Pressure: 175psi
Cylinders: Inside 18½" x 26"
Tractive Effort: 23635lbf
Valve Gear: Stephenson (slide valves)

Gresley added to the fleet of GNR 0-6-0Ts by the construction of this class which were known as the 'Ardsley Tanks' (GNR 'J23' class). They were designed for freight and shunting work. Introduced in 1922, most of the class were built at Doncaster. The total of 102 engines included thirty which were rebuilt from engines of Gresley's smaller 'J51' class.

The engines had distinctive side tanks. They ran the full length of the boiler and then sloped down at the front end. They were also fitted with a cut away section near the front which exposed the front splashers.

Thirty engines of this class were transferred to Hornsey in 1952 for working transfer freights to the Southern Region via the Metropolitan Widened lines. This was unusual as the engines were not fitted with condensing apparatus, which was normally required for this line. The width over the footplates was reduced by two inches to make them suitable for these duties.

Seven engines were transferred to work as departmental shunters at Doncaster Works in 1961-1962. They were renumbered in the service stock as 10-16, and they outlived the rest of the class by a couple of years.

1 'J50/1' consisted of ten 'J51' engines of 1913-1914. These were smaller Gresley GNR engines and they were rebuilt from 1929 as 'J50' engines. They originally had 18" diameter cylinders, 4ft 2in diameter boilers (rebuilt to 4ft 5in diameter as 'J50') and 3 ton bunkers (increased to 4¾ tons).

2 'J50/2' was Gresley's design for the GNR. They were built in 1914-1924 and also incorporated some earlier engines which were rebuilt (see 'r' below).

3 'J50/3' was a post-grouping development of the design. Introduced in 1926, they had some small detail differences (left-hand drive instead of right-hand drive and steam brakes instead of vacuum brakes). They also had a slightly less rounded cab roof.

4 The last batch of engines were built at Gorton in 1938-1939. They were classified as 'J50/4' and they were developed from the 'J50/3' class with a larger hopper type bunker.

r As well as the ten 'J50/1' engines, twenty of the 'J50/2's were also rebuilt from 'J51's (these built in 1915-1922).

Year End Totals: 'J50' class

'47	'48	'49	'50	'51	'52	'53	'54	'55	'56	'57	'58	'59	'60	'61	'62	'63	'64	'65	'66	'67
102	102	102	102	102	102	102	102	102	102	102	99	87	67	29	12					

Year End Totals: 'J50' (service) class

'47	'48	'49	'50	'51	'52	'53	'54	'55	'56	'57	'58	'59	'60	'61	'62	'63	'64	'65	'66	'67
														2	7	7	7			

Number	*Built*	*Renumbered*	*BR Dates*	*Scrap*	*Notes*
68890	12/13 Don	08/48 8890	-03/61	04/61	1
68891	02/14 Don	09/49 8891	-07/61	08/61	1
68892	02/14 Don	04/49 8892	-09/63	11/63	1
68893	02/14 Don	10/50 8893	-10/59	10/59	1
68894	02/14 Don	04/49 8894	-09/61	10/61	1
68895	02/14 Don	04/50 8895	-03/60	04/60	1
68896	03/14 Don	12/48 8896	-08/61	09/61	1
68897	03/14 Don	10/49 8897	-11/60	11/60	1
68898	03/14 Don	03/51 8898	-01/60	04/60	1
68899	04/14 Don	06/48 8899	-12/60	08/61	1
68900	12/14 Don	06/51 8900	-01/62	02/62	2r
68901	12/14 Don	12/49 8901	-10/60	11/60	2r
68902	12/14 Don	10/50 8902	-09/60	10/60	2r
68903	02/15 Don	03/49 8903	-04/61	05/61	2r
68904	02/15 Don	01/50 8904	-09/63	10/63	2r
68905	03/15 Don	05/49 8905	-12/60	06/61	2r
68906	04/15 Don	04/48 8906	-05/59	06/59	2r
68907	04/15 Don	02/49 8907	-04/61	05/61	2r
68908	06/15 Don	11/50 8908	-09/63	10/63	2r
68909	06/15 Don	08/49 8909	-04/60	04/60	2r
68910	06/19 Don	03/49 8910	-11/62	12/62	2r
68911	06/19 Don	01/50 8911	-11/60	09/65	2r
					04/61➲10
68912	07/19 Don	01/49 8912	-09/59	10/59	2r
68913	07/19 Don	10/50 8913	-08/60	09/60	2r
68914	07/19 Don	08/50 8914	-11/60	09/65	2r
					04/61➲11
68915	07/19 Don	12/50 8915	-10/60	11/60	2r
68916	07/19 Don	01/49 8916	-04/61	05/61	2r
68917	08/19 Don	08/48 8917	-09/62	09/65	2r
					09/62➲12
68918	08/19 Don	07/48 8918	-07/61	07/61	2r
68919	08/19 Don	11/49 8919	-09/59	10/59	2r
68920	10/22 Don	02/50 8920	-07/61	07/61	2
68921	11/22 Don	07/51 8921	-04/61	05/61	2
68922	11/22 Don	10/50 8922	-09/63	11/63	2
68923	11/22 Don	12/48 8923	-12/61	12/61	2
68924	11/22 Don	06/50 8924	-02/61	06/61	2
68925	12/22 Don	11/50 8925	-03/63	01/64	2
68926	12/22 Don	02/51 8926	-02/62	02/62	2
68927	12/22 Don	07/50 8927	-04/61	05/61	2
68928	12/22 Don	03/49 8928	-09/62	09/65	2
					09/62➲13
68929	12/22 Don	04/49 8929	-05/61	06/61	2
68930	02/24 Don	11/48 8930	-02/61	02/61	2
68931	02/24 Don	05/49 8931	-08/61	09/61	2
68932	03/24 Don	05/48 8932	-12/61	12/61	2
68933	03/24 Don	04/49 8933	-12/61	12/61	2
68934	03/24 Don	11/48 8934	-09/63	11/63	2
68935	04/24 Don	05/51 8935	-09/63	11/63	2
68936	04/24 Don	06/48 8936	-04/61	05/61	2
68937	05/24 Don	10/48 8937	-09/63	11/63	2
68938	05/24 Don	08/49 8938	-10/59	11/59	2
68939	06/24 Don	09/50 8939	-11/62	01/63	2
68940	03/26 Don	03/48 8940	-09/58	11/58	3
68941	03/26 Don	03/49 8941	-12/61	12/61	3
68942	04/26 Don	03/49 8942	-09/58	10/58	3
68943	04/26 Don	09/49 8943	-02/61	02/61	3
68944	04/26 Don	07/51 8944	-09/60	10/60	3
68945	04/26 Don	07/48 8945	-04/61	05/61	3
68946	04/26 Don	06/48 8946	-02/61	03/61	3
68947	05/26 Don	03/49 8947	-02/61	02/61	3
68948	05/26 Don	04/48 8948	-11/61	11/61	3
68949	06/26 Don	08/50 8949	-04/59	05/59	3
68950	08/26 Don	02/49 8950	-09/61	10/61	3
68951	08/26 Don	12/49 8951	-07/61	07/61	3
68952	08/26 Don	01/50 8952	-08/60	09/60	3
68953	08/26 Don	08/48 8953	-08/59	09/59	3
68954	08/26 Don	10/48 8954	-09/60	09/60	3
68955	09/26 Don	06/48 8955	-12/59	05/60	3
68956	09/26 Don	02/50 8956	-09/60	09/60	3
68957	09/26 Don	05/50 8957	-09/60	09/60	3
68958	10/26 Don	06/48 8958	-03/60	05/60	3
68959	11/26 Don	10/49 8959	-08/61	09/61	3
68960	11/26 Don	05/48 8960	-07/61	08/61	3
68961	11/26 Don	08/51 8961	-09/62	09/65	3
					09/62➲14
68962	12/26 Don	01/49 8962	-06/61	06/61	3
68963	12/26 Don	07/49 8963	-02/62	02/62	3
68964	12/26 Don	01/50 8964	-09/62	10/62	3
68965	12/26 Don	08/49 8965	-09/63	11/63	3
68966	12/26 Don	01/50 8966	-08/61	08/61	3
68967	01/27 Don	09/49 8967	-06/59	07/59	3
68968	01/27 Don	02/49 8968	-04/61	05/61	3
68969	03/27 Don	01/50 8969	-02/60	02/60	3
68970	04/27 Don	09/49 8970	-04/61	05/61	3
68971	05/27 Don	12/48 8971	-09/62	09/65	3
					09/62➲15
68972	03/30 Don	09/48 8972	-09/62	12/62	3
68973	03/30 Don	04/49 8973	-07/59	08/59	3
68974	03/30 Don	04/52 8974	-08/59	09/59	3
68975	04/30 Don	04/48 8975	-07/61	02/62	3
68976	04/30 Don	04/49 8976	-09/62	09/65	3
					09/62➲16
68977	04/30 Don	10/48 8977	-09/63	11/63	3
68978	11/38 Gor	04/48 8978	-11/58	12/58	4
68979	11/38 Gor	09/52 8979	-02/61	02/61	4
68980	12/38 Gor	10/50 8980	-02/60	03/60	4
68981	12/38 Gor	09/48 8981	-05/61	05/61	4
68982	12/38 Gor	05/49 8982	-09/62	12/62	4
68983	01/39 Gor	07/50 8983	-04/62	05/62	4
68984	02/39 Gor	03/49 8984	-03/63	04/63	4
68985	04/39 Gor	01/51 8985	-11/59	12/59	4
68986	04/39 Gor	08/51 8986	-07/62	07/62	4
68987	05/39 Gor	11/49 8987	-04/62	04/62	4
68988	06/39 Gor	11/48 8988	-09/63	11/63	4
68989	07/39 Gor	06/48 8989	-07/62	07/62	4
68990	07/39 Gor	05/49 8990	-04/61	05/61	4
68991	08/39 Gor	10/48 8991	-08/61	09/61	4

Class continued with 10 (Service Locomotives)

L1 67701-67800, (69000-69015)
2-6-4T LNER Thompson

Class continued from 67800

Number	*Built*	*Renumbered*	*BR Dates*	*Scrap*	*Notes*
69000	45 Don	9000	-12/60	09/61	
					05/48➲67701
69001	01/48 Dar	9001	01/48-10/60	11/60	
					05/48➲67702

Number	Built	Renumbered	BR Dates	Scrap	Notes
69002	01/48 Dar	9002	01/48-09/62	11/62	05/48➔67703
69003	02/48 Dar	9003	02/48-11/60	02/61	04/48➔67704
69004	02/48 Dar	9004	02/48-12/60	01/61	04/48➔67705
69005	02/48 Dar	9005	02/48-12/60	09/61	04/48➔67706
69006	02/48 Dar	9006	02/48-07/61	11/62	04/48➔67707
69007	03/48 Dar	9007	03/48-12/60	10/61	05/48➔67708
69008	03/48 Dar	9008	03/48-12/60	10/61	05/48➔67709
69009	03/48 Dar	9009	03/48-11/62	12/62	05/48➔67710
69010	03/48 Dar	9010	03/48-12/60	04/61	04/48➔67711
69011	03/48 Dar	9011	03/48-10/61	11/61	07/48➔67712
69012	04/48 Dar	9012	04/48-10/61	01/62	04/48➔67713
69013	04/48 Dar		04/48-12/60	01/61	05/48➔67714
69014	04/48 Dar		04/48-02/62	09/62	05/48➔67715
69015	04/48 Dar		04/48-09/62	12/62	05/48➔67716

J72 68670-68754, 69001-69028, 58-59
0-6-0T NER and BR Worsdell

Class continued from 68754

Number	Built	Renumbered	BR Dates	Scrap	Notes
69001	10/49 Dar		10/49-09/63	11/63	
69002	11/49 Dar		11/49-10/62	06/63	
69003	11/49 Dar		11/49-12/63	09/64	
69004	11/49 Dar		11/49-09/63	11/63	
69005	11/49 Dar		11/49-10/64	04/68	10/64➔58
69006	11/49 Dar		11/49-12/63	01/64	
69007	11/49 Dar		11/49-10/62	11/62	
69008	12/49 Dar		12/49-12/63	01/65	
69009	12/49 Dar		12/49-09/63	10/63	
69010	12/49 Dar		12/49-10/62	03/63	
69011	12/49 Dar		12/49-12/63	09/64	
69012	12/49 Dar		12/49-02/61	04/61	
69013	12/49 Dar		12/49-01/62	05/63	
69014	12/49 Dar		12/49-02/62	08/63	
69015	12/49 Dar		12/49-09/61	02/63	
69016	01/50 Dar		01/50-10/64	01/65	
69017	01/50 Dar		01/50-04/62	03/63	
69018	01/50 Dar		01/50-10/62	12/62	
69019	01/50 Dar		01/50-12/63	09/64	
69020	01/50 Dar		01/50-12/63	01/65	
69021	04/51 Dar		04/51-09/63	11/63	
69022	04/51 Dar		04/51-12/62	02/63	
69023 §	04/51 Dar		04/51-10/64		10/64➔59
69024	04/51 Dar		04/51-09/63	01/64	
69025	04/51 Dar		04/51-12/63	01/65	
69026	05/51 Dar		05/51-04/62	06/63	
69027	05/51 Dar		05/51-10/62	04/63	
69028	05/51 Dar		05/51-10/64	01/65	

Class continued with 58 (Service Locomotives)

L3 69050-69069
2-6-4T GCR Robinson

Power Classification:	5F
Introduced:	1914-1917
Designer:	Robinson
Company:	GCR
Weight:	97t 9cwt
Driving Wheel:	5' 1"
Boiler Pressure:	180psi superheated
Cylinders:	Inside 21" x 26" c Inside 20" x 26"
Tractive Effort:	28760lbf c 26085lbf
Valve Gear:	Stephenson (slide valves)

The 'L3' class was designed by Robinson for freight duties on the GCR. They were the GCR class '1B' and they were known as the LNER 'L1' class until 1945. A total of twenty engines were built between 1914 and 1917. They were the first 2-6-4Ts to appear in the country, and the only 2-6-4Ts to be built with inside cylinders.

Although designed for working goods trains they were known to have worked occasional passenger trains between Rickmansworth and Aylesbury, and in the Nottingham area.

They were fitted with flower-pot chimneys in LNER days, but most of the class received a later type of chimney and altered bunker before withdrawal.

The first engine was withdrawn in 1947. The remaining nineteen came into BR stock, and they had all been withdrawn by 1955.

c 69061 had smaller cylinders.

Year End Totals: 'L3' class

'47	'48	'49	'50	'51	'52	'53	'54	'55	'56	'57	'58	'59	'60	'61	'62	'63	'64	'65	'66	'67
19	19	15	12	7	7	6	3													

Number	Built	Renumbered	BR Dates	Scrap	Notes
69050	12/14 Gor	03/50 9050	-03/55	*11/55*	
69051	12/14 Gor	11/48 9051	-05/51	*51*	
69052	02/15 Gor	06/48 9052	-08/54	*11/55*	
69053	03/15 Gor	9053	-07/50	*08/50*	
69054	03/15 Gor	04/48 9054	-08/49	*49*	
69055	04/15 Gor	09/48 9055	-07/51	*07/51*	
69056	05/15 Gor	9056	-01/51	02/51	
69057	06/15 Gor	9057	-10/49	*49*	
69058	11/15 Gor	9058	-08/49	*49*	
69059	12/15 Gor	9059	-08/49	*49*	
69060	06/16 Gor	04/48 9060	-06/54	*08/54*	
69061	06/16 Gor	11/48 9061	-02/53	*53*	c
69062	06/16 Gor	06/48 9062	-05/51	*51*	
69064	01/17 Gor	08/50 9064	-01/55	*02/55*	
69065	02/17 Gor	08/50 9065	-05/54	*54*	
69066	03/17 Gor	9066	-04/50	*50*	
69067	03/17 Gor	9067	-02/51	*51*	
69068	04/17 Gor	9068	-07/50	*08/50*	
69069	05/17 Gor	09/49 9069	-07/55	*55*	

L2 69070-69071
2-6-4T Metropolitan Railway

Power Classification:	4MT
Introduced:	1925
Designer:	Hally
Company:	Metropolitan Railway
Weight:	87t 7cwt
Driving Wheel:	5' 6"
Boiler Pressure:	200psi superheated
Cylinders:	Outside 19" x 28"
Tractive Effort:	26035lbf
Valve Gear:	Walschaert (piston valves)

In the 1920s the Government was seeking to avoid unemployment at Woolwich Arsenal resulting from the decline of arms manufacture. They ordered one hundred complete sets of parts for SECR 'N' class locomotives (the boilers being built by the North British Locomotive Company and the remainder at Woolwich) in 1924-1925. It was hoped that other railways would purchase these to replenish their locomotive stock, but unfortunately there were no takers. In 1925 the Southern Railway purchased parts for fifty locomotives at a very cheap price and twenty-six sets of parts went to the Great Southern Railway of Ireland.

Another six sets of parts were converted by Armstrong Whitworth & Co. in 1925 as 2-6-4T engines for the Metropolitan Railway. They were numbered 111-116 and they were the last new steam engines to be built for the Metropolitan Railway. They were mainly used for working coal traffic from the junction with the LMS at Verney Junction to the power station at Neasden.

The six engines were acquired by the LNER from the London Passenger Transport Board in 1937, becoming LNER 6158-6163 (class 'L2'). The two survivors which came into BR stock were both taken out of service in 1948.

Year End Totals: 'L2' class

'47	'48	'49	'50	'51	'52	'53	'54	'55	'56	'57	'58	'59	'60	'61	'62	'63	'64	'65	'66	'67
2																				

Number	Built	Renumbered	BR Dates	Scrap	Notes
69070	03/25 AW	9070	-10/48	*10/48*	
69071	03/25 AW	9071	-10/48	*10/48*	

M2 69076-69077
0-6-4T Metropolitan Railway

Power Classification:	3MT
Introduced:	1915-1916
Designer:	Jones
Company:	Metropolitan Railway
Weight:	71t 1cwt
Driving Wheel:	5' 9"
Boiler Pressure:	160psi superheated
Cylinders:	Inside 20" x 26"
Tractive Effort:	20500lbf
Valve Gear:	Stephenson (piston valves)

These two engines were the survivors of four 0-6-4Ts which were built for the Metropolitan Railway by the Yorkshire Engine Company in 1915. They were numbered 94-97 and they were taken over by the LNER from the London Passenger Transport Board in 1937, becoming LNER 6154-6157 (class 'M2').

They were the only named locomotives on the Metropolitan Railway since the early days and the other two engines (94 and 97) were named LORD ABERCONWAY and BRILL. The two survivors were taken out of service in 1948.

Year End Totals: 'M2' class

'47	'48	'49	'50	'51	'52	'53	'54	'55	'56	'57	'58	'59	'60	'61	'62	'63	'64	'65	'66	'67
2																				

Number	Built	Renumbered	BR Dates	Scrap	Notes
69076 ROBERT H. SELBIE	01/16 YE	9076	-10/48	*10/48*	
69077 CHARLES JONES	02/16 YE	9077	-10/48	*10/48*	

N12 69089
0-6-2T H&BR

Power Classification:	4F
Introduced:	1901
Designer:	M Stirling
Company:	H&BR
Weight:	58t 0cwt
Driving Wheel:	4' 6"
Boiler Pressure:	175psi
Cylinders:	Inside 18" x 26"
Tractive Effort:	23205lbf
Valve Gear:	Stephenson (piston valves)

This was the last survivor of a class of nine 0-6-2Ts which had been built in 1901 for the Hull and Barnsley Railway. They were the H&BR class 'F2' and the first engine was withdrawn in 1936. The engines were originally built with domeless boilers, but they later carried domed boilers. The 'N13' class was built as an enlarged version of this class.

This engine was withdrawn from Hull Springhead in August 1948 without being renumbered.

Year End Totals: 'N12' class

'47	'48	'49	'50	'51	'52	'53	'54	'55	'56	'57	'58	'59	'60	'61	'62	'63	'64	'65	'66	'67
1																				

Number	Built	Renumbered	BR Dates	Scrap	Notes
69089	12/01 K	9089	-08/48	*48*	

N10 69090-69109
0-6-2T NER Worsdell

Power Classification:	3F
Introduced:	1902-1903
Designer:	W Worsdell
Company:	NER
Weight:	57t 14cwt
Driving Wheel:	4' 7¼"
Boiler Pressure:	160psi
Cylinders:	Inside 18½" x 26"
Tractive Effort:	21905lbf
Valve Gear:	Stephenson (slide valves)

Worsdell built twenty of these 0-6-2T engines (NER class 'U') in 1902-1903. Built as mixed traffic engines, they were tank engine versions of the 'J25' class. Like that class they had boilers which were interchangeable with the 'J21' class, but none of those fitted to these tank engines were superheated.

The NER also had two other classes of 0-6-2Ts (see 'N8' and 'N9') which were tank engine equivalents of the 'J21' class.

Year End Totals: 'N10' class

'47	'48	'49	'50	'51	'52	'53	'54	'55	'56	'57	'58	'59	'60	'61	'62	'63	'64	'65	'66	'67
20	19	19	19	19	19	19	19	18	16	9	6	4	4	3						

Number	Built	Renumbered	BR Dates	Scrap	Notes
69090	10/02 Dar	01/49 9090	-11/56	56	
69091	11/02 Dar	12/48 9091	-11/56	*01/57*	
69092	11/02 Dar	08/49 9092	-04/59	04/59	
69093	11/02 Dar	03/49 9093	-12/57	01/58	
69094	11/02 Dar	11/49 9094	-07/57	08/57	
69095	12/02 Dar	10/50 9095	-10/55	55	
69096	12/02 Dar	05/50 9096	-12/57	01/58	
69097	12/02 Dar	03/50 9097	-04/62	08/62	
69098	10/02 Dar	05/49 9098	-09/57	10/57	
69099	12/02 Dar	11/48 9099	-02/58	02/58	
69100	10/02 Dar	11/50 9100	-11/57	01/58	
69101	12/02 Dar	11/49 9101	-04/62	03/63	
69102	12/02 Dar	12/48 9102	-02/59	02/59	
69103	12/02 Dar	9103	-11/48	*12/48*	
69104	12/02 Dar	05/49 9104	-03/58	04/58	
69105	03/03 Dar	06/49 9105	-06/61	07/61	
69106	03/03 Dar	06/49 9106	-03/58	04/58	
69107	03/03 Dar	04/49 9107	-12/57	01/58	
69108	04/03 Dar	10/49 9108	-07/57	08/57	
69109	04/03 Dar	07/48 9109	-04/62	09/62	

N13 69110-69119
0-6-2T H&BR Stirling

Power Classification:	4F reclassified 3F in 1953
Introduced:	1913-1914
Designer:	M Stirling
Company:	H&BR
Weight:	61t 9cwt
Driving Wheel:	4' 6"
Boiler Pressure:	175psi
Cylinders:	Inside 18" x 26"
Tractive Effort:	23205lbf
Valve Gear:	Stephenson (slide valves)

These ten engines were built in 1913-1914 for the Hull and Barnsley Railway as an enlarged version of the 'N12' class. They were the H&BR class 'F3'. They were all withdrawn between 1948 and 1956.

Year End Totals: 'N13' class

'47	'48	'49	'50	'51	'52	'53	'54	'55	'56	'57	'58	'59	'60	'61	'62	'63	'64	'65	'66	'67
10	9	9	9	9	6	5	4	1												

Number	Built	Renumbered	BR Dates	Scrap	Notes
69110	11/13 HL	9110	-06/48	*06/48*	
69111	12/13 HL	05/49 9111	-08/52	52	
69112	12/13 HL	01/50 9112	-11/52	12/52	
69113	12/13 HL	12/49 9113	-05/53	53	
69114	01/14 HL	09/48 9114	-10/56	56	
69115	01/14 HL	09/50 9115	-05/55	06/55	
69116	02/14 HL	10/51 9116	-12/54	01/55	
69117	02/14 HL	06/50 9117	-07/55	08/55	
69118	03/14 HL	08/50 9118	-05/52	52	
69119	03/14 HL	07/50 9119	-06/55	55	

N14 69120-69125
0-6-2T NBR Reid

Power Classification:	4MT reclassified 3MT in 1953
Introduced:	1909
Designer:	Reid
Company:	NBR
Weight:	62t 19cwt
Driving Wheel:	4' 6"
Boiler Pressure:	175psi
Cylinders:	Inside 18" x 26"
Tractive Effort:	23205lbf
Valve Gear:	Stephenson (slide valves)

In 1909 W P Reid introduced six 0-6-2T engines with 4½ ton bunkers for banking duties on Cowlairs incline. They were the NBR class 'A'. They were fitted with safety valves on the dome. They were later rebuilt with 'N15' type boilers.

In 1910 six more engines were built with detail differences for the same duties. They were classified 'N15/2'.

The first three of the 'N14's were withdrawn in 1947 leaving three to come into BR stock. They were all withdrawn by 1954.

Year End Totals: 'N14' class

'47	'48	'49	'50	'51	'52	'53	'54	'55	'56	'57	'58	'59	'60	'61	'62	'63	'64	'65	'66	'67
3	3	3	2	2	2	2														

Number	Built	Renumbered	BR Dates	Scrap	Notes
69120	09/09 NB	03/49 9120	-03/54	*05/54*	
69124	09/09 NB	12/48 9124	-11/50	*50*	
69125	09/09 NB	04/50 9125	-03/54	*05/54*	

N15 69126-69224
0-6-2T NBR Reid

Power Classification:	4MT reclassified 3MT in 1953
Introduced:	1910-1924
Designer:	Reid
Company:	NBR
Weight:	1 60t 18cwt
	2 62t 1cwt
Driving Wheel:	4' 6"
Boiler Pressure:	175psi
Cylinders:	Inside 18" x 26"
Tractive Effort:	23205lbf
Valve Gear:	Stephenson (slide valves)

These engines were developed from the 'N14' class by Reid. They were known as NBR class 'A' and ninety-nine engines were built between 1910 and 1924.

1 The 'N15/1' class was a version of the 'N15/2's for general freight duties. They were fitted with smaller 3½ ton bunkers. Sixty-three engines were built between 1910 and 1920 and thirty more were built by the LNER in 1923-1924.

2 The 'N15/2' engines were fitted with larger 4½ ton bunkers for banking duties on Cowlairs incline. Six engines were built in 1910. They differed from the 'N14's by having the safety valves over the firebox, and by having larger cabs. They were fitted with Westinghouse brakes.

b One of the original 'N14' boilers with pop safety valves on the dome survived in BR days. It was carried by 69151 until 1951 and thereafter by 69222.

Year End Totals: 'N15' class

'47	'48	'49	'50	'51	'52	'53	'54	'55	'56	'57	'58	'59	'60	'61	'62	'63	'64	'65	'66	'67
99	99	99	99	99	99	99	99	99	99	96	75	54	30	21						

Number	Built	Renumbered	BR Dates	Scrap	Notes
69126	06/10 NB	06/48 9126	-02/62	09/62	2
69127	06/10 NB	01/51 9127	-06/59	08/59	2
69128	06/10 NB	10/50 9128	-10/62	12/64	2
69129	06/10 NB	08/49 9129	-12/58	01/59	2
69130	06/10 NB	07/48 9130	-12/57	03/58	2
69131	07/10 NB	10/50 9131	-02/62	11/62	2
69132	06/10 NB	06/49 9132	-11/60	01/61	1
69133	06/10 NB	12/49 9133	-08/60	09/60	1
69134	07/10 NB	08/48 9134	-03/61	04/61	1
69135	07/10 NB	08/48 9135	-10/62	02/63	1
69136	07/10 NB	01/49 9136	-05/61	07/61	1
69137	07/10 NB	06/48 9137	-05/62	07/62	1
69138	07/10 NB	01/51 9138	-10/62	06/64	1
69139	07/10 NB	10/48 9139	-06/58	07/58	1
69140	08/10 NB	03/49 9140	-06/58	04/59	1
69141	08/10 NB	11/48 9141	-09/60	09/60	1
69142	08/10 NB	07/48 9142	-01/58	03/58	1
69143	08/10 NB	52 9143	-09/60	02/61	1
69144	07/12 NB	08/48 9144	-02/60	04/60	1
69145	07/12 NB	06/48 9145	-03/60	05/60	1
69146	07/12 NB	04/49 9146	-07/59	09/59	1
69147	08/12 NB	01/49 9147	-06/58	02/59	1
69148	08/12 NB	12/50 9148	-06/58	03/59	1
69149	08/12 NB	04/48 9149	-03/60	05/60	1
69150	08/12 NB	08/48 9150	-10/62	02/63	1
69151	08/12 NB	05/50 9151	-02/59	02/60	1b
69152	08/12 NB	12/48 9152	-12/58	01/59	1
69153	08/12 NB	09/48 9153	-09/58	08/59	1
69154	08/12 NB	06/48 9154	-11/59	02/60	1
69155	08/12 NB	10/48 9155	-09/62	06/63	1
69156	08/12 NB	07/48 9156	-02/62	06/63	1
69157	08/12 NB	07/49 9157	-04/58	07/58	1
69158	08/12 NB	08/48 9158	-05/58	07/58	1
69159	08/12 NB	07/48 9159	-10/61	06/63	1
69160	08/12 NB	03/50 9160	-08/58	02/60	1
69161	08/12 NB	02/51 9161	-09/60	10/60	1
69162	08/12 NB	04/50 9162	-03/59	02/60	1
69163	08/12 NB	09/48 9163	-02/62	07/62	1
69164	05/13 NB	06/48 9164	-04/59	02/60	1
69165	05/13 NB	11/49 9165	-05/60	06/60	1
69166	05/13 NB	06/49 9166	-12/59	01/60	1
69167	05/13 NB	07/48 9167	-12/57	07/58	1
69168	05/13 NB	04/49 9168	-02/60	03/60	1
69169	05/13 NB	05/48 9169	-02/59	12/59	1
69170	05/13 NB	02/50 9170	-01/60	04/60	1
69171	05/13 NB	07/50 9171	-06/60	08/60	1
69172	08/16 NB	03/51 9172	-11/58	08/59	1
69173	08/16 NB	04/50 9173	-01/61	03/61	1
69174	09/16 NB	10/48 9174	-11/58	12/58	1
69175	09/16 NB	04/48 9175	-10/58	03/59	1
69176	10/16 NB	12/49 9176	-08/59	09/59	1
69177	12/16 NB	08/49 9177	-08/60	10/60	1
69178	12/23 Cow	06/48 9178	-12/62	10/63	1
69179	01/17 NB	06/48 9179	-09/60	11/60	1
69180	01/17 NB	08/50 9180	-03/61	04/61	1
69181	02/17 NB	04/51 9181	-02/62	11/62	1
69182	03/17 NB	12/50 9182	-09/59	09/59	1
69183	03/17 NB	03/49 9183	-11/61	09/63	1
69184	03/17 NB	10/48 9184	-11/60	01/61	1
69185	05/13 NB	04/48 9185	-07/59	09/59	1
69186	02/20 NB	03/48 9186	-07/59	10/59	1
69187	02/20 NB	04/48 9187	-12/59	03/60	1
69188	02/20 NB	12/49 9188	-10/62	12/62	1
69189	02/20 NB	11/50 9189	-04/58	06/58	1
69190	02/20 NB	06/48 9190	-08/60	10/60	1
69191	02/20 NB	05/51 9191	-10/62	10/62	1
69192	02/20 NB	07/49 9192	-03/59	09/59	1
69193	03/20 NB	12/49 9193	-08/58	12/58	1
69194	03/20 NB	03/50 9194	-10/60	11/60	1
69195	03/20 NB	12/49 9195	-03/58	05/58	1
69196	01/23 RS	03/49 9196	-10/62	10/63	1
69197	01/23 RS	10/48 9197	-12/59	03/60	1
69198	02/23 RS	05/48 9198	-06/60	06/60	1
69199	02/23 RS	04/48 9199	-05/61	09/61	1
69200	03/23 RS	12/48 9200	-06/58	02/59	1
69201	03/23 RS	05/48 9201	-01/58	03/58	1
69202	03/23 RS	02/49 9202	-05/60	06/60	1
69203	03/23 RS	11/48 9203	-06/58	06/60	1
69204	03/23 RS	11/48 9204	-07/62	11/62	1
69205	03/23 RS	12/49 9205	-02/60	04/60	1
69206	10/23 Cow	06/48 9206	-05/60	06/60	1
69207	11/23 Cow	03/49 9207	-02/60	03/60	1
69208	11/23 Cow	10/48 9208	-11/59	02/60	1
69209	11/23 Cow	06/49 9209	-10/60	11/60	1
69210	11/23 Cow	11/48 9210	-10/57	02/58	1
69211	11/23 Cow	09/48 9211	-10/62	06/64	1
69212	12/23 Cow	04/48 9212	-10/62	10/62	1
69213	12/23 Cow	06/48 9213	-10/59	02/60	1
69214	12/23 Cow	01/50 9214	-05/59	09/59	1
69215	12/23 Cow	10/48 9215	-11/59	04/60	1
69216	12/23 Cow	11/49 9216	-02/62	06/63	1
69217	02/24 Cow	03/51 9217	-10/59	02/60	1
69218	02/24 Cow	10/48 9218	-10/62	11/62	1
69219	02/24 Cow	05/48 9219	-12/61	09/63	1
69220	03/24 Cow	07/51 9220	-11/58	06/59	1
69221	03/24 Cow	04/48 9221	-07/61	08/61	1
69222	03/24 Cow	02/49 9222	-05/59	12/59	1 51⇨b
69223	03/24 Cow	08/48 9223	-08/60	11/60	1
69224	04/24 Cow	09/49 9224	-10/62	02/63	1

N4 69225-69247
0-6-2T MS&LR (GCR) Parker

Power Classification:	2MT
Introduced:	1889-1892
Designer:	Parker
Company:	MS&LR
Weight:	2 61t 10cwt
	4 61t 19cwt
Driving Wheel:	5' 1"
Boiler Pressure:	160psi
Cylinders:	Inside 18" x 26"
Tractive Effort:	18780lbf
Valve Gear:	Joy (slide valves)

The 'N4' class (GCR class '9A') was introduced by Parker on the Manchester Sheffield and Lincolnshire Railway in 1889. A total of fifty-five engines were built in 1889-1892 with round-topped boilers and Joy valve gear. They were all later rebuilt with Belpaire boilers. They were fitted with 'flower-pot' chimneys by Gresley during LNER days. The first engine was withdrawn in 1932.

The class was developed into the 'N5' class with Belpaire boilers and Stephenson valve gear in 1891.

2 'N4/2'. These were the original engines introduced in 1889.

4 'N4/4'. These engines were developed from 'N4/2' with larger bunkers.

1 & 3 'N4/1' and 'N4/3' were engines of 'N4/2' and 'N4/4' before the chimneys were shortened to fit the LNER loading gauge.

Year End Totals: 'N4' class

'47	'48	'49	'50	'51	'52	'53	'54	'55	'56	'57	'58	'59	'60	'61	'62	'63	'64	'65	'66	'67
22	22	19	16	16	11	9														

Number	Built	Renumbered	BR Dates	Scrap	Notes
69225	12/89 Gor	09/49 9225	-12/54	55	2
69226	01/90 Gor	9226	-10/49	*49*	2
69227	07/90 N	06/48 9227	-11/53	12/53	2

GNR Stirling 'J52' class 0-6-0ST No 68878 at King's Cross shed in October 1955.

NER Worsdell 'N10' class 0-6-2T No 69099.

Hull & Barnsley Railway Stirling 'N13' class 0-6-2T No 69113.

NBR Reid 'N15' class 0-6-2T No 69178, fitted with a stove-pipe chimney.

Number	Built	Renumbered	BR Dates	Scrap	Notes
69228	07/90 N	02/50 9228	-12/54	02/55	2
69229	08/90 N	04/50 9229	-06/52	07/52	2
69230	11/90 N	12/49 9230	-12/54	02/55	2
69231	11/90 N	02/50 9231	-10/54	54	2
69232	12/90 N	12/49 9232	-12/54	02/55	2
69233	12/90 N	01/50 9233	-11/54	54	2
69234	01/91 N	08/48 9234	-01/53	53	2
69235	01/91 N	10/49 9235	-08/54	08/54	2
69236	04/91 N	03/48 9236	-11/54	54	2
69237	04/91 N	05/48 9237	-07/50	08/50	2
69239	05/91 N	04/48 9239	-03/54	54	2
69240	05/91 N	06/50 9240	-11/52	52	2
69241	05/91 N	9241	-09/49	49	2
69242	02/92 N	02/49 9242	-01/52	52	4
69243	02/92 N	9243	-10/49	49	4
69244	02/92 N	08/49 9244	-02/52	52	4
69245	03/92 N	06/48 9245	-10/50	12/50	4
69246	03/92 N	09/49 9246	-04/52	52	4
69247	03/92 N	9247	-05/50	50	4

N5 69250-69370
0-6-2T MS&LR (GCR) Parker/Pollitt

Power Classification:	2MT
Introduced:	1891-1901 3 Rebuilt 1915 by Robinson
Designer:	Parker and Pollitt
Company:	MS&LR
Weight:	2 62t 7cwt 3 64t 13cwt
Driving Wheel:	5' 1"
Boiler Pressure:	160psi
Cylinders:	2 Inside 18" x 26" 3 Inside 18½" x 26"
Tractive Effort:	2 18780lbf 3 19840lbf
Valve Gear:	Stephenson (slide valves)

The 'N5' class of 0-6-2T was directly developed from the MS&LR 'N4' class. The only change was the fitting of Belpaire boilers and Stephenson valve gear instead of Joy valve gear.

The first three engines (GCR class '9C') appeared from Gorton in 1891. They were of considerable importance in that they were the first engines in the country to be fitted with Belpaire fireboxes. After this an 0-6-0 tender version appeared (GCR '9D', LNER 'J10'), before 124 more engines of the class appeared (mostly built by Beyer Peacock) between 1894 and 1901. They were identical with the first three engines but they were classified '9F' by the GCR (as the MS&LR was renamed in 1897).

They were all fitted with 'flower-pot' chimneys by Gresley during LNER days, in common with many other ex-GCR engines. The first engine was withdrawn in 1936.

1 The 'N5/1' classification was originally used for engines of 'N5/2' before the chimneys were shortened to fit the LNER loading gauge.

2 The standard engines were classified 'N5/2'.

3 69311 was rebuilt with larger tanks, bunker and cylinders in 1915. The side tanks flanked the whole length of the boiler and the water capacity was increased from 1360 gallons to 2000 gallons. It was reclassified 'N5/3'.

p 69257 was fitted with push-pull control apparatus.

w Two locomotives (69270 and one other which was withdrawn in 1936) were built new for the Wrexham, Mold and Connah's Quay Railway to the GCR design. They came into GCR stock when that line was taken over by the GCR in 1905.

Year End Totals: 'N5/2' class

'47	'48	'49	'50	'51	'52	'53	'54	'55	'56	'57	'58	'59	'60	'61	'62	'63	'64	'65	'66	'67
120	120	119	119	118	118	118	115	88	65	49	35	19								

Year End Totals: 'N5/3' class

'47	'48	'49	'50	'51	'52	'53	'54	'55	'56	'57	'58	'59	'60	'61	'62	'63	'64	'65	'66	'67
1	1	1	1	1																

Number	Built	Renumbered	BR Dates	Scrap	Notes
69250	09/91 Gor	02/51 9250	-08/56	10/56	2
69251	08/92 Gor	02/49 9251	-07/49	49	2
69252	11/92 Gor	01/49 9252	-08/51	51	2
69253	08/93 BP	03/48 9253	-11/55	55	2
69254	09/93 BP	10/48 9254	-03/56	05/56	2
69255	09/93 BP	07/48 9255	-06/56	56	2
69256	09/93 BP	06/48 9256	-11/55	55	2
69257	10/93 BP	10/50 9257	-12/59	04/60	2p
69258	10/93 BP	03/49 9258	-09/60	09/60	2
69259	10/93 BP	09/48 9259	-11/58	12/58	2
69260	10/93 BP	09/49 9260	-07/56	56	2
69261	10/93 BP	01/49 9261	-12/57	09/58	2
69262	10/93 BP	03/49 9262	-12/59	01/60	2
69263	11/93 BP	11/50 9263	-12/60	12/60	2
69264	11/93 BP	04/49 9264	-02/55	55	2
69265	11/93 BP	03/49 9265	-12/59	04/60	2
69266	12/93 BP	09/49 9266	-12/60	12/60	2
69267	12/93 BP	07/48 9267	-02/60	03/60	2
69268	01/94 BP	06/48 9268	-02/60	02/60	2
69269	01/94 BP	01/49 9269	-10/58	10/58	2
69270	96 BP	03/49 9270	-10/56	02/57	2w
69271	01/94 BP	04/53 9271	-03/58	05/58	2
69272	02/94 BP	03/49 9272	-04/56	56	2
69273	02/94 BP	06/52 9273	-06/55	55	2
69274	02/94 BP	03/49 9274	-12/60	12/60	2
69275	02/94 BP	03/49 9275	-11/55	55	2
69276	03/94 BP	02/49 9276	-12/59	04/60	2
69277	03/94 BP	05/49 9277	-11/56	56	2
69278	03/94 BP	04/50 9278	-11/55	55	2
69279	03/94 BP	05/49 9279	-06/55	55	2
69280	03/94 BP	04/48 9280	-11/55	55	2
69281	03/94 BP	04/48 9281	-08/58	10/58	2
69282	08/94 BP	06/48 9282	-07/55	03/56	2
69283	08/94 BP	08/51 9283	-06/58	07/58	2
69284	08/94 BP	10/48 9284	-02/58	06/58	2
69285	09/94 BP	08/49 9285	-11/55	55	2
69286	09/94 BP	04/49 9286	-12/60	12/60	2
69287	09/94 BP	06/49 9287	-07/55	55	2
69288	10/94 BP	03/49 9288	-04/55	55	2
69289	10/94 BP	06/49 9289	-01/54	54	2
69290	10/94 BP	07/50 9290	-10/59	12/59	2
69291	11/94 BP	03/49 9291	-11/55	55	2
69292	09/95 Gor	02/49 9292	-02/60	03/60	2
69293	05/95 Gor	03/49 9293	-12/60	12/60	2
69294	10/96 Gor	05/49 9294	-10/59	10/59	2
69295	12/96 Gor	03/49 9295	-03/58	03/58	2
69296	09/96 Gor	03/49 9296	-12/60	12/60	2
69297	02/96 Gor	01/51 9297	-08/58	08/58	2
69298	04/96 Gor	03/49 9298	-12/59	04/60	2
69299	05/96 Gor	03/50 9299	-02/60	03/60	2
69300	05/96 Gor	02/51 9300	-02/58	09/58	2
69301	06/96 Gor	03/48 9301	-12/55	56	2
69302	01/96 BP	11/50 9302	-12/57	09/58	2
69303	03/98 BP	04/50 9303	-11/55	55	2
69304	03/98 BP	04/48 9304	-02/55	55	2
69305	05/98 BP	09/50 9305	-02/58	05/58	2
69306	05/98 BP	06/49 9306	-10/55	55	2
69307	05/98 BP	01/49 9307	-12/60	01/61	2
69308	05/98 BP	03/49 9308	-03/60	04/60	2
69309	07/98 BP	05/50 9309	-12/60	12/60	2
69310	07/98 BP	01/50 9310	-11/55	55	2
69311	07/98 BP	08/48 9311	-02/52	52	3
69312	07/98 BP	01/49 9312	-10/57	12/57	2
69313	08/98 BP	03/52 9313	-03/55	55	2
69314	08/98 BP	03/52 9314	-02/60	07/60	2
69315	04/98 Gor	08/48 9315	-06/58	07/58	2
69316	05/98 Gor	10/48 9316	-03/57	03/57	2
69317	02/98 Gor	02/49 9317	-02/56	03/56	2
69318	03/99 Gor	11/50 9318	-11/56	02/57	2
69319	03/99 Gor	10/49 9319	-12/59	04/60	2
69320	04/99 Gor	11/50 9320	-10/59	10/59	2
69321	05/99 Gor	09/50 9321	-09/56	56	2
69322	06/99 Gor	11/50 9322	-07/59	09/59	2
69323	06/99 Gor	01/50 9323	-11/56	56	2
69324	07/99 Gor	05/49 9324	-11/54	01/55	2
69325	08/99 Gor	06/50 9325	-09/56	56	2
69326	09/99 Gor	01/49 9326	-10/57	10/57	2
69327	09/99 Gor	03/49 9327	-09/59	10/59	2
69328	10/99 Gor	02/49 9328	-01/57	03/57	2
69329	11/99 Gor	04/48 9329	-09/57	11/57	2
69330	11/99 Gor	06/49 9330	-02/55	55	2
69331	11/99 Gor	03/49 9331	-01/57	01/57	2
69332	12/99 Gor	11/48 9332	-02/59	03/59	2
69333	12/99 Gor	02/49 9333	-01/56	56	2
69334	12/99 Gor	10/50 9334	-07/56	56	2
69335	02/00 Gor	08/48 9335	-09/57	09/57	2
69336	03/00 Gor	09/48 9336	-12/54	55	2
69337	03/00 Gor	03/49 9337	-08/56	56	2
69338	02/00 Gor	04/48 9338	-03/55	02/56	2
69339	05/00 Gor	03/49 9339	-03/56	56	2
69340	06/00 Gor	05/49 9340	-05/56	06/56	2
69341	06/00 Gor	11/48 9341	-12/59	04/60	2
69342	07/00 Gor	03/49 9342	-08/59	09/59	2
69343	09/00 Gor	02/49 9343	-01/60	03/60	2
69344	10/00 Gor	03/49 9344	-12/59	01/60	2
69345	10/00 Gor	06/50 9345	-09/56	02/57	2
69346	12/00 Gor	06/49 9346	-09/57	09/57	2
69347	12/00 Gor	02/49 9347	-10/57	12/57	2
69348	12/00 Gor	08/50 9348	-01/57	03/57	2
69349	04/00 BP	06/49 9349	-08/58	10/58	2
69350	04/00 BP	12/50 9350	-01/57	04/57	2
69351	04/00 BP	01/50 9351	-09/56	56	2
69352	04/00 BP	04/48 9352	-06/55	55	2
69353	05/00 BP	01/51 9353	-11/55	03/56	2
69354	05/00 BP	03/48 9354	-02/60	04/60	2
69355	05/00 BP	10/48 9355	-04/58	09/58	2
69356	05/00 BP	03/49 9356	-02/57	03/57	2
69357	05/00 BP	01/50 9357	-11/55	55	2
69358	05/00 BP	11/50 9358	-11/56	56	2
69359	05/00 BP	02/49 9359	-04/56	56	2
69360	06/00 BP	11/48 9360	-04/60	04/60	2
69361	06/00 BP	04/48 9361	-06/59	09/59	2
69362	06/00 BP	06/49 9362	-08/58	09/58	2
69363	07/00 BP	06/49 9363	-07/56	56	2
69364	07/00 BP	01/49 9364	-08/55	55	2
69365	02/01 BP	04/49 9365	-02/57	03/57	2
69366	02/01 BP	06/48 9366	-08/56	56	2
69367	02/01 BP	08/48 9367	-11/55	55	2
69368	02/01 BP	09/48 9368	-05/55	55	2
69369	03/01 BP	12/50 9369	-02/57	03/57	2
69370	03/01 BP	01/49 9370	-09/60	09/60	2

N8 69371-69401
0-6-2T NER Worsdell

Power Classification:	3MT
Introduced:	1886-1890
Designer:	T W Worsdell
Company:	NER
Weight:	56t 5cwt s 58t 14cwt
Driving Wheel:	5' 1¼"
Boiler Pressure:	160psi s 160psi superheated
Cylinders:	Inside 18" x 24" sr Inside 19" x 24" c Inside 19" x 26"
Tractive Effort:	17265lbf sr 19235lbf c 20840lbf
Valve Gear:	Joy (slide valves) sr Stephenson (piston valves)

The 'N8' class originally consisted of sixty-two engines built by T W Worsdell in 1886-1890 for the NER. They were originally two-cylinder compounds and they were a tank engine version of the 'J21' class. They were all later converted as simples with Joy valve gear and slide valves. Twenty more engines were built new as simples (see 'N9' class).

Some engines retained the NER type of safety valve columns in BR days although most engines had acquired pop safety valves.

s Many engines were fitted with superheaters and extended smokeboxes. They were also fitted with larger cylinders and they had piston valves operated by Stephenson valve gear.

r Some of the superheated engines later had the superheaters removed, but they still retained the Stephenson valve gear, piston valves and larger cylinders.

c Some engines had the piston stroke increased from 24" to 26" when they were superheated.

Year End Totals: 'N8' class

'47	'48	'49	'50	'51	'52	'53	'54	'55	'56	'57	'58	'59	'60	'61	'62	'63	'64	'65	'66	'67
30	29	23	19	16	9	8	7	1												

Number	Built	Renumbered	BR Dates	Scrap	Notes
69371	07/86 Dar	04/48 9371	-03/52	05/52	s
69372	08/86 Dar	10/48 9372	-11/50	50	r
69373	10/86 Dar	9373	-03/50	50	s
69374	01/88 Ghd	9374	-03/49	03/49	r
69375	03/88 Ghd	9375	-03/49	49	rc
69376	10/88 Ghd	9376	-02/50	50	s
69377	10/88 Ghd	06/49 9377	-06/55	09/55	s
69378	11/88 Ghd	12/51 9378	-09/55	55	r
69379	11/88 Ghd	11/49 9379	-10/52	11/52	s
69380	11/88 Ghd	9380	-11/50	50	s
69381	12/88 Ghd	10/49 9381	-06/55	09/55	rc
69382	12/88 Ghd	11/49 9382	-07/52	08/52	rc
69383	02/89 Dar	9383	-08/49	49	r
69384	02/89 Dar	9384	-03/49	49	s
69385	04/89 Dar	11/49 9385	-10/54	01/55	s
69386	05/89 Dar	10/49 9386	-02/55	55	sc
69387	05/89 Dar	06/49 9387	-07/52	08/52	r
69389	06/89 Dar	09/49 9389	-07/52	08/52	
69390	11/89 Dar	06/50 9390	-09/56	56	s
69391	11/89 Dar	04/49 9391	-02/53	53	s
69392	12/89 Dar	10/48 9392	-05/55	55	
69393	12/89 Dar	07/49 9393	-10/52	52	s
69394	02/90 Dar	03/50 9394	-10/55	55	s
69395	02/90 Dar	10/49 9395	-08/52	52	s
69396	03/90 Dar	9396	-08/49	49	
69397	03/90 Dar	9397	-08/49	49	r
69398	04/90 Dar	01/50 9398	-10/51	51	s
69399	04/90 Dar	9399	-10/48	10/48	r
69400	04/90 Dar	9400	-10/51	51	rc
69401	05/90 Dar	03/49 9401	-09/51	51	sc

N9 69410-69429
0-6-2T NER Worsdell

Power Classification: 3MT
Introduced: 1893-1894
Designer: W Worsdell
Company: NER
Weight: 56t 10cwt
Driving Wheel: 5' 1¼"
Boiler Pressure: 160psi
Cylinders: Inside 19" x 26"
Tractive Effort: 20840lbf
Valve Gear: Stephenson (slide valves)

The 'N9' class consisted of twenty engines built by Wilson Worsdell in 1893-1894. They were the NER class 'N'. They were developed from the 'N8' class but they were all built as simples. The first engine was withdrawn in 1946.

n 69429 retained the NER type of safety valve columns in BR days. The others had acquired pop safety valves.

Year End Totals: 'N9' class

'47	'48	'49	'50	'51	'52	'53	'54	'55	'56	'57	'58	'59	'60	'61	'62	'63	'64	'65	'66	'67
17	16	12	6	4	4	3	3													

Number	Built	Renumbered	BR Dates	Scrap	Notes
69410	05/93 Dar	9410	-10/50	50	
69411	06/93 Dar	9411	-11/49	49	
69413	06/93 Dar	9413	-11/50	50	
69414	07/93 Dar	9414	-07/50	50	
69415	08/93 Dar	9415	-10/49	49	
69418	09/93 Dar	04/48 9418	-01/51	51	
69419	09/93 Dar	9419	-02/48	02/48	
69420	10/93 Dar	9420	-07/49	49	
69421	11/93 Dar	9421	-08/49	49	
69422	11/93 Dar	9422	-04/50	50	
69423	12/93 Dar	9423	-07/51	51	
69424	12/93 Dar	02/52 9424	-06/55	07/55	
69425	12/93 Dar	9425	-11/50	50	
69426	12/93 Dar	01/49 9426	-02/53	53	
69427	12/93 Dar	01/52 9427	-06/55	08/55	
69428	02/94 Dar	9428	-07/50	50	
69429	02/94 Dar	03/52 9429	-07/55	08/55	n

N1 69430-69485
0-6-2T GNR Ivatt

Power Classification: 2MT
Introduced: 1907-1912
Designer: Ivatt
Company: GNR
Weight: 65t 17cwt
t 64t 14cwt
Driving Wheel: 5' 8"
Boiler Pressure: 175psi
s 170psi superheated
Cylinders: Inside 18" x 26"
Tractive Effort: 18430lbf
s 17900lbf
Valve Gear: Stephenson (slide valves)

In 1907 Ivatt produced his first 0-6-2T engine for the London suburban services (69430). It was a tank engine version of the 'J1' class and the boiler was interchangeable with the 'D2', 'J1' and 'J5' classes. It was fitted with condensing apparatus for working through the Metropolitan tunnels to Moorgate. However the weight distribution proved to be unacceptable for the Metropolitan lines and the engine had the condensing apparatus removed and was transferred to work in the West Riding.

In 1907-1912 fifty-five more engines were built at Doncaster with the tanks cut back to correct the weight distribution. All except 69472-69475 (which were delivered new to the West Riding in 1912) were fitted with condensing apparatus and they were put to work on the Kings Cross and Moorgate suburban services. Many engines later had the condensing apparatus removed when they were replaced by more modern engines and sent to work in the Leeds and Bradford districts.

No. 9438 was withdrawn in 1947 leaving fifty-five engines to come into BR stock in 1948.

s Eleven engines were fitted with superheaters, but they still retained their slide valves.

c These engines were fitted with condensing apparatus in BR days, but changes did occur.

t 69430 was the original engine with longer side tanks than its successors.

Year End Totals: 'N1' class

'47	'48	'49	'50	'51	'52	'53	'54	'55	'56	'57	'58	'59	'60	'61	'62	'63	'64	'65	'66	'67
55	55	55	55	54	52	49	41	21	13	9	7									

Number	Built	Renumbered	BR Dates	Scrap	Notes
69430	04/07 Don	03/49 9430	-12/56	57	t
69431	12/07 Don	09/51 9431	-03/55	55	c
69432	12/07 Don	03/49 9432	-11/54	12/54	c
69433	12/07 Don	08/48 9433	-12/54	55	c
69434	12/07 Don	05/50 9434	-03/59	04/59	c
69435	12/07 Don	04/51 9435	-03/55	55	sc
69436	12/07 Don	01/49 9436	-07/55	55	s
69437	12/07 Don	11/48 9437	-06/54	08/54	sc
69439	12/07 Don	06/50 9439	-11/55	12/55	sc
69440	02/08 Don	02/50 9440	-03/57	05/57	
69441	03/10 Don	07/49 9441	-05/55	55	c
69442	03/10 Don	07/50 9442	-09/53	10/53	c
69443	03/10 Don	04/49 9443	-03/59	04/59	
69444	03/10 Don	04/50 9444	-10/56	56	
69445	04/10 Don	03/51 9445	-01/55	55	c
69446	04/10 Don	10/48 9446	-06/53	53	
69447	04/10 Don	12/48 9447	-10/56	56	
69448	05/10 Don	03/50 9448	-01/53	53	
69449	05/10 Don	06/48 9449	-04/55	55	
69450	05/10 Don	12/49 9450	-03/59	04/59	c
69451	12/10 Don	01/52 9451	-10/55	10/55	c
69452	12/10 Don	01/51 9452	-03/59	04/59	s
69453	12/10 Don	06/48 9453	-04/58	05/58	c
69454	12/10 Don	01/50 9454	-02/55	55	
69455	12/10 Don	02/49 9455	-05/55	55	c
69456	12/10 Don	04/48 9456	-11/54	12/54	c
69457	01/11 Don	02/49 9457	-04/57	05/57	c
69458	02/11 Don	09/51 9458	-11/55	12/55	c
69459	02/11 Don	05/48 9459	-03/55	55	
69460	03/11 Don	04/51 9460	-08/55	55	c
69461	12/11 Don	11/50 9461	-06/54	09/54	c
69462	12/11 Don	11/48 9462	-04/59	04/59	c
69463	12/11 Don	09/50 9463	-10/55	12/55	c
69464	02/12 Don	08/48 9464	-08/55	55	sc
69465	02/12 Don	07/48 9465	-12/55	02/56	c
69466	02/12 Don	05/51 9466	-07/55	55	c
69467	03/12 Don	06/49 9467	-07/56	56	c
69468	03/12 Don	05/48 9468	-03/54	54	c
69469	03/12 Don	09/51 9469	-04/57	05/57	c
69470	04/12 Don	10/48 9470	-08/56	56	c
69471	04/12 Don	09/50 9471	-01/56	02/56	c
69472	04/12 Don	09/49 9472	-08/58	10/58	s
69473	04/12 Don	04/49 9473	-09/52	52	
69474	04/12 Don	10/49 9474	-03/59	04/59	
69475	04/12 Don	05/51 9475	-04/55	55	c
69476	05/12 Don	05/48 9476	-03/55	55	c
69477	06/12 Don	09/51 9477	-04/59	04/59	c
69478	06/12 Don	04/49 9478	-12/56	57	sc
69479	06/12 Don	07/48 9479	-10/52	52	sc
69480	06/12 Don	9480	-06/51	51	c
69481	06/12 Don	05/48 9481	-05/56	06/56	c
69482	06/12 Don	05/50 9482	-08/54	09/54	sc
69483	06/12 Don	01/50 9483	-03/55	55	s
69484	06/12 Don	09/50 9484	-09/57	11/57	c
69485	06/12 Don	02/50 9485	-11/54	12/54	c

N2 69490-69596
0-6-2T GNR Gresley

Power Classification: 3MT
Introduced: 1920-1929
Designer: Gresley
Company: GNR
Weight: 2 70t 5cwt
3 70t 8cwt
4 71t 9cwt
Driving Wheel: 5' 8"
Boiler Pressure: 170psi superheated
Cylinders: Inside 19" x 26"
Tractive Effort: 19945lbf
Valve Gear: Stephenson (piston valves)

The 'N2' was Gresley's enlarged version of the 'N1' class with larger boilers, superheaters and piston valves. Introduced on the GNR in 1920, the first sixty engines were fitted with condensing apparatus for working the Metropolitan Widened Lines to Moorgate. The boiler was higher pitched than the 'N1's in order to clear the piston valves, and this meant that the engines had to have squat chimneys and domes to suit the Metropolitan loading gauge. They replaced the 'C12's on this duty and these were transferred away to other parts of the system.

More engines were built by the LNER after grouping, and some of these had taller chimneys and no condensing apparatus. In all 107 engines were built (fifteen at Doncaster and the rest by North British, Beyer Peacock, Hawthorn Leslie and Yorkshire Engine). They all came into BR stock in 1948.

1 The original GNR engines were 'N2/1' and they were later included in 'N2/2'. They were all built with right-hand drive unlike the post-grouping engines which had left-hand drive.

2 The 'N2/2's were introduced by the LNER in 1925. They later included the earlier 1920 'N2/1's. They were originally fitted with condensing apparatus. This was added to or removed from engines as they were transferred to or from the London area.

3 The 'N2/3's were introduced by the LNER in 1925. They were built for the Great Eastern Section and Scotland and they were non-condensing with taller chimneys and domes. They were fitted with Westinghouse brakes. Some were fitted with shorter chimneys.

4 The 'N2/4's were a final batch of condensing engines for the London area, which were introduced in 1928. They were heavier than the 'N2/2's.

c These engines were fitted with condensing apparatus in BR days.

Year End Totals: 'N2' class

'47	'48	'49	'50	'51	'52	'53	'54	'55	'56	'57	'58	'59	'60	'61	'62	'63	'64	'65	'66	'67
107	107	107	107	107	107	107	107	106	105	95	81	47	32	13						

Number	Built	Renumbered	BR Dates	Scrap	Notes
69490	12/20 Don	07/48 9490	-07/59	08/59	2c
69491	04/21 Don	04/48 9491	-02/59	03/59	2c
69492	05/21 Don	03/50 9492	-11/59	12/59	2c
69493	06/21 Don	06/48 9493	-12/58	01/59	2c
69494	06/21 Don	10/48 9494	-01/58	06/58	2c
69495	07/21 Don	07/50 9495	-09/58	10/58	2c
69496	08/21 Don	09/49 9496	-04/58	06/58	2c
69497	08/21 Don	05/49 9497	-03/58	04/58	2c
69498	08/21 Don	01/51 9498	-09/61	10/61	2c
69499	08/21 Don	10/49 9499	-09/58	10/58	2c
69500	12/20 NB	10/48 9500	-08/57	09/57	2
69501	12/20 NB	12/50 9501	-11/57	12/57	2
69502	12/20 NB	08/50 9502	-05/58	05/58	2
69503	12/20 NB	08/48 9503	-01/57	03/57	2
69504	12/20 NB	06/50 9504	-09/62	03/63	2c
69505	12/20 NB	04/50 9505	-11/60	11/60	2
69506	12/20 NB	11/48 9506	-05/61	06/61	2c
69507	12/20 NB	01/50 9507	-05/60	05/60	2
69508	01/21 NB	04/48 9508	-12/59	03/60	2
69509	01/21 NB	02/49 9509	-10/60	09/61	2
69510	01/21 NB	01/49 9510	-11/59	01/60	2
69511	01/21 NB	06/48 9511	-12/60	01/61	2
69512	01/21 NB	03/50 9512	-07/62	08/62	2c
69513	01/21 NB	02/49 9513	-05/61	06/61	2
69514	02/21 NB	05/49 9514	-09/55	55	2
69515	02/21 NB	08/48 9515	-07/59	08/59	2
69516	02/21 NB	01/50 9516	-01/61	02/61	2
69517	02/21 NB	06/50 9517	-08/59	09/59	2c
69518	02/21 NB	01/50 9518	-01/61	05/61	2
69519	02/21 NB	06/48 9519	-10/57	10/57	2
69520	02/21 NB	03/49 9520	-09/62	03/63	2c
69521	02/21 NB	11/48 9521	-06/61	06/61	2c
69522	02/21 NB	06/49 9522	-11/59	12/59	2c
69523 §	02/21 NB	01/49 9523	-07/62		2c
69524	02/21 NB	08/48 9524	-11/59	12/59	2c
69525	02/21 NB	04/48 9525	-03/59	04/59	2c
69526	03/21 NB	02/51 9526	-08/59	09/59	2c
69527	03/21 NB	10/49 9527	-06/58	07/58	2c
69528	03/21 NB	08/49 9528	-11/59	12/59	2c
69529	03/21 NB	06/48 9529	-09/62	03/63	2c
69530	03/21 NB	01/50 9530	-12/59	01/60	2c
69531	03/21 NB	11/49 9531	-06/61	07/61	2c
69532	03/21 NB	09/48 9532	-06/59	07/59	2c
69533	03/21 NB	07/49 9533	-09/61	10/61	2c
69534	03/21 NB	10/48 9534	-02/59	03/59	2c
69535	03/21 NB	10/50 9535	-09/62	02/63	2c
69536	03/21 NB	01/49 9536	-06/59	08/59	2c
69537	03/21 NB	08/48 9537	-04/59	05/59	2c
69538	04/21 NB	02/50 9538	-09/62	03/63	2c
69539	04/21 NB	01/49 9539	-07/59	08/59	2c
69540	04/21 NB	08/49 9540	-07/60	08/60	2c
69541	04/21 NB	10/50 9541	-08/59	09/59	2c
69542	04/21 NB	08/49 9542	-04/59	04/59	2c
69543	04/21 NB	12/48 9543	-09/61	10/61	2c
69544	04/21 NB	08/50 9544	-12/58	01/59	2c
69545	04/21 NB	12/48 9545	-07/59	08/59	2c
69546	04/21 NB	09/50 9546	-09/62	03/63	2c
69547	04/21 NB	11/49 9547	-06/59	07/59	2c
69548	04/21 NB	10/48 9548	-07/59	08/59	2c
69549	04/21 NB	02/49 9549	-09/61	10/61	2c
69550	05/25 BP	06/49 9550	-09/58	10/58	2
69551	02/25 BP	10/49 9551	-12/58	01/59	2
69552	03/25 BP	05/49 9552	-05/60	06/60	2
69553	03/25 BP	06/49 9553	-12/59	01/60	2

69554	03/25 BP	09/50 9554	-06/58	07/58	2
69555	03/25 BP	12/48 9555	-04/59	04/59	4c
69556	03/25 BP	05/49 9556	-12/59	01/60	4c
69557	04/25 BP	04/49 9557	-06/57	07/57	2
69558	03/25 BP	06/48 9558	-06/57	07/57	2
69559	03/25 BP	04/50 9559	-07/57	07/57	2
69560	04/25 BP	12/48 9560	-10/60	11/60	2
69561	04/25 BP	02/50 9561	-05/61	06/61	2
69562	11/25 Don	03/51 9562	-01/56	*08/56*	3
69563	11/25 Don	06/48 9563	-05/60	05/60	3
69564	11/25 Don	01/50 9564	-06/61	07/62	3
69565	12/25 Don	06/48 9565	-04/58	06/58	3
69566	12/25 Don	02/51 9566	-06/57	07/57	3
69567	12/25 Don	07/48 9567	-04/59	05/59	3
69568	10/28 HL	04/48 9568	-09/62	03/63	4c
69569	10/28 HL	12/48 9569	-03/59	04/59	4c
69570	10/28 HL	10/48 9570	-12/59	12/59	4c
69571	11/28 HL	11/48 9571	-06/61	06/61	4c
69572	11/28 HL	08/49 9572	-03/61	04/61	4c
69573	11/28 HL	07/50 9573	-12/58	01/59	4c
69574	11/28 HL	07/49 9574	-03/61	03/61	4c
69575	11/28 HL	05/48 9575	-09/62	03/63	4c
69576	12/28 HL	03/49 9576	-07/59	09/59	4c
69577	12/28 HL	01/49 9577	-05/59	06/59	4c
69578	01/29 HL	01/49 9578	-11/59	12/59	4c
69579	02/29 HL	04/48 9579	-09/62	11/62	4c
69580	03/29 HL	07/48 9580	-09/61	10/61	4c
69581	03/29 HL	03/48 9581	-12/60	01/61	4c
69582	03/29 HL	05/48 9582	-09/60	10/60	4c
69583	03/29 HL	12/49 9583	-09/62	03/63	4c
69584	03/29 HL	12/48 9584	-07/59	08/59	4c
69585	04/29 HL	06/50 9585	-09/61	10/61	4c
69586	05/29 HL	07/48 9586	-03/61	04/61	4c
69587	05/29 HL	04/48 9587	-07/60	07/60	4c
69588	09/28 YE	12/49 9588	-02/60	03/60	4c
69589	10/28 YE	06/49 9589	-03/60	04/60	4c
69590	11/28 YE	09/48 9590	-06/57	07/57	4c
69591	12/28 YE	08/49 9591	-08/59	09/59	4c
69592	12/28 YE	07/49 9592	-09/61	10/61	4c
69593	01/29 YE	11/48 9593	-09/62	03/63	4c
69594	01/29 YE	08/50 9594	-01/60	01/60	3
69595	02/29 YE	04/49 9595	-10/57	11/57	3
69596	03/29 YE	02/49 9596	-09/60	09/60	3

N7 69600-69733
0-6-2T GER & LNER Hill & Gresley

Power Classification:	3MT
Introduced:	1914-1928
Designer:	Hill and Gresley
Company:	GER and LNER
Weight:	N7 62t 5cwt 1 63t 13cwt 2 64t 17cwt 35 64t 0cwt 4 61t 16cwt
Driving Wheel:	4' 10"
Boiler Pressure:	180psi superheated
Cylinders:	Inside 18" x 24"
Tractive Effort:	20515lbf
Valve Gear:	Inside Walschaert (piston valves)

Hill designed the N7 class with the purpose of replacing the 2-4-2Ts, 0-4-4Ts and the 0-6-0Ts on the busy suburban services out of Liverpool Street. The first two engines appeared in 1914; 69600 was originally fitted with a saturated boiler for comparison with 69601 which was superheated. They were the GER class 'L'.

At grouping, twelve engines were in service with another ten under construction at Stratford. (69621 was the last engine to be constructed at Stratford and it has since been preserved.) Gresley continued to develop the design in LNER days and 112 more engines were built at Doncaster and Gorton and by Beardmore and R Stephenson.

N7 The original twenty-two GER engines (69600-69621) were classified 'N7'. They were fitted with Belpaire fireboxes and short-travel valves. They were later rebuilt with Gresley round-topped boilers and reclassified 'N7/4'.

1 The 'N7/1' class consisted of the LNER engines which were built in 1925-1926 (69622-69671). They had some detail differences from the 'N7's but they were also fitted with Belpaire fireboxes and short-travel valves. They were later rebuilt with Gresley round-topped boilers and reclassified 'N7/5'.

2 The 'N7/2' class consisted of thirty LNER engines which were built in 1927 (69672-69701). They were fitted with long-travel valves and redesigned Walschaert valve gear but they still retained Belpaire fireboxes. They were fitted with pony trucks instead of radial axle-boxes and they were fitted with higher bunkers without coal rails. Most were later rebuilt with Gresley round-topped boilers and reclassified 'N7/3'.

3 The last batch of engines (69702-69733) were built new at Doncaster with Gresley's round topped boilers in 1927-1928. They were classified 'N7/3'. The 'N7/2' engines were also classified 'N7/3' when they were fitted with round topped boilers from 1943 onwards.

4 These were the original 'N7' engines which were rebuilt from 1940 with Gresley round-topped boilers and reclassified 'N7/4'.

5 These were the 'N7/1' engines which were rebuilt from 1943 with Gresley round-topped boilers and reclassified 'N7/5' ('N7/3' until 1952).

p These engines were fitted with push-pull control apparatus.

Year End Totals: 'N7' class

'47	'48	'49	'50	'51	'52	'53	'54	'55	'56	'57	'58	'59	'60	'61	'62	'63	'64	'65	'66	'67
134	134	134	134	134	134	134	134	134	134	133	122	82	37	9						

Number	*Built*	*Renumbered*	*BR Dates*	*Scrap*	*Notes*
69600	01/14 Str	09/50 9600	-02/59	04/59	4
69601	02/14 Str	10/48 9601	-05/58	05/58	4
69602	07/21 Str	06/49 9602	-07/59	09/59	N7 06/49⇨4
69603	07/21 Str	05/49 9603	-07/59	09/59	4
69604	09/21 Str	03/48 9604	-08/59	09/59	4
69605	09/21 Str	08/48 9605	-10/58	11/58	4
69606	09/21 Str	06/49 9606	-08/58	09/58	4
69607	10/21 Str	09/48 9607	-07/58	09/58	4
69608	10/21 Str	07/48 9608	-08/58	01/59	4
69609	10/21 Str	08/48 9609	-04/58	06/58	N7 08/48⇨4
69610	11/21 Str	09/50 9610	-01/59	04/59	4
69611	11/21 Str	10/48 9611	-11/60	01/61	4
69612	12/23 Str	09/48 9612	-08/59	09/59	4
69613	12/23 Str	10/49 9613	-11/59	11/59	4
69614	12/23 Str	03/49 9614	-12/60	06/61	4
69615	01/24 Str	05/48 9615	-09/60	10/60	4
69616	01/24 Str	09/49 9616	-01/59	04/59	4
69617	01/24 Str	11/48 9617	-07/60	08/60	4
69618	01/24 Str	07/48 9618	-09/61	12/61	4
69619	02/24 Str	04/49 9619	-02/59	04/59	4
69620	02/24 Str	06/49 9620	-11/60	06/61	4
69621 §	03/24 Str	01/49 9621	-09/62		4
69622	08/25 Gor	09/50 9622	-11/59	12/59	5
69623	09/25 Gor	12/48 9623	-02/59	04/59	1 06/52⇨5
69624	10/25 Gor	11/49 9624	-12/58	01/59	1 12/55⇨5
69625	10/25 Gor	12/48 9625	-04/59	04/59	1 02/50⇨5
69626	10/25 Gor	06/49 9626	-06/59	07/59	1 04/54⇨5
69627	11/25 Gor	01/49 9627	-03/59	04/59	1 09/56⇨5
69628	11/25 Gor	08/51 9628	-12/58	12/58	1 08/51⇨5
69629	11/25 Gor	11/48 9629	-08/60	10/60	1 04/56⇨5
69630	11/25 Gor	07/50 9630	-11/60	06/61	1 06/50⇨5
69631	12/25 Gor	05/49 9631	-01/61	03/61	1 08/55⇨5
69632	01/26 Gor	12/50 9632	-09/62	03/63	5
69633	02/26 Gor	08/49 9633	-08/59	09/59	5
69634	02/26 Gor	05/48 9634	-01/59	04/59	1 02/51⇨5
69635	02/26 Gor	03/49 9635	-03/59	04/59	5
69636	03/26 Gor	10/50 9636	-11/60	06/61	5
69637	04/26 Gor	01/50 9637	-03/59	04/59	1 10/55⇨5
69638	04/26 Gor	01/50 9638	-05/59	11/59	1 01/50⇨5
69639	05/26 Gor	04/48 9639	-01/59	02/59	5
69640	06/26 Gor	08/50 9640	-09/62	01/63	1 08/50⇨5
69641	06/26 Gor	03/50 9641	-12/58	01/59	1 09/52⇨5
69642	07/26 Gor	06/48 9642	-11/60	01/61	1 03/51⇨5
69643	07/26 Gor	08/48 9643	-05/58	07/58	1 06/50⇨5
69644	09/26 Gor	06/50 9644	-01/59	02/59	1 06/50⇨5
69645	09/26 Gor	04/50 9645	-11/60	12/60	1 55⇨5
69646	10/26 Gor	09/48 9646	-09/62	01/63	1 06/54⇨5
69647	10/26 Gor	06/48 9647	-11/60	01/61	5
69648	11/26 Gor	05/48 9648	-08/60	10/60	5
69649	12/26 Gor	04/49 9649	-07/59	09/59	5
69650	12/26 Gor	09/49 9650	-05/59	06/59	5
69651	02/27 Gor	09/48 9651	-01/61	06/61	5p
69652	10/25 RS	09/50 9652	-12/60	06/61	5
69653	10/25 RS	07/48 9653	-05/62	05/62	1 09/52⇨5
69654	10/25 RS	04/51 9654	-12/60	06/61	1 04/51⇨5
69655	10/25 RS	08/49 9655	-08/59	09/59	1 02/53⇨5
69656	10/25 RS	10/50 9656	-04/61	06/61	5
69657	10/25 RS	12/48 9657	-06/59	09/59	1 01/51⇨5
69658	10/25 RS	09/50 9658	-04/61	05/61	1 08/50⇨5
69659	11/25 RS	03/48 9659	-01/59	04/59	1 11/50⇨5
69660	11/25 RS	09/48 9660	-05/59	06/59	5
69661	11/25 RS	05/48 9661	-10/59	11/59	1 01/51⇨5
69662	11/25 RS	02/50 9662	-05/59	09/59	1 02/50⇨5
69663	12/25 RS	05/49 9663	-11/60	12/60	5
69664	12/25 RS	08/48 9664	-11/60	01/61	5
69665	12/25 RS	08/49 9665	-02/60	04/60	1 06/52⇨5
69666	12/25 RS	09/48 9666	-03/59	04/59	5
69667	12/25 RS	09/49 9667	-02/59	04/59	1 09/49⇨5
69668	12/25 RS	10/50 9668	-09/61	10/61	1 10/50⇨5
69669	12/25 RS	04/50 9669	-04/59	04/59	5
69670	01/26 RS	11/50 9670	-09/61	10/61	1 11/50⇨5
69671	01/26 RS	01/50 9671	-09/62	01/63	1 01/50⇨5
69672	11/27 Gor	09/50 9672	-10/59	11/59	2 09/50⇨3
69673	11/27 Gor	02/50 9673	-09/61	10/61	2 02/50⇨3
69674	11/27 Gor	02/51 9674	-06/61	07/61	2 02/51⇨3
69675	11/27 Gor	07/49 9675	-06/61	08/61	3
69676	12/27 Gor	10/49 9676	-02/59	04/59	3
69677	12/27 Gor	06/49 9677	-11/60	01/61	3
69678	01/28 Gor	12/48 9678	-09/61	10/61	3
69679	01/28 Gor	09/48 9679	-01/61	08/61	3
69680	02/28 Gor	09/49 9680	-12/60	06/61	2 09/49⇨3
69681	02/28 Gor	09/49 9681	-12/60	06/61	2 04/52⇨3
69682	07/27 BM	11/48 9682	-12/60	08/61	3
69683	07/27 BM	05/50 9683	-02/60	03/60	2 12/54⇨3
69684	07/27 BM	05/50 9684	-08/60	10/60	2 05/50⇨3
69685	07/27 BM	12/49 9685	-12/60	06/61	3
69686	07/27 BM	06/48 9686	-09/61	10/61	3
69687	07/27 BM	09/49 9687	-12/60	06/61	3
69688	07/27 BM	10/48 9688	-11/60	06/61	2 05/51⇨3
69689	08/27 BM	02/49 9689	-03/57	04/57	2p
69690	08/27 BM	05/49 9690	-01/61	06/61	2p 01/55⇨3
69691	08/27 BM	10/50 9691	-12/60	06/61	3p
69692	08/27 BM	10/48 9692	-09/62	01/63	3p
69693	08/27 BM	01/49 9693	-09/61	10/61	3
69694	08/27 BM	07/48 9694	-11/60	01/61	2p 11/54⇨3
69695	08/27 BM	07/48 9695	-12/58	01/59	2p
69696	08/27 BM	05/49 9696	-04/61	06/61	3p
69697	09/27 BM	11/50 9697	-09/62	01/63	3
69698	09/27 BM	05/48 9698	-09/61	10/61	2p 09/50⇨3
69699	09/27 BM	07/48 9699	-11/60	01/61	3
69700	09/27 BM	01/51 9700	-12/60	08/61	2 01/51⇨3
69701	09/27 BM	06/50 9701	-12/60	06/61	3
69702	11/27 Don	11/48 9702	-03/61	04/61	3
69703	11/27 Don	04/48 9703	-01/59	02/59	3
69704	11/27 Don	03/49 9704	-10/60	12/60	3
69705	11/27 Don	07/48 9705	-06/59	09/59	3
69706	11/27 Don	06/48 9706	-12/60	01/61	3
69707	11/27 Don	52 9707	-04/61	06/61	3
69708	12/27 Don	09/48 9708	-01/61	08/61	3p
69709	12/27 Don	08/48 9709	-11/60	12/60	3
69710	12/27 Don	12/48 9710	-09/61	10/61	3
69711	12/27 Don	12/49 9711	-11/59	12/59	3
69712	12/27 Don	02/49 9712	-12/60	06/61	3
69713	01/28 Don	04/48 9713	-09/61	10/61	3
69714	01/28 Don	09/49 9714	-09/61	10/61	3
69715	01/28 Don	09/48 9715	-12/60	06/61	3
69716	02/28 Don	08/48 9716	-02/59	04/59	3
69717	02/28 Don	08/49 9717	-01/59	02/59	3
69718	02/28 Don	11/49 9718	-12/60	06/61	3
69719	03/28 Don	10/48 9719	-11/60	06/61	3
69720	04/28 Don	12/49 9720	-11/60	12/60	3

Number	Built		Renumbered		BR Dates	Scrap	Notes
69721	06/28	Don	03/49	9721	-12/60	06/61	3
69722	06/28	Don	02/49	9722	-12/60	06/61	3
69723	07/28	Don	08/49	9723	-09/61	10/61	3
69724	07/28	Don	09/49	9724	-09/61	10/61	3
69725	07/28	Don	10/48	9725	-09/62	12/62	3
69726	09/28	Don	03/49	9726	-12/60	01/61	3
69727	09/28	Don	02/49	9727	-11/60	06/61	3
69728	10/28	Don	10/48	9728	-09/61	10/61	3
69729	10/28	Don	08/49	9729	-12/60	01/61	3
69730	11/28	Don	04/49	9730	-09/61	10/61	3
69731	11/28	Don	06/49	9731	-02/59	04/59	3
69732	12/28	Don	12/49	9732	-09/61	10/61	3
69733	12/28	Don	07/49	9733	-10/60	12/60	3

A7 69770-69789
4-6-2T NER Raven

Power Classification: 5F reclassified 3F in 1953
Introduced: 1910-1911
Designer: Raven
Company: NER
Weight: 87t 10cwt
Driving Wheel: 4' 7¼"
Boiler Pressure: 180psi
s 160psi superheated
1 175psi superheated
n 175psi
Cylinders: Three 16½" x 26"
Tractive Effort: 29405lbf
s 26140lbf
1 28585lbf
Valve Gear: Stephenson (piston valves)

This was the only purpose-built 4-6-2T class on the NER (the other two classes, 'A6' and 'A8', were converted from other types). Twenty of these engines were built by Vincent Raven for heavy mineral traffic and shunting duties (NER class 'Y'). This was his first design for the NER and the engines appeared from Darlington in 1910.

In common with most of Raven's designs, the engines had three cylinders driving on the leading coupled axle, and three independent sets of Stephenson link motion. There was some variety in chimneys, domes and smokeboxes among different engines of this class.

s Most engines of the class were later rebuilt with superheated boilers and reduced boiler pressure.

1 'A7/1' These engines were rebuilt with Robinson type superheated boilers.

n 69787 was an 'A7/1' engine but not superheated.

Year End Totals: 'A7' class

'47	'48	'49	'50	'51	'52	'53	'54	'55	'56	'57	'58	'59	'60	'61	'62	'63	'64	'65	'66	'67
20	20	20	20	19	17	17	10	6	3											

Number	Built		Renumbered		BR Dates	Scrap	Notes
69770	10/10	Dar	07/48	9770	-10/54	*10/54*	s 07/50⇨1
69771	11/10	Dar	06/48	9771	-11/54	01/55	s 06/48⇨1
69772	11/10	Dar	02/49	9772	-12/57	*02/58*	s
69773	12/10	Dar	03/49	9773	-03/55	*04/55*	s 07/51⇨1
69774	12/10	Dar	05/50	9774	-08/54	*54*	s 05/50⇨1
69775	12/10	Dar	11/49	9775	-04/52	*52*	1
69776	01/11	Dar	11/48	9776	-06/54	*07/54*	s 01/52⇨1
69777	01/11	Dar	10/48	9777	-05/52	*05/52*	s
69778	02/11	Dar	01/50	9778	-05/55	*06/55*	
69779	02/11	Dar	12/49	9779	-11/54	*01/55*	s 12/49⇨1
69780	02/11	Dar	01/50	9780	-11/54	*01/55*	s 01/50⇨1
69781	03/11	Dar	08/48	9781	-11/56	*03/57*	s 04/51⇨1
69782	03/11	Dar	07/48	9782	-12/57	04/58	s
69783	03/11	Dar	04/48	9783	-12/56	*03/57*	s 04/48⇨1
69784	04/11	Dar	05/48	9784	-03/56	*03/56*	s 05/48⇨1
69785	04/11	Dar	10/49	9785	-11/55	*55*	1
69786	05/11	Dar	04/48	9786	-12/57	*03/58*	s 04/48⇨1
69787	05/11	Dar	09/48	9787	-08/54	*08/54*	08/51⇨1n
69788	05/11	Dar	07/48	9788	-11/55	*55*	s 07/48⇨1
69789	06/11	Dar		9789	-05/51	06/51	s

A6 69791-69799
4-6-2T NER Worsdell 'Whitby Tanks'

Power Classification: 4P
Introduced: 1907-1908
Rebuilt 1914-1916 by Raven
Designer: W Worsdell
Company: NER
Weight: 78t 0cwt
s 79t 0cwt
Driving Wheel: 5' 1¼"
Boiler Pressure: 175psi
s 175psi superheated
Cylinders: Inside 19" x 26"
Tractive Effort: 22795lbf
Valve Gear: Stephenson (piston valves)

Wilson Worsdell built ten class 'W' 4-6-0T engines in 1907-1908 for working the NER's steeply graded Whitby to Scarborough line. They were built to replace the 0-4-4Ts which were working on that line and they became known as the 'Whitby Tanks'.

In service it was found that the engines suffered from having insufficient coal capacity, and they were rebuilt in 1914-1916 as 4-6-2T engines with enlarged bunkers. There was some variety in chimneys, domes and smokeboxes among different engines of this class.

The first engine to be withdrawn was 9790 in 1947, leaving the remaining nine engines to come into BR stock in 1948.

s Most engines of the class were later rebuilt with superheated boilers.

Year End Totals: 'A6' class

'47	'48	'49	'50	'51	'52	'53	'54	'55	'56	'57	'58	'59	'60	'61	'62	'63	'64	'65	'66	'67
9	8	8	6	1	1															

Number	Built		Renumbered		BR Dates	Scrap	Notes
69791	12/07	Ghd	04/50	9791	-08/51	*51*	s
69792	12/07	Ghd		9792	-12/48	*49*	s
69793	01/08	Ghd	02/49	9793	-04/51	*51*	s
69794	02/08	Ghd	12/48	9794	-08/51	08/51	
69795	03/08	Ghd	08/48	9795	-07/50	*50*	
69796	03/08	Ghd	03/49	9796	-03/53	*04/53*	s
69797	03/08	Ghd	08/49	9797	-08/51	*51*	s
69798	04/08	Ghd	06/48	9798	-02/51	*51*	
69799	04/08	Ghd		9799	-02/50	*50*	s

A5 69800-69842
4-6-2T GCR & LNER Robinson & Gresley

Power Classification: 4P reclassified 3P in 1953
Introduced: 1 1911-1923
2 1925-1926
Designer: 1 Robinson
2 Robinson and Gresley
Company: 1 GCR
2 LNER
Weight: 1 85t 18cwt
2 90t 11cwt
Driving Wheel: 5' 7"
Boiler Pressure: 180psi superheated
Cylinders: Inside 20" x 26"
Tractive Effort: 23750lbf
Valve Gear: Stephenson (piston valves)

Robinson introduced this class of 4-6-2T engines for express suburban passenger workings on the Marylebone to Aylesbury and High Wycombe lines. Thirty-one engines were built at Gorton in 1911-1923 and they were the GCR class '9N'. The last ten engines were built after grouping and they had side-window cabs, the earlier engines later receiving these as well. The boilers were interchangeable with the GCR 'D9' class of 4-4-0s. They were fine engines and probably amongst the best express tank engines ever built.

Gresley recognised that this was a good design and a further batch of thirteen engines was built by Hawthorn Leslie in 1925-1926 for use in the North Eastern area around Middlesbrough.

One of the original batch of engines was scrapped in 1942, but all the others (a total of forty-three engines) came into BR stock in 1948.

1 The 'A5/1's were the original GCR engines.

2 The 'A5/2's were the LNER Gresley built engines. They had cut down chimneys and reduced boiler mountings and they were fitted with Westinghouse and vacuum brakes.

Year End Totals: 'A5' class

'47	'48	'49	'50	'51	'52	'53	'54	'55	'56	'57	'58	'59	'60	'61	'62	'63	'64	'65	'66	'67
43	43	43	43	43	43	43	43	43	43	41	18	10								

Number	Built		Renumbered		BR Dates	Scrap	Notes
69800	03/11	Gor	03/49	9800	-08/59	09/59	1
69801	04/11	Gor	11/48	9801	-04/60	04/60	1
69802	05/11	Gor	06/48	9802	-12/58	02/59	1
69803	05/11	Gor	04/49	9803	-07/59	07/59	1
69804	05/11	Gor	04/48	9804	-04/58	04/58	1
69805	06/11	Gor	02/49	9805	-09/59	10/59	1
69806	06/11	Gor	03/49	9806	-04/60	05/60	1
69807	06/11	Gor	05/49	9807	-07/58	09/58	1
69808	08/11	Gor	12/49	9808	-11/60	11/60	1
69809	10/12	Gor	09/48	9809	-05/59	05/59	1
69810	11/12	Gor	12/48	9810	-10/58	05/59	1
69811	11/12	Gor	04/48	9811	-10/58	10/58	1
69812	11/12	Gor	01/50	9812	-07/59	09/59	1
69813	12/12	Gor	08/48	9813	-04/60	05/60	1
69814	12/12	Gor	07/48	9814	-11/60	11/60	1
69815	06/17	Gor	07/48	9815	-07/57	07/57	1
69816	07/17	Gor	11/51	9816	-01/59	02/59	1
69817	08/17	Gor	11/50	9817	-04/60	04/60	1
69818	09/17	Gor	10/48	9818	-12/58	02/59	1
69819	10/17	Gor	09/49	9819	-03/58	04/58	1
69820	01/23	Gor	10/48	9820	-11/60	11/60	1
69821	02/23	Gor	02/49	9821	-05/60	06/60	1
69822	02/23	Gor	07/49	9822	-11/58	12/58	1
69823	03/23	Gor	10/48	9823	-04/60	05/60	1
69824	04/23	Gor	11/48	9824	-12/58	01/59	1
69825	04/23	Gor	01/49	9825	-11/59	12/59	1
69826	05/23	Gor	05/48	9826	-06/58	07/58	1
69827	05/23	Gor	04/48	9827	-11/59	11/59	1
69828	06/23	Gor	07/48	9828	-05/58	05/59	1
69829	06/23	Gor	09/48	9829	-05/60	06/60	1
69830	09/25	HL	05/48	9830	-11/58	12/58	2
69831	10/25	HL	09/48	9831	-11/58	05/59	2
69832	10/25	HL	08/48	9832	-10/58	*10/58*	2
69833	10/25	HL	06/48	9833	-04/57	*03/58*	2
69834	11/25	HL	04/48	9834	-10/58	12/58	2
69835	11/25	HL	04/49	9835	-11/58	07/59	2
69836	12/25	HL	05/48	9836	-08/58	09/58	2
69837	12/25	HL	05/48	9837	-12/58	*12/58*	2
69838	12/25	HL	03/49	9838	-11/58	*11/58*	2
69839	01/26	HL	04/49	9839	-09/58	10/58	2
69840	01/26	HL	05/48	9840	-09/58	10/58	2
69841	02/26	HL	04/48	9841	-09/58	10/58	2
69842	03/26	HL	12/48	9842	-10/58	*05/59*	2

A8 69850-69894
4-6-2T NER converted from 4-4-4T

Power Classification: 4P reclassified 3P in 1953
Introduced: 1913-1922
Rebuilt Gresley 1931-1936
Designer: Raven
Company: NER
Weight: 86t 18cwt
Driving Wheel: 5' 9"
Boiler Pressure: 175psi superheated
Cylinders: Three 16½" x 26"
Tractive Effort: 22890lbf
Valve Gear: Stephenson (piston valves)

Between 1913 and 1922 Raven put forty-five three-cylinder 4-4-4T engines into service on the NER. They were the NER class 'D' and later the LNER class 'H1'. They worked on fast passenger services, notably between Darlington and Newcastle and the North East Coast.

It was found that this double-bogie design could roll excessively at high speeds. For this reason they were all rebuilt by Gresley to 4-6-2Ts between 1931-1936. In this form they rode excellently, but they never appeared to be quite so fast as in their earlier days.

There was some variety in chimneys, domes and smokeboxes among different engines of this class. Many of the class were fitted with larger bunkers to increase the coal capacity, some of them with hoppers on the bunkers.

Year End Totals: 'A8' class

'47	'48	'49	'50	'51	'52	'53	'54	'55	'56	'57	'58	'59	'60	'61	'62	'63	'64	'65	'66	'67
45	45	45	45	45	45	45	45	45	45	43	26	21								

Number	Built		Renumbered		BR Dates	Scrap	Notes
69850	10/13	Dar	09/49	9850	-06/60	08/60	
69851	10/13	Dar	12/49	9851	-11/58	07/59	
69852	11/13	Dar	08/48	9852	-11/59	12/59	
69853	11/13	Dar	09/49	9853	-01/60	02/60	

69854	12/13 Dar	06/48 9854	-05/60	05/60	
69855	12/13 Dar	10/48 9855	-01/60	02/60	
69856	12/13 Dar	03/50 9856	-12/59	12/59	
69857	12/13 Dar	07/48 9857	-02/60	02/60	
69858	12/13 Dar	09/48 9858	-05/60	05/60	
69859	12/13 Dar	06/49 9859	-02/60	02/60	
69860	12/13 Dar	09/48 9860	-06/60	09/60	
69861	12/13 Dar	05/50 9861	-06/60	08/60	
69862	02/14 Dar	11/48 9862	-07/58	09/58	
69863	02/14 Dar	03/50 9863	-11/58	02/59	
69864	02/14 Dar	07/48 9864	-10/58	02/59	
69865	03/14 Dar	06/48 9865	-04/58	09/58	
69866	03/14 Dar	06/48 9866	-11/58	12/58	
69867	03/14 Dar	10/49 9867	-12/59	01/60	
69868	04/14 Dar	08/48 9868	-11/57	11/57	
69869	04/14 Dar	12/48 9869	-06/60	09/60	
69870	05/20 Dar	10/48 9870	-06/60	08/60	
69871	06/20 Dar	08/49 9871	-11/58	11/58	
69872	06/20 Dar	12/48 9872	-10/58	10/58	
69873	06/20 Dar	08/48 9873	-02/60	02/60	
69874	06/20 Dar	08/50 9874	-05/60	06/60	
69875	06/20 Dar	04/48 9875	-05/60	06/60	
69876	06/20 Dar	01/49 9876	-10/57	11/57	
69877	06/20 Dar	01/50 9877	-12/59	01/60	
69878	06/21 Dar	01/50 9878	-06/60	08/60	
69879	03/22 Dar	11/48 9879	-11/58	12/58	
69880	06/21 Dar	05/49 9880	-06/60	07/60	
69881	07/21 Dar	10/48 9881	-06/58	07/58	
69882	07/22 Dar	10/48 9882	-11/58	12/58	
69883	08/21 Dar	08/49 9883	-06/60	06/60	
69884	08/21 Dar	07/48 9884	-11/58	01/59	
69885	09/21 Dar	08/48 9885	-06/60	09/60	
69886	08/21 Dar	01/50 9886	-06/60	07/60	
69887	10/21 Dar	06/48 9887	-12/59	01/60	
69888	11/21 Dar	04/49 9888	-10/58	10/58	
69889	12/21 Dar	12/48 9889	-05/60	06/60	
69890	12/21 Dar	06/50 9890	-01/58	03/58	
69891	02/22 Dar	10/48 9891	-09/58	10/58	
69892	03/22 Dar	02/49 9892	-11/58	11/58	
69893	03/22 Dar	09/48 9893	-11/58	05/59	
69894	05/22 Dar	01/49 9894	-06/60	07/60	

S1 69900-69905
0-8-4T GCR & LNER Robinson & Gresley

Power Classification: 7F reclassified 6F in 1953
Introduced: 1 1907-1908
2 Rebuilt 1932 by Gresley
3 1932
Designer: Robinson
3 Gresley
Company: GCR
3 LNER
Weight: 1 99t 6cwt
2 99t 2cwt
3 99t 1cwt
Driving Wheel: 4' 8"
Boiler Pressure: 180psi superheated
Cylinders: Three 18" x 26"
Tractive Effort: 34525lbf
Valve Gear: Stephenson (slide valves)

In 1907-1908 Robinson put four 0-8-4T engines into service to work at the GCR's new hump shunting yard at Wath-on-Dearne. They were known as the GCR '8H' class and the boilers were interchangeable with the 'O4' 2-8-0s.

Although they were powerful engines they sometimes had difficulty shunting heavy trains over the hump in slippery weather. One engine was rebuilt in 1932 with a reversible booster on the trailing bogie, raising the tractive effort to 46895lbf. Two more engines were built in 1932 with boosters, but the boosters were removed from all three in 1943.

The engines spent most of their lives shedded at Mexborough for working in Wath Yard. Two worked for a while at Whitemoor Yard in March and also at Frodingham. They were made redundant by the coming of the diesel shunter and they were all scrapped between 1954 and 1957.

1 The original engines were classified 'S1/1'. They were later superheated.

2 The engine which was rebuilt with a booster and superheater in 1932 was classified 'S1/2'. The booster was removed in 1943.

3 The engines which were built with boosters and superheaters in 1932 were classified 'S1/3'. They also had altered tanks and side window cabs. The boosters were removed in 1943.

Year End Totals: 'S1' class

'47	'48	'49	'50	'51	'52	'53	'54	'55	'56	'57	'58	'59	'60	'61	'62	'63	'64	'65	'66	'67
6	6	6	6	6	6	6	5	5	2											

Number	*Built*	*Renumbered*	*BR Dates*	*Scrap*	*Notes*
69900	12/07 BP	03/49 9900	-01/56	*02/56*	1
69901	12/07 BP	10/48 9901	-01/57	03/57	2
69902	01/08 BP	11/50 9902	-01/56	*02/56*	1
69903	01/08 BP	04/51 9903	-03/54	54	1
69904	05/32 Gor	10/48 9904	-01/56	*02/56*	3
69905	06/32 Gor	02/49 9905	-01/57	*01/57*	3

T1 69910-69922
4-8-0T NER Raven

Power Classification: 7F reclassified 5F in 1953
Introduced: 1909-1925
Designer: Raven
Company: NER
Weight: 85t 8cwt
Driving Wheel: 4' 7¼"
Boiler Pressure: 175psi
s 175psi superheated
Cylinders: Three 18" x 26"
Tractive Effort: 34020lbf
Valve Gear: Stephenson (piston valves)

In 1909 Raven built ten three-cylinder 4-8-0T engines (to Wilson Worsdell's design) for heavy freight duties on the NER. They were the NER class 'X' and they were also used for hump shunting at various yards in the North East.

Gresley added another five engines for the LNER in 1925. Two of the original engines were scrapped in 1937, but the rest stayed in service into BR days, being scrapped in 1955-1961.

s 69914 was rebuilt with a superheater in 1935.

Year End Totals: 'T1' class

'47	'48	'49	'50	'51	'52	'53	'54	'55	'56	'57	'58	'59	'60	'61	'62	'63	'64	'65	'66	'67
13	13	13	13	13	13	13	13	11	10	7	6	1	1							

Number	*Built*	*Renumbered*	*BR Dates*	*Scrap*	*Notes*
69910	09/09 Ghd	04/48 9910	-10/59	11/59	
69911	09/09 Ghd	11/50 9911	-03/57	04/57	
69912	10/09 Ghd	12/50 9912	-10/59	12/59	
69913	11/09 Ghd	12/50 9913	-12/57	02/58	
69914	12/09 Ghd	08/49 9914	-08/55	08/55	s
69915	02/10 Ghd	10/49 9915	-03/59	03/59	
69916	03/10 Ghd	04/48 9916	-08/57	09/57	
69917	04/10 Ghd	05/48 9917	-11/59	11/59	
69918	11/25 Dar	01/50 9918	-10/58	11/58	
69919	11/25 Dar	08/50 9919	-02/55	04/55	
69920	11/25 Dar	12/50 9920	-01/59	02/59	
69921	12/25 Dar	01/51 9921	-06/61	07/61	
69922	12/25 Dar	12/49 9922	-10/56	10/56	

Q1 69925-69937
0-8-0T LNER Thompson rebuild of GCR 'Q4'

Power Classification: 5F
Introduced: 1902-1911, rebuilt 1942-1945 by Thompson
Designer: Robinson
Company: GCR/LNER
Weight: 1 69t 18cwt
2 73t 13cwt
Driving Wheel: 4' 8"
Boiler Pressure: 180psi
Cylinders: Outside 19" x 26"
Tractive Effort: 25645lbf
Valve Gear: Stephenson (slide valves)

In 1942 it was decided to convert twenty-five of Robinson's 0-8-0 tender engines ('Q4' class) to tanks to meet the need for wartime shunting engines. In the event only thirteen engines were converted in 1942-1945 and they were known as the 'Q1' class. The superheaters were removed when the engines were rebuilt.

1 The first four engines were classified 'Q1/1' and they were rebuilt in 1942-43 with 1500 gallon tanks.

2 The other engines were classified 'Q1/2' and they were rebuilt in 1943-45 with 2000 gallon tanks.

Year End Totals: 'Q1' class

'47	'48	'49	'50	'51	'52	'53	'54	'55	'56	'57	'58	'59	'60	'61	'62	'63	'64	'65	'66	'67
13	13	13	13	13	13	13	12	12	10	10	5									

Number	*Built*	*Renumbered*	*BR Dates*	*Scrap*	*Notes*
69925	10/03 K	03/51 9925	-08/54	*10/54*	1
69926	11/10 Gor	09/48 9926	-02/58	03/58	1
69927	03/07 K	07/48 9927	-04/56	07/57	1
69928	05/09 Gor	08/49 9928	-08/59	09/59	1
69929	11/03 K	10/48 9929	-08/59	09/59	2
69930	08/05 K	11/49 9930	-10/58	10/58	2
69931	04/09 Gor	01/49 9931	-11/58	05/59	2
69932	09/10 Gor	12/49 9932	-11/58	11/58	2
69933	12/03 K	06/48 9933	-12/58	01/59	2
69934	11/03 K	06/48 9934	-08/59	09/59	2
69935	03/04 K	09/48 9935	-09/59	09/59	2
69936	11/10 Gor	08/48 9936	-09/59	09/59	2
69937	02/04 K	08/48 9937	-11/56	56	2

U1 69999
2-8-8-2T LNER Gresley Beyer Garratt

Power Classification: Not classified
Introduced: 1925
Designer: Beyer-Garratt/Gresley
Company: LNER
Weight: 178t 1cwt
Driving Wheel: 4' 8"
Boiler Pressure: 180psi superheated
Cylinders: Six 18½" x 26"
Tractive Effort: 72940lbf
Valve Gear: Walschaert with derived motion (piston valves)

The 'Garratt' type of engine was an unmistakable design. They were in effect two engines in one, employing a single large boiler, and they were a patent of the Beyer Peacock Company in Manchester. The type achieved great success abroad, particularly in South Africa, but only two classes were built for working in Britain, the 'Garratt' engines on the LMS and this solitary LNER 'U1' class engine.

This 2-8-8-2T was the largest and most powerful steam engine ever to be seen in the British Isles. It consisted of two 2-8-0 three-cylinder units (identical with Gresley's 'O2' class) with a large 7ft diameter boiler slung between them. It made its debut at the Railway Centenary Exhibition in 1925.

The engine was designed by Gresley and Beyer Peacock for banking work on the Worsborough Incline. This consisted of three miles at 1 in 40 between Wentworth Junction and West Silkstone near Barnsley.

While the Wath-Penistone line was being electrified (completed in 1953) the engine was given trials in 1949 on the Lickey incline near Bromsgrove. The large grate proved beyond the capabilities of one fireman and in 1955 the engine was converted to work as an oil burner. It was, however, withdrawn later that year without being put into regular service.

Year End Totals: 'U1' class

'47	'48	'49	'50	'51	'52	'53	'54	'55	'56	'57	'58	'59	'60	'61	'62	'63	'64	'65	'66	'67
1	1	1	1	1	1	1	1													

Number	*Built*	*Renumbered*	*BR Dates*	*Scrap*	*Notes*
69999	06/25 BP	11/48 9999	-12/55	03/56	

Miscellaneous Locomotives

These locomotives were not included in the main number list.

Railcar 2136
Sentinel Railcar

Power Classification: Not classified
Introduced: 1928-1931
Designer: Sentinel
Company: LNER
Weight:
Driving Wheel:
Boiler Pressure:
Cylinders: Six
Tractive Effort:
Valve Gear:

Between 1903 and 1911 many railways in Britain attempted to reduce their costs on branch lines with little traffic by introducing steam railcars. These consisted of a single saloon coach, with a small engine unit (usually an 0-4-0T) forming the bogie at one end.

In some designs the engine was detachable, in others the engine was completely enclosed within the body.

Steam railcars were designed to avoid the need for turning at the end of each run. A driving cab was fitted at the other end of the unit which duplicated some of the controls, and there was a bell code system by which the driver could communicate with the fireman.

The LNER had fifty gear-driven six-cylinder railcars, built by the Sentinel company in 1928-1931 and all named after famous stage coaches. They were all withdrawn between 1943 and 1948 with only one surviving to come into BR stock.

Five more units were built in 1930-1932 with twin engines, but none of these survived to come into BR stock.

Year End Totals: 'Railcar' class

'47	'48	'49	'50	'51	'52	'53	'54	'55	'56	'57	'58	'59	'60	'61	'62	'63	'64	'65	'66	'67
1																				

Number	Built	Renumbered	BR Dates	Scrap	Notes
2136 HOPE	12/28 SC		-02/48	*02/48*	

J66 68370-68388, Mersey Railway No 3, 31, 32, 36
0-6-0T GER Holden

Mersey Railway number 3.

Class continued from 68388

Number	Built	Renumbered	BR Dates	Scrap	Notes
No 3	06/87 Str		-06/50	06/50	

Class continued with 31 (Service Locomotives)

Service Locomotives

Until 1952 service locomotives retained their original numbers. In 1952 a new scheme was introduced for all service locomotives which were numbered in a separate series from 1 upwards.

J52 68757-68889, 1-2, 9
0-6-0ST GNR Stirling and Ivatt

Class continued from 68889

Number	Built	Renumbered	BR Dates	Scrap	Notes
1	05/99 SS	12/52 *68845*	12/52-02/58	*58*	2
2	01/99 RS	12/52 68816	12/52-03/56	*56*	2
2	12/01 Don	03/56 68858	03/56-04/61	*61*	2

Class continued with 9

Y3 68154-68185, 3, 5, 7-8, 21, 38, 40-42, 57
0-4-0T LNER Sentinel Two-speed gearbox

Class continued from 68185

Number	Built	Renumbered	BR Dates	Scrap	Notes
3	04/31 S	12/52 68181	12/52-11/59	*59*	g

Class continued with 5

Y1 68130-68153, 4, 6, 37, 39, 51-54
0-4-0T LNER Sentinel Single-speed gearbox

Class continued from 68153

Number	Built	Renumbered	BR Dates	Scrap	Notes
4	10/26 S	12/52 68132	12/52-08/59	*59*	1

Class continued with 6

Y3 68154-68185, 3, 5, 7-8, 21, 38, 40-42, 57
0-4-0T LNER Sentinel Two-speed gearbox

Class continued from 3

Number	Built	Renumbered	BR Dates	Scrap	Notes
5	09/30 S	03/53 68165	03/53-11/58	*58*	

Class continued with 7

Y1 68130-68153, 4, 6, 37, 39, 51-54
0-4-0T LNER Sentinel Single-speed gearbox

Class continued from 4

Number	Built	Renumbered	BR Dates	Scrap	Notes
6	10/26 S	03/53 68133	03/53-11/55	*11/55*	1

Class continued with 37

Y3 68154-68185, 3, 5, 7-8, 21, 38, 40-42, 57
0-4-0T LNER Sentinel Two-speed gearbox

Class continued from 5

Number	Built	Renumbered	BR Dates	Scrap	Notes
7	09/30 S	03/53 68166	03/53-05/64	*64*	
8	05/31 S	09/55 68183	09/55-01/59	*59*	g

Class continued with 21

J52 68757-68889, 1-2, 9
0-6-0ST GNR Stirling and Ivatt

Class continued from 2

Number	Built	Renumbered	BR Dates	Scrap	Notes
9	05/99 SS	02/58 68840	02/58-04/61	04/61	2b

J50 68890-68991, 10-16
0-6-0T GNR and LNER Gresley

Class continued from 68991

Number	Built	Renumbered	BR Dates	Scrap	Notes
10	06/19 Don	04/61 68911	04/61-05/65	09/65	2r
11	07/19 Don	04/61 68914	04/61-05/65	09/65	2r
12	08/19 Don	09/62 68917	09/62-05/65	09/65	2r
13	12/22 Don	09/62 68928	09/62-05/65	09/65	2
14	11/26 Don	09/62 68961	09/62-09/65	09/65	3
15	05/27 Don	09/62 68971	09/62-05/65	09/65	3
16	04/30 Don	09/62 68976	09/62-05/65	09/65	3

B1 61000-61409, 17-32
4-6-0 LNER Thompson 'Bongo' or 'Antelope'

Class continued from 61409

Number	Built	Renumbered	BR Dates	Scrap	Notes
17	07/46 NB	12/63 61059	12/63-04/66	07/66	
18	07/47 VF	11/63 61181	11/63-12/65	02/66	
19	06/47 NB	12/63 61204	12/63-02/66	07/66	
20	06/47 NB	12/63 61205	12/63-12/65	07/66	
21	09/47 NB	11/63 61233	11/63-04/66	07/66	
22	11/47 NB	11/63 61252	11/63-05/64	07/66	
23	03/48 NB	11/63 61300	11/63-11/65	03/66	
24	05/48 NB	61323	11/63-11/63	03/64	
24	02/51 NB	11/63 61375	11/63-04/66	08/66	
25	12/47 NB	01/65 61272	01/65-11/65	04/66	
26	03/47 NB	01/65 61138	01/65-10/67	01/68	
27	12/46 NB	01/65 61105	01/65-07/66	08/66	
28	05/47 NB	08/65 61194	08/65-08/66	10/66	
29 §	12/47 NB	12/65 61264	12/65-07/67		
30	06/46 NB	02/66 61050	02/66-01/68	10/68	
31	06/46 NB	02/66 61051	02/66-05/66	05/66	
32	04/48 NB	02/66 61315	02/66-01/68	10/68	

Y3 68154-68185, 3, 5, 7-8, 21, 38, 40-42, 57
0-4-0T LNER Sentinel Two-speed gearbox

Class continued from 8

Number	Built	Renumbered	BR Dates	Scrap	Notes
21	09/30 S	01/56 68162	01/56-07/60	*60*	

Class continued with 38

J66 68370-68388, Mersey Railway No 3, 31, 32, 36
0-6-0T GER Holden

Class continued from Mersey Railway No 3

Number	Built	Renumbered	BR Dates	Scrap	Notes
31	08/88 Str	08/52 68382	08/52-01/59	01/59	
32	06/86 Str	10/52 68370	10/52-09/62	*62*	

Class continued with 36

Y4 68125-68129, 33
0-4-0T GER Hill

Class continued from 68129

Number	Built	Renumbered	BR Dates	Scrap	Notes
33	01/21 Str	09/52 68129	09/52-12/63	*64*	

Y7 68088-68089, 34
0-4-0T NER Worsdell

Class continued from 68089

Number	Built	Renumbered	BR Dates	Scrap	Notes
34 **§**	10/23 Dar	68088	-12/52		

J92 68667-68669, 35
0-6-0CT GER Stratford Works Crane Tanks

Class continued from 68669

Number	Built	Renumbered	BR Dates	Scrap	Notes
35	07/68 Str	09/52 68668	09/52-11/52	*52*	

J66 68370-68388, Mersey Railway No 3, 31, 32, 36
0-6-0T GER Holden

Class continued from 32

Number	Built	Renumbered	BR Dates	Scrap	Notes
36	06/88 Str	11/52 68378	11/52-01/59	*59*	

Y1 68130-68153, 4, 6, 37, 39, 51-54
0-4-0T LNER Sentinel Single-speed gearbox

Class continued from 6

Number	Built	Renumbered	BR Dates	Scrap	Notes
37	09/25 S	05/53 *68130*	05/53-04/56	*56*	1

Class continued with 39

Y3 68154-68185, 3, 5, 7-8, 21, 38, 40-42, 57
0-4-0T LNER Sentinel Two-speed gearbox

Class continued from 21

Number	Built	Renumbered	BR Dates	Scrap	Notes
38	09/30 S	05/53 *68168*	05/53-03/59	*59*	

Class continued with 40

Y1 68130-68153, 4, 6, 37, 39, 51-54
0-4-0T LNER Sentinel Single-speed gearbox

Class continued from 37

Number	Built	Renumbered	BR Dates	Scrap	Notes
39	12/26 S	08/53 *68131*	08/53-04/63	*63*	1

Class continued with 51

Y3 68154-68185, 3, 5, 7-8, 21, 38, 40-42, 57
0-4-0T LNER Sentinel Two-speed gearbox

Class continued from 38

Number	Built	Renumbered	BR Dates	Scrap	Notes
40	10/30 S	05/53 *68173*	05/53- 64	*64*	
41	10/30 S	05/53 *68177*	05/53-03/63	*63*	
42	10/30 S	03/53 *68178*	03/53-07/60	*60*	

Class continued with 57

J69 between 68490 & 68636, 43-45
0-6-0T GER Holden

Class continued from 68636

Number	Built	Renumbered	BR Dates	Scrap	Notes
43	03/92 Str	01/59 68532	01/59-08/59	11/59	J69/1
44	04/90 Str	08/59 68498	08/59-09/62	09/62	J69/2
45	04/94 Str	11/59 68543	11/59-09/62	09/62	J69/1

Y1 68130-68153, 4, 6, 37, 39, 51-54
0-4-0T LNER Sentinel Single-speed gearbox

Class continued from 39

Number	Built	Renumbered	BR Dates	Scrap	Notes
51	08/27 S	11/52 68136	11/52-11/56	*56*	4
53	09/30 S	04/54 68152	04/54-03/59	03/59	1
54 §	12/33 S	10/54 68153	10/54-07/61		2

Y8 68090-68091, 55
0-4-0T NER Worsdell

Class continued from 68091

Number	Built	Renumbered	BR Dates	Scrap	Notes
55	06/90 Ghd	07/54 *68091*	07/54-11/56	*11/56*	

Y3 68154-68185, 3, 5, 7-8, 21, 38, 40-42, 57
0-4-0T LNER Sentinel Two-speed gearbox

Class continued from 42

Number	Built	Renumbered	BR Dates	Scrap	Notes
57	08/29 S	11/56 68160	11/56-02/61	*61*	

J72 68670-68754, 69001-69028, 58-59
0-6-0T NER and BR Worsdell

Class continued from 69028

Number	Built	Renumbered	BR Dates	Scrap	Notes
58	11/49 Dar	10/64 69005	10/64-10/67	04/68	
59 §	04/51 Dar	10/64 69023	10/64-09/66		

Preserved Locomotives

Preserved locomotives which ran in service on BR.

D40 62260-62279, 49
4-4-0 GNOSR Pickersgill

Class continued from 62279

Number	Built	Renumbered	BR Dates	Scrap	Notes
49 § GORDON HIGHLANDER	10/20 NB	06/58 62277	06/58-10/65		

D34 62467-62498, 256
4-4-0 NBR Reid 'Glen'

Class continued from 62498

Number	Built	Renumbered	BR Dates	Scrap	Notes
256 § GLEN DOUGLAS	09/13 Cow	11/59 62469	11/59-10/65		

Historical surveys

Historical survey of Great Central 4-6-0 engines.

Robinson built a number of small classes of 4-6-0 engines for the Great Central Railway between 1902 and 1924 as follows:

1. The first batch consisted of outside cylinder engines built in 1902-1906. Two engines ('B1' class, later 'B18') were built with 6' 9" wheels and were both withdrawn in 1947. The 'B5' class with 6' 1" wheels and 'B9' class with 5' 4" wheels were mixed traffic engines. The 'B4' class was fitted with 6' 7" wheels and was designed for working fast goods and fish trains.

2. The second batch, built in 1912-1915, had inside cylinders. Six engines ('B2' class, later 'B19') were built with 6' 9" wheels for express running and they were all withdrawn by 1947. The 'B8' class was a goods version with 5' 7" wheels.

3. The third batch, comprising the 'B3', 'B6' and 'B7' classes, were built in 1917-1924, again with outside cylinders. The 'B6' class comprised three engines built with 5' 7" wheels for mixed traffic duties. They were all withdrawn by late 1947. The 'B7' class was a four-cylinder version of the 'B6's with 5' 8" wheels. The 'B3' class was an express version of the 'B7's with 6' 9" wheels.

Historical survey of Great Eastern 2-4-2T engines.

The Great Eastern Railway was a large user of the 2-4-2T type for branch lines and London suburban work. A total of 242 engines were built, of which 235 were still in service at Grouping in 1923. The classes are summarised below.

1. Worsdell built the first batch of engines with 5' 4" wheels in 1884-1887. The class was continued by James Holden in 1903-1909 and 160 were built in total. These were the LNER 'F4' class. These engines were heavy on coal consumption and this gave rise to the nickname 'Gobblers' which stuck with these engines and their successors (although not always with the same justification).

2. James Holden also built fifty engines with 5' 8" wheels between 1893 and 1902. These were the LNER 'F3' class.

3. S D Holden (James Holden's son) built a batch of twelve engines in 1909 with small 4' 10" wheels for push-pull operation. These were the 'F7' class.

4. The 'F5' class consisted of thirty-two 'F4' engines rebuilt by S D Holden from 1911 onwards with higher boiler pressure.

5. The 'F6' class was a new build version of the 'F5' class with some detail alterations. Twenty engines were built by S D Holden in 1911-1912.

Historical survey of Great Eastern 0-6-0T engines.

James Holden introduced his 0-6-0Ts to the Great Eastern in 1886. There were ultimately 249 engines of five different classes ('J65'-'J69'). They all had 4' 0" driving wheels but the other dimensions progressively increased over the years. A large number of them spent many years on the busy suburban services out of Liverpool Street in London (for which they were fitted with Westinghouse brakes) and others were used all over the system in East Anglia for goods and general shunting work.

GNR Ivatt 'N1' class 0-6-2T No 69482.

NER Raven 'A7' class 4-6-2T No 69788.

NER 'A8' class 4-6-2T No 69860.

NER Worsdell 'Y8' class 0-4-0T Departmental No 55 at York in June 1956.

Part 5
British Railways Standard and Austerity Locomotives

Locomotive Origins

At the start of 1948 BR acquired two hundred 'WD' 2-8-0 locomotives from the LNER. The remainder of the 'WD' 2-8-0 and 'WD' 2-10-0 locomotives were on loan to BR from the Ministry of Supply (War Department) and were purchased on 25th December 1948. All the other locomotives in this section are BR Standard Locomotives, built by BR.

Locomotive Numbering

All the BR standard locomotives received their numbers from new. The Ministry of Supply Austerity locomotives are shown with their previous War Department numbers (which they carried when on loan) or their previous LNER numbers.

Locomotive Classification

BR Standard Locomotives used the LMS type Power Classification which was adopted by BR. In this section a numerical suffix is given to the Power Classification to differentiate between different classes of engines when cross-referencing with the appendices.

Notes

70000 was the first BR standard locomotive to appear in 1951. 92220 was the last BR steam locomotive to be built. It appeared from Swindon in 1960.

'WD' 2-10-0 locomotive number 601 was loaned to BR from the Longmoor Military Railway from 1957 to 1959.

BR Standard 'Britannia' Pacific 7P6F No 70014 *Iron Duke*.

BR Standard Class 5
4-6-0 No 73001.

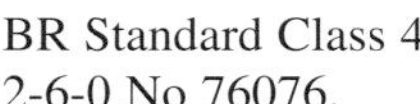

BR Standard Class 4
2-6-0 No 76076.

BR Standard Class 3
2-6-0 No 77001.

7P6F 70000-70054
4-6-2 BR Standard 'Britannia'

Power Classification: 7P6F/7MT
Introduced: 1951-54
Designer: Riddles, designed at Derby
Company: BR
Weight: Loco 94t 0cwt
x Tender 49t 3cwt
y Tender 52t 10cwt
z Tender 54t 10cwt
Driving Wheel: 6' 2"
Boiler Pressure: 250psi superheated
Cylinders: Outside 20" x 28"
Tractive Effort: 32160lbf
Valve Gear: Walschaert (piston valves)

This was the first of the new BR Standard classes to appear in 1951. The locomotives contained features which were standard throughout almost all of the BR Standard types, namely high running plates, two outside cylinders and Walschaert valve gear. Fifty-five engines were built at Crewe and they worked express passenger trains over most of the principal main lines. In particular they worked extremely well over the difficult main line of the old GER, where they revolutionised both timings and timekeeping.

70004 was exhibited at the Festival of Britain when it was new in 1951. Afterwards it was allocated at Stewarts Lane where it was kept in immaculate condition for many years for working the Golden Arrow Pullman service between London and Dover.

As steam locomotives were ousted from each of the BR Regions, all the 'Britannias' ultimately finished their days on the London Midland Region.

Several different types of tender were fitted, allocated as shown below.

x BR1 4250 gallon tender.

y BR1A 5000 gallon tender.

z BR1D 4725 gallon tender.

Year End Totals: '7P6F' class

'47	'48	'49	'50	'51	'52	'53	'54	'55	'56	'57	'58	'59	'60	'61	'62	'63	'64	'65	'66	'67
				25	38	45	55	55	55	55	55	55	55	55	55	55	55	53	42	1

Number	Built	Renumbered	BR Dates	Scrap	Notes
70000 § BRITANNIA	01/51 Crw		01/51-06/66		x
70001 LORD HURCOMB	02/51 Crw		02/51-08/66	01/67	x
70002 GEOFFREY CHAUCER	03/51 Crw		03/51-01/67	06/67	x
70003 JOHN BUNYAN	03/51 Crw		03/51-03/67	12/67	x
70004 WILLIAM SHAKESPEARE	03/51 Crw		03/51-12/67	04/68	x
70005 JOHN MILTON	04/51 Crw		04/51-07/67	01/68	x
70006 ROBERT BURNS	04/51 Crw		04/51-05/67	11/67	x
70007 COEUR-DE-LION	04/51 Crw		04/51-06/65	07/65	x
70008 BLACK PRINCE	04/51 Crw		04/51-01/67	06/67	x
70009 ALFRED THE GREAT	05/51 Crw		05/51-01/67	06/67	x
70010 OWEN GLENDOWER	05/51 Crw		05/51-09/67	01/68	x
70011 HOTSPUR	05/51 Crw		05/51-12/67	04/68	x
70012 JOHN OF GAUNT	05/51 Crw		05/51-12/67	04/68	x
70013 § OLIVER CROMWELL	05/51 Crw		05/51-08/68		x
70014 IRON DUKE	06/51 Crw		06/51-12/67	04/68	x
70015 APOLLO	06/51 Crw		06/51-08/67	02/68	x
70016 ARIEL	06/51 Crw		06/51-08/67	01/68	x
70017 ARROW	06/51 Crw		06/51-09/66	01/67	x
70018 FLYING DUTCHMAN	06/51 Crw		06/51-12/66	06/67	x
70019 LIGHTNING	06/51 Crw		06/51-03/66	08/67	x
70020 MERCURY	07/51 Crw		07/51-01/67	06/67	x
70021 MORNING STAR	08/51 Crw		08/51-12/67	05/68	x
70022 TORNADO	08/51 Crw		08/51-12/67	04/68	x
70023 VENUS	08/51 Crw		08/51-12/67	04/68	x
70024 VULCAN	08/51 Crw		10/51-12/67	04/68	x
70025 WESTERN STAR	09/52 Crw		09/52-12/67	01/68	y
70026 POLAR STAR	10/52 Crw		10/52-01/67	05/67	y
70027 RISING STAR	10/52 Crw		10/52-06/67	11/67	y
70028 ROYAL STAR	10/52 Crw		10/52-09/67	02/68	y
70029 SHOOTING STAR	11/52 Crw		11/52-10/67	03/68	y
70030 WILLIAM WORDSWORTH	11/52 Crw		11/52-06/66	10/66	x
70031 BYRON	11/52 Crw		11/52-11/67	03/68	x
70032 TENNYSON	11/52 Crw		11/52-09/67	03/68	x
70033 CHARLES DICKENS	12/52 Crw		12/52-07/67	06/68	x
70034 THOMAS HARDY	12/52 Crw		12/52-05/67	10/67	x
70035 RUDYARD KIPLING	12/52 Crw		12/52-12/67	04/68	x
70036 BOADICEA	12/52 Crw		12/52-10/66	02/67	x
70037 HEREWARD THE WAKE	12/52 Crw		12/52-10/66	02/68	x
70038 ROBIN HOOD	01/53 Crw		01/53-08/67	02/68	x
70039 SIR CHRISTOPHER WREN	02/53 Crw		02/53-09/67	02/68	x
70040 CLIVE OF INDIA	03/53 Crw		03/53-04/67	12/67	x
70041 SIR JOHN MOORE	03/53 Crw		03/53-04/67	10/67	x
70042 LORD ROBERTS	04/53 Crw		04/53-05/67	01/68	x
70043 LORD KITCHENER	06/53 Crw		06/53-08/65	11/65	x
70044 EARL HAIG	06/53 Crw		06/53-12/66	02/67	x
70045 LORD ROWALLAN	06/54 Crw		06/54-12/67	03/68	z
70046 ANZAC	06/54 Crw		06/54-07/67	01/68	z
70047	06/54 Crw		06/54-07/67	12/67	z
70048 THE TERRITORIAL ARMY, 1908-1958	07/54 Crw		07/54-05/67	10/67	z
70049 SOLWAY FIRTH	07/54 Crw		07/54-12/67	03/68	z
70050 FIRTH OF CLYDE	08/54 Crw		08/54-08/66	12/66	z
70051 FIRTH OF FORTH	08/54 Crw		08/54-12/67	03/68	z
70052 FIRTH OF TAY	08/54 Crw		08/54-04/67	11/67	z
70053 MORAY FIRTH	09/54 Crw		09/54-04/67	10/67	z
70054 DORNOCH FIRTH	09/54 Crw		09/54-11/66	06/67	z

8P 71000
4-6-2 BR Standard 'Duke of Gloucester'

Power Classification: 8P
Introduced: 1954
Designer: Riddles, designed at Derby
Company: BR
Weight: Loco 101t 5cwt
Tender 55t 10cwt, later 53t 14cwt
Driving Wheel: 6' 2"
Boiler Pressure: 250psi superheated
Cylinders: Three 18" x 28"
Tractive Effort: 39080lbf
Valve Gear: Caprotti

This locomotive was authorised as a replacement for LMSR pacific 46202 which was damaged beyond repair in the Harrow crash of 1952. The opportunity was taken to design a locomotive which was to be the prototype of a new standard design for main line duties. It was a three-cylinder machine with Caprotti valve gear and it was more powerful than the 'Britannias' and most other BR standard engines (only the '9F's had a higher tractive effort). In a sense it was the ultimate in British steam locomotive design, but it was disappointing in service. As the modernisation programme progressed it remained the sole example of its class, and most of the problems were never ironed out before its withdrawal. It attained the sad distinction of being the last new express steam engine to be built in Britain.

The locomotive was fitted with a BR1E 4725 gallon tender and was based on the West Coast main line. In November 1957 it was fitted with a new BR1J 4325 gallon tender.

After withdrawal in 1962 its cylinders and motion were removed for preservation. The engine itself was eventually sent to Barry scrapyard (having a very close brush with the cutter's torch when it was accidentally delivered to Cashmore's scrapyard in Newport en-route). It was rescued from Barry in 1974 and it underwent a major restoration to main-line condition.

Year End Totals: '8P' class

'47	'48	'49	'50	'51	'52	'53	'54	'55	'56	'57	'58	'59	'60	'61	'62	'63	'64	'65	'66	'67
							1	1	1	1	1	1	1	1	1					

Number	Built	Renumbered	BR Dates	Scrap	Notes
71000 § DUKE OF GLOUCESTER	05/54 Crw		05/54-11/62		

6P5F 72000-72009
4-6-2 BR Standard 'Clan'

Power Classification: 6P5F/6MT
Introduced: 1951-52
Designer: Riddles, designed at Derby
Company: BR
Weight: Loco 86t 19cwt
Tender 49t 3cwt
Driving Wheel: 6' 2"
Boiler Pressure: 225psi superheated
Cylinders: Outside 19½" x 28"
Tractive Effort: 27520lbf
Valve Gear: Walschaert (piston valves)

These ten locomotives, which were built at Crewe, were a lighter version of the 'Britannia' class, with higher running plates, smaller diameter boilers and taller domes and chimneys. As often happens when the proportions of a good design are altered, the result was far from satisfactory. The 'Clans' were generally poor machines, lacking the punch of the 'Britannias'. A further fifteen were ordered (five for use on the Southern Region and ten for use on the Scottish Region), but the order was cancelled.

All the locomotives were fitted with BR1 4250 gallon tenders and were based on the Scottish region (hence the Clan names). They actually did most of their work on the services from Liverpool and Manchester to Glasgow.

Year End Totals: '6P5F' class

'47	'48	'49	'50	'51	'52	'53	'54	'55	'56	'57	'58	'59	'60	'61	'62	'63	'64	'65	'66	'67
				2	10	10	10	10	10	10	10	10	10	10	5	5	5	2		

Number	Built	Renumbered	BR Dates	Scrap	Notes
72000 CLAN BUCHANAN	12/51 Crw		12/51-12/62	03/64	
72001 CLAN CAMERON	12/51 Crw		12/51-12/62	02/64	
72002 CLAN CAMPBELL	01/52 Crw		01/52-12/62	04/64	
72003 CLAN FRASER	01/52 Crw		01/52-12/62	03/64	
72004 CLAN MACDONALD	02/52 Crw		02/52-12/62	03/64	
72005 CLAN MACGREGOR	02/52 Crw		02/52-05/65	07/65	
72006 CLAN MACKENZIE	02/52 Crw		02/52-05/66	10/66	
72007 CLAN MACKINTOSH	03/52 Crw		03/52-12/65	03/66	
72008 CLAN MACLEOD	03/52 Crw		03/52-04/66	06/66	
72009 CLAN STEWART	04/52 Crw		04/52-08/65	12/65	

5MT 73000-73171
4-6-0 BR Standard 'Class 5'

Power Classification: 5MT
Introduced: 1951-57
Designer: Riddles, designed at Doncaster
Company: BR

Weight:	Loco 76t 4cwt
	u Tender 49t 3cwt
	v Tender 50t 5cwt
	w Tender 53t 5cwt
	x Tender 55t 5cwt
	y Tender 52t 10cwt
	z Tender 49t 3cwt
Driving Wheel:	6' 2"
Boiler Pressure:	225psi superheated
Cylinders:	Outside 19" x 28"
Tractive Effort:	26120lbf
Valve Gear:	Walschaert (piston valves)
	c Caprotti

One hundred and seventy-two of these standard class 5 mixed traffic locomotives were built at Derby and Doncaster. They were based largely on the LMS Stanier Class 5s ('44658' class), with a few modifications, the most noticeable being the exceptionally high running plate which had then become the fashion.

They were designed for mixed traffic duties comparable with those performed by the LMS 'Black Fives', the LNER 'B1's and the GWR 'Halls'. From 1959 a number of Southern Region based locomotives received names from withdrawn SR 'King Arthur' 'N15' locomotives.

c 73125-54 were built in 1956-57 with Caprotti valve gear.

Several different types of tender were fitted, allocated as shown below.

u BR1 4250 gallon tender.

v BR1B 4725 gallon tender.

w BR1C 4725 gallon tender.

x BR1F 5625 gallon tender.

y BR1G 5000 gallon tender.

z BR1H 4250 gallon tender.

Year End Totals: '5MT' class

'47	'48	'49	'50	'51	'52	'53	'54	'55	'56	'57	'58	'59	'60	'61	'62	'63	'64	'65	'66	'67
				29	30	50	75	119	149	172	172	172	172	172	172	172	156	115	76	23

Number	*Built*	*Renumbered*	*BR Dates*	*Scrap*	*Notes*
73000	04/51 Der		04/51-04/68	06/68	u
73001	05/51 Der		05/51-12/65	05/66	u
73002	05/51 Der		05/51-03/67	10/68	u
73003	06/51 Der		06/51-12/65	06/66	u
73004	06/51 Der		06/51-10/67	04/68	u
73005	06/51 Der		06/51-06/66	10/66	u
73006	06/51 Der		06/51-03/67	09/67	u
73007	07/51 Der		07/51-03/66	06/66	u
73008	07/51 Der		07/51-09/65	12/65	u
73009	07/51 Der		07/51-07/66	09/66	u
73010	08/51 Der		08/51-06/68	09/68	u
73011	08/51 Der		08/51-11/67	03/68	u
73012	08/51 Der		08/51-11/64	05/65	u
73013	08/51 Der		08/51-05/66	08/66	u
73014	09/51 Der		09/51-07/67	04/68	u
73015	09/51 Der		09/51-08/65	11/65	u
73016	09/51 Der		09/51-12/66	10/68	u
73017	09/51 Der		09/51-10/64	03/65	u
73018	10/51 Der		10/51-07/67	01/68	u
73019	10/51 Der		10/51-01/67	05/67	u
73020	10/51 Der		10/51-07/67	01/68	u
73021	10/51 Der		10/51-08/65	11/65	u
73022	10/51 Der		10/51-04/67	11/67	u
73023	11/51 Der		11/51-08/65	11/65	u
73024	11/51 Der		11/51-11/64	03/65	u
73025	11/51 Der		11/51-10/67	02/68	u
73026	12/51 Der		12/51-04/67	10/67	u
73027	12/51 Der		12/51-02/64	04/64	u
73028	12/51 Der		12/51-12/66	04/67	u
73029	01/52 Der		01/52-07/67	03/68	u
73030	06/53 Der		06/53-08/65	11/65	u
73031	07/53 Der		07/53-09/65	12/65	u
73032	07/53 Der		07/53-08/65	11/65	u
73033	08/53 Der		08/53-01/68	05/68	u
73034	08/53 Der		08/53-03/68	06/68	u
73035	08/53 Der		08/53-01/68	05/68	u
73036	09/53 Der		09/53-09/65	12/65	u
73037	09/53 Der		09/53-07/67	03/68	u
73038	09/53 Der		09/53-09/65	05/66	u
73039	09/53 Der		09/53-09/67	03/68	u
73040	10/53 Der		10/53-05/68	07/68	u
73041	10/53 Der		10/53-06/65	12/65	u
73042	10/53 Der		10/53-08/65	01/66	u
73043	10/53 Der		10/53-07/67	09/68	u
73044	11/53 Der		11/53-03/65	08/65	u
73045	11/53 Der		11/53-08/67	02/68	u
73046	11/53 Der		11/53-09/64	03/65	u
73047	12/53 Der		12/53-12/64	04/65	u
73048	12/53 Der		12/53-10/67	05/68	u
73049	12/53 Der		12/53-03/65	06/65	u
73050 §	06/54 Der		06/54-06/68		y
				☒04/64-05/64	
73051	06/54 Der		06/54-08/65	11/65	y
73052	06/54 Der		06/54-12/64	04/65	y
73053	06/54 Der		06/54-03/68	05/68	z
73054	06/54 Der		06/54-08/65	10/65	z
73055	06/54 Der		06/54-06/66	01/67	z
73056	07/54 Der		07/54-06/65	09/65	z
73057	07/54 Der		07/54-03/66	06/66	z
73058	07/54 Der		07/54-11/64	03/65	z
73059	08/54 Der		08/54-05/67	08/67	z
73060	08/54 Der		08/54-05/67	10/67	z
73061	09/54 Der		09/54-12/64	03/65	z
73062	09/54 Der		09/54-06/65	10/65	z
73063	09/54 Der		09/54-06/66	10/66	z
73064	10/54 Der		10/54-05/67	09/67	z
73065	10/54 Der		10/54-07/67	04/68	w
73066	10/54 Der		10/54-04/67	08/67	w
73067	10/54 Der		10/54-04/68	06/68	w
73068	10/54 Der		10/54-12/65	04/66	w
73069	11/54 Der		11/54-08/68	03/69	w
73070	11/54 Der		11/54-05/67	11/67	w
73071	11/54 Der		11/54-09/67	10/68	w
73072	12/54 Der		12/54-10/66	05/67	w
73073	12/54 Der		12/54-10/67	02/68	w
73074	12/54 Der		12/54-09/64	03/65	w
73075	04/55 Der		04/55-12/65	03/66	w
73076	04/55 Der		04/55-07/64	02/65	w
73077	05/55 Der		05/55-12/64	03/65	w
73078	05/55 Der		05/55-07/66	10/66	w
73079	05/55 Der		05/55-05/67	09/67	w
73080	06/55 Der		06/55-12/66	05/67	v
MERLIN					
73081	07/55 Der		07/55-07/66	10/66	v
EXCALIBUR					
73082 §	07/55 Der		07/55-06/66		v
CAMELOT					
73083	07/55 Der		07/55-09/66	02/67	v
PENDRAGON					
73084	08/55 Der		08/55-12/65	04/66	v
TINTAGEL					
73085	08/55 Der		08/55-07/67	04/68	v
MELISANDE					
73086	09/55 Der		09/55-10/66	02/67	v
THE GREEN KNIGHT					
73087	09/55 Der		09/55-10/66	03/67	v
LINETTE					
73088	09/55 Der		09/55-10/66	06/67	v
JOYOUS GARD					
73089	09/55 Der		09/55-09/66	06/67	v
MAID OF ASTOLAT					
73090	10/55 Der		10/55-10/65	01/66	w
73091	10/55 Der		10/55-05/65	08/65	w
73092	10/55 Der		10/55-07/67	01/68	w
73093	11/55 Der		11/55-07/67	03/68	w
73094	11/55 Der		11/55-05/67	02/68	w
73095	11/55 Der		11/55-09/66	01/67	w
73096 §	11/55 Der		11/55-11/67		w
73097	12/55 Der		12/55-05/67	10/67	w
73098	12/55 Der		12/55-03/66	06/66	w
73099	12/55 Der		12/55-10/66	06/67	w
73100	08/55 Don		08/55-01/67	05/67	v
73101	09/55 Don		09/55-08/66	11/66	v
73102	09/55 Don		09/55-12/66	04/67	v
73103	09/55 Don		09/55-10/65	02/66	v
73104	09/55 Don		09/55-10/65	02/66	v
73105	12/55 Don		12/55-09/66	02/67	v
73106	12/55 Don		12/55-06/65	10/65	v
73107	12/55 Don		12/55-09/66	06/67	v
73108	12/56 Don		12/55-12/66	04/67	v
73109	01/56 Don		01/56-10/64	02/65	v
73110	10/55 Don		10/55-01/67	06/67	x
THE RED KNIGHT					
73111	10/55 Don		10/55-09/65	02/66	x
KING UTHER					
73112	10/55 Don		10/55-06/65	12/65	x
MORGAN LE FAY					
73113	10/55 Don		10/55-01/67	05/67	x
LYONNESSE					
73114	11/55 Don		11/55-06/66	10/66	x
ETARRE					
73115	11/55 Don		11/55-03/67	11/67	x
KING PELLINORE					
73116	11/55 Don		11/55-11/64	02/65	x
ISEULT					
73117	11/55 Don		11/55-03/67	09/67	x
VIVIEN					
73118	12/55 Don		12/55-07/67	09/68	x
KING LEODEGRANCE					
73119	12/55 Don		12/55-03/67	10/67	x
ELAINE					
73120	01/56 Don		01/56-12/66	04/67	v
73121	01/56 Don		01/56-02/66	06/66	v
73122	01/56 Don		01/56-09/65	01/66	v
73123	02/56 Don		02/56-05/65	07/65	v
73124	02/56 Don		02/56-12/65	03/66	v
73125	06/56 Der		06/56-06/68	10/68	vc
73126	06/56 Der		06/56-04/68	07/68	vc
73127	08/56 Der		08/56-10/67	07/68	vc
73128	08/56 Der		08/56-05/68	08/68	vc
73129 §	08/56 Der		08/56-11/67		vc
73130	09/56 Der		09/56-01/67	09/67	vc
73131	09/56 Der		09/56-01/68	05/68	vc
73132	10/56 Der		10/56-04/68	07/68	vc
73133	10/56 Der		10/56-06/68	12/68	vc
73134	10/56 Der		10/56-06/68	10/68	vc
73135	10/56 Der		10/56-04/68	12/68	wc
73136	11/56 Der		11/56-03/68	06/68	wc
73137	11/56 Der		11/56-06/67	01/68	wc
73138	11/56 Der		11/56-05/68	09/68	wc
73139	11/56 Der		11/56-05/67	01/68	wc
73140	12/56 Der		12/56-10/67	02/68	wc
73141	12/56 Der		12/56-07/67	02/68	wc
73142	12/56 Der		12/56-05/68	12/68	wc
73143	12/56 Der		12/56-06/68	11/68	wc
73144	12/56 Der		12/56-08/67	02/68	wc
73145	01/57 Der		01/57-09/66	09/67	vc
73146	02/57 Der		02/57-05/67	11/67	vc
73147	02/57 Der		02/57-08/65	11/65	vc
73148	03/57 Der		03/57-09/65	01/66	vc
73149	03/57 Der		03/57-12/66	04/67	vc
73150	04/57 Der		04/57-12/66	04/67	vc
73151	04/57 Der		04/57-08/66	10/66	vc
73152	05/57 Der		05/57-12/65	02/66	vc
73153	05/57 Der		05/57-12/66	04/67	vc
73154	06/57 Der		06/57-12/66	05/67	vc
73155	12/56 Don		12/56-07/67	03/68	v
73156 §	12/56 Don		12/56-11/67		v
73157	12/56 Don		12/56-05/68	08/68	v
73158	12/56 Don		12/56-10/67	02/68	v
73159	01/57 Don		01/57-10/67	03/68	v
73160	01/57 Don		01/57-11/67	03/68	v
73161	01/57 Don		01/57-12/64	04/65	v
73162	02/57 Don		02/57-05/65	08/65	v
73163	02/57 Don		02/57-11/65	02/66	v
73164	03/57 Don		03/57-12/64	04/65	v
73165	03/57 Don		03/57-09/65	12/65	v
73166	03/57 Don		03/57-12/65	05/66	v
73167	04/57 Don		04/57-08/65	10/65	v
73168	04/57 Don		04/57-12/65	04/66	v
73169	04/57 Don		04/57-10/66	06/67	v
73170	05/57 Don		05/57-06/66	01/67	v
73171	05/57 Don		05/57-10/66	03/67	v

4MT [1] 75000-75079
4-6-0 BR Standard 'Class 4'

Power Classification:	4MT
Introduced:	1951-57
Designer:	Riddles, designed at Brighton
Company:	BR
Weight:	Loco 69t 0cwt
	x Tender 50t 5cwt
	yz Tender 42t 3cwt
Driving Wheel:	5' 8"
Boiler Pressure:	225psi superheated
Cylinders:	Outside 18" x 28"
Tractive Effort:	25515lbf
Valve Gear:	Walschaert (piston valves)

These locomotives were designed for cross-country and secondary passenger work. They were a smaller version of the '73000' class, and as they were lighter engines they had almost universal availability over main and secondary routes throughout Britain. Eighty of these engines were built at Swindon and they were based on the London Midland, Western and Southern Regions, including such routes as those of the former Cambrian Railways.

d From 1957 some locomotives (including all those allocated to the Southern Region) were fitted with double chimneys.

Several different types of tender were fitted, allocated as shown below.

x BR1B 4725 gallon tender.

y BR2 3500 gallon tender.

z BR2A 3500 gallon tender.

Year End Totals: '4MT [1]' class

'47	'48	'49	'50	'51	'52	'53	'54	'55	'56	'57	'58	'59	'60	'61	'62	'63	'64	'65	'66	'67
				16	20	45	50	63	68	80	80	80	80	80	80	80	78	67	46	10

Number	*Built*	*Renumbered*	*BR Dates*	*Scrap*	*Notes*
75000	05/51 Sdn		05/51-12/65	04/66	y
75001	08/51 Sdn		08/51-12/64	04/65	y
75002	08/51 Sdn		08/51-08/67	02/68	y
75003	08/51 Sdn		08/51-10/65	02/66	y
					12/59⇨d

Number	Built	Renumbered	BR Dates	Scrap	Notes
75004	08/51 Sdn		08/51-03/67	08/67	y
75005	09/51 Sdn		09/51-11/65	02/66	y
					01/62⇨d
75006	09/51 Sdn		09/51-08/67	02/68	y
					12/60⇨d
75007	09/51 Sdn		09/51-04/65	08/65	y
75008	10/51 Sdn		10/51-12/65	04/66	y
					09/62⇨d
75009	10/51 Sdn		10/51-08/68	11/68	y
75010	11/51 Sdn		11/51-10/67	02/68	y
75011	11/51 Sdn		11/51-10/66	02/67	y
75012	11/51 Sdn		11/51-01/67	06/67	y
75013	11/51 Sdn		11/51-08/67	02/68	y
75014 §	12/51 Sdn		12/51-12/66		y
75015	12/51 Sdn		12/51-12/67	06/68	y
75016	01/52 Sdn		01/52-07/67	06/68	y
75017	01/52 Sdn		01/52-01/67	05/67	y
75018	03/52 Sdn		03/52-06/67	11/67	y
75019	03/52 Sdn		03/52-08/68	11/68	y
75020	11/53 Sdn		11/53-08/68	11/68	y
					62⇨d
75021	11/53 Sdn		11/53-02/68	06/68	y
75022	12/53 Sdn		12/53-12/65	04/66	y
75023	12/53 Sdn		12/53-01/66	04/66	y
75024	12/53 Sdn		12/53-11/67	04/68	y
75025	04/54 Sdn		04/54-12/65	04/66	y
75026	05/54 Sdn		05/54-12/67	07/68	y
					07/62⇨d
75027 §	05/54 Sdn		05/54-08/68		y
75028	05/54 Sdn		05/54-12/65	04/66	y
75029 §	05/54 Sdn		05/54-08/67		y
					05/57⇨d
75030	06/53 Sdn		06/53-12/67	07/68	y
75031	06/53 Sdn		06/53-02/66	05/66	y
75032	06/53 Sdn		06/53-02/68	05/68	y
75033	07/53 Sdn		07/53-12/67	06/68	y
75034	07/53 Sdn		07/53-02/68	07/68	y
75035	08/53 Sdn		08/53-07/67	01/68	y
75036	08/53 Sdn		08/53-06/66	08/66	y
75037	08/53 Sdn		08/53-12/67	07/68	y
75038	08/53 Sdn		08/53-12/65	04/66	y
75039	08/53 Sdn		08/53-09/67	02/68	y
75040	09/53 Sdn		09/53-10/67	03/68	y
75041	09/53 Sdn		09/53-01/68	08/68	y
75042	09/53 Sdn		09/53-10/67	03/68	y
75043	09/53 Sdn		09/53-12/67	04/68	y
75044	09/53 Sdn		09/53-03/66	06/66	y
75045	09/53 Sdn		09/53-04/66	08/66	y
75046	10/53 Sdn		10/53-08/67	02/68	y
75047	10/53 Sdn		10/53-08/67	02/68	y
75048	10/53 Sdn		10/53-08/68	11/68	y
75049	10/53 Sdn		10/53-10/66	03/67	y
75050	11/56 Sdn		11/56-11/66	06/67	z
75051	11/56 Sdn		11/56-10/66	02/67	z
75052	12/56 Sdn		12/56-08/67	02/68	z
75053	01/57 Sdn		01/57-09/66	02/67	z
75054	01/57 Sdn		01/57-09/66	01/67	z
75055	01/57 Sdn		01/57-06/67	02/68	z
75056	03/57 Sdn		03/57-06/66	08/66	z
75057	03/57 Sdn		03/57-02/66	06/66	z
75058	04/57 Sdn		04/57-12/67	04/68	z
75059	04/57 Sdn		04/57-07/67	12/67	z
75060	05/57 Sdn		05/57-04/67	10/67	z
75061	05/57 Sdn		05/57-02/67	06/67	z
75062	05/57 Sdn		05/57-02/68	06/68	z
75063	06/57 Sdn		06/57-06/66	08/66	z
75064	06/57 Sdn		06/57-05/67	09/67	z
75065	08/55 Sdn		08/55-09/66	03/67	x
					04/61⇨d
75066	09/55 Sdn		09/55-01/66	04/66	x
					04/61⇨d
75067	09/55 Sdn		09/55-10/64	11/65	x
					12/60⇨d
75068	09/55 Sdn		09/55-07/67	02/68	x
					01/61⇨d
75069 §	09/55 Sdn		09/55-09/66		x
					10/60⇨d
75070	10/55 Sdn		10/55-09/66	03/67	x
					02/61⇨d
75071	10/55 Sdn		10/55-08/67	02/68	x
					03/61⇨d
75072	11/55 Sdn		11/55-12/65	04/66	x
					11/60⇨d
75073	11/55 Sdn		11/55-12/65	04/66	x
					08/61⇨d
75074	11/55 Sdn		11/55-07/67	02/68	x
					07/61⇨d
75075	11/55 Sdn		11/55-07/67	02/68	x
					09/61⇨d
75076	12/55 Sdn		12/55-07/67	12/67	x
					06/61⇨d
75077	12/55 Sdn		12/55-07/67	02/68	x
					06/61⇨d
75078 §	01/56 Sdn		01/56-07/66		x
					10/61⇨d
75079 §	01/56 Sdn		01/56-11/66		x
					11/61⇨d

4MT [2] 76000-76114
2-6-0 BR Standard 'Class 4'

Power Classification: 4MT
Introduced: 1952-57
Designer: Riddles, designed at Doncaster
Company: BR
Weight: Loco 59t 2cwt
x Tender 50t 5cwt
yz Tender 42t 3cwt
Driving Wheel: 5' 3"
Boiler Pressure: 225psi superheated
Cylinders: Outside 17½" x 26"
Tractive Effort: 24170lbf
Valve Gear: Walschaert (piston valves)

These locomotives were built for intermediate passenger and cross-country work, and were smaller than the '75000' class. They were based closely on the '43000' LMS Ivatt 2-6-0 class introduced in 1947. One hundred and fifteen engines were built at Horwich and Doncaster and they were based on all regions except the Western. They were widely used and always highly regarded.

Several different types of tender were fitted, allocated as shown below.

x BR1B 4725 gallon tender.

y BR2 3500 gallon tender.

z BR2A 3500 gallon tender.

Year End Totals: '4MT [2]' class

'47	'48	'49	'50	'51	'52	'53	'54	'55	'56	'57	'58	'59	'60	'61	'62	'63	'64	'65	'66	'67
					10	35	45	60	79	115	115	115	115	115	115	115	108	92	40	

Number	Built	Renumbered	BR Dates	Scrap	Notes
76000	12/52 Hor		12/52-05/67	09/67	y
76001	12/52 Hor		12/52-08/66	03/68	y
76002	12/52 Hor		12/52-01/67	05/67	y
76003	12/52 Hor		12/52-03/66	06/66	y
76004	12/52 Hor		12/52-10/66	01/67	y
76005	12/52 Hor		12/52-07/67	11/67	y
76006	02/53 Hor		02/53-07/67	11/67	y
76007	02/53 Hor		02/53-07/67	11/67	y
76008	02/53 Hor		02/53-05/67	12/67	y
76009	02/53 Hor		02/53-07/67	01/68	y
76010	02/53 Hor		02/53-09/66	03/67	y
76011	02/53 Hor		02/53-07/67	11/67	y
76012	02/53 Hor		02/53-09/66	03/67	y
76013	02/53 Hor		02/53-09/66	03/67	y
76014	02/53 Hor		02/53-09/66	01/67	y
76015	05/53 Hor		05/53-10/65	01/66	y
76016	05/53 Hor		06/53-10/66	06/67	y
76017 §	07/53 Hor		07/53-07/65		y
76018	07/53 Hor		07/53-10/66	06/67	y
76019	07/53 Hor		07/53-02/66	06/66	y
76020	12/52 Don		12/52-04/66	07/66	y
76021	12/52 Don		12/52-10/66	02/67	y
76022	12/52 Don		12/52-09/66	12/66	y
76023	12/52 Don		12/52-10/65	01/66	y
76024	01/53 Don		01/53-12/66	04/67	y
76025	09/53 Don		09/53-10/65	02/66	y
76026	11/53 Don		11/53-07/67	09/67	y
76027	11/53 Don		11/53-10/65	01/66	y
76028	11/53 Don		11/53-05/64	08/64	y
76029	11/53 Don		11/53-10/64	03/65	y
76030	11/53 Don		11/53-04/65	12/65	y
76031	11/53 Don		11/53-07/67	12/67	y
76032	12/53 Don		12/53-08/64	12/64	y
76033	12/53 Don		12/53-02/67	11/67	y
76034	12/53 Don		12/53-09/64	10/64	y
76035	05/54 Don		05/54-05/66	08/66	y
76036	06/54 Don		06/54-01/67	07/67	y
76037	06/54 Don		06/54-06/67	11/67	y
76038	07/54 Don		07/54-09/66	12/66	y
76039	07/54 Don		07/54-06/67	12/67	y
76040	07/54 Don		07/54-04/67	09/67	y
76041	07/54 Don		07/54-04/67	02/68	y
76042	08/54 Don		08/54-07/66	11/66	y
76043	08/54 Don		08/54-09/66	12/66	y
76044	08/54 Don		08/54-10/66	03/67	y
76045	03/55 Don		03/55-01/66	06/66	z
76046	03/55 Don		03/55-05/67	09/67	z
76047	03/55 Don		03/55-11/66	02/68	z
76048	03/55 Don		03/55-02/67	07/67	z
76049	04/55 Don		04/55-01/66	05/66	z
76050	08/56 Don		08/56-09/65	11/66	z
76051	08/56 Don		08/56-05/67	12/67	z
76052	09/56 Don		09/56-12/66	02/68	z
76053	04/55 Don		04/55-01/67	08/67	x
76054	04/55 Don		04/55-10/64	03/65	x
76055	04/55 Don		04/55-10/65	01/66	x
76056	06/55 Don		06/55-11/65	03/66	x
76057	06/55 Don		06/55-10/66	07/67	x
76058	06/55 Don		06/55-03/67	12/67	x
76059	06/55 Don		06/55-09/66	03/67	x
76060	06/55 Don		06/55-12/65	05/66	x
76061	06/55 Don		06/55-01/67	06/67	x
76062	06/55 Don		06/55-10/65	02/66	x
76063	07/56 Don		07/56-04/67	11/67	x
76064	07/56 Don		07/56-07/67	11/67	x
76065	07/56 Don		07/56-10/65	06/66	x
76066	07/56 Don		07/56-07/67	11/67	x
76067	08/56 Don		08/56-07/67	11/67	x
76068	08/56 Don		08/56-10/65	02/66	x
76069	08/56 Don		08/56-06/67	03/68	x
76070	09/56 Don		09/56-08/66	01/67	z
76071	10/56 Don		10/56-01/66	06/66	z
76072	10/56 Don		10/56-10/64	01/65	z
76073	10/56 Don		10/56-06/66	11/66	z
76074	11/56 Don		11/56-10/66	01/67	z
76075	12/56 Hor		12/56-10/67	04/68	z
76076	12/56 Hor		12/56-11/66	04/67	z
76077 §	12/56 Hor		12/56-11/67		z
76078	12/56 Hor		12/56-11/66	04/67	z
76079 §	02/57 Hor		02/57-11/67		z
76080	02/57 Hor		02/57-12/67	04/72	z
76081	02/57 Hor		02/57-07/67	12/67	z
76082	03/57 Hor		03/57-10/66	04/67	z
76083	03/57 Hor		03/57-10/66	03/67	z
76084 §	03/57 Hor		03/57-11/67		z
76085	04/57 Hor		04/57-08/66	11/66	z
76086	05/57 Hor		04/57-09/66	05/67	z
76087	05/57 Hor		05/57-01/67	09/67	z
76088	05/57 Hor		05/57-06/67	12/67	z
76089	05/57 Hor		05/57-09/66	12/66	z
76090	06/57 Hor		06/57-12/66	04/67	z
76091	06/57 Hor		06/57-12/66	04/67	z
76092	06/57 Hor		06/57-08/66	11/66	z
76093	07/57 Hor		07/57-02/67	04/67	z
76094	08/57 Hor		08/57-05/67	09/67	z
76095	08/57 Hor		08/57-03/67	05/68	z
76096	09/57 Hor		09/57-12/66	07/67	z
76097	09/57 Hor		09/57-07/64	01/65	z
76098	10/57 Hor		10/57-05/67	03/68	z
76099	11/57 Hor		11/57-08/66	11/66	z
76100	05/57 Don		05/57-08/66	04/68	z
76101	06/57 Don		06/57-12/66	05/67	z
76102	06/57 Don		06/57-12/66	05/67	z
76103	06/57 Don		06/57-07/66	11/66	z
76104	07/57 Don		07/57-05/67	09/67	z
76105	07/57 Don		07/57-01/66	04/66	z
76106	07/57 Don		07/57-09/65	11/65	z
76107	08/57 Don		08/57-10/65	06/66	z
76108	08/57 Don		08/57-07/66	11/66	z
76109	08/57 Don		08/57-09/66	01/67	z
76110	08/57 Don		08/57-12/66	04/67	z
76111	08/57 Don		08/57-01/66	04/66	z
76112	09/57 Don		09/57-10/65	02/66	z
76113	10/57 Don		10/57-12/66	04/67	z
76114	10/57 Don		10/57-12/66	04/67	z

3MT [1] 77000-77019
2-6-0 BR Standard 'Class 3'

Power Classification: 3MT
Introduced: 1954
Designer: Riddles, designed at Swindon
Company: BR
Weight: Loco 57t 9cwt
Tender 42t 3cwt
Driving Wheel: 5' 3"
Boiler Pressure: 200psi superheated
Cylinders: Outside 17½" x 26"
Tractive Effort: 21490lbf
Valve Gear: Walschaert (piston valves)

These locomotives were built as a tender version of the '82000' '3MT' class, designed for working on virtually any main or secondary line throughout Britain. They had a boiler based on the GWR Swindon number 2 boiler (as fitted to the '5600' class), and were fitted with BR2A 3500 gallon tenders. The class was distinctive in having a high running plate with small sized wheels. They were numerically the smallest of the new BR standard classes with only twenty engines being built at Swindon in 1954. The engines were divided mainly between the North Eastern and Scottish regions. An order for a further five of these locomotives was cancelled.

Year End Totals: '3MT [1]' class

'47	'48	'49	'50	'51	'52	'53	'54	'55	'56	'57	'58	'59	'60	'61	'62	'63	'64	'65	'66	'67
							20	20	20	20	20	20	20	20	20	20	20	19	3	

Number	Built	Renumbered	BR Dates	Scrap	Notes
77000	02/54 Sdn		02/54-12/66	03/67	
77001	02/54 Sdn		02/54-01/66	02/66	
77002	02/54 Sdn		02/54-06/67	02/68	

77003	02/54 Sdn		02/54-12/66	03/67	
77004	03/54 Sdn		03/54-12/66	03/67	
77005	03/54 Sdn		03/54-11/66	04/67	
77006	03/54 Sdn		03/54-03/66	06/66	
77007	03/54 Sdn		03/54-11/66	04/67	
77008	04/54 Sdn		04/54-06/66	10/66	
77009	06/54 Sdn		06/54-05/66	10/66	
77010	06/54 Sdn		06/54-11/65	02/66	
77011	06/54 Sdn		06/54-02/66	05/66	
77012	07/54 Sdn		07/54-06/67	02/68	
77013	07/54 Sdn		07/54-03/66	06/66	
77014	07/54 Sdn		07/54-07/67	02/68	
77015	07/54 Sdn		07/54-07/66	11/66	
77016	08/54 Sdn		08/54-03/66	06/66	
77017	08/54 Sdn		08/54-11/66	04/67	
77018	08/54 Sdn		08/54-11/66	04/67	
77019	09/54 Sdn		09/54-11/66	04/67	

2MT [1] 78000-78064
2-6-0 BR Standard 'Class 2'

Power Classification:	2MT
Introduced:	1952-56
Designer:	Riddles, designed at Derby
Company:	BR
Weight:	Loco 49t 5cwt Tender 36t 17cwt
Driving Wheel:	5' 0"
Boiler Pressure:	200psi superheated
Cylinders:	Outside 16½" x 24"
Tractive Effort:	18515lbf
Valve Gear:	Walschaert (piston valves)

These locomotives were designed for light passenger work. Sixty-five engines were built at Darlington and they were the smallest engines in the BR range of standard types. They were similar in design to the '46400' LMS Ivatt '2MT' class of 1946. They had a lower running plate than most of the BR Standard designs, and were fitted with BR3 3000 gallon tenders.

The 84000 class was a tank version of this design.

Year End Totals: '2MT [1]' class

'47	'48	'49	'50	'51	'52	'53	'54	'55	'56	'57	'58	'59	'60	'61	'62	'63	'64	'65	'66	'67
					4	12	45	55	65	65	65	65	65	65	65	64	60	43	12	

Number	Built	Renumbered	BR Dates	Scrap	Notes
78000	12/52 Dar		12/52-07/65	01/66	
78001	12/52 Dar		12/52-12/65	03/66	
78002	12/52 Dar		12/52-06/66	10/66	
78003	12/52 Dar		12/52-12/66	09/67	
78004	01/53 Dar		01/53-11/65	02/66	
78005	02/53 Dar		02/53-09/64	03/65	
78006	03/53 Dar		03/53-12/65	03/66	
78007	03/53 Dar		03/53-05/67	12/67	
78008	03/53 Dar		03/53-10/66	01/67	
78009	04/53 Dar		04/53-02/64	12/64	
78010	12/53 Dar		12/53-09/66	12/66	
78011	12/53 Dar		12/53-09/65	12/65	
78012	01/54 Dar		01/54-05/67	10/67	
78013	01/54 Dar		01/54-05/67	10/67	
78014	02/54 Dar		02/54-09/65	12/65	
78015	02/54 Dar		02/54-11/63	01/64	
78016	03/54 Dar		03/54-08/66	05/67	
78017	03/54 Dar		03/54-12/66	10/67	
78018 §	03/54 Dar		03/54-11/66		
78019 §	03/54 Dar		03/54-11/66		
78020	04/54 Dar		04/54-05/67	11/67	
78021	05/54 Dar		05/54-05/67	11/67	
78022 §	05/54 Dar		05/54-09/66		
78023	05/54 Dar		05/54-05/67	10/67	
78024	05/54 Dar		05/54-02/65	01/66	
78025	05/54 Dar		05/54-02/65	11/65	
78026	06/54 Dar		06/54-08/66	12/66	
78027	06/54 Dar		06/54-09/65	02/66	
78028	06/54 Dar		06/54-02/67	06/67	
78029	07/54 Dar		07/54-09/65	01/66	
78030	09/54 Dar		09/54-10/65	12/65	
78031	09/54 Dar		09/54-10/66	03/67	
78032	09/54 Dar		09/54-09/65	01/66	
78033	10/54 Dar		10/54-09/65	11/65	
78034	10/54 Dar		10/54-01/66	04/66	
78035	11/54 Dar		11/54-12/65	04/66	
78036	11/54 Dar		11/54-11/66	08/67	
78037	11/54 Dar		11/54-05/67	11/67	
78038	11/54 Dar		11/54-09/66	12/66	
78039	11/54 Dar		11/54-09/66	03/67	
78040	12/54 Dar		12/54-01/66	05/66	
78041	12/54 Dar		12/54-05/67	11/67	
78042	12/54 Dar		12/54-09/65	12/65	
78043	12/54 Dar		12/54-09/65	01/66	
78044	12/54 Dar		12/54-05/67	10/67	
78045	10/55 Dar		10/55-01/66	04/66	
78046	10/55 Dar		10/55-11/66	06/67	
78047	10/55 Dar		10/55-09/66	01/67	
78048	10/55 Dar		10/55-07/64	04/65	
78049	11/55 Dar		11/55-08/66	12/66	
78050	11/55 Dar		11/55-01/66	04/66	
78051	11/55 Dar		11/55-12/66	03/67	
78052	11/55 Dar		11/55-01/66	04/66	
78053	11/55 Dar		11/55-07/64	04/65	
78054	12/55 Dar		12/55-12/65	03/66	
78055	08/56 Dar		08/56-02/67	06/67	
78056	08/56 Dar		08/56-07/66	11/66	
78057	09/56 Dar		08/56-05/66	08/66	
78058	09/56 Dar		09/56-12/66	09/67	
78059 §	09/56 Dar		09/56-11/66		
78060	10/56 Dar		10/56-10/66	03/67	
78061	10/56 Dar		10/56-11/66	03/67	
78062	10/56 Dar		10/56-05/67	10/67	
78063	11/56 Dar		11/56-12/66	12/67	
78064	11/56 Dar		11/56-11/66	03/67	

4MT [3] 80000-80154
2-6-4T BR Standard 'Class 4 Tank'

Power Classification:	4MT
Introduced:	1951-57
Designer:	Riddles, designed at Brighton
Company:	BR
Weight:	88t 10cwt
Driving Wheel:	5' 8"
Boiler Pressure:	225psi superheated
Cylinders:	Outside 18" x 28"
Tractive Effort:	25515lbf
Valve Gear:	Walschaert (piston valves)

Refer to the Historical Survey of LMS 2-6-4T Engines in the LMS section of this book for more details of this class.

These locomotives were built for suburban and semi-express passenger work. They were based on the '42050' series of LMS Stanier and Fairburn 2-6-4T locomotives, but with the tank sides, cab and bunker sloping inwards to conform with the loading gauge. One hundred and fifty-five engines were built at Derby, Doncaster and Brighton and they were fitted with the same boilers as the '75000' class.

They were successful engines and they always steamed well, without the need for re-draughting. They were popular performers with an admirable turn of speed and good acceleration. They were based on all regions except the Western.

Year End Totals: '4MT [3]' class

'47	'48	'49	'50	'51	'52	'53	'54	'55	'56	'57	'58	'59	'60	'61	'62	'63	'64	'65	'66	'67
				17	54	72	108	131	151	155	155	155	155	155	154	154	123	79	25	

Number	Built	Renumbered	BR Dates	Scrap	Notes
80000	09/52 Der		09/52-12/66	04/67	
80001	10/52 Der		10/52-07/66	11/66	
80002 §	10/52 Der		10/52-03/67		
80003	10/52 Der		10/52-03/65	07/65	
80004	11/52 Der		11/52-05/67	09/67	
80005	11/52 Der		11/52-08/66	11/66	
80006	11/52 Der		11/52-09/66	12/66	
80007	12/52 Der		12/52-07/66	11/66	
80008	12/52 Der		12/52-07/64	04/65	
80009	12/52 Der		12/52-09/64	04/65	
80010	07/51 Bton		07/51-06/64	04/65	
80011	07/51 Bton		07/51-07/67	03/68	
80012	08/51 Bton		08/51-03/67	09/67	
80013	10/51 Bton		10/51-06/66	12/66	
80014	10/51 Bton		10/51-05/65	08/65	
80015	10/51 Bton		10/51-07/67	03/68	
80016	10/51 Bton		10/51-07/67	02/68	
80017	10/51 Bton		10/51-09/64	04/65	
80018	10/51 Bton		10/51-04/65	08/65	
80019	12/51 Bton		12/51-03/67	11/67	
80020	10/51 Bton		10/51-06/65	07/65	
80021	11/51 Bton		11/51-07/64	04/65	
80022	11/51 Bton		11/51-06/65	09/65	
80023	11/51 Bton		11/51-10/65	01/66	
80024	12/51 Bton		12/51-08/66	11/66	
80025	12/51 Bton		12/51-08/66	11/66	
80026	12/51 Bton		12/51-09/66	12/66	
80027	01/52 Bton		01/52-11/66	06/67	
80028	01/52 Bton		01/52-09/66	01/67	
80029	01/52 Bton		01/52-12/65	03/66	
80030	02/52 Bton		02/52-06/64	03/65	
80031	03/52 Bton		03/52-09/64	04/65	
80032	03/52 Bton		03/52-01/67	05/67	
80033	03/52 Bton		03/52-10/66	02/67	
80034	04/52 Bton		04/52-01/66	05/66	
80035	05/52 Bton		05/52-04/65	08/65	
80036	05/52 Bton		05/52-11/64	04/65	
80037	05/52 Bton		05/52-03/66	07/66	
80038	06/52 Bton		06/52-09/64	04/65	
80039	06/52 Bton		06/52-01/66	04/66	
80040	06/52 Bton		06/52-05/64	07/64	
80041	07/52 Bton		07/52-03/66	07/66	
80042	08/52 Bton		08/52-02/65	05/65	
80043	08/52 Bton		08/52-03/66	07/66	
80044	08/52 Bton		08/52-11/64	01/65	
80045	09/52 Bton		09/52-05/67	09/67	
80046	09/52 Bton		09/52-05/67	09/67	
80047	10/52 Bton		10/52-08/66	11/66	
80048	10/52 Bton		10/52-07/65	04/66	
80049	10/52 Bton		10/52-06/64	03/65	
80050	11/52 Bton		11/52-11/64	07/65	
80051	11/52 Bton		11/52-08/66	11/66	
80052	12/52 Bton		12/52-06/64	04/65	
80053	12/52 Bton		12/52-06/64	04/65	
80054	12/54 Der		12/54-07/66	10/66	
80055	12/54 Der		12/54-09/66	12/66	
80056	12/54 Der		12/54-10/64	11/64	
80057	12/54 Der		12/54-12/66	05/67	
80058	01/55 Der		01/55-07/66	11/66	
80059	03/53 Bton		03/53-11/65	03/66	
80060	03/53 Bton		03/53-02/66	06/66	
80061	04/53 Bton		04/53-12/66	05/67	
80062	05/53 Bton		05/53-10/64	03/65	
80063	05/53 Bton		05/53-08/66	11/66	
80064 §	06/53 Bton		06/53-09/65		
80065	09/53 Bton		06/53-09/66	02/67	
80066	07/53 Bton		07/53-06/65	10/65	
80067	08/53 Bton		08/53-06/65	09/65	
80068	08/53 Bton		08/53-10/66	02/67	
80069	09/53 Bton		09/53-01/66	04/66	
80070	10/53 Bton		10/53-06/65	10/65	
80071	12/53 Bton		12/53-07/64	03/65	
80072 §	11/53 Bton		11/53-07/65		
80073	11/53 Bton		11/53-07/64	03/65	
80074	11/53 Bton		11/53-07/64	03/65	
80075	12/53 Bton		12/53-07/64	03/65	
80076	12/53 Bton		12/53-07/64	03/65	
80077	01/54 Bton		01/54-10/64	04/65	
80078 §	02/54 Bton		02/54-07/65		
80079 §	03/54 Bton		03/54-07/65		
80080 §	03/54 Bton		03/54-07/65		
80081	04/54 Bton		04/54-06/65	10/65	
80082	04/54 Bton		04/54-09/66	02/67	
80083	05/54 Bton		05/54-08/66	02/67	
80084	05/54 Bton		05/54-06/65	10/65	
80085	05/54 Bton		05/54-07/67	02/68	
80086	06/54 Bton		06/54-05/67	02/68	
80087	07/54 Bton		07/54-06/64	04/65	
80088	07/54 Bton		07/54-06/65	10/65	
80089	08/54 Bton		08/54-10/66	03/67	
80090	08/54 Bton		08/54-03/65	05/65	
80091	09/54 Bton		09/54-11/66	04/67	
80092	09/54 Bton		09/54-09/66	01/67	
80093	10/54 Bton		10/54-09/66	01/67	
80094	10/54 Bton		10/54-07/66	02/67	
80095	11/54 Bton		11/54-10/66	03/67	
80096	11/54 Bton		11/54-12/65	03/66	
80097 §	12/54 Bton		12/54-07/65		
80098 §	12/54 Bton		12/54-07/65		
80099	01/55 Bton		01/55-05/65	07/65	
80100 §	01/55 Bton		01/55-07/65		
80101	02/55 Bton		02/55-07/65	04/66	
80102	03/55 Bton		03/55-12/65	03/66	
80103	03/55 Bton		03/55-09/62	09/62	
80104 §	03/55 Bton		03/55-07/65		
80105 §	04/55 Bton		04/55-07/65		
80106	10/54 Don		10/54-10/64	03/65	
80107	10/54 Don		10/54-09/64	03/65	
80108	11/54 Don		11/54-05/65	07/65	
80109	11/54 Don		11/54-11/65	02/66	
80110	11/54 Don		11/54-05/65	08/65	
80111	11/54 Don		11/54-11/66	04/67	
80112	12/54 Don		12/54-08/66	11/66	
80113	12/54 Don		12/54-09/66	12/66	
80114	12/54 Don		12/54-12/66	04/67	
80115	12/54 Don		12/54-10/64	03/65	
80116	05/55 Bton		05/55-05/67	09/67	
80117	05/55 Bton		05/55-03/66	06/66	
80118	06/55 Bton		06/55-11/66	04/67	
80119	06/55 Bton		06/55-05/65	10/65	
80120	07/55 Bton		07/55-05/67	09/67	
80121	07/55 Bton		07/55-06/66	08/66	
80122	08/55 Bton		08/55-12/66	04/67	
80123	09/55 Bton		09/55-08/66	11/66	
80124	09/55 Bton		09/55-12/66	04/67	
80125	10/55 Bton		10/55-10/64	06/65	
80126	10/55 Bton		10/55-11/66	02/67	
80127	11/55 Bton		11/55-07/64	11/64	
80128	11/55 Bton		11/55-04/67	09/67	
80129	12/55 Bton		12/55-10/64	11/64	
80130	12/55 Bton		12/55-08/66	11/66	
80131	03/56 Bton		03/56-05/65	07/65	
80132	03/56 Bton		03/56-01/66	04/66	
80133	03/56 Bton		03/56-07/67	03/68	
80134	04/56 Bton		04/56-07/67	02/68	
80135 §	04/56 Bton		04/56-07/65		
80136 §	05/56 Bton		05/56-07/65		

80137	05/56 Bton		05/56-10/65	02/66	
80138	06/56 Bton		06/56-10/66	02/67	
80139	06/56 Bton		06/56-07/67	01/68	
80140	07/56 Bton		07/56-07/67	12/67	
80141	07/56 Bton		07/56-01/66	04/66	
80142	08/56 Bton		08/56-03/66	07/66	
80143	09/56 Bton		09/56-07/67	01/68	
80144	09/56 Bton		09/56-05/66	10/66	
80145	10/56 Bton		10/56-06/67	11/67	
80146	10/56 Bton		10/56-07/67	03/68	
80147	11/56 Bton		11/56-06/65	01/66	
80148	11/56 Bton		11/56-06/64	04/65	
80149	12/56 Bton		12/56-03/65	07/65	
80150 §	12/56 Bton		12/56-10/65		
80151 §	01/57 Bton		01/57-05/67		
80152	02/57 Bton		02/57-07/67	03/68	
80153	02/57 Bton		02/57-03/65	07/65	
80154	03/57 Bton		03/57-04/67	10/67	

3MT [2] 82000-82044

2-6-2T BR Standard 'Class 3 Tank'

Power Classification: 3MT
Introduced: 1952-55
Designer: Riddles, designed at Swindon
Company: BR
Weight: 73t 10cwt
Driving Wheel: 5' 3"
Boiler Pressure: 200psi superheated
Cylinders: Outside 17½" x 26"
Tractive Effort: 21490lbf
Valve Gear: Walschaert (piston valves)

These locomotives were built for light passenger work and were derived from the GWR '6100' class with almost identical boilers. They were later developed into the '77000' class. Forty-five engines were built at Swindon. They were mainly based on the Western and Southern Regions.

Year End Totals: '3MT [2]' class

'47	'48	'49	'50	'51	'52	'53	'54	'55	'56	'57	'58	'59	'60	'61	'62	'63	'64	'65	'66	'67
					20	20	32	45	45	45	45	45	45	45	45	45	35	14	2	

Number	Built	Renumbered	BR Dates	Scrap	Notes
82000	04/52 Sdn		04/52-12/66	05/67	
82001	04/52 Sdn		04/52-12/65	04/66	
82002	04/52 Sdn		04/52-02/64	04/64	
82003	05/52 Sdn		05/52-12/66	10/68	
82004	05/52 Sdn		05/52-10/65	07/66	
82005	05/52 Sdn		05/52-09/65	02/66	
82006	05/52 Sdn		05/52-09/66	02/67	
82007	05/52 Sdn		05/52-07/64	12/64	
82008	06/52 Sdn		06/52-02/64	06/64	
82009	06/52 Sdn		06/52-10/66	03/67	
82010	06/52 Sdn		06/52-04/65	10/65	
82011	07/52 Sdn		07/52-08/64	11/64	
82012	07/52 Sdn		07/52-05/64	11/64	
82013	07/52 Sdn		07/52-06/64	11/64	
82014	08/52 Sdn		08/52-05/64	11/64	
82015	08/52 Sdn		08/52-12/64	04/65	
82016	08/52 Sdn		08/52-04/65	04/65	
82017	08/52 Sdn		08/52-04/65	08/65	
82018	09/52 Sdn		09/52-07/66	10/66	
82019	09/52 Sdn		09/52-07/67	03/68	
82020	09/54 Sdn		09/54-09/65	01/66	
82021	10/54 Sdn		10/54-10/65	03/66	
82022	10/54 Sdn		10/54-10/65	05/66	
82023	10/54 Sdn		10/54-10/66	03/67	
82024	10/54 Sdn		10/54-01/66	05/66	
82025	11/54 Sdn		11/54-08/64	12/64	
82026	11/54 Sdn		11/54-06/66	10/66	
82027	11/54 Sdn		11/54-01/66	04/66	
82028	12/54 Sdn		12/54-09/66	02/67	
82029	12/54 Sdn		12/54-07/67	01/68	
82030	12/54 Sdn		12/54-12/65	04/66	
82031	12/54 Sdn		12/54-12/66	10/68	
82032	01/55 Sdn		01/55-05/65	11/65	
82033	01/55 Sdn		01/55-09/65	02/66	
82034	01/55 Sdn		01/55-12/66	10/68	
82035	03/55 Sdn		03/55-08/65	11/65	
82036	04/55 Sdn		04/55-07/65	11/65	
82037	04/55 Sdn		04/55-08/65	11/65	
82038	05/55 Sdn		05/55-08/65	10/65	
82039	05/55 Sdn		05/55-07/65	11/65	
82040	05/55 Sdn		05/55-07/65	11/65	
82041	06/55 Sdn		06/55-12/65	07/66	
82042	06/55 Sdn		06/55-08/65	02/66	
82043	06/55 Sdn		06/55-02/64	05/64	
82044	08/55 Sdn		08/55-11/65	02/66	

2MT [2] 84000-84029

2-6-2T BR Standard 'Class 2 Tank'

Power Classification: 2MT
Introduced: 1953-57
Designer: Riddles, designed at Derby
Company: BR
Weight: 63t 5cwt
Driving Wheel: 5' 0"
Boiler Pressure: 200psi superheated
Cylinders: Outside 16½" x 24"
Tractive Effort: 18515lbf
Valve Gear: Walschaert (piston valves)

These locomotives were designed for light passenger work and were fitted for push-pull work. They were similar in design to the LMS Ivatt '2MT' class of 1946 ('41200' class), and were a tank version of the '78000' class.

The first twenty engines were built at Crewe in 1953 for use on the London Midland Region. They replaced older 2-4-2T and 0-4-4T engines of pre-grouping design on branch-line passenger trains. The last ten engines were built at Darlington in 1957 for use on the Southern Region.

In 1960, 84020 was taken to Eastleigh for conversion and trials for working on the Isle of Wight. This plan was abandoned before conversion could take place. However in 1965 the plans were revived and ten engines (84010/13-17/19/25/26/28) were transferred (on paper) from the London Midland Region to Eastleigh for transfer to the island. Again these plans were abandoned and the transfer was cancelled.

Year End Totals: '2MT [2]' class

'47	'48	'49	'50	'51	'52	'53	'54	'55	'56	'57	'58	'59	'60	'61	'62	'63	'64	'65	'66	'67
						20	20	20	20	30	30	30	30	30	30	29	20			

Number	Built	Renumbered	BR Dates	Scrap	Notes
84000	07/53 Crw		07/53-11/65	04/66	
84001	07/53 Crw		07/53-10/64	02/65	
84002	07/53 Crw		07/53-04/65	09/66	
84003	08/53 Crw		08/53-09/65	02/66	
84004	08/53 Crw		08/53-11/65	06/66	
84005	08/53 Crw		08/53-11/65	09/66	
84006	08/53 Crw		08/53-11/65	05/66	
84007	09/53 Crw		09/53-01/64	11/64	
84008	09/53 Crw		09/53-11/65	01/66	
84009	09/53 Crw		09/53-11/65	12/65	
84010	09/53 Crw		09/53-12/65	04/66	
84011	09/53 Crw		09/53-04/65	12/65	
84012	09/53 Crw		09/53-10/63	10/63	
84013	09/53 Crw		09/53-12/65	03/66	
84014	09/53 Crw		09/53-12/65	05/66	
84015	10/53 Crw		10/53-12/65	04/66	
84016	10/53 Crw		10/53-12/65	04/66	
84017	10/53 Crw		10/53-12/65	03/66	
84018	10/53 Crw		10/53-04/65	01/66	
84019	10/53 Crw		10/53-12/65	03/66	
84020	03/57 Dar		03/57-10/64	02/65	
84021	03/57 Dar		03/57-09/64	10/64	
84022	03/57 Dar		03/57-09/64	10/64	
84023	04/57 Dar		04/57-09/64	10/64	
84024	04/57 Dar		04/57-09/64	10/64	
84025	04/57 Dar		04/57-12/65	03/66	
84026	04/57 Dar		04/57-12/65	03/66	
84027	05/57 Dar		05/57-05/64	06/64	
84028	05/57 Dar		05/57-12/65	04/66	
84029	06/57 Dar		06/57-06/64	10/64	

WD [1] 90000-90732

2-8-0 MOS (WD) 'Austerity'

Power Classification: 8F
Introduced: 1943-46
Designer: Riddles
Company: Ministry of Supply
Weight: Loco 70t 5cwt
Tender 55t 10cwt
Driving Wheel: 4' 8½"
Boiler Pressure: 225psi superheated
Cylinders: Outside 19" x 28"
Tractive Effort: 34215lbf
Valve Gear: Walschaert (piston valves)

These war-time 'Austerity' locomotives were designed by Riddles and 934 were built by the North British Locomotive Company and Vulcan Foundry from 1943 onwards. The design was developed from the LMS Stanier 8F which was at first the standard type for war work. However it was thought that a simpler type of locomotive was needed and this class was developed to be built at minimal cost for short term service in the war. Many saw service in France, Holland and Belgium during the war.

The LNER purchased 200 locomotives in 1947 (which became their class 'O7') and 533 others were on loan to BR at nationalisation. These were purchased at the end of 1948 and from 1949 onwards they were all renumbered into one series. The North British engines were numbered 90000-90421 and the Vulcan Foundry engines 90422-90732. They were numbered in approximate order of construction, with the exception of the LNER engines which were kept in one series.

None of this large BR class have been preserved, but one engine which worked overseas has been preserved in this country. WD 79257 was built by the Vulcan Foundry in 1945 and went to Holland. It later became the Dutch State Railway number 4464 and then in 1952 it was sold to the Swedish State Railway numbered 1931. It was rescued and brought back to this country in 1976 and it now carries the fictitious BR number 90733.

Year End Totals: 'WD [1]' class

'47	'48	'49	'50	'51	'52	'53	'54	'55	'56	'57	'58	'59	'60	'61	'62	'63	'64	'65	'66	'67
	533	733	733	733	733	733	733	733	733	733	733	732	730	730	650	553	428	227	123	

Number	Built	Renumbered	BR Dates	Scrap	Notes
90000	02/43 NB	10/50 63000	01/49-06/65	11/65	
90001	01/43 NB	04/49 63001	01/49-04/66	08/66	
90002	03/43 NB	06/50 63002	01/49-04/66	08/66	
90003	03/43 NB	12/49 63003	01/49-06/64	08/64	
90004	04/43 NB	03/49 63004	01/49-12/63	05/64	
90005	04/43 NB	04/49 63005	01/49-04/65	07/65	
90006	05/43 NB	05/49 63006	01/49-09/63	09/63	
90007	05/43 NB	09/49 63007	01/49-07/65	02/66	
90008	05/43 NB	03/49 63008	01/49-04/67	06/67	
90009	06/43 NB	10/50 63009	01/49-09/67	11/67	
90010	07/43 NB	07/49 63010	01/49-02/65	08/65	
90011	07/43 NB	05/51 63011	01/49-06/66	10/66	
90012	08/43 NB	03/50 63012	01/49-02/64	04/64	
90013	08/43 NB	04/49 63013	01/49-04/66	08/66	
90014	09/43 NB	12/50 63014	01/49-04/67	07/67	
90015	08/43 NB	01/50 63015	01/49-05/63	07/63	
90016	08/43 NB	09/50 63016	01/49-06/67	01/68	
90017	08/43 NB	06/51 63017	01/49-09/63	12/63	
90018	08/43 NB	04/51 63018	01/49-04/66	08/66	
90019	09/43 NB	02/50 63019	01/49-12/63	12/63	
90020	09/43 NB	09/50 63020	01/49-04/67	09/67	
90021	10/43 NB	06/49 63021	01/49-10/62	03/63	
90022	10/43 NB	08/50 63022	01/49-10/62	12/62	
90023	09/43 NB	11/50 63023	01/49-09/62	12/62	
90024	09/43 NB	07/50 63024	01/49-02/66	06/66	
90025	09/43 NB	10/49 63025	01/49-08/65	10/65	
90026	10/43 NB	06/49 63026	01/49-12/63	01/64	
90027	10/43 NB	06/50 63027	01/49-05/63	06/63	
90028	11/43 NB	04/49 63028	01/49-12/62	04/63	
90029	11/43 NB	05/50 63029	01/49-07/65	11/65	
90030	11/43 NB	09/50 63030	01/49-04/67	08/67	
90031	10/43 NB	07/50 63031	01/49-05/63	07/63	
90032	11/43 NB	03/49 63032	01/49-02/66	06/66	
90033	11/43 NB	10/50 63033	01/49-05/63	09/63	
90034	12/43 NB	09/49 63034	01/49-09/62	01/63	
90035	11/43 NB	02/51 63035	01/49-02/66	07/66	
90036	01/44 NB	10/49 63036	01/49-12/65	04/66	
90037	01/44 NB	10/50 63037	01/49-04/66	08/66	
90038	01/44 NB	07/50 63038	01/49-08/65	11/65	
90039	01/44 NB	10/49 63039	01/49-09/66	12/66	
90040	02/44 NB	07/50 63040	01/49-07/65	12/65	
90041	02/44 NB	04/49 63041	01/49-12/66	04/67	
90042	02/44 NB	10/50 63042	01/49-01/65	04/65	
90043	03/44 NB	03/51 63043	01/49-12/65	04/66	
90044	03/44 NB	06/49 63044	01/49-12/66	02/67	
90045	03/44 NB	11/50 63045	01/49-10/65	02/66	
90046	04/44 NB	07/49 63046	01/49-03/63	06/63	
90047	04/44 NB	08/50 63047	01/49-06/67	02/68	
90048	04/44 NB	10/50 63048	01/49-05/63	06/63	
90049	04/44 NB	12/49 63049	01/49-09/63	12/63	
90050	04/44 NB	05/50 63050	01/49-05/63	07/63	
90051	05/44 NB	04/49 63051	01/49-10/65	01/66	
90052	05/44 NB	04/50 63052	01/49-03/64	04/64	
90053	05/44 NB	05/49 63053	01/49-07/65	02/66	
90054	05/44 NB	05/49 63054	01/49-01/67	03/67	
90055	05/44 NB	06/51 63055	01/49-03/65	06/65	
90056	05/44 NB	11/49 63056	01/49-05/67	08/67	
90057	05/44 NB	09/50 63057	01/49-06/67	01/68	
90058	05/44 NB	02/50 63058	01/49-12/63	02/64	
90059	05/44 NB	09/50 63059	01/49-04/65	10/65	
90060	06/44 NB	11/50 63060	01/49-06/62	08/63	
90061	06/44 NB	01/50 63061	01/49-06/67	10/67	
90062	06/44 NB	10/50 63062	01/49-01/60	02/60	
90063	06/44 NB	03/50 63063	01/49-04/66	08/66	
90064	06/44 NB	01/51 63064	01/49-01/64	03/64	
90065	06/44 NB	06/50 63065	01/49-04/64	05/64	
90066	07/44 NB	07/51 63066	01/49-05/63	09/63	
90067	07/44 NB	07/49 63067	01/49-10/64	01/65	
90068	07/44 NB	11/50 63068	01/49-07/66	10/66	

90069	07/44	NB	09/50	63069	01/49-01/66	05/66
90070	07/43	NB	08/50	63070	01/49-02/65	05/65
90071	07/44	NB	11/49	63071	01/49-04/67	09/67
90072	08/44	NB	07/50	63072	01/49-12/65	04/66
90073	08/44	NB	10/49	63073	01/49-02/66	08/66
90074	09/44	NB	09/49	63074	01/49-09/67	11/67
90075	08/44	NB	02/50	63075	01/49-04/66	09/66
90076	08/44	NB	07/50	63076	01/49-09/67	11/67
90077	08/44	NB	06/50	63077	01/49-05/63	07/63
90078	08/44	NB	09/50	63078	01/49-11/66	07/67
90079	08/44	NB	10/50	63079	01/49-01/64	02/64
90080	08/44	NB	10/49	63080	01/49-02/66	07/66
90081	09/44	NB	01/50	63081	01/49-06/67	12/67
90082	09/44	NB	11/50	63082	01/49-07/66	10/66
90083	09/44	NB	05/49	63083	01/49-12/59	02/60
90084	09/44	NB	02/51	63084	01/49-06/65	11/65
90085	10/44	NB	02/49	63085	01/49-05/65	08/65
90086	10/44	NB	08/49	63086	01/49-08/63	10/63
90087	09/44	NB	12/50	63087	01/49-10/62	11/62
90088	10/44	NB	08/50	63088	01/49-07/65	11/65
90089	10/44	NB	05/49	63089	01/49-01/67	06/67
90090	10/44	NB	10/50	63090	01/49-06/63	11/63
90091	10/44	NB	10/50	63091	01/49-06/67	12/67
90092	10/44	NB	10/50	63092	01/49-10/65	01/66
90093	11/44	NB	12/50	63093	01/49-08/62	11/62
90094	11/44	NB	05/50	63094	01/49-06/67	01/68
90095	11/44	NB	10/49	63095	01/49-06/63	09/63
90096	12/44	NB	12/51	63096	01/49-09/65	12/65
90097	12/44	NB	03/49	63097	01/49-08/63	09/63
90098	02/45	NB	07/49	63098	01/49-11/64	02/65
90099	02/45	NB	04/49	63099	01/49-06/67	01/68
90100	03/45	NB	11/51	63100	01/49-01/64	02/64
90101	01/43	NB	03/51	77000	12/48-05/64	09/64
90102	01/43	NB	10/51	77001	12/48-11/63	01/64
90103	02/43	NB	03/49	77003	12/48-11/65	04/66
90104	02/43	NB	09/50	77004	12/48-02/66	06/66
90105	02/43	NB	02/52	77005	12/48-12/62	05/63
90106	02/43	NB	08/50	77006	12/48-09/62	12/62
90107	02/43	NB	06/49	77007	12/48-11/63	12/63
90108	02/43	NB	04/49	77008	12/48-08/65	10/65
90109	02/43	NB	10/51	77010	12/48-05/64	09/64
90110	02/43	NB	02/52	77012	12/48-03/64	12/64
90111	02/43	NB	05/50	77013	12/48-04/64	07/64
90112	02/43	NB	03/51	77014	12/48-01/67	12/67
90113	02/43	NB	02/52	77015	12/48-09/66	11/66
90114	02/43	NB	03/50	77016	12/48-07/64	10/64
90115	03/43	NB	05/51	77017	12/48-05/65	08/65
90116	03/43	NB	03/49	77018	12/48-06/67	10/67
90117	03/43	NB	03/51	77019	12/48-01/67	05/67
90118	03/43	NB	12/49	77020	12/48-11/63	02/64
90119	03/43	NB	02/49	77022	12/48-01/65	05/65
90120	03/43	NB	11/49	77023	12/48-04/65	07/65
90121	03/43	NB	12/50	77024	12/48-06/65	09/65
90122	03/43	NB	12/49	77025	12/48-10/65	11/65
90123	03/43	NB	11/51	77026	12/48-03/65	07/65
90124	03/43	NB	08/51	77027	12/48-06/65	10/65
90125	03/43	NB	10/50	77028	12/48-07/65	11/65
90126	03/43	NB	03/49	77029	12/48-01/67	06/67
90127	03/43	NB	11/50	77030	12/48-10/64	12/65
90128	03/43	NB	06/49	77031	12/48-11/62	02/63
90129	03/43	NB	11/50	77032	12/48-07/64	01/65
90130	04/43	NB	11/49	77034	12/48-10/65	02/66
90131	04/43	NB	02/49	77035	12/48-03/65	07/65
90132	04/43	NB	08/49	77036	12/48-04/67	08/67
90133	04/43	NB	05/49	77037	12/48-10/65	04/66
90134	04/43	NB	10/49	77039	12/48-07/62	01/63
90135	04/43	NB	06/52	77040	12/48-09/67	11/67
90136	04/43	NB	10/50	77041	12/48-04/65	07/65
90137	04/43	NB	05/51	77042	12/48-12/62	05/63
90138	04/43	NB	06/51	77044	12/48-04/64	05/64
90139	04/43	NB	11/50	77047	12/48-05/65	07/65
90140	04/43	NB	03/50	77048	12/48-10/64	01/65
90141	05/43	NB	02/49	77049	12/48-02/64	08/64
90142	05/43	NB	05/51	77150	12/48-12/65	05/66
90143	05/43	NB	50	77151	12/48-06/64	09/64
90144	05/43	NB	03/49	77152	12/48-12/63	03/64
90145	05/43	NB	03/50	77155	12/48-06/64	10/64
90146	05/43	NB	02/49	77157	12/48-06/65	08/65
90147	05/43	NB	05/49	77160	12/48-05/64	01/65
90148	05/43	NB	02/49	77161	12/48-04/66	09/66
90149	05/43	NB	07/51	77162	12/48-01/66	05/66
90150	05/43	NB	05/49	77163	12/48-09/62	12/62
90151	05/43	NB	11/50	77164	12/48-05/63	07/63
90152	05/43	NB	03/51	77165	12/48-05/65	08/65
90153	05/43	NB	10/51	77166	12/48-02/66	05/66
90154	06/43	NB	02/49	77167	12/48-04/66	09/66
90155	06/43	NB	08/49	77169	12/48-01/67	05/67
90156	06/43	NB	09/51	77170	12/48-04/66	09/66
90157	06/43	NB	05/49	77171	12/48-07/64	04/65
90158	06/43	NB	02/51	77173	12/48-12/65	02/66
90159	06/43	NB	04/51	77174	12/48-11/63	07/64
90160	06/43	NB	12/50	77175	12/48-06/67	02/68
90161	06/43	NB	08/51	77176	12/48-02/64	03/64
90162	06/43	NB	05/49	77178	12/48-02/64	05/64
90163	06/43	NB	05/49	77179	12/48-12/62	10/63
90164	06/43	NB	05/49	77180	12/48-04/65	07/65
90165	06/43	NB	05/51	77181	12/48-04/64	01/65
90166	06/43	NB	08/51	77182	12/48-05/65	08/65
90167	07/43	NB	08/51	77184	12/48-05/62	05/62
90168	07/43	NB	09/50	77185	12/48-08/66	11/66
90169	07/43	NB	02/50	77186	12/48-08/65	11/65
90170	07/43	NB	05/51	77187	12/48-08/63	02/65
90171	07/43	NB	04/49	77192	12/48-07/65	10/65
90172	07/43	NB	11/50	77195	12/48-06/67	12/67
90173	07/43	NB	07/52	77196	12/48-07/64	01/65
90174	07/43	NB	03/50	77198	12/48-10/62	06/63
90175	07/43	NB	03/49	77199	12/48-04/65	08/65
90176	08/43	NB	09/51	77200	12/48-02/63	06/63
90177	08/43	NB	09/50	77201	12/48-06/63	07/63
90178	08/43	NB	03/49	77202	12/48-02/66	07/66
90179	08/43	NB	02/52	77203	12/48-05/64	10/64
90180	08/43	NB	03/51	77204	12/48-03/65	06/65
90181	08/43	NB	10/50	77205	12/48-05/65	08/65
90182	08/43	NB	03/50	77206	12/48-12/63	06/64
90183	08/43	NB	12/51	77207	12/48-08/65	11/65
90184	08/43	NB	05/49	77208	12/48-10/64	10/65
90185	08/43	NB	04/51	77209	12/48-03/65	06/65
90186	08/43	NB	02/49	77210	12/48-08/63	09/63
90187	08/43	NB	09/49	77212	12/48-02/66	07/66
90188	08/43	NB	02/51	77214	12/48-04/65	07/65
90189	08/43	NB	03/49	77215	12/48-11/65	03/66
90190	09/43	NB	03/49	77218	12/48-02/66	06/66
90191	09/43	NB	10/50	77221	12/48-01/60	02/60
90192	09/43	NB	01/51	77222	12/48-04/63	10/63
90193	09/43	NB	02/51	77225	12/48-08/63	09/63
90194	09/43	NB	50	77226	12/48-03/64	05/64
90195	09/43	NB	06/49	77227	12/48-10/65	01/66
90196	09/43	NB	10/49	77228	12/48-09/62	11/62
90197	09/43	NB	06/49	77229	12/48-05/64	12/64
90198	09/43	NB	08/50	77230	12/48-12/62	04/63
90199	09/43	NB	02/50	77231	12/48-11/66	05/67
90200	10/43	NB	06/49	77232	12/48-07/67	10/67
90201	10/43	NB	03/49	77234	12/48-07/64	02/65
90202	10/43	NB	11/50	77235	12/48-04/65	07/65
90203	10/43	NB	05/51	77237	12/48-10/65	04/66
90204	10/43	NB	01/50	77239	12/48-06/65	10/65
90205	10/43	NB	02/52	77241	12/48-03/64	07/65
90206	10/43	NB	03/49	77242	12/48-05/63	09/63
90207	11/43	NB	06/51	77247	12/48-05/65	08/65
90208	11/43	NB	03/50	77248	12/48-03/64	03/64
90209	11/43	NB	02/49	77249	12/48-07/64	02/65
90210	11/43	NB	03/49	77252	12/48-07/67	12/67
90211	11/43	NB	07/49	77253	12/48-07/65	10/65
90212	11/43	NB	02/49	77255	12/48-08/65	10/65
90213	11/43	NB	10/49	77256	12/48-02/66	06/66
90214	11/43	NB	01/51	77257	12/48-03/64	12/64
90215	11/43	NB	10/51	77258	12/48-04/65	08/65
90216	11/43	NB	02/50	77259	12/48-08/64	08/65
90217	11/43	NB	09/49	77260	12/48-06/65	10/65
90218	11/43	NB	05/51	77261	12/48-05/64	10/64
90219	04/43	NB	05/50	77302	12/48-05/64	01/65
90220	04/43	NB	12/50	77303	12/48-11/65	03/66
90221	04/43	NB	11/50	77305	12/48-01/65	04/65
90222	04/43	NB	08/49	77306	12/48-08/65	06/66
90223	04/43	NB	03/51	77307	12/48-08/65	10/65
90224	04/43	NB	11/50	77309	12/48-03/64	07/64
90225	04/43	NB	09/49	77310	12/48-04/65	07/65
90226	04/43	NB	07/49	77311	12/48-12/63	02/64
90227	04/43	NB	09/50	77312	12/48-09/65	02/66
90228	05/43	NB	09/49	77313	12/48-09/63	09/63
90229	05/43	NB	09/51	77314	12/48-09/66	12/66
90230	05/43	NB	06/49	77315	12/48-05/67	10/67
90231	05/43	NB	04/51	77317	12/48-09/63	10/63
90232	05/43	NB	11/51	77319	12/48-01/66	04/66
90233	05/43	NB	03/49	77320	12/48-05/67	12/67
90234	05/43	NB	05/50	77321	12/48-11/63	05/64
90235	05/43	NB	03/49	77323	12/48-10/65	01/66
90236	05/43	NB	10/49	77324	12/48-09/67	02/68
90237	06/43	NB	04/49	77325	12/48-01/64	07/64
90238	06/43	NB	09/51	77326	12/48-03/63	06/63
90239	06/43	NB	05/51	77327	12/48-11/63	01/64
90240	06/43	NB	05/51	77328	12/48-01/67	06/67
90241	06/43	NB	11/50	77329	12/48-01/66	05/66
90242	06/43	NB	05/49	77330	12/48-09/65	01/66
90243	06/43	NB	09/49	77332	12/48-06/67	11/67
90244	06/43	NB	07/51	77334	12/48-07/62	11/62
90245	06/43	NB	01/50	77335	12/48-05/64	08/65
90246	06/43	NB	02/51	77338	12/48-04/65	07/65
90247	07/43	NB	11/49	77340	12/48-10/62	03/63
90248	07/43	NB	12/49	77342	12/48-11/65	03/66
90249	07/43	NB	06/49	77348	12/48-12/63	02/64
90250	07/43	NB	02/49	77350	12/48-03/63	05/63
90251	07/43	NB	07/49	77351	12/48-05/63	10/63
90252	08/43	NB	02/49	77352	12/48-09/65	12/65
90253	08/43	NB	03/50	77353	12/48-12/62	05/63
90254	08/43	NB	11/50	77355	12/48-01/67	09/67
90255	08/43	NB	03/49	77356	12/48-12/65	03/66
90256	08/43	NB	05/49	77358	12/48-08/62	11/62
90257	08/43	NB	08/50	77359	12/48-08/64	01/65
90258	08/43	NB	12/50	77362	12/48-01/66	06/66
90259	08/43	NB	03/49	77364	12/48-10/65	01/66
90260	09/43	NB	02/51	77365	12/48-09/63	09/63
90261	09/43	NB	10/51	77368	12/48-07/65	12/65
90262	09/43	NB	12/49	77371	12/48-06/67	01/68
90263	09/43	NB	08/51	77372	12/48-01/64	05/64
90264	09/43	NB	09/50	77374	12/48-08/64	02/65
90265	09/43	NB	07/50	77375	12/48-06/67	12/67
90266	10/43	NB	03/49	77378	12/48-07/65	09/65
90267	10/43	NB	03/50	77379	12/48-03/65	06/65
90268	10/43	NB	12/51	77380	12/48-04/65	08/65
90269	10/43	NB	02/51	77381	12/48-05/63	07/63
90270	10/43	NB	08/49	77386	12/48-12/62	07/63
90271	10/43	NB	01/53	77388	12/48-07/65	11/65
90272	10/43	NB	03/49	77390	12/48-06/67	12/67
90273	11/43	NB	01/51	77392	12/48-10/65	02/66
90274	11/43	NB	09/50	77393	12/48-01/66	04/66
90275	11/43	NB	08/49	77394	12/48-07/65	11/65
90276	11/43	NB	12/50	77395	12/48-02/65	08/65
90277	11/43	NB	07/50	77398	12/48-10/65	03/66
90278	11/43	NB	05/50	77399	12/48-12/62	05/63
90279	11/43	NB	02/49	77401	12/48-06/65	10/65
90280	11/43	NB	05/49	77402	12/48-09/65	12/65
90281	12/43	NB	03/49	77404	12/48-06/67	11/67
90282	12/43	NB	04/49	77406	12/48-01/65	03/65
90283	12/43	NB	12/50	77407	12/48-10/65	01/66
90284	12/43	NB	01/52	77408	12/48-03/65	05/65
90285	12/43	NB	11/49	77411	12/48-06/65	09/65
90286	12/43	NB	02/51	77413	12/48-07/62	09/62
90287	12/43	NB	03/51	77414	12/48-12/62	04/63
90288	12/43	NB	02/51	77415	12/48-09/62	12/62
90289	12/43	NB	05/49	77416	12/48-11/64	05/65
90290	01/44	NB	03/51	77418	12/48-05/65	07/65
90291	01/44	NB	05/49	77419	12/48-02/65	05/65
90292	01/44	NB	04/49	77421	12/48-10/65	01/66
90293	01/44	NB	09/51	77424	12/48-09/65	10/65
90294	01/44	NB	12/49	77425	12/48-07/65	10/65
90295	01/44	NB	02/52	77426	12/48-01/66	05/66
90296	01/44	NB	09/49	77428	12/48-08/65	11/65
90297	01/44	NB	03/49	77429	12/48-08/64	02/65
90298	02/44	NB	06/49	77431	12/48-07/62	09/62
90299	02/44	NB	08/49	77432	12/48-05/64	10/64
90300	02/44	NB	05/49	77433	12/48-06/67	10/67
90301	02/44	NB	05/49	77434	12/48-09/65	01/66
90302	02/44	NB	12/50	77436	12/48-08/64	11/64
90303	02/44	NB	07/49	77439	12/48-12/62	04/63
90304	02/44	NB	09/49	77440	12/48-09/64	01/65
90305	02/44	NB	02/51	77441	12/48-03/66	08/66
90306	02/44	NB	08/49	77442	12/48-06/65	11/65
90307	03/44	NB	04/49	77443	12/48-12/62	06/63
90308	03/44	NB	01/51	77444	12/48-10/62	05/63
90309	03/44	NB	11/51	77445	12/48-07/67	10/67
90310	03/44	NB	05/49	77447	12/48-12/66	03/67
90311	03/44	NB	10/49	77449	12/48-08/64	11/64
90312	03/44	NB	01/52	70801	12/48-12/63	03/64
90313	03/44	NB	08/49	70802	12/48-04/64	07/64
90314	04/44	NB	05/51	70807	12/48-04/65	08/65
90315	04/44	NB	10/52	70808	12/48-11/65	05/66
90316	04/44	NB	01/50	70809	12/48-12/65	04/66
90317	04/44	NB	08/50	70811	12/48-03/65	05/65
90318	04/44	NB	12/49	70814	12/48-09/67	02/68
90319	04/44	NB	05/51	70817	12/48-06/64	01/65
90320	05/44	NB	04/49	70825	12/48-07/62	09/62
90321	05/44	NB	06/50	70829	12/48-07/67	12/67
90322	06/44	NB	03/50	70833	12/48-08/64	12/64
90323	06/44	NB	02/49	70834	12/48-05/64	10/64
90324	06/44	NB	05/49	70836	12/48-05/64	01/65
90325	06/44	NB	01/50	70838	12/48-09/65	11/65
90326	06/44	NB	04/52	70839	12/48-11/63	12/63
90327	06/44	NB	03/52	70843	12/48-01/65	05/65
90328	07/44	NB	03/49	70845	12/48-05/64	09/64
90329	07/44	NB	08/49	70849	12/48-10/65	12/65
90330	07/44	NB	06/49	70850	12/48-12/65	03/66
90331	07/44	NB	04/49	70851	12/48-11/63	02/64
90332	07/44	NB	12/49	70853	12/48-01/67	03/67
90333	07/44	NB	04/49	70857	12/48-10/65	03/66
90334	08/44	NB	08/49	70859	12/48-11/63	12/63
90335	08/44	NB	03/52	70860	12/48-11/63	12/63
90336	08/44	NB	01/50	70864	12/48-01/66	04/66
90337	08/44	NB	06/49	70865	12/48-01/67	08/67
90338	08/44	NB	11/49	70866	12/48-11/63	11/63
90339	08/44	NB	09/49	70867	12/48-07/67	10/67
90340	09/44	NB	11/49	70871	12/48-07/65	11/65
90341	09/44	NB	09/49	70874	12/48-07/65	11/65
90342	09/44	NB	05/49	70875	12/48-11/65	03/66
90343	09/44	NB	11/52	70876	12/48-12/63	01/64
90344	09/44	NB	02/49	70877	12/48-11/64	12/64
90345	09/44	NB	02/51	70878	12/48-06/67	11/67
90346	07/44	NB	09/50	77263	12/48-10/65	02/66
90347	07/44	NB	02/50	77270	12/48-05/67	09/67
90348	07/44	NB	01/51	77271	12/48-09/67	10/67
90349	08/44	NB	03/51	77274	12/48-06/65	02/66
90350	08/44	NB	12/50	77278	12/48-08/66	11/66
90351	08/44	NB	01/50	77280	12/48-09/67	12/67
90352	08/44	NB	01/52	77283	12/48-06/67	12/67
90353	08/44	NB	06/49	77285	12/48-02/65	08/65
90354	08/44	NB	08/49	77286	12/48-10/64	02/65
90355	09/44	NB	03/52	77288	12/48-10/62	11/62
90356	09/44	NB	10/51	77289	12/48-10/62	11/62
90357	09/44	NB	03/49	77291	12/48-09/66	12/66
90358	09/44	NB	11/49	77292	12/48-11/63	02/64
90359	09/44	NB	02/49	77294	12/48-10/64	01/65
90360	09/44	NB	11/50	77296	12/48-09/67	11/67
90361	09/44	NB	03/49	77297	12/48-04/67	08/67
90362	09/44	NB	06/49	77299	12/48-06/67	11/67

90363	09/44	NB	03/49	78510	12/48-06/67	11/67
90364	09/44	NB	11/49	78512	12/48-12/65	05/66
90365	09/44	NB	05/51	78514	12/48-06/65	11/65
90366	10/44	NB	06/52	78521	12/48-01/64	02/64
90367	10/44	NB	11/49	78522	12/48-02/66	07/66
90368	10/44	NB	05/49	78525	12/48-06/65	09/65
90369	10/44	NB	02/49	78526	12/48-04/66	09/66
90370	09/44	NB	06/49	78560	12/48-05/67	09/67
90371	09/44	NB	07/49	78561	12/48-05/64	01/65
90372	09/44	NB	03/50	78563	12/48-12/65	07/66
90373	10/44	NB	03/51	78564	12/48-09/66	11/66
90374	10/44	NB	10/49	78568	12/48-04/64	09/64
90375	10/44	NB	11/49	78569	12/48-07/64	11/64
90376	10/44	NB	09/49	78572	12/48-12/62	06/63
90377	10/44	NB	04/51	78575	12/48-02/66	06/66
90378	10/44	NB	04/49	78578	12/48-09/67	10/67
90379	11/44	NB	09/49	78580	12/48-03/66	06/66
90380	11/44	NB	08/49	78581	12/48-03/66	08/66
90381	11/44	NB	09/49	78583	12/48-10/65	03/66
90382	11/44	NB	04/49	78585	12/48-09/67	10/67
90383	11/44	NB	12/49	78587	12/48-04/65	07/65
90384	11/44	NB	11/49	78588	12/48-02/66	07/66
90385	11/44	NB	07/50	78590	12/48-03/67	06/67
90386	11/44	NB	03/49	78592	12/48-04/67	09/67
90387	11/44	NB	03/51	78594	12/48-09/62	09/62
90388	11/44	NB	11/49	78595	12/48-07/64	11/64
90389	12/44	NB	11/49	78596	12/48-10/64	03/65
90390	12/44	NB	04/51	78597	12/48-09/65	12/65
90391	12/44	NB	03/49	78598	12/48-08/62	10/62
90392	12/44	NB	02/49	78599	12/48-12/64	03/65
90393	12/44	NB	03/51	78600	12/48-08/65	01/66
90394	12/44	NB	08/51	78601	12/48-04/64	12/64
90395	12/44	NB	03/50	78602	12/48-10/66	03/67
90396	12/44	NB	04/49	78604	12/48-06/67	11/67
90397	12/44	NB	09/49	78605	12/48-05/67	08/67
90398	12/44	NB	03/49	78606	12/48-07/65	09/65
90399	12/44	NB	12/50	78607	12/48-03/65	08/65
90400	12/44	NB	02/49	78609	12/48-12/63	01/64
90401	12/44	NB	06/49	78610	12/48-11/65	03/66
90402	01/45	NB	04/49	78612	12/48-04/64	12/64
90403	01/45	NB	02/51	78614	12/48-05/64	01/65
90404	01/45	NB	08/49	78615	12/48-06/67	02/68
90405	01/45	NB	05/51	78616	12/48-09/67	12/67
90406	01/45	NB	07/50	78621	12/48-07/67	12/67
90407	01/45	NB	04/50	78624	12/48-05/67	08/67
90408	01/45	NB	06/50	78531	12/48-04/64	12/64
90409	01/45	NB	08/51	78532	12/48-06/67	11/67
90410	02/45	NB	12/51	78537	12/48-04/66	09/66
90411	02/45	NB	09/50	78538	12/48-08/64	11/64
90412	02/45	NB	08/49	78541	12/48-10/64	12/65
90413	02/45	NB	12/51	78542	12/48-02/66	06/66
90414	02/45	NB	04/49	78543	12/48-12/62	04/63
90415	02/45	NB	06/49	78544	12/48-01/67	06/67
90416	02/45	NB	03/49	78546	12/48-05/64	04/65
90417	03/45	NB	09/49	78551	12/48-09/67	10/67
90418	03/45	NB	09/51	78553	12/48-01/66	05/66
90419	03/45	NB	10/49	78554	12/48-04/65	07/65
90420	03/45	NB	10/49	78556	12/48-08/65	02/66
90421	03/45	NB	10/49	78559	12/48-08/65	12/65
90422	08/43	VF	03/50	63101	01/49-06/65	11/65
90423	08/43	VF	04/51	63102	01/49-12/65	04/66
90424	09/43	VF	11/49	63103	01/49-12/63	12/63
90425	09/43	VF	11/49	63104	01/49-12/62	12/63
90426	10/43	VF	11/50	63105	01/49-03/65	06/65
90427	10/43	VF	12/50	63106	01/49-06/67	01/68
90428	10/43	VF	10/50	63107	01/49-01/66	04/66
90429	11/43	VF	08/50	63108	01/49-04/67	09/67
90430	11/43	VF	06/51	63109	01/49-09/67	04/68
90431	11/43	VF	06/49	63110	01/49-12/62	04/63
90432	12/43	VF	02/49	63111	01/49-10/65	01/66
90433	01/44	VF	10/50	63112	01/49-05/64	10/64
90434	01/44	VF	08/50	63113	01/49-06/67	10/67
90435	02/44	VF	01/50	63114	01/49-09/63	09/63
90436	02/44	VF	07/50	63115	01/49-06/62	11/63
90437	02/44	VF	10/49	63116	01/49-04/66	09/66
90438	02/44	VF	06/49	63117	01/49-10/65	01/66
90439	03/44	VF	02/51	63118	01/49-11/65	03/66
90440	03/44	VF	03/49	63119	01/49-09/63	11/63
90441	03/44	VF	06/49	63120	01/49-10/66	05/67
90442	03/44	VF	11/50	63121	01/49-04/65	07/65
90443	03/44	VF	02/51	63122	01/49-06/65	10/65
90444	03/44	VF	06/50	63123	01/49-01/67	05/67
90445	03/44	VF	08/50	63124	01/49-07/66	10/66
90446	03/44	VF	09/49	63125	01/49-11/63	01/64
90447	03/44	VF	12/49	63126	01/49-11/63	11/63
90448	03/44	VF	01/51	63127	01/49-12/65	05/66
90449	03/44	VF	04/49	63128	01/49-01/66	05/66
90450	04/44	VF	12/49	63129	01/49-06/67	01/68
90451	04/44	VF	05/50	63130	01/49-12/66	03/67
90452	04/44	VF	04/49	63131	01/49-06/65	10/65
90453	04/44	VF	03/49	63132	01/49-09/63	12/63
90454	04/44	VF	08/51	63133	01/49-06/65	02/66
90455	04/44	VF	11/49	63134	01/49-09/62	09/62
90456	04/44	VF	10/50	63135	01/49-02/66	07/66
90457	04/44	VF	05/50	63136	01/49-01/66	05/66
90458	04/44	VF	06/50	63137	01/49-06/67	12/67
90459	04/44	VF	05/50	63138	01/49-06/67	10/67
90460	05/44	VF	04/49	63139	01/49-06/65	11/65
90461	05/44	VF	03/49	63140	01/49-09/63	09/63
90462	05/44	VF	02/49	63141	01/49-01/67	06/67
90463	05/44	VF	09/50	63142	01/49-11/63	07/64
90464	05/44	VF	04/50	63143	01/49-03/64	04/64
90465	05/44	VF	06/50	63144	01/49-01/67	03/67
90466	05/44	VF	12/50	63145	01/49-12/65	04/66
90467	05/44	VF	09/50	63146	01/49-11/63	01/64
90468	05/44	VF	10/49	63147	01/49-04/67	09/67
90469	05/44	VF	10/49	63148	01/49-11/64	03/65
90470	05/44	VF	11/49	63149	01/49-12/66	03/67
90471	05/44	VF	04/49	63150	01/49-04/66	09/66
90472	05/44	VF	06/50	63151	01/49-12/63	06/64
90473	05/44	VF	12/49	63152	01/49-09/62	12/62
90474	06/44	VF	08/50	63153	01/49-07/65	10/65
90475	06/44	VF	06/49	63154	01/49-08/63	09/63
90476	06/44	VF	11/50	63155	01/49-07/65	02/66
90477	06/44	VF	04/49	63156	01/49-03/66	06/66
90478	06/44	VF	11/49	63157	01/49-09/67	11/67
90479	06/44	VF	05/49	63158	01/49-10/66	11/66
90480	06/44	VF	03/49	63159	01/49-08/65	09/65
90481	07/44	VF	06/49	63160	01/49-10/66	12/66
90482	07/44	VF	11/50	63161	01/49-07/67	11/67
90483	07/44	VF	02/51	63162	01/49-03/64	03/64
90484	07/44	VF	09/49	63163	01/49-03/66	05/66
90485	07/44	VF	11/50	63164	01/49-08/64	11/64
90486	07/44	VF	09/51	63165	01/49-04/65	07/65
90487	07/44	VF	12/50	63166	01/49-08/63	10/63
90488	07/44	VF	12/50	63167	01/49-12/64	05/65
90489	07/44	VF	02/50	63168	01/49-04/67	09/67
90490	07/44	VF	05/50	63169	01/49-02/64	04/64
90491	08/44	VF	09/49	63170	01/49-09/65	12/65
90492	08/44	VF	11/49	63171	01/49-10/65	02/66
90493	08/44	VF	01/50	63172	01/49-02/66	07/66
90494	08/44	VF	50	63173	01/49-09/62	12/62
90495	08/44	VF	07/50	63174	01/49-12/62	01/64
90496	08/44	VF	10/49	63175	01/49-04/65	07/65
90497	08/44	VF	09/50	63176	01/49-03/63	05/63
90498	08/44	VF	06/49	63177	01/49-02/66	08/66
90499	08/44	VF	07/50	63178	01/49-12/63	12/63
90500	09/44	VF	08/49	63179	01/49-08/63	09/63
90501	09/44	VF	09/49	63180	01/49-11/65	01/66
90502	09/44	VF	03/49	63181	01/49-05/63	10/63
90503	09/44	VF	11/50	63182	01/49-01/67	04/67
90504	09/44	VF	09/50	63183	01/49-05/63	06/63
90505	09/44	VF	11/49	63184	01/49-06/62	02/64
90506	10/44	VF	05/51	63185	01/49-01/66	05/66
90507	10/44	VF	09/50	63186	01/49-07/63	09/63
90508	11/44	VF	10/50	63187	01/49-12/62	01/64
90509	11/44	VF	09/50	63188	01/49-08/65	10/65
90510	12/44	VF	11/50	63189	01/49-07/65	04/66
90511	12/44	VF	02/50	63190	01/49-06/64	10/64
90512	12/44	VF	02/51	63191	01/49-09/62	11/62
90513	01/45	VF	08/50	63192	01/49-07/62	09/62
90514	01/45	VF	09/50	63193	01/49-01/66	05/66
90515	01/45	VF	10/49	63194	01/49-11/65	02/66
90516	01/45	VF	12/49	63195	01/49-11/65	06/66
90517	03/45	VF	10/50	63196	01/49-05/66	08/66
90518	03/45	VF	10/51	63197	01/49-02/66	05/66
90519	04/45	VF	02/51	63198	01/49-09/64	05/65
90520	04/45	VF	03/49	63199	01/49-02/65	08/65
90521	05/43	VF	09/51	77050	12/48-10/64	01/65
90522	05/43	VF	09/49	77051	12/48-05/65	07/65
90523	05/43	VF	10/49	77052	12/48-12/62	10/63
90524	06/43	VF	02/49	77053	12/48-05/63	09/63
90525	06/43	VF	11/49	77054	12/48-05/64	01/65
90526	06/43	VF	11/49	77055	12/48-12/62	01/64
90527	06/43	VF	04/49	77056	12/48-05/63	06/63
90528	06/43	VF	08/49	77057	12/48-09/65	01/66
90529	06/43	VF	02/49	77058	12/48-11/65	02/66
90530	06/43	VF	01/50	77059	12/48-05/63	08/63
90531	06/43	VF	06/50	77060	12/48-09/63	09/63
90532	06/43	VF	07/49	77061	12/48-11/62	01/63
90533	06/43	VF	03/49	77062	12/48-02/66	06/66
90534	06/43	VF	10/49	77063	12/48-10/66	02/67
90535	07/43	VF	06/51	77064	12/48-10/64	03/65
90536	07/43	VF	04/50	77066	12/48-09/63	10/63
90537	07/43	VF	07/50	77067	12/48-02/66	07/66
90538	07/43	VF	08/49	77068	12/48-04/66	10/66
90539	07/43	VF	12/50	77070	12/48-11/63	06/64
90540	07/43	VF	01/50	77071	12/48-07/65	04/66
90541	07/43	VF	04/49	77072	12/48-05/65	08/65
90542	07/43	VF	11/50	77073	12/48-07/63	09/63
90543	07/43	VF	09/50	77074	12/48-02/65	08/65
90544	07/43	VF	05/51	77075	12/48-06/64	10/64
90545	07/43	VF	03/51	77076	12/48-10/65	01/66
90546	08/43	VF	10/50	77077	12/48-02/64	03/64
90547	08/43	VF	09/50	77078	12/48-10/66	02/67
90548	08/43	VF	06/51	77079	12/48-05/64	01/65
90549	08/43	VF	03/51	77080	12/48-12/62	12/63
90550	08/43	VF	08/49	77081	12/48-09/62	12/62
90551	08/43	VF	12/50	77085	12/48-04/66	10/66
90552	08/43	VF	04/49	77086	12/48-05/64	06/65
90553	08/43	VF	05/50	77087	12/48-11/65	02/66
90554	08/43	VF	03/49	77088	12/48-09/62	11/62
90555	08/43	VF	02/50	77089	12/48-06/64	12/64
90556	08/43	VF	12/50	77090	12/48-03/65	05/65
90557	09/43	VF	10/49	77092	12/48-09/65	11/65
90558	09/43	VF	04/49	77094	12/48-11/65	02/66
90559	09/43	VF	09/50	77095	12/48-12/62	12/63
90560	09/43	VF	11/50	77096	12/48-04/67	09/67
90561	09/43	VF	10/50	77097	12/48-03/65	08/65
90562	09/43	VF	05/50	77098	12/48-10/62	03/63
90563	09/43	VF	11/52	77099	12/48-08/65	06/66
90564	09/43	VF	11/50	77101	12/48-05/64	01/65
90565	09/43	VF	08/52	77102	12/48-10/62	01/64
90566	09/43	VF	01/50	77103	12/48-07/64	01/65
90567	09/43	VF	05/51	77104	12/48-11/64	03/65
90568	09/43	VF	04/49	77106	12/48-01/64	03/64
90569	09/43	VF	05/50	77107	12/48-10/65	03/66
90570	09/43	VF	11/50	77108	12/48-05/64	10/64
90571	10/43	VF	03/49	77111	12/48-11/63	12/63
90572	10/43	VF	10/50	77115	12/48-02/66	06/66
90573	10/43	VF	09/51	77116	12/48-08/65	10/65
90574	10/43	VF	11/50	77118	12/48-02/64	01/65
90575	10/43	VF	11/49	77119	12/48-07/62	03/63
90576	10/43	VF	11/51	77120	12/48-03/63	03/63
90577	10/43	VF	08/51	77121	12/48-05/65	07/65
90578	10/43	VF	11/50	77122	12/48-12/63	01/64
90579	10/43	VF	02/49	77123	12/48-02/65	07/65
90580	10/43	VF	09/51	77124	12/48-08/65	11/65
90581	10/43	VF	06/49	77126	12/48-11/64	04/65
90582	10/43	VF	04/49	77127	12/48-03/64	06/64
90583	11/43	VF	02/51	77128	12/48-04/64	07/64
90584	11/43	VF	03/51	77129	12/48-08/64	02/65
90585	11/43	VF	02/49	77130	12/48-04/65	07/65
90586	11/43	VF	08/49	77135	12/48-02/66	06/66
90587	11/43	VF	06/51	77138	12/48-11/65	02/66
90588	11/43	VF	06/50	77141	12/48-02/67	10/67
90589	11/43	VF	02/49	77142	12/48-05/64	06/64
90590	11/43	VF	09/51	77144	12/48-03/64	05/64
90591	11/43	VF	04/50	77145	12/48-10/62	08/63
90592	12/43	VF	10/50	77147	12/48-06/64	09/64
90593	12/43	VF	06/50	77148	12/48-07/66	10/66
90594	12/43	VF	04/51	77149	12/48-09/62	11/62
90595	12/43	VF	03/49	77451	12/48-02/64	01/65
90596	12/43	VF	03/49	77452	12/48-04/67	09/67
90597	12/43	VF	06/49	77453	12/48-07/63	07/63
90598	12/43	VF	03/49	77454	12/48-02/64	03/64
90599	12/43	VF	05/50	77455	12/48-08/64	12/64
90600	12/43	VF	06/50	77456	12/48-08/66	11/66
90601	12/43	VF	03/50	77457	12/48-06/65	12/65
90602	12/43	VF	04/49	77458	12/48-01/65	03/65
90603	12/43	VF	03/51	77459	12/48-02/62	02/62
90604	12/43	VF	05/50	77460	12/48-12/63	03/64
90605	12/43	VF	01/51	77461	12/48-09/67	04/68
90606	12/43	VF	03/49	77462	12/48-02/66	06/66
90607	12/43	VF	10/49	77463	12/48-10/62	12/62
90608	12/43	VF	08/50	77464	12/48-12/62	12/63
90609	01/44	VF	06/49	77465	12/48-08/63	10/63
90610	01/44	VF	05/49	77466	12/48-05/67	09/67
90611	01/44	VF	07/51	77467	12/48-07/67	06/68
90612	01/44	VF	09/51	77468	12/48-03/64	08/64
90613	01/44	VF	02/49	77469	12/48-05/65	08/65
90614	01/44	VF	04/49	77470	12/48-11/63	06/64
90615	01/44	VF	09/49	77471	12/48-09/67	01/68
90616	01/44	VF	07/49	77476	12/48-06/62	11/62
90617	01/44	VF	08/49	77479	12/48-06/67	11/67
90618	01/44	VF	06/51	77480	12/48-05/64	01/65
90619	02/44	VF	52	77481	12/48-10/65	03/66
90620	02/44	VF	08/49	77482	12/48-06/67	03/68
90621	02/44	VF	10/51	77484	12/48-12/65	05/66
90622	02/44	VF	11/49	77485	12/48-09/66	01/67
90623	02/44	VF	02/49	77488	12/48-12/63	03/64
90624	02/44	VF	03/49	77489	12/48-12/63	03/64
90625	02/44	VF	02/51	77492	12/48-05/67	12/67
90626	02/44	VF	06/50	77494	12/48-03/65	08/65
90627	03/44	VF	12/51	77497	12/48-09/67	11/67
90628	03/44	VF	04/49	77499	12/48-01/67	05/67
90629	03/44	VF	08/49	77503	12/48-09/65	12/65
90630	03/44	VF	02/49	77508	12/48-10/62	11/63
90631	03/44	VF	05/49	78626	12/48-01/67	04/67
90632	03/44	VF	05/49	78629	12/48-05/65	08/65
90633	04/44	VF	03/49	78632	12/48-07/67	01/68
90634	04/44	VF	02/51	78637	12/48-12/62	04/63
90635	04/44	VF	05/49	78638	12/48-01/64	03/64
90636	04/44	VF	04/49	78643	12/48-04/66	10/66
90637	04/44	VF	05/49	78644	12/48-10/62	08/63
90638	05/44	VF	08/49	78650	12/48-12/62	06/63
90639	05/44	VF	05/49	78652	12/48-01/67	05/67
90640	05/44	VF	03/49	78658	12/48-08/66	01/67
90641	05/44	VF	05/50	78666	12/48-08/65	06/66
90642	06/44	VF	03/49	78671	12/48-09/67	05/68
90643	06/44	VF	06/49	78672	12/48-02/64	08/64
90644	06/44	VF	09/49	78675	12/48-06/67	11/67
90645	06/44	VF	02/50	78681	12/48-01/67	04/67
90646	06/44	VF	06/50	78682	12/48-05/64	01/65
90647	06/44	VF	09/49	78683	12/48-03/65	07/65
90648	06/44	VF	08/50	78684	12/48-08/62	09/62
90649	06/44	VF	03/50	78685	12/48-01/67	05/67
90650	07/44	VF	04/49	78688	12/48-06/67	11/67
90651	07/44	VF	06/49	78689	12/48-10/66	12/66
90652	07/44	VF	03/49	78695	12/48-09/66	11/66
90653	07/44	VF	12/49	78700	12/48-09/62	03/63
90654	08/44	VF	05/49	78704	12/48-06/67	11/67
90655	08/44	VF	02/51	78705	12/48-04/67	09/67
90656	08/44	VF	03/49	78714	12/48-02/65	03/65

90657	*08/*44 VF	01/50 78715	12/48-09/62	10/62
90658	08/44 VF	03/49 78717	12/48-11/65	02/66
90659	*09/*44 VF	12/49 79178	12/48-05/63	07/63
90660	*09/*44 VF	01/50 79181	12/48-07/65	11/65
90661	*09/*44 VF	09/49 79182	12/48-12/63	02/64
90662	*09/*44 VF	06/49 79184	12/48-08/65	01/66
90663	*09/*44 VF	01/51 79186	12/48-04/64	05/64
90664	*09/*44 VF	02/50 79190	12/48-10/66	02/67
90665	*10/*44 VF	01/50 79194	12/48-12/65	04/66
90666	*10/*44 VF	02/50 79195	12/48-10/62	08/63
90667	*10/*44 VF	06/49 79196	12/48-05/64	09/65
90668	*10/*44 VF	11/50 79198	12/48-04/65	07/65
90669	*10/*44 VF	11/49 79199	12/48-02/66	06/66
90670	*10/*44 VF	03/49 79202	12/48-06/67	01/68
90671	*10/*44 VF	03/50 79203	12/48-09/63	12/63
90672	*10/*44 VF	06/49 79204	12/48-05/64	07/64
90673	*10/*44 VF	09/49 79205	12/48-03/64	09/64
90674	*10/*44 VF	05/49 79206	12/48-08/65	11/65
90675	11/44 VF	08/50 79207	12/48-04/66	10/66
90676	*11/*44 VF	05/51 79208	12/48-01/64	03/64
90677	*11/*44 VF	09/49 79209	12/48-09/67	11/67
90678	*11/*44 VF	07/49 79210	12/48-06/67	09/67
90679	*11/*44 VF	06/49 79213	12/48-09/66	03/67
90680	*11/*44 VF	10/49 79214	12/48-01/67	05/67
90681	*11/*44 VF	04/49 79215	12/48-07/65	10/65
90682	11/44 VF	03/49 79219	12/48-09/67	01/68
90683	11/44 VF	09/51 79220	12/48-02/66	08/66
90684	*11/*44 VF	02/50 79221	12/48-01/67	05/67
90685	*11/*44 VF	02/49 79224	12/48-11/64	03/65
90686	*11/*44 VF	12/51 79225	12/48-04/65	07/65
90687	*12/*44 VF	01/52 79226	12/48-01/66	04/66
90688	*12/*44 VF	10/51 79227	12/48-06/67	01/68
90689	*12/*44 VF	05/51 79228	12/48-02/66	06/66
90690	*12/*44 VF	03/49 79229	12/48-09/62	10/63
90691	*12/*44 VF	05/51 79232	12/48-07/62	07/62
90692	*12/*44 VF	09/49 79233	12/48-12/63	01/64
90693	*12/*44 VF	06/51 79234	12/48-10/62	11/63
90694	*12/*44 VF	03/49 79235	12/48-01/67	05/67
90695	*12/*44 VF	03/49 79239	12/48-09/67	11/67
90696	*12/*44 VF	02/51 79242	12/48-08/63	08/63
90697	12/44 VF	09/49 79243	12/48-11/65	04/66
90698	01/45 VF	04/50 79244	12/48-07/67	10/67
90699	*01/*45 VF	04/50 79254	12/48-09/67	04/68
90700	*01/*45 VF	03/49 79259	12/48-02/64	05/64
90701	*02/*45 VF	02/49 79261	12/48-11/62	06/63
90702	02/45 VF	03/50 79262	12/48-08/65	09/65
90703	02/45 VF	06/49 79263	12/48-07/65	04/66
90704	*02/*45 VF	08/51 79264	12/48-06/67	12/67
90705	*02/*45 VF	11/49 79265	12/48-07/64	10/64
90706	*02/*45 VF	11/49 79266	12/48-02/66	06/66
90707	*02/*45 VF	07/50 79268	12/48-01/67	05/67
90708	*02/*45 VF	11/49 79269	12/48-05/64	01/65
90709	*02/*45 VF	05/50 79271	12/48-04/66	10/66
90710	*02/*45 VF	06/49 79272	12/48-02/65	03/65
90711	*02/*45 VF	06/50 79273	12/48-01/67	07/67
90712	*02/*45 VF	04/49 79274	12/48-08/64	05/65
90713	*02/*45 VF	03/49 79275	12/48-11/63	02/64
90714	*02/*45 VF	05/50 79276	12/48-12/64	04/65
90715	*03/*45 VF	04/49 79278	12/48-05/64	01/65
90716	*03/*45 VF	02/49 79279	12/48-11/63	01/64
90717	*03/*45 VF	03/49 79280	12/48-03/64	01/65
90718	*03/*45 VF	07/49 79281	12/48-02/66	07/66
90719	*03/*45 VF	09/49 79282	12/48-02/66	06/66
90720	*03/*45 VF	08/50 79283	12/48-07/65	11/65
90721	*03/*45 VF	08/50 79294	12/48-09/67	04/68
90722	*04/*45 VF	09/49 79298	12/48-06/67	11/67
90723	*04/*45 VF	02/49 79301	12/48-11/66	04/67
90724	*04/*45 VF	07/50 79302	12/48-06/65	10/65
90725	*04/*45 VF	03/49 79303	12/48-08/65	01/66
90726	*04/*45 VF	08/50 79304	12/48-12/62	02/64
90727	*04/*45 VF	12/49 79306	12/48-09/65	11/65
90728	*04/*45 VF	08/50 79307	12/48-12/63	01/64
90729	*04/*45 VF	03/49 79309	12/48-04/63	05/63
90730	*04/*45 VF	03/50 79310	12/48-10/65	01/66
90731	*05/*45 VF	07/50 79311	12/48-11/66	04/67
90732 VULCAN	*05/*45 VF	05/50 79312	12/48-09/62	12/62

WD [2] 90750-90774 (601 on loan)
2-10-0 MOS (WD) 'Austerity'

Power Classification:	8F
Introduced:	1943
Designer:	Riddles
Company:	Ministry of Supply
Weight:	Loco 78t 6cwt Tender 55t 10cwt
Driving Wheel:	4' 8½"
Boiler Pressure:	225psi superheated
Cylinders:	Outside 19" x 28"
Tractive Effort:	34215lbf
Valve Gear:	Walschaert (piston valves)

These were an enlarged version of the 2-8-0 WD 'Austerity' locomotives and 150 were built by the North British Locomotive Company. They were given an extra set of wheels to enable them to work over lightly laid track. As such they were the first successful locomotives with ten coupled wheels to work in this country (the short-lived GER *'Decapod'* of 1902-1906 and the Midland 0-10-0 for the Lickey Bank were the only other ten coupled locomotives which had run in Britain). They paved the way for the development of Riddles' successful '9F' 2-10-0 of 1954. They also differed from the 2-8-0 engines in that they were fitted with wide fire-boxes.

Twenty-five of the locomotives were on loan to BR at nationalisation. These were purchased at the end of 1948. They worked mainly in Scotland. Two other locomotives worked on the Longmoor Military Railway, 600 GORDON and 601 KITCHENER. 601 was temporarily loaned to BR from 1957-59.

Unusually both 90773 and 90774 both carried the same name. The names were later removed from both locomotives, 90774 losing its name in July 1952.

None of this BR class have been preserved, but some of the others which worked overseas have been preserved in this country, together with 600 GORDON (WD 73651) from the Longmoor Military Railway.

Year End Totals: 'WD [2]' class

'47	'48	'49	'50	'51	'52	'53	'54	'55	'56	'57	'58	'59	'60	'61	'62	'63	'64	'65	'66	'67
	25	25	25	25	25	25	25	25	25	25	25	25	25	22						

Number	*Built*	*Renumbered*	*BR Dates*	*Scrap*	*Notes*
90750	*06/*45 NB	03/51 73774	12/48-05/62	06/62	
90751	*06/*45 NB	01/50 73775	12/48-12/62	12/63	
90752	*06/*45 NB	06/51 73776	12/48-12/61	06/62	
90753	*06/*45 NB	02/51 73777	12/48-07/61	08/61	
90754	*06/*45 NB	05/50 73778	12/48-07/61	06/62	
90755	*06/*45 NB	*50* 73779	12/48-12/62	01/64	
90756	*06/*45 NB	06/50 73780	12/48-12/62	11/63	
90757	*06/*45 NB	03/50 73781	12/48-12/62	11/63	
90758	*06/*45 NB	06/50 73782	12/48-12/62	12/63	
90759	*06/*45 NB	11/50 73783	12/48-12/62	06/63	
90760	*06/*45 NB	11/51 73784	12/48-05/62	07/62	
90761	*07/*45 NB	05/49 73785	12/48-11/62	11/63	
90762	*07/*45 NB	06/50 73786	12/48-12/62	11/63	
90763	*07/*45 NB	03/50 73787	12/48-12/62	11/63	
90764	*07/*45 NB	09/52 73788	12/48-05/62	06/62	
90765	*07/*45 NB	12/51 73789	12/48-12/62	01/64	
90766	*07/*45 NB	06/49 73790	12/48-12/62	11/63	
90767	*07/*45 NB	08/50 73791	12/48-12/62	12/63	
90768	*08/*45 NB	06/50 73792	12/48-07/62	12/63	
90769	*08/*45 NB	11/49 73793	12/48-12/62	12/63	
90770	*08/*45 NB	08/52 73794	12/48-12/62	11/63	
90771	*08/*45 NB	09/51 73795	12/48-12/62	12/63	
90772	*08/*45 NB	10/49 73796	12/48-12/62	12/63	
90773 NORTH BRITISH	*09/*45 NB	10/50 73798	12/48-12/62	12/63	
90774 NORTH BRITISH	*09/*45 NB	05/49 73799	12/48-12/62	12/63	

Class continued with 601 (Locomotive On Loan)

9F 92000-92250
2-10-0 BR Standard

Power Classification:	9F c 8F
Introduced:	1954-60
Designer:	Riddles, designed at Brighton
Company:	BR
Weight:	Loco 86t 14cwt f Loco 90t 4cwt v Tender 50t 5cwt w Tender 53t 5cwt x Tender 55t 5cwt y Tender 52t 10cwt z Tender 52t 7cwt
Driving Wheel:	5' 0"
Boiler Pressure:	250psi superheated
Cylinders:	Outside 20" x 28"
Tractive Effort:	39670lbf
Valve Gear:	Walschaert (piston valves)

This was the BR standard design for heavy mineral trains which was developed from the WD Austerity 2-10-0 class. A total of 251 engines were built at Crewe and Swindon. They were the last of the twelve BR standard types to appear and were probably the most successful. Ironically they were destined to have the shortest lives of any of the BR standard types, being the victims of BR's wholesale dieselisation programme. Some were scrapped when they were only five years old.

Although designed as freight locomotives they worked well on the occasional passenger train. 92220 was the last steam locomotive to be built for BR and it was turned out from Swindon in GWR green with a copper capped chimney.

There were several alterations to members of this class as follows:

a These locomotives were fitted with Westinghouse air pumps to work the power operated doors of the wagons used on the iron ore trains between Tyne Dock and Consett.

c Franco-Crosti locomotives rebuilt to conventional working (see f).

d These locomotives were either built or rebuilt with double chimneys.

f 92020-29 were introduced in 1955 with Franco-Crosti boilers. These were unusual boilers in which the chimney was only used for lighting up the locomotive, the normal exhaust coming from a separate outlet on the side of the boiler. This was designed to reduce coal consumption. The expected reduction in coal consumption did not, however, match predictions, and in addition the engines experienced problems with excessive corrosion. They were rebuilt along more conventional lines in 1959-62 (c) but still retained the preheat boiler (underneath the main boiler) although this was sealed off. In this form they were classified '8F' as the boiler was smaller than those on the standard members of the class.

g 92250 was fitted with a Giesl oblong ejector in place of an ordinary chimney. This was a specially designed blastpipe which was intended to reduce coal consumption.

m These locomotives were fitted with mechanical stokers which were not particularly successful.

Several different types of tender were fitted, allocated as shown below.

v BR1B 4725 gallon tender.

w BR1C 4725 gallon tender.

x BR1F 5625 gallon tender.

y BR1G 5000 gallon tender.

z BR1K 4325 gallon tender.

Year End Totals: '9F' class

'47	'48	'49	'50	'51	'52	'53	'54	'55	'56	'57	'58	'59	'60	'61	'62	'63	'64	'65	'66	'67
							32	70	115	172	233	248	251	251	251	251	235	170	125	18

Number	*Built*	*Renumbered*	*BR Dates*	*Scrap*	*Notes*
92000	01/54 Crw		01/54-07/65	11/65	y ⇨d
92001	01/54 Crw		01/54-01/67	05/67	y ⇨d
92002	01/54 Crw		01/54-11/67	04/68	y
92003	01/54 Crw		01/54-03/65	07/65	y
92004	01/54 Crw		01/54-03/68	07/68	y
92005	02/54 Crw		02/54-08/65	12/65	y
92006	02/54 Crw		02/54-04/67	11/67	y ⇨d
92007	02/54 Crw		02/54-12/65	02/66	y
92008	03/54 Crw		03/54-10/67	08/68	y
92009	03/54 Crw		03/54-03/68	07/68	y
92010	05/54 Crw		05/54-04/66	06/66	x
92011	05/54 Crw		05/54-11/67	01/68	x
92012	05/54 Crw		05/54-10/67	02/68	x
92013	05/54 Crw		05/54-09/66	05/67	x
92014	05/54 Crw		05/54-10/67	08/68	x
92015	09/54 Crw		09/54-05/67	11/67	w
92016	10/54 Crw		10/54-10/67	04/68	w
92017	10/54 Crw		10/54-12/67	04/68	w
92018	10/54 Crw		10/54-04/67	08/67	w
92019	10/54 Crw		10/54-06/67	01/68	w
92020	03/55 Crw		03/55-10/67	08/68	vf 61⇨c
92021	03/55 Crw		03/55-11/67	01/68	vf 60⇨c
92022	03/55 Crw		03/55-11/67	04/68	vf 62⇨c
92023	03/55 Crw		03/55-11/67	04/68	vf 61⇨c
92024	06/55 Crw		06/55-11/67	05/68	vf 60⇨c
92025	06/55 Crw		06/55-11/67	04/68	vf 60⇨c
92026	06/55 Crw		06/55-11/67	04/68	vf 59⇨c
92027	07/55 Crw		06/55-08/67	12/67	vf 60⇨c
92028	07/55 Crw		07/55-10/66	01/67	vf 59⇨c
92029	07/55 Crw		07/55-11/67	02/68	vf 60⇨c
92030	11/54 Crw		11/54-02/67	07/67	x

92031 11/54 Crw 11/54-01/67 05/67 x
92032 11/54 Crw 11/54-04/67 10/67 x
92033 11/54 Crw 11/54-09/65 12/65 x
92034 12/54 Crw 12/54-05/64 08/65 x
92035 12/54 Crw 12/54-02/66 04/66 x
92036 12/54 Crw 12/54-12/64 05/65 x
92037 12/54 Crw 12/54-02/65 06/65 x
92038 12/54 Crw 12/54-04/65 07/65 x
92039 12/54 Crw 12/54-10/65 01/66 x
92040 12/54 Crw 12/54-08/65 11/65 x
92041 12/54 Crw 12/54-08/65 11/65 x
92042 01/55 Crw 01/55-12/65 04/66 x
92043 01/55 Crw 01/55-07/66 10/66 x
92044 01/55 Crw 01/55-04/65 07/65 x
92045 02/55 Crw 02/55-09/67 02/68 w
92046 02/55 Crw 02/55-10/67 08/68 w
92047 02/55 Crw 02/55-11/67 04/68 w
92048 02/55 Crw 02/55-09/67 02/68 w
92049 03/55 Crw 03/55-11/67 06/68 w
92050 08/55 Crw 08/55-09/67 02/68 w
92051 08/55 Crw 08/55-10/67 02/68 w
92052 08/55 Crw 08/55-08/67 01/68 w
92053 09/55 Crw 09/55-02/66 12/66 w
92054 09/55 Crw 09/55-05/68 06/68 w
92055 09/55 Crw 09/55-12/67 04/68 w
92056 10/55 Crw 10/55-11/67 02/68 w
92057 10/55 Crw 10/55-09/65 12/65 w
92058 10/55 Crw 10/55-10/67 02/68 w
92059 10/55 Crw 10/55-09/66 01/67 w
92060 11/55 Crw 11/55-10/66 04/67 va
92061 11/55 Crw 11/55-09/66 11/66 va
92062 11/55 Crw 11/55-06/66 10/66 va
92063 11/55 Crw 11/55-11/66 04/67 va
92064 12/55 Crw 12/55-11/66 04/67 va
92065 12/55 Crw 12/55-04/67 08/67 va
92066 12/55 Crw 12/55-06/65 09/65 va
92067 12/55 Crw 12/55-10/66 02/67 x
92068 12/55 Crw 12/55-01/66 04/66 x
92069 12/55 Crw 12/55-05/68 10/68 x
92070 01/56 Crw 01/56-11/67 02/68 x
92071 01/56 Crw 01/56-11/67 02/68 x
92072 02/56 Crw 02/56-01/66 06/66 x
92073 02/56 Crw 02/56-11/67 02/68 x
92074 02/56 Crw 02/56-04/67 10/67 x
92075 03/56 Crw 03/56-09/66 01/67 x
92076 03/56 Crw 03/56-02/67 06/67 x
92077 03/56 Crw 03/56-07/68 10/68 w
92078 03/56 Crw 03/56-05/67 01/68 w
92079 03/56 Crw 03/56-11/67 04/68 w
92080 04/56 Crw 04/56-05/67 11/67 w
92081 04/56 Crw 04/56-02/66 06/66 w
92082 05/56 Crw 05/56-11/67 04/68 w
92083 05/56 Crw 05/56-02/67 07/67 w
92084 05/56 Crw 05/56-11/67 03/68 w
92085 05/56 Crw 05/56-12/66 07/80 w
92086 06/56 Crw 06/56-11/67 04/68 w
92087 08/56 Sdn 08/56-02/67 06/67 x
92088 10/56 Sdn 10/56-05/68 10/68 x
92089 09/56 Sdn 09/56-02/67 07/67 x
92090 11/56 Sdn 11/56-05/67 12/67 x
92091 11/56 Sdn 11/56-06/68 11/68 x
92092 12/56 Sdn 12/56-10/66 04/67 x
92093 01/57 Sdn 01/57-08/67 02/68 x
92094 02/57 Sdn 02/57-05/68 09/68 x
92095 03/57 Sdn 03/57-09/66 04/67 x
92096 04/57 Sdn 04/57-02/67 06/67 x
92097 06/56 Crw 06/56-10/66 04/67 va
92098 07/56 Crw 07/56-08/66 10/66 va
92099 07/56 Crw 07/56-09/66 11/66 va
92100 08/56 Crw 08/56-05/67 01/68 w
92101 08/56 Crw 08/56-10/67 08/68 w
92102 08/56 Crw 08/56-11/67 03/68 w
92103 08/56 Crw 08/56-06/67 06/68 w
92104 08/56 Crw 08/56-02/67 07/67 w
92105 09/56 Crw 09/56-01/67 05/67 w
92106 09/56 Crw 09/56-07/67 12/67 w
92107 09/56 Crw 09/56-02/67 07/67 w
92108 10/56 Crw 10/56-11/67 02/68 w
92109 10/56 Crw 10/56-11/67 03/68 w
92110 10/56 Crw 10/56-12/67 03/68 w
92111 11/56 Crw 11/56-10/67 02/68 w
92112 11/56 Crw 11/56-11/67 03/68 w
92113 11/56 Crw 11/56-10/67 08/68 w
92114 12/56 Crw 12/56-07/67 02/68 w
92115 12/56 Crw 12/56-02/66 06/66 w
92116 12/56 Crw 12/56-11/66 06/67 w
92117 12/56 Crw 12/56-12/67 04/68 w
92118 12/56 Crw 12/56-06/68 09/68 w
92119 01/57 Crw 01/57-09/67 02/68 w
92120 02/57 Crw 02/57-07/67 02/68 w
92121 02/57 Crw 02/57-07/67 01/68 w
92122 02/57 Crw 02/57-11/67 02/68 w
92123 03/57 Crw 03/57-10/67 02/68 w
92124 03/57 Crw 03/57-12/66 04/67 w
92125 03/57 Crw 03/57-12/67 04/68 w
92126 03/57 Crw 03/57-08/67 01/68 w
92127 03/57 Crw 03/57-09/67 12/67 w
92128 04/57 Crw 04/57-11/67 05/68 w
92129 04/57 Crw 04/57-06/67 11/67 w
92130 04/57 Crw 04/57-05/66 11/66 w
92131 05/57 Crw 04/57-09/67 02/68 w
92132 05/57 Crw 05/57-10/67 02/68 w
92133 05/57 Crw 05/57-07/67 01/68 w
92134 § 05/57 Crw 05/57-12/66 w
92135 06/57 Crw 06/57-06/67 03/68 w
92136 06/57 Crw 06/57-10/66 02/67 w
92137 06/57 Crw 06/57-09/67 02/68 w
92138 06/57 Crw 06/57-07/67 02/68 w
92139 06/57 Crw 06/57-09/67 02/68 w
92140 07/57 Crw 07/57-04/65 07/65 x
92141 07/57 Crw 07/57-12/65 04/66 x
92142 07/57 Crw 07/57-02/65 02/66 x
92143 08/57 Crw 08/57-02/65 05/65 x
92144 08/57 Crw 08/57-12/65 04/66 x
92145 08/57 Crw 08/57-02/66 04/66 x
92146 09/57 Crw 09/57-04/66 08/66 x
92147 09/57 Crw 09/57-04/65 08/65 x
92148 09/57 Crw 09/57-12/65 04/66 x
92149 10/57 Crw 10/57-06/65 10/65 x
92150 10/57 Crw 10/57-04/67 11/67 w
92151 10/57 Crw 10/57-04/67 04/68 w
92152 10/57 Crw 10/57-11/67 03/68 w
92153 10/57 Crw 10/57-01/68 06/68 w
92154 11/57 Crw 11/57-07/67 01/68 w
92155 11/57 Crw 11/57-11/66 04/67 w
92156 11/57 Crw 11/57-07/67 03/68 w
92157 11/57 Crw 11/57-09/67 01/68 w
92158 11/57 Crw 11/57-07/66 11/66 w
92159 11/57 Crw 11/57-07/67 01/68 w
92160 11/57 Crw 11/57-07/68 10/68 w
92161 12/57 Crw 12/57-12/66 05/67 w
92162 12/57 Crw 12/57-11/67 05/68 w
92163 03/58 Crw 03/58-11/67 05/68 w
92164 04/58 Crw 04/58-07/66 10/66 w
92165 04/58 Crw 04/58-03/68 06/68 zdm
92166 05/58 Crw 05/58-11/67 03/68 zdm
92167 05/58 Crw 05/58-07/68 11/68 zdm
92168 12/57 Crw 12/57-06/65 11/65 x
92169 12/57 Crw 12/57-05/64 01/65 x
92170 12/57 Crw 12/57-05/64 01/65 x
92171 02/58 Crw 02/58-05/64 03/65 x
92172 01/58 Crw 01/58-04/66 07/66 x
92173 02/58 Crw 02/58-03/66 05/66 x
92174 02/58 Crw 02/58-12/65 05/66 x
92175 02/58 Crw 02/58-05/64 02/65 x
92176 03/58 Crw 03/58-05/64 03/65 x
92177 03/58 Crw 03/58-05/64 08/64 x
92178 09/57 Sdn 09/57-10/65 12/65 xd
92179 10/57 Sdn 10/57-11/65 05/66 x
92180 11/57 Sdn 11/57-04/65 07/65 x
92181 11/57 Sdn 11/57-02/65 07/65 x
92182 12/57 Sdn 12/57-04/66 07/66 x
92183 12/57 Sdn 12/57-04/66 07/66 xd
92184 01/58 Sdn 01/58-02/65 06/65 xd
92185 01/58 Sdn 01/58-02/65 06/65 xd
92186 01/58 Sdn 01/58-08/65 02/66 xd
92187 02/58 Sdn 02/58-02/65 05/65 xd
92188 02/58 Sdn 02/58-02/65 05/65 xd
92189 03/58 Sdn 03/58-12/65 04/66 xd
92190 03/58 Sdn 03/58-10/65 01/66 xd
92191 04/58 Sdn 04/58-12/65 04/66 xd
92192 05/58 Sdn 05/58-02/65 05/65 xd
92193 05/58 Sdn 05/58-06/65 11/65 xd
92194 06/58 Sdn 06/58-12/65 03/66 xd
92195 06/58 Sdn 06/58-05/65 11/65 xd
92196 08/58 Sdn 08/58-12/64 01/66 xd
92197 09/58 Sdn 09/58-09/65 01/66 xd
92198 10/58 Sdn 10/58-08/64 06/65 xd
92199 10/58 Sdn 10/58-08/64 06/65 xd
92200 11/58 Sdn 11/58-10/65 12/65 xd
92201 12/58 Sdn 12/58-03/66 07/66 xd
92202 12/58 Sdn 12/58-12/65 03/66 xd
92203 § 04/59 Sdn 04/59-11/67 yd
92204 04/59 Sdn 04/59-12/67 03/68 yd
92205 05/59 Sdn 05/59-06/67 01/68 yd
92206 05/59 Sdn 05/59-05/67 09/67 yd
92207 § 06/59 Sdn 06/59-12/64 yd
92208 06/59 Sdn 06/59-10/67 02/68 yd
92209 06/59 Sdn 06/59-12/65 03/66 yd
92210 08/59 Sdn 08/59-11/64 03/65 yd
92211 09/59 Sdn 09/59-05/67 12/67 yd
92212 § 09/59 Sdn 09/59-01/68 yd
92213 10/59 Sdn 10/59-10/66 02/67 yd
92214 § 10/59 Sdn 10/59-08/65 yd
92215 11/59 Sdn 11/59-06/67 03/68 yd
92216 12/59 Sdn 12/59-10/65 04/66 yd
92217 12/59 Sdn 12/59-08/66 10/66 yd
92218 01/60 Sdn 01/60-05/68 07/68 yd
92219 § 01/60 Sdn 01/60-08/65 yd
92220 § 03/60 Sdn 03/60-03/65 yd
EVENING STAR
92221 05/58 Crw 05/58-05/65 09/65 yd
92222 06/58 Crw 06/58-03/65 07/65 yd
92223 06/58 Crw 06/58-04/68 09/68 yd
92224 06/58 Crw 06/58-09/67 06/68 yd
92225 06/58 Crw 06/58-07/65 09/65 yd
92226 06/58 Crw 06/58-09/65 02/66 yd
92227 07/58 Crw 07/58-10/67 01/68 yd
92228 07/58 Crw 07/58-01/67 06/67 yd
92229 07/58 Crw 07/58-11/64 02/65 yd
92230 08/58 Crw 08/58-12/65 07/66 yd
92231 08/58 Crw 08/58-11/66 04/67 yd
92232 08/58 Crw 08/58-12/64 03/65 yd
92233 08/58 Crw 08/58-02/68 08/68 yd
92234 08/58 Crw 08/58-11/67 02/68 yd
92235 08/58 Crw 08/58-11/65 04/66 yd
92236 09/58 Crw 09/58-04/65 10/65 yd
92237 09/58 Crw 09/58-09/65 11/65 yd
92238 09/58 Crw 09/58-09/65 12/65 yd
92239 09/58 Crw 09/58-11/66 04/67 yd
92240 § 10/58 Crw 10/58-08/65 yd
92241 10/58 Crw 10/58-07/65 12/65 yd
92242 10/58 Crw 10/58-05/65 08/65 yd
92243 10/58 Crw 10/58-12/65 04/66 yd
92244 10/58 Crw 10/58-12/65 07/66 yd
92245 § 11/58 Crw 11/58-12/64 yd
92246 11/58 Crw 11/58-12/65 04/66 yd
92247 12/58 Crw 12/58-10/66 04/67 yd
92248 12/58 Crw 12/58-05/65 08/65 yd
92249 12/58 Crw 12/58-05/68 09/68 yd
92250 12/58 Crw 12/58-12/65 07/66 yg

Locomotive On Loan

Locomotive on loan to BR from the Longmoor Military Railway.

WD [2] 90750-90774 (601 on loan)
2-10-0 MOS (WD) 'Austerity'

Class continued from 90774

Number	Built	Renumbered	BR Dates	Scrap	Notes
601	08/45 NB	73797	05/57-02/59	67	
KITCHENER					

BR Standard Class 4
tank 2-6-4T
N0 80012.

BR Standard Class 2
tank 2-6-2T
No 84016.

WD Riddles Austerity
'WD' class 2-8-0
No 90001.

Appendicies

Appendix 1. Statistics.

Two tables are given for each group, the Summary of Year End Totals by Type, and the Summary of Year End Totals by Class. In each table, the totals of locomotives are given at the year end for each year from the end of 1947 (all locomotives coming into BR stock) until the end of 1967. At the end of 1968 only three locomotives remained in BR stock, the three Vale of Rheidol narrow gauge 2-6-2Ts.

The totals given are the actual numbers of locomotives in stock on the 31st December of each year. In some years this does not agree exactly with the official BR totals, as the BR statistical year-end date did not always coincide exactly with the end of the year.

The Class Totals List also shows the number of the first member of each class to enable the reader to find the class details in the other sections.

Appendix 2. Chronological list of classes (listed by Railway Company).

In this appendix, all the Railway Companies that built locomotives which came into BR stock are listed. The Railway Companies are grouped together in the five main groups, and in each section the pre-grouping companies are shown first in alphabetical order. Under each Railway Company heading, the classes built by that company are shown, in the order of the date of introduction. (Dates marked with an asterisk are rebuilding dates.) This appendix can be used to trace the development of the locomotive classes which came into BR stock.

Appendix 3. Alphabetical list of locomotive names.

A full alphabetic list of names is given with the locomotive numbers. The names are shown in a font that reflects as closely as possible the style of the locomotive nameplate, or the painted locomotive name.

Appendix 4. Chronological list of additions to stock.

This list shows chronologically (within the period covered by this book) when locomotives were built or added to stock.

Appendix 5. Chronological list of withdrawals from stock.

This list shows chronologically (within the period covered by this book) when steam locomotives were withdrawn or removed from stock.

Appendix 6. Youngest and oldest locomotives at time of withdrawal.

This list shows the ages of all locomotives which were under ten years old, and all those that were seventy or more years old at the time of their withdrawal from service. The ages are shown in years and months separated by a colon (:). A plus sign (+) indicates that the engine concerned was at least this age – the actual month of entry into service not being known.

A list is also shown of the locomotives that held the title of being 'the oldest locomotive in British Railways stock' at various times between 1948 and 1968.

Appendix 7. Locomotives which survived for more than a year after withdrawal before scrapping.

Some locomotives survived for a long time after withdrawal. This list shows all locomotives which survived for a year or more before being scrapped.

Appendix 8. Locomotives which still carried their pre-nationalisation number after January 1951.

The vast majority of locomotives to be renumbered received their new numbers before the end of 1950, but a significant number of engines lingered on with their old numbers after that date. This list shows all engines carrying their old numbers after January 1951, listed in the order that they were renumbered, or scrapped carrying their old numbers (marked with an X) or renumbered into departmental stock (marked R).

Appendix 9. Ex-LNER locomotives 1946 renumbering scheme.

Although it is strictly outside the scope of this work, it was felt that the reader would appreciate a complete list of the pre-1946 numbers of LNER locomotives which came into BR stock. Numbers marked with an asterisk (*) are temporary intermediate numbers carried by the locomotives concerned, from 1942 onwards.

Appendix 1 Statistics.

Summary of year end totals by type – all British Railways steam locomotives.

Type	1947	1948	1949	1950	1951	1952	1953	1954	1955	1956	1957	1958	1959	1960	1961	1962	1963	1964	1965	1966	1967
Tender Locomotives																					
4-6-4	1	1	1	1	1	1	1	1	1	1	1	1	0	0	0	0	0	0	0	0	0
4-6-2	279	342	383	392	420	441	448	458	458	458	458	458	455	451	435	380	302	202	137	88	1
4-6-0	2503	2575	2599	2662	2683	2660	2681	2708	2755	2778	2781	2743	2661	2609	2526	2093	1784	1361	915	613	184
4-4-2	62	33	19	8	5	5	5	5	5	1	1	0	0	0	0	0	0	0	0	0	0
4-4-0	1615	1504	1354	1280	1078	1004	949	891	798	730	602	479	317	241	55	1	0	0	0	0	0
2-10-0	0	25	25	25	25	25	25	57	95	140	197	258	273	276	273	251	251	235	170	125	18
2-8-0	1469	1983	2022	2021	2011	2002	1999	1996	1993	1979	1981	1969	1895	1866	1838	1618	1407	1168	783	504	150
2-6-2	186	186	186	186	186	186	186	186	186	186	184	184	184	184	184	115	72	40	14	0	0
2-6-0	1009	1027	1110	1195	1277	1314	1357	1420	1443	1462	1485	1456	1379	1320	1251	963	813	604	419	189	6
2-4-0	24	23	22	21	21	19	19	16	10	5	3	1	0	0	0	0	0	0	0	0	0
0-10-0	1	1	1	1	1	1	1	1	1	0	0	0	0	0	0	0	0	0	0	0	0
0-8-0	952	890	702	566	483	462	455	449	445	434	383	370	281	271	222	127	91	62	40	17	0
0-6-0	4386	4210	4054	3935	3768	3663	3521	3411	3275	3159	3013	2821	2309	1938	1481	843	545	267	104	36	0
0-4-2	4	0	0	0	0	0	0	0	0	0	0	0	0	0	0	0	0	0	0	0	0
Total	12491	12800	12478	12293	11959	11783	11647	11599	11465	11333	11089	10740	9754	9156	8265	6391	5265	3939	2582	1572	359
Tank Locomotives																					
4-8-0T	17	17	17	17	17	17	17	17	15	14	11	10	3	3	2	0	0	0	0	0	0
4-6-2T	134	131	130	127	118	112	110	103	99	96	89	49	36	5	5	0	0	0	0	0	0
4-4-2T	267	250	241	232	180	171	160	139	110	80	65	38	21	6	0	0	0	0	0	0	0
2-8-2T	54	54	54	54	54	54	54	54	54	54	54	54	54	54	54	52	39	10	0	0	0
2-8-0T	151	151	151	151	151	151	151	151	151	151	151	151	136	134	129	110	65	18	0	0	0
2-6-4T	535	638	679	755	784	821	838	871	891	911	915	915	910	884	811	594	509	345	197	82	0
2-6-2T	766	785	818	839	836	869	871	882	877	871	856	815	750	686	574	361	298	181	53	10	0
2-4-2T	285	233	201	175	152	120	99	94	58	41	30	7	4	3	0	0	0	0	0	0	0
2-4-0T	17	11	4	4	4	3	3	3	3	3	3	3	3	3	3	0	0	0	0	0	0
0-8-4T	20	13	10	7	6	6	6	5	5	2	0	0	0	0	0	0	0	0	0	0	0
0-8-2T	10	5	5	3	1	1	0	0	0	0	0	0	0	0	0	0	0	0	0	0	0
0-8-0T	22	22	22	21	21	21	21	20	20	18	18	13	8	8	8	0	0	0	0	0	0
0-6-4T	7	5	4	2	0	0	0	0	0	0	0	0	0	0	0	0	0	0	0	0	0
0-6-2T	1246	1190	1139	1103	1059	1022	995	943	836	751	676	596	446	338	265	175	109	57	2	0	0
0-6-0T	3058	3010	2982	2988	2978	2968	2916	2872	2775	2662	2542	2324	2020	1723	1411	977	700	389	130	12	0
0-4-4T	590	562	539	518	484	449	411	395	351	321	289	248	205	188	96	60	35	16	14	10	0
0-4-2T	123	113	107	103	101	101	100	100	100	91	73	57	44	33	27	19	12	2	0	0	0
0-4-0T	196	187	175	172	164	156	151	139	119	110	93	79	64	47	37	24	13	6	6	0	0
2-8-8-2	1	1	1	1	1	1	1	1	0	0	0	0	0	0	0	0	0	0	0	0	0
2-6-6-2	33	33	33	33	33	33	33	33	26	13	1	0	0	0	0	0	0	0	0	0	0
Total	7532	7411	7312	7305	7144	7076	6937	6822	6490	6189	5866	5359	4704	4115	3422	2372	1780	1024	402	114	0
Narrow Gauge Locomotives																					
2-6-2T	3	3	3	3	3	3	3	3	3	3	3	3	3	3	3	3	3	3	3	3	3
0-6-0T	2	2	2	2	2	2	2	2	2	2	2	2	2	2	1	0	0	0	0	0	0
0-4-2T	2	0	0	0	0	0	0	0	0	0	0	0	0	0	0	0	0	0	0	0	0
Total	7	5	5	5	5	5	5	5	5	5	5	5	5	5	4	3	3	3	3	3	3
Service Locomotives																					
4-6-0	1	1	1	1	0	0	0	0	0	0	0	0	0	0	0	0	8	7	8	4	2
0-6-0	0	0	0	0	0	0	0	0	0	0	0	0	0	0	0	0	2	2	2	0	0
0-6-0T	21	21	20	19	19	19	19	18	18	18	17	17	13	12	11	14	14	15	6	5	0
0-4-0T	16	17	16	17	18	17	17	17	17	16	16	15	9	7	5	5	2	0	0	0	0
0-4-2T	2	2	1	1	0	0	0	0	0	0	0	0	0	0	0	0	0	0	0	0	0
Total	40	41	38	38	37	36	36	35	35	34	33	32	22	19	16	19	26	24	16	9	2
Miscellaneous Locomotives																					
2-4-2T	1	1	1	1	1	1	1	1	1	0	0	0	0	0	0	0	0	0	0	0	0
0-4-0T	2	2	2	2	2	2	2	2	1	1	1	1	1	1	1	0	0	0	0	0	0
Steam Rail Cars	3	0	0	0	0	0	0	0	0	0	0	0	0	0	0	0	0	0	0	0	0
Total	6	3	3	3	3	3	3	3	2	1	1	1	1	1	1	0	0	0	0	0	0
Grand Total	20076	20260	19836	19644	19148	18903	18628	18464	17997	17562	16994	16137	14486	13296	11708	8785	7074	4990	3003	1698	364

Summary of year end totals by type – GWR group steam locomotives.

Type	1947	1948	1949	1950	1951	1952	1953	1954	1955	1956	1957	1958	1959	1960	1961	1962	1963	1964	1965	1966	1967
Tender Locomotives																					
4-6-0	675	691	701	731	700	679	670	669	669	668	665	664	659	649	636	468	328	169	0	0	0
4-4-0	85	65	39	36	26	26	26	24	22	22	8	6	5	0	0	0	0	0	0	0	
2-8-0	221	205	205	205	205	205	202	199	196	182	181	170	141	127	126	116	81	35	0	0	0
2-6-0	253	236	231	230	224	220	217	217	216	210	205	182	149	122	113	68	35	0	0	0	0
2-4-0	3	3	3	3	3	1	1	0	0	0	0	0	0	0	0	0	0	0	0	0	0
0-6-0	183	183	180	178	175	165	137	124	122	121	120	119	92	82	73	53	34	15	0	0	0
Total	1420	1383	1359	1383	1333	1296	1253	1233	1225	1203	1179	1141	1046	980	948	705	478	219	0	0	0
Tank Locomotives																					
2-8-2T	54	54	54	54	54	54	54	54	54	54	54	54	54	54	54	52	39	10	0	0	0
2-8-0T	151	151	151	151	151	151	151	151	151	151	151	151	136	134	129	110	65	18	0	0	0
2-6-2T	455	454	457	448	435	418	400	399	381	375	350	309	286	234	208	151	120	61	0	0	0
2-4-0T	13	7	0	0	0	0	0	0	0	0	0	0	0	0	0	0	0	0	0	0	0
0-8-2T	1	0	0	0	0	0	0	0	0	0	0	0	0	0	0	0	0	0	0	0	0
0-6-2T	391	370	349	334	315	302	289	275	248	219	200	200	200	200	200	171	109	57	2	0	0
0-6-0T	1249	1236	1238	1262	1280	1294	1283	1288	1285	1281	1255	1199	1072	970	865	621	450	215	30	0	0
0-4-2T	98	98	95	95	95	95	95	95	95	88	70	54	42	33	27	19	12	2	0	0	0
0-4-0T	17	17	17	17	17	15	15	15	14	14	14	13	10	3	2	2	0	0	0	0	0
Total	2429	2387	2361	2361	2347	2329	2287	2277	2228	2182	2094	1980	1800	1628	1485	1126	795	363	32	0	0
Narrow Gauge Locomotives																					
2-6-2T	3	3	3	3	3	3	3	3	3	3	3	3	3	3	3	3	3	3	3	3	3
0-6-0T	2	2	2	2	2	2	2	2	2	2	2	2	2	2	1	0	0	0	0	0	0
0-4-2T	2	0	0	0	0	0	0	0	0	0	0	0	0	0	0	0	0	0	0	0	0
Total	7	5	5	5	5	5	5	5	5	5	5	5	5	5	4	3	3	3	3	3	3
Service Locomotives																					
0-4-0T	0	1	1	1	1	1	1	0	0	0	0	0	0	0	0	0	0	0	0	0	0
Total	0	1	1	1	1	1	1	0	0	0	0	0	0	0	0	0	0	0	0	0	0
Grand Total	3856	3776	3726	3750	3686	3631	3546	3515	3458	3390	3278	3126	2851	2613	2437	1834	1276	585	35	3	3

Summary of year end totals by type – SR group steam locomotives.

Type	1947	1948	1949	1950	1951	1952	1953	1954	1955	1956	1957	1958	1959	1960	1961	1962	1963	1964	1965	1966	1967
Tender Locomotives																					
4-6-2	90	117	130	139	140	140	140	140	140	140	140	140	140	140	140	140	130	93	70	46	0
4-6-0	177	174	172	170	168	168	167	167	159	148	136	131	106	96	67	41	23	6	0	0	0
4-4-2	9	9	8	8	5	5	5	5	5	1	1	0	0	0	0	0	0	0	0	0	0
4-4-0	372	351	318	299	185	167	159	151	144	134	130	119	96	85	27	1	0	0	0	0	0
2-6-0	174	174	174	174	174	174	174	174	174	174	174	174	174	174	174	130	87	22	10	0	0
0-6-0	325	312	289	284	265	264	255	253	246	240	230	219	194	169	101	60	40	10	3	0	0
0-4-2	4	0	0	0	0	0	0	0	0	0	0	0	0	0	0	0	0	0	0	0	0
Total	1151	1137	1091	1074	937	918	900	890	868	837	811	783	710	664	509	372	280	131	83	46	0
Tank Locomotives																					
4-8-0T	4	4	4	4	4	4	4	4	4	4	4	4	2	2	2	0	0	0	0	0	0
4-6-2T	7	7	7	7	5	5	5	5	5	5	5	5	5	5	5	0	0	0	0	0	0
4-4-2T	47	37	37	29	4	3	3	3	3	3	3	3	3	3	0	0	0	0	0	0	0
2-6-4T	15	15	15	15	15	15	15	15	15	15	15	15	15	15	15	15	5	0	0	0	0
2-4-0T	3	3	3	3	3	3	3	3	3	3	3	3	3	3	3	0	0	0	0	0	0
0-8-0T	9	9	9	8	8	8	8	8	8	8	8	8	8	8	8	0	0	0	0	0	0
0-6-4T	5	5	4	2	0	0	0	0	0	0	0	0	0	0	0	0	0	0	0	0	0
0-6-2T	142	142	138	138	128	128	124	120	105	85	70	59	39	34	18	4	0	0	0	0	0
0-6-0T	127	117	95	89	77	75	75	75	72	69	67	60	51	39	29	19	7	6	6	6	0
0-4-4T	287	275	260	258	241	227	212	209	197	194	186	175	144	129	87	60	35	16	14	10	0
0-4-2T	18	8	5	1	0	0	0	0	0	0	0	0	0	0	0	0	0	0	0	0	0
0-4-0T	29	25	14	14	14	14	14	13	13	13	9	8	4	3	3	3	0	0	0	0	0
Total	693	647	591	568	499	482	463	455	425	399	370	340	274	241	170	101	47	22	20	16	0
Service Locomotives																					
0-6-0	0	0	0	0	0	0	0	0	0	0	0	0	0	0	0	0	2	2	2	0	0
0-6-0T	4	4	3	4	4	4	4	4	4	4	4	4	3	3	3	4	6	6	4	4	0
0-4-2T	2	2	1	1	0	0	0	0	0	0	0	0	0	0	0	0	0	0	0	0	0
0-4-0T	1	1	1	1	1	1	1	1	1	1	1	1	0	0	0	0	0	0	0	0	0
Total	7	7	5	6	5	5	5	5	5	5	5	5	3	3	3	4	8	8	6	4	0
Grand Total	1851	1791	1687	1648	1441	1405	1368	1350	1298	1241	1186	1128	987	908	682	477	335	161	109	66	0

Summary of year end totals by type – LMS group steam locomotives.

Type	1947	1948	1949	1950	1951	1952	1953	1954	1955	1956	1957	1958	1959	1960	1961	1962	1963	1964	1965	1966	1967
Tender Locomotives																					
4-6-2	50	51	51	51	51	51	51	50	50	50	50	50	50	50	44	35	22	0	0	0	0
4-6-0	1104	1128	1151	1171	1166	1158	1155	1155	1155	1155	1155	1155	1155	1152	1139	1022	942	780	642	464	151
4-4-0	651	625	591	569	534	498	465	430	376	337	278	234	150	122	26	0	0	0	0	0	0
2-8-0	567	635	674	674	674	674	674	674	674	674	677	677	676	674	672	666	667	638	543	381	150
2-6-0	308	343	370	447	535	562	575	575	575	575	575	575	575	575	571	498	432	346	224	110	6
2-4-0	3	2	1	0	0	0	0	0	0	0	0	0	0	0	0	0	0	0	0	0	0
0-10-0	1	1	1	1	1	1	1	1	1	0	0	0	0	0	0	0	0	0	0	0	0
0-8-0	706	663	510	408	348	327	320	314	310	299	248	235	146	137	89	9	6	0	0	0	0
0-6-0	2180	2057	1988	1931	1853	1799	1726	1676	1596	1524	1426	1370	1151	994	785	519	321	128	11	0	0
Total	5570	5505	5337	5252	5162	5070	4967	4875	4737	4614	4409	4296	3903	3704	3326	2749	2390	1892	1420	955	307
Tank Locomotives																					
4-6-2T	10	8	7	6	5	1	0	0	0	0	0	0	0	0	0	0	0	0	0	0	0
4-4-2T	68	67	61	60	35	30	28	28	23	14	14	13	3	0	0	0	0	0	0	0	0
2-6-4T	498	544	574	628	645	645	645	645	645	645	645	645	640	626	577	425	350	222	118	57	0
2-6-2T	219	239	269	299	309	339	339	339	339	339	339	339	297	287	209	109	91	65	39	8	0
2-4-2T	167	138	116	99	87	59	43	39	29	23	20	7	4	3	0	0	0	0	0	0	0
2-4-0T	1	1	1	1	1	0	0	0	0	0	0	0	0	0	0	0	0	0	0	0	0
0-8-4T	14	7	4	1	0	0	0	0	0	0	0	0	0	0	0	0	0	0	0	0	0
0-8-2T	9	5	5	3	1	1	0	0	0	0	0	0	0	0	0	0	0	0	0	0	0
0-6-2T	94	64	52	45	37	31	29	19	15	15	15	11	1	1	1	0	0	0	0	0	0
0-6-0T	864	849	833	831	822	815	797	782	756	709	663	616	523	435	359	262	215	155	91	4	0
0-4-4T	193	178	170	153	141	127	111	106	95	85	81	73	61	59	9	0	0	0	0	0	0
0-4-2T	3	3	3	3	2	2	1	1	1	0	0	0	0	0	0	0	0	0	0	0	0
0-4-0T	62	62	62	60	60	60	63	64	59	56	50	45	41	35	28	19	13	6	6	0	0
2-6-6-2	33	33	33	33	33	33	33	33	26	13	1	0	0	0	0	0	0	0	0	0	0
Total	2235	2198	2190	2222	2178	2143	2089	2056	1988	1899	1828	1749	1570	1446	1183	815	669	448	254	69	0
Service Locomotives																					
0-6-0T	10	10	10	10	10	10	10	9	9	9	8	8	5	4	3	3	1	0	0	0	0
0-4-0T	1	1	0	0	0	0	0	0	0	0	0	0	0	0	0	0	0	0	0	0	0
Total	11	11	10	10	10	10	10	9	9	9	8	8	5	4	3	3	1	0	0	0	0
Miscellaneous Locomotives																					
2-4-2T	1	1	1	1	1	1	1	1	1	0	0	0	0	0	0	0	0	0	0	0	0
0-4-0T	2	2	2	2	2	2	2	2	1	1	1	1	1	1	1	0	0	0	0	0	0
Steam Rail Cars	2	0	0	0	0	0	0	0	0	0	0	0	0	0	0	0	0	0	0	0	0
Total	5	3	3	3	3	3	3	3	2	1	1	1	1	1	1	0	0	0	0	0	0
Grand Total	7821	7717	7540	7487	7353	7226	7069	6943	6736	6523	6246	6054	5479	5155	4513	3567	3060	2340	1674	1024	307

Summary of year end totals by type – LNER group steam locomotives.

Type	1947	1948	1949	1950	1951	1952	1953	1954	1955	1956	1957	1958	1959	1960	1961	1962	1963	1964	1965	1966	1967
Tender Locomotives																					
4-6-4	1	1	1	1	1	1	1	1	1	1	1	1	0	0	0	0	0	0	0	0	0
4-6-2	139	174	202	202	202	202	202	202	202	202	202	202	199	195	185	145	90	49	12	0	0
4-6-0	547	582	575	590	604	605	594	592	590	590	573	541	489	460	432	310	239	172	91	27	0
4-4-2	53	24	11	0	0	0	0	0	0	0	0	0	0	0	0	0	0	0	0	0	0
4-4-0	507	463	406	376	333	313	299	286	256	237	186	120	66	34	2	0	0	0	0	0	0
2-8-0	681	610	410	409	399	390	390	390	390	390	390	389	346	335	310	186	106	67	13	0	0
2-6-2	186	186	186	186	186	186	186	186	186	186	184	184	184	184	184	115	72	40	14	0	0
2-6-0	274	274	335	344	344	344	344	344	343	339	331	325	281	249	193	67	60	48	31	24	0
2-4-0	18	18	18	18	18	18	18	16	10	5	3	1	0	0	0	0	0	0	0	0	0
0-8-0	246	227	192	158	135	135	135	135	135	135	135	135	135	134	133	118	85	62	40	17	0
0-6-0	1698	1658	1597	1542	1475	1435	1403	1358	1311	1274	1237	1113	872	693	522	211	150	114	90	36	0
Total	4350	4217	3933	3826	3697	3629	3572	3510	3424	3359	3242	3011	2572	2284	1961	1152	802	552	291	104	0
Tank Locomotives																					
4-8-0T	13	13	13	13	13	13	13	13	11	10	7	6	1	1	0	0	0	0	0	0	0
4-6-2T	117	116	116	114	108	106	105	98	94	91	84	44	31	0	0	0	0	0	0	0	0
4-4-2T	152	146	143	143	141	138	129	108	84	63	48	22	15	3	0	0	0	0	0	0	0
2-6-4T	22	79	90	112	107	107	106	103	100	100	100	100	100	88	64	0	0	0	0	0	0
2-6-2T	92	92	92	92	92	92	92	92	92	92	92	92	92	90	82	26	13	0	0	0	0
2-4-2T	118	95	85	76	65	61	56	55	29	18	10	0	0	0	0	0	0	0	0	0	0
0-8-4T	6	6	6	6	6	6	6	5	5	2	0	0	0	0	0	0	0	0	0	0	0
0-8-0T	13	13	13	13	13	13	13	12	12	10	10	5	0	0	0	0	0	0	0	0	0
0-6-4T	2	0	0	0	0	0	0	0	0	0	0	0	0	0	0	0	0	0	0	0	0
0-6-2T	619	614	600	586	579	561	553	529	468	432	391	326	206	103	46	0	0	0	0	0	0
0-6-0T	818	808	816	806	799	784	761	727	662	603	557	449	374	279	158	75	28	13	3	2	0
0-4-4T	110	109	109	107	102	95	88	80	59	42	22	0	0	0	0	0	0	0	0	0	0
0-4-2T	4	4	4	4	4	4	4	4	4	3	3	3	2	0	0	0	0	0	0	0	0
0-4-0T	88	83	82	81	73	67	59	47	33	27	20	13	9	6	4	0	0	0	0	0	0
2-8-8-2	1	1	1	1	1	1	1	1	0	0	0	0	0	0	0	0	0	0	0	0	0
Total	2175	2179	2170	2154	2103	2048	1986	1874	1653	1493	1344	1060	830	570	354	101	41	13	3	2	0
Service Locomotives																					
4-6-0	1	1	1	1	0	0	0	0	0	0	0	0	0	0	0	0	8	7	8	4	2
0-6-0T	7	7	7	5	5	5	5	5	5	5	5	5	5	5	5	7	7	9	2	1	0
0-4-0T	14	14	14	15	16	15	15	16	16	15	15	14	9	7	5	5	2	0	0	0	0
Total	22	22	22	21	21	20	20	21	21	20	20	19	14	12	10	12	17	16	10	5	2
Miscellaneous Locomotives																					
Steam Rail Cars	1	0	0	0	0	0	0	0	0	0	0	0	0	0	0	0	0	0	0	0	0
Total	1	0	0	0	0	0	0	0	0	0	0	0	0	0	0	0	0	0	0	0	0
Grand Total	6548	6418	6125	6001	5821	5697	5578	5405	5098	4872	4606	4090	3416	2866	2325	1265	860	581	304	111	2

Summary of year end totals by type – BR standard and Austerity steam locomotives.

Type	1947	1948	1949	1950	1951	1952	1953	1954	1955	1956	1957	1958	1959	1960	1961	1962	1963	1964	1965	1966	1967
Tender locomotives																					
4-6-2	0	0	0	0	27	48	55	66	66	66	66	66	66	66	66	60	60	60	55	42	1
4-6-0	0	0	0	0	45	50	95	125	182	217	252	252	252	252	252	252	252	234	182	122	33
2-10-0	0	25	25	25	25	25	25	57	95	140	197	258	273	276	273	251	251	235	170	125	18
2-8-0	0	533	733	733	733	733	733	733	733	733	733	733	732	730	730	650	553	428	227	123	0
2-6-0	0	0	0	0	0	14	47	110	135	164	200	200	200	200	200	200	199	188	154	55	0
Total	0	558	758	758	830	870	955	1091	1211	1320	1448	1509	1523	1524	1521	1413	1315	1145	788	467	52
Tank Locomotives																					
2-6-4T	0	0	0	0	17	54	72	108	131	151	155	155	155	155	155	154	154	123	79	25	0
2-6-2T	0	0	0	0	0	20	40	52	65	65	75	75	75	75	75	75	74	55	14	2	0
Total	0	0	0	0	17	74	112	160	196	216	230	230	230	230	230	229	228	178	93	27	0
Grand Total	0	558	758	758	847	944	1067	1251	1407	1536	1678	1739	1753	1754	1751	1642	1543	1323	881	494	52

GER Hill 'N7' class 0-6-2T No 69635 at Stratford in October 1955.

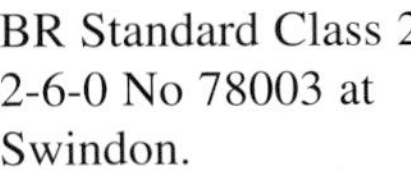

BR Standard Class 2 2-6-0 No 78003 at Swindon.

Summary of year end totals by class – GWR group steam locomotives.

Class	Lowest number	1947	1948	1949	1950	1951	1952	1953	1954	1955	1956	1957	1958	1959	1960	1961	1962	1963	1964	1965	1966	1967
655	1742	21	14	12																		
1000	1000	30	30	30	30	30	30	30	30	30	30	30	30	30	30	30	21	8				
1101	1101	6	6	6	6	6	6	6	6	6	6	6	6	5								
1159	3574	3	3																			
1361	1361	5	5	5	5	5	5	5	5	5	5	5	5	5	5	2						
1366	1366	6	6	6	6	6	6	6	6	6	6	6	6	6	4	3	3	3				
1400	1400	75	75	75	75	75	75	75	75	75	68	61	49	41	32	27	19	12	2			
1500	1500			10	10	10	10	10	10	10	10	10	10	9	9	7	5					
1501	1531	4	2	1	1																	
1600	1600			20	30	50	50	50	55	70	70	70	70	64	55	50	39	33	15	3		
1813	1835	1	1																			
1854	906	36	25	10	2																	
1901	992	44	44	31	25	13	7	3	3	3	2	2										
2021	2021	110	110	100	85	61	38	27	21	9	4	1	1									
2181	2181	10	10	10	8	7	3	3	3													
2251	2200	118	120	120	120	120	120	120	120	120	120	120	119	92	82	73	53	34	15			
2301	2322	54	52	49	47	44	36	12	4	2	1											
2600	2612	12	4																			
2721	2721	44	27	15																		
2800	2800	72	75	83	84	84	84	84	84	84	84	84	78	49	35	34	28	10	1			
2800 (oil burning)	4800	12	9	1																		
2884	2884	75	77	83	83	83	83	83	83	83	83	83	83	83	83	83	82	67	34			
2884 (oil burning)	4850	8	6																			
2900	2902	47	39	31	26	13	4															
3100	3100	5	5	5	5	5	5	5	5	5	5	2	1	1								
3150	3150	33	30	26	23	22	17	15	15	15	13	3										
3252	9054	11	11	4	2																	
3300	3335	45	28	9	8																	
3500	3561	10	7																			
4000	4003	47	46	43	36	20	8	4	3	3	2											
4073	100A1	141	151	161	170	168	168	167	167	167	167	166	165	162	155	152	97	49	12			
4200	4200	91	91	91	91	91	91	91	91	91	91	91	91	76	74	70	54	33	8			
4300	4303	220	212	211	210	204	200	197	197	196	193	194	178	149	122	113	68	35				
4400	4400	11	11	10	10	8	7	4	3													
4500	4500	75	75	75	71	68	63	52	52	39	39	36	28	22	17	11	6	2				
4575	4575	100	100	100	100	100	100	100	100	100	98	93	77	67	40	32	16	11				
4700	4700	9	9	9	9	9	9	9	9	9	9	9	9	9	9	9	6	4				
4900	4900	247	252	255	258	258	258	258	258	258	258	258	258	256	254	246	173	106	50			
4900 (oil burning)	3900	11	6	3																		
5101	4100	149	151	159	157	151	145	143	143	141	140	137	125	119	104	93	71	57	29			
5205	5205	60	60	60	60	60	60	60	60	60	60	60	60	60	60	59	56	32	10			
5400	5400	25	25	25	25	25	25	25	25	25	24	17	14	9	6	5	3					
5600	5600	200	200	200	200	200	200	200	200	200	200	200	200	200	200	200	171	109	57	2		
5700	3600	751	762	772	772	772	772	772	772	772	768	757	728	678	621	563	405	305	166	27		
5800	5800	20	20	20	20	20	20	20	20	20	20	9	5	1	1							
6000	6000	30	30	30	30	30	30	30	30	30	30	30	30	30	30	30						
6100	6100	70	70	70	70	70	70	70	70	70	70	70	69	68	65	65	53	47	31			
6400	6400	40	40	40	40	40	40	40	40	40	40	40	37	28	25	20	13	7				
6700	6700	60	66	70	80	80	80	80	80	80	80	75	56	39	29	23	13	3				
6800	6800	80	80	80	80	80	80	80	80	80	80	80	80	80	79	77	76	71	45			
6959	6959	22	37	48	71	71	71	71	71	71	71	71	71	71	71	71	71	65	43			
7200	7200	54	54	54	54	54	54	54	54	54	54	54	54	54	54	54	52	39	10			
7400	7400	30	40	40	50	50	50	50	50	50	50	50	50	43	41	35	27	18	2			
7800	7800	20	20	20	30	30	30	30	30	30	30	30	30	30	30	30	30	29	19			
8100	8100	10	10	10	10	10	10	10	10	10	10	9	9	9	8	7	5	3	1			
8300	8393	1																				
9000	9000	29	26	26	26	26	26	26	24	22	22	8	6	5								
9300	9300	20	20	20	20	20	20	20	20	20	17	11	4									
9400	3400	10	10	23	76	119	169	180	198	201	210	210	210	181	165	150	108	78	32			
9700	9700	11	11	11	11	11	11	11	11	11	11	11	11	10	10	7	5	3				
AD[1]	190	1																				
AD[2]	666	2	2	2	2	2	2	2	1													
AD[3]	680	1																				
AD[4]	1205	2	2	2	2	1	1	1	1	1												
BM[1]	421	7	6	4	1																	
BM[2]	431	6	6	6	6	5	5	2														
BPGV[1]	2162	5	5	5	5	5	5	4	4	1												
BPGV[2]	2176	1	1	1	1	1	1	1	1													
BPGV[3]	2192	2	2	2	2	1																
BPGV[4]	2194	2	2	2	2	2	2															
BPGV[5]	2196	1	1	1	1	1	1	1	1	1												
BPGV[6]	2197	1	1	1	1	1																
BPGV[7]	2198	1	1	1	1	1	1	1	1	1	1	1	1									
BR[1]	198	4	2																			
BR[2]	238	20	14	9	7																	
BR[3]	783	2	1																			
Cam[1]	844	11	11	11	11	11	9	5														
Cam[2]	1196	2																				
Car[1]	155	1	1	1	1	1	1															
Car[2]	681	4	4	4	4	4	4	3	1													
Car[3]	1338	1	1	1	1	1	1	1	1	1	1	1	1	1	1	1	1					
CMDP	28	2	2	2	2	2	2	1														
Cor	3	2																				
L&L	1308	1																				
LMM[1]	359	1	1	1	1	1	1	1														
LMM[2]	803	1	1	1	1																	
MSWJ	1334	3	3	3	3	3	1	1														
PM[1]	1150	3	3	3	3	3	2	2	2	2	2	2	2	2	2	1	1					
PM[2]	1153	1	1	1	1	1	1	1	1													
PT[1]	184	1																				
PT[2]	1358	1																				
ROD	3002	45	29	29	29	29	29	26	23	20	6	5										
RR[1]	30	5	5	3	1																	
RR[2]	33	3	2	1	1																	
RR[3]	35	10	10	10	10	10	10	9	9	8	4											
RR[4]	52	24	21	19	17	15	10	7	4													
RR[5]	76	2	2	2	1	1	1															
RR[6]	78	4	4	4	4	4	4	4	2													
RR[7]	82	2	2	2	2	2	2	2	1													
RR[8]	90	3	3	3	3	3	3	3														
RR[9]	93	4	4	4	4	4	4	3														
SHT[1]	1140	1	1	1	1	1	1	1	1	1	1	1										
SHT[2]	1141	3	3	3	3	3	2	2	2	2	2	2	2	1								
SHT[3]	1142	1	1	1	1	1	1	1	1	1	1	1	1									
SHT[4]	1144	1	1	1	1	1	1	1	1	1	1	1	1	1								
SHT[5]	1146	2	2	2	2																	
TV[1]	193	3	3	3	3	2	1															
TV[2]	200	41	37	30	25	19	12	10	7													

Class	Lowest number	1947	1948	1949	1950	1951	1952	1953	1954	1955	1956	1957	1958	1959	1960	1961	1962	1963	1964	1965	1966	1967
TV[3]	303	58	58	58	58	58	57	55	52	40	15											
TV[4]	410	2																				
VoR	7	3	3	3	3	3	3	3	3	3	3	3	3	3	3	3	3	3	3	3	3	3
W&C	1331	1	1	1																		
W&L	822	2	2	2	2	2	2	2	2	2	2	2	2	2	2	1						
WCP	5	2	1	1	1	1	1	1														
YTW (service)	1		1	1	1	1	1	1														

Summary of year end totals by class – SR group steam locomotives.

Class	Lowest number	1947	1948	1949	1950	1951	1952	1953	1954	1955	1956	1957	1958	1959	1960	1961	1962	1963	1964	1965	1966	1967
A1 (service)	DS680	1	1	1	1	1	1	1	1	1	1	1	1	1	1	1						
A1X	32635	12	12	12	12	10	10	10	10	10	10	10	10	10	9	9	9					
A1X (service)	DS377	2	2	2	2	2	2	2	2	2	2	2	2	1	1	1	1					
A12	30618	4																				
B1	31013	16	9	3	1																	
B4[1]	30081	25	21	11	11	11	11	11	11	11	11	9	8	4	3	3	3					
B4[2]	32044	7	6	5	4																	
B4X	32043	12	12	12	12																	
BB & WC	34001	70	89	100	109	110	110	110	110	110	110	101	86	80	59	50	50	40	20	14	7	
BB & WC Rebuilt	34001											9	24	30	51	60	60	60	50	40	29	
C	31004	106	106	104	104	104	104	98	96	89	88	85	81	64	53	21	3					
C (service)	DS239																	2	2	2		
C2	32435	3	2	2																		
C2X	32434	45	45	45	45	45	45	45	45	45	45	43	40	38	27	3						
C3	32300	8	7	5	5	1																
C14	30588	2	2	2	2	2	2	2	2	2	2											
C14 (service)	77S	1	1	1	1	1	1	1	1	1	1	1	1									
D	31057	28	28	28	27	18	18	13	10	6												
D1[1]	31145	20	20	20	19	17	17	17	17	17	17	17	17	15	11							
D1[2]	32286	2	1	1	1																	
D1/M	32215	16	7	4																		
D1/M (service)	700S	2	2	1	1																	
D3	32364	28	23	16	16	13	7	1	1													
D3X	32397	1																				
D15	30463	10	10	10	10	8	4	4	2	1												
E	31036	15	15	15	15	3	3	2	1													
E1[1]	31019	11	11	10	8	7	7	7	7	7	7	7	5	4	3							
E1[2]	32097	30	27	21	19	13	11	11	11	11	8	7	6	4	1							
E1R	32094	10	10	10	10	10	10	10	10	9	5	3	3									
E2	32100	10	10	10	10	10	10	10	10	10	10	10	10	10	10	6	2					
E3	32165	16	16	15	15	15	15	15	15	12	9	5	3									
E4	32463	70	70	70	70	70	70	70	70	63	56	50	45	33	28	14	4					
E4X	32466	4	4	4	4	4	4	4	4	3	2	2	1									
E5	32399	24	24	21	21	11	11	7	4	3												
E5X	32401	4	4	4	4	4	4	4	3	1												
E6	32408	10	10	10	10	10	10	10	10	10	10	9	6	6	6	4						
E6X	32407	2	2	2	2	2	2	2	2	2	2	1	1									
EKR	30948	1	1																			
F1	31002	9	4																			
G6	30160	34	28	14	11	10	10	10	10	10	10	10	8	6	3							
G6 (service)	DS682				1	1	1	1	1	1	1	1	1	1	1	1						
G16	30492	4	4	4	4	4	4	4	4	4	4	4	4	2	2	2						
H	31005	64	64	64	64	59	59	59	58	54	54	52	51	40	33	15	7	3				
H1	32037	3	3	3	3																	
H2	32421	6	6	5	5	5	5	5	5	5	1	1										
H15	30330	26	26	26	26	26	26	26	26	24	23	20	18	10	9							
H16	30516	5	5	5	5	5	5	5	5	5	5	5	5	5	5	5						
I1X	32001	18	8	8	8																	
I3	32021	26	26	26	18	1																
J	31595	5	5	4	2																	
J1	32325	1	1	1	1																	
J2	32326	1	1	1	1																	
K	32337	17	17	17	17	17	17	17	17	17	17	17	17	17	17	17						
K10	30135	31	23	8	2																	
KESR	30949	1	1	1																		
L	31760	22	22	22	22	22	22	22	22	22	20	20	18	10	8							
L1	31753	15	15	15	15	15	15	15	15	15	15	15	15	13	10	1						
L11	30134	40	40	34	28	6																
L12	30415	20	20	20	20	2	2	1	1													
LN	30850	16	16	16	16	16	16	16	16	16	16	16	16	16	16	10						
M7	30021	104	103	103	103	103	103	103	103	103	103	99	91	75	69	49	35	14				
MN	35001	20	28	30	30	30	30	30	30	30	24	15	10									
MN Rebuilt	35001										6	15	20	30	30	30	30	30	23	16	10	
N	31400	80	80	80	80	80	80	80	80	80	80	80	80	80	80	80	78	53	12	6		
N1	31822	6	6	6	6	6	6	6	6	6	6	6	6	6	6	6						
N15	30448	74	74	74	74	74	74	73	73	69	63	55	52	35	26	12						
N15X	32327	7	7	7	7	7	7	7	7	5	1											
O1	31003	55	44	25	23	8	8	8	8	8	8	8	7	4	2							
O2	30177	48	48	48	48	48	48	43	43	39	37	35	33	29	27	23	18	18	16	14	10	
P	31027	8	8	8	8	8	8	8	8	7	7	6	5	5	2							
Q	30530	20	20	20	20	20	20	20	20	20	20	20	20	20	20	20	17	13	3			
Q1	33001	40	40	40	40	40	40	40	40	40	40	40	40	40	40	40	40	27	7	3		
R	31658	15	15	14	14	11	6	3	2													
R1[1]	31010	13	13	12	12	12	12	12	12	10	10	10	7	2								
R1[2]	31696	13	13	11	10	7	4	3	2	1												
S	31685	1	1	1	1																	
S11	30395	10	10	10	10	1	1	1														
S15	30496	45	45	45	45	45	45	45	45	45	45	45	45	45	45	45	41	23	6			
T	31602	2	2	2	1																	
T (service)	500S	1	1																			
T1	30001	14	9	4	3																	
T9	30113	66	66	66	66	46	38	37	36	36	35	31	24	14	13	1	1					
T14	30443	9	6	4	2																	
U	31610	50	50	50	50	50	50	50	50	50	50	50	50	50	50	50	48	34	10	4		
U1	31890	21	21	21	21	21	21	21	21	21	21	21	21	21	21	21	4					
USA	30061	14	14	14	14	14	14	14	14	14	14	14	14	14	14	14	8	7	6	6	6	
USA (service)	DS233																3	6	6	4	4	
V	30900	40	40	40	40	40	40	40	40	40	40	40	40	40	40	25						
W	31911	15	15	15	15	15	15	15	15	15	15	15	15	15	15	15	15	5				
Z	30950	8	8	8	8	8	8	8	8	8	8	8	8	8	8	8						
700	30306	30	30	30	30	30	30	30	30	30	30	29	29	28	27	17						
756	30756	1	1	1	1																	
757	30757	2	2	2	2	2	2	2	2	2	1											
1302	31302	1	1																			
0298	30585	3	3	3	3	3	3	3	3	3	3	3	3	3	3	3						

Class	Lowest number	1947	1948	1949	1950	1951	1952	1953	1954	1955	1956	1957	1958	1959	1960	1961	1962	1963	1964	1965	1966	1967
0330	KESR 4	1																				
0395	30564	18	18	18	17	17	17	14	14	14	9	5	2									
0415	30582	3	3	3	3	3	3	3	3	3	3	3	3	3	3							
0458	30458	1	1	1	1	1	1	1														

Summary of year end totals by class – LMS group steam locomotives.

Class	Lowest number	1947	1948	1949	1950	1951	1952	1953	1954	1955	1956	1957	1958	1959	1960	1961	1962	1963	1964	1965	1966	1967
0F[1]	41509	3	3	3	3	3	3	3	3	1	1	1										
0F[1] (service)	41509	1	1																			
0F[2]	41528	10	10	10	10	10	10	10	10	10	10	8	8	8	8	5	5	3	2	2		
0F[3]	47000	5	5	5	5	5	5	9	10	10	10	10	10	10	10	10	10	9	4	4		
0F[4]	51202	23	23	23	23	23	23	23	23	23	22	19	16	15	13	10	4	1				
0F[5]	56010	14	14	14	12	12	12	12	12	11	11	10	9	7	3	3						
0P	55051	2	2	2	2	2	2	2	2	2	1											
1F[1]	41660	95	85	80	78	69	64	55	50	41	32	24	22	15	11	11	9	7	5	5		
1F[2]	47862	2	2	2	2	2	2	1	1	1												
1F[3]	51535	5	5	5	5	5	5	4	4	4	3	3	3	1	1							
1P[1]	46601	43	30	21	18	15	12	4	2													
1P[2]	58020	1	1	1																		
1P[3]	58021	1																				
1P[4]	58022	1	1																			
1P[5]	58030	9	8	5	1	1	1	1														
1P[6]	58039	56	48	45	38	32	28	19	17	12	5	4	3	1								
1P[7]	58092	1	1	1	1	1																
2F[1]	47160	10	10	10	10	10	10	10	10	10	10	10	10	8	7	7	5	2				
2F[2]	51307	96	90	79	79	79	79	76	70	61	45	31	25	16	10	3						
2F[2] (service)	11304	5	5	5	5	5	5	5	5	5	5	5	5	5	4	3	3	1				
2F[3]	52016	25	20	19	14	11	9	8	6	3	1	1	1									
2F[4]	56151	23	23	23	23	23	23	23	23	23	23	23	19	11	8	1						
2F[5]	57230	238	219	198	188	174	165	154	154	150	144	140	134	118	115	58	16					
2F[6]	58110	1	1	1	1																	
2F[7]	58111	3	3	1																		
2F[8]	58114	96	92	91	87	84	81	76	70	60	51	43	41	34	23	12	3	1				
2F[9]	58188	109	92	84	79	70	65	62	54	48	40	33	29	19	10	3						
2F[10]	58320	46	28	25	20	18	10															
2F[11]	58362	75	50	43	31	25	17	9	7													
2F[12]	58850	15	14	14	14	14	13	11	10	8	5	2	1	1								
2F[13]	58870	1																				
2F[14]	58880	64	41	33	26	21	16	15	5	1	1	1										
2F[15] (service)	CD3	5	5	5	5	5	5	5	4	4	4	3	3									
2P[1]	40322	5	5	5	5	4	4	2	2	2												
2P[2]	40332	160	156	138	125	113	98	86	77	69	59	41	34	22	16	3						
2P[3]	40563	136	136	136	136	136	136	136	135	135	135	134	134	91	81	15						
2P[4]	41900	10	10	10	10	10	10	10	10	10	10	10	10	1	1	1						
2P[5]	41910	17	16	10	9	3	2															
2P[6]	46762	1	1	1	1	1																
2P[7]	46876	15	9	5	5	2	1															
2P[8]	50621	109	100	88	78	70	47	39	37	29	23	20	7	4	3							
2P[8] (misc.)	10897	1	1	1	1	1	1	1	1	1												
2P[9]	54363	1																				
2P[10]	54379	2	1	1																		
2P[11]	54397	10	7	4	2	2	1															
2P[12]	55116	26	22	22	19	16	9	6	5	4	4	3	2	2	2							
2P[13]	55159	76	74	72	69	66	63	59	58	53	51	50	44	43	42	6						
2P[14]	55237	4	4	4	4	4	4	4	4	4	4	4	4	4	4							
2P[15]	55260	10	10	10	10	10	10	10	10	10	10	10	10	10	10	2						
2MT[1]	41200	10	30	60	90	100	130	130	130	130	130	130	130	130	130	130	109	91	65	39	8	
2MT[2]	46400	20	35	35	65	95	115	128	128	128	128	128	128	128	128	127	115	111	103	82	42	
3F[1]	41980	14	14	14	14	14	14	14	14	14	14	14	11	1	1	1						
3F[2]	43137	11	11	11	11	11	11	11	11	11	11	10	10	6	1							
3F[3]	43191	324	319	317	314	312	309	302	295	275	259	240	218	145	100	54	7	3				
3F[4]	43765	63	60	59	52	47	44	40	36	30	28	24	21	16	12	6						
3F[5]	47200	60	60	60	60	60	60	60	58	54	50	44	40	31	26	18	13	11	4	3		
3F[6]	47260	412	417	417	417	417	417	417	417	417	417	417	417	392	344	310	235	195	146	83	4	
3F[7]	52088	245	233	221	219	191	184	166	150	136	118	89	75	58	32	16						
3F[8]	52494	6	6	6	5	5	5	5	5	5	3											
3F[9]	52528	37	31	26	25	22	17	11	7	2	2											
3F[10]	56230	147	145	145	145	145	144	141	140	138	124	109	79	48	28	9						
3F[11]	56905	1																				
3F[12]	57550	76	71	68	68	68	68	68	68	68	67	65	63	58	53	37	10					
3F[13]	57629	17	13	13	13	13	13	13	13	13	13	13	13	12	12	8	2					
3F[14]	57650	29	29	29	29	29	29	29	29	29	29	29	29	29	29	22	8					
3F[15]	57693	7	7	4	3	1																
3P[1]	40711	22	17	10	8	3																
3P[2]	41928	51	51	51	51	32	28	28	28	23	14	14	13	3								
3P[3]	50835	14	7	6	2	1																
3P[4]	54434	1																				
3P[5]	54438	22	22	22	22	22	21	18	16	7	7	1										
3P[6]	54461	48	48	48	48	48	48	47	47	47	47	47	47	31	23	8						
3P[7]	58010	1	1																			
3P[8]	58011	3																				
3MT[1]	40001	70	70	70	70	70	70	70	70	70	70	70	70	38	29	7						
3MT[2]	40071	139	139	139	139	139	139	139	139	139	139	139	139	129	128	72						
4F[1]	43835	192	192	192	192	192	192	192	191	186	178	159	156	120	112	97	77	56	21			
4F[2]	44027	580	580	580	580	580	580	580	580	580	580	580	580	536	495	472	396	261	107	11		
4F[3]	48801	3	1	1																		
4F[4]	57950	6	5	5	4	3																
4P[1]	40900	195	195	195	195	195	189	176	153	116	89	55	19	6	2							
4P[2]	41000	45	37	32	28	11	1															
4P[3]	54630	23	17	14	12	7	3															
4P[4]	54764	2	1	1																		
4P[5]	55350	10	8	7	6	5	1															
4P[6]	58000	6	2																			
4MT[1]	42050	130	176	206	260	277	277	277	277	277	277	277	277	277	277	274	231	201	144	90	42	
4MT[2]	42300	125	125	125	125	125	125	125	125	125	125	125	125	120	109	87	50	34	14	2		
4MT[3]	42425	206	206	206	206	206	206	206	206	206	206	206	206	206	204	187	144	115	64	26	15	
4MT[4]	42500	37	37	37	37	37	37	37	37	37	37	37	37	37	36	29						
4MT[5]	43000	3	23	50	97	155	162	162	162	162	162	162	162	162	162	162	162	156	141	99	65	6
5P	50412	7	5	2	1																	
5MT[1]	42700	245	245	245	245	245	245	245	245	245	245	245	245	245	245	242	181	129	75	27	2	
5MT[2]	42945	40	40	40	40	40	40	40	40	40	40	40	40	40	40	40	40	36	27	16	1	
5MT[3]	44658	742	782	814	840	842	842	842	842	842	842	842	842	842	842	841	820	791	724	627	456	151
5XP	46004	1	1																			
6F[1]	47875	9	5	5	3	1	1															
6F[2]	48892	123	85	48	25	14	5	2	1													

Class	Lowest number	1947	1948	1949	1950	1951	1952	1953	1954	1955	1956	1957	1958	1959	1960	1961	1962	1963	1964	1965	1966	1967
6F³	52727	12	11	5	1																	
6P5F¹	45500	44	35	34	34	34	34	34	34	34	34	34	34	34	32	24						
6P5F²	45552	189	189	189	189	189	188	188	188	188	188	188	188	188	187	184	143	112	48	15	8	
7F¹	47930	14	7	4	1																	
7F²	48893	319	319	273	242	221	215	215	212	212	207	168	155	96	91	62	3	3				
7F³	49395	60	60	60	60	60	60	60	60	60	60	60	60	41	41	26	6	3				
7F⁴	49500	175	175	114	77	53	47	43	41	38	32	20	20	9	5	1						
7F⁵	52841	17	13	10	3																	
7F⁶	53800	11	11	11	11	11	11	11	11	11	11	11	11	10	9	7	5	4				
7P¹	45512	8	17	18	18	18	18	18	18	18	18	18	18	18	18	17	16	11	3			
7P²	45735	2	2	2	2	2	2	2	2	2	2	2	2	2	2	2	2	2				
7P³	46100	27	24	18	12	10	7	3	1													
7P³ Rebuilt	46100	44	47	53	59	61	64	68	70	71	71	71	71	71	71	71	41	26	5			
8F	48000	556	624	663	663	663	663	663	663	663	663	666	666	666	665	665	661	663	638	543	381	150
8P¹	46200	13	13	13	13	13	13	13	12	12	12	12	12	12	12	6						
8P²	46220	37	38	38	38	38	38	38	38	38	38	38	38	38	38	38	35	22				
0-10-0	58100	1	1	1	1	1	1	1	1	1												
Garratt	47967	33	33	33	33	33	33	33	33	26	13	1										
Crane	58865	1	1	1	1																	
NG¹	Wren	1	1	1	1	1	1	1	1	1	1	1	1	1	1	1						
NG²	10	1	1	1	1	1	1	1	1													
Rail Motor¹	50617	1																				
Rail Motor²	29988	1																				
Sentinel¹	47180	4	4	4	4	4	4	3	3	2												
Sentinel²	47184	1	1	1	1	1	1	1	1													
Sentinel³	47190	2	2	2	2	2	2	2	2	2	2	2	2	1	1							

Summary of year end totals by class – LNER group steam locomotives.

Class	Lowest number	1947	1948	1949	1950	1951	1952	1953	1954	1955	1956	1957	1958	1959	1960	1961	1962	1963	1964	1965	1966	1967
A1	60114		21	49	49	49	49	49	49	49	49	49	49	49	49	49	43	37	26	2		
A1/1	60113	1	1	1	1	1	1	1	1	1	1	1	1	1	1	1						
A2	60525	1	15	15	15	15	15	15	15	15	15	15	15	15	15	15	7	5	5	3		
A2/1	60507	4	4	4	4	4	4	4	4	4	4	4	4	4	1							
A2/2	60501	6	6	6	6	6	6	6	6	6	6	6	6	4	3							
A2/3	60500	15	15	15	15	15	15	15	15	15	15	15	15	15	15	15	7	3	3			
A3	60035	77	78	78	78	78	78	78	78	78	78	78	78	77	77	71	59	26	3	1		
A4	60001	34	34	34	34	34	34	34	34	34	34	34	34	34	34	34	29	19	12	6		
A5	69800	43	43	43	43	43	43	43	43	43	43	41	18	10								
A6	69791	9	8	8	6	1	1															
A7	69770	20	20	20	20	19	17	17	10	6	3											
A8	69850	45	45	45	45	45	45	45	45	45	45	43	26	21								
A10	60068	1																				
B1	61000	274	342	360	383	402	409	409	409	409	409	409	409	409	409	408	288	226	172	91	27	
B1 (service)	17																	8	7	8	4	2
B2	61603	9	9	10	10	10	10	10	10	10	10	10	7									
B3	61497	1	1																			
B4	61482	4	3	1																		
B5	61680	7	3	1																		
B7	61360	38	18	4																		
B8	61353	5	2																			
B9	61469	4	2																			
B12/1	61500	13	13	12	11	10	7	2														
B12/3	61509	50	48	47	47	44	44	44	44	42	42	25	16	1	1							
B12/4	61500	9	8	8	7	6	4															
B13 (service)	61699	1	1	1	1																	
B16/1	61400	47	46	45	45	45	45	45	45	45	45	45	44	38	26							
B16/2	61406	7	7	7	7	7	7	7	7	7	7	7	7	7	7	7	7	5				
B16/3	61403	15	16	17	17	17	17	17	17	17	17	17	17	17	17	17	15	8				
B17/1, B17/4	61600	60	53	43	34	28	26	21	18	12	11	7	3	1								
B17/5	61659	2	2	1	1																	
B17/6	61600	2	9	19	28	35	36	39	42	48	49	53	38	16								
C1	62808	17	10	5																		
C4	62903	20	14	6																		
C6	62933	2																				
C7	62954	14																				
C12	67350	49	43	40	40	38	37	33	32	20	17	16	1	1								
C13	67400	40	40	40	40	40	39	36	29	24	16	10	1	1								
C14	67440	12	12	12	12	12	12	12	12	12	12	4	3	1								
C15	67452	30	30	30	30	30	29	27	14	9	2	2	2	2								
C16	67482	21	21	21	21	21	21	21	21	19	16	16	16	11	3							
D1	62203	7	5	4																		
D2	62150	31	21	6	1																	
D3	62000	19	13	5	1																	
D9	62300	26	26	7																		
D10	62650	10	10	10	10	10	10	6	3													
D11	62660	35	35	35	35	35	35	35	35	35	35	35	33	24	14	1						
D15	62501	13	12	12	10	5																
D16/2	62542	16	10	4	3	1																
D16/3	62510	88	89	94	94	94	92	90	90	75	67	39	17	4								
D17	62111	2																				
D20	62340	50	48	47	47	28	28	27	17	14	7											
D29	62400	12	9	5	3	2																
D30	62417	25	25	25	25	24	24	24	24	24	24	16	6	2								
D31	62059	7	4	3	2	1																
D32	62443	10	2	1	1																	
D33	62455	10	9	7	7	3	1															
D34	62467	30	30	28	27	27	27	27	27	27	27	27	26	14	6	1						
D40	62260	18	18	18	18	18	18	15	15	6	2	1										
D41	62225	22	21	19	16	9	3															
D49/1	62700	34	34	34	34	34	34	34	34	34	34	32	22	12	9							
D49/2	62726	41	41	41	41	41	41	41	41	41	41	36	16	10	5							
D49/4	62768	1	1	1	1	1																
E4	62780	18	18	18	18	18	18	18	16	10	5	3	1									
F1	67097	3	2																			
F2	67104	9	7	2																		
F3	67114	15	8	5	1	1	1															
F4	67151	37	26	26	23	12	8	4	3	1												
F5	67188	30	32	32	32	32	32	32	32	18	12	5										
F6	67220	22	20	20	20	20	20	20	20	10	6	5										
F7	67093	2																				
G5	67240	110	109	109	107	102	95	88	80	59	42	22										
J1	65002	11	11	11	11	10	5	2														
J2	65015	9	9	9	8	8	8	2														
J3	64105	33	29	26	25	14	7	3														

Class	Lowest number	1947	1948	1949	1950	1951	1952	1953	1954	1955	1956	1957	1958	1959	1960	1961	1962	1963	1964	1965	1966	1967
J4	64109	8	7	5	2																	
J5	65480	20	20	20	20	20	20	10	3													
J6	64170	110	110	110	110	110	110	110	110	107	107	105	75	40	23	7						
J10	65126	78	77	77	75	75	60	53	53	53	37	35	15	4	2							
J11	64280	174	174	174	174	174	174	174	171	146	136	117	100	76	56	30						
J15	65350	127	114	92	80	65	62	62	62	59	53	52	41	26	14	11						
J17	65500	89	89	89	89	89	89	89	86	78	78	75	58	41	20	12						
J19	64640	35	35	35	35	35	35	35	35	35	35	35	34	22	13	4						
J20	64675	25	25	25	25	25	25	25	25	25	25	25	25	22	13	5						
J21	65025	83	75	56	43	29	28	27	15	12	11	9	5	4	2	1						
J24	65600	34	28	21	9																	
J25	65645	76	74	66	59	54	53	52	39	38	36	34	23	15	11	8						
J26	65730	50	50	50	50	50	50	50	50	50	50	50	44	25	24	14						
J27	65780	115	115	115	115	115	115	115	115	115	115	115	115	94	93	91	79	61	55	44	26	
J35	64460	70	70	70	70	70	70	70	70	70	70	70	64	44	34	14						
J36	65210	123	118	118	114	104	96	96	96	95	93	87	86	82	75	67	32	11	9	8	3	
J37	64536	104	104	104	104	104	104	104	104	104	104	104	104	101	100	95	67	47	25	17	4	
J38	65900	35	35	35	35	35	35	35	35	35	35	35	35	35	35	35	33	31	25	21	3	
J39	64700	289	289	289	289	289	289	289	289	289	289	289	289	241	178	128						
J50	68890	102	102	102	102	102	102	102	102	102	102	102	99	87	67	29	12					
J50 (service)	10															2	7	7	7			
J52	68757	132	132	132	127	126	122	113	97	65	45	27	7	3	2							
J52 (service)	1	1	1	1	2	2	2	2	2	2	2	2	2	2	2							
J55	68317	1																				
J55 (service)	68319	1	1	1																		
J60	68366	2																				
J62	68200	3	3	1	1																	
J63	68204	7	7	7	7	7	7	6	6	4	1											
J65	68211	4	3	2	2	2	2	1	1	1												
J66	68370	18	18	18	14	9	3	3	1													
J66 (service)	31	2	2	2	1	1	3	3	3	3	3	3	3	1	1	1						
J67	68490	45	44	44	39	36	34	34	30	20	11	7										
J68	68638	29	29	29	29	29	29	29	29	29	29	29	22	10	3							
J69	68490	89	90	90	95	98	100	96	96	95	92	87	62	43	29	11						
J69 (service)	43													2	2	2						
J70	68216	11	11	10	10	9	8	4	4													
J71	68230	81	80	80	76	71	67	64	58	49	39	30	23	14	4							
J72	68670	85	85	100	105	113	113	113	113	113	113	113	108	100	78	34	18	4				
J72 (service)	58																		2	2	1	
J73	68355	10	10	10	10	10	10	10	10	9	9	8	5	3								
J75	68365	1	1																			
J77	68390	46	43	42	40	38	38	37	32	28	21	16	7	5	1							
J83	68442	39	39	39	39	39	39	39	39	39	34	32	21	18	16	11						
J88	68320	35	35	35	35	35	35	35	34	33	32	31	20	16	10	7						
J92 (service)	68667	3	3	3	2	2																
J93	68484	3	1																			
J94	68006	75	75	75	75	75	75	75	75	75	75	75	75	75	69	66	45	24	13	3	2	
K1	62001			61	70	70	70	70	70	70	70	70	70	70	70	70	67	60	48	31	24	
K1/1	61997	1	1	1	1	1	1	1	1	1	1	1	1	1	1							
K2	61720	75	75	75	75	75	75	75	75	74	70	62	56	24	10	2						
K3	61800	192	192	192	192	192	192	192	192	192	192	192	192	180	163	121						
K4	61993	5	5	5	5	5	5	5	5	5	5	5	5	5	5							
K5	61863	1	1	1	1	1	1	1	1	1	1	1	1	1								
L1	67701	1	60	75	100	100	100	100	100	100	100	100	100	100	88	64						
L2	69070	2																				
L3	69050	19	19	15	12	7	7	6	3													
M2	69076	2																				
N1	69430	55	55	55	55	54	52	49	41	21	13	9	7									
N2	69490	107	107	107	107	107	107	107	107	106	105	95	81	47	32	13						
N4	69225	22	22	19	16	16	11	9														
N5/2	69250	120	120	119	119	118	118	118	115	88	65	49	35	19								
N5/3	69311	1	1	1	1	1																
N7	69600	134	134	134	134	134	134	134	134	134	134	133	122	82	37	9						
N8	69371	30	29	23	19	16	9	8	7	1												
N9	69410	17	16	12	6	4	4	3	3													
N10	69090	20	19	19	19	19	19	19	19	18	16	9	6	4	4	3						
N12	69089	1																				
N13	69110	10	9	9	9	9	6	5	4	1												
N14	69120	3	3	3	2	2	2	2														
N15	69126	99	99	99	99	99	99	99	99	99	99	96	75	54	30	21						
O1	63571	51	53	58	58	58	58	58	58	58	58	58	58	58	58	58	30	18	10			
O2	63921	67	66	66	66	66	66	66	66	66	66	66	66	66	62	56	40					
O3	63475	17	15	15	14	4																
O4/1, O4/6	63571	213	212	209	209	209	202	197	191	179	163	145	130	96	92	83	34	20	13	1		
O4/5	63579	8	7	6	6	6	6	6	6	4	4	3	2									
O4/7	63570	41	41	40	40	40	40	40	40	40	39	35	34	27	24	18	7	4	3			
O4/8	63573	16	16	16	16	16	18	23	29	43	60	83	99	99	99	95	75	64	41	12		
O6	63554	68																				
O7	63000	200	200																			
Q1	69925	13	13	13	13	13	13	13	12	12	10	10	5									
Q4	63200	34	34	25	13																	
Q5	63250	77	58	32	10																	
Q6	63340	120	120	120	120	120	120	120	120	120	120	120	120	120	119	118	118	85	62	40	17	
Q7	63460	15	15	15	15	15	15	15	15	15	15	15	15	15	15	15						
S1	69900	6	6	6	6	6	6	6	5	5	2											
T1	69910	13	13	13	13	13	13	13	13	11	10	7	6	1	1							
U1	69999	1	1	1	1	1	1	1	1													
V1	67600	78	78	78	78	78	72	62	59	57	48	42	34	28	20	16						
V2	60800	184	184	184	184	184	184	184	184	184	184	184	184	184	184	184	115	72	40	14		
V3	67600	14	14	14	14	14	20	30	33	35	44	50	58	64	70	66	26	13				
V4	61700	2	2	2	2	2	2	2	2	2	2											
W1	60700	1	1	1	1	1	1	1	1	1	1	1	1									
Y1	68130	15	15	15	15	14	12	11	6	5	5	3	2									
Y1 (service)	4	9	7	7	7	7	7	7	7	6	4	4	4	2	2	1	1					
Y3	68154	28	26	25	24	18	17	13	11	6	3	1										
Y3 (service)	3	3	5	5	6	7	7	7	7	8	10	10	9	6	4	3	3	2				
Y4	68125	4	4	4	4	4	4	4	4	3	1											
Y4 (service)	33	1	1	1	1	1	1	1	1	1	1	1	1	1	1	1	1					
Y5 (service)	68081	1																				
Y6	68082	2	2	2	2	1																
Y7	68088	2	1	1	1	1																
Y7 (service)	34		1	1	1	1																
Y8	68090	2	1	1	1	1	1	1														
Y8 (service)	55								1	1												
Y9	68092	33	33	33	33	33	33	30	26	19	18	16	11	9	6	4						
Y10	68186	2	1	1	1	1																
Z4	68190	2	2	2	2	2	2	2	2	2	2	2	2	1								
Z5	68192	2	2	2	2	2	2	2	2	2	1	1	1	1								
Railcar	2136	1																				

Summary of year end totals by class – BR standard and Austerity steam locomotives.

Class	Lowest number	1947	1948	1949	1950	1951	1952	1953	1954	1955	1956	1957	1958	1959	1960	1961	1962	1963	1964	1965	1966	1967
2MT[1]	78000						4	12	45	55	65	65	65	65	65	65	65	64	60	43	12	
2MT[2]	84000							20	20	20	20	30	30	30	30	30	30	29	20			
3MT[1]	77000								20	20	20	20	20	20	20	20	20	20	20	19	3	
3MT[2]	82000						20	20	32	45	45	45	45	45	45	45	45	45	35	14	2	
4MT[1]	75000					16	20	45	50	63	68	80	80	80	80	80	80	80	78	67	46	10
4MT[2]	76000						10	35	45	60	79	115	115	115	115	115	115	115	108	92	40	
4MT[3]	80000					17	54	72	108	131	151	155	155	155	155	155	154	154	123	79	25	
5MT	73000					29	30	50	75	119	149	172	172	172	172	172	172	172	156	115	76	23
6P5F	72000					2	10	10	10	10	10	10	10	10	10	10	5	5	5	2		
7P6F	70000					25	38	45	55	55	55	55	55	55	55	55	55	55	55	53	42	1
8P	71000								1	1	1	1	1	1	1	1						
9F	92000								32	70	115	172	233	248	251	251	251	251	235	170	125	18
WD[1]	90000		533	733	733	733	733	733	733	733	733	733	733	732	730	730	650	553	428	227	123	
WD[2]	90750		25	25	25	25	25	25	25	25	25	25	25	25	25	22						

LMS Stanier 'Black Five' 4-6-0 No 45389 at Ferryhill in July 1954.

GCR Robinson 'C13' class 4-4-2T No 67434 at Penistone Station on a Barnsley train in April 1950.

Appendix 2. Chronological List of Classes (listed by Railway Company).

Dates marked with an asterisk are rebuilding dates.

Great Western Railway Group

Alexandra Docks & Railway

1886	AD[3]	680	0-6-0ST	Peckett
1908	AD[1]	190	0-6-2ST	Andrew Barclay
1917	AD[2]	666	0-6-0T	Kerr Stuart
1920	AD[4]	1205	2-6-2T	Hawthorn Leslie

Barry Railway

1888	BR[1]	198	0-6-2T	Hosgood 'B'
1889	BR[3]	783	0-6-0T	Hosgood 'D'
1890	BR[2]	238	0-6-2T	Hosgood 'B1'

Brecon & Merthyr Railway

1909	BM[1]	421	0-6-2T	Dunbar 4ft 6in
1915	BM[2]	431	0-6-2T	Dunbar 5ft

Burry Port & Gwendraeth Valley Railway

1900	BPGV[3]	2192	0-6-0ST	Carr
1903	BPGV[4]	2194	0-6-0ST	Eager
1906	BPGV[5]	2196	0-6-0ST	Avonside Engine
1907	BPGV[2]	2176	0-6-0ST	Avonside Engine
1909	BPGV[1]	2162	0-6-0T	Hudswell Clarke
1909	BPGV[6]	2197	0-6-0T	Hudswell Clarke
1910	BPGV[7]	2198	0-6-0T	Hudswell Clarke

Cambrian Railways

1866	Cam[2]	1196	2-4-0T	Sharp Stewart
1903	Cam[1]	844	0-6-0	Jones '15'

Cardiff Railway

1898	Car[3]	1338	0-4-0ST	Kitson
1908	Car[1]	155	0-6-2T	Ree
1920	Car[2]	681	0-6-0PT	Hope

Cleobury Mortimer & Ditton Priors Light Railway

1908	CMDP	28	0-6-0PT	Manning Wardle

Corris Railway

1878	Cor	3	0-4-2ST	Falcon (Narrow Gauge)
1921	Cor	4	0-4-2ST	Kerr Stuart (Narrow Gauge)

Liskeard & Looe Railway

1902	L&L	1308	2-4-0T	Andrew Barclay

Llanelly & Mynydd Mawr Railway

1911	LMM[2]	803	0-6-0T	Hudswell Clarke
1917	LMM[1]	359	0-6-0ST	Hudswell Clarke

Midland & South Western Junction Railway

1894	MSWJ	1334	2-4-0	Dübs

Port Talbot Railway & Docks Co.

1898	PT[1]	184	0-6-2T	Stephenson
1902	PT[2]	1358	0-8-2T	Sharp Stewart

Powlesland & Mason, Swansea Docks

1903	PM[2]	1153	0-4-0T	Hawthorn Leslie
1907	PM[1]	1150	0-4-0T	Peckett

Railway Operating Division of the Royal Engineers

1917	ROD	3002	2-8-0	Robinson

Rhymney Railway

1904	RR[2]	33	0-6-2T	Jenkins'M'
1907	RR[1]	30	0-6-2T	Hurry Riches 'R'
1908	RR[5]	76	0-6-2T	Hurry Riches 'P1'
1908	RR[7]	82	0-6-2T	Hurry Riches 'P'
1908	RR[9]	93	0-6-0T	Hurry Riches 'S'
1910	RR[4]	52	0-6-2T	Hurry Riches 'A'
1920	RR[8]	90	0-6-0T	Hurry Riches 'S1'
1921	RR[3]	35	0-6-2T	Hurry Riches 'R1'
1921	RR[6]	78	0-6-2T	Hudswell Clarke 'AP'

Shropshire & Montgomery Railway

1893	S&M	1	0-4-2WT	'Gazelle'

Swansea Harbour Trust Railways

1905	SHT[1]	1140	0-4-0ST	Barclay
1906	SHT[2]	1141	0-4-0ST	Peckett
1909	SHT[4]	1144	0-4-0ST	Hawthorn Leslie
1911	SHT[3]	1142	0-4-0ST	Hudswell Clarke
1912	SHT[5]	1146	0-6-0ST	Peckett

Taff Vale Railway

1884	TV[1]	193	0-6-0T	Hurry Riches 'H'
1902	TV[4]	410	0-6-2T	Hurry Riches 'O3'
1907	TV[2]	200	0-6-2T	Hurry Riches 'O4'
1914	TV[3]	303	0-6-2T	Cameron 'A'

Vale of Rheidol Railway

1923	VoR	7	2-6-2T	Swindon (Narrow Gauge)

Welshpool & Llanfair Light Railway

1902	W&L	822	0-6-0T	Beyer Peacock (Narrow Gauge)

Weston, Clevedon & Portishead Railway

1872	WCP	5	0-6-0T	Stroudley 'Terrier'

Whitland & Cardigan Railway

1877	W&C	1331	0-6-0T	Fox Walker

Ystalyfera Tin Works

1900	YTW	1	0-4-0ST	Peckett

Great Western Railway

1872	1501	1531	0-6-0PT	Armstrong Wolverhampton 4ft 7½in
1874	1901	992	0-6-0PT	Dean & Armstrong Wolverhampton 4ft 1½in
1882	1813	1835	0-6-0PT	Dean Swindon ex Side Tank 4ft 7½in
1883	2301	2322	0-6-0	Dean Goods
1890	1854	906	0-6-0PT	Dean Swindon 4ft 7½in
1892	655	1742	0-6-0PT	Dean Wolverhampton 4ft 7½in
1895	1159	3574	0-4-2T	Armstrong
1895	3252	9054	4-4-0	Dean 'Duke'
1897	2021	2021	0-6-0PT	Dean Wolverhampton 4ft 1½in
1897	2181	2181	0-6-0PT	Dean 2021 with modified brakes
1897	2721	2721	0-6-0PT	Dean Swindon 4ft 7½in
1899	3300	3335	4-4-0	Dean & Churchward 'Bulldog'
1899	3500	3561	2-4-0T	Dean 'Metropolitan Tank'
1900	2600	2612	2-6-0	Dean 'Aberdare'
1902	2900	2902	4-6-0	Churchward 'Saint'
1903	2800	2800	2-8-0	Churchward
1903	City	3440	4-4-0	Churchward 'City'
1904	4400	4400	2-6-2T	Churchward 4ft 1½in
1906	3150	3150	2-6-2T	Churchward 5ft 8in
1906	4000	4000	4-6-0	Churchward 'Star'
1906	4500	4500	2-6-2T	Churchward 4ft 7½in
1910	1361	1361	0-6-0ST	Churchward
1910	4200	4200	2-8-0T	Churchward
1911	4300	4303	2-6-0	Churchward
1919	4700	4700	2-8-0	Churchward
1923	4073	100A1	4-6-0	Collett 'Castle'
1923	5205	5205	2-8-0T	Collett 4200 with enlarged cylinders
1924	5600	5600	0-6-2T	Collett
1926	1101	1101	0-4-0T	Collett & Avonside Dock Shunters
1927	4575	4575	2-6-2T	Collett Modified 4500
1927	6000	6000	4-6-0	Collett 'King'
1928	4900	4900	4-6-0	Collett 'Hall'
1928 *	8300	8393	2-6-0	Modified Churchward design with ballast weights fitted
1929	5700	3600	0-6-0PT	Collett 4ft 7½in
1929	5101	4100	2-6-2T	Churchward & Collett 5ft 8in
1930	2251	2200	0-6-0	Collett
1930	6700	6700	0-6-0PT	Collett 5700 class without vacuum brakes
1931	5400	5400	0-6-0PT	Collett 5ft 2in
1931	6100	6100	2-6-2T	Collett
1932	1400	1400	0-4-2T	Collett Motor Fitted
1932	6400	6400	0-6-0PT	Collett 4ft 7½in
1932	9300	9300	2-6-0	Modified Churchward design with ballast weights fitted
1933	5800	5800	0-4-2T	Collett Non-motor fitted
1933	9700	9700	0-6-0PT	Collett 5700 class with condensing apparatus
1934	1366	1366	0-6-0PT	Collett
1934 *	7200	7200	2-8-2T	Collett 4200/5205 rebuilds
1936	6800	6800	4-6-0	Collett 'Grange'
1936	7400	7400	0-6-0PT	Collett Non motor fitted
1936 *	9000	9000	4-4-0	Collett 'DukeDog' or 'Earl'
1938	2884	2884	2-8-0	Collett Modified 2800 class
1938 *	3100	3100	2-6-2T	Collett 3150 rebuilds 5ft 3in
1938	7800	7800	4-6-0	Collett 'Manor'
1938	8100	8100	2-6-2T	Collett 5100 rebuilds 5ft 6in
1944	6959	6959	4-6-0	Hawksworth 'Modified Hall'
1945	1000	1000	4-6-0	Hawksworth 'County'
1947	9400	3400	0-6-0PT	Hawksworth 4ft 7½in

British Railways

1949	1500	1500	0-6-0PT	Hawksworth
1949	1600	1600	0-6-0PT	Hawksworth

Southern Railway Group

East Kent Light Railway

1917	EKR	30948	0-6-0T	Kerr Stuart

Kent & East Sussex Light Railway

1876	0330	KESR 4	0-6-0ST	Beattie ex-LSWR
1905	KESR	30949	0-8-0T	Hawthorn Leslie

London, Brighton & South Coast Railway

1872	A1	DS680	0-6-0T	Stroudley 'Terrier'
1873	D1[2] & D1/M	32215	0-4-2T	Stroudley
1874	E1[2]	32097	0-6-0T	Stroudley
1892	D3	32364	0-4-4T	Billinton
1893	C2	32435	0-6-0	Billinton 'Vulcan'
1894	E3	32165	0-6-2T	Billinton
1897	E4	32463	0-6-2T	Billinton
1899	B4[2]	32044	4-4-0	Billinton
1902	E5	32399	0-6-2T	Billinton
1904	E6	32408	0-6-2T	Billinton
1905	H1	32037	4-4-2	Marsh Atlantics
1906	C3	32300	0-6-0	Marsh
1907	I3	32021	4-4-2T	Marsh
1908 *	C2X	32434	0-6-0	Marsh rebuilt from 'C2'
1909 *	D3X	32397	0-4-4T	Marsh rebuilt from 'D3'
1909 *	E4X	32466	0-6-2T	Marsh rebuilt from 'E4'
1910	J1	32325	4-6-2T	Marsh
1911 *	E5X	32401	0-6-2T	Marsh rebuilt from 'E5'
1911 *	E6X	32407	0-6-2T	Marsh rebuilt from 'E6'
1911	H2	32421	4-4-2	Marsh Later Atlantics
1911 *	A1X	32635	0-6-0T	Marsh reb. Stroudley 'Terrier'
1912	J2	32326	4-6-2T	Marsh
1913	E2	32100	0-6-0T	Billinton
1913	K	32337	2-6-0	Billinton
1922 *	B4X	32043	4-4-0	Billinton rebuilt from 'B4[2]'
1925 *	I1X	32001	4-4-2T	Maunsell rebuilt from Marsh 'I1'
1927 *	E1R	32094	0-6-2T	Maunsell rebuilt from 'E1[2]'
1934 *	N15X	32327	4-6-0	Maunsell rebuilt from Billinton 'Remembrance'

London, Chatham & Dover Railway (became part of SECR)

1879	T	31602	0-6-0T	Kirtley
1881	1302	31302	0-4-0CT	Neilson Crane Engine
1891	R	31658	0-4-4T	Kirtley

London & South Western Railway

1874	0298	30585	2-4-0WT	Beattie
1881	0395	30564	0-6-0	Adams
1882	0415	30582	4-4-2T	Adams
1887	A12	30618	0-4-2	Adams
1889	O2	30177	0-4-4T	Adams
1891	B4[1]	30081	0-4-0T	Adams & Drummond
1894	T1	30001	0-4-4T	Adams
1894	G6	30160	0-6-0T	Adams
1897	M7	30021	0-4-4T	Drummond
1897	700	30306	0-6-0	Drummond
1899	T9	30113	4-4-0	Drummond
1901	K10	30135	4-4-0	Drummond
1903	L11	30134	4-4-0	Drummond
1903	S11	30395	4-4-0	Drummond
1904	L12	30415	4-4-0	Drummond
1906	C14	30588	0-4-0T	Drummond
1911	T14	30443	4-6-0	Drummond
1912	D15	30463	4-4-0	Drummond
1914	H15	30330	4-6-0	Urie & Maunsell
1918	N15	30448	4-6-0	Urie & Maunsell 'King Arthur'
1920	S15	30496	4-6-0	Urie & Maunsell
1921	G16	30492	4-8-0T	Urie
1921	H16	30516	4-6-2T	Urie

Plymouth, Devonport & South Western Junction Railway

1907	756	30756	0-6-0T	Hawthorn Leslie
1907	757	30757	0-6-2T	Hawthorn Leslie

Southampton Dock Company

1890	0458	30458	0-4-0ST	Hawthorn Leslie

South Eastern Railway (became part of SECR)

1878	O1	31003	0-6-0	Built as Stirling 'O' class, rebuilt in 1903
1883	F1	31002	4-4-0	Built as Stirling 'F' class, rebuilt in 1903
1888	R1[1]	31010	0-6-0T	Built as Stirling 'R' class, rebuilt in 1910
1898	B1	31013	4-4-0	Built as Stirling 'B' class, rebuilt in 1910

South Eastern & Chatham Railway

1900	C	31004	0-6-0	Wainwright
1900	R1[2]	31696	0-4-4T	Wainwright version of Kirtley LCDR 'R' class
1901	D	31057	4-4-0	Wainwright
1903 *	F1	31002	4-4-0	Wainwright rebuilt from SER Stirling 'F' class of 1883
1903 *	O1	31003	0-6-0	Wainwright rebuilt from SER Stirling 'O' class of 1878
1904	H	31005	0-4-4T	Wainwright
1905	E	31036	4-4-0	Wainwright
1909	P	31027	0-6-0T	Wainwright
1910 *	R1[1]	31010	0-6-0T	Wainwright rebuilt from SER Stirling 'R' class of 1888
1910 *	B1	31013	4-4-0	Wainwright rebuilt from SER Stirling 'B' class of 1898
1913	J	31595	0-6-4T	Wainwright
1914	L	31760	4-4-0	Wainwright
1917	N	31400	2-6-0	Maunsell
1917 *	S	31685	0-6-0ST	Maunsell rebuilt from 'C' class
1919 *	E1[1]	31019	4-4-0	Maunsell rebuilt from 'E' class
1921 *	D1[1]	31145	4-4-0	Maunsell rebuilt from 'D' class
1922	N1	31822	2-6-0	Maunsell 3-cylinder version of 'N' class

United States War Department

1942	USA	30061	0-6-0T	'USA' Tank

Southern Railway

1926	LN	30850	4-6-0	Maunsell 'Lord Nelson'
1926	L1	31753	4-4-0	Maunsell
1928 *	U	31610	2-6-0	Maunsell Converted from SECR 'River' 2-6-4T of 1917
1928 *	U1	31890	2-6-0	Maunsell 3-cylinder version of 'U' class
1929	Z	30950	0-8-0T	Maunsell
1930	V	30900	4-4-0	Maunsell 'Schools'
1931	W	31911	2-6-4T	Maunsell
1938	Q	30530	0-6-0	Maunsell
1941	MN	35001	4-6-2	Bulleid 'Merchant Navy' Pacific
1942	Q1	33001	0-6-0	Bulleid 'Austerity'
1945	BB & WC	34001	4-6-2	Bulleid 'Battle of Britain' & 'West Country' Pacific

British Railways

1949	Leader	36001	0-6-6-0T	Bulleid 'Leader'
1956 *	MN Reb	35001	4-6-2	Rebuilt 'Merchant Navy'
1957 *	BB Reb & WC Reb	34001	4-6-2	Rebuilt 'Battle of Britain' & 'West Country'

London, Midland & Scottish Railway Group

Caledonian Railway

1883	2F[5]	57230	0-6-0	Drummond
1885	0F[5]	56010	0-4-0ST	Drummond
1886	CR Single	123	4-2-2	Neilson & Co. (Preserved)
1895	2P[12]	55116	0-4-4T	McIntosh
1895	3F[10]	56230	0-6-0T	McIntosh
1899	3P[4]	54434	4-4-0	McIntosh 'Dunalastair III' Superheated
1899	3F[12]	57550	0-6-0	McIntosh Class '812'
1899	3F[13]	57629	0-6-0	McIntosh Class '652'
1900	2P[13]	55159	0-4-4T	McIntosh & Pickersgill Class '439'
1904	2P[9]	54363	4-4-0	McIntintosh 'Dunalastair IV'
1904	3P[5]	54438	4-4-0	McIntosh 'Dunalastair IV' Superheated
1912	2F[4]	56151	0-6-0T	McIntosh
1916	3P[6]	54461	4-4-0	Pickersgill
1916	4P[3]	54630	4-6-0	Pickersgill Class '60'
1917	4P[5]	55350	4-6-2T	Pickersgill
1918	3F[14]	57650	0-6-0	Pickersgill Class '294'
1922	2P[14]	55237	0-4-4T	Pickersgill Class '431'
1925	2P[15]	55260	0-4-4T	McIntosh Class '439' (built by LMS)

Furness Railway

1913	3F[8]	52494	0-6-0	Pettigrew

Glasgow & South Western Railway

1915	3F[11]	56905	0-6-2T	Drummond

Highland Railway

1894	Jones Goods	103	4-6-0	Jones (Preserved)
1896	2P[10]	54379	4-4-0	Jones 'Loch'
1898	2P[11]	54397	4-4-0	Drummond 'Ben'
1900	3F[15]	57693	0-6-0	Drummond 'Barney'
1905	0P	55051	0-4-4T	Drummond
1917	4F[4]	57950	4-6-0	Cumming 'Clan Goods'
1919	4P[4]	54764	4-6-0	Cumming 'Clan'

Lancashire & Yorkshire Railway

1876	2F[3]	52016	0-6-0	Barton Wright Class '25'
1887	NG[1]	Wren	0-4-0ST	Beyer Peacock Horwich Works Narrow Gauge
1889	2P[8]	50621	2-4-2T	Aspinall Class '5'
1889	3F[7]	52088	0-6-0	Aspinall Class '27'
1891	0F[4]	51202	0-4-0ST	Aspinall 'Pug' Class '21'
1891 *	2F[2]	51307	0-6-0ST	Aspinall Rebuilt Saddle Tank Class '23'
1897	1F[3]	51535	0-6-0T	Aspinall Side Tank Class '24'
1898	3P[3]	50835	2-4-2T	Aspinall & Hughes Class '6'
1900	6F[3]	52727	0-8-0	Aspinall Class '30'
1906	Rail Motor[1]	50617	0-4-0T	Hughes
1908	5P	50412	4-6-0	Hughes
1912	7F[5]	52841	0-8-0	Hughes Class '31'
1913 *	3F[9]	52528	0-6-0	Hughes Class '28'

London & North Western Railway

1870	2F[15]	CD3	0-6-0ST	Webb 'Special Tank'
1873	2F[10]	58320	0-6-0	Webb 'Coal Engine'
1876	1P[7]	58092	2-4-0T	Webb
1880	2F[11]	58362	0-6-0	Webb '18in Goods Cauliflower'
1881	2F[14]	58880	0-6-2T	Webb 'Coal Tank'
1890	1P[1]	46601	2-4-2T	Webb
1898	2P[7]	46876	0-6-2T	Webb
1901	1F[2]	47862	0-4-2ST	Webb 'Bissel Truck'
1904	3P[7]	58010	4-4-0	Whale 'Precursor'
1905	Rail Motor[2]	29988	0-4-0T	Whale
1905 *	2F[13]	58870	0-6-0ST	Whale Saddle Tank rebuilt from Webb 'Coal Engine'
1906	4F[3]	48801	4-6-0	Whale '19in Goods'
1910	3P[8]	58011	4-4-0	Bowen Cooke 'George the Fifth'
1911	6F[1]	47875	0-8-2T	Bowen Cooke
1911	4P[6]	58000	4-6-0	Bowen Cooke 'Prince of Wales'
1912 *	6F[2]	48892	0-8-0	Bowen Cooke 'G1' Class rebuilt from earlier engines
1913	5XP	46004	4-6-0	Bowen Cooke Rebuilt 'Claughton'
1921	7F[3]	49395	0-8-0	Bowen Cooke 'G2' Class
1923	7F[1]	47930	0-8-4T	Beames
1936 *	7F[2]	48893	0-8-0	'G2A' Class rebuilt from earlier engines to Bowen Cooke 'G2' design by LMS

London, Tilbury & Southend Railway

1897	3P[2]	41928	4-4-2T	Whitelegg
1900	2P[5]	41910	4-4-2T	Whitelegg 'Intermediate'
1903	3F[1]	41980	0-6-2T	Whitelegg

Midland Railway

1863	2F[6]	58110	0-6-0	Kirtley Double Framed
1868	2F[7]	58111	0-6-0	Kirtley Double Framed with Belpaire Boiler
1874	1F[1]	41660	0-6-0T	Johnson
1875	1P[5]	58030	0-4-4T	Johnson 5ft 7in
1875	2F[8]	58114	0-6-0	Johnson 4ft 11in
1876	1P[2]	58020	2-4-0	Johnson 6ft 3in
1876	1P[3]	58021	2-4-0	Johnson 6ft 6in
1876	1P[4]	58022	2-4-0	Johnson 6ft 9in
1878	2F[9]	58188	0-6-0	Johnson 5ft 3in
1881	1P[6]	58039	0-4-4T	Johnson 5ft 4in
1882	2P[2]	40332	4-4-0	Johnson & Fowler
1883	0F[1]	41509	0-4-0ST	Johnson
1885	3F[2]	43137	0-6-0	Johnson 4ft 11in
1885	3F[3]	43191	0-6-0	Johnson 5ft 3in
1899	3F[5]	47200	0-6-0T	Johnson 'Jinty'
1900	3P[1]	40711	4-4-0	Johnson
1902	4P[2]	41000	4-4-0	Deeley Compound
1906	3F[4]	43765	0-6-0	Deeley
1907	0F[2]	41528	0-4-0T	Deeley
1911	4F[1]	43835	0-6-0	Fowler
1919	0-10-0	58100	0-10-0	Fowler 'Lickey Banker'

North London Railway

1858	Crane	58865	0-4-2ST	Sharp Stewart & Park Crane Tank
1880	2F[12]	58850	0-6-0T	Park

Somerset & Dorset Joint Railway

1885	3F[3]	43191	0-6-0	Johnson 5ft 3in
1911	4F[1]	43835	0-6-0	Fowler
1914	2P[1]	40322	4-4-0	Fowler
1914	7F[6]	53800	2-8-0	Fowler
1922	4F[2]	44027	0-6-0	Fowler
1924	3F[6]	47260	0-6-0T	Fowler 'Jinty'
1928	2P[3]	40563	4-4-0	Fowler
1929	Sentinel[3]	47190	0-4-0T	Sentinel

Wirral Railway

1889	2P[6]	46762	2-4-2T	Aspinall (ex LYR Class 5)

London, Midland & Scottish Railway

1924	4P[1]	40900	4-4-0	Fowler Compound
1924	4F[2]	44027	0-6-0	Fowler
1924	3F[6]	47260	0-6-0T	Fowler 'Jinty'
1925	2P[15]	55260	0-4-4T	McIntosh CR Class '439'
1926	5MT[1]	42700	2-6-0	Hughes/Fowler Horwich 'Crab'
1927	4MT[2]	42300	2-6-4T	Fowler
1927	7P[3]	46100	4-6-0	Fowler 'Royal Scot'
1927	Garratt	47967	2-6-6-2T	Fowler & Beyer Peacock 'Garratt'
1928	2P[3]	40563	4-4-0	Fowler
1928	2F[1]	47160	0-6-0T	Fowler 'Dock Tank'
1929	7F[4]	49500	0-8-0	Fowler
1930	3MT[1]	40001	2-6-2T	Fowler
1930	6P5F[1]	45500	4-6-0	Fowler 'Patriot'
1930	Sentinel[1]	47180	0-4-0T	Sentinel two speed shunter
1932	2P[4]	41900	0-4-4T	Stanier
1932	0F[3]	47000	0-4-0ST	Stanier
1932	Sentinel[2]	47184	0-4-0T	Sentinel single speed shunter
1933	5MT[2]	42945	2-6-0	Stanier
1933	8P[1]	46200	4-6-2	Stanier 'Princess Royal'
1934	4MT[4]	42500	2-6-4T	Stanier 3-Cylinder
1934	5MT[3]	44658	4-6-0	Stanier 'Black Five'
1934	6P5F[2]	45552	4-6-0	Stanier 'Jubilee'
1935	3MT[2]	40071	2-6-2T	Stanier
1935	4MT[3]	42425	2-6-4T	Stanier 2-Cylinder
1935	8F	48000	2-8-0	Stanier
1937	8P[2]	46220	4-6-2	Stanier 'Princess Coronation'
1942 *	7P[2]	45735	4-6-0	Stanier 'Rebuilt Jubilee'
1943	7P[3] Reb	46100	4-6-0	Stanier 'Rebuilt Royal Scot'
1945	4MT[1]	42050	2-6-4T	Fairburn
1946	2MT[1]	41200	2-6-2T	Ivatt
1946	2MT[2]	46400	2-6-0	Ivatt
1946 *	7P[1]	45512	4-6-0	Ivatt 'Rebuilt Patriot'
1947	4MT[5]	43000	2-6-0	Ivatt 'Mogul'

London & North Eastern Railway Group

Great Central Railway

1897	J62	68200	0-6-0ST	Pollitt
1898	F2	67104	2-4-2T	Pollitt
1901	D9	62300	4-4-0	Robinson
1901	J11	64280	0-6-0	Robinson
1902	B5	61680	4-6-0	Robinson 'Fish'
1902	Q4	63200	0-8-0	Robinson
1903	C4	62903	4-4-2	Robinson 'Atlantic'
1903	C13	67400	4-4-2T	Robinson
1906	B9	61469	4-6-0	Robinson
1906	B4	61482	4-6-0	Robinson 'Immingham'
1906	J63	68204	0-6-0T	Robinson
1907	C14	67440	4-4-2T	Robinson
1907	S1	69900	0-8-4T	Robinson
1911	O4	63570	2-8-0	Robinson
1911	A5	69800	4-6-2T	Robinson
1913	B8	61353	4-6-0	Robinson 'Glenalmond'
1913	D10	62650	4-4-0	Robinson 'Director'
1914	L3	69050	2-6-4T	Robinson
1920	B3	61497	4-6-0	Robinson 'Lord Faringdon'
1920	D11	62660	4-4-0	Robinson 'Large Director'
1921	B7	61360	4-6-0	Robinson

Great Eastern Railway

1868	J92	68667	0-6-0CT	Ruston & Proctor Stratford Works Crane Tanks
1874	Y5	68081	0-4-0ST	Neilson
1883	J15	65350	0-6-0	Worsdell, Holden & Hill
1883	Y6	68082	0-4-0T	Worsdell Tram
1884	F4	67151	2-4-2T	Worsdell
1886	J66	68370	0-6-0T	Holden
1889	J65	68211	0-6-0T	Holden
1890	J67	68490	0-6-0T	Holden
1891	E4	62780	2-4-0	Holden
1893	F3	67114	2-4-2T	Holden
1900	D15	62501	4-4-0	Holden 'Claud Hamilton'
1900	J17	65500	0-6-0	Holden
1902	J69	68490	0-6-0T	Holden
1903	J70	68216	0-6-0T	Holden Tram
1909	F7	67093	2-4-2T	Holden 'Crystal Palace Tanks'
1911	B12	61500	4-6-0	Holden
1911 *	F5	67188	2-4-2T	Holden
1911	F6	67220	2-4-2T	Holden
1912	J19	64640	0-6-0	Hill
1912	J68	68638	0-6-0T	Hill
1913	Y4	68125	0-4-0T	Hill
1914	N7	69600	0-6-2T	Hill
1920	J20	64675	0-6-0	Hill
1923 *	D16	62510	4-4-0	'Super Claud', 'Rebuilt Claud' (rebuilt & developed from D15)

Great North of Scotland Railway

1893	D41	62225	4-4-0	Johnson
1899	D40	62260	4-4-0	Pickersgill
1915	Z4	68190	0-4-2T	Manning Wardle Aberdeen Harbour Shunters
1915	Z5	68192	0-4-2T	Manning Wardle Aberdeen Harbour Shunters

Great Northern Railway

1874	J55	68317	0-6-0ST	Stirling
1892	J52	68757	0-6-0ST	Stirling
1896	D3	62000	4-4-0	Ivatt
1896	J4	64109	0-6-0	Ivatt
1897	D2	62150	4-4-0	Ivatt
1898	C12	67350	4-4-2T	Ivatt
1902	C1	62808	4-4-2	Ivatt 'Large Atlantic'
1907	N1	69430	0-6-2T	Ivatt
1908	J1	65002	0-6-0	Ivatt
1909	J5	65480	0-6-0	Ivatt
1911	D1	62203	4-4-0	Ivatt
1911	J6	64170	0-6-0	Ivatt & Gresley
1912 *	J3	64105	0-6-0	Ivatt 'J4' rebuilt with larger boiler
1912	J2	65015	0-6-0	Gresley
1913	O3	63475	2-8-0	Gresley 2-cylinder
1913	J50	68890	0-6-0T	Gresley
1914	K2	61720	2-6-0	Gresley
1920	K3	61800	2-6-0	Gresley
1920	N2	69490	0-6-2T	Gresley
1921	O2	63921	2-8-0	Gresley 3-cylinder
1922	A10	60068	4-6-2	Gresley Pacific

Hull & Barnsley Railway

1901	J75	68365	0-6-0T	Stirling
1901	N12	69089	0-6-2T	Stirling
1913	N13	69110	0-6-2T	Stirling

Lancashire, Derbyshire & East Coast Railway (later part of GCR)

1897	J60	68366	0-6-0T	Kitson

Manchester, Sheffield & Lincolnshire Railway (renamed GCR in 1897)

1889	F1	67097	2-4-2T	Parker
1889	N4	69225	0-6-2T	Parker
1891	N5	69250	0-6-2T	Parker & Pollitt
1892	J10	65126	0-6-0	Parker

Metropolitan Railway

1915	M2	69076	0-6-4T	Jones
1925	L2	69070	2-6-4T	Hally

Midland & Great Northern Joint Railway

1896	J4	64109	0-6-0	Ivatt
1897	J93	68484	0-6-0T	Marriott
1912 *	J3	64105	0-6-0	Ivatt 'J4' rebuilt with larger boiler

Ministry of Supply (War Department)

1943	O7	63000	2-8-0	Riddles 'Austerity'
1943	O6	63554	2-8-0	Stanier '8F'
1943	J94	68006	0-6-0ST	Riddles

North British Railway

1882	Y9	68092	0-4-0ST	Holmes
1884	D31	62059	4-4-0	Holmes
1888	J36	65210	0-6-0	Holmes
1900	J83	68442	0-6-0T	Holmes
1904	J88	68320	0-6-0T	Reid
1906	D32	62443	4-4-0	Reid 'Intermediates'
1906	J35	64460	0-6-0	Reid
1909	D29	62400	4-4-0	Reid 'Scott'
1909	D33	62455	4-4-0	Reid
1909	N14	69120	0-6-2T	Reid
1910	N15	69126	0-6-2T	Reid
1911	C15	67452	4-4-2T	Reid
1912	D30	62417	4-4-0	Reid 'Scott'
1913	D34	62467	4-4-0	Reid 'Glen'
1914	J37	64536	0-6-0	Reid
1915	C16	67482	4-4-2T	Reid

North Eastern Railway

1886	J21	65025	0-6-0	Worsdell
1886	J71	68230	0-6-0T	Worsdell
1886	N8	69371	0-6-2T	Worsdell
1888	Y7	68088	0-4-0T	Worsdell
1890	Y8	68090	0-4-0T	Worsdell
1891	J73	68355	0-6-0T	Worsdell
1893	N9	69410	0-6-2T	Worsdell
1894	J24	65600	0-6-0	Worsdell
1894	G5	67240	0-4-4T	Worsdell
1896	D17	62111	4-4-0	Worsdell
1898	J25	65645	0-6-0	Worsdell
1898	J72	68670	0-6-0T	Worsdell
1899	B13	61699	4-6-0	Worsdell
1899	D20	62340	4-4-0	Worsdell
1899 *	J77	68390	0-6-0T	Worsdell rebuilt from 1874 Fletcher Well Tanks
1901	Q5	63250	0-8-0	Worsdell
1902	N10	69090	0-6-2T	Worsdell
1903	C6	62933	4-4-2	Worsdell Atlantic
1904	J26	65730	0-6-0	Worsdell
1906	J27	65780	0-6-0	Worsdell & Raven
1909	T1	69910	4-8-0T	Worsdell
1910	A7	69770	4-6-2T	Raven
1911	C7	62954	4-4-2	Raven Atlantic

1913	Q6	63340	0-8-0	Raven 2-cylinder
1914 *	A6	69791	4-6-2T	Raven 'Whitby Tanks' rebuilt from Worsdell 4-6-0Ts of 1907
1919	B16	61400	4-6-0	Raven
1919	Q7	63460	0-8-0	Raven 3-cylinder
1931 *	A8	69850	4-6-2T	Raven, rebuilt by Gresley
London & North Eastern Railway				
1925	Y1	68130	0-4-0T	Sentinel (Single-speed gearbox)
1925	U1	69999	2-8-8-2T	Gresley & Beyer Garratt
1926	J39	64700	0-6-0	Gresley
1926	J38	65900	0-6-0	Gresley
1927	A3	60035	4-6-2	Gresley Pacific
1927	D49	62700	4-4-0	Gresley 'Shire' & 'Hunt'
1927	Y3	68154	0-4-0T	Sentinel (Two-speed gearbox)
1928	Railcar	2136		Sentinel Railcar
1928	B17	61600	4-6-0	Gresley 'Sandringham'
1930	V1	67600	2-6-2T	Gresley
1930	Y10	68186	0-4-0T	Sentinel Tram
1935	A4	60001	4-6-2	Gresley Streamlined Pacific
1936	V2	60800	2-6-2	Gresley 'Green Arrow'
1937 *	W1	60700	4-6-4	Gresley Streamlined
1937	K4	61993	2-6-0	Gresley
1939	V3	67600	2-6-2T	Gresley
1941	V4	61700	2-6-2	Gresley
1942	B1	61000	4-6-0	Thompson
1942 *	Q1	69925	0-8-0T	Thompson rebuild of GCR 'Q4'
1943 *	A2/2	60501	4-6-2	Thompson Pacific
1944	A2/1	60507	4-6-2	Thompson Pacific
1944 *	O1	63571	2-8-0	Thompson rebuild of GCR Robinson 'O4'
1945 *	A1/1	60113	4-6-2	Thompson Pacific
1945 *	B2	61603	4-6-0	Thompson Rebuilt 'Sandringham'
1945 *	K5	61863	2-6-0	Thompson 2-cylinder rebuild from 'K3'
1945 *	K1/1	61997	2-6-0	Thompson 'K4' rebuilt as 'K1' prototype
1945	L1	67701	2-6-4T	Thompson
1946	A2/3	60500	4-6-2	Thompson Pacific
1947	A2	60525	4-6-2	Peppercorn Pacific
British Railways				
1948	A1	60114	4-6-2	Peppercorn Pacific
1949	K1	62001	2-6-0	Peppercorn

British Railways Group

Ministry of Supply (War Department)				
1943	WD [1]	90000	2-8-0	Riddles 'Austerity'
1943	WD [2]	90750	2-10-0	Riddles 'Austerity'
British Railways				
1951	7P6F	70000	4-6-2	Riddles Standard 'Britannia'
1951	5MT	73000	4-6-0	Riddles Standard Class 5
1951	4MT [1]	75000	4-6-0	Riddles Standard Class 4
1951	4MT [3]	80000	2-6-4T	Riddles Standard Class 4 Tank
1951	6P5F	72000	4-6-2	Riddles Standard Clan
1952	3MT [2]	82000	2-6-2T	Riddles Standard Class 3 Tank
1952	4MT [2]	76000	2-6-0	Riddles Standard Class 4
1952	2MT [1]	78000	2-6-0	Riddles Standard Class 2
1953	2MT [2]	84000	2-6-2T	Riddles Standard Class 2 Tank
1954	9F	92000	2-10-0	Riddles Standard '9F'
1954	3MT [1]	77000	2-6-0	Riddles Standard Class 3
1954	8P	71000	4-6-2	Riddles Standard 'Duke of Gloucester'

LSWR Urie 'H16' class 4-6-2T No 30516.

NBR Reid 'J35' class 0-6-0 No 64491.

Appendix 3. Alphabetical list of locomotive names.

Name	Number
3RD CARABINIER	46125
17 SQUADRON	34062
25 SQUADRON	34060
41 SQUADRON	34076
46 SQUADRON	34074
66 SQUADRON	34110
73 SQUADRON	34061
74 SQUADRON	34080
92 SQUADRON	34081
141 SQUADRON	34079
145 SQUADRON	34087
213 SQUADRON	34088
219 SQUADRON	34086
222 SQUADRON	34078
229 SQUADRON	34063
249 SQUADRON	34073
253 SQUADRON	34084
257 SQUADRON	34072
264 SQUADRON	34075
501 SQUADRON	34085
601 SQUADRON	34071
602 SQUADRON	34089
603 SQUADRON	34077
605 SQUADRON	34083
615 SQUADRON	34082
A. H. PEPPERCORN	60525
A. HAROLD BIBBY	61250
A. S. HARRIS	30756
ABBERLEY HALL	4981
ABBOTSBURY CASTLE	4083
ABBOTSFORD	60141
ABERDEEN COMMONWEALTH	35007
ABERDEENSHIRE	62713
ABERDONIAN	60158
ABERGAVENNY CASTLE	5013
ABERPORTH GRANGE	6860
ABERYSTWYTH CASTLE	4084
ABNEY HALL	6900
ABOUKIR	45681
ABOYEUR	60148
ACHILLES	45697
ACTON BURNELL HALL	6991
ACTON HALL	4982
ADAM WOODCOCK	62437
ADDAX	61024
ADDERLEY HALL	4901
ADEN	45633
AGAMEMNON	45693
AIRBORNE	60511
AJAX	45689
ALBERT HALL	4983
ALBERTA	45562
ALBRIGHTON HALL	4984
ALCAZAR	60136
ALDBOROUGH HALL	6931
ALDENHAM HALL	4902
ALDERNEY	30085
ALDERSEY HALL	6930
ALEXANDER REITH GRAY	61242
ALFRED BALDWIN	3363
ALFRED THE GREAT	70009
ALLAN-BANE	62692
ALLENBY	65268
ALLESLEY HALL	4985
ALNWICK CASTLE	61622
ALVERSTONE	W29
AMADIS	60149
AMETHYST	45700
ANDREW BAIN	62276
ANDREW K. MCCOSH	60003
ANSON	45672
ANTHONY MANOR	7801
ANTI-AIRCRAFT COMMAND	34049
ANZAC	70046
APOLLO	70015
APPLEDORE	34100
ARBORFIELD HALL	6992
ARBURY HALL	3954
ARBURY HALL	5986
ARCHIBALD STURROCK	60118
ARDINGLY	30917
ARETHUSA	45696
ARGYLL AND SUTHERLAND HIGHLANDER	46107
ARGYLLSHIRE	62708
ARIEL	70016
ARLEY HALL	6901
ARLINGTON COURT	2931
ARLINGTON GRANGE	6800
ARMADA	45679
ARROW	70017
ARSENAL	61648
ARTHOG HALL	6993
ASHBURNHAM	2192
ASHEY	W28
ASHFORD HALL	5966
ASHLEY GRANGE	6824
ASHTON COURT	2932
ASHWICKE HALL	3951
ASHWICKE HALL	5976
ASKE HALL	61627
ASSAM	45583
ASTLEY HALL	4903
ASTON HALL	4986
ATHELHAMPTON HALL	6971
ATHELNEY CASTLE	7009
ATLAS	45737
AUDLEY END	61606
AULD REEKIE	60160
AUSTRALIA	3393
AUSTRALIA	45563
AVONDALE CASTLE	7010
AXMINSTER	34018
AYLBURTON GRANGE	6801
AYRSHIRE YEOMANRY	45156
BACHELORS BUTTON	60537
BAGGRAVE HALL	6994
BAGLAN HALL	4913
BAHAMAS	45596
BAHRAM	60531
BAILIE MACWHEEBLE	62671
BALMORAL	60140
BAMPTON GRANGE	6802
BANBURY CASTLE	7011
BANFFSHIRE	62717
BANGOR	45523
BANTAM COCK	61700
BARBADOS	45597
BARBURY CASTLE	5095
BARCOTE MANOR	7803
BARFLEUR	45685
BARHAM	45653
BARNINGHAM HALL	6920
BARNSLEY	61669
BARNSTAPLE	34005
BARODA	45587
BARON OF BRADWARDINE	62672
BARRY CASTLE	7012
BARTON HALL	4905
BASUTOLAND	45598
BATH ABBEY	5083
BATLEY	10
BAYARDO	60079
BAYDON MANOR	7804
BEACHAMWELL HALL	6934
BEACHY HEAD	32424
BEARLEY GRANGE	6831
BEATTIE	32331
BEATTY	45677
BEAUFORT	5078
BECHUANALAND	45599
BECKFORD HALL	5977
BEDFORDSHIRE	62724
BEENHAM GRANGE	6808
BELGIAN MARINE	35017
BELLEROPHON	45694
BELMONT HALL	6903
BELVOIR CASTLE	61632
BEMBRIDGE	W33
BEN A'BHUIRD	54416
BEN ALDER	54398
BEN ALISKY	54409
BEN ATTOW	54403
BEN BHACH ARD	54415
BEN CLEBRIG	54404
BEN DEARG	54410
BEN VRACKIE	54401
BEN WYVIS	54399
BENACHIE	62274
BENGAL	45577
BENINGBROUGH HALL	6972
BENTHALL HALL	6995
BEN-Y-GLOE	54397
BERE ALSTON	34104
BERKELEY CASTLE	4085
BERKSHIRE	62730
BERMUDA	45600
BERRINGTON HALL	4912
BERRY POMEROY CASTLE	5012
BERWICKSHIRE	62709
BEVERSTON CASTLE	5068
BHOPAL	45594
BIBBY LINE	35020
BIBURY COURT	2933
BICKMARSH HALL	5967
BIDEFORD	34019
BIGGIN HILL	34057
BIHAR AND ORISSA	45581
BINGLEY HALL	5921
BINNEGAR HALL	4904
BIRCHWOOD GRANGE	6807
BIRTLES HALL	6933
BISHOP'S CASTLE	5064
BITTERN	60019
BLACK DUNCAN	62441
BLACK PRINCE	70008
BLACK WATCH	46102
BLACKBIRD	3441
BLACKBUCK	61006
BLACKMOOR VALE	34023
BLACKMORE VALE	34023
BLACKPOOL	45524
BLACKTAIL	61038
BLACKWELL GRANGE	6806
BLACKWELL HALL	6996
BLAIR ATHOL	60058
BLAISDON HALL	4910
BLAKE	45650
BLAKEMERE GRANGE	6810
BLAKESLEY HALL	4909
BLANDFORD	34107
BLANDFORD FORUM	34107
BLASIUS	3341
BLENHEIM	5073
BLENHEIM	60087
BLICKLING	61607
BLINK BONNY	60051
BLUE FUNNEL CERTUM PETE FINUM	35013
BLUE PETER	60532
BLUE STAR	35010
BLUNDELL'S	30932
BOADICEA	70036
BODICOTE GRANGE	6870
BODINNICK HALL	5978
BODMIN	34016
BOIS ROUSSEL	60117
BOMBAY	3408
BOMBAY	45576
BON ACCORD	60154
BONCHURCH	W32
BONGO	61005
BONGRACE	60128
BONNIE DUNDEE	60159
BOOK LAW	60088
BORDERER	60155
BORWICK HALL	6921
BOSCASTLE	34039
BOSCAWEN	45642
BOSTOCK HALL	5988
BOSWELL	60138
BOURTON GRANGE	6871
BRADFIELD	30923
BRADFIELD HALL	4906
BRADFORD	61667
BRADFORD CITY	61668
BRADING	W22
BRADLEY MANOR	7802
BRADSHAW	45518
BRANCEPETH CASTLE	61626
BRAUNTON	34046
BRECCLES HALL	6936
BRECON CASTLE	5023
BRENTOR	34095
BRICKLEHAMPTON HALL	6973
BRIDE OF LAMMERMOOR	2987
BRIDGWATER CASTLE	5096
BRIGHTON	30915
BRISTOL CASTLE	7013
BRITANNIA	45700
BRITANNIA	70000
BRITISH COLUMBIA	45559
BRITISH GUIANA	45601
BRITISH HONDURAS	45602
BRITISH INDIA LINE	35018
BRITISH LEGION	46170
BRITISH MONARCH	4021
BRITTANY	30097
BROCKET HALL	5987
BROCKINGTON GRANGE	6804
BROCKLEBANK LINE	35025
BROCKLEY HALL	4987
BROCKTON GRANGE	6832
BRONZINO	60539
BROOME HALL	4908
BROOME MANOR	7805
BROUGHTON CASTLE	5033
BROUGHTON GRANGE	6805
BROUGHTON HALL	3903
BROUGHTON HALL	4907
BROWN JACK	60043
BROWSHOLME HALL	6935
BRYNGWYN HALL	6974
BRYN-IVOR HALL	6997
BUCKENHILL GRANGE	6830
BUCKLEBURY GRANGE	6803
BUDE	34006
BUDLEIGH SALTERTON	34014
BUILTH CASTLE	4086
BULLFINCH	3442
BULWELL HALL	4988
BUNSEN	45512
BURGHCLERE GRANGE	6809
BURMA	45580
BURMINGTON GRANGE	6829
BURRY PORT	2193
BURTON AGNES HALL	6998
BURTON HALL	6922
BURWARTON HALL	6932
BUSHBUCK	61017
BUTLEIGH COURT	2934
BUTLER-HENDERSON	62660
BUTLERS HALL	6902
BYNG	65216
BYRON	70031
CADBURY CASTLE	7028
CAEN	30090
CAERHAYS CASTLE	7014
CAERNARVON	45515
CAERPHILLY CASTLE	4073
CALBOURNE	W24
CALCOT GRANGE	6833
CALCUTTA	3406
CALDICOT CASTLE	4074
CALEB BALDERSTONE	62422
CALL BOY	60099
CALLINGTON	34047
CALSTOCK	34103
CALVELEY HALL	6939
CAMBRIDGESHIRE	62720
CAMELFORD	34032
CAMELOT	30742
CAMELOT	73082
CAMERON HIGHLANDER	46105
CAMERON OF LOCHIEL	61995
CAMERONIAN	46113
CAMERONIAN	60040
CAMPERDOWN	45680
CAMPION HALL	5941
CANADA	45553
CANADIAN PACIFIC	35005
CAPEL DEWI HALL	6999
CAPESTHORNE HALL	6975
CAPTAIN CRAIGENGELT	62681
CAPTAIN CUTTLE	60091
CARADOC GRANGE	6873
CARDIFF CASTLE	4075
CARDIGAN CASTLE	4087
CAREW CASTLE	5024
CARISBROOKE	W13
CARISBROOKE	W36
CARMARTHEN CASTLE	4076
CARN BREA CASTLE	7015
CASTLE HEDINGHAM	61614
CAXTON HALL	5922
CAYNHAM COURT	2935
CEFNTILLA COURT	2936
CENTENARY	60056
CENTRAL PROVINCES	45582
CEYLON	45604
CHAFFINCH	3443
CHALE	W31
CHAMOIS	61029
CHAMOSSAIRE	60514
CHAMPION LODGE	61643
CHANNEL PACKET	35001
CHARD	34033
CHARFIELD HALL	6904
CHARLES DICKENS	70033
CHARLES JONES	69077
CHARTERHOUSE	30903
CHELTENHAM	30925
CHEPSTOW CASTLE	4077
CHERBOURG	30098
CHERWELL HALL	4989
CHESFORD GRANGE	6812
CHESHIRE	62728
CHESTER CASTLE	7016
CHICHELEY HALL	6906
CHILDREY MANOR	7809
CHIRK CASTLE	5025
CHIRU	61034
CHRIST'S HOSPITAL	30913
CICERO	60101
CITY OF BIRMINGHAM	46235
CITY OF BRADFORD	46236
CITY OF BRISTOL	46237
CITY OF CARLISLE	46238
CITY OF CHESTER	46239
CITY OF COVENTRY	46240
CITY OF EDINBURGH	46241
CITY OF GLASGOW	46242
CITY OF HEREFORD	46255
CITY OF LANCASTER	46243
CITY OF LEEDS	46248
CITY OF LEICESTER	46252
CITY OF LICHFIELD	46250
CITY OF LIVERPOOL	46247
CITY OF LONDON	46245
CITY OF LONDON	61670
CITY OF MANCHESTER	46246
CITY OF NOTTINGHAM	46251
CITY OF SALFORD	46257
CITY OF SHEFFIELD	46249
CITY OF ST. ALBANS	46253
CITY OF STOKE-ON-TRENT	46254
CITY OF TRURO	3440
CITY OF WELLS	34092
CIVIL SERVICE RIFLEMAN	46163
CLAN BUCHANAN	72000
CLAN CAMERON	72001
CLAN CAMPBELL	72002
CLAN FRASER	72003
CLAN LINE	35028
CLAN MACDONALD	72004
CLAN MACGREGOR	72005
CLAN MACKENZIE	72006
CLAN MACKINNON	54767
CLAN MACKINTOSH	72007
CLAN MACLEOD	72008
CLAN MUNRO	54764
CLAN STEWART	72009
CLAUD HAMILTON	62546
CLAUGHTON HALL	6905
CLAVERHOUSE	62424
CLEEVE ABBEY	5091
CLEEVE GRANGE	6850
CLEVEDON COURT	2937
CLIFFORD CASTLE	5098
CLIFTON	30927
CLIFTON HALL	4990
CLIVE OF INDIA	70040
CLOVELLY	34037
CLUMBER	61620
CLUN CASTLE	7029
CLYFFE HALL	5951
COBHAM HALL	4991
COCHRANE	45656
COCK O' THE NORTH	60501
COCKINGTON MANOR	7806
CODRINGTON	45676
CŒUR DE LION	2980
COEUR-DE-LION	70007
COGAN HALL	5952
COITY CASTLE	5035
COLDSTREAM GUARDSMAN	46114
COLDSTREAMER	60873
COLLINGWOOD	45645
COLOMBO	60036
COLONEL GARDINER	62675
COLORADO	60094
COLOSSUS	45702
COLSTON HALL	5923
COLWYN BAY	45525
COMBE MARTIN	34043
COMET	9083
COMET	45735
COMMONWEALTH OF AUSTRALIA	60012
COMPTON CASTLE	5099
COMPTON MANOR	7807
CONDOVER HALL	4915
CONEY HALL	7920
CONNAUGHT	45742
CONQUEROR	45701
CONYNGHAM HALL	6937
COOKHAM MANOR	7808
CORFE CASTLE	5034
CORMORANT	3444
CORNDEAN HALL	6938
CORNUBIA	9054
CORNWALLIS	45666
CORONACH	60093
CORONATION	46220
CORSHAM COURT	2938
CORY HALL	5968
COUNTESS	823
COUNTY OF BERKS	1002
COUNTY OF BRECKNOCK	1007
COUNTY OF BUCKS	1001
COUNTY OF CARNARVON	1010
COUNTY OF CAERNARVON	1010
COUNTY OF CARDIGAN	1008
COUNTY OF CARMARTHEN	1009
COUNTY OF CHESTER	1011
COUNTY OF CORNWALL	1006
COUNTY OF DENBIGH	1012
COUNTY OF DEVON	1005
COUNTY OF DORSET	1013
COUNTY OF GLAMORGAN	1014
COUNTY OF GLOUCESTER	1015
COUNTY OF HANTS	1016
COUNTY OF HEREFORD	1017
COUNTY OF LEICESTER	1018
COUNTY OF MERIONETH	1019
COUNTY OF MIDDLESEX	1000
COUNTY OF MONMOUTH	1020
COUNTY OF MONTGOMERY	1021
COUNTY OF NORTHAMPTON	1022
COUNTY OF OXFORD	1023
COUNTY OF PEMBROKE	1024
COUNTY OF RADNOR	1025
COUNTY OF SALOP	1026
COUNTY OF SOMERSET	1004
COUNTY OF STAFFORD	1027

COUNTY OF WARWICK 1028
COUNTY OF WILTS 1003
COUNTY OF WORCESTER 1029
COURAGEOUS 45711
COWES W15
CRANBOURNE GRANGE 6811
CRANBROOK CASTLE 7030
CRANLEIGH 30936
CRANMORE HALL 4914
CRANSLEY HALL 5989
CRAWLEY GRANGE 6872
CREDITON 34048
CREWKERNE 34040
CRICCIETH CASTLE 5026
CROMWELL'S CASTLE 7031
CROOME COURT 2939
CROSBY HALL 4992
CROSSWOOD HALL 4917
CROXTETH HALL 6923
CROYDON 34056
CRUCKTON HALL 5979
CRUMLIN HALL 4916
CRYNANT GRANGE 6861
CUDDIE HEADRIGG 62426
CUDWORTH 32330
CULFORD HALL 61615
CUMBERLAND 62734
CUNARD WHITE STAR 35004
CURLEW 60122
CYCLOPS 45692
CYPRUS 45605
DALTON HALL 4993
DANDIE DINMONT 62401
DANTE 60513
DARLINGTON 61652
DARTINGTON HALL 4918
DARTMOOR 34021
DARTMOUTH CASTLE 4088
DAUNTLESS 45717
DAVENHAM HALL 6907
DE ROBECK 45678
DEFENCE 45722
DEFIANCE 45728
DEFIANT 5080
DENBIGH CASTLE 7001
DENBIGH CASTLE 7032
DERBY COUNTY 61651
DERBYSHIRE 62701
DERWENT GRANGE 6862
DEVIZES CASTLE 7002
DIAMOND JUBILEE 60046
DIBATAG 61033
DICK TURPIN 60080
DIDLINGTON HALL 6940
DINAN 30101
DINARD 30147
DINGLEY HALL 5980
DINMORE MANOR 7820
DINTON HALL 5924
DIRK HATTERAICK 62412
DITCHEAT MANOR 7821
DODINGTON HALL 7901
DOLDOWLOD HALL 5942
DOLHYWEL GRANGE 6863
DOMINIE SAMPSON 62420
DOMINION OF CANADA 3391
DOMINION OF CANADA 60010
DOMINION OF NEW ZEALAND 60013
DONCASTER 60048
DONCASTER ROVERS 61657
DONNINGTON CASTLE 4089
DONNINGTON HALL 4919
DONOVAN 60047
DORCHESTER 34042
DORCHESTER CASTLE 4090
DORFORD HALL 5990
DORNEY COURT 2940
DORNOCH FIRTH 70054
DOVER 30911
DOWNHAM HALL 6908
DOWNSIDE 30912
DOWNTON HALL 4994
DRAKE 45659
DRAYCOTT MANOR 7810
DREADNOUGHT 45718
DRYSLLWYN CASTLE 7018
DUCHESS OF ABERCORN 46234
DUCHESS OF ATHOLL 46231
DUCHESS OF BUCCLEUCH 46230
DUCHESS OF DEVONSHIRE 46227
DUCHESS OF GLOUCESTER 46225
DUCHESS OF HAMILTON 46229
DUCHESS OF KENT 46212
DUCHESS OF MONTROSE 46232
DUCHESS OF NORFOLK 46226
DUCHESS OF RUTLAND 46228
DUCHESS OF SUTHERLAND 46233
DUDLEY CASTLE 4091
DUGALD DALGETTY 62423
DUIKER 61015
DUKE OF GLOUCESTER 71000
DUKE OF ROTHESAY 60508

DUKE OF SUTHERLAND 45541
DULWICH 30907
DUMBARTONSHIRE 62711
DUMBIEDYKES 62427
DUMBLETON HALL 4920
DUMFRIES-SHIRE 62732
DUMMER GRANGE 6834
DUNCAN 45674
DUNLEY HALL 5953
DUNLEY MANOR 7811
DUNRAVEN CASTLE 4092
DUNSTER CASTLE 4093
DURHAM SCHOOL 60860
DWIGHT D. EISENHOWER 60008
DYMOCK GRANGE 6864
DYNEVOR CASTLE 4094
E. C. TRENCH 45539
E. TOOTAL BROADHURST 45534
EARL BALDWIN 5063
EARL BATHURST 5051
EARL CAIRNS 5053
EARL CAWDOR 5046
EARL HAIG 70044
EARL KITCHENER OF KHARTOUM 61358
EARL MARISCHAL 60502
EARL OF BERKELEY 5060
EARL OF BIRKENHEAD 5061
EARL OF CLANCARTY 5058
EARL OF DARTMOUTH 5047
EARL OF DEVON 5048
EARL OF DUCIE 5054
EARL OF DUDLEY 5045
EARL OF DUNRAVEN 5044
EARL OF ELDON 5055
EARL OF MOUNT EDGCUMBE 5043
EARL OF MOUNT EDGCUMBE 30757
EARL OF PLYMOUTH 5049
EARL OF POWIS 5056
EARL OF RADNOR 5052
EARL OF ST. GERMANS 5050
EARL OF SHAFTESBURY 5062
EARL ROBERTS OF KANDAHAR 61357
EARL ST. ALDWYN 5059
EARL WALDEGRAVE 5057
EARLESTOWN CD8
EARLHAM HALL 61644
EAST ANGLIAN 61659
EAST ASIATIC COMPANY 35024
EASTBOURNE 30914
EASTBURY GRANGE 6813
EASTCOTE HALL 5925
EASTHAM GRANGE 6835
EASTNOR CASTLE 7004
EASTON COURT 2941
EASTON HALL 4995
EATON HALL 4921
EATON MASCOT HALL 7902
EDDYSTONE 34028
EDEN HALL 4996
EDIE OCHILTREE 62677
EDSTONE HALL 7921
EDWARD FLETCHER 60142
EDWARD THOMPSON 60500
EDWIN A. BEAZLEY 62652
EIRE 45572
ELAINE 30747
ELAINE 73119
ELAND 61001
ELDER-DEMPSTER LINES 35030
ELDERS FYFFES 35016
ELLANGOWAN 62425
ELLEN DOUGLAS 62688
ELLERMAN LINES 35029
ELMDON HALL 5943
ELMLEY CASTLE 7003
ELTON HALL 4997
ELVEDEN 61604
EMPIRE OF INDIA 60011
ENBORNE GRANGE 6814
ENTERPRISE 60111
ENVILLE HALL 4922
EPSOM 30937
ERLESTOKE MANOR 7812
ESHTON HALL 6942
ESTEVARNEY GRANGE 6836
ETARRE 30751
ETARRE 73114
ETON 30900
EVAN DHU 62673
EVENING STAR 92220
EVENLEY HALL 4923
EVERTON 61663
EVESHAM ABBEY 5085
EXCALIBUR 30736
EXCALIBUR 73081
EXETER 34001
EXMOOR 34022
EXMOUTH 34015

EXPRESS 45706
EYDON HALL 4924
EYNSHAM HALL 4925
EYTON HALL 4998
FAENDRE HALL 5954
FAIREY BATTLE 5077
FAIRLEIGH HALL 4926
FAIRWAY 60092
FALCON 60025
FALKLAND ISLANDS 45606
FALLODON 61616
FARLEIGH CASTLE 5027
FARNBOROUGH HALL 4927
FARNLEY HALL 6943
FATHER AMBROSE 62439
FAWLEY COURT 2942
FEARLESS 45723
FELSTEAD 60089
FIGHTER COMMAND 34064
FIGHTER PILOT 34055
FIJI 45607
FILLONGLEY HALL 6941
FIRDAUSSI 60038
FIRTH OF CLYDE 70050
FIRTH OF FORTH 70051
FIRTH OF TAY 70052
FISHBOURNE W14
FISHER 45669
FITZHERBERT WRIGHT 61249
FLAMBOYANT 60153
FLAMINGO 3445
FLAMINGO 60095
FLEDBOROUGH HALL 6944
FLEETWOOD 45546
FLORA MACIVOR 62674
FLYING DUTCHMAN 70018
FLYING FOX 60106
FLYING SCOTSMAN 60103
FORD CASTLE 61617
FOREMARKE HALL 7903
FORFARSHIRE 62706
FORTHAMPTON GRANGE 6837
FOUNTAINS HALL 7904
FOWEY CASTLE 7019
FOWEY HALL 7905
FOXCOTE MANOR 7822
FOXHUNTER 60134
FRAMLINGHAM 61603
FRANK BIBBY 3364
FRANKTON GRANGE 6816
FRENCH 65217
French Line C.G.T. 35019
FRENSHAM HALL 5981
FRESHFORD MANOR 7813
FRESHWATER W35
FRESHWATER W8
FREWIN HALL 6909
FRILFORD GRANGE 6815
FRILSHAM MANOR 7816
FRINGFORD MANOR 7814
FRITWELL MANOR 7815
FROBISHER 45640
FRON HALL 7906
FURIOUS 45729
G. J. CHURCHWARD 7017
GAINSBOROUGH 60086
GALATEA 45699
GALOPIN 60076
GALTEE MORE 60049
GANNET 60032
GARSINGTON MANOR 7817
GARTH HALL 3950
GARTH HALL 5955
GATACRE HALL 4928
GAY CRUSADER 60108
GAYTON HALL 61641
GAZELLE 1
GAZELLE 61003
GEMSBOK 61020
GENERAL STEAM NAVIGATION 35011
GEOFFREY CHAUCER 70002
GEOFFREY GIBBS 61248
GEOFFREY H. KITSON 61237
GEORGE DAVIDSON 62273
GERARD POWYS DEWHURST 62661
GHANA 45610
GIBRALTAR 45608
GIGGLESWICK 45538
GILBERT AND ELLICE ISLANDS 45609
GILWELL PARK 61646
GLADIATEUR 60070
GLADIATOR 5076
GLASFRYN HALL 6945
GLASGOW YEOMANRY 45158
GLASTONBURY ABBEY 4061
GLEN ALADALE 62488
GLEN ARKLET 62487
GLEN BEASDALE 62475
GLEN CROE 62474
GLEN DESSARY 62489
GLEN DOCHART 62477

GLEN DOUGLAS 256
GLEN DOUGLAS 62469
GLEN FALLOCH 62471
GLEN FINTAIG 62490
GLEN FRUIN 62480
GLEN GARRY 62483
GLEN GARVIN 62492
GLEN GLOY 62493
GLEN GOUR 62494
GLEN GRANT 62279
GLEN LOY 62496
GLEN LUSS 62495
GLEN LYON 62484
GLEN MALLIE 62497
GLEN MAMIE 62482
GLEN MOIDART 62498
GLEN MURRAN 62485
GLEN NEVIS 62472
GLEN OGLE 62481
GLEN ORCHY 62468
GLEN QUOICH 62478
GLEN ROY 62470
GLEN SHEIL 62479
GLEN SLOY 62476
GLEN SPEAN 62473
GLENFINNAN 62467
GLORIOUS 45719
GLOUCESTER CASTLE 7020
GNU 61018
GODSHILL W25
GOLD COAST 45610
GOLDEN EAGLE 60023
GOLDEN FLEECE 60030
GOLDEN PLOVER 60031
GOLDFINCH 3446
GOODMOOR GRANGE 6838
GOODRICH CASTLE 5014
GOPSAL HALL 4999
GORDON HIGHLANDER 49
GORDON HIGHLANDER 46106
GORDON HIGHLANDER 62277
GOSSINGTON HALL 6910
GOUGH 65235
GOYTREY HALL 4929
GRAND PARADE 60090
GRANTLEY HALL 6924
GRANVILLE 30102
GRANVILLE MANOR 7818
GRAYTHWAITE HALL 6976
GREAT CENTRAL 60156
GREAT EASTERN 60157
GREAT NORTHERN 60113
GREAT WESTERN 7007
GREEN ARROW 60800
GRENADIER GUARDSMAN 46110
GRESHAM HALL 5991
GRIMSBY TOWN 61650
GROTRIAN HALL 5926
GRUNDISBURGH HALL 6977
GUERNSEY 30176
GUILD HALL 5927
GUILLEMOT 60020
GUNTON 61608
GUY MANNERING 60129
GUY MANNERING 62413
GWALIOR 45589
GWENDDWR GRANGE 6817
GWENDRAETH 2196
H. A. IVATT 60123
H.L.I. 46121
HABERFIELD HALL 3955
HABERFIELD HALL 6949
HACKNESS HALL 6925
HACKWORTH 32328
HADDON HALL 5928
HAGLEY HALL 4930
HAIG 65226
HAIG 65311
HAILEYBURY 30924
HAL O' THE WYND 60116
HAL O' THE WYND 62417
HAMPDEN 5074
HAMPTON COURT 2943
HANBURY HALL 4931
HANHAM HALL 5929
HANNINGTON HALL 5930
HAPPY KNIGHT 60533
HARDWICK GRANGE 6818
HARDY 45675
HAREWOOD HOUSE 61628
HARLAXTON MANOR 61636
HARLECH CASTLE 4095
HAROLDSTONE HALL 6978
HARRINGTON HALL 5982
HARROW 30919
HARRY HINCHLIFFE 61240
HART HALL 7907
HARTEBEESTE 61009
HARTLAND 34101
HARTLAND POINT 32039
HARTLEBURY CASTLE 7033
HARVESTER 60074

HATFIELD HOUSE 61621
HATHERLEY HALL 5931
HATHERTON HALL 4932
HATTON CASTLE 62278
HAUGHTON GRANGE 6874
HAVERFORDWEST CASTLE 7021
HAVRE 30086
HAWKE 45652
HAWKINGE 34069
HAWKINS 45649
HAYDON HALL 5932
HAYSTOUN OF BUCKLAW 62682
HAZEL HALL 5901
HAZELEY GRANGE 6840
HEADBOURNE GRANGE 6852
HEATHERDEN HALL 6946
HECATE 30949
HELEN MACGREGOR 62409
HELMINGHAM HALL 6947
HELMINGHAM HALL 61647
HELMSTER HALL 6912
HELPERLY HALL 6979
HENGRAVE HALL 5970
HENLEY HALL 5983
HENSHALL HALL 7908
HERCULES 1
HEREFORD CASTLE 7022
HEREWARD THE WAKE 70037
HERMIT 60109
HERRINGBONE 60524
HERTFORDSHIRE 62703
HEVENINGHAM HALL 7909
HEWELL GRANGE 6839
HIGHCLERE CASTLE 4096
HIGHLAND CHIEFTAN 60507
HIGHLAND LIGHT INFANTRY, CITY OF GLASGOW REGIMENT 46121
HIGHNAM COURT 2944
HIGHNAM GRANGE 6819
HILDA 359
HILLINGDON COURT 2945
HIMLEY HALL 4933
HINCHINGBROOKE 61634
HINDERTON HALL 5900
HINDFORD GRANGE 6875
HINDLIP HALL 4934
HINTON MANOR 7819
HIROLA 61023
HOBBIE ELLIOTT 62683
HOGUE 45683
HOLBROOKE HALL 6948
HOLKER HALL 6911
HOLKHAM 61601
HOLKHAM HALL 6926
HOLLAND-AFRIKA LINE 35023
HOLLAND AMERICA LINE 35022
HOLSWORTHY 34097
HOLYHEAD 45514
HOLYROOD 60152
HOME GUARD 45543
HONEYWAY 60519
HONFLEUR 30095
HONG KONG 45611
HONINGHAM HALL 61610
HONINGTON HALL 5969
HONITON 34034
HONOURABLE ARTILLERY COMPANY 46144
HOOD 45654
HOOK NORTON MANOR 7823
HOPE 2136
HOPTON GRANGE 6865
HORNE 65236
HORNET'S BEAUTY 60535
HORSLEY HALL 5956
HORTON HALL 5992
HOTSPUR 70011
HOUGHTON HALL 61612
HOWARD OF EFFINGHAM 30854
HOWARD OF EFFINGHAM 45670
HOWE 45644
HOWICK HALL 5902
HOWN HALL 7910
HUDDERSFIELD TOWN 61653
HULL CITY 61660
HUMORIST 60097
HUNTINGDONSHIRE 62722
HURRICANE 5072
HURRICANE 34065
HURST GRANGE 6851
HURSTPIERPOINT 30918
HUTTON HALL 5957
HYCILLA 60516
HYDERABAD 45585
HYPERION 60037
ICKENHAM HALL 5944
IFORD MANOR 7824
ILFRACOMBE 34017
ILLUSTRIOUS 45532
IMMINGHAM 61482
IMPALA 61002

IMPLACABLE	45709
IMPNEY HALL	6951
IMPREGNABLE	45721
INCE CASTLE	7034
INCHCAPE	3430
INDIA	45574
INDOMITABLE	45720
INDORE	45592
INFLEXIBLE	45727
INVERNESS-SHIRE	62725
INVINCIBLE	45715
INYALA	61016
IRISH ELEGANCE	60534
IRISH GUARDSMAN	46116
IRON DUKE	70014
IRONSIDE	30458
IRRESISTIBLE	45710
ISAMBARD KINGDOM BRUNEL	5069
ISEULT	30749
ISEULT	73116
ISINGLASS	60063
ISLE OF JERSEY	9084
ISLE OF MAN	45511
IVANHOE	2981
IVANHOE	62410
JACKDAW	3447
JAIROU	61037
JAMAICA	45612
JAMES FITZJAMES	62694
JEANIE DEANS	62404
JELLICOE	45667
JERSEY	30081
JERVIS	45663
JINGLING GEORDIE	62430
JOFFRE	65253
JOHN BUNYAN	70003
JOHN MILTON	70005
JOHN OF GAUNT	70012
JONATHAN OLDBUCK	62676
JOYOUS GARD	30741
JOYOUS GARD	73088
JUTLAND	45684
JUTLAND	62668
KASHMIR	45588
KEELE HALL	5903
KEITH	45655
KELHAM HALL	5904
KEMPENFELT	45662
KENILWORTH	60124
KENILWORTH	62431
KENILWORTH CASTLE	4097
KENLEY	34068
KENYA	45613
KEPPEL	45673
KESTREL	60130
KETLEY HALL	4935
KETTLEDRUMMLE	62434
KEYES	45658
KIDWELLY	2194
KIDWELLY CASTLE	4098
KILGERRAN CASTLE	4099
KILVERSTONE HALL	61642
KIMBERLEY HALL	6952
KIMBOLTON CASTLE	61633
KINCARDINESHIRE	62716
KING ARTHUR	30453
KING CHARLES I	6010
KING CHARLES II	6009
KING EDWARD I	6024
KING EDWARD II	6023
KING EDWARD III	6022
KING EDWARD IV	6017
KING EDWARD V	6016
KING EDWARD VI	6012
KING EDWARD VII	6001
KING EDWARD VIII	6029
KING GEORGE I	6006
KING GEORGE II	6005
KING GEORGE III	6004
KING GEORGE IV	6003
KING GEORGE V	6000
KING GEORGE VI	6028
KING GEORGE VI	46244
KING HENRY III	6025
KING HENRY IV	6020
KING HENRY V	6019
KING HENRY VI	6018
KING HENRY VII	6014
KING HENRY VIII	6013
KING JAMES I	6011
KING JAMES II	6008
KING JOHN	6026
KING LEODEGRANCE	30739
KING LEODEGRANCE	73118
KING PELLINORE	30738
KING PELLINORE	73115
KING RICHARD I	6027
KING RICHARD II	6021
KING RICHARD III	6015
KING UTHER	30737
KING UTHER	73111
KING WILLIAM III	6007
KING WILLIAM IV	6002
KINGFISHER	3448
KINGFISHER	60024
KING'S-CANTERBURY	30933
KING'S COURIER	60144
KING'S OWN	46161
KING'S OWN YORKSHIRE LIGHT INFANTRY	60872
KING'S-WIMBLEDON	30931
KINGSLAND GRANGE	6876
KINGSTHORPE HALL	6950
KINGSTONE GRANGE	6820
KINGSWAY HALL	5933
KINGSWEAR CASTLE	5015
KINLET HALL	4936
KINROSS-SHIRE	62718
KIRBY HALL	5993
KITCHENER	601
KITTIWAKE	60120
KLIPSPRINGER	61007
KNELLER HALL	5934
KNIGHT COMMANDER	4020
KNIGHT OF LIÉGE	4017
KNIGHT OF ST. JOHN	4015
KNIGHT OF ST. PATRICK	4013
KNIGHT OF THE GRAND CROSS	4018
KNIGHT OF THE THISTLE	4012
KNIGHT OF THISTLE	60065
KNIGHT TEMPLAR	4019
KNOLTON HALL	5958
KNOWSLEY HALL	5905
KOLHAPUR	45593
KUDU	61008
LADAS	60067
LADY GODIVA	45519
LADY MACBETH	2905
LADY MARGARET	1308
LADY MARGARET HALL	7911
LADY OF AVENEL	62411
LADY OF LYNN	2906
LADY OF LYONS	2903
LADY OF QUALITY	2908
LADY OF THE LAKE	2902
LADY PATRICIA	46210
LAIRD O' MONKBARNS	62421
LAIRD OF BALMAWHAPPLE	62691
LAMBTON CASTLE	61623
LAMPHEY CASTLE	7005
LAMPORT & HOLT LINE	35026
LANARKSHIRE	62705
LANARKSHIRE YEOMANRY	45154
LANCASHIRE	62707
LANCASHIRE FUSILIER	46119
LANCING	30904
LANELAY HALL	4937
LANGFORD COURT	2946
LANGTON HALL	6914
LAPFORD	34102
LAUNCESTON	34012
LAUNCESTON CASTLE	5000
LAWTON HALL	5906
LEANDER	45690
LEATHERHEAD	30939
LEATON GRANGE	6821
LECHLADE MANOR	7825
LECKHAMPTON HALL	5945
LEEDS UNITED	61656
LEEWARD ISLANDS	45614
LEICESTER CITY	61665
LEIGHTON HALL	3953
LEIGHTON HALL	6953
LEINSTER	45741
LEMBERG	60045
LESLIE RUNCIMAN	61238
LEVENS HALL	6913
LEVIATHAN	45704
LIDDINGTON HALL	4938
LIGHTNING	70019
LILFORD HALL	6927
LINCOLNSHIRE	62710
LINCOLNSHIRE REGIMENT	61605
LINDEN HALL	5984
LINETTE	30752
LINETTE	73087
LITTLE LINFORD HALL	7912
LITTLE WYRLEY HALL	7913
LITTLETON HALL	4939
LIVERPOOL	61664
LLANDOVERY CASTLE	5001
LLANDUDNO	45520
LLANFAIR GRANGE	6877
LLANFRECHFA GRANGE	6827
LLANGEDWYN HALL	4941
LLANRUMNEY HALL	6980
LLANSTEPHAN CASTLE	5004
LLANTHONY ABBEY	5088
LLANTILIO CASTLE	5028
LLANVAIR GRANGE	6825
LLEWENI HALL	7914
LLOYD'S	100A1
LLYWELYN	8
LOCH ARKAIG	61764
LOCH EIL	61782
LOCH GARRY	61774
LOCH INSH	54379
LOCH LAGGAN	61791
LOCH LAIDON	61789
LOCH LOCHY	61772
LOCH LOMOND	61790
LOCH LONG	61993
LOCH MORAR	61781
LOCH OICH	61794
LOCH QUOICH	61787
LOCH RANNOCH	61788
LOCH SHEIL	61783
LOCH TAY	54385
LOCH TREIG	61775
LOCKHEED HUDSON	5081
LODE STAR	4003
LONDON RIFLE BRIGADE	46166
LONDON SCOTTISH	46124
LONGFORD GRANGE	6878
LONGWORTH MANOR	7826
LORD ANSON	30861
LORD BALFOUR OF BURLEIGH	61246
LORD BEAVERBROOK	34054
LORD BURGHLEY	61247
LORD COLLINGWOOD	30862
LORD DOWDING	34052
LORD DUNCAN	30858
LORD FARINGDON	60034
LORD GLENALLAN	62679
LORD GLENVARLOCH	62436
LORD HAWKE	30860
LORD HOOD	30859
LORD HOWE	30857
LORD HURCOMB	70001
LORD JAMES OF DOUGLAS	62687
LORD KITCHENER	70043
LORD LOCH	25321
LORD MILDMAY OF FLETE	3417
LORD NELSON	30850
LORD OF THE ISLES	61996
LORD PRESIDENT	60503
LORD RATHMORE	45533
LORD ROBERTS	70042
LORD RODNEY	30863
LORD ROWALLAN	70045
LORD RUTHERFORD OF NELSON	45665
LORD ST. LEVAN	30758
LORD ST. VINCENT	30856
LOTHERTON HALL	6954
LUCKIE MUCKLEBACKIT	62678
LUCY ASHTON	62680
LUDFORD HALL	4940
LUDLOW CASTLE	5002
LULWORTH CASTLE	5003
LUMLEY CASTLE	61624
LUNDY	34029
LUSITANIA	58001
LYDCOTT HALL	6955
LYDFORD	34106
LYDFORD CASTLE	7006
LYDHAM MANOR	7827
LYME REGIS	34009
LYNMOUTH	34099
LYNTON	34038
LYONNESSE	30743
LYONNESSE	73113
LYONSHALL CASTLE	5036
LYSANDER	5079
LYTHAM ST. ANNES	45548
MACCAILIN MÓR	61997
MACLEOD OF MACLEOD	61998
MADDEN	45668
MADGE WILDFIRE	60135
MADOQUA	61027
MADRAS	3407
MADRAS	45575
MADRESFIELD COURT	2947
MAID OF ASTOLAT	30744
MAID OF ASTOLAT	73089
MAID OF LORN	62689
MAINDY HALL	4942
MALAY STATES	45615
MALCOLM GRAEME	62685
MALLARD	60022
MALMESBURY ABBEY	4062
MALTA, G.C.	45616
MALVERN	30929
MANCHESTER UNITED	61662
MANITOBA	45558
MANNA	60085
MANORBIER CASTLE	5005
MANSTON	34070
MANTON GRANGE	6822
MARBLE HALL	5907
MARBURY HALL	6981
MARLAS GRANGE	6841
MARLBOROUGH	30922
MARMION	60132
MARNE	62670
MARRINGTON HALL	4943
MARS	45698
MARWELL HALL	5946
MAUDE	65243
MAUNSELL	DS237
MAURITIUS	45617
MAWLEY HALL	5959
MAYFLOWER	61379
MEDINA	W1
MEG DODS	62419
MEG MERRILIES	60115
MEG MERRILIES	62406
MELISANDE	30753
MELISANDE	73085
MELMERBY HALL	6982
MELTON	60044
MELTON HALL	61638
MERCHANT TAYLORS	30910
MERCURY	9087
MERCURY	70020
MERE HALL	7915
MEREVALE HALL	5971
MERLIN	30740
MERLIN	60027
MERLIN	73080
MERRY HAMPTON	60066
MERSTONE	W27
METEOR	45734
MIDDLESBROUGH	61655
MIDDLETON HALL	4944
MIDLOTHIAN	60151
MILES BEEVOR	60026
MILLIGAN HALL	4945
MILTON	61635
MINORU	60062
MINOTAUR	45695
MISTERTON HALL	6916
MOBBERLEY HALL	7916
MONMOUTH CASTLE	5037
MONS	62665
MONS	65224
MONS MEG	60504
MONTGOMERY CASTLE	5016
MORAY FIRTH	70053
MORAYSHIRE	62712
MORECAMBE AND HEYSHAM	45526
MOREHAMPTON GRANGE	6853
MORETON HALL	5908
MORFA GRANGE	6866
MORGAN LE FAY	30750
MORGAN LE FAY	73112
MORLAIS CASTLE	5038
MORNING STAR	4004
MORNING STAR	70021
MORTEHOE	34094
MOSELEY HALL	4946
MOSTYN HALL	5985
MOTTRAM HALL	6956
MOUNTS BAY	9073
MUNSTER	45740
MURRAY OF ELIBANK	61245
MURSLEY HALL	6915
MYSORE	45586
MYTTON HALL	5996
NANHORAN HALL	4947
NANNERTH GRANGE	6826
NAPIER	45646
NATAL COLONY	3396
NAWORTH CASTLE	61629
NEATH ABBEY	5090
NEDERLAND LINE	35014
NEIL GOW	60082
NELSON	45664
NEPTUNE	45687
NEW BRUNSWICK	45557
NEW HEBRIDES	45618
NEW SOUTH WALES	45564
NEW ZEALAND	45570
NEW ZEALAND LINE	35021
NEWFOUNDLAND	45573
NEWPORT	W34
NEWPORT CASTLE	5065
NEWTON HALL	5909
NIGERIA	45619
NIGHT HAWK	60078
NIGHTINGALE	3449
NILGHAI	61019
NINGWOOD	W18
NORCLIFFE HALL	3952
NORCLIFFE HALL	6957
NORMANDY	30096
NORNA	62435
NORTH ASTON HALL	7917
NORTH BORNEO	45620
NORTH BRITISH	60161
NORTH BRITISH	90773
NORTH BRITISH	90774
NORTH EASTERN	60147
NORTH FORELAND	32422
NORTH STAR	4000
NORTH WEST FRONTIER	45584
NORTHERN RHODESIA	45621
NORTHUMBERLAND	62733
NORTHWICK HALL	3902
NORTHWICK HALL	4948
NORTON HALL	5935
NORWICH CITY	61639
NOTTINGHAM FOREST	61666
NOTTINGHAMSHIRE	62723
NOVA SCOTIA	45556
NOVELTY	45733
NUNHOLD GRANGE	6842
NUNNEY CASTLE	5029
NYALA	61030
NYASALAND	45622
OAKLEY GRANGE	6823
OAKLEY HALL	5936
OCEAN	45730
OCEAN SWELL	60517
ODNEY MANOR	7828
OGMORE CASTLE	7007
OGMORE CASTLE	7035
OKEHAMPTON	34013
OLD CONTEMPTIBLES 1914 AUG. 5 TO NOV. 22	46127
OLDLANDS HALL	6917
OLIVER BURY	61251
OLIVER CROMWELL	70013
OLTON HALL	5972
ONTARIO	45554
ORIBI	61014
ORIENT LINE	35008
ORION	45691
ORMONDE	60057
ORYX	61004
OSBORNE	W19
OSPREY	60131
OTTERINGTON HALL	6983
OTTERY ST. MARY	34045
OUREBI	61026
OVERTON GRANGE	6879
OWAIN GLYNDŴR	7
OWEN GLENDOWER	70010
OWEN TUDOR	60520
OWSDEN HALL	6984
OXBURGH HALL	6958
OXFORDSHIRE	62702
PACKWOOD HALL	4949
PADSTOW	34008
PALESTINE	45623
PALLAH	61025
PAPYRUS	60096
PARK HALL	5910
PARWICK HALL	6985
PATRICK STIRLING	60119
PATRIOT	45500
PATSHULL HALL	4950
PAVILAND GRANGE	6845
PEACOCK	3450
PEARL DIVER	60529
PEATLING HALL	6959
PEEBLES-SHIRE	62719
PELICAN	3451
PEMBROKE CASTLE	4078
PENDEFORD HALL	4951
PENDENNIS CASTLE	4079
PENDRAGON	30746
PENDRAGON	73083
PENGUIN	3452
PENHYDD GRANGE	6844
PENINSULAR & ORIENTAL S.N. CO.	35006
PENRHOS GRANGE	6868
PENRICE CASTLE	7023
PEPLOW HALL	4952
PEREGRINE	60034
PEREGRINE	60146
PERSEVERANCE	45731
PERSIMMON	60050
PERTHSHIRE	62714
PETER POUNDTEXT	62438
PETERSTON GRANGE	6867
PHOENIX	45736
PIONEER	2197
PITCHFORD HALL	4953
PLAISH HALL	4954
PLANET	45545
PLASPOWER HALL	4955
PLOWDEN HALL	4956
PLUMER	65233
PLYMOUTH	34003
POLAR STAR	70026
POLYPHEMUS	45688
POMMERN	60133
PORT LINE	35027
PORTISHEAD	5
PORTLAND BILL	32038
POSTLIP HALL	4957
POULTON GRANGE	6843
POWDERHAM CASTLE	4080
POWIS CASTLE	7024
PRESTATYN	45522
PRESTON HALL	5911
PRETTY POLLY	60061
PRINCE ALBERT	4042

PRINCE ALBERT 62663
PRINCE EDWARD ISLAND 45560
PRINCE GEORGE 4044
PRINCE GEORGE 62658
PRINCE HENRY 4043
PRINCE HENRY 62650
PRINCE JOHN 4045
PRINCE OF WALES 9
PRINCE OF WALES 4041
PRINCE OF WALES 60054
PRINCE OF WALES 62662
PRINCE PALATINE 60052
PRINCE RUPERT 45671
PRINCESS ALEXANDRA 4053
PRINCESS ALEXANDRA 46224
PRINCESS ALICE 4050
PRINCESS ALICE 46223
PRINCESS ANNE 46202
PRINCESS ARTHUR OF CONNAUGHT 46207
PRINCESS AUGUSTA 4058
PRINCESS BEATRICE 4052
PRINCESS BEATRICE 46209
PRINCESS CHARLOTTE 4054
PRINCESS ELIZABETH 4057
PRINCESS ELIZABETH 46201
PRINCESS EUGENIE 4060
PRINCESS HELENA 4051
PRINCESS HELENA VICTORIA 46208
PRINCESS LOUISE 4047
PRINCESS LOUISE 46204
PRINCESS MARGARET 4056
PRINCESS MARGARET ROSE 46203
PRINCESS MARIE LOUISE 46206
PRINCESS MARY 4046
PRINCESS MARY 62664
PRINCESS MAUD 4049
PRINCESS PATRICIA 4059
PRINCESS SOPHIA 4055
PRINCESS VICTORIA 4048
PRINCESS VICTORIA 46205
PRIORY HALL 4958
PRIVATE E. SYKES V.C. 45537
PRIVATE W. WOOD V.C. 45536
PRONGHORN 61035
PTARMIGAN 58012
PUKU 61012
PUNJAB 45579
PURDON VICCARS 62651
PURLEY HALL 4959
PYLE HALL 4960
PYRLAND HALL 4961
QUEBEC 45555
QUEEN ADELAIDE 4034
QUEEN ALEXANDRA 4032
QUEEN BERENGARIA 4038
QUEEN BOADICEA 4040
QUEEN CHARLOTTE 4035
QUEEN ELIZABETH 4036
QUEEN ELIZABETH 46221
QUEEN GUINEVERE 30454
QUEEN MARY 4031
QUEEN MARY 46222
QUEEN MARY 62307
QUEEN MATILDA 4039
QUEEN MAUD 46211
QUEEN OF THE BELGIANS 58000
QUEEN VICTORIA 4033
QUEEN VICTORIA'S RIFLEMAN 46160
QUEEN'S HALL 5912
QUEEN'S WESTMINSTER RIFLEMAN 46162
QUEENSLAND 45566
QUENTIN DURWARD 2979
QUENTIN DURWARD 62432
QUICKSILVER 60015
QUIDENHAM 61609
R.E.M.E. 45528
RABY CASTLE 61625
RADLEY 30930
RAGLAN CASTLE 5008
RAGLEY HALL 4962
RALEIGH 45639
RALPH ASSHETON 61036
RAMSBURY MANOR 7829
RAVENINGHAM HALL 6960
RAYNHAM HALL 61611
READING ABBEY 5084
REDGAUNTLET 60137
REDGAUNTLET 62402
REEDBUCK 61031
REITBOK 61021
REMEMBRANCE 32333
RENOWN 45713
REPTON 30926
REPULSE 45725
RESOLUTION 45708
RESOLVEN GRANGE 6869
RESTORMEL CASTLE 5010
REVENGE 45714
RHOSE WOOD HALL 7918
RHUDDLAN CASTLE 5039
RHYL 45521
RIGNALL HALL 4963
RIPON HALL 5914
RISING STAR 70027
RIVER FAL 3379
RIVER PLYM 3376
ROB ROY 2988
ROB ROY 62400
ROBERT BLAKE 30855
ROBERT BURNS 70006
ROBERT H. SELBIE 69076
ROBERT THE BRUCE 60510
ROBERT THE DEVIL 60110
ROBIN HOOD 70038
RODERICK DHU 62693
RODNEY 45643
RODWELL HALL 4964
ROEDEER 61040
ROLLESTON HALL 5973
ROOD ASHTON HALL 4965
ROOKE 45660
ROTTERDAM LLOYD 35015
ROUGEMONT CASTLE 5007
ROUNDHILL GRANGE 6854
ROXBURGHSHIRE 62715
ROYAL ARMY SERVICE CORPS 46126
ROYAL ENGINEER 46109
ROYAL FUSILIER 46111
ROYAL INNISKILLING FUSILIER 46120
ROYAL IRISH FUSILIER 46123
ROYAL LANCER 60107
ROYAL MAIL 35003
ROYAL NAVAL DIVISION 45502
ROYAL OBSERVER CORPS 34050
ROYAL SCOT 46100
ROYAL SCOTS FUSILIER 46103
ROYAL SCOTS GREY 46101
ROYAL SIGNALS 45504
ROYAL SOVEREIGN 61632
ROYAL SOVEREIGN 61671
ROYAL STAR 70028
ROYAL TANK CORPS 45507
ROYAL ULSTER RIFLEMAN 46122
ROYAL WELCH FUSILIER 46118
ROYDON HALL 5994
RUCKLEY GRANGE 6846
RUDYARD KIPLING 70035
RUGBY 30920
RUNTER HALL 7919
RUSHTON HALL 5913
RUTLANDSHIRE 62729
RYDAL HALL 6986
RYDE W3
SAIGHTON GRANGE 6855
SAINT AMBROSE 2912
SAINT ANDREW 2913
SAINT BARTHOLOMEW 2915
SAINT BENEDICT 2916
SAINT BENET'S HALL 5947
SAINT BRIDES HALL 3904
SAINT BRIDES HALL 4972
SAINT DAVID 2920
SAINT EDMUND HALL 5960
SAINT HELENA 2924
SAINT JOHNSTOUN 60162
SAINT MARTIN 4900
SAINT MUNGO 60145
SAINT NICHOLAS 2926
SAINT PATRICK 2927
SAINT PETER'S HALL 7900
SAINT SEBASTIAN 2928
SAINT STEPHEN 2929
SAINT VINCENT 2930
ST. ALBAN'S HEAD 32426
ST. DONATS CASTLE 5017
ST. DUNSTAN'S 45501
ST. FAGANS CASTLE 5067
ST. FRUSQUIN 60075
ST. GATIEN 60073
ST. HELENA 45624
ST. LAWRENCE 30934
ST. MALO 30093
ST. MAWES CASTLE 5018
ST. OLAVE'S 30938
ST. PAUL'S 30909
ST. PETER'S SCHOOL, YORK, A.D. 627 60847
ST. SIMON 60112
ST. VINCENT 45686
SALFORD HALL 7922
SALISBURY 34002
SALMON TROUT 60041
SAMSON 45738
SANDON HALL 6918
SANDOWN W21
SANDRINGHAM 61600
SANDWICH 45641
SANDWICH 60039
SANSOVINO 60053
SANSPAREIL 45732
SARAWAK 45625
SARUM CASTLE 5097
SASKATCHEWAN 45561
SASSABY 61022
SAUNTON 34093
SAYAJIRAO 60530
SCEPTRE 60069
SCOTS GUARDSMAN 46115
SCOTTISH BORDERER 46104
SCOTTISH UNION 60125
SEA EAGLE 60139
SEAFORTH HIGHLANDER 46108
SEAGULL 3453
SEAGULL 60033
SEAHORSE 45705
SEATON 34020
SEAVIEW W17
SELKIRKSHIRE 62731
SELSEY BILL 32037
SERLBY HALL 61631
SEVENOAKS 30935
SEYCHELLES 45626
SHAFTESBURY 34035
SHAKENHURST HALL 4966
SHANKLIN W20
SHAW SAVILL 35009
SHEFFIELD UNITED 61649
SHEFFIELD WEDNESDAY 61661
SHERBORNE 30906
SHERVINGTON HALL 6987
SHERWOOD FORESTER 46112
SHIRBURN CASTLE 5030
SHIRENEWTON HALL 4967
SHOOTING STAR 70029
SHORWELL W30
SHOTOVER 60081
SHOTTON HALL 3900
SHOTTON HALL 4968
SHOVELL 45651
SHREWSBURY 30921
SHREWSBURY CASTLE 5009
SHRUGBOROUGH HALL 4969
SIDDINGTON HALL 5948
SIDMOUTH 34010
SIERRA LEONE 45627
SILURIAN 60121
SILVER FOX 60017
SILVER JUBILEE 45552
SILVER KING 60016
SILVER LINK 60014
SIMON GLOVER 62442
SINGAPORE 60042
SIR AGLOVALE 30781
SIR AGRAVAINE 30775
SIR ALEXANDER ERSKINE-HILL 61221
SIR ARCHIBALD SINCLAIR 34059
SIR ARTHUR YORKE 3418
SIR BALAN 30769
SIR BALIN 30768
SIR BEDIVERE 30457
SIR BERKELEY SHEFFIELD 62657
SIR BLAMOR DE GANIS 30797
SIR BORS DE GANIS 30763
SIR BRIAN 30782
SIR CADOR OF CORNWALL 30804
SIR CHARLES NEWTON 60005
SIR CHRISTOPHER WREN 70039
SIR CLEMENT ROYDS 62656
SIR COLGREVANCE 30779
SIR CONSTANTINE 30805
SIR DANIEL GOOCH 5070
SIR DAVID STEWART 62275
SIR DINADAN 30795
SIR DODINAS LE SAVAGE 30796
SIR DURNORE 30802
SIR ECTOR DE MARIS 30794
SIR EDWARD ELGAR 7005
SIR EDWARD FRASER 62653
SIR EUSTACE MISSENDEN, SOUTHERN RAILWAY 34090
SIR FELIX POLE 5066
SIR FRANCIS DRAKE 30851
SIR FRANK REE 45530
SIR FREDERICK BANBURY 60102
SIR FREDERICK HARRISON 45531
SIR FREDERICK PILE 34058
SIR GAHERIS 30774
SIR GALAGARS 30776
SIR GALAHAD 30456
SIR GALLERON 30806
SIR GARETH 30765
SIR GAWAIN 30764
SIR GERAINT 30766
SIR GILLEMERE 30783
SIR GUY 30789
SIR HAROLD MITCHELL 61243
SIR HARRY LE FISE LAKE 30803
SIR HECTIMERE 30798
SIR HERBERT WALKER, K.C.B. 45535
SIR HERVIS DE REVEL 30792
SIR HUGO 60083
SIR IRONSIDE 30799
SIR JAMES MILNE 7001
SIR JOHN HAWKINS 30865
SIR JOHN MOORE 70041
SIR KAY 30450
SIR KEITH PARK 34053
SIR LAMIEL 30777
SIR LAMORAK 30451
SIR LAUNCELOT 30455
SIR LAVAINE 30773
SIR LIONEL 30786
SIR MADOR DE LA PORTE 30785
SIR MARTIN FROBISHER 30864
SIR MELEAUS DE LILE 30800
SIR MELIAGRANCE 30452
SIR MELIOT DE LOGRES 30801
SIR MENADEUKE 30787
SIR MURROUGH WILSON 60002
SIR NEROVENS 30784
SIR NIGEL GRESLEY 60007
SIR ONTZLAKE 30793
SIR PELLEAS 30778
SIR PERCIVALE 30772
SIR PERSANT 30780
SIR PRIANIUS 30770
SIR RALPH WEDGWOOD 60006
SIR RICHARD GRENVILLE 30853
SIR ROBERT TURNBULL 45540
SIR RONALD MATTHEWS 60001
SIR SAGRAMORE 30771
SIR TORRE 30449
SIR TRAFFORD LEIGH-MALLORY 34109
SIR TRISTRAM 30448
SIR URRE OF THE MOUNT 30788
SIR UWAINE 30791
SIR VALENCE 30767
SIR VILLIARS 30790
SIR VINCENT RAVEN 60126
SIR VISTO 60068
SIR WALTER RALEIGH 30852
SIR WALTER SCOTT 60143
SIR WALTER SCOTT 62403
SIR WILLIAM A. STANIER, F.R.S. 46256
SIR WILLIAM GRAY 61189
SIROCCO 58010
SKETTY HALL 4970
SKYLARK 3454
SOLARIO 60104
SOLOMON ISLANDS 45603
SOLWAY FIRTH 70049
SOMALILAND 45628
SOMERLEYTON HALL 61640
SOMME 62667
SOMME 65222
SOUGHTON HALL 6962
SOUTH AFRICA 45571
SOUTH AUSTRALIA 45567
SOUTH FORELAND 32421
SOUTHERN RHODESIA 45595
SOUTHPORT 45527
SPARKFORD HALL 5997
SPARROW HAWK 60018
SPEARMINT 60100
SPEKE HALL 7923
SPION KOP 60098
SPITFIRE 5071
SPITFIRE 34066
SPRINGBOK 61000
STACKPOLE COURT 2948
STANFORD COURT 2949
STANFORD HALL 5937
STANLEY HALL 5938
STANWAY HALL 3901
STANWAY HALL 4971
STARLING 3455
STEADY AIM 60512
STEDHAM HALL 6961
STEINBOK 61039
STEMBOK 61032
STEPHENSON 32329
STEPHENSON 45529
STIRLINGSHIRE 62704
STOKESAY CASTLE 5040
STOWE 30928
STOWE GRANGE 6856
STRAIGHT DEAL 60522
STRAITS SETTLEMENTS 45629
STRANG STEEL 61244
STROUDLEY 32332
STURDEE 45647
SUDELEY CASTLE 7025
SUGAR PALM 60526
SUN CASTLE 60523
SUN CHARIOT 60527
SUN STREAM 60515
SUNDERLAND 61654
SUNSTAR 60072
SWALLOWFIELD PARK 4007
SWANAGE 34105
SWANSEA CASTLE 7008
SWAZILAND 45630
SWEENEY HALL 4973
SWIFTSURE 45716
SWINDON 7037
SWITHLAND HALL 6988
SWORDFISH 5082
TAGALIE 60064
TALGARTH HALL 4974
TALISMAN 2989
TAMAR VALLEY 34024
TANGANYIKA 45631
TANGLEY HALL 5939
TANGMERE 34067
TAPLOW COURT 2950
TASMANIA 3395
TASMANIA 45569
TAUNTON CASTLE 7036
TAVISTOCK 34011
TAW VALLEY 34027
TAWSTOCK COURT 2951
TEHRAN 60518
TEMPLECOMBE 34098
TENBY CASTLE 7026
TENNYSON 70032
THAMES 9091
THANE OF FIFE 60505
THE ABBOT 62429
THE ALBRIGHTON 62751
THE ARTISTS' RIFLEMAN 46164
THE ATHERSTONE 62752
THE BADSWORTH 62739
THE BEDALE 62740
THE BEDFORDSHIRE AND HERTFORDSHIRE REGIMENT 45516
THE BELVOIR 62753
THE BERKELEY 62754
THE BILSDALE 62755
THE BLANKNEY 62741
THE BORDER REGIMENT 46136
THE BOY SCOUT 46169
THE BRAES OF DERWENT 62742
THE BRAMHAM MOOR 62736
THE BROCKLESBY 62756
THE BURTON 62757
THE CATTISTOCK 62758
THE CHESHIRE REGIMENT 46134
THE CLEVELAND 62743
THE COTSWOLD 62760
THE COTTESMORE 62749
THE CRAVEN 62759
THE DERBYSHIRE YEOMANRY 45509
THE DERWENT 62761
THE DUKE OF WELLINGTON'S REGT. (WEST RIDING) 46145
THE DURHAM LIGHT INFANTRY 60964
THE EARL 822
THE EARL OF KERRY 62655
THE EAST LANCASHIRE REGIMENT 46135
THE ESSEX REGIMENT 61658
THE FAIR MAID 62405
THE FERNIE 62762
THE FIERY CROSS 62686
THE FITZWILLIAM 62763
THE GARTH 62764
THE GIRL GUIDE 46168
THE GLASGOW HIGHLANDER 45157
THE GLOUCESTERSHIRE REGIMENT 28TH/61ST 5017
THE GOATHLAND 62765
THE GRAFTON 62766
THE GREAT MARQUESS 61994
THE GREEN HOWARD, ALEXANDRA, PRINCESS OF WALES'S OWN YORKSHIRE REGIMENT 60835
THE GREEN HOWARDS 46133
THE GREEN KNIGHT 30754
THE GREEN KNIGHT 73086
THE GROVE 62767
THE HERTFORDSHIRE REGIMENT 46167
THE HOLDERNESS 62744
THE HURWORTH 62745
THE HUSSAR 46154
THE KING'S DRAGOON GUARDSMAN 46152
THE KING'S REGIMENT, LIVERPOOL 46132
THE KING'S ROYAL RIFLE CORPS 46140
THE LADY OF THE LAKE 62690
THE LANCER 46155
THE LEICESTERSHIRE REGIMENT 45503
THE LIFE GUARDSMAN 46150
THE LONDON IRISH RIFLEMAN 46138
THE LOVAT SCOUTS 46128
THE LOYAL REGIMENT 46158
THE MANCHESTER REGIMENT 46148
THE MEYNELL 62726
THE MIDDLESEX REGIMENT 46149
THE MIDDLETON 62746
THE MORPETH 62768
THE NEEDLES 32423
THE NORTH STAFFORDSHIRE REGIMENT 46141
THE NORTHAMPTONSHIRE REGIMENT 46147
THE OAKLEY 62769
THE PERCY 62747
THE PIRATE 62418

Name	No.
THE PRINCE OF WALES'S VOLUNTEERS SOUTH LANCASHIRE	46137
THE PRINCESS ROYAL	46200
THE PUCKERIDGE	62770
THE PYTCHLEY	62750
THE QUORN	62727
THE RANGER 12TH LONDON REGT.	46165
THE RED KNIGHT	30755
THE RED KNIGHT	73110
THE RIFLE BRIGADE	46146
THE ROYAL AIR FORCE	46159
THE ROYAL ARMY ORDNANCE CORPS	45505
THE ROYAL ARTILLERYMAN	46157
THE ROYAL DRAGOON	46153
THE ROYAL HORSE GUARDSMAN	46151
THE ROYAL LEICESTERSHIRE REGIMENT	45503
THE ROYAL PIONEER CORPS	45506
THE ROYAL WARWICKSHIRE REGIMENT	46131
THE RUFFORD	62771
THE SCOTTISH HORSE	46129
THE SINNINGTON	62772
THE SNAPPER, THE EAST YORKSHIRE REGIMENT, THE DUKE OF YORK'S OWN	60809
THE SOMERSET LIGHT INFANTRY (PRINCE ALBERT'S)	4016
THE SOUTH DURHAM	62773
THE SOUTH STAFFORDSHIRE REGIMENT	46143
THE SOUTH WALES BORDERER	46156
THE SOUTH WALES BORDERERS	4037
THE SOUTHWOLD	62748
THE STAINTONDALE	62774
THE SUFFOLK REGIMENT	61645
THE TALISMAN	62428
THE TERRITORIAL ARMY, 1908-1958	70048
THE TETRARCH	60060
THE TYNEDALE	62775
THE WELCH REGIMENT	46139
THE WEST YORKSHIRE REGIMENT	46130
THE WHITE KNIGHT	60077
THE YORK & LANCASTER REGIMENT	46142
THE YORK AND AINSTY	62737
THE ZETLAND	62738
THIRLESTAINE HALL	6965
THOMAS HARDY	70034
THORNBRIDGE HALL	6964
THORNBURY CASTLE	7027
THORNYCROFT HALL	7924
THORPE HALL	61637
THROWLEY HALL	6963
THUNDERER	45703
THUNDERSLEY	80
TIDMARSH GRANGE	6847
TINTAGEL	30745
TINTAGEL	73084
TINTAGEL CASTLE	5011
TINTERN ABBEY	5087
TITLEY COURT	2953
TIVERTON CASTLE	5041
TOBAGO	45635
TOCKENHAM COURT	2954
TODDINGTON GRANGE	6848
TONBRIDGE	30905
TONGA	45632
TOPI	61013
TORNADO	70022
TORQUAY MANOR	7800
TORRINGTON	34031
TORTWORTH COURT	2955
TOTLAND	W23
TOTNES CASTLE	5031
TOTTENHAM HOTSPUR	61630
TOYNBEE HALL	5961
TRACERY	60059
TRAFALGAR	45682
TRANQUIL	60071
TRAVANCORE	45590
TRE POL AND PEN	9065
TREAGO CASTLE	5019
TREGENNA CASTLE	5006
TRELLECH GRANGE	6828
TREMATON CASTLE	5020
TREMATON HALL	5949
TRENTHAM HALL	5915
TRESCO ABBEY	5092
TRETOWER CASTLE	5094
TREVITHICK	9064
TREVITHICK	32327
TREVONE	34096
TREVOR HALL	5998
TREVOSE HEAD	32425
TRIGO	60084
TRIMBUSH	60536
TRINIDAD	45634
TRINITY HALL	5916
TROUVILLE	30089
TUDOR GRANGE	6857
TUDOR MINSTREL	60528
TWINEHAM COURT	2952
TYLNEY HALL	6919
TYRWHITT	45657
UDAIPUR	45591
UGANDA	45636
ULSTER	45739
UMBERSLADE HALL	4975
UMSEKE	61028
UNDERLEY HALL	6928
UNION CASTLE	35002
UNION OF SOUTH AFRICA	60009
UNITED PROVINCES	45578
UNITED STATES LINE	35012
UPTON CASTLE	5093
USK CASTLE	5032
VALIANT	45707
VANCOUVER	3401
VELOCITY	60538
VENTNOR	W16
VENUS	70023
VERNON	45661
VICTOR WILD	60105
VICTORIA	45565
VICTORY	45712
VINDICTIVE	45726
VISCOUNT CHURCHILL	111
VISCOUNT HORNE	5086
VISCOUNT PORTAL	7000
VISCOUNT RIDLEY	61241
VIVIEN	30748
VIVIEN	73117
VULCAN	70024
VULCAN	90732
W.P. ALLEN	60114
WADEBRIDGE	34007
WAINWRIGHT	DS238
WALLSWORTH HALL	5974
WALSINGHAM	61602
WALTER BURGH GAIR	62654
WALTER K. WHIGHAM	60028
WALTON GRANGE	6849
WALTON HALL	5918
WANDERING WILLIE	62440
WANTAGE HALL	5962
WARDLEY HALL	5950
WARDOUR CASTLE	5066
WARFIELD HALL	4976
WARSPITE	45724
WARWICK CASTLE	4081
WARWICKSHIRE	62721
WATCOMBE HALL	4977
WATERBUCK	61011
WATERSMEET	34030
WATLING STREET	60521
WAVERLEY	60509
WELBECK ABBEY	61619
WELLINGTON	5075
WELLINGTON	30902
WELLS	34092
WELSH GUARDSMAN	46117
WEMYSS	45648
WEST HAM UNITED	61672
WESTERN AUSTRALIA	45568
WESTERN STAR	70025
WESTMINSTER	30908
WESTMINSTER ABBEY	5089
WESTMINSTER HALL	5917
WESTMORLAND	62735
WESTOL HALL	7925
WESTWARD HO	34036
WESTWOOD HALL	4978
WEYMOUTH	34091
WHADDON HALL	6970
WHIMPLE	34025
WHITBOURNE HALL	5940
WHITGIFT	30916
WHITTINGTON CASTLE	5021
WHITWELL	W26
WHORLTON HALL	6929
WICK HALL	5995
WIGHTWICK HALL	6989
WIGMORE CASTLE	5022
WILD SWAN	60021
WILDEBEESTE	61010
WILLBROOK	60150
WILLESLEY HALL	6967
WILLEY HALL	7926
WILLIAM HENTON CARVER	61215
WILLIAM SHAKESPEARE	70004
WILLIAM WHITELAW	60004
WILLIAM WORDSWORTH	70030
WILLINGTON HALL	7927
WILSON WORSDELL	60127
WILTON	34041
WIMPOLE HALL	5963
WINCANTON	34108
WINCHESTER	30901
WINCHESTER CASTLE	5042
WINDSOR CASTLE	4082
WINDSOR LAD	60035
WINDWARD ISLANDS	45637
WINNIPEG	3400
WINSLOW HALL	5975
WINSTON CHURCHILL	34051
WITCHINGHAM HALL	6966
WITHERSLACK HALL	6990
WIZARD OF THE MOOR	62684
WOLF HALL	7928
WOLF OF BADENOCH	60506
WOLLATON HALL	5999
WOLSELEY HALL	5964
WOODBASTWICK HALL	61613
WOODCOCK	60029
WOODCOCK HALL	6968
WOOLACOMBE	34044
WOOLLAS HALL	5965
WOOLSTON GRANGE	6858
WOOLWINDER	60055
WOOTTON HALL	4979
WORSLEY HALL	5919
WORSLEY-TAYLOR	62659
WRAYSBURY HALL	6969
WREN	
WROTTESLEY HALL	4980
WROXALL	W4
WYCLIFFE HALL	5920
WYKE HALL	7929
WYNYARD PARK	61618
YARMOUTH	W2
YEOVIL	34004
YES TOR	34026
YIEWSLEY GRANGE	6859
YORKSHIRE	62700
YPRES	62669
ZANZIBAR	45638
ZEEBRUGGE	62666

Vale of Rheidol 2-6-2T No 9 *Prince of Wales* at Devil's Bridge in June 1963.

Appendix 4. Chronological list of additions to stock.

Jan-48
3218
3219
6982
42190
42191
42192
42193
43003
43004
43005
43006
43007
43008
60526
60527
61274
61275
61276
61277
61278
61279
61280
61281
61282
69001
69002

Feb-48
6981
6983
6984
6985
42194
42195
42196
44748
44749
44750
60528
60529
61283
61284
61285
61286
61287
61288
61289
61290
61291
61292
61293
69003
69004
69005
69006

Mar-48
6986
6987
6988
6989
42197
42198
42199
43009
43010
43011
44751
44752
44753
60530
60531
60532
61294
61295
61296
61297
61298
61299
61300
61301
61302
61303
61304
69007
69008
69009
69010
69011

Apr-48
6990
9662
9663
9664
9665
9666
42147
43012
43013
43014
44754
44755
60533
60534
61305
61306
61307
61308
61309
61310
61311
61312
61313
61314
61315
67717
69012
69013
69014
69015

May-48
7008
7009
9667
9668
9669
9670
34071
34072
34073
34074
34075
34076
42148
42149
42150
42151
42152
43015
43016
43017
43018
44740
46257
60535
60536
61316
61317
61318
61319
61320
61321
61322
61323
67718
67719
67720
67721

Jun-48
7010
7011
7012
9671
9672
42153
42154
42155
42156
42157
43019
44738
44739
44741
44742
44743
44756
60537
60538
61324
61325
61326
61327
61328
61329
61330
61331
61332
67722
67723
67724
67725

Jul-48
1
7014
7015
34077
34078
34079
42158
42159
42160
44698
44699
44700
44744
44745
44747
61333
61334
61335
67726
67727
67728
67729

Aug-48
7016
7430
7431
7432
7433
7434
34080
34081
41210
41211
41212
42161
42162
42163
42164
44701
44702
44703
44746
60114
60539
61336
61337
61338
67730

Sep-48
4160
4161
4162
4163
4164
7017
7435
7436
7437
34082
35021
35022
41213
41214
41215
41216
41217
41218
41219
41220
41221
41222
42165
42166
42167
42168
42169
44704
44705
44706
44707
60115
60130
61339

Oct-48
4165
4166
4167
7438
7439
34083
34084
35023
35024
41223
41224
41225
41226
41227
41228
41229
42170
42171
42172
42173
42174
44708
44709
44710
44711
44712
47589
47611
47660
60116
60117
60131
60132
60133
67731
67732

Nov-48
4168
4169
6760
6761
6762
6763
6764
6991
6992
42175
42176
42177
42178
44713
44714
44715
44716
46420
46421
46422
46423
46424
46425
47607
47659
60118
60119
60134
60135
60136
61340
67733
67734
67735
67736
67737
67738
67739
67740
67741
67742
67743
67744
67745

Dec-48
6765
6993
6994
6995
34085
34086
34087
34088
34089
35025
35026
35027
35028
42179
42180
42181
42182
43020
43021
43022
44717
44757
46426
46427
46428
46429
46430
46431
46432
46433
46434
60120
60121
60122
60137
60138
60139
60140
60141
61341
67746
67747
67748
67749
67750
67751
67752
67753
67754
67755
67756
67757
67758
67759
67760
90101
90102
90103
90104
90105
90106
90107
90108
90109
90110
90111
90112
90113
90114
90115
90116
90117
90118
90119
90120
90121
90122
90123
90124
90125
90126
90127
90128
90129
90130
90131
90132
90133
90134
90135
90136
90137
90138
90139
90140
90141
90142
90143
90144
90145
90146
90147
90148
90149
90150
90151
90152
90153
90154
90155
90156
90157
90158
90159
90160
90161
90162
90163
90164
90165
90166
90167
90168
90169
90170
90171
90172
90173
90174
90175
90176
90177
90178
90179
90180
90181
90182
90183
90184
90185
90186
90187
90188
90189
90190
90191
90192
90193
90194
90195
90196
90197
90198
90199
90200
90201
90202
90203
90204
90205
90206
90207
90208
90209
90210
90211
90212
90213
90214
90215
90216
90217
90218
90219
90220
90221
90222
90223
90224
90225
90226
90227
90228
90229
90230
90231
90232
90233
90234
90235
90236
90237
90238
90239
90240
90241
90242
90243
90244
90245
90246
90247
90248
90249
90250
90251
90252
90253
90254
90255
90256
90257
90258
90259
90260
90261
90262
90263
90264
90265
90266
90267
90268
90269
90270
90271
90272
90273
90274
90275
90276
90277
90278
90279
90280
90281
90282
90283
90284
90285
90286
90287
90288
90289
90290
90291
90292
90293
90294
90295
90296
90297
90298
90299
90300
90301
90302
90303
90304
90305
90306
90307
90308
90309
90310
90311
90312
90313
90314
90315
90316
90317
90318
90319
90320
90321
90322
90323
90324
90325
90326
90327
90328
90329
90330
90331
90332
90333
90334
90335
90336
90337
90338
90339
90340
90341
90342
90343
90344
90345
90346
90347
90348
90349
90350
90351
90352
90353
90354
90355
90356
90357
90358
90359
90360
90361
90362
90363
90364
90365
90366
90367
90368
90369
90370
90371
90372
90373
90374
90375
90376
90377
90378
90379
90380
90381
90382
90383
90384
90385
90386
90387
90388
90389
90390
90391
90392
90393
90394
90395
90396
90397
90398
90399
90400
90401
90402
90403
90404
90405
90406
90407
90408
90409
90410
90411
90412
90413
90414
90415
90416
90417
90418
90419
90420
90421
90521
90522
90523
90524
90525
90526
90527
90528
90529
90530
90531
90532
90533
90534
90535
90536
90537
90538
90539
90540
90541
90542
90543
90544
90545
90546
90547
90548
90549
90550
90551
90552
90553
90554
90555
90556
90557
90558
90559
90560
90561
90562
90563
90564
90565
90566
90567
90568
90569
90570
90571
90572
90573
90574
90575
90576
90577
90578
90579
90580
90581
90582
90583
90584
90585
90586
90587
90588
90589
90590
90591
90592
90593
90594
90595
90596
90597
90598
90599
90600
90601
90602
90603
90604
90605
90606
90607
90608
90609
90610
90611
90612
90613
90614
90615
90616
90617
90618
90619
90620
90621
90622
90623
90624
90625
90626
90627
90628
90629
90630
90631
90632
90633
90634
90635
90636
90637
90638
90639
90640
90641
90642
90643
90644
90645
90646
90647
90648
90649
90650
90651
90652
90653
90654
90655
90656
90657
90658
90659
90660
90661
90662
90663
90664
90665
90666
90667
90668
90669
90670
90671
90672
90673
90674
90675
90676
90677
90678
90679
90680
90681
90682
90683
90684
90685
90686
90687
90688
90689
90690
90691
90692
90693
90694
90695
90696
90697
90698
90699
90700
90701
90702
90703
90704
90705
90706
90707
90708
90709
90710
90711
90712
90713
90714
90715
90716
90717
90718
90719
90720
90721
90722
90723
90724
90725
90726
90727
90728
90729
90730
90731
90732
90750
90751
90752
90753
90754
90755
90756
90757
90758
90759
90760
90761
90762
90763
90764
90765
90766
90767
90768
90769
90770
90771
90772
90773
90774

Jan-49
6766
6767
6768
6769
6996
6997
6998
34090
35029
35030
42183
42184
43023
43024
43025
44728
44729
61342
67761
67762
67763

Feb-49
6999
9673
42185
42186
43026
43027
44730
44731
44732
44733
44734
44735
60123
60142
60143
61343
67764
67765

Mar-49
7901
7902
9674
9675
9676
9677
42107
42108
43028
43029
43030
44718
44719
44720
44721
44736
44737
60124
60144
60145
61344

Apr-49
7900
7903
7904
7905
9678
9679
9680
42109
43031
43032
44722
44723
44724
44725
60125
60126
60146
60147
61345
61346
W35
W36

May-49
7018
7019
7020
9681
9682
42110
43033
43034
43035
44658
44659
44660
44726
44727
60127
60128
60148
60149
61347
62001

Jun-49
1500
7021
7022
7023
7024
42111
42112
42113
42114
43036
43037
43038
44661
44662
44663
44664
44665
60129
60150
60151
61348
62002
62003
62004
62005
62006
62007
62008
62009
62010
62011

Jul-49
1501
1502
42115
42116
43039
43040
44666
44667
48045
60152
61349
61350
62012
62013
62014
62015
62016
62017
62018
62019

Aug-49
1503
1504
1505
7025
7026
7027
8400
8401
8450
41230
41231
41232
41233
41234
41235
42117
42118
42119
42120
43041
43042
48046
48288
60153
61351
61352
62020
62021
62022
62023
62024
62025
62026
62027
62028
62029
62030
62031
62032
62033

Sep-49
1506
1507
1508
1509
8402
8403
8404
8451
32646
32677
34091
34092
41236
41237
41238
41239
41240
41241
41242
42121
42122
43043
43044
48061
48247
48257
48258
48262
48263
48287
48290
48292
60154
60155
61353
61354
61355
61356
62034
62035
62036
62037
62038
62039
67766
67767

Oct-49
1600
1601
1602
1603
1604
4170
4171
4172
4173
8452
34093
34094
34095
41243
41244
41245
41246
41247
42123
42124
42125
43045
43046
48016
48039
48250
48253
48256
48260
48296
60156
61357
61358
61359
62040
62041
62042
62043
62044
62045
62046
62047
62048
62049
62050
67768
67769
69001

Nov-49
1605
1606
1607
1608
1609
1610
1611
1612
4174
4175
4176
4177
4178
8453
34096
34097
34098
41248
41249
41250
41251
41252
41253
41254
41255
42126
42127
42128
43047
43048
43049
48248
48249
48252
48289
48294
48295
48297
60157
60158
60159
62051
62052
62053
62054
62055
62056
62057
67770
67771
67772
69002
69003
69004
69005
69006
69007

Dec-49
1613
1614
1615
1616
1617
1618
1619
4179
7906
8405
8406
8407
8454
34099
34100
41256
41257
41258
41259
42129
42130
42131
42132
44668
44669
48012
48018
48020
48077
48094
48246
48251
48254
48255
48259
48261
48286
48291
60160
60161
60162
62058
62059
62060
62061
67773
67774
67775
69008
69009
69010
69011
69012
69013
69014
69015

Jan-50
7440
7441
7907
7908
7909
7910
8408
8409
8410
8411
8412
8413
8414
8455
42133
42134
42135
44670
46435
46436
46437
46438
46439
62062
62063
62064
62065
62066
67776
67777
69016
69017
69018
69019
69020

Feb-50
7442
7443
7444
7911
8456
9410
9411
34101
34102
34103
34105
42136
42137
44671
44672
44673
46440
46441
46442
46443
46444
46445
62067
62068
62069
67778
67779
67780

Mar-50
7445
7446
7447
7912
7913
7914
7915
8415
8416
8417
8418
8457
9412
9413
34104
34106
42138
42139
44674
44675
46446
46447
46448
46449
61360
61361
61362
61400
62070
67781
67782
67783
67784

Apr-50
7448
7449
7916
7917
8419
8458
9414
34107
34108
34109
42140
42141
44676
44677
46450
46451
46452
46453
46454
46455
61363
61364
61365
61366
61367
61401
61402
61403
67785
67786
67787

May-50
7028
7029
7918
7919
8459
9415
9416
9417
9418
42142
42143
44678
44679
46456
46457
46458
46459
46460
61404
61405
61406
67788
67789
67790
M8108
M8182
M8236
S&M 1

Jun-50
1620
1621
1622
1623
1624
7030
7031
7032
8460
8461
9419
9420
41260
42144
42145
44680
44681
44682
46461
46462
46463
46464
61368
61369
61407
61408
61409
67791
67792
67793

Jul-50
7033
8420
8421
8462
9421
9422
9423
41261
41262
41263
41264
42096
42097
42098
43050
44683
44684
67794
67795

Aug-50
1625
1626
1627
1628
7034
7035
7036
7037
9424
42146
41265

41266
41267
41268
41269
42099
42100
43051
43052
43053
43054
43070
44685
44688
67796
67797
67798

Sep-50
1629
7920
7921
7922
7923
7924
8463
9425
9426
9427
9428
41270
41271
41272
41273
41274
42050
42051
42052
42101
42102
42103
42104
42105
43055
43056
43057
43058
43059
43060
43061
43071
43072
43073
43074
43075
44689
67799
67800

Oct-50
6770
6771
7925
7926
7927
7928
8422
8423
8464
9429
9430
41275
41276
41277
41278
41279
41280
41281
41282
42053
42054
42055
42066
42067
42068
42069
42106
43076
43077
43078
43079
43080
43081
44690
44691
44692
61370
61371

Nov-50
6772
6773
6774
6775
6776
7820
7821
7929
8465
8466
9431
9432
41283
41284
41285
41286
41287
42056
42057
42058
42059
42070
42071
42072
42073
42074
42075
43062
43063
43064
43065
43082
43083
43084
43085
43086
43087
44693

Dec-50
6777
6778
6779
7822
7823
7824
7825
7826
7827
7828
7829
8424
9433
41288
41289
42060
42061
42062
42063
42064
42065
42076
42077
42078
43066
43067
43068
43069
43088
43089
43090
43091
43092
43093
43094
43095
43096
44694
44695
44696
44697
61372
61373

Jan-51
1630
1631
1632
1633
8426
9434
9435
9436
9437
34110
42079
42080
42081
42082
43097
70000

Feb-51
1634
1635
1636
1637
8425
8427
8428
8467
8468
9438
9439
9440
42083
42084
42085
43098
43099
43100
43101
61374
70001

Mar-51
1638
1639
1640
1641
8429
8469
9441
9442
9443
42086
42087
42088
43102
43103
43104
43105
43112
61375
70002
70003
70004

Apr-51
1642
1643
1644
1645
9444
9445
42089
42090
42091
43106
43113
44686
61376
69021
69022
69023
69024
69025
70005
70006
70007
70008
73000

May-51
1646
1647
1648
1649
8470
8471
9446
9447
9448
42092
42093
42094
43107
43108
43114
43115
44687
61377
61378
69026
69027
69028
70009
70010
70011
70012
70013
73001
73002
75000

Jun-51
9449
9450
42095
43109
43110
43116
43117
43118
43119
46465
46466
46467
61379
70014
70015
70016
70017
70018
70019
73003
73004
73005
73006

Jul-51
8472
9451
9452
9453
43111
43120
43137
43138
43139
46468
46469
46470
46471
46472
70020
73007
73008
73009
80010
80011

Aug-51
8473
43121
43122
43123
43140
43141
43142
43143
46473
46474
46475
61380
70021
70022
70023
73010
73011
73012
73013
75001
75002
75003
75004
80012

Sep-51
9454
9455
9456
41290
41291
41292
43124
43125
43126
43144
43145
43146
46476
46477
46478
46479
46480
61381
61382
73014
73015
73016
73017
75005
75006
75007

Oct-51
8474
9457
9458
41293
41294
41295
41296
41297
41298
43127
43128
43147
43148
43149
46481
46482
46483
46484
61383
61384
61385
61386
70024
73018
73019
73020
73021
73022
75008
75009
80013
80014
80015
80016
80017
80018
80020

Nov-51
8475
9459
9460
41299
43129
43130
43131
43150
43151
43152
46485
46486
46487
46488
46489
46490
61387
61388
61389
73023
73024
73025
75010
75011
75012
75013
80021
80022
80023

Dec-51
9461
9462
43132
43133
43134
43135
43153
43154
43155
46491
46492
46493
46494
61390
61391
61392
72000
72001
73026
73027
73028
75014
75015
80019
80024
80025
80026

Jan-52
9463
9464
9465
41320
43136
43156
46495
61393
61394
72002
72003
73029
75016
75017
80027
80028
80029

Feb-52
9466
9467
9468
41321
41322
46496
46497
46498
61395
61396
72004
72005
72006
80030

Mar-52
8476
8477
8480
8481
9469
9470
41300
41301
41302
41303
41304
41323
41324
41325
46499
46500
46501
46502
61397
72007
72008
75018
75019
80031
80032
80033

Apr-52
8482
9471
9472
41305
41306
41307
41308
41326
41327
61398
61399
72009
80034
82000
82001
82002

May-52
8478
8483
8484
9473
9474
41309
41310
41311
41312
41313
41314
41315
41328
41329
80035
80036
80037
82003
82004
82005
82006
82007

Jun-52
8479
8485
8486
9475
9476
41316
41317
41318
41319
80038
80039
80040
82008
82009
82010

Jul-52
8487
8488
8489
8490
9477
9478
9479
43157
43158
80041
82011
82012
82013

Aug-52
8491
8492
9480
9481
43159
43160
80042
80043
80044
82014
82015
82016
82017

Sep-52
8493
8494
9482
43161
70025
80000
80045
80046
82018
82019

Oct-52
8495
8496
9483
9484
9485
70026
70027
70028
80001
80002
80003
80047
80048
80049

Nov-52
8497
8498
8499
9486
9487
46503
46504
46505
46506
46507
70029
70030
70031
70032
80004
80005
80006
80050
80051

Dec-52
9488
46508
46509
46510
46511
46512
46513
46514
70033
70034
70035
70036
70037
76000
76001
76002
76003
76004
76005
76020
76021
76022
76023
78000
78001
78002
78003
80007
80008
80009
80052
80053

Jan-53
8430
8431
9489
46515
46516
46517
46518
70038
76024
78004

Feb-53
8432
8434
46519
46520
46521
70039
76006
76007
76008
76009
76010
76011
76012
76013
76014
78005

Mar-53
8433
46522
46523
46524
46525
46526
46527
70040
70041
78006
78007
78008
80059
80060

Apr-53
8435
70042
78009
80061

May-53
8436
8437
76015
80062
80063

Jun-53
8438
8439
70043
70044
73030
75030
75031
75032
76016
80064
80065

Jul-53
73031
73032
75033
75034
76017
76018
76019
80066
84000
84001
84002

Aug-53
73033
73034
73035
75035
75036
75037
75038
75039
80067
80068
84003
84004
84005
84006

Sep-53
73036
73037
73038
73039
75040
75041
75042
75043
75044
75045
76025
80069
84007
84008
84009
84010
84011
84012
84013
84014

Oct-53
47005
73040
73041
73042
73043
75046
75047
75048
75049
80070
84015
84016
84017
84018
84019

Nov-53
47006
47007
73044
73045
73046
75020
75021
76026
76027
76028
76029
76030
76031
80072
80073
80074

Dec-53
47008
73047
73048
73049
75022
75023
75024
76032
76033
76034
78010
78011
80071
80075
80076

Jan-54
47009
78012
78013
80077
92000
92001
92002
92003
92004

Feb-54
9490
77000
77001
77002
77003
78014
78015
80078
92005
92006
92007

Mar-54
8440
8442
8443
9491
77004
77005
77006
77007
78016
78017
78018
78019
80079
80080
92008
92009

Apr-54
8441
8444
75025
77008
78020
80081
80082

May-54
9492
71000
75026
75027
75028
75029
76035
78021
78022
78023
78024
78025
80083
80084
80085
92010
92011
92012
92013
92014

Jun-54
8445
8446
8447
8448
8449
9493
70045
70046
70047
73050
73051
73052
73053
73054
73055
76036
76037
77009
77010
77011
78026
78027
78028
80086

Jul-54
70048
70049
73056
73057
73058
76038
76039
76040
76041
77012
77013
77014
77015
78029
80087
80088

Aug-54
9494
70050
70051
70052
73059
73060
76042
76043
76044
77016
77017
77018
80089
80090

Sep-54
70053
70054
73061
73062
73063
77019
78030
78031
78032
80091
80092
82020
92015

Oct-54
9495
9496
73064
73065
73066
73067
73068
78033
78034
80093
80094
80106
80107
82021
82022
82023
82024
92016
92017
92018
92019

Nov-54
1650
73069
73070
73071
78035
78036
78037
78038
78039
80095
80096
80108
80109
80110
80111
82025
82026
82027
92030
92031
92032
92033

Dec-54
1651
1652
1653
1654
9497
73072
73073
73074
78040
78041
78042
78043
78044
80054
80055
80056
80057
80097
80098
80112
80113
80114
80115
82028
82029
82030
82031
92034
92035
92036
92037
92038
92039
92040
92041

Jan-55
1655
1656
1657
80058
80099
80100
82032
82033
82034
92042
92043
92044

Feb-55
1658
1659
1660
80101
92045
92046
92047
92048

Mar-55
1661
1662
1663
1664
9498
76045
76046
76047
76048
80102
80103
80104
82035
92020
92021
92022
92023
92049

Apr-55
1665
1666
73075
73076
76049
76053
76054
76055
80105
82036
82037

May-55
1667
1668
1669
73077
73078
73079
80116
80117
82038
82039
82040

Jun-55
73080
76056
76057
76058
76059
76060
76061
76062
80118
80119
82041
82042
82043
92024
92025
92026
92027

Jul-55
9499
73081
73082
73083
80120
80121
92028
92029

Aug-55
73084
73085
73100
75065
80122
82044
92050
92051
92052

Sep-55
73086
73087
73088
73089
73101
73102
73103
73104
75066
75067
75068
75069
80123
80124
92053
92054
92055

Oct-55
73090
73091
73092
73110
73111
73112
73113
75070
75071
78045
78046
78047
78048
80125
80126
92056
92057
92058
92059

Nov-55
73093
73094
73095
73096
73114
73115
73116
73117
75072
75073
75074
75075
78049
78050
78051
78052
78053
80127
80128
92060
92061
92062
92063

Dec-55
3400
73097
73098
73099
73105
73106
73107
73108
73118
73119
75076
75077
78054
80129
80130
92064
92065
92066
92067
92068
92069

Jan-56
3401
73109
73120
73121
73122
75078
75079
92070
92071

Feb-56
3402
3403
73123
73124
92072
92073
92074

Mar-56
3404
80131
80132
80133
92075
92076
92077
92078
92079

Apr-56
3405
80134
80135
92080
92081

May-56
3406
80136
80137
92082
92083
92084
92085

Jun-56
73125
73126
80138
80139
92086
92097

Jul-56
76063
76064
76065
76066
80140
80141
92098
92099

Aug-56
3407
3408
73127
73128
73129
76050
76051
76067
76068
76069
78055
78056
78057
80142
92087
92100
92101
92102
92103
92104

Sep-56
73130
73131
76052
76070
78058
78059
80143
80144
92089
92105
92106
92107

Oct-56
3409
73132
73133
73134
73135
76071
76072
76073
78060
78061
78062
80145
80146
92088
92108
92109
92110

Nov-56
73136
73137
73138
73139
75050
75051
76074
78063
78064
80147
80148
92090
92091
92111
92112
92113

Dec-56
73140
73141
73142
73143
73144
73155
73156
73157
73158
75052
76075
76076
76077
76078
80149
80150
92092
92114
92115
92116
92117
92118

Jan-57
73145
73159
73160
73161
75053
75054
75055
80151
92093
92119

Feb-57
73146
73147
73162
73163
76079
76080
76081
80152
80153
92094
92120
92121
92122

Mar-57
73148
73149
73164
73165
73166
75056
75057
76082
76083
76084
80154
84020
84021
84022
92095
92123
92124
92125
92126
92127

Apr-57
73150
73151
73167
73168
73169
75058
75059
76085
76086
84023
84024
84025
84026
92096
92128
92129
92130
92131

May-57
73152
73153
73170
73171
75060
75061
75062
76087
76088
76089
76100
84027
84028
92132
92133
92134

Jun-57
73154
75063
75064
76090
76091
76092
76101
76102
76103
84029
92135
92136
92137
92138
92139

Jul-57
76093
76104
76105
76106
92140
92141
92142

Aug-57
76094
76095
76107
76108
76109
76110
76111
92143
92144
92145

Sep-57
48773
48774
48775
76096
76097
76112
92146
92147
92148
92178

Oct-57
76098
76113
76114
92149
92150
92151
92152
92153
92179

Nov-57
76099
92154
92155
92156
92157
92158
92159
92160
92180
92181

Dec-57
92161
92162
92168
92169
92170
92182
92183

Jan-58
92172
92184
92185
92186

Feb-58	**Mar-58**	92165	**Jun-58**	**Jul-58**	92232	92238	92243	**Dec-58**	**Apr-59**	**Jun-59**	**Sep-59**	**Nov-59**	**Jan-60**
92171	92163	92191	92194	92227	92233	92239	92244	92201	92203	92207	92211	92215	92218
92173	92176		92195	92228	92234			92202	92204	92208	92212		92219
92174	92177	**May-58**	92222	92229	92235	**Oct-58**	**Nov-58**	92247		92209		**Dec-59**	
92175	92189	92166	92223			92198	92200	92248	**May-59**		**Oct-59**	92216	**Mar-60**
92187	92190	92167	92224	**Aug-58**	**Sep-58**	92199	92245	92249	92205	**Aug-59**	92213	92217	92220
92188		92192	92225	92196	92197	92240	92246	92250	92206	92210	92214		
	Apr-58	92193	92226	92230	92236	92241							
	92164	92221		92231	92237	92242							

Bulleid 'Leader' 0-6-6-0T No 36001.

BR-built Stanier 'OF' 0-4-0ST No 47006. It is one of the later engines with shortened saddle tanks and increased coal capacity in front of the cab.

Appendix 5. Chronological list of withdrawals from stock.

Jan-48
6, 198, 424, 2612, 2665, 2793, 3585, 40715, 40736, 41759, 43573, 46682, 46718, 48910, 49175, 49251, 52032, 52401, 55355, 57313, 57406, 62367, 62876, 62924, 65380, 67358, 67370, 67378, 68488, M1307, M1385, M3602, M7715, M7812, M27648, M28095, M28230, M28415, M28586, M28597

Feb-48
411, 1358, 2623, 3004, 30146, 30150, 30343, 30618, 31042, 31445, 31459, 32601, 32699, 41668, 46679, 46747, 46878, 46926, 47892, 47938, 49231, 49273, 50903, 52046, 52256, 52417, 54643, 54764, 57408, 62111, 62112, 62122, 62155, 62195, 62450, 62808, 62870, 62920, 63252, 63268, 63279, 63298, 63339, 65063, 65195, 65383, 65400, 65410, 65612, 65639, 67119, 68134, 68213, 69419, M1361, M3050, M3473, M7796, M7841, M25321, M28097, M28153, M28350, M28441, M28542, R/C2136

Mar-48
410, 2656, 2752, 3396, 32239, 32259, 32361, 43338, 46691, 46692, 46909, 49225, 49236, 49272, 50617, 50667, 50901, 52152, 52337, 52422, 52568, 52841, 54379, 54637, 57333, 58931, 61354, 61685, 62062, 62143, 62403, 62443, 62463, 62914, 62933, 62937, 62993, 63315, 63321, 63494, 64136, 64145, 65220, 65289, 65328, 65399, 65418, 65421, 67097, 67114, 67355, 68366, M3021, M3153, M3195, M3424, M7700, M23016, M25722, M25827, M27525

Apr-48
54, 190, 202, 268, 275, 906, 1196, 1197, 1726, 1753, 1762, 1769, 1900, 2728, 2730, 2748, 2749, 2751, 2774, 2776, 2785, 2905, 3002, 3019, 3158, 3366, 3408, 3417, 3421, 3452, 4004, 4365, 4386, 31450, 41870, 46673, 49038, 49250, 49274, 49286, 50429, 51320, 52837, 54434, 54644, 56905, 57327, 57343, 57380, 57641, 58044, 58263, 58292, 58301, 58345, 58918, 58937, 61394, 61690, 62157, 62921, 64152, 65069, 65256, 65337, 67159, 67161, 67168, 67169, 67170, 67172, 67173, 67179, 67180, 67181, 67185, 68081

May-48
1308, 2669, 2714, 2739, 2913, 2980, 2988, 3027, 3391, 5127, 5146, 5302, 5349, 30090, 30672, 31028, 31031, 31215, 32122, 32435, 40757, 41674, 41714, 41842, 43265, 43269, 43831, 46605, 46686, 46738, 46740, 46883, 46920, 49013, 49197, 49233, 49383, 50875, 52457, 52467, 52618, 52873, 54415, 54631, 55116, 57301, 57308, 57374, 57616, 58003, 58011, 58012, 58037, 58227, 58266, 58339, 58387, 58395, 58408, 58936, 61383, 62066, 62453, 62871, 63921, 65352, 65368, 65394, 65625, 67115, 67117, 67134, 67141, 68484

Jun-48
238, 1706, 1713, 2680, 2781, 2797, 3006, 3009, 3379, 3440, 5119, 5374, 30176, 30340, 30363, 31002, 31014, 31397, 32164, 32609, 40748, 41002, 41029, 41818, 43439, 43769, 46661, 46681, 47959, 49095, 49103, 49201, 50952, 52127, 52253, 52935, 55117, 55190, 57290, 57304, 57330, 57422, 57574, 58055, 58205, 58210, 58337, 58358, 58423, 58909, 61363, 61364, 61397, 61500, 61681, 62504, 62600, 62922, 62954, 62973, 63250, 63254, 63264, 63310, 65031, 65049, 65115, 65704, 67306, 68441, 69110

Jul-48
200, 212, 248, 298, 1532, 2356, 2643, 2662, 2746, 2764, 2916, 3021, 3030, 3165, 3184, 3442, 5343, 9007, 30009, 31388, 32001, 32003, 32006, 32010, 32269, 32286, 32289, 32397, 32598, 41018, 46881, 47948, 49131, 49309, 49362, 50423, 57371, 57442, 57551, 58320, 58357, 58366, 58370, 58405, 58428, 58901, 58922, 62169, 62821, 62829, 62849, 62975, 62981, 62982, 62983, 62988, 62995, 63489, 64167, 65674, 67143, 67388

Aug-48
259, 261, 783, 1730, 1745, 1780, 2734, 2755, 2928, 3005, 3035, 3037, 3039, 3046, 3395, 3589, 3597, 5130, 9006, 30010, 30091, 30348, 31051, 31396, 31426, 41026, 41033, 41718, 47875, 47887, 47930, 48912, 48913, 49056, 49136, 49295, 50728, 50800, 50835, 50934, 50950, 54416, 55180, 58021, 58150, 58250, 58297, 58324, 58325, 58374, 58390, 58905, 58914, 58920, 61358, 61369, 61373, 61378, 61380, 61384, 61393, 61476, 62064, 62126, 62144, 62198, 62238, 62400, 62563, 62972, 62978, 62989, 65032, 67105, 68187, 68368, 69089

Sep-48
2709, 2989, 3008, 3013, 3376, 5320, 5340, 30139, 30143, 30271, 31013, 32007, 32044, 32370, 32377, 32599, 32604, 41027, 41036, 41762, 41893, 41910, 43796, 49165, 51342, 52063, 52170, 52374, 55130, 57471, 57606, 57629, 57639, 57953, 58081, 58141, 58255, 58284, 58359, 58361, 58385, 58391, 58425, 58885, 58930, 61355, 61360, 61372, 61374, 62444, 62446, 62448, 62454, 62560, 62602, 65641, 68135, 68390

Oct-48
3, 4, 51, 184, 1749, 2569, 2706, 2717, 3335, 3445, 5111, 5121, 5131, 30003, 30145, 30239, 30366, 30392, 30636, 31046, 31386, 31437, 31453, 32371, 41024, 47954, 49152, 50899, 51487, 52049, 52574, 52877, 54363, 54401, 56270, 57421, 58000, 58039, 58074, 58331, 58353, 58386, 58401, 58414, 58893, 58898, 58907, 61368, 61488, 61509, 61517, 62116, 62160, 62163, 62187, 62409, 64107, 65104, 65411, 68285, 68400, 69070, 69071, 69076, 69077, 69399

Nov-48
1538, 1867, 3049, 4353, 5128, 9019, 30101, 30261, 30445, 30459, 30460, 31378, 31438, 31440, 31454, 32004, 32283, 32308, 32358, 32373, 32605, 47956, 48801, 48939, 49128, 49303, 50631, 51427, 51467, 52036, 52528, 52545, 52602, 54641, 54652, 56351, 57469, 57578, 58356, 58402, 58884, 58906, 61370, 61390, 61395, 61470, 61680, 62124, 62175, 62189, 62205, 62207, 62390, 62449, 62583, 62916, 62992, 63253, 63263, 63292, 63295, 63323, 63327, 65381, 65626, 67093, 67094, 68090, 69103, 29988

Dec-48
62, 71, 201, 680, 1889, 2935, 3430, 3431, 3446, 30278, 30279, 30627, 30629, 32383, 40408, 40492, 40494, 40545, 40731, 47888, 47958, 48834, 48924, 48962, 49012, 49179, 49349, 49384, 50801, 50823, 50896, 50943, 51405, 55133, 55351, 57636, 58355, 58372, 58403, 58870, 61366, 61376, 62970, 63301, 63306, 65056, 65385, 65607, 67106, 67351, 68317, 69792

Jan-49
213, 246, 421, 1835, 1897, 2570, 2767, 2795, 3448, 4320, 31003, 31106, 31109, 31127, 31371, 32309, 32589, 40400, 47951, 48892, 49184, 50945, 51468, 58001, 58113, 58256, 58342, 58886, 58896, 61371, 61385, 62137, 62145, 62152, 62156, 62197, 62306, 62322, 62875, 64163, 67099, 67100, 68201, 68365

Feb-49
1894, 2724, 3441, 3562, 9091, 30081, 30085, 30098, 30099, 30100, 30147, 30152, 30257, 30264, 30267, 30361, 30385, 30393, 30948, 31105, 31372, 31389, 31457, 31460, 31707, 32367, 32374, 40496, 40735, 41874, 43783, 48894, 48909, 48935, 49072, 49217, 49227, 50412, 50696, 51318, 52518, 54397, 54403, 57286, 57305, 57699, 58270, 58294, 61379, 61389, 62167, 62329, 62910, 62923, 63206, 63224, 63291, 63297, 63299, 63308, 63317, 63322, 63331, 65086, 65606, 67107, 68203

Mar-49
283, 1758, 2769, 3175, 30002, 30013, 30097, 30135, 30153, 30237, 30240, 30273, 30351, 31078, 31151, 31231, 31428, 31449, 32051, 32366, 32387, 32389, 32398, 32572, 40394, 40466, 40711, 41676, 46931, 48906, 48918, 49003, 49016, 49110, 49111, 49166, 49195, 49259, 49263, 49290, 49329, 49363, 49517, 49518, 49525, 49542, 49551, 49565, 49577, 49616, 49630, 49632, 49633, 49646, 50432, 51325, 52821, 52834, 54646, 57382, 58344, 58416, 58894, 61353, 61361, 62165, 62179, 62594, 63273, 63332, 65649, 65668, 65715, 67140, 69374, 69375, 69384

Apr-49
47, 277, 3592, 30092, 30095, 30103, 30181, 30198, 40555, 41788, 43458, 46004, 46917, 49040, 49042, 49052, 49054, 49055, 49086, 49185, 49297, 49305, 49338, 49372, 49504, 49507, 49521, 49549, 49559, 49562, 49601, 49669, 50670, 51438, 51495, 52586, 52952, 57393, 57466, 58030, 58222, 61357, 61362, 61469, 61497, 62065, 62151, 62153, 62881, 62902, 62925, 63275, 63286, 63316, 64127, 65109, 65633, 65684, 65703, 67113

May-49
30, 280, 2756, 2789, 3400, 3443, 3577, 5117, 30008, 30383, 30394, 30439, 30440, 30443, 31007, 31163, 31398, 31439, 32153, 32235, 32299, 32307, 32423, 32457, 40437, 40510, 40756, 41042, 41756, 46711, 49015, 49060, 49159, 49242, 49248, 49256, 49360, 49512, 49522, 49527, 49597, 49626, 49629, 49644, 50813, 51443, 51469, 52103, 52828, 57231, 57358, 57624, 58002, 58057, 58078, 58223, 58251, 58407, 61475, 62150, 62314, 62377, 62473, 62810, 62917, 63212, 63214, 63277, 63300, 63305, 63307, 63334, 64106, 64110, 65029, 65107, 65114, 65351, 65392, 65395, 65415, 65602, 65629, 67104, 67112, 68215

Jun-49
53, 1731, 2651, 2655, 3364, 9072, 30380, 31316, 31455, 32395, 40517, 41008, 41013, 41913, 41920, 46639, 46663, 47936, 48931, 48954, 49004, 49019, 49123, 49170, 49283, 49530, 49581, 49604, 49606, 49614, 50711, 50732, 52181, 52806, 57584, 57693, 58010, 58031, 58243, 58424, 61386, 61485, 61510, 61702, 61704, 61707, 61712, 62139, 62193, 62194, 62402, 62903, 62915, 63318, 65364, 65376

Jul-49
2708, 9087, 30001, 30144, 30169, 31238, 31302, 31446, 40500, 40720, 41010, 48948, 49102, 49207, 49299, 49337, 49365, 49533, 49607, 49613, 49622, 49642, 49647, 49670, 50738, 51492, 52229, 52541, 52886, 52971, 54653, 57400, 57427, 57452, 57561, 62199, 62311, 62315, 62317, 62319, 65051, 67149, 67377, 69251, 69420

Aug-49
289, 784, 1884, 1930, 1969, 2620, 2902, 3182, 3418, 3419, 5135, 30137, 30265, 30386, 31039, 31080, 31257, 31448, 40385, 40391, 40483, 40554, 41912, 46876, 49238, 49285, 49526, 49528, 49550, 49584, 49599, 49611, 49658, 50665, 52294, 52439, 52454, 52578, 52827, 55354, 57351, 57381, 57402, 58208, 62125, 62133, 62303, 62308, 62330, 62404, 62828, 62912, 63228, 63296, 63312, 63335, 65052, 65059, 65060, 65363, 65387, 65393, 65428, 65608, 67359, 68489, 69054, 69058, 69059, 69383, 69396, 69397, 69421

Sep-49
296, 1863, 2523, 2713, 3189, 30167, 30263, 30345, 31374, 31385, 31429, 32253, 46637, 46669, 46710, 47932, 48903, 48925, 49026, 49043, 49084, 49091, 49188, 49211, 49221, 49269, 49280, 49534, 49564, 49572, 49639, 49652, 49656, 52019, 52442, 57399, 58111, 58399, 58417, 61483, 61703, 61713, 62190, 62332, 62458, 62481, 63200, 63216, 63338, 65093, 65357, 65372, 65379, 65397, 68218, 69241

Oct-49
269, 1715, 1764, 2667, 2987, 3363, 3438, 3561, 3575, 3599, 4012, 4019, 30141, 30269, 30276, 30391, 31599, 31709, 32141, 40456, 40544, 40734, 41509, 43260, 48897, 48904, 49194, 49379, 49513, 49539, 49546, 49576, 50448, 50692, 50880, 50889, 51482, 52607, 52839, 54642, 57316, 57403, 57420, 57702, 58048, 58334, 58882, 58927, 58934, 61689, 62131, 62177, 62188, 62214, 62240, 62313, 62321, 62406, 63210, 63294, 64109, 65026, 65044, 65108, 65609, 65665, 67150, 68415, 69057, 69226, 69243, 69415

Nov-49
34, 52, 231, 258, 265, 1878, 1909, 1919, 1945, 1990, 2029, 2059, 2064, 2065, 2102, 2772, 2794, 2798, 2903, 2930, 2946, 3159, 3341, 3382, 3386, 3393, 3401, 3582, 3586, 4017, 9076, 30262, 30354, 31380, 32162, 32567, 40479, 40506, 40739, 40740, 41031, 49036, 49135, 49192, 49325, 49351, 51400, 51475, 52192, 55184, 57294, 57415, 57449, 58022, 58379, 61688, 62234, 62300, 62309, 62318, 62324, 62401, 62877, 63255, 63313, 65058, 65066, 65079, 65112, 65375, 65409, 65412, 65414, 65632, 65724, 67109, 67399, 68167, 69411, 500S

Dec-49
206, 287, 297, 423, 1531, 1720, 1754, 1799, 1888, 1891, 1896, 1912, 1973, 2000, 2006, 2007, 2018, 2019, 2022, 2045, 2047, 2114, 2137, 2464, 2738, 2786, 2787, 2929, 2941, 2942, 3383, 3407, 3426, 3432, 3450, 3574, 3588, 4402, 9064, 9065, 9073, 30275, 30341, 30410, 30435, 30447, 31384, 31451, 31672, 32097, 32112, 32127, 40459, 41768, 41918, 41923, 41924, 46676, 46687, 46742, 46924, 48911, 49011, 49067, 49169, 49237, 49294, 49298, 49320, 49353, 49573, 49588, 49643, 49645, 49654, 50675, 50750, 52184, 52326, 52403, 52609, 54410, 55159

57310
58032
58253
58380
58883
58890
61536
61706
62123
62128
62333
62445
62455
63219
63330
65036
65121
65353
65371
65416
65436
65721

Jan-50

291
1331
1907
1965
2702
2745
30005
30140
30142
31123
31377
31699
32025
32436
32690
40490
40512
40533
41873
43813
43830
48896
49039
49075
49083
49124
49176
49529
49569
49621
50951
52047
52956
54767
55123
57409
58035
58329
58351
58367
58404
58406
58923
61709
62304
62839
62885
63293
65081
65367
65386
65603
65707
67126

Feb-50

32
61
1742
2757
4026
4531
30151
30161
30168
30444
30462
32074
32215
32234
32274
32533
48824
48966
49059
49080
49133
49190
49220
49235
49279
49553
49567
49605
50793
50804
50849
52913
57401
57467
57694
58064
58134
58917
61529
61705
61710
62135
62215
62282
62325
62476
63233
63238
63276
65027
65072
65073
65094
65116
65120
65123
65127
65419
69376
69799

Mar-50

100 A1
262
272
288
426
1752
1773
2113
2704
2712
2761
2799
2924
2955
30949
32080
40516
40561
40745
41895
43772
47885
48934
49058
49065
49097
49127
49255
49284
49317
49324
49501
49519
49655
50676
50891
52542
52782
52825
54409
54651
55127
56010
58049
58112
58155
58267
58282
58348
58371
58384
58397
58422
58929
62302
63231
65294
67124
68243
69373

Apr-50

1949
2039
2091
2382
2791
30329
31452
41022
41034
43408
46635
49107
49356
49369
49556
49596
49615
50893
50953
52023
54385
57298
58082
58202
58341
58369
58373
61057
62301
62312
62591
62854
63241
65037
65083
65101
65215
65634
65646
65669
65681
67160
67183
68384
68386
68396
68416
69066
69422

May-50

64
1747
2013
2052
2096
2130
4013
4030
40427
40468
40727
41914
43818
48941
49029
49053
49076
49100
49291
49333
49520
49537
49575
52110
52856
57390
57440
58239
58245
58338
62173
62180
62235
62817
67299
69247

Jun-50

422
2071
2771
2790
2792
3455
5373
9054
30272
31217
32085
40403
40446
41039
43297
43805
47933
49032
49069
49183
49232
49500
49561
49579
49628
49634
50743
52962
55356
56026
57342
58036
58275
58411
61504
62307
63256
63260
63281
67285

Jul-50

46
294
1760
2037
2110
2124
2707
2715
2780
3169
30166
48929
49332
49541
50755
50798
54645
55183
57950
61686
61711
62140
62161
62208
62305
63213
63232
63272
63290
65084
65365
67108
69053
69068
69237
69414
69428
69795
S&M 1
M 8108
M 8182
M 8236

Aug-50

281
428
1979
2132
2721
4025
4543
30382
40498
40515
41017
46632
49041
49085
49514
49516
49543
49574
49583
49619
49636
49653
49665
50442
55129
58079
62203
62413
62512
63207
63262
63278
63287
63289
65658

Sep-50

1989
2126
2716
3168
5114
5122
32252
48908
49101
49219
49307
50748
50844
52022
52508
52906
52910
58033
58034
58881
62412
63274
63285
65437
65621
65624
65651

Oct-50

286
1789
1858
1870
2141
2189
2743
2754
2760
2915
3154
4051
4513
31179
31738
40478
47937
49050
49257
49319
49331
49531
49609
50630
52041
52727
52822
54404
55192
57391
58020
58041
58059
58307
58916
62247
62249
62508
63226
63261
63280
63336
65057
65128
65373
65402
65427
65600
65611
65725
68379
68381
68669
68763
69245
69410

Nov-50

76
1705
1709
1782
2155
2184
2719
2722
2744
4039
4045
30390
30407
31597
32079
32087
32088
32142
43802
47896
49535
49635
52208
52916
55191
57425
57453
58061
58388
58410
58897
61482
62148
62154
62181
62209
62822
62900
62901
62908
62909
62919
63203
63257
63271
64120
64121
64128
65021
65291
65374
65413
65423
65429
65628
65631
65642
67156
68277
68288
68310
68767
68801
69124
69372
69380
69413
69425

Dec-50

1855
1862
2153
2386
2908
2939
4528
9083
30158
30259
30268
30412
30576
31511
31598
31604
31736
32076
32090
40488
43319
43827
46658
47939
48933
49074
49090
49334
49364
49641
49649
49651
52064
58912
62132
62918
63205
63221
63229
63251
63282
63283
63333
63491
64162
65274
65604
65627
65636
67111
67128
67139
68319
68782
Dep 3323

Jan-51

74
1146
1206
2009
2055
2943
2979
3178
3406
4503
40370
40406
40530
41012
49071
49264
49282
49347
49623
49625
52407
58262
58928
62243
62357
62417
63201
63328
65043
67165
69056
69418

Feb-51

31
33
433
992
1542
1941
2912
2931
4015
4055
4409
30405
31160
31477
31546
31547
32027
32078
32584
40477
40762
41011
41824
41955
41960
41962
41963
41964
41965
41968
43811
49156
49208
49523
49585
49673
50815
52092
52831
57283
57379
57697
58043
58364
58392
58865
62283
62340
62348
62361
62376
62382
62405
62503
62547
63486
63493
64135
64137
65041
65292
65350
65354
65369
65377
65622
65659
68372
68387
69067
69798

Mar-51

60
425
803
907
1917
1943
2017
2033
2054
2056
2075
2981
3377
4020
5365
30134
30159
30353
30402
30408
30413
30430
31036
31157
31275
31443
31502
31532
31696
31730
31740
31745
31748
32029
32039
32077
32084
32301
32402
32594
40397
40758
41003
41037
41916
41917
41919
41921
41926
41931
49218
49258
49261
49292
49388
49580
49660
50642
50909
52111
52280
52444
54647
55188
57334
62227
62341
62342
62344
62363
62366
62369
62451
63217
63220
63234
63480
64115
64151
65111
65279
65396
65431
67177
67373

Apr-51

220
240
263
267
274
276
1147
1925
1957
1993
2026
2095
2190
2192
2936
2947
3447
3451
4018
4041
4058
4400
5134
9084
30121
30122
30154
30155
30165
30286
30428
30441
30713
30714
30722
31057
31383
31541
31667
31670
32089
32603
32644
40424
40462
41745
41852
41854
41915
46688
48936
49022
49178
49204
49205
49312
49558
49631
49663
50654
52219
55134
57277
58052
58151
58352
58363
62353
62354
62362
62365
62370
62379
63303
63319
63481
63483
64148
65030
65095
65226
65254
65298
65355
65378
65406
65407
65640
67166
68404
69793

May-51

270
271
278
2063
2098
2104
5303
5346
30113
30114
30115
30116
30118
30156
30173
30280
30303
30305
30314
30414
30446
30731
31041
31093
31379
31381
31390
31595
32009
32022
32062
32156
40470
40549
41006
41020
41690
43582
43765
46906
48920
49006
49062
49098
49540
49568
49590
49593
49610
49650
52059
52126
52945
54638
58063
58274
58289
61699
63227
63235
63236
63259
63479
64123
65426
65614
65653
65672
65679
65718
67255
68082
68163
68221
68377
68433
69051
69062
69789

Jun-51

219
295
299
1967
2021
2032
2073
2117
2322
2932
3444
3449
4031
4033
4040
4509
30007
30020
30367
30384
30406
30409
30416
30418
30461
30723
31044
31066
31092
31248
31391
31395
31432
31705
31710
31731
32005
32008
32054
32063
32068
32082
32083
32129
32145
32325
32326
32574
32595
32596
32602
40546
40729
40747
41005
41856
47884
49014
49030
49031
49296
49370
49502
49571
49587
49589
49617
52088
52296
52460
52590
57323
57455
57951
58285
61503
62172
62251
62391
62461
62501
62528
63204
63223
63240
63267
63284
64150
65076
65245
65308
65623
67245
68248
68385
69480

Jul-51

293
2044
2051
4003
4047
5129
5364
9089
30389
30423
30424
30436
31016
31108
31182
31373
31515
31587
31602
32002
32023
32037
32038
32300
32359
40508
41781
46603
46628
46922
47881
52238
52446
58237
58296
58302
58368
65006
65238
65362
67264
68231
68376
69055
69423

Aug-51

2159
5132
41023
41030
41933
41953
41954
43824
50766
50842
52056
52583
55138
55353
57306
58201
58349
61525
62246
62460
63270
63475
64119
64142
65255
65322
67151
67153
67155
67164
67171
67175
67313
68175
68247
68311
68762
69252
69791
69794
69797

Sep-51

1968
2066
2089
2926
2952
4007
4016
4032
30171
30174
30401
30420
30421
30422
30425
31369
31490
31659
31732
32026
32030
32070
32073
32081
32406
32590
40741
41000
41767
41929
41932
41934
41935
41956
41957
41959
43777
43801
49213
49222
49510
49594
52034
52100
52112
52284
52428
52433
52557
52870
57312
58400
58895
61526
61559
62000
62232
62466
62520
62603
63202
63225
63243
63311
63314
63477
63478
63485
64124
65028
65105
65122
65401
65644
67154
67317
68139
68302
69401

Oct-51

2050
2076
2385
4035
4502
5136
5137
5359
30164
30395
30403
30404
30429
30431
30432
30438
30704
30716
31175
31176
31516
31596
31685
32021
32028
32050
32067
32086
32303
32393
32647
40325
40497
41001
41015
41016
41019
41793
50455
52288
54649
55132
57272
57352
58045
58268
58935
62459
63326
67356
69398
69400

Nov-51

195
1861
2014
2083
2131
2152
2431
2944
2948
3453
3454
4028
4042
4046
4337
30396
30426
30427
30756
32056
41009
41041
43747
49193
49300
49302
52176
52233
52250
52363
52448
54648
55171
55181
57289
57318
57394
58110
58420
58908
61515
62252
62505
65025
65067
65102
65118
65439
65615
65619
68171
68200
DS3191

Dec-51

2927
5143
30163
30175
30281
30397
30398
30399
30417
30419
30433
30442
30463
30469
31159
31273
31514
32043
32045
32052
32055
32060
32071
32072
32075
32147
32160
32306
32388
32394
32400
32404
32405
32575
32691
41043
41958
46912
47931
49163
49595
50720
50736
50886
52191
52330
52353
52414
52430
52857
54630
57344
57698
58042
58046
58248
58252
58933
62229
64112
64158
64160
65080
65408
65601
65617
67163
68172
68179

Jan-52

203
2004
2016
2023
2093
2150
2154
2407
2940
2949
4043
4054
5144
5348
32302
40471
40514
40532
41829
49371
49548
49661
50749
54635
54654
55122
55186
57372
57695
58226
58322
58333
62410
62590
63482
64105
65278
65340
67381
68089
68373
68766
69242

Feb-52

72
193
1964
2002
2030
2109
2148
2181
2187
2188
2193
2953
4022
4050
4057
40417
41004
46656
46749
46762
49138
49171
49187
49359
50806
50840
50898
55360
56268
57468
58304
58398
62228
62502
63580
63627
63778
63809
63849
65007
65286
65398
67152
68141
68147
68186
69244
69311

Mar-52

2080
2339
2349
3151
4036
4404
4529
30148
30157
30312
30468
30472
32128
40558
41032
41727
41890
41937
49253
49671
50671
50872
50873
55352
58092
58254
58335
58340
58346
61505
62230
63476
63488
65008
65009
65382
68224
68380
69371

Apr-52

57
292
4038
40430
49096
49244
49265
50640
55350
57255
58360
61511
61560
62506
62507
62538
65183
65231
65240
68388
68789
69246
69775

May-52

2025
2048
2086
2094
2140
2151
5142
41007
41014
41035
41040
41794
41925
48901
49346
50639
50697
50812
54399
57433
58069
58350
58365
58892
62598
64153
65005
65137
65151
68268
68667
69118
69777

Jun-52

73
1141
1903
2100
2115
2121
2934
2951
2954
4023
4318
4504
5305
30170
30172
30411
30437
30733
31674
32091
32386
40415
49017
49563
50735
50892
55121
55361
57956
58327
58393
58913
58932
62255
62457
64116
64117

64118 65155 65264 65366 68286 68775 68792 69229

Jul-52

5125 40383 40507 40728 40743 43820 46899 50623 50633 50681 50695 50802 55144 57955 58060 58377 58381 58418 58910 61521 61552 62527 69382 69387 69389

Aug-52

209 2001 2106 2906 2938 3167 30311 32378 40499 41038 41820 41930 43336 49151 50622 50689 50799 50925 52037 52357 52598 55139 57280 58047 58149 58231 65130 65188 65193 65271 67178 67292 68255 68382 69111 69395

Sep-52

63 67 217 1334 1335 2127 2483 2950 4034 4059 4544 40726 41021 41028 41044 43807 49092 49241 52588 55136 55140 61628 62509 64129 65040 65141 65161 65189 65664 67167 67275 68129 68668 69473

Oct-52

2123 2197 2452 3157 4021 4060 4518 5141 30302 30466 30703 31665 31673 31700 31708 32364 40503 40523 41961 43228 49506 50634 52030 52231 52554 52579 54640 55170 57954 58058 58426 62231 62248 62411 62768 64114 67276 68370 69379 69393 69479

Nov-52

207 284 344 864 887 1150 2067 2079 2122 2444 3188 4303 5138 5139 41967 50625 52362 52587 54634 55172 57332 57387 57458 58259 58421 62462 65004 65179 65204 67244 67252 67260 68083 68136 68375 68378 69112 69240 Dep 35

Dec-52

218 2185 2482 2572 3161 4516 30119 30307 30470 30725 31658 31675 31706 32133 32365 32379 32391 40423 40528 40560 40911 40918 40922 41109 41171 41182 43724 43804 45637 46727 49591 52169 52266 52285 52386 54445 55142 57337 58147 58280 58863 58919 62256 62281 63484 65126 65163 65168 65283 67184 67330 67435 67471 68088 68132 68157 68181 68299 68816 68845

Jan-53

236 1991 1996 2031 2068 2135 2195 2350 2401 2408 2449 2462 2468 2534 2537 2933 4048 4403 4408 4520 5147 5300 5309 40324 40547 41025 41046 41125 41869 46643 46680 50852 52102 52262 52304 52440 52559 58053 58067 58076 58161 58383 58389 58419 64133 65003 65010 65660 67158 67182 67331 67348 68249 68398 69234 69448

Feb-53

55 309 337 893 2156 2167 2194 2343 2351 2515 2543 2573 3034 3153 4044 4512 4514 4517 30197 30204 30213 30336 30415 30565 30754 31491 31750 40322 40410 41055 41780 43540 46620 46683 46701 46757 46900 47877 48902 50703 50778 52107 52156 52246 54398 54636 55175 56237 56276 57388 57410 57439 57464 58050 58070 58088 58090 58249 58328 58330 58347 58362 58429 61513 62225 62373 62616 62651 62657 65136 65149 65172 65190 67242 67291 67303 67404 68220 69061 69391 69426

Mar-53

2010 2111 2129 2146 2147 2414 2445 4407 4501 4510 4527 30231 30581 31697 32368 41148 41911 41922 57322 57397 57423 57450 57454 58354 61507 61624 62241 62242 62261 62581 65019 65201 65484 67127 67287 67406 67410 68092 68111 68133 68165 68166 68174 68178 68217 69796

Apr-53

892 894 896 2038 2042 2327 2354 2409 4515 41052 41695 52157 52279 52333 52525 52581 55143 56258 58861 61563 65499 68773 68779

May-53

432 2568 3033 4381 31260 31291 31486 31501 31728 31744 32372 32376 32380 32592 41057 41660 43792 49162 52105 52382 52404 58240 58323 58326 58858 61501 61508 64122 65154 65164 67372 67393 68130 68168 68173 68177 69113

Jun-53

111 2323 2556 2937 2945 3047 3160 4049 4052 4525 5140 41184 41666 43797 52243 54447 54481 57438 58211 61543 65487 67390 69446

Jul-53

30571 31663 32385 32399 40353 40444 41092 41770 43653 43662 49326 49608 52091 52615 55135 58321 58336 58378 61528 61532 67176 67186 67354 68533 68774

Aug-53

285 2085 4500 30221 31090 31234 31580 32573 32659 40401 40484 43283 43833 47180 49600 49612 51348 51490 52043 52255 52572 55119 58145 58396 58889 61604 62260 62654 62655 65014 65077 67335 67464 68131 68161 68176 68219 68770 68803 68825

Sep-53

56 95 155 434 2551 2578 41145 43767 46654 50687 50714 54650 55166 55179 58075 58332 58343 62270 62464 64141 65492 68208 69442

Oct-53

40 75 431 682 1935 2920 31662 40422 40432 40505 40551 41056 41846 52098 54444 55161 55359 58068 58180 65016 65481 65488 65491 67468 68154 68282 68776

Nov-53

28 77 194 4511 32384 40905 41099 41664 47865 50859 51514 52616 54449 58229 58303 58415 61524 65018 65023 65482 68211 68216 68281 68505 68548 68786 69227 DS515

Dec-53

2426 31660 31733 32588 40351 40425 41178 41833 43293 43364 43604 46601 49524 50678 50762 51536 52619 54639 57395 64125 65015 65022 65489 65497 68107 68137 68525 68794

Jan-54

1 29 65 80 359 435 436 2579 40919 41080 43448 43782 52124 52309 56250 58258 58265 58382 58413 64367 65017 65676 67453 67479 68780 69289

Feb-54

31493 40359 40480 41047 41058 41174 43819 49602 51489 52321 52365 52580 58264 62650 65496

Mar-54

5 94 335 873 1336 30282 30471 31038 31315 31572 31703 43296 43779 52138 58911 65692 67295 68509 69120 69125 69239 69468 69903

Apr-54

96 2053 2411 2460 9001 41082 43667 43821 49089 51410 58880 61502 62388 65716 67257 67349 67475 68109 68146 68152 68371

May-54

81 82 90 93 279 684 2458 2484 2532 9002 31729 40529 41096 41115 41813 43191 52024 58038 58172 58232 58244 58272 58899 62392 62652 65689 67408 68096 68140 68143 68271 68413 68421 69065

Jun-54

68 91 92 282 2099 2340 2541 3020 30458 32585 40901 41084 46202 46666 50765 55146 58903 62352 64131 64132 65068 65075 67267 67288 67412 67454 67462 68103 68156 68374 68422 69060 69437 69461 69776

Jul-54

205 3025 4053 40455 40524 52137 52435 52558 54455 58234 58921 65020 65042 67369 68091 68256 68401 68854

Aug-54

844 32401 40438 40539 41074 41110 43299 43862 46712 52258 52524 52592 65002 65493 65495 67283 67402 68234 68440 68534 68859 69052 69235 69482 69774 69787 69925

Sep-54

58 322 849 855 895 2081 2112 4401 40395 40436 40662 40914 41054 41133 41134 41139 41141 41811 49389 49503 50621 51375 51460 51519 52118 52174 52189 52299 52349 58056 58195 58200 58278 58290 58888 58900 58915 58924 62380 62389 64335 65547 65667 65671 65688 67422 67456 67469 67476 67477 68772

Oct-54

40923 41051 41087 41146 41711 41853 43683 48893 51471 52549 58089 58853 62358 62371 62374 64339 65480 65490 65661 65705 68153 68292 68304 68493 68799 68844 68850 69231 69385 69770

Nov-54

375 667 30400 30464 31671 32587 43661 52245 55197 61539 62347 62351 62659 62782 65013 65038 65579 65585 65686 65694 65710 67272 67465 67470 68144 68151 68184 68258 68341 68572 68757 68760 68764 68777 68791 68798 68802 69233 69236 69324 69432 69456 69485 69771 69779 69780

Dec-54

683 2060 2108 3026 31311 31746 32591 41138 41747 47244 47245 49339 52031 52334 54459 58235 58242 58902 62783 64140 65047 65062 65089 65092 65097 65098 65100 65119 65485 65486 65690 67174 67247 67426 67429 67432 67461 67473 68098 68781 68788 69116 69225 69228 69230 69232 69336 69433

Jan-55

216 356 371 2043 40906 41124 41176 41682 47252 56248 62273 62656 64391 65082 65494 65552 67360 67383 68112 68209 68222 69064 69445

Feb-55

360 372 681 4522 4532 4534 4535 4537 31555 32328 32568 41067 41183 41938 41971 41972 41973 41974 43454 50715 52220 52561 52608 54448 54457 55187 58084 58129 58375 58851 62793 65569 67213 67271 67304 67327 67387 67455 68428 68544 69264 69304 69330 69386 69454 69919

Mar-55

210 352 2035 2090 2097 2162 2165 2176 4506 4530 4533 9000 30434 31513 40405 40924 41523 50656 51436 52053 52150 52215 52522 55194 56020 58040 58376 58430 61523 62272 62531 62579 62795 64342 64347 65384 65510 65516 65524 65723 67196 67197 67241 67249 67296 67301 67309 67336 67467 68206 68225 68300 68358 68606 69050 69313 69338 69431 69435 69459 69476 69483 69773

Apr-55

666 2061 2136 2186 2474 30485 31158 31531 31687 31713 32465 32586 40912 41091 41175 41889 43810 47232 47237 51376 51379 51472 52272 52569 55145 55193 58164 58887 62585 62791 64282 65574 67268 67293 67350 67353 67361 67371 67375 67382 67385 67389 67403 68094 68105 68185 68420 69288 69449 69475

May-55

83 211 2144 2166 2183 31166 32094 32489 41076 41117 41129 43568 43600 50807 54438 58300 62279 62784 64301 64390 65517 65543 67307 67405 67411 68093 68432 68889 69115 69368 69392 69441 69455 69778

Jun-55

2082 31225 31309 31591 32518 41061 41865 43252 47253 47985 47990 52164 52317 52582 55177 58087 58241 58852 64289 64370 67414 67457 68289 68303 68307 69119 69273 69279 69352 69377 69381 69424 69427

Jul-55

59 66 69 70 78 79 204 208 215 290 2513 30490 31335 32576 40908 40916 41104 41154 41169 41749 43581 47970 47975 52397 52416 52465 62278 62536 64307 64360 64374 65422 67210 67220 67498 68121 68169 68223 68393 68514 68592 68611 68790 69069 69117 69282 69287 69429 69436 69466

Aug-55

39 345 374 2034 2070 2088 2092 2182 4405 4406 4410 4542 32169 32330 32453 32501 40903 40913 41127 41130 41135 41149 41713 41725 43909 46604 51477 52045 52194 54446 58394 61562 62274 62384 62658 62794 64242 64326 64350 64356 65314 67162 67187 67198 67222 67236 67237 68120 68122 68155 68226 68584 69364 69460 69464 69914

Sep-55

30467 31154 31277 31496 31586 31661 31718 40377 40419 40472 40535 41107 41136 43723 43803 43817 43894 46616 47183 49140 49554 49570 50686 52021 52331 52408 54451 58077 58162 58207 58891 58904 58925 61722 62269 62525 62653 62780 67204 67206 67215 67243 67310 67463 68125 68158 68183 68238 68259 68590 68769 68807 68812 68873 68879 68883 68884 69378 69514 W23 W34

Oct-55

343 346 365 366 1153 3014 3023 3032 4523 4539 4541 5112 5113 5395 9003 30743 31294 31698 32167 32390 32516 40522 41072 41516 43273 43317 43524 43676 43835 43867 44006 50731 50869 51470 51510 51511 54443 54450 54454 54460 57235 57260 58236 58257 58273 58286 62262 62276 62359 62541 62552 62557 62573 62620 64286 64323 64358 64369 64415 67368 67459 68284 68383 68531 68597 68771 68787 68804 68805 68861 68865 68868 69095 69306 69394 69451 69463

Nov-55

30746 31734 32482 32496 40448 40562 40921 41059 41069 41070 41081 41161 41177 41188 41198 41671 43298 43331 43494 43497 43544 43636 43686 43755 43775 43781 43791 47989 49557 50648 51530 57282 58054 58125 58127 58152 58230 58277 62355 62554 62607 64194 64291 64299 64334 64400 64413 64436 65088 67205 67217 67226

67232
67238
67300
67308
67328
67401
67499
68236
68270
68337
68594
68758
68795
68796
68797
68806
68810
68814
68818
68856
68858
68881
69253
69256
69275
69278
69280
69285
69291
69303
69310
69353
69357
69367
69439
69458
69785
69788
Dep 6

Dec-55

308
4521
30203
30740
30752
31320
31666
32490
40915
41672
41859
43310
43351
47184
47991
47993
50651
52447
52575
55196
56263
57315
58133
58409
58412
58427
62275
62549
62559
62574
64212
65090
65359
65483
65498
67188
67190
67191
67207
67223
67233
67239
67266
67314
67316
67345
68148
68523
68765
68783
68820
68852
68864
69301
69465
69999
W19

Jan-56

357
389
1205
2196
30465
30579
30744
32168
32327
32332
32513
32570
32571
32583
32593
32696
40527
43275
47215
47220
47983
47999
49620
52099
52300
52453
57456
58073
58080
62781
62790
64426
65430
67235
68162
68429
68437
68504
68540
68589
68827
69333
69471
69562
69900
69902
69904

Feb-56

379
384
1404
1425
1460
3185
30577
30741
30745
31488
32464
41943
43770
43936
47182
47984
47997
48899
49028
50653
51396
52051
52239
52381
55174
58062
58309
62349
67344
67415
67436
67452
67478
67480
67481
68407
68833
69317

Mar-56

307
367
1413
2101
3010
3164
5700
5762
6321
40521
41065
41128
41147
41191
41777
41814
43334
43874
47992
49322
49354
49603
51488
52104
52167
52450
56231
57320
57457
58117
58159
58194
58212
58862
65165
67251
67290
67334
67347
67458
68446
68476
68517
68821
68876
69254
69339
69784
Dep 2

Apr-56

306
382
386
4586
5159
31063
31704
31769
32333
32460
32610
40556
40900
41131
41137
41170
41805
41940
43313
43462
47976
49212
55162
56271
57412
58179
58193
58269
65236
65370
65647
67240
67302
67312
67332
67430
67466
67472
67483
67493
68127
68193
68204
68205
68207
68291
68547
68559
69272
69359
69927
Dep 37

May-56

41
303
348
362
377
2138
2168
2516
3012
3029
3031
3048
6383
40326
41097
41838
43633
43875
43956
49666
51323
51513
52437
52494
58100
65035
65197
65248
65708
67225
67364
67384
67495
68180
68297
68455
68473
68492
68496
68586
68793
68878
69340
69481

Jun-56

312
2107
3022
3040
5316
30569
32459
32561
40364
40910
41050
41053
41826
41839
41966
43607
43790
47974
47977
47996
49532
50655
51439
52369
56273
56317
56319
58126
58154
58233
58276
61720
61727
62792
67157
68395
68430
68436
68819
69255
W15

Jul-56

44
316
351
394
2072
3038
5327
40463
40526
40902
40909
40929
40938
41142
41187
43838
43895
43974
49638
50764
50788
51390
51425
51504
52343
55051
57230
58071
58176
58855
61734
62268
62551
62786
65205
68759
68830
68853
69260
69334
69363
69467

Aug-56

2011
3028
30230
30737
32329
32421
32426
32478
32606
40518
40531
40932
43232
43598
43698
47233
47988
47998
49552
51535
52390
56303
56339
62267
62523
64309
64380
65143
65417
67234
67425
68214
68521
68562
68838
68872
68880
69250
69337
69366
69470

Sep-56

37
391
399
3043
40323
41160
41166
41686
43204
43226
43943
47256
50650
51345
51464
51479
52197
58091
62542
64431
64449
65425
65435
67269
67392
67407
67431
68128
68240
68293
68313
68417
68809
68813
68822
68836
68885
69321
69325
69345
69351
69390

Oct-56

368
380
388
1402
1411
1416
2040
3016
3017
3042
3044
5792
30728
30736
30747
31549
31574
31737
32422
32425
32511
32514
32582
41079
41132
41885
43246
43748
47862
47981
50652
51313
51361
51462
51516
51521
52016
52166
52273
56233
56249
56261
56307
56358
57589
58051
58072
58184
58224
62343
62345
62360
62386
62577
65171
65404
67194
67211
67284
67286
67333
68323
68469
69114
69270
69444
69447
69922
W2

Nov-56

35
387
4062
5307
5317
30332
30573
32095
32096
32138
32558
40434
41720
43546
47181
47971
58139
58310
58854
61737
62271
62372
62378
62532
62569
62787
64398
64408
65182
67219
67224
67279
67322
68099
68160
68239
68276
68287
68294
68301
68855
68877
69090
69091
69277
69318
69323
69358
69781
69937
Dep 51
Dep 55

Dec-56

347
378
4598
5408
7711
30570
30758
31075
31577
31761
40362
40917
40939
41088
41126
41942
41944
41951
41952
41970
41976
43281
43550
51216
52177
52358
52405
52509
56355
56366
57459
62265
62567
62587
64366
64378
64410
65139
65148
65153
65162
65173
65176
65180
65181
65185
65203
67189
67201
67216
67289
67298
67400
67409
68511
69430
69478
69783

Jan-57

361
376
3018
30572
30574
31711
32520
40414
40418
41064
41085
41108
41151
43891
43959
44024
49035
49051
49068
49189
49316
51447
52196
52418
54440
55053
55125
56230
56299
57460
58142
61512
61538
61541
61545
61550
61557
61565
61569
61574
61578
61579
61735
61744
62430
62519
62553
62556
62565
62601
62608
62611
64327
64432
65537
67208
67294
67321
67451
68145
68351
68434
68503
68515
68595
68610
69328
69331
69348
69350
69503
69901
69905

Feb-57

43
1415
2027
2160
5401
5512
5808
30742
31712
40458
40486
41155
41699
41753
43259
43463
43912
43992
47979
47980
49024
49657
49664
51491
51500
52499
52576
54456
56243
56257
57234
58299
58306
62397
62609
64303
64312
64330
64448
65250
65324
67199
67209
67346
68210
68232
68266
68412
69356
69365
69369

Mar-57

349
364
4061
4326
5391
5752
30094
30753
32434
32458
40450
40904
40934
41180
41860
43469
43595
43889
47240
47978
49046
49341
49659
49672
52132
52203
52336
52412
52529
52551
56342
58156
61700
62264
62514
65078
67318
67337
67339
67395
68159
68298
68826
69316
69440
69689
69911

Apr-57

385
397
1414
5161
32461
32476
32537
32695
40930
41075
41077
41706
43181
43201
43402
43795
43857
47972
47973
49161
49223
49254
49555
51240
51503
52165
52376
52379
56294
58188
61537
61732
65213
65356
67256
68252
68512
68808
68841
68843
69457
69469
69833
W1

May-57

305
393
2134
2538
3100
4000
4538
5505
5811
30330
30739
30755
32462
32492
32608
40525
41140
41197
41530
43401
43476
43596
43852
47987
48940
48952
49057
49547
51506
52094
52521
55168
56028
58121
58216
58860
61726
61736
62375
62383
62420
62526
62558
62575
62617
62796
65523
67273
67282
67446
68142
68280
68516
68598
68761
68811
68851

Jun-57

1400
1422
1443
3104
3163
3186
5107
5109
5513
5535
5741
5806
5807
5812
5814
5817
5819
8105
30042
30207
30483
30580
30589
30749
30751
32488
32499
40509
41045
41098
41192
41534
43684
43717
43847
51474
51499
52338
61520
61729
62546
62605
67419
67443
68279
68551
68823
69557
69558
69566
69590

Jul-57

3171
5314
5415
5803
5816
6737
9008
9009
9010
9011
9012
9016
9020
9023
30082
30750
32170
32331
40404
40409
40482
40495
40927
41089
41710
41779
43898
43980
43993
47227
47986
47995
48914
49393
49545
51353
52160
52217
52501
56350
58114
58140
58187
58206
64414
67278
67440
67444
68115
68391
68778
69094
69108
69559
69815

Aug-57

304
370
373
381
383
390
398
1439
3101
5325
5403
5710
5724
6710
9022
9024
9025
9026
9027
9028
30041
30250
30578
30730
40356
40485
40676
40926
41073
41172
43396
43690
43851
44017
47969
49005
49148
49172
49214
49538
49566
50636
50752
51212
51338
51432
52186
52235
52368
52510
54441
54452
54453
56329
57346
58189
61730
62424
62516
65186
65242
65244
67338
67437
67441
68106
68426
68465
68567
69500
69916

Sep-57

42
3150
4596
5406
6713
6730
30304
30688
30748
31508
31557
32412
41105
41150
41186
41194
41748
43286
43901
43941
47242
47968
48951
49186
49648
51526
52123
52136
52163
52236
52293
56346
57430
57582
58136
61555
62387
62419
62429
62510
62533
62548
62562
62576
62578
62593
62619
62713
64295
64300
65650
65680
67250
68164
68253
68362
68887
69098
69329
69335
69346
69484

Oct-57

36
38
3172
3177
3180
3183
4056
4505
5405
5413
5712
5729
5760
30244
40520
41048
43341
43837
47206
47243
48907
48944
49202
49239
49536
51234
52175
58083
58288
58856
61540
61701
61733
62539
62596
64320
64322
64349
64372
64399
64401
64411
64412
64453
65091
65225
67221
67258
67277
67326
67423
67434
68126
68768
68832
68874
68888
69210
69312
69326
69347
69519
69595
69876
CD8

Nov-57

1403
3176
3187
4548
5334
5723
5735
5813
7792
30216
30487
31274
31321
32407
40426
40433
41103
41112
41116
41153
41179
41181
41185
41195
41803
43224
43776
43786
43806
43916
43927
47258
47967
48917
49066
49088
49108
49230
49247
49271
49318
49367
51307
51381
51481
52125
52143
52172
52328
52449
56297
56320
56369
57573
58238
58859
62381
62395
62396
62438
62535
67193
67324
67343
67428
67442
68267
68273
68423
68784
68886
69100
69501
69868

Dec-57

5404
6708
8755
30283
30588
30708
30757
32485
40519
40559
43239
43290
43443
47982
49033
49167
49385
49390
49560
50887
54458
56234
56280
56357
61519
61556
62423
62435
62584
62724
62726
62748
62757
62758
62761
62789
64193
64204
64293
65159
65572
67200
67202
67203
67254
67259
67319
67413
67449
68450
68849
68860
69093
69096
69107
69130
69167
69261
69302
69772
69782
69786
69913

Jan-58

4375
4526
4546
4583
4597
5701
5711
5714
5732
5736
6703
6705
6706
6709
6722
6740
6748
8703
30705
30721
32409
41118
41190
41199
41752
43312
43367
43392
43978
49047
49073
49145
49168
51202
56274
56334
57588
58203
58247
61601
61602
61724
62521
62737
64186
64187
64195
64221
64230
64264
64424
65191
65433
65501
65509
67270
67362
67391
67427
67433
67438
68113
68149
68182
68357
68397
68427
68593
68785
68882
69142
69201
69494
69890

Feb-58

4551
5165
5419
7795
30038
30224
30233
31059
31504
31593
32413
32455
32493
32502
32524
41095
41518
43491
43892
47222
47234
49146
49174
49345
51321
56314
56354
61474
61725
62561
62706
64200
64353
64526
65156
65270
65571
65575
67265
68116
68340
68438
68451
68518
68536
68628
68828
68829
68835
68840
68867
68871
69099
69284
69300
69305
69926
Dep 1

Mar-58

1406
1408
2008
3036
3041
3174
3190
5716
5730
5805
6396
6704
6771
30162
30675
30738
31184
32454
32540
40464
40541
40928
41060
41071
41144
41152
43193
43710
43823
49376
52388
56275
61638
62555
62564
62586
62788
62797
64211
65144
65147
65175
65202
65432
65500
65699
67218
67229
67231
67447
68328
68333
68464
68475
68576
68603
68870
69104
69106
69195
69271
69295
69497
69819

Apr-58

2800
4581
4582
5347
5751
5786
6727
30284
30564
30568
32424
32467
32481
40337
40933
40935
40937
41159
41988
41989
43656
43879
47994
48921
49260
49358
50660
50829
52356
52366
56254
56277
57556
58857
61570
61774
62515
62568
62592
64199
65135
65200

67192
67228
67340
67366
67374
67386
68244
68399
68474
68494
68583
68817
68839
68857
69157
69189
69355
69453
69496
69565
69609
69804
69865

May-58

1140
1461
5313
5379
5506
6715
6718
6731
6733
30022
30037
31064
40447
40920
41066
41086
41111
41114
41980
43332
43575
52387
52399
52517
55182
55213
56030
56244
56284
56286
56315
56330
57396
61605
61765
61775
62434
62703
62756
64244
64290
64464
65061
65132
65442
65529
65534
65535
65654
67195
67212
67227
67230
67357
67365
67376
67380
68308
68402
68490
68495
68546
68555
68568
68588
68607
68632
68651
68815
68863
69158
69502
69601
69643
69828

Jun-58

2012
4524
4580
5323
5411
5772
5777
30242
30285
30334

31069
31178
31339
31582
32414
40407
41093
41724
43323
52159
52427
57368
61609
61667
62277
62437
62442
62580
62736
62746
64220
64243
64344
64495
65160
65170
65196
65438
65508
65673
65683
65746
65752
65754
65765
65767
67214
67379
67394
68296
68321
68424
68452
68461
68491
68527
68537
68585
68718
69139
69140
69147
69148
69200
69203
69283
69315
69527
69554
69826
69881

Jul-58

4138
4139
5108
5157
5162
5171
5310
5328
5362
5371
5372
5397
5501
5502
5718
5800
6726
6732
6744
6747
41106
41189
41196
43356
43757
43798
51512
52120
55141
56267
56353
57437
58196
61516
61542
61600
61643
62572
62614
62749
64225
64227
64252
64263
64267
64296
65466
68306
68324

68327
68561
68605
68617
68631
68653
68800
68842
69607
69807
69862

Aug-58

2814
2827
3170
4578
5168
5338
5390
5392
5507
5715
5725
5733
5739
6407
6423
6427
6746
31461
32560
43208
43631
43742
47251
54439
56265
56283
56375
57443
61553
61617
61634
62425
62440
62522
62752
62773
64255
64275
64285
64306
64340
65562
67367
68242
68330
68347
68348
68356
68519
68529
68541
68618
68657
68659
68662
68666
68847
69160
69193
69281
69297
69349
69362
69472
69606
69608
69836

Sep-58

1405
1430
1446
1459
1465
1469
3793
4545
4554
4576
4579
5156
5344
5360
5367
5368
5377
5402
5722
5742
5767
5781
5797
5801
6100
7710
30243
30727
31147
31506

32113
41078
41156
41936
43419
43815
49121
52212
56155
56238
56328
57405
61554
61561
61603
61606
61619
61622
61630
61642
61650
61669
61671
62441
62468
62530
62545
62599
62679
62700
62704
62721
62735
62766
62769
62772
64202
64218
64302
64422
64486
64528
65064
65167
65456
65515
65518
65522
65568
65648
67297
68449
68664
68866
68940
68942
69153
69495
69499
69550
69839
69840
69841
69891

Oct-58

1418
1436
3011
3015
3024
3102
4590
5105
5172
5312
5335
5386
7779
30333
30454
31767
32440
40931
41167
43231
43522
50725
50757
50777
50818
50831
50855
50865
51424
51453
55160
55176
56251
56272
56301
56323
56345
57413
58066
58157
61547
61567
61621
61640
62513
62518

62534
62543
62588
62615
62683
62702
62732
62741
62742
62750
62754
62755
62764
62767
62771
62774
64189
64205
64249
64271
64276
64338
64517
65103
65142
65178
65405
65441
65444
65504
65573
65677
65717
65734
67253
67263
67325
68097
68118
68339
68435
68608
68735
68848
68862
69175
69269
69605
69810
69811
69832
69834
69842
69864
69872
69888
69918
69930

Nov-58

1401
2820
5086
5160
5719
5782
30260
30322
30337
30712
40420
40553
41163
41164
41193
43301
43441
43745
47249
50643
50644
50646
50705
51235
51415
52360
52432
56164
56253
56255
56281
56293
58192
58926
61564
62431
62725
64183
64201
64281
64343
64416
65039
65145
65209
65657
65697
67246
67320
67329
67341
67352

67363
67398
67424
67439
68246
68305
68460
68463
68478
68978
69172
69174
69220
69259
69822
69830
69831
69835
69838
69851
69863
69866
69871
69879
69882
69884
69892
69893
69931
69932
Dep 5

Dec-58

2258
2801
2802
4553
4572
4595
5517
5574
5785
5802
9013
9021
30087
30356
30575
30766
31774
32466
41068
41083
41090
41102
41113
41119
41122
43300
49276
51230
51423
52216
52350
55178
55212
56157
56161
56236
56306
58225
61648
61781
62422
62428
62432
62566
62730
62775
63668
64216
64274
64345
64392
64409
64645
65146
65199
65208
65390
65391
65587
65655
65696
67248
67261
67262
67274
67280
67281
67305
67311
67315
67323
67342
67397
67416
67418
67420
67421
68102
68322

68355
68405
68414
68466
68532
68553
68616
68699
68700
68746
69129
69152
69493
69544
69551
69573
69624
69628
69641
69695
69802
69818
69824
69837
69933

Jan-59

1423
2254
2263
2269
2279
2812
2828
2830
3740
4091
4377
5083
5394
5566
5743
5810
6318
6322
6328
7416
7714
7750
7754
8758
9708
9772
30054
30270
30376
30776
31018
31523
32124
32139
32477
32486
40413
41094
43180
43186
43244
43274
43612
43712
43787
43984
47208
47219
49113
49598
51316
51546
56011
56247
56288
56311
61549
61566
61573
61576
61635
61646
61749
61768
61898
62571
62582
62610
63667
64217
64522
64649
64651
64662
64672
64688
65730
65733
65740
65748
65758
65759
65771
68138
68251

68290
68574
68625
68630
68636
68712
68748
68831
69610
69616
69634
69639
69644
69659
69703
69717
69816
69920
Dep 8
Dep 31
Dep 36

Feb-59

1417
1437
1456
1457
2829
4224
4519
4568
4584
5315
5398
5703
6354
6716
6717
6721
6723
6734
6736
7415
7438
7738
30046
30086
30252
30492
30566
30787
30792
31340
31585
31681
31772
32135
32411
40005
40461
41121
41173
41928
41939
41941
41945
41946
41948
41950
41977
41978
41982
41983
41984
41985
41986
41987
41990
41991
41992
41993
43357
43553
43578
43771
43890
43946
43970
44145
47246
49177
50647
55164
56152
56162
56262
61615
61632
61645
61649
61739
61746
61757
61793
62490
63581
63620
63629
63797
63835
64262
64492

65117
65187
65467
65738
65739
65742
65744
65750
65766
65770
65775
68295
68312
68329
68837
69102
69151
69169
69332
69491
69534
69600
69619
69623
69667
69676
69716
69731

Mar-59

1429
1600
2198
2817
2825
2833
4200
4226
4261
4540
4599
5388
5522
5707
5765
5790
5796
6355
6409
6428
6432
7730
8417
30710
41049
41100
41143
41165
43292
48945
49109
49117
49180
49226
49301
49330
49368
50712
51397
51404
51457
52237
52268
56245
61580
61776
62678
62745
62751
63638
63682
63714
63729
63751
63769
63790
63855
63876
64176
64198
64215
64248
64261
64328
64361
64381
64388
64485
65131
65675
65749
65764
65829
68191
68331
68480
68638
68710
69162
69192
69434
69443

69450
69452
69474
69525
69569
69627
69635
69637
69666
69915
Dep 38
Dep 53

Apr-59

1467
2069
2259
2803
2823
4536
4900
5355
5382
5400
5424
5708
6303
6331
6334
6743
7447
7731
7734
7770
30026
30160
30455
30478
30488
30801
32507
32566
40600
43324
43629
47331
49132
49181
49200
49228
49308
56287
57414
57465
58085
58308
61558
61575
61631
61655
61665
61785
62427
62483
62494
62731
63614
63625
63673
63696
63745
63839
63851
63905
64266
64283
64304
64428
64475
64521
65447
65525
65527
65531
65538
65540
65553
65557
65780
65793
65803
65836
65843
68245
68250
68639
68640
68658
68949
69092
69164
69462
69477
69537
69542
69555
69567
69625
69669
77s

May-59

5734
7411
7735
30256
30310
30481
30482
30484
30706
30724
30778
31165
31295
31430
31554
40412
40416
40536
40538
40573
40590
40599
40606
40610
41062
41795
41857
41878
43253
43355
43506
47214
47226
47329
48922
49509
49511
49578
49582
49592
49640
49662
49667
51458
51497
54461
56038
56252
56352
56359
56365
57241
57407
57419
58119
58130
58132
58178
58204
58281
61546
61639
61777
61991
62470
62665
62708
63640
63812
63847
64210
64224
64258
64287
64430
64536
64714
64715
64734
64768
64829
64873
65388
65454
65542
65840
68150
68263
68751
68846
68906
69214
69222
69577
69638
69650
69660
69662
69809
CD6

Jun-59

1428
1603
2205
2208
2225
2228
2237
2238
2284

2290
2840
2843
2848
2863
2864
2868
2869
2870
2878
2880
4212
4260
5345
5409
5423
5740
5784
5804
6402
6404
6405
6414
6417
6701
6707
6711
6729
6735
6745
6779
8434
8442
8443
8447
8450
8485
8492
9403
9417
9427
9438
9439
9443
9491
9492
30123
30335
30352
30767
30797
31270
31470
31683
31781
32437
32517
40550
41120
43223
43237
43584
43731
43873
43939
47210
47538
48905
49010
49409
49436
51231
51484
51544
52044
56153
56163
56166
56256
56290
56318
57243
57339
57462
60700
61614
61731
61743
61748
61750
61751
61758
61762
61783
61879
62436
62475
62492
62715
63583
63654
63699
63756
63761
64246
64280
64297
64516
64752
64762
64763
64785

64787
64788
65783
65785
65798
65866
67448
68334
68468
68524
68824
68967
69127
69361
69532
69536
69547
69626
69657
69705

Jul-59

1145
2293
2804
4217
5341
5799
7420
7742
8412
8432
9005
30088
30473
30477
30486
30671
30779
30780
31252
31779
40493
40534
40607
40616
40666
40688
40693
41661
41726
43183
43222
43241
43381
43727
43836
43904
49315
53800
56154
56160
56291
57247
58246
58279
61623
61627
61644
61661
61738
61770
61855
61931
61983
62673
63710
64321
64336
64466
64584
64644
64731
64799
64900
65221
65247
65259
65806
65827
68283
68741
68973
69146
69185
69186
69322
69490
69515
69539
69545
69548
69576
69584
69602
69603
69649
69803
69812
W3

Aug-59

1509
2226
2235
2272
2824
2838
4211
4221
4223
4358
4560
4686
5186
5189
5321
5705
5721
5809
6102
6308
7401
7705
7743
7769
8448
8462
9402
30084
30301
30452
30711
30726
30786
31010
31107
31128
31174
31221
31245
31272
31425
31434
31503
31548
31755
31773
31775
31778
32456
40030
40542
40567
40587
40675
41101
41158
42308
43192
43210
43248
43258
43315
43318
43335
43339
43369
43558
43619
43623
43651
43674
43926
44144
44385
47191
47216
47247
47315
48926
48943
49018
49063
49120
49157
49340
49586
52278
52348
52527
56296
57307
58167
58171
58213
61568
61651
61878
62418
62540
62589
62677
62714
63582
64181
64228
64259
64279
64319
64365
64501
64648

64661
64735
64737
64753
64755
64773
64776
65138
65526
65656
65687
65700
65784
65826
65856
65886
68265
68498
68520
68535
68648
68739
68953
68974
69176
69342
69517
69526
69541
69591
69604
69612
69633
69655
69800
69928
69929
69934
Dep 4
Dep 43

Sep-59

2270
2278
2280
2299
2808
2810
2826
5378
5381
5738
5747
5753
5818
6305
6359
6397
8408
9459
9499
30177
30232
30324
30567
31071
31191
31279
31297
31741
31777
32166
32463
32471
32494
32519
32677
40021
40052
40332
40608
40611
41797
43388
43630
43860
43877
44201
47169
47205
52232
52458
56285
56321
56322
56327
56344
58198
61426
61577
61612
61616
61629
61633
61637
61652
61753
61789
61876
62439
62472
62480

62487
62517
62606
62701
62738
62753
62770
63660
63680
64190
64272
64294
64460
64484
64498
64513
64520
64702
64766
64797
64803
64832
64876
64881
64905
65177
65184
65451
65468
65475
65502
65685
65698
65848
68124
68467
68510
68581
68912
68919
69182
69327
69805
69935
69936

Oct-59
1616
1635
1644
2266
2296
2811
2816
4201
4215
4508
4585
5010
5356
5375
5393
5414
5500
5726
5737
5788
6358
6725
6773
7746
7751
7797
30030
30083
30374
30702
30732
30784
30785
31164
31219
31227
31243
31253
31758
32529
32577
40513
40605
42341
43308
43531
43587
43750
47370
49044
49143
49278
49311
49366
52108
52289
54467
54468
54471
54472
54473
54474
54479
54496
54497

54503
54504
56156
56264
56316
56332
56333
56340
56373
56374
57279
57553
57575
57638
58191
58217
61430
61441
61514
61611
61636
61778
61780
61787
62477
62675
62676
62684
62707
62720
62722
62728
62760
63694
63749
64188
64197
64207
64214
64229
64238
64239
64247
64250
64254
64269
64351
64382
64496
64509
64511
64530
64805
64841
64894
64913
64961
65333
65545
65702
65737
65781
65816
67482
67487
67488
67497
67500
68326
68363
68528
68557
68587
68601
68602
68652
68893
68938
69213
69217
69290
69294
69320
69661
69672
69910
69912

Nov-59
1101
1142
2281
2285
2832
4208
4577
4940
5163
5319
5528
5745
6325
6399
6420
7763
7768
7774
7789
9432
30027
30212
30289

30805
31259
31327
31329
31576
31770
32165
32480
32497
32579
32697
40002
40004
40008
40017
40023
40027
40043
40044
40045
40046
40047
40048
40055
40056
40058
40059
40065
40066
40084
40096
40125
40127
40139
40160
40163
40169
40172
40204
40565
40568
40576
40589
40594
40598
40617
40633
40636
40644
40649
40653
40655
40656
40658
40660
40667
40673
40674
40677
40679
40680
40925
41901
41902
41903
41904
41905
41906
41907
41908
41909
41975
42321
42354
43219
43233
43247
43294
43370
43379
43665
43759
43785
43829
43841
43842
43864
43886
43896
43934
43998
44032
44050
44058
44064
44072
44073
44116
44120
44225
44291
44306
44357
44361
44365
44372
44382
44383
44423
47299
47309
49009

49027
49048
49105
49112
49115
49116
49149
49150
49153
49160
49198
49203
49252
49266
49268
49270
49289
49306
49327
49348
49355
49378
49386
49387
49395
49396
49397
49398
49400
49410
49417
49418
49419
49420
49424
49427
49429
49435
49442
49445
49450
49515
51319
51358
52095
52135
52183
52269
52389
52431
52443
52455
54469
54484
56235
56266
57276
57444
57595
57599
58065
58190
60503
60505
61433
61458
61470
61530
61533
61647
61654
61723
61755
61772
61790
61885
61911
61988
62692
62694
62705
63572
63642
63723
64184
64241
64376
64640
64658
64670
64683
64750
64761
64793
64834
64973
64976
64983
65434
65463
65505
65544
65559
65580
65732
68108
68406
68409
68543
68596
68599
68629

68641
68643
68645
68655
68985
69154
69208
69215
69492
69510
69522
69524
69528
69578
69613
69622
69711
69825
69827
69852
69917
Dep 3
CD7

Dec-59
1610
2252
2262
2815
4206
4231
5148
5170
5196
5350
5533
5556
5794
6774
7716
7752
7773
7778
7791
8421
8423
9400
9496
30130
30179
30318
30323
30449
30493
30789
31269
40013
40019
40025
40039
40040
40060
40061
40067
40068
40069
40582
40601
40654
40699
41123
41754
42312
43205
43249
43251
43271
43278
43287
43327
43378
43387
43398
43433
43440
43490
43502
43520
43538
43622
43638
43660
43675
43678
43693
43711
43728
43753
43799
43858
43866
43878
43881
43907
43910
43919
43930
43961
43965
43966
43990
43997

44000
44005
44014
44018
44021
44084
44095
44103
44108
44136
44140
44142
44161
44173
44175
44204
44217
44227
44230
44285
44293
44298
44313
44316
44317
44326
44369
47162
47274
47291
47296
47301
47337
47339
47346
47363
47364
47382
47387
47394
47407
47409
47411
47440
47477
47489
49245
49249
49304
50795
54470
54508
56269
56295
57354
57361
57424
57552
58199
60104
61535
61571
61607
61613
61625
61658
61662
61721
61752
61754
61786
61823
62478
62489
62511
62529
62544
62570
62612
62618
62785
63753
63804
63889
64234
64235
64237
64273
64298
64407
64421
64429
64451
64473
64490
64506
64538
64665
64668
64675
64751
64912
64972
64980
64984
64985
64988
65133
65134
65140
65158
65166

65194
65424
65443
65449
65452
65470
65472
65512
65561
65706
65824
67445
68359
68661
68665
68682
68694
68955
69166
69187
69197
69257
69262
69265
69276
69298
69319
69341
69344
69508
69530
69553
69556
69570
69856
69867
69877
69887
90083

Jan-60
1102
1103
1104
1105
1106
1144
1370
1652
2809
2831
2877
2881
3103
4164
4592
5155
5361
5530
5551
5559
5567
5713
5915
6311
6393
6750
7727
8410
8419
8429
8455
8463
9445
30182
30236
30319
30774
31239
31319
31492
31785
31788
32151
32508
43828
43897
47238
51221
51343
52410
55218
56165
56241
56371
58116
58118
58146
58183
58261
61610
61618
61620
61626
61641
61653
61656
61759
62597
62604
62709
62719

63733
64331
64389
64438
64641
64654
64694
64695
64769
64777
64780
64800
64838
64887
64959
65514
65530
65533
65546
65558
65563
67417
67450
68230
68262
68264
68425
68444
68579
68591
68670
68898
69170
69343
69594
69853
69855
90062
90191

Feb-60
2275
2844
2850
4547
5005
7701
8704
30047
30769
30775
31337
31370
31540
31558
31688
31743
31762
31784
32447
32526
32551
32554
32689
43174
43256
43337
43406
43431
44510
47229
49544
49624
49674
50781
52139
56170
56367
57273
57435
57448
57628
58219
60501
61442
61465
61477
61663
61836
61928
62497
64172
64213
64396
64712
64721
64722
64724
64728
64771
64826
64827
64830
64890
64891
64898
64937
64960
64967
64977
64981
65169

65342
65343
65459
65474
65477
65551
65584
65847
68360
68431
68697
68722
68727
68752
68834
68969
68980
69144
69168
69205
69207
69267
69268
69292
69299
69314
69354
69588
69665
69683
69857
69859
69873

Mar-60
2806
2847
4562
5102
5106
5178
5185
5709
6105
7703
7706
7717
7737
7759
7767
31033
31047
31325
31581
32442
32444
40057
40070
41847
41879
43178
43509
43664
43749
43839
44077
44093
44343
44360
44366
44391
44406
44410
44412
44415
44427
44430
44438
44453
44459
44471
44473
44480
44483
44488
44495
44496
44498
44502
44503
44506
44507
44511
44513
44515
44546
44555
44563
44600
47323
47352
47374
47486
47498
47525
47527
47528
47563
47575
47585
47586
47591

47595
47600
47636
47639
47650
47672
53802
54476
56304
56349
61427
61608
61659
61666
61672
61741
61791
61802
61806
61838
61900
62471
62482
62485
62498
62524
64180
64348
64383
64433
64567
64759
64774
64781
64782
64828
64883
64902
64951
64952
64953
64954
64956
64957
64958
64962
64965
64968
65448
65455
65473
65519
65536
65548
65555
67491
67492
67496
68260
68457
68654
68671
68895
68958
69145
69149
69308
69589

Apr-60
5795
6759
7793
30093
30474
31692
31763
41949
41969
42418
43188
43305
43314
43429
43456
43989
52162
61670
61881
61909
61937
63888
64178
64192
64270
64315
64357
64405
64487
64642
64647
64659
64807
64824
64948
65389
65461
65565
65570
67460
67474
67484

67486
67490
67501
67502
68656
68714
68725
68909
69360
69801
69806
69813
69817
69823

May-60
2282
2805
2835
2837
4073
4097
5028
5079
5333
5353
5396
5702
5704
5717
5727
5731
5750
5763
5764
5769
5776
6439
7728
7733
8468
8708
9673
11394
30456
30791
31102
31223
31310
31509
32655
40014
40652
41157
41855
42345
42490
43207
43218
43344
43773
43843
44031
52141
54462
54477
54490
54498
54499
56025
56292
56348
57554
57605
58144
58158
61779
61882
61955
62663
62743
63372
63970
64179
64256
64368
64397
64468
64656
65192
65229
65252
68100
68190
68192
68309
68314
68364
68392
68731
69165
69202
69206
69507
69552
69563
69821
69829
69854
69858
69874
69875

69889

Jun-60
1407
1412
1427
1441
1448
1449
1452
1464
1620
1625
1629
1637
3202
4556
5407
5418
5422
5519
5523
5524
5527
5754
6104
6300
6401
6406
6728
7400
7708
7758
8411
9004
9015
9018
9428
9434
9449
30266
32532
32559
40036
40552
41162
42450
43329
43457
43570
43627
44019
44052
47541
49064
51445
52452
56331
58173
61657
61660
61664
61782
61863
61992
62421
62426
62493
64175
64257
64387
64452
64483
65662
65666
67671
68320
68352
68507
68569
68679
69171
69198
69850
69860
69861
69869
69870
69878
69880
69883
69885
69886
69894

Jul-60
1604
4162
5179
5197
5543
5561
5755
6121
6307
6323
6702
6712
6719
6756
7419
7712

7781
9436
31323
41773
42326
43212
43394
43484
43973
44029
44163
47167
47260
47560
47652
49234
49321
52140
56259
56335
56363
57609
58168
61794
61815
63716
63894
64403
64684
64741
64789
64802
64893
64966
65110
65317
65471
65566
69540
69587
69617
Dep 21
Dep 42

Aug-60
1601
3609
4575
4587
5150
5529
5540
6751
6766
6775
7709
7723
7725
7726
8778
9414
9468
30448
30673
30794
31054
31265
31494
31520
31725
32562
40011
40489
40501
40698
43243
43307
43326
43373
47203
47561
52179
52322
54480
54494
56035
58086
58153
58287
60509
61440
61456
61668
62467
62662
62664
62667
62669
62740
64240
64660
64686
64693
64708
64717
64765
64775
64784
64889
64896
64974
65479

65503
65506
65539
65564
65712
65713
68123
68332
68349
68501
68573
68749
68753
68913
68952
69133
69177
69190
69223
69629
69648
69684
DS3152

Sep-60
1602
2203
2264
2265
2274
2297
2821
4170
4589
4901
5169
5324
5370
5534
5546
5565
5748
5759
6332
6343
6371
6389
7702
7719
7757
8427
30058
30255
30450
30687
30763
32443
32484
32495
32543
40041
40402
40454
40583
40631
42346
42365
42390
42399
43187
43235
43359
43399
43523
43639
43652
43735
43840
44585
45502
45609
47265
47303
47537
47576
51227
51486
51524
52351
57558
58165
58209
58850
61471
61769
61933
64196
64206
64209
64463
64502
64504
64512
64529
64678
64682
64778
65070
65777
67624
68022
68028

68072
68076
68114
68343
68354
68676
68902
68944
68954
68956
68957
69141
69143
69161
69179
69258
69370
69582
69596
69615

Oct-60
1659
2202
4084
4550
4559
5009
5311
5337
5384
5504
5510
5552
5557
5558
6333
6377
6398
6801
9014
9017
30274
31048
31086
31266
31287
31497
40491
40581
40588
40630
40690
40907
41063
43203
43340
43644
43650
43784
44375
47241
47670
48616
49082
52161
52429
52466
56027
56032
56308
58170
58220
61410
61424
61428
61990
62488
62660
62710
62739
62762
63959
64251
64434
64650
64663
64685
64764
64770
65249
65440
67702
68033
68269
68316
68410
68497
68513
68526
68563
68575
68650
68663
68685
68701
68706
68901
68915
69194
69209
69509

69560
69704
69733

Nov-60
1143
1371
2213
2813
2846
4288
4594
5104
5331
5339
5514
6351
6352
6360
6382
7707
7722
7766
7775
7777
7794
8108
8754
9462
9749
9795
30238
31298
32446
32527
40012
40028
40062
40584
40671
41947
42300
42373
42398
43189
43361
43572
43574
43594
43634
43814
43868
45508
47347
47401
47510
47523
47567
49229
49505
51336
51498
52089
52154
52244
52252
52290
52305
52319
52341
52378
52400
52411
52445
56172
56279
56289
56300
56310
56343
56361
58197
58295
58298
60510
61469
61745
61792
62613
62661
62668
62670
63643
63669
63950
63953
64182
64222
64288
64325
64425
64440
64462
64493
64681
64726
64738
64783
65233
65511
67704
67726
68235
68254
68361
68577
68644
68681
68705
68730
68738
68897
68911
68914
69132
69184
69505
69611
69620
69630
69636
69642
69645
69647
69663
69664
69677
69688
69694
69699
69709
69719
69720
69727
69808
69814
69820
W4

Dec-60
1454
4281
5103
5110
5536
5757
7704
7740
9737
30288
40161
42380
42512
43194
43444
43579
43705
47254
47262
47271
47282
47311
47335
47436
47443
47446
47463
47509
47568
47569
47573
47635
52133
52225
56260
56364
58260
60507
61478
61728
61747
61760
61771
61773
61916
61924
62666
62744
63700
65446
65549
67701
67705
67706
67708
67709
67711
67714
67725
67736
68027
68571
68633
68647
68660
68691
68724
68899
68905
69263
69266
69274
69286
69293
69296
69307
69309
69511
69581
69614
69652
69654
69680
69681
69682
69685
69687
69691
69700
69701
69706
69712
69715
69718
69721
69722
69726
69729

Jan-61
1364
1366
1433
1501
1502
2819
3638
3649
3704
3799
4203
4287
5176
5207
5417
6425
6752
6753
6761
6776
7410
7761
7776
8406
8413
8424
8454
8457
8460
8473
8476
9447
9458
9481
9701
30128
30489
30491
31787
32491
40001
40421
40439
40443
40452
40487
40504
40511
40543
40548
40627
40628
40936
42397
43234
43333
43800
45616
47212
47607
50721
51229
52270
56309
57653
58293
60504
61446
61740
61761
61766
61767
62717
62723
62727
62759
62763
62765
64173
64232
64268
64311
64371
64652
64653
64666
64674
64679
64680
64689
64743
64767
64823
65239
65589
65714
65727
65762
67612
67750
68275
68278
68344
68456
68500
68558
68560
68578
68719
69173
69516
69518
69631
69651
69679
69690
69708

Feb-61
7429
7433
7747
8740
30059
30355
30524
30584
30667
30783
30799
30919
30932
31037
31258
31276
31328
31487
31519
31550
31590
31764
31765
31766
31776
31782
32107
32541
40003
40054
40396
40411
40502
40580
40585
40632
40635
40682
40691
42438
42539
43321
43325
43405
43562
43715
43737
45511
47369
47484
50746
52201
52355
54488
55233
55265
56158
56370
58131
58169
58186
58291
60508
61763
63709
64231
64341
64363
64404
64439
64441
64523
64746
64808
64878
64885
65520
65736
67489
67494
67768
67790
68272
68408
68443
68447
68502
68508
68530
68545
68623
68678
68690
68696
68716
68924
68930
68943
68946
68947
68979
69012
Dep 57

Mar-61
4229
4571
5768
5771
6411
6426
6805
7745
8101
9735
30229
30300
30331
30707
30718
30719
30729
30771
31027
31193
31246
31495
31545
31694
31727
32505
32528
32536
40015
40557
40683
40695
41532
41536
43266
43306
43395
43474
43515
43548
43762
43778
45500
47190
47204
47312
47619
49243
51371
51441
51496
52415
52526
53805
54487
56169
56171
56239
56324
56338
56341
56376
58115
58215
58221
58283
61784
61828
61971
62734
62747
63649
63954
64260
64278
64310
64317
64446
64524
64560
64698
64723
64729
64908
64987
65276
65339
65513
65556
65779
68026
68233
68522
68683
68684
68869
68890
69134
69180
69572
69574
69586
69702

Apr-61
1419
1431
1463
1647
2207
2227
5158
5175
5194
5791
5815
7748
8705
8722
8726
8769
8777
8796
30338
30357
30479
30806
31019
31322
31735
32546
32578
40051
40574
40586
40629
41529
43245
43267
43309
43386
43459
43482
43580
43809
43944
43948
44067
47200
47209
47540
52230
52240
52260
52464
54505
56167
56168
56246
60095
60506
61849
61858
61967
62495
62716
62718
62733
63573
63595
63944
63947
63952
64185
64223
64236
64359
64447
64596
64700
64710
64716
64804
64874
64882
64906
64909
64964
65295
67485
68080
68875
68903
68907
68916
68921
68927
68936
68945
68968
68970
68990
69656
69658
69696
69707
Dep 2
Dep 9

May-61
1361
1362
3657
3667
3670
3676
3724
5166
5177
5503
5949
6902
6949
7700
7798
9762
9771
9781
30043
30104
30124
30327
30457
30865
31517
32512
32515
40092
40126
40155
40171
40622
42377
42507
43200
43225
43250
43605
43624
43729
43962
44148
45514
47277
47398
47513
47559
47571
47605
47625
47626
47637
51429
52171
52182
52207
55169
55198
55219
55235
56173
56372
57232
57324
57434
61416
61462
61874
62474
62479
62671
62711
62729
63597
63608
63662
63747
63782
63958
64208
64313
64444
64476
64534
64892
64970
65588
65753
65868
68325
68459
68673
68929
68981
69136
69199
69506
69513
69561

Jun-61
1410
1615
1634
5195
5198
5351
6700
7756
7787
8789
8798
9736
9745
9751
9767
30040
30109
30694
30939
31065
31500
31512
31553
31556
31578
31693
31695
31760
32108
32410
32449
32475
32506
32552
32565
40050
40595
40604
42344
43214
43268
43284
43411
43468
43812
43911
43921
44206
44371
47418
49637
52393
54475
54483
55195
55209
55231
56337
57356
57431
57473
57586
57591
57619
58271
58305
61788
61844
61850
61865
61904
61919
61997
63626
63845
63915
64337
64384
64471
64482
64489
64494
64500
64810
64831
67610
67665
68612
68726
68962
69105
69521
69531
69564
69571
69674
69675
69921

Jul-61
1640
6720
8706
8721
9739
30060
30117
30248
30258
30313
30317
30349
30453
30582
30583
30669
30676
30691
30693
30699
30701
30709
30715
30717
30764
30802
30904
30914
30938
31061
31113
31162
31247
31256
31480
31498
31507
31575
31583
31714
31780
32694
40016
40020
40075
40077
40571
40572
40577
40579
40603
40678
40684
40685
41168
43211
43277
43374
43427
43846
43900
43922
44141
44477
53801
54478
55126
55167
55185
55199
55210
55237
55239
56240
56242
57349
57373
57416
58181
60502
61432
61445
61466
61803
61824
61852
61902
61921
61925
61927
61941
61964
62674
62681
62682
62686
62688
62689
62690
62712
63957
64170
64233
64265
64364
64402
64427
64531
64736
64748
64772
64845
64914
64928
64930
64932
65281
65760
65774
65778
67707
67717
67719
67732
67738
67740
68550
68554
68715
68740
68891
68918
68920
68951
68960
68975
69221
90753
90754
Dep 54

Aug-61
822
4573
5516
6802
7409
8762
8772
8774
8787
30192
30674
30696
30800
30803
30858
31307
32553
32563
40007
40010
40018
40029
40032
40034
40035
40037
40038
40042
40049
40053
40064
40097
40107
40142
40570
40575
40593
40597
40623
40624
40659
40692
42307
42349
42864
42893
42930
43905
43920
45503
45509
45516
45619
47268
51413
52271
55200
55202
56360
56362
57570
61764
61842
61978
62672
62680
62687
63719
64316
64352
64417
64435
64539
64655
64707
64732
64815
64916
65157
65198
65227
67627
67650
67670
67760
68073
68110
68471
68686
68693
68702
68708
68711
68721
68737
68896
68931
68959
68966
68991

Sep-61
1606
4117
4552
4926
5318
5706
5756
7417
30044
30183
30287
30308
30523
30668
30772
30854
30855
30907
30908
30931
31242
31255
31505
32415
32556
32564
40033
40118
40124
40566
40596
40618
40637
40640
40648
40650
40663
40669
42328
42360
42506
42510
42524
42531
43185
43330
43371
43507
43529
43673
43751
43863
43872
43883
44002
44037
44082
44107
44111
44147
44152
44547
44590
45501
45539
47239
47255
47334
47403
47405
47420
47421
47438
47448
47462
47508
47570
47580
47620
47624
47632
47634
49422
51419
51444
51537
52129
55206
55207
55211
55214
55222
55223
55226
55228
55229
55230
55232
55236
55238
55261
55266
55268
56151
57236
57238
57244
57250
57411
57426
57429
57472
58122
58135
58137
60035
60055
60064
60079
61411
61412
61413
61414
61415
61419
61422
61423
61425
61429
61431
61436
61443
61447
61450
61451
61452
61459
61473
61572
61808
61833
61888
61891
61920
61975
63891
64171
64174
64308
64667
64669
64676
64677
64692
64697
64720
64779
65507
65554
67669
67728
67758
67769
67775
68338
68538
68552
68570
68613
68642
68646
68649
68687
68720
68744
68745
68894
68950
69015
69498
69533
69543
69549
69580
69585
69592
69618
69668
69670
69673
69678
69686
69693
69698
69710
69713
69714
69723
69724
69728
69730
69732

Oct-61
2215
4207
4563
4565
4997
5332
5538
5780
6329
6392
9705
30023
30223
30246
30247
30253
30522
30768
30777
30790
30918
31068
31145
31150
31177
31229
31244
31261
31326
31579
31682
31684
31691
31716
31720
31753
31756
32102
32441
32448
32450
32469
32522
32534
40076
40079
40081
40091
40094
40095
40101
40102
40103
40111
40115
40121
40123
40129
40130
40131
40132
40133
40134
40136
40141
40143
40149
40156
40162
40165
40166
40167
40168
40175
40178
40182
40183
40184
40194
40199
40208
40209
40602
40609
40612
40613
40614
40615
40619
40620
40621
40625
40626
40641
40642
40643
40645
40647
40668
40686
40687
40689
42217
42302
42325
42329
42332
42348
42356
42364
42382
42383
42386
42404
42423
42427
42428
42467
42471
42475
42479
42545
42552
42570
42627
42635
42637
42648
42669
42683
43295
43681
44033
44090
44105
46204
46210
46211
46212
47218
47529
48915
48932
48942
48953
49007
49020
49021
49023
49061
49077
49119
49137
49158
49164
49191
49196
49209
49210
49275
49288
49310
49342
49343
49357
49392
49399
49401
49405
49411
49412
49413
49414
49421
49433
49441
49443
49444
49453
49618
49627
50850
51246
54464
54485
55124
55165
55201
55208
55215
55216
55220
55221
55224
55262
55264
55267
56298
56326
57233
57245
57246
57256
57257
57262
57263
57264
57268
57271
57303
57335
57377
57404
57418
57432
57436
57446
57451
57461
57470
57557
57559
57560
57564
57576
58163
61460
61866
61892
61894
61961
61968
61979
61993
61995
61996
61998
63860
64385
64461
64474
64488
64505
64542
64565
64646
64725
64733
64825
64839
64862
64901
64904
64931
65099
65232
65235
65450
65458
65478
65691
65741
65769
67712
67713
67722
67762
67794
68119
68619
68672
68674
68675
68677
68680
68688
68689
68692
68698
68703
68704
68713
68728
68729
68732
68734
68742
68743
68747
69159

Nov-61
2233
2260
2267
4075
4123
4945
5174
5515
5553
5907
5950
6306
6313
6341
6413
6415
7322
7421
7771
7772
8404
8451
8782
9474
9714
9720
30277
30910
30920
30922
30933
31004
31067
31161
31481
31489
31552
31573
31589
31715
31739
31749
31754
31759
31783
31789
32100
32445
32451
32498
32504
32539
32544
32547
32548

32549
40074
40108
40140
40195
40569
40578
40651
40661
42395
42521
42549
43368
43826
43832
44319
44324
45401
45544
45630
46205
46207
47221
47263
48927
49423
49668
51217
54492
54493
54506
54507
55240
55263
57239
57285
57287
57288
57292
57317
57321
57350
57353
57366
57389
57441
57579
57580
57583
57585
57593
57623
57632
57640
57650
57651
57659
57663
57665
57669
60102
61851
61860
61936
61959
62484
63757
63799
63904
64219
64418
64477
64515
64518
64532
64535
64643
64745
64837
64920
65528
65782
67681
67718
67739
67748
67772
67782
68717
68948
69183

Dec-61

1152
2206
2220
2288
4083
4092
4549
5509
5511
5542
5770
7741
7760
8441
8775
9703
9765
11304
30475
30476
30521
30851
30859
30905
31306
31757
31768
31771
32438
32521
32538
32545
32550
40071
40144
40192
40592
42220
42330
42363
42534
43884
44088
44249
44409
44474
46407
48950
49313
52459
54489
54491
54501
55203
55227
56305
56356
56368
57319
57325
57363
57364
57367
57392
57463
57563
57633
57637
58174
58175
61085
61814
61901
61903
61938
61994
62496
62691
62693
63457
63570
64479
64816
65745
68923
68932
68933
68941
69219
90752

Jan-62

1435
1642
2216
2230
3726
4126
4632
5167
5549
5720
5920
5921
6152
6153
6166
8470
8494
8735
8760
9416
9454
9738
30050
30692
30864
30913
30924
30927
31723
32500
32525
40093
40152
40154
40158
40170
40180
42412
42448
42764
43679
43714
44166
44196
47678
49246
49391
49508
51241
55173
55225
56313
61201
61222
61368
61839
61861
61862
61908
61976
62685
63648
63833
63870
64395
64507
64533
64792
64809
64863
64870
64963
64979
65246
65751
65763
65839
67601
67613
67623
67679
67727
67774
68063
68442
68458
68900
69013

Feb-62

1605
1624
1626
3602
3636
3656
3713
5069
5547
6006
6348
6408
7796
8435
8467
8483
8489
8700
8733
8753
8779
8792
9421
9460
9465
9740
30326
30773
30788
30796
30804
30852
30853
30863
30900
30909
31317
31584
31717
31786
32416
32523
32535
40024
40185
40206
40207
40540
40564
40697
42375
43849
43996
44224
46476
47353
47404
47473
47475
47516
49277
51408
51446
53803
53804
54466
54482
54486
54495
54500
57314
57345
57626
58214
60850
60960
60977
61265
61376
61913
61932
61945
61966
62031
62034
62052
63599
63623
64177
64191
64245
64470
64514
64671
64867
65296
65305
65457
65521
65532
65577
65583
67609
67648
67659
67660
67661
67666
67715
67720
67743
67753
68064
68342
68353
68454
68472
68481
68549
68709
68926
68963
69014
69126
69131
69156
69163
69181
69216
90603

Mar-62

1468
3614
4094
4957
4965
5326
5783
6101
6127
6162
6168
6302
6429
7406
7422
7784
8711
8713
8734
8736
9469
30350
31530
31689
31721
32509
40082
40179
41769
41900
42452
42797
43400
43410
43618
43721
43763
43793
43859
44001
44087
44550
44606
45504
45506
45519
47213
47259
47275
47340
47483
47601
49440
51207
51222
51244
52248
52311
55269
57338
57347
57357
57359
57370
57603
57618
57635
57673
57686
58166
58228
60875
60928
61000
61217
61290
61804
61818
61829
61841
61887
61918
61948
61953
61987
63677
63681
63762
63775
64423
64472
64553
64628
64703
64705
64706
64718
64744
64811
64817
64843
64858
64884
64915
65258
65578
67603
67622
67631
67655
67751
67752
67756
67799

Apr-62

1426
2860
3723
4086
4566
4974
4987
4990
5004
5006
5012
5044
5412
5521
5539
5560
5572
5744
5793
6120
6123
6324
6336
7328
7334
7718
7753
8715
8727
8784
8797
30193
30306
31112
31218
31268
31293
31686
31722
31724
32580
32581
40181
42387
42514
43435
43446
43464
43621
43760
43825
43938
43985
44154
44256
44397
44487
44561
46453
47310
47504
48964
49134
52438
56031
56159
56232
56282
57267
57274
57275
57571
57597
57612
57621
57654
57655
60811
60826
60849
60857
60917
61046
61063
61380
61801
61809
61813
61837
61923
61926
61949
63779
64443
64450
64497
64519
64566
64696
64713
64836
64842
64868
64903
64939
65033
65216
65315
65320
65581
65586
65645
65663
65693
65720
65728
65747
65757
65786
67634
68030
68695
68707
68754
68983
68987
69017
69026
69097
69101
69109

May-62

1505
1618
2223
2234
2239
2255
2853
3624
3640
3645
3684
3697
3703
3718
3722
3732
3743
3774
4085
4561
4625
4641
4685
4977
4982
4986
5024
5035
5090
5182
5183
5187
5212
5636
5639
5682
5728
5758
5761
5766
5779
5789
5906
5913
5928
5935
6157
6376
6390
6687
6778
6865
7720
7736
7755
7762
7764
7785
7786
7799
8107
8719
8741
8750
8761
8764
8788
8790
9409
9467
9497
9643
9702
9709
9718
9728
9750
9758
9783
30049
30063
30339
30698
30781
31521
31719
40009
40110
40563
40634
40638
40646
42352
42371
42420
42433
42779
42818
42889
43213
43510
44245
44258
44482
45265
45520
46478
47224
47332
47342
47366
47414
47425
47514
47572
47621
47642
49404
52218
56312
57365
57386
57398
57562
57682
60093
60823
60829
60867
60907
60953
61077
61137
61742
61816
61834
61868
61873
61896
61922
61940
61958
61986
63635
63758
63798
63955
64253
64578
64590
64711
64806
64820
64947
65266
65280
65318
65787
65807
67602
67629
67637
67644
67778
67788
67795
68336
68626
69137
69653
90167
90750
90760
90764

Jun-62

2240
2292
4274
4702
4963
4995
5059
5193
5376
5526
6003
6004
6008
6010
6013
6023
6024
6387
6739
6755
6758
7425
8499
9476
9721
30451
30798
31267
31510
31588
31690
32470
32472
40122
40174
40665
40696
41702
41981
42219
42223
42254
42255
42257
42323
42340
42342
42362
42370
42393
42500
42501
42502
42503
42504
42505
42508
42509
42511
42513
42515
42516
42517
42518
42519
42520
42522
42523
42525
42526
42527
42528
42529
42530
42532
42533
42535
42536
42538
42576
42579
42593
42672
42677
42678
42679
42684
42687
42822
42825
42829
42847
42868
42939
43263
43436
43565
43789
43844
43848
43869
43902
44036
44104
44267
44573
44576
45179
45505
45510
45515
45517
45537
45541
45542
45546
45548
45549
45551
47261
47290
47304
47328
47351
47424
47455
47470
47536
47542
47555
49155
49403
56278
57295
57300
57362
57385
57620
60815
60820
60863
60890
60908
60909
61079
61247
61298
61756
61946
61989
63743
63787
63917
63951
64203
64226
64277
64393
64420
64437
64527
64545
64971
65330
65560
65670
65695
65726
65731
65735
65743
65755
65756
65761
65768
65772
65773
65776
65867
67649
68052
68057
90060
90436
90505
90616
DS680

Jul-62

823
1434
1609
2295
3404
3785
4078
4558
4588
4931
4968
4973
5013
5053
5067
5077
5082
5084
5180
5188
5358
5385
5532
5541
5600
5657
5661
5778
5909
5916
5941
5946
5947
5965
5989
5997
6017
6020
6029
6310
6316
6339
6340
7313
7402
7721
7729
7765
7788
8422
8440
8477
8724
8730
8731
8771
8780
9407
9410
9433
9448
9451
9478
9486
9487
9627
9719
9722
9723
30795
31324
40085
40088
40090
40105
40109
40113
40128
40173
40197
40198
40201
40203
41255
41256
41257
41259
42396
42749
42811
42824
42850
42927
44016
44070
44138
44158
44187
47546
49099
49141
58123
58124
58185
58218
60848
61043
61170
61183
61203
61231
61800
61870
61877
61884
61895
61910
61929
61935
61974
63603
63895
63929
63934
64284
64292
64305
64355
64377
64525
64742
64955
65211
65300
65306
65310
65313
65818
67614
67676
67746
67747
67757
68009
68055
68117
68350
68733
68986
68989
69204
69512
69523
90134
90244
90286
90298
90320
90513
90575
90691
90768

Aug-62

1473
2209
2250
2849
3611
3641
4077
4112
4146
4235
4266
4293
4912
4925
4971
5003
5048
5062
5095
5151
5173
5181
5537
5663
5664
5969
5996
6109
6374
6600
6645
7302
7323
7338
7408
7713
8763
9741
9757
30200
30377
30793
30850
30860
40063
40072
40073
40080
40089
40100
40146
40681
42304
42318
42331
42351
42367
42385
42596
42929
43242
43254
43389
43496
43499
43583
43586
43608
43668
43680
43687
43709
43766
43822
44314
44329
47392
47422
47479
47522
47545
47548
47604
47610
47630
48898
55217
56347
57242
57249
57254
57265
57341
57383
57445
57577
57587
57622
57642
57666
57667
57671
57691
60068
60800
60874
61234
61239
61379
61439
61810
61914
61947
63584
63588
63605
63633
63713
63724
63766
63823
63857
63864
63885
63920
64318
64329
64333
64394
64419
64445
64478
64604
64607
64637
64673
64794
64855
64949
65420
65445
65453
65469
65567
65799
65863
67617
67667
67730
67737
67764
68018
68565
90093
90256
90391
90648

Sep-62

1004
1018
1026
1462
1508
2200
2229
2256
2271
2276
2294
3211
3408
3623
3630
3688
3694
3741
3750
3760
3783
4037
4099
4102
4106
4116
4118
4129
4152
4218
4230
4236
4250
4270
4291
4557
4567
4906
4909
4913
4917
4921
4934
4937
4944
4947
4948
4952
4960
4967
4969
4984
4999
5007
5008
5011
5016
5017
5019
5021
5030
5032
5033
5034
5036
5045
5046
5047
5052
5061
5064
5066
5068
5075
5088
5094
5190
5357
5399
5421
5520
5525
5544
5550
5562
5617
5631
5642
5646
5652
5698
5746
5773
5798
5910
5911
5917
5918
5926
5930
5931
5940
5959
5960
5964
5966
5968
5973
5980
5981
5982
5999
6001
6002
6007
6009
6012
6014
6015
6016
6019
6021
6022
6026
6027
6146
6312
6330
6342
6362
6366
6386
6388
6391
6422
6436
6616
6617
6630
6640
6641
6647
7300
7301
7305
7309
7311
7316
7321
7330
7331
7336
7341
7724
7744
7783
8445
8449
8482
8709
8742
8748
8757
8765
9712
9756
9785
9797
30028
30051
30321
30375
30765
30782
30856
30857
31533
32101
32105
32510
40104
40119
40138
40145
40148
40191
40193
40202
40537
40664
40700
41246
42305
42347
42537
42724
42742
42903
43216
43449
43585
43682
43734
43756
43808
43914
43932
44008
44020
44062
44122
44129
44216
44273
44338
44368
44407
44508
44509
44518
44521
44557
45513
45524
45533
45538
45547
46209
46466
46469
47217
47269
47270
47302
47319
47348
47356
47381
47426
47433
47457
47466
47474
47497
47554
47593
47633
49002
49025
49034
49087
49125
49126
49139
49147
49199
49240
49323
49352
49382
49416
49425
49426
49437
51204
51206
51412
52093
52312
52345
52441
52523
57311
57331
57378
57613
58160
60845
60893
60896
60914
60930
60936
60938
60943
60956
60983
61005
61009
61027
61036
61045
61047
61048
61052
61054
61060
61066
61091
61096
61111
61114
61124
61130
61139
61149
61150
61151
61154
61163
61164
61166
61171
61182
61187
61193
61202
61206
61209
61226
61228
61235
61236
61253
61254
61266
61271
61280
61282
61283
61284
61286
61287
61301
61311

61317
61335
61362
61363
61364
61371
61373
61377
61391
61405
61805
61812
61817
61821
61825
61826
61827
61831
61835
61840
61845
61848
61864
61880
61886
61890
61907
61912
61915
61942
61943
61944
61954
61956
61957
61960
61963
61972
61977
61982
63574
63587
63609
63616
63621
63631
63634
63641
63657
63664
63686
63708
63759
63900
63979
64314
64324
64332
64346
64362
64373
64375
64379
64386
64406
64442
64480
64598
64630
64657
64664
64687
64690
64691
64699
64740
64798
64819
64866
65361
65460
65462
65464
65465
65476
65541
65576
65582
65800
67703
67716
67723
67724
67729
67731
67734
67735
67793
68069
68499
68542
68556
68566
68600
68609
68621
68635
68917
68928
68961
68964
68971
68972
68976
68982
69155
69504
69520
69529
69535
69538
69546
69568
69575
69579
69583
69593
69621
69632
69640
69646
69671
69692
69697
69725
80103
90023
90034
90106
90150
90196
90288
90387
90455
90473
90494
90512
90550
90554
90594
90653
90657
90690
90732
Dep 32
Dep 44
Dep 45

Oct-62

1003
1007
1022
1470
1633
1645
3407
3637
3755
3769
3773
4163
4267
4289
4605
4647
4700
4708
4941
5072
5774
5925
5953
6301
6629
6738
6749
6770
7324
7428
7434
7440
7732
8100
8407
8416
8428
8438
8439
8453
8490
8725
8744
8756
8773
9759
9761
30061
30065
30070
30861
30862
31278
31409
31877
31878
31879
31897
32103
32106
40006
40099
40120
40164
40453
40657
40672
41236
41247
41258
41266
41271
41288
42088
42094
42146
42227
42303
42324
42336
42358
42388
42402
42407
42429
42470
42472
42473
42476
42483
42540
42553
42575
42578
42591
42599
42615
42621
42641
42642
42646
42653
42658
42661
42666
42685
42714
42726
42775
42786
42874
42887
42891
43240
43257
43282
43514
43593
43615
43645
43657
43754
43899
44011
44143
44159
44193
44234
44251
44253
44254
44257
44307
44312
44318
44320
44323
44325
44330
44393
44417
44435
44491
44537
44553
44579
44594
45507
45518
45559
45566
45713
45718
45724
45728
45729
45731
46100
46123
46131
46137
46139
46201
46203
46206
46208
46415
46494
47168
47235
47316
47417
47431
47552
47588
49335
49377
49394
49434
52119
52275
52456
52461
54465
54502
56039
57237
57240
57251
57253
57258
57259
57284
57299
57329
57369
57417
57447
57596
57614
57617
57631
57643
57644
57672
57681
58128
58177
60069
60072
60076
60078
60081
60115
60123
60135
60137
60153
60511
60515
60516
60517
60518
60521
60526
60538
60539
60801
60839
60842
60860
60878
60918
60926
60934
60947
60979
61028
61078
61136
61192
61211
61381
61395
61811
63948
63965
64354
64701
64856
64871
64923
64926
64945
65210
65217
65218
65230
65241
65257
65260
65304
65334
65344
65837
67639
67641
67673
67677
67759
67797
68007
68048
68056
68074
68101
68104
68335
68346
68445
68448
68453
68470
68479
69002
69007
69010
69018
69027
69128
69135
69138
69150
69188
69191
69196
69211
69212
69218
69224
90021
90022
90087
90174
90247
90308
90355
90356
90562
90565
90591
90607
90630
90637
90666
90693

Nov-62

1438
2834
2883
3827
4601
5020
5027
5078
6005
6028
6410
6418
6438
7016
8799
30131
30132
30245
30346
30502
30504
30505
30516
30517
30518
30519
30520
30540
30689
30697
30700
30770
30826
30912
30917
30928
30950
30951
30952
30957
31305
31414
31542
31630
31822
31876
31880
31892
31902
31904
32339
32344
32346
32348
32349
32350
32351
32352
32473
40026
40031
40078
40083
40086
40087
40098
40106
40116
40135
40137
40157
40205
40694
41235
41277
41278
42122
42298
42320
42376
42443
42457
42544
42580
42585
42600
42624
42674
42773
42781
42830
42866
42881
43933
45543
45550
45607
45651
45662
45686
45722
46117
46134
46146
46147
46154
46159
46161
46170
46200
46408
46471
46493
47488
47526
47562
47608
47644
49049
49070
49079
49081
49093
49094
49104
49114
49122
49129
49130
49144
49154
49216
49224
49267
49287
49293
49314
49328
49344
49381
49402
49408
49415
49431
49432
49438
49447
49451
52121
52413
57252
57340
57555
57569
57611
57615
57645
57674
57684
58120
60122
61020
61064
61106
61295
61297
61339
61352
61807
61820
61822
61830
61832
61843
61854
61859
61867
61889
61905
61917
61934
61939
61950
61951
61970
61973
61981
61984
63467
63468
63575
63598
63600
63712
63721
63755
63760
63767
63777
63792
63794
63796
63805
63838
63848
63856
63862
63874
63886
63922
64499
64510
64727
64730
64739
64749
64754
64757
64758
64760
64791
64801
64814
64821
64833
64840
64846
64847
64849
64872
64875
64877
64879
64880
64886
64888
64895
64899
64907
64911
64918
64938
64969
65797
65877
67710
67721
67733
67754
67761
67763
67765
67771
67781
67784
67789
67796
68017
68034
68044
68058
68910
68939
71000
90128
90532
90701
90761

Dec-62

1015
1017
1029
1363
1365
1646
1649
1653
2212
2855
3207
3606
3632
3655
3663
3666
3674
3780
4095
4145
4246
4269
4276
4656
4938
4961
5204
5219
5258
5604
5630
5695
5902
5912
6000
6011
6018
6025
6601
6669
6754
6757
6767
7224
7241
7739
7749
7790
8729
8737
8746
8751
8770
8776
8781
9424
9604
9717
9725
9727
9775
30033
30045
30062
30125
30199
30225
30309
30315
30316
30325
30368
30378
30494
30495
30534
30537
30585
30586
30587
30690
30695
30901
30902
30903
30906
30911
30915
30916
30921
30923
30925
30926
30929
30930
30934
30935
30936
30937
30953
30954
30955
30956
31308
31610
31893
31894
31895
31896
31898
31899
31900
31903
31905
31906
31907
31908
31909
32337
32338
32340
32341
32342
32343
32345
32347
32353
32408
32417
32418
32487
32557
40022
40112
40114
40117
40147
40150
40151
40153
40159
40176
40177
40186
40187
40188
40189
40190
40196
40200
40670
41252
41254
41263
41265
41267
41269
41280
42097
42111
42117
42130
42144
42162
42164
42172
42173
42175
42191
42193
42203
42205
42207
42211
42215
42237
42248
42258
42268
42272
42276
42290
42306
42314
42315
42372
42403
42415
42422
42454
42541
42568
42638
42671
42692
42713
42720
42743
42744
42745
42752
42766
42784
42804
42807
42808
42809
42833
42834
42835
42836
42837
42857
42862
42875
42876
42877
42882
42883
42884
42899
42906
42915
42918
43261
43428
43599
43876
44004
44128
44189
44194
44199
44228
44255
44281
44328
44340
44388
44404
45030
45036
45085
45086
45098
45119
45151
45152
45157
45165
45266
45355
45453
45458
45536
45570
45576
45582
45587
45594
45603
45615
45621
45628
45636
45656
45665
45673
45677
45678
45679
45683
45687
45688
45691
45692
45693
45707
45711
45715
45720
45725
45727
46102
46103
46104
46105
46106
46107
46109
46113
46121
46124
46127
46130
46135
46145
46151
46153
46164
46227
46231
46232
46477
46481
47163
47292
47358
47376
47402
47491
47556
47574
48009
48930
49008
49037
49045
49078
49106
49142
49262
49281
49350
49373
49375
49428
49439
49449
49452
52515
54463
55189
55204
55234
55260
56029
56302
56325
56336
57266
57550
57565
57594
57601
57602
57604
57608
57658
58138
60003
60014
60028
60030
60033
60049
60059
60067
60109
60111
60113
60514
60519
60529
60531
60534
60536
60537
60807
60819
60821
60827
60832
60840
60851
60866
60873
60879
60888
60894
60911
60915
60920
60927
60933
60937
60949
60951
60958
60965
60971
60978
60980
61011
61015
61025
61067
61082
61086
61100
61108
61112
61128
61184
61186
61200
61230
61241
61246
61260
61267
61296
61316
61332
61333
61366
61408
61417
61819
61846
61847
61853
61856
61857
61869
61871
61872
61875
61883
61893
61897
61899
61906
61930
61952
61962
61965
61969
61980
61985
63460
63461
63462
63463
63464
63465
63466
63469
63470
63471
63472
63473
63474
63578
63579
63591
63602
63610
63617
63624
63637
63655
63656
63658
63659
63666
63676
63689
63690
63693
63695
63698
63711
63718
63735
63737
63740
63748
63752
63771
63776
63783
63789
63806
63808
63817
63821
63832
63837
63854
63865
63867
63869
63881
63883
63901
63911
63912
63923
63930
63933
63961
63966
63967
63971
63982
64491
64540
64543
64544
64556
64574
64581
64594
64609
64622
64638
64639
64704
64709
64719
64747
64756
64786
64790
64795
64796
64812
64813
64818
64822
64835
64844
64848
64850
64851
64852
64853
64854
64857
64859
64860
64861
64864
64865
64869
64897
64910
64917
64919
64921
64922
64924
64925
64927
64929
64933
64934
64935
64936
64940
64941
64942
64943
64944
64946
64950
64975
64978
64982
64986
65228
65237
65268
65275
65293
65303
65312
65316
65321
65923
65928
67600
67604
67605
67606
67607
67608
67611
67615
67616
67618
67619
67621
67625
67626
67630
67632
67633
67657
67664
67668
67672
67674
67675
67680
67685
67687
67688
67689
67741
67742
67744
67745
67749
67755
67766
67767
67770
67773
67776
67777
67779
67780
67783
67785
67786
67787
67791
67792
67798
67800
68065
68066
68075
68077
68095
68345
68477
68750
69022
69178
72000
72001
72002
72003
72004
90028
90105
90137
90163
90198
90253
90270
90278
90287
90303
90307
90376
90414
90425
90431
90495
90508
90523
90526
90549
90559
90608
90634
90638
90726
90751
90755
90756
90757
90758
90759
90762
90763
90765
90766
90767
90769
90770
90771
90772
90773
90774
W25

Jan-63

1621
2243
2858
2865
3215
3628
3629
3639
3719
3764
3771
3787
4081
4096
4127
4225
4280
4570
5065
5232
5568
5611
5653
5693
6356
6369
6370
6421
6431
6433
6610
6642
6677
6693
6962
7033
7329
8478
8712
8752
8759
9652
9744
9747
30539
30846
31522
31923
32468
41289
42136
42270
42466
42480
42655
42759
42895
42935
44112
44150
44519
44524
44559
45528
45650
45680
46108
46234
46246
46253
47459
57384
57668
60103
61053
61383
65871
67647
67662

Feb-63

1009
1019
1025
2888
3204
3627
4076
4290
4574
4915
4939
5001
5023
5099
5227
5247
5628
7007
7017
7030
7314
9423
9665
30034
30035
30039
30112
30320
33028
41274
42067
42098
42101
42316
42392
42728
42928
43855
43915
44341
44475
45648
45701
46133
46138
46438
47539
47551
47581
47654
60903
61071
63618
63742
63887
64617
65881
68031
68067
90176

Mar-63

1023
2807
2861
2866
2897
3679
3729
3736
3756
3786
4141
4149
4677
4935
4994
5049
5058
5097
5199
5260
5649
5956
5994
6119
6607
6619
6673
6698
6762
7009
7037
7247
8472
8701
8710
8738
8791
9412
9419
9444
9628
9769
30024
30066
30089
30328
30513
30533
30670
31891
32635
42100
42310
42357
42389
42391
42747
42767
42821
42870
42921
43453
44053
44205
44268
44335
44374
44413
44455
44545
45719
47281
47583
57348
57360
57607
57670
60039
60525
61033
63704
63772
63774
63803
63880
63890
65830
65875
68070
68078
68925
68984
90046
90238
90250
90497
90576
Dep 41

Apr-63
2857
2889
3651
3660
4253
4633
4953
5015
5060
5080
5164
5224
5239
5253
5612
5627
5645
5697
5944
5945
5995
6662
6676
7015
7448
7809
9455
30074
32104
32109
32503
32661
42182
42206
42293
42659
42890
42944
43945
44100
44153
44351
44378
44469
44485
44740
44747
45159
45540
46220
47283
47449
47481
47532
57326
57328
60013
60015
60022
60047
60074
60101
60144
60513
60814
60883
60900
60912
60981
61475
63364
63374
63396
63425
63428
63430
63447
63452
63705
63946
64601
64615
64635
65850
65857
65883
90192
90729
Dep 39

May-63
1001
1504
1619
1648
2245
2871
2874
2892
3710
3711
3795
4074
4134
4248
5051
5217
5229
5255
5548
5938
5993
6353
6615
6835
8430
9408
9731
9755
9784
30031
30105
30110
31612
31815
31861
31872
32474
42188
42281
42294
42333
42469
42543
42547
42582
42592
42603
42636
42838
42843
42933
43861
44071
44094
44101
44114
44198
44252
44299
44331
44472
44476
44532
44551
45125
45169
45174
45525
45634
45669
45702
46169
46221
47166
47264
47386
47413
47460
51237
60053
60056
60110
60136
60906
60968
61273
63622
63897
63898
63899
63972
63978
64631
65820
65849
65887
65890
90015
90027
90031
90033
90048
90050
90066
90077
90151
90206
90251
90269
90502
90504
90524
90527
90530
90659

Jun-63
1005
2851
4090
4251
4265
4298
4918
4946
5022
5101
5192
5201
5234
5622
5644
5650
5943
6384
6623
6636
6663
6675
7215
7227
7237
7449
7715
8783
30057
30496
30498
30500
30501
30503
30510
31403
31636
31794
31795
31890
31901
31921
32479
33005
34035
34043
34055
34074
41531
41739
42485
42632
42853
43853
43995
44097
44209
44231
44272
44445
44470
45452
45575
45659
46247
46252
47225
47278
47465
49406
49448
49454
51232
57278
57572
57625
60018
60044
60046
60050
60058
60105
60500
60520
60523
60533
60803
60817
60830
60854
60862
60869
60889
60897
60921
60935
60966
61068
61453
63350
63365
63601
63824
63986
64589
64612
65224
65253
65261
65277
65287
90090
90095
90177
DS681

Jul-63
1432
2845
2867
3668
3765
3803
3833
4264
4672
4922
4956
4970
4980
5092
5555
5615
5620
5640
5643
5666
5679
5749
5905
5908
6314
6335
6437
6666
6674
6809
6828
7031
7200
7228
7412
7426
7780
8444
8491
8496
8728
8766
8786
8794
9401
9440
9479
9483
9713
9715
30032
30120
30241
30249
30251
30497
30509
30511
30514
30515
30538
30549
30845
31271
31280
31407
31543
31592
31863
31867
31910
31916
31920
33002
33013
33025
41875
42140
42157
42178
42231
42253
42279
42401
42556
42681
42718
42790
42852
42976
43521
43845
43882
43937
43987
44026
44034
44164
44176
44241
44282
44283
44309
44322
44359
44398
44416
44442
44447
44465
44494
44542
45087
45175
45189
45714
46120
47322
47360
47490
47638
51253
60008
60870
60881
60959
61449
62016
63340
63353
63355
63369
63373
63376
63380
63408
63416
63418
63442
63449
63592
63678
63744
63780
63801
63983
64600
65341
68020
90507
90542
90597

Aug-63
1151
2872
2894
3626
3766
3781
4907
5050
5087
5154
5225
5233
5262
5416
5554
5608
5614
5690
5775
5919
5948
5977
6319
6379
6919
8458
9764
9793
31402
31805
31918
31922
33008
33011
33016
33021
33024
42384
44132
44292
44523
45010
45049
45244
45555
45625
47161
47300
47458
47502
47582
47679
57269
57291
57566
57592
57634
57689
57690
60073
60097
60861
61069
63375
63390
63400
63596
63736
63784
64568
65290
65331
68015
68071
90086
90097
90170
90186
90193
90475
90487
90500
90609
90696

Sep-63
1002
1006
1016
1338
1608
2224
2842
3650
3811
3831
3858
4119
4252
4282
4629
4651
4682
4701
4902
4927
4975
4996
5038
5093
5380
5616
5672
5903
5985
5986
6138
6327
6375
6416
6609
6631
6632
6968
7001
7018
7021
7036
7246
7326
7335
9763
30055
30102
31005
31544
31631
31637
31818
31820
31823
31825
31826
31851
31852
31865
32640
33031
42151
42425
42486
42487
42668
42711
42723
42750
42873
43342
44015
44046
44074
44126
44190
44202
44262
44297
44303
44370
44419
44434
44444
44539
44596
44750
45022
45023
45099
45123
45166
45199
45315
45457
45521
45649
45706
45730
46101
46111
46114
46116
46126
46149
47248
57336
57590
57661
60048
60060
60061
60066
60082
60096
60107
60841
60852
60853
60871
60872
60880
60899
60902
60905
60924
60948
60950
61001
61006
61073
61074
61075
61083
61088
61090
61113
61126
61135
61142
61159
61160
61177
61227
61270
61279
61305
61318
61325
61328
61331
61336
61374
61393
61399
61409
61420
61455
61461
61464
61468
61476
62032
63433
63434
63722
63840
63925
63926
63927
63928
63931
63932
63935
63936
63937
63938
63939
63940
63941
63942
63943
63945
63949
63956
63960
63962
63963
63964
63968
63973
63974
63976
63977
63980
63985
63987
64551
67635
67645
67653
67654
67658
67663
67682
67683
67686
68029
68045
68049
68723
68892
68904
68908
68922
68934
68935
68937
68965
68977
68988
69001
69004
69009
69021
69024
90006
90017
90049
90228
90231
90260
90435
90440
90453
90461
90531
90536
90671

Oct-63
1008
1027
1409
1471
2818
2852
2854
3212
3214
3633
3652
3653
3843
3846
4087
4232
4257
4272
4507
4617
4618
4644
4690
4908
4924
4955
4964
4981
4998
5031
5040
5071
5081
5216
5221
5236
5248
5249
5410
5420
5625
5787
5929
5954
5978
6365
6639
6659
6670
6694
6929
6939
7216
7234
7239
7333
8456
9633
9636
9645
9700
9799
11324
30096
30379
31611
31615
31813
31824
31847
31911
31915
32678
33037
41203
41240
41292
41297
41318
41537
42063
42091
42120
42166
42228
42238
42288
42301
42319
42339
42440
42458
42491
42557
42595
42698
42704
42770
42771
42774
42798
42865
42871
42984
43142
43658
43870
43935
43969
44010
44013
44047
44066
44068
44069
44085
44168
44183
44184
44186
44208
44237
44239
44261
44308
44342
44352
44354
44363
44387
44411
44418
44424
44432
44454
44493
44504
44517
44530
44535
44574
44592
44595
44598
45100
45320
45485
45639
46222
46223
46224
46242
47160
47287
47294
47412
47518
47618
47657
57302
60017
60021
60025
60029
60032
60057
60087
60088
60089
60090
60098
60099
60108
60159
60161
60162
60858
62013
62036
62038
63385
63619
63687
63731
63795
63859
63908
63924
63969
63975
63981
63984
64557
64627
64629
68021
68025
68035
68039
68040
68041
68736
84012

Nov-63
1021
1424
1617
3706
4114
4140
4555
4905
4966
5025
5152
5369
5904
5937
5970
6118
6151
6164
6317
6320
6344
6381
6385
6618
6627
6724
7236
7304
8103
8425
8426
8461
8465
8487
9413
9425
9441
9482
9704
11368
30127
30129
30829
30831
31614
31860
31871
31919
31925
32636
32646
32650
32662
32670
34011
34049
34067
34069
34110
41250
41281
41282
41302
42180
42313
42355
42419
42561
42563
42571
42598
42617
42706
42721
42729
42735
42746
42758
42762
42785
42792
42794
42796
42805
42813
42854
42910
42911
42949
42973
43114
43977
44012
44022
44055
44133
44207
44219
44223
44232
44270
44448
44526
44541
44562
44568
44582
44584
44744
44755
45317
45367
45535
45560
45591
45624
45644
45645
45671
45709
45712
45717
45740
46119
46150
46158
46230
46249
46483
46489
47267
47379
47496
57261
57270
57296
57309
57355
57375
57568
57581
57600
57627
57630
57652
57679
57688
58143
60038
60086
60892
60898
60954
60972
61059
61119
61122
61156
61181
61204
61205
61233
61252
61300
61323
61375
61378
63392
63448
63576
63652
63853
64548
64559
64562
64582
64593
64626
65214
65222
65251
65273
65285
65311
65325
65335
65900
68038
78015
90102
90107
90118
90159
90234
90239
90326
90331
90334
90335
90338
90358
90446
90447
90463
90467
90539
90571
90614
90713
90716

Dec-63
1028
1421
1440
1466
1500
1503
1506
1507
1662
2204
2246
2251
2273
2277
2283
2298
2841
2882
3203
3206
3213
3216
3219
3600
3604
3648
3678
3712
3714
3716
3720
3733
3762
3777
3779
3791
3806
3839
3853
4098
4142
4228
4238
4271
4296
4299
4640
4654
4661
4681
4688
4705
4904
4910
4914
4928
4930
4942
4943
4979
4983
4991
5029
5041
5043
5203
5205
5220
5246
5250
5263
5570
5607
5610
5626
5654
5680
5687
5900
5923
5924
5942
5972
6133
6347
6368
6372
6373
6380
6403
6620
6652
6653
6664
6696
6699
6714
6741
6742
6760
6763
6764
6769
6772
6807
6814
6920
6943
6948
6975
6977
7000
7006
7027
7028
7203
7214
7312
7315
7317
7405
7407
7430
7441
7442
7911
7921
8106
8464
8785
9422
9429
9603
9612
9618
9638
9668
9752
9760
9770
30056
30507
30508
31404
31623
31633
31634
31635
31836
31839
31844
33019
34068
41213
41245
41273
41276
41279
41306
41309
42068
42337
42643
42768
42806
42810
42872
42885
42914
43083
43107
43110
43131
43942
44083
44089
44098
44119
44151
44162
44174
44212
44238
44265
44274
44280
44287
44336
44345
44395
44426
44437
44457
44556
44706
44885
44969
45251
45358
45646
45668
45734
45738
46143
46473
47007
47419
47441
47547
47589
47651
48407
53810
58148
60037
60160
60804
60805
60974
61004
61095
61125
61169
61174
61175
61207
61269
61314
61334
61341
61358
61359
61369
62039
62053
63342
63356
63441
63577
63585
63665
63672
63684
64550
64575
64579
64583
64603
64616
64619
65265
65307
65323
65329
65338
65810
65852
65854
65864
65884
65888
65891
65902
67652
67656
68008
68042
68059
68061
69003
69006
69008
69011
69019
69020
69025
90004
90019
90026
90058
90144
90182
90226
90249
90312
90343
90400
90424
90472
90499
90578
90604
90623
90624
90661
90692
90728
Dep 33

Jan-64
2885
3665
3822
4105
4213
4256
4275
4279
4642
4936
5238
5251
5573
5671
5678
5914
5922
5987
6304
6350
6605
6768
6832
6852
7004
7219
7251
7403
9748
9791
30036
30048
30111
30499
30506
30532
30536
30544
30547
30825
30827
30828
30832
30841
30847
31263
31518
31551
31613
31617
31618
31622
31625
31626
31629
31638
31796
31797
31806
31807
31808
31817
31819
31829
31830
31832
31850
31857
31864
31868
31917
33007
33010
33014
33017
33022
33029
33032
33034
33038
41262
41311
42124
42137
42229
42338
42409
42441
42463
42562
42569
42572
42612
42628
42633
42923
43061
43068
43094
43104
43152
43955
44167
44279
44296
44364
44520
44538
44604
45476
45523
45610
45614
46142
46144
46157
47004
47223
47430
47469
47609
48144
48150
48216
48396
48508
48772
53806
58182
60075
60120
60838
61143
61258
61288
63424
63451
63632
63715
63827
63852
63872
64554
64613
64634
68024
84007
90064
90079
90100
90237
90263
90366
90568
90635

90676

Feb-64

1020
1614
1650
1666
2241
2247
4263
4706
4972
4988
5073
5085
5240
5623
5638
5656
5685
6682
6843
6912
7204
7212
7901
9779
31833
31838
31848
35002
35015
42123
42135
42234
42261
42361
42607
42623
42719
42731
42769
42823
42888
42962
43620
43637
43669
43885
43923
43986
44091
44106
44156
44295
44399
44428
44512
44533
44578
44746
44976
45032
45066
45361
45465
45484
45487
45497
45529
45532
45572
45695
45741
46110
46132
46229
46233
47207
47228
47368
47557
60094
60967
61007
61117
61178
62018
62068
62069
63352
63727
63746
63754
63763
65889
73027
78009
82002
82008
82043
90012
90141
90161
90162
90490
90546
90574
90595
90598
90643
90700

Mar-64

1447
2219
3778
3829
3841
3847
3857
4242
4259
4626
5018
5037
5057
5070
5259
5647
5683
5958
5998
6603
6875
6972
6981
7002
7010
7445
9420
30021
30068
30133
30512
31810
31841
31874
31913
41205
42168
42280
42902
43972
44060
44302
45170
45605
45618
45638
45640
45690
45708
45732
46236
47503
47550
47558
53808
60005
60020
60802
60834
60864
61044
61080
61146
61155
61312
63358
63388
63399
63611
63685
63720
63750
63822
63829
63841
65876
90052
90110
90194
90205
90208
90214
90224
90464
90483
90582
90590
90612
90673
90717

Apr-64

1012
1014
1024
2856
2862
2875
2884
3672
3685
3698
3702
3721
3727
3734
3832
3834
3852
4109
4237
4241
4247
4255
4262
4603
4652
4667
4693
5228
5231
5322
5674
5951
6400
6634
6680
6686
6688
6818
6824
6844
6914
6941
7208
7235
7238
7325
7332
8414
8452
8716
8732
9431
9456
9484
9489
9607
9674
9732
9746
9788
9792
31870
34065
34075
42311
42366
42378
42408
42417
42434
42461
42550
42560
42709
42820
42897
42922
43053
43971
43976
44030
44038
44078
44110
44180
44288
44301
44321
44436
44439
44440
44467
44531
44752
44754
44996
45122
45366
45612
45685
46136
46141
46167
47003
47385
47478
47511
47623
47648
48140
48209
48210
48341
48420
48524
48642
49446
60825
60855
60910
61041
61056
61104
61144
61152
61213
61251
61401
63383
63401
63415
63439
63594
63645
63726
63836
90065
90111
90138
90165
90313
90374
90394
90402
90408
90583
90663

May-64

1455
2289
3613
3618
3646
3664
3673
3680
3689
3692
3701
3731
3748
3757
3761
3768
3815
4079
4088
4104
4135
4167
4214
4243
4622
4628
4637
4658
4659
4703
4704
4707
4923
4950
4976
5074
5211
5222
5244
5518
5629
5934
6361
6646
6765
6777
6839
6940
6954
7211
7225
7307
7825
7905
8102
8702
8747
9634
9655
9664
9730
9743
9777
9786
30025
30029
30052
30053
30107
30108
30254
30480
30546
30667
31793
31821
33001
34028
41210
41231
41253
41326
41327
41844
42185
42192
42278
42292
42335
42444
42446
42453
42493
42594
42614
42652
42686
42858
42943
43038
43880
43903
43957
44109
44124
44171
44172
44221
44242
44286
44304
44315
44327
44333
44337
44464
44479
44492
44540
44543
44549
44701
44742
44783
44801
44922
44957
44967
44968
45008
45121
45153
45172
45356
45400
45459
45468
45479
45534
45568
45569
45571
45585
46112
46168
47320
47380
47434
47476
48008
48172
48431
60002
60011
60043
60070
60083
60119
60143
60833
60856
60925
60932
60942
60964
60969
60975
61037
61038
61243
61467
61472
63422
63604
63647
63800
63907
63914
64546
64561
65828
67651
68016
68032
68036
76028
80040
82012
82014
84027
90101
90109
90147
90179
90197
90218
90219
90245
90299
90323
90324
90328
90371
90403
90416
90433
90525
90548
90552
90564
90570
90589
90618
90646
90667
90672
90708
90715
92034
92169
92170
92171
92175
92176
92177
Dep 7
Dep 22

Jun-64

1622
1627
1630
1636
1654
1656
2201
2836
2839
2886
2887
2896
3209
3824
3845
4122
4128
4132
4136
4143
4159
4166
4174
4277
4695
4699
4951
5039
5096
5098
5306
5330
5619
5624
5637
5901
5952
5963
5967
6124
6144
6149
6158
6338
6378
6394
6608
6624
6635
6637
6638
6660
6690
6800
6825
6834
6873
6901
6905
6909
6913
6946
6950
6960
6970
6989
6992
7035
7202
7242
7308
7310
7339
7340
7404
7427
7436
7817
7902
7903
8743
9450
9635
30836
30844
31400
31413
31616
31621
31624
31628
31801
31804
31827
31854
33003
33023
33030
33033
33035
33036
33039
33040
34016
34045
34062
34073
41239
42059
42077
42090
42163
42167
42171
42186
42190
42200
42226
42239
42244
42246
42256
42275
42353
42413
42416
42437
42619
42695
42738
42756
42757
42761
42763
42802
42839
42842
42867
43854
43925
44009
44039
44041
44213
44289
44290
44392
44396
44403
44452
44567
44738
44784
44785
44923
44961
45144
45384
45462
45482
45496
45545
45564
45578
45606
45682
45710
45737
46118
46129
46162
46403
47297
47517
53809
60054
60063
60065
60139
60149
60916
61084
61197
61219
61229
61249
61277
61346
61355
61402
61418
61421
61434
61437
61438
61444
61448
61454
61457
61463
63345
63348
63370
63393
63670
63802
63846
63884
64537
64564
64586
64587
64605
64633
65309
65346
65924
67642
68046
68051
68054
80010
80030
80049
80052
80053
80087
80148
82013
84029
90003
90143
90145
90319
90511
90544
90555
90592
W36

Jul-64

1000
1010
1013
1451
1661
1665
3603
3634
3693
3695
3746
3752
3804
4101
4130
4278
4569
4591
4600
4614
4657
4660
4678
5191
5215
5230
5254
5634
5635
5957
5975
5976
5991
6130
6140
6337
6349
6357
6695
6811
7206
7209
7217
7229
7230
7243
7423
7435
7444
7446
7823
8466
8480
8497
8707
8717
8723
9442
9457
9466
9473
9485
9620
9648
9734
9766
30531
30830
31812
31814
31849
31856
31924
34083
41228
41268
41315
41322
41323
41328
41329
42054
42057
42201
42208
42242
42263
42708
42776
42851
43136
44007
44080
44569
44676
44994
45007
45158
45173
45700
46409
46435
46461
46467
46474
46475
47515
47579
47594
47622
48306
48463
60040
60042
60077
60125
60809
60812
60882
60887
60904
60922
60941
60945
61081
61109
61118
61242
61351
61356
61435
62019
63403
64541
64549
65904
73076
76097
78048
78053
80008
80021
80071
80073
80074
80075
80076
80127
82007
90114
90129
90157
90173
90201
90209
90375
90388
90566
90705

Aug-64

2879
3800
3801
3860
4080
4124
4916
4933
6804
6808
6867
6982
7003
7218
7418
7800
8409
8418
8431
31412
31869
31875
31912
31914
34027
34061
34070
34081
34094
35006
35018
42092
42153
42379
42411
42584
42682
42965
42966
43917
43931
44048
44059
44165
44191
44259
44284
44348
44380
44554
44583
45623
45696
47236
47308
47349
47375
47492
47549
47584
47628
49173
60012
60147
61062
61321
62058
62063
63367
65913
65919
76032
82011
82025
90216
90257
90264
90297
90302
90311
90322
90411
90485
90584
90599
90712
92198
92199

Sep-64

1445
1474
2232
2248
2249
2257
2261
2286
2291
3403
3617
3622
3707
3737
3805
3825
4082
4093
4103
4131
4284
4286
4294
4564
4593
4608
4619
4624
4634
4648
4649
4691
4692
4949
4958
4978
4985
5002
5055
5076
5210
5214
5218
5237
5264
5336
5563
5602
5603
5632
5641
5648
5668
5669
6122
6131
6142
6148
6309
6326
6345
6346
6363
6424
6434
6685
6822
6845
6846
6945
6966
6985
6987
6988
7005
7008
7020
7025
7032
7213
7220
7233
7240
7245
7250
7303
7306
7337
7413
7414
7424
7431
7432
7443
7810
8400
8401
8405
8446
8475
8720
8768
9406
9435
9470
9471
9493
9498
9637
9663
9707
9742
9787
9794
11305
30840
30843
31406
31632
31792
31798
31802
31828
31834
31835
31837
31840
31843
31845
31846
31853
31855
31859
34003
34020
34029
34030
34054
34078
34080
34091
34096
34106
34107
34109
35009
35025
41225
41226
41227
41237
41260
42282
42309
42421
42424
42481
42559
42589
42608
42620
42630
42631
42639
42640
42651
42696
42703
42707
42760
42788
42815
42816
42826
42840
42845
42846
42855
42860
42931
42952
42956
43856
43888
43928
43951
43958
44092
44102
44117
44182
44197
44220
44226
44240
44248
44332
44362
44367
44379
44381
44431
44441
44461
44463
44468
44499
44514
44516
44529
44552
44564
44565
44566
44572
44577
44581
44586
44588
44602
44605
44660
44748
44749
44751
44756
45088
45103
45413
45470
45522
45552
45556
45557
45558
45561
45577
45579
45584
45592
45599
45601
45611
45613
45620
45622
45631
45635
45641
45657
45676
45681
45716
45723
45733
45735
45736
46163
46241
46248
47002
47008
47009
47164
47165
47257
47284
47343
47344
47345
47355
47372
47390
47461
47467
47501
47524
47640
48654
48657
48734
51218
61065
63382
63402
63615
63702
63786
63807
64572
65908
68013
73046
73074
76034
78005
80009
80017
80031
80038
80107
84021
84022
84023
84024
90304
90519

Oct-64

1367
1368
1444
2891
2898
3409
3601
3612
3683
3739
3798
3809
3821
3828
3856
4089
4108
4133
4137
4171
4222
4233
4273
4283
4292
4610
4615
4616
4627
4670
4903
4919
5000
5054
5091
5184
5213
5245
5257
5571
5609
5660
5670
5927
5939
6114
6430
6435
6602
6806
6810
6900
6971
6996
7026
7231
7319
7782
7815
8479
8749
9621
9629
9654
9710
9729
9798
34058
34072
34105
41300
41303
41310
41535
41712
42056
42089
42126
42127
42143
42218
42221
42245
42262
42359
42405
42414
42445
42451
42474
42588
42629
42717
42725
42748
42755
42907
42926
42934
42970
43940
43947
43988
44042
44096
44236
44244
44260
44275
44384
44460
44603
44719
44745
45136
45183
45526
45583
45598
45663
45670
45674
46122
46125
46156
46166
46225
46226
46228
46235
46237
46238
46239
46240
46243
46244
46245
46250
46251
46254
46255
46256
46257
47354
47653
53807
60001
60023
60071
60080
60085
60091
60092
60141
60150
60808
60891
60913
60939
60982
61185
62029
63765
63773
64552
64555
64563
64573
64591
64636
65791
65870
65878
68014
68019
69005
69016
69023
69028
73017
73109
75067
76029
76054
76072
80056
80062
80077
80106
80115
80125
80129
84001
84020
90067
90127
90140
90184
90354
90359
90389
90412
90521
90535
W32

Nov-64

1011
1369
1420
1453
1458
1472
1631
1639
1641
1657
1658
1664
1667
2211
2217
2218
2221
2822
2893
3210
3217
3400
3401
3402
3405
3406
3621
3730
3742
3797
3810
3838
4120
4153
4602
4653
4674
4687
4932
4954
4989
5026
5056
5089
5153
5243
5545
5662
5694
5699
5962
5979
6107
6115
6137
6139
6364
6367
6395
6412
6678
6684
6821
6842
6863
6878
6925
6933
6936
6994
6997
7012
7207
7221
7223
7226
7318
7320
7327
7806
7807
7824
8402
8437
8469
8493
8495
8714
8739

9453
9494
9606
9632
9642
9660
9661
9677
9679
9706
9778
9782
30541
30823
30834
30835
31410
33012
33015
34092
34099
35001
41248
42449
42489
42565
42573
42586
42654
42657
42754
42856
42880
42925
42969
43908
43929
43954
43960
43963
43979
44025
44027
44040
44045
44079
44131
44134
44146
44149
44177
44178
44185
44222
44229
44233
44478
44481
44484
44497
44534
44575
44580
44589
44591
45035
45155
45553
45554
45617
45672
45699
45703
46148
46165
47211
47230
47288
47333
47587
48069
48179
48455
60036
60045
60051
60084
61031
61165
61212
61274
61294
61398
62009
63341
63423
63438
63456
63663
67620
67628
67636
67638
67640
67643
67646
67678
67684
67690
67691
73012
73024

73058
73116
80036
80044
80050
90098
90289
90344
90469
90567
90581
90685
92210
92229

Dec-64

2859
2873
3745
3794
3814
3819
4173
4295
4613
4959
5242
5508
5531
5564
5569
5651
5675
5974
6103
6419
6621
6622
6850
6942
7805
7900
7916
7926
8104
8793
9490
9601
9650
9768
30530
30542
30543
41317
42084
42099
42148
42250
42284
42286
42291
42551
42602
42605
42662
42670
42701
42705
42793
42894
42920
42971
42979
43058
43060
43072
43086
43087
43147
43154
43850
43871
43949
44023
44049
44051
44054
44130
44179
44214
44235
44246
44344
44373
44376
44421
44433
44501
44558
44571
44593
44789
44793
44849
45456
45527
45580
45689
46155
46525
47306
47365

48611
48895
49361
49407
49430
60062
60106
60112
60114
60158
60822
60957
61034
61105
61162
61167
61268
61382
61400
62037
62054
62055
62061
63571
63636
63728
64585
64614
65927
68050
73047
73052
73061
73077
73161
73164
75001
82015
90392
90488
90714
92036
92196
92207
92232
92245

Jan-65

1663
1668
2876
3200
3725
3753
3826
3835
4172
5601
5936
5984
5990
6125
6606
7222
7818
9624
33004
35024
41215
42400
42459
42634
42722
42791
42799
43032
43059
43065
43081
43085
43093
43127
43145
43146
43150
43155
43156
43157
43158
43160
43950
43975
44065
44121
44127
44358
44402
44486
44548
44739
45102
45178
45306
45327
45567
45586
45595
45597
45642
45652
45667
45704

46420
46423
46472
47468
47485
47616
47664
48001
48006
48007
48387
48461
48761
60126
60128
60140
60157
61097
61120
61138
61153
61179
61272
61338
62020
62033
62040
62051
62066
62070
63351
63703
63906
90042
90119
90221
90282
90327
90602

Feb-65

2231
3610
3699
3700
3747
3807
3862
4179
4227
4297
4606
4993
5014
5063
6649
6812
6840
6860
6904
6907
6915
6935
6955
6969
6979
7011
7013
7014
7019
7023
7024
7244
7910
7918
9796
31799
34031
35020
41308
42165
42209
42214
42350
42465
42478
42488
42590
42609
42649
42667
42733
43134
43887
43918
44035
44099
44137
44215
44353
44425
44921
45313
45337
45414
46524
47305
47669
48095
48217
48312
48649

60524
61327
63692
63861
65845
65926
78024
78025
80042
90010
90070
90276
90291
90353
90520
90543
90579
90656
90710
92037
92142
92143
92181
92184
92185
92187
92188
92192

Mar-65

1613
2253
2899
3705
3715
3796
3865
4929
5223
5226
5256
5261
5618
5673
5686
6128
6150
6655
6877
6938
6995
7437
7906
7913
7928
9602
9671
30548
34010
34014
41293
42179
42299
42430
42447
42567
42680
42832
42841
42848
42896
43952
43994
44125
44195
44211
44263
44266
44347
44456
44527
44741
45286
45378
45380
45387
45512
45589
45602
45726
47442
47452
47564
47577
47578
48027
48409
60016
61215
61221
62047
63683
63813
63877
63878
65808
65822
73044
73049
80003
80090
80149

80153
90055
90123
90131
90180
90185
90267
90284
90317
90399
90426
90556
90561
90626
90647
92003
92220
92222

Apr-65

1632
2890
2895
3635
3642
3661
3691
3728
3770
4151
4254
4258
4285
4643
4992
5200
5955
5983
6658
6817
6906
6911
6922
6986
7201
7210
7253
7439
7803
7826
9480
9488
9611
30535
30545
31620
31831
31862
34022
42050
42060
42158
42435
42456
42482
42554
42558
42601
42660
42716
42751
42778
42787
42817
42886
42972
43037
43067
43090
43092
43144
43148
43913
44135
44192
44305
44544
45142
45194
45653
45655
45666
46152
46497
47295
47395
47645
48430
60156
60527
60961
61198
61310
63359
63378
63391
63411
63717
63741
63842
63902
65933

75007
76030
80018
80035
82010
82016
82017
84002
84011
84018
90005
90059
90120
90136
90164
90175
90188
90202
90215
90225
90246
90268
90314
90383
90419
90442
90486
90496
90585
90668
90686
92038
92044
92140
92147
92180
92236

May-65

1442
1450
2214
2222
2236
2242
2268
2287
3201
3205
3208
3218
3818
3849
3859
4169
4177
4609
4679
5206
5252
5613
5633
5681
5689
5696
6612
6628
6648
6650
6826
6866
6974
7232
7813
8474
8488
9426
9446
9452
9461
9472
9475
9646
9753
30833
31790
34039
41238
41242
41270
42062
42075
42103
42106
42147
42155
42160
42198
42202
42222
42289
42369
42381
42494
42555
42564
42566
42604
42688
42741
42772
42892

42901
42904
42932
42937
42941
43075
43865
43893
43991
43999
44003
44118
44250
44276
44277
44386
44414
44429
44450
44466
44528
44587
44673
45163
45588
45629
45661
45664
45742
46128
46160
46404
47361
47512
47647
48419
48737
60010
61214
61291
62056
63354
63357
63404
63414
63432
63444
63679
63793
63882
64621
65792
68010
68011
68023
68037
68043
68047
68053
68060
68062
72005
73091
73123
73162
80014
80099
80108
80110
80119
80131
82032
90085
90115
90139
90152
90166
90181
90207
90290
90522
90541
90577
90613
90632
92195
92221
92242
92248
Dep 10
Dep 11
Dep 12
Dep 13
Dep 15
Dep 16

Jun-65

1623
2210
2244
3608
3620
3644
3647
3687
3690
3717
3763
3772
3784
3790
3812

3830
3854
4107
4110
4115
4121
4125
4144
4150
4156
4157
4158
4160
4611
4623
4631
4638
4639
4655
4663
4665
4666
4669
4673
4675
4694
5042
5202
5208
5241
5621
5655
5665
5688
5691
6110
6116
6154
6159
6614
6633
6654
6657
6661
6689
6691
6823
6841
6862
6926
6928
6958
7022
7034
7205
7248
7249
7252
7920
7923
8109
8403
8415
8420
8433
8436
8459
8471
8481
8484
8486
8498
9404
9405
9411
9415
9418
9430
9437
9463
9464
9477
9495
9617
9625
9631
9644
9647
9659
9667
9670
9676
9678
9716
9726
9754
41305
41325
42053
42064
42082
42114
42368
42492
42732
42916
43062
43064
43080
43091
43111
43143

43153
43159
43161
43924
44061
44063
44123
44334
44401
44422
44702
45146
45460
45498
46488
46507
47250
47606
48116
48145
48148
48478
48601
48733
60100
60116
60117
60127
60132
60142
60148
60152
60512
60522
60535
60847
60865
60901
60929
60963
61039
61094
61190
61225
61276
61357
61372
61392
61397
62003
62014
62049
63343
63361
63419
63427
63606
63650
63671
63691
63850
63863
63893
63913
65794
68068
70007
73041
73056
73062
73106
73112
80020
80022
80066
80067
80070
80081
80084
80088
80147
90000
90084
90121
90124
90146
90204
90217
90279
90285
90306
90349
90365
90368
90422
90443
90452
90454
90460
90601
90724
92066
92149
92168
92193

Jul-65

1612
1655
3631
3671
3686

3708
3808
3813
3816
3820
3823
3837
3840
3842
3848
3851
3861
3864
3866
4604
4620
4621
4650
4664
4668
4684
4697
5209
5667
5684
5692
6644
6672
6816
6820
6837
6869
6908
6963
6978
7801
7811
8795
9615
9619
9622
9623
9649
9651
9653
9711
9780
31401
31811
33018
41200
41201
41208
41209
41214
41218
41221
41243
41261
41314
41321
42051
42065
42070
42109
42112
42113
42296
42322
42477
42542
42618
42626
42730
42849
42869
42905
42936
43128
43982
44043
44044
44076
44115
44157
44200
44349
44389
44716
44753
44769
44799
44827
44924
44959
44978
44979
44980
45002
45113
45301
45334
45335
45379
45416
45471
45491
45604
46444
46479
47359
47423

47454
47500
47596
47614
47665
47680
48039
48097
48099
48173
48183
48184
48189
48259
48297
48333
48360
48403
48416
48446
48518
48624
48630
48658
48660
48688
48689
48774
60133
61093
61098
61141
61218
61245
61299
61365
61370
62015
62035
62043
63589
63590
63613
63630
63646
63651
63707
63725
63768
63868
63879
64592
76017
78000
80048
80072
80078
80079
80080
80097
80098
80100
80101
80104
80105
80135
80136
82036
82039
82040
90007
90029
90040
90053
90088
90125
90171
90211
90261
90266
90271
90275
90294
90340
90341
90398
90474
90476
90510
90540
90660
90681
90703
90720
92000
92225
92241

Aug-65

1607
3654
3662
3738
3802
3817
3850
3855
4268
4612
5933
5961
5992

6108
6643
6836
6851
6916
6973
6983
7917
7929
8745
9616
9681
9682
34050
34063
35016
35021
41232
42119
42131
42174
42194
42212
42230
42243
42247
42327
42432
42439
42442
42460
42464
42673
42710
42753
42777
42783
42814
42827
42844
42961
43967
43981
43983
44139
44169
44181
44443
44449
44489
44490
44536
44721
44901
44955
45077
45192
45230
45245
45293
45351
45429
45443
45499
46482
47285
47286
47330
47399
47400
47432
47487
47499
47505
47646
47676
47681
48020
48078
48102
48156
48273
48290
48378
48389
48427
48607
48610
48634
48653
48656
48716
48719
48769
61070
61107
61127
61157
61191
61194
61259
61320
61353
61367
62030
63661
63697
63701
63734
63738
63828
65841

65906
70043
72009
73015
73021
73023
73030
73032
73042
73051
73054
73147
73167
82035
82037
82038
82042
90025
90038
90108
90169
90183
90212
90222
90223
90296
90393
90420
90421
90480
90509
90563
90573
90580
90641
90662
90674
90702
90725
92005
92040
92041
92186
92214
92219
92240
DS235
DS236

Sep-65

3616
3658
3669
3735
3751
4111
4147
4148
4155
4168
4607
4636
4662
5235
6112
6117
6129
6656
6679
6692
6803
6813
6827
6854
6870
6874
6903
6917
6918
6961
6964
7804
7814
9600
9605
9639
9662
9666
9733
9790
30824
30837
30838
30839
30842
31842
33009
33026
34051
34085
34103
35019
42061
42104
42118
42129
42199
42285
42317
42374
42406
42468

42645
42675
42819
42878
42879
42898
42912
42938
42940
42974
43025
43964
44081
44243
44355
44420
44505
44560
44597
44763
44764
44970
44973
44975
45074
45180
45184
45229
45237
45360
45398
45573
45608
45721
46425
46456
46459
46498
46510
46511
47325
47371
47439
47451
47464
47480
47495
47519
47666
48094
48135
48198
48285
48295
48328
48330
48355
48401
48406
48429
48490
48661
48682
48704
60006
60027
60859
60884
60885
60931
60944
60962
61061
61076
61129
61196
61208
61292
61396
62064
63607
63628
63688
63706
63732
63791
64558
64625
73008
73031
73036
73038
73111
73122
73148
73165
76050
76106
78011
78014
78027
78029
78032
78033
78042
78043
80064
82005
82020
82033
84003
90096

90227
90242
90252
90280
90293
90301
90325
90390
90491
90528
90557
90629
90727
92033
92057
92197
92226
92237
92238
Dep 14
W30

Oct-65
1611
1643
1651
1669
3615
3659
3767
3789
3844
3863
4154
4165
4175
4176
4178
4676
4683
4962
5932
5988
6132
6155
6161
6163
6167
6604
6613
6651
6665
6671
6681
6683
6830
6831
6833
6853
6855
6857
6858
6861
6864
6868
6871
6879
6910
6921
6924
6927
6930
6931
6934
6947
6957
6965
6976
6980
7827
7828
7908
7912
7915
9609
9613
9675
31627
31800
34007
34042
34046
34053
34084
35004
35005
41219
41275
41324
42170
42259
42265
42295
42343
42597
42780
42800
42900
44155
44210
44522
44931
45026
45078
45117
45171
45272
45362
45389
45632
45658
46413
46430
46468
46527
47338
47428
48525
48558
60118
60121
60129
60130
60131
60134
60138
60146
60154
60155
60816
60828
60835
60843
60846
60876
60895
60923
60940
60946
60952
61016
61023
61110
61134
61168
61220
61244
61257
61275
61304
61385
61387
62010
63347
63371
63398
63443
63586
63593
63739
64571
64580
64599
65846
65858
65862
65916
73090
73103
73104
75003
76015
76023
76025
76027
76055
76062
76065
76068
76107
76112
78030
80023
80137
80150
82004
82021
82022
90045
90051
90092
90122
90130
90133
90195
90203
90235
90259
90273
90277
90283
90292
90329
90333
90346
90381
90432
90438
90492
90545
90569
90619
90730
92039
92178
92190
92200
92216

Nov-65
3643
3696
3749
3754
3788
3792
3836
4100
4113
4161
4630
4645
4671
4698
5606
5658
5659
5676
5677
6113
6143
6169
6611
6625
6626
6667
6815
6819
6829
6838
6856
6859
6876
7802
7812
7816
7819
7820
7821
7822
7909
9656
41212
41272
41313
42241
42828
42946
42948
42950
42958
42964
42982
43005
43013
43035
43082
43089
43108
43109
43149
43906
43953
43968
44028
44056
44057
44075
44086
44170
44188
44264
44294
44346
44356
44390
44400
44408
44446
44458
44462
44570
44599
44601
44686
44757
44787
44823
45009
45037
45081
45093
45257
45291
45314
45354
45439
45531
45563
45626
45633
45698
45705
46140
47321
47362
47378
47408
47520
47543
47597
47655
47677
48004
48016
48096
48112
48138
48260
48262
48366
48413
48732
48759
60031
60041
60151
60810
60837
60844
61010
61018
61049
61176
61188
61195
61248
61256
61313
61324
61389
61394
61404
63362
63612
63819
63843
65327
73163
75005
76056
77010
78004
80059
80109
82044
84000
84004
84005
84006
84008
84009
90103
90189
90220
90248
90315
90342
90401
90439
90501
90515
90516
90529
90553
90558
90587
90658
90697
92179
92235
Dep 23
Dep 25

Dec-65
3675
3677
3682
3759
3775
4680
4689
4920
5971
6106
6111
6126
6134
6135
6136
6141
6145
6147
6156
6160
6165
6668
6847
6848
6849
6872
6923
6932
6937
6944
6951
6952
6953
6956
6959
6967
6984
6990
6991
6993
6998
6999
7029
7808
7829
7904
7907
7914
7919
7922
7924
7925
7927
9626
9672
9680
9773
9789
31619
31858
34033
42139
42334
42426
42831
42947
42959
44160
44247
44269
44271
44300
44339
44350
44451
44904
44939
45011
45020
45068
45090
45108
45143
45148
45300
45486
45530
45590
45600
45684
46115
47350
47429
47544
47656
47660
48037
48248
48314
48391
48434
48500
48771
60026
61003
61087
61147
61172
61264
61285
61348
61361
63386
63389
63639
63770
64632
65844
65851
72007
73001
73003
73068
73075
73084
73124
73152
73166
73168
75000
75008
75022
75025
75028
75038
75072
75073
76060
78001
78006
78035
78054
80029
80096
80102
82001
82030
82041
84010
84013
84014
84015
84016
84017
84019
84025
84026
84028
90036
90043
90072
90142
90158
90255
90316
90330
90364
90372
90423
90448
90466
90621
90665
92007
92042
92141
92144
92148
92174
92189
92191
92194
92202
92209
92230
92243
92244
92246
92250
Dep 18
Dep 20
W18

Jan-66
9669
9724
31809
31816
31866
31873
33006
33020
33027
34041
34076
42213
42232
42484
42702
42740
42909
42953
42957
42960
42980
42983
44113
44278
44670
44687
44707
44743
44762
44960
45181
45235
45643
46450
47535
47602
47662
48109
48120
48134
48207
48246
48302
48383
48447
48452
48515
48539
48555
48638
48644
60052
60973
61145
61223
61384
63384
63644
63674
63675
63730
63788
63816
63873
64624
65282
65297
65805
75023
75066
76045
76049
76071
76105
76111
77001
78034
78040
78045
78050
78052
80034
80039
80069
80132
80141
82024
82027
90069
90149
90232
90241
90258
90274
90295
90336
90418
90428
90449
90457
90506
90514
90687
92068
92072

Feb-66
1660
34079
35011
41291
42156
42169
42712
42715
42924
43016
43042
44310
45216
45248
45396
45418
46463
47393
48065
48089
48175
48181
48331
48444
48479
48523
48543
48608
48615
48762
60007
60877
61026
61050
61051
61055
61058
61092
61210
61232
61281
61315
61322
61390
63417
63764
64610
65821
65831
73121
75031
75057
76019
77011
80060
90024
90032
90035
90073
90080
90104
90153
90178
90187
90190
90213
90367
90377
90384
90413
90456
90493
90498
90518
90533
90537
90572
90586
90606
90669
90683
90689
90706
90718
90719
92035
92053
92081
92115
92145
Dep 19

Mar-66
3681
3758
31803
34048
41206
41216
41223
41249
41283
41290
41296
41307
42107
42266
42581
42700
42734
42945
42951
42975
43031
44203
44218
45182
45252
45433
45574
46410
46518
47231
47276
47506
47592
48003
48005
48050
48129
48309
48422
48530
48619
48627
48633
48667
48691
48694
48706
48713
48760
60124
60970
61326
61343
63785
64595
65832
65932
70019
73007
73057
73098
75044
76003
77006
77013
77016
80037
80041
80043
80117
80142
90305
90379
90380
90477
90484
92173
92201

Apr-66
3776
9657
9776
31411
34082
34097
42195
42240
42455
42610
42955
43014
43126
44668
45210
45218
46416
46496
47280
47317
47415
47445
47450
47453
47565
47627
47675
48195
48203
48250
48277
48398
48647
48698
48718
61042
61089
61121
61158
61250
61302
61329
61360
61406
63653
63781
63818
63858
72008
75045
76020
90001
90002
90013
90018
90037
90063
90075
90148
90154
90156
90369
90410
90437
90471
90538
90551
90636
90675
90709
92010
92146
92172
92182
92183
Dep 17
Dep 21
Dep 24

May-66
5605
6697
34059
34064
35022
42197
42260
42431
42462
42625
42967
42978
42981
43036
44692
44731
45233
46401
47611
48064
48092
48188
48280
48472
48521
48659
48748
61024
65796
65905
72006
73013
76035
77009
78057
80144
90517
92130
Dep 31
W21
W26
W29

Jun-66
31405
31408
31639
31791
34038
34086
42078
42095
42110
42132
42142
42176
42225
42394
42436
42676
42977
43116
44405
44908
44956
44974
45097
45654
45660
46414
46514
47272
47336
47631
48118
48426
48541
48625
60009
60145
60528
63349
63360
63410
63421
63435
63445
63446
63454
64588
65788
65814
65825
70000
70030
73005
73055
73063
73082
73114
73170
75036
75056
75063
76073
77008
78002
80013
80121
82026
90011
92062

Jul-66
3625
4635
8718
8767
9608
9614
9640
34101
35017
41287
42121
42159
42216
42249
42264
42801
42812
42861
42913
42963
43074
44311
44394
44500
44698
44700
44850
44881
45016
45047
45082
45177
45185
45195
45333
45596
46429
46445
46513
46526
47341
47389
47416
47598
48147
48215
48264
48284
48291
48303
48326
48346
48405
48511
48621
60004
61040
61103
61116
61224
61345
61403
63406
63412
64606
65243
65801
65893
65910
73009
73078
73081
75078
76042
76103
76108
77015
78056
80001
80007
80054
80058
80094
82018
90068
90082
90445
90593
92043
92158
92164
Dep 27

Aug-66
1638
3709
3744
42058
42277
42863
42908
42917
44786
44810
45164
45176
45348
45364
45370
45461
45477
45480
45581
46412
46460
46462
47006
47437
48415
48554
48605
48736
60034
60818
60886
61293
61349
64577
64597
64608
65790
65802
65874
65907
70001
70050
73101
73151
76001
76070
76085
76092
76099
76100
78016
78026
78049
80005
80024
80025
80047
80051
80063
80083
80112
80123
80130
90168
90350
90600
90640
92098
92217
Dep 28

Sep-66
1628
3619
9610
9630
34026
34066
35010
35027
35029
41211
41294
42074
42183
42273
42410
42691
43026
43045
43069
43113
44688
44704
44705
44797
44798
44813
44869
44925
44954
44966
44999
45004
45091
45128
45129
45138
45140
45160
45168
45220
45309
45322
45325
45344
45393
45403
45410
45419
45422
45427
45430
45434
45438
45442
45472
45474
45475
45627
46419
46426
46434
46464
47266
47307
47397
47410
47427
47507
48002
48101
48155
48213
48254
48263
48274
48286
48296
48311
48342
48353
48357
48358
48367
48404
48418
48428
48457
48477
48512
48520
48526
48606
48628
48629
48680
48726
48747
48755
60019
60024
60806
60919
61099
61132
61133
61148
61261
61344
62006
62022
63363
63379
63409
65809
65859
65930
65931
70017
73083
73089
73095
73105
73107
73145
75053
75054
75065
75069
75070
76010
76012
76013
76014
76022
76038
76043
76059
76086
76089
76109
78010
78022
78038
78039
78047
80006
80026
80028
80055
80065
80082
80092
80093
80113
82006
82028
90039
90113
90229
90357
90373
90622
90652
90679
92013
92059
92061
92075
92095
92099
Dep 59

Oct-66
3605
3607
3782
9641
9658
34005
34009
34017
34032
41299
41301
41316
42087
42181
42583
42606
42693
43020
43052
44377
44525
44720
44723
44724
44726
44729
44760
44811
44841
44935
44945
44952
44987
45012
45029
45044
45045
45058
45105
45112
45118
45205
45207
45311
45338
45385
45432
45464
46421
46427
46442
46454
46495
46504
46509
46519
46521
47000
47318
47377
47384
47391
47396
47435
47482
47494
47521
47530
47566
47615
47643
47649
47658
47661
47668
48103
48127
48137
48186
48196
48225
48251
48289
48318
48339
48349
48361
48388
48397
48414
48432
48475
48514
48527
48623
48635
48670
48679
62002
62021
63453
63459
64618
65819
65873
65922
68079
70036
70037
73072
73086
73087
73088
73099
73169
73171
75011
75049
75051
76004
76016
76018
76021
76044
76057
76074
76082
76083
78008
78031
78060
80033
80068
80089
80095
80138
82009
82023
90395
90441
90479
90481
90534
90547
90651
90664
92028
92060
92067
92092
92097
92136
92213
92247
W35

Nov-66
4646
4696
9774
41202
41204
41207
41220
41229
41233
41234
41244
41251
41286
41304
42069
42115
42128
42919
43018
43030
43135
43141
44712
44714
44718
44788
44791
44847
44880
44941
44972
44977
44984
44995
45051
45053
45063
45084
45115
45127
45154
45161
45162
45217
45224
45289
45329
45332
45372
45408
45451
45463
45469
45473
45488
45489
47444
47472
47533
47590
47603
47659
47667
47671
47673
48080
48083
48133
48139
48142
48143
48178
48223
48255
48354
48370
48385
48443
48502
48600
48651
48662
48663
48672
48686
60530
60813
60824
60868
60955
60976
61017
61022
61032
61303
61307
61308
61330
61350
62028
63377

64570
64623
65267
65319
65815
65903
65909
65912
65914
65915
65917
65918
65920
65921
65925
70054
75050
75079
76047
76076
76078
77005
77007
77017
77018
77019
78018
78019
78036
78046
78059
78061
78064
80027
80091
80111
80118
80126
90078
90199
90723
90731
92063
92064
92116
92155
92231
92239

Dec-66
34012
41217
41222
41241
41264
41285
41528
41533
41708
41734
41763
41804
41835
42096
42102
42105
42108
42125
42150
42161
42177
42184
42204
42271
42664
42690
42694
42736
42737
42739
42765
42782
42789
42795
42803
42859
42968
43009
43022
43039
43040
43054
43056
43057
43078
43079
43095
43099
43102
43103
43124
43132
43133
44703
44710
44779
44782
44808
44820
44839
44919
44951
44953
44992
45018
45033
45137
45213
45214
45223
45238
45249
45357
45365
45399
45467
45478
45483
45490
45492
46405
46422
46424
46428
46446
46447
46451
46458
46508
46512
46517
47001
47005
47201
47202
47273
47279
47293
47298
47314
47324
47326
47327
47357
47367
47373
47388
47406
47447
47471
47493
47599
47612
47641
47674
48079
48088
48219
48249
48270
48372
48412
48462
48516
48641
48668
48738
60532
60831
60836
61008
61013
61014
61029
61035
61101
61131
61140
61161
61237
61240
61263
61319
61342
61386
62004
62008
63368
63381
63405
63440
63450
64547
64569
65934
70018
70044
73016
73028
73080
73102
73108
73120
73149
73150
73153
73154
75014
76024
76052
76090
76091
76096
76101
76102
76110
76113
76114
77000
77003
77004
78003
78017
78051
78058
78063
80000
80057
80061
80114
80122
80124
82000
82003
82031
82034
90041
90044
90310
90451
90470
92085
92124
92134
92161

Jan-67
30073
42080
42154
42224
42577
42697
42727
42942
43051
43066
43097
44737
44860
44918
44981
45106
45130
45197
45204
45240
45276
45283
45336
45341
45565
45694
45739
46406
46411
46418
46500
48146
48149
48187
48536
48711
48739
48756
61173
61199
61216
61309
62067
63413
65835
65838
65842
65872
70002
70008
70009
70020
70026
73019
73100
73110
73113
73130
75012
75017
76002
76036
76053
76061
76087
80032
90054
90089
90112
90117
90126
90155
90240
90254
90332
90337
90415
90444
90462
90465
90503
90628
90631
90639
90645
90649
90680
90684
90694
90707
90711
92001
92031
92105
92228
W14
W16
W17
W20
W22
W27
W28
W33

Feb-67
42548
42622
42954
43011
43100
43151
44666
44671
44856
44989
45094
45222
45277
45383
45441
45446
45466
46417
46502
47531
48029
48122
48130
48185
48199
48221
48288
48343
48436
48440
48545
48751
48766
61238
62017
62024
62046
62059
63420
65853
65865
65869
75061
76033
76048
76093
78028
78055
90588
92030
92076
92083
92087
92089
92096
92104
92107

Mar-67
34006
34019
34077
34088
35014
35026
41284
42071
42076
42644
42663
43071
43096
43122
44689
44771
44790
44958
45028
45060
45064
45079
45132
45141
45228
45250
45326
45369
45495
46431
46439
46440
46443
46465
47534
48000
48035
48053
48098
48105
48123
48136
48152
48159
48165
48177
48180
48301
48320
48379
48513
48538
48547
48690
48701
48705
48728
48743
48753
61019
62027
62065
65823
65911
70003
73002
73006
73115
73117
73119
75004
76058
76095
80002
80012
80019
90385
W24
W31
DS233
DS234

Apr-67
34002
34015
34071
35012
41230
41295
42086
42133
42134
42546
42613
43101
43138
44685
44691
44722
44794
44879
44892
44998
45062
45109
45247
45340
45352
45371
45402
45647
46441
48073
48082
48114
48121
48316
48458
48459
48494
48548
48685
48693
48707
48708
48717
48770
61102
61262
61278
61340
61347
61354
61407
62001
62025
62041
63436
64576
64602
64611
64620
65234
65901
65929
70040
70041
70052
70053
73022
73026
73066
75060
76040
76041
76063
80128
80154
90008
90014
90020
90030
90071
90132
90361
90386
90429
90468
90489
90560
90596
90655
92006
92018
92032
92065
92074
92150
92151

May-67
34044
34056
34057
42052
42079
42081
42187
42196
42210
42233
42236
42267
42274
42297
42611
42647
42656
42699
43012
43048
43077
44693
44696
44699
44796
44863
44875
44930
44937
44982
44986
44991
44997
45019
45024
45070
45124
45126
45147
45167
45211
45274
45319
45359
45404
45423
46400
46432
46433
46436
46437
46448
46449
46452
46455
46457
46470
46480
46486
46487
46490
46491
46499
46501
46503
46506
46515
46516
46520
46522
46523
48057
48075
48126
48141
48157
48174
48256
48417
48435
48449
48466
48509
48552
48604
48640
61072
61115
61123
61180
61189
62012
62057
62062
63346
63366
63397
65813
65817
65833
65834
65861
68006
70006
70034
70042
70048
73059
73060
73064
73070
73079
73094
73097
73139
73146
75064
76000
76008
76046
76051
76094
76098
76104
78007
78012
78013
78020
78021
78023
78037
78041
78044
78062
80004
80045
80046
80086
80116
80120
80151
90056
90230
90233
90347
90370
90397
90407
90610
90625
92015
92078
92080
92090
92100
92206
92211

Jun-67
34008
34047
34098
34104
34108
42116
42587
42650
42665
43024
43034
43098
43105
43115
43140
44659
44695
44733
44768
44821
44853
44867
44870
44900
44928
44946
45003
45014
45031
45069
45120
45242
45278
45303
45339
45343
45346
45675
46402
46484
46485
46492
46505
47313
48011
48106
48110
48128
48131
48163
48265
48266
48275
48287
48324
48603
48643
48645
48712
48754
61002
61012
61021
61255
61289
61388
62023
62048
65288
65345
65812
65880
65885
70027
73137
75018
75055
76037
76039
76069
76088
77002
77012
80145
90016
90047
90057
90061
90081
90091
90094
90099
90116
90160
90172
90243
90262
90265
90272
90281
90300
90345
90352
90362
90363
90396
90404
90409
90427
90434
90450
90458
90459
90617
90620
90644
90650
90654
90670
90678
90688
90704
90722
92019
92103
92129
92135
92205
92215

Jul-67
30064
30067
30069
30071
30072
34001
34004
34013
34018
34021
34023
34024
34025
34034
34036
34037
34040
34052
34060
34087
34089
34090
34093
34095
34100
34102
35003
35007
35008
35013
35023
35028
35030
41224
41298
41312
41319
41320
42055
42149
42235
42269
42287
43015
43055
43117
43123
43129
43130
44732
44795
44835
44862
44882
44883
44913
45040
45059
45071
45116
45188
45191
45302
45406
45417
48104
48154
48162
48202
48269
48347
48376
48394
48411
48454
48501
48542
48557
48602
48613
48648
48681
48709
62026
62042
62044
63394
63407
63426
63429
63437
63455
63458
65789
65795
65804
65860
70005
70033
70046
70047
73014
73018
73020
73029
73037
73043
73065
73085
73092
73093
73118
73141
73155
75016
75035
75059
75068
75074
75075
75076
75077
76005
76006
76007
76009
76011
76026
76031
76064
76066
76067
76081
77014
80011
80015
80016
80085
80133
80134
80139
80140
80143
80146
80152
82019
82029
90200
90210
90309
90321
90339
90406
90482
90611
90633
90698
92106
92114
92120
92121
92133
92138
92154
92156
92159
Dep 29

Aug-67
43041
43049
43073
43119
43120
44661
44667
44717
44766
44774
44817
44830
44914
44936
45039
45050
45056
45057
45089
45139
45256
45304
45308
45324
45405
45409
45412
45448
45454
45455
48085
48108
48160
48176
48194
48204
48208
48220
48258
48261
48271
48315
48386
48456
48464
48522
48528
48535
48556
48636
48650
48655
48671
48695
48725
48731
48742
48768
62060
63431
65892
70015
70016
70038
73045
73144
75002
75006
75013
75029
75046
75047
75052
75071
92027
92052
92093
92126

Sep-67
42066
42138
42145
42189
42283
43000
43001
43003
43004
43007
43021
43029
43044
43050
43063
43070
43076
43084
43112
43125
43137
43139
44675
44679
44680
44681
44684
44736
44765
44792
44805
44812
44814
44828
44832
44833
44837
44843
44852
44865
44866
44872
44896
44909
44912
44927
44934
44944
44948
45006
45015
45021
45042
45052
45072
45075
45107
45186
45193
45198
45226
45234
45239
45241
45243
45264
45270
45271
45297
45298
45323
45328
45373
45440
45481
45494
45697
48054
48061
48100
48158
48161
48171
48218
48281
48283
48313
48337
48350
48359
48364
48375
48395
48399
48450
48460
48474
48506
48531
48550
48618
48637
48675
48699
48721
48767
61030
61306
61337
62007
62011
62045
62050
63344
63387
63395
65811
65855
65879
65882
65894
70010
70028
70032
70039
73039
73071
75039
90009
90074
90076
90135
90236
90318
90348
90351
90360
90378
90382
90405
90417
90430
90478
90605
90615
90627
90642
90677
90682
90695
90699
90721
92045
92048
92050
92119
92127
92131
92137
92139
92157
92224
DS237
DS238

Oct-67
42072
42073
42083
42085
42093
42141
42152
42251
42252
42574
42616
42689
43043
44662
44669
44677
44694
44725
44727
44770
44772
44775
44776
44822
44824
44825
44826
44854
44857
44886
44898
44902
44907
44911
44933
44938
44943
44964
44983
44985
44990
45000
45067
45080
45111
45135
45208
45215
45219
45225
45261
45263
45267
45273
45275
45307
45321
45363
45374
45415
45425
45428
45437
45593
47289
47383
47629
48017
48018
48067
48113
48125
48164
48166
48268
48279
48332
48371
48377
48382
48425
48439
48473
48495
48505
48534
48537
48540
48622
48664
48669
48673
48676
48703
48710
48714
48724
48735
48741
68012
70029
73004
73025
73048
73073
73127
73140
73158
73159
75010
75040
75042
76075
92008
92012
92014
92016
92020
92046
92051
92058
92101
92111
92113
92123
92132
92208
92227
Dep 26
Dep 58

Nov-67
43017
43028
43046
43118
43121
44658
44678
44682
44697
44730
44759
44778
44819
44831
44840
44844
44859
44861
44873
44876
44893
44905
44917
44920
45043
45048
45061
45145
45232
45280
45281
45288
45292
45299
45331
45347
45349
45368
45431
45449
45450
45562
48024
48055
48070
48074
48076
48084
48093
48119
48169
48211
48214
48222
48276
48352
48363
48381
48408
48438
48470
48517
70031
73011
73096
73129
73156
73160
75024
76077
76079
76084
92002
92011
92021
92022
92023
92024
92025
92026
92029
92047
92049
92056
92070
92071
92073
92079
92082
92084
92086
92102
92108
92109
92112
92122
92128
92152
92162
92163
92166
92203
92234

Dec-67
43002
43010
43023
43047
43088
44674
44734
44767
44773
44834
44858
44887
44895
44915
44916
44962
44988
44993
45041
45083
45092
45196
45221
45236
45246
45259
45285
45295
45377
48190
48205
48310
48336
48362
48402
48469
48674
48696
48697
48729
48757
48758
48764
62005
70004
70011
70012
70014
70021
70022
70023
70024
70025
70035
70045
70049
70051
75015
75026
75030
75033
75037
75043
75058
76080
92017
92055
92110
92117
92125
92204

Jan-68
44708
44715
44728
44842
44846
44889
45005
45114
45227
45375
45493
48010
48046
48151
48193
48200
48305
48334
48351
48510
48559
48609
48626
48677
48750
73033
73035
73131
75041
92153
92212
Dep 30
Dep 32

Feb-68
44815
44848
45034
45038
45054
45133
45296
45391
45421
48421
48424
48492
48631
48639
48683
75021
75032
75034
75062
92233

Mar-68
43006
43008
43033
44665
44672
44800

44804	48201	73053	48107	**May-68**	48045	73040	44890	45420	48374	73133	92167	45055	45386	48493
44807	48224	73136	48192	43019	48056	73128	44891	45435	48380	73134		45073	45388	48519
44838	48272	92004	48197	43027	48124	73138	44910	45445	48384	73143	**Aug-68**	45095	45390	48665
44906	48304	92009	48292	44663	48182	73142	44929	48026	48392	92091	44690	45096	45397	48666
44940	48307	92165	48308	44664	48206	73157	44942	48033	48467	92118	44709	45110	45407	48715
45001	48317		48335	44711	48252	92054	44947	48132	48491		44713	45134	45444	48723
45101	48345	**Apr-68**	48344	44829	48322	92069	44949	48168	48504	**Jul-68**	44735	45156	45447	48727
45150	48442	44683	48433	44836	48325	92088	45046	48170	48529	44758	44781	45206	48062	48730
45258	48465	44761	48437	44855	48329	92094	45076	48212	48549	44816	44806	45212	48167	48752
45279	48468	44851	48441	44864	48365	92218	45104	48267	48612	44878	44809	45231	48191	48765
45294	48503	44903	48453	44868	48390	92249	45149	48282	48620	44899	44871	45260	48247	48773
45316	48507	44926	48749	45013	48445		45187	48293	48646	44963	44874	45262	48253	48775
45395	48532	44965	48763	45027	48451	**Jun-68**	45202	48319	48652	45200	44877	45268	48278	70013
45426	48544	45131	73000	45065	48471	43106	45203	48321	48678	45353	44888	45269	48294	73069
48036	48553	45253	73067	45190	48533	44777	45209	48323	48687	45394	44894	45287	48340	75009
48063	48617	45376	73126	45201	48551	44780	45255	48327	48692	48115	44897	45305	48348	75019
48077	48632	45424	73132	45254	48614	44802	45290	48338	48720	48257	44932	45310	48393	75020
48081	48700	45436	73135	45282	48684	44803	45312	48356	48746	48448	44950	45318	48400	75027
48111	48740	48012	92223	45284	48702	44818	45345	48368	73010	48546	44971	45330	48410	75048
48117	48744	48060		45381	48722	44845	45382	48369	73050	92077	45017	45342	48423	
48153	73034	48090		45392	48745	44884	45411	48373	73125	92160	45025	45350	48476	

BR(GWR) Hawksworth '1500' class 0-6-0PT No 1507 at Newport Pill in July 1959.

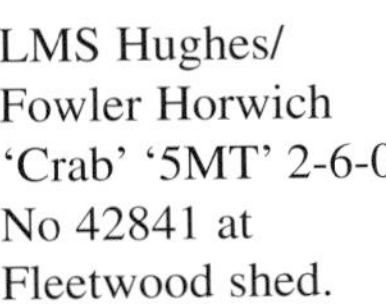

LMS Hughes/ Fowler Horwich 'Crab' '5MT' 2-6-0 No 42841 at Fleetwood shed.

Appendix 6. Youngest and oldest locomotives at time of withdrawal.

The ages are shown in years and months separated by a colon (:). A plus sign (+) indicates that the engine concerned was at least this age – the actual month of entry into service not being known.

Under 10 years old

36001 1:5
61057 3:9
9499 4:2
8447 5:0
92220 5:0
1652 5:1
9492 5:1
8448 5:2
9496 5:2
8442 5:3
8443 5:3
9491 5:3
92210 5:3
92207 5:6
92219 5:7
1659 5:8
92198 5:10
92199 5:10
92214 5:10
92216 5:10
3408 6:1
92245 6:1
3407 6:2
92176 6:2
92177 6:2
92171 6:3
92175 6:3
3404 6:4
8434 6:4
92196 6:4
92229 6:4
92232 6:4
8432 6:5
92169 6:5
92170 6:5
92248 6:5
92209 6:6
92236 6:7
92242 6:7
92217 6:8
92192 6:9
92222 6:9
92241 6:9
8492 6:10
76097 6:10
92240 6:10
92195 6:11
92200 6:11
8485 7:0
84027 7:0
84029 7:0
92187 7:0
92188 7:0
92197 7:0
92202 7:0
92213 7:0
92221 7:0
92237 7:0
92238 7:0
92250 7:0
92184 7:1
92185 7:1
92193 7:1
92225 7:1
92246 7:1
92243 7:2
92244 7:2
92181 7:3
92201 7:3
92226 7:3
92235 7:3
92230 7:4
6771 7:5
9497 7:5
84023 7:5
84024 7:5
92180 7:5
80103 7:6
84021 7:6
84022 7:6
92143 7:6
92168 7:6

92194 7:6
80148 7:7
84020 7:7
92142 7:7
92147 7:7
92186 7:7
92190 7:7
92215 7:7
8441 7:8
92149 7:8
92191 7:8
92211 7:8
73164 7:9
92140 7:9
92189 7:9
9459 7:10
92174 7:10
92247 7:10
73161 7:11
1653 8:0
3409 8:0
76072 8:0
92206 8:0
76112 8:1
80153 8:1
92173 8:1
92178 8:1
92179 8:1
92205 8:1
76106 8:2
76107 8:2
92239 8:2
8445 8:3
8449 8:3
9443 8:3
73162 8:3
80149 8:3
92148 8:3
92164 8:3
92172 8:3
92231 8:3
8440 8:4
9438 8:4
9439 8:4
73167 8:4
92144 8:4
92182 8:4
92183 8:4
92208 8:4
92212 8:4
92218 8:4
9481 8:5
76111 8:5
92141 8:5
1644 8:6
3406 8:6
6779 8:6
9468 8:6
71000 8:6
73147 8:6
73148 8:6
73165 8:6
76105 8:6
92145 8:6
92228 8:6
3403 8:7
3405 8:7
73152 8:7
80147 8:7
84028 8:7
92146 8:7
92203 8:7
1635 8:8
73168 8:8
78053 8:8
80127 8:8
82043 8:8
84025 8:8
84026 8:8
92158 8:8
92204 8:8
1662 8:9
3402 8:9
9427 8:9

9445 8:9
73109 8:9
73163 8:9
73166 8:9
76099 8:9
78048 8:9
1666 8:10
3401 8:10
8429 8:10
8435 8:10
8476 8:10
80129 8:10
80150 8:10
3400 8:11
6773 8:11
9462 8:11
75057 8:11
76108 8:11
8417 9:0
9432 9:0
9449 9:0
73116 9:0
75063 9:0
80125 9:0
92155 9:0
92161 9:0
6774 9:1
7447 9:1
8462 9:1
9417 9:1
73170 9:1
75067 9:1
76050 9:1
76103 9:1
76109 9:1
92130 9:1
8423 9:2
76068 9:2
76092 9:2
76113 9:2
76114 9:2
80131 9:2
80136 9:2
92115 9:2
1650 9:3
1665 9:3
8444 9:3
8468 9:3
9458 9:3
73076 9:3
73123 9:3
75056 9:3
76065 9:3
76071 9:3
76096 9:3
76100 9:3
80135 9:3
92224 9:3
92227 9:3
92234 9:3
1637 9:4
1661 9:4
8438 9:4
8439 9:4
8463 9:4
8494 9:4
73151 9:4
76085 9:4
76086 9:4
76089 9:4
76110 9:4
92136 9:4
1600 9:5
1656 9:5
8421 9:5
8473 9:5
9434 9:5
73171 9:5
80137 9:5
92034 9:5
92249 9:5
1654 9:6
1667 9:6
8412 9:6

9436 9:6
9474 9:6
9498 9:6
73106 9:6
73154 9:6
73169 9:6
76054 9:6
76090 9:6
76091 9:6
76101 9:6
76102 9:6
80141 9:6
92066 9:6
92095 9:6
92150 9:6
92151 9:6
92166 9:6
92233 9:6
8427 9:7
8489 9:7
8499 9:7
73077 9:7
73091 9:7
73153 9:7
76082 9:7
76083 9:7
76093 9:7
76095 9:7
76098 9:7
80142 9:7
92134 9:7
1603 9:8
1664 9:8
1668 9:8
8408 9:8
9447 9:8
9486 9:8
9487 9:8
73112 9:8
73122 9:8
73145 9:8
73150 9:8
75053 9:8
75054 9:8
76073 9:8
76087 9:8
78057 9:8
80144 9:8
92154 9:8
92156 9:8
92159 9:8
92163 9:8
1629 9:9
1658 9:9
6775 9:9
8419 9:9
8483 9:9
9428 9:9
73074 9:9
73149 9:9
75061 9:9
76094 9:9
78015 9:9
82025 9:9
92124 9:9
1616 9:10
1625 9:10
1657 9:10
1663 9:10
8450 9:10
73124 9:10
76104 9:10
80056 9:10
80115 9:10
80132 9:10
92081 9:10
92092 9:10
92096 9:10
92157 9:10
92223 9:10
1509 9:11
1647 9:11
73111 9:11
75051 9:11

75060 9:11
75064 9:11
76070 9:11
76074 9:11
76076 9:11
76078 9:11
78056 9:11
80087 9:11
80107 9:11
80119 9:11
92057 9:11
92072 9:11
92116 9:11
92162 9:11
92165 9:11

Over 70 years old

41747 70:0
43428 70:0+
56025 70:0
57341 70:0
58022 70:0
58042 70:0
58900 70:0
58902 70:0
68269 70:0
30225 70:1
43234 70:1+
57325 70:1
58247 70:1+
58899 70:1
65099 70:1
65246 70:1
68232 70:1
68507 70:1
M28153 70:1
32156 70:2
32274 70:2
40351 70:2
58926 70:2
65235 70:2
65288 70:2
68110 70:2
68522 70:2
30579 70:3
41676 70:3
41773 70:3
52129 70:3
57340 70:3
57360 70:3
58202 70:3
65227 70:3
65232 70:3
68092 70:3+
68242 70:3
68501 70:3
1531 70:4
30089 70:4
43245 70:4+
51490 70:4
65268 70:4
68542 70:4
40364 70:5
43200 70:5+
43225 70:5+
43250 70:5+
51320 70:5
51477 70:5
58051 70:5
68100 70:5+
68254 70:5
Dep 3170:5
43214 70:6+
43263 70:6+
58233 70:6+
68497 70:6
32141 70:7
41749 70:7
51514 70:7
65260 70:7
65420 70:7

Dep 3670:7
M8182 70:7
58904 70:8
65257 70:8
65273 70:8
68500 70:8
1903 70:9
30192 70:9
51204 70:9
51206 70:9
57331 70:9
58346 70:9
68502 70:9
68508 70:9
43282 70:10+
57329 70:10
58363 70:10
68097 70:10+
68245 70:10
43192 70:11
52089 70:11
58238 70:11+
58889 70:11
65241 70:11
68433 70:11
1542 71:0
40362 71:0
43261 71:0+
51488 71:0
30200 71:1
43180 71:1+
43186 71:1+
Pres 103 71:1
32127 71:2
51504 71:2
57336 71:2
65237 71:2
32609 71:3
57324 71:3
58340 71:3
65261 71:3
M23016 71:3+
30183 71:4
57328 71:4
57348 71:4
65253 71:4
30193 71:5
41844 71:5
43213 71:5+
51479 71:5
51516 71:5
57326 71:5
65230 71:5
65265 71:5
30199 71:6
30580 71:6
32094 71:6
52119 71:6
52121 71:6
57260 71:6
30571 71:7
41690 71:7
43183 71:7+
51325 71:7
58201 71:7
58246 71:7+
65228 71:7
31337 71:8
32142 71:8
32145 71:8
43242 71:8+
43254 71:8+
58334 71:8
58880 71:8
43342 71:9+
65251 71:9
43240 71:10+
43257 71:10+
51318 71:10
51491 71:10
52044 71:10
57321 71:10

57235 71:11
57319 71:11
58211 71:11
68104 71:11
W32 71:11
41769 72:0
57317 72:0
68415 72:0
6 72:1
51506 72:1
58037 72:1
58888 72:1
W25 72:1
32147 72:2
41725 72:2
41753 72:2
58354 72:2
43178 72:3+
57314 72:3
65216 72:3
43174 72:4
43188 72:4+
58021 72:4
58343 72:4
65224 72:4
30564 72:5
41711 72:5
58150 72:5
68093 72:5+
68416 72:5
68499 72:5
Dep 4472:5
51510 72:6
57307 72:6
65217 72:6
65218 72:6
Dep 3323 72:6
52093 72:7
32112 72:8
32129 72:8
57230 72:8
58891 72:8
W8 72:8
30577 72:9
41748 72:9
43187 72:9+
58141 72:9+
65222 72:9
57279 72:10
58224 72:10
58329 72:10
65211 72:10
68101 72:10+
32096 72:11
43189 72:11+
1331 73:0
32095 73:0
W30 73:0
30569 73:1
32283 73:1
41752 73:1
65033 73:1
30566 73:2
58335 73:2
65361 73:2
68230 73:2
W36 73:2
41713 73:3
57234 73:3
W18 73:3
41695 73:4
51436 73:4
51460 73:4
58887 73:4
68400 73:4
32128 73:5
58030 73:5
58040 73:5
58331 73:5
51439 73:6
56011 73:6
58031 73:6
30570 73:7

30573 73:7
41720 73:7
68235 73:7
30574 73:9
40356 73:9
43185 73:9+
32644 73:10
43750 73:10+
51410 73:10
58035 73:10
65214 73:10
57276 73:11
58032 73:11
58155 73:11
32133 74:0
51471 74:0
51472 74:0
51489 74:0
51511 74:1
58113 74:1+
68233 74:1
41835 74:2
57273 74:2
57303 74:2
58134 74:2+
65210 74:2
WREN 74:2+
30578 74:3
58036 74:3
58216 74:3
58336 74:3
51390 74:4
65267 74:4
51396 74:5
51470 74:5
58092 74:5
58324 74:5
58325 74:5
68390 74:5
W26 74:5
W33 74:5
58020 74:6
58034 74:6
58195 74:6
58200 74:6
51376 74:7
58212 74:7
65243 74:7
W16 74:7
W22 74:7
51375 74:8
51530 74:8
58033 74:8
M28095 74:8
W21 74:8
32215 74:9
M28097 74:9
W29 74:9
32605 74:10
32647 74:10
51348 74:10
57300 74:10
58225 74:10
58333 74:10
W20 74:10
41666 74:11
51464 74:11
68396 74:11
30572 75:0
41660 75:0
41724 75:0
41754 75:0
51513 75:0
57295 75:0
68095 75:0+
30568 75:1
51503 75:1
58151 75:1
W17 75:1
30584 75:2
57285 75:2
57287 75:2

57292 75:2
58320 75:2
68437 75:2
41710 75:3
57299 75:3
57311 75:3
W24 75:3
32299 75:4
41664 75:4
51379 75:4
57288 75:4
992 75:5
40337 75:5
57241 75:5
58207 75:5
68432 75:5
57243 75:6
30575 75:7
51498 75:7
57247 75:7
68404 75:7
M8108 75:7
51499 75:8
68428 75:8
68436 75:8
68438 75:8
51447 75:9
51453 75:9
58111 75:9+
65234 75:9
68422 75:9
30582 75:10
68421 75:10
41682 75:11
41804 76:0
51462 76:0
51496 76:0
51526 76:0
W2 76:0
41726 76:1
57284 76:1
58161 76:1
51404 76:2
51521 76:2
57302 76:2
58112 76:3+
Dep 3276:3
30583 76:4
51425 76:4
51500 76:4
57274 76:4
57275 76:4
51432 76:5
51512 76:5
57296 76:5
58149 76:5
W35 76:5
30567 76:6
57278 76:6
57309 76:6
68429 76:6
68430 76:6
68434 76:6
W14 76:6
W28 76:6
W27 76:7
58213 76:8
58217 76:8
5 76:9
32689 76:9
51474 76:9
58147 76:9
41706 76:10
51481 76:10
58180 76:10+
58332 76:10
68413 76:10
40332 76:11
57291 76:11
DS515 76:11
W31 76:11
41763 77:0
58219 77:0
58220 77:0

68420 77:0
41671 77:1
41672 77:1
51457 77:1
41699 77:2
51484 77:3
58194 77:3+
58206 77:3
58193 77:4+
57268 77:5
58172 77:5+
58221 77:5
58330 77:5
51424 77:6
57232 77:6
57257 77:6
57262 77:6
57263 77:6
57264 77:6
57271 77:6
58327 77:6
41686 77:7
51524 77:7
57256 77:7
68398 77:7
57250 77:8
58145 77:8+
58328 77:8
51345 77:9
51423 77:9
57236 77:9
57238 77:9
57244 77:9
32138 77:10
32659 77:10
51381 77:10
57245 77:10
57233 77:11
57239 77:11
57246 77:11
57267 77:11
58038 78:0
58203 78:0
58228 78:0
51497 78:1
58215 78:1
51441 78:2
68426 78:2
68435 78:2
51415 78:3
W1 78:3
57265 78:4
58164 78:4+
58188 78:4+
58196 78:4
W3 78:4
57254 78:5
51397 78:6
57258 78:6
57259 78:6
41739 78:7
51323 78:7
57253 78:7
58322 78:7
68427 78:7
51361 78:8
57242 78:8
57252 78:8
57266 78:8
58189 78:8+
51353 78:9
57249 78:9
57251 78:9
58162 78:9
57240 78:10
68417 78:10
Pres 123 78:10+
51458 78:11
57237 78:11
32151 79:1
58214 79:1
58323 79:1
68401 79:1

68423 79:1
32677 79:2
51445 79:2
58129 79:2+
58204 79:2
32696 79:3
51313 79:3
51429 79:3
58159 79:3
58209 79:3
68424 79:3
58179 79:4+
58326 79:4
51486 79:5
57269 79:5
58218 79:5
58198 79:6
57261 79:7
58176 79:7+
68412 79:7
57270 79:8
58152 79:8
58127 79:9
58199 79:9
58850 79:9
32139 79:10
32606 79:10
51338 79:10
58125 79:10
58184 79:10+
58192 79:11+
11394 79:11
58133 80:0+
32135 80:1
51444 80:2
58154 80:2
68431 80:2
51413 80:4
68407 80:4
32124 80:5
58126 80:5
58321 80:5
32608 80:6
32695 80:7
51321 80:7
58187 80:7+
51307 80:8
58197 80:8
68425 80:9
DS377 80:9
58191 80:10+
51446 80:11
58110 80:11+
58139 80:11+
58156 80:11
58190 80:11+
68393 80:11
58117 81:0
41661 81:1
58142 81:1+
68395 81:1
68414 81:3
32113 81:4
32610 81:4
51419 81:4
51412 81:6
58140 81:7+
51358 81:9
58136 81:9+
51316 81:10
1196 81:11
1197 81:11
51343 81:11
58121 81:11
41702 82:0
51408 82:0
W4 82:0
68669 82:1
41734 82:2
51319 82:2
41712 82:5
51371 82:5
58114 82:5
58178 82:5+

68409 82:5
58157 82:6
58167 82:8+
58171 82:8+
68397 82:8
68399 82:10
68391 82:11
68402 82:11
58183 83:1+
32697 83:2
32678 83:3
68405 83:3
51336 83:4
58130 83:5+
58132 83:5+
58158 83:5
68410 83:5
58173 83:6+
58168 83:7+
58165 83:9+
58170 83:10+
58119 83:11
58146 83:11
68667 84:0
58169 84:2+
58186 84:2+
68406 84:2
68668 84:2
58153 84:4
11304 84:4
Dep 3584:4
32655 84:5
58144 84:5+
11368 84:6
58181 84:7+
32635 84:9
58118 84:9
58116 84:10
58163 84:10
58174 85:0+
58175 85:0+
58131 85:2+
58166 85:3+
68408 85:3
32640 85:6
58185 85:7+
58135 85:9+
58137 85:9+
58160 85:9
68392 85:9
58177 85:10+
58115 86:0
58122 86:1
32694 86:4
11324 86:4
DS680 86:4
41708 86:6
58124 86:6
58128 86:8
32646 86:10
58123 86:10
32650 86:11
58138 87:0+
30586 87:1
58182 87:1+
9 87:3
11305 87:3
58120 87:5
32661 87:6
DS681 87:8
58148 87:9
58143 87:11+
32662 88:1
30587 88:6
30585 88:7
32670 90:11
32636 91:2
58865 93:0

Oldest engines in stock (until date shown)

58865 02/51
68667 05/52
68668/Dep 35 11/52
32636 11/63
58148 12/63
58182 01/64
11305 09/64
41708 12/66
W31 03/67
65234 04/67
65288 06/67
65789 07/67
65811 09/67
7 04/89

(not including narrow gauge)

47289 10/67
45025 08/68

Appendix 7. Locomotives which survived for more than one year after withdrawal before scrapping.

The length of time is shown in years and months. When the exact scrapping date is unknown, the length of time is in years only.

1 yr 0 m
203 298 1017 1401 1470 1504 1626 1633 2122 2229 2245 2841 2869 2884 3213 3215 3219 3442 3623 3764 3853 4090 4106 4116 4230 4238 4242 4246 4250 4259 4691 4956 4960 4980 4999 5006 5022 5155 5202 5255 5260 5410 5525 5546 5551 5612 5787 5905 5908 5940 5943 6133 6312 6406 6607 6610 6698 6738 6749 7031 7329 7780 7790 8421 8423 8746 9024 9307 9414 9444 30032 30199 30368 30837 31880 31907 32353 32413 32696 33002 33013 34005 34032 34066 34074 34088 40010 40054 40151 40153 40186 40493 40534 40607 40656 41158 41203 41293 41795 41946 41948 41950 41977 41978 41982 41983 41984 41985 41986 41987 41990 41991 41992 41993 42164 42267 42341 42472 42473 42479 42621 42626 42627 42641 42642 42752 42804 42871 42873 43213 43241 43257 43282 43292 43308 43327 43335 43339 43369 43378 43558 43587 43615 43619 43623 43674 43800 43902 43930 43935 43966 44018 44161 44234 44273 44279 44285 44312 44316 44323 44330 44345 44368 44395 44418 44708 44808 44820 44912 44930 45240 45266 45271 45286 45336 45417 45495 45589 45665 45673 45677 45687 45692 45693 45707 45711 45720 45727 46109 46508 47007 47163 47228 47235 47247 47339 47409 47612 47672 48053 48149 48217 48407 48450 48945 48953 49104 49109 49117 49180 49226 49330 49342 49368 49397 49424 49445 50644 52120 52510 55233 55234 56162 56313 56325 56336 56364 57267 57288 57350 57389 57441 57593 57618 57670 57673 57682 57686 58112 58163 60041 60927 60965 60971 61041 61056 61262 61981 62032 62034 62038 62490 62678 62679 63233 63880 63923 63926 63930 63933 63956 63971 64477 64500 64518 64527 64535 64540 64601 64615 64622 64631 64691 64699 64703 64843 64858 64915 65216 65315 65582 65695 67613 67622 67631 67648 67672 67782 68329 68331 68344 68480 69151 69162 69196 69828 70033 73145 75016 78063 90184 90216 90425 90549 90559 90608 90611 90751 90758 90761 90767 90769 90771 90772 90773 90774 92103 92142 92151 W21 W29 W32

1 yr 1 m
212 1007 1473 2069 2250 2271 2281 2851 2871 3170 3655 3674 4280 4906 4928 5173 5190 5390 5550 5631 6011 6012 6302 6353 6393 6418 6669 7224 7311 7321 7324 7775 7829 8405 8428 8439 8490 8738 9302 9432 9493 9604 31725 31868 32553 34009 34026 40028 40049 40117 40134 40208 40566 40601 40638 41106 41246 41264 41726 42280 42303 42386 42436 42569 42570 42862 42952 43147 43210 43223 43584 43651 43899 44090 44105 44159 44162 44256 44317 44325 44419 45102 45107 45182 45242 45373 45623 45678 45728 45731 46117 46161 46477 47210 47216 47226 47231 47466 47556 47572 47621 48061 48436 49113 49310 49413 49443 49618 52387 52399 52517 54465 55053 56298 56302 56312 56326 56347 57237 57271 57299 57303 57329 57335 57418 57461 57564 57571 57635 57654 57668 58137 58167 58213 60535 61269 61756 61950 61970 62468 62588 62686 63587 63616 63772 63925 63939 63980 63985 64470 67427 67433 67447 67617 67636 69008 69020 69025 69564 73071 75067 90495 90508 90526 90552 90630 90690 90693 90755 90765 92196 W18

1 yr 2 m
322 683 8752 30320 40396 44399 45130 46132 46411 63241 64342 64507 64514 67679

1 yr 3 m
35 906 1005 1018 1152 1462 1610 1645 2064 3386 2789 2882 3212 3622 3630 3641 3688 3741 3750 3769 4118 4129 4605 4708 4967 5001 5259 5360 5407 5649 5687 5693 5746 5773 5910 5911 5926 5944 5959 5960 5966 5981 6016 6026 6144 6388 6616 6640 6641 6856 7334 7911 8407 8756 9312 9749 9757 30059 30089 30125 30586 30826 30903 31757 31879 34024 34060 34087 34089 34102 40147 40158 40190 40193 40553 40624 40628 40670 41083 41113 41120 41122 41123 41205 41724 42144 42175 42268 42276 42692 42863 42917 43258 43300 43580 43926 44005 44230 44351 44365 44445 44473 44474 44480 44762 44860 45142 45458 45536 45655 45683 45718 45725 46408 47293 47392 47641 49252 49270 56232 57366 57447 57552 57594 57601 57602 57604 57608 57658 58115 58196 60980 61052 61054 61066 61096 61149 61166 61171 61194 61272 61278 61280 61286 61369 61411 61817 61907 61915 61942 61944 61957 61963 61977 62422 62428 62432 62691 62693 63488 63656 63693 63776 63832 63948 63966 64515 64519 64544 64574 64638 64639 65275 65693 65741 67462 67649 67676 67775 68050 68322 68350 68458 68750 69026 69052 69927 72000 72001 72003 72004 73043 73118 76050 76052 76095 90060 90127 90412 90726

1 yr 4 m
35 1022 1435 1604 3679 3755 4289 4976 5049 5092 5151 5774 5903 6109 6348 6708 9665 9741 9769 30035 30689 30697 30951 31407 34008 34047 34098 35008 40053 40091 40093 40166 40194 40199 40543 41661 41907 41908 42165 42729 42801 42830 42861 43381 43400 43618 43721 43763 43793 43939 44120 44432 44506 45139 45179 45304 47214 47249 47374 47527 47575 47598 48386 48556 49112 49149 49150 49442 54495 54500 55267 56278 57245 57284 57285 57357 57359 57555 57569 57579 57580 57611 57615 57623 57640 57667 57669 57674 58192 58281 60101 62431 63238 64532 65305 68460 68463 68478 68481 69013 69156 69216 76047 90245 90565 92034

1 yr 5 m
246 271 1015 1026 1616 1635 1644 2212 2256 2832 3611 3629 3694 4095 4112 4236 4700 4806 4944 4952 5250 5392 5555 5568 5646 5798 5917 5918 5930 6025 6101 6356 6368 6370 6379 6380 6600 7033 7309 7336 8448 8462 8701 8757 8763 8765 9314 9402 9457 9480 9609 30518 30534 30537 30538 30700 30902 30921 30930 30935 31409 31893 31894 31896 32337 32340 34104 34108 35030 40103 40111 40143 40149 40152 42364 42383 42407 43237 43789 43914 43984 44093 44338 44471 44513 45576 46105 46107 46121 46415 47550 47650 49153 49348 50712 55201 57364 57392 57470 57576 57596 57614 57643 57644 57672 57681 58132 61182 61254 61363 61373 61443 61450 61460 61982 62418 63421 63659 63698 63837 63883 63911 67667 67707 68119 68336 68339 68442 69006 70037 72002 90205 90667 W36

1 yr 6 m
1428 1652 2148 3901 4176 4672 4921 4947 4971 5160 5397 5399 5423 5562 6374 6617 6711 6727 8412 8432 8449 30540 31822 35012 40065 40148 40182 40204 40538 40589 40685 41062 41078 41121 42302 42329 42742 43324 43355 43553 43864 43890 43946 44062 44072 44216 44357 45730 47246 47600 51397 51404 51457 52455 55265 57295 57650 57651 58178 58308 61413 61415 62441 62484 62685 63574 64479 64486 65393 65541 68449 68591 69014 69015 70019 84002 90436 90768

1 yr 7 m
1003 3207 3654 3902 4269 4570 4909 4913 4948 5258 5548 5733 5968 5982 6391 6779 7411 7735 8434 8442 8443 8447 8450 8485 8492 9403 9417 9427 9496 40002 40030 40084 40115 40165 40592 40611 40658 41090 41102 41857 42921 43253 43271 43506 43629 43785 43910 43961 43990 44014 44119 44186 44225 44246 44293 44438 46102 46104 47301 47477 49452 51423 51546 54506 54507 57262 57263 57353 57550 58085 60529 60534 60537 61144 61451 62425 62440 64497 68353 68477 69160 76001 90170

1 yr 8 m
240 1004 1151 1438 2852 4102 4941 5357 5424 6301 6339 6743 7016 7428 7434 8416 9752 31305 31542 40020 40094 40184 40613 40642 40651 40653 40655 40660 40661 40679 41165 42927 43205 43251 43799 43919 43970 44064 44175 44291 45040 45071 47337 47352 47363 51316 51415 55225 56029 58130 58865 61105 61419 63657 63900 65235 65344 67623 69138 69159 69211 73002 76100

1 yr 9 m
1416 1457 2200 4218 4574 4917 5060 5544 5707 6028 6438 6736 7316 7758 8429 8744 9459 30090 30133 32235 40004 40055 40056 40154 40420 40620 40621 40687 40689 42179 42909 43474 47528 47552 47586 47639 52443 54466 54482 54486 54501 55203 55269 57249 57451 61009 61235 61284 62442 64282 68461 69219 90505

1 yr 10 m
337 1001 2276 4276 4934 4984 5980 7438 8482 9628 32343 40127 40181 40195 40578 40602 40640 40688 43387 44173 47387 47440 48249 49357 52389 67750 69183 73016 82003 82031 82034

1 yr 11 m
2022 2047 2294 3954 4119 4567 4701 4987 5986 6146 6330 7302 7305 9425 34083 40017 40059 40156 40175 40615 40625 40668 41903 41904 44364 46200 52183 52269 54489 55124 55221 55240 55262 55264

2 yr 0 m
205 1603 5067 5421 9438 9439 9443 34062 40124 40513 40669 43180 43357 43578 43771 43897 47291 49078 54463 55204 55206 55263 55266 58225 61200 63629 63635 64747 69203

2 yr 1 m
6737 43244 43274 43612 43712 43787 47585 51512 58157 58246 60026 62031 62821 64528 65287 68704

2 yr 2 m
309 58377 62052

2 yr 3 m
5182 5253 5935 30952 34017 34075 40674 42702 44340 44361 46450 47370 49375 61412 65293 67373 67650 69128 Dep 22 W30

2 yr 4 m
1429 3102 5097 5247 5537 5723 5994 7247 31231 40168 40635 40693 47591 49640 52431 57258 57653 58119 58204 65239 68091

2 yr 5 m
1991 7015 31231 40565 40677 41902 41909 43873 44000 44483 45486 49511 49582 49592 49667 51458 51497 62877

2 yr 6 m
394 6730 7009 7037 7408 41173

2 yr 7 m
2066 41905 41906 43278

2 yr 8 m
6734 47364 49509

2 yr 9 m
9492 40125 58116

2 yr 10 m
42439 43502 68332

2 yr 11 m
47539

3 yrs
9424

3 yr 0 m
1468 1709 43249 43622 43904 49662

3 yr 1 m
5547 30722 40519

3 yr 2 m
258 47305

3 yr 3 m
5815 40163

3 yr 4 m
6010

3 yr 5 m
42148 57361 Dep 3323

3 yr 6 m
61943

3 yr 7 m
3101

3 yr 8 m
2534

3 yr 10 m
1150 3100

3 yr 11 m
68089

4 yr 0 m
67 7415 8497

4 yr 1 m
1607 8466

4 yr 2 m
285

4 yr 4 m
5752 30103 65099

4 yr 5 m
68179 76080

4 yr 6 m
5510 9462

4 yr 7 m
7723 54508

4 yr 8 m
6325

9449

4 yr 9 m
5422
7722

4 yr 10 m
1600
5557
5558

65658

4 yr 11 m
8408

5 yrs
56250
68159
68396

5 yr 0 m
9445
9468
62829
62849

5 yr 1 m
7711

5 yr 2 m
8419
30101

5 yr 5 m
195

5 yr 6 m
9499

5 yr 8 m
5794

5 yr 9 m
7741
9491

6 yr 1 m
8417

6 yr 4 m
6771

6 yr 5 m
68382

6 yr 7 m
7734
68070

6 yr 8 m
68020

6 yr 11 m
2053

7 yrs
3663

7 yr 1 m
7739
7749

7 yr 7 m
1422
3817

7 yr 8 m
65626

7 yr 11 m
193

8 yr 6 m
30095

8 yr 7 m
2034

8 yr 10 m
2794

9 yr 0 m
9792

9 yr 1 m
2092
5757

9 yr 4 m
68067

9 yr 5 m
30097

9 yr 6 m
30098
30099
30100

30147

9 yr 9 m
1502

10 yrs
68416

10 yr 0 m
7779

11 yr 3 m
1509

11 yr 6 m
30237

12 yr 2 m
30092

12 yr 8 m
30176

13 yrs
30081

13 yr 2 m
54398

13 yr 7 m
92085

15 yr 1 m
4156

LNER Gresley 'A3' Pacific No 60041 *Salmon Trout* at Edinburgh Haymarket in June 1960, fitted with a double chimney.

GWR Collett '7400' class 0-6-0PT No 7428 at Snow Hill in April 1957. Note that it is still lettered 'GWR' on the tank sides, nine years after coming into BR stock.

Appendix 8. Locomotives which still carried their pre-nationalisation number after January 1951.

x Scrapped carrying its old number.
R Renumbered into departmental stock.

1951
30064
30223
30253
30498
30693
30863
31321
31337
31623
31758
31778
31809
32075
32091
32407
42835

Jan-51
30063
30174
30229
30308
31150
31712
31735
32168
32342
40406 x
40509
40530 x
40536
40547
41205
42299
42899
43392
47236
47371
47502
47503
49347 x
49377
50831
52119
52299
52376
52515
54399
56242
58071
58135
61458
63359
63384
63437
63806
64207
64217
64403
64521
64805
64819
64841
65043 x
65275
65512
65513
65702
65755
65760
65773
65850
67238
67385
68119
68185
68244
68729
68985
69056 x
69127
69138
69297
69353
69452
69498
69700
69921
90064
90192
90214
90273
90308
90348
90448
90605
90663

Feb-51
30127
30256
31547 x
31611
31714
32104
32694
40326
40580
40762 x
41661
41990
41992
42297
42690
43679
44143
46418
47165
47211
47295
47331
47339
47351
47645
47676
49005
49009
49063
49070
49155
49208 x
49450
50815 x
50909
52524
54467
54487
55164
55169
55195
56030
56172
56234
56255
56354
58145
61426
62361 x
62376 x
62382 x
62785
63405
63611
63648
63693
64125
64135 x
64189
64214
64275
64344
64353
64378
64379
64687
64714
64783
64802
64910
64979
65002
65270
65350 x
65354 x
65369 x
65377 x
65444
65548
65622 x
65772
67357
67367
67374
68211
68316
68351
68355
68387 x
68417
68505
68512
68517
68823
68848
68870
68926
69067 x
69161
69250
69300
69526
69566
69674
90035
90084
90158
90188
90193
90246
90260
90269
90286
90288
90305
90345
90403
90439
90443
90483
90512
90519
90583
90625
90634
90655
90696
90753

Mar-51
30203
30251
30353 x
30408 x
30413 x
30430 x
30670
31157 x
31252
31443 x
31519
31730 x
31740 x
31748 x
31825
32447
32487
32570
32640
40038
40622
41916 x
41917 x
41919 x
41921 x
41926 x
43010
43257
43334
43449
43656
43855
44091
44203
44224
44334
44409
45148
46415
47180
47286
47391
47508
47555
48763
49044
49218 x
49258 x
49292 x
49326
49388 x
51241
52179
52215
55122
55188 x
55216
55264
56363
56376
63842
63870
64115 x
64151 x
64177
64221
64728
64907
65396 x
65454
65500
65511
65578
65736
67296
67309
67322
68115
68279
68326
68341
68354
68500
68665
68760
68898
69172
69217
69445
69562
69925
90043
90101
90112
90117
90152
90180
90223
90287
90290
90349
90373
90387
90393
90545
90549
90584
90603
90750

Apr-51
30049
30154 x
30155 x
30165 x
30441 x
30698
30713 x
30722 x
30769
31107
31174
31245
31274
31544
32473
32603 x
40501
40676
41140
41915 x
43186
43669
43776
43991
44232
44236
46688 x
46900
47290
47334
48936 x
49007
49020
49114
49205 x
49312 x
49359
52219 x
52458
55230
58076
58151 x
62370 x
63303 x
63400
63683
64148 x
64232
64693
64886
65226 x
65355 x
65406 x
65508
65661
65700
65796
65802
67353
68122
68404 x
68534
68610
68623
68658
68764
69181
69435
69460
69654
69903
90018
90159
90185
90231
90377
90390
90423
90594

May-51
30061
30082
30113 x
30114 x
30116 x
30118 x
30280 x
30303 x
30305 x
30314 x
30356
30414 x
30577
30731 x
31041 x
31093 x
31178
31291
31335
31339
31379 x
31381 x
31390 x
32009 x
32062 x
32138
32156 x
32608
32661
32695
33003
40031
40487
40549 x
40568
40569
41690 x
43829
43942
44279
46414
46906 x
47169
47261
49023
49034
49203
49444
51244
52162
55262
56293
58063 x
58139
58169
61425
61429
61431
61699 x
63235 x
63259 x
64123 x
64650
64677
65018
65614 x
65694
65769
67197
67457
68012
68151
68152
68153
68258
68377 x
68433 x
68444
68480
68575
68707
68759
68816
68871
68935
69191
69466
69475
69789 x
90011
90115
90137
90142
90165
90170
90203
90218
90239
90240
90314
90319
90365
90405
90506
90544
90567
90676
90689
90691

Jun-51
30007 x
30020 x
30068
30250
30255
30367 x
30384 x
30723 x
31044 x
31066 x
31248 x
31271
31391 x
31395 x
31432 x
31542
32008 x
32054 x
32063 x
32068 x
32101
32391
32595 x
32596 x
32602 x
40566
40619
40691
40729 x
41749
41856 x
43282
43890
44404
44435
47239
47420
47624
47678
49031 x
49239
50799
52182
52590 x
63267 x
63284 x
63342
63460
64150 x
64688
64801
64824
65022
65076 x
65577
65623 x
65663
67216
67456
68181
68312
68397
68509
68900
69480 x
90017
90055
90138
90207
90430
90535
90548
90587
90618
90693
90752

Jul-51
30034
30212
30238
30389 x
30436 x
30770
31108 x
31147
31373 x
31602 x
32002 x
32359 x
32697
41781 x
43351
43840
46628 x
46922 x
47412
47505
49049
49344
55182
56035
56309
58288
58296 x
58368 x
64216
64404
64934
65006 x
65362 x
65549
65667
67220
68231 x
68327
68345
68376 x
68574
68632
68645
68748
68921
68944
69220
69423 x
90066
90149
90244
90611

Aug-51
30069
30070
30084
30246
30564
40666
40681
41185
47603
49021
57688
58072
58120
58140
58349 x
61433
63270 x
64174
64708
64924
64929
64952
65541
65574
65686
67153 x
68148
68175 x
68214
68247 x
68298
68311 x
68650
68961
68986
69283
69628
90124
90161
90166
90167
90263
90394
90409
90454
90577
90704

Sep-51
30304
30311
30401 x
31369 x
31577
31732 x
32070 x
32073 x
41702
43463
45552
47238
47357
49120
49213 x
49246
50887
55234
56031
56296
58895 x
61419
62672
63311 x
63314 x
64124 x
64768
65339
65401 x
65644 x
65894
68098
68139 x
68183
68337
68339
68672
68681
68829
69431
69458
69469
69477
90156
90176
90229
90238
90293
90418
90486
90521
90573
90580
90590
90612
90683
90771

Oct-51
30395 x
31175 x
31685 x
32050 x
32067 x
32647 x
40404
41811
44401
47550
54454
58354
58935 x
63326 x
65890
67304
68230
68254
68304
68528
68562
68654
68856
69116
69400 x
90102
90109
90153
90215
90261
90356
90518
90621
90688

Nov-51
30756 x
32056 x
40677
43208
43747 x
44032
44098
44248
44568
46683
47531
49047
49132
49193 x
49254
49302 x
49304
49433
55174
58420 x
64773
64810
65025 x
65439 x
67494
68102
68112
68144
68251
68383
68546
68793
69816
90100
90123
90232
90309
90576
90760

Dec-51
1150
30282
30463 x
30691
31513
31755
32045 x
32052 x
32055 x
32060 x
32160 x
32306 x
32691 x
40364
43799
49051
49441
50736 x
52353 x
55236
58248 x
62795
64158 x
68172 x
68272
68438
68808
69378
90096
90183
90268
90410
90413
90627
90686
90765

1952
30042
30087
30088
30093
30162
31064
31065
31191
31276
31558
31574
31711
31718
32418
32485
32560
43731
62620
63647
63913
64642
65565
67606
68110
68494
68664
69143
69707
90619

Jan-52
31480
40539
43750
43904
44335
47491
48926
49437
56011
58333 x
62783
65727
68328
68579
69427
69451
90284
90312
90352
90687

Feb-52
31229
44457
47246
49068
49171 x
56029
56164
58143
65117
68147 x
68186 x
68795
69424
90105
90110
90113
90179
90205
90295

Mar-52
30148 x
30157 x
32408
40493
41878
44003
47381
49061
58335 x
58340 x
58346 x
65343
65382 x
65554
68158
68174
68239
68380 x
69313
69314
69429
90327
90335
90355

Apr-52
43622
47597
49265 x
50807
52123
58360 x
61423
65331
68974
90326

May-52
44245
47191
52203
52293
58350 x
68142
68405
68504
68788

Jun-52
30170 x
30172 x
30411 x
30437 x
48951
50735 x
50892 x
58327 x
58913 x
58932 x
64117 x
67488
69273
90135
90366

Jul-52
43301
43514
43820 x
46899 x
49129
49270
58114
58167
58418 x
62360
68145
68514
90173

Aug-52
48278
48745
58171
64140
90565
90770

Sep-52
43332
43436
47496
47625
48921
49010
65213
68138
68979
90764

Oct-52
31673 x
31708 x
32573
40407
48510
49199
62372
64114 x
90315

Nov-52
47419
49108
49116
56039
58421 x
68108
68136
90343
90563

Dec-52
32133 x
49330
49385
58147 x
67471 x
68157 x
68845 R

Jan-53
43253
58067 x
58419 x
65297
67500
68249 x
90271

Feb-53
31491 x
44436
48310
49277
52269
58050 x
58330 x

Mar-53
41911 x
47407
68178 R

Apr-53
30224
48602
69271

May-53
49275
68130 R
68168 R
68173 R
68177 R

Jun-53
58206
68619

Jul-53
43662 x
49417
62395

Aug-53
32650
43749
68131 R
68149
68161 x
68176 x

Sep-53
47377

Oct-53
68154 x

Dec-53
47423
50725
68137 x
68525 x

Feb-54
31493 x
68124

Apr-54
40682
68109 x

May-54
68096 x
68143 x

Jun-54
68103 x

Jul-54
68091 R

Sep-54
51537

Nov-54
67465 x
67470 x

Dec-54
67461 x

Apr-56
68568

Appendix 9. Ex-LNER Locomotives 1946 renumbering scheme.

* Temporary intermediate numbers carried from 1942 onwards.

Listed in BR number order	
60001	4500
60002	4499
60003	4494
60004	4462
60005	4901
60006	605*
	4466
60007	4498
60008	4496
60009	4488
60010	4489
60011	4490
60012	4491
60013	4492
60014	2509
60015	2510
60016	2511
60017	2512
60018	4463
60019	4464
60020	4465
60021	4467
60022	4468
60023	4482
60024	585*
	4483
60025	586*
	4484
60026	587*
	4485
60027	588*
	4486
60028	4487
60029	4493
60030	4495
60031	4497
60032	4900
60033	4902
60034	4903
60035	570*
	2500
60036	2501
60037	2502
60038	2503
60039	2504
60040	575*
	2505
60041	2506
60042	2507
60043	2508
60044	2543
60045	2544
60046	2545
60047	2546
60048	2547
60049	517*
	2548
60050	518*
	2549
60051	2550
60052	520*
	2551
60053	521*
	2552
60054	522*
	2553
60055	2554
60056	2555
60057	2556
60058	2557
60059	2558
60060	528*
	2559
60061	2560
60062	2561
60063	531*
	2562
60064	2563
60065	2564
60066	2565
60067	2566
60068	2567
60069	537*
	2568
60070	538*
	2569
60071	2570
60072	2571
60073	2572
60074	542*
	2573
60075	2574
60076	2575
60077	545*
	2576
60078	2577
60079	2578
60080	2579
60081	2580
60082	2581
60083	2582
60084	2595
60085	2596
60086	2597
60087	565*
	2598
60088	2599
60089	2743
60090	2744
60091	2745
60092	2746
60093	2747
60094	2748
60095	558*
	2749
60096	2750
60097	2751
60098	561*
	2752
60099	2795
60100	2796
60101	2797
60102	4471
60103	502*
	4472
60104	4473
60105	4474
60106	4475
60107	4476
60108	507*
	4477
60109	508*
	4478
60110	4479
60111	4480
60112	511*
	4481
60113	4470
60501	2001
60502	2002
60503	2003
60504	2004
60505	994*
	2005
60506	2006
60507	3696
60508	3697
60509	3698
60510	3699
60700	10000
60800	4771
60801	701*
	4772
60802	4773
60803	4774
60804	4775
60805	4776
60806	4777
60807	4778
60808	4779
60809	709*
	4780
60810	710*
	4781
60811	711*
	4782
60812	4783
60813	4784
60814	714*
	4785
60815	4786
60816	4787
60817	4788
60818	718*
	4789
60819	719*
	4790
60820	720*
	4791
60821	721*
	4792
60822	722*
	4793
60823	4794
60824	4795
60825	4796
60826	4797
60827	4798
60828	4799
60829	4800
60830	4801
60831	4802
60832	4803
60833	733*
	4804
60834	4805
60835	4806
60836	4807
60837	4808
60838	4809
60839	4810
60840	4811
60841	4812
60842	4813
60843	4814
60844	4815
60845	4816
60846	4817
60847	4818
60848	4819
60849	4820
60850	750*
	4821
60851	4822
60852	4823
60853	4824
60854	4825
60855	4826
60856	4827
60857	4828
60858	4829
60859	4830
60860	4831
60861	4832
60862	762*
	4833
60863	4834
60864	4835
60865	4836
60866	4837
60867	4838
60868	4839
60869	4840
60870	4841
60871	771*
	4842
60872	4843
60873	4844
60874	4845
60875	775*
	4846
60876	4847
60877	4848
60878	4849
60879	779*
	4850
60880	4851
60881	4852
60882	4853
60883	4854
60884	4855
60885	4856
60886	4857
60887	4858
60888	4859
60889	4860
60890	4861
60891	4862
60892	4863
60893	4864
60894	4865
60895	4866
60896	4867
60897	4868
60898	4869
60899	4870
60900	4871
60901	4872
60902	4873
60903	4874
60904	4875
60905	805*
	4876
60906	4877
60907	4878
60908	4879
60909	809*
	4880
60910	4881
60911	4882
60912	4883
60913	4884
60914	4885
60915	4886
60916	4887
60917	4888
60918	4889
60919	4890
60920	4891
60921	4892
60922	4893
60923	4894
60924	4895
60925	4896
60926	4897
60927	4898
60928	3655
60929	3656
60930	3657
60931	3658
60932	3659
60933	3660
60934	3661
60935	3662
60936	3663
60937	3664
60938	4899
60939	3641
60940	3642
60941	3643
60942	3644
60943	3645
60944	3646
60945	3647
60946	3648
60947	3649
60948	3650
60949	3651
60950	3652
60951	3653
60952	3654
60953	3665
60954	3666
60955	3667
60956	3668
60957	3669
60958	3670
60959	3671
60960	3672
60961	3673
60962	3674
60963	3675
60964	3676
60965	3677
60966	3678
60967	3679
60968	3680
60969	3681
60970	3682
60971	871*
	3683
60972	3684
60973	3685
60974	3686
60975	3687
60976	3688
60977	3689
60978	3690
60979	3691
60980	3692
60981	3693
60982	3694
60983	3695
61000	8301
61001	8302
61002	8303
61003	8304
61004	8305
61005	8306
61006	8307
61007	8308
61008	8309
61009	8310
61353	5442
61354	5443
61355	5444
61357	5446
61358	5279
61360	5072
61361	5073
61362	5078
61363	5036
61364	5037
61365	5038
61366	5458
61367	5459
61368	5460
61369	5461
61370	5462
61371	5463
61372	5464
61373	5465
61374	5466
61375	5467
61376	5468
61377	5469
61378	5470
61379	5471
61380	5472
61381	5473
61382	5474
61383	5031
61384	5032
61385	5033
61386	5034
61387	5035
61388	5475
61389	5476
61390	5477
61391	5478
61392	5479
61393	5480
61394	5481
61395	5482
61396	5483
61397	5484
61400	840
61401	841
61402	842
61403	843
61404	844
61405	845
61406	846
61407	847
61408	848
61409	849
61410	906
61411	908
61412	909
61413	911
61414	914
61415	915
61416	920
61417	921
61418	922
61419	923
61420	924
61421	926
61422	927
61423	928
61424	929
61425	930
61426	931
61427	932
61428	933
61429	934
61430	936
61431	937
61432	942
61433	943
61434	2363
61435	2364
61436	2365
61437	2366
61438	2367
61439	2368
61440	2369
61441	2370
61442	2371
61443	2372
61444	2373
61445	2374
61446	2375
61447	2376
61448	2377
61449	2378
61450	2379
61451	2380
61452	2381
61453	2382
61454	1371
61455	1372
61456	1373
61457	1374
61458	1375
61459	1376
61460	1377
61461	1378
61462	1379
61463	1380
61464	1381
61465	1382
61466	1383
61467	1384
61468	1385
61469	6105
61470	6106
61475	6111
61476	6112
61482	6097
61483	6098
61485	6100
61488	6103
61497	6166
61500	8500
61501	8501
61502	8502
61503	8503
61504	8504
61505	8505
61507	8507
61508	8508
61509	8509
61510	8510
61511	8511
61512	8512
61513	8513
61514	8514
61515	8515
61516	8516
61517	8517
61519	8519
61520	8520
61521	8521
61523	7437*
	8523
61524	8524
61525	8525
61526	8526
61528	8528
61529	8529
61530	8530
61532	8532
61533	8533
61535	7449*
	8535
61536	8536
61537	8537
61538	8538
61539	8539
61540	8540
61541	8541
61542	8542
61543	8543
61545	8545
61546	8546
61547	8547
61549	8549
61550	8550
61552	8552
61553	7467*
	8553
61554	8554
61555	8555
61556	7470*
	8556
61557	8557
61558	7472*
	8558
61559	8559
61560	8560
61561	8561
61562	7476*
	8562
61563	8563
61564	8564
61565	7479*
	8565
61566	8566
61567	8567
61568	7482*
	8568
61569	8569
61570	8570
61571	8571
61572	8572
61573	8573
61574	7488*
	8574
61575	8575
61576	8576
61577	7491*
	8577
61578	8578
61579	8579
61580	8580
61600	2800
61601	2801
61602	2802
61603	2803
61604	2804
61605	2805
61606	2806
61607	2807
61608	2808
61609	2809
61610	2810
61611	2811
61612	2812
61613	2813
61614	2814
61615	2815
61616	2816
61617	2817
61618	2818
61619	2819
61620	2820
61621	2821
61622	2822
61623	2823
61624	2824
61625	2825
61626	2826
61627	2827
61628	2828
61629	2829
61630	2830
61631	2831
61632	2832
61633	2833
61634	2834
61635	2835
61636	2836
61637	2837
61638	2838
61639	2839
61640	2840
61641	2841
61642	2842
61643	2843
61644	2844
61645	2845
61646	2846
61647	2847
61648	2848
61649	2849
61650	2850
61651	2851
61652	2852
61653	2853
61654	2854
61655	2855
61656	2856
61657	2857
61658	2858
61659	2859
61660	2860
61661	2861
61662	2862
61663	2863
61664	2864
61665	2865
61666	2866
61667	2867
61668	2868
61669	2869
61670	2870
61671	2871
61672	2872
61680	6069
61681	6071
61685	5182
61686	5183
61688	5185
61689	1311*
	5186
61690	1312*
	5187
61699	761
61700	3401
61701	3402
61720	4630
61721	4631
61722	4632
61723	4633
61724	4634
61725	4635
61726	4636
61727	4637
61728	4638
61729	4639
61730	4640
61731	4641
61732	4642
61733	4643
61734	4644
61735	4645
61736	4646
61737	4647
61738	4648
61739	4649
61740	4650
61741	4651
61742	4652
61743	4653
61744	4654
61745	4655
61746	4656
61747	4657
61748	4658
61749	4659
61750	4660
61751	4661
61752	4662
61753	4663
61754	4664
61755	4665
61756	4666
61757	4667
61758	4668
61759	4669
61760	4670
61761	4671
61762	4672
61763	4673
61764	4674
61765	4675
61766	4676
61767	4677
61768	4678
61769	4679
61770	4680
61771	4681
61772	4682
61773	4683
61774	4684
61775	4685
61776	4686
61777	4687
61778	4688
61779	4689
61780	4690
61781	4691
61782	4692
61783	4693
61784	4694
61785	4695
61786	4696
61787	4697
61788	4698
61789	4699
61790	4700
61791	4701
61792	4702
61793	4703
61794	4704
61800	4000
61801	4001
61802	4002
61803	4003
61804	4004
61805	4005
61806	4006
61807	4007
61808	4008
61809	4009
61810	17
61811	28
61812	32
61813	33
61814	36
61815	38
61816	39
61817	46
61818	52
61819	53
61820	58
61821	69
61822	73
61823	75
61824	80
61825	91
61826	92
61827	109
61828	111
61829	112
61830	113
61831	114
61832	116
61833	118
61834	120
61835	121
61836	125
61837	126
61838	127
61839	134
61840	135
61841	140
61842	141
61843	143
61844	146
61845	153
61846	156
61847	158
61848	159
61849	163
61850	167
61851	170
61852	178
61853	180
61854	184
61855	186
61856	188
61857	191
61858	195
61859	200
61860	203
61861	202
61862	204
61863	206
61864	207
61865	208
61866	227
61867	228
61868	229
61869	231
61870	1300
61871	1312
61872	1318
61873	1331
61874	1345
61875	1364
61876	1365
61877	1367
61878	1368
61879	1386
61880	1387
61881	1388
61882	1389
61883	1391
61884	1392
61885	1394
61886	1395
61887	1396
61888	1397
61889	1398
61890	2761
61891	2762
61892	2763
61893	2764
61894	2765
61895	2766
61896	2767
61897	2768
61898	2769
61899	1100
61900	1101
61901	1102
61902	1106
61903	1108
61904	1117
61905	1118
61906	1119
61907	1121
61908	1125
61909	1133
61910	1135
61911	1137
61912	1141
61913	1154
61914	1156
61915	1158
61916	1162
61917	1164
61918	1166
61919	1302
61920	1304
61921	1308
61922	1310
61923	1324
61924	1306
61925	2934
61926	2935
61927	2936
61928	2937
61929	1325
61930	1332
61931	1333
61932	1339
61933	1399
61934	1307
61935	1322
61936	2938
61937	2939
61938	2940
61939	2425
61940	2426
61941	2427
61942	2428
61943	2438
61944	2439
61945	2440
61946	2442
61947	2443
61948	2447
61949	2448
61950	2449
61951	2450
61952	2451
61953	2459
61954	2461
61955	2463
61956	2466
61957	2467
61958	2468
61959	2417
61960	2429
61961	2445
61962	2446
61963	2453
61964	2455
61965	2458
61966	2465
61967	2471
61968	2472
61969	2470
61970	2473
61971	2498
61972	2499
61973	3813
61974	3814
61975	3815
61976	3816
61977	3817
61978	3818
61979	3819
61980	3820
61981	3821
61982	3822
61983	3823
61984	3824
61985	3825
61986	3826
61987	3827
61988	3828
61989	3829
61990	3830
61991	3831
61992	3832
61993	3441
61994	3442
61995	3443
61996	3444
61997	3445
61998	3446
62000	1*
	4075
62059	9635
62060	9642
62062	9404
62064	9731
62065	9732
62066	9733
62072	9768
62111	1873
62112	1902
62116	4071
62122	4302
62123	4303
62124	4306
62125	4307
62126	4309
62128	4311
62131	4316
62132	4317
62133	4318
62135	4343
62137	4345
62139	4347
62140	4348
62143	4351
62144	4352
62145	4355
62148	4359
62150	4305
62151	4320
62152	4321
62153	4323
62154	4324
62155	4326
62156	4327
62157	4329
62160	4332
62161	4333
62163	4337
62165	4339
62167	4361
62169	4365
62172	4369
62173	4370
62175	4373
62177	4377
62179	4380
62180	4381
62181	4383
62187	4392
62188	4393
62189	4394
62190	4395
62193	4180
62194	3041
62195	3042
62197	3045
62198	3047
62199	3048
62203	3052
62205	3054
62207	3056
62208	3057
62209	3058
62214	3063
62215	3064
62225	6878
62227	6880
62228	6881
62229	6882
62230	6883
62231	6819
62232	6820
62234	6822
62235	6823
62238	6894
62240	6896
62241	6897
62242	6898
62243	6899
62246	6902
62247	6903
62248	6904
62249	6905
62251	6907
62252	6908
62255	6911
62256	6912
62260	6825
62261	6826
62262	6913
62264	6915
62265	6827
62267	6829
62268	6831
62269	6833
62270	6834
62271	6835
62272	6836
62273	6845
62274	6846
62275	6847
62276	6848
62277	6849
62278	6850
62279	6852
62300	6013
62301	6014
62302	6015
62303	6016
62304	6017
62305	6018
62306	6019
62307	6021
62308	6023
62309	6024
62311	6026
62312	6027
62313	6029
62314	6030
62315	6031
62317	6033
62318	6034
62319	6035
62321	6037
62322	6038
62324	6040
62325	6041
62329	5107
62330	5108
62332	5111
62333	5112
62340	2011
62341	2012
62342	2013
62343	2014
62344	2015
62345	2016
62347	2018
62348	2019
62349	2020
62351	2022
62352	2023
62353	2024
62354	2025
62355	2026
62357	2028
62358	2029
62359	2030
62360	2101
62361	2102
62362	2103
62363	2104
62365	2106
62366	2107
62367	2108
62369	2110
62370	476
62371	592
62372	707
62373	708
62374	711
62375	712
62376	713
62377	723
62378	724
62379	725
62380	1026
62381	1042
62382	1051
62383	1078
62384	1184
62386	1207
62387	1209
62388	1210
62389	1217
62390	1223
62391	1232
62392	1235
62395	1260
62396	1665
62397	1672
62400	9895
62401	9896
62402	9897
62403	9898
62404	9899
62405	9900
62406	9243
62409	9338
62410	9339
62411	9340
62412	9359
62413	9360
62417	9363
62418	9409
62419	9410
62420	9411
62421	9412
62422	9413
62423	9414
62424	9415
62425	9416
62426	9417
62427	9418
62428	9419
62429	9420
62430	9421
62431	9422
62432	9423
62434	9425
62435	9426
62436	9427
62437	9428
62438	9497
62439	9498
62440	9499
62441	9500
62442	9501
62443	9882
62444	9883
62445	9884
62446	9885
62448	9887
62449	9888
62450	9889
62451	9890
62453	9892
62454	9893
62455	9864
62457	9866
62458	9867
62459	9894
62460	9331
62461	9332
62462	9333
62463	9382
62464	9383
62466	9385
62467	9149
62468	9221
62469	9256
62470	9258
62471	9266
62472	9307
62473	9405
62474	9406
62475	9407
62476	9408
62477	9100
62478	9291
62479	9298
62480	9153
62481	9241
62482	9242
62483	9270
62484	9278
62485	9281
62487	9503
62488	9504
62489	9490
62490	9502
62492	9034
62493	9035
62494	9492
62495	9493
62496	9494
62497	9495
62498	9496
62501	8890
62502	8891
62503	8892
62504	8893
62505	7764*
	8894
62506	8895
62507	8896
62508	8897
62509	8898
62510	8899
62511	8880
62512	8881
62513	8882
62514	8883
62515	8884
62516	8885
62517	8886
62518	8887
62519	8888
62520	8889
62521	7740*
	8870
62522	8871
62523	8872
62524	8873
62525	8874
62526	8875
62527	8876
62528	8877
62529	8878
62530	8879
62531	8860
62532	8861
62533	8862
62534	8863
62535	8864
62536	8865
62538	8867
62539	8868
62540	8869
62541	8850
62542	8851
62543	8852
62544	8853
62545	8854
62546	8855
62547	8856
62548	7727*
	8857
62549	7728*
	8858
62551	8840
62552	8841
62553	7712*
	8842
62554	8843
62555	8844
62556	8845
62557	8846
62558	8847
62559	8848
62560	8849
62561	8830
62562	8831
62563	8832
62564	8833
62565	8834
62566	8835
62567	8836
62568	7707*
	8837
62569	7708*
	8838
62570	8839

62571	8820
62572	8821
62573	7692*
	8822
62574	8823
62575	8824
62576	7695*
	8825
62577	8826
62578	8827
62579	8828
62580	8829
62581	8810
62582	8811
62583	8812
62584	8813
62585	8814
62586	8815
62587	8816
62588	8817
62589	8818
62590	8819
62591	8800
62592	8801
62593	8802
62594	8803
62596	8805
62597	8806
62598	8807
62599	8808
62600	8809
62601	8790
62602	8791
62603	8792
62604	8793
62605	8794
62606	8795
62607	8796
62608	8797
62609	8798
62610	8799
62611	8780
62612	8781
62613	8782
62614	8783
62615	8784
62616	8785
62617	8786
62618	8787
62619	8788
62620	8789
62650	5429
62651	5430
62652	5431
62653	5432
62654	5433
62655	5434
62656	5435
62657	5436
62658	5437
62659	5438
62660	5506
62661	5507
62662	5508
62663	5509
62664	5510
62665	5501
62666	5502
62667	5503
62668	5504
62669	5505
62670	5511
62671	6378
62672	6379
62673	6380
62674	6381
62675	6382
62676	6383
62677	6384
62678	6385
62679	6386
62680	6387
62681	6388
62682	6389
62683	6390
62684	6391
62685	6392
62686	6393
62687	6394
62688	6395
62689	6396
62690	6397
62691	6398
62692	6399
62693	6400
62694	6401
62700	234
62701	251
62702	253
62703	256
62704	264
62705	265
62706	266
62707	236
62708	270
62709	277
62710	245
62711	281
62712	246
62713	249
62714	250
62715	306
62716	307
62717	309
62718	310
62719	311
62720	318
62721	320
62722	322
62723	327
62724	335
62725	329
62726	352
62727	336
62728	2753
62729	2754
62730	2755
62731	2756
62732	2757
62733	2758
62734	2759
62735	2760
62736	201
62737	211
62738	220
62739	232
62740	235
62741	247
62742	255
62743	269
62744	273
62745	282
62746	283
62747	288
62748	292
62749	297
62750	298
62751	205
62752	214
62753	217
62754	222
62755	226
62756	230
62757	238
62758	258
62759	274
62760	279
62761	353
62762	357
62763	359
62764	361
62765	362
62766	363
62767	364
62768	365
62769	366
62770	368
62771	370
62772	374
62773	375
62774	376
62775	377
62780	7797*
	7427
62781	7463
62782	7466
62783	7477
62784	7478
62785	7802*
	7490
62786	7492
62787	7494
62788	7805*
	7496
62789	7497
62790	7503
62791	7506
62792	7791*
	7407
62793	7408
62794	7409
62795	7794*
	7411
62796	7414
62797	7416
62808	3279
62810	3281
62817	3288
62821	3293
62822	3294
62828	3300
62829	3301
62839	4409
62849	4419
62854	4424
62870	4440
62871	4441
62875	4445
62876	4446
62877	4447
62881	4451
62885	4455
62900	5192
62901	5194
62902	5263
62903	5264
62908	6084
62909	6085
62910	6086
62912	6088
62914	6091
62915	6092
62916	6093
62917	6094
62918	5260
62919	5261
62920	5262
62921	5358
62922	5360
62923	5361
62924	5362
62925	5363
62933	742
62937	1792
62954	716
62970	2164
62972	2166
62973	2167
62975	2169
62978	2193
62981	2196
62982	2197
62983	2198
62988	2203
62989	2204
62992	2207
62993	2208
62995	2210
63000	77009
63001	77002
63002	77021
63003	77300
63004	77033
63005	77046
63006	77316
63007	77318
63008	77322
63009	77336
63010	77339
63011	77343
63012	77211
63013	77213
63014	77220
63015	77354
63016	77357
63017	77360
63018	77363
63019	77367
63020	77223
63021	77233
63022	77236
63023	77369
63024	77370
63025	77373
63026	77382
63027	77243
63028	77250
63029	77251
63030	77254
63031	77385
63032	77391
63033	77397
63034	77410
63035	77412
63036	77420
63037	77422
63038	77423
63039	77427
63040	77430
63041	77435
63042	77437
63043	77448
63044	70800
63045	70804
63046	70810
63047	70813
63048	70815
63049	70816
63050	70818
63051	70821
63052	70822
63053	70823
63054	70824
63055	70826
63056	70827
63057	70828
63058	70830
63059	70831
63060	70832
63061	70837
63062	70840
63063	70841
63064	70842
63065	70844
63066	70846
63067	70847
63068	70848
63069	70854
63070	77265
63071	70852
63072	70858
63073	70870
63074	70872
63075	77272
63076	77276
63077	77277
63078	77279
63079	77281
63080	77284
63081	77290
63082	77298
63083	78513
63084	78515
63085	78516
63086	78520
63087	78562
63088	78565
63089	78527
63090	78528
63091	78570
63092	78577
63093	78582
63094	78584
63095	78591
63096	78603
63097	78608
63098	78534
63099	78540
63100	78550
63101	77083
63102	77091
63103	77093
63104	77100
63105	77110
63106	77112
63107	77113
63108	77131
63109	77133
63110	77136
63111	77146
63112	77473
63113	77474
63114	77486
63115	77487
63116	77491
63117	77493
63118	77496
63119	77498
63120	77501
63121	77502
63122	77504
63123	77505
63124	77506
63125	77507
63126	78625
63127	78627
63128	78628
63129	78630
63130	78633
63131	78634
63132	78635
63133	78639
63134	78641
63135	78642
63136	78645
63137	78646
63138	78648
63139	78649
63140	78651
63141	78653
63142	78654
63143	78655
63144	78656
63145	78661
63146	78662
63147	78663
63148	78664
63149	78665
63150	78667
63151	78668
63152	78670
63153	78673
63154	78674
63155	78676
63156	78677
63157	78679
63158	78680
63159	78686
63160	78687
63161	78690
63162	78691
63163	78692
63164	78696
63165	78697
63166	78698
63167	78699
63168	78702
63169	78703
63170	78706
63171	78707
63172	78708
63173	78709
63174	78710
63175	78711
63176	78712
63177	78713
63178	78716
63179	78718
63180	79177
63181	79180
63182	79185
63183	79187
63184	79191
63185	79192
63186	79200
63187	79211
63188	79216
63189	79236
63190	79240
63191	79241
63192	79245
63193	79247
63194	79251
63195	79253
63196	79285
63197	79288
63198	79305
63199	79308
63200	6052
63201	6054
63202	5056
63203	5057
63204	5059
63205	5064
63206	5065
63207	5067
63210	5085
63212	5092
63213	5136
63214	5137
63216	5142
63217	5146
63219	5152
63220	5153
63221	6076
63223	6132
63224	6133
63225	6134
63226	6135
63227	6136
63228	6140
63229	5039
63231	5159
63232	5160
63233	5161
63234	5162
63235	5163
63236	5164
63238	5962
63240	6176
63241	6177
63243	6180
63250	2116
63251	2117
63252	2118
63253	2119
63254	2120
63255	2121
63256	2122
63257	2123
63259	2125
63260	130
63261	527
63262	1002
63263	1320
63264	1700
63267	1709
63268	1717
63270	1682
63271	1684
63272	1685
63273	1694
63274	83
63275	162
63276	1696
63277	410
63278	474
63279	1186
63280	650
63281	651
63282	1009
63283	1731
63284	1757
63285	715
63286	785
63287	792
63289	1218
63290	1110
63291	1669
63292	411
63293	430
63294	443
63295	444
63296	1111
63297	1149
63298	1150
63299	1173
63300	578
63301	660
63303	1031
63305	1054
63306	1062
63307	1177
63308	1178
63310	644
63311	645
63312	646
63313	647
63314	648
63315	652
63316	653
63317	654
63318	655
63319	656
63321	643
63322	657
63323	658
63326	669
63327	764
63328	767
63330	770
63331	771
63332	772
63333	773
63334	774
63335	781
63336	783
63338	793
63339	794
63340	1247
63341	1248
63342	1249
63343	1250
63344	1251
63345	1252
63346	1253
63347	1254
63348	1257
63349	1261
63350	1262
63351	1264
63352	1271
63353	1276
63354	1278
63355	1279
63356	1280
63357	1283
63358	1284
63359	1285
63360	1288
63361	1291
63362	1292
63363	1293
63364	1294
63365	1311
63366	1335
63367	1361
63368	1362
63369	1363
63370	2213
63371	2214
63372	2215
63373	2216
63374	2217
63375	2218
63376	2219
63377	2220
63378	2221
63379	2222
63380	2223
63381	2224
63382	2225
63383	2226
63384	2227
63385	2228
63386	2229
63387	2230
63388	2231
63389	2232
63390	2233
63391	2234
63392	2235
63393	2236
63394	2237
63395	2238
63396	2239
63397	2240
63398	2241
63399	2242
63400	2243
63401	2244
63402	2245
63403	2246
63404	2247
63405	2248
63406	2249
63407	2250
63408	2251
63409	2252
63410	2253
63411	2254
63412	2255
63413	2256
63414	2257
63415	2258
63416	2259
63417	2260
63418	2261
63419	2262
63420	2263
63421	2264
63422	2265
63423	2266
63424	2267
63425	2268
63426	2269
63427	2270
63428	2271
63429	2272
63430	2273
63431	2274
63432	2275
63433	2276
63434	2277
63435	2278
63436	2279
63437	2280
63438	2281
63439	2282
63440	2283
63441	2284
63442	2285
63443	2286
63444	2287
63445	2288
63446	2289
63447	2290
63448	2291
63449	2292
63450	2293
63451	2294
63452	2295
63453	2296
63454	2297
63455	2298
63456	2299
63457	2300
63458	2301
63459	2302
63460	901
63461	902
63462	903
63463	904
63464	905
63465	624
63466	625
63467	626
63468	628
63469	629
63470	630
63471	631
63472	632
63473	633
63474	634
63475	3456
63476	3457
63477	3458
63478	3459
63479	3460
63480	3462
63481	3463
63482	3464
63483	3465
63484	3466
63485	3467
63486	3468
63488	3470
63489	3471
63491	3473
63493	3475
63494	3476
63554	3154*
63570	6223
63571	6224
63572	3500*
	5966
63573	6226
63574	6227
63575	6228
63576	6229
63577	3501*
	5026
63578	6231
63579	6232
63580	3502*
	5069
63581	6234
63582	3503*
	5093
63583	6236
63584	6237
63585	3504*
	5331
63586	3505*
	5332
63587	6240
63588	6241
63589	6242
63590	6243
63591	6244
63592	6245
63593	6246
63594	3506*
	5333
63595	6248
63596	6249
63597	6250
63598	3507*
	5334
63599	6252
63600	3508*
	5335
63601	3509*
	5102
63602	5377
63603	5378
63604	5379
63605	5380
63606	5381
63607	3510*
	5133
63608	3511*
	5155
63609	5384
63610	5385
63611	5386
63612	5387
63613	5388
63614	5389
63615	5390
63616	5391
63617	3513*
	5347
63618	5393
63619	5394
63620	5395
63621	5396
63622	5397
63623	5398
63624	5399
63625	3514*
	5348
63626	5001
63627	5005
63628	5008
63629	6554
63630	6555
63631	6556
63632	3515*
	5349
63633	6536
63634	3516*
	5350
63635	3517*
	5351
63636	6376
63637	6558
63638	6375
63639	6559
63640	3518*
	5352
63641	6561
63642	6538
63643	3519*
	5353
63644	6543
63645	6366
63646	6374
63647	6544
63648	6372
63649	6365
63650	6545
63651	6539
63652	6371
63653	6370
63654	3521*
	5355
63655	6364
63656	6363
63657	6546
63658	3522*
	5400
63659	6360
63660	3524*
	5403
63661	6540
63662	6358
63663	6359
63664	3525*
	5404
63665	6357
63666	6542
63667	6367
63668	6361
63669	3526*
	5405
63670	6356
63671	3527*
	5406
63672	6354
63673	6352
63674	6351
63675	6353
63676	6350
63677	3528*
	5407
63678	3529*
	5408
63679	6325
63680	3531*
	6184
63681	6347
63682	6548
63683	3533*
	6186
63684	3534*
	6187
63685	6344
63686	6495
63687	6324
63688	6343
63689	6341
63690	3535*
	6188
63691	6342
63692	3536*
	6189
63693	3537*
	6190
63694	6349
63695	6496
63696	6323
63697	6338
63698	3538*
	6191
63699	6337
63700	3539*
	6192
63701	6498
63702	6321
63703	6336
63704	6550
63705	6320
63706	6319
63707	3540*
	6193
63708	6318
63709	6552
63710	3541*
	6194
63711	3542*
	6195
63712	6334
63713	6553
63714	6316
63715	6333
63716	6310
63717	6314
63718	6313
63719	3545*
	6198
63720	6311
63721	6331
63722	3546*
	6199
63723	3547*
	6200
63724	6329
63725	6328
63726	6500
63727	3548*
	6201
63728	6308
63729	6309
63730	6326
63731	6307
63732	6501
63733	6502
63734	6503
63735	6562
63736	3550*
	6203
63737	6564
63738	3552*
	6205
63739	6285
63740	6566
63741	6567
63742	6568
63743	3553*
	6206
63744	6284
63745	3554*
	6207
63746	6571
63747	6572
63748	6258
63749	6573
63750	6278
63751	6574
63752	6575
63753	6576
63754	6577
63755	6578
63756	6255
63757	3555*
	6208
63758	6276
63759	6282
63760	6579
63761	3556*
	6209
63762	3557*
	6210
63763	6272
63764	6581
63765	6271
63766	6582
63767	6274
63768	6513
63769	6583
63770	6584
63771	6270
63772	3558*
	6211
63773	3560*
	6213
63774	6268
63775	6586
63776	6267
63777	3561*
	6214
63778	3562*
	6215
63779	6588
63780	6505
63781	6269
63782	6506
63783	6589
63784	6507
63785	6590
63786	6515
63787	6591
63788	6592
63789	3563*
	6216
63790	6594
63791	6510
63792	6283
63793	6280
63794	6277
63795	6595
63796	6596
63797	3565*
	6218
63798	6275
63799	3566*
	6219
63800	6511
63801	6598
63802	6281
63803	3567*
	6220
63804	6512
63805	3568*
	6221
63806	6601
63807	6518
63808	6519
63809	3569*
	6222
63812	6265
63813	6604
63816	6606
63817	6263
63818	6264
63819	6262
63821	6521
63822	6259
63823	6608
63824	6516
63827	6306
63828	6609
63829	6304
63832	6303
63833	6531
63835	6611
63836	6522
63837	6523
63838	6261
63839	6305
63840	6524
63841	6302
63842	6257
63843	6612
63845	6614
63846	6256
63847	6290
63848	6291
63849	6615
63850	6294
63851	6299
63852	6289
63853	6292
63854	6526
63855	6616
63856	6617
63857	6618
63858	6619
63859	6620
63860	6621
63861	6622
63862	6532
63863	6533
63864	6534
63865	6535
63867	6624
63868	6625
63869	6626
63870	6627
63872	6525
63873	6629
63874	6630
63876	6528
63877	6529
63878	6631
63879	6288
63880	6286
63881	6632
63882	6287
63883	6298
63884	6633
63885	6634
63886	6635
63887	6636
63888	6637
63889	6638
63890	6639
63891	6295
63893	6293
63894	6300
63895	6296
63897	6254
63898	6253
63899	6640
63900	6641
63901	6642
63902	5412
63904	5414
63905	5415
63906	5417
63907	5418
63908	5419
63911	5422
63912	5010
63913	5011
63914	5012
63915	5013
63917	5015
63920	5022
63921	3461
63922	3477
63923	3478
63924	3479
63925	3480
63926	3481
63927	3482
63928	3483
63929	3484
63930	3485
63931	3486
63932	3487
63933	3488
63934	3489
63935	3490
63936	3491
63937	3492
63938	3493
63939	3494
63940	3495
63941	3496
63942	3497
63943	3498
63944	3499
63945	3500
63946	3501
63947	2954
63948	2955
63949	2956
63950	2957
63951	2958
63952	2959
63953	2960
63954	2961
63955	2430
63956	2431
63957	2432
63958	2433
63959	2434
63960	2435
63961	2436
63962	2437
63963	3833
63964	3834
63965	3835
63966	3836
63967	3837
63968	3838
63969	3839
63970	3840
63971	3841
63972	3842
63973	3843
63974	3844
63975	3845
63976	3846
63977	3847
63978	3848
63979	3849
63980	3850
63981	3851
63982	3852
63983	3853
63984	3854
63985	3855
63986	3856
63987	3857
64105	3313
64106	4035
64107	4036
64109	4040
64110	4041
64112	4090
64114	4093
64115	4094
64116	4097
64117	4100
64118	4103
64119	4105
64120	4106
64121	4107
64122	4109
64123	4113
64124	4114
64125	4125
64127	4129
64128	4131
64129	4133
64131	3329
64132	3331
64133	3332
64135	3345
64136	3350
64137	3375
64140	3306
64141	3387
64142	3388
64145	4137
64148	4146
64150	4153
64151	4160
64152	4162
64153	4166
64158	083
64160	085
64162	087
64163	088
64167	092
64170	3521
64171	3522
64172	3523
64173	3524
64174	3525
64175	3526
64176	3527
64177	3528
64178	3529
64179	3530
64180	3531
64181	3532
64182	3533
64183	3534
64184	3535
64185	3536
64186	3537
64187	3538
64188	3539
64189	3540
64190	3541
64191	3542
64192	3543
64193	3544
64194	3545
64195	3546
64196	3547
64197	3548
64198	3549
64199	3550
64200	3551
64201	3552
64202	3553
64203	3554
64204	3555
64205	3556
64206	3557
64207	3558
64208	3559
64209	3560
64210	3561
64211	3562
64212	3563
64213	3564
64214	3565
64215	3566
64216	3567
64217	3568
64218	3569
64219	3570
64220	3571
64221	3572
64222	3573
64223	3574
64224	3575
64225	3576
64226	3577
64227	3578
64228	3579
64229	3580
64230	3581
64231	3582
64232	3583
64233	3584
64234	3585
64235	3586
64236	3587
64237	3588
64238	3589
64239	3590
64240	3591
64241	3592
64242	3593
64243	3594
64244	3595
64245	3596
64246	3597
64247	3598
64248	3599
64249	3600
64250	3601
64251	3602
64252	3603
64253	3604
64254	3605
64255	3606
64256	3607
64257	3608
64258	3609
64259	3610
64260	3621
64261	3622
64262	3623
64263	3624
64264	3625
64265	3626
64266	3627
64267	3628
64268	3629
64269	3630
64270	3631
64271	3632
64272	3633
64273	3634
64274	3635
64275	3636
64276	3637
64277	3638
64278	3639
64279	3640
64280	5973
64281	5974
64282	5975
64283	5976
64284	5977
64285	5978
64286	5979
64287	5980
64288	5981
64289	5982
64290	5983
64291	5984
64292	5985
64293	5986
64294	5987
64295	5988
64296	5989
64297	5990
64298	5991
64299	5992
64300	5993
64301	5994
64302	5995
64303	5996
64304	5997
64305	5998

64306 5999
64307 6000
64308 6001
64309 6002
64310 6003
64311 6004
64312 6005
64313 6006
64314 6007
64315 6008
64316 6009
64317 6010
64318 6011
64319 6012
64320 6043
64321 6044
64322 6045
64323 6046
64324 6047
64325 6048
64326 6049
64327 6050
64328 6051
64329 5198
64330 5201
64331 5203
64332 5205
64333 5206
64334 5209
64335 5210
64336 5211
64337 5214
64338 5215
64339 5216
64340 5218
64341 5219
64342 5221
64343 5222
64344 5223
64345 5224
64346 5225
64347 5226
64348 5227
64349 5228
64350 5229
64351 5230
64352 5231
64353 5234
64354 5177
64355 5197
64356 5202
64357 5204
64358 5207
64359 5208
64360 5217
64361 5220
64362 5232
64363 5233
64364 5240
64365 5241
64366 5235
64367 5236
64368 5237
64369 5238
64370 5239
64371 5242
64372 5243
64373 5244
64374 5245
64375 5246
64376 5247
64377 5248
64378 5249
64379 5250
64380 5252
64381 5253
64382 5254
64383 5255
64384 5256
64385 5257
64386 6078
64387 6079
64388 6080
64389 6081
64390 6082
64391 6115
64392 6116
64393 6117
64394 6118
64395 6119
64396 5281
64397 5282
64398 5283
64399 5284
64400 5285
64401 5286
64402 5287
64403 5288
64404 5289
64405 5290
64406 5291
64407 5292
64408 5293
64409 5294
64410 5295
64411 5296
64412 5297
64413 5298
64414 5299
64415 5300
64416 5301
64417 5302

64418 5303
64419 5304
64420 5305
64421 5306
64422 5307
64423 5308
64424 5309
64425 5311
64426 5312
64427 5313
64428 5314
64429 5315
64430 5316
64431 5317
64432 5318
64433 5319
64434 5320
64435 5322
64436 5323
64437 5324
64438 5325
64439 5326
64440 5327
64441 5328
64442 5329
64443 5330
64444 5016
64445 5947
64446 5948
64447 5949
64448 5950
64449 5951
64450 5952
64451 5953
64452 5954
64453 5955
64460 9848
64461 9849
64462 9850
64463 9851
64464 9852
64466 9854
64468 9856
64470 9329
64471 9330
64472 9185
64473 9186
64474 9187
64475 9188
64476 9189
64477 9190
64478 9191
64479 9192
64480 9193
64482 9195
64483 9196
64484 9197
64485 9198
64486 9199
64487 9200
64488 9201
64489 9202
64490 9203
64491 9204
64492 9205
64493 9206
64494 9364
64495 9365
64496 9366
64497 9367
64498 9368
64499 9369
64500 9370
64501 9371
64502 9372
64504 9374
64505 9375
64506 9376
64507 9377
64509 9379
64510 9380
64511 9381
64512 9207
64513 9208
64514 9038
64515 9056
64516 9057
64517 9058
64518 9059
64519 9115
64520 9120
64521 9335
64522 9336
64523 9337
64524 9347
64525 9348
64526 9226
64527 9228
64528 9220
64529 9253
64530 9254
64531 9086
64532 9124
64533 9126
64534 9127
64535 9129
64536 9008
64537 9013
64538 9044
64539 9062
64540 9113
64541 9136

64542 9222
64543 9255
64544 9260
64545 9261
64546 9263
64547 9429
64548 9430
64549 9431
64550 9432
64551 9433
64552 9434
64553 9435
64554 9436
64555 9437
64556 9088
64557 9089
64558 9123
64559 9139
64560 9151
64561 9157
64562 9158
64563 9161
64564 9162
64565 9167
64566 9274
64567 9292
64568 9295
64569 9297
64570 9304
64571 9305
64572 9314
64573 9315
64574 9454
64575 9455
64576 9456
64577 9457
64578 9458
64579 9459
64580 9460
64581 9461
64582 9462
64583 9463
64584 9464
64585 9465
64586 9466
64587 9467
64588 9468
64589 9469
64590 9476
64591 9477
64592 9478
64593 9479
64594 9480
64595 9313
64596 9470
64597 9471
64598 9472
64599 9473
64600 9485
64601 9486
64602 9487
64603 9488
64604 9489
64605 9296
64606 9300
64607 9301
64608 9302
64609 9303
64610 9306
64611 9401
64612 9402
64613 9403
64614 9491
64615 9046
64616 9072
64617 9073
64618 9084
64619 9109
64620 9110
64621 9111
64622 9171
64623 9175
64624 9272
64625 9273
64626 9299
64627 9506
64628 9507
64629 9508
64630 9517
64631 9098
64632 9101
64633 9103
64634 9033
64635 9104
64636 9128
64637 9105
64638 9143
64639 9518
64640 8240
64641 8241
64642 8242
64643 8243
64644 8244
64645 8245
64646 8246
64647 8247
64648 8248
64649 8249
64650 8140
64651 8141
64652 8142
64653 8143

64654 8144
64655 8145
64656 8146
64657 8147
64658 8148
64659 8149
64660 8260
64661 8261
64662 8262
64663 8263
64664 8264
64665 8265
64666 8266
64667 8267
64668 8268
64669 8269
64670 8250
64671 8251
64672 8252
64673 8253
64674 8254
64675 8270
64676 8271
64677 8272
64678 8273
64679 8274
64680 8275
64681 8276
64682 8277
64683 8278
64684 8279
64685 8280
64686 8281
64687 8282
64688 8283
64689 8284
64690 8285
64691 8286
64692 8287
64693 8288
64694 8289
64695 8290
64696 8291
64697 8292
64698 8293
64699 8294
64700 1448
64701 1449
64702 1450
64703 1451
64704 1452
64705 1454
64706 1455
64707 1456
64708 1457
64709 1458
64710 1459
64711 1481
64712 1484
64713 1492
64714 1493
64715 1494
64716 1495
64717 1270
64718 1496
64719 1497
64720 1498
64721 1233
64722 1255
64723 1263
64724 1259
64725 1265
64726 1266
64727 1267
64728 1272
64729 1273
64730 1268
64731 1269
64732 1274
64733 1277
64734 1275
64735 1281
64736 1282
64737 1286
64738 1287
64739 1289
64740 1290
64741 1295
64742 1296
64743 1298
64744 2691
64745 2692
64746 2693
64747 2694
64748 2695
64749 2696
64750 2697
64751 2698
64752 2699
64753 2700
64754 2701
64755 2702
64756 2703
64757 2704
64758 2705
64759 2706
64760 2707
64761 2708
64762 2709
64763 2710
64764 2711
64765 2712

64766 2713
64767 2714
64768 2715
64769 2716
64770 2717
64771 2718
64772 2719
64773 2720
64774 2721
64775 2722
64776 2723
64777 2724
64778 2725
64779 2726
64780 2727
64781 2728
64782 2729
64783 2730
64784 2731
64785 2732
64786 2733
64787 2734
64788 2735
64789 2736
64790 2737
64791 2738
64792 2739
64793 2740
64794 2741
64795 2742
64796 2770
64797 2771
64798 2772
64799 2773
64800 2774
64801 2775
64802 2776
64803 2777
64804 2778
64805 2779
64806 2780
64807 2781
64808 2782
64809 2783
64810 2784
64811 2785
64812 1418
64813 1425
64814 1466
64815 1429
64816 1470
64817 1487
64818 1489
64819 1491
64820 2786
64821 2787
64822 2788
64823 2962
64824 2963
64825 2964
64826 2965
64827 2966
64828 2967
64829 2968
64830 2969
64831 2970
64832 2971
64833 2972
64834 2973
64835 2974
64836 2975
64837 2976
64838 2977
64839 2978
64840 2979
64841 2980
64842 1453
64843 1469
64844 1471
64845 1480
64846 1482
64847 1483
64848 1412
64849 1463
64850 1467
64851 1468
64852 1472
64853 1488
64854 1490
64855 1475
64856 1476
64857 1477
64858 1478
64859 1479
64860 1436
64861 1460
64862 1464
64863 1465
64864 1473
64865 1474
64866 1485
64867 1486
64868 1504
64869 1505
64870 1506
64871 1584
64872 2941
64873 2942
64874 2943
64875 2944
64876 2945
64877 2946

64878 2947
64879 2948
64880 2949
64881 2950
64882 2951
64883 2952
64884 2953
64885 2981
64886 2982
64887 2983
64888 2984
64889 2985
64890 2986
64891 2987
64892 2988
64893 2989
64894 2990
64895 2991
64896 2992
64897 2993
64898 2994
64899 2995
64900 2996
64901 2997
64902 2998
64903 2999
64904 3000
64905 1803
64906 1813
64907 1824
64908 1828
64909 1854
64910 1856
64911 1857
64912 1869
64913 1870
64914 1532
64915 1533
64916 1534
64917 1536
64918 1539
64919 1540
64920 1543
64921 1544
64922 1545
64923 1547
64924 1563
64925 1577
64926 1580
64927 1585
64928 1586
64929 1587
64930 1875
64931 1880
64932 1894
64933 1508
64934 1509
64935 1535
64936 1537
64937 1538
64938 1541
64939 1542
64940 1546
64941 1548
64942 1551
64943 1558
64944 1560
64945 1804
64946 1808
64947 1835
64948 1862
64949 1896
64950 1863
64951 1898
64952 1903
64953 1922
64954 1926
64955 1927
64956 1928
64957 1930
64958 1933
64959 1940
64960 1942
64961 1943
64962 1952
64963 1965
64964 1971
64965 1974
64966 1977
64967 1980
64968 1984
64969 1996
64970 1997
64971 3081
64972 3082
64973 3083
64974 3084
64975 3085
64976 3086
64977 3087
64978 3088
64979 3089
64980 3090
64981 3091
64982 3092
64983 3093
64984 3094
64985 3095
64986 3096
64987 3097
64988 3098
65002 3003

65003 3004
65004 3005
65005 3006
65006 3007
65007 3008
65008 3009
65009 3010
65010 3011
65013 3014
65014 3015
65015 3071
65016 3072
65017 3073
65018 3074
65019 3075
65020 3076
65021 3077
65022 3078
65023 3079
65025 16
65026 1305
65027 1315
65028 1323
65029 1337
65030 800
65031 874
65032 875
65033 876
65035 613
65036 619
65037 944
65038 993
65039 1507
65040 1510
65041 1511
65042 1512
65043 1513
65044 1514
65047 973
65049 981
65051 806
65052 899
65056 470
65057 294
65058 432
65059 582
65060 123
65061 312
65062 97
65063 313
65064 314
65066 68
65067 139
65068 300
65069 810
65070 26
65072 147
65073 997
65075 1550
65076 1552
65077 1553
65078 1554
65079 1555
65080 1556
65081 665
65082 807
65083 1557
65084 1559
65086 513
65088 570
65089 1561
65090 1562
65091 1564
65092 1565
65093 1566
65094 1567
65095 1569
65097 1574
65098 1575
65099 1576
65100 1122
65101 1588
65102 1589
65103 1590
65104 1591
65105 1593
65107 1595
65108 1596
65109 1608
65110 1609
65111 1610
65112 1611
65114 1614
65115 1615
65116 1805
65117 1806
65118 1810
65119 1811
65120 1812
65121 1814
65122 1819
65123 1820
65126 5643
65127 5673
65128 5675
65130 5680
65131 5787
65132 5788
65133 5789
65134 5792
65135 5793
65136 5794

65137 5795
65138 5797
65139 5798
65140 5799
65141 5802
65142 5803
65143 5805
65144 5807
65145 5808
65146 5809
65147 5811
65148 5812
65149 5815
65151 5819
65153 5821
65154 5823
65155 5824
65156 5827
65157 5828
65158 5831
65159 5832
65160 5835
65161 5836
65162 5837
65163 5838
65164 5839
65165 5841
65166 5846
65167 5847
65168 5848
65169 5849
65170 5850
65171 5851
65172 5074
65173 5075
65175 5077
65176 5080
65177 5081
65178 5082
65179 5083
65180 5090
65181 5094
65182 5095
65183 5096
65184 5097
65185 5098
65186 5099
65187 5100
65188 5101
65189 5103
65190 5116
65191 5117
65192 5118
65193 5119
65194 5120
65195 5121
65196 5122
65197 5123
65198 5124
65199 5125
65200 5126
65201 5130
65202 5131
65203 5132
65204 5134
65205 5141
65208 5175
65209 5176
65210 9604
65211 9617
65213 9622
65214 9623
65215 9625
65216 9628
65217 9176
65218 9632
65220 9644
65221 9645
65222 9646
65224 9648
65225 9649
65226 9650
65227 9651
65228 9652
65229 9653
65230 9654
65231 9655
65232 9656
65233 9657
65234 9658
65235 9659
65236 9660
65237 9663
65238 9664
65239 9667
65240 9668
65241 9669
65242 9670
65243 9673
65244 9675
65245 9677
65246 9045
65247 9068
65248 9183
65249 9678
65250 9679
65251 9680
65252 9681
65253 9682
65254 9683
65255 9684
65256 9685

65257 9686
65258 9687
65259 9688
65260 9689
65261 9690
65264 9247
65265 9248
65266 9357
65267 9358
65268 9611
65270 9181
65271 9182
65273 9280
65274 9177
65275 9180
65276 9705
65277 9706
65278 9707
65279 9708
65280 9709
65281 9710
65282 9711
65283 9712
65285 9714
65286 9715
65287 9716
65288 9717
65289 9718
65290 9719
65291 9720
65292 9721
65293 9722
65294 9723
65295 9724
65296 9725
65297 9726
65298 9727
65300 9742
65303 9745
65304 9746
65305 9747
65306 9748
65307 9749
65308 9750
65309 9751
65310 9752
65311 9753
65312 9754
65313 9755
65314 9756
65315 9757
65316 9758
65317 9759
65318 9760
65319 9761
65320 9762
65321 9763
65322 9764
65323 9771
65324 9772
65325 9773
65327 9775
65328 9776
65329 9777
65330 9778
65331 9779
65333 9781
65334 9782
65335 9783
65337 9785
65338 9786
65339 9787
65340 9788
65341 9789
65342 9790
65343 9791
65344 9792
65345 9793
65346 9794
65350 7813
65351 7821
65352 7825
65353 7828
65354 7527
65355 7530
65356 7532
65357 7540
65359 7833
65361 7836
65362 7837
65363 7840
65364 7843
65365 7846
65366 7847
65367 7848
65368 7849
65369 7850
65370 7852
65371 7853
65372 7854
65373 7855
65374 7857
65375 7860
65376 7865
65377 7866
65378 7869
65379 7871
65380 7872
65381 7874
65382 7875
65383 7876
65384 7877

65385 7878
65386 7880
65387 7881
65388 7883
65389 7886
65390 7887
65391 7888
65392 7892
65393 7893
65394 7894
65395 7895
65396 7897
65397 7898
65398 7901
65399 7902
65400 7904
65401 7906
65402 7907
65404 7910
65405 7911
65406 7913
65407 7914
65408 7915
65409 7918
65410 7920
65411 7921
65412 7922
65413 7924
65414 7925
65415 7926
65416 7927
65417 7928
65418 7929
65419 7931
65420 7932
65421 7934
65422 7937
65423 7940
65424 7941
65425 7942
65426 7943
65427 7945
65428 7508
65429 7509
65430 7510
65431 7511
65432 7512
65433 7514
65434 7515
65435 7516
65436 7517
65437 7520
65438 7523
65439 7526
65440 7640
65441 7641
65442 7642
65443 7643
65444 7644
65445 7645
65446 7646
65447 7647
65448 7648
65449 7649
65450 7552
65451 7553
65452 7554
65453 7555
65454 7556
65455 7557
65456 7558
65457 7559
65458 7560
65459 7561
65460 7562
65461 7563
65462 7564
65463 7565
65464 7566
65465 7567
65466 7568
65467 7569
65468 7570
65469 7571
65470 7542
65471 7543
65472 7544
65473 7545
65474 7546
65475 7547
65476 7548
65477 7549
65478 7550
65479 7551
65480 3021
65481 3022
65482 3023
65483 3024
65484 3025
65485 3026
65486 3027
65487 3028
65488 3029
65489 3030
65490 3031
65491 3032
65492 3033
65493 3034
65494 3035
65495 3036
65496 3037
65497 3038

65498 3039
65499 3040
65500 8150
65501 8151
65502 8152
65503 8153
65504 8154
65505 8155
65506 8156
65507 8157
65508 8158
65509 8159
65510 8160
65511 8161
65512 8162
65513 8163
65514 8164
65515 8165
65516 8166
65517 8167
65518 8168
65519 8169
65520 8170
65521 8171
65522 8172
65523 8173
65524 8174
65525 8175
65526 8176
65527 8177
65528 8178
65529 8179
65530 8180
65531 8181
65532 8182
65533 8183
65534 8184
65535 8185
65536 8186
65537 8187
65538 8188
65539 8189
65540 8190
65541 8191
65542 8192
65543 8193
65544 8194
65545 8195
65546 8196
65547 8197
65548 8198
65549 8199
65551 8201
65552 8202
65553 8203
65554 8204
65555 8205
65556 8206
65557 8207
65558 8208
65559 8209
65560 8210
65561 8211
65562 8212
65563 8213
65564 8214
65565 8215
65566 8216
65567 8217
65568 8218
65569 8219
65570 8220
65571 8221
65572 8222
65573 8223
65574 8224
65575 8225
65576 8226
65577 8227
65578 8228
65579 8229
65580 8230
65581 8231
65582 8232
65583 8233
65584 8234
65585 8235
65586 8236
65587 8237
65588 8238
65589 8239
65600 1821
65601 1822
65602 1823
65603 1825
65604 1826
65606 1829
65607 1830
65608 1843
65609 1844
65611 1847
65612 1850
65614 1852
65615 1853
65617 1858
65619 1860
65621 1892
65622 1895
65623 1897
65624 1899
65625 1900
65626 1931

65627 1932
65628 1934
65629 1935
65631 1937
65632 1941
65633 1945
65634 1946
65636 1948
65639 1951
65640 1954
65641 1955
65642 1956
65644 1960
65645 1961
65646 1962
65647 1963
65648 1964
65649 1967
65650 1969
65651 1970
65653 1973
65654 1976
65655 1979
65656 1981
65657 1982
65658 1983
65659 1985
65660 1986
65661 1987
65662 1988
65663 1989
65664 1990
65665 1991
65666 1992
65667 1993
65668 1994
65669 1995
65670 2050*
2000

65671 536
65672 1725
65673 1726
65674 2032
65675 2033
65676 2034
65677 2037
65679 2040
65680 2041
65681 2042
65683 2044
65684 2045
65685 2046
65686 2047
65687 2048
65688 25
65689 463
65690 2061
65691 2065
65692 2067
65693 2068
65694 2069
65695 2070
65696 2071
65697 2072
65698 2073
65699 2075
65700 2076
65702 2079
65703 2080
65704 2051
65705 2053
65706 2055
65707 2056
65708 2057
65710 2059
65712 29
65713 257
65714 459
65715 2126
65716 2128
65717 2130
65718 2131
65720 2134
65721 2135
65723 2138
65724 2139
65725 2140
65726 2141
65727 2142
65728 1723
65730 132
65731 243
65732 342
65733 434
65734 442
65735 543
65736 554
65737 555
65738 1159
65739 1172
65740 1043
65741 1057
65742 1098
65743 1130
65744 1369
65745 1671
65746 1674
65747 1676
65748 1678
65749 1773
65750 1360
65751 1670

65752	816
65753	835
65754	881
65755	1146
65756	1673
65757	1698
65758	67
65759	233
65760	379
65761	406
65762	1139
65763	1390
65764	1194
65765	1200
65766	1202
65767	1208
65768	1370
65769	1781
65770	412
65771	1366
65772	438
65773	517
65774	525
65775	765
65776	818
65777	831
65778	1131
65779	1777
65780	790
65781	814
65782	836
65783	839
65784	880
65785	883
65786	888
65787	891
65788	917
65789	938
65790	1006
65791	1016
65792	1018
65793	1052
65794	1189
65795	1227
65796	1256
65797	1393
65798	1402
65799	1686
65800	1001
65801	1003
65802	1004
65803	1005
65804	1007
65805	1013
65806	1008
65807	1010
65808	1011
65809	1012
65810	1014
65811	1015
65812	1017
65813	1022
65814	1023
65815	1024
65816	1025
65817	1027
65818	1028
65819	1029
65820	1030
65821	1034
65822	1035
65823	1036
65824	1039
65825	1040
65826	1044
65827	1046
65828	1047
65829	1048
65830	1049
65831	1050
65832	1053
65833	1056
65834	1060
65835	1061
65836	1064
65837	1065
65838	1066
65839	1067
65840	1201
65841	1203
65842	1204
65843	1205
65844	1211
65845	1212
65846	1213
65847	1214
65848	1216
65849	1219
65850	1220
65851	1221
65852	1222
65853	1224
65854	1225
65855	1226
65856	1228
65857	1229
65858	1230
65859	1231
65860	2338
65861	2339
65862	2340
65863	2341
65864	2342
65865	2343
65866	2344
65867	2345
65868	2346
65869	2347
65870	2348
65871	2349
65872	2350
65873	2351
65874	2352
65875	2353
65876	2354
65877	2355
65878	2356
65879	2357
65880	2358
65881	2359
65882	2360
65883	2361
65884	2362
65885	2383
65886	2384
65887	2385
65888	2386
65889	2387
65890	2388
65891	2389
65892	2390
65893	2391
65894	2392
65900	1400
65901	1401
65902	1403
65903	1404
65904	1405
65905	1406
65906	1407
65907	1408
65908	1409
65909	1410
65910	1411
65911	1413
65912	1414
65913	1415
65914	1416
65915	1417
65916	1419
65917	1420
65918	1421
65919	1422
65920	1423
65921	1424
65922	1426
65923	1427
65924	1428
65925	1434
65926	1437
65927	1440
65928	1441
65929	1442
65930	1443
65931	1444
65932	1445
65933	1446
65934	1447
67093	7597* 8308
67094	7598* 8310
67097	5577
67099	5582
67100	5598
67104	5776
67105	5777
67106	5778
67107	5779
67108	5780
67109	5781
67111	5783
67112	5784
67113	5785
67114	8092
67115	8093
67117	8095
67119	8097
67124	8075
67126	8078
67127	8079
67128	8081
67134	8061
67139	8067
67140	8068
67141	8040
67143	8042
67149	8048
67150	8049
67151	7236
67152	7244
67153	7573
67154	7574
67155	7578
67156	7579
67157	7581
67158	7584
67159	7586
67160	7588
67161	7111
67162	7214
67163	7219
67164	7222
67165	7232
67166	7233
67167	7171
67168	7172
67169	7173
67170	7174
67171	7175
67172	7177
67173	7178
67174	7180
67175	7184
67176	7185
67177	7186
67178	7187
67179	7189
67180	7071
67181	7072
67182	7074
67183	7075
67184	7076
67185	7077
67186	7078
67187	7079
67188	7141
67189	7142
67190	7143
67191	7144
67192	7145
67193	7147
67194	7781
67195	7782
67196	7783
67197	7784
67198	7785
67199	7786
67200	7787
67201	7788
67202	7091
67203	7094
67204	7095
67205	7096
67206	7100
67207	7103
67208	7104
67209	7108
67210	7109
67211	7110
67212	7780
67213	7589
67214	7590
67215	7170
67216	7179
67217	7188
67218	7789
67219	7790
67220	7061
67221	7062
67222	7063
67223	7064
67224	7065
67225	7066
67226	7067
67227	7068
67228	7069
67229	7070
67230	7001
67231	7002
67232	7003
67233	7004
67234	7005
67235	7006
67236	7007
67237	7008
67238	7009
67239	7010
67240	1096
67241	1687
67242	1691
67243	1701
67244	1702
67245	1765
67246	1783
67247	1788
67248	1769
67249	1791
67250	1837
67251	1838
67252	1772
67253	1839
67254	1840
67255	1169
67256	1703
67257	1730
67258	1793
67259	1795
67260	1316
67261	1778
67262	1865
67263	1866
67264	1867
67265	1868
67266	1748
67267	1751
67268	1762
67269	1780
67270	529
67271	1713
67272	1779
67273	1737
67274	1786
67275	394
67276	505
67277	405
67278	1881
67279	1882
67280	1740
67281	1883
67282	1884
67283	1885
67284	1886
67285	1887
67286	1888
67287	1889
67288	1890
67289	1911
67290	1912
67291	1913
67292	1914
67293	1915
67294	1916
67295	1917
67296	1918
67297	1919
67298	1920
67299	1752
67300	1692
67301	1693
67302	1739
67303	1745
67304	526
67305	1755
67306	1759
67307	1754
67308	1775
67309	1764
67310	2081
67311	2082
67312	2083
67313	2084
67314	2085
67315	2086
67316	2087
67317	2088
67318	2089
67319	2090
67320	2091
67321	2092
67322	2093
67323	2094
67324	2095
67325	2096
67326	2097
67327	2098
67328	2099
67329	2100
67330	381
67331	439
67332	468
67333	540
67334	580
67335	1319
67336	1334
67337	1695
67338	149
67339	380
67340	387
67341	384
67342	408
67343	413
67344	427
67345	433
67346	435
67347	436
67348	437
67349	441
67350	4009A
67351	4010
67352	4013
67353	4014
67354	4015
67355	4016
67356	4018
67357	4019
67358	4020
67359	4501
67360	4502
67361	4503
67362	4504
67363	4505
67364	4506
67365	4507
67366	4508
67367	4509
67368	4510
67369	4511
67370	4513
67371	4514
67372	4517
67373	4518
67374	4519
67375	4520
67376	4521
67377	4523
67378	4524
67379	4525
67380	4527
67381	4528
67382	4529
67383	4530
67384	4531
67385	4534
67386	4536
67387	4537
67388	4538
67389	4539
67390	4540
67391	4541
67392	4542
67393	4543
67394	4544
67395	4545
67397	4547
67398	4548
67399	4549
67400	6055
67401	6056
67402	6057
67403	6058
67404	6059
67405	6060
67406	6061
67407	6062
67408	6063
67409	6064
67410	6065
67411	6066
67412	5171
67413	5178
67414	5179
67415	5188
67416	5190
67417	5191
67418	5193
67419	5199
67420	5002
67421	5009
67422	5018
67423	5020
67424	5027
67425	5028
67426	5047
67427	5029
67428	5050
67429	5055
67430	5457
67431	5454
67432	5455
67433	5456
67434	5310
67435	5357
67436	5359
67437	5114
67438	5115
67439	5453
67440	6120
67441	6121
67442	6122
67443	6123
67444	6124
67445	6125
67446	6126
67447	6127
67448	6128
67449	6129
67450	6130
67451	6131
67452	9001
67453	9002
67454	9003
67455	9004
67456	9005
67457	9122
67458	9131
67459	9134
67460	9135
67461	9141
67462	9155
67463	9164
67464	9006
67465	9012
67466	9015
67467	9025
67468	9041
67469	9043
67470	9048
67471	9053
67472	9265
67473	9267
67474	9309
67475	9016
67476	9026
67477	9039
67478	9051
67479	9064
67480	9102
67481	9133
67482	9438
67483	9439
67484	9440
67485	9441
67486	9442
67487	9443
67488	9444
67489	9445
67490	9446
67491	9447
67492	9448
67493	9449
67494	9450
67495	9451
67496	9452
67497	9511
67498	9512
67499	9513
67500	9514
67501	9515
67502	9516
67600	2900
67601	2901
67602	2902
67603	2903
67604	2904
67605	2905
67606	2906
67607	2907
67608	2908
67609	2909
67610	2910
67611	2911
67612	2912
67613	2913
67614	2914
67615	2915
67616	2916
67617	2917
67618	2918
67619	2919
67620	2920
67621	2921
67622	2922
67623	2923
67624	2924
67625	2925
67626	2926
67627	2927
67628	2928
67629	2929
67630	2930
67631	2931
67632	2932
67633	2933
67634	417
67635	446
67636	477
67637	479
67638	481
67639	484
67640	486
67641	487
67642	497
67643	498
67644	402
67645	414
67646	415
67647	416
67648	418
67649	2897
67650	419
67651	422
67652	423
67653	428
67654	440
67655	2898
67656	454
67657	455
67658	461
67659	465
67660	466
67661	2899
67662	404
67663	407
67664	420
67665	424
67666	425
67667	447
67668	448
67669	451
67670	467
67671	469
67672	472
67673	478
67674	480
67675	483
67676	485
67677	488
67678	489
67679	490
67680	491
67681	496
67682	390
67683	391
67684	392
67685	393
67686	395
67687	396
67688	397
67689	398
67690	399
67691	401
68006	75094
68007	75097
68008	75101
68009	75108
68010	75117
68011	75119
68012	75124
68013	75125
68014	75134
68015	75139
68016	75148
68017	75149
68018	75150
68019	75153
68020	75164
68021	75183
68022	75184
68023	75190
68024	71509
68025	71498
68026	71506
68027	71440
68028	71447
68029	71451
68030	71452
68031	75272
68032	75281
68033	75287
68034	75297
68035	75320
68036	75321
68037	75322
68038	75323
68039	75324
68040	75325
68041	75326
68042	75327
68043	75328
68044	75329
68045	75330
68046	75331
68047	75258
68048	75259
68049	75260
68050	75261
68051	75262
68052	75263
68053	75265
68054	75266
68055	75267
68056	75268
68057	75269
68058	75270
68059	75271
68060	71467
68061	71468
68062	71469
68063	71470
68064	71471
68065	71472
68066	71473
68067	71474
68068	71475
68069	71476
68070	71486
68071	71532
68072	71533
68073	71534
68074	71535
68075	71536
68076	71462
68077	71466
68078	71463
68079	71464
68080	71465
68081	7230
68082	7133
68083	7134
68088	985
68089	986
68090	559
68091	560
68092	10101
68093	10102
68094	10092
68095	10094
68096	10097
68097	10098
68098	10100
68099	10083
68100	10084
68101	10088
68102	10089
68103	10093
68104	9009
68105	9010
68106	9011
68107	9014
68108	9017
68109	10090
68110	10091
68111	10095
68112	10096
68113	9032
68114	9040
68115	9042
68116	9050
68117	9063
68118	9144
68119	9146
68120	9308
68121	9310
68122	9546
68123	9547
68124	9610
68125	7227
68126	7228
68127	7226
68128	7229
68129	7210
68130	7772* 8400
68131	7773* 8401
68132	4991
68133	4992
68134	4993
68135	7774* 8402
68136	44
68137	79
68138	9529
68139	19
68140	100
68141	106
68142	108
68143	119
68144	124
68145	142
68146	150
68147	171
68148	174
68149	175
68150	183
68151	187
68152	45
68153	59
68154	81
68155	90
68156	189
68157	192
68158	193
68159	196
68160	197
68161	198
68162	21
68163	23
68164	35
68165	42
68166	49
68167	60
68168	61
68169	87
68171	55
68172	62
68173	63
68174	64
68175	65
68176	78
68177	96
68178	98
68179	94
68180	117
68181	154
68182	148
68183	155
68184	172
68185	86
68186	7775* 8403
68187	7776* 8404
68188	8430
68189	8431
68190	6843
68191	6844
68192	6830
68193	6832
68200	5883
68201	5885
68203	5890
68204	5060
68205	5061
68206	5089
68207	5157
68208	5321
68209	5538
68210	5277
68211	7155
68213	7247
68214	7250
68215	7253
68216	7135
68217	7136
68218	7137
68219	7139
68220	7130
68221	7127
68222	7128
68223	7131
68224	7125
68225	7126
68226	7129
68230	165
68231	299
68232	261
68233	326
68234	533
68235	70
68236	168
68238	347
68239	494
68240	499
68242	286
68243	403
68244	541
68245	1123
68246	1167
68247	221
68248	224
68249	492
68250	495
68251	501
68252	1083
68253	239
68254	50
68255	241
68256	244
68258	260
68259	338
68260	400
68262	103
68263	176
68264	177
68265	179
68266	181
68267	248
68268	482
68269	802
68270	77
68271	161
68272	252
68273	280
68275	449
68276	450
68277	452
68278	572
68279	577
68280	1085
68281	1103
68282	1140
68283	1142
68284	1153
68285	1157
68286	237
68287	240
68288	1084
68289	1095
68290	1143
68291	1151
68292	1155
68293	1196
68294	1197
68295	1198
68296	1199
68297	972
68298	137
68299	977
68300	978
68301	980
68302	1735
68303	1796
68304	1797
68305	1831
68306	1832
68307	1833
68308	1834
68309	1836
68310	1134
68311	1789
68312	1688
68313	1689
68314	1690
68316	1864
68317	3859
68319	4990
68320	9836
68321	9837
68322	9838
68323	9839
68324	9840
68325	9841
68326	9842
68327	9843
68328	9844
68329	9845
68330	9846
68331	9847
68332	9233
68333	9234
68334	9235
68335	9236
68336	9237
68337	9238
68338	9066
68339	9114
68340	9116
68341	9117
68342	9118
68343	9119
68344	9121
68345	9130
68346	9132
68347	9152
68348	9277
68349	9290
68350	9087
68351	9271
68352	9279
68353	9288
68354	9289
68355	544
68356	545
68357	546
68358	547
68359	548
68360	549
68361	550
68362	551
68363	552
68364	553
68365	2532
68366	6411
68368	6409
68370	7281
68371	7288
68372	7289
68373	7290
68374	7293
68375	7296
68376	7298
68377	7304
68378	7307
68379	7309
68380	7310
68381	7311
68382	7313
68383	7319
68384	7320
68385	7321
68386	7322
68387	7323
68388	7324
68390	948
68391	953
68392	954
68393	956
68395	1340
68396	1341
68397	1342
68398	1344
68399	1346
68400	1347
68401	1348
68402	1349
68404	1431
68405	1432
68406	1433
68407	1435
68408	1438
68409	1115
68410	354
68412	15
68413	614
68414	43
68415	47
68416	71
68417	607
68420	324
68421	276
68422	105
68423	344
68424	37
68425	612
68426	1116
68427	597
68428	319
68429	199
68430	57
68431	151
68432	604
68433	1000
68434	1313
68435	1461
68436	1462
68437	623
68438	166
68440	290
68441	305
68442	9795
68443	9796
68444	9797
68445	9798
68446	9799
68447	9800
68448	9801
68449	9802
68450	9803
68451	9804
68452	9805
68453	9806
68454	9807
68455	9808
68456	9809
68457	9810
68458	9811
68459	9812
68460	9813
68461	9814
68463	9816
68464	9817
68465	9818
68466	9819
68467	9820
68468	9821
68469	9822
68470	9823
68471	9824
68472	9825
68473	9826
68474	9827
68475	9828
68476	9829
68477	9830
68478	9831
68479	9832
68480	9833
68481	9834
68484	096
68488	094
68489	016
68490	7327
68491	7328
68492	7329
68493	7330
68494	7331
68495	7332
68496	7334
68497	7335
68498	7336
68499	7337
68500	7338
68501	7339
68502	7340
68503	7341
68504	7342
68505	7343
68507	7345
68508	7346
68509	7397
68510	7398
68511	7399
68512	7400
68513	7401
68514	7403
68515	7405
68516	7011
68517	7012
68518	7013
68519	7014
68520	7015
68521	7016
68522	7018
68523	7019
68524	7347
68525	7348
68526	7349
68527	7350
68528	7351
68529	7352
68530	7353
68531	7354
68532	7355
68533	7356
68534	7357
68535	7358
68536	7359
68537	7360
68538	7361
68540	7363
68541	7365
68542	7366
68543	7367
68544	7368
68545	7369
68546	7370
68547	7371
68548	7372
68549	7373
68550	7374
68551	7375
68552	7376
68553	7377
68554	7378
68555	7379
68556	7380
68557	7381
68558	7382
68559	7383
68560	7384
68561	7385
68562	7386
68563	7387
68565	7389
68566	7390
68567	7391
68568	7392
68569	7393
68570	7394
68571	7395
68572	7396
68573	7265
68574	7266
68575	7267
68576	7268
68577	7269
68578	7270
68579	7271
68581	7273
68583	7256
68584	7257
68585	7258
68586	7260
68587	7261
68588	7262
68589	7263
68590	7264
68591	7203
68592	7204
68593	7206
68594	7207
68595	7208
68596	7305
68597	7190
68598	7191
68599	7192
68600	7193
68601	7194
68602	7195
68603	7196
68605	7198
68606	7200
68607	7160
68608	7161
68609	7162
68610	7163
68611	7164
68612	7165
68613	7166
68616	7169
68617	7051
68618	7052
68619	7053
68621	7055
68623	7057
68625	7059
68626	7060
68628	7082
68629	7083
68630	7084
68631	7085
68632	7086
68633	7087
68635	7089
68636	7090
68638	7042
68639	7043
68640	7044
68641	7045
68642	7046
68643	7047
68644	7048
68645	7049
68646	7050
68647	7021
68648	7022
68649	7023
68650	7024
68651	7025
68652	7026
68653	7027
68654	7028
68655	7029
68656	7030
68657	7031
68658	7032
68659	7033
68660	7034
68661	7035
68662	7036
68663	7037
68664	7038
68665	7039
68666	7040
68667	B
68668	C
68669	D
68670	462
68671	1715
68672	1718
68673	1721
68674	1722
68675	1732
68676	1744
68677	1746
68678	1761
68679	1770
68680	1720
68681	1728
68682	1733
68683	1734
68684	1736
68685	1741
68686	1742
68687	1747
68688	1749
68689	1763
68690	2173
68691	2174
68692	2175
68693	2176
68694	2177
68695	2178
68696	2179
68697	2180
68698	2181
68699	2182
68700	2183
68701	2184
68702	2185
68703	2186
68704	2187
68705	2188
68706	2189
68707	2190
68708	2191
68709	2192
68710	2303
68711	2304
68712	2305
68713	2306
68714	2307
68715	2308
68716	2309
68717	2310
68718	2311
68719	2312
68720	2313
68721	2314
68722	2315
68723	2316
68724	2317
68725	2318
68726	2319
68727	2320
68728	2321
68729	2322
68730	2323
68731	2324
68732	2325
68733	2326
68734	2327
68735	2328
68736	2329
68737	2330
68738	2331
68739	2332
68740	2333
68741	2334
68742	2335
68743	2336
68744	2337

68745	500
68746	512
68747	516
68748	524
68749	542
68750	566
68751	571
68752	574
68753	576
68754	581
68757	3922
68758	3923
68759	3925
68760	3926
68761	3927
68762	3929
68763	3930
68764	3961
68765	3962
68766	3963
68767	3965
68768	3966
68769	3967
68770	3968
68771	3969
68772	3970
68773	3971
68774	3972
68775	3973
68776	3974
68777	3975
68778	3976
68779	3977
68780	3978
68781	3979
68782	3980
68783	4046
68784	4047
68785	4048
68786	4049
68787	4050
68788	4051
68789	4052
68790	4053
68791	4054
68792	4055
68793	4056
68794	4057
68795	4058
68796	4059
68797	4060
68798	4211
68799	4212
68800	4213
68801	4214
68802	4215
68803	3111
68804	3155A
68805	4201
68806	4202
68807	4203
68808	4204
68809	4205
68810	4206
68811	4207
68812	4208
68813	4209
68814	4210
68815	4216
68816	4217
68817	4218
68818	4219
68819	4220
68820	4221
68821	4222
68822	4223
68823	4224
68824	4225
68825	4226
68826	4227
68827	4228
68828	4229
68829	4230
68830	4231
68831	4232
68832	4233
68833	4234
68834	4235
68835	4236
68836	4237
68837	4238
68838	4239
68839	4240
68840	4241
68841	4242
68842	4243
68843	4244
68844	4245
68845	4246
68846	4247
68847	4248
68848	4249
68849	4250
68850	4251
68851	4252
68852	4253
68853	4254
68854	4255
68855	4256
68856	4257
68857	4258
68858	4259

68859	4260
68860	4261
68861	4262
68862	4263
68863	4264
68864	4265
68865	4266
68866	4267
68867	4268
68868	4269
68869	4270
68870	4271
68871	4272
68872	4273
68873	4274
68874	4275
68875	4276
68876	4277
68877	4278
68878	4279
68879	4280
68880	4281
68881	4282
68882	4283
68883	4284
68884	4285
68885	4286
68886	4287
68887	4288
68888	4289
68889	4290
68890	3180* 3157
68891	3181* 3158
68892	3182* 3159
68893	3183* 3160
68894	3184* 3161
68895	3185* 3162
68896	3186* 3163
68897	3187* 3164
68898	3188* 3166
68899	3189* 3167
68900	3168
68901	3169
68902	3170
68903	3171
68904	3172
68905	3173
68906	3174
68907	3175
68908	3176
68909	3178
68910	3211
68911	3212
68912	3213
68913	3214
68914	3215
68915	3216
68916	3217
68917	3218
68918	3219
68919	3220
68920	3221
68921	3222
68922	3223
68923	3224
68924	3225
68925	3226
68926	3227
68927	3228
68928	3229
68929	3230
68930	3231
68931	3232
68932	3233
68933	3234
68934	3235
68935	3236
68936	3237
68937	3238
68938	3239
68939	3240
68940	583
68941	586
68942	588
68943	589
68944	591
68945	593
68946	594
68947	596
68948	601
68949	603
68950	609
68951	610
68952	616
68953	617
68954	618
68955	621
68956	622
68957	635
68958	636
68959	1037
68960	1041

68961	1045
68962	1058
68963	1063
68964	1068
68965	1069
68966	1070
68967	1074
68968	1079
68969	1081
68970	1082
68971	1086
68972	2789
68973	2790
68974	2791
68975	2792
68976	2793
68977	2794
68978	599
68979	600
68980	602
68981	605
68982	606
68983	608
68984	611
68985	615
68986	584
68987	585
68988	587
68989	590
68990	595
68991	598
69050	5272
69051	5273
69052	5274
69053	5275
69054	5276
69055	5336
69056	5337
69057	5338
69058	5339
69059	5340
69060	5341
69061	5342
69062	5343
69064	5345
69065	5366
69066	5367
69067	5368
69068	5369
69069	5370
69070	6158
69071	6160
69076	6155
69077	6156
69089	2486
69090	1321
69091	1667
69092	1683
69093	1697
69094	1774
69095	89
69096	429
69097	1109
69098	1112
69099	1132
69100	1138
69101	1148
69102	1317
69103	1706
69104	1710
69105	1699
69106	1707
69107	1711
69108	1785
69109	1716
69110	2405
69111	2407
69112	2410
69113	2415
69114	2419
69115	2533
69116	2534
69117	2535
69118	2536
69119	2537
69120	9858
69124	9862
69125	9863
69126	9007
69127	9154
69128	9209
69129	9210
69130	9251
69131	9282
69132	9386
69133	9387
69134	9388
69135	9389
69136	9390
69137	9391
69138	9392
69139	9393
69140	9396
69141	9397
69142	9398
69143	9399
69144	9907
69145	9908
69146	9909
69147	9910
69148	9911
69149	9912

69150	9913
69151	9914
69152	9915
69153	9916
69154	9917
69155	9918
69156	9919
69157	9920
69158	9921
69159	9922
69160	9923
69161	9924
69162	9925
69163	9926
69164	9223
69165	9224
69166	9229
69167	9230
69168	9246
69169	9252
69170	9257
69171	9264
69172	9047
69173	9054
69174	9061
69175	9065
69176	9069
69177	9070
69178	9071
69179	9276
69180	9453
69181	9142
69182	9165
69183	9166
69184	9259
69185	9219
69186	9020
69187	9022
69188	9029
69189	9049
69190	9096
69191	9097
69192	9106
69193	9107
69194	9108
69195	9240
69196	9519
69197	9520
69198	9521
69199	9522
69200	9523
69201	9524
69202	9525
69203	9526
69204	9527
69205	9528
69206	9019
69207	9023
69208	9031
69209	9052
69210	9055
69211	9060
69212	9067
69213	9074
69214	9075
69215	9076
69216	9077
69217	9078
69218	9079
69219	9099
69220	9125
69221	9147
69222	9174
69223	9225
69224	9227
69225	5513
69226	5514
69227	5605
69228	5606
69229	5611
69230	5614
69231	5620
69232	5622
69233	5623
69234	5625
69235	5628
69236	5629
69237	5632
69239	5635
69240	5636
69241	5637
69242	5713
69243	5716
69244	5718
69245	5720
69246	5721
69247	5724
69250	5515
69251	5516
69252	5517
69253	5518
69254	5519
69255	5520
69256	5522
69257	5523
69258	5524
69259	5525
69260	5526
69261	5527
69262	5528
69263	5529
69264	5530

69265	5532
69266	5533
69267	5534
69268	5535
69269	5127
69270	5409
69271	5537
69272	5539
69273	5540
69274	5541
69275	5542
69276	5543
69277	5544
69278	5545
69279	5546
69280	5547
69281	5548
69282	5744
69283	5745
69284	5746
69285	5747
69286	5748
69287	5749
69288	5750
69289	5751
69290	5752
69291	5753
69292	5200
69293	5536
69294	5021
69295	5025
69296	5054
69297	5757
69298	5759
69299	5760
69300	5761
69301	5762
69302	5755
69303	5763
69304	5764
69305	5765
69306	5766
69307	5767
69308	5768
69309	5769
69310	5770
69311	5771
69312	5772
69313	5773
69314	5775
69315	5051
69316	5173
69317	5189
69318	5894
69319	5895
69320	5896
69321	5897
69322	5898
69323	5899
69324	5900
69325	5901
69326	5902
69327	5903
69328	5904
69329	5905
69330	5906
69331	5907
69332	5908
69333	5909
69334	5910
69335	5911
69336	5912
69337	5913
69338	5914
69339	5915
69340	5916
69341	5917
69342	5918
69343	5919
69344	5920
69345	5921
69346	5922
69347	5923
69348	5924
69349	5925
69350	5926
69351	5927
69352	5928
69353	5929
69354	5930
69355	5931
69356	5932
69357	5933
69358	5934
69359	5935
69360	5936
69361	5937
69362	5938
69363	5939
69364	5940
69365	5941
69366	5942
69367	5943
69368	5944
69369	5945
69370	5946
69371	210
69372	212
69373	535
69374	503
69375	74
69376	856

69377	859
69378	861
69379	862
69380	863
69381	864
69382	219
69383	346
69384	348
69385	1152
69386	1127
69387	136
69389	1105
69390	345
69391	515
69392	573
69393	1072
69394	76
69395	267
69396	271
69397	780
69398	961
69399	1091
69400	1104
69401	293
69410	1617
69411	1618
69413	1641
69414	1642
69415	1643
69418	1646
69419	1647
69420	1648
69421	1649
69422	1650
69423	1651
69424	1652
69425	1653
69426	1654
69427	1655
69428	383
69429	1705
69430	3190
69431	4551
69432	4552
69433	4553
69434	4554
69435	4555
69436	4556
69437	4557
69439	4559
69440	4560
69441	4561
69442	4562
69443	4563
69444	4564
69445	4565
69446	4566
69447	4567
69448	4568
69449	4569
69450	4570
69451	4571
69452	4572
69453	4573
69454	4574
69455	4575
69456	4576
69457	4577
69458	4578
69459	4579
69460	4580
69461	4581
69462	4582
69463	4583
69464	4584
69465	4585
69466	4586
69467	4587
69468	4588
69469	4589
69470	4590
69471	4591
69472	4592
69473	4593
69474	4594
69475	4595
69476	4596
69477	4597
69478	4598
69479	4599
69480	4600
69481	4601
69482	4602
69483	4603
69484	4604
69485	4605
69490	4606
69491	4607
69492	4608
69493	4609
69494	4610
69495	4611
69496	4612
69497	4613
69498	4614
69499	4615
69500	4721
69501	4722
69502	4723
69503	4724
69504	4725
69505	4726

69506	4727
69507	4728
69508	4729
69509	4730
69510	4731
69511	4732
69512	4733
69513	4734
69514	4735
69515	4736
69516	4737
69517	4738
69518	4739
69519	4740
69520	4741
69521	4742
69522	4743
69523	4744
69524	4745
69525	4746
69526	4747
69527	4748
69528	4749
69529	4750
69530	4751
69531	4752
69532	4753
69533	4754
69534	4755
69535	4756
69536	4757
69537	4758
69538	4759
69539	4760
69540	4761
69541	4762
69542	4763
69543	4764
69544	4765
69545	4766
69546	4767
69547	4768
69548	4769
69549	4770
69550	2583
69551	2584
69552	2585
69553	2586
69554	2587
69555	2588
69556	2589
69557	2590
69558	2591
69559	2592
69560	2593
69561	2594
69562	892
69563	893
69564	894
69565	895
69566	896
69567	897
69568	2662
69569	2663
69570	2664
69571	2665
69572	2666
69573	2667
69574	2668
69575	2669
69576	2670
69577	2671
69578	2672
69579	2673
69580	2674
69581	2675
69582	2676
69583	2677
69584	2678
69585	2679
69586	2680
69587	2681
69588	2682
69589	2683
69590	2684
69591	2685
69592	2686
69593	2687
69594	2688
69595	2689
69596	2690
69600	7978* 8000
69601	7979* 8001
69602	7980* 8002
69603	7981* 8003
69604	7982* 8004
69605	7983* 8005
69606	7984* 8006
69607	7985* 8007
69608	7986* 8008
69609	7987* 8009

69610	7988* 8010
69611	7989* 8011
69612	7990
69613	7991
69614	7992
69615	7993
69616	7994
69617	7995
69618	7996
69619	7997
69620	7998
69621	7999
69622	409
69623	421
69624	426
69625	456
69626	457
69627	460
69628	464
69629	471
69630	473
69631	475
69632	826
69633	827
69634	828
69635	829
69636	830
69637	832
69638	833
69639	834
69640	837
69641	838
69642	850
69643	851
69644	852
69645	853
69646	865
69647	866
69648	867
69649	868
69650	870
69651	873
69652	907
69653	912
69654	913
69655	916
69656	918
69657	919
69658	935
69659	940
69660	941
69661	947
69662	950
69663	952
69664	964
69665	966
69666	967
69667	968
69668	970
69669	971
69670	987
69671	988
69672	2632
69673	2633
69674	2634
69675	2635
69676	2636
69677	2637
69678	2638
69679	2639
69680	2640
69681	2641
69682	2642
69683	2643
69684	2644
69685	2645
69686	2646
69687	2647
69688	2648
69689	2649
69690	2650
69691	2651
69692	2652
69693	2653
69694	2654
69695	2655
69696	2656
69697	2657
69698	2658
69699	2659
69700	2660
69701	2661
69702	2600
69703	2601
69704	2602
69705	2603
69706	2604
69707	2605
69708	2606
69709	2607
69710	2608
69711	2609
69712	2610
69713	2611
69714	2612
69715	2613
69716	2614
69717	2615
69718	2616
69719	2617

69720	2618
69721	2619
69722	2620
69723	2621
69724	2622
69725	2623
69726	2624
69727	2625
69728	2626
69729	2627
69730	2628
69731	2629
69732	2630
69733	2631
69770	1113
69771	1114
69772	1126
69773	1129
69774	1136
69775	1170
69776	1174
69777	1175
69778	1176
69779	1179
69780	1180
69781	1181
69782	1182
69783	1183
69784	1185
69785	1190
69786	1191
69787	1192
69788	1193
69789	1195
69791	687
69792	688
69793	689
69794	690
69795	691
69796	692
69797	693
69798	694
69799	695
69800	5165
69801	5166
69802	5167
69803	5168
69804	5169
69805	5170
69806	5023
69807	5024
69808	5448
69809	5449
69810	5450
69811	5451
69812	5452
69813	5128
69814	5129
69815	5371
69816	5372
69817	5373
69818	5374
69819	5411
69820	5003
69821	5006
69822	5007
69823	5030
69824	5045
69825	5046
69826	5088
69827	5154
69828	5156
69829	5158
69830	1712
69831	1719
69832	1738
69833	1750
69834	1756
69835	1760
69836	1766
69837	1767
69838	1768
69839	1771
69840	1782
69841	1784
69842	1790
69850	2143
69851	2144
69852	2145
69853	2146
69854	2147
69855	2148
69856	2149
69857	2150
69858	2151
69859	2152
69860	2153
69861	2154
69862	2155
69863	2156
69864	2157
69865	2158
69866	2159
69867	2160
69868	2161
69869	2162
69870	1517
69871	1518
69872	1519
69873	1520
69874	1523
69875	1528

69876	1529
69877	1531
69878	1499
69879	1500
69880	1501
69881	1502
69882	1503
69883	1524
69884	1525
69885	1526
69886	1527
69887	1327
69888	1329
69889	1330
69890	1521
69891	1328
69892	1326
69893	1522
69894	1530
69900	6170
69901	6171
69902	6172
69903	6173
69904	2798
69905	2799
69910	1350
69911	1351
69912	1352
69913	1353
69914	1354
69915	1356
69916	1357
69917	1359
69918	1656
69919	1657
69920	1658
69921	1659
69922	1660
69925	5058
69926	5961
69927	6139
69928	5048
69929	5070
69930	6077
69931	5044
69932	5959
69933	5087
69934	5068
69935	5147
69936	6179
69937	5138
69999	2395

Listed in pre-1946 number order

B	68667
C	68668
D	68669
016	68489
083	64158
085	64160
087	64162
088	64163
092	64167
094	68488
096	68484
1*	62000
15	68412
16	65025
17	61810
19	68139
21	68162
23	68163
25	65688
26	65070
28	61811
29	65712
32	61812
33	61813
35	68164
36	61814
37	68424
38	61815
39	61816
42	68165
43	68414
44	68136
45	68152
46	61817
47	68415
49	68166
50	68254
52	61818
53	61819
55	68171
57	68430
58	61820
59	68153
60	68167
61	68168
62	68172
63	68173
64	68174
65	68175
67	65758
68	65066
69	61821
70	68235
71	68416
73	61822
74	69375

75	61823
76	69394
77	68270
78	68176
79	68137
80	61824
81	68154
83	63274
86	68185
87	68169
89	69095
90	68155
91	61825
92	61826
94	68179
96	68177
97	65062
98	68178
100	68140
103	68262
105	68422
106	68141
108	68142
109	61827
111	61828
112	61829
113	61830
114	61831
116	61832
117	68180
118	61833
119	68143
120	61834
121	61835
123	65060
124	68144
125	61836
126	61837
127	61838
130	63260
132	65730
134	61839
135	61840
136	69387
137	68298
139	65067
140	61841
141	61842
142	68145
143	61843
146	61844
147	65072
148	68182
149	67338
150	68146
151	68431
153	61845
154	68181
155	68183
156	61846
158	61847
159	61848
161	68271
162	63275
163	61849
165	68230
166	68438
167	61850
168	68236
170	61851
171	68147
172	68184
174	68148
175	68149
176	68263
177	68264
178	61852
179	68265
180	61853
181	68266
183	68150
184	61854
186	61855
187	68151
188	61856
189	68156
191	61857
192	68157
193	68158
195	61858
196	68159
197	68160
198	68161
199	68429
200	61859
201	62736
202	61861
203	61860
204	61862
205	62751
206	61863
207	61864
208	61865
210	69371
211	62737
212	69372
214	62752
217	62753
219	69382
220	62738
221	68247
222	62754

224	68248
226	62755
227	61866
228	61867
229	61868
230	62756
231	61869
232	62739
233	65759
234	62700
235	62740
236	62707
237	68286
238	62757
239	68253
240	68287
241	68255
243	65731
244	68256
245	62710
246	62712
247	62741
248	68267
249	62713
250	62714
251	62701
252	68272
253	62702
255	62742
256	62703
257	65713
258	62758
260	68258
261	68232
264	62704
265	62705
266	62706
267	69395
269	62743
270	62708
271	69396
273	62744
274	62759
276	68421
277	62709
279	62760
280	68273
281	62711
282	62745
283	62746
286	68242
288	62747
290	68440
292	62748
293	69401
294	65057
297	62749
298	62750
299	68231
300	65068
305	68441
306	62715
307	62716
309	62717
310	62718
311	62719
312	65061
313	65063
314	65064
318	62720
319	68428
320	62721
322	62722
324	68420
326	68233
327	62723
329	62725
335	62724
336	62727
338	68259
342	65732
344	68423
345	69390
346	69383
347	68238
348	69384
352	62726
353	62761
354	68410
357	62762
359	62763
361	62764
362	62765
363	62766
364	62767
365	62768
366	62769
368	62770
370	62771
374	62772
375	62773
376	62774
377	62775
379	65760
380	67339
381	67330
383	69428
384	67341
387	67340
390	67682
391	67683
392	67684

393	67685
394	67275
395	67686
396	67687
397	67688
398	67689
399	67690
400	68260
401	67691
402	67644
403	68243
404	67662
405	67277
406	65761
407	67663
408	67342
409	69622
410	63277
411	63292
412	65770
413	67343
414	67645
415	67646
416	67647
417	67634
418	67648
419	67650
420	67664
421	69623
422	67651
423	67652
424	67665
425	67666
426	69624
427	67344
428	67653
429	69096
430	63293
432	65058
433	67345
434	65733
435	67346
436	67347
437	67348
438	65772
439	67331
440	67654
441	67349
442	65734
443	63294
444	63295
446	67635
447	67667
448	67668
449	68275
450	68276
451	67669
452	68277
454	67656
455	67657
456	69625
457	69626
459	65714
460	69627
461	67658
462	68670
463	65689
464	69628
465	67659
466	67660
467	67670
468	67332
469	67671
470	65056
471	69629
472	67672
473	69630
474	63278
475	69631
476	62370
477	67636
478	67673
479	67637
480	67674
481	67638
482	68268
483	67675
484	67639
485	67676
486	67640
487	67641
488	67677
489	67678
490	67679
491	67680
492	68249
494	68239
495	68250
496	67681
497	67642
498	67643
499	68240
500	68745
501	68251
502*	60103
503	69374
505	67276
507*	60108
508*	60109
511*	60112
512	68746
513	65086
515	69391
516	68747
517*	60049
517	65773
518*	60050
520*	60052
521*	60053
522*	60054
524	68748
525	65774
526	67304
527	63261
528*	60060
529	67270
531*	60063
533	68234
535	69373
536	65671
537*	60069
538*	60070
540	67333
541	68244
542*	60074
542	68749
543	65735
544	68355
545*	60077
545	68356
546	68357
547	68358
548	68359
549	68360
550	68361
551	68362
552	68363
553	68364
554	65736
555	65737
558*	60095
559	68090
560	68091
561*	60098
565*	60087
566	68750
570*	60035
570	65088
571	68751
572	68278
573	69392
574	68752
575*	60040
576	68753
577	68279
578	63300
580	67334
581	68754
582	65059
583	68940
584	68986
585*	60024
585	68987
586*	60025
586	68941
587*	60026
587	68988
588*	60027
588	68942
589	68943
590	68989
591	68944
592	62371
593	68945
594	68946
595	68990
596	68947
597	68427
598	68991
599	68978
600	68979
601	68948
602	68980
603	68949
604	68432
605*	60006
605	68981
606	68982
607	68417
608	68983
609	68950
610	68951
611	68984
612	68425
613	65035
614	68413
615	68985
616	68952
617	68953
618	68954
619	65036
621	68955
622	68956
623	68437
624	63465
625	63466
626	63467
628	63468
629	63469
630	63470
631	63471
632	63472
633	63473
634	63474
635	68957
636	68958
643	63321
644	63310
645	63311
646	63312
647	63313
648	63314
650	63280
651	63281
652	63315
653	63316
654	63317
655	63318
656	63319
657	63322
658	63323
660	63301
665	65081
669	63326
687	69791
688	69792
689	69793
690	69794
691	69795
692	69796
693	69797
694	69798
695	69799
701*	60801
707	62372
708	62373
709*	60809
710*	60810
711*	60811
711	62374
712	62375
713	62376
714*	60814
715	63285
716	62954
718*	60818
719*	60819
720*	60820
721*	60821
722*	60822
723	62377
724	62378
725	62379
733*	60833
742	62933
750*	60850
761	61699
762*	60862
764	63327
765	65775
767	63328
770	63330
771*	60871
771	63331
772	63332
773	63333
774	63334
775*	60875
779*	60879
780	69397
781	63335
783	63336
785	63286
790	65780
792	63287
793	63338
794	63339
800	65030
802	68269
805*	60905
806	65051
807	65082
809*	60909
810	65069
814	65781
816	65752
818	65776
826	69632
827	69633
828	69634
829	69635
830	69636
831	65777
832	69637
833	69638
834	69639
835	65753
836	65782
837	69640
838	69641
839	65783
840	61400
841	61401
842	61402
843	61403
844	61404
845	61405
846	61406
847	61407
848	61408
849	61409
850	69642
851	69643
852	69644
853	69645
856	69376
859	69377
861	69378
862	69379
863	69380
864	69381
865	69646
866	69647
867	69648
868	69649
870	69650
871*	60971
873	69651
874	65031
875	65032
876	65033
880	65784
881	65754
883	65785
888	65786
891	65787
892	69562
893	69563
894	69564
895	69565
896	69566
897	69567
899	65052
901	63460
902	63461
903	63462
904	63463
905	63464
906	61410
907	69652
908	61411
909	61412
911	61413
912	69653
913	69654
914	61414
915	61415
916	69655
917	65788
918	69656
919	69657
920	61416
921	61417
922	61418
923	61419
924	61420
926	61421
927	61422
928	61423
929	61424
930	61425
931	61426
932	61427
933	61428
934	61429
935	69658
936	61430
937	61431
938	65789
940	69659
941	69660
942	61432
943	61433
944	65037
947	69661
948	68390
950	69662
952	69663
953	68391
954	68392
956	68393
961	69398
964	69664
966	69665
967	69666
968	69667
970	69668
971	69669
972	68297
973	65047
977	68299
978	68300
980	68301
981	65049
985	68088
986	68089
987	69670
988	69671
993	65038
994*	60505
997	65073
1000	68433
1001	65800
1002	63262
1003	65801
1004	65802
1005	65803
1006	65790
1007	65804
1008	65806
1009	63282
1010	65807
1011	65808
1012	65809
1013	65805
1014	65810
1015	65811
1016	65791
1017	65812
1018	65792
1022	65813
1023	65814
1024	65815
1025	65816
1026	62380
1027	65817
1028	65818
1029	65819
1030	65820
1031	63303
1034	65821
1035	65822
1036	65823
1037	68959
1039	65824
1040	65825
1041	68960
1042	62381
1043	65740
1044	65826
1045	68961
1046	65827
1047	65828
1048	65829
1049	65830
1050	65831
1051	62382
1052	65793
1053	65832
1054	63305
1056	65833
1057	65741
1058	68962
1060	65834
1061	65835
1062	63306
1063	68963
1064	65836
1065	65837
1066	65838
1067	65839
1068	68964
1069	68965
1070	68966
1072	69393
1074	68967
1078	62383
1079	68968
1081	68969
1082	68970
1083	68252
1084	68288
1085	68280
1086	68971
1091	69399
1095	68289
1096	67240
1098	65742
1100	61899
1101	61900
1102	61901
1103	68281
1104	69400
1105	69389
1106	61902
1108	61903
1109	69097
1110	63290
1111	63296
1112	69098
1113	69770
1114	69771
1115	68409
1116	68426
1117	61904
1118	61905
1119	61906
1121	61907
1122	65100
1123	68245
1125	61908
1126	69772
1127	69386
1129	69773
1130	65743
1131	65778
1132	69099
1133	61909
1134	68310
1135	61910
1136	69774
1137	61911
1138	69100
1139	65762
1140	68282
1141	61912
1142	68283
1143	68290
1146	65755
1148	69101
1149	63297
1150	63298
1151	68291
1152	69385
1153	68284
1154	61913
1155	68292
1156	61914
1157	68285
1158	61915
1159	65738
1162	61916
1164	61917
1166	61918
1167	68246
1169	67255
1170	69775
1172	65739
1173	63299
1174	69776
1175	69777
1176	69778
1177	63307
1178	63308
1179	69779
1180	69780
1181	69781
1182	69782
1183	69783
1184	62384
1185	69784
1186	63279
1189	65794
1190	69785
1191	69786
1192	69787
1193	69788
1194	65764
1195	69789
1196	68293
1197	68294
1198	68295
1199	68296
1200	65765
1201	65840
1202	65766
1203	65841
1204	65842
1205	65843
1207	62386
1208	65767
1209	62387
1210	62388
1211	65844
1212	65845
1213	65846
1214	65847
1216	65848
1217	62389
1218	63289
1219	65849
1220	65850
1221	65851
1222	65852
1223	62390
1224	65853
1225	65854
1226	65855
1227	65795
1228	65856
1229	65857
1230	65858
1231	65859
1232	62391
1233	64721
1235	62392
1247	63340
1248	63341
1249	63342
1250	63343
1251	63344
1252	63345
1253	63346
1254	63347
1255	64722
1256	65796
1257	63348
1259	64724
1260	62395
1261	63349
1262	63350
1263	64723
1264	63351
1265	64725
1266	64726
1267	64727
1268	64730
1269	64731
1270	64717
1271	63352
1272	64728
1273	64729
1274	64732
1275	64734
1276	63353
1277	64733
1278	63354
1279	63355
1280	63356
1281	64735
1282	64736
1283	63357
1284	63358
1285	63359
1286	64737
1287	64738
1288	63360
1289	64739
1290	64740
1291	63361
1292	63362
1293	63363
1294	63364
1295	64741
1296	64742
1298	64743
1300	61870
1302	61919
1304	61920
1305	65026
1306	61924
1307	61934
1308	61921
1310	61922
1311*	61689
1311	63365
1312	61871
1312*	61690
1313	68434
1315	65027
1316	67260
1317	69102
1318	61872
1319	67335
1320	63263
1321	69090
1322	61935
1323	65028
1324	61923
1325	61929
1326	69892
1327	69887
1328	69891
1329	69888
1330	69889
1331	61873
1332	61930
1333	61931
1334	67336
1335	63366
1337	65029
1339	61932
1340	68395
1341	68396
1342	68397
1344	68398
1345	61874
1346	68399
1347	68400
1348	68401
1349	68402
1350	69910
1351	69911
1352	69912
1353	69913
1354	69914
1356	69915
1357	69916
1359	69917
1360	65750
1361	63367
1362	63368
1363	63369
1364	61875
1365	61876
1366	65771
1367	61877
1368	61878
1369	65744
1370	65768
1371	61454
1372	61455
1373	61456
1374	61457
1375	61458
1376	61459
1377	61460
1378	61461
1379	61462
1380	61463
1381	61464
1382	61465
1383	61466
1384	61467
1385	61468
1386	61879
1387	61880
1388	61881
1389	61882
1390	65763
1391	61883
1392	61884
1393	65797
1394	61885
1395	61886
1396	61887
1397	61888
1398	61889
1399	61933
1400	65900
1401	65901
1402	65798
1403	65902
1404	65903
1405	65904
1406	65905
1407	65906
1408	65907
1409	65908
1410	65909
1411	65910
1412	64848
1413	65911
1414	65912
1415	65913
1416	65914
1417	65915
1418	64812
1419	65916
1420	65917
1421	65918
1422	65919
1423	65920
1424	65921
1425	64813
1426	65922
1427	65923
1428	65924
1429	64815
1431	68404
1432	68405
1433	68406
1434	65925
1435	68407
1436	64860
1437	65926
1438	68408
1440	65927
1441	65928
1442	65929
1443	65930
1444	65931
1445	65932
1446	65933
1447	65934
1448	64700
1449	64701
1450	64702
1451	64703
1452	64704
1453	64842
1454	64705
1455	64706
1456	64707
1457	64708
1458	64709
1459	64710
1460	64861
1461	68435
1462	68436
1463	64849
1464	64862
1465	64863
1466	64814
1467	64850
1468	64851
1469	64843
1470	64816
1471	64844
1472	64852
1473	64864
1474	64865
1475	64855
1476	64856
1477	64857
1478	64858
1479	64859
1480	64845
1481	64711
1482	64846
1483	64847
1484	64712
1485	64866
1486	64867
1487	64817
1488	64853
1489	64818
1490	64854
1491	64819
1492	64713
1493	64714
1494	64715
1495	64716
1496	64718
1497	64719
1498	64720
1499	69878
1500	69879
1501	69880
1502	69881
1503	69882
1504	64868
1505	64869
1506	64870
1507	65039
1508	64933
1509	64934
1510	65040
1511	65041
1512	65042
1513	65043
1514	65044
1517	69870
1518	69871
1519	69872
1520	69873
1521	69890
1522	69893
1523	69874
1524	69883
1525	69884
1526	69885
1527	69886
1528	69875
1529	69876
1530	69894
1531	69877
1532	64914
1533	64915
1534	64916
1535	64935
1536	64917
1537	64936
1538	64937
1539	64918
1540	64919
1541	64938
1542	64939
1543	64920
1544	64921
1545	64922
1546	64940
1547	64923
1548	64941
1550	65075
1551	64942
1552	65076
1553	65077
1554	65078
1555	65079
1556	65080
1557	65083
1558	64943
1559	65084
1560	64944
1561	65089
1562	65090
1563	64924
1564	65091
1565	65092
1566	65093
1567	65094
1569	65095
1574	65097
1575	65098
1576	65099
1577	64925
1580	64926
1584	64871
1585	64927
1586	64928
1587	64929
1588	65101
1589	65102
1590	65103
1591	65104
1593	65105
1595	65107
1596	65108
1608	65109
1609	65110
1610	65111
1611	65112
1614	65114
1615	65115
1617	69410
1618	69411
1641	69413
1642	69414
1643	69415
1646	69418
1647	69419
1648	69420
1649	69421
1650	69422
1651	69423
1652	69424
1653	69425
1654	69426
1655	69427
1656	69918
1657	69919
1658	69920
1659	69921
1660	69922
1665	62396
1667	69091
1669	63291
1670	65751
1671	65745
1672	62397
1673	65756
1674	65746
1676	65747
1678	65748
1682	63270
1683	69092
1684	63271
1685	63272
1686	65799
1687	67241
1688	68312
1689	68313
1690	68314
1691	67242
1692	67300
1693	67301
1694	63273
1695	67337
1696	63276
1697	69093
1698	65757
1699	69105
1700	63264
1701	67243
1702	67244
1703	67256
1705	69429
1706	69103
1707	69106
1709	63267
1710	69104
1711	69107
1712	69830
1713	67271
1715	68671
1716	69109
1717	63268
1718	68672
1719	69831
1720	68680
1721	68673
1722	68674
1723	65728
1725	65672
1726	65673
1728	68681
1730	67257
1731	63283
1732	68675
1733	68682
1734	68683
1735	68302
1736	68684
1737	67273
1738	69832
1739	67302
1740	67280
1741	68685
1742	68686
1744	68676
1745	67303
1746	68677
1747	68687
1748	67266
1749	68688
1750	69833
1751	67267
1752	67299
1754	67307
1755	67305
1756	69834
1757	63284
1759	67306
1760	69835
1761	68678
1762	67268
1763	68689
1764	67309
1765	67245
1766	69836
1767	69837
1768	69838
1769	67248
1770	68679
1771	69839
1772	67252
1773	65749
1774	69094
1775	67308
1777	65779
1778	67261
1779	67272
1780	67269
1781	65769
1782	69840
1783	67246
1784	69841
1785	69108
1786	67274
1788	67247
1789	68311
1790	69842
1791	67249
1792	62937
1793	67258
1795	67259
1796	68303
1797	68304
1803	64905
1804	64945
1805	65116
1806	65117
1808	64946
1810	65118
1811	65119
1812	65120
1813	64906
1814	65121
1819	65122
1820	65123
1821	65600
1822	65601
1823	65602
1824	64907
1825	65603
1826	65604
1828	64908
1829	65606
1830	65607
1831	68305
1832	68306
1833	68307
1834	68308
1835	64947
1836	68309
1837	67250
1838	67251
1839	67253
1840	67254
1843	65608
1844	65609
1847	65611
1850	65612
1852	65614
1853	65615
1854	64909
1856	64910
1857	64911
1858	65617
1860	65619
1862	64948
1863	64950
1864	68316
1865	67262
1866	67263
1867	67264
1868	67265
1869	64912
1870	64913
1873	62111
1875	64930
1880	64931
1881	67278
1882	67279
1883	67281
1884	67282
1885	67283
1886	67284
1887	67285
1888	67286
1889	67287
1890	67288
1892	65621
1894	64932
1895	65622
1896	64949
1897	65623
1898	64951
1899	65624
1900	65625
1902	62112
1903	64952
1911	67289
1912	67290
1913	67291
1914	67292
1915	67293
1916	67294
1917	67295
1918	67296
1919	67297
1920	67298
1922	64953
1926	64954
1927	64955
1928	64956
1930	64957
1931	65626
1932	65627
1933	64958
1934	65628
1935	65629
1937	65631
1940	64959
1941	65632
1942	64960
1943	64961
1945	65633
1946	65634
1948	65636
1951	65639
1952	64962
1954	65640
1955	65641
1956	65642
1960	65644
1961	65645
1962	65646
1963	65647
1964	65648
1965	64963
1967	65649
1969	65650
1970	65651
1971	64964
1973	65653
1974	64965
1976	65654
1977	64966
1979	65655
1980	64967
1981	65656
1982	65657
1983	65658
1984	64968
1985	65659
1986	65660
1987	65661
1988	65662
1989	65663
1990	65664
1991	65665
1992	65666
1993	65667
1994	65668
1995	65669
1996	64969
1997	64970
2000	65670
2001	60501
2002	60502
2003	60503
2004	60504
2005	60505
2006	60506
2011	62340
2012	62341
2013	62342
2014	62343
2015	62344
2016	62345
2018	62347
2019	62348
2020	62349
2022	62351
2023	62352
2024	62353
2025	62354
2026	62355
2028	62357
2029	62358
2030	62359
2032	65674
2033	65675
2034	65676
2037	65677
2040	65679
2041	65680
2042	65681
2044	65683
2045	65684
2046	65685
2047	65686
2048	65687
2050*	65670
2051	65704
2053	65705
2055	65706
2056	65707
2057	65708
2059	65710
2061	65690
2065	65691
2067	65692
2068	65693
2069	65694
2070	65695
2071	65696
2072	65697
2073	65698
2075	65699
2076	65700
2079	65702
2080	65703
2081	67310
2082	67311
2083	67312
2084	67313
2085	67314
2086	67315
2087	67316
2088	67317
2089	67318
2090	67319
2091	67320
2092	67321
2093	67322
2094	67323
2095	67324
2096	67325
2097	67326
2098	67327
2099	67328
2100	67329
2101	62360
2102	62361
2103	62362
2104	62363
2106	62365
2107	62366
2108	62367
2110	62369
2116	63250
2117	63251
2118	63252
2119	63253
2120	63254
2121	63255
2122	63256
2123	63257
2125	63259
2126	65715
2128	65716
2130	65717
2131	65718
2134	65720
2135	65721
2138	65723
2139	65724
2140	65725
2141	65726
2142	65727
2143	69850
2144	69851
2145	69852
2146	69853
2147	69854
2148	69855
2149	69856
2150	69857
2151	69858
2152	69859
2153	69860

2154	69861	2283	63440	2407	69111	2589	69556	2701	64754	2813	61613	2949	64880	3089	64979	3470	63488	3556*	63761	3666	60954	4006	61806
2155	69862	2284	63441	2410	69112	2590	69557	2702	64755	2814	61614	2950	64881	3090	64980	3471	63489	3556	64205	3667	60955	4007	61807
2156	69863	2285	63442	2415	69113	2591	69558	2703	64756	2815	61615	2951	64882	3091	64981	3473	63491	3557*	63762	3668	60956	4008	61808
2157	69864	2286	63443	2417	61959	2592	69559	2704	64757	2816	61616	2952	64883	3092	64982	3475	63493	3557	64206	3669	60957	4009	61809
2158	69865	2287	63444	2419	69114	2593	69560	2705	64758	2817	61617	2953	64884	3093	64983	3476	63494	3558*	63772	3670	60958	4009A	67350
2159	69866	2288	63445	2425	61939	2594	69561	2706	64759	2818	61618	2954	63947	3094	64984	3477	63922	3558	64207	3671	60959	4010	67351
2160	69867	2289	63446	2426	61940	2595	60084	2707	64760	2819	61619	2955	63948	3095	64985	3478	63923	3559	64208	3672	60960	4013	67352
2161	69868	2290	63447	2427	61941	2596	60085	2708	64761	2820	61620	2956	63949	3096	64986	3479	63924	3560*	63773	3673	60961	4014	67353
2162	69869	2291	63448	2428	61942	2597	60086	2709	64762	2821	61621	2957	63950	3097	64987	3480	63925	3560	64209	3674	60962	4015	67354
2164	62970	2292	63449	2429	61960	2598	60087	2710	64763	2822	61622	2958	63951	3098	64988	3481	63926	3561*	63777	3675	60963	4016	67355
2166	62972	2293	63450	2430	63955	2599	60088	2711	64764	2823	61623	2959	63952	3111	68803	3482	63927	3561	64210	3676	60964	4018	67356
2167	62973	2294	63451	2431	63956	2600	69702	2712	64765	2824	61624	2960	63953	3154*	63554	3483	63928	3562*	63778	3677	60965	4019	67357
2169	62975	2295	63452	2432	63957	2601	69703	2713	64766	2825	61625	2961	63954	3155A	68804	3484	63929	3562	64211	3678	60966	4020	67358
2173	68690	2296	63453	2433	63958	2602	69704	2714	64767	2826	61626	2962	64823	3157	68890	3485	63930	3563*	63789	3679	60967	4035	64106
2174	68691	2297	63454	2434	63959	2603	69705	2715	64768	2827	61627	2963	64824	3158	68891	3486	63931	3563	64212	3680	60968	4036	64107
2175	68692	2298	63455	2435	63960	2604	69706	2716	64769	2828	61628	2964	64825	3159	68892	3487	63932	3564	64213	3681	60969	4040	64109
2176	68693	2299	63456	2436	63961	2605	69707	2717	64770	2829	61629	2965	64826	3160	68893	3488	63933	3565*	63797	3682	60970	4041	64110
2177	68694	2300	63457	2437	63962	2606	69708	2718	64771	2830	61630	2966	64827	3161	68894	3489	63934	3565	64214	3683	60971	4046	68783
2178	68695	2301	63458	2438	61943	2607	69709	2719	64772	2831	61631	2967	64828	3162	68895	3490	63935	3566*	63799	3684	60972	4047	68784
2179	68696	2302	63459	2439	61944	2608	69710	2720	64773	2832	61632	2968	64829	3163	68896	3491	63936	3566	64215	3685	60973	4048	68785
2180	68697	2303	68710	2440	61945	2609	69711	2721	64774	2833	61633	2969	64830	3164	68897	3492	63937	3567*	63803	3686	60974	4049	68786
2181	68698	2304	68711	2442	61946	2610	69712	2722	64775	2834	61634	2970	64831	3166	68898	3493	63938	3567	64216	3687	60975	4050	68787
2182	68699	2305	68712	2443	61947	2611	69713	2723	64776	2835	61635	2971	64832	3167	68899	3494	63939	3568*	63805	3688	60976	4051	68788
2183	68700	2306	68713	2445	61961	2612	69714	2724	64777	2836	61636	2972	64833	3168	68900	3495	63940	3568	64217	3689	60977	4052	68789
2184	68701	2307	68714	2446	61962	2613	69715	2725	64778	2837	61637	2973	64834	3169	68901	3496	63941	3569*	63809	3690	60978	4053	68790
2185	68702	2308	68715	2447	61948	2614	69716	2726	64779	2838	61638	2974	64835	3170	68902	3497	63942	3569	64218	3691	60979	4054	68791
2186	68703	2309	68716	2448	61949	2615	69717	2727	64780	2839	61639	2975	64836	3171	68903	3498	63943	3570	64219	3692	60980	4055	68792
2187	68704	2310	68717	2449	61950	2616	69718	2728	64781	2840	61640	2976	64837	3172	68904	3499	63944	3571	64220	3693	60981	4056	68793
2188	68705	2311	68718	2450	61951	2617	69719	2729	64782	2841	61641	2977	64838	3173	68905	3500*	63572	3572	64221	3694	60982	4057	68794
2189	68706	2312	68719	2451	61952	2618	69720	2730	64783	2842	61642	2978	64839	3174	68906	3500	63945	3573	64222	3695	60983	4058	68795
2190	68707	2313	68720	2453	61963	2619	69721	2731	64784	2843	61643	2979	64840	3175	68907	3501*	63577	3574	64223	3696	60507	4059	68796
2191	68708	2314	68721	2455	61964	2620	69722	2732	64785	2844	61644	2980	64841	3176	68908	3501	63946	3575	64224	3697	60508	4060	68797
2192	68709	2315	68722	2458	61965	2621	69723	2733	64786	2845	61645	2981	64885	3178	68909	3502*	63580	3576	64225	3698	60509	4071	62116
2193	62978	2316	68723	2459	61953	2622	69724	2734	64787	2846	61646	2982	64886	3180*	68890	3503*	63582	3577	64226	3699	60510	4075	62000
2196	62981	2317	68724	2461	61954	2623	69725	2735	64788	2847	61647	2983	64887	3181*	68891	3504*	63585	3578	64227	3813	61973	4090	64112
2197	62982	2318	68725	2463	61955	2624	69726	2736	64789	2848	61648	2984	64888	3182*	68892	3505*	63586	3579	64228	3814	61974	4093	64114
2198	62983	2319	68726	2465	61966	2625	69727	2737	64790	2849	61649	2985	64889	3183*	68893	3506*	63594	3580	64229	3815	61975	4094	64115
2203	62988	2320	68727	2466	61956	2626	69728	2738	64791	2850	61650	2986	64890	3184*	68894	3507*	63598	3581	64230	3816	61976	4097	64116
2204	62989	2321	68728	2467	61957	2627	69729	2739	64792	2851	61651	2987	64891	3185*	68895	3508*	63600	3582	64231	3817	61977	4100	64117
2207	62992	2322	68729	2468	61958	2628	69730	2740	64793	2852	61652	2988	64892	3186*	68896	3509*	63601	3583	64232	3818	61978	4103	64118
2208	62993	2323	68730	2470	61969	2629	69731	2741	64794	2853	61653	2989	64893	3187*	68897	3510*	63607	3584	64233	3819	61979	4105	64119
2210	62995	2324	68731	2471	61967	2630	69732	2742	64795	2854	61654	2990	64894	3188*	68898	3511*	63608	3585	64234	3820	61980	4106	64120
2213	63370	2325	68732	2472	61968	2631	69733	2743	60089	2855	61655	2991	64895	3189*	68899	3513*	63617	3586	64235	3821	61981	4107	64121
2214	63371	2326	68733	2473	61970	2632	69672	2744	60090	2856	61656	2992	64896	3190	69430	3514*	63625	3587	64236	3822	61982	4109	64122
2215	63372	2327	68734	2486	69089	2633	69673	2745	60091	2857	61657	2993	64897	3211	68910	3515*	63632	3588	64237	3823	61983	4113	64123
2216	63373	2328	68735	2498	61971	2634	69674	2746	60092	2858	61658	2994	64898	3212	68911	3516*	63634	3589	64238	3824	61984	4114	64124
2217	63374	2329	68736	2499	61972	2635	69675	2747	60093	2859	61659	2995	64899	3213	68912	3517*	63635	3590	64239	3825	61985	4125	64125
2218	63375	2330	68737	2500	60035	2636	69676	2748	60094	2860	61660	2996	64900	3214	68913	3518*	63640	3591	64240	3826	61986	4129	64127
2219	63376	2331	68738	2501	60036	2637	69677	2749	60095	2861	61661	2997	64901	3215	68914	3519*	63643	3592	64241	3827	61987	4131	64128
2220	63377	2332	68739	2502	60037	2638	69678	2750	60096	2862	61662	2998	64902	3216	68915	3521*	63654	3593	64242	3828	61988	4133	64129
2221	63378	2333	68740	2503	60038	2639	69679	2751	60097	2863	61663	2999	64903	3217	68916	3521	64170	3594	64243	3829	61989	4137	64145
2222	63379	2334	68741	2504	60039	2640	69680	2752	60098	2864	61664	3000	64904	3218	68917	3522*	63658	3595	64244	3830	61990	4146	64148
2223	63380	2335	68742	2505	60040	2641	69681	2753	62728	2865	61665	3003	65002	3219	68918	3522	64171	3596	64245	3831	61991	4153	64150
2224	63381	2336	68743	2506	60041	2642	69682	2754	62729	2866	61666	3004	65003	3220	68919	3523	64172	3597	64246	3832	61992	4160	64151
2225	63382	2337	68744	2507	60042	2643	69683	2755	62730	2867	61667	3005	65004	3221	68920	3524*	63660	3598	64247	3833	63963	4162	64152
2226	63383	2338	65860	2508	60043	2644	69684	2756	62731	2868	61668	3006	65005	3222	68921	3524	64173	3599	64248	3834	63964	4166	64153
2227	63384	2339	65861	2509	60014	2645	69685	2757	62732	2869	61669	3007	65006	3223	68922	3525*	63664	3600	64249	3835	63965	4180	62193
2228	63385	2340	65862	2510	60015	2646	69686	2758	62733	2870	61670	3008	65007	3224	68923	3525	64174	3601	64250	3836	63966	4201	68805
2229	63386	2341	65863	2511	60016	2647	69687	2759	62734	2871	61671	3009	65008	3225	68924	3526*	63669	3602	64251	3837	63967	4202	68806
2230	63387	2342	65864	2512	60017	2648	69688	2760	62735	2872	61672	3010	65009	3226	68925	3526	64175	3603	64252	3838	63968	4203	68807
2231	63388	2343	65865	2532	68365	2649	69689	2761	61890	2897	67649	3011	65010	3227	68926	3527*	63671	3604	64253	3839	63969	4204	68808
2232	63389	2344	65866	2533	69115	2650	69690	2762	61891	2898	67655	3014	65013	3228	68927	3527	64176	3605	64254	3840	63970	4205	68809
2233	63390	2345	65867	2534	69116	2651	69691	2763	61892	2899	67661	3015	65014	3229	68928	3528*	63677	3606	64255	3841	63971	4206	68810
2234	63391	2346	65868	2535	69117	2652	69692	2764	61893	2900	67600	3021	65480	3230	68929	3528	64177	3607	64256	3842	63972	4207	68811
2235	63392	2347	65869	2536	69118	2653	69693	2765	61894	2901	67601	3022	65481	3231	68930	3529*	63678	3608	64257	3843	63973	4208	68812
2236	63393	2348	65870	2537	69119	2654	69694	2766	61895	2902	67602	3023	65482	3232	68931	3529	64178	3609	64258	3844	63974	4209	68813
2237	63394	2349	65871	2543	60044	2655	69695	2767	61896	2903	67603	3024	65483	3233	68932	3530	64179	3610	64259	3845	63975	4210	68814
2238	63395	2350	65872	2544	60045	2656	69696	2768	61897	2904	67604	3025	65484	3234	68933	3531*	63680	3621	64260	3846	63976	4211	68798
2239	63396	2351	65873	2545	60046	2657	69697	2769	61898	2905	67605	3026	65485	3235	68934	3531	64180	3622	64261	3847	63977	4212	68799
2240	63397	2352	65874	2546	60047	2658	69698	2770	64796	2906	67606	3027	65486	3236	68935	3532	64181	3623	64262	3848	63978	4213	68800
2241	63398	2353	65875	2547	60048	2659	69699	2771	64797	2907	67607	3028	65487	3237	68936	3533*	63683	3624	64263	3849	63979	4214	68801
2242	63399	2354	65876	2548	60049	2660	69700	2772	64798	2908	67608	3029	65488	3238	68937	3533	64182	3625	64264	3850	63980	4215	68802
2243	63400	2355	65877	2549	60050	2661	69701	2773	64799	2909	67609	3030	65489	3239	68938	3534*	63684	3626	64265	3851	63981	4216	68815
2244	63401	2356	65878	2550	60051	2662	69568	2774	64800	2910	67610	3031	65490	3240	68939	3534	64183	3627	64266	3852	63982	4217	68816
2245	63402	2357	65879	2551	60052	2663	69569	2775	64801	2911	67611	3032	65491	3279	62808	3535*	63690	3628	64267	3853	63983	4218	68817
2246	63403	2358	65880	2552	60053	2664	69570	2776	64802	2912	67612	3033	65492	3281	62810	3535	64184	3629	64268	3854	63984	4219	68818
2247	63404	2359	65881	2553	60054	2665	69571	2777	64803	2913	67613	3034	65493	3288	62817	3536*	63692	3630	64269	3855	63985	4220	68819
2248	63405	2360	65882	2554	60055	2666	69572	2778	64804	2914	67614	3035	65494	3293	62821	3536	64185	3631	64270	3856	63986	4221	68820
2249	63406	2361	65883	2555	60056	2667	69573	2779	64805	2915	67615	3036	65495	3294	62822	3537*	63693	3632	64271	3857	63987	4222	68821
2250	63407	2362	65884	2556	60057	2668	69574	2780	64806	2916	67616	3037	65496	3300	62828	3537	64186	3633	64272	3859	68317	4223	68822
2251	63408	2363	61434	2557	60058	2669	69575	2781	64807	2917	67617	3038	65497	3301	62829	3538*	63698	3634	64273	3922	68757	4224	68823
2252	63409	2364	61435	2558	60059	2670	69576	2782	64808	2918	67618	3039	65498	3306	64140	3538	64187	3635	64274	3923	68758	4225	68824
2253	63410	2365	61436	2559	60060	2671	69577	2783	64809	2919	67619	3040	65499	3313	64105	3539*	63700	3636	64275	3925	68759	4226	68825
2254	63411	2366	61437	2560	60061	2672	69578	2784	64810	2920	67620	3041	62194	3329	64131	3539	64188	3637	64276	3926	68760	4227	68826
2255	63412	2367	61438	2561	60062	2673	69579	2785	64811	2921	67621	3042	62195	3331	64132	3540*	63707	3638	64277	3927	68761	4228	68827
2256	63413	2368	61439	2562	60063	2674	69580	2786	64820	2922	67622	3045	62197	3332	64133	3540	64189	3639	64278	3929	68762	4229	68828
2257	63414	2369	61440	2563	60064	2675	69581	2787	64821	2923	67623	3047	62198	3345	64135	3541*	63710	3640	64279	3930	68763	4230	68829
2258	63415	2370	61441	2564	60065	2676	69582	2788	64822	2924	67624	3048	62199	3350	64136	3541	64190	3641	60939	3961	68764	4231	68830
2259	63416	2371	61442	2565	60066	2677	69583	2789	68972	2925	67625	3052	62203	3375	64137	3542*	63711	3642	60940	3962	68765	4232	68831
2260	63417	2372	61443	2566	60067	2678	69584	2790	68973	2926	67626	3054	62205	3387	64141	3542	64191	3643	60941	3963	68766	4233	68832
2261	63418	2373	61444	2567	60068	2679	69585	2791	68974	2927	67627	3056	62207	3388	64142	3543	64192	3644	60942	3965	68767	4234	68833
2262	63419	2374	61445	2568	60069	2680	69586	2792	68975	2928	67628	3057	62208	3401	61700	3544	64193	3645	60943	3966	68768	4235	68834
2263	63420	2375	61446	2569	60070	2681	69587	2793	68976	2929	67629	3058	62209	3402	61701	3545*	63719	3646	60944	3967	68769	4236	68835
2264	63421	2376	61447	2570	60071	2682	69588	2794	68977	2930	67630	3063	62214	3441	61993	3545	64194	3647	60945	3968	68770	4237	68836
2265	63422	2377	61448	2571	60072	2683	69589	2795	60099	2931	67631	3064	62215	3442	61994	3546*	63722	3648	60946	3969	68771	4238	68837
2266	63423	2378	61449	2572	60073	2684	69590	2796	60100	2932	67632	3071	65015	3443	61995	3546	64195	3649	60947	3970	68772	4239	68838
2267	63424	2379	61450	2573	60074	2685	69591	2797	60101	2933	67633	3072	65016	3444	61996	3547*	63723	3650	60948	3971	68773	4240	68839
2268	63425	2380	61451	2574	60075	2686	69592	2798	69904	2934	61925	3073	65017	3445	61997	3547	64196	3651	60949	3972	68774	4241	68840
2269	63426	2381	61452	2575	60076	2687	69593	2799	69905	2935	61926	3074	65018	3446	61998	3548*	63727	3652	60950	3973	68775	4242	68841
2270	63427	2382	61453	2576	60077	2688	69594	2800	61600	2936	61927	3075	65019	3456	63475	3548	64197	3653	60951	3974	68776	4243	68842
2271	63428	2383	65885	2577	60078	2689	69595	2801	61601	2937	61928	3076	65020	3457	63476	3549	64198	3654	60952	3975	68777	4244	68843
2272	63429	2384	65886	2578	60079	2690	69596	2802	61602	2938	61936	3077	65021	3458	63477	3550*	63736	3655	60928	3976	68778	4245	68844
2273	63430	2385	65887	2579	60080	2691	64744	2803	61603	2939	61937	3078	65022	3459	63478	3550	64199	3656	60929	3977	68779	4246	68845
2274	63431	2386	65888	2580	60081	2692	64745	2804	61604	2940	61938	3079	65023	3460	63479	3551	64200	3657	60930	3978	68780	4247	68846
2275	63432	2387	65889	2581	60082	2693	64746	2805	61605	2941	64872	3081	64971	3461	63921	3552*	63738	3658	60931	3979	68781	4248	68847
2276	63433	2388	65890	2582	60083	2694	64747	2806	61606	2942	64873	3082	64972	3462	63480	3552	64201	3659	60932	3980	68782	4249	68848
2277	63434	2389	65891	2583	69550	2695	64748	2807	61607	2943	64874	3083	64973	3463	63481	3553*	63743	3660	60933	4000	61800	4250	68849
2278	63435	2390	65892	2584	69551	2696	64749	2808	61608	2944	64875	3084	64974	3464	63482	3553	64202	3661	60934	4001	61801	4251	68850
2279	63436	2391	65893	2585	69552	2697	64750	2809	61609	2945	64876	3085	64975	3465	63483	3554*	63745	3662	60935	4002	61802	4252	68851
2280	63437	2392	65894	2586	69553	2698	64751	2810	61610	2946	64877	3086	64976	3466	63484	3554	64203	3663	60936	4003	61803	4253	68852
2281	63438	2395	69999	2587	69554	2699	64752	2811	61611	2947	64878	3087	64977	3467	63485	3555*	63757	3664	60937	4004	61804	4254	68853
2282	63439	2405	69110	2588	69555	2700	64753	2812	61612	2948	64879	3088	64978	3468	63486	3555	64204	3665	60953	4005	61805	4255	68854

4256	68855	4488	60009	4611	69495	4753	69532	4865	60894	5089	68206	5227	64348	5353	63643	5508	62662	5802	65141	5987	64294	6131	67451
4257	68856	4489	60010	4612	69496	4754	69533	4866	60895	5090	65180	5228	64349	5355	63654	5509	62663	5803	65142	5988	64295	6132	63223
4258	68857	4490	60011	4613	69497	4755	69534	4867	60896	5092	63212	5229	64350	5357	67435	5510	62664	5805	65143	5989	64296	6133	63224
4259	68858	4491	60012	4614	69498	4756	69535	4868	60897	5093	63582	5230	64351	5358	62921	5511	62670	5807	65144	5990	64297	6134	63225
4260	68859	4492	60013	4615	69499	4757	69536	4869	60898	5094	65181	5231	64352	5359	67436	5513	69225	5808	65145	5991	64298	6135	63226
4261	68860	4493	60029	4630	61720	4758	69537	4870	60899	5095	65182	5232	64362	5360	62922	5514	69226	5809	65146	5992	64299	6136	63227
4262	68861	4494	60003	4631	61721	4759	69538	4871	60900	5096	65183	5233	64363	5361	62923	5515	69250	5811	65147	5993	64300	6139	69927
4263	68862	4495	60030	4632	61722	4760	69539	4872	60901	5097	65184	5234	64353	5362	62924	5516	69251	5812	65148	5994	64301	6140	63228
4264	68863	4496	60008	4633	61723	4761	69540	4873	60902	5098	65185	5235	64366	5363	62925	5517	69252	5815	65149	5995	64302	6155	69076
4265	68864	4497	60031	4634	61724	4762	69541	4874	60903	5099	65186	5236	64367	5366	69065	5518	69253	5819	65151	5996	64303	6156	69077
4266	68865	4498	60007	4635	61725	4763	69542	4875	60904	5100	65187	5237	64368	5367	69066	5519	69254	5821	65153	5997	64304	6158	69070
4267	68866	4499	60002	4636	61726	4764	69543	4876	60905	5101	65188	5238	64369	5368	69067	5520	69255	5823	65154	5998	64305	6160	69071
4268	68867	4500	60001	4637	61727	4765	69544	4877	60906	5102	63601	5239	64370	5369	69068	5522	69256	5824	65155	5999	64306	6166	61497
4269	68868	4501	67359	4638	61728	4766	69545	4878	60907	5103	65189	5240	64364	5370	69069	5523	69257	5827	65156	6000	64307	6170	69900
4270	68869	4502	67360	4639	61729	4767	69546	4879	60908	5107	62329	5241	64365	5371	69815	5524	69258	5828	65157	6001	64308	6171	69901
4271	68870	4503	67361	4640	61730	4768	69547	4880	60909	5108	62330	5242	64371	5372	69816	5525	69259	5831	65158	6002	64309	6172	69902
4272	68871	4504	67362	4641	61731	4769	69548	4881	60910	5111	62332	5243	64372	5373	69817	5526	69260	5832	65159	6003	64310	6173	69903
4273	68872	4505	67363	4642	61732	4770	69549	4882	60911	5112	62333	5244	64373	5374	69818	5527	69261	5835	65160	6004	64311	6176	63240
4274	68873	4506	67364	4643	61733	4771	60800	4883	60912	5114	67437	5245	64374	5377	63602	5528	69262	5836	65161	6005	64312	6177	63241
4275	68874	4507	67365	4644	61734	4772	60801	4884	60913	5115	67438	5246	64375	5378	63603	5529	69263	5837	65162	6006	64313	6179	69936
4276	68875	4508	67366	4645	61735	4773	60802	4885	60914	5116	65190	5247	64376	5379	63604	5530	69264	5838	65163	6007	64314	6180	63243
4277	68876	4509	67367	4646	61736	4774	60803	4886	60915	5117	65191	5248	64377	5380	63605	5532	69265	5839	65164	6008	64315	6184	63680
4278	68877	4510	67368	4647	61737	4775	60804	4887	60916	5118	65192	5249	64378	5381	63606	5533	69266	5841	65165	6009	64316	6186	63683
4279	68878	4511	67369	4648	61738	4776	60805	4888	60917	5119	65193	5250	64379	5384	63609	5534	69267	5846	65166	6010	64317	6187	63684
4280	68879	4513	67370	4649	61739	4777	60806	4889	60918	5120	65194	5252	64380	5385	63610	5535	69268	5847	65167	6011	64318	6188	63690
4281	68880	4514	67371	4650	61740	4778	60807	4890	60919	5121	65195	5253	64381	5386	63611	5536	69293	5848	65168	6012	64319	6189	63692
4282	68881	4517	67372	4651	61741	4779	60808	4891	60920	5122	65196	5254	64382	5387	63612	5537	69271	5849	65169	6013	62300	6190	63693
4283	68882	4518	67373	4652	61742	4780	60809	4892	60921	5123	65197	5255	64383	5388	63613	5538	68209	5850	65170	6014	62301	6191	63698
4284	68883	4519	67374	4653	61743	4781	60810	4893	60922	5124	65198	5256	64384	5389	63614	5539	69272	5851	65171	6015	62302	6192	63700
4285	68884	4520	67375	4654	61744	4782	60811	4894	60923	5125	65199	5257	64385	5390	63615	5540	69273	5883	68200	6016	62303	6193	63707
4286	68885	4521	67376	4655	61745	4783	60812	4895	60924	5126	65200	5260	62918	5391	63616	5541	69274	5885	68201	6017	62304	6194	63710
4287	68886	4523	67377	4656	61746	4784	60813	4896	60925	5127	69269	5261	62919	5393	63618	5542	69275	5890	68203	6018	62305	6195	63711
4288	68887	4524	67378	4657	61747	4785	60814	4897	60926	5128	69813	5262	62920	5394	63619	5543	69276	5894	69318	6019	62306	6198	63719
4289	68888	4525	67379	4658	61748	4786	60815	4898	60927	5129	69814	5263	62902	5395	63620	5544	69277	5895	69319	6021	62307	6199	63722
4290	68889	4527	67380	4659	61749	4787	60816	4899	60938	5130	65201	5264	62903	5396	63621	5545	69278	5896	69320	6023	62308	6200	63723
4302	62122	4528	67381	4660	61750	4788	60817	4900	60032	5131	65202	5272	69050	5397	63622	5546	69279	5897	69321	6024	62309	6201	63727
4303	62123	4529	67382	4661	61751	4789	60818	4901	60005	5132	65203	5273	69051	5398	63623	5547	69280	5898	69322	6026	62311	6203	63736
4305	62150	4530	67383	4662	61752	4790	60819	4902	60033	5133	63607	5274	69052	5399	63624	5548	69281	5899	69323	6027	62312	6205	63738
4306	62124	4531	67384	4663	61753	4791	60820	4903	60034	5134	65204	5275	69053	5400	63658	5577	67097	5900	69324	6029	62313	6206	63743
4307	62125	4534	67385	4664	61754	4792	60821	4990	68319	5136	63213	5276	69054	5403	63660	5582	67099	5901	69325	6030	62314	6207	63745
4309	62126	4536	67386	4665	61755	4793	60822	4991	68132	5137	63214	5277	68210	5404	63664	5598	67100	5902	69326	6031	62315	6208	63757
4311	62128	4537	67387	4666	61756	4794	60823	4992	68133	5138	69937	5279	61358	5405	63669	5605	69227	5903	69327	6033	62317	6209	63761
4316	62131	4538	67388	4667	61757	4795	60824	4993	68134	5141	65205	5281	64396	5406	63671	5606	69228	5904	69328	6034	62318	6210	63762
4317	62132	4539	67389	4668	61758	4796	60825	5001	63626	5142	63216	5282	64397	5407	63677	5611	69229	5905	69329	6035	62319	6211	63772
4318	62133	4540	67390	4669	61759	4797	60826	5002	67420	5146	63217	5283	64398	5408	63678	5614	69230	5906	69330	6037	62321	6213	63773
4320	62151	4541	67391	4670	61760	4798	60827	5003	69820	5147	69935	5284	64399	5409	69270	5620	69231	5907	69331	6038	62322	6214	63777
4321	62152	4542	67392	4671	61761	4799	60828	5005	63627	5152	63219	5285	64400	5411	69819	5622	69232	5908	69332	6040	62324	6215	63778
4323	62153	4543	67393	4672	61762	4800	60829	5006	69821	5153	63220	5286	64401	5412	63902	5623	69233	5909	69333	6041	62325	6216	63789
4324	62154	4544	67394	4673	61763	4801	60830	5007	69822	5154	69827	5287	64402	5414	63904	5625	69234	5910	69334	6043	64320	6218	63797
4326	62155	4545	67395	4674	61764	4802	60831	5008	63628	5155	63608	5288	64403	5415	63905	5628	69235	5911	69335	6044	64321	6219	63799
4327	62156	4547	67397	4675	61765	4803	60832	5009	67421	5156	69828	5289	64404	5417	63906	5629	69236	5912	69336	6045	64322	6220	63803
4329	62157	4548	67398	4676	61766	4804	60833	5010	63912	5157	68207	5290	64405	5418	63907	5632	69237	5913	69337	6046	64323	6221	63805
4332	62160	4549	67399	4677	61767	4805	60834	5011	63913	5158	69829	5291	64406	5419	63908	5635	69239	5914	69338	6047	64324	6222	63809
4333	62161	4551	69431	4678	61768	4806	60835	5012	63914	5159	63231	5292	64407	5422	63911	5636	69240	5915	69339	6048	64325	6223	63570
4337	62163	4552	69432	4679	61769	4807	60836	5013	63915	5160	63232	5293	64408	5429	62650	5637	69241	5916	69340	6049	64326	6224	63571
4339	62165	4553	69433	4680	61770	4808	60837	5015	63917	5161	63233	5294	64409	5430	62651	5643	65126	5917	69341	6050	64327	6226	63573
4343	62135	4554	69434	4681	61771	4809	60838	5016	64444	5162	63234	5295	64410	5431	62652	5673	65127	5918	69342	6051	64328	6227	63574
4345	62137	4555	69435	4682	61772	4810	60839	5018	67422	5163	63235	5296	64411	5432	62653	5675	65128	5919	69343	6052	63200	6228	63575
4347	62139	4556	69436	4683	61773	4811	60840	5020	67423	5164	63236	5297	64412	5433	62654	5680	65130	5920	69344	6054	63201	6229	63576
4348	62140	4557	69437	4684	61774	4812	60841	5021	69294	5165	69800	5298	64413	5434	62655	5713	69242	5921	69345	6055	67400	6231	63578
4351	62143	4559	69439	4685	61775	4813	60842	5022	63920	5166	69801	5299	64414	5435	62656	5716	69243	5922	69346	6056	67401	6232	63579
4352	62144	4560	69440	4686	61776	4814	60843	5023	69806	5167	69802	5300	64415	5436	62657	5718	69244	5923	69347	6057	67402	6234	63581
4355	62145	4561	69441	4687	61777	4815	60844	5024	69807	5168	69803	5301	64416	5437	62658	5720	69245	5924	69348	6058	67403	6236	63583
4359	62148	4562	69442	4688	61778	4816	60845	5025	69295	5169	69804	5302	64417	5438	62659	5721	69246	5925	69349	6059	67404	6237	63584
4361	62167	4563	69443	4689	61779	4817	60846	5026	63577	5170	69805	5303	64418	5442	61353	5724	69247	5926	69350	6060	67405	6240	63587
4365	62169	4564	69444	4690	61780	4818	60847	5027	67424	5171	67412	5304	64419	5443	61354	5744	69282	5927	69351	6061	67406	6241	63588
4369	62172	4565	69445	4691	61781	4819	60848	5028	67425	5173	69316	5305	64420	5444	61355	5745	69283	5928	69352	6062	67407	6242	63589
4370	62173	4566	69446	4692	61782	4820	60849	5029	67427	5175	65208	5306	64421	5446	61357	5746	69284	5929	69353	6063	67408	6243	63590
4373	62175	4567	69447	4693	61783	4821	60850	5030	69823	5176	65209	5307	64422	5448	69808	5747	69285	5930	69354	6064	67409	6244	63591
4377	62177	4568	69448	4694	61784	4822	60851	5031	61383	5177	64354	5308	64423	5449	69809	5748	69286	5931	69355	6065	67410	6245	63592
4380	62179	4569	69449	4695	61785	4823	60852	5032	61384	5178	67413	5309	64424	5450	69810	5749	69287	5932	69356	6066	67411	6246	63593
4381	62180	4570	69450	4696	61786	4824	60853	5033	61385	5179	67414	5310	67434	5451	69811	5750	69288	5933	69357	6069	61680	6248	63595
4383	62181	4571	69451	4697	61787	4825	60854	5034	61386	5182	61685	5311	64425	5452	69812	5751	69289	5934	69358	6071	61681	6249	63596
4392	62187	4572	69452	4698	61788	4826	60855	5035	61387	5183	61686	5312	64426	5453	67439	5752	69290	5935	69359	6076	63221	6250	63597
4393	62188	4573	69453	4699	61789	4827	60856	5036	61363	5185	61688	5313	64427	5454	67431	5753	69291	5936	69360	6077	69930	6252	63599
4394	62189	4574	69454	4700	61790	4828	60857	5037	61364	5186	61689	5314	64428	5455	67432	5755	69302	5937	69361	6078	64386	6253	63898
4395	62190	4575	69455	4701	61791	4829	60858	5038	61365	5187	61690	5315	64429	5456	67433	5757	69297	5938	69362	6079	64387	6254	63897
4409	62839	4576	69456	4702	61792	4830	60859	5039	63229	5188	67415	5316	64430	5457	67430	5759	69298	5939	69363	6080	64388	6255	63756
4419	62849	4577	69457	4703	61793	4831	60860	5044	69931	5189	69317	5317	64431	5458	61366	5760	69299	5940	69364	6081	64389	6256	63846
4424	62854	4578	69458	4704	61794	4832	60861	5045	69824	5190	67416	5318	64432	5459	61367	5761	69300	5941	69365	6082	64390	6257	63842
4440	62870	4579	69459	4721	69500	4833	60862	5046	69825	5191	67417	5319	64433	5460	61368	5762	69301	5942	69366	6084	62908	6258	63748
4441	62871	4580	69460	4722	69501	4834	60863	5047	67426	5192	62900	5320	64434	5461	61369	5763	69303	5943	69367	6085	62909	6259	63822
4445	62875	4581	69461	4723	69502	4835	60864	5048	69928	5193	67418	5321	68208	5462	61370	5764	69304	5944	69368	6086	62910	6261	63838
4446	62876	4582	69462	4724	69503	4836	60865	5050	67428	5194	62901	5322	64435	5463	61371	5765	69305	5945	69369	6088	62912	6262	63819
4447	62877	4583	69463	4725	69504	4837	60866	5051	69315	5197	64355	5323	64436	5464	61372	5766	69306	5946	69370	6091	62914	6263	63817
4451	62881	4584	69464	4726	69505	4838	60867	5054	69296	5198	64329	5324	64437	5465	61373	5767	69307	5947	64445	6092	62915	6264	63818
4455	62885	4585	69465	4727	69506	4839	60868	5055	67429	5199	67419	5325	64438	5466	61374	5768	69308	5948	64446	6093	62916	6265	63812
4462	60004	4586	69466	4728	69507	4840	60869	5056	63202	5200	69292	5326	64439	5467	61375	5769	69309	5949	64447	6094	62917	6267	63776
4463	60018	4587	69467	4729	69508	4841	60870	5057	63203	5201	64330	5327	64440	5468	61376	5770	69310	5950	64448	6097	61482	6268	63774
4464	60019	4588	69468	4730	69509	4842	60871	5058	69925	5202	64356	5328	64441	5469	61377	5771	69311	5951	64449	6098	61483	6269	63781
4465	60020	4589	69469	4731	69510	4843	60872	5059	63204	5203	64331	5329	64442	5470	61378	5772	69312	5952	64450	6100	61485	6270	63771
4466	60006	4590	69470	4732	69511	4844	60873	5060	68204	5204	64357	5330	64443	5471	61379	5773	69313	5953	64451	6103	61488	6271	63765
4467	60021	4591	69471	4733	69512	4845	60874	5061	68205	5205	64332	5331	63585	5472	61380	5775	69314	5954	64452	6105	61469	6272	63763
4468	60022	4592	69472	4734	69513	4846	60875	5064	63205	5206	64333	5332	63586	5473	61381	5776	67104	5955	64453	6106	61470	6274	63767
4470	60113	4593	69473	4735	69514	4847	60876	5065	63206	5207	64358	5333	63594	5474	61382	5777	67105	5959	69932	6111	61475	6275	63798
4471	60102	4594	69474	4736	69515	4848	60877	5067	63207	5208	64359	5334	63598	5475	61388	5778	67106	5961	69926	6112	61476	6276	63758
4472	60103	4595	69475	4737	69516	4849	60878	5068	69934	5209	64334	5335	63600	5476	61389	5779	67107	5962	63238	6115	64391	6277	63794
4473	60104	4596	69476	4738	69517	4850	60879	5069	63580	5210	64335	5336	69055	5477	61390	5780	67108	5966	63572	6116	64392	6278	63750
4474	60105	4597	69477	4739	69518	4851	60880	5070	69929	5211	64336	5337	69056	5478	61391	5781	67109	5973	64280	6117	64393	6280	63793
4475	60106	4598	69478	4740	69519	4852	60881	5072	61360	5214	64337	5338	69057	5479	61392	5783	67111	5974	64281	6118	64394	6281	63802
4476	60107	4599	69479	4741	69520	4853	60882	5073	61361	5215	64338	5339	69058	5480	61393	5784	67112	5975	64282	6119	64395	6282	63759
4477	60108	4600	69480	4742	69521	4854	60883	5074	65172	5216	64339	5340	69059	5481	61394	5785	67113	5976	64283	6120	67440	6283	63792
4478	60109	4601	69481	4743	69522	4855	60884	5075	65173	5217	64360	5341	69060	5482	61395	5787	65131	5977	64284	6121	67441	6284	63744
4479	60110	4602	69482	4744	69523	4856	60885	5077	65175	5218	64340	5342	69061	5483	61396	5788	65132	5978	64285	6122	67442	6285	63739
4480	60111	4603	69483	4745	69524	4857	60886	5078	61362	5219	64341	5343	69062	5484	61397	5789	65133	5979	64286	6123	67443	6286	63880
4481	60112	4604	69484	4746	69525	4858	60887	5080	65176	5220	64361	5345	69064	5501	62665	5792	65134	5980	64287	6124	67444	6287	63882
4482	60023	4605	69485	4747	69526	4859	60888	5081	65177	5221	64342	5347	63617	5502	62666	5793	65135	5981	64288	6125	67445	6288	63879
4483	60024	4606	69490	4748	69527	4860	60889	5082	65178	5222	64343	5348	63625	5503	62667	5794	65136	5982	64289	6126	67446	6289	63852
4484	60025	4607	69491	4749	69528	4861	60890	5083	65179	5223	64344	5349	63632	5504	62668	5795	65137	5983	64290	6127	67447	6290	63847
4485	60026	4608	69492	4750	69529	4862	60891	5085	63210	5224	64345	5350	63634	5505	62669	5797	65138	5984	64291	6128	67448	6291	63848
4486	60027	4609	69493	4751	69530	4863	60892	5087	69933	5225	64346	5351	63635	5506	62660	5798	65139	5985	64292	6129	67449	6292	63853
4487	60028	4610	69494	4752	69531	4864	60893	5088	69826	5226	64347	5352	63640	5507	62661	5799	65140	5986	64293	6130	67450	6293	63893

6294	63850	6526	63854	6852	62279	7125	68224	7329	68492	7532	65356	7877	65384	8160	65510	8278	64683	8784	62615	8899	62510	9132	68346
6295	63891	6528	63876	6878	62225	7126	68225	7330	68493	7540	65357	7878	65385	8161	65511	8279	64684	8785	62616	9001	67452	9133	67481
6296	63895	6529	63877	6880	62227	7127	68221	7331	68494	7542	65470	7880	65386	8162	65512	8280	64685	8786	62617	9002	67453	9134	67459
6298	63883	6531	63833	6881	62228	7128	68222	7332	68495	7543	65471	7881	65387	8163	65513	8281	64686	8787	62618	9003	67454	9135	67460
6299	63851	6532	63862	6882	62229	7129	68226	7334	68496	7544	65472	7883	65388	8164	65514	8282	64687	8788	62619	9004	67455	9136	64541
6300	63894	6533	63863	6883	62230	7130	68220	7335	68497	7545	65473	7886	65389	8165	65515	8283	64688	8789	62620	9005	67456	9139	64559
6302	63841	6534	63864	6894	62238	7131	68223	7336	68498	7546	65474	7887	65390	8166	65516	8284	64689	8790	62601	9006	67464	9141	67461
6303	63832	6535	63865	6896	62240	7133	68082	7337	68499	7547	65475	7888	65391	8167	65517	8285	64690	8791	62602	9007	69126	9142	69181
6304	63829	6536	63633	6897	62241	7134	68083	7338	68500	7548	65476	7892	65392	8168	65518	8286	64691	8792	62603	9008	64536	9143	64638
6305	63839	6538	63642	6898	62242	7135	68216	7339	68501	7549	65477	7893	65393	8169	65519	8287	64692	8793	62604	9009	68104	9144	68118
6306	63827	6539	63651	6899	62243	7136	68217	7340	68502	7550	65478	7894	65394	8170	65520	8288	64693	8794	62605	9010	68105	9146	68119
6307	63731	6540	63661	6902	62246	7137	68218	7341	68503	7551	65479	7895	65395	8171	65521	8289	64694	8795	62606	9011	68106	9147	69221
6308	63728	6542	63666	6903	62247	7139	68219	7342	68504	7552	65450	7897	65396	8172	65522	8290	64695	8796	62607	9012	67465	9149	62467
6309	63729	6543	63644	6904	62248	7141	67188	7343	68505	7553	65451	7898	65397	8173	65523	8291	64696	8797	62608	9013	64537	9151	64560
6310	63716	6544	63647	6905	62249	7142	67189	7345	68507	7554	65452	7901	65398	8174	65524	8292	64697	8798	62609	9014	68107	9152	68347
6311	63720	6545	63650	6907	62251	7143	67190	7346	68508	7555	65453	7902	65399	8175	65525	8293	64698	8799	62610	9015	67466	9153	62480
6313	63718	6546	63657	6908	62252	7144	67191	7347	68524	7556	65454	7904	65400	8176	65526	8294	64699	8800	62591	9016	67475	9154	69127
6314	63717	6548	63682	6911	62255	7145	67192	7348	68525	7557	65455	7906	65401	8177	65527	8301	61000	8801	62592	9017	68108	9155	67462
6316	63714	6550	63704	6912	62256	7147	67193	7349	68526	7558	65456	7907	65402	8178	65528	8302	61001	8802	62593	9019	69206	9157	64561
6318	63708	6552	63709	6913	62262	7155	68211	7350	68527	7559	65457	7910	65404	8179	65529	8303	61002	8803	62594	9020	69186	9158	64562
6319	63706	6553	63713	6915	62264	7160	68607	7351	68528	7560	65458	7911	65405	8180	65530	8304	61003	8805	62596	9022	69187	9161	64563
6320	63705	6554	63629	7001	67230	7161	68608	7352	68529	7561	65459	7913	65406	8181	65531	8305	61004	8806	62597	9023	69207	9162	64564
6321	63702	6555	63630	7002	67231	7162	68609	7353	68530	7562	65460	7914	65407	8182	65532	8306	61005	8807	62598	9025	67467	9164	67463
6323	63696	6556	63631	7003	67232	7163	68610	7354	68531	7563	65461	7915	65408	8183	65533	8307	61006	8808	62599	9026	67476	9165	69182
6324	63687	6558	63637	7004	67233	7164	68611	7355	68532	7564	65462	7918	65409	8184	65534	8308	67093	8809	62600	9029	69188	9166	69183
6325	63679	6559	63639	7005	67234	7165	68612	7356	68533	7565	65463	7920	65410	8185	65535	8308	61007	8810	62581	9031	69208	9167	64565
6326	63730	6561	63641	7006	67235	7166	68613	7357	68534	7566	65464	7921	65411	8186	65536	8309	61008	8811	62582	9032	68113	9171	64622
6328	63725	6562	63735	7007	67236	7169	68616	7358	68535	7567	65465	7922	65412	8187	65537	8310	67094	8812	62583	9033	64634	9174	69222
6329	63724	6564	63737	7008	67237	7170	67215	7359	68536	7568	65466	7924	65413	8188	65538	8310	61009	8813	62584	9034	62492	9175	64623
6331	63721	6566	63740	7009	67238	7171	67167	7360	68537	7569	65467	7925	65414	8189	65539	8400	68130	8814	62585	9035	62493	9176	65217
6333	63715	6567	63741	7010	67239	7172	67168	7361	68538	7570	65468	7926	65415	8190	65540	8401	68131	8815	62586	9038	64514	9177	65274
6334	63712	6568	63742	7011	68516	7173	67169	7363	68540	7571	65469	7927	65416	8191	65541	8402	68135	8816	62587	9039	67477	9180	65275
6336	63703	6571	63746	7012	68517	7174	67170	7365	68541	7573	67153	7928	65417	8192	65542	8403	68186	8817	62588	9040	68114	9181	65270
6337	63699	6572	63747	7013	68518	7175	67171	7366	68542	7574	67154	7929	65418	8193	65543	8404	68187	8818	62589	9041	67468	9182	65271
6338	63697	6573	63749	7014	68519	7177	67172	7367	68543	7578	67155	7931	65419	8194	65544	8430	68188	8819	62590	9042	68115	9183	65248
6341	63689	6574	63751	7015	68520	7178	67173	7368	68544	7579	67156	7932	65420	8195	65545	8431	68189	8820	62571	9043	67469	9185	64472
6342	63691	6575	63752	7016	68521	7179	67216	7369	68545	7581	67157	7934	65421	8196	65546	8500	61500	8821	62572	9044	64538	9186	64473
6343	63688	6576	63753	7018	68522	7180	67174	7370	68546	7584	67158	7937	65422	8197	65547	8501	61501	8822	62573	9045	65246	9187	64474
6344	63685	6577	63754	7019	68523	7184	67175	7371	68547	7586	67159	7940	65423	8198	65548	8502	61502	8823	62574	9046	64615	9188	64475
6347	63681	6578	63755	7021	68647	7185	67176	7372	68548	7588	67160	7941	65424	8199	65549	8503	61503	8824	62575	9047	69172	9189	64476
6349	63694	6579	63760	7022	68648	7186	67177	7373	68549	7589	67213	7942	65425	8201	65551	8504	61504	8825	62576	9048	67470	9190	64477
6350	63676	6581	63764	7023	68649	7187	67178	7374	68550	7590	67214	7943	65426	8202	65552	8505	61505	8826	62577	9049	69189	9191	64478
6351	63674	6582	63766	7024	68650	7188	67217	7375	68551	7597*	67093	7945	65427	8203	65553	8507	61507	8827	62578	9050	68116	9192	64479
6352	63673	6583	63769	7025	68651	7189	67179	7376	68552	7598*	67094	7978*	69600	8204	65554	8508	61508	8828	62579	9051	67478	9193	64480
6353	63675	6584	63770	7026	68652	7190	68597	7377	68553	7640	65440	7979*	69601	8205	65555	8509	61509	8829	62580	9052	69209	9195	64482
6354	63672	6586	63775	7027	68653	7191	68598	7378	68554	7641	65441	7980*	69602	8206	65556	8510	61510	8830	62561	9053	67471	9196	64483
6356	63670	6588	63779	7028	68654	7192	68599	7379	68555	7642	65442	7981*	69603	8207	65557	8511	61511	8831	62562	9054	69173	9197	64484
6357	63665	6589	63783	7029	68655	7193	68600	7380	68556	7643	65443	7982*	69604	8208	65558	8512	61512	8832	62563	9055	69210	9198	64485
6358	63662	6590	63785	7030	68656	7194	68601	7381	68557	7644	65444	7983*	69605	8209	65559	8513	61513	8833	62564	9056	64515	9199	64486
6359	63663	6591	63787	7031	68657	7195	68602	7382	68558	7645	65445	7984*	69606	8210	65560	8514	61514	8834	62565	9057	64516	9200	64487
6360	63659	6592	63788	7032	68658	7196	68603	7383	68559	7646	65446	7985*	69607	8211	65561	8515	61515	8835	62566	9058	64517	9201	64488
6361	63668	6594	63790	7033	68659	7198	68605	7384	68560	7647	65447	7986*	69608	8212	65562	8516	61516	8836	62567	9059	64518	9202	64489
6363	63656	6595	63795	7034	68660	7200	68606	7385	68561	7648	65448	7987*	69609	8213	65563	8517	61517	8837	62568	9060	69211	9203	64490
6364	63655	6596	63796	7035	68661	7203	68591	7386	68562	7649	65449	7988*	69610	8214	65564	8519	61519	8838	62569	9061	69174	9204	64491
6365	63649	6598	63801	7036	68662	7204	68592	7387	68563	7692*	62573	7989*	69611	8215	65565	8520	61520	8839	62570	9062	64539	9205	64492
6366	63645	6601	63806	7037	68663	7206	68593	7389	68565	7695*	62576	7990	69612	8216	65566	8521	61521	8840	62551	9063	68117	9206	64493
6367	63667	6604	63813	7038	68664	7207	68594	7390	68566	7707*	62568	7991	69613	8217	65567	8523	61523	8841	62552	9064	67479	9207	64512
6370	63653	6606	63816	7039	68665	7208	68595	7391	68567	7708*	62569	7992	69614	8218	65568	8524	61524	8842	62553	9065	69175	9208	64513
6371	63652	6608	63823	7040	68666	7210	68129	7392	68568	7712*	62553	7993	69615	8219	65569	8525	61525	8843	62554	9066	68338	9209	69128
6372	63648	6609	63828	7042	68638	7214	67162	7393	68569	7727*	62548	7994	69616	8220	65570	8526	61526	8844	62555	9067	69212	9210	69129
6374	63646	6611	63835	7043	68639	7219	67163	7394	68570	7728*	62549	7995	69617	8221	65571	8528	61528	8845	62556	9068	65247	9219	69185
6375	63638	6612	63843	7044	68640	7222	67164	7395	68571	7740*	62521	7996	69618	8222	65572	8529	61529	8846	62557	9069	69176	9220	64528
6376	63636	6614	63845	7045	68641	7226	68127	7396	68572	7764*	62505	7997	69619	8223	65573	8530	61530	8847	62558	9070	69177	9221	62468
6378	62671	6615	63849	7046	68642	7227	68125	7397	68509	7772*	68130	7998	69620	8224	65574	8532	61532	8848	62559	9071	69178	9222	64542
6379	62672	6616	63855	7047	68643	7228	68126	7398	68510	7773*	68131	7999	69621	8225	65575	8533	61533	8849	62560	9072	64616	9223	69164
6380	62673	6617	63856	7048	68644	7229	68128	7399	68511	7774*	68135	8000	69600	8226	65576	8535	61535	8850	62541	9073	64617	9224	69165
6381	62674	6618	63857	7049	68645	7230	68081	7400	68512	7775*	68186	8001	69601	8227	65577	8536	61536	8851	62542	9074	69213	9225	69223
6382	62675	6619	63858	7050	68646	7232	67165	7401	68513	7776*	68187	8002	69602	8228	65578	8537	61537	8852	62543	9075	69214	9226	64526
6383	62676	6620	63859	7051	68617	7233	67166	7403	68514	7780	67212	8003	69603	8229	65579	8538	61538	8853	62544	9076	69215	9227	69224
6384	62677	6621	63860	7052	68618	7236	67151	7405	68515	7781	67194	8004	69604	8230	65580	8539	61539	8854	62545	9077	69216	9228	64527
6385	62678	6622	63861	7053	68619	7244	67152	7407	62792	7782	67195	8005	69605	8231	65581	8540	61540	8855	62546	9078	69217	9229	69166
6386	62679	6624	63867	7055	68621	7247	68213	7408	62793	7783	67196	8006	69606	8232	65582	8541	61541	8856	62547	9079	69218	9230	69167
6387	62680	6625	63868	7057	68623	7250	68214	7409	62794	7784	67197	8007	69607	8233	65583	8542	61542	8857	62548	9084	64618	9233	68332
6388	62681	6626	63869	7059	68625	7253	68215	7411	62795	7785	67198	8008	69608	8234	65584	8543	61543	8858	62549	9086	64531	9234	68333
6389	62682	6627	63870	7060	68626	7256	68583	7414	62796	7786	67199	8009	69609	8235	65585	8545	61545	8860	62531	9087	68350	9235	68334
6390	62683	6629	63873	7061	67220	7257	68584	7416	62797	7787	67200	8010	69610	8236	65586	8546	61546	8861	62532	9088	64556	9236	68335
6391	62684	6630	63874	7062	67221	7258	68585	7427	62780	7788	67201	8011	69611	8237	65587	8547	61547	8862	62533	9089	64557	9237	68336
6392	62685	6631	63878	7063	67222	7260	68586	7437*	61523	7789	67218	8040	67141	8238	65588	8549	61549	8863	62534	9096	69190	9238	68337
6393	62686	6632	63881	7064	67223	7261	68587	7449*	61535	7790	67219	8042	67143	8239	65589	8550	61550	8864	62535	9097	69191	9240	69195
6394	62687	6633	63884	7065	67224	7262	68588	7463	62781	7791*	62792	8048	67149	8240	64640	8552	61552	8865	62536	9098	64631	9241	62481
6395	62688	6634	63885	7066	67225	7263	68589	7466	62782	7794*	62795	8049	67150	8241	64641	8553	61553	8867	62538	9099	69219	9242	62482
6396	62689	6635	63886	7067	67226	7264	68590	7467*	61553	7797*	62780	8061	67134	8242	64642	8554	61554	8868	62539	9100	62477	9243	62406
6397	62690	6636	63887	7068	67227	7265	68573	7470*	61556	7802*	62785	8067	67139	8243	64643	8555	61555	8869	62540	9101	64632	9246	69168
6398	62691	6637	63888	7069	67228	7266	68574	7472*	61558	7805*	62788	8068	67140	8244	64644	8556	61556	8870	62521	9102	67480	9247	65264
6399	62692	6638	63889	7070	67229	7267	68575	7476*	61562	7813	65350	8075	67124	8245	64645	8557	61557	8871	62522	9103	64633	9248	65265
6400	62693	6639	63890	7071	67180	7268	68576	7477	62783	7821	65351	8078	67126	8246	64646	8558	61558	8872	62523	9104	64635	9251	69130
6401	62694	6640	63899	7072	67181	7269	68577	7478	62784	7825	65352	8079	67127	8247	64647	8559	61559	8873	62524	9105	64637	9252	69169
6409	68368	6641	63900	7074	67182	7270	68578	7479*	61565	7828	65353	8081	67128	8248	64648	8560	61560	8874	62525	9106	69192	9253	64529
6411	68366	6642	63901	7075	67183	7271	68579	7482*	61568	7833	65359	8092	67114	8249	64649	8561	61561	8875	62526	9107	69193	9254	64530
6495	63686	6819	62231	7076	67184	7273	68581	7488*	61574	7836	65361	8093	67115	8250	64670	8562	61562	8876	62527	9108	69194	9255	64543
6496	63695	6820	62232	7077	67185	7281	68370	7490	62785	7837	65362	8095	67117	8251	64671	8563	61563	8877	62528	9109	64619	9256	62469
6498	63701	6822	62234	7078	67186	7288	68371	7491*	61577	7840	65363	8097	67119	8252	64672	8564	61564	8878	62529	9110	64620	9257	69170
6500	63726	6823	62235	7079	67187	7289	68372	7492	62786	7843	65364	8140	64650	8253	64673	8565	61565	8879	62530	9111	64621	9258	62470
6501	63732	6825	62260	7082	68628	7290	68373	7494	62787	7846	65365	8141	64651	8254	64674	8566	61566	8880	62511	9113	64540	9259	69184
6502	63733	6826	62261	7083	68629	7293	68374	7496	62788	7847	65366	8142	64652	8260	64660	8567	61567	8881	62512	9114	68339	9260	64544
6503	63734	6827	62265	7084	68630	7296	68375	7497	62789	7848	65367	8143	64653	8261	64661	8568	61568	8882	62513	9115	64519	9261	64545
6505	63780	6829	62267	7085	68631	7298	68376	7503	62790	7849	65368	8144	64654	8262	64662	8569	61569	8883	62514	9116	68340	9263	64546
6506	63782	6830	68192	7086	68632	7304	68377	7506	62791	7850	65369	8145	64655	8263	64663	8570	61570	8884	62515	9117	68341	9264	69171
6507	63784	6831	62268	7087	68633	7305	68596	7508	65428	7852	65370	8146	64656	8264	64664	8571	61571	8885	62516	9118	68342	9265	67472
6510	63791	6832	68193	7089	68635	7307	68378	7509	65429	7853	65371	8147	64657	8265	64665	8572	61572	8886	62517	9119	68343	9266	62471
6511	63800	6833	62269	7090	68636	7309	68379	7510	65430	7854	65372	8148	64658	8266	64666	8573	61573	8887	62518	9120	64520	9267	67473
6512	63804	6834	62270	7091	67202	7310	68380	7511	65431	7855	65373	8149	64659	8267	64667	8574	61574	8888	62519	9121	68344	9270	62483
6513	63768	6835	62271	7094	67203	7311	68381	7512	65432	7857	65374	8150	65500	8268	64668	8575	61575	8889	62520	9122	67457	9271	68351
6515	63786	6836	62272	7095	67204	7313	68382	7514	65433	7860	65375	8151	65501	8269	64669	8576	61576	8890	62501	9123	64558	9272	64624
6516	63824	6843	68190	7096	67205	7319	68383	7515	65434	7865	65376	8152	65502	8270	64675	8577	61577	8891	62502	9124	64532	9273	64625
6518	63807	6844	68191	7100	67206	7320	68384	7516	65435	7866	65377	8153	65503	8271	64676	8578	61578	8892	62503	9125	69220	9274	64566
6519	63808	6845	62273	7103	67207	7321	68385	7517	65436	7869	65378	8154	65504	8272	64677	8579	61579	8893	62504	9126	64533	9276	69179
6521	63821	6846	62274	7104	67208	7322	68386	7520	65437	7871	65379	8155	65505	8273	64678	8580	61580	8894	62505	9127	64534	9277	68348
6522	63836	6847	62275	7108	67209	7323	68387	7523	65438	7872	65380	8156	65506	8274	64679	8780	62611	8895	62506	9128	64636	9278	62484
6523	63837	6848	62276	7109	67210	7324	68388	7526	65439	7874	65381	8157	65507	8275	64680	8781	62612	8896	62507	9129	64535	9279	68352
6524	63840	6849	62277	7110	67211	7327	68490	7527	65354	7875	65382	8158	65508	8276	64681	8782	62613	8897	62508	9130	68345	9280	65273
6525	63872	6850	62278	7111	67161	7328	68491	7530	65355	7876	65383	8159	65509	8277	64682	8783	62614	8898	62509	9131	67458	9281	62485

9282	69131	9383	62464	9448	67492	9517	64630	9686	65257	9781	65333	9844	68328	10091	68110	71473	68066	77002	63001	77430	63040	78667	63150
9288	68353	9385	62466	9449	67493	9518	64639	9687	65258	9782	65334	9845	68329	10092	68094	71474	68067	77009	63000	77435	63041	78668	63151
9289	68354	9386	69132	9450	67494	9519	69196	9688	65259	9783	65335	9846	68330	10093	68103	71475	68068	77021	63002	77437	63042	78670	63152
9290	68349	9387	69133	9451	67495	9520	69197	9689	65260	9785	65337	9847	68331	10094	68095	71476	68069	77033	63004	77448	63043	78673	63153
9291	62478	9388	69134	9452	67496	9521	69198	9690	65261	9786	65338	9848	64460	10095	68111	71486	68070	77046	63005	77473	63112	78674	63154
9292	64567	9389	69135	9453	69180	9522	69199	9705	65276	9787	65339	9849	64461	10096	68112	71498	68025	77083	63101	77474	63113	78676	63155
9295	64568	9390	69136	9454	64574	9523	69200	9706	65277	9788	65340	9850	64462	10097	68096	71506	68026	77091	63102	77486	63114	78677	63156
9296	64605	9391	69137	9455	64575	9524	69201	9707	65278	9789	65341	9851	64463	10098	68097	71509	68024	77093	63103	77487	63115	78679	63157
9297	64569	9392	69138	9456	64576	9525	69202	9708	65279	9790	65342	9852	64464	10100	68098	71532	68071	77100	63104	77491	63116	78680	63158
9298	62479	9393	69139	9457	64577	9526	69203	9709	65280	9791	65343	9854	64466	10101	68092	71533	68072	77110	63105	77493	63117	78686	63159
9299	64626	9396	69140	9458	64578	9527	69204	9710	65281	9792	65344	9856	64468	10102	68093	71534	68073	77112	63106	77496	63118	78687	63160
9300	64606	9397	69141	9459	64579	9528	69205	9711	65282	9793	65345	9858	69120			71535	68074	77113	63107	77498	63119	78690	63161
9301	64607	9398	69142	9460	64580	9529	68138	9712	65283	9794	65346	9862	69124	Ex War		71536	68075	77131	63108	77501	63120	78691	63162
9302	64608	9399	69143	9461	64581	9546	68122	9714	65285	9795	68442	9863	69125	Department		75094	68006	77133	63109	77502	63121	78692	63163
9303	64609	9401	64611	9462	64582	9547	68123	9715	65286	9796	68443	9864	62455	Locomotives		75097	68007	77136	63110	77504	63122	78696	63164
9304	64570	9402	64612	9463	64583	9596	63796	9716	65287	9797	68444	9866	62457	70800	63044	75101	68008	77146	63111	77505	63123	78697	63165
9305	64571	9403	64613	9464	64584	9604	65210	9717	65288	9798	68445	9867	62458	70804	63045	75108	68009	77211	63012	77506	63124	78698	63166
9306	64610	9404	62062	9465	64585	9610	68124	9718	65289	9799	68446	9882	62443	70810	63046	75117	68010	77213	63013	77507	63125	78699	63167
9307	62472	9405	62473	9466	64586	9611	65268	9719	65290	9800	68447	9883	62444	70813	63047	75119	68011	77220	63014	78513	63083	78702	63168
9308	68120	9406	62474	9467	64587	9617	65211	9720	65291	9801	68448	9884	62445	70815	63048	75124	68012	77223	63020	78515	63084	78703	63169
9309	67474	9407	62475	9468	64588	9622	65213	9721	65292	9802	68449	9885	62446	70816	63049	75125	68013	77233	63021	78516	63085	78706	63170
9310	68121	9408	62476	9469	64589	9623	65214	9722	65293	9803	68450	9887	62448	70818	63050	75134	68014	77236	63022	78520	63086	78707	63171
9313	64595	9409	62418	9470	64596	9625	65215	9723	65294	9804	68451	9888	62449	70821	63051	75139	68015	77243	63027	78527	63089	78708	63172
9314	64572	9410	62419	9471	64597	9628	65216	9724	65295	9805	68452	9889	62450	70822	63052	75148	68016	77250	63028	78528	63090	78709	63173
9315	64573	9411	62420	9472	64598	9632	65218	9725	65296	9806	68453	9890	62451	70823	63053	75149	68017	77251	63029	78534	63098	78710	63174
9329	64470	9412	62421	9473	64599	9635	62059	9726	65297	9807	68454	9892	62453	70824	63054	75150	68018	77254	63030	78540	63099	78711	63175
9330	64471	9413	62422	9476	64590	9642	62060	9727	65298	9808	68455	9893	62454	70826	63055	75153	68019	77265	63070	78550	63100	78712	63176
9331	62460	9414	62423	9477	64591	9644	65220	9731	62064	9809	68456	9894	62459	70827	63056	75164	68020	77272	63075	78562	63087	78713	63177
9332	62461	9415	62424	9478	64592	9645	65221	9732	62065	9810	68457	9895	62400	70828	63057	75183	68021	77276	63076	78565	63088	78716	63178
9333	62462	9416	62425	9479	64593	9646	65222	9733	62066	9811	68458	9896	62401	70830	63058	75184	68022	77277	63077	78570	63091	78718	63179
9335	64521	9417	62426	9480	64594	9648	65224	9742	65300	9812	68459	9897	62402	70831	63059	75190	68023	77279	63078	78577	63092	79177	63180
9336	64522	9418	62427	9485	64600	9649	65225	9745	65303	9813	68460	9898	62403	70832	63060	75258	68047	77281	63079	78582	63093	79180	63181
9337	64523	9419	62428	9486	64601	9650	65226	9746	65304	9814	68461	9899	62404	70837	63061	75259	68048	77284	63080	78584	63094	79185	63182
9338	62409	9420	62429	9487	64602	9651	65227	9747	65305	9816	68463	9900	62405	70840	63062	75260	68049	77290	63081	78591	63095	79187	63183
9339	62410	9421	62430	9488	64603	9652	65228	9748	65306	9817	68464	9907	69144	70841	63063	75261	68050	77298	63082	78603	63096	79191	63184
9340	62411	9422	62431	9489	64604	9653	65229	9749	65307	9818	68465	9908	69145	70842	63064	75262	68051	77300	63003	78608	63097	79192	63185
9347	64524	9423	62432	9490	62489	9654	65230	9750	65308	9819	68466	9909	69146	70844	63065	75263	68052	77316	63006	78625	63126	79200	63186
9348	64525	9425	62434	9491	64614	9655	65231	9751	65309	9820	68467	9910	69147	70846	63066	75265	68053	77318	63007	78627	63127	79211	63187
9357	65266	9426	62435	9492	62494	9656	65232	9752	65310	9821	68468	9911	69148	70847	63067	75266	68054	77322	63008	78628	63128	79216	63188
9358	65267	9427	62436	9493	62495	9657	65233	9753	65311	9822	68469	9912	69149	70848	63068	75267	68055	77336	63009	78630	63129	79236	63189
9359	62412	9428	62437	9494	62496	9658	65234	9754	65312	9823	68470	9913	69150	70852	63071	75268	68056	77339	63010	78633	63130	79240	63190
9360	62413	9429	64547	9495	62497	9659	65235	9755	65313	9824	68471	9914	69151	70854	63069	75269	68057	77343	63011	78634	63131	79241	63191
9363	62417	9430	64548	9496	62498	9660	65236	9756	65314	9825	68472	9915	69152	70858	63072	75270	68058	77354	63015	78635	63132	79245	63192
9364	64494	9431	64549	9497	62438	9663	65237	9757	65315	9826	68473	9916	69153	70870	63073	75271	68059	77357	63016	78639	63133	79247	63193
9365	64495	9432	64550	9498	62439	9664	65238	9758	65316	9827	68474	9917	69154	70872	63074	75272	68031	77360	63017	78641	63134	79251	63194
9366	64496	9433	64551	9499	62440	9667	65239	9759	65317	9828	68475	9918	69155	71440	68027	75281	68032	77363	63018	78642	63135	79253	63195
9367	64497	9434	64552	9500	62441	9668	65240	9760	65318	9829	68476	9919	69156	71447	68028	75287	68033	77367	63019	78645	63136	79285	63196
9368	64498	9435	64553	9501	62442	9669	65241	9761	65319	9830	68477	9920	69157	71451	68029	75297	68034	77369	63023	78646	63137	79288	63197
9369	64499	9436	64554	9502	62490	9670	65242	9762	65320	9831	68478	9921	69158	71452	68030	75320	68035	77370	63024	78648	63138	79305	63198
9370	64500	9437	64555	9503	62487	9673	65243	9763	65321	9832	68479	9922	69159	71462	68076	75321	68036	77373	63025	78649	63139	79308	63199
9371	64501	9438	67482	9504	62488	9675	65244	9764	65322	9833	68480	9923	69160	71463	68078	75322	68037	77382	63026	78651	63140		
9372	64502	9439	67483	9506	64627	9677	65245	9768	62072	9834	68481	9924	69161	71464	68079	75323	68038	77385	63031	78653	63141		
9374	64504	9440	67484	9507	64628	9678	65249	9771	65323	9836	68320	9925	69162	71465	68080	75324	68039	77391	63032	78654	63142		
9375	64505	9441	67485	9508	64629	9679	65250	9772	65324	9837	68321	9926	69163	71466	68077	75325	68040	77397	63033	78655	63143		
9376	64506	9442	67486	9511	67497	9680	65251	9773	65325	9838	68322	10000	60700	71467	68060	75326	68041	77410	63034	78656	63144		
9377	64507	9443	67487	9512	67498	9681	65252	9775	65327	9839	68323	10083	68099	71468	68061	75327	68042	77412	63035	78661	63145		
9379	64509	9444	67488	9513	67499	9682	65253	9776	65328	9840	68324	10084	68100	71469	68062	75328	68043	77420	63036	78662	63146		
9380	64510	9445	67489	9514	67500	9683	65254	9777	65329	9841	68325	10088	68101	71470	68063	75329	68044	77422	63037	78663	63147		
9381	64511	9446	67490	9515	67501	9684	65255	9778	65330	9842	68326	10089	68102	71471	68064	75330	68045	77423	63038	78664	63148		
9382	62463	9447	67491	9516	67502	9685	65256	9779	65331	9843	68327	10090	68109	71472	68065	75331	68046	77427	63039	78665	63149		

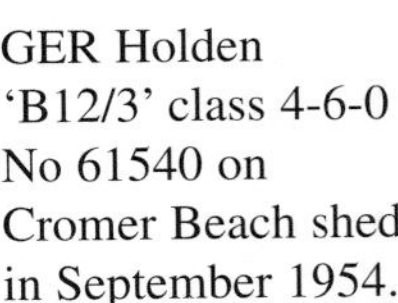

GER Holden 'B12/3' class 4-6-0 No 61540 on Cromer Beach shed in September 1954.

BR Standard Class 7 4-6-2 No 70039 *Sir Christopher Wren*.